# American History: A Survey

Pictorial essays on ''The Course of American Art''
by **Gerald Bernstein**, *Brandeis University*

**Third Edition**

**Alfred•A•Knopf   New York**

# American History:

# A Survey

## Richard N. Current,
### University of North Carolina at Greensboro

## T. Harry Williams,
### Louisiana State University

## Frank Freidel,
### Harvard University

**This is a Borzoi Book**
**Published by Alfred A. Knopf, Inc.**

Third edition
9876

Copyright © 1959, 1961, 1964, 1966,
1971 by Richard N. Current, T. Harry
Williams, Frank Freidel
All rights reserved under International and
Pan-American Copyright Conventions.
Published in the United States by Alfred
A. Knopf, Inc., New York, and simultane-
ously in Canada by Random House of
Canada Limited, Toronto. Distributed by
Random House, Inc., New York.

Library of Congress Catalog Card Number: 76–103725

Manufactured in the United States of
America

Composed by Westcott & Thomson, Inc.,
Philadelphia, Pa.
Printed and bound
by American Book-Stratford Press

Published 1961, reprinted five times
Second edition, 1966; reprinted three times
Third edition, 1971

Permission for the use of
"The Visit" by Marisol
The Dr. Peter Ludwig Collection
Wallraf-Richartz Museum, Cologne
Courtesy, Sidney Janis Gallery

Cartographic consultants:
David Ward
Randall Sale
*University of Wisconsin*

Douglas McManis
*Columbia University*

Cartography by:
Francis & Shaw

To the Memory of **William Best Hesseltine** (1902–1963)

# Preface

This is a thoroughly reorganized and extensively rewritten edition of a textbook that was last revised five years ago. We have again extended our account to keep up with the new history that has been made during the past five years—new history both in the sense of actual events and in the sense of scholarly writings. By dividing the book into thirty chapters of fairly uniform length (each of them having a theme-setting introduction), we have now simplified the instructor's task of making assignments, whether he teaches a one-semester, a two-semester, or a two-quarter or three-quarter course. We have enlarged as well as reorganized our treatment of the colonial period, and we have increased our attention to the role that black Americans have played throughout the nation's history. We have also corrected persisting errors, provided fresh illustrations and new color maps, and brought the appendices and lists of suggested readings up to date. On these lists we have indicated the books that are available in comparatively low-priced paperback editions. Since the variety of paperbacks continually grows and changes, we recommend that current issues of the quarterly publication *Paperbound Books in Print* also be consulted.

Besides drastically revising our textbook, we have added some wholly new features to it. One of these is a series of brief, simplified historiographical essays with the heading "Where Historians Disagree." These are intended to introduce the student to some of the most important conflicts of historical interpretation and thus help him understand that the study of history involves far more than merely collecting and memorizing "facts." Another new feature consists of pictorial essays, groups of illustrations in full color, with commentary. These contain a synopsis history of American art and architecture and thus strengthen our coverage of cultural history.

In the work of revision we have been immeasurably aided by historical scholars, experts in their respective fields, who have examined and criticized parts of our earlier edition. In the interests of objectivity, some of these scholars have made their critiques without our being informed of their names. Since it is impossible to identify all the critics, we have decided to identify none of them, but we cannot forgo this opportunity to extend to all of them our most sincere thanks. We have been greatly helped also by users of the text, students as well as instructors, who have sent us criticisms and corrections. To these sharp-eyed and well-informed readers, too, we wish to express our profound gratitude. We shall continue to be grateful for suggestions regarding corrections or other improvements to be incorporated in future reprintings and revisions.

We urge the student taking up this volume for the first time to look at it as a whole and make himself familiar, at the outset, with all its features, including the index, the appendices, and the table of contents. We counsel him also to bear in mind that the whole of American history is not contained in this or in any other book. This one is intended to open the subject, not to close it. The book will have succeeded if, with the indispensable aid of the instructor, it arouses a desire to learn more about the history of the United States than is included between these covers.

R. N. C.

T. H. W.

F. F.

# Contents

1. **From the Old World to the New**
   **The Epoch of Discovery** / **4**
   The Quickening of Europe / **4**
   Westward to the East / **6**
   **The Colonizing Impulse** / **9**
   The Spanish Colonies / **10**
   England Against Spain / **12**
   Englishmen Look Overseas / **14**
   **The Wilderness Setting** / **16**
   The Eastern Woodlands / **16**
   The Woods Indians / **17**
   European Rivals / **19**
   **The First English Settlements** / **20**
   Early Attempts / **21**
   Jamestown and Virginia / **22**
   Plymouth Plantation / **25**
   **Selected Readings** / **27**

2. **Transplanted Englishmen**
   **New England** / **30**
   Massachusetts Bay / **30**
   Exodus From the Bay Colony / **31**
   Frontier Defense / **34**
   Changing Ways / **35**
   **The Chesapeake Country** / **37**
   Maryland / **37**
   Tobacco and Society / **38**
   Political Turbulence / **39**
   **More Proprietary Colonies** / **42**
   Carolina / **42**
   New York / **45**
   The Quaker Colonies / **46**
   **Experiment in Union** / **48**
   The Mercantile System / **49**
   The Dominion of New England / **49**
   The "Glorious Revolution" / **50**
   **Selected Readings** / **52**

3. **Provincial Americans**
   **The Expanding Settlements** / **56**

   The Founding of Georgia / **56**
   The Labor Supply / **56**
   Population Growth / **58**
   **The Economic Basis** / **61**
   Agriculture / **62**
   Industries / **63**
   Money and Commerce / **65**
   **Aspects of Society** / **69**
   The Class Structure / **69**
   Home and Family / **71**
   **The Mind and Spirit** / **73**
   The Pattern of Religions / **73**
   The Great Awakening / **75**
   Reading and Writing / **76**
   The Higher Learning / **78**
   Concepts of Law / **80**
   **Selected Readings** / **80**

4. **The Empire Under Strain**
   **A Loosening of Ties** / **83**
   Toward Self-Rule / **84**
   Intercolonial Disunity / **85**
   **The Struggle for a Continent** / **86**
   New France / **86**
   Anglo-French Conflict / **88**
   The Great War for the Empire / **89**
   **The New Imperialism** / **91**
   Burdens of Empire / **92**
   Policies of George III / **93**
   Colonial Self-Interest / **94**
   **Stirrings of Revolt** / **96**
   The Stamp Act Crisis / **97**
   The Townshend Program / **98**
   The Philosophy of Revolt / **101**
   The Tea Excitement / **102**
   **Cooperation for War** / **105**
   The Continental Congress / **106**
   Lexington and Concord / **107**
   **Selected Readings** / **108**

**5.  The American Revolution**
**The States United / 112**
Original War Aims / **112**
Declaration of Independence / **113**
State Governments / **114**
The Confederation / **115**
Mobilizing for War / **117**
**The War for Independence / 118**
The Fighting, to 1777 / **120**
Foreign Friends / **122**
Victory at Yorktown / **124**
Winning the Peace / **127**
**The Confederation's Problems / 129**
A Disputed Treaty / **129**
Failures in Foreign Affairs / **130**
The Needs of the West / **131**
Planning for the Territories / **133**
Debts, Taxes, and Daniel Shays /
**135**
**Selected Readings / 136**

**6.  Beginnings Under the Constitution**
**Toward a New Government / 140**
Advocates of Centralization / **140**
A Divided Convention / **142**
Differences Compromised / **144**
The Constitution of 1787 / **145**
**Adoption and Adaptation / 146**
"Federalists," "Antifederalists" /
**146**
Filling in the Gaps / **148**
**Hamilton Against Jefferson / 150**
Hamilton's Financial Plans / **150**
Enacting the Program / **152**
Rise of Political Parties / **153**
**Asserting National Sovereignty /
154**
Securing the Frontier / **154**
Maintaining Neutrality / **156**
Jay's Treaty / **158**
**Downfall of the Federalists / 159**
Election of 1796 / **159**
Quasi-War With France / **160**
Repression and Protest / **162**
Election of 1800 / **163**
**Selected Readings / 165**

**7.  The Jeffersonian Era**
**Spirit of the Young Republic / 168**

Education and the Professions .
/ **168**
Literature and Music / **171**
Churches and Religion / **172**
**Emerging Industrialism / 175**
Some New Technology / **175**
Transportation and Trade / **177**
City and Country / **179**
**Jefferson in Power / 180**
President and Party Leader / **180**
Conflict With the Courts / **182**
Dollars and Ships / **184**
**Doubling the National Domain / 185**
Jefferson and Napoleon / **185**
The Louisiana Purchase / **187**
Exploring the West / **190**
The Burr Conspiracy / **191**
**Selected Readings / 192**

**8.  Free Seas and Fresh Lands**
**Causes of Conflict / 195**
Neutral Rights / **195**
Impressment / **196**
"Peaceable Coercion" / **198**
Red Men and Redcoats / **200**
The War Hawks / **202**
**The Course of American Art:
Part One / follows 202**
**The War of 1812 / 203**
The Course of Battle / **203**
New England Objections / **206**
The Peace Settlement / **208**
Free Seas Again / **209**
**Postwar Expansion / 210**
Banks, Tariffs, Roads / **210**
"Era of Good Feelings" / **213**
Florida and the Far West / **214**
The Great Migration / **216**
The Panic of 1819 / **220**
**Selected Readings / 221**

**9.  Sectionalism and Patriotism**
**The Canal Age / 224**
The People 1820–1840 / **224**
New Waterways / **226**
The First Railroads / **229**
Broadening of Business / **231**
Workers and Unions / **232**
**Sectional and National Trends / 234**
The Missouri Compromise / **234**

Marshall and the Court / **237**
Latin American Independence / **239**
Origin of the Monroe Doctrine / **240**
**The Two-Party System Revived / 242**
''Corrupt Bargain!'' / **242**
The Second President Adams / **244**
Jackson Vindicated / **246**
**Selected Readings / 247**

10. **Jacksonian Democracy**
**Advent of Mass Politics / 250**
The Common Man's President
/ **250**
More and More Voters / **251**
**''Our *Federal* Union''**
Calhoun: His Theory / **254**
Van Buren to the Fore / **256**
The Webster-Hayne Debate / **257**
State Rights, Indians, Georgia / **259**
South Carolina Interposes / **260**
**Jackson and the Bank / 262**
Biddle's Institution / **263**
The ''Monster'' Destroyed / **265**
**Whigs Against Democrats / 266**
Party Principles / **266**
Three Against One 1836 / **267**
The Panic of 1837 / **268**
The Van Buren Program / **271**
The Log Cabin Campaign / **272**
The Taney Court / **273**
**Selected Readings / 274**

11. **The North and National Unity**
**The Northern Economy / 278**
The Northeast: Business / **278**
The Northeast: Farms and Labor /
**280**
The Northwest / **281**
**Unifying and Divisive Forces / 283**
Rising Immigration / **284**
The Nativist Movement / **285**
Development of Railroads / **285**
The Telegraph / **288**
The New Journalism / **289**
**Persisting Cultural Nationalism**
/ **290**
Democracy and Civilization / **290**
Literature: A Golden Age / **292**
The Flowering of New England /
**293**

Arts and Sciences / **295**
**Selected Readings / 297**

12. **Slavery and the South**
**Freedom's Ferment / 299**
Spirit of Social Reform / **300**
Free Public Schools / **302**
Higher Education / **303**
Model Communities / **304**
Remedying Social Ills / **305**
**The Antislavery Crusade / 308**
The Negro in the North / **308**
The White Abolitionists / **310**
The Campaign for Liberation / **312**
**The Southern Way of Life / 313**
Elements of Southernism / **313**
Gradations of White Society / **314**
King Cotton / **316**
The Mind of the South / **317**
**The ''Peculiar Institution'' / 318**
The Regimen of Slavery / **319**
The Slave's Response / **322**
The Proslavery Reaction / **323**
**Selected Readings / 325**

13. **Fruits of Manifest Destiny**
**The Tyler Administration / 328**
Frustration of the Whigs / **328**
Webster's Diplomacy / **329**
**Polk and Expansion / 330**
Election of 1844 / **330**
**The Course of American Art:**
**Part Two / follows 330**
Partitioning of Oregon / **331**
Annexation of Texas / **332**
Lands Beyond Texas / **334**
War With Mexico / **336**
**A New Sectional Crisis / 339**
Settlers in the Far West / **339**
Wartime and Postwar Politics / **340**
Taylor and the Territories / **341**
The Compromise of 1850 / **343**
**An Uneasy Truce / 345**
Renewed Agitation / **345**
''Young America'' / **346**
**Selected Readings / 349**

14. **The Breaking of the Union**
**New Territorial Controversy / 352**
The Kansas-Nebraska Act / **352**

''Bleeding Kansas'' / **353**
Buchanan and Depression / **355**
The Dred Scott Case / **355**
Deadlock Over Kansas / **356**
Lincoln Against Douglas / **357**
**The Separation of the Sections / 358**
John Brown's Raid / **359**
Election of Lincoln / **360**
Secession of the South / **362**
The Opposing Sides / **365**
**The North Mobilizes / 367**
Economic Measures / **367**
Raising the Union Armies / **369**
Politics and Emancipation / **370**
**The South Mobilizes / 373**
The Confederate Government / **373**
Money and Men / **374**
State Rights in the Confederacy /
**375**
**Selected Readings / 376**

15. **The War of the Rebellion**
**Strategy and Diplomacy / 380**
The Commanders in Chief / **380**
The Role of Sea Power / **381**
Europe and the Disunited States /
**383**
**Campaigns and Battles / 384**
The Opening Clashes  1861 / **385**
The Western Theater  1862 / **385**
The Virginia Front  1862 / **388**
Year of Decision  1863 / **390**
The Ending  1864–1865 / **394**
**The Problem of Peacemaking / 396**
The War's Aftermath / **398**
Reconstruction: The Issues / **399**
Lincoln's Plan / **401**
Johnson and ''Restoration'' / **403**
**Selected Readings / 404**

16. **Reconstructing the Nation**
**Radical Reconstruction / 408**
Congress Takes Over / **408**
The Congressional Plan / **409**
Congressional Supremacy / **410**
The Reconstructed States / **413**
**The Grant Administration / 415**
A Soldier President / **415**
Successes in Foreign Affairs / **417**
The Liberals Defect / **419**

The Greenback Question / **422**
**A Return to White Supremacy / 423**
Southern Republicans Lose / **423**
The Compromise of 1877 / **425**
Discrimination Made Legal / **428**
The ''New South'' / **430**
**Selected Readings / 432**

17. **Industrialization and Urbanization**
**The Rise of Big Business / 436**
Some Basic Inventions / **436**
Steel and Oil / **437**
Other Industries / **441**
Railroad Expansion / **441**
The Transcontinental Lines / **443**
**Growth of Cities / 444**
The City's Lure / **445**
The Newer Immigrants / **445**
The Urban Scene / **447**
**Capitalism and Its Critics / 450**
Self-Made Men / **450**
Survival of the Fittest / **451**
Doubt and Dissent / **452**
Socialists and Single-Taxers / **453**
**Industrial Conflict / 454**
Labor Organizes / **454**
The Knights and the AFL / **455**
The Homestead Strike / **457**
The Pullman Strike / **458**
**Selected Readings / 460**

18. **The End of the Old Frontier**
**The Last West / 464**
Delayed Settlement / **464**
The Miners Arrive / **466**
The Day of the Cowboy / **467**
**The Taming of the Tribes / 470**
The Plains Indians / **470**
The Warriors' Last Stand / **472**
**Decline of the Farmer / 475**
Farming on the Plains / **475**
Changes in Agriculture / **476**
The Farmers' Grievances / **477**
**Knowledge for a New Society / 478**
The Pragmatic Approach / **478**
Toward Universal Schooling / **479**
Expanding Higher Education / **480**
The Publishing Business / **482**
**Culture in the Gilded Age / 483**
Reflections in Literature / **483**

Art and Architecture / **485**
New Uses of Leisure / **486**
**Selected Readings / 489**

19. **The Swell of Agrarian Protest**
   **The Politics of Complacency / 492**
   Republicans and Democrats / **492**
   Hayes and the Patronage / **493**
   The Martyrdom of Garfield / **495**
   Arthur and Reform / **496**
   Return of the Democrats / **496**
   Cleveland Finds an Issue / **498**
   **The Farmers Organize / 500**
   The Grangers and the Railroads /
     **500**
   The Farmers' Alliances / **501**
   The People's Party / **502**
   **A Negative Response / 504**
   Regulating the Railroads / **504**
   Disposing of the Trusts / **505**
   Revising the Tariff / **507**
   **"Battle of the Standards" / 508**
   The Panic of 1893 / **508**
   The Silver Question / **509**
   "A Cross of Gold" / **510**
   Bryan is Beaten / **513**
   McKinley and Prosperity / **514**
   **Selected Readings / 515**

20. **Emergence of a World Power**
   **Imperialist Stirrings / 518**
   The New Manifest Destiny / **518**
   Hemispheric Hegemony / **519**
   Hawaii and Samoa / **520**
   **War With Spain / 522**
   Controversy Over Cuba / **522**
   **The Course of American Art:**
   **Part Three / follows 522**
   "A Splendid Little War" / **524**
   Decision for Imperialism / **526**
   **The Republic as an Empire / 527**
   Governing the Colonies / **528**
   The Open Door / **529**
   A Modern Military System / **530**
   **Life in the Imperial Republic / 531**
   Automobiles and Airplanes / **531**
   Mass Production / **534**
   Social and Cultural Advances / **535**
   High Noon of Monopoly / **538**

The Rich and the Poor / **538**
**Selected Readings / 543**

21. **The Progressive Movement**
   **Local and State Beginnings / 546**
   The Urban Progressives / **546**
   Social Justice / **548**
   Municipal Reform / **550**
   In the Statehouse / **551**
   The Neglected Negro / **552**
   **The Square Deal / 553**
   The First Roosevelt / **553**
   Trust Busting / **556**
   Government and Labor / **558**
   Regulation and Conservation / **560**
   **A Rift in the Republican Ranks / 562**
   Taft and the Tariff / **562**
   T. R. Against Taft / **564**
   **The New Freedom / 567**
   Woodrow Wilson Wins / **567**
   Presidential Leadership / **569**
   The Trusts Again / **570**
   Retreat and Advance / **571**
   **Selected Readings / 572**

22. **The War to End War**
   **Progressivism by the Sword / 576**
   T. R. and World Politics / **576**
   The Iron-Fisted Neighbor / **578**
   Taft and Dollar Diplomacy / **580**
   Wilsonian Intervention / **580**
   Making Mexico Behave / **581**
   **Unneutral Neutrality / 583**
   War in Europe / **583**
   Blockade and Submarine Warfare
     / **583**
   Preparedness—or Pacifism / **587**
   "A Fearful Thing" / **588**
   **War Without Stint / 589**
   Controlling the Economy / **589**
   Delivering the Goods / **592**
   Peace Ideals and War Hatreds / **592**
   The AEF in France / **594**
   **A Frustrated Peace / 597**
   Repudiation at the Polls / **597**
   The Armistice / **598**
   Wilson at Versailles / **599**
   The League Rejected / **601**
   **Selected Readings / 602**

23. **The Illusion of Normalcy**
    **The Postwar Reaction / 606**
      The Red Scare / **606**
      The KKK and the Negro / **608**
      Persisting Progressivism / **609**
    **Republican Prosperity / 610**
      The Harding Tragedy / **610**
      Keeping Cool With Coolidge / **612**
      Favored Business / **613**
      The Decline of Unions / **614**
      No Parity for Farmers / **615**
    **The U.S. and the World / 616**
      Steps Toward Peace / **617**
      Economic Nationalism / **618**
      Immigration Restriction / **618**
    **The Course of American Art:**
    **Part Four / follows 618**
    **Life in the Twenties / 619**
      The Jazz Age / **619**
      Writers, Artists, Musicians / **622**
      A Search for Values / **624**
    **The Great Depression / 625**
      Election of 1928 / **625**
      The Wall Street Crash / **626**
      The Hoover Program / **627**
      Deepening Despair / **630**
    **Selected Readings / 633**

24. **Experimenting With a New Deal**
    **A Change of Leadership / 636**
      The Interregnum of 1932–1933
        / **636**
      F. D. R. Takes Command / **637**
    **Tentative Beginnings / 640**
      Emergency Relief / **640**
      The First AAA / **641**
      The NRA / **643**
      TVA and Conservation / **644**
      Money and Banking / **646**
    **A Shift to the Left / 647**
      The Pressure of Politics / **647**
      The Workers' Welfare / **648**
      Encouraging Unions / **649**
      More for Farmers / **651**
      Less for Big Business / **652**
    **The Limits of Reform / 654**
      Mandate From the People / **654**
      Storm Over the Court / **655**
      Recovery and Recession / **656**
    **Culture in the Depression / 659**

      Expression and Escape / **659**
      Education and the Professions / **661**
    **Selected Readings / 662**

25. **The Abandonment of Isolation**
    **Depression Diplomacy / 666**
      Hoover-Stimson Policies / **667**
      Seeking Friends and Customers
        / **668**
      Legislating Neutrality / **669**
    **World War Again / 670**
      Facing Japan and Germany / **670**
      Aiding the Allies / **671**
      "Intervention" or "Isolation"? / **673**
      Arsenal of Democracy / **675**
      Pearl Harbor / **676**
    **The Battle for Production / 679**
      Mobilizing for Defense / **679**
      Materials for Victory / **680**
      Transporting the Supplies / **682**
      Scientists Against the Axis / **683**
    **The Impact on Civilians / 684**
      Manpower and Womanpower / **684**
      Restraining Labor Unions / **685**
      Price Controls, War Finance / **686**
      Information and Misinformation
        / **689**
    **Selected Readings / 691**

26. **Victory Without Peace**
    **Fighting a Global War / 694**
      The American War Machine / **694**
      On the Defensive  1914–1942
        / **695**
      The Mediterranean Offensive / **696**
      The Liberation of Europe / **698**
      The Pacific Offensive / **700**
      Atomic Triumph Over Japan / **702**
    **Frustrations of Peacemaking / 704**
      The Dangerous Alliance / **704**
      The Yalta Conference / **706**
      The U.N. Organization / **707**
      A Fourth Term for F. D. R. / **708**
      Truman Takes Over / **710**
    **Postwar Readjustments / 712**
      Military Reorganization / **712**
      Reconversion and Inflation / **713**
      "Had Enough?" / **715**
      Truman Beats Dewey / **716**
    **Selected Readings / 718**

27. **A Balance of Terror**
   **Start of the Cold War  /  722**
      Containment of Communism  /  **722**
      The North Atlantic Alliance  /  **723**
      China Turns Red  /  **725**
      Defending South Korea  /  **727**
      Retreat From North Korea  /  **728**
   **The Politics of Fright  /  730**
      Hysterical Loyalty  /  **730**
      A Troubled Electorate  /  **732**
      Eisenhower Elected  /  **733**
   **New Hands at the Helm  /  735**
      A Korean Armistice  /  **735**
      "Massive Retaliation"  /  **736**
      China and IndoChina  /  **737**
      Our German Ally  /  **738**
      The Geneva Spirit  /  **739**
      Menace in the Middle East  /  **740**
   **The Communists Gain  /  741**
      The Rocket Race  /  **741**
      Friendly Overtures Fail  /  **745**
      Disgruntled Neighbors  /  **747**
   **Selected Readings  /  749**

28. **The Politics of Plenty**
   **The "Middle of the Road"  /  752**
      Businessmen in Government  /  **752**
      "Eisenhower Prosperity"  /  **752**
      An End to McCarthyism  /  **754**
      Desegregation Begins  /  **755**
      A Second Term for Ike  /  **757**
   **The "New Frontier"  /  759**
      Kennedy Over Nixon  /  **759**
      The Kennedy Program  /  **761**
      "Let Us Continue"  /  **763**
      Commitment to Equal Rights  /  **766**
      One Man, One Vote  /  **767**
   **The "Great Society"  /  768**
      Johnson Thrashes Goldwater  /  **768**
      The Johnson Program  /  **770**
      War on Poverty  /  **771**
      Black Power  /  **772**
      Resort to Riot  /  **774**
   **Selected Readings  /  776**

29. **National Security in the 1960s**
   **The Kennedy Approach  /  780**
      Continuing Foreign Aid  /  **780**
      Reshaping Defense Policies  /  **782**
   **Perilous Encounters  /  783**
      Heightening Tension  /  **783**
      Confrontation Over Cuba  /  **785**
      Loosening of Alliances  /  **787**
   **Johnson's Dilemmas  /  788**
      Dominican Intervention  /  **789**
      Involvement in Vietnam  /  **790**
      Escalating the War  /  **792**
      Deescalation Begins  /  **794**
   **Nixon's Inheritance  /  795**
      Election of 1968  /  **795**
      Appeal for Consensus  /  **799**
      Revising the Constitution  /  **799**
      The General Welfare  /  **800**
      A Doomsday Game  /  **802**
      A Way Out of Vietnam?  /  **803**
   **Selected Readings  /  805**

30. **Entering the Space Age**
   **The Crowding Country  /  808**
      Levels of Living  /  **808**
      The Rise of the Megalopolis  /  **810**
      Urban Renewal and Reform  /  **812**
      Transportation  /  **814**
   **Leisure and Learning  /  815**
      Television  /  **816**
      Music  /  **816**
      Art and Architecture  /  **818**
      Writing  /  **819**
      Youth and Education  /  **820**
   **The Promise of Technology  /  821**
      Innovations and Resources  /  **821**
      Scientific Research  /  **824**
      The Space Race Begins  /  **825**
      To the Moon and Beyond  /  **826**
   **Selected Readings  /  827**

**Appendices**
The Declaration of Independence  /  **829**
The Constitution of the United States
   of America  /  **833**
Sovereigns of England and
   Great Britain, 1485–1820  /  **849**
Admission of States to the Union  /  **850**
Presidential Elections  /  **851**
Presidents, Vice Presidents,
   and Cabinet Members  /  **856**
Chief Justices of the United States  /  **862**
Speakers of the House of Representatives  /  **862**
Population of the United States  /  **864**
**General Bibliography  /  869**
**Index  /  follows 874**

# Illustrations

Housing the First Settlers / **2**

Pilgrims Going to Church / **2**

Tenochtitlán—The Aztec Capital / **10**

Florida Indians / **20**

Arrival at Roanoke / **22**

Tobacco Preparation: Eighteenth Century / **41**

A City in the Wilderness / **44**

Penn's Treaty With the Indians / **47**

*Detail* / **28**

The John Ward House / **54**

The John Ward House: Kitchen / **54**

An Eighteenth-Century Indenture / **57**

Charleston in 1740 / **67**

A Slave Coffle / **70**

Westover / **72**

Christ Church, Cambridge, Massachusetts / **74**

Harvard College, About 1740 / **79**

The Need for Colonial Unity / **85**

The Taking of Quebec / **92**

The Bloody Massacre / **103**

*Detail* / **82**

Taking the Pledge / **104**

The Battle of Lexington / **107**

*Common Sense* / **112**

The Continental Army at Valley Forge / **123**

*Detail* / **110**

John Paul Jones / **126**

The Peacemakers of 1783 / **128**

The Constitutional Convention / **138**

A Federalist Cartoon / **147**

Federal Hall, New York / **155**

The First Bank of the United States / **155**

John Adams / **160**

Building the Navy / **162**

Thomas Jefferson / **166**

A School in Session About 1800 / **169**

Brooklyn, New York, in the Early 1800s / **170**

A Camp Meeting / **173**

Whitney's Gun Factory / **176**

Washington City / **180**

The Lewis and Clark Expedition / **190**

Impressment / **194**

Seaman's Protection Paper / **197**

Victory at Sea / **204**

James Monroe / **214**

From Forest to Farm / **218**

Fourth of July / **222**

New York Port 1828 / **226**

The Erie Canal / **227**

Cotton Mills, Lowell, Massachusetts / **233**

John Quincy Adams / **244**

King Andrew the First / **248**

Webster Replying to Hayne / **258**

The Second Bank of the United States / **263**

The Bank Cartooned 1833 / **264**

The Panic of 1837 / **270**

Whig Broadside of 1840 / **272**

Two Views of Immigration / **276**

St. Louis in the 1850s / **282**

McCormick and the Evolution of Farm Machinery / **283**

Niagara Suspension Bridge / **287**

Dancing the Quadrille / **290**

Walt Whitman / **293**

Plantation Life on the Mississippi / **298**

A Lyceum Lecture / **304**

The "Cold Water" Pledge / **306**

The Bloomer Costume / **307**

Negro Leader / **310**

Slave Scenes / **321**

Westward Movement / **326**

Taylor at Buena Vista / **338**

Mormon Leader / **340**

Washing for Gold / **342**

The Technique of Ostend / **348**

A Union Army Camp / **350**

A Recruiting Poster for Negro Soldiers / **350**

Violence in Congress / **354**

Lincoln and Douglas in Debate / **357**

The Hanging of John Brown / **359**

A Northern View of Emancipation / **371**

The North's Greatest General / **378**

The South's Greatest General / **378**

Battle of Ironclads / **382**

Union Dead at Gettysburg / **389**

The Impact of the War on the South / **397**

Andrew Johnson / **403**

A Damaging Victory / **406**

The Impeachment of Andrew Johnson / **412**

Hiram R. Revels / **414**

The "Strong" Government / **416**

Hamilton Fish / **419**

Grant Wants to Go to the Horse Races / **420**

The Ku Klux Klan: A Southern View / **423**

The Ku Klux Klan: A Northern View / **424**

Tenement Street / **434**

An Early Typewriter / **436**

Brooklyn Bridge / **440**

New York's Elevated Railroad / **449**

The Modern Robber Barons / **452**

The Haymarket Tragedy / **457**

The Pullman Strike / **459**

Mining in Colorado / **462**

A Sod House on the Plains / **466**

The Slaughter of the Buffalo / **471**

Apache Warrior / **472**

Threshing Wheat on the Great Plains / **476**

Mark Twain With His Friends / **484**

An Early Football Game / **487**

A Party of Patches / **490**

The Stalwart Boss of the Republicans / **493**

President and Mrs. Hayes / **494**

Blaine and Gould / **497**

Grover Cleveland / **498**

Sockless Jerry Simpson / **504**

The Cross of Gold / **511**

The Orator of the Silver Crusade / **512**

The Victors of San Juan Hill / **516**

Wreck of the *Maine* / **523**

McKinley Measures Uncle Sam for a New Suit / **528**

Herald Square   1910 / **532**

The Wright Brothers' First Flight / **533**

The Ford Assembly Line / **534**

The Duryea Car / **536**

Child at Spindles / **539**

"The Steerage" by Stieglitz / **541**

Suffragettes in Action / **544**

Chicago's Ghetto / **549**

Slum Dwellers, About 1910 / **549**

President Roosevelt in Yosemite / **554**

Poor People Waiting for Coal / **559**

La Follette Campaigning in Wisconsin / **561**

"New Wine in Old Bottles" / **564**

"Revising the Tariff Downward (?)" / **565**

Woodrow Wilson and Champ Clark / **567**

World War I Recruiting Poster / **574**

"Here No One Dares Lay a Hand but Myself" / **578**

The *Lusitania* Sailing From New York City / **586**

Fourth Liberty Loan Parade / **590**

Captain Edward Rickenbacker / **595**

The Big Four in Paris / **600**

"Lindbergh Speeds Across North Atlantic" / **604**

Sacco and Vanzetti Being Taken Into Court / **607**

Ku Klux Klan Parading in Washington, D.C. / **608**

The Seized Tug *Geronimo* / **620**

The Sinclair Lewises Go Camping / **622**

Hoover Dam / **629**

Shacks of the Unemployed / **631**

An Apple Seller in New York City / **631**

The NRA Eagle / **634**

The Ride to Roosevelt's Inauguration / **638**

A Sharecropper's Family   1936 / **642**

An NLRB Election   1941 / **649**

Dust Storm, Oklahoma / **652**

"American Gothic" by Wood / **660**

"A Good Time to Look at Them" / **664**

Secretary of State Cordell Hull / **668**

The U.S.S. *Shaw* Exploding / **678**

The Mushrooming of War Plants / **681**

Waiting to Purchase Meat / **687**

Japanese-Americans Being Evacuated From the Pacific Coast / **690**

The Mushroom Cloud Over Nagasaki / **692**

The Invasion of Normandy / **698**

Hiroshima, Japan   1945 / **703**

Stalin, Roosevelt, and Churchill at Teheran / **705**

Stalin and Truman at Potsdam / **711**

President Harry S Truman / **717**

U.S. Fighting Chinese Communists / **720**
U.S.S. *New Jersey* in Korean War / **720**
The Berlin Airlift / **725**
Eisenhower Versus Taft / **733**
Dulles and Eisenhower / **735**
Launching the First American Satellite / **744**
Broadcasting a VOA Program / **746**
President John F. Kennedy / **750**
Desegregation in Washington, D.C. / **755**
Two Presidential Candidates Debate / **760**
The March on Washington / **763**
President Johnson Takes the Oath of
    Office / **764**
Voter Registration, Selma, Alabama / **766**
Martin Luther King / **775**
Peace March   1968 / **778**
A Cuban Ballistic Missile Launch Site / **786**
Training Vietnamese Troops / **791**
The 1968 Democratic Contenders / **796**
President Nixon / **798**
". . . One Giant Leap for Mankind" / **806**
Two Kitchens / **811**
Air Pollution in New York / **814**
The Robert Joffrey Ballet / **817**

# Maps

Early Voyages of Discovery / **5**
The Lands That Columbus Saw on His
    Four Voyages / **7**
Explorations of Sixteenth-Century America
    / **9**
New England   1660 / **33**
The Carolinas and Georgia / **43**
The Middle Colonies in the Seventeenth
    Century / **45**
Distribution of Major Immigrant Groups in
    Colonial America / **59**
Regional Economic Specialization and Foreign
    Markets in Colonial America / **66**
Overseas Trades of Colonial America / **68**
The French in America / **87**
North America in 1700 / **90**
North America After 1713 / **90**
North America After 1763 / **91**
English Mainland Colonies / **96**

The War in the North   1775 / **120**
Washington's Retreat   1776 / **121**
British Campaigns   1777 / **122**
Road to Yorktown   1780–1781 / **125**
State Claims to Western Lands   1781
    / **132**
Land Survey Under the Ordinance of 1785
    / **133**
Election of 1800 / **164**
The United States at the Time of the
    Louisiana Purchase / **188**
Election of 1812 / **202**
War of 1812 / **207**
The National Road / **212**
Boundary Settlements   1818–1819 / **216**
Canals in the Northeast   1840 / **228**
The Missouri Compromise   1820–1821
    / **235**
Election of 1824 / **243**
Election of 1828 / **246**
Election of 1836 / **268**
Centers of Population   1790–1860 / **279**
Railroads in Operation   1850;
    Railroad Construction   1850–1860
    / **286**
Major Centers of Cotton Production in the
    Antebellum South / **317**
American Expansion in Oregon / **332**
Western Trails / **334**
American Expansion Into the Southwest
    / **335**
The Mexican War   1846–1848 / **337**
Slave and Free Territory   1850 / **346**
Election of 1860 / **362**
The Process of Secession / **363**
The War in the West   1861–1862 / **386**
Vicksburg Campaign   1863 / **391**
Gettysburg Campaign   1863 / **393**
Virginia Campaigns   1864–1865 / **394**
Sherman's March Through the Confederacy
    1864–1865 / **395**
Railroads in Operation   1870;
    Railroad Construction
    1870–1890 / **442**
The Last Frontier / **464**
Mining Towns / **467**
The Cattle Kingdom / **469**
Election of 1896 / **513**
The Spanish-American War: Pacific Front
    / **525**

The Spanish-American War: Caribbean
  Front / **526**
Election of 1904 / **556**
Election of 1908 / **563**
Election of 1912 / **568**
The U.S. in Mexico  1914–1917 / **581**
Election of 1916 / **588**
Major German Offensives  1918 / **596**
U.S. Participation in Allied Offensives  1918
  / **597**
Election of 1920 / **611**
Election of 1924 / **613**
Farm Tenancy: 1910 and 1930 / **616**
Election of 1928 / **626**
Election of 1932 / **636**
The Tennessee Valley Authority / **645**
Election of 1936 / **654**
Election of 1940 / **674**
The North African and Sicilian Campaigns
  / **697**
The Normandy Landings / **699**
The War in the Pacific / **701**
Election of 1944 / **709**
Election of 1948 / **718**
Divided Germany and Austria / **724**
The Korean War  1950–1953 / **728**
Election of 1952 / **734**
Election of 1956 / **758**
Election of 1960 / **761**
Election of 1964 / **769**
The Range of Cuban-Based Soviet Missiles
  / **785**
Vietnam / **793**
Election of 1968 / **797**
Population Density in the United States  1900
  and 1960 / **809**

# Charts

Estimated Colonial Population Growth
  (English Mainland Colonies)  1620–1780
  / **61**
Exports to and Imports From England
  by American Colonies  1763–1776
  / **100**
Ratification of the Constitution / **146**

Balance of Trade  1790–1820 / **211**
Population Growth  1620–1840 / **224**
Business Activity  1790–1839 / **269**
Slaveholders in 1860 / **314**
Comparison of North and South  1860
  / **366**
Protective Tariff Levels  1860–1900 / **368**
Deaths in the Civil War and Other Wars
  / **369**
Business Activity  1840–1879 / **430**
Business Activity  1880–1920 / **438**
Population Growth  1840–1900 / **446**
Effect of the Quota Acts on Immigration
  / **619**
Prices of Common Stocks 1920–1937
  / **627**
Unemployment  1929–1942 / **640**
The National Debt  1910–1968 / **688**
U.S. Armed Forces  1898–1968 / **694**
Organized Labor  1900–1966 / **714**
U.S. Foreign Aid  1949–1967 / **780**
Business Activity  1921–1966 / **822**

# Where Historians Disagree

The American Revolution / **119**
Background of the Constitution / **141**
Jacksonian Democracy / **255**
The Abolitionists / **309**
The Causes of the Civil War / **361**
The Nature of Reconstruction / **411**
The Motivation and Methods of Business
  / **439**
The Meaning of Populism / **503**
The Nature of Progressivism / **547**
The Causes of American Entrance Into
  World War I / **585**
The Nature of the New Deal / **657**
The Background of Pearl Harbor / **677**
Origins of the Cold War / **743**

# American History: A Survey

# Chapter 1
# From
# the Old World
# to the New

The history of the United States from its colonial beginnings is fairly short. It covers a period of less than 400 years, a period that can be spanned by the overlapping lifetimes of a mere half-dozen men. Yet the roots of American civilization go deep into the human past. These roots are to be traced mostly to the Old World, not the New.

There is no evidence that human life originated in the New World. No bones or fossils of the apelike ancestors of man, such as those unearthed on other continents, have ever been found in either North or South America. The earliest remains of humanity so far discovered here are, at the most, only about 25,000 years old.

The American continents were peopled as a result of two long-continuing immigration movements, the first from Asia, the second from Europe and Africa. Probably the first began thousands of years ago when Siberian tribes, in search of new hunting grounds or of refuge from pursuing enemies, crossed over the Bering Strait to Alaska. Crossings by Asians, a few at a time, went on for centuries, then finally ceased. From Alaska the new-comers and their descendants fanned out to populate both the continents. By 1492 there were perhaps a million people north of Mexico, 3 million in Mexico and Central America, and 6 million (some estimates run much higher) in South America.

The Stone Age forefathers of these people brought little with them from Asia. Over the centuries the first Americans developed for themselves such tools and customs as they possessed when the Europeans arrived. Cultures ranged all the way from those of primitive, acorn-gathering tribes to that of the Maya, who by A.D. 1000 had created in Central America one of the most brilliant civilizations then existing anywhere in the world. Even the most complex of the aboriginal cultures, however, remained limited in comparison with the civilization that was developing in Europe. Though the Mayas and others had forms of picture writing, none of the American Indians had a true alphabet and— strange to say—none had any conception of the wheel. They had little chance to show

---

## Housing the First Settlers

When the English first landed at Jamestown, Plymouth, and elsewhere in America, they had neither time nor facilities to build substantial frame or brick houses. Nor were these colonists familiar with the log cabin that later became typical of the American frontier. So they constructed temporary shelters of various kinds, including wigwams patterned after those of the Indians and cottages similar to those of some of the poorer folk in England. The Pioneer Village at Salem, Massachusetts, is a reconstruction of Salem village as it may have looked during its earliest years. The photograph shows, at the left, one of the reconstructed Salem cottages with a dirt floor, a thatched roof, and a chimney made of small logs daubed with plaster. Such houses were far from fireproof. In 1626,

as a fire-prevention measure, Plymouth Colony adopted a law prohibiting thatched roofs. (Top left, Essex Institute, Salem, Mass.)

## Pilgrims Going to Church

This picture, often reproduced, was at one time familiar to practically every schoolchild in the United States. It was painted, about 1870, by George Henry Broughton, who had been born in England, had grown up in Albany, New York, and had studied art in England and France. He was particularly fond of scenes of Puritan life, picturesque costumes, and winter landscapes. This painting combines all three. (Bottom left, Library of Congress) whether they would ever have invented such things, once the Europeans had brought in a far superior technology.

The second peopling of the Americas began with the expansion of Europe at the end of the medieval and the start of the modern period. The history of the United States is an extension of European and particularly English history. The new Americans had much to learn from those already here, and they were to be influenced a good deal by the wilderness environment they found, but their way of life was to be based mainly on the European traditions they brought with them.

## THE EPOCH OF DISCOVERY

Between the time when those first Siberian tribesmen descried the headlands of Alaska and the time thousands of years later when Christopher Columbus sighted a West Indian island, no doubt other wanderers from abroad—certainly from Scandinavia and possibly from Egypt and elsewhere—caught at least a glimpse of some part of America. If so, these "discoveries" did not lead to any general knowledge that such a place existed, and still less to any systematic effort to explore it. The rest of the world was not yet ready for such an enterprise. The great age of exploration had to wait for developments in Europe.

### The Quickening of Europe

During the Middle Ages (roughly from A.D. 500 to A.D. 1500) the civilization of Western Europe was in many ways inferior to that of ancient Greece or Rome. After Germanic barbarians had overrun the Roman Empire, the dream of Roman peace and unity lingered on. The countries of medieval Europe were thought to form a single whole, under the spiritual authority of the Roman Catholic Church and the political authority of what was called the Holy Roman Empire. But kings often asserted power independently of the emperor, and nobles asserted power independently of the kings. Ordinary people, the serfs, tied by custom to the soil, worked the fields while their lords engaged in desultory warfare and chivalric games. Merchants and craftsmen were handicapped by the disorders that prevailed much of the time. Except within the Church, art and learning had few practitioners, and it was left to the monasteries to keep alive the memory of past greatness.

Medieval Europe was backward even by comparison with certain other areas of the contemporary world. Though India and China, like the Roman Empire, had suffered from invasion and conquest, they had fallen upon no "dark age" comparable to that of Europe. The land of the Moslems, extending around the southern rim of the Mediterranean and on to the east of it, supported science, industry, and commerce such as no country of Christian Europe could match. Moslem scholars were familiar with classical learning and far surpassed it in such fields as mathematics, with their Arabic numerals and their decimal system (based on a concept of early India). The wonders of the Far East dazzled the few Europeans who, like the Venetian merchant Marco Polo, got a chance to visit them, and the wonders of the Near East amazed the crusading knights who set out to recover the Holy Land from the infidels.

Forces leading to the awakening of Europe and the discovery of America were set in motion around A.D. 1000 by an outpouring of the Norsemen from Denmark, Norway, and Sweden. These Vikings made conquests as far east as Russia, as far south as France and the British Isles, and as far west as Iceland and Greenland. Two of them, Biarni Heriulfson and Leif Ericson, on separate voyages, even touched upon the coast of North America, but later attempts at colonization failed, and neither of these men is generally considered the effective discoverer of the New World. Indirectly, however, the Norse did contribute to the subsequent discovery or rediscovery by Columbus. They pioneered in the construction of ocean-going ships, stimulated trade over the area of their widespread conquests, and infused into the life of Europe much of their own energy and daring. Their descendants in France, the Normans

**GREENLAND**
**ICELAND**
**NEWFOUNDLAND**
**ENGLAND EUROPE**
**NORTH AMERICA**
**FRANCE**
**PORTUGAL**
**SPAIN**
Cabot 1497-1498
Drake 1577-1580
Columbus 1492
**ASIA**
**CHINA**
**CUBA** **BAHAMAS**
**HISPANIOLA**
**CAPE VERDE I.**
Vespucius 1499
**INDIA**
**AFRICA**
**PHILIPPINES**
**PACIFIC OCEAN**
Magellan 1519-1522
**SOUTH AMERICA**
Equator
**INDIAN OCEAN**
**SPICE I.**
**PACIFIC OCEAN**
Da Gama 1497-1498
**BRAZIL**
Cabral 1500
Drake 1577-1580
Magellan 1519-1522
**AUSTRALIA**
Spain Portugal
DEMARCATION LINE OF 1493
**ATLANTIC OCEAN**

← **English**
←-- **Spanish**
←-- **Portuguese**
☐ **World as Known to Europeans 1492**

## Early Voyages of Discovery

(who set up kingdoms in England, Italy and Sicily, and northern Africa), provided outstanding leadership in the Crusades.

The Crusades further encouraged shipbuilding and commerce. In Syria and Egypt the Crusaders got acquainted with a number of exotic goods—spices, perfumes, drugs, silks, china, glassware, gems—which were brought by land and by sea all the way from the Orient. In the Near East some Europeans, especially the Italians, set up trading posts where they exchanged for Oriental commodities the gold, silver, copper, lead, and tin from the mines of Western Europe. These traders sent their imports on to such wholesaling centers as Pisa, Genoa, and Venice, which distributed the goods among merchants from other towns and ultimately among the consumers, remote from the original sources of supply in China, India, or the "Spice Islands" of the East Indies.

This commerce fostered the growth of towns and gave a new importance to town life in Europe. The townsmen or bourgeoisie came to form a substantial "middle" class between the nobles and the clergy above them and the serfs below. They accumulated capital in larger and larger amounts, making possible trading ventures of increasing size and profit. Desiring peace and security, such as would be good for business, the merchants breathed a spirit quite out of harmony with feudalism and its disorders. In the contests between kings and turbulent nobles, the bourgeoisie came to the support of the kings and thus aided in the rise of centralized national governments.

Increased wealth, leisure, and security made possible a greater cultivation of the things of the mind and prepared the way for the Renaissance in Europe. The Renaissance was marked by a changing outlook on life. Formerly, preoccupied with their own sinfulness and weakness, men had viewed their earthly lives as contemptible and had tried to concentrate their thoughts upon eternity. Now, with increasing human self-confidence, they began to show more and more interest in the world about them. Formerly they had relied for their ideas mostly on the authority of the Bible and the works of Aristotle as expounded by the churchmen. Now many became willing to observe, experiment, and test truths for themselves. This changing attitude was involved both in the renewed study of Greek and Roman classics and in the creation of vernacular literatures. It was related also to the multiplication of efforts to control the natural environment through applied science and technology rather than through prayer or magic.

Among the inventions coming into use after the twelfth century were guns and gunpowder, bellows and blast furnaces, various machines powered by water or wind, movable type and the printing press, the mechanical clock, improvements in ship design and construction, and several devices intended to aid the art of navigation. The compass, at first only a needle magnetized with lodestone and floated in water, told the navigator his direction. He could obtain his latitude by sighting a fixed star with the quadrant, the cross staff, or the astrolabe. Theoretically he could calculate his longitude by means of the clock, but in actual practice this was not accurate enough to help him much (until the invention of the chronometer in the eighteenth century). So he continued to follow the coasts when feasible, and when he ventured out of sight of land he proceeded (as Columbus did) mainly by dead reckoning, setting his course by the compass, and finding his position by elapsed time and estimated speed.

Geographical knowledge was still, as in ancient times, a mixture of fable and fact, even though map making had improved remarkably. Mariners, foremost among them the Italians, carefully charted the shorelines along which they sailed, until the coastal areas of almost all the known world had been accurately mapped. On the high seas away from the familiar routes, however, everything remained a matter of speculation. Practical sailors and educated men believed that the earth was a sphere, but many of them underestimated its size. The first globe ever made, the work of a Nuremberg cartographer in 1492, showed an unbroken ocean stretching westward from Europe around to Asia and occupying only about a third of the earth's surface.

On the European edge of this sea of darkness stood the rising nation-states of England, France, Holland, Portugal, and Spain, each with a strong government and a consciousness of national unity. These countries, while the most powerful in Europe, were also the most distant from the rich sources of the Oriental trade. In the process of this trade, Italian and Arab mer-

chants added their profits and commissions, and various rulers added their tolls and taxes, so that by the time Oriental wares reached the Atlantic nations the price was outrageously high, and excessive amounts of money were drained away to the east. If the middlemen somehow could be by-passed, the Western merchants could gain larger profits for themselves and the Western nations could end the troublesome loss of specie. Here was an adequate motive for finding new routes, entirely by sea, that could be controlled from home. The search for new approaches to the East led to the discovery of new lands in the West, in that presumably empty ocean that lay at the back of Europe.

## Westward to the East

Without the wealth of the merchants and the organizing power of the nation-states, the glorious age of exploration would have been unthinkable. But it would also have been inconceivable without patriotic and religious zeal, skillful seamanship, bold imagination, and courageous leadership.

Portugal early took the lead as an exploring nation. Its maritime supremacy owed a great deal to one man, Prince Henry the Navigator, who devoted his life to nautical studies and to the promotion of exploration. Concentrating upon the western coast of Africa, with the visionary aim of establishing a Christian empire to aid in war against the Moors, and with the more practical object of finding gold, Prince Henry sent out expedition after expedition, some of his mariners going as far south as Cape Verde. After his death in 1460 his work was carried on by intrepid explorers advancing still farther south. At last, in 1486, Bartholomeu Diaz went clear around the southern tip of the continent, and in 1497–1498 Vasco da Gama proceeded all the way to India. In 1500 the next fleet bound for India, that of Pedro Cabral, was blown off its southward course and happened upon the coast of Brazil. So America would have been discovered within a decade even if Columbus had never made his famous voyage of 1492.

Christopher Columbus, who was born and reared in Genoa, got most of his seafaring knowledge and experience in the service of the Portuguese. He was not the first man to think of reaching the East by sailing west, but he was the first to do something about it. Though an industrious student of geography, he was convinced of the feasibility of his plan as a result of errors rather than special insight. From his reading of Marco Polo's wondrous travel book, from his correspondence with the Florentine geographer Toscanelli, and from other studies and his own calculations, he gathered that the world was smaller than it actually is and that the Asian continent extended farther eastward than it actually does. So he concluded that the western ocean was narrow enough to be crossed on a relatively brief voyage. But he failed to convince the King of Portugal, and as the Portuguese progressed with their own route to the East around Africa, they completely lost interest in the idea of a westward crossing.

Columbus then turned from Portugal to Spain. Though not a maritime people like the Portuguese, the Spaniards were proud, energetic, and zealous. They were being unified under the strongest monarchy in Europe after the marriage of Ferdinand of Aragon and Isabella of Castile. To Queen Isabella the importunate Columbus appealed for money, men, and ships with which to carry out his project and thereby extend the sway of Christianity and the power and glory of Spain. For several years the Queen withheld her aid, partly because her advisers doubted Columbus' theories and partly because she was busy with Christianizing and conquering Spain itself. In 1492, with the fall of the Moorish stronghold of Granada, the Mohammedans were practically eliminated from Spanish soil, and during that same year the Jews who rejected conversion were forced to leave the country. At last Isabella granted Columbus his request.

On his first voyage, with the *Pinta*, the *Niña*, and the *Santa Maria* and with ninety men, Columbus steered as straight as he could for Japan. He thought he had arrived there when, ten weeks after embarking, he landed on Watling Island in the Bahamas, and he thought he had reached the China coast when he pushed on to

**The Lands That Columbus Saw on His Four Voyages**

Cuba. He returned to Spain with a few natives —he called them "Indians"—but he brought no news of the great Khan's court in China and no samples of the famous wealth of the Indies. The next year, with a much larger expedition, he discovered other islands and left a colony on one of them, Hispaniola. On a third voyage, in 1498, cruising along the northern coast of South America, he passed the mouth of the Orinoco River and surmised that such a large fresh-water stream must emerge from a continent, one separate from Asia. On his last voyage, in 1502, he tried to sail around the northwestern end of the continent so as to find the rich and civilized part of the Indies, but he was blocked by the Isthmus of Panama and succeeded only in exploring the Caribbean coast of Central America. He died still thinking he had been in at least the fringes of the Far East.

At first a hero, then a man in disgrace, Columbus was not even honored in the naming of the land he had discovered. Disregarding Columbus' promised monopoly, Spain itself licensed numerous explorers after him, and rival governments sent out expeditions of their own. The Portuguese, who claimed the whole region of his discoveries, promptly dispatched a fleet to the scene (1501). A Florentine merchant, Americus Vespucius, who was aboard, afterward wrote partly fictitious letters describing several visits to the new continent, and a German geographer, Martin Waldseemüller, published one of the letters with the suggestion that the land be named for Americus. The name stuck.

Yet Columbus, for all his misconceptions, deserved the fame that ultimately came to him. He dispelled the terrors of the unknown ocean and led the way to the New World. The explorers of many nations who followed him were only carrying on the work he had begun. Just as he had done on his final voyage, they concentrated their efforts mainly on the search for a water passage that would lead through or around the new lands and on to the riches of the Far East. They never found the kind of passage they sought (because it did not exist until 1914, when the Panama Canal was opened), but they revealed the outlines of both continents and made known the vastness of the territory available for European use.

Spain, turning to the sea as a result of Columbus' initiative, replaced Portugal as the foremost exploring nation. Vasco de Balboa fought his way across the Isthmus of Panama (1513) and gazed upon the great ocean that separated America from China and the Indies. Seeking access to that ocean, Ferdinand Magellan, a Portuguese in Spanish employ, found the strait that now bears his name at the southern end of South America, struggled through the stormy narrows and into the ocean, so calm by contrast that he christened it the Pacific, then proceeded to the Philippines. There Magellan himself fell at the hands of natives, but his expedition went on to complete the first circumnavigation of the globe (1519–1522). By 1550 the Spaniards had explored the coasts of North America as far north as Oregon and Labrador.

England followed Spain as a sponsor of voyages westward in search of the East. John Cabot, Genoa-born like Columbus and inspired by the latter's unsuccessful efforts to reach the Orient, sailed twice to the northeastern coast of North America under the auspices of King Henry VII, the first time in 1497. Columbus never laid eyes upon the North American continent; Cabot was the first to leave a record of having viewed it, and he may therefore be considered its effective discoverer. Much later, after failing to find a northeast passage around Europe, Englishmen began to look for a northwest passage around North America. Martin Frobisher made three trips, the last one in 1578, and discovered Frobisher's Bay, Baffin's Land, and the Eskimos, but not the strait he was after. Year after year, other Englishmen kept up the search.

Meanwhile, under Francis I, the government of France promoted a series of expeditions to the New World. In 1523–1524 Giovanni Verrazano, a Florentine navigator, followed the shore northward from North Carolina in quest of an opening to Asia for France. Between 1534 and 1541 Jacques Cartier and Jean François Roberval, on separate voyages, tried to find the much-sought passage by pushing up the St. Lawrence River. The Dutch government, a latecomer, commissioned the Englishman Henry Hudson to find an all-Dutch route to Asia. He was looking for it when, in 1609, he entered the river that afterward was named for him. Though much

**Explorations of Sixteenth-Century America**

Map labels:

BAFFIN ISLAND

HUDSON BAY

LABRADOR

NEWFOUNDLAND

NORTH AMERICA

St. Lawrence R.

Drake's Bay

Missouri R.

Mississippi R.

Santa Fe 1609

Arkansas R.

Ohio R.

Red R.

ATLANTIC OCEAN

Rio Grande

St. Augustine 1565

GULF OF MEXICO

FLORIDA

Havana 1515

AZTECS

Tenochtitlán (Mexico City)

Vera Cruz

MAYAS

NEW SPAIN

Santiago 1515

Santo Domingo

San Juan 1509

CARIBBEAN SEA

Panama 1519

Orinoco R.

PACIFIC OCEAN

SOUTH AMERICA

Amazon R.

Tumbes

INCAS

**French Explorers**
◄●●●● Verrazano 1524
◄━ ━ Cartier 1534-1535

**Spanish Explorers**
◄●●●● Balboa 1513
◄━━━ Ponce De León 1513
◄━━━ Cortés 1519
◄━ ━ Pizarro 1531-1533
◄━ ━ De Soto 1539-1542
◄━ ━ Coronado 1540-1542

**English Explorers**
◄━━━ Frobisher 1576-1578
◄━ ━ Drake 1577-1580
◄● ● ● Hawkins 1580
◄●●●● Gilbert 1583

valuable information came from all this activity by men of several nationalities sailing under diverse flags, often not their own, the precise relationship of the Asian and North American continents remained something of a mystery until 1728, when Vitus Bering, a Dane in Russian employ, voyaged through the strait that separates the two.

## THE COLONIZING IMPULSE

While remaining an obstacle to those preoccupied with routes to the East, the New World became for others a goal in itself, a possible source of wealth rivaling and even surpassing the original Indies. The Spaniards soon were building themselves an American empire. On the basis of Columbus' discoveries and a papal decree, they claimed the whole of the New World, except for a chunk of it (Brazil) which they left to the Portuguese. Other nations waited a century or more to grow into successful colonizing powers. During this time the English (and the French as well) were developing the national strength and unity that would enable them to compete with Spain. Finally the English and others challenged the Spanish monopoly at least in North America.

## The Spanish Colonies

Awaiting the Spaniards were the riches of the native Aztec and Inca empires. The Aztecs were the heirs of Mayan civilization, which had reached its height at about A.D. 1000. In Central America the Mayas had built elaborately carved stone temples and pyramids, bred corn from a kind of wild grass, devised an accurate calendar from astronomical observations, and invented a number system similar to the Arabic and su-

### Tenochtitlan—The Aztec Capital

This is a model reconstructing the central square. Tenochtitlán, located on the site of the present Mexico City, had a population of about 100,000 in 1502 when the last of the emperors, Montezuma II, began his reign. His empire, covering much of central and southern Mexico, was a rather loose association of city-states from which he collected heavy tribute. The Aztecs developed a complex and magnificent civilization, made up largely of elements adapted from the Mayas and other neighboring peoples. In Tenochtitlán there were surgeons and physicians who are believed to have been as skillful as the best in contemporary Europe, and there were hospitals and nurses. There were also human sacrifices. To appease the Aztec gods, young men and women captives were slaughtered on top of the pyramids. These structures, like those of the Mayas, were comparable in size to the pyramids of ancient Egypt but were used as temples rather than burial monuments. When Hernando Cortés, the Spanish conqueror of Mexico, entered Tenochtitlán in 1519, he found in the central square a rack which held the skulls of about 100,000 sacrificial victims. (Courtesy of The American Museum of Natural History) perior to the Roman. After conquering the Mayas and other, less highly civilized peoples, the Aztecs ruled them all through their emperor, whose capital was on the present site of Mexico City. From Cuzco in the mountains of Peru the Incas ruled a more highly centralized and even larger empire, one of the largest of all history, and they constructed thousands of miles of paved roads (or rather pathways, for they had no wheeled vehicles) to hold their empire together.

The early Spanish colonists, beginning with those Columbus brought on his second voyage, settled in the islands of the Caribbean, where they tried without much luck to enslave the Indians and uncover gold. Then (during the same years, 1519–1522, that Magellan's fleet was on its way around the world) Hernando Cortés destroyed the Aztec empire and looted its treasure. The news of silver to be found in Mexico turned the attention of the Spaniards to the mainland. From the island colonies and from the mother country fortune hunters descended upon Mexico in a movement comparable in some ways to the nineteenth-century gold rushes elsewhere in the world. When Francisco Pizarro conquered Peru and revealed the wealth of the Incas (1532–1538), the way was opened for a similar advance into South America.

Exploration and colonization in Spanish America was primarily a work of private enterprise, carried on by individual leaders, with little direct support from the government at home. Before a man could undertake the job he had to get a royal license. By its terms the King was to have a tenth of the wealth to be produced in the new colony, and the colonizer was to have a tenth in addition to a generous estate, other lands to divide among his followers, and the right for himself and for them to the use of native labor. But he had to equip and finance his own expedition and take the risk of loss or ruin. He might succeed and make a fortune, or through shipwreck or other accident he might lose everything including his life, as many an adventurer did.

The colonial population came only in small part from Spain itself and scarcely at all from other countries in Europe, for few Spaniards were able or willing to emigrate, and foreigners with a few exceptions were excluded from the colonies. Colonial officials were supposed to bring their wives with them, but among the ordinary settlers men outnumbered women by at least ten to one. Naturally, then, most of the Spanish men married Indian women, and a sizable mixed population grew up. There was nevertheless a manpower shortage, which the Spaniards tried to overcome by forcing the Indians to work for wages. The first experiments with forced labor, as on the island of Hispaniola, resulted in the near extermination of the natives, but Indians continued to work in the mines or on the ranches of the mainland for centuries. As workers on the plantations of the islands and coastal areas, Negro slaves began to be imported as early as 1502, the African slave trade having been established by the Portuguese more than fifty years before that.

The whites exploited the colored peoples, yet the Spanish conquerors were not peculiarly cruel and predatory, no more so than the later English colonists. The millions of Indians who died in Spanish America were mostly victims of the white man's diseases. The Spanish reputation for harsh treatment of the natives arose originally from the writings of a sensitive friend of the Indians in the colonies who was himself a Spaniard—Bartolomeo de las Casas.

And if the Spaniards seemed at times to have a monomania for gold and silver, they were in this respect little different from Englishmen such as those at Jamestown who spent their first precious weeks prospecting feverishly for gold. The difference was that the Spaniards, or many of them at least, were fabulously successful. Over a period of three centuries the mines in Spanish America yielded more than ten times as much gold and silver as all the rest of the mines in the world.

The Spanish settlers farmed as well as mined, and they brought in elements of European civilization which, over the centuries, proved far more valuable to the New World than all the gold and silver they took out. They transferred their language and learning, their tools and mechanical arts, from the homeland to the colonies. They transplanted grains and fruits and vegetables, including wheat, oranges, lemons, grapes, bananas, olives, and sugar cane. They introduced domestic animals such as cows, pigs, mules, and especially horses, which soon multiplied and ran wild even beyond the colonial frontiers, becoming accessible to the Indians far north on the Great Plains and revolutionizing their way of life. And though the Spaniards brought the sword, they also brought the cross. Priests or friars accompanied every colonizing venture, making each settlement a Christian community and carrying the gospel bravely to the heathen.

The government of the colonies was reasonably efficient and highly centralized. But the Spanish empire did have weaknesses. For one thing, its commercial policy was unusually inflexible and strict. To enforce the collection of duties and provide protection against pirates, the government required all trade with the colonies to be carried on through a single Spanish port and only a few colonial ports, in fleets making but two voyages a year. This system checked the prosperity of many of the colonists, such as those in Argentina, who had to import their European manufactures and export their own agricultural products through distant Porto Bello on the Isthmus of Panama.

One of the most serious weaknesses of the empire resulted from the facts of geography. Above Mexico the colonial domain widened out into the whole continent of North America, with no natural barrier such as would limit the aspirations of the Spaniards or provide them with an easily defensible boundary. They could not people the area within this wide border arc thickly enough to make it secure, yet they kept expending energy and resources in trying to hold and even to advance beyond it. The motives for this northward push varied. Such early explorers as Coronado, De Soto, and Ponce de Leon looked for fabled treasures in the wilderness. Men of religious orders, Jesuit or Franciscan, went out to save souls, the Franciscans establishing a chain of missions, which by 1776 extended through California as far north as San Francisco Bay. Frontiersmen moved into New Mexico and Texas to prospect for silver or engage in the Indian trade. Viceroyal expeditions set up remote military outposts, as at St. Augus-

tine in Florida (1565). Indeed, the requirements of defense were always a consideration—defense against the raids of wild tribes and against the colonial thrusts of rival European nations—and *presidios* or fortresses dotted the frontier. But it was a wasting struggle, and in the end a losing one.

These outer reaches of the empire, eventually incorporated into the United States, brought elements of Spanish culture directly into the amalgam of American civilization. Many of these elements are indicated by Spanish words that have become Americanized, words like *ranch*, *rodeo*, *corral*, *lariat*, *patio*, and *calaboose*.

## England Against Spain

While Spain was building her American empire, the religious unity of Western Europe disappeared, with profound consequences for the colonization of America. As of 1500, the Christian world already was divided between East and West, between the Church of Constantinople and the Church of Rome. But virtually all of Western Europe was Roman Catholic and, in spiritual matters, recognized the supremacy of the Pope. Soon Western Europe itself was divided, between Catholics and those who protested, or Protestants, of whom there came to be many sects. The Protestant leaders intended to reform the Church, and so their movement is known as the Reformation.

The Reformation began in 1517 when Martin Luther, a German professor of theology, challenged the right of the Pope to sell "indulgences" for the remission of sins. Before long, Luther broke completely with the Roman Church. He concluded that man could not find salvation through the Church, its priests, or its sacraments, that man could be saved only by faith, by a thoroughgoing belief in redemption through Christ. Advancing beyond strictly religious matters, Luther advised German rulers to seize Church lands. Rapidly he won converts among both rulers and people.

While Luther was getting his revolt under way, a second great Protestant leader arose, one who was to have a far more direct and important influence upon American civilization. This man was John Calvin. A Frenchman by birth, Calvin studied law and theology in Paris. About 1533 he left the Catholic Church, and then the country. Fleeing to Switzerland, he settled in Geneva, and there he set up a kind of church-state.

In his *Institutes of the Christian Religion* (1536), one of the great theological works of all time, Calvin expounded his religious views. The main points, much simplified, were these: God is all-knowing, all-powerful. Man is weak, helpless, born in sin, and cannot save himself by his own efforts: he must rely upon God. The future of every soul is foreordained from the beginning of things, long before the soul is born. God's elect would give evidence of their future glory by the upright, moral life they lived in this world. Others had a duty to honor God and, regardless, had no choice but to conform. Calvin insisted upon hard work and strict morality. The Calvinist doctrines, stern and even terrifying as they appear, appealed to many people because of their very forthrightness and puritanical austerity.

Neither Calvin nor Luther, however, caused England to leave the Church of Rome. England broke away because of the political ambitions and marital difficulties of one of her kings, Henry VIII. He coveted the monastery wealth, disliked the loss of money in English contributions to the Pope, desired a male heir (which his wife Catherine, daughter of Ferdinand and Isabella of Spain, failed to give him), and fell in love with Anne Boleyn. When the Pope refused to grant a dispensation permitting him to marry Anne, Henry VIII with the cooperation of Parliament made himself (1534) "the supreme head of the Church of England." He was no theological reformer: he kept the main tenets of Roman Catholic doctrine.

After the death of Henry VIII (1547) the Church of England went first to Protestant and then, under "Bloody Mary," to Catholic extremes, with persecutions and martyrdoms on both sides. Finally the Anglican Church straightened out upon a steady middle course during the long and glorious reign of Anne Boleyn's fiery, red-headed, able daughter, Elizabeth I (1558–1603). Under Elizabeth, the Church was given a theology more Protestant than it had had under her father, Henry VIII.

While losing many lands to Lutheranism, Calvinism, or Anglicanism, the Church of Rome undertook to reform itself and win back as much of the world as possible. This undertaking is known as the Catholic Reformation or the Counter Reformation. King Philip II of Spain assumed the task of leading the Roman Catholic forces of the world against the Protestants.

In 1568 the Dutch revolted against Philip II, their Spanish overlord. They fought as Dutchmen for national independence, and as Calvinists for religious freedom. They were an industrial and maritime people, noted for their linen and woolen cloth, their ships, their fisheries, and their trade. Holding an advantage upon the sea, they robbed the galleons bringing treasure from the New World to Spain. When Spain agreed to a truce (1609), the Dutch turned to planning American colonies of their own.

In their forays against Spanish shipping the Dutch received encouragement and aid from England. Queen Elizabeth had to fend against the machinations of Philip II as he sought to enhance the power of Spain and win back for Rome the areas of Christendom that had been lost. English Catholics were ready to collaborate with a foreign king in forwarding this presumably holy work. With Philip's encouragement they plotted to get rid of Elizabeth and put Mary Stuart, "Queen of Scots," on the throne. Elizabeth, foiling them, had Mary executed.

In this undeclared war England did not remain on the defensive. Seamen loyal to the Queen—urged on by patriotism, piety, and plunder—struck at the colonial sources of Spanish strength in every way they could. Roving the waters of Spanish America, these "sea dogs" smuggled slaves, pirated treasure ships, and robbed unprotected towns. The greatest of them all, Francis Drake, followed Magellan's route into the Pacific, looted his way northward along the American coast, went on around the world, and returned a profit of several thousand percent to the Queen, who secretly had backed his venture. When she knighted him, instead of rebuking him as the Spanish ambassador demanded, she indicated plainly enough that England was ready to challenge Spain upon the sea.

The decisive test soon came. After England had made an alliance with the rebels of the United Netherlands, Philip II declared war. Determining to invade and conquer England, he assembled an unprecedented fleet of his best and largest warships, an "Invincible Armada." But the Spaniards thought of themselves as soldiers more than sailors, and they applied their ideas of land warfare to naval combat, loading troops on their unwieldly vessels to board the enemy craft and grapple at close range with the latter's men. The English, islanders that they were, relied upon their navy and their privateers, not upon an army. They had fast, maneuverable ships which could sail into the Spanish fleet, fire destructive broadsides, and escape to return and fire again. When, in 1588, the Armada appeared in the English Channel, the new naval tactics did not have a chance to show fully their superiority, for a terrible storm helped to scatter the invaders and destroy most of their ships.

England, having become the world's foremost sea power, could not be kept from colonial enterprises of her own on the other side of the Atlantic. Already Englishmen had made their first, rather tentative efforts to start settlements in the New World. Soon the English were to people the Atlantic coast of North America with colonies which eventually would grow into a great continental nation.

## Englishmen Look Overseas

The dream of America as a place of unique opportunity—for liberty, abundance, security, and peace—appeared in England soon after Columbus' discovery. This dream found a classic expression in *Utopia*, a book written by Sir Thomas More and published in Latin in 1516 (translated, 1551), which described society on an imaginary island supposedly discovered by a companion of Americus Vespucius in the waters of the New World. Life in Utopia was as nearly perfect as human beings guided by reason and good will could make it. Though the Utopians lived comfortably enough, they scorned the mere accumulation of material things, and while all were expected to keep busy, none was oppressed or overworked. They enjoyed complete freedom of thought but were careful not to offend one another in the expression of their beliefs. True lovers of peace, they went to war only to defend their neighbors and thereby ensure their own ultimate safety. In presenting

such a picture of an ideal community, the book commented by indirection upon the social and economic evils of More's England.

The Tudor age, for all its literary glory and its swashbuckling spirit, was not a happy time for most of the common people, who suffered not only from war and religious strife but also from the effects of economic change. While the population of England grew steadily—from 3 million in 1485 to 4 million in 1603—the food supply did not increase proportionately. Landowners concentrated on the production of wool. Neither cotton nor silk being yet in general use, wool was in great demand for making cloth. Land tilled at one time by serfs and later by rent-paying tenants, much of it better suited to sheep raising than to the production of crops, was steadily enclosed for sheep runs and taken away from the farmers on it.

Thousands of evicted tenants roamed the countryside in gangs, to the alarm of more fortunate householders, whose feelings are preserved in the nursery rhyme: "Hark, hark! The dogs do bark: the beggars are coming to town." The Elizabethan government passed rather ineffectual laws for halting enclosures, relieving the worthy poor, and compelling the able-bodied or "sturdy beggars" to work. Relatively few of these could find reemployment in raising or manufacturing wool. All the while the cost of living rose, mainly because of an increased money supply arising from the output of Spanish gold and silver mines in America. England, it seemed, contained either too many sheep or too many people.

Amid the widespread distress, a rising class of merchant capitalists prospered from the expansion of foreign trade as they turned from the export of raw wool to the export of woolen cloth. These merchant capitalists gathered up the raw material, put it out for spinning and weaving in individual households, and then sold the finished product both in England and abroad.

At first each exporter did business on his own, though he might belong to the Company of Merchant Adventurers. This company regulated the activities of its members, secured trading privileges for them, and provided protection for their voyages. In time chartered companies sprang up, each with a monopoly from the sovereign of England for trading in a particular region, among them the Muscovy Company (1555), the Levant Company (1581), the Barbary Company (1585), the Guinea Company (1588), and the East India Company (1600). Some of these were regulated companies, similar to the Merchant Adventurers, each member doing business separately. Others were joint-stock companies, much like modern corporations, with stockholders sharing risk and profit either on single ventures or, as became more common, on a permanent basis. These investors often made fantastic profits from the exchange of English manufactures, especially woolens, for exotic goods, and they felt a powerful urge to continue with the expansion of their profitable trade.

To further this drive, spokesmen for the merchant capitalists developed a set of ideas about the proper relation of government and business —ideas supporting the argument that (notwithstanding the sufferings of the dispossessed) the whole nation benefited from the activities of the overseas traders. The trade of England as a whole, it was said, was basically like that of any individual or firm: transactions were worthwhile if sales exceeded purchases in value. The difference in value would have to be paid in money (gold and silver), and the inflow of money into England would stimulate business and strengthen the national economy by raising commodity prices and lowering interest rates. Merchant capitalists depended upon loans to carry on their business, and interest was considered now as a cost of production, whereas in medieval times it had been regarded as sinful usury. According to their theory, the government should act to encourage a "favorable" balance of trade— that is, an excess of exports over imports.

This economic philosophy, restated by Thomas Mun in his book *England's Treasure by Forraign Trade* (1664), came to be known in the eighteenth century as "mercantilism." It guided the economic policies not only of England but also of Spain, France, and other nation-states.

Colonies would fit well into this mercantilistic program, would also alleviate poverty and unemployment, and would serve other useful purposes, or so it seemed to a number of thoughtful Englishmen in the late sixteenth and early seventeenth centuries. The Oxford clergyman Richard Hakluyt, who published a series of explorers' narratives and an essay (1584) on "western planting," made himself the outstanding propagandist for the establishment of colonies. He and others argued that colonies would provide an additional market for English manufacturers and that the colonial demand would give employment in the mother country to the poor who lived there "idly to the annoy of the whole state." Colonial commerce, while yielding profit for shipowners and customs duties for the government, would bring from the colonies products for which England previously had depended upon foreigners—products such as lumber, naval stores, and above all, silver and gold.

Colonies might also serve as bases for finding and controlling a westward passage to Asia, attacking the Spanish empire, and converting the Indians to Protestantism so that the Catholic revival, the Counter Reformation, would not spread to the New World.

There was yet another reason for the growing interest in colonies. The Church of England, in the form it took under Queen Elizabeth, by no means satisfied all her subjects. It was much too Protestant to suit those Englishmen who held on to the Roman Catholic faith, and at the same time it seemed too "popish" to many who opposed the ways and influence of Rome. Among these were the Puritans, who, affected in varying degrees by the teachings of John Calvin, wished to "purify" the Church. The majority of the Puritans were content to remain within the Anglican fold but hoped to simplify the forms of worship and lessen the power of the bishops, who were appointed by the throne. A minority, the Separatists, were determined to worship as they pleased in their own independent congregations. Like all subjects, however, they were forbidden by law to absent themselves from regular Anglican services or to hold unauthorized religious meetings, and they were taxed to support the established Church.

The discontent of the Puritans and other dissenters increased after the death of Queen Elizabeth, the last of the Tudors, and the accession of James I, the first of the Stuarts, in 1603. A Scotsman, James I was looked upon as a foreigner. He was a learned man but a poor politician—the "wisest fool in Christendom," it was said. Convinced that kings ruled by divine right, he let his subjects know at the outset that he intended to govern as he pleased. He soon antagonized the Puritans, who included most of the rising businessmen, by resorting to illegal and arbitrary taxation and also by favoring English Catholics and supporting "high church" forms of elaborate ceremony. More and more religious nonconformists began to look for places of refuge outside the kingdom.

## THE WILDERNESS SETTING

The fate of the English colonies—their success or failure, the kind of development they took—was to depend in large measure upon the environment in which they were planted along the Atlantic seaboard of North America. This environment consisted not only of geographical conditions such as soil and climate, flora and fauna, but also of the human inhabitants apart from the English themselves, that is, the Indian natives and the European intruders.

### The Eastern Woodlands

Three thousand miles and more from England, the colonies were to be separated from the mother country, and yet connected with it, by the Atlantic Ocean. The overseas crossing took from four to twelve weeks or more, in close-packed and often disease-ridden ships which sailed at irregular intervals depending on wind and weather. The distance and the difficulty of ocean travel put the colonists very much upon their own resources once they had landed on the American shore. Nevertheless, the nature of the shoreline and of the terrain behind it inclined them toward the sea, and they kept in touch with the homeland by means of the same ocean they had crossed.

Along much of its extent the coast had been submerged, and the rivers emptying into the ocean had been "drowned" by the prehistoric sinking of the continent's edge. So there was, and is, an indented coastline with a number of bays and harbors, into each of which flows one or more rivers, giving access for varying dis-

tances to and from the interior. For instance, the Charles leads to Boston harbor at its mouth, the much longer Hudson to New York harbor, the Delaware to Delaware Bay, the Susquehanna and the Potomac and the York and the James (among others) to Chesapeake Bay, and the Ashley and the Cooper to Charleston harbor. At a time when travel and transportation by water were easier and more economical than by land, the rivers with their tributaries largely determined the lines of settlement and the course of trade.

The topography of the area in which the colonies were located divides it lengthwise into three belts at different levels: the coastal plain, the piedmont plateau, and the Appalachian highland. The plain, very narrow in New England but increasing southward from New York to a width of 200 miles in Georgia, is so low that the rivers traversing it flow backward with the incoming tides, and hence it is known (in the South) as the "tidewater" region. The piedmont, 150 miles across at its widest, is several hundred or more feet higher than the plain and is set off from it by the "fall line," an imaginary line drawn through the points at which the rivers descend to the lowland over falls or rapids. From the piedmont the Appalachian Mountains rise to elevations as high as 6,000 feet in New Hampshire and North Carolina. The mountain barrier is unbroken from New England to Georgia except along the course of the Hudson and the Mohawk rivers, but between the various parallel ranges are valleys that allow fairly easy movement along the highland southwestward from Pennsylvania.

Depending upon latitude, elevation, and distance from the sea, the climate in what was English America varies a great deal from place to place, providing most though not all kinds of weather to be found within the Temperate Zone. There is a remarkable contrast between the steamy summers of the South Carolina coast and the snowy winters of the New England interior. Yet the climate on the whole was fairly similar to what Englishmen had known at home, similar enough that they could easily adapt themselves to it. The unfamiliar features—the more dramatic weather changes, the more violent storms, the more brilliant and abundant sunshine—generally appealed to the newcomers and no doubt stimulated them to unwonted activity.

Soils in America resembled those in England enough to permit the growing of most of the familiar crops, in one place or another. But the soils varied considerably, from the silted river bottoms of the tidewater to the sandy pine barrens on the edge of the upcountry in the South, and from the rich lands of the Susquehanna Valley to the thin topsoil of glacier-scoured New England in the North. Subsoil minerals abounded, especially in the mountains, but most of them—coal, oil, gas—were left for later exploitation, Available in the colonial period were widely scattered deposits of iron ore, both in the mountains and in the lowland bogs. But at that time the most valuable natural resource, other than the soil itself, was the wood that grew upon it and that then served hundreds of industrial uses.

To the first colonists, America was trees. From the Atlantic to the Appalachians and beyond stretched a great forest, unbroken except for occasional small clearings made by the elements or by the Indians, and thick with tall pines, maples, oaks, and countless other varieties of trees as well as shrubs. Even before sighting land the early voyagers to America could sometimes smell the fresh and invigorating forest scent, and once they had disembarked they found themselves in a veritable Garden of Eden, full of birds and beasts for game; flowers, berries, and fruits; and infinite resources of wood. All this made a refreshing contrast with comparatively treeless England, rapidly being deforested to meet the needs of industry.

And yet the friendly forest—so green and beautiful, so rich in materials for food and shelter and manufactures of many kinds—also had its uninviting and even hostile aspects. In its shadows lurked the wolves and panthers that devoured the settler's livestock, lurked also the red men who often threatened his and his family's lives. It stood in the way of the frontiersman eager to cultivate the soil, and he had to convert forest into fields by the slow and laborious effort of girdling or else chopping down the trees, burning the dead or downed timber, and eventually uprooting the stumps. The song

"Woodman, Spare That Tree," popular with a later generation of Americans, would have appealed to few of the first settlers or the frontiersmen who followed the receding forest. Their object was to get rid of the trees, and unceasingly the ax resounded.

Apart from the great forest, the geographical fact that most distinguished the new from the old country and most influenced the economic development of the colonies was sheer space, the vast extent of the land. Not that all the land was readily accessible. The need for clearing the forest, the presence of hostile tribes, the dependence upon water transport, and ultimately the difficulty of crossing the mountain barrier—all these considerations hindered the actual occupation of the land, and they operated more and more effectively in proportion to remoteness from the seaports. Hence the English settlements, scattered though they might seem, remained on the whole fairly compact throughout the colonial period, at least in comparison with the Spanish and French settlements in the New World, though not in comparison with the crowded towns and countryside of the Old World. There populations teemed and lacked sufficient room. Here land was plentiful and people relatively scarce.

## The Woods Indians

The North American Indians had the general features of their Mongoloid ancestors—yellow or brown skin, straight and coarse black hair, and high cheekbones—but there were minor variations in physical appearance among the numerous tribes. There were greater differences in modes of living and ways of speaking. Hundreds of languages were spoken, but most of these belonged to one or another of about a dozen linguistic stocks. Men of different tribes with related languages could not always understand each other, any more than Frenchmen could understand Spaniards, nor were such tribes necessarily alike in their cultural patterns.

In 1600 along the Atlantic seaboard south of the St. Lawrence River there lived about 125,000 Indians. They were most heavily concentrated in southern New England and around Chesapeake Bay. The largest group, as classified by language type, were the Algonquins, who

## Indians Greet the White Man [1524]

In most cases the American natives were very hospitable to the European upon his first approach. Thus Verrazano, exploring for the King of France, reported of his visit to the North Carolina coast:

*While at anchor on this coast, there being no harbor to enter, we sent the boat on shore with twenty-five men, to obtain water; but it was not possible to land without endangering the boat, on account of the immense high surf thrown up by the sea, as it was an open roadstead. Many of the natives came to the beach, indicating by various friendly signs that we might trust ourselves on shore. One of their noble deeds of friendship deserves to be made known to your Majesty. A young sailor was attempting to swim ashore through the surf, to carry them some knick-knacks, as little bells, looking glasses, and other like trifles; when he came near three or four of them he tossed the things to them, and turned about to get back to the boat; but he was thrown over by the waves; and so dashed by them that he lay, as it were, dead upon the beach. When these people saw him in this situation, they ran and took him by the head, legs, and arms, and carried him to a distance from the surf. The young man, finding himself borne off in this way, uttered very loud shrieks in fear and dismay, while they answered as they could in their own language, showing him that he had no cause for fear. Afterwards they laid him down at the foot of a little hill, when they took off his shirt and trousers and examined him, expressing the greatest astonishment at the whiteness of his skin. Our sailors in the boat, seeing a great fire made up and their companion placed near it— full of fear, as in all cases of novelty— imagined that the natives were about to roast him for food. But as soon as he had recovered his strength, after a short stay with them, showing by signs that he wished to return aboard, they hugged him with great affection, and accompanied him to the shore, then leaving him that he might feel more secure, they withdrew to a little hill, from which they watched him until he was safe in the boat.*

were scattered from Canada south to Virginia. Next in numbers were the Iroquois, centering in New York and forming a wedge between the northern and the southern Algonquins. The Iroquois included the "five nations"—Seneca, Cayuga, Onondaga, Oneida, and Mohawk—and also, far to the south, the Cherokees and the Tuscaroras. Still farther south roamed the tribes of the third largest language group, the Muskogean. These were the Chickasaws, Choctaws, Creeks, and Seminoles.

Most of the tribes carried on a primitive form of agriculture. They made clearings by cutting into trees to kill them and by setting fires in the forest. Among the dead and blackened trunks they planted pumpkins, squash, beans, and corn —crops they had learned of indirectly from the Indians of Mexico and South America. A tribe abandoned its clearing and made a new one when the yields fell, or when the accumulated filth of the village became too deep to endure. The Indian "old fields," especially in New England, attracted incoming settlers as convenient places to begin settlement, and the newcomers eagerly adopted the cultivation of native crops, above all corn. Without the clearings and the crops that the Indians provided, the Englishmen would have had much greater difficulty than they did in getting a start in the New World.

None of the Indians of the eastern woodlands (or, for that matter, of the entire continent north of Mexico) showed a talent for political organization at all comparable to that of the Aztecs or the Incas. The nearest thing to it was found in the Iroquois league of five nations (which became six nations in 1713 when the Tuscaroras moved north and joined the league). Other tribes had their own separate and rudimentary governments and were often at war with one another or with the Iroquois. From time to time they made alliances or temporary confederations.

The primitive tribal system offered both advantages and disadvantages for the invading Englishmen. On the one hand, the divisions and rivalries among the red men made it easier for the whites to deal with them than would otherwise have been the case. If the Indians had been united they could have driven out the invaders. On the other hand, the disunity of the tribes prevented the English from making such a quick and easy conquest as the Spaniards had made when they got control of Mexico and Peru by killing or capturing the native imperial rulers.

To Englishmen the Indians were of interest as customers for English goods and as suppliers of woodland commodities, especially hides and skins. Trade brought the white man and the red man together. It weakened the Indian, for while he obtained guns, knives, blankets, and iron pots, he also received firewater, and he became increasingly dependent upon the white man and his commerce.

As viewed from a distance in England, the Indian in the American wilderness seemed like a strong and innocent creature, a noble savage, awaiting only an opportunity to be civilized and Christianized. Some of the colonists, after their arrival in America, continued to look upon him in that way, and by 1619 about fifty missionaries had already entered the wilds to convert native souls. But most of the colonists soon changed their image of the Indian. After a few massacres they began to consider him a wild beast fit only to be slaughtered.

In English America there was not to be the fusion of Indian and European people and culture that developed in the Spanish empire. The reasons for this were various, but one of them was the fact that the Englishmen, unlike the Spaniards (and the Frenchmen), almost always came as family men, with their womenfolk, and hence had much less occasion to intermarry with the aborigines.

Nevertheless, American history without the Indians would have lacked much of its special character. Not only did the colonists receive from them a number of new things to eat, such as corn, but the English language in America was enriched by words of native origin (*moccasin* and *succotash*, to mention only two), and American thought was colored by numerous elements of Indian lore. Yet on the whole the aboriginal influence on American civilization was more negative than positive. Despite their kindly aid to the first European arrivals, the Indians formed an obstacle to the advance of white settlement, and life on the frontier derived many of its peculiarly "American" qualities from the Indian danger and the Indian wars.

## European Rivals

In the wilderness the English were to encounter threats not only from the Indians but also from rival Europeans. To the south and southwest were scattered the outposts of the Spaniards who, despite a peace that Spain and England made in 1604, continued to look upon the English as intruders. The English in their settlements along the coast could not for many years feel entirely safe from attack by Spanish ships.

On the north and northwest were beginning to appear the outposts of another and eventually even more dangerous rival, France. The French founded their first permanent settlement in America at Quebec in 1608, less than a year after the English had started their first at Jamestown. New France grew in population very slowly. Few Roman Catholics felt any inclination to leave their beloved homeland, and the discontented Protestants who desired to emigrate were excluded from the colony. To the English in America, however, the French presented a danger disproportionate to their numbers, largely because of their influence upon the Algonquin Indians.

In the Indian trade the English had the advantage of cheaper goods, but the French had an offsetting advantage. While the English in the region generally bought from the Iroquois, who as middlemen secured furs from more remote tribes, the French by-passed the Iroquois and dealt directly with the Algonquins. *Coureurs de bois,* footloose and fearless fur traders and trappers, penetrated deep into the interior, made friends with the Indians, lived among them, and took squaws for wives. Thus the

French gained the backing of the Hurons and other Algonquin tribes.

At the same time the French antagonized the Algonquins' traditional foes, the Iroquois. When Samuel de Champlain, founder of Quebec, discovered Lake Champlain and came upon a band of Iroquois (1609), some of his men fired. Terrified by their first experience with guns, the Indians fled. Thus began a historic enmity between the Iroquois and the French. The anti-French feeling of the Iroquois persisted because the Iroquois as middlemen resented the competition of the French in the fur trade. For many years the Iroquois were to look upon their English customers as allies.

Besides the Spaniards and the Frenchmen, the English were soon to find in the New World another European rival, the Dutch. Shortly after the planting of the first two English colonies, at Jamestown and Plymouth, the Dutch began to wedge themselves in between, when the Dutch West India Company established posts on the Hudson, Delaware, and Connecticut rivers.

## THE FIRST ENGLISH SETTLEMENTS

The English colonies in America did not result from deliberate governmental planning. They originated in a variety of responses to the economic changes and religious and political struggles going on in England at the end of the sixteenth and the beginning of the seventeenth century. England was advancing out of feudalism and into capitalism faster than any other

**Florida Indians　1564**

This drawing by the Frenchman Jacques Le Moyne de Morguer is the earliest known eye-witness depiction of aborigines of the New World in their native habitat. The Indians have presented offerings to and are worshiping a column which the French had set up in 1562. (Library of Congress)

country. Her colonization was essentially a business enterprise, a product of the new age. But it was motivated by ideals of a better life as well as by the search for power and profit.

## Early Attempts

The pioneers of English colonization were Sir Humphrey Gilbert and his half-brother Sir Walter Raleigh, though neither of them succeeded in founding a permanent colony. Both were friends of Queen Elizabeth. While Drake and other sea dogs were harrying the Spaniards in the New World and on the high seas, Gilbert kept insisting at court that English bases in America would give still greater opportunities for sapping the power of Spain. In 1578 he obtained from Elizabeth a patent conferring upon him, for six years, the exclusive right "to inhabit and possess at his choice all remote and heathen lands not in the actual possession of any Christian prince."

That same year Gilbert and Raleigh, with seven ships and nearly 400 men, set out to establish a base in the New World. Storms turned them back before they had crossed the ocean. Gilbert waited five years while he sought to raise enough money to try again. Then, in 1583, he sailed with a second and smaller expedition, reached Newfoundland, and took possession of it in the Queen's name. He proceeded southward along the coast, looking for a good place to build a military outpost that might eventually grow into a profitable colony, of which he would be proprietor. Once more a storm defeated him; this time his ship sank and he was lost at sea.

The next year Raleigh, securing from Elizabeth a six-year grant similar to Gilbert's, sent out men to look over the American coast. They returned with two Indians and with glowing reports of an island the natives called Roanoke, and of its environs (in what is now North Carolina). With her permission Raleigh named the area "Virginia" in honor of Elizabeth, the "Virgin Queen." He expected financial aid in return, but she said she could not afford it. So he had to raise money from private investors to finance another voyage to Roanoke. The hundred men he sent out in 1585 spent a year in America, exploring as far north as Chesapeake

Bay, which they recommended as the best location for a settlement.

In 1587 Raleigh sponsored still another expedition, this one carrying ninety-one men, seventeen women (two of them pregnant), and nine children as colonists. He directed them to Chesapeake Bay, but the pilot nevertheless landed them on Roanoke Island. Here one of the women gave birth to Virginia Dare, the first American-born child of English parents. A relief ship, delayed until 1590 by the hostilities with Spain, found the island utterly deserted. What had become of the "lost colony" is still a mystery.

The colonizing efforts of Gilbert and Raleigh taught lessons and set examples for later and more successful promoters of colonization. After sending out his ill-fated settlers, Raleigh again sought financial aid from merchants, to whom he sold rights of trading with his proposed colony. He realized that the undertaking was too big for the purse of one man alone. Some of the colonizers after him raised funds for their ventures by forming companies and selling stock, but others, as individuals or unincorporated groups, depended on their own resources.

After the accession of James I, Raleigh was accused of plotting against the King. Raleigh was deprived of his monopoly, imprisoned, and eventually executed. None of his successors received grants so vast and undefined as both his and Gilbert's had been. Thereafter the crown, in theory the owner as well as the sovereign of lands to be occupied by Englishmen, granted and regranted territory to companies or proprietors, on terms that imposed varying conditions, and set boundaries that often were conflicting and vague.

A group of London merchants, to whom Raleigh had assigned his charter rights, planned to renew his attempts at colonization in Virginia, which still consisted of an undefined stretch along the Atlantic seaboard. A rival group of merchants, who lived in Plymouth and other West Country towns, were also interested in American ventures. They were already sponsoring voyages of exploration to the coast farther north, up to Newfoundland, where West Country fishermen had been going for many years.

### Arrival at Roanoke

John White, a "skilful painter," sailed with the first colonizing expedition to Roanoke Island, in 1585. He recorded the country and its inhabitants in a series of pictures which Thomas Hariot, another member of the expedition, published in a *Briefe and True Report of the New Found Land of Virginia*. The illustration reproduced above was entitled "The Arrival of the Englishmen." It shows the sheltered positon of Roanoke Island behind the Outer Banks of the North Carolina coast. After the failure of the first colonizing attempt, White went to Roanoke as governor of the second colony, in 1587. Returning to England for supplies, he was unable to get back to Roanoke again until 1590. He then could find no trace of the colonists, including his daughter and his granddaughter, Virginia Dare.

In 1606 James I issued a new charter, which divided America between the two groups. The London Company got the exclusive right to colonize in the south (between the 34th and the 41st parallels), and the Plymouth Company the same right in the north (between the 38th and the 45th parallels). These areas overlapped, but neither company was allowed to start a colony within a hundred miles of where the other already had put a settlement. Each company, as soon as it had begun actual colonization, was to receive a grant of land a hundred miles wide and a hundred miles deep. The settlers themselves were to retain all the "liberties, franchises, and immunities" that belonged to Englishmen at home.

Through the efforts of the London Company (or Virginia Company of London, its full name), the first enduring English colony was about to be planted in America. The merchants, taking the East India Company as their model, intended at the outset to found not an agricultural settlement but a trading post. To it they expected to send English manufactures for barter with the Indians, and from it they hoped to bring back American commodities procured in exchange or produced by the labor of their own employees.

### Jamestown and Virginia

The London Company's first expedition of three small ships (the *Godspeed*, the *Discovery*, and the *Sarah Constant*), with about 100 men, the survivors among 144 who had embarked from

England, sailed into Chesapeake Bay and up the James River in the spring of 1607. The men had instructions from the company to avoid the mistakes of Roanoke and pick an easily defended site well inland and on high ground. They disembarked and began to build a palisaded town —which, like the river, they named for their King—at a point that seemed to meet most of the requirements. But the place was low and swampy, it was surrounded by thick woods which were hard to clear for cultivation, and it was soon threatened by hostile Indians of a confederation led by the imperial chief Powhatan.

The colonists, too many of whom were adventurous gentlemen and too few of whom were willing laborers, ran into serious difficulties from the moment they landed. They faced an overwhelming task in trying to sustain themselves, and the promoters in London complicated the task by demanding a quick return on their investment. When the men in Jamestown ought to have been growing food, they were required to hunt for gold and to pile up lumber, tar, pitch, and iron ore for export. By January 1608, when ships appeared with additional men and supplies, all but thirty-eight of the first arrivals were dead.

Jamestown, already facing extinction, was carried through the crisis mainly by the efforts of twenty-seven-year-old Captain John Smith, hero of his own narratives of hairbreadth escapes from both Turks and Indians but a sensible and capable man nevertheless. Leadership in the colony had been divided among the several members of a council who quarreled continually until Smith, as council president, asserted his will. He imposed work and order on the community. During the next winter, fewer than a dozen (in a population of about 200) succumbed. By the summer of 1609, when Smith was deposed from the council and returned to England for the treatment of a serious powder burn, the colony was showing promise of survival, though in fact its worst trials were yet to come.

Already the promoters in London were making a strenuous effort to build up the Virginia colony. To raise money and men, they sold company stock to "adventurers" remaining at home, gave shares to "planters" willing to migrate at their own expense, and provided passage for

### Suffering at Jamestown [1607–1608]

An expedition under Captain Christopher Newport began the Jamestown settlement in May 1607. In June, Captain Newport sailed for England, leaving behind 104 settlers. In September only 46 of these were still living. One of the survivors, George Percy, wrote an account of the terrible time at Jamestown:

*There were never Englishmen left in a foreign country in such misery as we were in this new discovered Virginia. We watched every three nights, lying on the bare cold ground, what weather soever came; and warded all the next day; which brought our men to be most feeble wretches. Our food was but a small can of barley, sodden in water, to five men a day. Our drink, cold water taken out of the river; which was at flood very salt; at low tide full of slime and filth, which was the destruction of many of our men. Thus we lived for the space of five months [from August 1607 to January 1608] in this miserable distress, not having five able men to man our bulwarks upon any occasion. If it had not pleased God to put a terror in the savages' hearts we had all perished by those wild and cruel pagans, being in that weak estate as we were; our men night and day groaning in every corner of the fort most pitiful to hear. . . .*

*It pleased God after a while to send those people which were our mortal enemies, to relieve us with victuals, as bread, corn, fish, and flesh in great plenty, which was the setting up of our feeble men; otherwise we had all perished.*

poor men agreeing to serve the company for seven years. Under a new communal plan, the company would hold all land and carry on all trade for a seven-year period. The settlers would contribute their labor to the common enterprise and draw upon a company storehouse for their subsistence. At the end of the period the profits would be divided among the stockholders. The London merchants obtained a new charter

(1609), which increased their power over the colony and enlarged its area (to a width of 400 miles north and south and a length extending all the way "from sea to sea, west and northwest"). In the spring of 1609 the company sent off to Virginia a "great fleet" of nine vessels with about 600 men, women, and children aboard.

Disaster followed. One of the Virginia-bound ships sank in a hurricane and another ran aground on the island of Bermuda. Many of those who reached Jamestown, still weak from their long and stormy voyage, succumbed to fevers before winter came. That winter of 1609–1610 turned into a "starving time" worse than anything before. While Indians killed off the livestock in the woods and kept the settlers within the palisade, these unfortunates were reduced to eating "dogs, cats, rats, snakes, toadstools, horsehides," and even the "corpses of dead men," as one survivor recalled. When the migrants who had been stranded on Bermuda arrived at Jamestown the following May, they found about 60 scarcely human wretches still alive (there had been nearly 500 people there the previous summer). No one could see much point in staying, and soon all were on their way downriver, leaving the town to its decay.

Yet the colony was to begin again. The refugees met a relief ship coming up the river and were persuaded to go back to Jamestown. This ship was part of a fleet bringing supplies and the colony's first governor, Lord De La Warr. He reestablished the settlement and imposed strict discipline, then went home on account of illness, while new relief expeditions with hundreds of colonists began to arrive. De La Warr's successors Thomas Dale and Thomas Gates continued his harsh rule, sentencing offenders to be flogged, hanged, or broken on the wheel. Under Dale and Gates the colony spread, with new settlements lining the river above and below Jamestown. The communal system of labor was not functioning very well, for despite the governors' strictness the lazy often evaded work, "presuming that howsoever the harvest prospered, the general store must maintain them." Before the seven years of the system were up, Dale changed it to allow the private ownership and cultivation of land, in return for part-time work

for the company and contributions of grain to its storehouse. Meanwhile the cultivators were discovering, in tobacco, a saleable crop.

Tobacco had come into use in Europe soon after Columbus' first return from the West Indies, where he had seen the Cuban natives smoking small cigars *(tabacos)*, which they inserted in the nostril. In England Sir Walter Raleigh popularized the smoking habit, and the demand for tobacco soared despite objections on both hygienic and economic grounds. Some critics denounced it as a poisonous weed, the cause of many diseases. King James I himself led the attack with *A Counterblaste to Tobacco* (1604), in which he urged his people not to imitate "the barbarous and beastly manners of the wild, godless, and slavish Indians, especially in so vile and stinking a custom." Other critics were concerned because England's tobacco imports came from the Spanish colonies and resulted in the loss of English gold. In 1612 the Jamestown planter John Rolfe began to experiment with the West Indian plant. It grew well in Virginia soil and, though rated less desirable than the Spanish-grown, found ready buyers in England. Tobacco cultivation quickly spread up and down the James.

When the seven-year communal period was up (1616), the company had no profits to divide, but only land and debts. Still, the promoters were rather optimistic because of their success with tobacco. In 1618 they launched a last great campaign to attract settlers and make the colony profitable. They offered a "headright" of fifty acres to anyone who paid his own or someone else's passage to Virginia, and another fifty for each additional migrant whose way he paid. Thus a wealthy man could send or take servants to work for him and receive, in turn, a sizable plantation. The company expected to add to its income by charging the headright landholder a small quitrent (one shilling a year for every fifty acres). Old investors and settlers were given grants of one hundred acres apiece. To make life in the colony more attractive, the company promised the colonists the rights of Englishmen (as provided in the original charter of 1606), an end to the strict and arbitrary rule, and even a share in self-government. To diversify the colonial economy, the company undertook to transport ironworkers and other skilled craftsmen to Virginia.

On July 30, 1619, in the Jamestown church, delegates from the various communities met as the House of Burgesses to consider, along with the governor and his council, the enactment of laws for the colony. This was a bright example for the future—the first meeting of an elected legislature, a representative assembly, within what was to become the United States. A month later there occurred in Jamestown another event with a far less happy forecast. "About the last of August," John Rolfe recorded, "came in a Dutch man of war that sold us twenty negars." These black men were bought, it seems, not as slaves but as servants to be held for a term of years and then freed, like the white servants with whom the planters already were familiar. In any case, a start had been made toward the enslavement of Africans within what was to be the American republic.

For several years the Indians had given the Virginia colonists little trouble. A kind of truce had resulted from the capture of the great chief Powhatan's daughter Pocahontas and her marriage (1614) to John Rolfe. Going with her husband on a visit to England, Pocahontas as a Christian convert and a gracious lady stirred up interest in projects to civilize the Indians. She died while abroad. Then Powhatan also died, and his brother Opechancanough replaced him as head of the native confederacy. Under Opechancanough the Indians pretended to be friendly while he laid plans to eliminate the English intruders. On a March morning in 1622 the tribesmen called on the white settlements as if to offer goods for sale, then suddenly turned to killing and were not stopped until 347 whites of both sexes and all ages, including Rolfe, lay dead or dying. The surviving Englishmen struck back with merciless revenge and gave up all thought of civilizing the savages.

The massacre came as a final blow to the London Company, which soon faced bankruptcy. In 1624 James I revoked the company's charter and took control of the colony. By that time the white population of Virginia was less than 1,300; thousands more had come over, but most of these had died and many had gone back to England. Still, the remaining colonists had a cash crop, a representative government (which was to continue), and a hope for future growth and prosperity. Though a failure as a profit-making enterprise, Virginia was at last succeeding as a colonizing venture.

## Plymouth Plantation

While the London Company was starting the colonization of Jamestown, the Plymouth Company attempted to found a colony far to the north, at the mouth of the Kennebec River (on the coast of what is now Maine), but in a year the surviving colonists returned to England. The Plymouth Company made no further effort to colonize. The most it did was to send Captain John Smith, after his return from Jamestown, to look over its territory. He drew a map of the area, wrote an enthusiastic pamphlet about it, and named it "New England." Eventually the Plymouth merchants reorganized as the Council for New England and, with a new, sea-to-sea land grant from the King, proceeded to deal in real estate on a tremendous scale.

The first enduring settlement in New England —the second in English America—resulted from the discontent of a congregation of Puritan Separatists. From time to time Separatists had been imprisoned and even executed for persisting in their defiance of the government and the Church of England. A band of them in the hamlet of Scrooby looked to Holland as a country where they might worship as they pleased, though it was against the law to leave the realm without the King's consent. Slipping away a few at a time, members of the Scrooby congregation crossed the English Channel and began their lives anew in Holland. Here they were allowed to meet and hold their services without interference. But, as aliens, they were not allowed to join the Dutch guilds of craftsmen, and so they had to work long and hard at unskilled and poorly paid jobs. They were further troubled as their children began to speak Dutch, marry into Dutch families, and lose their Englishness. Some of the Puritans decided to move again, this time across the Atlantic, where they might find opportunity for happier living and also for spreading "the gospel of the Kingdom of Christ in those remote parts of the world."

Leaders of this group got permission from the London Company to settle as an independent community with land of its own in Virginia. They tried, and failed, to get from James I a guarantee of religious freedom, but they were assured that he would "not molest them, provided they carried themselves peaceably." This was a historic concession on the part of the King, for it opened English America to settlement by dissenting Protestants. The next step was to arrange financing for the voyage. Several English merchants agreed to advance the necessary funds, on the condition that a communal plan like that of Jamestown be put into effect, with the merchants to share the profits at the end of seven years.

The migrating Puritans "knew they were pilgrims" when they left Holland, their leader and historian William Bradford later wrote. The sailing from Plymouth was delayed, and it was not until September that the *Mayflower*, with thirty-five "saints" (Puritan Separatists) and sixty-seven "strangers" aboard, finally put out to sea. Their destination was probably the mouth of the Hudson River, in the northeast corner of the London Company's Virginia grant, but when they sighted Cape Cod in November, it was too late in the year to go on. After reconnoitering, they chose a site in an area that John Smith had labeled "Plymouth" on his map. Since this lay outside the London Company's territory, they would be without a government once ashore, and some of the "strangers" began to show a lawless spirit. One of the "saints" therefore drew up an agreement, which forty-one of the passengers signed. This Mayflower Compact was like the church covenant by which the Separatists formed congregations, except that it set up a civil government, and it professed allegiance to the King. Then, December 21, 1620, the Pilgrims landed at Plymouth Rock.

Here they settled on cleared land that had been an Indian village until, several years earlier, an epidemic swept the place. During the first winter half of the colonists perished from scurvy and exposure, but the rest managed to put the colony on its feet. Among the neighboring Indians, whose military power had been weakened

## The Mayflower Compact [1620]

*In the name of God, Amen. We, whose names are underwritten, the Loyal Subjects of our dread Sovereign Lord King James, by the Grace of God, of Great Britain, France, and Ireland, King, Defender of the Faith, &c. Having undertaken for the Glory of God, and Advancement of the Christian Faith, and the Honour of our King and Country, a Voyage to plant the first colony in the northern Parts of Virginia; Do by these presents, solemnly and mutually in the Presence of God and one another, covenant and combine ourselves together into a civil Body Politick, for our better Ordering and Preservation, and Furtherance of the Ends aforesaid; And by Virtue hereof do enact, constitute, and frame, such just and equal Laws, Ordinances, Acts, Constitutions, and Offices, from time to time, as shall be thought most meet and convenient for the general Good of the Colony; unto which we promise all due Submission and Obedience.*

by the recent plague, the Pilgrims discovered friends—the Squanto, Samoset, Massasoit—who showed them how to gather seafood and cultivate corn. After the first harvest the settlers invited the Indians to join them in an October festival, the original Thanksgiving. They could not aspire to rich farms on the sandy and marshy soil, but they soon developed a profitable trade in fish and furs. From time to time new colonists arrived from England, and in a decade the population reached the modest total of 300.

The people of "Plymouth Plantation" elected their own governor, and they chose the great-hearted William Bradford again and again. As early as 1621 he cleared their land title with a patent from the Council for New England, but he never succeeded in his efforts to secure a royal charter giving them indisputable rights of government. Terminating the communal labor plan ahead of schedule, the governor distributed land among the families, thus making "all hands very industrious." He and a group of fellow "undertakers" assumed the colony's debt to its financiers in England and, with earnings from the fur trade, finally paid it off, even though the financiers had not lived up to their agreement to keep on sending supplies.

The Pilgrims remained poor ; as late as the 1640s they had only one plow among them. Yet they clung to the belief that God had put them in the New World for a reason. Governor Bradford wrote in retrospect: "As one small candle may light a thousand, so the light here kindled hath shone to many, yea in some sort to our whole nation."

# Selected Readings

**The American Indians** W. T. Hagan, *American Indians* (1961); Kenneth MacGowan, *Early Man in the New World*° (1950); Clark Wissler, *Indians of the United States: Four Centuries of Their History and Culture* (1940); Paul Radin, *The Story of the American Indian* (1927).

**The European Background** W. H. McNeill, *The Rise of the West* (1963); Wallace Notestein, *The English People on the Eve of Colonization, 1603–1630*° (1954); Alan Simpson, *Puritanism in Old and New England* (1955); K. E. Knorr, *British Colonial Theories, 1570–1850* (1944); Maurice Powicke, *The Reformation in England*° (1941); R. H. Tawney, *Religion and the Rise of Capitalism*° (1926); J. U. Nef, *Industry and Government in France and England, 1540–1640* (1940); Lawrence Stone, *The Crisis of Aristocracy* (1965).

**Discovery and Exploration** C. E. Nowell, *The Great Discoveries and the First Colonial Empires*° (1954); J. B. Brebner, *The Explorers of North America, 1492–1806*° (1933); Gwyn

Jones, *The Norse Atlantic Saga* (1964); R. A. Skelton, T. E. Marston, and G. D. Painter, *The Vinland Map and the Tartar Relation* (1965); S. E. Morison, *Admiral of the Ocean Sea* (2 vols., 1942), a classic biography of Columbus; Paul Horgan, *Conquistadors in North American History* (1963); Charles Gibson, *Spain in America* (1966).

**Early English Colonizing Efforts** A. L. Rowse, *Sir Walter Raleigh* (1962); D. B. Quinn, *The Roanoke Voyages, 1584–1590* (2 vols., 1955).

**Jamestown** G. F. Willison, *Behold Virginia* (1951); Bradford Smith, *Captain John Smith: His Life and Legend* (1953); Philip L. Barbour, *The Three Worlds of Captain John Smith* (1964).

**Plymouth** William Bradford, *Of Plymouth Plantation*, ed. by S. E. Morison (1952); George Langdon, *Pilgrim Colony: A History of New Plymouth, 1620–1691* (1966); G. F. Willison, *Saints and Strangers*° (1945).

---

° Titles available in paperback.

# Chapter 2
# Transplanted Englishmen

The colonists who came to English America in the seventeenth century were transplanted Englishmen. They had no desire to lose their Englishness. Rather, they hoped to build in the New World a better England, one that would be free from the imperfections of their native land, one that would give them greater opportunities for personal happiness. They disagreed among themselves as to what was good and what was bad at home. Depending on their religion and their station in life, they saw their fortunes and prospects in England rising or falling as one side or the other gained the upper hand in a long-continuing struggle between King and Parliament.

King James I died in 1625, before actually coming to blows with Parliament, but his son Charles I was more extreme in his autocratic tendencies and in his Roman Catholic sympathies. From 1629 to 1640, Charles I ruled as an absolute monarch, refusing to call Parliament into session, imposing high-church forms upon the people, and imprisoning Puritan leaders. Finally he called Parliament because he needed money and hoped the members would vote taxes for him. This ''Long Parliament'' remained in session almost twenty years.

During that time, civil war broke out between the King's followers, the Cavaliers, and the Parliament forces, the Roundheads, who were largely Puritans. After Charles I had been defeated and beheaded, the stern Roundhead leader Oliver Cromwell governed England as ''Protector'' from 1649 until his death in 1658. There was no strong man to succeed him, and after his son had been Protector for less than a year, the Protectorate came to an end.

In 1660 the Stuart dynasty was restored. Parliament accepted Charles II as King on the condition that he govern in partnership with its members and not in the high-handed way of his father and grandfather. The handsome and debonair Charles II, tired of his travels in exile, desired above all to stay in England and keep his throne. His less clever brother James II, who succeeded him in 1685, appointed Catholics to high office and attempted to dictate to Parliament and the courts. He quickly lost popular support.

James II fled to France, without resisting, when Parliament offered the throne to his Protestant daughter Mary and her husband William of Orange, ruler of the Netherlands and Protestant champion of Europe. William and Mary became joint sovereigns of England in 1688. By this ''Glorious Revolution'' the long struggle between King and Parliament was finally settled in Parliament's favor.

These events of seventeenth-century England form an essential part of the background of colonization during the period when most of her American colonies were founded.

---

**Penn's Treaty With the Indians**
*Detail.*

## NEW ENGLAND

New England from the 1620s to the 1670s took its character as a colony in part from the Pilgrims who settled at Plymouth, but in a much larger measure from the Puritans who later landed at nearby Massachusetts Bay and then spread out from there. These Puritans would have liked to remake the institutions of England, but they faced too much opposition there. In the wilderness of America they saw an opportunity to create society anew.

### Massachusetts Bay

Englishmen were first attracted to Massachusetts Bay by its fisheries, and as early as 1623 a group of merchants tried to set up a permanent fishing and trading post on Cape Ann. Some of the settlers later moved to Salem. In 1628 another group of merchants—Puritans—obtained from the Council for New England a grant of land lying between the Merrimac and Charles rivers and extending from sea to sea. These wealthy Puritans bought the equipment of the defunct fishing and trading business and sent to Salem a ship with supplies and forty passengers to lay the groundwork for a large settlement. In 1629 the new enterprisers organized the Massachusetts Bay Company, secured a royal charter confirming their land grant and giving the company the right to govern its colony, and sent out nearly 400 additional settlers.

Some members of the company, alarmed by the high-church and anti-Parliament attitudes of the new King, Charles I, were beginning to look upon the colony less as a business venture and more as a Puritan refuge. Some were eager to migrate themselves if they could do so and still control the company. They arranged to buy the stock of those who preferred to stay at home. Then, in 1630, they sailed under the lead of the company's governor, John Winthrop, a gentleman of means, with a university education, a deep but narrow piety, a cool and calculating way, and a remarkably forceful and stubborn character. The expedition, with seventeen ships and 1,000 people, was the largest of its kind in the seventeenth century. These colonists founded a number of new towns, among them Boston, which was to be both the company's headquarters and the colony's capital.

The Massachusetts Bay Company soon was transformed into the Massachusetts colonial government. Governor Winthrop brought with him the company charter. According to its terms, the "freemen" (the stockholders) were to meet as a General Court to choose officers and adopt rules for the corporation. After their arrival in America the freemen proceeded to elect officials and pass laws for the colony. At their first meeting the freemen, eight of them, voted to concentrate power in their own and the governor's hands. At their next meeting, in 1631, they increased the number of freemen (the word now meaning voters or citizens, not necessarily stockholders) by more than a hundred, so as to include about half of the family heads in the colony at that time. Governor Winthrop continued to dominate colonial politics, but in 1634 he agreed to an arrangement by which the freemen would elect from year to year the governor, the deputy governor, the council of governor's assistants, and two "deputies" from each town— all of whom would constitute the General Court. In 1644 this became a bicameral legislature, with a lower House of Deputies and an upper chamber consisting of the governor and his council.

To be a freeman, to take any part in the colonial government, a man had to be a member of the Puritan Church. This was not easy. The Puritans in England (and the Pilgrims in Plymouth) had required for church membership only that a person profess the faith, sign the covenant, and live an upright life. The Puritans in Massachusetts, however, soon began to limit membership to the "visible saints," that is, to those who could demonstrate that they had experienced God's saving grace and hence belonged to the elect, the group whom He had chosen for eventual salvation. Churches were formed by persons covenanting with one another and with God, and these members, once in, decided who else could enter the fold. Whether admitted to membership or not, everyone in the community was a part of the congregation and was required by law to attend religious services.

Unlike the Separatist founders of Plymouth, the Puritan founders of Massachusetts had come with no intention of breaking away from the Church of England. They only wished, at first, to rescue the Church from what they saw as the evil influence of Rome. Nevertheless, they soon were acting as if they were religiously independent. As the prominent preacher John Cotton said, the Church in every town had "complete liberty to stand alone." Each congregation chose its own minister and regulated its own affairs. Thus there arose in Massachusetts—as well as in Plymouth—what came to be known as the Congregational Church.

These Massachusetts Puritans were not necessarily grim, joyless, or "puritanical," despite their belief in predestination. They enjoyed the ordinary pleasures of life, and they appreciated beauty in plain and simple forms. They strove to lead a useful, conscientious life of thrift and hard work. They honored material success, for if a person did well it was possible evidence that God favored him as one of the elect. If his ways were upright, this was another possible indication of divine grace. Many were hopeful that they were among the chosen, but no one could be entirely sure. So people searched their hearts, and those of their neighbors so far as possible, to look for signs of salvation.

"We here enjoy God and Jesus Christ," Winthrop wrote to his wife soon after his arrival; "is this not enough?" He and the other Massachusetts founders saw themselves as starting a holy commonwealth, a model for the corrupt world to see. The problem was to keep it holy. In this effort the preachers and the politicians worked together. The ministers did not run the government, but they supported it, and they exerted great influence upon the church members who alone could vote or hold office in it. The government in turn protected the ministers, taxed the people (members and nonmembers alike) to support the Church, and enforced the law requiring attendance at services. In this Puritan oligarchy the dissidents had no more freedom of worship than the Puritans themselves had had in England.

The Lord seemed to smile upon the Massachusetts enterprise. After the first winter (1629–1630), when nearly 200 died and many others decided to leave, the colony grew and prospered. The nearby Pilgrims helped with food

and advice. Incoming settlers, many of them well-to-do, brought needed tools and other goods, which they exchanged for the cattle, corn, and other produce of the established colonists. During the 1630s, while Charles I ruled England without a Parliament, Puritans escaping from his tyranny migrated in such numbers that by 1643 the colony had a population of about 15,000. Then, during the war against King and Cavaliers, quite a few of the colonists went back to aid the Puritan cause at home, and for a while those returning to England outnumbered those newly arriving in Massachusetts.

## Exodus From the Bay Colony

Meanwhile, an outpouring from Massachusetts Bay to various parts of New England (and to other places in English America) had begun. This exodus was motivated generally by one or both of two considerations: the unproductiveness of the stony soil around Boston, and the oppressiveness of the Massachusetts government. Not all the incoming settlers were saints, and as the population increased, the proportion of those who could vote or hold office declined. To the Puritan authorities, opposition to their Church seemed like a threat to the government, like both heresy and treason. Independent thinkers—and Puritanism somehow bred them —had little choice but to give in or get out. Such thinkers were responsible for new settlements north and south, in New Hampshire and Rhode Island. Families seeking richer lands as well as greater religious and political independence began new settlements in the west, in Connecticut.

The Connecticut Valley, one hundred miles beyond the settled frontier, contained fertile meadows that invited pioneering despite the presence of warlike Indians and the claims of the already fortified Dutch. By the early 1630s a few Englishmen were already living there. Well up the river was a post that Pilgrims going out from Plymouth had founded. Near the river's mouth was the post of Saybrook, started by a group of English Puritans who had a large though vague land grant from the Council for New England.

The Connecticut Valley appealed to Thomas Hooker, a minister of Newtown (Cambridge), who questioned the fairness of government by the General Court, arguing that "a general council, chosen by all," would be "most suitable to rule and most safe for the relief of the whole people." When, in 1634, Newtown petitioned the General Court for permission to occupy the Connecticut Valley before it was "possessed by others," Governor Winthrop and his associates turned down the request. In 1635 a number of families from other Massachusetts towns moved west with the General Court's approval, on the understanding that they would "continue still under this government." The next year Hooker led his congregation through the wilds and established the town of Hartford.

Disregarding the claims of the Dutch, the English grantees, and the Massachusetts General Court, the people of Hartford and two other newly-founded upriver towns, Windsor and Wethersfield, decided to set up a colonial government of their own. In 1639 they adopted a kind of constitution known as the Fundamental Orders of Connecticut. This provided for a government similar to that of Massachusetts Bay, but gave a larger proportion of the people the right to vote and hold office.

A separate colony, the project of a Puritan minister and a wealthy merchant from England, grew up around New Haven on the Connecticut coast. The Fundamental Articles of New Haven (1639) set up a Bible-based government even stricter than that of Massachusetts Bay. Eventually the governor of Connecticut obtained a royal charter (1662) that not only authorized his colony but also extended its jurisdiction over the New Haven settlements.

Rhode Island had its origin in the religious dissent of Roger Williams, a likeable but troublesome young minister of Massachusetts Bay. Even John Winthrop, who considered him a heretic, called Williams a "sweet and amiable" man, and William Bradford described him thus: "A man godly and zealous, having many precious parts, but very unsettled in judgement." Williams was an extreme Separatist who at first advocated not religious freedom but rather a church made even more pure and strict. Making friends with the neighboring Indians, he concluded that the land belonged to them and not to the King or to the Massachusetts Bay Company. The colonial government, considering

Williams a dangerous man, decided to deport him, but he escaped. He took refuge with Narragansett tribesmen during a bitter winter, then bought a tract of land from them and in 1636, with a few of his friends, created the town of Providence on it.

By that time another menace to the established order had appeared in Massachusetts Bay. Anne Hutchinson, the charming and strong-minded wife of a substantial Bostonian, attracted many more followers than Williams with her heretical doctrine that the Holy Spirit dwelled within and guided every true believer. If this were so, the Bible would have no more authority than anyone's personal revelation, and both the church and the government would be exposed to anarchy, or so it seemed to Governor Winthrop and his associates. Mrs. Hutchinson's followers were numerous and influential enough to prevent Winthrop's reelection as governor in 1636, but the next year he got back into office and set the orthodox ministers to proving that she was a heretic. In 1638, after a trial at which Winthrop himself presided, she was convicted of sedition and banished as "a woman not fit for our society." With her family and some of her followers she moved to a point on Narragansett Bay not far from Providence.

In time other communities of dissidents arose in that vicinity. They quarreled with one another and with Roger Williams, who, having paid the Indians for the land, looked upon himself as its proprietor. As he matured he modified some of his views on religion. He began to advocate complete freedom of worship and absolute separation of church and state. Eventually he turned into a "seeker," one who respected but doubted all religions while he sought the true one. Rhode Island reflected his changing ideas. In 1644 he got from Parliament a charter authorizing a government for the combined settlements. The government, though based on the Massachusetts pattern, did not restrict the vote to church members nor did it tax the people for church support. A royal charter of 1663 confirmed the existing arrangement and added a guarantee of "liberty in religious concernments."

New Hampshire and Maine had become the separate possessions of two proprietors, Captain

Grant to Mason 1629

Grant to Gorges 1639

Grant to Duke of York by Charles II 1664

**New England 1660**

John Mason and Sir Ferdinando Gorges. In 1629 they divided their grant from the Council for New England along the Piscataqua River. Despite lavish promotional efforts, especially on the part of Gorges, few settlers were drawn to these northern regions until the religious disrup-tion of Massachusetts Bay. In 1639 John Wheel-wright, a disciple of Anne Hutchinson, led some of his fellow heretics to Exeter, in New Hamp-shire. Thereafter a number of towns in that prov-ince and in Maine were peopled by orthodox and unorthodox Puritans from Massachusetts or

## The New England Confederation [1643]

*The said United Colonies [Massachusetts, Plymouth, Connecticut, and New Haven] for themselves and their posterities do jointly and severally hereby enter into a firm and perpetual league of friendship and amity for offence and defence, mutual advice and succor upon all just occasions both for preserving and propagating the truth and liberties of the Gospel and for their own mutual safety and welfare.*

The United States Colonies further agreed:

1. To provide men and provisions and to share in all costs in proportion to their abilities.
2. To send immediate aid to any of their confederates that might be invaded or in danger.
3. To appoint two commissioners apiece for managing the affairs of the confederation.
4. To begin no war, and to involve the confederation in no war, without the consent of at least six of the eight commissioners.

by new colonists from abroad. The Massachusetts Bay Company extended its authority over the whole territory in the north but ultimately lost its cases against the heirs of both Mason and Gorges in the highest courts of England. New Hampshire was then set up as a separate colony in 1679. The Gorges family having sold their rights to it, Maine remained a part of Massachusetts until admitted to the Union as a state in 1820.

### Frontier Defense

As New England spread, the settlers ran into trouble with the Indians. With a few exceptions like Roger Williams and John Eliot, a saintly missionary who translated the Bible into an Indian language, the Puritans viewed the red men as "pernicious creatures" who deserved exter-

mination unless they would adopt the white man's ways. In 1637 the exasperated Pequots went on the warpath in the Connecticut Valley. The Connecticut frontiersmen marched against a palisaded Pequot stronghold and set it afire. About 400 Indians were burned to death or killed when trying to escape, and most of the survivors were hunted down, captured, and sold as slaves. The Pequot tribe was almost wiped out.

The New England colonies faced danger not only from the Indians but also from the Dutch and the French, who claimed the territory on which some of the outlying settlements were made. The colonies could not expect help from England at the time when the mother country was distracted by the civil war between Cavaliers and Roundheads. To provide frontier protection, to adjust boundary disputes among themselves, and to further their mutual interests in other ways, four of the colonies joined to form "The Confederation of the United Colonies of New England" (1643). These four were Massachusetts, Plymouth, Connecticut, and New Haven. The other settlements—those of Rhode Island, New Hampshire, and Maine—were excluded, since Massachusetts aspired to annex them and objected to recognizing them as equals.

By 1675, when King Philip's War began, the New England Confederation had deteriorated so much that it could no longer be relied upon for organizing frontier defense. King Philip and the Wampanoags, with their Indian allies, destroyed or depopulated twenty towns and caused the deaths of a sixteenth of the white male population in three years of gloom and terror for New England. The war did not end until Massachusetts had called upon the aid of "praying" Indians, thousands of whom John Eliot and other missionaries had converted and who had settled down in or near the white man's towns. One of these Indians shot and killed King Philip. Other leaders were executed after their surrender, and many warriors again were sold into slavery (in the West Indies), but danger still remained. The French, who had given little aid to King Philip's hosts, were later to back the Indians in revengeful attacks upon the New England frontier.

## Changing Ways

In New England the early settlers almost always took up land in groups. A congregation arriving from England received from the General Court the grant of a town (township), an area of twenty-five square miles or so. Its distribution was left to the leaders of the new settlement. They laid out a village, in which they set aside a "common" as pasture and timberland, chose a site for a meeting house (church) and for a fort, and assigned each family a strip of land as a home lot on either side of the one village street. They also divided up the outlying fields in the town, the size of a field and the desirability of its location depending on the family's numbers, wealth, and social standing. Wherever he went to work his fields, the typical seventeenth-century New Englander lived not in a lonely farmhouse but in a village with neighbors close by, and he maintained a strong sense of community.

Once established, the town was left to go pretty much its own way, with little interference from the colonial government except in cases where the townspeople could not agree among themselves. They held a yearly "town meeting" in the meeting house to decide important local questions and to choose a group of "selectmen" who governed the town until the next general gathering. The town meeting itself decided who could participate in its sessions and who was eligible for election to a town office. As a rule it qualified all adult males, even in Massachusetts, instead of limiting the local suffrage to church members. The town (not the county) was the basic unit of local government.

One thing the Massachusetts government attempted to require of the towns was provision for education. An early statute called upon parents to see to their children's "ability to read and understand the principles of religion and the capital laws of the country." A law of 1647—designed to circumvent "that old deluder Satan"—required each town of fifty householders to hire a schoolmaster to teach reading and writing, and each town of one hundred householders to set up a Latin grammar school (high school). Connecticut adopted somewhat similar legislation. The laws could not always be enforced, especially in the frontier settlements, which often preferred paying a fine to undergoing the expense of maintaining schools.

The villagers were fairly self-sufficient, producing most of what they consumed. They needed crops, however, that they could sell or exchange for goods they could not themselves produce. They experimented unsuccessfully with hemp, wine grapes, and sassafras (then in demand abroad as a supposed cure for syphilis). Some trapped or traded for furs, and others set up sawmills, both furs and lumber being valuable items for export. The Massachusetts government helped to promote an iron furnace at Saugus, to lessen the need for imports by making possible the colonial manufacture of pots, kettles, plows, and guns. This experiment lasted only from 1652 to 1676.

Coastal towns meanwhile developed an overseas trade through fishing, shipping, shipbuilding, and related enterprises. For New England, the ocean proved more productive than the land. Locally built vessels soon were busy taking ship's timbers and naval stores to England, fish to Spain, and lumber products and African slaves to the West Indies; in return they brought back sugar and a variety of manufactured goods. Since money was scarce, imports were commonly bartered for domestic products. Massachusetts, alone among all the English colonies, minted a coin of its own, the "pine-tree shilling," but only for about three decades (1652–1684).

With the growth of commerce, the colonial shipowning merchants came to dominate the New England economy. Some of these merchants diversified their holdings, investing part of their profits in timberlands, sawmills, shipyards, rum distilleries, and properties of various kinds. The rich businessmen might be good Puritans—though many were not—and yet their way to wealth inevitably created tensions within Puritan society. Such men looked outward to the world of the Atlantic, and their activities brought in sophisticated, cosmopolitan attitudes as well as exotic commodities. These activities changed New England life, especially in the port towns. Here dwelled not only the merchants in their mansions but also the upstart blacksmiths, carpenters, and other artisans who demanded and got higher and higher pay for their indispensable skills. The ports were over-run, besides, with rowdy sailors and longshore-men and with the gaudy women who catered to them. Old and orthodox Puritans resented the changes taking place, and at the same time the rising merchants longed for further changes of a kind that would give them a greater voice in colonial government.

The Puritan oligarchy gradually lost some of its political power, even in Massachusetts, and the ministers lost some of their authority, while the merchants gained in influence. John Win-throp, the dominant figure of early Massachu-setts and most of the time its governor, died in 1649. As he and others of the first generation of American Puritans passed away, the number of church members declined, for few of the second generation could show the saving grace that church membership required.

The Puritans faced a dilemma. If they con-tinued to admit no one except "visible saints," the Church would go on shrinking, but if they opened the door to others, the Church would lose its purity. To meet this problem, the Puri-tans allowed the children of saints to be baptized as partial members even without proof of a con-version experience. But what about the uncon-verted children of these partial members? By the Half-Way Covenant, which a conference of ministers approved in 1662, such men and wom-en of the third generation were given the right to be baptized, though not the right to partake of communion or vote in church affairs. As time passed, the difference between full and half membership was forgotten, and in most com-munities the Congregational Church came to include all who cared to join and could profess the faith. As the number of church members rose, so did the number of men who could take part in colonial politics as voters and office-holders.

Orthodox Puritans continued to oppose the transformation that was coming over the erst-while land of the saints. Sabbath after Sabbath the ministers preached sermons (as of course ministers still do) deploring the signs of waning piety. "Truly so it is," one minister lamented in 1674, "the very heart of New England is changed and exceedingly corrupted with the sins

## Day of Doom [1662]

The earliest book-publishing centers in English America were Cambridge and Boston. From their presses came more than two hundred titles between 1640 and 1700. The very first of these was *The Whole Book of Psalms*, popularly known as the "Bay Psalm Book." Another best seller, published in 1662 and reprinted many times thereafter, was *The Day of Doom, Or a Poetical Description of the Great and Last Judg-ment*, written by Michael Wiggles-worth, a Harvard graduate and Puritan divine. Two of its 224 dreary stanzas describe the eternal punishment of the damned as follows:

Whom having brought, as they are taught,
    unto the brink of Hell,
(That dismal place far from Christ's face
    where Death and Darkness dwell;
Where God's fierce ire kindleth the fire,
    and vengeance feeds the flame
With piles of Wood, and Brimstone Flood,
    that none can quench the same,)

With Iron bands they bind their hands
    and cursed feet together,
And cast them all, both great and small,
    into that Lake for ever,
Where day and night, without respite,
    they wail, and cry, and howl
For tort'ring pain, which they sustain
    in Body and in Soul.

of the times." There was, he said, a growing spirit of profaneness, pride, worldliness, sensu-ality, gainsaying and rebellion, libertinism, car-nality, formality, hypocrisy, "and a spiritual idolatry in the worship of God."

Yet Puritanism remained an important ele-ment in the life of New Englanders, and it was in some degree to affect the outlook of most Americans for many generations. It left its last-ing mark not in the form of theological doctrines or religious practices but in the form of attitudes that were real though hard to define—a sense of duty, of hard work and of success as its reward, and of mission to make the world a better place.

# THE CHESAPEAKE COUNTRY

The Massachusetts Bay Colony began as a planned society, and early New England continued to be characterized by a sense of collective interest and social purpose. The Chesapeake Bay colonies—Virginia and Maryland—developed in a somewhat different way. "The most noticeable feature of the Chesapeake settlements," the historian Wesley Frank Craven has written, "is the absence of a common purpose and goal except such as was dictated principally by the requirements of individual interest."

## Maryland

One of the stockholders of the London Company, George Calvert, Lord Baltimore, after taking part in the promotion of Virginia, conceived the idea of undertaking a new colony on his own. Himself a convert to the Roman Catholic faith, Calvert had in mind primarily a gigantic speculation in real estate, and incidentally the establishment of a refuge for Roman Catholics, victims of political discrimination in England. After getting a Newfoundland grant from James I and spending a winter on it, he looked over Virginia and decided to relocate his colony in the warmer climate to the south of his previous location. From Charles I he obtained a patent to a wedge of Virginia's territory which lay north of the Potomac and east of Chesapeake Bay, and which the King now christened Maryland in honor of his Roman Catholic wife, the Frenchwoman Henrietta Maria. George Calvert died before the grant was made official, and it was then issued (1632) to his son Cecilius, the second Lord Baltimore.

The Maryland charter contained some curious provisions which revived in the colony a feudal concept long dead in the mother country. Calvert and his heirs were to hold their province as "true and absolute lords and proprietaries," acknowledging the suzerainty of the King by the annual payment of two Indian arrowheads and a fifth of all the gold and silver to be mined. The proprietor, exercising within Maryland a power comparable to that of the King in England, was to have the privilege of subinfeudating his land—that is, granting it in parcels to men who would become his vassals. But he was to make no laws incompatible with those of England, and none without the consent of the freemen or their representatives.

Since the London Company (which still claimed its land rights in Virginia) objected to the Calvert grant, Lord Baltimore remained at home to defend his interests at court. He appointed his brother Leonard Calvert governor and sent him with another brother to see to the settlement of the family's province. In March of 1643 the *Ark* and the *Dove*, bearing 200 or 300 passengers, most of them Protestants, entered the Potomac and turned into one of its eastern tributaries. On a high and dry bluff these first arrivals laid out the village of St. Mary's, while the neighboring Indians, already withdrawing to avoid native enemies, assisted by selling land and providing stocks of corn. The early Marylanders knew no massacres, no plagues, no starving time.

Spending a large part of the family fortune in the development of their American possessions, the Calverts had to attract many thousands of settlers if their venture was to pay. They encouraged the immigration of Protestants as well as Roman Catholics, and since relatively few of the latter were inclined to leave England, the Protestant settlers (mostly Anglicans) soon far outnumbered the Catholics.

The Calverts drew on the experience and example of Virginia. To the early arrivals they offered land on even more generous terms—one hundred acres for each man, another one hundred for his wife and for every servant he brought along, and fifty for each of his children. The landholders were expected to pay the same modest quitrent as those in Virginia (one shilling for every fifty acres). The Virginia governor welcomed the newcomers and offered them his aid, but not all the Virginians were so friendly. One of them, William Claiborne, made continual trouble for the Maryland proprietors by his claim to Kent Island, which lay within the Maryland boundaries. In Claiborne's absence Leonard Calvert invaded the island and took it by force (1637).

At the insistence of Maryland settlers, the proprietor agreed (1635) to the calling of a representative assembly—the House of Delegates, as it came to be known—which based its proceedings on the rules of Parliament. By the 1650s Maryland had a bicameral legislature, with the governor and his council constituting the upper house. The governor was appointed by the proprietor, Lord Baltimore. This was similar to the government that was developing in Virginia, except that there the governor was appointed by the King.

Politics in Maryland from the beginning were complicated by the hostility of the Protestants toward the Catholic minority and the Catholic proprietor. To appease the majority, he appointed a Protestant as governor in 1648. To further calm the colony, he sent over from England the draft of an "Act Concerning Religion," which assured freedom of worship to all who believed in Jesus Christ. Before passing this as part of the Maryland Toleration Act (1649), the legislature added a series of religious offenses with drastic penalties for them, including the death penalty for cursing God. The act did not end the political turbulence in Maryland.

## Tobacco and Society

Tobacco growing quickly spread throughout the Chesapeake settlements—in Maryland as well as Virginia—and provided the basis for the society that grew up in the region. Accounting for tobacco's primacy were not only the soil and climate but also the long and irregular shoreline, with dozens of deep creeks and rivers emptying into the bay. To transport heavy hogsheads overland was difficult and damaging to the leaf, but for the man with a farm on one of the natural waterways it was easy enough to roll the hogsheads to his own landing, from which ocean-going ships could carry them to markets abroad. The early settlers therefore took up land along the bay and the navigable streams, and many acquired extensive tracts. Thus most of the people came to be widely scattered, living on isolated farms. Villages or towns were few.

Even if a man owned a thousand acres or more, he actually farmed only a small part of his land, because of the difficulty of clearing it. On his clearing he raised not only tobacco but also corn, fruit, vegetables, cattle, hogs, and other things for his own and his family's use, so that the farm was fairly self-sufficient. His life was hard. He lived in no elegant mansion but in a small and often crude house, and he worked in his fields alongside his boys and his servants or slaves—if he had any.

His servants might have come with him from England. If he brought them along and paid their way, he received not only a headright of land for each of them but also their services for a term of years, usually four or five. Or the servants might have come later, binding themselves to their master in return for their passage over. Some were sold into servitude against their will. From time to time, beginning as early as 1617, the English government dumped shiploads of convicts in America, though according to Captain John Smith "some did chuse to be hanged ere they would go thither, and were." The government also transported prisoners taken in battles with the Scots and with the Irish in the 1650s. Likewise it got rid of other groups deemed undesirable: orphans, vagrants, paupers, and those who were simply "lewd and dangerous." Still other involuntary immigrants were neither dangerous nor dependent but were victims of kidnaping, or "impressment."

The system of temporary servitude grew naturally out of existing practices in England, such as that of apprenticeship by which a youth bound himself to a master for seven years to learn a trade. Men and women binding themselves to a master in America were commonly known as "indentured" servants because of the papers recording the contract, papers which were cut or torn with an indented or indentured edge, so that the two copies, one going to the master and the other to the servant, would correspond. Upon completing his term the servant was entitled to certain benefits—clothing, tools, and occasionally land—in addition to his freedom and the privilege, if he could afford it, of acquiring servants of his own.

Relatively few of the indentured servants landed in New England, where the economy was not such as to create much of a demand for them. During the seventeenth century they flocked to Virginia and Maryland, where the laborious processes of cultivating tobacco required many hands.

Throughout this period, the number of black workers on the tobacco farms increased rather slowly. "Most of the Negroes came from the

Spanish Indies or directly from Africa," the historian David Hawke explains, "and were of small use to a farmer with little time to spare in directing an untrained man who spoke a strange tongue." In Virginia there were fewer than 300 Negroes in 1640, and only about 2,000 in 1670, when the total population of the colony had reached 40,000. By that time blacks were being treated as permanent slaves and no longer as temporary servants. But the day of the great tobacco plantation, with its labor force consisting almost entirely of Negro slaves, still lay in the future.

As early as 1640 the price of tobacco had begun to fall because of overproduction and because of the poor quality of much of the product. In that year the Virginia government made an attempt at crop control, ordering the farmers of the colony to plant less. This directive was hard to enforce throughout Virginia, and it had no effect at all in Maryland, which refused to cooperate. While Virginians complained about the "trash" that Marylanders were exporting, the price continued on a fluctuating downward trend. To maintain their incomes, planters tried to grow more tobacco, not less. Those who could acquired additional land and labor and enlarged their fields. Thus the price decline contributed to the eventual development of great plantations.

In the Chesapeake region, with its scattered population, the English county was adapted as the basic unit of local government. In Virginia the House of Burgesses created eight counties in 1634. The governor and his council appointed the sheriffs, justices of the peace, and other county officials. In Maryland the proprietor originally intended to set up vast feudalistic estates, each with a baron who would be responsible for governing the settlers on his land. But a county system similar to that of Virginia grew up instead. Though Virginians and Marylanders did not elect their county officers, they could exert considerable influence in county affairs. Still, these people had a smaller role in local government than did contemporary New Englanders.

Though there was more religious diversity in Maryland than in Virginia, Anglicans predominated in both colonies, but in both of them Anglicanism soon ceased to be quite the same thing

that it was in England. Virginia laws dating from 1643 directed all members to conform to the Church of England, ordered the expulsion of nonconformists, and required the payment of tithes to support the established church. The Bishop of London was supposed to watch over the far-flung American parishes, but he left the responsibility to the colonial governors, who most of the time were preoccupied with political affairs. Actual control gravitated to the parishes themselves. They worked out relatively democratic and independent church organizations of their own. Local vestries (governing boards of laymen) hired pastors on a yearly basis and provided salaries. These were paid in tobacco, and the amount remained the same while the price fluctuated. The living was uncertain, and to qualify as a pastor a candidate had to cross the ocean and be ordained by a bishop in England, there being no bishops in America. Fewer and fewer able and well-trained men were attracted to the ministry, and the numbers of idle and profligate "fox-hunting parsons" increased. Even the most conscientious parsons found it next to impossible to give adequate care to the souls of their parishioners, so far apart did the planters live and so extensive were the parish boundaries. Often the elaborate rituals of the Church had to be simplified or omitted altogether.

In Virginia, as in Massachusetts, laws were passed as early as the 1640s to encourage schooling. A Virginia statute ordered county officials to "take up" children whose parents were "disabled to maintain and educate them." In promoting schools, Massachusetts had the advantages of fairly compact settlement, a comparatively large number of university graduates among the early settlers, and a religion that strongly emphasized the ability to read the Bible. Education in the seventeenth-century tobacco colonies was left mainly to individual families, who, when they could afford to do so, imported servants as tutors or endowed "old field schools" on worn-out tobacco lands.

## Political Turbulence

The political history of Virginia from the 1640s to the 1670s centered around the career of Sir William Berkeley, a strong-willed Oxford graduate who at the age of thirty-six arrived in 1642 with an appointment as governor from King Charles I.

In the beginning Governor Berkeley was popular. He helped to open up the interior by sending out explorers who crossed the Blue Ridge Mountains. He directed a force that put down the Indians in 1644 when old Chief Opechancanough led them in a bloody attack comparable to the massacre of twenty-two years earlier. Opechancanough was captured and, against Berkeley's orders, was shot and killed. The defeated Indians agreed to a treaty ceding all the land between the York and the James rivers to the east of the fall line, and prohibiting white settlement to the west of that line.

This attempt to delimit Indian territory—like many such attempts later in American history—was a failure from the start. Virginia was growing fast, especially after Cromwell's victory in the English civil war and the flight of many of the defeated Cavaliers to the colony. By 1650 its population (16,000) was twice as large as in

1640, and by 1660 five times as large (40,000). As the choice lands along the tidewater were taken up, new arrivals and servants completing their terms or escaping from their masters pressed on beyond the falls into the piedmont. By 1652 three counties had been formed in the territory recently set aside for the Indians. Clashes frequently occurred between the Indians and the frontiersmen.

When Cromwell seized power in England, Berkeley had to give up the governorship of Virginia, but King Charles II reappointed him after the Stuart Restoration. Once back in office, Berkeley, by the force of his personality, and by corrupting the council and the House of Burgesses, made himself practically an autocrat. Originally the Virginia government had been remarkably democratic. When the first burgesses were elected in 1619, all men aged seventeen or older were entitled to vote. After 1670 the vote was restricted to landowners, and elections were seldom held, the same burgesses re-

## Virginia Tobacco Land [1686]

In 1686 the Reverend John Clayton of Yorkshire, England, visited the Virginia tobacco country. Two years later he reported to the Royal Society of London (a society of Englishmen and colonials devoted to scientific inquiry):

*And yet in truth 'tis only the barrenest parts that they have cultivated, by tilling and planting only the highlands, leaving the richer vales unstirred, because they understand not anything of draining. So that the richest meadow lands, which is one third of the country, is boggy, marsh, and swamp, whereof they make little advantage, but lose in them abundance of their cattle, especially at the first of the spring, when the cattle are weak, and venture too far after young grass. Whereas vast improvements might be made thereof, for the generality of Virginia is sandy land with a shallow soil, so that after they have cleared a fresh piece of ground out of the woods, it will not bear tobacco past two or three years, unless cow-penned [and thus manured]. . . . Therefore every three or four years they must be for clearing a new piece of ground out of the woods, which requires much labour and toil, it being so thick grown all over with massy timber. Thus their plantations run over vast tracts of ground, each ambitious of engrossing as much as they can, that they may be sure to have enough to plant, and for their stocks and herds of cattle to range and to feed in. Plantations of 1,000, 2,000 or 3,000 acres are common, whereby the country is thinly inhabited, the living solitary and unsociable, trading confused and dispersed, besides other inconveniences. Whereas they might improve 200 or 300 acres to more advantage, and would make the country much more healthy. For those that have 3,000 acres have scarce cleared 600 acres thereof, which is peculiarly termed the plantation, being surrounded with the 2,400 acres of wood, so that there can be no free or even motion of the air.*

## Tobacco Preparation: Eighteenth Century

When tobacco was harvested, the stalks were hung in a well-ventilated barn to cure. After several months, in damp weather when the leaves were pliable, they were stripped from the stalks, sorted, and tied into "hands," then packed tightly in hogsheads. These were stored in public warehouses until examined by official inspectors.

Eventually the hogsheads were carried by boat or wagon or were rolled to the nearest ship landing. Ships from England ascended the rivers of the tobacco country to pick up cargoes. From William Tatham, *An Historical and Practical Essay on the Culture and Commerce of Tobacco* (London, 1800).

maining in office year after year. Each county continued to have only two representatives, even though the new counties of the back country contained many more people than some of the old ones of the tidewater area. Thus the more recent settlers on the frontier were under-represented—if indeed they were represented at all.

Popular discontent, made worse by the low price of tobacco, was already widespread when, in 1673, the young, bold, handsome Cambridge

graduate Nathaniel Bacon arrived in Virginia. His wealthy family gave him the money to buy a good farm in the back country and got him a place on the governor's council. A few years later the Indians raised the war cry on the frontier, killing several hundred whites, among them Bacon's overseer. Bacon and other concerned landholders demanded that Governor Berkeley send the militia out to pursue and chastise the marauders. But Berkeley preferred not to antagonize the Indians—he and many of his political associates were profiting from a large-scale trade with them—and so he ordered the militia merely to guard the edge of settlement. Bacon then led a force of his own to attack the Indians, whereupon Berkeley dismissed him from the governor's council and proclaimed him and his men rebels.

Thus, in 1676, began Bacon's Rebellion. When Berkeley, to gain popular support, called for a new election of burgesses, Bacon ran and was overwhelmingly elected. Going to Jamestown for the session, the rebel, not yet thirty years old, confronted the governor, now seventy. Berkeley had Bacon arrested but, hesitating to hang such a "darling of the people," pardoned him and gave him a commission to fight the Indians. While Bacon went off with his army, the House of Burgesses passed a series of reforms, known as Bacon's Laws, to lessen the authority of the governor and give greater powers of self-government to the counties. Now Berkeley again denounced Bacon as a rebel, and Bacon turned back from the frontier and marched with his army toward Jamestown, while Berkeley fled. Bacon captured the town and burned it, but when he was on the point of taking command of Virginia, he died of dysentery. Berkeley returned, recovered control, secured the repeal of most of Bacon's Laws, and saw to the execution of thirty-seven of the leading rebels before he was recalled to England, where he too died.

Later generations of Americans, looking back and finding a parallel between 1676 and 1776, were to view Bacon as a forerunner of the Patriots who championed the cause of Independence. He was not that, though his example helped to inspire the rebels who came long after him. He had advocated reform of the colonial government, not separation from England. He represented a disaffected group of the ruling class, but he also gained a following among the common people of Virginia.

His rebellion aroused the discontented of Maryland also. These people objected not only to Lord Baltimore's religion but also to his economic exploitation and arbitrary rule of his domain. From quitrents, export duties, and other sources, the proprietor was making out of the colony the present-day equivalent of more than a third of a million dollars a year. In 1670 he copied Virginia and limited the suffrage to landholders, then undertook to get control of the legislature. At the time Bacon was burning Jamestown, two Marylanders tried to rouse a mob to overthrow the proprietor's government. Both men were hanged.

## MORE PROPRIETARY COLONIES

After Lord Baltimore had received his Maryland grant, no new colonization projects got under way from England for approximately thirty years, until the Stuart Restoration. Then Charles II, having returned from his wandering exile (1660) to reign as the Merry Monarch, proceeded to reward his faithful courtiers with truly regal gifts of American land. He not only acknowledged with royal charters the various colonies that had broken off from the (to him) detestable Puritan commonwealth of Massachusetts, but he also gave rise within a quarter of a century to four additional colonies: Carolina, New York, New Jersey, and Pennsylvania. All these, like Maryland, were founded by proprietors rather than companies. By this time, companies had lost interest in colonization and had turned to more profitable ventures; meanwhile, because of the presence of already thriving settlements, proprietors were finding colonization much easier than it had been in the days of Sir Humphrey Gilbert and Sir Walter Raleigh.

### Carolina

Carolina (after the Latin *Carolinus*, meaning Charles), partly taken like Maryland from the Virginia grant, was awarded by Charles II to a group of eight of his favorites, all prominent politicians active in colonial affairs. One was the Virginia governor, Sir William Berkeley, but the man who was to do the most for the development of Carolina was Sir Anthony Ashley Cooper, about to become the Earl of Shaftesbury. In successive charters (1663, 1665) the eight proprietors received joint title to a vast territory stretching south to the Florida peninsula and west to the Pacific Ocean. Like Lord Baltimore in respect to Maryland, they were given almost kingly powers over their grant.

Like him, they expected to profit as landlords and land speculators, reserving tremendous estates for their own development, selling or giving away the rest in smaller tracts, and collecting annual payments as quitrents from the settlers. Though committed to the advancement of the Church of England, the Carolina proprietors welcomed customers whether Anglican or not. Indeed, the charter guaranteed religious freedom to all who would worship as Christians. The proprietors also promised political freedom —at least as much of it as was to be found anywhere else in America—with laws to be made by a representative assembly. They hoped to attract settlers from the existing American colonies and thus to avoid the expense of financing expeditions from England.

The proprietors, four of whom had investments in the African slave trade, also intended to introduce slaves into the colony so as to profit both from selling them and from using their labor. Early settlers were offered a bonus of extra land for every black bondsman or woman they brought in. Negro slavery existed from the outset in Carolina, with no transitional period of temporary servitude as in Virginia.

The leading proprietor, the Earl of Shaftesbury, desired a planned society and a uniform pattern of settlement for the colony. With the aid of the philosopher John Locke he drew up the Fundamental Constitution for Carolina in 1669. According to this document, the territory was to be divided into 12,000-acre squares, with counties consisting of forty squares apiece. In each county, eight of the squares would belong to the proprietors, or "seigneurs," eight others would go to newly created nobles, who would bear the title of "landgrave" or "cacique," and the remaining twenty-four would be distributed among ordinary settlers, or "leet-men." At the bottom of this stratified society would be the blacks, whose subjection would be complete, regardless of their possible conversion to Christianity: "Every freeman of Carolina shall have absolute power and authority over his Negro slaves, of what opinion or religion soever." Proprietors, nobles, and other landholders would have a voice in the colonial parliament in proportion to the size of their land holdings.

While the Fundamental Constitution, with

The Carolinas and Georgia

occasional revisions, remained in effect (at least on paper) for thirty years, Carolina was slow to develop, and when it did, it took a pattern much less regular and artificial. In fact, the colony developed along two natural but quite different lines in its two widely separated areas of settlement—the one in its northeastern corner, around Albemarle Sound; and the other far to the southwest, on the Ashley and Cooper rivers and in their hinterland.

The northern part of Carolina, the first part to be settled, suffered in the early years from geographical handicaps, the coastal region being isolated by the Dismal Swamp, by the southeastwardly flow of the rivers, and by the lack of natural harbors usable for ocean-going ships. As a Carolina proprietor, Virginia's Governor Berkeley worked hard to induce Virginians to take up land on the other side of the colonial boundary, and gradually the Albemarle settlements grew. Virginians were inclined to look upon the neighboring Carolinians as a lazy and immoral set of runaway servants, debtors, thieves, and pirates. Actually, most of these people—like many in the Virginia they had left behind—were honest but poor tobacco-growing farmers, though they showed the marks of their primitive, backwoods existence, having few roads and practically no villages, churches, schools—or slaves. The settlers disliked paying quitrents, and when one of Nathaniel Bacon's

(REFERENCES.)

| | | | | | |
|---|---|---|---|---|---|
| A. Granville Bastion. | G. Half Moon. | N. Kea:L.Smiths Bridge. | T. Quaker Meeting house. | 4. Chevaliers house | 10. Tradds house. |
| B. Craven D.º | H. Draw-bridge to the line. | O. Ministers House. | V. Court of Guard | 5. Geo.Logan d.º | 11. Nat: Law d.º |
| C. Carteret D.º | I. Johnsons covered half Moon. | P. English Church. | W. first Rice patch in Carolina | 6. Poinsett d.º | 12. Landgrave Smith d.º |
| D. Colleton D.º | K. Draw-bridge in half moon | Q. French........D.º | 1. Pasquero & Garrets house. | 7. Elicott d.º | 13. Col: Rhetts. d.º |
| E. Ashley D.º | L. Palisades. | R. Independent D.º | 2. Lowndacks d.º | 8. Starling d.º | 14. Ben: Skenking d.º |
| F. Blakes D.º | M. L. Col.Rhetts Bridge. | S. Ana baptist D.º | 3. Mr Croskeys d.º | 9. M.Boone d.º | 15. Bindery d.º |

## A City in the Wilderness: Charleston in 1704

Lord Ashley, the most active of the Carolina proprietors, gave instructions to divide Charleston "into regular streets, for be the buildings never so mean and thin at first, yet as the town increases in riches and people, the void places will be filled up and the buildings will grow more beautiful." Thus, from the beginning, Charleston grew according to an orderly, rectangular plan. To hasten

settlement, the proprietors in 1694 directed the Carolina governor to fortify the town. This map of 1704 shows Charleston (population, about 2,000) with its completed fortifications. Inside the walls were four churches, a few warehouses and shops, and several fine houses in addition to more modest dwellings. Outside were a Quaker meeting house and several rice plantations.

lieutenants, John Culpeper, took refuge in Albemarle County, some of them followed him in overthrowing the Albemarle governor, in 1677, and took temporary control themselves.

The southern part of Carolina was favored with an excellent harbor at the point where the Ashley and Cooper rivers joined (as local boosters eventually were to say) "to form the Atlantic Ocean." Here in 1670 a fleet bringing colonists arrived whom the Earl of Shaftesbury had sent out after realizing that settlers from existing colonies were not going to flock in. Then in 1680 he saw to the laying-out of the city of Charleston, which soon had its wharves, forti-

fications, and fine houses, and its wide streets running at right angles to one another. Settlers took up land along the two rivers, down which they began to send large quantities of corn, lumber, cattle, pork, and (in the 1690s) some rice to Charleston, for shipment to Barbados in the British West Indies. To Charleston also came furs, hides, and Indian slaves obtained by traders who were advancing farther and farther into the interior, around the southern end of the Appalachians, to deal with the southwestern tribes.

In Charleston and its vicinity there developed a stratified society that embodied the spirit, though not the letter, of Shaftesbury's Fundamental Constitution. Many of the early inhabitants had moved here from the declining sugar plantations of Barbados and other West Indian islands. These people, already familiar with African slavery, brought their blacks with them. Large planters, often with homes in Charleston as well as plantations nearby, and city merchants occupied more or less the position of the nobles in the Shaftesbury plan. Ordinary farmers, many of them located at some distance inland, corresponded roughly to the "leet-men." The wealthy planters and merchants, centering in Charleston, dominated the region's economy, social life, and politics. Charleston became the capital of Carolina in 1690, when the governor took up his residence there, leaving a deputy to take charge of the Albemarle settlements.

Already there were in fact two Carolinas, each having a distinctive way of life, long before the colony was formally divided (1729) into North and South Carolina, with completely separate governments.

## New York

The year after making his Carolina grant, Charles II bestowed (1664) upon his brother, the Duke of York, all the territory lying between the Connecticut and Delaware rivers. A large part of this land presumably belonged to the Massachusetts Bay Company by virtue of the company's sea-to-sea grant. The whole region was claimed by the Dutch, who occupied strategic points within it.

The Dutch republic, after winning independence from Spain, had launched upon its own career of overseas trading and empire building in Asia, Africa, and America. On the basis of Hudson's explorations, the Dutch staked an American claim and proceeded promptly to exploit it with a busy trade in furs. To add permanence to the business, the Dutch West India Company began to encourage settlement, transporting whole families on such voyages as that of the *New Netherland* in 1624, and later offering vast feudal estates to "patroons" who would bring over immigrants to work the land. So developed the colony of New Netherland. It centered around New Amsterdam with its blockhouse on Manhattan Island and included thinly

**The Middle Colonies in the Seventeenth Century**

scattered settlements on the Hudson, the Delaware, and the Connecticut, with forts for their protection. In 1655 the Dutch extended their sway over the few Swedes and Finns settled along the lower Delaware. In the Connecticut Valley, they had to give in to the superior numbers of the English moving out from Massachusetts Bay.

Three Anglo-Dutch wars arose from the commercial and colonial rivalry of England and the Netherlands throughout the world and particularly in America, where the English resented the foreign stronghold that wedged apart their own northern and southern colonies and provided smuggling bases for the Dutch. In 1664 troop-carrying vessels of the English navy put in at New Amsterdam and extracted a surrender from the arbitrary and unpopular governor, the peg-legged Peter Stuyvesant. During the final conflict the Dutch reconquered and briefly held their old provincial capital (1673–1674), then lost it again for good.

New York, formerly New Netherland, already the property of the Duke of York and renamed by him, was his to rule as virtually an absolute monarch. Since he was himself a Roman Catholic, and the inhabitants of his province included Anglicans from England and Puritans from New England as well as Calvinists from Holland, he found it expedient to be broad-minded with regard to religion and politics.

Like other proprietors before him, instead of going to America he delegated powers to a governor and a council. The Duke's Laws, which the first governor issued, basing them on some of the laws of Massachusetts and Connecticut, provided for no town meetings but for the election of certain local officials and for the gubernatorial appointment of others. These laws also directed each town to set up a church and to give tax support both to it and to any other church that residents of the town might organize. Thus there was to be a variety of established churches. On the Duke's instructions, a later governor, who took office in 1683, consulted with representatives of the people and with them adopted a Charter of Liberties and Privileges, which guaranteed the rights of Englishmen and called for an elected assembly.

The Duke's concessions failed to satisfy all New Yorkers. Many people complained about the inequality of property holding and political power. The Duke confirmed the Dutch patroonships already in existence, the most notable of them being Rensselaerswyck with its 700,000 acres around Albany, and he gave comparable estates to Englishmen in order to create a class of influential landowners loyal to him. Wealthy English and Dutch landlords, shipowners, and fur traders, along with the Duke's political appointees, actually dominated the colonial government.

The system of landholding turned away from New York some settlers who preferred living on their own farms to working as a tenant on someone else's estate. Under English rule the population nevertheless grew much faster than under the Dutch regime. By 1685, when the Duke ascended to the throne as James II, New York contained about four times as many people (around 30,000) as when he had taken it over some twenty years before. Most of them still lived within the Hudson Valley, close to the river itself, with the largest settlement at its mouth, in the town of New York. The colony had become predominantly English in both population and customs, yet Dutch traditions lingered on to leave a distinctive regional flavor.

On the north and west the Duke's dominions were extended as far as Lake Ontario by means of a protectorate over the Iroquois. On the east, however, his territory was trimmed in a boundary compromise with Massachusetts and Connecticut. On the south it was enlarged somewhat by his claim (based on conquest from the Dutch) to land west of the lower Delaware, but was diminished even more by his generosity in parting with his possessions. He gave what became New Jersey to a couple of cronies, both Carolina proprietors, Sir George Carteret and Sir John Berkeley. The latter sold his half interest to two enterprising members of the Society of Friends, thus bringing the Quakers into the colonization business. The Duke gave what became Delaware to another Quaker, the greatest of all the colonizers, William Penn.

## The Quaker Colonies

The Society of Friends originated in mid-seventeenth-century England in response to the preachings of George Fox, a Notingham shoemaker, whose followers came to be known as Quakers from his admonition to them to "tremble at the name of the Lord." The essence of Fox's teachings was the doctrine of the Inner Light, the illumination from God within each soul, the divine conscience, which when rightly heeded could guide human beings along the paths of righteousness.

Of all the Protestant sectarians of the time, the Quakers were the most anarchistic and the most democratic. They had no church government except for their monthly, quarterly, and annual meetings at which the congregations were represented on a local, regional, and national basis. They had no traditional church buildings—only meeting houses. They had no paid clergy, and in their worship they spoke up one by one as the spirit moved them. Disregarding social distinctions such as those of sex and class, they treated women as equals and addressed one another with the "thee" and "thou" then commonly used in speaking to servants and inferiors. Defying other accepted conventions, they refused to participate in taking oaths or in fighting wars. The Quakers were unpopular enough as a result of these beliefs and practices, and they increased their unpopularity by occasionally breaking up other religious groups at worship. Many of them were jailed from time to time.

Naturally, like the Puritans earlier, George Fox and his followers looked to America for asylum. A few of them went to New England, but there (except in Rhode Island) they were greeted with fines, whippings, and orders to leave, and three men and a woman who persisted in staying were actually put to death. Many migrated to northern Carolina, and there, as the fastest-growing religious community, they soon were influential in colonial politics. Yet the Quakers desired a colony of their own, and Fox himself visited America (1671–1672) to look over the land. As the head of a sect despised in England, however, he could not get the necessary grant without the aid of someone influential at

the court. Fortunately for his cause, his teachings had struck the hearts of a number of wealthy and prominent men, one of whom in particular made possible a large-scale effort to realize the Quaker dream.

William Penn—whose father was Sir William Penn, an admiral in the Royal Navy and a landlord of valuable Irish estates—received a gentleman's education at his father's expense but could not overcome his mystical inclinations despite his father's discipline. Converted to the doctrine of the Inner Light, the younger Penn took up evangelism and, though always moderate and soft-spoken, was repeatedly put in prison, where he wrote a powerful tract, *No Cross, No Crown*. With George Fox he visited the European continent and found Quakers there, as in the British Isles, who longed to emigrate.

New Jersey, half of which two of his fellow

### Penn's Treaty With the Indians

William Penn entered into a number of treaties with the Indians for the purchase of land. These treaties, unlike many agreements between red men and whites, were scrupulously observed by the Pennsylvania Quakers. Benjamin West's painting, one of the best known of his

many historical canvases, probably represents negotiations that were carried on in June 1683. This engraving made from the painting was first published in 1775. (Library of Congress)

Quakers owned, received Penn's attention when he was asked to assist them with their debts. In their behalf he helped to see to the division of the province into East and West Jersey, Carteret as one of the original proprietors keeping the East, and the Quakers the West. West Jersey soon began to fill up with Friends from England while East Jersey was being populated mostly by Puritans from New England. Before long Penn together with other wealthy Quakers purchased the eastern property from Carteret (1682), and eventually the two Jerseys were reunited as one colony (1702), second in Quaker population only to Pennsylvania itself.

Pennsylvania—which Charles II insisted on naming for his old ally the admiral—was based on the King's grant of 1681. Penn, reconciled with his father, had inherited the latter's Irish lands and also his claim to a small fortune owed by the King. Charles II, possessing more real estate than ready cash, paid the debt with a grant of territory, between New York and Maryland, which was larger than England and Wales combined and which (unknown to him) contained more value in soil and minerals than any other province of English America. Within this fabulous estate Penn was to have the rights of both landlord and ruler while acknowledging the feudal suzerainty of the King by the token payment of two beaver skins a year.

Like the Calverts, the Carolina proprietors, and the Duke of York, Penn intended to make money from land sales and quitrents and from private property to be worked for him. He promptly sold several large tracts to rich Quaker associates and one tract of 15,000 acres to a group of German immigrants led by Francis Daniel Pastorius. Through his informative and honest advertising—as in his pamphlet entitled *A Brief Account of the Province of Pennsylvania*, which was translated into several European languages—Penn made Pennsylvania the best-known and most cosmopolitan of all the colonies. But he and his descendants were to find almost hopeless the task of collecting quitrents.

Much more than a mere real-estate promoter, Penn undertook in Pennsylvania what he called a Holy Experiment. Colonies, he said, were the "seeds of nations," and he proposed to plant the seeds of brotherly love. Closely supervising the planting, he devised a liberal Frame of Government with a representative assembly. He personally voyaged to Pennsylvania (1682) to oversee the laying-out, between the Delaware and Schuylkill rivers, of the city he appropriately named Philadelphia ("Brotherly Love"), which with its rectangular streets, like those of Charleston, helped to set the pattern for most later cities in America. Penn believed, as had Roger Williams, that the land belonged to the Indians, and he was careful to see that they were reimbursed for it, as well as to see that they were not debauched by the fur traders' firewater. With the Indians, who honored him as a rarity, an honest white man, his colony had no trouble during his lifetime. It prospered from the outset because of his thoughtful planning and also because of favorable circumstances, including the mildness of the climate and the fertility of the soil. The settlers were well-to-do and well-equipped, and they received assistance from the people of other colonies and from the Hollanders and Swedes and Finns already there—for Pennsylvania when Penn first saw it was no such wilderness as Virginia had been when John Smith arrived.

Delaware, after its transfer to Penn from the Duke of York (1682), was treated as a part of Pennsylvania (and was known as "the lower counties") but was given the privilege of setting up its own representative assembly. The three counties did so in 1703, and thereafter Delaware was considered a separate colony, though until the Revolution it continued to have the same governor as Pennsylvania.

## EXPERIMENT IN UNION

The colonies, for the most part, had originated as quite separate projects and had grown up in rather independent ways, with little thought for a long time that they belonged, or ought to belong, to a unified empire. To be sure, a step toward intercolonial union had been taken with the forming of the New England Confederation, but that was the doing of some of the colonies themselves for their own purposes, and these did not include the strengthening of imperial control. A very different kind of union, one imposing the King's authority on the colonies, was attempted in the 1680s with the establishment of the Dominion of New England. This was intended to help enforce the mercantile system.

## The Mercantile System

One of the arguments for colonization in the first place had been that colonies would increase the wealth of the mother country and lessen her dependence on other nations. According to the mercantile theory, she would prosper and grow strong by exporting more and more to foreigners and importing less and less from them. Colonies would aid by providing a market for her manufactured goods and a source of supply for raw materials she could not produce at home. To get the full benefit, she would have to exclude foreigners (as Spain had done) from her colonial trade.

On the whole, such a mercantile system would meet the needs of the colonies as well as those of the mother country. The colonies stood to gain by concentrating on the crude products of the field and forest, and exchanging these for the finer goods of manufacturers abroad who had the capital and skilled labor to produce them economically. In actual practice, the colonies did turn out products that the mother country needed for her own consumption or for resale to foreigners—products such as tobacco, furs, lumber, and naval stores. But the colonies also produced surpluses of commodities like wheat, flour, and fish that competed with commodities produced in the mother country. And whether the goods were complementary or competitive, the colonial producers sometimes found that they could make a better bargain with Spaniards, Frenchmen, or Hollanders than with Englishmen. Hence a considerable trade early developed between the English colonists and foreigners, especially the Dutch.

At first the English government, distracted as it was by the conflict between King and Parliament, made only half-hearted efforts to regulate the colonial trade in accordance with mercantilist principles. Once Oliver Cromwell was in power, he secured laws from Parliament (1650, 1651) to keep Dutch ships out of the English colonies. After the Restoration, under Charles II, the government went much further, adopting legislation that had the positive aim of directing colonial trade as well as the negative one of excluding foreigners from it.

This legislation consisted of three Navigation Acts. The first of these (1660) closed the colonies to all trade except that carried in English ships, which were defined as ships built in England or the colonies and manned by sailors of whom three-fourths were Englishmen or colonists. This law also required that certain enumerated items, among them tobacco, be exported from the colonies only to England or to an English possession. The second act (1663) provided that all goods sent from Europe to the colonies had to go by way of England and that taxes could be put on the goods during their transshipment. The third act (1673) was designed to prevent colonists from evading the export control (in regard to the enumerated items) by clearing from one colonial port for another and then actually heading for a foreign port. The new act levied a duty on cargoes bound for the intercolonial coastal trade. It also provided for the appointment of customs officials to collect the duties and administer the Navigation Acts. These acts, with later amendments and additions, were to form the legal basis of England's mercantile system for a century.

## The Dominion of New England

If the Navigation Acts were to be strictly enforced, the King would have to do more than dispatch customs officials to America. With the cooperation of Parliament, he would have to set up in London some kind of agency to oversee colonial affairs. He would also have to get more direct control over the colonial governments than he had.

Only in Virginia, a "royal colony" since 1624, did the King as yet have the right to appoint the governor. In Massachusetts, a "corporate colony," the people elected their own governor, as they also did in Plymouth. In Maryland, a "proprietary colony," the appointing power had been delegated to the proprietor. When Charles II created other proprietary colonies—Carolina, New York, New Jersey, Pennsylvania—he himself followed the Maryland example. And when he gave royal charters to Connecticut and Rhode Island, he accepted these two as "corporate colonies" by allowing them to go on choosing their officials. Moreover, he and his predecessors had permitted the development of an assembly representing the people (or some of the people) in each of the colonies—royal, corporate, or proprietary. And the assemblies were claiming more and more power for themselves.

For help in enforcing the new trade regulations, Charles II could not place much reliance on the colonial governments. Least of all could he depend on Massachusetts, the worst offender, which dared to behave practically like an independent republic, even usurping the sovereign's prerogative of coining money. The Puritan oligarchs, whose religion in itself was obnoxious to him, persisted in maintaining their own established church instead of the Church of England, thus violating the terms of the Massachusetts Bay Company's charter, which obliged the colony to conform to English law. Many of the Massachusetts merchants, disregarding the Navigation Acts as well, evaded the payment of duties and made smuggling a regular business.

After a royal investigating commission had visited the Bay Colony and reported back to London the extent of the colony's illegal business, Charles II decided to take action for controlling and chastising Massachusetts in particular, and tightening control over the American empire in general. In 1675 he set up a special committee, the Lords of Trade (consisting of some of his official advisers on the Privy Council), to make recommendations for imperial reform. The Lords of Trade recommended that the King participate more directly in colonial government. He did so, and at the same time struck a blow at Massachusetts when, in 1679, he denied her authority over New Hampshire and chartered a separate, royal colony whose governor he would himself appoint.

Charles II wished to make a royal colony of Massachusetts as well, but her corporate charter was one he could not revoke without a lawsuit. He soon had grounds for action. When the Lords of Trade ordered Massachusetts to see that the Navigation Acts were obeyed, the General Court replied that, in view of the charter's provisions for self-government, Parliament had no power to legislate for the colony. When the Lords of Trade sent over a customs official to see to the enforcement of the acts, the General Court not only refused to recognize him but arrested the local agents he appointed. Finally the King started legal proceedings that led, in 1684, to the revocation of the charter.

His brother and successor, James II, went much further when he came to the throne in 1685. He combined Massachusetts and the rest of the New England colonies into one Dominion of New England, and later he added New York and New Jersey to it. Within this dominion he eliminated the existing assemblies, and over it he placed a single governor, Sir Edmund Andros, with headquarters in Boston. An able but stern and tactless administrator, Andros thoroughly antagonized the people as he proceeded to levy taxes and enforce the Navigation Acts. When colonists protested on the basis of their rights as Englishmen—especially their right to be taxed only with the consent of their representatives—he retorted that they had no rights.

## The "Glorious Revolution"

Soon after the Bostonians heard of the 1688 movement to overthrow James II in England, they determined to overthrow his viceroy in New England. A mob set out after Andros and other royal officials; he escaped but later surrendered and was imprisoned.

The Massachusetts leaders now hoped to get back their old corporate charter, but they were to be disappointed. Despite the persuasive efforts of Increase Mather, an outstanding Puritan divine who was on a lobbying mission in London, the new sovereigns, William and Mary, combined Plymouth with Massachusetts and claimed the land as a royal colony (1691). Under the new charter, they themselves appointed the governor, but they restored the General Court with its elected lower house and allowed the General Court to choose the members of the upper house. This charter also did away with the religious test for voting and officeholding. Though there remained a property requirement, the great majority of Massachusetts men could meet it. Thus the Massachusetts government, no longer a Puritan oligarchy, began to be fairly democratic. Quakers, Baptists, and other sectarians now were free to worship as they pleased

## Confession of a Witch [1692]

Mrs. Mary Osgood, of Andover, Massachusetts, was examined for witchcraft, September 8, by a group of judges. They reported:

*She confesses that, about 11 years ago, when she was in a melancholy state and condition, she used to walk abroad in her orchard; and upon a certain time she saw the appearance of a cat, at the end of the house, which yet she thought was a real cat. However, at that time, it diverted her from praying to God, and instead thereof she prayed to the devil; about which time she made a covenant with the devil, who, as a black man, came to her and presented her a book, upon which she laid her finger, and that left a red spot: and that upon her signing, the devil told her he was her God, and that she should serve and worship him, and she believes she consented to it. She says, further, that about two years agone, she was carried through the air, in company with deacon Frye's wife, Ebenezer Baker's wife, and Goody Tyler, to five mile pond, where she was baptised by the devil, who dipped her face in the water and made her renounce her former baptism, and told her she must be his, soul and body, forever, and that she must serve him, which she promised to do.*

About six weeks later, on October 19, she was visited by Increase Mather, who reported:

*Mrs. Osgood freely and relentingly said that the confession which she made upon her examination for witchcraft, and afterwards acknowledged before the honourable judges, was wholly false, and that she was brought to the said confession by the violent urging and unreasonable pressings that were used toward her; she asserted that she never signed the devil's book, was never baptised by the devil, never afflicted any of the accusers, or gave her consent for their being afflicted.*

in what once had been the exclusive land of the Puritans, though all had to pay tithes in support of the established (Congregational) church.

The politico-religious crisis in Massachusetts gave rise to an atmosphere of tension and uncertainty in which public hysteria could thrive. This, together with the efforts of preachers to revive the Puritan sense of sin, led to the worst witch craze ever to occur in the English colonies (though others as bad or worse occurred in various part of contemporary Europe).

None of the seventeenth-century ministers labored harder to keep up the old faith than did Increase Mather and his son Cotton. Puritanism demanded a well-educated ministry, and the Mathers were intellectual giants. Like most scientists of the period, they believed in witches. In one of the many learned books he wrote, *Illustrious Providences* (1684), Increase Mather undertook to show that God had a special concern for New England and that the people should note carefully any evidence of "Witchcrafts, Diabolical Possessions, Remarkable Judgements upon noted Sinners," and the like. There later arose a widespread hysteria, which went to its greatest extremes in the Massachusetts town of Salem, where it was stimulated by the antics of two West Indian slaves who were steeped in voodoo lore. Hundreds of people were accused as witches, many of them were sentenced to die, and nineteen actually put to death before the witchcraft trials were stopped in 1692.

Afterward almost all the witch hunters publicly repented their part in the affair. The Mathers often were blamed for it, though in fact they had pleaded for moderation during the trials and had helped to bring them to an end. Still, the net effect was to diminish the prestige and authority of the Church and its leaders.

Andros had been ruling New York through a lieutenant governor, Captain Francis Nicholson, who enjoyed the support of the wealthy merchants and fur traders of the province. The same groups had shared in political power while New York was a proprietary colony of the Duke of York and after it became a royal colony upon the Duke's accession to the English throne as James II. The groups that were excluded from a fair share in the government—farmers, mechanics, small traders, and shopkeepers—already had a long accumulation of grievances when news came of James' fall and Andros' arrest. Rebellious militiamen promptly seized the New York City fort, and Lieutenant Governor Nicholson sailed away to England.

The leadership of the New York rebels fell to Jacob Leisler, who had come from Germany, succeeded as a merchant, and married into a prominent Dutch family, but had never gained acceptance as one of the colony's ruling class. Leisler's followers proclaimed him commander in chief, and he declared his loyalty to William and Mary. He claimed, as intended for him, the dispatches arriving from the King and Queen and addressed to "Our Lieutenant-Governor and Commander-in-Chief of our Province of New York, or in his absence to such as for the time being take care to keep the peace and administer the laws." Assuming the title of lieutenant governor, Leisler with the aid of the militia kept the peace and administered the laws for two years (1689–1691), until William and Mary finally appointed a new governor, who was given authority to call an elected assembly. When, ahead of the new governor, a British officer appeared with a contingent of troops, Leisler refused to surrender the fort to him. Leisler afterward yielded, but the delay gave his political enemies, soon back in power, a pretext for charging him with treason. He and a son-in-law were hanged, drawn, and quartered.

In Maryland the people at first assumed (erroneously) that the Catholic Lord Baltimore had sided with the Catholic James II and had opposed the accession of William and Mary. So, in 1689, an old opponent of the proprietor's government, John Coode, started a new revolt as head of an organization calling itself "An Association in Arms for the Defense of the Protestant Religion, and for Asserting the Right of King William and Queen Mary to the Province of Maryland and All the English Dominions." The insurgents drove out Lord Baltimore's officials and, through an elected convention, chose a committee to run the government for the time being. In 1691 William and Mary took advantage of their opportunity to deprive the proprietor of his authority and transform Maryland into a royal colony. (It became a proprietary colony again in 1715, after the fifth Lord Baltimore had joined the Anglican Church.)

Thus the Glorious Revolution of 1688 in England touched off revolutions, mostly bloodless, in the colonies. Under the new regime the representative assemblies that had been abolished were revived, but not the scheme for colonial unification from above. Several of the provinces, however, were now royal colonies in which the King appointed the governor, and over which he potentially had greater direct control than he once had had. The colonists had not yet challenged the ultimate authority of the King. "What had been won (possibly the word should be 'preserved')," W. F. Craven has written, "was the practical right of the colonists to determine very largely for themselves questions of public policy fundamentally affecting their domestic life. In this large measure of self-government the colonists were to find with time good cause for remembering the Revolution as a glorious one and, by remembering it, fresh and potent defenses for their rights of self-government."

# Selected Readings

General Accounts C. M. Andrews, *The Colonial Period of American History*° (4 vols., 1934–1938); Clarence L. Ver Steeg, *The Formative Years, 1607–1763* (1964).

New England C. M. Andrews, *The Fathers of New England* (1919); S. E. Morison, *Builders of the Bay Colony*° (1930); A. T. Vaughan, *New England Frontier: Puritans and Indians, 1620–*

1675 (1965); Perry Miller, *The New England Mind: The Seventeenth Century*° (1939); Bernard Bailyn, *The New England Merchants in the Seventeenth Century*° (1955); E. S. Morgan, *The Puritan Dilemma: The Story of John Winthrop*° (1958); S. H. Brockunier, *The Irrepressible Democrat: Roger Williams* (1940); Edith Curtis, *Anne Hutchinson* (1930); M. J. A. Jones, *Congregational Commonwealth: Connecticut, 1636–1662* (1968).

**The Middle Colonies** T. J. Wertenbaker, *The Founding of American Civilization: The Middle Colonies* (1938); T. J. Condon, *New York Beginnings: The Commercial Origins of New Netherland* (1968); A. W. Trelease, *Indian Affairs in Colonial New York: The Seventeenth Century* (1960); E. B. Bronner, *William Penn's "Holy Experiment": The Founding of Pennsylvania, 1681–1701* (1962); M. M. Dunn, *William Penn: Politics and Conscience* (1967); W. W. Comfort, *William Penn, 1644–1718* (1944); J. E. Pomfret, *The Province of West New Jersey, 1609–1702* (1956) and *The Province of East New Jersey* (1962).

**The South** W. F. Craven, *The Southern Colonies in the Seventeenth Century, 1607–1689* (1949); Verner Crane, *The Southern Frontier, 1670–1732*° (1956); M. P. Andrews, *The Founding of Maryland* (1933); R. L. Morton, *Colonial Virginia* (2 vols., 1960); T. J. Wertenbaker, *Torchbearer of the Revolution* (1940), on Nathaniel Bacon as a democratic hero; W. E. Washburn, *The Governor and the Rebel: A History of Bacon's Rebellion in Virginia* (1958), a less sympathetic account.

**Imperial Control** G. L. Beer, *The Origins of the British Colonial System* (1908) and *The Old Colonial System* (2 vols., 1912); L. A. Harper, *The English Navigation Laws* (1939); Viola Barnes, *The Dominion of New England* (1923); J. R. Reich, *Leisler's Rebellion* (1953); M. G. Hall, L. H. Leder, and M. G. Kammen, eds., *The Glorious Revolution*° (1964), a collection of contemporary writings.

---

° Titles available in paperback.

# Chapter 3
# Provincial Americans

The seventeenth-century colonists remained essentially transplanted Englishmen, though even the first arrivals had begun to depart from many of their accustomed ways. As new generations grew up in America they developed a more and more distinctive character. In the course of the eighteenth century they became provincial "Americans"—a term that had been applied to them even before 1700 but did not come into general use until after 1750.

There were three main reasons for the divergence between the culture of the colonies and that of the homeland. First, English society was not transplanted as a whole. The people who left for America were not entirely typical of England: usually they were the more discontented or the more adventurous; they were themselves in some degree "different." Second, they found in the New World a new environment with new challenges and opportunities. Certain elements of the English inheritance flourished and adapted themselves to the strange surroundings, while others withered or never took root at all. Third, some of the early colonists (the Dutch, for example) had come from countries other than England, and during the eighteenth century new arrivals in much larger numbers came from others places—from Scotland and Ireland, the European continent, and Africa. Hence, in America, there was a mixture of peoples and cultures, though the English continued to predominate.

Provincial Americans were affected by new currents of thought coming from abroad during the eighteenth century. This was the Age of the Enlightenment, when the ideas of the Englishman Sir Isaac Newton and other scientists (or "natural philosophers") gave a fresh conception of God's universe. They saw it as a universe that God had fashioned like a clock and had set going to operate with regularity. It followed natural laws that could be understood by the use of man's reason. The spirit of the Enlightenment spread from England and Europe to America.

## The John Ward House

The left-hand portion of this house in Salem, Massachusetts, was built in 1684. The right-hand portion, with another gable, was added later, and the lean-to in the rear still later. Note the second-story overhang. This was characteristic of many seventeenth-century dwellings in New England. It was copied from medieval English houses, but its origin and purpose are uncertain. The most likely theories are these: (1) It was a technical matter of construction: separate, offset posts for the two stories made possible a stronger framing than did one long post; (2) It was a matter of aesthetics: people liked the way the overhang looked. Note too the casement windows with their diamond-shaped panes, also typical of the time. (Top left, Essex Institute, Salem, Mass.)

## The John Ward House: Kitchen

In colonial New England the kitchen usually was located either in an ell of the house or in a lean-to at the rear (in the South, the kitchen often was located in a separate outbuilding). The kitchen, with its large fireplace, was used not only for the preparation of meals but also as a dining room, a general workroom, and to a considerable extent a living room. Its furniture included a trestle table, chairs, a wash-bench, meat tubs, a cheese press, a churn, a spinning wheel, often a loom, and sometimes a pallet bed for an indentured servant or an apprentice. (Bottom left, Essex Institute, Salem, Mass.)

In the developing American character there were variations from colony to colony and from region to region. The New England colonies had much in common with one another, less in common with the middle colonies (Pennsylvania, New Jersey, New York), and still less in common with the Southern colonies. These last fell into two subgroups with important differences between the two: the tobacco colonies (Maryland, Virginia, and North Carolina) and the others (South Carolina and, after its founding in 1733, Georgia).

## THE EXPANDING SETTLEMENTS

The population of English America increased tenfold between 1700 and 1776. This mainly reflected the growth of existing colonies; only one new colony was founded during these years.

### The Founding of Georgia

Georgia, the last of the mainland colonies, was unique in its origins. It was founded by neither a corporation nor a proprietorship, and its guiding purpose was neither to make profits nor to create a sectarian refuge. In the beginning Georgia was the work of trustees serving without pay. Their main purpose was twofold: to provide a new start in life for Englishmen imprisoned for debt, and to erect a military barrier against the Spaniards on the southern border of English America.

As claimants to the whole continent, the Spaniards had looked suspiciously upon the encroachment at Jamestown, and had taken one captive while giving up three of their own men in a half-hearted attempt to frighten the English away. In a treaty of 1676 Spain recognized England's title to lands already occupied by English subjects. Ten years later Spanish forces from Florida attacked and destroyed an outlying South Carolina settlement south of the treaty line. When Spain and England went to war in Europe (1701–1713) hostilities were renewed in America, and thereafter another European conflict with American repercussions was continually expected.

General James Oglethorpe, a hero of the late war with Spain, was much concerned about the need for a buffer colony between South Carolina and Florida. As head of a parliamentary committee investigating English prisons, Oglethorpe also knew at first hand the plight of honest debtors rotting in confinement. He conceived the idea of solving both problems at once by resettling such prisoners as farmer-soldiers on the faraway frontier.

The charter from George II (1732) transferred the land between the Savannah and Altamaha rivers to the administration of Oglethorpe and his fellow trustees for a period of twenty-one years. In their colonization policies they were to keep in mind the needs of military security. Landholdings were limited in size so as to make settlement compact. Negroes—free or slave—were excluded, and Roman Catholics also, to forestall the danger of wartime insurrection and of collusion with enemy coreligionists. And the Indian trade was strictly regulated, with rum prohibited, to lessen the risk of Indian complications.

Oglethorpe himself led the first expedition, building a fortified town at the mouth of the Savannah in 1733, and later constructing additional forts south of the Altamaha. Only a few debtors were released from jail and sent to Georgia, but hundreds of needy tradesmen and artisans from England and Scotland and religious refugees from Switzerland and Germany were brought to the new colony at the expense of the trustees, who raised funds from charitable individuals as well as from Parliament. Though other settlers came at their own expense, immigrants were not attracted in large numbers during the early years. Newcomers generally preferred to settle in South Carolina, where there were no laws against big plantations, slaves, and rum. Before the twenty-one years of the trusteeship were up, these restrictions were repealed, and after 1750 Georgia developed along lines similar to those of South Carolina.

### The Labor Supply

After 1700 few white servants headed for the South, even for Virginia or Maryland, where they once had flocked. The largest numbers now went to Pennsylvania, where opportunities and working conditions were most attractive, and they continued to go to Pennsylvania and New York, though in dwindling numbers, until long after the American Revolution. Many of these people were "free willers" or "redemptioners" from Europe, who gave their indentures to the captain of the ship they boarded. He auctioned off their contracts after putting in at an American port, and each buyer then claimed his servants.

In Virginia and Maryland white servitude was being replaced by Negro slavery, which had advantages for the master. It gave him a constant labor supply and practically complete control over it. Identifiable by their color, black slaves could not run away and merge themselves with the mass of free humanity as white servants could. Nor could slaves rise out of their bondage

to compete with their masters for wealth and political influence as the servants sometimes did. Moreover, considering the length of their service, slaves were cheaper, especially with the fall of slave prices after 1697, when the monopoly of the Royal African Company was broken and the slave trade was opened to English and colonial merchants on a competitive basis.

This trade was dominated by ships owned in England but was shared by others owned in New England. The latter often followed a "triangular" route. That is, a ship took rum and other items from a New England port to the Guinea Coast of Africa, slaves from Africa to the West Indies, and sugar and molasses as well as specie and bills from the West Indies to the home port. There some of the cargo would be

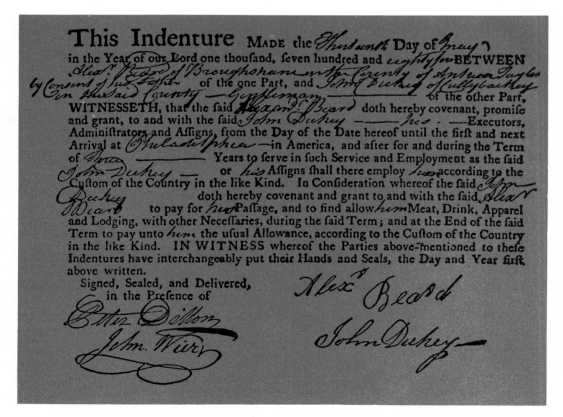

## An Eighteenth–Century Indenture

This contract, dated May 13, 1784, was made late in the history of indentured servitude and typifies the standardized form that developed. Note that it is printed, with spaces left blank to be filled in. In this particular case, the contract was made between the master and his servant before either of them sailed for America. Originally, a contract was written in two identical parts on a single sheet, which was torn in two, leaving an indented or indentured edge—hence the term "indenture."

distilled into rum for another voyage of the same kind. On the African coast the slave marts were kept supplied by native chieftains who made a business of capturing enemy tribesmen in warfare and bringing them, tied together in long lines known as "coffles," out of the jungle. Then, after some haggling on the seashore, came the horrors of the "middle passage"—so called because it was the second of the three legs of the voyage—during which the slaves were packed in the dark and stinking hold, with no sanitary facilities, no room to stand up, and scarcely air enough to breathe. Those who died en route were thrown overboard, and the losses from disease were generally high. Those who survived were "seasoned" for a time in the West Indies before being shipped on to the mainland.

Slavery in colonial times was not confined to any single region. Slaves labored as domestics and occasionally as farm hands for wealthy families in the North. As of 1763 there were about 230,000 Negroes in all the colonies, most of them slaves. About 16,000 lived in New England, 29,000 in the middle colonies, and the rest in the South. By 1775 nearly half of the people of Virginia and more than two-thirds of those of South Carolina were black.

## Population Growth

Besides the Africans, other non-English peoples came in large numbers to the colonies after the end of the seventeenth century, while immigration from England itself fell off. Recovering from a prolonged depression in the 1630s, England thereafter began to develop more and more industries which demanded workmen, so that the talk of overpopulation ceased to be heard. Instead of encouraging emigration from its own shores, the government tried to check the loss of English manpower by prohibiting the departure of skilled artisans, while continuing to unload the unemployable or the undesirable upon the defenseless colonies. Although, during the eighteenth century, the colonies received relatively few newcomers from England, the populations of several of them were swelled by vast numbers of arrivals from France, Germany, Switzerland, Ireland, and Scotland.

Of these immigrants the earliest though not the most numerous were the French Calvinists,

or Huguenots. Under the Edict of Nantes (1598) they had enjoyed liberties and privileges that enabled them to constitute practically a state within the state in Roman Catholic France. In 1685 the edict was revoked, and singly and in groups the Huguenots took the first opportunity to leave the country, until a total of about 300,000 had left for England, the Netherlands, America, and elsewhere, only a small minority of them going to the English colonies. These émigrés were mostly artisans, merchants, and men of letters and science who enriched their new homes with both their talents and their wealth. In America they settled in the towns along the coast from Charleston to Boston, to become the ancestors of Americans like Paul Revere (Rivoire).

Like the French Protestants, many German Protestants suffered from the arbitrary enactments of their rulers, and German Catholics as well as Protestants suffered even more from the devastating wars of the Sun King of France, Louis XIV. The Rhineland of southwestern Germany, the area known as the Palatinate, was especially exposed to the slaughter of its people and the ruin of its farms. For the Palatine Germans, the unusually cold winter of 1708–1709 came as the last straw, and more than 12,000 of them sought refuge in England. The Catholics among them were shipped back to Germany and the rest were resettled in England, Ireland, or the colonies.

Arriving in New York, approximately 3,000 of them tried to make homes in the Mohawk Valley, only to be ousted by rapacious colonial landlords. Some of the Palatines moved farther up the Mohawk, but most of them made their way to Pennsylvania, where they received a hearty welcome. After that, the Quaker colony was the usual destination of Germans, who sailed for America in growing numbers, including some Moravians and Mennonites with religious views similar to those of the Quakers. But quite a few of the German Protestants went to North Carolina, especially after the founding of New Bern (1710) by a company of 600 German-speaking Swiss. All together, the Germans comprised the largest body of eighteenth-century white immigrants except for the Scotch-Irish.

The Scotch-Irish, the most numerous of the

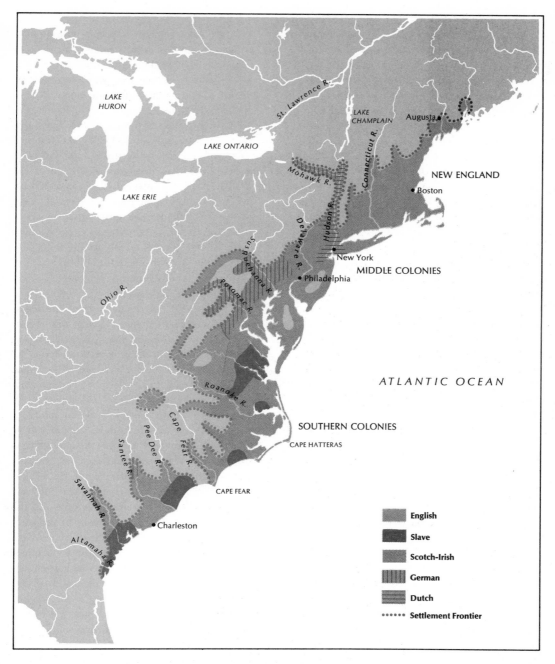

**Distribution of Major Immigrant Groups in Colonial America**

newcomers, were not Irishmen at all, though
coming from Ireland, and they were distinct
from the Scots who came to America directly
from Scotland. In the early 1600s King James I,
to further the conquest of Ireland, had seen to

the peopling of the northern county of Ulster
with his subjects from the Scottish Lowlands,
who as good Presbyterians might be relied upon
to hold their ground against the Irish Catholics.
These Ulster colonists—the Scotch-Irish—even-

tually prospered despite the handicap of a barren soil and the necessity of border fighting with the Irish tribesmen. Then, after about a century, the English government destroyed their prosperity by prohibiting the export of their woolens and other products, and at the same time threatened their religion by virtually outlawing it and insisting upon conformity with the Anglican Church. As the long-term leases of the Scotch-Irish terminated, in the years after 1710, the English landlords doubled and even tripled the rents. Rather than sign new leases, thousands upon thousands of the ill-used tenants embarked in successive waves of emigration.

Understandably a cantankerous and troublesome lot, these people often were coldly received at the colonial ports, and most of them pushed out to the edge of the American wilderness. There they occupied land with scant regard for ownership, believing that "it was against the laws of God and nature that so much land should be idle while so many Christians wanted it to labor on and to raise bread." There also they fought the Indians as earlier they had fought the Irish. Among their illustrious descendants was the characteristically Scotch-Irish Andrew Jackson.

The Scots and the Irish, as migrants to America, had no connection with the Scotch-Irish. Scottish Highlanders, some of them Roman Catholics frustrated in the rebellions of 1715 and 1745, went with their tartans and kilts and bagpipes to more than one of the colonies, but mostly to North Carolina. Presbyterian Lowlanders, afflicted with high rents in the country and unemployment in town, left in largest numbers shortly before the American Revolution. These Scots, Lowlanders and Highlanders alike, with few exceptions became Loyalists after the outbreak of the Revolutionary War, but the Scotch-Irish were Patriots almost to the man, as were the Irish. The Irish had migrated in trickles over a long period and, by the time of the Revolution, were about as numerous as the Scots, though less conspicuous, many of them having lost their Roman Catholic religion and their identity as Irishmen.

All these various immigrants contributed to the remarkable growth of the colonies. In 1700 the colonial population totaled a quarter of a million or less; by 1775 it was nearly ten times as large, more than two million. The number practically doubled every twenty-five years, as Benjamin Franklin observed, leading the English clergyman Thomas Malthus to his pessimistic conclusion (1798) that any population, if unchecked, would increase in a geometrical progression while the means of subsistence (except in a new and favored country like America) could not be increased nearly so fast. Important as the continuing immigration was, the rapid growth of the colonial population was mainly due to natural increase, to the excess of births over deaths. In the colonies, with their abundance of land and opportunity, large families were an asset rather than a liability, and husbands and wives heeded the Biblical advice: "Be ye fruitful and multiply."

Hence the colonists of English origin, those who had arrived earliest and had had the longest time to multiply, continued greatly to outnumber those of non-English origin. Yet the proportion of non-English ancestry increased year by year, from a tenth in 1700 to a third (including the people from Africa) in 1760. The most homogeneous and most purely English part of the colonies was New England, while the most cosmopolitan part was the middle colonies, above all Pennsylvania. By the 1770s the Pennsylvania population was in origin roughly a third English, a third German, and a third Scotch-Irish. These groups did not intermix very much but were concentrated in separate areas—the English around Philadelphia, the Germans to the north and west, and the Scotch-Irish still farther out on the frontier. Many of the Germans continued to speak their native language, which eventually was corrupted into a German-English dialect known as "Pennsylvania Dutch." Nevertheless, in the colonies as a whole, there was a good deal of intermarriage between the different nationalities, and even before the Revolution thousands of Americans could trace their ancestry to two or more nations of the Old World.

As compared with the population of England, that of the colonies was not only mixed but also youthful and masculine, containing somewhat fewer old persons and women, especially along the frontier. And the colonial population was surprisingly mobile, New Englanders resettling

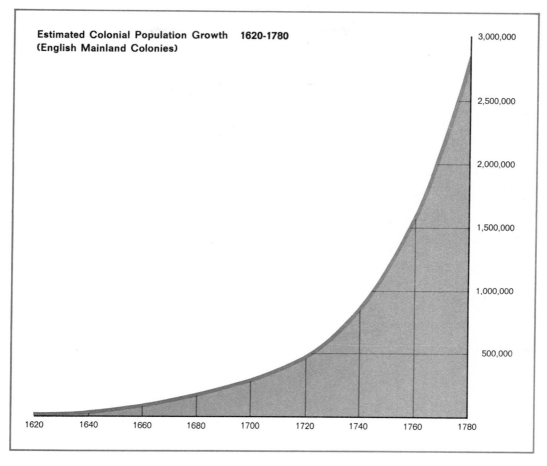

Estimated Colonial Population Growth   1620-1780
(English Mainland Colonies)

in New Jersey and other colonies to the south, and Pennsylvanians (Scotch-Irish and Germans) swarming up the Shenandoah Valley to people the back country of the Carolinas. In all the colonies men and women pushed upstream toward the unsettled wilderness, until with Daniel Boone leading the way into Kentucky (1769) they began even to occupy the land beyond the mountains.

Along the seacoast a number of villages grew into small cities. For more than a century after its founding, Boston remained the largest town, but eventually it was overtaken by both Philadelphia and New York. In 1760 Philadelphia had more than 23,000 people, New York about 18,000, and Boston nearly 16,000. Next in order were Charleston, S.C., with approximately 8,000 and Newport, R.I., with 7,500. After 1700 these colonial towns increased more rapidly than most English cities, yet not always so rapidly as did

the American population as a whole. Eight out of a hundred Americans lived in towns in 1720, and only about five or six out of a hundred in 1742. The rest of the people—the overwhelming majority throughout the colonial period—were scattered over the countryside and lived upon farms of one description or another.

## THE ECONOMIC BASIS

In the shaping of the provincial economy—that is, in the determination of the ways the colonists made their living—three forces were especially important. One of these was the policy of the British government, which discouraged certain occupations and encouraged others, in accordance with mercantilist principles. A second and more important influence derived from the geographical conditions in America, which favored some lines of activity and made others impracticable. A third consisted of the aims and energies of the individual settlers, who brought with them from the British Isles and the European Continent (and, in the case of the slaves, from Africa) their own skills and habits and aspirations for personal success. As a result of these diverse factors, there flourished in the eighteenth century a variety of agricultural, industrial, and commercial pursuits, not all of which conformed to the broad mercantilistic plan.

## Agriculture

Though there were regional differences, farming throughout the colonies had certain characteristics in common. In all the colonies it was a matter of adapting European plants and animals to American conditions or applying European techniques to the cultivation of native crops. The colonist's tools and methods, while an improvement on those of the Indian, continued to be extremely primitive. The ground was still broken with hoe and mattock or with a crude wooden plow, usually drawn by oxen because of their slower and steadier pull than horses could provide, and often requiring two men to hold and guide it. Harvesting was backbreaking work with sickle or scythe. Grain was threshed with a flail or by the trampling of oxen, and it was winnowed by being tossed in the air for the breeze to carry away the chaff. In George Washington's time these processes were not much advanced beyond what they had been in the day of the Pharaohs, and in colonial America there was even less care of the soil than there had been in ancient Egypt. Most of the colonists gave little thought to conserving their land by rotating crops, applying fertilizers, or checking erosion. Their attitude was reasonable enough in their circumstances: it paid them to economize on labor, not on land.

Near the frontier—that ever-expanding arc from Maine to Georgia, which bounded the area of settlement—subsistence farming was the rule. The frontiersman planted his corn and beans amid the stumps in patches he had incompletely reclaimed from the forest, and with his crops and his catch of wild game he fed himself and his family. Eventually some of the backwoodsmen went in for cattle raising on a fairly large scale, especially in Pennsylvania and the Carolinas. In these areas, long before the day of the cowboy on the Great Plains, herders let their branded cattle roam over an open range and, after the annual roundup, drove them to distant cities. The town of Cowpens, South Carolina, derived its name from its origin as a cattle-raising center. As the line of settlement moved outward, so did the frontier kind of farm and ranch life. Within that line—in areas that, beginning with the seacoast itself, had shared most of the frontier characteristics at one time or another—arose patterns of agriculture increasingly more elaborate, more productive, and more diverse.

In New England—where farmers once had lived on village lots, shared the "commons" as pasture and timberland, and tilled outlying fields—the system of landholding gradually changed. After 1700 the commons were partly divided into private property, and the fields were consolidated into separate farms. The typical farm became one that was small enough to be worked by the farmer, his sons, and perhaps an occasional hired hand, with the aid of neighbors at harvests and at house or barn raisings. It was bounded by fences made of stones that had been laboriously cleared off the fields. A fairly self-sufficient unit, producing mainly for use rather than for sale, it contained a variety of scrawny livestock, apple and other orchards, and fields devoted chiefly to hay and corn, the prevalence of the "blast" or black-stem rust having discouraged the cultivation of wheat.

An exception to the usual New England farm scene was to be found on the shores and islands of Narragansett Bay. Here were rich and extensive farms on which were bred fine sheep, cattle, and horses, notably the Narragansett pacer. And here gangs of Negro slaves were used.

In New York, despite the abundance of excellent soil, agricultural productivity lagged because of the engrossment of the land in great estates, running to thousands and even hundreds of thousands of acres, on which few people were willing to work as tenants when they could get farms of their own in other colonies. The Dutch and their descendants set examples of careful tillage on the freeholds they had acquired at an early date.

In Pennsylvania, of all the colonies the most

favored by nature for farming, the Germans likewise applied the intensive cultivation they had learned in the old country. Their neat and substantial barns were their pride, but the work of their womenfolk in the fields was sometimes shocking to non-Germans. With fairly large holdings, these farmers needed all the labor they could get, and in addition to their wives and daughters they employed indentured servants, women as well as men.

In New York and Pennsylvania the farmers concentrated upon the production of staples to be sold abroad and at home. After ceasing to produce enough food to feed all its own people, New England depended upon these "bread colonies" for its wheat. So, to some extent, did those Southern colonies that were preoccupied with the growing of tobacco.

In the Chesapeake region there still existed tobacco farms as small as a hundred acres, cultivated by the owners, their families, and perhaps a servant or a slave or two. Such farms, however, had come to be overshadowed by large plantations with thousands of acres and dozens of Negroes. The Maryland plantation of Charles Carroll of Carrollton, reputedly the wealthiest man in the colonies, covered 40,000 acres and contained 285 slaves. On the tobacco plantations slave labor was easily adapted to the simple and repetitive round of tasks that the crop required—sowing, transplanting, weeding, worming, picking, curing, stripping, and packing.

Slave labor was also fairly well suited to rice culture along the Georgia and Carolina coasts. Here dikes and ditches leading from the tidal rivers permitted the necessary flooding and draining of the paddies, while care was taken to see that no salt water reached the rice with the incoming tide. To cultivate the growing rice, men had to stand knee-deep in mud, their bare backs exposed to malarial mosquitoes and to the broiling sun. Since white men could not be hired to do it, Negroes were compelled to perform this torturing and unhealthful work. But the rice plantations were smaller than the tobacco plantations and did not provide a similar year-round routine that would utilize slave labor to the full.

Indigo supplemented rice after the successful cultivation of the dye plant (1743) by Eliza Lucas, the daughter of a West Indian planter. Grown on high ground, the indigo did not get in the way of the rice on the river bottoms, and it occupied the slaves at times when they were not busy with the rice. They tended the indigo fields, cut the leaves, soaked them in vats, and extracted the residue as a blue powder. Glad for a chance to be freed from foreign sources of the dye, Parliament granted a bounty of sixpence a pound.

The British government tried to encourage the production of other crops that would meet the needs of mercantilism. It gave bounties for hemp, and a little was grown in the colonies, particularly in North Carolina, but not enough to make the experiment pay. The government also attempted to force the growth of grapes for wine and of mulberry trees for silk, but had even less success with these than with hemp. Too much skilled labor was required for such products. Obstinately the colonial farmers and planters stuck to those lines of production in which they had a comparative advantage over producers elsewhere in the world. In some cases, as with tobacco and indigo, the colonial products happened to supplement those grown in England and thus fit the mercantilistic pattern. In other cases, as with wheat, the produce of the colonies competed with that of the mother country and was either irrelevant to the mercantile system or incompatible with it.

## Industries

In the 1700s, as in earlier times, most families produced nearly all their necessities within the household, but an increasing quantity of goods was manufactured outside the home, in shops. Specialists in various arts and crafts had come to America in the seventeenth century but found it hard to make a living from their specialties. These men had to turn to farming, and their skills deteriorated from disuse. Even after 1700 there were few opportunities for craftsmen in rural areas, particularly in the colonies to the south of Pennsylvania. On many a plantation, slaves were trained to produce the needed manufactures that it was not feasible to import from England.

In the rising towns, artisans of many kinds appeared—carpenters, chandlers (candlemak-

ers), coopers (barrelmakers), cordwainers (shoe-
makers), weavers, tailors, wheelwrights, and
dozens of others. Except in such lines as mil-
linery and dressmaking, women artisans were
rare, though now and then a widow took over
her husband's work and succeeded as a cobbler,
tinworker, or even blacksmith. By 1750 almost
a third of the people of Philadelphia owed their
living to a craft of some kind.

The craft usually was a family enterprise, and
the shop was on the ground floor of the master
craftsman's home. The master was assisted by
his sons and by one or more journeymen and
apprentices, who lived as members of his household, and who aspired eventually to become
masters with shops of their own. In some ways
the craftsman was like the small businessman of
the present. He had to procure and train workers, provide materials, supervise the work (while
taking an active part in it), and find a market.
When possible, he made goods to order, or, as
he called them, "bespoke" goods, but in slack
times he might produce a stock of articles for
general sale. In newspaper advertisements he
sometimes made exaggerated and even fraudulent claims for his wares, while running down
the wares of his competitors. He sold on credit
or for barter, seldom for cash.

In America the guild, or association of craftsmen, which in England regulated each of the
trades, did not take root. Regulations regarding
apprenticeship, the quality of goods, and other
matters were provided by the colonial and municipal governments. Despite the laws intended
to maintain high standards, some of the products
were shoddy and most of them were inferior to
the machine-made goods of today. By 1750,
however, American artisans were turning out
some articles that compared with the best of
that time or of any time. For instance, the gunsmiths of Lancaster, Pennsylvania, were justly
famous for the Pennsylvania rifle (also known as
the Kentucky rifle), and the wagonmakers of
the same town for the Conestoga wagon (the
original "covered wagon," with ends up-curved
to hold the load securely on hills and rough
roads). American silversmiths, such as Paul
Revere, did work as fine as that of England or
France and finer than that of the rest of Europe.
The same was true of American cabinetmakers.

Colonial craftsmanship became notable for
quantity as well as quality. As late as 1700 all
but a tiny fraction of the manufactures that the
colonists bought were made in England. Before
the Revolution, more than half of the manufactures were made in America. The rise of the
colonial craftsman was watched with concern
by men in London who took the doctrines of
mercantilism seriously.

When colonial merchants began to organize
the work of shops and households on a larger
and more efficient scale, there arose the "putting-out" system, which was a forerunner of the
later factory system. The merchant supplied
materials to workers in homes or shops, then
gathered up and marketed the finished product.
Before the Revolution, Lynn, Massachusetts,
was already famous for shoemaking and
Germantown, Pennsylvania, for producing knit
goods. Under the putting-out system the workers were not drawn together as in post-Revolutionary factories.

Water power was widely used in various kinds
of colonial mills. At the rapids of streams small
enough to be easily dammed, grist and fulling
mills were set up to take some of the heavier
labor out of the household, grinding grain and
fulling cloth (shrinking and tightening the weave
by a process of soaking and pounding) for the
farmers in the area. The millowner was usually
a farmer himself in his spare time. He frequently
used his water wheel to power a sawmill for
cutting his neighbors' logs. Other and busier
sawmills accompanied the lumber industry,
which followed the retreating forest. Circular
saws were as yet unknown, and the up-and-
down powered saw, while it would do the work
of twenty men in cutting soft pine, was not very
efficient in cutting hardwoods, particularly if
the trees were large. So it had to be supplemented by the large "pit saw" operated by two
men, one down in a pit and the other on the
ground above, and also by the ax and the adze,
the hammer and the wedge. Other forest industries yielded pitch, tar, resin, turpentine, and
potash for a number of industrial uses.

Like lumbering, the fur trade and the fisheries
were extractive industries, depending closely
upon the resources provided by nature. Both
fishing and fur trading became big businesses

employing what were, by colonial standards, large amounts of capital. It was expensive to provide fur traders with goods for bartering with Indian trappers—guns, knives, blankets, looking-glasses, and beads to exchange for furs and hides—and most of the business came to be controlled by English merchants in London and colonial merchants in Albany, Philadelphia, and Charleston. It was costly also to outfit fleets for the fishing industry, which concentrated mainly in New England waters, though almost every farmer near a stream or pond was at least a part-time fisherman.

The fisheries led to shipbuilding, the first colonial-built ships being put together on the New England coast for the use of fishermen, and the abundance of timber and naval stores enabled the industry in the colonies to expand to the point of outdoing that of England itself. So cheap and yet so seaworthy were the materials that, despite the high wages of colonial labor, excellent ships could be produced at as little as half the cost of those built in English yards. Usually a master shipwright contracted for the construction of a vessel, and he procured, paid, and directed the laborers who did the work. While New England kept its early lead in shipbuilding, New York and Pennsylvania also had their shipyards, and Virginia and the Carolinas, with their fine supply of live-oak timber, became important centers of the industry in the latter half of the eighteenth century.

Some undertakings on a still-larger scale than ship construction were to be found in the iron industry. From almost the very beginnings of Virginia and Massachusetts, small bloomeries and forges were erected to utilize the bog ores in those colonies, and eventually sizable furnaces were erected to smelt either bog or rock ores in almost all the colonies. The most extensive industrial enterprise anywhere in English America was that of the German ironmaster Peter Hasenclever, in northern New Jersey. It was founded in 1764 with British capital and was operated thereafter with a labor force of several hundred, many of whom were brought over from ironworks in Germany. It included not only furnaces and forges but also sawmills and a gristmill.

From the beginning of colonization, the home government encouraged the colonial production of iron in a crude form, as a raw material for English mills and foundries. When colonial ironmakers began to produce more than merely the crude metal, their competitors in England induced Parliament to pass the Iron Act of 1750, which removed the English duty on pig and bar iron but forbade the colonists to erect new mills for the secondary processing of iron or steel. This prohibition was in line with other acts intended to limit the rise of advanced manufactures in America. The Woolen Act (1699) prohibited the export of wool or woolens from a colony to any place outside its boundaries, and the Hat Act (1732) similarly prohibited the export of hats, which could be cheaply made in America because of the availability of beaver skins. But the colonists usually disregarded such legislation when it was in their interest to do so.

## Money and Commerce

Though the colonists produced most of what they consumed, they by no means achieved economic self-sufficiency. The colonies as a whole could not supply their entire wants from their own agriculture and industry. Neither could any of the separate colonies, nor could an individual household except at an extremely low level of living. To maintain and raise their living standards the mainland colonists had to have the benefits of trade with one another and with people overseas.

Intercolonial trade was fairly extensive and diversified. In the busy coastal traffic the surplus products of each region were exchanged—such products as the fish and rum of New England, the flour and meat of the middle colonies, and the tobacco and indigo of the South. The trade between the seaports and their hinterland involved some of these same products, besides many others, including the variety of small articles carried by the packhorse peddler. A large proportion of the commodities distributed upriver from the seaports had their origin abroad, and a large proportion of those gathered in the interior were destined for export. Much of the intercolonial and inland trade was thus a part of overseas commerce.

Foreign trade provided indispensable consumer and capital goods that the colonists could

**Regional Economic Specialization and Foreign Markets in Colonial America**

not manufacture for themselves in suitable quantity or quality. From abroad the millowner had to get his machinery, the shipwright his hardware and navigating instruments, the farmer his spades and other tools, the Indian trader most of his supplies. Even a modest home included kitchen utensils, tableware, needles and thread, lanterns, and other equipment of European make. Wealthier families bought additional imports, luxury items such as mirrors, paper, books, fine furniture, and fancy cloth. The more the colonists prospered, whether individually or collectively, the more they demanded goods of foreign manufacture.

The central problem in the overseas commerce of the colonies was to find the means of payment for these increasing imports. Money was scarce in the colonies. They did not mine their own gold or silver, and the mercantilist policy was intended to drain them of such specie as they might acquire. They did obtain a motley collection of Spanish and other European coins from their dealings with pirates and from certain routes of overseas trade. Generally, in their transactions with one another, the colonists resorted to barter or else used money substitutes, though always calculating in terms of pounds, shillings, and pence. Beaver skins circulated widely as a medium of exchange and so did tobacco—not the leaves but warehouse certificates representing tobacco in storage. All the colonies experimented at one time or another with paper currency, often securing it with land. But Parliament suppressed this expedient by legislating against the Massachusetts land bank in 1740, and by outlawing paper money as legal tender in New England in 1751 and in the rest of the colonies later on. Anyhow,

this kind of paper was not acceptable in payment for imported goods and services, which had to be bought with specie or with bills of exchange arising from colonial exports. In short, the colonies had to sell abroad in order to buy from abroad, but British policy attempted to limit and control their selling opportunities.

Though the tobacco planters had an abundant staple for export, they were not allowed to dispose of it to the highest bidder in the markets of the world. According to the Navigation Acts, tobacco was one of the "enumerated items" that must be exported only to the British Isles, whence more than half of it was reexported to other places. The laws also prohibited the growing of tobacco in the British Isles, but protection against competition in the mother country did not quite offset the disadvantages of the colonial planter.

He usually sold his annual crop to an English merchant (or after the mid-eighteenth century to a Scottish merchant) either directly or through a factor in the colonies, and the merchant credited him with its value, after deducting charges for shipping, insurance, and a merchant's commission. Through the merchant he bought slaves and manufactured goods, and the merchant deducted the cost of these from the

### Charleston in 1740

This painting by a Charlestonian shows the busy waterfront on the Cooper River. The prominent steeple is that of St. Philip's Church. At this time, with a population of nearly 7,000, Charleston was the fourth largest of the colonial towns. Its merchants prospered by trading in the South Carolina staples, deerskins and rice. These were carried away in English ships, which brought in cargoes of furniture, shoes, linen, hardware, and other manufactured goods. Flour and foodstuffs were imported from the North, chiefly from Philadelphia, but Charleston had more commerce with the West Indies than with the Northern colonies. It had far more trade with England than did any Northern port. The city had developed remarkably in a space of less than forty years. Compare this picture with the 1704 map of Charleston on page 44.

planter's credit on the books. After tobacco prices had begun to fall, the planter often found at the end of a year that his crop did not pay for all the goods he had ordered in return. The merchant then carried him until the next year and charged interest on the extension of credit. As the years went by, the planter went more and more deeply into debt, eventually leaving his indebtedness to his heirs.

The colonial merchant in such ports as Boston, New York, and Philadelphia did not have the same difficulties as the tobacco planter, though he had others of his own. He was favored by the Navigation Acts, passed in 1650 and after, which excluded foreign ships from practically all of the colonial carrying trade. And he found a market in England for the furs, timber, naval stores, and vessels produced in the Northern colonies. But he could not profitably sell in England all the fish, flour, wheat, and meat which the colonies produced for export. He had to find other markets for these commodities if he was to obtain adequate means of paying for his imports from England.

Wherever he traded, his profits would be reduced if he obeyed the laws and paid the duties imposed on most of the colonial goods that went to England and on all the European goods that went through England to the colonies.

In the English island colonies of the West Indies the colonial merchant found a ready outlet for mainland products. In the French, Dutch, and Spanish islands of the Caribbean he also got eager customers—and often better prices. Responding to pressure from English sugar planters, who wished to monopolize the mainland trade, Parliament in the Molasses Act of 1733 put a high duty on foreign sugar taken to the continental colonies. The molasses duty was intended to discourage commerce with the foreign islands. But the Northern merchant could evade the tax by smuggling, and he often did.

From the ports of New England and the middle colonies went cargo after cargo of lumber, horses, wheat, flour, biscuits, corn, peas, potatoes, beef, pork, bacon, and fish. From the West Indies were obtained sugar, molasses,

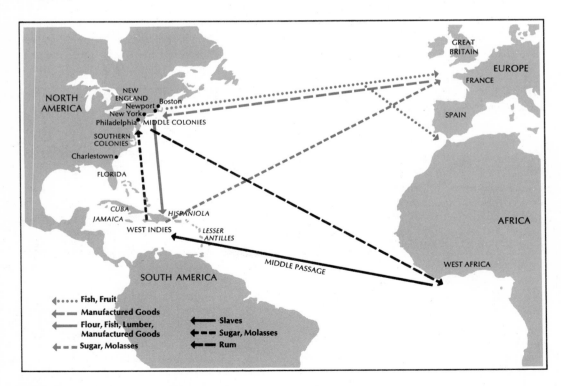

**Overseas Trades of Colonial America**

rum, dyewoods, cotton, ginger, coffee, Spanish coins and bills of exchange (these were drafts drawn by planters in the West Indies on merchants in England; they served much the same purpose as checks drawn on a bank). Sometimes West Indian products were carried directly to England; more commonly they were brought back to American ports, where part was sold in the domestic market and the rest exported to England. These exports, together with bills of exchange and Spanish money, helped to pay for the English goods imported into the thirteen colonies.

To and from England, to and from the West Indies—these were much the most important routes of trade for the Northern merchant. He also worked out a number of routes of indirect trade with the mother country, some of them complex and frequently changing, others fairly stable and somewhat "triangular" in their simplicity. Thus he might direct his ships to Catholic southern Europe with fish, then to England with wine and other proceeds in cash or bills of exchange, and then back home with manufactured goods.

## ASPECTS OF SOCIETY

In provincial America the generous economic basis of life supported a society in which the benefits of physical well-being were more widely diffused than anywhere else in the world. It was a comparatively open society, in which people had more opportunity than elsewhere to rise in economic and social status. Yet it was also a society with great inequalities, one that offered only hardship and poverty to many of its members and especially to those of African descent.

### The Class Structure

In England, as in Europe, class lines were sharply marked during the seventeenth and eighteenth centuries. The chances for any Englishman to rise above the station of his father and grandfather were rather slim—unless he went to America.

In the colonies the English class arrangement was not reproduced. Few or none of the nobility became colonists, though some of them were colonial enterprisers. A relatively small number of untitled gentlemen and a great many members of the middle and lower orders migrated to Virginia, Massachusetts, and other colonies. Some of these arrivals doubtless hoped to reconstruct in America something like the social system they had known in England, only here they hoped to occupy the higher levels themselves. A fortunate few did acquire extensive landholdings and proceeded to mimic the aristocrats back home, but no true aristocracy was transplanted to the colonies.

A colonial class system nevertheless grew up. Once social differentiation was well developed, as it was by the middle of the eighteenth century, the upper classes in the colonies consisted of the royal officials, the proprietary families, the great landholders in the North and the planters in the South, and the leading merchants with their investments mostly in forms of property other than land. The middle classes included most of the landowning farmers and, in the towns, the lesser merchants, shopkeepers, ship captains, professional men, and self-employed artisans. The lower classes comprised the indentured servants and the poorest farmers, together with the comparatively small number of wage earners, including farm hands, sailors, and fishermen. Forming a separate class or caste, though often working in the fields alongside white servants and even alongside men of the master class, were the Negro slaves, the lowliest of all.

All except the slaves could aspire to a higher place for themselves or at least for their children. Once a man had made a fortune, he was usually accepted by those who theretofore had considered him their social inferior. The colonists, believing in enterprise and material success, honored the self-made man. Afterward his descendants were inclined to forget the humble and even grubby origins of the family fortune and to think of themselves as thoroughgoing aristocrats. For example, one of the "first families" of eighteenth-century Virginia, the Byrds, enjoyed a fortune that William Byrd I had put together in the seventeenth century by selling pots, pans, guns, and rum to the Indians in exchange for furs and hides, as well as by dealing in Indian and African slaves.

### A Slave Coffle

A slave ship off the African coast awaits her cargo. One slave trader wrote: "The negroes are so wilful and loth to leave their own country, that they have often leap'd out of the canoos, boat and ship, into the sea, and kept under water till they were drowned, to avoid being taken up and saved by our boats. . . ." All together, 5 million or more slaves were shipped from Africa. Though nearly half this number died en route, more Negro than white colonists crossed the Atlantic before 1800. From *Freedman's National and Family Record* (1873). (Library of Congress)

Class consciousness and class distinctions came to be quite noticeable in provincial America. Usually a person's place in society was obvious from his appearance and dress. An ordinary farmer in his coarse linen homespun or a town craftsman in his leather apron made a sharp contrast with a planter or merchant in buckle shoes, knee breeches, colorful waistcoat, starched ruffles, and powdered wig. A farm girl, her face parched by winter fire or summer sun, her buxom figure clothed in homemade linsey-woolsey, was not likely to be mistaken for a planter's or merchant's daughter, whose delicate form was clad in imported silks and satins, and whose complexion was protected by a dainty parasol.

As some of the rich grew richer, some of the poor became more impoverished. There was a widening of extremes. If many of the early indentured servants acquired valuable land and respectable status after completing their servitude, many of the later ones either took up subsistence farming on the frontier or sank to the level of the "poor whites" on worn-out lands in the neighborhood of the planters. Yet, especially in New England, the vast majority of the people came to form a self-respecting, property-owning middle class.

A few humanitarians began to take note of what they considered the wrongs of the society they knew. Of these reformers the foremost was a New Jersey Quaker, John Woolman, who wrote appealingly and traveled widely in a patient effort to better the condition of workers, especially slaves. In *Some Considerations on the Keeping of Negroes* (Part I, 1754; Part II, 1762) he took up an antislavery crusade which had been preached before him, but never so earnestly.

The pleas of Woolman and other reformers did little to soften the institution of slavery, which during the first half of the eighteenth century had become more and more rigid, with slave codes that were more and more severe. This was especially true in South Carolina, where whites had reason to fear the blacks who greatly outnumbered them. There, slave conspiracies or mere rumors of them brought savage retribution and further tightenings of the already strict laws governing slavery. Near Charleston several slaves accused of conspiring to revolt were burned to death in 1720. In the city itself fifty were hanged in 1740, and when a disastrous fire followed, two more were executed for arson.

Such events were not confined to the South. In New York City a Negro insurrection led in 1712 to the execution of twenty-one participants, one of whom was chained up without food or drink until he died. Again, in 1741, 101 Negroes were convicted of plotting with poor whites to burn the city; 18 of the blacks were hanged, 13 burned alive, and the rest banished; 4 whites, 2 of them women, went to the gallows. Even in New England, where slaves were relatively few and slavery relatively mild, there were occasional instances of blacks attacking whites. In 1723 several Negroes were suspected of starting a series of fires in Boston, and in 1741 a black man and woman schemed to set the torch to neighboring Charlestown. But the threat from Negroes caused no mass hysteria or wholesale vengeance in New England.

## Home and Family

From the beginning, the family shelters of the colonists were fairly close imitations of those already familiar to them, yet houses (like almost everything else) were more or less altered by Americanizing trends. The first English pioneers built thatched huts rather than log cabins of the kind now considered peculiarly American. Introduced by the early Swedish settlers along the Delaware, the log cabin did not become the typical frontier dwelling until the eighteenth century. By that time a variety of building materials and architectural styles had appeared in the older settled areas. Though a higher proportion of colonial than of English houses were built of wood, a considerable number were built of stone or brick, some of which was imported. In New England a common type of farmhouse was the "salt-box," two stories high in front and one in back, and sided with unpainted clapboards. In the middle colonies the redbrick house with a Dutch gambrel roof and the substantial farmhouse of native stone were characteristic. In the South the more prosperous planters erected Georgian mansions, which as a rule were copies of English models, reduced in size and simplified in ornament.

Crowded into the generally small houses were comparatively large families, at least in the early years of settlement. The family often included not only numerous children but also a varying number of dependent relatives, such as elderly grandparents or unmarried aunts. The household was further enlarged in many cases by the presence of servants, domestic slaves, or hired hands living under the same roof.

As head of the household, the father traditionally wielded strong authority over its members. He was entitled to whatever property his wife had owned before her marriage to him, but he was responsible also for her debts and misdeeds. Discipline was strict: children were expected to speak only when spoken to, and the rod was seldom spared.

The patriarchal family, with its enlarged household, proved difficult to maintain under the conditions of life in eighteenth-century America. Here, where land was so much more abundant and labor so much scarcer than in England, separate and smaller families could manage to survive much more easily. "Dependent kin, servants, and sons soon left the patriarchal household, setting up their own reduced establishments which would never grow to the old proportions," as the historian Bernard Bailyn has observed. Elders were shocked by what seemed to them the breakup of the very foundation of the social order. In a futile effort to restore parental authority, the colonies passed laws demanding obedience from children and providing severe penalties for filial disrespect.

Immorality in provincial America would be

hard to measure. Among their contemporaries in neighboring colonies, the countryfolk of North Carolina had a reputation for loose morals, but as a whole these Carolinians were probably no worse than their critics. The church and court records of New England contain much evidence of premarital relations in that part of the country, but what the evidence most likely proves is that the Puritans were prone to confess their sins and to keep careful records, rather than that these people were especially given to fornication. Furthermore, the Puritan betrothal was itself such a solemn and binding ceremony that some New Englanders doubted whether intercourse between engaged couples was really wrong, and in the early eighteenth century Harvard students discussed that very question in public debate. In the rural South, as in the rural North, prostitutes were almost unheard of, but in the seaports commercialized vice grew with the growth of commerce itself.

Among indentured servants nonmarital relations were a common evil, or so it was believed —and no doubt correctly, since servants usually were forbidden to marry during their servitude. As for the slaves, their marriages were not recognized by law, and few masters were as much concerned with the identity of a slave father as they were with the fecundity of a slave mother. The offspring of white fathers and black mothers, and vice versa, began to appear at an early date and, despite the intensification of race prejudice, became more numerous as time went on. Though indentured servants were blamed for the racial intermixture, men of the master class were responsible for much of it.

## Westover

In 1688 William Byrd I began the construction of a house on land he had bought along the James River, not far from the place where Richmond, Virginia, later was to be located. His son, the brilliant William Byrd II, lived here during much of his life (when he was not in England). In 1749 the house burned down, and William Byrd III had it rebuilt. He failed, however, to maintain the fortune his father and grandfather had accumulated, and eventually the estate passed out of the family's possession. A French traveler, the Marquis de Chastellux, who was a guest at Westover in 1782, wrote: "There are magnificent houses at every view, for the banks of the James River form the garden of Virginia. That of Mrs. Byrd surpasses them all in the magnificence of the buildings, the beauty of its situation, and the pleasures of society." Westover is one of the finest examples of the Georgian style, as applied to domestic architecture, in America. (Photograph by Thomas T. Waterman, Library of Congress)

# THE MIND AND SPIRIT

The new scientific spirit of the Enlightenment was quite out of keeping with old beliefs, such as the notion of witchcraft or even the idea of a personal God who kept watch over individual lives. Nevertheless old attitudes persisted and often were intermingled with the new. In provincial America the diverging points of view were represented by two outstanding figures: Benjamin Franklin, a perfect example of the Enlightenment man, and Jonathan Edwards, a latter-day expounder of the old-time Puritan faith. Yet Edwards, along with many other religious leaders, also shared the growing interest in science and reason.

## The Pattern of Religions

Though originating abroad, religions developed a new and distinctive pattern in America. With the immigration of diverse sectarians from several countries, the colonies became an ecclesiastical patchwork made up of a great variety of churches. Toleration flourished to a degree remarkable for the time, not because it was deliberately sought but because conditions favored its growth. No single religious establishment predominated in the colonies as the Church of England did in the British Isles and as other state churches, Lutheran or Roman Catholic, did in Western Europe.

By law, the Church of England was established in Virginia, Maryland, New York, the Carolinas, and Georgia. In these colonies everyone regardless of belief or affiliation was supposed to be taxed for the support of the Church. Actually, except in Virginia and Maryland, the Church of England succeeded in maintaining its position as the established church only in certain localities.

To strengthen Anglicanism in America, the Bishop of London began in 1689 to delegate the supervision of the colonial churches to his personal representatives, or commissaries. When the first commissary, James Blair, was appointed in Virginia, more than half of the parishes in the colony had no minister. When Blair died in 1743, after more than fifty years of devoted labor, there were only two unsupplied parishes. Further to strengthen Anglicanism, in America and elsewhere, the Church of England in 1701 set up the Society for the Propagation of the Gospel in Foreign Parts. Missionaries of the SPG founded a number of new Anglican communions in the colonies, especially in Massachusetts and Connecticut. Seeing that Anglicanism in America was handicapped by the lack of a bishop, the missionaries agitated for the appointment of one. But Congregationalists and others opposed this as a step toward tyranny, and the Anglican clergy of Virginia and Maryland agreed with them. No bishop was appointed.

Not all the Puritans were Congregationalists: some of them became Presbyterians. In belief, these two groups were essentially the same, but they differed in ecclesiastical organization, the Presbyterians having a more highly centralized government, with a governing body of presbyters (made up of ministers and lay elders) for the churches of each district. In the early 1700s many of the Puritan churches of Connecticut, and most of those founded in other colonies by emigrants from New England, adopted the Presbyterian form of government. The number of Presbyterians in America was greatly increased by the immigration of the Scotch-Irish. At first, most of these people lacked churches and pastors. Francis Makemie, often called the father of Presbyterianism in America, organized the first American presbytery (1705) and for twenty years traveled up and down the coast from New York to South Carolina to set up churches for the churchless.

Another Calvinist group, numerous in parts of New York and New Jersey, was the Dutch Reformed. Originally the American Baptists, of whom Roger Williams is considered the first, were also Calvinistic in their theology. Then, in Rhode Island and in other colonies, a bewildering variety of Baptist sects sprang up. They had in common a belief that infant baptism did not suffice and that rebaptism, usually by total immersion, was necessary. Some remained Calvinists, believers in predestination, and others came to believe in salvation by man's free will.

Quite different from the Calvinists were the Quaker mystics and the German pietists, such as the Mennonites, Dunkers, and Moravians. The Quakers (Society of Friends) abandoned their early enthusiasm, which once had caused

## Christ Church, Cambridge, Massachusetts

Peter Harrison, who designed Christ Church, has been called "America's first architect." Born in England, Harrison became a ship captain when only twenty-three. He married an American woman with considerable property and prospered as a merchant of Newport, Rhode Island. In versatility, though not in genius, he rivaled Benjamin Franklin. He was not a jack of all trades, according to his biographer Carl Bridenbaugh, but was "rather a master of ten—ship-handling, navigation, ship-building, woodcarving, drafting, cartography, surveying, military engineering and construction, commerce, and the new agriculture," in addition to architecture. He acquired the largest and best selected architectural library in colonial America. Among the notable structures he designed were King's Chapel in Boston, Touro Synagogue in Newport, St. Michael's in Charleston, and Christ Church in Cambridge. The building committee for Christ Church insisted upon the most simple and inexpensive construction. Though he did not manage to keep within the cost limit, Harrison succeeded in creating a charmingly original design, in the spirit of the late Georgian style, at a remarkably low cost. On the interior, he produced an effect of considerable spaciousness for so small a church by leaving out the usual gallery, or balcony, on each side. (Library of Congress)

them to disturb other religious gatherings when they first settled in America. As their wealth increased, many of the Friends lost still more of their old-time fervor, the rich Philadelphia merchants dividing their allegiance between meeting house and counting house. Though politically dominant in Pennsylvania from the beginning, the Quakers did not use their power to compel conformity. Of all the colonies, Rhode Island and Pennsylvania were characterized by the greatest religious diversity and freedom. In Pennsylvania and other places where Germans settled, the Lutherans as well as the pietist sects added variety to the colonial religious scene.

Protestants extended toleration to one another more readily than to Roman Catholics. To strict Puritans the Pope seemed no less than Antichrist. Their border enemies in New France, being "papists," seemed agents to the devil bent on frustrating the divine mission of the wilderness Zion in New England. In most of the English colonies, however, the Roman Catholics were far too small a minority to occasion serious conflict. They were most numerous in Maryland, and even there they numbered no more than 3,000. Ironically, they suffered their worst persecution in that colony, which had been founded as a refuge for them and had been distinguished by its Toleration Act of 1649. According to Maryland laws passed after 1691, Catholics not only were deprived of political rights but also were forbidden to hold religious services except in private houses.

Even fewer than the Catholics, the Jews in provincial America totaled no more than about 2,000 at any time. The largest community lived in New York City, smaller groups in Newport and Charleston, and dispersed families in all the colonies. There was relatively little social discrimination against the Jews, but there was political discrimination: in no colony could they vote or hold office. In New England they enjoyed a certain esteem because of the Puritans' interest in the Old Testament and in Hebrew culture.

## The Great Awakening

During the early 1700s the pious outlook gave way more and more to a worldly view. With the westward movement and the wide scattering of the colonial population, many of the frontiersmen lost touch with organized religion. With the rise of towns and the multiplication of material comforts, the inhabitants of the more densely settled areas were inclined toward an increasingly secular outlook. With the appearance of numerous and diverse sects, some people were tempted to doubt whether any particular denomination, even their own, possessed a monopoly of truth and grace. And with the progress of science and free thought in Europe, at least a few Americans began to adopt a rational and skeptical philosophy.

For thousands of the colonists, the trend away from religion was reversed by a revival movement known as the Great Awakening, which reached a climax in the 1740s. Wandering exhorters from abroad did much to stimulate the

**"Sinners in the Hands of an Angry God" [1741]**

Jonathan Edwards (1703–1758) was the most original and systematic theologian of colonial America. Edwards argued that God's grace is the only way that any man can be redeemed from the original sin committed by Adam; poor sinners could yield themselves up to God's grace if their hearts were "filled with love to him who has loved them." The extremes of terror and salvation that he posed were undeniably effective: when he preached this sermon at Enfield, Connecticut, in 1741, it produced great "breathing of distress, and weeping."

*Your wickedness makes you as it were heavy as lead, and to tend downwards with great weight and pressure towards hell; and if God should let you go, you would immediately sink and swiftly descend and plunge into the bottomless gulf . . .*

*O sinner! Consider the fearful danger you are in: it is a great furnace of wrath, a wide and bottomless pit, full of the fire of wrath, that you are held over in the hand of God . . . You hang by a slender thread, with the flames of divine wrath flashing about it, and ready every moment to singe it, and burn it asunder . . .*

*And now you have an extraordinary opportunity, a day wherein Christ has thrown the door of mercy wide open, and stands in the door calling and crying with a loud voice to poor sinners . . .*

*And let everyone that is yet out of Christ, and hanging over the pit of hell, . . . now hearken to the loud calls of God's word and providence. This acceptable year of the Lord, a day of such great favours to some, will doubtless be a day of as remarkable vengeance to others. . . .*

revivalistic spirit. John and Charles Wesley, founders of Methodism, which began as a reform movement within the Church of England, visited Georgia and other colonies in the 1730s with the intention of revitalizing religion and converting Indians and Negroes. George White-field, a powerful open-air preacher from England and for a time an associate of the Wesleys, made several evangelizing tours through the colonies. Everywhere he went, Whitefield drew tremendous crowds, and it was said (with some exaggeration) that he could make his hearers weep merely by uttering, in his moving way, the word "Mesopotamia."

Though itinerants like Whitefield contributed to the rousing of religious excitement, the Great Awakening could hardly have occurred without the work of regular ministers with an evangelizing bent. One of the most important of these was Theodore J. Frelinghuysen, a youthful German-born pastor of three Dutch Reformed congregations in central New Jersey. Frelinghuysen preached the necessity of spiritual rebirth not only to the Dutch Reformed but also to the Scotch-Irish Presbyterian settlers of the Raritan Valley. His emotional preaching divided his own parishioners. The older and more well-to-do among them were scandalized; the young and the poor rallied to his support.

The Puritans of New England also were divided on the issue of revivalism. A majority of the Congregational ministers of Massachusetts denounced the "errors" and "disorders" arising from revival meetings. Among the errors and disorders was the practice of uneducated men "taking upon themselves to be preachers of the word of God," creating confusion and tumult, and leading members away from their regular churches.

Yet the outstanding preacher of the Great Awakening in New England was Jonathan Edwards—a Puritan of the Puritans and one of the most profound theologians in the history of American religious thought. From his pulpit in Northampton, Massachusetts, Edwards attacked the new doctrines of easy salvation for all. He called upon his people to return to the faith of their fathers. He preached afresh the old Puritan ideas of the absolute sovereignty of God, the depravity of man, predestination, the necessity of experiencing a sense of election, and election by God's grace alone. Describing hell as vividly as if he had been there, he brought his listeners to their knees in terror of divine wrath. Day after day the agonized sinners crowded his par-

sonage to seek his aid; at least one committed suicide.

The Great Awakening spread over the colonies like a religious epidemic. It was most contagious in frontier areas and among the comparatively poor and uneducated folk, especially in the South. In the Southern back country it affected the largest number of people, prevailed the longest, and had the most lasting consequences. The Presbyterian Church was split by the formation of a large and rapidly growing group of revivalistic, "New Light" Presbyterians. Converts flocked to various free-will Baptist sects; the Baptists were on the way to eventually becoming one of the two most numerous denominations in the United States.

The Great Awakening not only led to the division of existing congregations and the founding of new sects, but it also had a number of other results. Some of the revivalists denounced book learning as a snare and a delusion, a positive hindrance to salvation, but others saw education as a means of furthering their own brand of religion, and so they founded schools for the preparation of ministers. Many believed that revivalism, through its emphasis on righteous conduct, brought about an improvement in manners and morals, and no doubt it did so, at least temporarily. To some extent, too, it aroused a spirit of humanitarianism, a concern for the physical as well as the spiritual welfare of the poor and oppressed. The widely preached doctrine of salvation for all—of equal opportunity to share in God's grace—encouraged the notion of equal rights to share also in the good things on earth. Thus it stimulated feelings of democracy.

Though the Great Awakening had these important and lasting consequences, many of the converted soon backslid, and by the end of the colonial period English America contained fewer church members for its population than did any other Christian country of the time, and fewer than the United States has today.

## Reading and Writing

As an American variant of English culture developed in the colonies, it was reflected in the partial Americanization of the English language. New words originated in borrowings from the

Indians (such as *skunk* and *squash*), from the French (*portage, prairie*), and from the Dutch (*boss, cooky*). Americanisms also arose from the combining of words already in the English language (*bull-frog, snow-plow*), from the formation of new adjectives based on existing nouns (*kinky, chunky*), from the adoption of unfamiliar uses for familiar words (*branch,* meaning *stream; ordinary,* meaning *inn*), and from the retention of old English expressions that were being dropped in England (*cater-corner; bub,* for *boy*). After 1700 English travelers in America began to notice a strangeness in accent as well as vocabulary, and in 1756 the great lexicographer Dr. Samuel Johnson mentioned the existence of an "American dialect."

Dr. Johnson thought of Americans as barbarians, and some no doubt were, but from the beginning many had been concerned lest civilization be lost in the wilderness. They continued to provide schooling for their children as best they could, particularly in New England. In various colonies, the advancement of religion being one motive for education, the Quakers and other sects operated church schools. Here and there a widow or an old maid conducted a "dame school," holding private classes in her home. In some of the cities master craftsmen set up evening schools for their apprentices, at least a hundred such schools appearing between 1723 and 1770. To the end of the colonial period (and beyond it) numberless children with no school available were still learning to read and write from their father or mother at the family fireside.

Far more people learned to read than ever attended school, yet a great many never learned to read at all. The literacy rate, which is unknown, must have varied a good deal from place to place. It seems to have been very low in some of the thinly settled areas, especially in the South. It was highest in the towns, especially in New England. Nevertheless, the Connecticut legislature stated in 1690 that many people in Connecticut were "unable to read the English tongue," and of the thirteen town proprietors of Manchester, New Hampshire, in 1716, eight could not write. Colonial wills and other legal documents often were signed with a mark, by people who could not write even their own names. On the whole, literacy doubtless improved during the eighteenth century, and by the time of the Revolution probably a majority of Americans could read.

Books were available in numerous collections. Several of the wealthy colonists owned hundreds of volumes apiece; William Byrd II had one of the largest private libraries, with more than 3,600 volumes, at Westover, his plantation home. A dozen or more subscription libraries were established, most of them in Pennsylvania, and a few small endowed public libraries, one of the earliest at Bath, North Carolina. Harvard College, in 1723, possessed 3,200 volumes. Much the larger proportion of all these books were printed abroad and imported, but several American cities were active book-publishing centers.

Founded in 1704, the first regular newspaper in the colonies, though not a very newsy one, was the weekly Boston *News-Letter,* a small folded sheet of four pages with two columns to a page. By the 1760s one or more weekly papers were being published in each of the colonies except New Jersey and Delaware, both of which were well enough supplied by the presses of New York and Philadelphia. Several monthly magazines, notably the *American Magazine* of Philadelphia, were started after about 1750, with hopes of wide circulation. One after another they appeared for a year or two and then expired. More successful and more widely read were the yearly almanacs. Originally mere collections of weather data, these turned into small magazines of a sort, containing a great variety of literary fare. *Poor Richard's Almanac,* now well remembered, was only one of many, though a superior one.

Its publisher, Benjamin Franklin, was one of a few colonial-born men of letters who wrote works of lasting literary merit. The titles of some of his essays—*Advice to a Young Man on Choosing a Mistress* (1745), *Reflections on Courtship and Marriage* (1746), *Observations Concerning the Increase of Mankind* (1755), and *Advice to a Young Tradesman* (1762)—suggest his pragmatic and worldly-wise outlook. Quite different was the sternly logical and otherworldly view of Jonathan Edwards, whose treatise *On the Freedom of the Will* (1754) is considered, by those who can understand it, as perhaps the most brilliant of American theological studies. John Woolman in his *Journal* (published in 1775, after his death) related a life as spiritual as Edwards' and as humanitarian as Franklin's but more humble and sensitive than either. A writer rivaling Franklin in charm, though not in productivity, was William Byrd II, whose breezy *History of the Dividing Line* (not published till 1841) recounted his experiences as one of the commissioners who, in 1728, marked off the boundary between Virginia and North Carolina.

As a rule, colonial authors had no time for belles-lettres, for fiction, poetry, drama, and the like. Writers concentrated upon sermons, religious tracts, and subjects of urgent, practical concern. Puritans, Quakers, and many other Protestants condemned play acting as sinful. The first theaters opened in the South, one at Williamsburg in 1718 and the famous Dock Street Theater at Charleston in 1736. By the middle of the century plays could be seen in all the larger seaport cities except Boston, where the Puritan ban remained.

## The Higher Learning

Of the six colleges in actual operation by 1763, all but two were founded by religious groups primarily for the training of preachers. Harvard (1636) was established by Congregationalists, William and Mary (1693) by Anglicans, and Yale (1701) by conservative Congregationalists who were dissatisfied with the growing religious liberalism of Harvard. The College of New Jersey (1746), later known as Princeton, was set up by Presbyterians in response to the Great Awakening. At any of these institutions a student with secular interests could derive something of a liberal education from the prevailing curricula, which included logic, ethics, physics, geometry, astronomy, rhetoric, Latin, Hebrew, and Greek. From the beginning Harvard was intended not only to provide an educated ministry but also to "advance learning and perpetuate it to posterity." King's College (1754), afterward Columbia, had no theological faculty and was interdenominational from the start. The Academy and College of Philadelphia (1755), which grew into the University of Pennsylvania, was a completely secular institution,

founded by a group of laymen under the inspiration of Benjamin Franklin. It offered courses in utilitarian subjects as well as the liberal arts—in mechanics, chemistry, agriculture, government, commerce, and modern languages. Though the colonies thus were well supplied with colleges, at least in comparison with other countries at the time, some Americans continued to go to English universities. But the great majority of colonial leaders, after 1700, received their entire education in America.

Until a medical school was opened in Philadelphia (1765) there was no opportunity for aspiring physicians to get academic training on this side of the Atlantic. Those who desired to attend a medical school had to go abroad, and usually they went to the University of Edinburgh. Most of the practicing physicians had no medical degrees. Some put in a sort of internship with an older practitioner, and others took up the healing art entirely on their own. Some colonial physicians and, surprising though it seems, churchmen like Cotton Mather and Jonathan Edwards advocated as earnestly as anyone in the world the most controversial medical innovation of their time—inoculation against smallpox. There was no law school in the colonies, and men prepared themselves for a legal career by independent study, by working with an established lawyer, or, in comparatively few cases, by attending one of the Inns of Court (law schools) in London.

In the colonial colleges, considerable attention was given to scientific subjects. Chairs in "natural philosophy," or physical science, were endowed at William and Mary and at Harvard. The most advanced scientific thought of Europe—Copernican astronomy and Newtonian physics—eventually made its way into American teaching. But scientific speculation and experiment were not the exclusively academic, professional occupations that they later became.

Mather, Edwards, and many other ministers, merchants, and planters in America were active as amateur scientists. The Royal Society of London, founded in 1662 for the advancement of science, honored a number of them by electing them as fellows. To this society the American members and nonmember correspondents

## Harvard College, About 1740

At the left is Harvard Hall, built in 1675; in the center Stoughton Hall, 1699; at the right Massachusetts Hall, 1720. In 1641 an anonymous writer put down the essential facts regarding the beginnings of higher education in America, as follows: "After God had carried us safe to *New-England,* and wee had builded our houses, provided necessaries for our liveli-hood, rear'd convenient places for God's worship, and settled the Civill Government: One of the next things we longed for and looked after was to advance *Learning* and perpetuate it to Posterity; dreading to leave an illiterate Ministry to the Churches, when our present Ministers shall lie in the Dust. And as

wee were thinking and consulting how to effect this great Work, it pleased God to stir up the heart of one Mr. *Harvard* (a godly Gentlemen and a lover of Learning, there living amongst us) to give the one halfe of his Estate (it being in all about 1700. l.) towards the erecting of a Colledge, and all his Library: after him another gave 300. l. others after them cast in more, and the publique hand of the State added the rest: The Colledge was, by common consent, appointed to be at *Cambridge* (a place very pleasant and accommodate) and is called (according to the name of the first founder) *Harvard Colledge.*"

sent samples and descriptions of plants, animals, and remarkable phenomena. By means of their contributions the colonial amateurs added a good deal to the accumulation of data upon which later scientific progress was to be based. They also sent in plans for mechanical inventions and helped to start the reputation of Americans as a mechanically ingenious people.

The greatest of colonial scientists and inventors, Benjamin Franklin, gained world-wide

fame with his kite experiment (1752) which demonstrated that lightning and electricity were one and the same. Showing their respect for experimental science, Harvard, Yale, and William and Mary honored themselves by honoring Franklin as a Master of Arts. The University of St. Andrews in Scotland and Oxford University in England conferred doctoral degrees upon him. Thereafter he took satisfaction in being known as "Dr. Franklin." He interested himself in countless subjects besides electricity, and he was a theoretical or "philosophical" scientist as well as a practical one. He also was a promoter of science. In 1727 he and his Philadelphia friends organized the Junto, a club for the discussion of intellectual and practical matters of mutual interest. In 1744 he led in the founding of the American Philosophical Society, the first learned society in America.

## Concepts of Law

As with social and intellectual life, the legal and political institutions inherited from England also were more or less modified in their transmission to the colonies. Changes in the law resulted in part from the scarcity of English-trained lawyers, who were almost unknown in America before 1700. Not till a generation after that did the authorities in England make a deliberate effort to impose the common law and the statutes of the realm upon the provinces. By that time the legal standards on this side of the ocean had become pretty well fixed, and a number of variant legal systems had come into being through a lack of acquaintance or sym-

pathy with English law, though all these systems embodied many of its essentials, including such ancient rights as trial by jury.

Pleading and court procedure were simplified in America, and punishments were made less severe. Instead of the gallows or the prison, the colonists more commonly resorted to the whipping post, the branding iron, the stocks, and the ducking stool (for gossipy women). Crimes were redefined. In England a printed attack on a public official, whether true or false, was considered libelous. In the colonies, at the trial (1734) of the New York publisher John Peter Zenger, who was powerfully defended by the Philadelphia lawyer Andrew Hamilton, it was held that criticisms of the government were not libels if factually true—a verdict which brought some progress toward freedom of the press. Legal philosophy itself was changed as colonists came to think of law as a reflection of the divine will or the natural order, not as an expression of the power of an earthly sovereign. Provincial lawyers, who became an influential class during the eighteenth century, were less closely attached to English tradition than the legal profession in the United States was afterward to be.

# Selected Readings

**Expanding Settlements** T. R. Reese, *Colonial Georgia: A Study in British Imperial Policy in the Eighteenth Century* (1963); R. L. Meriwether, *The Expansion of South Carolina, 1729–1765* (1940); A. H. Hirsch, *The Huguenots of Colonial South Carolina* (1928); I. C. C. Graham, *Colonists from Scotland* (1956); J. G. Leyburn, *The Scotch-Irish: A Social History* (1962); A. B. Faust, *The German Element in the United States* (2 vols., 1909); Frederic Klees, *The Pennsylvania Dutch* (1950).

**Labor** M. W. Jernegan, *Laboring and Dependent Classes in Colonial America, 1607–1783* (1932); R. B. Morris, *Government and Labor in Early America* (1946); A. E. Smith, *Colonists in Bondage* (1947); Samuel McKee, *Labor in Colonial New York, 1664–1776* (1935); C. A. Herrick, *White Servitude in Pennsylvania*

(1926); J. C. Ballagh, *A History of Slavery in Virginia* (1902); L. J. Greene, *The Negro in Colonial New England* (1942); W. D. Jordan, *White Over Black: American Attitudes Toward the Negro, 1550–1812°* (1968).

**Economic Life** Lyman Carrier, *The Beginnings of Agriculture in America* (1923); A. C. Bining, *British Regulation of the Colonial Iron Industry* (1933) and *Pennsylvania Iron Manufacture in the Eighteenth Century* (1938); R. McFarland, *A History of the New England Fisheries* (1911); R. G. Albion, *Forests and Sea Power* (1926); F. B. Tolles, *Meeting House and Counting House°* (1948).

**Aspects of Society** Carl Bridenbaugh, *Myths and Realities: Societies of the Colonial South°* (1952), *The Colonial Craftsman* (1950), *Cities in the Wilderness, 1625–1742°* (1938), *Cities in*

*Revolt, 1743–1776°* (1955), and, with Jessica Bridenbaugh, *Rebels and Gentlemen: Philadelphia in the Age of Franklin* (1942); E. S. Morgan, *Virginians at Home°* (1952); L. B. Wright, *The First Gentlemen of Virginia°* (1940); T. J. Wertenbaker, *The Planters of Colonial Virginia* (1922); Sumner Powell, *Puritan Village°* (1963).

**Culture in General** L. B. Wright, *The Cultural Life of the American Colonies, 1607–1763°* (1957) and *The Atlantic Frontier: Colonial American Civilization* (1947); D. J. Boorstin, *The Americans: The Colonial Experience°* (1958); C. M. Andrews, *Colonial Folkways* (1919); Hugh Morrison, *Early American Architecture from the First Colonial Settlements to the Early National Period* (1952).

**Religion** W. W. Sweet, *Religion in Colonial America* (1942); Perry Miller, *The New England Mind: From Colony to Province°* (1953);

M. L. Starkey, *The Devil in Massachusetts°* (1949); E. S. Gaustad, *The Great Awakening in New England* (1957); Perry Miller, *Jonathan Edwards°* (1949); O. E. Winslow, *Jonathan Edwards, 1703–1758* (1940); Janet Whitman, *John Woolman, American Quaker* (1942); J. T. Ellis, *Catholics in Colonial America* (1965); J. R. Marcus, *Early American Jewry* (1951).

**Science** Brook Hindle, *The Pursuit of Science in Revolutionary America, 1735–1789* (1956); Carl Van Doren, *Benjamin Franklin°* (1938), an extensive biography; V. W. Crane, *Benjamin Franklin and a Rising People°* (1954), a compact account; O. T. Beall, Jr., and R. H. Shryock, *Cotton Mather, First Significant Figure in American Medicine* (1954); John Duffy, *Epidemics in Colonial America* (1953).

_____

° Titles available in paperback.

# Chapter 4
# The Empire
# Under Strain

Looking back two centuries later, it is easy enough to see that the people of the thirteen colonies, for all their diversity, had come to share some distinctive characteristics by the middle of the eighteenth century. From the point of view of England at that time, these people seemed already to be Americans rather than, in a strict sense, Englishmen. As yet, however, few of the colonists thought of themselves as Americans. Their "country," as they saw it, was first of all their particular colony, and then perhaps their region (at least in the case of Southerners and New Englanders), and finally the British Empire.

As of 1763 the Empire appeared to be an imposing success, having just disposed of its last great imperial rival in America—France. Yet it was about to prove a failure, at least so far as its ability to hold the thirteen colonies was concerned. After the great victory over the French, the policy makers in London undertook to bind the outlying provinces more closely than ever to the metropolitan center. Instead of consolidating the Empire, however, its rulers unwittingly prepared the way for its early disruption.

The colonies by then had long been used to a large measure of self-rule, and to preserve this they resisted the imperial program of George III's government. In the course of their resistance they developed a new sense of common cause and new forms of political cooperation. They were not yet conscious of belonging to, or of desiring to create, a separate country, but they eventually found themselves engaged in the first battles of a war that was to lead to independence.

War came in consequence of a real clash of interests, economic and political, between the groups dominant in England and those dominant in the colonies. This conflict was the result of a century and a half of divergence in the development of English and American ways. As the historian Charles M. Andrews has said, "New soil had produced new wants, new desires, new points of view, and the colonists were demanding the right to live their own lives in their own way."

## A LOOSENING OF TIES

After England's Glorious Revolution of 1688 and the collapse of the Dominion of New England, the English government (or, after 1707, the British government when Great Britain was created by the union of England and Scotland) made no serious or sustained effort for more than seventy years to tighten its control over the colonies. During that time, it is true,

---

**The "Bloody Massacre"**
*Detail.*

additions were made to the list of royal colonies (New Jersey, 1702; North and South Carolina, 1729; Georgia, 1754) until they numbered eight, in all of which the King had the power of appointing governors and other colonial officials. During that time, also, Parliament passed new laws supplementing the original Navigation Acts and elaborating on the mercantilist program— laws restricting colonial manufactures, prohibiting paper currency, and regulating trade. Nevertheless, the British government itself remained uncertain and divided about the extent to which it ought to interfere in colonial affairs. The colonies were left, within broad limits, to go their separate ways, and they were able to assert fairly extensive rights of self-government.

## Toward Self-Rule

During the first half of the eighteenth century, though the colonies continued to be governed in the King's name, Parliament more and more asserted its supremacy over the King. Theoretically Parliament represented the interests of the whole kingdom and indeed the whole Empire. Actually it represented best the interests of the great merchants and landholders in England. Most of them objected to any ambitious scheme for imperial reorganization that would require large expenditures, increase taxes, and diminish the profit of the colonial trade.

During the reigns of George I (1714–1727) and George II (1727–1760), both of whom were German-born, the real executive in England was beginning to be the prime minister and his fellow cabinet ministers, who held their places not by the King's favor but by their ability to control a majority in Parliament. The first of the prime ministers, Robert Walpole, believed that a relaxation of trade restrictions against the colonies would enable them to buy more English goods and would thus benefit England and her merchants. Walpole therefore deliberately refrained from attempting a very strict enforcement of all Navigation Acts. His policy of "salutary neglect" was to continue until after the outbreak of the French and Indian War.

Meanwhile the day-to-day administration of colonial affairs remained decentralized and inefficient. In England there was no separate and full-fledged colonial office. The nearest equivalent was the Board of Trade and Plantations, set up in 1696. The board, a mere advisory body, made recommendations to the Privy Council (the central agency of all administration), while the Privy Council, the war department, the lords of the admiralty, or the treasury officials made most of the actual decisions. All these agencies, except for the board itself, had responsibility for administering laws at home as well as overseas; none could concentrate upon colonial affairs alone. To complicate matters further, there was a certain amount of overlapping and confusion

of authority among the departments. And very few of the London officials ever visited America and obtained first-hand knowledge of conditions there.

Some information could be obtained from colonial agents in England. Though the colonists did not elect official representatives to sit in Parliament, some of the assemblies sent unofficial representatives or lobbyists to London to encourage the passage of desired legislation and discourage the enactment of unwanted laws. The best known of these colonial agents, Benjamin Franklin, looked out for the interests of not only Pennsylvania but also Georgia, New Jersey, and Massachusetts.

The conflicts of administrative authority in London, together with the ministerial policy of salutary neglect, weakened the hold of England upon the colonies, and so did the character of the officials who were sent to America. These included the officials placed in charge of each royal colony—governor, councillors, secretary, attorney general, receiver general, surveyor general, supreme court justices—and the agents of the London administrative departments, such as collectors of customs and naval officers, who were located in all the colonies. Some of these officeholders were able and devoted men, but the majority were not. There being no merit system, appointments often were made on the basis of bribery or favoritism rather than ability or integrity. Many an appointee remained in England and, with part of his salary, hired another man to take his place in America. Such a deputy, poorly paid as he was, found it hard to resist opportunities to augment his income with bribes. For example, a customs collector seldom hesitated, for a fee smaller than the duty itself, to pass the goods of a smuggling colonial merchant. Even honest and well-paid officials, desiring to get along with the people among whom they had to live, usually found it expedient to yield to popular resistance in the colonies.

This resistance to imperial authority centered in the colonial assemblies. By the 1750s they had established the right to levy taxes, make appropriations, approve appointments, and pass laws for their respective colonies. Their legislation was subject to veto by the governor and to disallowance by the Privy Council, but they could often sway the governor by means of their money powers, and they could get around the Privy Council by repassing disallowed laws in slightly altered form. The assemblies came to look upon themselves as little parliaments, each practically as sovereign within its colony as Parliament itself was in England. In 1754 the Board of Trade reported to the King, regarding the members of the New York assembly: They "have wrested from Your Majesty's governor the nomination of all offices of government, the custody and direction of the public military stores, the mustering and direction of troops raised for Your Majesty's service, and in short almost every other part of executive government."

## Intercolonial Disunity

Despite their frequent resistance to British authority and evasion of British laws, the colonists continued to think of themselves as loyal British subjects. They had much to gain from keeping their imperial connection. They enjoyed access to the markets of the Empire, bounties on the production of certain goods, the protection afforded by British naval and military forces, and the pride of belonging to the most powerful aggregation of peoples on the globe.

In some respects the colonists had more in common with Englishmen than with one another. To New Englanders Virginia seemed almost a foreign land, and to Virginians New England was just as strange. A Connecticut man denounced the merchants of New York for their "frauds and unfair practices," while a New Yorker condemned Connecticut because of the "low craft and cunning so incident to the people of that country." An English traveler wrote: "Fire and water are not more heterogeneous than the different colonies in North America."

Meanwhile some developments were laying a basis for the eventual growth of a sense of intercolonial community. The increase of population, which produced an almost continuous line of settlement along the seacoast, brought the people of the various colonies into closer and closer contact, as did the gradual construction of roads, the rise of intercolonial trade, and the improvement of the colonial post office. In 1691 the postal service operated only from Massachusetts

### The Need for Colonial Unity

Probably the first American editorial cartoon, this sketch appeared in Benjamin Franklin's newspaper, the *Pennsylvania Gazette* of Philadelphia, for May 9, 1754. The cartoon was intended to illustrate the need for colonial unity and, in particular, for the adoption of Franklin's Albany Plan.

to New York and Pennsylvania. In 1711 it was extended to New Hampshire on the north, in 1732 to Virginia on the south, and ultimately all the way to Georgia. After 1753 Franklin, a deputy postmaster, improved the service, providing weekly instead of biweekly posts and speeding them up so that, for example, mail was delivered from Boston to Philadelphia in about three weeks instead of six. Post riders carried newspapers as well as letters and thus enlarged and unified the colonial reading public.

Still, the colonists were loath to cooperate even when, in 1754, they faced a new threat from old and dreaded enemies, the French and their Indian allies. At the call of the Board of Trade, a conference of colonial leaders—with delegates on hand from Pennsylvania, Maryland, New York, and the New England colonies—was meeting in Albany to negotiate a treaty with the Iroquois. The delegates stayed on to talk about forming a colonial federation for defense. Benjamin Franklin proposed to his fellow delegates a plan by which Parliament would set up in America "one general government" for all the colonies, each of which would "retain its present constitution" except for the powers to be given the general government. The King would appoint a President-General, and the colonial assemblies would elect representatives to a Grand Council. The President-General in consultation with the Council would take charge of all relations with the Indians; the Council, subject to his veto, would make laws and levy taxes for raising troops, building forts, waging war and carrying on other Indian affairs.

War with the French and Indians was already beginning when this Albany Plan was presented to the colonial assemblies for their consideration. Yet none of them approved it, and none except the Massachusetts assembly even gave it very serious attention. "Everyone cries, a union is necessary," Franklin wrote to the Massachusetts governor, "but when they come to the manner and form of the union, their weak noodles are perfectly distracted."

## STRUGGLING FOR A CONTINENT

Spacious though it was, the continent of North America seemed too small to contain both the English and the French. The English, as Protestants, and the French, as Roman Catholics, eyed each other with suspicion and fear. As fishermen and fur traders they competed for the profits of the forest and the sea. Each national group began ultimately to feel that its very survival in America depended upon the elimination of the other's influence.

### New France

The French greatly extended their sway in America after the Grand Monarch, Louis XIV, took the government into his own hands (1661) and, with a program of centralization at home and expansion abroad, proceeded to live up to his supposed remark, "I am the state." His finance minister and economic planner, Jean Colbert, conceived of an integrated empire consisting of four parts: France itself as the center and the source of capital and manufactured goods; her West Indian islands (especially Martinique and Guadeloupe) as suppliers of sugar and other exotic products; posts along the African coast as aids in carrying on the slave trade; and the settlements in Canada as a market for exports from France and a granary for provisioning the West Indies. The colonies were to be governed directly from Paris, pretty much as if they were local subdivisions of France itself. New France was to have a governor, an intendant, and a bishop, each to be appointed by the King and each to serve as a check upon the other two. In practice this arrangement led to jealousies and

cross-purposes which often frustrated the colonial administration—except when some individual official in America had the character and will to assert his preeminence. Such a man was Jean Talon, the first of the intendants, and even more outstanding was Count Frontenac, the greatest of the governors (1672–1698).

Though Colbert intended to make Canada a compactly settled agricultural province, the aspirations of Talon and Frontenac for the glory of France caused them to expand New France beyond Colbert's limits; other forces also tended to disperse the colonial population. The lure of the forest and its furs drew immigrant peasants into the wilderness where they often married Indian squaws and adopted tribal ways. Another group, the Jesuits, were impelled onward by their missionary zeal in the search for savage souls to save. And the bottom lands of the Mississippi attracted farmers discouraged by the short growing season in Canada.

The nature of the Illinois country had been made known by adventuresome explorers. In 1673 Louis Joliet and Father Marquette journeyed together by canoe from Green Bay along the Fox, Wisconsin, and Mississippi rivers as far as the mouth of the Arkansas, then returned with assurance that the Mississippi empties into the Gulf of Mexico, not the Gulf of California as previously thought. The next year René Robert Cavelier, Sieur de La Salle, a supremely romantic and at the same time a shrewdly practical man, began the explorations that finally, in 1682, took him to the delta of the Mississippi, where he took possession of the surrounding country for the King of France, naming it Louisiana in the King's honor. Subsequently traders and missionaries wandered to the southwest as far as the Rio Grande, and the explorer La Vérendrye (1743) pushed westward from Lake Superior to a point within sight of the Rocky Mountains. Eventually Frenchmen revealed the outlines of the whole continental interior and marked its boundaries with the cross and the fleur-de-lis.

To secure their hold upon the territory thus staked out, they founded a string of widely separated communities, strategically located fortresses, and far-flung missions and trading posts. On Cape Breton Island they established Fort Louisbourg, one of the most redoubtable strongholds in all the New World, to guard the ap-

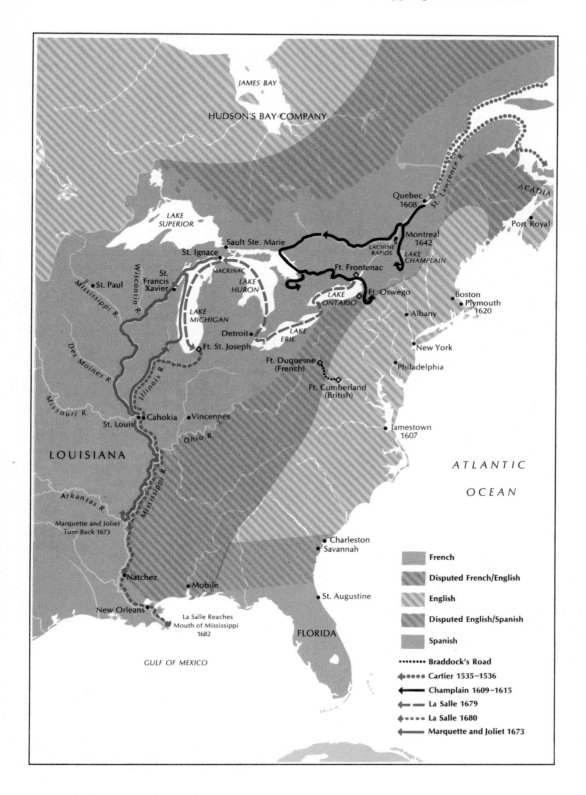

JAMES BAY

HUDSON'S BAY COMPANY

ACADIA

Quebec
1608
St. Lawrence R.

Port Royal

LAKE
SUPERIOR

Montreal
1642

Sault Ste. Marie

LACHINE
RAPIDS

St. Ignace

LAKE
CHAMPLAIN

St. Paul

Wisconsin R.

St.
Francis
Xavier

MACKINAC

Ft. Frontenac

LAKE
HURON

LAKE
ONTARIO

Ft. Oswego

Boston
Plymouth
1620

Mississippi R.

LAKE
MICHIGAN

Albany

Des Moines R.

Detroit

LAKE
ERIE

New York

Ft. St. Joseph

Illinois R.

Philadelphia

Ft. Duquesne
(French)

Missouri R.

St. Louis

Cahokia

Vincennes

Ft. Cumberland
(British)

Ohio R.

Jamestown
1607

LOUISIANA

ATLANTIC

OCEAN

Arkansas R.

Marquette and Joliet
Turn Back 1673

Mississippi R.

Charleston
Savannah

Natchez

Mobile

St. Augustine

New Orleans

La Salle Reaches
Mouth of Mississippi
1682

FLORIDA

GULF OF MEXICO

French

Disputed French/English

English

Disputed English/Spanish

Spanish

••••••• Braddock's Road

◄•••• Cartier 1535–1536

◄— Champlain 1609–1615

◄— — La Salle 1679

◄•••• La Salle 1680

◄— Marquette and Joliet 1673

**The French in America**

## Advantages of the French Threat [1748–1749]

Peter Kalm, a university professor in Swedish Finland, toured some of the English colonies during 1748–1749. He concluded (exaggerating somewhat the restrictions on the colonists):

*It is . . . of great advantage to the crown of England that the North American colonies are near a country under the government of the French, like Canada. . . . For the English colonies in this part of the world have increased so much in their number of inhabitants, and in their riches, that they almost vie with Old England. Now in order to keep up the authority and trade of their mother country, and to answer several other purposes, they are forbidden to establish new manufactures which would turn to the disadvantage of the British commerce: they are not allowed to dig for any gold or silver, unless they send them to England immediately: they have not the liberty of trading to any parts that do not belong to the British dominions, excepting some settled places, and foreign traders are not allowed to send their ships to them. These and some other restrictions occasion the inhabitants of the English colonies to grow less tender for their mother country. . . .*

*I have been told by Englishmen . . . that the English colonies in North America, in the space of thirty or fifty years, would be able to form a state by themselves, entirely independent of Old England. But as the whole country which lies along the sea-shore is unguarded, and on the land side is harassed by the French, in times of war these dangerous neighbors are sufficient to prevent the connection of the colonies with their mother country from being quite broken off. The English government has therefore sufficient reason to consider the French in North America as the best means of keeping their colonies in due submission.*

proach to the Gulf of St. Lawrence. From both banks of the St. Lawrence River the strips of land ("seigneuries") of would-be feudal lords stretched to the edge of the clearings. On a high bluff above the river stood Quebec, the pride of the French empire in America. Farther up the river was Montreal, even more "provincial" and less sophisticated than Quebec. Hundreds of miles to the northwest, near the juncture of Lake Superior with Lakes Michigan and Huron, was the tiny outpost of Sault Sainte Marie. Hundreds of miles to the southwest, at the juncture of Lakes Huron and Erie, was the well-fortified Detroit. Still farther in the same direction, along the Mississippi between the Missouri and the Ohio, was a cluster of hamlets—Cahokia, Kaskaskia, Fort Chartres, Sainte Genevieve—each with its outlying common fields of black earth under cultivation. Over on the Wabash was the fifth tiny settlement of the Illinois country, Vincennes.

On the lower Mississippi were plantations much like those in the Southern colonies of English America, plantations worked by Negro slaves and supporting a race-conscious class of "Creoles," who had far more pretensions to grandeur than did the comparatively poor and necessarily democratic seigneurs of Canada. Louisiana became relatively populous, especially after thousands of settlers had been brought in by the land-speculation schemes of John Law, whose "Mississippi Bubble" burst in 1721, to the ruin of investors in Europe and the disillusionment of recently arrived Louisianans. Founded in 1718, New Orleans soon grew into a city comparable in size with some of those on the Atlantic seaboard but quainter than most, with its houses built of cypress logs and bark roofs and set upon stilts above the swampy ground. To the east of New Orleans, along the Gulf of Mexico, were the towns of Biloxi (founded 1699) and Mobile (1702), completing the string of mainland settlements which stretched all the way around from Fort Louisbourg.

## Anglo-French Conflict

No serious trouble between English and French colonists occurred so long as their homelands remained at peace. Charles II and James II of England persisted in their friendship for Louis

XIV of France despite the fact that Louis, with his wars of French aggrandizement, ran directly counter to the traditional English policy of maintaining a balance of power on the European continent. In the Treaty of Whitehall (1686) James II and Louis XIV pledged themselves to refrain from hostilities in America even if ("which God forbid") they should find themselves at war with one another in Europe. This was an early and interesting attempt to keep America out of Europe's wars, but in just a few years it was a dead letter.

When James II was deposed, he was replaced by Louis XIV's enemy, William III, who continued to be stadholder (chief magistrate) of the Netherlands as well as King of England, and who soon resumed his stubborn resistance to the European aggressions of the French. His successor, Queen Anne, with the aid of alliances he had formed before his death, carried on the struggle against France and its new-found ally, Spain.

These wars spread from Europe to America, where they were known to the English colonists as King William's War (1689–1697) and Queen Anne's War (1701–1713). The first, which involved few of the colonists except in northern New England, led to no decisive result. The second, which entailed border fighting with the Spaniards in the South as well as the French and their Indian allies in the North, ended in one of the great and far-reaching international settlements of modern history—the Treaty of Utrecht (1713). At Utrecht the English were awarded some sizable territorial gains in North America at the expense of the French: Acadia (Nova Scotia), Newfoundland, and the shores of Hudson Bay.

After about a quarter of a century of European and American peace, England went to war with Spain over the question of English trading rights in the Spanish colonies, and the English in Georgia came to blows with the Spaniards in Florida. The Anglo-Spanish conflict soon merged in a general European war when Frederick the Great of Prussia seized some of the territory of Maria Theresa of Austria. Louis XV of France joined the Prussians against the Austrians in the hope of getting the Austrian Netherlands (Belgium), and George II of England came to the aid of Maria Theresa so as to keep the French out of the Low Countries. Again New England and New France were involved in the hostilities —in what the English colonists referred to as King George's War (1744–1748). New Englanders captured the French bastion at Louisbourg on Cape Breton Island, but to their bitter disappointment they had to abandon it in accordance with the peace treaty, which provided for the mutual restoration of conquered territory.

This war and the two preceding it had arisen primarily from European causes, and only a small fraction of the people in the English colonies had taken any part. To the colonists these were foreign wars—King William's, Queen Anne's, King George's—rather than their own. But the next conflict was different. Known to the colonists as the French and Indian War, it was in fact a "Great War for the Empire." Unlike the preliminaries, this climactic struggle originated in the interior of North America.

## The Great War for the Empire

Within the American wilderness a number of border disputes arose, but the most serious of them concerned the ownership of the Ohio Valley. The French, desiring to control this direct route between Canada and Louisiana, began to build a chain of fortifications to make good their claim. Pennsylvania fur traders and Virginia land speculators (the latter organized as the Ohio Company) looked to the country across the Alleghenies as a profitable field for their operations, and the British government, aroused to the defense of its territorial rights, gave instructions to the colonial governors to resist French encroachments. Acting on these instructions, the governor of Virginia sent George Washington, then only twenty-one, to protest to the commanders of the French forts newly built between Lake Erie and the Allegheny River, but these commanders politely replied that the land was French. While Washington was on his fruitless mission, a band of Virginians tried to forestall the French by erecting a fort of their own at the strategic key to the Ohio Valley—the forks of the Ohio, where the Allegheny and Monongahela rivers join. A stronger band of Canadians drove the Virginians away, completed the work, and named it Fort Duquesne.

**North America in 1700**

**North America After 1713**

Arriving with the advance guard of a relief force from Virginia, Washington met a French detachment in a brief but bloody skirmish. He then fell back to a hastily constructed stockade, Fort Necessity, where he was overwhelmed by troops from Fort Duquesne and compelled to surrender (July 4, 1754). The first shots of the French and Indian War had been fired.

For the English colonists, the war had begun inauspiciously, and it continued to go badly for them during the next few years. They received aid from the home government, but this aid was inefficiently and unintelligently applied. The British fleet failed to prevent the landing of large French reinforcements in Canada, and the newly appointed commander in chief of the British army in America, General Edward Braddock, failed to retake the forks of the Ohio. Brave but aged, wise in the ways of European warfare but unused to the American woods, Braddock wore out his men by having them cut a long military road through the forest toward Fort Duquesne, and he exposed them to attack from the tree-hidden enemy by marching them in the accepted European formation. Seven miles from the fort he ran into a French and

Indian ambush (July 9, 1755); he himself and large numbers of his men were killed, and the survivors fled all the way back to Fort Cumberland in Maryland. The frontier from Pennsylvania to Virginia was left exposed to Indian raids, and many frontier settlers withdrew to the east of the Allegheny Mountains.

After about two years of fighting in America, the governments of France and England finally declared hostilities, and a world war (known in Europe as the Seven Years' War, 1756–1763) began. France and England now changed partners, France allying herself with her former enemy, Austria, and England joining France's former ally, Prussia. Henceforth battles were fought not only on the American mainland but also in the West Indies, in Europe, and around the world in India.

In this global contest the British had the advantage of the mightiest navy on the seas and, with Frederick the Great on their side, the finest army in Europe. In America the people of the English colonies outnumbered those of the French colonies by approximately 15 to 1, but were by no means that much stronger militarily. The French had numerous and powerful Indian

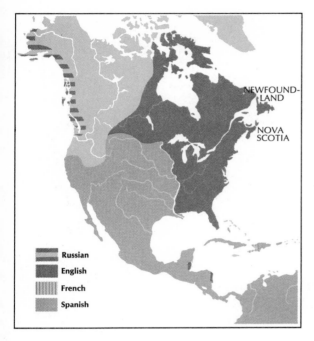

**North America After 1763**

Legend:
- Russian
- English
- French
- Spanish

to drive the French out of the continent.

With Pitt as organizer, the British regulars in America, together with colonial troops, proceeded to take one French stronghold after another, including Fort Duquesne in 1758. The next year, after a siege of Quebec, supposedly impregnable atop its towering cliff, the army of General James Wolfe struggled up a hidden ravine, surprised the larger forces of the Marquis de Montcalm, and defeated them in a battle in which both commanders were slain. The fall of Quebec marked the climax of the American phase of the war, and the decisive battle was afterward remembered as a romantic and tragic encounter between two high-minded, able men.

Some other phases of the war were less romantic, less high-minded. In the course of it the British resorted to such expedients as population dispersal. Fearing trouble from the French inhabitants of Nova Scotia, the British uprooted several thousand of them and scattered them throughout the English colonies; some of these Acadians eventually made their way to Louisiana, where they became the ancestors of the present-day Cajuns. Meanwhile the French and their savage allies were committing worse atrocities, and hundreds of defenseless families along the English frontier fell before the hatchet and the scalping knife.

Peace finally came after the accession of the peace-minded George III and the resignation of Pitt, who disagreed with the new King and wished to continue hostilities. Yet Pitt's aims were pretty well realized in the treaty signed at Paris in 1763. By its terms the French ceded to Great Britain some of their West Indian islands and all their colonies in India except two. The French also transferred Canada and all other French territory east of the Mississippi, except the island of New Orleans, to Great Britain, and New Orleans and the French claims west of the Mississippi to Spain. Thus the French gave up all their title to the mainland of North America.

## THE NEW IMPERIALISM

As the war ended, the London policy makers faced a dilemma, though they were not fully aware of it. On the one hand, they could revert

allies, many of them newly attracted to the French by the latter's early victories in the war. The English had few such allies; the Iroquois, traditionally friendly to the English and hostile to the French, now remained firmly neutral. Furthermore, the French government kept its colonists in a fairly good state of military discipline and readiness, and could count upon the loyal services of a high proportion of its colonial manpower. The British government, on the other hand, exercised much less control over its thirteen colonies, which often acted as if they were autonomous. Only where and when they were exposed to immediate danger did the English colonists wholeheartedly support the war effort.

At first the overall direction of British strategy was weak. Then, in 1757, William Pitt, as prime minister, was allowed to act as practically a wartime dictator of the Empire. Pitt reformed the army and the navy, replacing bureaucratic deadwood with young and eager officers. He gave generous subsidies to Frederick the Great, who thus was enabled to keep the French fairly busy in Europe. And he turned from the defensive to the offensive in America, with a determination

### The Taking of Quebec

In 1759 the capture of Quebec, was the main objective of the British campaign in America. General James Wolfe, only thirty-two, commanded an army that proceeded up the St. Lawrence River on navy transports. General Jeffrey Amherst, commander in chief of the British armies in America, was to take forts Crown Point and Ticonderoga, then join Wolfe before Quebec. Amherst was delayed, and Wolfe decided to go ahead alone, though his army was smaller than that of the French at Quebec, under the Marquis de Montcalm. The Quebec defenses were too strong for a direct attack from the river. After a few months' siege, Wolfe daringly landed his troops above the town, led them up an insufficiently guarded ravine, and reached the heights known as the Plains of Abraham. Now the cautious Montcalm had no choice but to fight. He attacked without waiting to assemble all his available forces, and in about fifteen minutes he was compelled to retreat. The contemporary English engraving portrays in the one scene a whole succession of events—the landings, the climb up the ravine, and the battle itself. (Library of Congress)

to the old colonial system with its half-hearted enforcement of the mercantilist program, but that would mean virtual independence for the colonies. On the other hand, the men in London could renew their efforts to reform the Empire and enforce the laws, but that would lead to revolt and absolute independence. The problem was further complicated by both the costs and the rewards of the war—the debts and the territory that it brought.

## Burdens of Empire

So strong had grown the colonial feeling against direct legislation by Parliament that, during the French and Indian War, the English government did not attempt to tax or draft the colonists directly but called upon the assemblies to provide quotas of soldiers and supplies. This requisition system, itself a concession to provincial prejudice, heightened the self-importance of the assemblies, and most of them further asserted their autonomy by complying in a slow and niggardly way. Some of them, unwilling to be taxed by Parliament, also refused to tax themselves; they issued paper money instead.

In Virginia the legislature not only issued paper money but, when the price of tobacco rose, also passed a law to deprive the Anglican clergy (who were paid in tobacco) of the benefits of the price rise. When this law was disallowed (1759), one of the ministers sued his vestrymen for his full pay. At the trial of the "parson's cause" the young lawyer Patrick Henry, defending the vestrymen, denounced the Privy Council for its tyranny and told his fellow Virginians to ignore its action. Roused by Henry's oratory, the jurors awarded the parson damages of only one penny. Thus did they defy the authority of the British government.

In Massachusetts the merchants disregarded the laws of the Empire even more flagrantly than did the planters in Virginia. Throughout the war these merchants persisted in trading with the enemy in Canada and in the French West Indies. British officials resorted to general search warrants—"writs of assistance"—for discovering smuggled goods and stamping out the illegal and unpatriotic trade. As attorney for the Massachusetts merchants, James Otis maintained that these searches violated the ancient rights of Englishmen and that the law of Parliament authorizing the warrants was therefore null and void. With eloquence as stirring as Henry's, Otis insisted that Parliament had only a limited power of legislating for the colonies.

The thirteen continental colonies were only a part of the British possessions scattered throughout the Americas and the world, and before 1763 they were not considered (except in their own eyes) as the most valuable part. Some of them, such as Virginia and Maryland with their tobacco production, fitted in fairly well with the aims of mercantilism; but on the whole the island colonies contributed a great deal more than those of the mainland to the profits of English merchants and the prosperity of the English homeland. The "sugar islands" in particular—Barbados and the Windward Islands, the Leeward Islands, Jamaica—yielded remarkable opportunities for the investment of English capital. They also complemented the economies of some of the mainland colonies by providing a market for the output of fisheries, farms, and forest industries.

Believing in a kind of commercial imperialism, most English merchants opposed the acquisition of territory for its own sake. But some Englishmen and Americans began to believe that land itself should be acquired for the Empire because of the population the land would support, the taxes it would produce, and the sense of imperial greatness it would confer. Both William Pitt and Benjamin Franklin were among the advocates of this new territorial imperialism. Franklin wrote powerfully upon the future greatness of the British Empire in America, stressing the need for vast spaces to accommodate the rapid and limitless growth of the American people. Old-fashioned mercantilists, however, continued to think of trade as the essence of empire, and of island and coastal possessions as bases for trade. The issue came to a head with the peacemaking at the end of the French and Indian War. Commercial imperialists urged that Canada be returned to France in exchange for the most valuable of her sugar islands, Guadeloupe. Territorial imperialists, Franklin among them, argued in favor of keeping Canada. The decision to retain Canada marked a change in the emphasis of imperial policy.

With the acquisition of Canada and the other fruits of war in 1763, the area of the British Empire was more than doubled and the problems of governing it were made many times more complex. The war had left the British government with a staggering burden of debt, and English landlords and merchants objected violently to increased taxes. The rather half-hearted war effort of the colonists had shown the cumulative evils of salutary neglect. And, by giving Great Britain undisputed title to the transmontane West as well as Canada, the peace had brought new problems of administration and defense. British statesmen feared that France, by no means crushed, might soon launch an attack somewhere in America for the recovery of her lost territories and prestige.

## Policies of George III

Responsibility for the solution of these postwar problems fell to the young monarch George III, who had come to the throne in 1760. Unlike the first two Georges, who had remained essentially German in point of view, George III was thoroughly British and proud of it. He was determined to follow the advice of his mother to be King in fact as well as name. Shrewdly, he took care not to upset the recently developed constitutional practice according to which the party controlling Parliament made and unmade ministries. Instead, becoming a politician himself, the King created a party of his own through patronage and bribes and thus took control of

Parliament away from the Whigs. Though not at all the ogre he was once pictured in American schoolbooks, George III achieved his aim of personal government and therefore deserves much of the credit or blame for the acts that followed.

More immediately responsible was George Grenville, whom the King made prime minister in 1763. Grenville, a brother-in-law of William Pitt, did not share Pitt's sympathy with the colonial point of view. He agreed with the prevailing British opinion that the colonists should be compelled to obey the laws and to pay a part of the cost of defending and administering the Empire. He fancied himself something of an efficiency expert, and he was indeed an able administrator. Furthermore, as chancellor of the exchequer and first lord of the treasury, he was well acquainted with matters of public finance. Promptly he undertook to impose system upon what had been a rather unsystematic aggregation of colonial possessions in America.

The Western problem was the most urgent. With the repulse of the French, frontiersmen from the English colonies had begun promptly to move over the mountains and into the upper Ohio Valley. Objecting to this intrusion, an alliance of Indian tribes, under the remarkable Ottawa chieftain Pontiac, raised the war cry. As an emergency measure the British government issued a proclamation forbidding settlers to advance beyond a line drawn along the mountain divide between the Atlantic and the interior.

Though the emergency passed, the principle of the Proclamation Line of 1763 remained— the principle of controlling the westward movement of population. This was something new. Earlier the government had encouraged the rapid peopling of the frontier for reasons of both defense and trade. In time the official attitude had begun to change, because of a fear that the interior might draw away so many people as to weaken markets and investments nearer the coast, and because of a desire to reserve land-speculating and fur-trading opportunities for English rather than colonial enterprisers. Then, having tentatively announced a new policy in 1763, the government soon extended and elaborated it. A definite Indian boundary was to be

located, and from time to time relocated, in agreement with the various tribes. Western lands were to be opened for occupation gradually, and settlement was to be carefully supervised to see that it proceeded in a compact and orderly way.

To provide further for the defense of the colonies, and to raise revenue and enforce imperial law within them, the Grenville ministry with the cooperation of Parliament meanwhile instituted a series of measures, some of which were familiar in principle and others fairly novel. Regular troops were now to be stationed permanently in the provinces, and by the Mutiny Act (1765) the colonists were called upon to assist in provisioning and maintaining the army. Ships of the navy were assigned to patrol American waters and look out for smugglers. The customs service was reorganized and enlarged, and vice-admiralty courts were set up in America to try accused smugglers without the benefit of sympathetic local juries. Royal officials were ordered to take up their colonial posts in person instead of sending substitutes. The Sugar Act (1764), designed in part to eliminate the illegal trade between the continental colonies and the foreign West Indies, lowered the high molasses duty of the Molasses Act of 1733, but imposed new duties on a number of items and made provision for more effective collection. The Currency Act (1764) forbade the colonial assemblies to issue any more paper money and required them to retire on schedule all the paper money issued during the war. And, most momentous of all, the Stamp Act (1765) imposed a tax to be paid on every legal document in the colonies, every newspaper, almanac, or pamphlet, and every deck of cards or pair of dice.

Thus the new imperial program with its reapplication of old mercantilist principles began to be put into effect. In a sense it proved highly effective. British officials soon were collecting more than ten times as much annual revenue in America as before 1763. But the new policy was not a lasting success.

## Colonial Self-Interest

The colonists still had much to gain by remaining within the Empire and enjoying its many benefits. They still held grievances against one another as well as against the authorities in London. In 1763, for example, a band of Pennsylvania frontiersmen known as the Paxton Boys descended on Philadelphia to demand defense money and changes in the tax laws, and bloodshed was averted only by concessions from the colonial government.

In 1771 a small-scale civil war broke out as a consequence of the Regulator movement in North Carolina. The Regulators were farmers of the Carolina upcountry who organized to oppose the extortionate taxes that the sheriffs collected. These sheriffs, along with other local officials, were appointed by the governor. At first the Regulators tried to redress their grievances peaceably, by electing their leaders to the colonial assembly. The western counties were badly underrepresented in the assembly, and the Regulators were unable to get control of it. They finally armed themselves and undertook to resist tax collections by force. To suppress the revolt, Governor William Tryon raised an army of militiamen, mostly from the eastern counties. The militiamen met and defeated the Regulators, some 2,000 strong, in the Battle of Alamance, in which nine on each side were killed and many others wounded. Afterward, six Regulators were hanged for treason.

Though such bloodshed was exceptional, the people of the colonies were divided by numerous conflicts of interest. After 1763, however, the policies of the British government increasingly offset the divisive tendencies within the colonies and caused Americans to look at the disadvantages of empire more closely than at its benefits. These policies threatened, in some degree or other, the well-being of nearly all classes in America.

Northern merchants would suffer from the various restraints upon their commerce, from the closing of the West to their ventures in land speculation and fur trading, from the denial of opportunities in manufacturing, and from the increased load of taxation. Southern planters, already burdened with debts to English merchants, would not only have to pay additional taxes but would also be deprived of the chance to lessen their debts by selling Western land, in which George Washington and others were much interested. Professional men—preachers,

lawyers, and professors—considered the interests of merchants and planters to be identical with their own. Small farmers, clearly the largest group in the colonies, stood to lose as a result of reduced markets and hence lower prices for their crops, together with an increase in their taxes and other costs, not to mention the difficulty of getting paper-money loans. Town workers faced the prospect of narrowing opportunities, particularly because of the restraints on manufacturing and paper money.

At the end of the French and Indian War, the colonists already were beginning to feel the pinch of a postwar depression. Previously the British government, pouring money into their midst to finance the fighting, had stimulated a wartime boom. Now the government was going to take money out of the colonies instead of putting it in. If the government's measures should be strictly enforced, the immediate effect would be to aggravate the hard times. The long-run effect would be to confine the enterprising spirit of the colonists and condemn them to a fixed or even a declining level of living.

Grievous as were the economic consequences of George III's program, its political consequences would be as bad or worse. While colonial democracy was far from all-inclusive, the colonists were used to a remarkably wide latitude in self-government. Nowhere else in the world at that time did so large a proportion of the people take an active interest in public affairs. The chief centers of American political activity were the provincial assemblies, and here the people (through their elected representatives) were able to assert themselves because the assemblies had established the right to give or withhold appropriations for the costs of government within the colonies. If, now, the British authorities should succeed in raising extensive revenues directly from America, the colonial voters and their representatives would lose control over public finance, and without such control their participation in politics would be very nearly meaningless.

Home rule was not something new and different that these Americans were striving to get. It was something old and familiar that they desired to keep. They would lose it if the London authorities were allowed to carry out the pro-

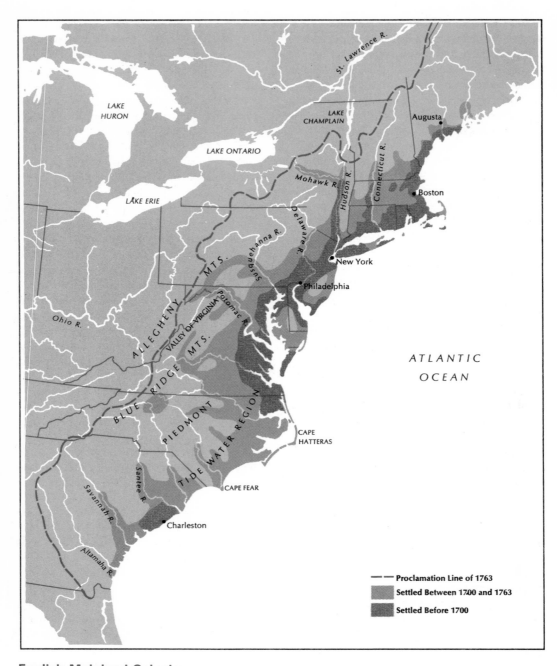

**English Mainland Colonies**

gram of raising revenues from colonial taxation and providing unconditional salaries for royal officials. The discontented Americans eventually prepared themselves to lay down their lives for a movement that was both democratic and conservative—a movement to conserve the liberties they already possessed.

## STIRRINGS OF REVOLT

The experience of the French and Indian War, while convincing prominent Englishmen of the need for tighter imperial control, had exerted an opposite effect on the attitude of colonials. Rightly or wrongly, they had gained a heightened sense of self-confidence in their own military prowess, along with a certain contempt for British regulars and especially their officers, such as the unfortunate General Braddock. The French threat having been removed from the frontier forest, many of the colonists felt a new surge of expansive energy and daring. In short, they concluded that they needed not more but rather less of imperial guidance and protection than they had previously received.

Through its very different influences on the thinking of English and colonial leaders, the grand victory of the Empire led to a period of unprecedented tension between the mother country and the colonies.

## The Stamp Act Crisis

If Prime Minister Grenville had wished deliberately to antagonize and unify some of the most influential groups in the colonies (which, of course, he did not) he could have chosen no means more effective than the Stamp Act. The tax fell upon all Americans, of whatever section, colony, or class. In particular, the stamps required for ship's papers and legal documents offended merchants and lawyers. Tavern owners, often the political oracles of their neighborhoods, now were supposed to buy stamps for their licenses; and printers, for their newspapers and other publications. Thus the tax antagonized those who could play most effectively upon public opinion.

Nevertheless, it occurred to few colonists that they could do more than grumble and buy the stamps, until the Virginia House of Burgesses sounded a "trumpet of sedition" that aroused Americans to action almost everywhere. In the House of Burgesses a group of young aristocrats aspired to exert themselves against the oligarchy of tidewater planters who, with the royal governor, dominated Virginia politics. Foremost among these young malcontents was Patrick Henry, who was ambitious to enlarge the fame he had gained in the "parson's cause." Henry made a fiery speech in the House (May 1765), concluding with a hint that George III like earlier tyrants might lose his head. There were shocked cries of "Treason!" and, according to a man who was present, Henry apologized, though many years afterward he was

quoted as having made the defiant reply: "If *this* be treason, make the most of it." In any case, he proceeded to introduce a set of resolutions declaring that Americans possessed all the rights of Englishmen, especially the right to be taxed only by their own representatives; moreover, that Virginians should pay no taxes except those voted by the Virginia assembly, and that anyone advocating the right of Parliament to tax Virginians should be deemed an enemy of the colony. The House of Burgesses did not adopt the most extreme of Henry's resolutions, but all of them were printed and circulated as the "Virginia Resolves," thus giving the impression in other colonies that the people of Virginia were both more daring and better unified than was the fact.

Stirred by the Virginia Resolves, mobs in various places began to take the law into their own hands, and during the summer of 1765 riots broke out in various places, the worst of them in Boston. Men belonging to the newly organized "Sons of Liberty" went about terrorizing stamp agents and burning the stamps. The agents, themselves Americans, hastily resigned, and very few stamps were sold in the continental colonies. In Boston the mob got out of hand and went about harrying pro-British "aristocrats" such as the lieutenant governor, Thomas Hutchinson, whose house was wrecked (though privately he had opposed the passage of the Stamp Act).

At about the time that Patrick Henry presented his resolutions to the Virginia assembly, James Otis proposed to his fellow legislators in Massachusetts that they call an intercolonial congress for concerted action against the new tax. In October 1765 the Stamp Act Congress met in New York, with delegates from nine of the colonies present. The delegates decided to petition both the King and the two houses of Parliament. Though admitting that Americans owed to Parliament "all due subordination," the congress denied that they could rightfully be taxed except by their provincial assemblies.

If the British government had tried to enforce the Stamp Act, possibly the Revolutionary War would have begun ten years earlier than it actually did. The government was not deterred by resolves, riots, and petitions, but the Americans also used something more persuasive than

## The Stamp Act Congress: Resolutions [1765]

*I. That His Majesty's subjects in these colonies owe the same allegiance to the Crown of Great Britain that is owing from his subjects born within the realm, and all due subordination to that august body the Parliament of Great Britain.*

*II. That His Majesty's liege subjects in these colonies are intitled to all the inherent rights and liberties of his natural born subjects within the kingdom of Great Britain.*

*III. That it is inseparably essential to the freedom of a people, and the undoubted right of Englishmen, that no taxes be imposed on them but with their own consent, given personally or by their representatives.*

*IV. That the people of these colonies are not, and from their local circumstances cannot be, represented in the House of Commons in Great Britain.*

*V. That the only representatives of the people of these colonies are persons chosen therein by themselves, and that no taxes ever have been, or can be constitutionally imposed on them, but by their respective legislatures. . . .*

any of these—economic pressure. Already, in response to the Sugar Act of 1764, many New Englanders had quit buying English goods. Now the colonial boycott spread, and the Sons of Liberty intimidated those colonists who were reluctant to participate in it. The merchants of England, feeling the loss of much of their colonial market, begged Parliament to repeal the Stamp Act, while stories of unemployment, poverty, and discontent arose from English seaports and manufacturing towns.

Having succeeded Grenville as prime minister, the Marquis of Rockingham used his influence in favor of appeasing both the English merchants and the American colonists, and King George III himself finally was convinced that the act must be repealed. Opponents of repeal, and they were strong and vociferous,

insisted that unless the colonists were compelled to obey the Stamp Act, they would soon cease to obey any laws of Parliament. So Parliament passed the Declaratory Act, asserting parliamentary authority over the colonies in "all cases whatsoever," and then repealed the Stamp Act (1766). In their rejoicing over the repeal, most Americans paid little attention to the sweeping declaration of Parliament's power.

## The Townshend Program

The appeasement policy of the Rockingham government was not so well received in England as in America. English landlords protested that the government had "sacrificed the landed gentlemen to the interests of traders and colonists." Soon the King dismissed the unpopular Rockingham and called upon William Pitt to form a new ministry. A critic of the Stamp Act, Pitt had a reputation in America as the colonists' friend, though his reputation suffered somewhat when he accepted a peerage as Lord Chatham. He continued as prime minister after gout and mental illness had laid him low, and the actual leadership of his administration fell to the chancellor of the exchequer, Charles Townshend, "Champagne Charlie," a brilliant man but a sort of playboy of British politics.

Townshend had to deal with imperial problems and colonial grievances still left over from the Grenville ministry. Now that the Stamp Act was gone, the worst of these grievances was the Mutiny Act of 1765, which required the colonists to provide quarters and supplies for the British troops in America. The Massachusetts assembly, refusing to vote the supplies, was the first to defy the Mutiny Act, but the New York assembly, when it did the same thing, presented a more serious challenge to imperial authorities, since the army headquarters were in New York.

To enforce the Mutiny Act and raise a revenue in the colonies, Townshend proposed two measures to Parliament. First, New York was to be punished by the suspension of its assembly until the law was obeyed there. By thus singling out New York, Townshend thought he would avoid Grenville's mistake of arousing all the colonies at once. Second, duties were to be laid upon colonial imports of glass, lead, paint, paper, and tea. Townshend reasoned that the colonists could not logically object to taxation of this kind. For Benjamin Franklin, as a colonial agent in London trying to prevent the passage of the Stamp Act, had drawn a distinction between "internal" and "external" taxes and had denounced the stamp duties as internal taxation. While Townshend laughed at this distinction he was now recommending duties that, without question, were to be collected externally. In 1767 Parliament approved the Townshend duties and suspended the New York assembly.

To the colonists, however, the Townshend duties were scarcely more acceptable than the stamp tax, and the suspension of the one assembly threatened the annihilation of all. Taking up New York's cause as well as its own, the Massachusetts assembly sent out a circular letter urging all the rest to stand up against every tax, external or internal, imposed by Parliament. At first the Massachusetts circular evoked little response in some of the legislatures and ran into strong opposition in at least one of them, that of Pennsylvania. Then Lord Hillsborough, in the new office of Secretary of State for the Colonies, issued a circular letter of his own in which he warned that assemblies endorsing the Massachusetts letter would be dissolved. Promptly the other colonies, even Pennsylvania, rallied to the support of Massachusetts.

Besides inducing Parliament to levy import duties and suspend the New York assembly, Townshend also took steps to enforce commercial regulations in the colonies more effectively than ever. The most fateful of these steps was the establishment of a board of customs commissioners in America. In doing so, he intended to stop the leaks in the colonial custom houses. His commissioners, with headquarters in Boston, virtually ended the smuggling at that place, though smugglers continued to carry on a busy trade in other colonial seaports.

Naturally the Boston merchants were the most indignant, and they took the lead in organizing another boycott. In 1768 the merchants of Philadelphia and New York joined those of Boston in a nonimportation agreement, and later some of the Southern merchants and planters also agreed to cooperate. Throughout

## The Declaratory Act [1766]

While repealing the Stamp Act, Parliament denied the arguments put forth by Americans at the meeting of the Stamp Act Congress and on other occasions. The constitutional issue was sharply drawn, as may be seen by comparing the resolutions of the Stamp Act Congress with these words of Parliament's "declaratory" act:

*Whereas several of the houses of representatives in his Majesty's colonies and plantations in America have of late, against law, claimed to themselves, or to the general assemblies of the same, the sole and exclusive right of imposing duties or taxes upon his Majesty's subjects in the said colonies and plantations; and have, in pursuance of such claim, passed certain votes, resolutions, and orders, derogatory to the legislative authority of parliament, and inconsistent with the dependency of said colonies and plantations upon the crown of Great Britain: . . . be it declared . . . That the said colonies and plantations in America have been, are, and of right ought to be subordinate unto and dependent upon the imperial crown and parliament of Great Britain; and that the King's majesty, by and with the advice and consent of the lords spiritual and temporal and commons of Great Britain in parliament assembled, had, hath, and of right ought to have full power and authority to make laws and statutes of sufficient force and validity to bind the colonies and people of America, subjects of the crown of Great Britain, in all cases whatsoever.*

the colonies, crude American homespun became suddenly fashionable, while English luxuries were frowned upon. Some enthusiasts, advocating the development of colonial manufactures of all kinds, looked forward to the creation of a self-sufficient America, with an economy independent of the Empire's.

Before the consequences of his program were fully apparent, Townshend died, leaving the

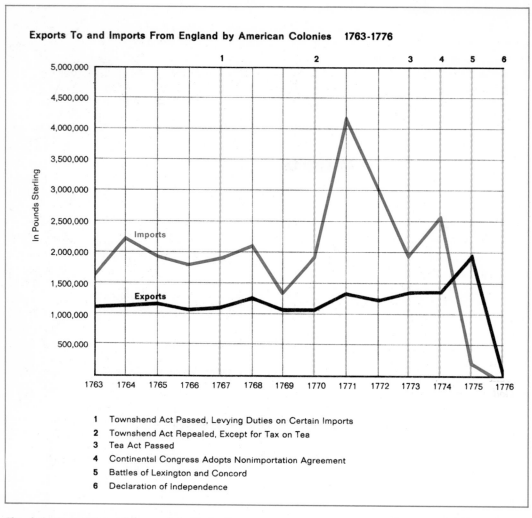

Exports To and Imports From England by American Colonies   1763-1776

1 Townshend Act Passed, Levying Duties on Certain Imports
2 Townshend Act Repealed, Except for Tax on Tea
3 Tea Act Passed
4 Continental Congress Adopts Nonimportation Agreement
5 Battles of Lexington and Concord
6 Declaration of Independence

Though the Stamp Act (1765) apparently had little effect on imports from England, the Townshend Act (1767) led to a considerable reduction in them in 1769. After this law's almost complete repeal (1770), imports rose dramati-cally in 1771. The Tea Act (1773) and the nonimportation agreement (1774) helped to bring on another decline, and the subsequent outbreak of hostilities resulted in an almost complete stoppage of trade.

question of revising his import duties to his successor, Lord North. Hoping to break the nonimportation agreement and divide the colonists, Lord North secured the repeal (1770) of all the Townshend duties except the tea tax.

Meanwhile the presence of the customs commissioners in Boston led to violence. The Boston mob had the most aggressive leader of all, Samuel Adams. The impoverished son of a once wealthy brewer, Adams had taken to politics after he himself had failed in business. As a rabble-rouser he had no equal in the colonies,

and from the time of the Stamp Act troubles he was the guiding spirit of Massachusetts radical-ism, even outdoing James Otis. Adams' success as a politician depended upon his finding suit-able topics for agitation, and the British govern-ment, having repeatedly supplied him with topics, obliged him again by locating the customs commissioners in Boston and then stationing troops there.

To the Boston "liberty boys," the presence of the customs commissioners was a standing invitation to violence, and before long the terrified officials were driven to take refuge in Castle William, out in the harbor. So that they could return safely to their duties, the British government placed four regiments (afterward reduced to two) within the city. The presence of the redcoats antagonized Samuel Adams and his followers more than ever. While his men ragged the soldiers and engaged them in brawls, Adams filled the newspapers with imaginary stories of rapes and other atrocities committed by the troops, and he spread throughout Boston a rumor that the soldiers were preparing for a concerted attack upon the citizens. On the night of March 5, 1770, a mob of dockworkers and other "liberty boys" fell upon the sentry at the custom house. Hastily Captain Preston lined up several of his men in front of the building to protect it. There was some scuffling, and one of the soldiers was knocked down. Other soldiers then fired into the crowd, killing five of its members.

These events quickly became known as the "Boston Massacre" through the efforts of Samuel Adams and his adherents, who published an account bearing the title *Innocent Blood Crying to God from the Streets of Boston* and giving the impression that the dead were victims of a deliberate plot. The soldiers, tried before a jury of Bostonians and defended by Samuel Adams' cousin John Adams, were found guilty of no more than manslaughter and were given only a token punishment. Nevertheless, through newspapers and pamphlets, Samuel Adams convicted the redcoats of murder in the minds of many contemporary Americans, and year after year on March 5 he revived the people's memory with orations recalling the events of 1770. Later generations accepted his version of the "massacre" and thus, without knowing it, honored his skill as the foremost propagandist of the pre-Revolutionary decade.

## The Philosophy of Revolt

Though America quieted down for a while after 1770, Americans did not abandon their principles, and these principles were revolutionary, at least in implication. "The Revolution was effected before the war commenced," one of the greatest of the Revolutionary leaders, John Adams, afterward remarked. "The Revolution was in the minds and hearts of the people." Of course, very few of the people thought of outright independence till after the war had begun, and even those few (among them Samuel Adams) considered it best not to admit that independence was their ultimate aim. For the time being, most politically conscious Americans desired no more, and no less, than autonomy within the Empire. They argued that the English Constitution, correctly interpreted, supported their claims to individual liberty and colonial self-rule, and that the laws of nature and of God justified them in resisting infringements upon their rights.

In the course of the argument the Americans came to the conclusion that they were better Englishmen than the English themselves, better acquainted with the Constitution and more devoted to the liberties it guaranteed. Some of the Whig politicians in England, such as William Pitt and above all Edmund Burke, who spoke eloquently in favor of conciliation, were more or less inclined to agree. But other Englishmen, like the famous lexicographer and literary critic Samuel Johnson, looked upon the Americans as a deluded and indeed a barbarized offshoot of the English people. The majority in England were outraged rather than convinced by all the speechmaking and pamphleteering on the other side of the Atlantic.

To Englishmen the Constitution, though worthy of the highest respect, was an assortment of laws and usages that had developed through many centuries and that were rather elastic and vague. To Americans, on the other hand, it was a fixed and definite body of principles, which ought to be written down so as to avoid disagreements. Americans believed the colonies did have written constitutions—the colonial charters, which supposedly guaranteed to Americans all the traditional rights of Englishmen.

Of these rights the most fundamental, according to the colonists, was the right to be taxed only with their own consent. When Townshend levied his "external" duties, the Philadelphia lawyer John Dickinson maintained in the *Letters of a Pennsylvania Farmer* that even external taxation was legal only when designed to regulate trade and not to raise a revenue. But Americans did not like trade regulations, either, when the regulations began to be enforced. Eventually the discontented colonists took an unqualified stand upon the slogan "No taxation without representation."

This clamor about "representation" made little sense to Englishmen. Only about one in twenty-five of them was entitled to vote for members of Parliament, and some populous boroughs in England had no representatives at all. According to the prevailing English theory, however, Parliament did not represent individuals or geographical areas. Instead, it represented the interests of the whole nation and indeed the whole Empire, no matter where the members happened to come from. The unenfranchised boroughs of England, the whole of Ireland, and the colonies 3,000 miles away—all were represented in the Parliament at London.

That was the theory of "virtual" representation, but Americans believed in actual representation. They felt they could be represented in Parliament only if they sent their quota of members to it. Some of them, even James Otis, considered proposals for electing American representatives, but most of the colonists realized that if they should participate in the action of Parliament they would be bound by that action, even though they were outnumbered and outvoted. So they reverted to the argument that they could be fairly represented only in their own colonial assemblies.

According to the American view of the Empire, and according to actual fact, these assemblies were little parliaments, as competent to legislate for their respective colonies as Parliament was for England. The Empire was a sort of federation of commonwealths, each with its own legislative body, all tied together by common loyalty to the King (much as in the British Commonwealth of Nations today). This being their conception of the Empire, the Americans protested bitterly against the pretensions of Parliament but had nothing except kind words for George III—until they decided to cut their imperial ties completely and declare for independence. According to the English view, the Empire was a single, undivided unit, and everywhere within it the King and Parliament together were supreme.

The American doctrine of resistance to unconstitutional and tyrannical laws was based chiefly upon the Bible and the writings of John Locke. For generations the preachers of New England had taught that no man need obey a government when it violated the will of God as set forth in the Scriptures. Now, to show that rebellion against tyranny was lawful in God's sight, they retold such Bible stories as the one about a King of Israel who burdened his people with unjust taxes and was overthrown.

John Locke (1632–1704) would probably have been shocked if he had lived to see the use that Americans made of his doctrines. In his *Two Treatises of Government* (1690) Locke attempted to justify the English revolution of 1688–1689 by which Parliament had won supremacy over the King. According to Locke's theory, men originally lived in a state of nature and enjoyed complete liberty, then agreed to a "compact" by which they set up a government to protect their "natural rights," especially their right to the ownership and enjoyment of private property. The government was limited by the terms of the compact and by "natural law." It was contrary to natural law for a government to take property without the consent of the owners, Locke wrote, and Americans noted in particular his sentence: "If any one shall claim a power to lay and levy taxes on the people by his own authority, and without such consent of the people, he thereby invades the fundamental law of property, and subverts the end of government." To Americans of the 1760s and 1770s it was clear that the British government was flouting the law of nature as well as the will of God. And, according to Locke, if a government should persist in exceeding its rightful powers, men would be released from their obligation to obey it. What was more, they would have the right to make a new compact and establish another government.

## The Tea Excitement

From time to time after 1770 Americans resisting British law broke the comparative stillness in America with such deeds as the seizure of a revenue ship on the lower Delaware, the burning of another (the *Gaspee*) in Narragansett Bay, and the tarring and feathering of a customs

## The "Bloody Massacre"

This broadside, "Engrav'd Printed & Sold by Paul Revere, Boston," pictures the Patriot version of the Boston incident of March 5, 1770. At the extreme right, Captain Thomas Preston, in command of the Custom House guards, leers as he orders his grinning men to fire on the unarmed citizens. The Custom House, Preston's headquarters, is sarcastically labeled "Butcher's Hall." Accompanying the picture were the names of the dead and eighteen lines of verse. One of

the dead was Crispus Attucks, a tall, brawny, forty-seven-year-old man, reputed to be a Negro with some Indian blood who had escaped from slavery and taken up the life of a sailor. When, in 1888, a monument was erected to the fallen, a poem was recited honoring Attucks as "leader and voice that day;/The first to defy and the first to die. . . ." (Courtesy of the Metropolitan Museum of Art, Rogers Fund, 1923)

officer on the streets of Boston. Not till 1773, however, did Americans reassert their revolutionary principles with anything approaching the unity and vigor of former years.

Tea revived the dispute. The East India

Company, with a large stock of unsalable tea on hand, was nearly bankrupt, and Lord North induced Parliament to go to the company's relief with the Tea Act of 1773. This law permitted the company to export its product to

## Taking the Pledge

This British caricature, entitled "A Society of Patriotic Ladies, at Edenton in North Carolina," was published in London in March 1775. It ridicules the American buy-at-home movement. The women are emptying their tea canisters and signing a pledge, which reads: "We the Ladies of Edenton do hereby Solemnly Engage not to Conform to that Pernicious Custom of Drinking Tea, or that we the aforesaid Ladies will not promote the Wear of any Manufacture from England until such time that all Acts which tend to Enslave this our Native Country shall be Repealed." (Courtesy of the Metropolitan Museum of Art)

America without paying any of the usual taxes except the tea tax still remaining from the original Townshend duties. With these privileges the company could undersell American merchants who bought their tea supplies in England.

Lord North, like others in his office before him, was surprised by the reaction of the Americans. He had not expected the tea-importing merchants in the colonies to like the new law, for it threatened to drive them out of business and replace them with a giant monopoly. But the colonists—especially the women—were excessively fond of tea. Lord North thought they would be so glad to get it cheap that they would swallow the hated tea tax along with it. Instead, they renounced their beloved beverage and turned for the time being to such substitutes as coffee and chocolate.

Meanwhile, with strong popular support, leaders in various colonies made plans to prevent the East India Company from landing its cargoes in colonial ports. In Philadelphia and New York determined men kept the tea from leaving the company's ships, and in Charleston they stored it away in a public warehouse. In Boston, having failed to turn back the three ships in the harbor, the followers of Samuel Adams staged a spectacular drama. On the evening of December 16, 1773, three companies of fifty men each, masquerading as "Mohawks," passed between the protecting lines of a tremendous crowd of spectators, went aboard, broke open the tea chests, and heaved them into the water. As the electrifying news of the Boston "tea party" spread, other seaports followed the example and held tea parties of their own.

When the Bostonians refused to pay for the property they had destroyed, George III and Lord North decided upon a policy of coercion, to be applied not against all the colonies but only against Massachusetts—the chief center of resistance. In four acts of 1774 Parliament proceeded to put this policy into effect. One of the laws closed the port of Boston, another drastically reduced the local and provincial powers of self-government in Massachusetts, still another permitted royal officers to be tried in other colonies or in England when accused of crimes, and the last provided for the quartering of

troops in the colonists' barns and empty houses.

These Coercive Acts were followed by the Quebec Act, which was separate from them in origin and quite different in purpose. Its object was to provide a civil government for the French-speaking, Roman Catholic inhabitants of Canada and the Illinois country. The law extended the boundaries of Quebec to include the French communities between the Ohio and Mississippi rivers. It also granted political rights to Roman Catholics and recognized the legality of the Roman Catholic Church within the enlarged province. In many ways it was a liberal and much-needed piece of legislation.

To many Protestants in the thirteen colonies, however, the Quebec Act was anathema. They were already alarmed by rumors that the Church of England schemed to appoint a bishop for America with the intention of enforcing Anglican authority upon all the various sects. To them the line between the Church of England and the Church of Rome always had seemed dangerously thin. When Catholics ceased to be actively persecuted in the mother country, alarmists in the colonies began to fear that Catholicism and Anglicanism were about to merge, and at the passage of the Quebec Act they became convinced that a plot was afoot in London for subjecting Americans to the tyranny of the Pope. Moreover, those interested in Western lands believed that the act, by extending the boundaries of Quebec, would reinforce the land policy of the Proclamation Line of 1763 and put an additional obstacle in the way of westward progress.

Had it not been for the Quebec Act, Lord North might have come close to succeeding in his effort to divide and rule the colonies by isolating Massachusetts. As it was, the colonists generally lumped the Quebec law with the Massachusetts measures as the fifth in a set of "Intolerable Acts." From New Hampshire to South Carolina the people prepared to take a united stand.

## COOPERATION FOR WAR

Revolutions do not just happen: they must be led and organized. From 1765 on, colonial leaders provided a variety of organizations for converting popular discontent into action, organizations which in time formed the basis for an independent government.

## The Continental Congress

Some of these organizations were local, some colony-wide, and some intercolonial. In many cases the provincial assemblies themselves served as centers of resistance, and sometimes they were replaced or supplemented by extralegal meetings, as when (in 1768) Sam Adams called a convention of delegates from the Massachusetts towns to sit in place of the General Court, which the royal governor had dissolved. Adams and others in various places organized mobs as Sons of Liberty and also set up committees of prominent citizens for a number of specific objects. The most famous and most effective were the committees of correspondence. Massachusetts took the lead (1772) with such committees on the local level, a network of them connecting Boston with the rural towns, but Virginia was the first to establish committees of correspondence on an intercolonial basis. These made possible cooperation among the colonies in a more continuous way than had the Stamp Act Congress, the first effort at intercolonial union for resistance against imperial authority. Virginia took the greatest step of all toward united action in 1774 when, the governor having dissolved the assembly, a rump session met in the Raleigh Tavern at Williamsburg, declared that the Intolerable Acts menaced the liberties of every colony, and issued a call for a Continental Congress.

Variously elected by the assemblies or by extralegal meetings, delegates from all the thirteen colonies except Georgia were present when, in September 1774, the Continental Congress convened in Philadelphia. The delegates divided into moderates and extremists, and the more extreme members seized the upper hand. At the outset they showed their strength by designating Carpenters' Hall as the meeting place. This was the headquarters of the Philadelphia Carpenters' Company, and some members complained that its selection was an unseemly attempt to curry favor with the city's artisans. In the ensuing sessions of the Congress,

however, the extremists were unable to carry through a program quite so thorough as some of them would have liked.

A majority of the delegates in Carpenters' Hall agreed upon five major decisions. First, in a very close vote, they defeated the plan of Joseph Galloway for a colonial union under British authority, a plan (much like the Albany Plan) which included a legislative council made up of representatives from the colonial assemblies and a president-general to be appointed by the King. Second, they drew up a somewhat self-contradictory statement of grievances, conceding to Parliament the right to regulate colonial trade but demanding the elimination of all oppressive legislation passed since 1763, and they addressed a petition to George III as their "Most Gracious Sovereign." Third, they approved a series of resolutions from a Suffolk County (Massachusetts) convention recommending, among other things, that military preparations be made for defense against possible attack by the British troops in Boston. Fourth, they agreed to nonimportation, nonexportation, and nonconsumption as means of stopping all trade with Great Britain, and they formed a "Continental Association" to see that these agreements were carried out. Fifth, the delegates adjourned to meet again the next spring, thus indicating that they conceived of the Continental Congress as a continuing organization.

Through their representatives in Philadelphia the colonies had, in effect, reaffirmed their autonomous status within the Empire and declared economic war to maintain that position. The more optimistic of the Americans supposed that economic warfare alone would win a quick and bloodless victory, but the more pessimistic had their doubts. "I expect no redress, but, on the contrary, increased resentment and double vengeance," John Adams said to Patrick Henry; "we must fight." And Henry replied, "By God, I am of your opinion." During the winter of 1774–1775 the enforcement of the nonimportation, nonexportation, and nonconsumption agreements proved increasingly difficult as people in the middle colonies and in the South, viewing the Continental Association as hardly less tyrannical than the British government, began to complain against the sacrifices they were compelled to make—all for the sake of those troublemakers in Massachusetts!

During the winter the Parliament in London debated proposals for conciliating the colonists. Lord Chatham (William Pitt) urged the withdrawal of troops from America, Edmund Burke urged the repeal of the Coercive Acts, but in vain; and not even Chatham and Burke thought of renouncing parliamentary authority over the colonies. Lord North, conceding less than Burke or Chatham, introduced a set of proposals of his own, and Parliament approved them early in 1775. The essence of these so-called Conciliatory Propositions was that the colonies, instead of being taxed directly by Parliament, should tax themselves at Parliament's demand. With this offer Lord North intended to redivide Americans by appealing to the disgruntled moderates. But his offer was too grudging, and it came too late. It did not reach America till after the first shots of war had been fired.

## Lexington and Concord

For months the farmers and townspeople of Massachusetts had been gathering arms and ammunition and training as "minutemen," ready to fight on a minute's notice. The Continental Congress had approved preparations for a defensive war, and these citizen-soldiers only waited for an aggressive move by the British regulars in Boston.

In Boston, General Thomas Gage, commanding the British garrison, knew of the warlike bustle throughout the countryside but thought his army too small to do anything until reinforcements should arrive, though some of his less cautious officers assured him that Americans were cowards, and Major John Pitcairn insisted that a single "small action" with the burning of a few towns would "set everything to rights." When General Gage received orders to arrest the rebel leaders Sam Adams and John Hancock, known to be in the vicinity of Lexington, he still hesitated, but when he heard that the minutemen

### The Battle of Lexington

A contemporary engraving by Amos Doolittle. It pictures the American version of the affair of April 19, 1775, at Lexington. In the center is shown "the party who fired first," at the command of Major Pitcairn, on horseback. In the foreground are some of the fallen and the fleeing members of the "Provincial Company of Lexington" (minute-men). The more prominent buildings on the edge of the square, or green, are the Public Inn at the left of the large tree and the Meeting House at the right of it. Behind the Meeting House are companies of British regulars marching along the road to Concord. (Courtesy of the New York Public Library, Stokes Collection) had stored a large supply of gunpowder in Concord (eighteen miles from Boston) he at last decided to act. On the night of April 18, 1775, he sent a detachment of about 1,000 men out from Boston on the road to Lexington and Concord. He intended to surprise the colonials with a bloodless coup.

But during the night the hard-riding horsemen William Dawes and Paul Revere warned the villages and farms, and when the redcoats arrived in Lexington the next day, several dozen minutemen awaited them on the common. Shots were fired and some of the minutemen fell, eight of them killed and ten more wounded. Advancing to Concord, the British burned what was left of the powder supply after the Americans hastily had removed most of it to safety. On the road from Concord back to Boston the 1,000 troops, along with 1,500 more who met them at Lexington, were harassed by the continual gunfire of farmers hiding behind trees, rocks, and stone fences. Before the day was over, the British had lost almost three times as many men as the Americans.

The first shots had been fired, but who had fired the first shot? According to the Lexington minutemen, Major Pitcairn upon his arrival had shouted, "Disperse, ye rebels!" and when this command was disregarded he had given the order to fire. According to the British officers and soldiers, one of the American guns had flashed first. The truth is still unknown, but the fact remains that the rebels succeeded in circulating their account well ahead of the British version, and they adorned it with horrible tales of redcoat atrocities. The effect was to rally to the rebel cause thousands of colonists, North and South, who previously had been lukewarm in its support. A war was on, and most Americans believed the enemy had started it.

# Selected Readings

**The French and the Frontier** H. I. Priestley, *France Overseas Through the Old Regime* (1939); J. A. Caruso, *The Mississippi Valley Frontier: The Age of French Exploration and Settlement* (1966); Francis Parkman, *A Half Century of Conflict* (2 vols., 1892) and *The Parkman Reader* ed. by S. E. Morison (1955); L. H. Gipson, *The British Empire Before the American Revolution* (13 vols., 1936–1967), vols. 6 and 7: *The Great War for the Empire;* H. H. Peckham, *The Colonial Wars, 1689–1762* (1964) and *Pontiac and the Indian Uprising* (1947); C. H. Ambler, *George Washington and the West* (1936); D. E. Leach, *The Northern Colonial Frontier, 1607–1763* (1966) and *Flintlock and Tomahawk* (1958); J. M. Sosin, *Whitehall and the Wilderness: The Middle West in British Colonial Policy, 1760–1775* (1961); T. P. Abernethy, *Western Lands and the American Revolution* (1937); C. W. Alvord, *The Mississippi Valley in British Politics* (2 vols., 1916).

**Revolutionary Backgrounds in General** J. C. Miller, *Origins of the American Revolution* (1957); L. H. Gipson, *The Coming of the Revolution, 1763–1775* (1954); C. M. Andrews, *The Colonial Background of the American Revolution* (1924).

**Commercial Policy and Colonial Government** Sir Lewis B. Namier, *England in the Age of the American Revolution* (1930); Herbert Butterfield, *George III and the Historians* (1959); L. W. Labaree, *Royal Government in America: A Study of the British Colonial System Before 1783* (1930); F. B. Wickwire, *British Subministers and Colonial America, 1763–1783* (1966); G. L. Beer, *British Colonial Policy, 1754–1765* (1907); J. P. Greene, *The Quest for Power: The Lower Houses of Assembly in the Southern Royal Colonies, 1689–1776* (1963); O. M. Dickerson, *American Colonial Government, 1696–1765* (1912) and *The Navigation Acts and the American Revolution* (1951); A. M. Schlesinger, *The Colonial Merchants and the American Revolution, 1763–1776* (1917); J. M. Sosin, *Agents and Merchants: British Colonial Policy and the Origins of the American Revolution, 1763–1776*

(1965); R. L. Schuyler, *Parliament and the British Empire* (1929), a defense of British policy; C. H. McIlwain, *The American Revolution: A Constitutional Interpretation* (1923), a brief for the discontented colonists.

**Developments in Individual States** Carl Becker, *The History of Political Parties in the Province of New York, 1760–1776°* (1909); C. A. Barker, *The Background of the Revolution in Maryland* (1940); Oscar Zeichner, *Connecticut's Years of Controversy, 1750–1776* (1949); Theodore Thayer, *Pennsylvania Politics and the Growth of Democracy, 1740–1776* (1953); R. E. Brown, *Middle-Class Democracy and the Revolution in Massachusetts, 1691–1780* (1955) and, with B. K. Brown, *Virginia, 1705–1786: Democracy or Aristocracy?* (1964); D. S. Lovejoy,

*Rhode Island and the American Revolution, 1760–1776* (1958).

**The Revolutionary Crisis** E. S. and H. M. Morgan, *The Stamp Act Crisis°* (1953); A. M. Schlesinger, *Prelude to Independence: The Newspaper War on Britain, 1764–1776°* (1958); J. C. Miller, *Sam Adams, Pioneer in Propaganda°* (1936); Jacob Axelrod, *Patrick Henry, The Voice of Freedom* (1947); D. S. Freeman, *George Washington* (7 vols., 1949–1957), vols. 1 and 2; C. C. Currey, *Road to Revolution: Benjamin Franklin in England, 1765–1775°* (1968); B. W. Labaree, *The Boston Tea Party* (1964); John Shy, *Toward Lexington: The Role of the British Army in the Coming of the American Revolution* (1965).

—————

°Titles available in paperback.

# Chapter 5
# The American Revolution

"The Revolution was effected before the war commenced," the Patriot leader John Adams said afterward. "The Revolution was in the minds and hearts of the people." What Adams meant was that long before 1775 Americans had come to take for granted a high degree of political and economic liberty, and they were bound to resist, by force if necessary, any serious infringement of it. He did not mean they had already decided upon complete independence, for that decision was not made until after the fighting had begun. Nor did he mean that all the people ever made up their minds in favor of the revolutionary cause, for according to his own estimate a third of the people opposed it.

The actual fighting seems insignificant in comparison with more recent wars. Battle deaths on the American side totaled less than 5,000. Cannons tossed out iron balls that did no damage unless they made a direct hit, and an alert soldier could see them coming and get out of the way. The Pennsylvania rifle, which some of the Patriots carried, was fairly accurate at a range of one hundred yards, but the more common smoothbore musket was not, and its flintlock misfired when wet. A military campaign was almost out of the question except in good weather.

Yet the war as the Patriots fought it, old-fashioned though it was in some respects, had one feature that made it new and revolutionary in itself. In previous wars comparatively small numbers of professional soldiers had served for pay. In this one the people on the American side took up arms in their own cause. Though their armies seldom numbered more than a few thousand at any one time, a total of almost 400,000 men enlisted (most of them for short terms) during the eight years that the war lasted.

Its consequences also were revolutionary. The first of the modern wars against colonialism, it brought into being a new nation which, though weak and insecure at the start, was eventually to grow into one of the greatest powers of all time. The ideals the war aroused provided inspiration for future generations not only in the United States but also in other countries. One of the leading revolutionaries of 1776, Thomas Paine, averred that the war "contributed more to enlighten the world, and diffuse a spirit of freedom and liberality among mankind, than any human event . . . that ever preceded it."

**The Continental Army at Valley Forge**

Detail from a painting by Edwin A. Abbey which hangs in the Pennsylvania House of Representatives. (Courtesy of the Pennsylvania Department of Commerce)

## THE STATES UNITED

In the American Revolution a war for autonomy on the part of the united colonies soon turned into a war for independence on the part of the United States. This inchoate nation, with a population less than a third as large as the nine million of Great Britain, and with economic and military resources proportionately still smaller, faced a tremendous task of mobilizing for the war. The task was further complicated by divisions among the people, who persisted in disagreeing about war aims.

### Original War Aims

Three weeks after the battles of Lexington and Concord, when the Second Continental Congress met in the State House in Philadelphia, the delegates (again from every colony except Georgia, which was not represented until the following autumn) agreed in their determination to support the war but disagreed about its objects. At one extreme the Adams cousins, John and Samuel, leaned toward independence (though they did not yet avow it), and at the other extreme John Dickinson of Pennsylvania hoped for an early reconciliation with Great Britain. Most of the delegates, holding views that ranged between those of Dickinson and the Adamses, disregarded Lord North's Conciliatory Propositions as insincere but voted reluctantly for one last appeal to the King in the Olive Branch Petition. Then, on July 6, 1775, they adopted a Declaration of the Causes and Necessity of Taking up Arms, announcing that the British government had left the American people with only two alternatives, "unconditional submission to the tyranny of irritated ministers or resistance by force," and that the people had decided to resist.

So, for the first year of the war, the Americans were fighting for a redress of grievances within the British Empire, not for independence. During that year, however, many of them began to change their minds, for various reasons. For one thing, they were making sacrifices so great—as in the Battle of Bunker Hill, the bloodiest engagement of the entire war and one of the most sanguinary anywhere in the eighteenth century —that their original war aims seemed incom-

**COMMON SENSE;**

ADDRESSED TO THE

**INHABITANTS**

O F

**A M E R I C A,**

On the following interesting

**S U B J E C T S.**

I. Of the Origin and Design of Government in general, with concise Remarks on the English Constitution.

II. Of Monarchy and Hereditary Succession.

III. Thoughts on the present State of American Affairs.

IV. Of the present Ability of America, with some miscellaneous Reflections.

Man knows no Master save creating HEAVEN,
Or those whom choice and common good ordain.
THOMSON.

PHILADELPHIA;
Printed, and Sold, by R. BELL, in Third-Street.
MDCCLXXVI.

*Common Sense*

Title page of the first edition of Thomas Paine's pamphlet, published anonymously in Philadelphia on January 10, 1776. Afterward Paine enlisted as a soldier and accompanied Washington's army on its retreat across New Jersey. During that time he wrote a series of essays under the collective title of *The Crisis*, to arouse support for the Patriot cause. The first of the *Crisis* papers contains the sentence: "These are the times that try men's souls." After the American Revolution Paine went to France and took an active part in the French Revolution, which began in 1789. In support of the French revolutionary cause he wrote *The Rights of Man* (1791–1792). He also wrote *The Age of Reason*, in which he attacked some aspects of conventional Christianity and expounded his own rationalistic beliefs. Returning to America in 1802, he spent his last years as a lonely, obscure man. (Library of Congress)

mensurate with the cost. For another thing, they lost much of their lingering affection for the mother country when she prepared to use Indians, Negro slaves, and foreign mercenaries (the hated "Hessians") against them. And, most important, they felt that they were being forced into independence when the British government replied to the Olive Branch Petition with the Prohibitory Act, which closed the colonies to all overseas trade and made no concession except an offer of pardon to repentant rebels. The Americans desperately needed miltary supplies to continue the war, and now they could get them from abroad in adequate amounts only if they broke completely with Great Britain and proceeded to behave in all respects as if they comprised a sovereign nation.

These feelings in America were not caused, but were clarified and crystallized, by the publication, in January 1776, of the pamphlet *Common Sense.* Its author, unmentioned on the title page, was Thomas Paine, who with letters of introduction from Benjamin Franklin had emigrated from England to America less than two years before. Though long a failure in various trades, Paine now proved a brilliant success as a revolutionary propagandist. In his pamphlet he argued with flashing phrases that it was plain common sense for Americans to separate from an England rotten with the corrupt monarchy of George III, brutal as an unnatural parent toward her colonies, responsible for dragging them in to fight her wars in the past, and no more fit as an island kingdom to rule the American Continent than a satellite was fit to rule the sun. "O! ye that love mankind! ye that dare oppose not only the tyranny but the tyrant, stand forth!" Month after month the pamphlet was reprinted until many thousands of copies were in circulation, passing from hand to hand and being read and reread.

## Declaration of Independence

Despite the persuasion of *Common Sense,* the American people were far from unanimous, and they entered upon a bitter debate over the merits of dependence and independence. While the debate raged, the Continental Congress advanced step by step toward a final break. Congress opened the ports of America to all the world except Great Britain, entered into communication with foreign powers, and recommended to the various colonies that they establish governments without the authority of the Empire, as in fact they already were doing. Congress also appointed a committee to draft a formal declaration and, on July 2, 1776, before approving the declaration, adopted a resolution "That these United Colonies are, and, of right, ought to be, free and independent states; that they are absolved from all allegiance to the British crown, and that all political connexion between them and the state of Great Britain is, and ought to be, totally dissolved." Two days later Congress approved the Declaration of Independence, which gave reasons for the action already taken.

The thirty-three-year-old Virginian Thomas Jefferson wrote the Declaration of Independence, his fellow committeemen Benjamin Franklin and John Adams revised the wording a little, and Congress made more drastic changes, striking out passages that condemned the British people and the slave trade. As Adams afterward observed, Jefferson said nothing new in composing the document. Its very virtue, in fact, lay in his noble phrasing of beliefs already widespread in America. He planned the document in two main parts. In the first part he restated the familiar contract theory of John Locke, who had held that governments were formed to protect the rights of life, liberty, and property, but Jefferson gave the theory a more humane twist by referring instead to the rights of "life, liberty and the pursuit of happiness." In the second part he listed the alleged crimes of the King who, with the backing of Parliament, had violated his contract with the colonists and thus had forfeited all claim to their loyalty.

Once adopted, the Declaration of Independence exerted an incalculable influence upon later history. With its democratic principle that "all men are created equal," it stimulated humanitarian movements of various kinds in the United States, and abroad it helped to inspire the French Revolution with its Declaration of the Rights of Man. More immediately, it led to increased foreign aid for the struggling rebels and prepared the way for France's all-out intervention on their side. It steeled American Patriots to carry on without regard to offers of a peace short of the stated goal. And at the same time it divided Americans more cruelly and more extensively than they ever had been divided before.

At the news of the Declaration of Independence, crowds gathered to cheer, fire guns and cannons, and ring church bells in Philadelphia, Boston, and other places, but there were many people in America who did not rejoice. Some had disapproved of the war from the beginning, and others had been willing to support it only so long as its aims did not conflict with their basic loyalty to the King. These people, numerous but in the minority, refused to cross the new line that had been drawn. Either openly or secretly they remained Loyalists, as they chose to call themselves, or Tories, as they were known to the Whig or Patriot majority. Among the Loyalists were rich families and poor ones, highly educated men (like the scientist Benjamin Thompson) and illiterates, townspeople and backwoodsmen. Among the Loyalist leaders were royal officials and Anglican clergymen who had sided with the British government throughout the prewar decade of controversy, plus a few of the wealthy merchants and large planters who earlier had belonged to the Patriot party but who seceded from it after the Declaration of Independence.

The remaining Patriots continued to be divided among themselves. On the one hand were men like John Adams and George Washington who wished to see independence achieved with comparatively little social change in America, but whose ranks were thinned by the loss of their former allies, now Loyalists. On the other hand were men like Thomas Jefferson who desired to accomplish democratic and humanitarian reforms along with independence. Thus (as in other wars, including World War II) patriotic Americans held different as well as common aims, some intending only to smite the foreign enemy, others aspiring also to lead a popular crusade at home.

## State Governments

While waging war, the Patriots also busied themselves with providing a government for the new nation. With the outbreak of war they set up provisional governments based upon existing assemblies or emergency conventions as the royal officials fled from their positions in one colony after another. When the colonies became states, the Patriots formed permanent governments with written constitutions. The constitution-making procedure varied from state to state. In Rhode Island and Connecticut the legislatures merely revised the old colonial charters, and in most of the other states the legislatures, though not elected for that purpose, took it upon themselves to draft new constitutions. Thomas Jefferson, for one, insisted that the fundamental law should come from the people of each state, who should elect constitutional conventions and then vote on ratification. Actually, conventions were held in only three states, referendums in only five, and both a convention and a referendum in only one—Massachusetts.

The new constitutions, all pretty much alike in general outline though different in detail, were both conservative and democratic. They were conservative in retaining essentially the same structure as the old colonial governments. Except in Georgia and Pennsylvania, both of which experimented with a unicameral legislature, each constitution provided for a two-house legislature, with an elected senate taking the place of the former governor's council. All the constitutions except Pennsylvania's continued the office of governor, though most of them denied the holder of this position the bulk of the executive powers he had enjoyed in colonial days. All of the new documents confirmed and extended the ideas of popular rule that long had been put into practice; every one of them included a bill of rights, and some had preambles stating that sovereignty (the ultimate power of government) resided in the people. To vote in any state a man had to own only a modest amount of property, in some states just enough so that he could qualify as a taxpayer. To hold office he had to meet a somewhat higher property requirement, essentially as in pre-Revolutionary times. Only in New Jersey were women allowed to vote, and eventually they were deprived of the suffrage even there. But, considering the widespread ownership of property, something approaching universal manhood suffrage existed from the beginning in all the states.

Once in operation, the new states proceeded

## Slavery in Massachusetts [1783]

In the case of Quork Walker, who was a slave suing his master, the Chief Justice of Massachusetts gave the following charge to the jury:

*As to the doctrine of slavery and the right of Christians to hold Africans in perpetual servitude, and sell and treat them as we do our horses and cattle, that (it is true) has been heretofore countenanced by the Province Laws formerly, but nowhere is it expressly enacted or established. It has been a usage—a usage which took its origin from the practice of some of the European nations, and the regulations of British government respecting the then Colonies, for the benefit of trade and wealth. But whatever sentiments have formerly prevailed in this particular or slid in upon us by the example of others, a different idea has taken place with the people of America, more favorable to the natural rights of mankind, and to that natural, innate desire of Liberty, with which Heaven (without regard to color, complexion, or shape of noses) has inspired all the human race. And upon this ground our Constitution of Government, by which the people of this Commonwealth have solemnly bound themselves, sets out with declaring that all men are born free and equal—and that every subject is entitled to liberty, and to have it guarded by the laws, as well as life and property—and in short is totally repugnant to the idea of being born slaves. This being the case, I think the idea of slavery is inconsistent with our own conduct and Constitution; and there can be no such thing as perpetual servitude of a rational creature, unless his liberty is forfeited by some criminal conduct or given up by personal consent or contract.*

to make advances in social as well as political democracy. In one way or another they multiplied opportunities for land ownership and thus enlarged the voting population. For instance, they eliminated the legal rights of primogeniture and entail, which before the war had helped to maintain a landed aristocracy by transferring an entire estate to the oldest son (when a man died without a will) and by keeping the estate intact from generation to generation (when a man by entailment willed that the property never be sold). The new states also made considerable progress toward religious freedom, though some retained religious tests for officeholding. New York and the Southern states, in which the Church of England had been tax-supported, soon saw to its complete disestablishment, and the New England states stripped the Congregational Church of some of its privileges. Virginia, in its Declaration of Rights, boldly announced the principle of complete toleration and, in 1786, enacted the principle in the Statute of Religious Liberty, which Jefferson long had championed.

The new states took steps toward personal as well as religious freedom. All of them except South Carolina and Georgia prohibited the importation of slaves, and even South Carolina laid temporary wartime bans on the slave trade. After the first antislavery society in America (founded in 1775) began its agitation, and prominent Southerners including Jefferson and Washington declared their opposition to slavery, Virginia and other Southern states changed their laws so as to encourage manumission, Pennsylvania passed a gradual-emancipation act (1780), and Massachusetts through a decision of its highest court (1783) held that the state's bill of rights outlawed the ownership of slaves. Besides all this, five of the new states put provisions into their constitutions for the establishment of public schools, and all soon began to revise their criminal codes so as to make the punishment more nearly fit the crime.

## The Confederation

While the separate states were fashioning constitutions and recasting their legal systems, the Second Continental Congress tried to create a written form of government for the states as a whole. No sooner had the Congress appointed

## The Articles of Confederation [1781]

1. [Article II] "Each state retains its sovereignty, freedom and independence, and every Power, Jurisdiction and right, which is not by this confederation expressly delegated to the United States, in Congress assembled."

2. [Article IV] The free inhabitants of each state "shall be entitled to all privileges and immunities of free citizens in the several states," and "full faith and credit" shall be given by each state to the judicial and other official proceedings of other states.

3. [Article V] Each state shall be represented in Congress by no less than two and no more than seven members, shall pay its own delegates, and shall have one vote (regardless of the number of members).

4. [Article VI] No state, without the consent of Congress, shall enter into diplomatic relations or make treaties with other states or with foreign nations, or engage in war except in case of actual invasion.

5. [Article VIII] A "common treasury" shall be supplied by the states in proportion to the value of their land and improvements; the states shall levy taxes to raise their quotas of revenue.

6. [Article IX] Congress shall have power to decide on peace and war, conduct foreign affairs, settle disputes between states, regulate the Indian trade, maintain post offices, make appropriations, borrow money, emit bills of credit, build a navy, requisition soldiers from the states, etc.—but nine states must agree before Congress can take any important action.

7. [Article X] A "Committee of the States," consisting of one delegate from each state, shall act in the place of Congress when Congress is not in session.

8. [Article XIII] No change shall be made in these Articles unless agreed to by Congress and "afterwards confirmed by the legislatures of every state."

a committee to draft a declaration of independence than it appointed another to draft a plan of union, and after much debate and many revisions the Congress, in November 1777, adopted the committee's plan, the Articles of Confederation.

The Articles of Confederation provided for a central government very similar to the one already in actual operation, though it increased the powers of Congress somewhat. Congress was to have the powers of conducting war, carrying on foreign relations, and appropriating, borrowing, and issuing money, but not the powers of regulating trade, levying taxes, or drafting troops. For troops and taxes it would have to make requisitions upon the states. There was to be no separate, single, strong executive (the "President of the United States" was to be merely the presiding officer at the sessions of Congress), but Congress itself was to see to the execution of the laws through an executive committee of thirteen, made up of one member from each state, through ad hoc and standing committees for specific functions, and through such administrative departments as it might choose to create. There were to be no Confederation courts, except for courts of admiralty, but disputes between the states were to be settled by a complicated system of arbitration. The states were to retain their individual sovereignty, each of the legislatures electing and paying the salaries of two to seven delegates to Congress, and each delegation, no matter how numerous, having only one vote. At least nine of the states (through their delegations) would have to approve any important measure, such as a treaty, before Congress could pass it, and all thirteen state legislatures would have to approve before the Articles could be ratified or amended.

Ratification was delayed by differences of opinion about the proposed plan. Some Americans were willing enough to accept a relatively weak central government, but others preferred to see it strengthened. The people of all the small states insisted upon equal state representation, but those of the large states thought they should be represented in proportion to their population. Above all, the states claiming Western lands wished to keep them, but the rest of the states demanded that the whole territory be turned over to the Confederation government. The "landed" states, among which Virginia had the largest and best claim, founded their claims upon colonial charters, with the exception of New York, which based its rights upon a protectorate over the Iroquois Indians. The "landless" states, particularly Maryland, maintained that as the fruit of common sacrifices in war the Western land had become the rightful property of all the states. In this dispute selfish interests as well as high principles were involved, for rival groups of land speculators schemed to secure the cancellation or confirmation of private grants already made. At last New York gave up its rather hazy claim, and Virginia made a qualified offer to cede its lands to Congress. Then Maryland, the only state still holding out against ratification, approved the Articles of Confederation, and they went into effect in 1781.

The Confederation government came into being in time to conclude the war and make the peace. Meanwhile, during the years of fighting from 1775 to 1781, the Second Continental Congress served as the agency for directing and coordinating the war effort of the people of the thirteen states.

## Mobilizing for War

Congress and the states faced overwhelming tasks in raising and organizing armies, providing the necessary supplies and equipment, and paying the costs of war.

Supplies of most kinds were scarce at the outset, and shortages persisted to the end. Though America, being a land of hunters, contained numerous gunsmiths, they were not able to meet the wartime demand for guns and ammunition, nor were they able to produce heavy arms. Some of the states offered bounties for the encouragement of manufactures, especially for the production of guns and powder, and Congress in 1777 established a government arsenal at Springfield, Massachusetts. Even so, the Americans themselves managed to manufacture only a small fraction of the equipment they used. They supplemented their own manufactures with matériel that fell into their hands upon the seizure of forts like Crown Point and Ticonderoga (in 1775), the surrender of British

armies, and the capture of supply ships by American privateers. But they got most of their war materials through importations from Europe, particularly from France.

In trying to meet the expenses of war, Congress had no power to tax the people, and the states had little inclination to do so. Indeed, cash was scarce in the country, as it always had been. When Congress requisitioned the states for money, none of them contributed more than a tiny part of its share. At first Congress hesitated to requisition goods directly from the people, but finally allowed army purchasing agents to take supplies from farmers and pay with certificates of indebtedness. Congress could not raise much money by floating long-term loans at home, since few Americans could afford war bonds and those few usually preferred to invest their funds in more profitable ventures, such as privateering. So Congress had no choice but to issue paper money, and Continental currency came from the printing presses in large and repeated batches. The states added sizable currency issues of their own.

With goods and coin so scarce and paper money so plentiful, prices rose to fantastic heights and the value of paper money fell proportionately. There quickly appeared all the usual evils of wartime profiteering, and more too. One reason why Washington's men suffered from shortages of food and clothing at Valley Forge during the terrible winter of 1777–1778 was that American farmers and merchants preferred to do business with the British forces occupying nearby Philadelphia, since the British could pay in gold or silver coin. To check the inflationary trend, Congress advised the states to pass laws for price control, but soon saw the futility of such measures and recommended that they be dropped. Eventually, in 1780, Congress decided that the states should accept Continental currency from taxpayers at the rate of forty paper dollars to one silver dollar, then send it to Congress to be destroyed. If the currency was not turned in for taxes at a fortieth of its face value, it became utterly worthless, hence the expression, "Not worth a Continental." By this time Congress was able to meet the most pressing of its financial needs by borrowing from abroad.

The states added to their financial resources by seizing lands belonging to the Crown and to colonial proprietors. In 1777 Congress recommended that the states also confiscate and sell the property of Loyalists active in the British cause, then lend the proceeds to the central government. The states were eager enough to expropriate the Loyalists, though not to make the requested loan. Already Patriots were punishing Tories in various ways, taking from them the rights of citizenship, barring them from certain occupations, and imposing special taxes and heavy fines upon them. The seizure and sale of Loyalist property, resulting incidentally in a widened distribution of land ownership among the buyers, netted the states a total of several million pounds, in value if not in actual cash. Around 100,000 of the Loyalists themselves, either voluntarily or because of banishment, left the country during the course of the war, the most numerous group going to Quebec and laying the foundations of English-speaking Canada.

The willingness of the remaining Tories to aid the British depended somewhat on the proximity of British troops and the prospects for the British cause. As for the Patriots, only a small proportion of them were willing to volunteer for the American armies once the first surge of patriotism at the start of the war had passed. The states had to resort to persuasion and force, to bounties and the draft, the bounties being commonly in the form of land scrip, since land was an asset with which the states were well supplied. Thus recruited, militiamen remained under the control of their respective states. Many of the recruits were expert marksmen and on the average they were physically bigger and stronger than the British regulars. Yet man for man they were no match for the redcoats in battle since they lacked the regulars' fine training, discipline, and esprit de corps.

Foreseeing some of the disadvantages of separately organized militias, Congress called upon the states (while they were still colonies) to raise troops for a regular force, the Continental army, and agreed that it should have a single commander in chief. George Washington, forty-three years old, sober and responsible by nature, possessed more command experience than any other American-born officer available. And he had political as well as military qualifications. An early advocate of independence, he was admired and trusted by nearly all the Patriots. A Virginian, he had the support not only of Southerners but also of Northerners who feared that the appointment of a New Englander might jeopardize sectional harmony. As the unanimous choice of the delegates, he took command in June 1775.

Congress chose well. Throughout the war Washington kept faithfully at his task, despite difficulties and discouragements that would have daunted a lesser man. With the aid of foreign military experts such as the Marquis de Lafayette and the Baron von Steuben he succeeded in building and holding together the Continental army, though at no time did it number as many as 10,000 men (not counting the militia of the separate states). The morale of the soldiers, who were getting short rations and low pay, became so bad that mutinies broke out (in 1781) among the Pennsylvania and New Jersey troops. Meanwhile, during the dark winter of Valley Forge, some congressmen and army officers, conspiring together in the so-called Conway Cabal, hinted at replacing Washington as commander in chief. He, on the other hand, complained often and bitterly against his employers, the delegates in Congress, who seemed to do too little in supplying him with manpower and equipment, and too much in interfering with his conduct of military operations. The faults were not all on the side of Congress, which had its difficulties too. Washington had his shortcomings as a military commander and he lost more battles than he won. Yet he was a great war leader. For all his faults and failures, he led the army and the nation to ultimate victory with his supreme steadiness and courage, his sacrificial devotion to the cause of independence.

## THE WAR FOR INDEPENDENCE

In their war for independence the Americans had the advantage of fighting on their home terrain, far from the center of British might. They also had the benefit of tremendous foreign aid, especially after the American war merged with a world contest in which Great Britain

# Where Historians Disagree

## The American Revolution

In their accounts of the American Revolution, historians at one time concentrated on the Patriot aim of autonomy within the British Empire and then complete independence from it. These historians differed among themselves in regard to revolutionary motivation; some of them emphasized political ideals, others stressed economic interests. But all of them took as their central theme the struggle between the American colonies and the British government.

Eventually, a number of writers began calling attention to struggles *within* the colonies as well. These writers maintained that the Revolution involved not only the question of home rule but also the question who should rule at home. It was, according to them, a movement toward both independence and democracy. Thus, in a study of New York politics from 1770 to 1776 (1909) and in *The Eve of the Revolution* (1918), Carl L. Becker described the Revolution as, in part, a kind of civil war, a contest for power between American radicals and conservatives, one that led to the "democratization of American politics and society." J. F. Jameson elaborated upon the idea in his slim but influential volume *The American Revolution Considered as a Social Movement* (1926). "The stream of revolution, once started, could not be confined within narrow banks, but spread abroad upon the land," Jameson wrote. "Many economic desires, many social aspirations were set free by the political struggle, many aspects of colonial society profoundly altered by the forces thus let loose." The social changes tended "in the direction of levelling democracy."

This view long prevailed, but recently it has been sharply challenged. The most forceful attack on it comes from Robert E. Brown, who shows in *Middle Class Democracy and the Revolution in Massachusetts, 1691–1780* (1955) that, before 1776, Massachusetts was already "very close to a complete democracy," with practically all men enjoying the right to vote. Brown argues that, at least in Massachusetts and probably also in other colonies, the aim of the Revolutionary leaders was to preserve the democratic liberties that already existed. And E. S. Morgan, in a bold and concise reinterpretation, *The Birth of the Republic, 1763–1789* (1956), holds that most Americans were in basic agreement on political principles; thus he endorses the older view of the Revolution as a struggle between the colonies and the British government.

The debate goes on, with no final decision on points of interpretation, but the net result is greatly to broaden our knowledge of the Revolutionary period.

faced the strongest powers of Europe as actual or potential foes. But the success of the Americans was also due to their own patriotic effort. Though losing battle after battle, they avoided catastrophes and gained at least a few decisive victories through the exertions of thousands of armed men under the majestic generalship of George Washington. And, having held their own in war, they won the peace because their diplomats shrewdly made the most of the opportunities that the world situation offered.

## The Fighting, to 1777

For about the first year of the fighting (1775–1776) the colonial armed forces took the offensive. After the British retreat from Concord and Lexington, the Americans besieged the army of General Gage in Boston, and though suffering severe casualties in the Battle of Bunker Hill (actually fought on Breed's Hill, June 17, 1775), they inflicted even greater losses upon the enemy and thereafter they continued to tighten the siege. Far to the south, at Moore's Creek Bridge in North Carolina, a band of Patriots crushed an uprising of Tories (February 27, 1776) and thereby discouraged British plans for

invading the Southern states with Loyalist aid. Far to the north the Americans themselves undertook an invasion of Canada. The fearless Benedict Arnold threatened Quebec after a winter march of incredible hardship. He was joined by Richard Montgomery, who took command of the combined forces. When they launched an attack, Montgomery was killed and Arnold wounded; though the latter kept up a siege for a time, the Quebec campaign ended in frustration. In the spring a civilian commission headed by the seventy-year-old Franklin returned from the north without success in its efforts to secure the allegiance of Canada as the fourteenth state. Already, however, the British had given up their attempt to hold Boston and had departed with hundreds of Loyalist refugees (March 17, 1776) for Halifax. Within a year from the firing of the first shots, the enemy had been driven from American soil.

The enemy soon returned, to put the Americans on the strategic defensive for the remainder of the war. During the summer of 1776, in the weeks immediately following the Declaration of Independence, the waters around the city of New York became filled with the most formi-

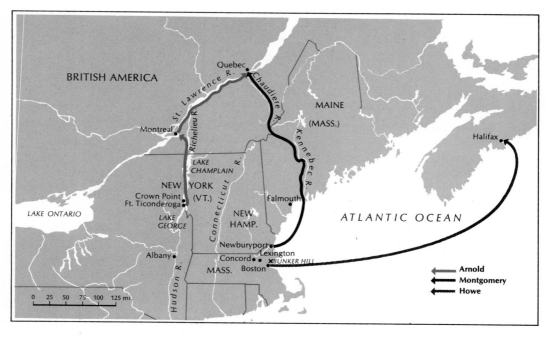

**The War in the North   1775**

dable military force Great Britain ever had sent abroad. Here were hundreds of men-of-war and troopships and a host of 32,000 disciplined soldiers under the command of the tall and affable Sir William Howe. Having no grudge against the Americans, Howe would rather awe them into submission than shoot them, and he believed that most of them, if given a chance, would show that they were at heart loyal to the King. In a parley with commissioners from Congress he offered the alternatives of submission with royal pardon or battle against overwhelming odds.

To oppose Howe's awesome array, Washington could muster only about 19,000 poorly armed and trained soldiers, including both Continentals and state troops, and he had no navy at all. Yet without hesitation the Americans chose continued war, which meant inevitably a succession of defeats. The British pushed the defenders off Long Island, compelled them to abandon Manhattan Island, and drove them in slow retreat over the plains of New Jersey, across the Delaware River, and into Pennsylvania.

Warfare being for eighteenth-century Europeans a seasonal activity, the British settled down for the winter with occupation forces at various points in New Jersey and with an outpost of Hessians at Trenton on the Delaware. But Washington did not content himself with sitting still. On Christmas night 1776, he daringly recrossed the icy river, surprised and scattered the Hessians, and occupied the town. Then he advanced and drove off a force of redcoats at Princeton. Unable to hold either Princeton or Trenton, he finally took refuge for the rest of the winter in the hills around Morristown. As the campaign of 1776 came to an end, the Americans could console themselves with the thought that they had won two minor victories, that their main army was still intact, and that the invaders were really no nearer than ever to the decisive triumph that Howe so confidently had anticipated.

For the campaign of 1777 the British devised a strategy that, if Howe had stuck to it, might have cut the United States in two and prepared the way for final victory by Great Britain. According to this plan, Howe would move from

**Washington's Retreat    1776**

New York up the Hudson to Albany, while another force, in a gigantic pincers movement, would come down from Canada to meet him. One of Howe's ambitious younger officers, the dashing John Burgoyne, "Gentleman Johnny," secured command of this northern force and elaborated upon the plan by preparing for a two-pronged attack along both the Mohawk and the upper Hudson approaches to Albany.

Then, fortunately for the United States, Howe adopted a different plan for himself, intending to dispirit the Patriots and rally the Loyalists by seizing the rebel capital, Philadelphia. Taking the bulk of his forces away from New York by sea, Howe landed at the head of Chesapeake Bay, brushed Washington aside at the Battle of Brandywine (September 11), and proceeded to occupy Philadelphia. Meanwhile, Washington after an unsuccessful attack at Germantown (October 4) went into winter quarters at Valley Forge, and the scattered Congress resumed its sittings in York, Pennsylvania.

Up north, Burgoyne was left to carry out his twofold campaign without aid from Howe. Sending Colonel Barry St. Leger with a fast-moving force up the St. Lawrence River toward Lake Ontario and the headwaters of the Mohawk, Burgoyne with his own army advanced directly down the upper Hudson Valley. He got

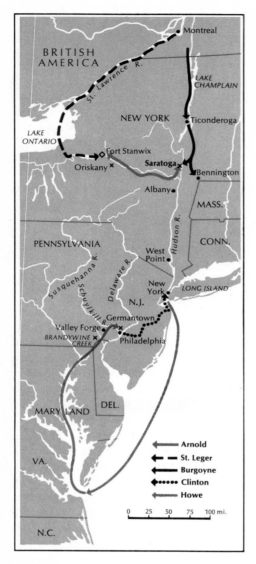

**British Campaigns 1777**

(August 6), Nicholas Herkimer with his German farmers checked a force of St. Leger's Indians and Tories, so that Benedict Arnold had time to go to the relief of Fort Stanwix and close off the Mohawk Valley to St. Leger's advance. In the other battle, at Bennington, Vermont (August 16), the Bunker Hill veteran John Stark with his New England militiamen severely mauled a detachment that Burgoyne had sent out to seek supplies. Short of materials, with all help cut off, Burgoyne fought a couple of costly engagements and then withdrew to Saratoga, where Gates surrounded him. Burgoyne was through, and he knew it. On October 17, 1777, he ordered what was left of his army, nearly 5,000 men, to lay down their arms.

Not only the United States but also Europe took note of the amazing news from the woods of upstate New York, and France in particular was impressed. The British surrender at Saratoga, a great turning point in the war, led directly to an alliance between the United States and France.

## Foreign Friends

Shortly after the fighting had begun, Congress appointed a secret committee with Franklin as chairman for the purpose of corresponding with "our friends" in Great Britain and, more significantly, in "other parts of the world." Later Congress replaced this agency with a Committee for Foreign Affairs and then (1781) with a Department of Foreign Affairs, the immediate ancestor of the State Department. As far as possible, however, Congress as a whole conducted foreign relations, often overruling or by-passing the agencies it created.

Even before the Declaration of Independence, Congress drew up a treaty plan for liberal commercial arrangements with other countries and prepared to send representatives to the capitals of Europe for negotiating treaties—which necessarily would mean European recognition of the United States as one of the sovereign nations of the world. "Militia diplomats," John Adams called the early American representatives abroad, and unlike the diplomatic regulars of Europe they knew little of the formal art and etiquette of Old World diplomacy. Yet most of them were well acquainted with certain

off to a flying start, easily taking Fort Ticonderoga and an enormous store of powder and supplies, and causing such consternation that Congress removed General Philip Schuyler from command in the north and replaced him with Horatio Gates, in response to the demands of New Englanders.

By the time Gates took command, Burgoyne already faced a sudden reversal of his military fortunes in consequence of two staggering defeats. In one of them, at Oriskany, New York fundamentals, for they had gained much diplomatic experience through their dealings with one another in intercolonial affairs, with the Indian tribes in war and peace, and with the British government as colonial agents in London. Since overseas communication was slow and uncertain (it took from one to three months to cross the Atlantic), these representatives abroad sometimes had to interpret the instructions of Congress very freely and make crucial decisions entirely on their own.

Of all the possible foreign friends of the United States, the most promising and most powerful was France, who still resented her defeat at the hands of Great Britain in 1763. France, under King Louis XVI, who came to the throne in 1774, had an astute and determined foreign minister in the Count de Vergennes, an expert practitioner of Machiavellian principles, thoroughly trained in the cutthroat diplomacy of eighteenth-century Europe. Ver-

gennes soon saw that France had a vital interest in the outcome of the American war. If the colonies should assert and maintain their independence, the power of Great Britain would be seriously weakened by the loss of a good part of her empire, and the power of France would be correspondingly increased.

From the start of the troubles between England and her colonies, the French had maintained observers in America to report the course of events, and after the shooting began both Americans and Frenchmen put out diplomatic feelers. In London the Massachusetts colonial agent Arthur Lee met the French dramatist and political genius Caron de Beaumarchais, and the two discussed the possibilities of secret assistance to the colonies. Beaumarchais reported to Vergennes, and Vergennes dispatched an army officer to America to encourage the rebellion, urge independence, and promise supplies. After several meetings with Vergennes' spokesman,

## The Continental Army at Valley Forge

Many foreigners served as officers in the Continental army—too many, it seemed to General Washington. Most of them received their commissions from Congress, not from the commander in chief. Once he referred to the foreigners as "hungry adventurers." But he deeply appreciated the assistance of a few of the volunteers from abroad, especially the Marquis de Lafayette and the Baron von Steuben. A veteran of the Prussian army, Steuben came to the United States in 1777, and Washington appointed him inspector general, with overall charge of military discipline, instruc-

tion, and supply. Steuben reorganized the Continental army, provided for improved training and drill of soldiers, and wrote a manual of army regulations. The painting by Edwin A. Abbey, which hangs in the Pennsylvania House of Representatives, shows Steuben instructing troops in Washington's camp at Valley Forge, near Philadelphia, during the winter of 1777–1778. After the war he settled in New York. (Courtesy of the Pennsylvania Department of Commerce)

Franklin's committee of secret correspondence sent Silas Deane to France as a "merchant" to make "commercial" arrangements. In consequence of these arrangements, Beaumarchais shipped large quantities of munitions to America through a fictitious trading firm that he had rigged up to disguise the fact that most of the shipments were financed by the King of France and the King of Spain. Whether this sort of lend-lease was a gift or a loan later became a question of bitter dispute between Congress and Beaumarchais.

After the Declaration of Independence, Franklin himself went to France to get further aid and outright recognition of the United States. A natural diplomat, the equal if not the superior of the world's best at that time, Franklin immediately captivated Frenchmen of all classes—and Frenchwomen too. But Vergennes hesitated. At the first news of the American Declaration, he was inclined to make a treaty recognizing United States independence, but he did not wish to act without Spain; and when reports came of Washington's defeat on Long Island he decided to wait and watch the military developments in America. If and when the Americans should show that they had a real chance of winning, then France would intervene. Meanwhile Vergennes was willing to go on financing the American war. He initiated a series of subsidies which in time amounted to nearly $62 million and a series of loans which totaled over $6 million.

The news that Vergennes and Franklin were waiting for—the news from Saratoga—arrived in London on December 2 and in Paris on December 4, 1777. In London the knowledge of Burgoyne's surrender caused Lord North to decide in favor of a peace offensive, an offer of complete home rule within the Empire for Americans if they would quit the war. In Paris, learning of Lord North's intentions from a British spy, Franklin let the word get out for Vergennes to hear. Vergennes worried. If the Americans should accept the British offer, his opportunity to weaken France's traditional enemy would be gone, and if they could not get what they wanted from France, they might accept. Without waiting for Spain to go along with France, Vergennes on February 6, 1778,

signed two treaties with Franklin and Deane, one a treaty of commerce and amity, and the other, which was supposed to be secret, a treaty of conditional and defensive alliance, to take effect if Great Britain should go to war with France. Congress and the King quickly ratified the treaties, and Congress received and banqueted a minister from France while the King welcomed Franklin as minister from the United States.

France soon drifted into war with Great Britain, and in 1779 Spain, with objectives of her own, declared war as an ally of France though not of the United States; Spain refused even to receive officially the American representative in Madrid, John Jay. A year later the Netherlands, persisting in its profitable trade with both the French and the Americans, found itself also at war with Britain and agreed to a treaty with the United States. The League of Armed Neutrals—Russia, Denmark, Sweden—assumed a defiant attitude toward Britain, but refrained from considering war and refused to have any official dealings with the upstart nation in America.

Indirectly all the countries arrayed in hostility to Britain contributed to the ultimate success of the United States by complicating the task of the latter's foe. Directly, the Netherlands provided loans to the Americans but was powerless to give military or naval support, and Spain gave unofficial subsidies but confined her military and naval activities to strictly Spanish objectives. France (for her own reasons, of course) was the true friend in need of the Americans. Not only did she furnish them most of their money and munitions, but she also provided a navy and an expeditionary force that, with Washington's army, made possible the decisive victory at Yorktown.

## Victory at Yorktown

During the first two years of the war the important campaigns and battles had taken place in the North, but after Saratoga the fighting in that part of the country developed into a stalemate. Replacing General Howe, Sir Henry Clinton withdrew from Philadelphia and took what had been Howe's army back to New York.

Washington used most of his army to keep watch around New York while (1778–1779) sending part of it to chastise the Indians along the frontier for their horrible massacres in the Cherry Valley (New York) and the Wyoming Valley (Pennsylvania). During that same winter George Rogers Clark, with orders from the state of Virginia and not from Washington or Congress, led a heroic expedition over the mountains and redeemed the settlements of the Illinois country from the British and their Indian allies. In 1779 the treason of Benedict Arnold shocked Washington and Patriots everywhere but did little military damage except for the transfer of Arnold's services to the British, since his scheme for betraying the Hudson River stronghold of West Point was frustrated in the nick of time. During the final two years of fighting, all the significant action occurred in the South.

Sir Henry Clinton, a rather timid strategist, planned a Southern offensive that was supposed to end the American will to resist, but he put the command of the operation in the hands of Lord Cornwallis, an able general but one as rash as Clinton himself was cautious, and capable of changing plans and disobeying orders in mid-campaign. Clinton and Cornwallis based their strategy on assumptions that were not to prove facts. They assumed that seapower would enable them to move their troops from point to point along the coast with ease, that the difficulties of overland travel would make American counter-action ineffectual, and that Loyalists would rise en masse to welcome and assist the redcoats as liberators. With the conquered South as a base, Clinton and Cornwallis thought they could dispose of the rest of the country at their leisure.

While it was true that in Georgia and the Carolinas there were numerous Tories, some of them disgruntled veterans of the Regulator movement, it was also true that in Virginia as in Massachusetts the mass of the people were fiercely patriotic and that even in the lower South the Loyalist strength was grossly overestimated. Actually, having the support of most of the countryside, the Patriot forces were to be better off than the British in matters of logistics and supply. And the French, while far from able to maintain consistent control of the coastal

**Road to Yorktown   1780–1781**

waters, were finally to have a fleet in the right place at the right time.

The British succeeded in taking Savannah (December 29, 1778) and Charleston (May 20, 1780), inspiring many Loyalists to take up arms, and advancing far into the interior. At every turn they were harassed, however, by Patriot guerrillas led by such resourceful fighters as Thomas Sumter, Andrew Pickens, and Francis Marion, the "Swamp Fox." Penetrating to Camden, well up the Wateree River in South Carolina, Cornwallis met and crushed (August 16, 1780) a combined force of militiamen and Continentals under Horatio Gates, who did not quite deserve his fame as the hero of Saratoga. Congress recalled Gates, and Washington gave the Southern command to Nathanael Greene, a former Quaker blacksmith of Rhode Island and probably the ablest of all the American generals of the time next to Washington himself.

Before Greene arrived in the war theater along the North and South Carolina line, the tide of battle already had begun to turn against Cornwallis. At King's Mountain (October 7, 1780) a band of Patriot riflemen from the backwoods killed, wounded, or captured an entire

### John Paul Jones

A Scot by birth, a Virginian by adoption, Jones became for Americans the greatest naval hero of the Revolutionary War. As captain of the sloop of war *Ranger*, he took to France the official news of the Saratoga victory and then proceeded to harry the British coast, boldly sinking ships within sight of land and occasionally going ashore to raid. In France, through Franklin's influence, he obtained a small fleet with the *Bonhomme Richard* (named for the "Poor Richard" of Franklin's famous almanac) as the flagship. The *Bonhomme Richard* under Jones' command defeated the British frigate *Serapis* in a spectacular duel (September 23, 1779). Captain Jones created such a nuisance for the British that he compelled them to keep a part of their naval force close to home, yet they managed to maintain supremacy in American waters during most of the war. Though Congress had begun to build a navy as early as December 1775, few of the American-built warships were even able to get out to sea. General Washington believed that ultimate victory would depend upon superior sea power; this the Americans achieved only through the presence of the French fleet, and only temporarily, at Yorktown. This painting of John Paul Jones directing his men against the *Serapis* is by a modern artist, N. C. Wyeth (1882–1945). (The Bettmann Archive)

force of 1,100 New York and South Carolina Tories, upon whom Cornwallis had depended as auxiliaries. Once arrived, Greene confused and exasperated Cornwallis by dividing the American forces into fast-moving contingents while refraining from a showdown in open battle. One of the contingents inflicted what Cornwallis

admitted was "a very unexpected and severe blow" at Cowpens (January 17, 1781). At last, having received the reinforcements he awaited, Greene combined all his forces and arranged to meet the British on ground of his own choosing at Guilford Court House, North Carolina. After a hard-fought battle (March 15, 1781) Greene was driven from the field, but Cornwallis lost so many men that he decided at last to abandon the Carolina campaign.

For a while Cornwallis thought of joining with the forces of Benedict Arnold, now in command of British raiders in Virginia, and undertaking the conquest of that state. In Virginia he sent out new raiding parties, drove off a Patriot army under Lafayette, and then— despite the expostulations of his superior officer, General Clinton—retreated to the peninsula between the York and James rivers and began to build fortifications at Yorktown. While Clinton worried about Cornwallis' moves, Washington made plans with the Count de Rochambeau, commander of the French expeditionary force in America, and with Admiral de Grasse, commander of a French fleet in American waters, for trapping Cornwallis. Washington and Rochambeau marched a Franco-American army from the New York vicinity to join Lafayette in Virginia while de Grasse sailed with additional troops for Chesapeake Bay and the York River. These joint operations, perfectly timed and executed, caught Cornwallis between land and sea. After a few shows of resistance, he asked for terms on October 17, 1781, four years to the day after the capitulation of Burgoyne, and two days later he surrendered his whole army of more than 7,000.

The fighting was over, but the war was not quite won. The United States continued to be something of an occupied country, with British forces holding the seaports of Savannah, Charleston, Wilmington, and New York. Before long a British fleet met and defeated Admiral de Grasse's fleet in the West Indies, ending Washington's hopes for further seapower assistance. So far as the naval and military situation was concerned, the British still held the upper hand in America. And peace was not yet to be made.

## Winning the Peace

Until Yorktown, peace had been for Americans an illusory and at times a dangerous proposition; and the prospects even after that victory, though improved, were not ideal. The trouble was with Spain. She entered the war solely to recover lost territories in America and Europe, above all Gibraltar, and she had an alliance binding France to make no separate peace. The United States had promised in its treaty of alliance to conclude no peace without France. Now, if Spain should fight on till she won Gibraltar back, and if France should stick by Spain, and the United States by France, the Americans might be at war forever. That, however, was not the real danger to American interests. The danger was that Spain, to get Gibraltar or American territory, might enter into a deal with Great Britain at the expense of the United States and that France might feel compelled to go along with Spain. In making peace, the United States had as much to fear from its allies as from its enemy.

When, in 1779, Spain in the role of mediator proposed a peace conference, Congress promptly named John Adams as the American delegate and sent him instructions to enter into no negotiations unless Great Britain first recognized the United States as "sovereign, free, and independent." Adams, already abroad as a militia diplomat, proceeded to Paris and remained there waiting for new peace opportunities after the Spanish proposal had been forgotten. The blustery Adams did not get along with Vergennes as well as the soft-spoken Franklin did. Vergennes sent to America a new minister, La Luzerne, to do something about the Adams nuisance. Lobbying with congressmen and playing up to the Secretary for Foreign Affairs, La Luzerne secured the replacement of the single delegate with a whole delegation, including Franklin and John Jay as well as Adams, and La Luzerne virtually dictated the delegation's instructions. These instructions told the prospective peacemakers to keep in close touch with the French government, tell it everything, follow its advice. Thus the United States was put into the hands of Vergennes by the time (1781) Austria and Russia made their

### Treaty of Paris [1783]

1. "His Britannic Majesty acknowledges the said United States . . . to be free, sovereign and independent States."

2. Boundaries shall run, as described in some detail, from Nova Scotia to and through the Great Lakes and the Lake of the Woods, "thence on a due west course to the river Mississippi," down the Mississippi to the thirty-first parallel, and then east to the Atlantic Ocean.

3. The people of the United States shall have fishing rights and liberties in the waters of British North America.

4. Creditors on either side "shall meet with no lawful impediment to the recovery of the full value, in sterling money, of all *bona fide* debts heretofore contracted."

5. Congress "shall earnestly recommend to the legislatures of the respective States" that they make restitution for confiscated Loyalist property.

6. There shall be no future confiscations or prosecutions on account of the part that anyone may have taken in the war.

7. Hostilities shall cease, and "His Britannic Majesty shall, with all convenient speed, and without causing any destruction, or carrying away any negroes or other property of the American inhabitants, withdraw all his armies, garrisons and fleets from the said United States, and from every post, place and harbour within the same."

joint mediation offer that led eventually to a general peace settlement.

Then the victory at Yorktown, by giving the Americans new bargaining power, rescued them from the worst of their dependence upon Vergennes. In England, Cornwallis' defeat provoked outcries against continuing the war and demands for cultivating American friendship as an asset in international politics. Lord

North resigned and Lord Shelburne emerged from the political wreckage as prime minister. British emissaries appeared in France to talk informally with Franklin. He suggested what he called "necessary" terms of peace, including independence and the establishment of the Mississippi as the western boundary of the United States, and "desirable" terms including the cession of Canada for the purpose of "reconciliation," a "sweet word," as he said. But John Jay, recently arrived from his fruitless mission to Spain, where he had acquired reason to be suspicious of Spaniards and all Europeans,

objected to continuing the negotiations on the grounds that the Americans were addressed not as plenipotentiaries of a sovereign nation but as "persons" from "colonies or plantations." The negotiations were delayed until Jay was satisfied.

All along Franklin, Jay, and Adams had kept Vergennes informed of their conversations with British agents, in accordance with the instructions from Congress. Then, one day, Jay learned that Vergennes' private secretary was off on a secret mission to England. Jay feared that Vergennes was going to leave the United States in

## The Peacemakers of 1783

Only John Jay, John Adams, and Benjamin Franklin actually took part in the peace negotiations, though two other commissioners (Henry Laurens and Thomas Jefferson) were appointed. Jay, Adams, and Franklin are pictured in that order, from left to right, in **Benjamin West's** unfinished painting. West, born in Pennsylvania, had studied art in Italy and, in 1763, had settled in England, where he became one of the leading artists. His "grand historic style" was highly esteemed by English patrons of art, including King

George III, who appointed him a court painter. In his historical paintings West exhibited considerable realism despite his grand manner. He left his mark upon all of the first generation of notable American painters—John Singleton Copley, Gilbert Stuart, Charles Willson Peale, John Trumbull, Washington Allston, and others who studied under him. (Courtesy of the H. F. Du Pont Winterthur Museum) the lurch and make a separate peace by which Great Britain and Spain would divide between themselves the territory west of the Alleghenies and east of the Mississippi. Such a deal, as Franklin exclaimed, would have "cooped us up within the Allegheny Mountains." Though Jay was mistaken as to the details of the secret mission, he was right in thinking that Vergennes was suggesting separate negotiations that were to be kept from the American peacemakers and that might have proved disadvantageous to the United States. From that day on, Franklin, Jay, and Adams ceased to inform Vergennes of their diplomacy but went ahead on their own and soon drew up a preliminary treaty with Great Britain. In doing so, they may have violated the spirit but they did not violate the letter of the Franco-American alliance, since they were not making a separate final peace. Of course, they disregarded their instructions from Congress, but those instructions had come originally from Vergennes himself.

After the preliminary articles were signed (November 30, 1782), Jay and Adams left to Franklin the delicate task of telling Vergennes what had been done. Franklin admitted to Vergennes that the Americans perhaps had violated etiquette in failing to keep the French informed, but he trusted that the incident would cause no rift in the Franco-American alliance. Cleverly Franklin observed: "The English, I just now learn, flatter themselves they have already divided us. I hope this little misunderstanding will therefore be kept a secret, and that they will find themselves totally mistaken." Vergennes, dealing with a fellow master of diplomacy, could not say much and was doubtless glad to have an excuse for ending the war regardless of the wishes of his Spanish ally. Franklin coolly asked for another loan from France—and got it!

The final treaty was signed September 3, 1783, when Spain as well as France agreed to end hostilities. It included a number of provisions that Franklin and Jay and Adams had opposed, and some of these were to lead to serious friction with Great Britain and with Spain in the years ahead. Yet it also included essentially the "necessary" terms that Franklin originally had indicated, though not his "desir-

able" ones such as the cession of Canada. On the whole the peace was remarkably favorable to the United States in granting a clear-cut recognition of independence and a generous, though ambiguous, delimitation of territory—from the southern boundary of Canada to the northern boundary of Florida and from the Atlantic to the Mississippi. Indeed, by playing off the powers of Europe against one another, Franklin and his colleagues had achieved the greatest diplomatic success in the history of the United States. With good reason the American people celebrated as the last of the British occupation forces embarked from New York and General Washington at the head of his troops rode triumphantly in.

## THE CONFEDERATION'S PROBLEMS

As usually happens at the end of a long and hard-fought war, peace in 1783 brought to the American people tasks almost as trying as those of the war itself. Congress, with the inadequate powers granted to it in the Articles of Confederation, did not quite succeed in solving its postwar problems of diplomacy and public finance, though it made a good beginning toward organizing its territories in the West. The states, too, had difficulties with debts and taxes and, in the case of Massachusetts, with an armed uprising.

### A Disputed Treaty

The peace treaty of 1783 recognized the independence of the United States and granted the new nation a vast domain—on paper—but Americans found it hard to exercise their full sovereignty in fact. At once they ran into serious conflict with both Great Britain and Spain, yet they could not count upon the support of France even though France remained technically America's ally.

Despite the treaty provision calling upon the British to evacuate American soil, British forces continued to occupy a string of frontier posts along the Great Lakes within the United States. Secret orders to hold these forts went from the Colonial Office in London to the governor general of Canada on April 8, 1784, just one day before King George III proclaimed the peace treaty as being in final effect and called upon all his subjects to obey its terms! The real reason for the secret orders was the Canadian and British desire to maintain points of contact with Indian tribes in the Northwest for the conduct of the fur trade and the continuance of defensive alliances with them. The avowed reason, which was an afterthought, was the alleged failure of the United States to carry out its treaty obligations, particularly in regard to private debts.

These debts, dating from pre-Revolutionary days, were owed by American citizens, mostly Southern planters, to merchants and other creditors in England. The American debtors had no intention of paying—many of them had supported the Revolution in order to gain independence and thus throw off their old obligations. The treaty provided only that the United States should place no obstacle in the way of the collection of the debts, and the United States did place no obstacle in the way. True, the individual states interfered with debt collections, through the passage of debtor stay laws, the issuance of paper money as legal tender, and the rulings of courts sympathetic with local debtors.

According to the ill-founded British complaints, the United States was violating not only the article regarding private debts but also the one regarding Loyalist property. On this point the treaty said merely that Congress should recommend to the various states that they make restitution to certain categories of Loyalists whose possessions had been confiscated during the war. Congress did recommend, but the states did not respond. The British had not really expected them to. The article was put into the treaty as a gesture of the King's concern for the fate of his faithful subjects. Anticipating that the states would do little or nothing for Loyalist refugees, Parliament itself appropriated money for their relief.

To British allegations of bad faith, Americans countered with the charge that Great Britain, besides refusing to abandon the frontier posts, was disregarding the treaty provision that obligated her to compensate American slaveowners whose slaves had been carried off by the British armies at the end of the war. And the two countries disputed the meaning and application of still another article, the one defining the northeastern boundary of the United States. Over part of its course the boundary was supposed to follow the St. Croix River, but unfortunately the river had two major branches, and the treaty did not specify which of the two was meant.

The peace arrangements led also to a boundary dispute between the United States and Spain. In her settlement with Spain, Great Britain gave back Florida (which had been British from 1763 to 1783) with the Atlantic and the Mississippi specified as its eastern and western limits but with no precise definition of its northern border. In the preliminary treaty with the United States, however, Great Britain had agreed secretly that, if she herself were to keep Florida, its boundary would be set at latitude 32° 28′ and that, if she ceded it to Spain, its boundary would be located farther south, at the thirty-first parallel. Afterward the United States insisted upon the more southerly of these lines, but Spain demanded the additional northern strip as rightfully a part of Florida. Spain also claimed extensive territory even north of that, as belonging to her by virtue of her (rather small-scale) military operations in the American West during the Revolutionary War.

There was another conflict between Anglo-American arrangements and the claims of Spain. In their treaty of peace Great Britain and the United States recognized the right of subjects and citizens of both countries to navigate the Mississippi River to its mouth. But Spain, possessing Louisiana as well as Florida and thus occupying both banks of the lower Mississippi, denied that Great Britain had any rights there to grant to the United States. In 1784 Spain exercised her lawful power over her territorial waters by closing the lower Mississippi to American navigation.

## Failures in Foreign Affairs

Thus several provisions of the peace with Great Britain failed to give Americans the benefits they desired and expected, and the treaty omitted entirely still other provisions they had hoped for. Above all, American shippers and traders wanted commercial arrangements that would give them privileges of trading and shipping on equal terms with British subjects in all parts of the British Empire.

No longer colonists, these businessmen, it is true, now had opportunities for exploiting worldwide routes of trade, which before the war had been legally closed to them. Congress proceeded to make satisfactory commercial treaties with the nations of Europe—with France (1778), the Netherlands (1782), Sweden (1783), and Prussia (1785). Congress also agreed to pay protection money to the Sultan of Morocco (1786) so that American merchantmen in the Mediterranean would be free from the depredations of at least some of the Barbary pirates. Without benefit of treaty, American enterprisers opened fabulously profitable trade routes to the Orient, beginning with the voyage of the *Empress of China* in 1784–1785.

Yet, though commerce flourished in new directions, most American trade persisted as much as possible in the old, prewar patterns. In the United States the bulk of imports continued to come from British sources, for Americans were used to British goods, and British merchants knew and catered to American tastes, offered attractive prices, and extended long and easy credit. To earn the British funds needed to pay for these imports, Americans desired free access to more British markets than were open to them after the war.

In 1784 Congress sent John Adams as minister to London with instructions to get a commercial treaty and speed up the evacuation of the frontier posts. Taunted by the query whether he represented one nation or thirteen, Minister Adams made no headway in England, partly because Congress had no power to retaliate against the kind of commercial warfare that Great Britain was pursuing against the United States. Throughout the 1780s the British government refused even to return the courtesy of sending a minister to the American capital.

The Spanish government, by contrast, was willing to negotiate its differences with the United States, and in 1785 its representative, Don Diego de Gardoqui, arrived in New York (where Congress had moved from Philadelphia)

to deal with the Secretary for Foreign Affairs, John Jay. After months of the most friendly conversations, Jay and Gardoqui initialed a treaty (1786). By its terms, the Spanish government would have granted Americans the right to trade with Spain but not with her colonies; would have conceded the American interpretation of the Florida boundary; and (in a secret article) would have joined in an alliance to protect American soil from British encroachments. The United States, besides guaranteeing Spanish possessions in America, would have agreed to "forbear" the navigation of the Mississippi for twenty years, though not to abandon the right of navigation. Jay found it hopeless, however, to secure the necessary nine state votes for the ratification of his treaty by Congress, since the delegates from the five Southern states objected bitterly and correctly that the interests of Southerners in Mississippi navigation were being sacrificed to the interests of Northerners in Spanish trade.

## The Needs of the West

Into the areas of postwar border conflict with Great Britain and Spain moved an unprecedented horde of American settlers during and after the Revolution. When the war began, only a few thousand lived west of the Appalachian divide; by 1790 their numbers had increased to 120,000. Most of the migrants made the mountain crossing under the auspices of able and farseeing land promoters. James Robertson and John Sevier led pioneers from North Carolina to the Watauga settlements (1770) and later to the Cumberland Valley (1779), thus laying the foundations for the future state of Tennessee. Richard Henderson, promoter of the Transylvania Company and employer of Daniel Boone, stimulated the growth of Kentucky by selling lands, organizing a provisional government (1776), and having the Wilderness Road hewn out. The managers of the Vandalia Company encouraged migration to what eventually became West Virginia. And the Allen brothers—Ethan, Ira, and Levi—attracted purchasers for their regal holdings of real estate in the Green Mountains of Vermont. The frontiersman usually had to depend upon such speculators for his land title and for other favors, yet he was characteristi-

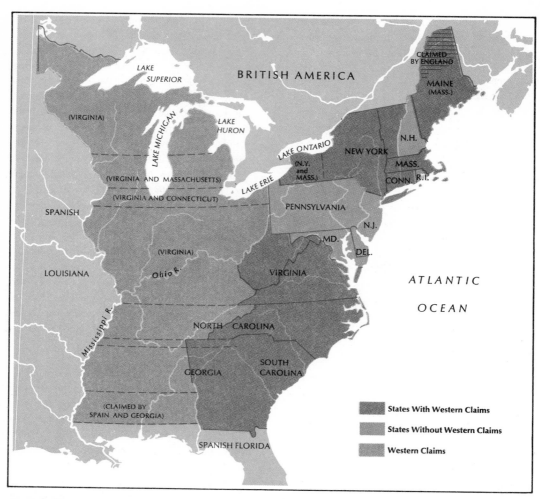

**State Claims to Western Lands   1781**

cally an individualist determined to make a future for himself. He and his family, together with thousands of others like him, comprised what was potentially the strongest single factor for redeeming the West for the United States.

But the United States could realize this potentiality only if the government were able to meet the needs of the frontier settler and keep him loyal to its distant authority. The settler needed protection from the Indians, access to outside markets for his surplus crops, and courts with orderly processes of law. In dealing with the West, Congress inherited responsibilities that formerly had baffled King and Parliament.

At first Congress lacked clear-cut jurisdiction over the trans-Appalachian region, and for several years conflicts of authority persisted among Congress, the states, and the frontier settlements themselves. Of course, with Virginia's cession in 1781, the landed states had begun to yield their Western claims to the Confederation. But Virginia had ceded her territory to the north of the Ohio River on the condition that private grants within it be canceled, and for a few years the grantees lobbied successfully to keep Congress from accepting the territory with that stipulation. North Carolina temporarily took back its ceded land, other states postponed their cessions, and not till 1802 did the last of them, Georgia, give up its claim. Meanwhile these states transferred the actual ownership of most of the land south of the Ohio River to private individuals and companies, and impatient settlers proceeded to set up their own state governments for Frankland or Franklin (Tennessee) and for Kentucky. North Carolina attempted to incorporate Tennessee, and Virginia tried to make Kentucky a Virginia county.

## Planning for the Territories

In 1784, having persuaded Virginia to make a new cession without specific restrictions, Congress accepted Virginia's Western lands (not including Kentucky), and began to make policy for the national domain. The most momentous decision, already resolved upon, was that settlements in the territory should not be held in permanent subjection as colonies but should be transformed ultimately into states equal with the original thirteen. In the Ordinance of 1784 Congress temporarily adopted Thomas Jefferson's very democratic plan for the transition to statehood of the territory between the Ohio River and the Great Lakes. This territory was to have been divided into ten districts, each to be self-governing from the start, to be represented by a delegate in Congress as soon as its population reached 20,000, and to be admitted as a state when its population equaled the number of free inhabitants of the smallest existing state.

Having thus prepared a scheme of territorial government, Congress in the Ordinance of 1785 provided a system of land survey and sale. The land to the north of the Ohio was to be surveyed and marked off in a rectangular pattern before any of it was sold. This program derived from the practice of New England towns rather than from that of the South, where the settler located a choice plot and afterward determined its boundaries, usually following topographical irregularities. The land ordinance of Congress provided for east-west base lines, north-south "ranges," and townships with sides paralleling the ranges and base lines. Each township was to contain thirty-six square-mile sections. In every township four sections were to be set aside for the United States and one for a public school. The rest of the sections were to be sold at auction for not less than $1 an acre. Since there were 640 acres in a section, the prospective

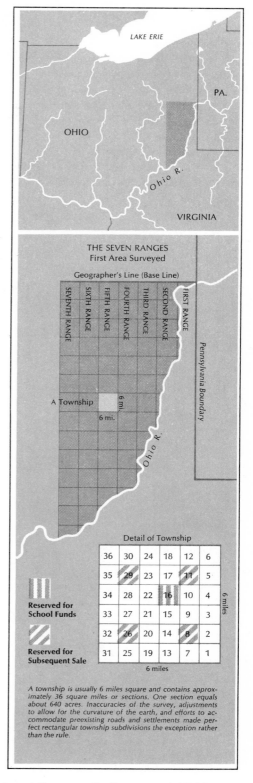

Land Survey: Ordinance of 1785

buyer of government land had to have at least $640 in ready cash or in United States certificates of indebtedness.

These terms favored the large speculators too much and the ordinary frontiersman too little to suit Jefferson, who believed that the West ought to belong to actual settlers on the ground. But the large speculators desired still further advantages, and Congress, in a hurry to realize returns from its domain, soon gave in to lobbying groups composed of some of its own members and various former army officers. To the Ohio and Scioto companies and the associates of John Cleves Symmes, Congress disposed of several million acres at only a few cents an acre. Millions of acres besides had been reserved at the time of cession by Virginia and Connecticut as bounty lands for their Revolutionary soldiers. Thus, before the government surveys had been well started, most of the choicest land north of the Ohio River was already spoken for (as was all the land south of the Ohio, to which the ordinances of Congress did not apply).

To protect their interests in the Northwest, the directors of the Ohio and Scioto companies demanded a territorial government that would give less influence to the inhabitants than would the one outlined in Jefferson's Ordinance of 1784, and the companies' skillful lobbyist Manasseh Cutler carried their case to Congress. Some of the congressmen themselves disliked Jefferson's idea of creating as many as ten new states north of the Ohio, since these states in time might gain political ascendancy. Soon Congress replaced the original law—which had never gone into actual effect—with the Ordinance of 1787. This famous "Northwest Ordinance" established one Northwest Territory for the time being, provided for its subsequent division into several territories, not fewer than three nor more than five, and laid out three stages for the evolution of each territory into a state. In the first stage, Congress-appointed officials would govern the territory, in the second an elected legislature would share power with them, and in the third, when the people numbered 60,000 or more, they might frame a constitution and apply for statehood. The Northwest Ordinance, embodying as it did the views of conservative Easterners, failed to satisfy the restless inhabitants of the Ohio country.

The Indian policy of Congress fell short of the requirements of land speculators as well as of frontier settlers. In 1785 and 1786 congressional commissioners made treaties with representatives of the Iroquois and other tribes, who thereby surrendered their claims to a stretch of land north of the Ohio in return for comparatively worthless trinkets. Repudiating the treaties, many of the tribesmen went on the warpath. Congress vainly instructed Colonel Josiah Harmar, commanding the federal troops in the Ohio country, to drive the Indians back, then in des-

## The Northwest Ordinance [1787]

1. Congress shall appoint a governor, a secretary, and three judges for the Northwest Territory. These officials shall adopt suitable laws from the original states. When the territory has "five thousand free male inhabitants of full age," they shall be allowed to elect representatives. These, together with the governor and a legislative council of five, shall form a general assembly to make laws for the territory.

2. The inhabitants shall be entitled to the benefits of trial by jury and other judicial proceedings according to the common law.

3. "Religion, morality, and knowledge being necessary to good government and the happiness of mankind, schools and the means of education shall forever be encouraged."

4. "There shall be formed in the said territory not less than three nor more than five States. . . . And, whenever any of the said States shall have sixty thousand free inhabitants therein, such State shall be admitted, by its delegates, into the Congress of the United States, on an equal footing with the original States."

5. "There shall be neither slavery nor involuntary servitude in the said territory, otherwise than in the punishment of crimes whereof the party shall have been duly convicted."

peration called upon the aging hero George Rogers Clark to save the frontier. While the campaign against the Indians in the Northwest faltered, a new threat arose in the Southwest, where the Creeks under the half-breed Alexander McGillivray not only repudiated their treaties ceding land but also formed an alliance with the Spaniards to resist the advance of American frontiersmen.

Some of the frontier leaders in the Southwest, instead of fighting the Spaniards, turned to collaborating with them. These leaders and their followers thought for a time that they saw advantages for themselves in the possible creation of a Southwestern confederacy under Spanish tutelage. They might thus get what the United States seemed unable to give them—protection from the Indians, cheap or free land, and an outlet to Eastern and foreign markets through the navigation of the Mississippi. After the collapse of the Jay-Gardoqui negotiations, the "Spanish Conspiracy" began to hum, attracting not only unscrupulous adventurers like General James Wilkinson but also such prominent politicians as William Blount of Kentucky and John Sevier of Tennessee. At the same time another underground separatist movement was afoot on the far northern frontier. The aspirations of Vermont for statehood having been frustrated by the rival claims of New York and New Hampshire to its soil, the Allen brothers intrigued with British agents for returning the Green Mountain country to the British Empire.

## Debts, Taxes, and Daniel Shays

At the end of the war foreign ships crowded into American seaports with cargoes of all kinds, and the American people bought extravagantly with cash or credit. In consequence the wartime accumulations of specie were drained out of the country, consumer indebtedness to importing merchants was multiplied, and a postwar depression lasting from 1784 to 1787 was made worse than it might otherwise have been. The depression, with its money scarcity, bore heavily upon debtors both public and private, complicating the financial problems of many citizens and of the Confederation and state governments.

The Confederation government had canceled most of its war debt to Americans by repudiating hundreds of millions of dollars in Continental currency. Yet it still owed a domestic debt estimated at about $34 million in 1783; and through continued borrowings from abroad, mostly from the Netherlands, its foreign debt increased to more than $10 million by 1788. During the 1780s the government had to make do with uncertain and fluctuating revenues. It could only make requisitions on the states; it never got around to assessing the real property in the states but merely estimated the proper quota for each of them to contribute. Often the states complained of unfairness and refused to comply; as a whole, they paid an average of only about one-sixth of the total that was requested. This was barely enough to meet the government's ordinary operating expenses. To pay the interest on the foreign debt, the Secretary of the Treasury, Robert Morris, used the proceeds from the new loans. Thus he maintained an excellent credit rating with Dutch and other foreign bankers. But he could not keep up with the domestic obligations, and the government lost credit at home. At a fraction of the face value, shrewd speculators bought up Confederation certificates of indebtedness from former Revolutionary soldiers and others who lost hope of payment from Congress and who needed ready cash.

The states, too, came out of the war with large debts, and one by one they added to their obligations by taking over parts of the Confederation debt owed to their respective citizens. Taxable resources varied a good deal from state to state. The chief reliance everywhere was upon the direct tax on land and its improvements, the income tax then being exceptional, though Maryland had one. The states supplemented their revenues by means of customs duties and harbor fees, though these tariff and navigation laws served also to protect the states' manufacturers and shippers from foreign competition. To some extent the tariffs interfered with trade between states, but with a few exceptions they were designed to limit importations of foreign and not American goods.

Suffering seriously from the postwar deflation and from the tax burden upon their land, the debtor farmers of the country demanded relief in the form of paper money, and seven of the states responded by issuing such currency. Of these seven, Rhode Island went to the greatest extremes, not only designating its paper as legal tender but compelling creditors to accept it or lose the right to collect their debts. While creditors fled from debtors eager to pay in Rhode Island currency, the highest court in the state, in the case of *Trevett* v. *Weeden* (1786), held that the monetary legislation was unconstitutional, and the legislature summoned the judges before it and censured them for their action.

The other six states refused to yield to the advocates of inflation and pursued policies of unrelieved taxation to support their public debts. To the state creditors—that is, the bondholders—all this was sound and honest public finance. But it seemed like robbery and tyranny to many of the poverty-stricken farmers, especially in New England, who felt that money was being extorted from them to swell the riches of the wealthy bondholders in Boston and other towns. At a time when cash was not to be had, these farmers were called upon to pay in specie not only state tax collectors but also mortgage holders and other private creditors. When debtors failed to pay they found their mortgages foreclosed and their property seized, and sometimes they found themselves in jail.

Mobs of distressed farmers rioted in various parts of New England but caused the most serious trouble in Massachusetts. There the malcontents of the Connecticut Valley and the Berkshire Hills, many of them Revolutionary veterans, found a leader in Daniel Shays, himself a former captain in the Continental army. Organizing and drilling his followers, Shays put forth a program of demands including paper money, tax relief, a moratorium on debts, the removal of the state capital from Boston to the interior, and the abolition of imprisonment for debt. During the summer of 1786 the Shaysites concentrated upon the immediate task of preventing the collection of debts, private or public, and went in armed bands from place to place to break up court sittings and sheriff's sales. In Boston, members of the legislature, including Samuel Adams, denounced Shays and his men as rebels and traitors. When winter came these rebels, instead of laying down their arms, advanced upon Springfield to get more of them from the arsenal there. From Boston approached an army of state militiamen financed by a loan from wealthy merchants who feared a new revolution. In January 1787, this army met the ragged troops of Shays, killed several of them, captured many more, and scattered the rest to the hills in a blinding snowstorm.

As a military enterprise, Shays' Rebellion was a fiasco, yet it had important consequences for the future of the United States. In Massachusetts it resulted in a few immediate gains for the discontented groups. Shays and his lieutenants, at first sentenced to death, were soon pardoned, and some concessions to Shays' earlier demands were granted in the way of tax relief and the postponement of debt payments. Far more significant, the rebellion also affected the country as a whole by giving added urgency to the movement for a new Constitution.

# Selected Readings

**The Revolution in General** J. R. Alden, *The American Revolution, 1775–1783°* (1954); J. C. Miller, *Triumph of Freedom, 1775–1783°* (1949); J. F. Jameson, *The American Revolution Considered as a Social Movement* (1926).

**Independence and Loyalism** C. L. Becker, *The Declaration of Independence°* (1922); R. G. Adams, *The Political Ideas of the American Revolution* (1922); P. H. Smith, *Loyalists and Redcoats: A Study in British Revolutionary Pol-*

*icy* (1964); W. H. Nelson, *The American Tory°* (1961); C. H. Van Tyne, *The Loyalists in the American Revolution* (1905).

**Campaigns and Battles** Christopher Ward, *The War of the Revolution* (2 vols., 1952); W. M. Wallace, *Appeal to Arms°* (1951); Lynn Montross, *Rag, Tag, and Bobtail* (1952); H. H. Peckham, *The War for Independence: A Military History* (1958); G. F. Scheer and H. F. Rankin, *Rebels and Redcoats°* (1957); Bernard Knollenberg, *Washington and the Revolution* (1940); Carl Berger, *Broadsides and Bayonets: The Propaganda War of the American Revolution* (1961).

**The Naval War** G. W. Allen, *Naval History of the American Revolution* (2 vols., 1913); S. E. Morison, *John Paul Jones: A Sailor's Biography°* (1959); W. B. Clark, *Ben Franklin's Privateers* (1956).

**Diplomacy** S. F. Bemis, *The Diplomacy of the American Revolution°* (1935); R. B. Morris, *The Peacemakers: The Great Powers and American Independence* (1965); A. O. Aldridge, *Franklin and His French Contemporaries* (1957); Gerald Stourzh, *Benjamin Franklin and American Foreign Policy* (1954).

**War Finance** C. L. Ver Steeg, *Robert Morris, Revolutionary Financier* (1954); E. J. Ferguson, *The Power of the Purse: A History of American Public Finance, 1776–1790* (1961).

**The Continental Congress** Lynn Montross, *The Reluctant Rebels: The Story of the Continental Congress, 1774–1789* (1950); E. C. Burnett, *The Continental Congress°* (1941).

**The "Critical Period"** Merrill Jensen, *The Articles of Confederation°* (1948) and *The New Nation: A History of the United States During the Confederation, 1781–1789°* (1950); E. P. Douglass, *Rebels and Democrats: The Struggle for Equal Political Rights and Majority Rule During the American Revolution°* (1955); R. P. McCormick, *Experiment in Independence: New Jersey in the Critical Period, 1781–1789* (1950); Irving Brant, *James Madison: The Nationalist, 1780–1787* (1948); M. L. Starkey, *A Little Rebellion* (1955), on the Shays uprising.

**From Independence to the Constitution** G. S. Wood, *The Creation of the American Republic, 1776–1787* (1969); B. F. Wright, *Consensus and Continuity, 1776–1787* (1958); E. S. Morgan, *The Birth of the Republic, 1763–89°* (1956).

°Titles available in paperback.

# Chapter 6
# Beginnings Under the Constitution

William E. Gladstone, a nineteenth-century British statesman, once described the Constitution of the United States as the "most wonderful work ever struck off at a given time by the brain and purpose of man." Of course, the Constitution was not the result of a sudden stroke of genius. It was the product of years of experience with colonial and state governments and with the Articles of Confederation. It took form in the heat of political controversy and was adopted in the face of bitter opposition. Yet, though far from flawless, it was indeed a wonderful work. Certainly it created, as it was intended to do, a "more perfect union" than existed at the time it was written. More than that, it provided a fundamental law capable of growth and adaptation to meet the needs of the nation for centuries to come.

From the beginning the Constitution took on some of the characteristics of a sacred writing, a holy mystery of the Americans. Among its virtues was its brevity (only about 7,000 words), but the defect of that virtue was a considerable ambiguity, which left room at certain points for a variety of interpretations. Political differences, no matter what the interests that underlay them, came to be expressed in constitutional terms. In discussing a governmental policy, men asked not only whether it was to their particular advantage, or whether it contributed to the public good, but also whether it was in accord with the Constitution. Those who had opposed the adoption of the Constitution joined the discussion instead of advocating repeal. All were willing to obey the fundamental law, but not all agreed on just what it permitted them to do.

Two basic lines of interpretation quickly appeared. According to one of them, the words of the document were to be liberally construed, so as to give the new government "implied powers" beyond those literally specified. According to the other line of interpretation, the words were to be strictly followed, so as to leave to the states all powers not plainly delegated to the new government. Alexander Hamilton was the first great exponent of liberal or loose construction, and Thomas Jefferson of strict construction and state rights.

It has been said that the shadows of Hamilton and Jefferson fall across the whole of subsequent American history, that to this day all Americans are either Hamiltonians or Jeffersonians. That is an oversimplification. Hamilton and Jefferson and their respective followers disagreed on other things besides the reading of the Constitution, and even on that subject their views changed before long. It would be nearer the truth to say that, over the years, the men of whichever party who have happened to be in control of the federal government have wished to use its powers to achieve their aims and hence have favored a liberal construction. To oppose those aims the men out of power have resorted to the doctrine of state rights.

**The Constitutional Convention**
*Detail.* A nineteenth-century depiction of George Washington presiding at the constitutional convention, by Junius Brutus Stearns. (The Granger Collection)

## TOWARD A NEW GOVERNMENT

During the 1780s the Confederation Congress steadily lost prestige while leading a rather waif-like existence. Its members timidly withdrew from Philadelphia in 1783 to escape the clamor of army veterans demanding back pay. After taking refuge for a while in Princeton, the delegates moved on to Annapolis and then to New York (1785), which for the time being remained the capital. With some difficulty a quorum had been rounded up to ratify the treaty ending the Revolutionary War. Only eighteen members, representing eight of the states, were on hand to pass the Northwest Ordinance.

### Advocates of Centralization

Weak though the Confederation government was, it satisfied a great many—probably a majority—of the people. They did not want a strong central government. Having just fought the Revolutionary War to avert the danger of remote and, to them, tyrannical authority, they desired to keep the centers of political power close to home in the thirteen states.

Others, however, either disliked the Articles of Confederation from the outset or came eventually to desire something different. Disgruntled at the refusal of Congress to grant them half pay for life, some of the military men through their exclusive and hereditary Society of the Cincinnati hoped to control and to invigorate the government, some of them even aspiring to a kind of army dictatorship. Artisans or "mechanics," the manufacturers of the time, preferred a uniformly high national tariff to the varying state tariffs. Merchants and shippers preferred a single and effective commercial policy to thirteen different and ineffective ones. Land speculators wished to see the "Indian menace" finally removed from their Western tracts, and creditors desired to stop the state issues of paper money. Investors in Confederation securities hoped to have the Confederation debt made good and the value of their securities enhanced. Large property owners in general looked for a reliable means of safety from the threat of mobs.

The issue was not whether the Confederation should be changed but how drastic the changes should be. Even its defenders reluctantly came to agree that the government needed strengthening at its weakest point—its lack of power to tax. To save the Articles of Confederation, its friends backed the impost amendment of 1782, which would have authorized Congress to levy customs duties. All the states ratified the amendment except Rhode Island, whose single veto was enough to kill it. The next year a similar amendment was accepted by Rhode Island but defeated by New York. Later the state-rights advocates proposed that the states make to Congress a temporary and qualified grant of taxing authority (not an amendment to the Articles), but most of the centralizers had begun to lose interest in such remedies. They insisted upon a much more thoroughgoing change.

The most resourceful of the reformers was the political genius, New York lawyer, one-time military aide to General Washington, and illegitimate son of a Scottish merchant in the West Indies—Alexander Hamilton. From the beginning he had been dissatisfied with the Articles of Confederation, had seen little to be gained by piecemeal amendments, and had urged the holding of a national convention to overhaul the entire document. To achieve his aim he took advantage of a movement for interstate cooperation which began in 1785 when a group of Marylanders and Virginians met in Alexandria to settle differences between their two states.

One of the Virginians, James Madison, who was as eager as Hamilton to see a stronger government, induced the Virginia legislature to invite all the states to send delegates to a larger conference on commercial questions. This group met at Annapolis in 1786, but representatives from only five states appeared at the meeting. Hamilton, a delegate from New York, took satisfaction in seeing the conference adopt his report and send copies to the state legislatures and to Congress. His report recommended that Congress call a convention of special delegates from all the states to gather in Philadelphia the next year and consider ways to "render the constitution of the Federal government adequate to the exigencies of the union."

At the moment, in 1786, there seemed little possibility that the Philadelphia convention would be any better attended or would accom-

# Where Historians Disagree

## Background of the Constitution

The 1780's once seemed to historians like a "critical period," one of impending collapse and chaos from which the newly independent republic was rescued only by the timely adoption of the Constitution. This was the theme of a widely read book that John Fiske, a popularizer of both science and history, wrote a century afterward (1888). Fiske and other writers emphasized the difficulties and failures of the 1780's—the business depression, the weaknesses of the central government under the Articles of Confederation, the threats to American territory from Great Britain and Spain, the debts of the Confederation and of the states, the interstate jealousies and barriers to trade, the widespread resort to paper-money inflation, and the disorders and lawlessness culminating in Shays' Rebellion. All this, according to Fiske and those who followed him, represented the darkness before the dawn. The dawn supposedly came with the establishment of the new government under the Constitution, when conditions suddenly began to improve.

One of the greatest of American historians, Charles A. Beard, challenged the prevailing view in an arresting and controversial work, *An Economic Interpretation of the Constitution of the United States* (1913). Beard maintained that the 1780's had been a "critical period" only for certain business interests, not for the people as a whole. According to him, these interests desired a central government strong enough to promote industry and trade, safeguard private property, and make good the public debt. Many of the delegates to the constitutional convention, he said, stood to gain directly as well as indirectly from their efforts, for they had bought up the Confederation's "certificates of indebtedness" cheaply, and these would rise in value if a strong central government were set up. He added that the advocates of the Constitution succeeded in obtaining its ratification despite the indifference or opposition of a majority of the people. In a later book (1927) Beard suggested that the Articles of Confederation might still be serving quite satisfactorily as our twentieth-century frame of government if a comparatively small group of impatient and determined men had not managed to bring about a drastic change in 1787–1788.

Most historians promptly adopted Beard's conclusions, and some proceeded to elaborate upon his work. Merrill Jensen, for one, in *The Articles of Confederation* (1940) and *The New Nation* (1950), produced additional evidence to show that the 1780's were a time of hopeful striving rather than black despair, of economic recovery and not persisting depression, of governmental progress under the Articles despite temporary failures. Other historians disagreed with Beard, however, and in recent years the dissenters, notably Robert E. Brown and Forrest McDonald, have criticized his methods and findings with increasing effectiveness. Today, few if any historians accept the Beard thesis without qualification.

plish any more than the previous meeting at Annapolis. The leadership of Washington would be essential for success. One of the wealthiest men in the country, but temporarily short of cash, Washington doubted whether he would undertake the trouble and expense of a trip to Philadelphia.

Then, early in 1787, the news of commotion and bloodshed in Massachusetts spread throughout the country and the world, news which seemed to foretell other and more dangerous insurrections than that of Shays. In Paris the American minister, Thomas Jefferson, was not alarmed. "I hold," he confided in a letter to his Virginia friend James Madison, "that a little rebellion, now and then, is a good thing, and as necessary in the political world as storms in the physical." At Mount Vernon, however, Washington did not take the news so calmly. "There are combustibles in every State which a spark might set fire to," he exclaimed. "I feel infinitely more than I can express for the disorders which have arisen. Good God!" Washington refused to listen to renewed suggestions that he make himself a military dictator, but after Congress had issued its call for a constitutional convention he borrowed money for the journey and, in May, left Mount Vernon for Philadelphia.

## A Divided Convention

Fifty-five men, representing all the states except Rhode Island, attended one or more sessions of the convention that sat in the Philadelphia State House from May to September, 1787. Never before or since has there been a more distinguished gathering in America. These "Founding Fathers," instead of being graybearded ancients as the term implies, were on the whole relatively young men, many of them in their twenties and thirties and only one (Benjamin Franklin) extremely old; his eighty-one years raised the average age from forty-three to forty-four. Despite their comparative youth, the delegates were men of vast practical experience in business, plantation management, and politics; and they were well educated for their time, more than a third of them being college graduates. Practically all of them represented, both directly and indirectly, the great property interests of the

### The Virginia Plan [1787]

The following branches of government were recommended in the Virginia Plan:

1. A "National Legislature," with the states represented in proportion either to their "quotas of contribution" or to "the number of free inhabitants." Two branches, the members of the first to be elected by the people, the members of the second to be nominated by the state legislatures and elected by the first. Powers: To "legislate in all cases to which the separate states are incompetent," to "negative all laws passed by the several states, contravening in the opinion of the National Legislature the articles of Union," and to use force against recalcitrant states.

2. A single "National Executive" to be chosen by the National Legislature.

3. A "National Judiciary" to be chosen by the National Legislature.

4. A "Council of Revision," consisting of the National Executive and part of the National Judiciary, with power to "examine" and reject state and national laws before they went into effect.

country. Many feared what one of them called the "turbulence and follies" of democracy.

Most of the constitution-makers agreed that the United States needed a stronger central government. There were differences of opinion, however, as to how much stronger the government should be, what specific powers it should have, and what structure it should be given. There were differences, in particular, over the relative influence the large and small states should exert in the new system, and over the provisions to be included for the protection and promotion of economic interests in different sections of the country.

Among the states, Virginia was then much the largest in population—more than twice as large as New York, more than four times as large as New Jersey, more than ten times as large as

Delaware. Among the delegations at Philadelphia, the Virginians were also the best prepared for the work of the convention. And among the Virginians, James Madison (aged thirty-six) was the intellectual leader. Already, before the convention met, he had done his homework well, having devised in some detail a plan for a new "national" government. The Virginians took the initiative from the moment the convention began.

Washington was easily elected to preside, and then a resolution was passed to keep the proceedings absolutely secret. Next, Edmund Randolph of Virginia proposed that "a *national* government ought to be established, consisting of a *supreme* Legislative, Executive, and Judiciary." This being approved, Randolph introduced the plan that Madison already had worked out. The Virginia Plan, if adopted, would give the larger influence to the richer and more populous states. It would also mean abandoning the Articles of Confederation and building the government anew.

But the existing Congress had called the convention "for the sole and express purpose of revising the Articles of Confederation," and the states in commissioning their "deputies" had authorized them to do no more than revise the Articles. Some of the delegates—especially those from the smaller states—now raised doubts whether the convention properly could entertain such proposals as were embodied in the Virginia Plan. At first, however, these men had nothing to offer in its stead. After some delay, William Paterson of New Jersey submitted an alternative scheme for a "federal" as opposed to a "national" government. The New Jersey Plan was intended only to revise and strengthen the Articles.

The stage was now set for a full debate between large-state and small-state delegates—between advocates of a national system (nationalists) and of a federal system (federalists). The Virginia Plan went much too far to suit the federalists. To them, one of its worst features was the system of representation in the proposed two-house legislature. In the lower house, if the states were to be represented in proportion to their population, the largest state (Virginia) would have about ten times as many representa-

## The New Jersey Plan [1787]

The main features of the New Jersey Plan were:
1. The continuance of the existing one-house Congress, with one vote for each state, but with the following additional powers: to raise a revenue from import duties, stamp taxes, and postage; to regulate interstate and foreign commerce; and to provide for the collection of taxes within any state failing to pay its share of the requisitions upon the states.
2. A plural "Federal Executive" to be elected by Congress.
3. A "Federal Judiciary" to be appointed by the Executive.
4. The establishment of acts of Congress and federal treaties as the "supreme law" of the states, and the authorization of the Federal Executive to "call forth the power of the Confederated States . . . to enforce and compel an obedience."

tives as the smallest (Delaware). In the upper house, if its members were to be elected by the lower house, some of the smaller states at any given time might have no members at all! To the small-state delegates the Congress of the Articles of Confederation, as well as the Congress of the New Jersey Plan, at least had the merit of equal representation for all the states, regardless of size. But the New Jersey Plan gained the support of only a minority in the convention and, after much argument, was tabled.

The Virginia Plan was left as the basis for discussion. Its proponents realized that they would have to make concessions to the small-state men if the convention were ever to reach a general agreement. The majority soon conceded an important point by consenting that the members of the upper house should be elected by the state legislatures rather than by the lower house of the national legislature. Thus each state would be sure of always having at least one member in the upper house, but there remained the question of how many members each state should have.

There remained also the question of the number of representatives each state should have in the lower house. If the number was to depend upon population, were slaves to be included in the population figure? The delegates from the states where slavery seemed a permanent institution—especially those from South Carolina—insisted that slaves should be counted as persons (though not, of course, entitled to vote) in determining a state's representation. But these delegates argued that slaves ought to be considered as property, not as persons, when it was proposed that the new legislature be allowed to levy a direct tax (such as a land or poll tax) upon each state in proportion to its population. Men who came from states where slavery had disappeared or was expected to disappear argued that slaves should be included in calculating taxation but not representation. Thus an issue between slave and free states was added to the one between large and small states.

## Differences Compromised

On these and other matters, the delegates bickered day after day. By the end of June, as both temperature and tempers rose to uncomfortable heights, the convention seemed in danger of breaking up, with nothing accomplished. If this should happen, the men at Philadelphia would "become a reproach and by-word down to future ages," said the venerable Franklin, the voice of calmness and conciliation throughout the summer. "And what is worse, mankind may hereafter, from this unfortunate instance, despair of establishing governments by human wisdom, and leave it to chance, war and conquest."

Through the calming influence of Franklin and others, especially Oliver Ellsworth of Connecticut, the delegates managed to settle the most serious of their disputes and go on with their work. A committee of twelve, with one member from each state, brought in a report that culminated in what afterwards was known as the "Great Compromise" (adopted on July 16, 1787). One part of this report provided that the states should be represented in the lower house in proportion to their population, and that three-fifths of the slaves should be included in determining the basis for both representation and direct taxation. The three-fifths formula, though seemingly rather arbitrary, gained some degree of logic from the assumption that, in contributing his labor to the wealth of a state, a slave was on the average three-fifths as productive as a freeman. Another part of the Great Compromise provided that in the upper house, the states should be represented equally with two members apiece.

In the ensuing weeks, while committees busied themselves with various parts of the document that was beginning to take shape, the convention as a whole effected another compromise, this one having to do with the legislative power to impose tariffs and regulate commerce. The men from some of the Southern states feared that this power might be used for levying export duties on their crops, interfering with the slave trade, and making commercial agreements (as in the recent Jay-Gardoqui treaty) which would sacrifice the interests of rice and tobacco growers. The South Carolinians proposed that a two-thirds vote in the legislature be required not only to approve commercial treaties but also to pass commercial laws. Though not accepting that proposal, the convention made concessions by forbidding the legislature to levy a tax on exports, to put a duty of more than ten dollars a head on imported slaves, or to prohibit slave importations until twenty years had elapsed.

Some differences of opinion the convention was unable to harmonize, and it disposed of them by evasion or omission. One of these concerned the question whether the new courts or some special agency should be empowered to review legislative acts and set them aside. The "council of revision," a part of the original Virginia Plan, was dropped, and no provision was added to confer the power of judicial review explicitly upon the courts.

The Constitution, as it finally took form at the end of summer in 1787, though an outgrowth of the Virginia Plan, was in some respects so different that Randolph himself refused to sign it. Yet it differed even more from the New Jersey Plan, and several refused on that account to give it their approval. Indeed, the completed document did not entirely satisfy any of the delegates. Nevertheless, thirty-nine of them affixed their signatures to it, doubtless with much the same feeling that Franklin expressed. "Thus I consent, Sir, to this Constitution," he said, *"because I expect no better, and because I am not sure that it is not the best."*

## The Constitution of 1787

Madison, who was responsible for most of the actual drafting, observed that it was, "in strictness, neither a national nor a federal Constitution, but a composition of both."

Certainly it possessed some strongly national features. The Constitution and all laws and treaties made under it were to be the "supreme law" of the land, regardless of anything to the contrary in the constitution or laws of any state. Broad powers were granted to the central government, including the congressional powers of taxation, regulation of commerce, control of money, and the passage of laws "necessary and proper" for carrying out its specific powers. At the same time, the individual states were deprived of a number of the powers—such as the issuance of money and the passage of laws "impairing the obligation of contracts," for example, laws postponing the payment of debts—which the states had been free to exercise under the Articles of Confederation. Now all state officials were to be required to take an oath of allegiance to the Constitution, and the state militias were to be made available, upon call, for enforcing the new "supreme law." Nowhere were the former claims of the states to individual sovereignty recognized. Gone was the stipulation of the Articles that "each State shall retain every power, jurisdiction, and right not *expressly* delegated to the United States in Congress assembled." Lacking was any bill of rights to limit the central government as the state bills limited the state governments.

On the other hand, the Constitution was federal in setting up a government that presupposed the existence of separate states and left wide powers to them. For instance, the states were to be represented as separate and equal entities in one of the two branches of the new legislature.

Within the allotted sphere of its powers, the new government was authorized to act directly upon the people of the United States. It would not have to act upon them solely through the member states, as the previous Confederation government, and indeed all confederation governments of the past, had done. Here, then, was something new and unique, something for which old terms were hardly adequate. It was a combination of two kinds of government, state and central, with each of them intended to be supreme within its respective sphere.

Next to the distinctive federal arrangement (the "division of powers"), the most striking feature of the new system was the complex organization and operation of the central government itself, with its checks and balances among the legislative, executive, and judicial branches (the "separation of powers"). There was the new Congress, with its two chambers, the Senate and the House of Representatives, each of the two with members elected in a different way and for different terms, and each checking the other, since both must agree before any law could be passed. There was the single executive, the President, who was to be chosen in a roundabout way, by special electors who themselves were to be chosen in whatever way the separate states might designate. The electors, meeting in isolated groups, state by state, were to cast their ballots as they saw fit, and if any man should receive a majority of the electoral votes, he would be President. It was assumed, however, that usually no man would get a majority, and then the final selection among the leading candidates would be up to the House of Representatives. Thus the election of a President would be far removed from the mass of the people. Yet the President, in addition to other powers, would have the power of vetoing acts of Congress. There was also the Supreme Court, which was still further removed from the ordinary voters since the President with the consent of the Senate was to appoint the judges for life. And while nothing was said in the Constitution itself about the power of reviewing and disallowing presidential actions or congressional acts, the Supreme Court could be expected to have some authority over them.

This complicated structure resulted from accident—that is, from the compromising of contradictory views—as much as from deliberate planning. Nevertheless, the complexity was such as to give the Founding Fathers hope that no single group or combination of groups in the country could ever gain absolute and unchecked power. A government so divided against itself ought to frustrate tyranny from whatever source. When the Founding Fathers spoke of tyranny, they usually had in mind the rule of mobs and demagogues—the threat of such leaders as Daniel Shays.

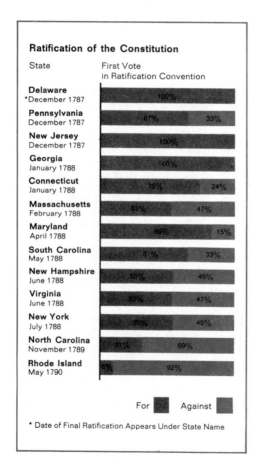

**Ratification of the Constitution**

| State | First Vote in Ratification Convention |
|---|---|
| **Delaware** *December 1787 | 100% |
| **Pennsylvania** December 1787 | 67% / 33% |
| **New Jersey** December 1787 | 100% |
| **Georgia** January 1788 | 100% |
| **Connecticut** January 1788 | 76% / 24% |
| **Massachusetts** February 1788 | 53% / 47% |
| **Maryland** April 1788 | 85% / 15% |
| **South Carolina** May 1788 | 67% / 33% |
| **New Hampshire** June 1788 | 55% / 45% |
| **Virginia** June 1788 | 53% / 47% |
| **New York** July 1788 | 55% / 45% |
| **North Carolina** November 1789 | 31% / 69% |
| **Rhode Island** May 1790 | 8% / 92% |

For ■   Against ■

\* Date of Final Ratification Appears Under State Name

The Constitution was promptly and overwhelmingly approved by the ratifying conventions of some of the smaller states, such as Delaware, New Jersey, and Georgia. But it barely got by in the large states of Massachusetts, Virginia, and New York. It was approved by North Carolina and Rhode Island only after it had already gone into effect. The conventions in these two states waited until they were sure a bill of rights would be added.

## ADOPTION AND ADAPTATION

Since the delegates at Philadelphia had exceeded their instructions from Congress and the states, they had reason to doubt whether the Constitution would ever be ratified if they followed the procedures laid down in the Articles of Confederation, which required *all* of the state *legislatures* to approve alterations in the form of the government. So the convention changed the rules, specifying in the Constitution that the new government should go into effect among the ratifying states when only *nine* of the thirteen had ratified, and recommending to Congress that the Constitution be submitted to specially called state *conventions* rather than to the legislatures of the states.

### "Federalists," "Antifederalists"

The Congress in New York, completely overshadowed by the convention in Philadelphia, accepted the latter's work and submitted it to the states for their approval or disapproval. The state legislatures, again with the exception of Rhode Island, arranged for the election of delegates to ratifying conventions, and sooner or later each of these conventions got down to business. Meanwhile, from the fall of 1787 to the summer of 1788, the merits and demerits of the new Constitution were debated in the legislatures, in mass meetings, and in the columns of newspapers, as well as in the convention halls. For the most part the struggle, though intense, was peaceful and deliberative, yet the opposing factions sometimes came to blows, and death and injury resulted in at least one place (Albany, New York).

Despite the reference of its preamble to "We the people," the Constitution was not in literal fact ordained and established by the whole people of the United States. As is shown by the elections for the state conventions, something like three-fourths of the adult white males in the country as a whole failed to vote for delegates, mainly because of indifference, and therefore exercised no real influence upon the outcome. Of those who did vote, a large majority favored ratification. The voters, however, did not have a clear-cut choice between a "federal" and a "national" government. The issues were con-

REDEUNT SATURNIA REGNA.

*On the erection of the Eleventh PILLAR of the great Na-*

*tional DOME, we beg leave most sincerely to felicitate* " OUR DEAR COUNTRY."

Rise it will.

The foundation good—it may yet be SAVED.

The FEDERAL EDIFICE.

ELEVEN STARS, in quick fucceffion rife—
ELEVEN COLUMNS ftrike our wond'ring eyes,
Soon o'er the *whole*, fhall fwell the beauteous DOME,
COLUMBIA's boaft—and FREEDOM's hallow'd home.
Here fhall the ARTS in glorious fplendour fhine!
And AGRICULTURE give her ftores divine!
COMMERCE refin'd, difpenfe us more than gold,
And this new world, teach WISDOM to the old—
RELIGION here fhall fix her bleft abode,
Array'd in *mildnefs*, like its parent GOD!
JUSTICE and LAW, fhall endlefs PEACE maintain,
And *the* " SATURNIAN AGE," *return again.*

## A Federalist Cartoon

The *Massachusetts Centinel* of Boston, in its issue for August 2, 1788, thus commented on New York's ratification of the new Constitution. Only two of the thirteen states have yet to ratify. A hand is shown lifting the North Carolina "pillar" into place, and the optimistic caption says, "Rise it will." The Rhode Island pillar is broken, but "The foundation [is] good—it may yet be SAVED." (Courtesy of the New-York Historical Society, New York City)

fused, both because of the "mixed" character of the Constitution itself and because of the terminology that was employed in the ratification debates. Since the idea of a strongly national government was thought to be unpopular, the advocates of the new Constitution chose to call themselves "Federalists" and to call their opponents "Antifederalists." These misnomers stuck, despite the insistence of opponents of ratification that they were "Federal Republicans," the true federalists of the time.

The friends of the Constitution had a number of advantages. They possessed a positive program and an appealing name, while the Antifederalists by that very word were made to stand for nothing constructive, for chaos itself. The Federalists were the better-organized group and had the weight of fame and superior leadership on their side. They could point to the support of the two most eminent men in America, Franklin and Washington. And Washington himself de-

clared that the choice lay between the Constitution and disunion. The Federalists also included some of the most profound political philosophers of any period or place in Hamilton, Madison, and Jay, who under the joint pseudonym "Publius" wrote a long series of newspaper essays expounding the meaning and virtues of the Constitution. Afterwards published in book form as *The Federalist*, these papers have been considered as the most authoritative of all constitutional commentaries and, indeed, as one of the greatest of all treatises on political science.

The opponents of ratification produced no comparable set of Antifederalist papers, yet these men too were able and sincere and they made a vigorous case for themselves in their own speeches and newspaper propaganda. Necessarily, the Antifederalists resorted mainly to negative argument. The Constitution, they protested, was illegal—as indeed it was if judged by the Articles of Confederation, the existing fundamental law. The new government would increase taxes, obliterate the states, wield dictatorial powers, favor the "well-born" over the common people, and put an end to individual liberty, the Antifederalists added. Of all their specific criticisms the most compelling was this: the Constitution lacked a bill of rights.

For all the efforts of the Antifederalists, ratification proceeded during the winter of 1787–1788. Delaware, the first to act, did so unanimously, as did two others of the smallest states, New Jersey and Georgia. In the large states of Pennsylvania and Massachusetts the Antifederalists put up a determined struggle but lost in the final vote. By June 1788, when the New Hampshire convention at last made up its mind, nine of the states had ratified and thus had made it possible for the Constitution to go into effect among themselves.

A new government could hardly hope to succeed, however, without the participation of Virginia and New York, whose conventions remained closely divided. Before the end of the month Virginia and then New York consented to the Constitution by rather narrow votes. The New York convention yielded to expediency—even some of the most staunchly Antifederalist delegates feared that the state's commercial interests would suffer if, once the other states had got together under the "New Roof," New York were to remain outside. Massachusetts, Virginia, and New York all ratified on the assumption, though not on the express condition, that certain desired amendments would be added to the Constitution, above all a bill of rights. Deciding to wait and see what became of these hopes for amendment, the North Carolina convention adjourned without taking action. Rhode Island, for the time being, did not even call a convention to consider ratification.

## Filling in the Gaps

When the first elections under the Constitution were held, in the early months of 1789, the results showed that the new government was to be in the hands of its friends. Few if any of the newly elected congressmen and senators had been extreme Antifederalists; almost all had favored ratification, and many had served as delegates to the Philadelphia convention. The President-elect, George Washington, had presided at the convention; many who had favored ratification did so because they expected him to preside over the new government also. He received the votes of all the presidential electors whom the states, either by legislative action or by popular election, had named. John Adams, a firm Federalist, though not a member of the convention, received the next highest number of electoral votes and hence was to be Vice President.

For the time being the seat of government was to continue to be the city of New York, and thus the sensibilities of the geographical sections were neatly balanced, the President being from the South, the Vice President from New England, and the capital in one of the middle states. Congressmen were so slow to reach New York that not until April was a quorum on hand to make an official count of the electoral vote and send a messenger to notify General Washington of his election. After a journey from Mount Vernon marked by elaborate celebrations along the way, Washington was inaugurated on April 30.

The responsibilities facing the first President and the first Congress were in some ways greater than those facing any President or Congress to follow. Though these men of 1789 had the Constitution as a guide, that document provided only a general plan that had yet to be applied to specific situations as they arose. It left many questions unanswered. What, for example, should be the rules of the two houses for the conduct of their business? What code of etiquette should govern the relations between the President on the one hand and Congress and the people on the other? Should he have some high-sounding title, such as "His Highness the President of the United States and Protector of Their Liberties"? (John Adams, who would have been horrified at the thought of a later Vice President being called "The Veep," thought both he and the President ought to have dignified forms of address.) What was the true meaning of various ambiguous phrases in the Constitution? In answering these and other questions, Washington and his colleagues knew they were setting precedents that, in many cases, would give lasting direction to the development of the Constitution in actual practice.

By filling certain gaps in the Constitution, the first Congress served almost as a continuation of the constitutional convention. The work of the convention had been incomplete in various respects, especially in that it had omitted a bill of rights. Dozens of amendments intended to make up for this lack had been proposed in the state ratifying conventions, and Congress now undertook the task of sorting these, reducing them to a manageable number, and sending them to the states for ratification. Of the twelve sent out, ten were ratified, and these took effect in 1791. The first nine of them limited Congress by forbidding it to infringe upon certain basic rights, such as freedom of religion, of speech, and of the press, immunity from arbitrary arrest, and trial by jury. The Tenth Amendment, reserving to the states all powers except those specifically withheld from them or delegated to the federal government, bolstered state rights and changed the emphasis of the Constitution from nationalism to federalism.

In regard to the structure of the federal courts, the Constitution had only this to say: "The judicial power of the United States shall be vested in one Supreme Court, and in such inferior courts as the Congress may from time to time ordain and establish." Thus the convention had left up to Congress the number of Supreme Court judges to be appointed and the kinds of lower courts to be organized. In the Judiciary Act of 1789 Congress provided for a Supreme Court of six members, with one chief justice and five associate justices; for thirteen district courts with one judge apiece; and for three circuit courts, each to consist of one of the district judges sitting with two of the Supreme Court justices. In the same act Congress gave the Supreme Court the power to make the final decision in cases involving the constitutionality of state laws. If the Constitution was in fact to be the "supreme law of the land," the various state courts could not be left to decide for themselves whether the state legislatures were violating that supreme law.

As for executive departments, the Constitution referred indirectly to them but did not specify what or how many they should be. The first Congress created three such departments— state, treasury, and war—and also the offices of attorney general and postmaster general.

In appointing department heads and other high officials, President Washington selected men who were qualified by character and experience, who were well disposed toward the Constitution (no Antifederalists) and who as a group would provide a balanced representation of the different sections of the country. To the office of secretary of the treasury he appointed Alexander Hamilton of New York, who had taken the lead in calling the constitutional convention and who, though only thirty-two, was an expert in public finance. For secretary of war he chose the Massachusetts Federalist, General Henry Knox. As attorney general he named Edmund Randolph of Virginia, sponsor of the plan upon which the Constitution had been based. He picked as secretary of state another Virginian, Thomas Jefferson, who had not opposed the Constitution though he had had nothing to do with its framing or adoption, having been away from the country as minister to France.

From time to time Washington called upon these four men for advice, usually as individuals. They did not form a cabinet in the sense of a group of presidential counselors holding regular meetings (the cabinet in this sense began to develop during the Presidency of Jefferson). When Washington took office he supposed, as did many others, that the Senate would act for certain purposes as an advisory council, since according to the Constitution the Senate was to give its advice and consent for the appointment of high officials and for the ratification of treaties. With only twenty-two members in the beginning, the Senate was small enough so that Washington could expect to consult personally with it. He changed his mind, however, after taking a treaty draft to the senators for their advice. They demanded that he leave the document for them to inspect and change at their leisure, and he refused, resolving never again to submit a treaty to the senators until its negotiation had been completed. Thus he set a precedent in treaty-making which for the most part his successors have followed.

## HAMILTON AGAINST JEFFERSON

During George Washington's first term he and his followers infused vigor into the government —the *national* government, as he always called it. As President, he thought it his duty to see that the laws of Congress, if constitutional, were faithfully carried out. A man of strong will, he was the master of his own administration, but (unlike later Presidents such as Andrew Jackson and Franklin D. Roosevelt) he did not conceive of himself as a popular leader who should find out the will of the people and then see that Congress enacted it into law. One of his department heads, Secretary of the Treasury Hamilton, provided the legislative leadership that Washington himself lacked. Hamilton exerted a greater positive influence than anyone else upon both domestic and foreign policies during Washington's Presidency, continuing to be influential even after his resignation in 1794.

### Hamilton's Financial Plans

Of all the leading men of his time, Hamilton was one of the most aristocratic in his personal tastes and in his political philosophy. He distrusted the common people. An admirer of the British political system, with its rule by King and upper classes, he wished to adapt its principles as closely as he could to government in the United States. What the country most needed, he thought, was order and stability; the people already had enough liberty, indeed too much of it. He thought the new government could be strengthened and made to succeed if the support of the wealthy men of the country could be brought to it. And, believing that all men were motivated by self-interest, he assumed that the way to gain the support of the wealthy was to give them a stake in the success of the new government. He therefore planned a program of financial legislation which, among other things, was intended to cause the propertied classes to look to the federal government for profitable investments and for the protection and promotion of their property interests.

If men of means were to have faith in the government, then it must keep faith with them by paying its debts and establishing its credit on a sound basis. Therefore, first of all, Hamilton

### Constitutionality of the Bank: Jefferson

*The incorporation of a bank, and the powers assumed by this bill, have not, in my opinion, been delegated to the United States by the Constitution.*

*I. They are not among the powers specially enumerated. . . .*

*II. Nor are they within either of the general phrases, which are the two following:—*

*1. "To lay taxes to provide for the general welfare of the United States."*
*. . . They [Congress] are not to do anything they please, to provide for the general welfare, but only to lay taxes for that purpose. . . . It was intended to lace them up straitly within the enumerated powers, and those without which, as means, these powers could not be carried into effect. . . .*

*2. The second general phrase is, "to make all laws necessary and proper for carrying into execution the enumerated powers." But they can all be carried into execution without a bank. A bank, therefore, is not necessary, and consequently not authorized by this phrase.*

*It has been much urged that a bank will give great facility or convenience in the collection of taxes. Suppose this were true; yet the Constitution allows only the means which are "necessary," not those which are merely "convenient," for effecting the enumerated powers.*

proposed that the existing public debt be "funded," or in other words that the miscellaneous, uncertain, depreciated certificates of indebtedness that the old Congress had issued during and since the Revolution be called in and exchanged for uniform, interest-bearing bonds, payable at definite dates. Next he recommended that the Revolutionary state debts be "assumed" or taken over by the United States, his object being to cause the state as well as the federal bondholders to look to the central government for eventual payment. His plan was not to pay off and thus eliminate the debt, either state or federal, but just the opposite: to create a large and permanent public debt, new bonds being issued as old ones were paid off.

Hamilton also planned the establishment of a national bank. At the time, there were only a few banks in the country, located in Boston, Philadelphia, and New York. A new, national bank would serve several purposes. It would aid business by providing loans and currency—in the form of bank notes, which in those days were used instead of checks. It would aid the government by making a safe place available for the deposit of federal funds, by facilitating the collection of taxes and the disbursement of the government's expenditures, and by keeping up the price of government bonds through judicious bond purchases. The kind of institution that Hamilton had in mind was to be "national" in the sense that it was to be chartered by the federal government, was to have a monopoly of the government's own banking business, and was to be government-controlled to some degree, one-fifth of the directors being appointed by the government.

The funding and assumption of the debts, together with the payment of regular interest on them, would cost a great deal of money, and so Hamilton had to find adequate sources of revenue. He thought the government should depend mainly upon two kinds of taxes (in addition to the receipts to be anticipated from the sales of public land). One of these was an excise to be paid by distillers of alcoholic liquors. This tax would hit most heavily the whiskey distillers of the back country, especially in Pennsylvania, Virginia, and North Carolina. These were small farmers who converted part of their corn and rye crop into whiskey, so as to have a concentrated and valuable product that they could conveniently take to market by horseback or muleback over poor mountain roads.

The other tax upon which Hamilton relied was the tariff on imports. Such a tax would not only raise a revenue, but also protect and encourage American manufactures by raising the price of competing manufactured goods brought in from abroad. In the old Articles of Confederation, according to its defenders as well as its critics, the worst defect had been Congress' lack of power to levy customs duties. One of the first acts of the new Congress, in 1789, was the pas-

## Constitutionality of the Bank: Hamilton

*It is conceded that implied powers are to be considered as delegated equally with express ones. Then it follows, that as a power of erecting a corporation may as well be implied as any other thing, it may as well be employed as an instrument or mean of carrying into execution any of the specified powers, as any other instrument or mean whatever. . . .*

*It is objected that none but necessary and proper means are to be employed; and the Secretary of State maintains that no means are to be considered as necessary but those without which the grant of the power would be nugatory. . . .*

*It is certain that neither the grammatical nor popular sense of the term requires that construction. According to both, necessary often means no more than needful, requisite, incidental, useful, or conducive to. . . .*

*If the end be clearly comprehended within any of the specified powers, and if the measure have an obvious relation to that end, and is not forbidden by any particular provision of the Constitution, it may safely be deemed to come within the compass of the national authority. . . .*

*A bank has a natural relation to the power of collecting taxes—to that of regulating trade—to that of providing for the common defence. . . . [Therefore] the incorporation of a bank is a constitutional measure. . . .*

sage of a tariff law designed to foster industries while raising a revenue, but the average level of duties under this law was extremely low. Hamilton advocated a higher and more decidedly protective tariff. In his Report on Manufactures he glowingly set forth the advantages, as he saw them, of stimulating the growth of industry in the United States. Factories, he said, would make the nation more nearly self-sufficient in wartime, would increase prosperity by creating a home market for the produce of the farms, and would make possible the fuller utilization of all kinds of labor, including the labor of women and children, even those (to quote Hamilton himself) of "tender years."

## Enacting the Program

Between 1789 and 1792 Hamilton succeeded in persuading Congress to pass the necessary laws for erecting his financial system—but only after a bitter struggle with a rising opposition group.

As for the funding of the public debt, very few of the congressmen objected to the plan itself, for they agreed with Hamilton that the government must make its credit good. Many of them disagreed, however, with his proposal to fund the debt *at par,* that is, to exchange new bonds for old certificates of indebtedness on a dollar-for-dollar basis. These old certificates had been issued to merchants and farmers in payment for war supplies during the Revolution, or to officers and soldiers of the Revolutionary army in payment for their services. Many of these original holders had been forced to sell at a sacrifice during the hard times of the 1780s, to speculators who bought up the securities at a fraction of their face value.

Admitting that the government should arrange to pay every cent it owed, to *whom* should it arrange to pay? Many congressmen believed that the original holders deserved some consideration, and James Madison, now a representative from Virginia, argued for a plan by which the new bonds would be divided between the original holders and the later purchasers. But the friends of Hamilton insisted that such a plan was impracticable and that the honor of the government required a literal fulfillment of its earlier promises to pay. Congress finally passed the funding bill in the form that Hamilton desired.

His assumption bill ran into even greater difficulty. Its opponents had a very good case, for if the federal government took over the state debts, the people of one state would have to pay federal taxes for servicing the debts of other states, and some of these debts, such as that of Massachusetts, were much larger than others,

such as that of Virginia. Naturally, Virginians did not think it fair for them to have to pay a share of the large Massachusetts debt, and their representatives in Congress balked at the assumption bill.

Finally the bill got the support of some of them and so managed to pass, but only because of a logrolling deal. The Virginians wanted the national capital to be permanently located near them in the South. After Jefferson's return from France, Hamilton appealed to him, and Jefferson held a dinner at which arrangements were made to barter Virginia votes for the assumption bill in return for Northern votes for a Southern location of the capital. In 1790 the capital was changed back to Philadelphia for a ten-year period, and after that a new capital city was to be built on the banks of the Potomac River, on land to be selected by Washington himself.

When Hamilton's bank bill was introduced into Congress, Madison and others opposed it on the grounds that it was unconstitutional, and though a majority voted for it, President Washington himself had his doubts. He therefore asked his official advisers for written opinions on the subject. In Hamilton's opinion the establishment of a bank was a fitting exercise of the powers of Congress, though the Constitution nowhere explicitly gave Congress the right. But Jefferson, with the support of his fellow Virginian, Randolph, argued that the Constitution should be construed in a strict sense and that Congress should be allowed no powers not clearly given to it. Washington found Hamilton's case more convincing, and he signed the bank bill when it came to him. The Bank of the United States began operations in 1791, under a charter that granted it the right to continue in business for twenty years.

Hamilton also had his way with the excise tax, though after its passage the law was altered somewhat, in response to protests from farmers, so as to bear less heavily on the smaller distillers. He did not succeed in getting from Congress a tariff as highly protective as he had hoped for, yet the tariff law of 1792 did raise the rates somewhat.

Once enacted, Hamilton's program worked as he had intended. The public credit quickly was restored; the bonds of the United States were soon selling at home and abroad at prices even above their par value.

At the same time, speculators got rich and corruption was rife. Many congressmen had bought up large amounts of the old certificates of indebtedness, and these men profited by their own legislation in funding the debt at par. Directly or indirectly, properly or improperly, thousands of wealthy merchants in the seaports also gained from the Hamilton program.

The mass of the people—the farmers scattered over the countryside—profited much less. While these people shared some of the benefit of national strength and prosperity, they bore most of the burden of paying for it. The financial program required taxes, and these came mostly from the farmers, who had to pay not only land taxes to their state governments but also the excise and, indirectly, the tariff to the federal government. The feeling grew that the Washington administration was not treating all the people fairly, and out of this feeling an organized political opposition arose.

## Rise of Political Parties

The Constitution made no reference to political parties, and the Founding Fathers, George Washington in particular, believed that such organizations were evil and should be avoided. Yet parties soon arose from a division between the followers of Hamilton and those of Madison and Jefferson.

Jefferson and Madison were such close collaborators that it is sometimes difficult to separate the contributions of the two. To describe the political philosophy of one is, in the main, to describe the political philosophy of both. Jefferson, himself a farmer, believed that farmers were God's chosen people and that an ideal republic would consist of sturdy citizens each tilling his own soil. Though an aristocrat by birth, his mother belonging to one of the first families of Virginia, the Randolphs, he had faith in the good intentions of such farmer-citizens and thought that, if properly educated, they could be trusted to govern themselves through the election of able and qualified men. But, in the 1790s, he feared city mobs as "sores upon the body politic." He then opposed the development of extensive manufactures because they would lead to the growth of cities packed with propertyless workers. While Hamilton emphasized the need for order and stability, Jefferson stressed the importance of individual freedom.

As a member of President Washington's official circle, Jefferson differed so strongly with his colleague Hamilton on particular issues such as the Bank that he soon offered to resign. But Washington preferred to keep both men in office to preserve national unity if possible. His became a coalition government, though he himself agreed more often with Hamilton than with Jefferson. The two secretaries continued to work against each other, and each began to organize a following in Congress and in the country at large. Hamilton's followers came to be known as Federalists, Jefferson's as Republicans.

The Federalists of the 1790s were not entirely the same men as the Federalists of 1787–1788 who had campaigned for the ratification of the Constitution, nor were the Republicans exactly the same men as the old Antifederalists. There were numerous exceptions, the most noteworthy being Madison, who had played a leading role at the constitutional convention and in the ratification effort, then had broken with Hamilton on the questions of funding and the Bank, and had become one of the founders of the Republican party. Both of the parties contained members in all sections of the country, but the Federalists were most numerous in the commercial centers of the Northeast, though also strong in such Southern seaports as Charleston, while the Republicans were most numerous in the rural areas of the South and the West.

Unlike the old Antifederalists, the new Republicans did not denounce the Constitution. On the contrary, they professed to be its special friends and accused their opponents of violating it.

Republicans and Federalists differed in their social philosophies as well as in their economic interests and their constitutional views. Their differences in social outlook are seen in their reactions to the progress of the revolution in France. When that revolution first began, as a rather mild movement in favor of constitutional monarchy and the rights of man, practically all Americans hailed it as a step in the right direction. But when the revolution went to radical extremes, with attacks on organized religion, the overthrow of the monarchy, and eventually the guillotining of the King and Queen, Americans adopted different views about the events in France, the Federalists denouncing and the Republicans applauding them. Indeed, many of the Republicans imitated the French radicals (the Jacobins) by cutting their hair short, wearing pantaloons, and addressing one another as "Citizen" Smith or "Citizeness" Jones. Thus, for a time, it was possible to tell a man's party by his manners and appearance, for the Federalists kept the old-fashioned long hair or powdered wig, knee breeches, and traditional etiquette of the gentleman. Republicans accused the Federalists of being aristocratic and even "monarchical." Federalists referred to the Republicans, in horrified tones, as "Jacobins" and as "Jacobinical rabble"—terms that then had much the same implication as the word "Communist" was to have many years later.

The two parties had different leanings in foreign affairs. Both were pro-American, but Jefferson and the Republicans believed that American interests would best be served by maintaining close relations with France, while Hamilton and the Federalists believed that friendship with Great Britain was essential for the success of the United States.

When the time came for the election of 1792, the Republicans had no candidate to put up against Washington. Jefferson as well as Hamilton urged him to run for a second term, and the President consented for the good of the country, though he would have preferred to retire to Mount Vernon.

# ASSERTING NATIONAL SOVEREIGNTY

Under the Federalists the new government disposed of questions that the old government of the Confederation had scarcely begun to deal with, questions not only of public finance but also of the frontier and diplomacy.

## Securing the Frontier

While during the early 1790s, the American people began to be divided between two political parties, they became more strongly united than ever in their loyalty to the government itself. Previously, during the 1780s, the old Congress had been powerless to tie the outlying parts of the country firmly to the United States, as farmers in western Massachusetts rose in revolt and settlers in Vermont, Kentucky, and Tennessee toyed with the idea of separating these territories from the Union. Now, however, the Washington administration made the power of the federal government felt even on the farthest reaches of the frontier.

The federal authority was challenged when, in 1794, the farmers of western Pennsylvania refused to pay the whiskey excise and terrorized the would-be tax collectors, much as the colonists had done throughout America at the time of the Stamp Act. The so-called Whiskey Rebellion was not left to the authorities of Pennsylvania as Shays' Rebellion had been left to the authorities of Massachusetts. Urged on by Hamilton, Washington took drastic steps. Calling out the militia of three states, he raised an army of nearly 15,000, a larger force than he had

## Federal Hall, New York

Here George Washington was inaugurated as President on April 30, 1789, taking his oath of office on the balcony that overlooks Wall Street. The building was originally constructed as the City Hall in 1699–1700. It was extensively remodeled and enlarged after the Revolution and was renamed Federal Hall when it served as the temporary capitol of the United States, in 1789–1790. At the end of Wall Street is the Gothic-styled Trinity Church (Anglican). It was built in 1688, destroyed in a great fire following the British occupation of the city in 1776, and rebuilt in 1788. Behind the church was a meadow sloping down to the Hudson River. (Top right)

## The First Bank of the United States

The headquarters of the Bank of the United States, which was founded through Alexander Hamilton's efforts, were in Philadelphia. The bank building on Third Street was completed in 1795. It is a good example of Early Republican architecture, with its rather boxlike shape, its balustrade along the roof edge, its quoins at the angle of the walls, and its Roman pediment and columns in front. From a drawing and engraving by W. Birch & Son of Philadelphia, published in 1799. (Bottom right)

commanded against the British during most of the Revolution, and he personally accompanied this army as far as the town of Bedford. At the approach of the militiamen, the farmers around Pittsburgh, where the rebellion centered, either ran for cover or stayed home and professed to be law-abiding citizens. The rebellion quickly collapsed.

While the whiskey rebels were intimidated into obedience, other frontiersmen were made loyal to the government by its acceptance of new states as members of the Union. First to be admitted were two of the original thirteen, North Carolina (1789) and Rhode Island (1790), both of which had ratified the Constitution when they found that a bill of rights was definitely to be added and that they could not conveniently go on as independent commonwealths. Then Vermont, which had had its own state government since the Revolution, was accepted as the fourteenth state (1791) after New York and New Hampshire finally agreed to give up their claims to sovereignty over the Green Mountain country. Next came Kentucky (1792) with the consent of Virginia, which previously had governed the Kentucky counties as its own. After North Carolina finally ceded its Western lands to the Union, these were given a territorial government similar to that of the Northwest Territory and after six years became the state of Tennessee (1796). With the admission of these frontier states, the schemes for separating Vermont, Kentucky, and Tennessee from the Union soon came to an end.

In the more remote areas of the Northwest and the Southwest, meanwhile, the government had to contend with the Indians and their foreign allies, British and Spanish, in order to get a firm grasp upon all the territory belonging to the United States. The Indians of the Southwest —Cherokees, Creeks, Choctaws, and Chickasaws—were led by the colorful and vengeful Alexander McGillivray, a half-breed Creek chieftain who had fought as a Tory during the Revolution and who continued to hate Americans. In his efforts to resist the advance of American frontiersmen into the lower Mississippi Valley, McGillivray received the support and encouragement of Spain. In 1790 President Washington tried to buy peace with the South-

western Indians by inviting McGillivray to New York and agreeing to pay him $100,000. Despite McGillivray's treaty with the United States, the Indians continued to accept subsidies from the Spaniards and to raid American settlements along the border. At last, in 1793–1794, the Tennesseans went on the warpath themselves, their militia invading the Indian country and chastising several of the tribes. Thus the Southwestern frontier was made safe for the time being.

In the Northwest the government pursued a policy of force against the Indians, even at some risk of becoming involved in hostilities with their protector and ally, Great Britain. Two expeditions failed before a third one finally succeeded in the conquest of the Ohio country. Washington gave the frontier command to General Wayne, who, despite his nickname "Mad Anthony," was a careful planner as well as a dashing soldier. With over 4,000 men, including a large contingent of Kentucky sharpshooters, Wayne moved cautiously toward the Maumee River, building forts as he went. The British officials in Canada, who were providing the Indians with supplies, themselves ordered the construction of a fort about twenty miles from the mouth of the river, well within the boundary of the United States. Near the British fort, at a place where trees had been blown over by a windstorm, Wayne in the summer of 1794 met and decisively defeated the Indians in the Battle of Fallen Timbers, the British garrison prudently keeping out of the fight. Next summer the Indians agreed in the Treaty of Greenville to abandon to the white men most of what afterwards became the state of Ohio.

Before the government could be sure of its hold upon the border areas, it had to bring to terms the foreign powers that persisted in exerting influence there—Great Britain and Spain. In its diplomacy the Washington administration, by taking advantage of the opportunities that arose from the accidents of international politics, managed to reassert American independence and redeem the West.

## Maintaining Neutrality

When Washington became President, Great Britain had not yet sent a minister to the United States, though all the other powers of Europe (except Russia) had entered into normal diplomatic relations with the young republic. In Congress Madison and the Republicans argued that Great Britain, in refusing to make a commercial treaty with the United States, was waging a kind of economic warfare against this country, and that the United States should retaliate by imposing special customs duties and harbor dues, in excess of the regular rates, upon her goods and ships. Though this legislation did not pass, the threat of it induced the British government finally, in 1791, to dispatch a regular minister to America.

A new crisis in foreign affairs faced the Washington administration when the French revolutionary government, after guillotining King Louis XVI, went to war in 1793 with Great Britain and her allies. Should the United States recognize the radical government of France by accepting a diplomatic representative from it? Was the United States obligated by the alliance of 1778 to go to war on the side of France? These questions Washington put to his official advisers, and both Hamilton and Jefferson recommended a policy of neutrality, though they presented quite different arguments for it. Washington decided to recognize the French government and to issue a proclamation announcing the determination of the United States to remain at peace. The proclamation (1793), though it did not mention the word "neutrality," was generally interpreted as a neutrality statement, which it actually was. Next year Congress passed a Neutrality Act, forbidding American citizens to participate in the war and prohibiting the use of American soil as a base of operations for either side.

The first challenge to American neutrality came from France. Not that the French revolutionaries asked for a declaration of war: they did not, for they supposed that the United States would be of more use to them as a nonbelligerent. Their purposes became apparent when their first minister to this country arrived. Instead of landing at Philadelphia and presenting himself immediately to the President, the youthful and brash Citizen Edmond Genêt disembarked at Charleston. There he made plans for using American ports to outfit French warships, issued letters of marque and reprisal authorizing American shipowners to serve as French privateers, and commissioned the aging George Rogers Clark to undertake an overland expedition against the possessions of Spain, which at the moment was an ally of Great Britain and an enemy of France. In all these steps, Genêt brazenly disregarded Washington's proclamation and flagrantly violated the Neutrality Act. When he finally reached Philadelphia, after being acclaimed by pro-French crowds on a tour through the interior, he got a stony reception from the President. He then assumed that the people were behind him, and he repeatedly appealed to them over the President's head. His conduct not only infuriated Washington and the Federalists but also embarrassed all except the most ardent Francophiles among the Republicans. At last Washington demanded that the French government recall him, but by that time Genêt's party, the Girondins, were out of power in France and the still more extreme Jacobins in control, so it would not have been safe for him to return. Generously the President granted him political asylum in the United States, and he settled down to live to a ripe old age with his American wife on a Long Island farm. Meanwhile the neutrality policy had survived its first great test.

The second challenge, an even greater one, came from Great Britain. Early in 1794 the Royal Navy suddenly seized hundreds of American ships engaged in trade in the French West Indies. The pretext for these seizures was a British interpretation of international law—known as the Rule of 1756—which held that a trade prohibited in peacetime (as American trade between France and the French overseas possessions had been) could not be legally opened in time of war. At the news of the seizures, the prevalent opinion in the United States became as strongly anti-British as it had recently been anti-French, and the anti-British feeling rose still higher at the report that the Governor-General of Canada had delivered a rousing and warlike speech to the Indians on the northwestern frontier. With peace thus endangered, Hamilton grew concerned, for war would mean an end to imports from England, and most of the revenue for maintaining his financial system came from duties on those imports.

## Jay's Treaty

To Hamilton and to other Federalists it seemed that this was no time for ordinary diplomacy. Jefferson had resigned in 1793 to devote himself to organizing a political opposition, and the State Department was now in the hands of an even more ardently pro-French Virginian, Edmund Randolph. By-passing the State Department, Washington named as a special commissioner to England the staunch New York Federalist, former Secretary for Foreign Affairs under the old Confederation and current Chief Justice of the Supreme Court, John Jay. Jay was instructed to secure damages for the recent spoliations, withdrawal of British forces from the frontier posts, and a satisfactory commercial treaty, without violating the terms of the existing treaty of amity and commerce with France, signed at the time of the alliance in 1778.

The treaty that Jay negotiated (1794) was a long and complex document, dealing with frontier posts, boundaries, debts, commerce, ship seizures, and neutral rights. It yielded more to Great Britain and obtained less for the United States than Jay had been authorized to give or instructed to get. When the terms were published in the United States, the treaty was denounced more than any treaty before or since, and Jay himself was burned in effigy in various parts of the country. The Republicans were unanimous in decrying it; they said it was a departure from neutrality, favoring Great Britain and unfair to France. Even some of the Federalists were outraged by its terms, those in the South objecting to its provision for the payment of the pre-Revolutionary debts. Opponents of the treaty went to extraordinary lengths to defeat it in the Senate, and French agents aided them and cheered them on. The American minister to France, James Monroe, and even the Secretary of State, Edmund Randolph, cooperated closely with the French in a desperate attempt to prevent ratification. Nevertheless, after amending the treaty a bit, the Senate gave its consent.

There was much to be said for Jay's Treaty, despite its very real shortcomings. By means of it the United States gained valuable time for continued peaceful development, obtained undisputed sovereignty over all the Northwest, and secured a reasonably satisfactory commercial agreement with the nation whose trade was most important. More than that, the treaty led immediately to a settlement of the worst of the outstanding differences with Spain.

In Madrid the Spanish foreign minister feared that the understanding between Great Britain and the United States might prove a prelude to joint operations between those two countries against Spain's possessions in North America. Spain was about to change sides in the European war, abandoning Great Britain for France, and it was therefore to Spain's interest to appease

### Jay's Treaty [1794]

**Frontier Posts.** "His Majesty will withdraw all his troops and garrisons from all posts and places within the boundary lines assigned by the treaty of peace to the United States."

**Boundaries.** Joint surveys will be made to locate the United States-Canadian boundary west of the Lake of the Woods and at the northeast, between Maine and New Brunswick.

**Debts.** The United States "will make full and complete compensation" for uncollectable debts owed by Americans to British creditors.

**Commerce.** There shall be freedom of commerce and navigation between the United States and Great Britain and the British East Indies. (Article XII, permitting the United States to trade with the British West Indies also, but only in relatively small ships, was stricken out before ratification.)

**Ship Seizures.** The British government will compensate Americans for ships and cargoes illegally captured in the past, the amount of payment to be determined by arbitration.

**Neutral Rights.** American ships carrying enemy (French) property, when captured by the British, shall be taken to British ports and the enemy property removed. (This was inconsistent with the usual American principle that "free ships make free goods.")

the United States. The relentless pressure of American frontiersmen advancing toward the Southwest made it doubtful whether Spain could long hold her borderlands in any event. And so, when Thomas Pinckney arrived in Spain as a special negotiator, he had no difficulty in gaining practically everything that the United States had sought from the Spaniards for over a decade. Pinckney's Treaty (1795) recognized the right of Americans to navigate the Mississippi to its mouth and to deposit goods at New Orleans for reloading on ocean-going ships; fixed the northern boundary of Florida where Americans always had insisted it should be, along the thirty-first parallel; and bound the Spanish authorities to prevent the Indians in Florida from raiding across the border.

Thus, before Washington had completed his second term in office, the United States had freed itself from the encroachments of both Great Britain and Spain.

## DOWNFALL OF THE FEDERALISTS

After George Washington had left the Presidency, the Federalists overreached themselves in their grasp for power. They faced the dilemma of all rulers in a government that depends upon the will of the people—that is, the dilemma of choosing between governmental strength and individual freedom—and they made their choice in favor of strong government at the expense of popular liberty and popular support. The Federalists never won another presidential election after 1796, yet their main achievements endured and, in one form or another, still endure.

### Election of 1796

As the time approached for the election of 1796, some of the party friends of Washington urged him to run again. Already twice elected without a single vote cast against him in the electoral college, he could be counted upon to hold the Federalist party together and carry it to a third great victory. But Washington, weary of the burdens of the presidential office, disgusted with the partisan abuse that was being heaped upon him, longed to retire to his beloved home,

Mount Vernon. Though he did not object to a third term in principle, he did not desire one for himself. To make his determination clear, he composed, with Hamilton's assistance, a long letter to the American people and had it published in a Philadelphia newspaper.

When Washington in this "Farewell Address" referred to the "insidious wiles of foreign influence," he was not writing merely for rhetorical effect. He had certain real evils in mind. Lately he had dismissed the Secretary of State, Edmund Randolph, and had recalled the minister to France, James Monroe, for working hand in hand with the French to defeat Jay's Treaty. The French were still interfering in American politics with the hope of defeating the Federalists in the forthcoming presidential election.

There was no doubt that Jefferson would be the candidate of the Republicans, and he chose as his running mate the New York Republican leader, Aaron Burr. With Washington out of the running, there was some question as to who the Federalist candidate would be. Hamilton, the very personification of Federalism, was not "available" because his forthright views had aroused too many enemies. John Jay was too closely identified with his unpopular treaty, and Thomas Pinckney, though *his* treaty had been enthusiastically received, had the handicap of being a South Carolinian at a time when party leaders thought the next candidate should be a Northerner. John Adams, who as Vice President was directly associated with none of the Federalist measures, finally got the nomination for President at a caucus of the Federalists in Congress, and Pinckney received the nomination for Vice President.

With Washington stepping aside, the Federalist party became torn by fierce factional rivalries. Hamilton disliked Adams and preferred Pinckney, as did many other Federalists especially in the South. New Englanders, on the other hand, had no particular liking for Pinckney and feared a plot to make him President instead of Adams. The result was a near disaster for the Federalists. They elected a majority of their presidential electors, despite the electioneering tactics of the French government, whose efforts may have boomeranged and helped the Federalists. But when the electors balloted in the

### John Adams

When elected to the Presidency, Adams was almost thirty years younger than the man depicted in this portrait, painted when he was past eighty. The artist was **Samuel F. B. Morse**. Afterward best known as the inventor of the magnetic telegraph, Morse did not give up painting for invention until he was in his forties. He was born in Massachusetts, the son of Jedidiah Morse, who was America's foremost geographer of the late eighteenth and early nineteenth century. The younger Morse graduated from Yale, studied art under Benjamin West and Washington Allston in England, and in 1823 opened a studio in New York. He helped to found and was the first president of the National Academy of Design. (In the Brooklyn Museum Collection)

various states, some of the Pinckney men declined to vote for Adams, and a still larger number of the Adams men declined to vote for Pinckney. So Pinckney received fewer votes than Jefferson, and Adams only three more than Jefferson. The next President was to be a Federalist, but the Vice President was to be a Republican!

By virtue of his diplomatic services during the Revolution, his writings as a conservative political philosopher, and his devotion to the public weal as he saw it, "Honest John" Adams ranks as one of the greatest American statesmen. Like most prominent members of the illustrious Adams family afterwards, however, he lacked the politician's touch which is essential for successful leadership in a republican society. Even Washington, remote and austere as he sometimes seems to have been, was fairly adept at conciliating factions and maintaining party har-

mony. Unwisely, the new President chose to continue Washington's department heads in office. Most of them were friends of Hamilton, and they looked to him for advice, though he held no official post.

## Quasi-War With France

As American relations with Great Britain and Spain improved in consequence of Jay's and Pinckney's treaties, relations with France, now under the government of the Directory, went from bad to worse. Despite the victory of the Federalists in the election of 1796, the leaders of the Directory assumed that France had the sympathy and support of the mass of the American people and could undermine the Adams administration by frustrating it in foreign affairs. Therefore the French, asserting that they were applying the same principles of neutral rights as the United States and Great Britain had adopted in Jay's Treaty, continued to capture American ships on the high seas and, in many cases, to imprison the crews. When Minister Monroe left France after his recall, the French went out of their way to show their affection for him and for the Republican party. When the South Carolina Federalist Charles Cotesworth Pinckney, a brother of Thomas Pinckney, arrived in France to replace Monroe, the Directory considered him *persona non grata* and refused to receive him as the official representative of the United States.

War seemed likely unless the Adams administration could settle the difficulties with France. Some of the President's advisers, in particular his Secretary of State, the stiff-backed New England Francophobe Timothy Pickering, favored war. Others urged a special effort for peace, and even Hamilton approved the idea of appointing commissioners to approach the Directory. Adams, himself a peace man, appointed a bipartisan commission of three: C. C. Pinckney, the recently rejected minister; John Marshall, a Virginia Federalist, afterwards famous as the great Chief Justice of the United States; and Elbridge Gerry, a Massachusetts Republican but a personal friend of the President's. In France, in 1797, the three Americans were met by three agents of the Directory's foreign minister, Prince Talleyrand, who had a reputation as the wizard of European diplomacy but who did not understand the psychology of Americans, even though he had lived for a time in the United States. Talleyrand's agents demanded a loan for France and a bribe for French officials before they would deal with Adams' commissioners. The response of the commissioners was summed up in Pinckney's laconic words: "No! No! Not a sixpence!"

When Adams received the commissioners' report, he sent a message to Congress in which he urged readiness for war, denounced the French for their insulting treatment of the United States, and vowed he would not appoint another minister to France until he knew the minister would be "received, respected and honored as the representative of a great, free, powerful and independent nation." The Republicans, doubting the President's charge that the United States had been insulted, asked for proof. Adams then turned the commissioners' report over to Congress, after deleting the names of the three Frenchmen and designating them only as Messrs. X., Y., and Z. When the report was published, the "X. Y. Z. Affair" provoked even more of a reaction than Adams had bargained for. It aroused the martial spirit of most Americans, made the Federalists more popular than ever as the party of patriotism, and led to a limited and undeclared war with France (1798–1800).

With the cooperation of Congress, which quickly passed the necessary laws, Adams cut off all trade with France, abrogated the treaties of 1778, and authorized public and private vessels of the United States to capture French armed ships on the high seas. Congress set up a Department of the Navy (1798) and appropriated money for the construction of warships to supplement the hundreds of privateers and the small number of government vessels already built for the protection of American shipping in the Mediterranean against the Barbary pirates. The new United States Navy soon gave a good account of itself. Its warships won a number of duels with French vessels of their own class and captured a total of eighty-five ships including armed merchantmen.

Having abandoned neutrality, the United States now was cooperating so closely with Great Britain as to be virtually a cobelligerent, though technically at peace. When the British offered to lend a part of their fleet to the United States, President Adams declined to borrow, since he preferred to build up a navy of his own. Nevertheless, the British provided shot and shell to make up for the deficient American supplies, furnished officers to help with the training and direction of American crews, and exchanged signaling information so that British and American ships could communicate readily with one another. Thus the United States was involved in the world war as a kind of associate member of the coalition against France.

The French foreign minister, Talleyrand, finally began to see the wisdom of an accommodation with the Americans. He took notice of the rapprochement between the United States and Great Britain, the successes of the American Navy, and the failure of the American people to show the expected enthusiasm for the cause of France. He was enlightened in regard to American public opinion by George Logan, a Philadelphia Quaker who, with no official authorization but with a letter of introduction from Vice President Jefferson, visited France to work for peace in the midst of the undeclared war. After Logan returned, President Adams gave him a sympathetic hearing, though the Federalists in Congress passed a law, the so-called Logan Act, to prohibit citizens from engaging in private and unofficial diplomacy with foreign governments in the future.

When, in 1800, Adams' new three-man commission arrived in France, Napoleon Bonaparte was in power as First Consul. The Americans requested that France terminate the treaties of 1778 and pay damages for seizures of American ships. Napoleon replied that, if the United States had any claim to damages, the claim must rest upon the treaties, and if the treaties were ended, the claim must be abandoned. Napoleon had his way. The Americans agreed to a new treaty that canceled the old ones, arranged for reciprocity in commerce, and ignored the question of damages. When Adams submitted this treaty to the Senate, the extreme Federalists raised so many objections that its final ratification was delayed until after he had left office. Nevertheless, the "quasi-war" had come to an honorable end, and the United States at last had freed itself

## Building the Navy

After the Revolutionary War the United States abandoned the warships it had accumulated, and from 1783 to 1798 there was no American navy. Then, with the outbreak of undeclared hostilities with France, the Department of the Navy was established and a naval building program begun. In that age of wooden sailing ships, there were three main categories of war vessels: (1) ships of the line, or line-of-battle ships, which were the largest and most heavily armed (roughly corresponding to twentieth-century battleships or dreadnoughts); (2) frigates, which were smaller and faster and had fewer guns (comparable to modern cruisers); (3) corvettes, sloops of war, and other relatively small craft (somewhat like the light cruisers, destroyers, and gunboats of the present). At the outset the United States navy

eschewed line-of-battle ships and placed its chief reliance on specially designed frigates which were faster, more maneuverable, and more heavily gunned than their European counterparts. In 1798 the frigates *United States, Constitution,* and *Constellation,* already partly built, were completed, and the *Philadelphia* and several others were started. The illustration shows work in progress on the *Philadelphia* in a Philadelphia shipyard. This frigate was not finished in time to be used against the French, but it saw plenty of action later (1803) in the war with Tripoli. Tripolitan pirates captured the ship, and Americans in a daring raid destroyed her to prevent the enemy's using her against them. (The Historical Society of Pennsylvania)

from the entanglements and embarrassments of the "perpetual" alliance with France.

## Repression and Protest

The outbreak of hostilities in 1798 had given the Federalists an advantage over the political opposition, and in the congressional elections of that year they increased their majorities in both houses. Meanwhile their new-found power went to their heads. Some of them schemed to go on winning elections by passing laws to weaken and to silence the opposition. They had

as an excuse the supposed necessity of protecting the nation from dangerous foreign influence in the midst of the undeclared war. By persecuting their critics, the Federalists produced a crop of Republican martyrs, gave rise to protests against their disregard of the Constitution, and provoked a reaction that helped to bring their party to defeat.

Since many Republican critics of the administration were foreigners by birth, especially Irish or French, the Federalists in Congress thought it desirable to limit the political rights of aliens and make it more difficult for them to become citizens of the United States. The Federalists struck at the civil liberties of both native Americans and the foreign-born in a series of laws commonly known as the Alien and Sedition Acts.

President Adams did not invoke the Alien Act nor deport any aliens, but this law together with the Naturalization Act doubtless had some effect in discouraging immigration and encouraging many foreigners already here to leave. The administration did enforce the Sedition Act, arresting about two dozen men and convicting ten of them. Most of these were Republican newspaper editors whose writings, while tending to bring the Federalists into disrepute, were not truly seditious at all. One of the editors merely had expressed the wish that, when a salute was fired in honor of the President, the wadding of the cannon had "struck him in the rear bulge of the breeches."

The Republicans had no reason to look to the Supreme Court for relief. Indeed, the Court never yet had declared an act of Congress unconstitutional, and the Republicans denied that it had the power to do so. They believed, however, that the recent Federalist legislation, particularly the Sedition Act, was unconstitutional, for the First Amendment stated that Congress should pass no law abridging freedom of speech or of the press.

What agency of government should decide the question of constitutionality? The Republican leaders Jefferson and Madison concluded that the state legislatures should decide. They ably expressed their view in two sets of resolutions, one written (anonymously) by Jefferson and adopted by the Kentucky legislature (1798, 1799), and the other drafted by Madison and approved by the Virginia legislature (1798). These Kentucky and Virginia resolutions asserted the following doctrines. The federal government had been formed by a "compact" or contract among the states. It was a limited government, possessing only certain delegated powers. Whenever it exercised any additional and undelegated powers, its acts were "unauthoritative, void, and of no force." The parties to the contract, the states, must decide for themselves when and whether the central govern-

ment exceeded its powers. And "nullification" by the states was the "rightful remedy" whenever the general government went too far. The resolutions urged all the states to join in declaring the Alien and Sedition Acts null and void and in requesting their repeal at the next session of Congress, but none of the others went along with Virginia and Kentucky.

## Election of 1800

In the election of 1800 Jefferson and Burr, representing the alliance of Virginia and New York, were again the Republican candidates. Adams was running for reelection on the Federalist ticket, and his running mate was C. C. Pinckney, brother of the Thomas Pinckney who had been the Federalist vice-presidential candidate in 1796.

During the nearly twelve years of Federalist rule, the party had created numerous political enemies in consequence of Hamilton's financial program, the suppression of the Whiskey Rebellion, Jay's Treaty, and the Alien and Sedition Acts. Denouncing these measures, and especially the last of them, the Republicans made state rights and constitutional liberties the main issues of their campaign in 1800. They pictured Adams as a tyrant and a man who wanted to be King. The Federalists, on the other hand, described Jefferson as a dangerous radical and his followers as wild men who, if they got into power, would bring on a reign of terror comparable to that of the French Revolution at its worst.

The contest was close, and the outcome in the electoral college depended upon the voting in one state, New York. In New York City the vice-presidential candidate, Burr, was the organizer of Republican victory. The Revolutionary veterans of the city had formed the Tammany Society to maintain their wartime fellowship and to combat the pretensions of the Society of the Cincinnati, the exclusive and aristocratic organization of Revolutionary officers. Though not himself a member of Tammany, Burr converted it into a political machine and, with its aid, carried the city for the Republicans by such a large majority as to carry the state also. The Republicans gained control of the legislature, and since New York was one of the states in which the legislature cast the electoral vote, the Republicans could count upon that vote in the presidential election.

When the state electors cast their votes, Adams received a total of 65 and Pinckney 64. Jefferson got 73 and so did Burr. To avoid such a tie, Republican leaders had meant for at least one of their electors to refrain from giving Burr his vote. But through a misunderstanding—some said that Burr himself was secretly responsible—the plan went awry. And so the election was not yet over: in accordance with the Constitution the decision between the two highest—between Burr and Jefferson—was up to the House of Representatives, with the delegation from each state casting a single vote.

Since the Federalists controlled a majority of the states' votes in the existing Congress, they had the privilege of deciding which of their opponents was to be the next President, though the Republicans, in making their nominations, had clearly intended for Jefferson to have the first place on their ticket. Some of the more extreme of the Federalists now hoped to postpone or to prevent any breaking of the tie and, instead, to make new arrangements for the presidential succession so that the highest office in the land would still fall to a Federalist. Others, fearing chaos and possible civil war if no election were made, thought it would be better to come to an understanding with Burr and elect him. Hamilton disapproved of both proposals. Though he had a low opinion of Jefferson, he had a still-lower one of Burr, his bitter rival in law and politics in New York. Burr himself remained strangely silent, neither electioneering openly for himself nor publicly refusing to accept office at the hands of the Federalists.

During the winter of 1800–1801 the House balloted again and again without mustering a majority for either candidate. Finally, only a few weeks before inauguration day, some of the Federalist die-hards gave in, the tie was broken, and Jefferson was named as President, Burr as Vice President. Afterwards one of the Federalists claimed that he had given in because Jefferson's friends had assured him that Jefferson, if elected, would appoint him to a government job and would preserve the main Federalist policies with respect to commerce, the navy, and the

**Election of 1800**

public debt, while making no wholesale removals of Federalists from the lower offices of the government.

In addition to winning a majority of the presidential electors in 1800, the Republicans also won a majority of the seats in both houses of the next Congress. The only branch of the government left in Federalist hands was the judiciary, and Adams and his fellow partisans during his last months in office took steps to make their hold upon the courts secure.

By the Judiciary Act of 1801 the Federalists succeeded in reducing the number of Supreme Court justiceships by one but at the same time greatly increasing the number of federal judgeships as a whole. The act created a separate system of circuit courts of appeal, between the federal district courts and the Supreme Court. Formerly (in accordance with the Judiciary Act of 1789) a district judge had sat with two Supreme Court justices to hear appeals on the circuit. The new law also provided for ten additional district judgeships.

To these newly created positions Adams proceeded to appoint deserving Federalists. It was said that he stayed up until midnight on his last day in office, March 3, 1801, in order to complete the signing of the judges' commissions, and so these officeholders were known as his "mid-night appointments." Since federal judges held office for life—that is, with good behavior—Jefferson as the incoming President would be powerless to remove Adams' appointees. Or so the Federalists assumed.

# Selected Readings

**The Constitution** Max Ferrand, *The Framing of the Constitution of the United States*° (1913); C. A. Beard, *An Economic Interpretation of the Constitution of the United States*° (1913); R. E. Brown, *Charles Beard and the Constitution*° (1956); Forrest McDonald, *We the People: The Economic Origins of the Constitution*° (1958) and *E Pluribus Unum: The Formation of the American Republic, 1776–1790* (1965); Clinton Rossiter, *The Grand Convention* (1966); Max Farrand, ed., *Records of the Federal Convention of 1787*° (4 vols., 1911–1937).

**Ratification** J. T. Main, *The Anti-Federalists: Critics of the Constitution, 1781–1788* (1961); A. T. Mason, *The State Rights Debate: Anti-federalism and the Constitution* (1964); R. A. Rutland, *The Ordeal of the Constitution: The Antifederalists and the Ratification Struggle of 1787–1788* (1966); L. G. DePauw, *The Eleventh Pillar: New York State and the Federal Constitution* (1966); J. E. Cooke, ed., *The Federalist*° (1961).

**The Federalist Regime** J. C. Miller, *The Federalist Era, 1789–1801*° (1960); Leonard White, *The Federalists*° (1948); M. J. Dauer, *The Adams Federalists* (1953); Nathan Schachner, *The Founding Fathers*° (1954); Stephen Kurtz, *The Presidency of John Adams*° (1957).

**The Jeffersonian Opposition** C. A. Beard, *The Economic Origins of Jeffersonian Democracy*° (1915); Joseph Charles, *The Origins of the American Party System*° (1956); W. N. Chambers, *Political Parties in a New Nation: The American Experience, 1776–1809*° (1963); Noble Cunningham, *The Jeffersonian Republicans* (1957).

**Rights and Repression** Irving Brant, *The Bill of Rights* (1965); L. W. Levy, *Legacy of Suppression: Freedom of Speech and Press in Early American History*° (1960); J. M. Smith, *Freedom's Fetters: The Alien and Sedition Laws and American Civil Liberties* (1956); J. C. Miller, *Crisis in Freedom: The Alien and Sedition Acts*° (1951); L. D. Baldwin, *Whiskey Rebels: The Story of a Frontier Uprising* (1939).

**Diplomacy** S. F. Bemis, *Jay's Treaty*° (1923) and *Pinckney's Treaty*° (1926); A. P. Whitaker, *The Spanish-American Frontier, 1783–1795* (1927) and *The Mississippi Question, 1795–1803* (1934); Alexander De Conde, *Entangling Alliance: Politics and Diplomacy under George Washington* (1958) and *The Quasi-War: The Politics and Diplomacy of the Undeclared War with France, 1797–1801* (1966); Bradford Perkins, *The First Rapprochement: England and the United States, 1795–1805* (1955); P. A. Varg, *Foreign Policies of the Founding Fathers* (1963); Felix Gilbert, *To the Farewell Address*° (1961); L. S. Kaplan, *Jefferson and France* (1967).

**Biographies** D. S. Freeman, *George Washington* (7 vols., 1948–1957); C. P. Smith, *John Adams* (1962); Gilbert Chinard, *Honest John Adams*° (1933); J. C. Miller, *Alexander Hamilton: Portrait in Paradox* (1959); Dumas Malone, *Jefferson and His Time* (3 vols., 1948–1962); Irving Brant, *James Madison: Father of the Constitution, 1787–1800* (1950); F. B. Tolles, *George Logan of Philadelphia* (1953).

---

° Titles available in paperback.

# Chapter 7
# The
# Jeffersonian Era

Thomas Jefferson and the Republicans, while out of power, had championed the rights of the states against the powers of the federal government. They denounced the Federalists for stretching those powers too far and interpreting the Constitution too loosely. Jefferson stood for governmental principles that were appropriate to the kind of country he envisaged—a country made up mostly of independent farmers and happily free from the workshops, the industrial towns, and the city mobs of Europe. He favored France and the French influence against England and English ways. A man of the Enlightenment like Franklin, he took a rational and skeptical approach to life both here and hereafter.

But during those years the young republic was beginning to develop in directions that would eventually make some (but by no means all) of Jefferson's views seem obsolete. New machinery, derived from England or devised at home, gave a little start to the growth of an industrial society, with factories and factory towns dotting the American countryside. The English tone prevailed over the French in most things of the mind. To the extent that American writers resisted the English influence, they tended to arouse a national feeling and thus to diminish the particularist sentiment, the sense of identification with an individual state. And a renewal of religious revivalism, coinciding with Jefferson's taking office, almost submerged the rational philosophy that had been rampant for some time.

Moreover, once Jefferson and his party followers were in control of the government, they had to deal with situations that seemed to demand strong, unfettered action. Soon the Republicans were going even further, in some respects, than the Federalists had gone in the exercise of federal authority. If Jefferson appeared to be inconsistent, so did many of his opponents, for they now adopted the theory of state rights and turned his former arguments against him.

But the idea of state rights was not the whole of the Jeffersonian philosophy. He stood primarily for the interests of the majority as he conceived them. As President, he did much to advance those interests, his greatest achievement being to double the territory of the United States.

**Thomas Jefferson**

Jefferson was sixty-one years old when this portrait was painted, in 1805, at the President's mansion in Washington, by Rembrandt Peale, son of Charles Willson Peale. (Courtesy of the New-York Historical Society, New York City)

## SPIRIT OF THE YOUNG REPUBLIC

Having won political independence, the American people—or at least some of them—also aspired to a kind of cultural independence. More than that, they looked forward to a time when (as a "Poem on the Rising Glory of America" had foretold in 1772) their "happy land" would be the "seat of empire" and the "final stage" of civilization, with "glorious works of high invention and of wond'rous art." The United States, as Joel Barlow saw it in his *Vision of Columbus* (1787), was destined to be "the last and greatest theatre for the improvement of mankind."

### Education and the Professions

In certain respects the Revolutionary War temporarily handicapped American intellectual life. Some learned men turned from science and scholarship to military or political service. The noted astronomer David Rittenhouse, for example, left his telescopes and devoted himself to a Revolutionary committee, the Pennsylvania Council of Safety, while advising his countrymen to abandon schools and concentrate on defense. Many schools did close, especially in rural areas, and most of the colleges were disrupted. Harvard buildings were used as American army barracks; Nassau Hall at Princeton was damaged during Washington's New Jersey campaign; and the William and Mary campus became the military headquarters of Cornwallis before the Battle of Yorktown.

But the Revolution also stimulated intellectual activity and brought forth ideas that were to have lasting consequences. Through military service thousands of young men got better acquainted with their own country, and by reading patriotic pamphlets, or at least hearing them discussed, these soldiers received something of a political education. With the French alliance there came from France not only troops and supplies but also ideas—giving further spread to the skeptical, experimental, scientific notions of the Enlightenment. And, with independence as an accomplished fact, it seemed to thoughtful Americans that widespread literacy and learning were absolutely essential to the success of the new republic. Thomas Jefferson, for one, called for a "crusade against ignorance."

The friends of learning advocated not merely education as such but a special kind of education, one that would fill the minds of youth with patriotic, republican thoughts. The Massachusetts geographer Jedidiah Morse, author of *Geography Made Easy* (1784), said the country must have its own textbooks so that the people would not be infected with the monarchical and aristocratic ideas of England. The Connecticut schoolmaster and lawyer Noah Webster likewise contended that the American schoolboy should be educated as a patriot. "As soon as he opens his lips," Webster wrote, "he should rehearse the history of his own country; he should lisp the praise of liberty, and of those illustrious heroes and statesmen who have wrought a revolution in her favor."

To foster a distinctive culture and unify the nation, Webster insisted upon a simplified and Americanized spelling—"honor" instead of "honour," for example. His *American Spelling Book* (1783), commonly known as the "blue-backed speller," eventually sold over 100 million copies to become the best-selling book (except for the Bible) in the entire history of American publishing. Webster also wrote grammars and other schoolbooks. His school dictionary (1806) was republished in many editions and eventually was much enlarged to form *An American Dictionary of the English Language* (1828). By means of his speller and his dictionary he succeeded in establishing a national standard of words and usages for the United States.

In their first constitutions, several of the states endorsed the principle of public education, but none actually required the establishment of free schools. A Massachusetts law of 1789 reaffirmed the colonial laws providing for the support of schools by the various towns. Jedidiah Morse observed later that the enforcement of the law was lax in many places. Even in Boston only seven public schools existed in 1790, and most of these were poorly housed; more than twice as many private schools were in operation. In Virginia, Jefferson as wartime governor proposed a plan by which the elements of reading and writing should be provided for all children, and secondary and higher educa-

## A School in Session About 1800

In such a one-room school, children of practically all ages were brought together. While one group recited, the rest learned their lessons—or were supposed to. Paper and ink were scarce; a slate and a slate pencil were commonly used instead. There was little in the way of furnishings except for backless benches and a few desks, usually placed under the windows, where the light was best. The teacher had to look out for the fire and perform the other chores of a janitor. Often the teacher was a college student, earning money during the long winter vacation from his own studies, or he was a recent college graduate supporting himself while he prepared for the law and politics. Daniel Webster and Thaddeus Stevens once taught school, and so did many another young men who afterward became prominent in public life. (Library of Congress)

tion for the gifted, with state scholarships for the needy. The plan was not enacted into law. As late as 1815 none of the states (not even Massachusetts) had a comprehensive public school system in actual operation.

Outside of New England, schooling continued to be viewed as the responsibility of the family and the church rather than the state. In the Middle Atlantic region and the South, most schools were run by religious groups, by proprietary schoolmasters, or by philanthropic societies. Though requiring tuition from parents who could afford it, many schools accepted the poor without pay. In the cities, special organizations were formed for the education of the poor. One of these, the New York Free School Society, introduced the Lancastrian method from England (1806), to economize on instruction costs: the teacher taught a lesson to several superior pupils, and then these "monitors" drilled groups of their fellow pupils.

During and after the Revolution, private academies sprang up in increasing numbers. Many were patterned after the academies founded by the Phillips family at Andover, Massachusetts (1778), and at Exeter, New Hampshire (1781). By 1815 there were thirty private secondary schools in Massachusetts, thirty-seven in New York, and more than one hundred in the country as a whole. Most of these admitted only boys, but a few academies or seminaries were provided for girls. Salem Female Academy, established in 1772 by North Carolina Moravians, was one of the earliest.

At the outbreak of the Revolution there had been a total of nine colleges in all the colonies;

in 1800 there were twenty-two in the various states, and the number continued steadily to increase thereafter. Whereas all but two of the colonial colleges were sectarian in origin and spirit, a majority of those founded during the first three decades of independence were nondenominational. Especially significant in foreshadowing the future pattern of higher education was the fact that five were state institutions: the universities of Georgia (1785), North Carolina (1789), Vermont (1791), Ohio (1804), and South Carolina (1805). For the time being, none of these was either quite public or a university in the modern sense. Their offerings were limited, and their financial support was derived mainly from private endowments, gifts, and tuition fees rather than appropriations by the rather niggardly legislatures. Scarcely more than one man in a thousand (and no women at all) had the benefit of such college education as was available.

Jefferson, John Adams, and a few other statesmen nourished the ideal of a true university, providing the best of training in the professions as well as the liberal arts. Nothing came of Jefferson's hope that a national university might be established. As wartime governor of Virginia, he managed to expand the work of William and Mary by adding professorships of law, medicine, and modern languages. George Wythe, the first law professor at the college, taught a remarkable number of youths who afterwards became distinguished lawyers and statesmen. Before 1800 the University of Pennsylvania and Columbia College instituted law courses, and Judge Tapping Reeve opened a private law school in Litchfield, Connecticut. As a rule, lawyers got their training, as in colonial times, by "reading law" in the office of a practicing attorney.

Most physicians likewise still studied medicine and gained experience by working with an established practitioner, but several medical schools were in existence by the early 1800s, the oldest of them at the University of Pennsylvania. Its most distinguished professor, and the outstanding physician in America, was Benjamin Rush, who had received his medical degree at Edinburgh. As an army surgeon during the Revolutionary War, Dr. Rush protested against improper sanitation and medical care, which

### Brooklyn, New York, in the Early 1800s

Settled by the Dutch, Brooklyn was not incorporated as a city until almost two centuries later, in 1834. It became a part of New York City in 1898. During the early 1800's, Brooklyn, on the tip of Long Island, retained a village atmosphere, though separated only by the East River from the bustling city of New York on Manhattan Island. Note the village pump—the water supply of the surrounding householders. From "Winter Scene in Brooklyn," a contemporary painting by Francis Guy. (In the Brooklyn Museum Collection) caused many more soldiers to die of camp diseases than of battle wounds. Afterwards he interested himself in the effects of diet and drink upon health, and he also made pioneering studies of psychosomatic and psychiatric disorders. As educators, Rush and other physicians had to struggle against age-old superstitions and against popular hostility to the dissection of corpses. In 1788 a riot was provoked when a human limb was hung out of a New York hospital window to dry, and from time to time medical students got into trouble for body-snatching, since cadavers seldom were available by legal means.

The science of public as well as private health remained in its infancy. In the summer of 1793 an epidemic of yellow fever raged unchecked in Philadelphia, bringing death to a tenth of the population in one of the worst disasters ever to befall an American city. The physicians were helpless, though Dr. Rush came near to guessing the cause of the epidemic when he explained it as being due to the miasma arising from decomposed matter. The Philadelphia experience stimulated programs for improving sanitation and making cities cleaner, and thus unwittingly the number of breeding places for the mosquito that transmits yellow fever were reduced. In many cases the prevailing medical practices hastened death instead of prolonging life. George Washington need not have died from a throat infection in 1799, but his physicians, doing their best according to their knowledge, bled and purged him so thoroughly as to impair his resistance to the disease.

## Literature and Music

During the first decades of independence, the most widely read American writings—and some of the greatest ones (such as *The Federalist*)—were polemical and political, not esthetic. In pamphlets and newspapers the literate American followed the arguments about British colonial policy, the aims of the Revolution, the question of a new Constitution, and the party contests of the young republic. He became a "newspaper-reading animal," as an English visitor observed. This preoccupation with the news of the day drew attention away from literature of a more artistic and permanent kind. Thus, in

one way, the newspapers handicapped literary development. Yet, in another way, they helped it, for they created a reading public and produced a potential market for literary works.

There was a more serious handicap to the rise of American authorship. An aspiring author found it hard to get his manuscript published, or to get it sold after it was in print. Until well into the nineteenth century, there were in America no book publishers in the modern sense, no firms that would bear the cost and take the risk of publishing. The author himself had to pay all or at least the larger part of the expenses. He could find few printers willing to share the burden with him, for they could reprint the works of popular English authors without paying a royalty. No author in the young republic could support himself by means of his writing alone. The first to try it was the novelist Charles Brockden Brown. He produced a series of well-written horror stories but had to take a job as a magazine editor in order to supplement his income.

The American author, if he looked to periodicals or the theater for a market, did little if any better than with books. In the late eighteenth century, several magazines were published in the United States, the most important being the *Columbian,* the *American Museum,* the *Massachusetts Magazine,* and the *New-York Magazine.* All of these filled their pages chiefly by clipping material from English publications. Meanwhile the theater had grown into an accepted, permanent institution in American cities, with substantial buildings and regular schedules of performances. George Washington himself attended plays, and opposition to the theater as "the house of the devil" declined, though it by no means disappeared. But the American dramatist, like the writer of books and the contributor to magazines, had to compete with English authors, who did not have to be paid royalties.

Under the circumstances, it is surprising that the young republic contained so many able and active poets, essayists, novelists, and playwrights as it did. Among the most active poets and essayists were the "Hartford Wits," a group of Connecticut writers who met together for sociability and mutual encouragement. The leaders were Joel Barlow, Timothy Dwight, and John Trumbull (not to be confused with the contemporary painter of the same name). These men wrote epics on American greatness and satires on American foibles—as seen from a solid, Federalist, New England point of view. Barlow eventually went over to the Jeffersonian side, but the ablest and most thoroughgoing Jeffersonian poet, a hardy foe of the Hartford Wits, was Philip Freneau of New Jersey.

Novels became the rage in England during the last half of the eighteenth century, and their popularity spread to the United States, where the latest English successes were promptly imported, reprinted, and eagerly read. The most fashionable themes were sex and sentimentality, satire, and terror. When novelists finally appeared in America, they hoped to produce a native, original kind of fiction, but they had to appeal to the prevailing taste. They used essentially the same themes as the English novelists, though substituting American scenes and situations for English ones.

Most of the songs popular during and after the Revolution consisted of new and patriotic words set to familiar English tunes. "Yankee Doodle" was written during the French and Indian War by a British army surgeon with the intention of poking fun at the ragged colonial troops. It became a favorite with the Yankees themselves, and during the Revolution they added many variations, some of them unsuitable for polite company. Other popular music was written by Francis Hopkinson, the first notable American composer and a man of amazing versatility. The first student to be graduated from the College of Philadelphia, Hopkinson practiced law, served in the first Continental Congress and signed the Declaration of Independence, wrote verse, essays, and Revolutionary pamphlets, painted, gave public performances on the harpsichord, and sat as a judge in Pennsylvania and federal courts, besides composing music. A collection of his best work was published under the title of *Seven Songs* (1788). His son, the eminent lawyer Joseph Hopkinson, wrote the words for "Hail, Columbia" during the undeclared war with France (1798); for many years, this stirring song remained the nearest equivalent to a national anthem.

## Churches and Religion

Americans of the young republic might have been patriotic enough but, from the point of view of many a religious leader, they were insufficiently pious. The religious excitement of the Great Awakening had passed, and sermons of the Revolutionary era lamented the "decay of vital piety," the "degeneracy of manners," and the luxurious growth of "vice."

Certainly large numbers of the people were turning away from familiar faiths. Many interested themselves in deism, the rational religion of Enlightenment philosophers, especially those in France. The deists believed in God but considered Him a rather remote being who had created the universe, not an intimate presence who was concerned with human individuals and their sins. Franklin, Jefferson, and others among the Founding Fathers held deistic views. Such views, at first confined to the well-educated, finally spread among the people at large. By 1800, books and articles attacking religious "superstitions" found eager readers all over the country. The most influential of such writings, Thomas Paine's *The Age of Reason* (1794–1796), was discussed in homes, colleges, taverns, stagecoaches, everywhere. Paine once declared that Christianity was the "strangest religion ever set up," for "it committed a murder upon Jesus in order to redeem mankind from the sin of eating an apple." No wonder the preachers regularly denounced Paine and deism and called for a new revival of religious faith.

While resisting the spread of free thought, the churches also had to deal with other problems. After the Declaration of Independence the groups with foreign ties had to reconsider their position, and even those without such ties faced the task of reorganizing on a national basis. As population moved westward, the churches had to follow the frontier if they were to grow with the country's growth. In responding to the challenges of the time, some denominations succeeded much better than others. New sects arose. The grim doctrines of Calvinism gave way to more optimistic faiths, and the religious pattern of the young republic became even more variegated than that of colonial America had been.

## A Camp Meeting

Originating in 1800, the camp meeting soon became a popular American religious institution in rural areas, especially in the South and West. By 1820, about 1,000 meetings a year were held. The painting reproduced here was made in the 1830's. A typical camp meeting (in Maryland, in 1806) was described by a participant who wrote of the tents, the wagons, the plank seats, the covered stand for the preacher, and the daily schedule. "At day break the trumpets were blown round the camp for the people to rise 20 minutes afterward for family prayer at the door of every tent—if fair weather—at sunrise they blew at the stand for public prayer, and then breakfasted. At

10 oclock they blew for preaching—by 2 ocl. dinner was to be over in every tent. At 3 ocl. preaching again, and again at night." After several days of this, "hundreds were prostrate upon the earth before the Lord. . . . Will I ever see anything more like the day of Judgment on this side of eternity—to see the people running, yes, running, from every direction to the stand, weeping, shouting, and shouting for joy. Prayer was then made—and every Brother fell upon the neck of his Brother, and the Sisters did likewise. Then we parted. O! glorious day they went home singing and shouting." (Courtesy of the New-York Historical Society, New York City)

The Congregationalists, who led in numbers and influence at the close of the colonial period, soon lost their preeminence. They continued to be tax-supported in Massachusetts, Connecticut, and New Hampshire even after those colonies were transformed into states. But the Congregationalists lacked the missionary zeal, appealing theology, and strong, centralized organization that were essential for winning and holding converts.

In New England, its home ground, the Congregational Church was weakened by the growing popularity of universalist and unitarian doctrines. Many of its members rejected not only the idea of predestination but also the idea of the Trinity. They believed that salvation was available to all, and that God was one (not

three), Jesus being only a great religious teacher and not the son of God. The Universalist Church came into existence (1779) when believers in universal salvation began to hold meetings in Gloucester, Massachusetts. A little later the Unitarian Church was founded in Boston (1782).

American Presbyterians adopted a constitution (1789) by which the whole country was divided into sixteen presbyteries and four synods, with a general assembly that served as the highest ecclesiastical court. Already well entrenched on the frontier, where so many of the Scotch-Irish had settled before the Revolution, the Church expanded with the expanding nation. Indeed, it grew too fast for the maintenance of internal harmony. Bickering reappeared between Old and New Lights, between traditional Calvinists and believers in salvation for all. New sects splintered off, as did the followers of Thomas and Alexander Campbell, who in the early 1800s rejected the Calvinist dogma of limited election. Later the Campbellites formed a separate church known as the Disciples of Christ.

Among the Baptists, as among the Presbyterians, there were disputes about the question of predestination or free will, but theological differences did not prevent the Baptists from growing more rapidly than any other denomination except one (the Methodist) during the late eighteenth and early nineteenth century. Scattered over the whole country, they were especially numerous in Virginia and the Carolinas. Long the most militant advocates of the separation of church and state, they ceased to impress others as dangerous radicals after this principle was adopted in the Virginia statute of religious liberty and in the federal Bill of Rights.

More than the Baptists or any other religious group, the Roman Catholics gained in prestige (though not in numbers) as a consequence of the Revolution. On the advice of Charles Carroll of Carrollton, a Maryland statesman and Catholic lay leader, most of the Catholics in America supported the Patriot cause during the war. The French alliance brought Catholic troops and chaplains to this country. In such times as these, Catholic Americans no longer seemed, as in colonial days, like agents of the devil. After the war the Vatican provided for the United States a church government separate from that of England. In 1784 Father John Carroll was appointed head of Catholic missions in this country, and with the elaboration of the American hierarchy he was made the first American bishop (1789) and finally Archbishop of Baltimore (1808).

The Anglicans suffered more than any other religious group as a result of the Revolution. They were badly divided on the issues of the war, the clergy being mostly Loyalist in the states where Anglicans were few, and partly Loyalist in Virginia and Maryland. In these two states the Anglican Church had benefited from tax support, which was lost when the Church

was disestablished. In other states the Church had depended upon aid from the mother country, and that aid was withdrawn. By the end of the war a large proportion of the parishes lacked clergymen, for there were few recruits to take the places of those who had died or had left the country as Loyalist refugees. Since there never had been an American bishop or an intercolonial organization of the Church, postwar Anglican leaders had to start from scratch in setting up an independent, national hierarchy. By 1789 they had succeeded in organizing the Protestant Episcopal Church. Until after the War of 1812 the Church remained weak, gaining few members and losing many with the departure of the Methodists.

John Wesley, the founder of Methodism, did not set up a new church in England, nor did he intend to do so in America. In 1776, ten years after his lay ministers had begun to organize Methodist "classes" in the colonies, American Methodists insisted that they were not "common dissenters" but " a religious society in communion with the Church of England." But the war changed their attitude. When peace came, the greatest of Wesley's agents in America, Francis Asbury, concluded that American conditions required the formation of a separate body. In 1784 Asbury called a meeting of Methodist preachers at Baltimore, and launched the Methodist Church, with himself as the first bishop.

The Methodists had a unique and effective organization. It was authoritarian, with power concentrated at the top in the hands of the bishops. The preachers were itinerants: each of them had charge of several widely scattered congregations and rode the rounds from one to another. Every year the preachers met in a conference (by 1796 there were six annual conferences in different parts of the country) where a bishop conferred with them, ordained new ministers, and assigned all the riders to their circuits, making frequent changes. This system was well adapted to a growing, moving, frontier society. As the historian W. W. Sweet has said, the Presbyterian minister in the West "was called by the people," the Baptist farmer-preacher "came with the people," and the Methodist circuit-rider "was sent to the people."

The circuit-rider brought a message of individual responsibility for eternal happiness. It was a welcome message. The Methodist Church, within sixty years after its foundation, became the largest in the United States.

Along with the Baptists and the Presbyterians, the Methodists gained many converts in the Second Awakening, a new wave of revivalism that swept the country at the turn of the century. This revivalism had two distinct phases. It began among the Presbyterians in certain colleges of the East and South, reaching its height at Yale under the leadership of President Timothy Dwight (1797–1817). Then, with zealous graduates carrying the evangelical spirit to the West, it went to even greater extremes on the frontier. In 1800, in Kentucky, the Presbyterians held the first camp meeting, an outdoor revival that lasted several days. The Methodists soon took up the camp-meeting technique, and the circuit-rider Peter Cartwright won fame as the most effective soul-saver of all backwoods revivalists. The camp meeting was a Methodist "harvest time," as Bishop Asbury said. It became increasingly popular, the bishop noting with satisfaction in 1811 that 400 camp meetings were to be held that year. Crowds of sinners as well as salvation seekers attended these open-air get-togethers, and the atmosphere sometimes was far from church-like. Many Presbyterians, especially Campbellites, came to frown on the camp meeting. Even Cartwright deplored the worst outbreaks of frenzy, when men and women had fits, rolled in the dust, and lay twitching with the "holy jerks."

After 1800 the devil and the deists were on the run. Freethinkers by no means disappeared (the young Abraham Lincoln took up free thought in frontier Illinois) but they were put upon the defensive. The great majority of Americans subscribed to some variant of revealed Christianity, though it usually was not quite the same as the predominant faith of their forefathers. The churches in the nineteenth century placed more emphasis on the New Testament and the saving grace of Jesus and less emphasis on the Old Testament and the stern decrees of Jehovah than those of the seventeenth or even the eighteenth century had done.

## EMERGING INDUSTRIALISM

While religious patterns were changing, so were industrial techniques, even more fundamentally. A new technology was developing, which was to have profound effects upon the future of the United States.

### Some New Technology

In part, the new technology came from England, where the Industrial Revolution was beginning at the time the American Revolution occurred. The essence of the Industrial Revolution was simply this: more rapidly and extensively than ever before, power-driven machines were taking the place of hand-operated tools. To tend the machines, workers were brought together in factories or mills located at the sources of power. New factory towns arose, with a new class of dependent laborers and another of millowners or industrial capitalists. The factory system was adapted most readily to the manufacture of cotton thread and cloth. In textile making, invention called forth invention. Improvements in weaving made necessary improvements in spinning so that the spinners could keep up with the weavers, and these improvements required new devices for carding, that is, combing and straightening the fibers for the spinner. Water, wind, and animal power continued to be used but began to be supplemented and replaced by steam. This was especially true after the appearance of James Watt's steam engine (patented in 1769), which, though cumbersome and inefficient, was a great improvement upon Thomas Newcomen's earlier "atmospheric" engine.

Though Americans copied all they could from England, the Industrial Revolution in the United States was largely an indigenous growth, with roots extending far back into the colonial period.

When English imports were cut off by the prewar boycott and then by the Revolutionary War, desperate efforts were made to stimulate the manufacture of certain necessities in America. Homespun became both patriotic and fashionable, and to speed up the output of linens and woolens a few of the states gave loans or

## Whitney's Gun Factory

The factory, construction of which began in 1798, was well located on Mill River and on the new turnpike from New Haven to Hartford, in Connecticut. At the right of the picture is a covered wooden truss bridge by which the turnpike crossed the river. At the left of the bridge are two large buildings (with a flume for water power) that housed the machine shops. Farther to the left, on the opposite side of the road, is a row of stone dwellings for the workmen. In the right foreground are the forging shop and a group of storehouses. From a painting made about 1825 by William Giles Munson, a resident of New Haven. (Courtesy of Yale University Art Gallery)

bounties for the making of wire for card teeth. Several of the states offered loans or bounties for the production of cannon, gunpowder, camp kettles, and other war material. Public efforts to encourage industry continued after the war, and to these a bit of tariff protection was added after the adoption of the Constitution. Private companies were formed, and one of these with Alexander Hamilton as a sponsor founded the town of Paterson, New Jersey (1791), to exploit the available water power for manufacturing.

Still, the American textile industry lagged behind that of England. Capital was scarce in the United States, even after certain American shipowners began to invest some of their shipping profits in textile mills. For years, prospects of profit were dim because of the abundance of cheap English imports, and the machinery available remained inferior to the steadily progressing English inventions. To protect England's superior position as a manufacturing nation, the British government tried to prevent the export of textile machinery and the emigration of skilled mechanics. Nevertheless, a number of mechanics and mill-wrights made their way to the United States, the most important of them being Samuel Slater. In 1790, with the aid of American mechanics, Slater built a spinning mill for the Quaker merchant Moses Brown at Pawtucket, Rhode Island. Though a few inferior spinning mills already were in operation, Slater's work is generally considered as the beginning of the factory system in America.

In textiles and in some other manufactured goods the young republic did not measure up to England. Americans generally produced the coarser kinds of yarn and cloth, and though they supplied their own needs in common metalware, they still imported the finer grades of cutlery and other metal products. Yet in certain respects American industry was neither imitative nor inferior, and some American inventors and engineers were equal to the greatest in the world. They were especially advanced in certain new techniques of mass production.

One of the most ingenious mechanics of his time was Oliver Evans, a Delaware farmer's son. Evans invented a card-making machine, constructed an automatic flour mill, improved upon the steam engine, and combined theory and practice in America's first textbook of mechanical engineering, *The Young Mill-Wright's and Miller's Guide* (1795). In his flour mill, which he put into operation the same year the constitutional convention met (1787), all the work was done by a variety of machines geared to the same water wheel. Only two men were needed. At one end of the mill a man emptied bags of wheat, and at the other end a man closed and rolled away barrels full of flour. Here was history's first continuous automatic production line, the beginning of automation.

Another pioneer in mass production was the Massachusetts-born, Yale-educated Eli Whitney. He is best known for the cotton gin, but he is even more important for the revolution he accomplished in the manufacture of guns.

The rise of the textile industry in England and America created a tremendous demand for the cotton that planters had begun to grow in the American South. But the planters were faced with the problem of separating the seeds from the cotton fast enough to meet the demand. There was a variety of cotton with smooth black seeds and long fibers that were easily cleaned, but this "long-staple" or "sea-island" variety could be grown successfully only along the coast or on the offshore islands of Georgia and South Carolina. There was also a short-staple cotton that could be raised almost anywhere in the South, but its sticky green seeds were very difficult to remove, a skilled slave being able to clean no more than a few pounds a day by hand. The planters were casting about for a machine or "gin" (that is, an engine) to clean the short-staple cotton when Whitney, then serving as a tutor on the Georgia plantation of General Nathanael Greene's widow, made his famous invention in 1793.

The gin was quite simple. A toothed roller caught the fibers of the cotton boll and pulled them between the wires of a grating, which held back the seeds, and a revolving brush re-moved the lint from the roller's teeth. But the gin had momentous consequences. With it, one slave could clean cotton as fast as several could by hand. Soon cotton growing spread into the upland South, and within a decade the total crop increased eightfold. Slavery, which with the decline of tobacco production had become a dying institution, was now revived, expanded, and firmly fixed upon the South.

During the undeclared war with France (1798–1800) all-out war was expected, and so the army needed many thousands of muskets in a hurry. Muskets then were made one at a time, and no two of them exactly alike, by skilled gunsmiths. There were not enough gunsmiths, and there was not enough time to meet the army's anticipated need. But Whitney had a plan. He made a contract with the government for the delivery of 10,000 muskets within two years. He designed a machine to make each of the parts exactly according to a pattern. Then all he had to do was to assemble the guns. This was the beginning of standardized quantity production through the manufacture of interchangeable parts. Before long, the same system was used for making clocks, and eventually it was applied to sewing machines and many other complicated products.

By fastening cotton and slavery upon the South, Whitney's gin contributed to the coming of the Civil War. His techniques of mass production, by building up the industrial strength of the North, helped the Union to win the war that the gin did so much to bring on. Such were some of the aftereffects of the industrial developments in the period of the young republic. There were also other political and social consequences of the changes then just getting under way. In America as in England, though somewhat more slowly, the Industrial Revolution created new classes and class conflicts, hastened the growth of crowded manufacturing towns, and gave rise to troublesome political issues, such as the perennial issue of the protective tariff.

## Transportation and Trade

Before the full potential of the Industrial Revolution could be realized in the United States, transportation had to be improved. What was needed was a system of roads and waterways that would connect all parts of the country and create a market extensive enough to justify production on a reasonably large scale. In the late eighteenth and early nineteenth century, goods still moved far more cheaply by water than by land. For the Atlantic seaports, ocean commerce with other continents was more easily carried on than overland trade with American settlements west of the Appalachian range. As Charles and Mary Beard have written, "the streets of London, the quays of Lisbon, and the Hong of Canton were more familiar sights to the merchants of the coast than were the somber forests and stump-studded clearings of Western America."

Temporarily, the Revolutionary War unsettled merchant shipping, as the British navy drove American merchantmen and fishing vessels from the seas. But, before the war was over, Americans learned to evade the enemy with light, fast, maneuverable ships. Indeed, the Yankees began to prey upon British commerce with hundreds of privateers. For many a shipowner, privateering proved to be more profitable than ordinary peacetime trade.

When, in 1785, the *Empress of China* returned to New York from Canton, she brought back a cargo of silk and tea, which yielded a fabulous profit. Within five years Yankee ships were trading regularly with the Far East. Generally these ships carried various manufactured goods around Cape Horn to California, exchanged them for hides and furs, and with these proceeded on across the Pacific, to barter them in China.

Not only in China but also in Europe and the Near East enterprising Yankees from Salem and other ports sought out every possible opportunity for commerce. These Yankees were aided by two acts of the new Congress (1789) giving preference in tariff rates and port duties to homeowned ships. American shipping was greatly stimulated (despite the loss of ships and cargoes seized by the belligerents) by the outbreak of European war in the 1790s. Yankee vessels took over most of the carrying trade between Europe and the European colonies in the Western Hemisphere.

As early as 1793, the young republic had come to possess a merchant marine and a foreign trade larger than those of any other country except England. In proportion to its population, the United States had more ships and commerce than any other nation in the world. And the shipping business was growing fast. Between 1789 and 1810 the total tonnage of American vessels engaged in overseas traffic rose from less than 125,000 to nearly 1 million. The country's exports carried in American ships increased from 30 to 90 per cent, and imports from 17.5 to 93 per cent.

Transportation and trade within the United States labored under handicaps, but improvements were steadily being made. In river transportation a new era began with the development of the steamboat. Oliver Evans' high-pressure engine, lighter and more efficient than James Watt's, made steam more feasible for powering boats as well as mill machinery and eventually the locomotive. Even before the high-pressure engine was available, a number of inventors experimented with steam-powered craft, and John Fitch exhibited to some of the delegates at the constitutional convention a forty-five-foot vessel with paddles operated by steam. The perfecting of the steamboat was chiefly the work of the inventor Robert Fulton and the promoter Robert R. Livingston. Their *Clermont,* equipped with paddle wheels and an English-built engine, voyaged up the Hudson in the summer of 1807, demonstrating the practicability of steam navigation even though taking thirty hours to go 150 miles. In 1811 a partner of Livingston's, Nicholas J. Roosevelt, introduced the steamboat to the West by sending the *New Orleans* from Pittsburgh down the Ohio and Mississippi. The next year this vessel entered upon a profitable career of fairly regular service between New Orleans and Natchez.

Meanwhile, in land transportation, the turnpike era had begun. In 1792 a corporation constructed a toll road the sixty miles from Philadelphia to Lancaster, with a hard-packed surface of crushed rock. This venture proved so successful that similar turnpikes (so named from the kind of tollgate frequently used) were laid out from other cities to neighboring towns. Since the turnpikes were built and operated for private profit, construction costs had to be low

## Fulton's Famous Voyage [1807]

In August, 1807, Robert Fulton wrote this letter to his friend Joel Barlow, a diplomat and poet, one of the group of authors known as the "Hartford Wits":

*My steamboat voyage to Albany and back has turned out rather more favourable than I had calculated. The distance from New York to Albany is 150 miles; I ran it up in thirty-two hours, and down in thirty hours; the latter is just five miles an hour. I had a light breeze against me the whole way going and coming, so that no use was made of my sails, and the voyage has been performed wholly by the power of the steam engine. I overtook many sloops and schooners beating to windward, and passed them as if they had been at anchor.*

*The power of propelling boats by steam is now fully proved. The morning I left New York, there were not perhaps thirty persons in the city who believed that the boat would ever move one mile an hour, or be of the least utility; and while we were putting off from the wharf, which was crowded with spectators, I heard a number of sarcastic remarks. This is the way, you know, in which ignorant men compliment what they call philosophers and projectors.*

*Having employed much time, and money and zeal, in accomplishing this work, it gives me, as it will you, great pleasure to see it so fully answer my expectations. It will give a cheap and quick conveyance to merchandise on the Mississippi and Missouri, and other great rivers, which are now laying open their treasures to the enterprise of our countrymen. And although the prospect of personal emolument has been some inducement to me, yet I feel infinitely more pleasure in reflecting with you on the immense advantage that my country will derive from the invention.*

enough and the prospective traffic heavy enough to assure an early and ample return. Therefore these roads, radiating from Eastern cities, ran for comparatively short distances and through rather thickly settled areas. If similar highways were to be extended over the mountains, the state governments or the federal government would have to finance the construction, at least in part.

## City and Country

The young republic was a land of remarkable diversity—in learning, in literary tastes, in religion, and in economic and social development. Much of the country remained a wilderness, yet its leading cities ranked in size and urban sophistication with the largest of England and Europe, except for such national capitals as London and Paris. The United States had no comparable capital of politics, science, literature, and art.

The total population rose from less than 4 million by the first census (1790) to well over 5 million by the second (1800). At this time, only three people in a hundred lived in towns of more than 8,000. Ten in a hundred lived west of the Appalachian Mountains. Though Virginia was still the most populous of the states, it contained none of the largest cities. Philadelphia (70,000) ranked first; New York (60,000) was close behind; and next in order were Baltimore (26,000), Boston (24,000), and Charleston (20,000).

Washington City, the newly founded national capital, was only a raw and straggling village, the entire District of Columbia containing no more than 3,200 people. Its broad but unpaved avenues radiated from the uncompleted Capitol and the President's house in accordance with the elaborate plan of the French architect, P. C. L'Enfant. This small town provided a new focus for the growing nationalism of Americans, and it symbolized their grand hopes for the future of their country. President Adams and his wife Abigail, sacrificing the comforts and attractions of Philadelphia, moved to Washington in 1800. And here President-elect Jefferson was inaugurated the following year.

## JEFFERSON IN POWER

Long afterwards Jefferson referred to his party's victory as "the revolution of 1800," but in his inaugural address of 1801, trying to sweeten the bitterness of the recent campaign, he emphasized the common principles of the two parties while restating the principles of his own. Noting that the country was separated by a wide ocean from the "devastating havoc" of the European war, he recommended a foreign policy of "peace, commerce, and honest friendship with all nations, entangling alliances with none"— much as George Washington had done in his Farewell Address. With respect to domestic affairs, Jefferson proposed a "wise and frugal government" that would leave men free to "regu-

late their own pursuits of industry." Yet he also favored the "encouragement of agriculture and of commerce as its handmaid."

### President and Party Leader

From the outset Jefferson acted in a spirit of democratic simplicity, which was quite in keeping with the frontier-like character of the raw city of Washington, but which was very different from the ceremonial splendor of former Federalist administrations in the metropolis of Philadelphia. He walked like an ordinary citizen to and from his inauguration at the capital, instead of riding in a coach at the head of a procession. In the presidential mansion he disregarded the courtly etiquette of his predecessors, widower that he was, without a First Lady to take charge of social affairs. At state dinners, adopting the "rule of pell-mell," he let his guests scramble for places at the table. He did not always bother to dress up, and the fastidious minister from Great Britain complained of being received by the President in slippers that

**Washington City**

A sketch of the neighborhood into which President and Mrs. Adams moved in 1800. The President's residence is the most distant building, to the left of the center of the picture. The building was not to be known as the White House until after it had been burned during the War of

1812 and then had been reconstructed and painted white. This drawing by N. King, made probably in 1799 and published in 1805, is the earliest known picture of what was to become the White House. (Culver)

were down at the heels, and coat and pantaloons that were "indicative of utter slovenliness and indifference to appearances."

Even at his best, the tall, freckle-faced sandy-haired Jefferson did not make a very impressive appearance, what with his shyness, his awkward posture, and his shambling gait. Yet, though a rather ineffective public speaker, he charmed his guests in conversation and he wrote with greater literary skill than any President before or since, with the possible exceptions of Abraham Lincoln and Woodrow Wilson. More than that, he was a genius with a wider diversity of talents than any other President, without exception. Besides being a politician and a diplomat, he was an architect, educator, inventor, scientific farmer, and philosopher-scientist, who diverted himself with such pastimes as sorting the bones of prehistoric animals. As a shrewd and practical politician, he was excelled by no other President, though he was equaled by Lincoln and by Franklin D. Roosevelt.

Jefferson was a strong executive, but neither his principles nor his nature inclined him to dictate to Congress. To avoid even the semblance of dictation, and to indulge his distaste for public speaking, he decided not to deliver his messages to Congress in person as Presidents Washington and Adams had done. Instead, he submitted his messages in writing, thus setting a precedent which was followed for more than a century, until President Wilson revived the practice of addressing Congress in person. Yet Jefferson, as party leader, gave direction to his fellow partisans among the senators and representatives, by quiet and sometimes by rather devious means.

To his cabinet he appointed a group of Republicans who were like-minded with him but were more than mere yes-men. Two of the ablest were the Secretary of State, James Madison, and the Secretary of the Treasury, Albert Gallatin. Madison, Jefferson's long-time neighbor and friend, continued to be so close a collaborator that, throughout Jefferson's Presidency, it is hard to tell how much of the impetus to policy came from the President himself and how much from the Secretary of State, particularly in foreign affairs. Gallatin, born in Switzerland, his speech marked by a French accent, was as

## Jefferson's First Inaugural [1801]

*We are all Republicans, we are all Federalists. If there be any among us who would wish to dissolve this Union or to change its republican form, let them stand undisturbed as monuments of the safety with which error of opinion may be tolerated where reason is left free to combat it. I know, indeed, that some honest men fear that a republican government can not be strong, that this Government is not strong enough; but would the honest patriot, in the full tide of successful experiment, abandon a government which has so far kept us free and firm on the theoretic and visionary fear that this Government, the world's best hope, may by possibility want energy to preserve itself? I trust not. I believe this, on the contrary, the strongest Government on earth. I believe it the only one where every man, at the call of the law, would fly to the standard of the law, and would meet invasions of the public order as his own personal concern. Sometimes it is said that man can not be trusted with the government of himself. Can he, then, be trusted with the government of others? Or have we found angels in the forms of kings to govern him? Let history answer this question.*

able a public financier as the great Hamilton had been and was, in addition, a thoroughgoing democrat, who at the time of the Whiskey Rebellion had used his talents as a lawyer to defend the tax-resisting farmers of the Pennsylvania frontier.

Jefferson used patronage as a political weapon. Like Washington before him, he believed that federal offices should be filled with men loyal to the principles and policies of the administration. True, he did not attempt a sudden and drastic removal of Federalist officeholders, possibly because of assurances to the contrary that had been given in his name when Federalist votes in Congress were needed to break the tie with Burr. Yet, at every convenient opportunity, he replaced the holdovers from the Adams administration with his own trusted followers. By the end of his first term about half the government jobs, and by the end of his second term practically all of them, were held by good Republicans. The President punished Burr and the Burrites by withholding patronage from them; he never forgave the man whom he believed guilty of plotting to frustrate the intentions of the party and the ambitions of its rightful candidate.

A tie vote between the presidential and vice-presidential candidates of the same party could not occur again. The Twelfth Amendment, added to the Constitution in 1804 before the election of that year, by implication recognized the function of political parties; it stipulated that the electors should vote for President and Vice President as separate and distinct candidates. Burr had no chance to run on the ticket with Jefferson a second time. In place of Burr, the congressional caucus of Republicans nominated his New York factional foe, George Clinton. The Federalist nominee, C. C. Pinckney, made a poor showing against the popular Jefferson, who carried even the New England states except Connecticut and was reelected by the overwhelming electoral majority of 162 to 14, while the Republican membership of both houses of Congress was increased.

During his second term Jefferson lost some of his popularity, and he had to deal with a revolt within the party ranks. His brilliant but erratic relative John Randolph of Roanoke, the House leader, turned against him, accused him of acting like a Federalist instead of a state-rights Republican, and mustered a handful of anti-Jefferson factionalists who called themselves "Quids."

Randolph became a fanatic on the subject of the Yazoo land claims. These arose from the action of the Georgia legislature, which, before ceding its territorial rights to the federal government, had made and then canceled a grant of millions of acres along the Mississippi to the Yazoo Land Companies. Jefferson favored a compromise settlement that would have satisfied both the state of Georgia and the Yazoo investors, many of whom were Northern Republicans whose support he needed. But Randolph, insisting that the claims were fraudulent, charged the President and the President's friends with complicity in corruption. A number of Randolph's colleagues in Congress were investors in the land companies or supporters of their claims, and time and again the tall, skinny Virginian would point his bony finger at one or another of these men and shriek "Yazoo!" He prevented the government from making any settlement of the question until after both he and Jefferson were out of office.

Randolph had a special antipathy toward Madison, whom he considered as one of the worst of the Yazoo men. He did all he could, which was not enough, to prevent Madison's nomination for the Presidency in 1808. Jefferson refused to consider a third term for himself, for he was opposed to it in principle, unlike Washington, who had declined to run again in 1796 only because he was weary of public office. Jefferson's refusal established a tradition against a third term for any President, a tradition that remained unbroken until Franklin D. Roosevelt was elected for a third time in 1940 (and then for a fourth time in 1944). Though unwilling himself to be a candidate in 1808, Jefferson was determined that his *alter ego*, Madison, should succeed him and carry on his policies without a break.

## Conflict With the Courts

The Federalists had used the courts as a means of strengthening their party and persecuting the opposition, or so it seemed to the Republicans, and soon after Jefferson's first inauguration his followers in Congress launched a counterattack against the Federalist-dominated judiciary. They repealed the Naturalization Act, changing the residence period for citizenship of foreigners from fourteen to five years, and they allowed the hated Alien and Sedition Acts to expire. Then they repealed the Judiciary Act of 1801, abolishing the new circuit courts and arranging for each of the Supreme Court justices to sit with a district judge on circuit duty. As President, Jefferson did not have the power to remove Adams' "midnight appointees" from their newly created jobs, but Congress achieved the same object by pulling their benches out from under them, despite Federalist protests that the repeal violated the constitutional provision that judges should hold office during good behavior for life.

In the debate on the question of the Judiciary Act of 1801 the Federalists maintained that the Supreme Court had the power of reviewing acts of Congress and disallowing those that conflicted with the Constitution. The Constitution itself said nothing about such a power of judicial review, but Hamilton in one of *The Federalist* papers had argued that the Supreme Court should have the power, and the Court actually had exercised it as early as 1796, though upholding the law of Congress then in question. In 1803, in the case of *Marbury* v. *Madison,* the Court for the first time declared a congressional act, or part of one, unconstitutional. (Not for more than half a century, in the Dred Scott case of 1857, did the Court do so a second time.)

William Marbury, one of President Adams' "midnight appointments," had been named as a justice of the peace in the District of Columbia, but his commission, though duly signed and sealed, had not been delivered to him at the time Adams left the Presidency. Madison, as Jefferson's secretary of state, refused to hand over the commission, and so Marbury applied to the Supreme Court for an order (writ of mandamus) directing Madison to perform his official duty.

The Chief Justice of the United States was John Marshall, a leading Federalist and prominent lawyer of Virginia, whom President Adams had appointed in 1801. (For the remainder of Adams' term, Marshall had continued to serve also as secretary of state. It was he himself who, in that capacity, had neglected to see that Marbury's commission was delivered.) Marshall never forgot his experiences with Washington's army during the Revolution. Having shared the sufferings at Valley Forge, he retained a vivid impression of the evils of a weak, divided, and inefficient form of government. As chief justice, he did his best to give the government unity and strength.

In the case of *Marbury* v. *Madison,* Marshall decided that Marbury had a right to the commission but that the Court had no power to issue

## Marbury v. Madison [1803]

Chief Justice Marshall:

*It is emphatically the province and duty of the judicial department to say what the law is. Those who apply the rule to particular cases must of necessity expound and interpret that rule. If two laws conflict with each other, the courts must decide on the operation of each.*

*So if a law be in opposition to the constitution; if both the law and the constitution apply to a particular case, so that the court must either decide that case conformably to the law, disregarding the constitution, or conformably to the constitution, disregarding the law, the court must determine which of these conflicting rules governs the case. This is of the very essence of judicial duty.*

*If, then, the courts are to regard the constitution, and the constitution is superior to any ordinary act of the legislature, the constitution, and not such ordinary act, must govern the case to which they both apply.*

the order. True, the original Judiciary Act of 1789 had conferred such a power upon the Court, but, said Marshall, the powers of the Court had been defined in the Constitution itself, and Congress could not rightfully enlarge them. Marshall did not claim, however, that only the federal judges could decide what the Constitution meant; he implied that each of the three branches of the federal government could decide for itself. In delivering his opinion, he went out of his way to discredit the Jefferson administration, yet shrewdly avoided an open conflict. Since he decided the immediate question (whether Madison should be ordered to deliver Marbury's commission) in Madison's favor, the administration had no opportunity to defy the Chief Justice by disobeying his decision.

While the case of *Marbury* v. *Madison* was

still pending, President Jefferson prepared for a renewed assault upon that Federalist stronghold, the judiciary. If he could not remove the most obnoxious of the judges directly, perhaps he could do so indirectly through the process of impeachment. According to the Constitution, the House of Representatives was empowered to bring impeachment charges against any civil officer for "high crimes and misdemeanors," and the Senate sitting as a court was authorized to try the officer on the charges. Jefferson sent evidence to the House to show that one of the district judges, John Pickering of New Hampshire, was unfit for his position. The House accordingly impeached him, and the Senate, despite his obvious insanity, found him guilty of high crimes and misdemeanors. He was removed.

Later the Republicans went after bigger game, one of the justices of the Supreme Court itself. Justice Samuel Chase, a rabidly partisan Federalist, had applied the Sedition Act with seeming brutality and had delivered political speeches from the bench, insulting President Jefferson and denouncing the Jeffersonian doctrine of equal liberty and equal rights. In doing so, Chase was guilty of no high crime or misdemeanor in the constitutional sense, and he was only saying what thousands of Federalists believed. Some of the Republicans came to the conclusion, however, that impeachment should not be viewed merely as a criminal proceeding, and that a judge could properly be impeached for political reasons—for obstructing the other branches of the government and disregarding the will of the people. As for Justice Chase, he could easily be shown to be out of step with Congress, the President, and public opinion, especially after the overwhelming victory of the Republicans in the election of 1804.

At Jefferson's own suggestion, the House of Representatives set up a committee to investigate Chase's conduct. Impeached on the basis of the committee's findings, the justice was brought to trial before the Senate early in 1805. Jefferson did his best to secure a conviction, even temporarily cultivating the friendship of Aaron Burr, who as Vice President presided over the trial. But Burr performed his duties with aloof impartiality, and John Randolph as the impeachment manager bungled the prosecution for the House of Representatives. A majority of the senators finally voted for conviction, but not the necessary two-thirds majority. Chase was acquitted.

From the Republican point of view, the Pickering and Chase impeachments, though only half successful, did considerable good, for they caused the federal judges as a whole to be more discreet and less partisan in statements from the bench. If the Republicans had succeeded in getting rid of Chase, they might have been emboldened to take action against the Chief Justice himself. As things stood, Marshall remained secure in his position, and the political duel between the Chief Justice and the President continued.

## Dollars and Ships

According to the Republicans, the administrations of Washington and Adams had been extravagant. Yearly expenditures had risen so much that by 1800 they were almost three times as high as they had been in 1793, and the public debt also had grown, though not so fast, since revenues had increased considerably. A part of these revenues came from internal taxation, including the hated whiskey excise. In 1802 the Republicans in Congress abolished the whole system of internal taxes, leaving customs duties and land sales as practically the only sources of revenue. Despite the tax cut, the new administration was determined to reduce the public debt by economizing on federal expenses. Secretary of the Treasury Gallatin proceeded to carry out a drastic retrenchment plan, scrimping as much as possible on expenditures for the ordinary operations of the government and effecting what Jefferson called a "chaste reformation" in the army and the navy. The tiny army of 4,000 men was reduced to only 2,500. The navy was pared down from twenty-five ships in commission to seven, and the number of officers and men was cut accordingly.

These reductions in the armed forces reflected other Jeffersonian principles as well as the desire for government economy. Jefferson feared that anything except the smallest of standing armies might become a menace to civil liberties and to civilian control of government. He believed that the navy, while no such threat to the principle of civilian supremacy, was likely to be misused as a means of forcing the expansion of overseas commerce, which he thought should be kept subordinate to agriculture. Yet, though he once said "peace is our passion," Jefferson was far from being a pacifist fanatic. He desired an efficient if small military force, and his administration deserves credit for founding the United States Military Academy at West Point (1802). He also contributed to the efficiency of the navy, even while reducing the size of it, for most of the decommissioned ships were outmoded, and many of the discharged officers were incompetent. And, in spite of himself, he was compelled to reverse his small-navy policy and build up the fleet because of trouble with pirates in the Mediterranean.

For years the Barbary states of North Africa —Morocco, Algiers, Tunis, and Tripoli—had made piracy a national enterprise. They demanded protection money from all nations whose ships sailed the Mediterranean, and even the mistress of the seas, Great Britain, gave regular contributions (she did not particularly desire to eliminate the racket, since it hurt her naval rivals and maritime competitors more seriously than it did her). During the 1780s and 1790s the United States agreed to treaties providing for annual tribute to Morocco and the rest, and from time to time the Adams administration ransomed American sailors who had been captured by the corsairs and were being held as slaves. Jefferson doubted the wisdom of continuing the appeasement policy. "Tribute or war is the usual alternative of these Barbary pirates," he said. "Why not build a navy and decide on war?"

The decision was not left to Jefferson. In 1801 the Pasha of Tripoli, dissatisfied with the American response to his extortionate demands, had the flagpole of the American consulate chopped down, that being his way of declaring war on the United States. Jefferson concluded that, as President, he had a constitutional right to defend the United States without a war declaration by Congress, and he sent a squadron to the relief of the ships already at the scene. Not until 1803, however, was the fleet in the Mediterranean strong enough to take effective action, under Commodores Edward Preble and Samuel

Barron. In 1805 the Pasha, by threatening to kill captive Americans, compelled Barron to agree to a peace that ended the payment of tribute but exacted a large ransom ($60,000) for the release of the prisoners. This was hardly a resounding victory for the United States.

Though the war in Tripoli cost money, Secretary Gallatin pressed on with his plan for diminishing the public debt. He was aided by an unexpected increase in tariff revenues. By the time Jefferson left office, the debt had been cut almost in half (from $83 million to $45 million), despite the expenditure of $15 million to buy Louisiana from Napoleon Bonaparte.

## DOUBLING THE NATIONAL DOMAIN

In the year that Jefferson was elected President of the United States, Napoleon made himself dictator of France with the title of First Consul, and in the year that Jefferson was reelected, Napoleon assumed the name and authority of Emperor. These two men, the democrat and the dictator, had little in common, yet they were good friends in international politics until Napoleon's ambitions leaped from Europe to America and brought about an estrangement.

### Jefferson and Napoleon

Napoleon failed in a grandiose plan to seize the British Empire in India, though he succeeded in the conquest of Italy. Then he was reminded that France at one time had possessed a vast empire of her own in North America. In 1763 her possessions east of the Mississippi had gone to Great Britain, and those west of it to Spain. The former were lost for good, but the latter might be recovered. In 1800 (on the very day after the signing of the peace settlement with the United States) Napoleon arranged for Spain to cede these possessions to him in the secret treaty of San Ildefonso. Thus he got title to Louisiana, which included roughly the whole of the Mississippi Valley to the west of the river, plus New Orleans to the east of the river near its mouth. He intended Louisiana to form the continental heartland of his proposed empire.

Other essential parts of his empire-to-be were

the sugar-rich and strategically valuable West Indian islands which still belonged to France—Guadeloupe, Martinique, and above all Santo Domingo. Unfortunately for his plans, the slaves on Santo Domingo had been inspired by the French Revolution to rise in revolt and create a republic of their own, under the leadership of the remarkable Negro, Toussaint L'Ouverture. Taking advantage of a truce in his war with England, Napoleon sent to the West Indies an army led by his brother-in-law, Charles Leclerc, to put down the insurrection and restore French authority.

Meanwhile, unaware of Napoleon's ultimate aim, Jefferson pursued the kind of foreign policy that was to be expected of such a well-known friend of France. He appointed as the American minister to Paris the ardently pro-French Robert R. Livingston. Continuing and hastening the peace policy of Adams, he carried through the ratification of the Franco-American settlement of 1800 and put it into effect even before it was ratified. With respect to Santo Domingo, however, he did not continue the policy of Adams, who had cooperated with the British in recognizing and supporting the rebel regime of Toussaint. Jefferson assured the French minister in Washington that the American people, especially those of the slaveholding states, did not approve of the Negro revolutionary who was setting a bad example for their own slaves. He even led the French minister to believe that the United States would join with France in putting down the rebellion.

Jefferson began to reappraise the whole subject of American relations with France when he heard rumors of the secret retrocession of Louisiana. "It completely reverses all the political relations of the U.S.," he wrote to Minister Livingston (April 18, 1802). Always before, we had looked to France as our "natural friend." But there was on the earth "one single spot" the possessor of which was "our natural and habitual enemy." That spot was New Orleans, the outlet through which the produce of the fast-growing West was shipped to the markets of the world. If France should actually take and hold New Orleans, Jefferson said, then "we must marry ourselves to the British fleet and nation."

Jefferson was even more alarmed when, in the fall of 1802, he learned that the Spanish intendant in charge at New Orleans had prohibited Americans from continuing to deposit their goods at that port for transshipment from river craft to ocean-going vessels. By the Pinckney Treaty (of 1795) Spain had guaranteed to Americans the right to deposit either at New Orleans or at some other suitable place. Without such a right, Spain's permission to use the lower Mississippi was of little value to the United States.

Westerners suspected, as did Jefferson himself, that Napoleon had procured the closing of the river for sinister purposes of his own. They demanded that something be done to reopen the river, and some of the more extreme among them clamored for war with France, the supposed source of all their troubles. The Federalists of the Northeast, though they had no real concern for the welfare of the West, played upon the discontent of the frontiersmen and encouraged the war cry for political reasons. The more the Federalists could arouse the West, the more they could embarrass the Jefferson administration. The President faced a dilemma. If he yielded to the frontier clamor and sought satisfaction through force, he would run the risk of renewed war with France. If on the other hand, he disregarded the clamor, he would stand to lose the political support of the West.

There was possibly a way out of the dilemma, and that was to purchase from Napoleon the port so indispensable to the United States. Or, assuming that the First Consul should prove unwilling to sell New Orleans, and assuming also that he had acquired East and West Florida along with Louisiana in the secret treaty with Spain, it might be possible to obtain from him all or part of the Floridas, or at least the rights of navigation and deposit on some river flowing into the Gulf of Mexico to the east of New Orleans. Jefferson did not think of trying to buy any part of Louisiana to the west of the Mississippi; he was content, for the time being, to let that river form the boundary between the French empire and the United States. Soon after hearing rumors of the Louisiana retrocession, he instructed Livingston in Paris to negotiate for the purchase of New Orleans, and Livingston on his own authority proceeded to suggest to the French that they might be glad to be rid of the upper part of Louisiana as well.

Jefferson also induced Congress to provide an army and a river fleet, and he allowed the impression to get out that American forces, despite his own desire for peace, might soon descend upon New Orleans. Then he sent a special envoy to work with Livingston in persuading the French to sell. For this extraordinary mission he chose an ideally suited man, James Monroe, who was well remembered in France and who, at the same time, had the confidence of the American frontiersmen; his appointment would reassure them that the President was looking after their interests. Jefferson told Monroe that if he and Livingston could not obtain even the minimum needs of the United States—even the use of the Mississippi or some other river emptying into the Gulf—they were to cross the Channel to England and there discuss some kind of understanding with the British government. Whether Jefferson, in his hints at an attack on New Orleans and an alliance with Great Britain, merely meant to bluff the French, he had no chance to show. While Monroe's coach was still rumbling on its way to Paris, Napoleon suddenly made up his mind to dispose of the entire Louisiana Territory.

Startling though this decision seemed to some of his advisers, Napoleon had good reasons for it. His plans for an American empire had gone awry partly because of certain mischances, which might be summarized in two words—*mosquitoes* and *ice*. The mosquitoes brought yellow fever and death to General Leclerc and to thousands of the soldiers whom Napoleon had sent to reconquer Santo Domingo. The ice, forming earlier than expected in a Dutch harbor as winter came in 1802, delayed the departure of an expeditionary force that Napoleon was readying to reinforce Leclerc's army and also to take possession of Louisiana. By the spring of 1803 it was too late. Napoleon then was expecting a renewal of the European war, and he feared that he would not be able to hold Louisiana if the British, with their superior naval power, should attempt to take it. He also realized that, quite apart from the British threat, there was danger from the United States: he could not prevent the Americans, who were pushing steadily into the Mississippi Valley, from sooner or later overrunning Louisiana.

## The Louisiana Purchase

Napoleon left the negotiations over Louisiana to his finance minister, Barbé-Marbois, rather than his foreign minister, Talleyrand, since Talleyrand was remembered for the X. Y. Z. Affair and was distrusted by Americans, while Barbé-Marbois had their respect, having lived for some time in the United States and having married an American girl. Livingston and Monroe, after the latter's arrival in Paris, had to decide first of all whether they should even consider making a treaty for the purchase of the entire Louisiana Territory, since they had not been authorized by their government to do so. They dared not wait until they could get new instructions from home, for Napoleon in the meantime might change his mind as suddenly as he had made it up. They decided to go ahead, realizing that Jefferson could reject their treaty if he disapproved what they had done. After a little haggling over the price that Barbé-Marbois asked—and he asked and got somewhat more than Napoleon's minimum—Livingston and Monroe put their signatures to the treaty, on April 30, 1803.

By the terms of the purchase arrangement, the United States was to pay 60 million francs directly to the French government and up to 20 million more to American citizens who held claims against France for ship seizures in the past—or a total of approximately $15 million. The United States was also to give France certain commercial privileges in the port of New Orleans, privileges not extended to other countries. Moreover, the United States was to incorporate the people of Louisiana into the Union and grant them as soon as possible the same rights and privileges as other citizens. This seemed to imply that the Louisiana inhabitants were to have the benefits of statehood in the near future. The boundaries were not defined, Louisiana being transferred to the United States simply with the "same extent" as when owned by France and earlier by Spain. When Livingston and Monroe appealed to Talleyrand for his opinion about the boundary, he merely replied: "You have made a noble bargain for

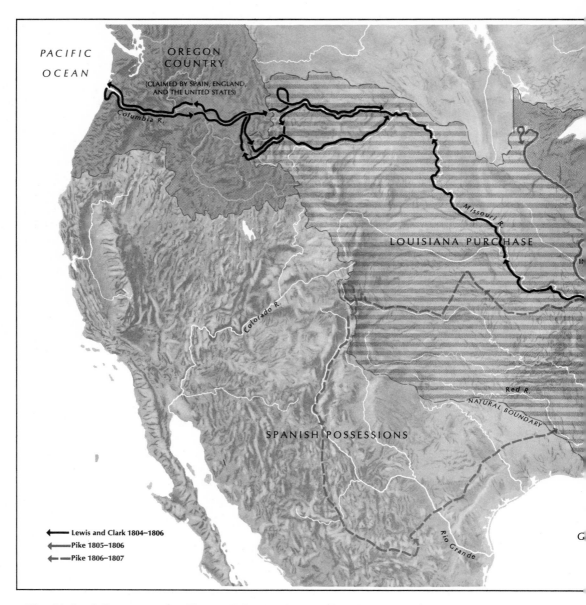

**The United States at the Time of the Louisiana Purchase**

yourselves, and I suppose you will make the most of it."

In Washington, the President was both pleased and embarrassed when he received the treaty. He was glad to get such a "noble bargain," but, according to his oft-repeated views on the Constitution, the United States lacked the constitutional power to accept the bargain. In the past he had always insisted that the fed-

eral government could rightfully exercise only those powers assigned to it in so many words, and nowhere did the Constitution say anything about the acquisition of new territory. Now he thought, at first, that an amendment should be adopted to give the government the specific right to buy additional land; he even went so far as to draft a suitable amendment. But his advisers cautioned him that ratification might

BRITISH AMERICA

MAINE

VERMONT

NEW HAMPSHIRE

NEW YORK

MASSACHUSETTS

RHODE ISLAND

CONNECTICUT

NORTHWEST TERRITORY

PENNSYLVANIA

NEW JERSEY

TORY

DELAWARE

MARYLAND

Ohio R.

VIRGINIA

KENTUCKY

TENNESSEE

NORTH CAROLINA

SOUTH CAROLINA

SSIPPI TORY

GEORGIA

ATLANTIC OCEAN

SPANISH FLORIDA

MEXICO

about it. Finally he gave in, trusting, as he said, "that the good sense of our country will correct the evil of loose construction when it shall produce ill effects." Thus, by implication, he left the question of constitutional interpretation to public opinion, and he cut the ground from under his doctrine of state rights.

When Jefferson called Congress into special session, a few of the die-hard Federalists of New England raised constitutional and other objections to the treaty, but the Senate promptly gave its consent and the House soon passed the necessary appropriation bill. The Spanish minister in Washington protested to Secretary Madison that the transaction was illegal, since Napoleon when acquiring Louisiana had promised never to part with it and also had agreed to provide an Italian kingdom for the son of the Spanish king but had never done so. Madison easily disposed of the protest by reminding the Spanish minister that the latter once had advised the United States to apply to France, not Spain, in response to a query whether Spain would be willing to sell a part of Louisiana.

Though Madison and Jefferson had a good case for the American title to Louisiana itself, they had considerably less justification when, taking advantage of the vagueness of the boundaries, they also claimed part of West Florida as American by virtue of the treaty with France. The Spaniards denied that any of Florida was included in Louisiana, and indeed the two provinces had had separate histories and had been separately administered. To persuade the Spaniards to give up Florida, Jefferson tried both promises of money and threats of force. Despite John Randolph's outraged opposition, the President obtained from Congress an appropriation for secret purposes, one of which was to bribe France to bring pressure upon Spain. It was no use. All of Florida remained in Spanish hands until after Jefferson left the Presidency.

When the United States concluded the purchase treaty with France, Spain was still administering Louisiana, the French never having taken actual possession. They did not take possession until late in 1803, and then only to turn the territory over to General James Wilkinson, the commissioner of the United States and the commander of a small occupation force. In New

be long delayed or possibly defeated, and they assured him that he already possessed all the constitutional power he needed: the President with the consent of the Senate obviously could make treaties, and the treaty-making power would justify the purchase of Louisiana. Years afterward (in 1828) the Supreme Court upheld this view, but Jefferson—strict constructionist that he had been—continued to have doubts

Orleans, beneath a bright December sun, the recently raised French tricolor was brought down and the Stars and Stripes run up. For the time being, Louisiana Territory was given a semimilitary government with officials appointed by the President; later it was organized on the general pattern of the Northwest Territory, with the assumption that it would be divided into states. The first of these was admitted to the Union as the state of Louisiana in 1812.

## Exploring the West

Meanwhile the geography of the far-flung territory was revealed by a series of explorations. Even before he became President, Jefferson as a scientist had been interested in finding out all he could about the nature and extent of the North American continent, and he had encouraged explorers interested in the Far West. After becoming President he renewed his efforts. In 1803, before Napoleon's offer to sell Louisiana, Jefferson planned an expedition that was to cross all the way to the Pacific Ocean

and gather not only geographical facts but also information about the prospects for Indian trade. Congress having secretly provided the necessary funds, Jefferson named as leader of the expedition his private secretary and Virginia neighbor, the thirty-two-year-old Meriwether Lewis, who as a veteran of Indian wars was skilled in wilderness ways. Lewis chose as a colleague the twenty-eight-year-old William Clark, who, like George Rogers Clark, his older brother, and like Lewis himself, was an experienced frontiersman and Indian fighter.

Lewis and Clark, with a chosen company of four dozen hardy men, set up winter quarters in St. Louis at about the time the United States took formal possession of Louisiana. In the spring of 1804 they started up the Missouri River, and with the Shoshoni squaw Sacajawea as their guide, her papoose on her back, they eventually crossed the Rocky Mountains, descended the Snake and the Columbia rivers, and in the late autumn of 1805 encamped on the Pacific coast. In September 1806 they were back again in St. Louis, bringing with them carefully

### The Lewis and Clark Expedition 1804–1806

Patrick Gass, one of the men who accompanied Lewis and Clark, wrote *A Journal of the Voyages and Travels of a Corps of Discovery* (1811), which was the first account of the expedition to be published. This book was illustrated with crude drawings. The one here reproduced was captioned "Captain Lewis & Clark holding a Council with the Indians."

kept records of what they had observed along the way. No longer was the Far West a completely unknown country.

While Lewis and Clark were on their epic journey, Jefferson sent out other explorers to fill in the picture of the Louisiana Territory. The most important of these was Lieutenant Zebulon Montgomery Pike. In the fall of 1805, then only twenty-six, Pike led an expedition from St. Louis up the Mississippi River in search of its source, and though he did not find it, he learned a good deal about the upper Mississippi Valley. In the summer of 1806 Pike was sent out again, this time by Wilkinson instead of Jefferson, to proceed up the valley of the Arkansas. He discovered, but failed in his attempt to climb, the peak that now bears his name. Then he turned southward into Mexico and ran into a Spanish army; he was compelled to surrender his maps and papers and return to the United States. His account of his Western travels left the impression that the land between the Missouri and the Rockies was a desert that American farmers could never cultivate and that ought to be left forever to the nomadic Indian tribes.

## The Burr Conspiracy

In the long run the Louisiana Purchase prepared the way for the growth of the United States as a great continental power. Immediately, however, the Purchase provoked reactions that threatened or seemed to threaten the very existence of the Union. From both the Northeast and the Southwest there soon arose rumors of secession plots.

Most of the American people heartily approved the acquisition of the new territory, as they indicated by their presidential votes in 1804, but some of the New England Federalists raged against it. Their feelings are understandable enough. Both their party and their section stood to lose in importance with the growth of the West. From their point of view the existence of the Northwest Territory was bad enough, for they would soon be outnumbered in national politics with the creation of new states, the first of which in that area was admitted to the Union as the state of Ohio in 1803. The addition of

Louisiana Territory, with its potential for still more new states, only made the evil worse in the minds of New England Federalists. A group of the most extreme of these men, known as the Essex Junto, concluded that the only recourse for New England was to secede from the Union and form a separate "Northern Confederacy." They justified such action by means of state-rights arguments similar to those Jefferson had used only about five years earlier in opposition to the Alien and Sedition Acts.

If a Northern Confederacy were to have any hope for lasting success as a separate nation, it would have to include New York as well as New England, or so the prospective seceders believed. But the prominent New York Federalist Alexander Hamilton had no sympathy with the secessionist scheme. He wrote: "Dismemberment of our empire will be a clear sacrifice of great positive advantages without any counterbalancing good, administering no relief to our real disease, which is *democracy*." He feared that disorders like those of the French Revolution were about to sweep over the United States. Then, he thought, the country would need a military dictator, a sort of American Napoleon, to bring order out of chaos, and he imagined that he himself would emerge as the man of the hour. He had no future so far as ordinary politics was concerned.

His New York Republican rival, Aaron Burr, was another politician without prospects, at least within the party of the vengeful Jefferson. When some of the Federalists approached Burr, he agreed to run with their support for governor in 1804. Rumor had it that he was implicated in the disunion plot and that, if elected, he would lead the state into secession along with New England, but the rumor lacked proof and the plot itself was fantastic, an impossible dream. Nevertheless, Hamilton accused Burr of plotting treason and cast slurs upon his personal character. Burr lost the election, then challenged Hamilton to a duel. Hamilton dared not refuse; if he did, he would sacrifice his reputation for honor and manliness, a reputation that would be indispensable to the career supposedly awaiting him as the savior of his country. And so the two men with their seconds met at Weehawken, New Jersey, across the Hudson River from New

York City, on a July morning in 1804. Hamilton was mortally wounded; he died the next day.

Burr, indicted for murder in both New Jersey and New York, presided over the United States Senate the following winter and then, at the end of his term as Vice President, faced a political outlook more hopeless than ever. He was ambitious and resourceful, with almost magical powers of attracting people to him. What could he do? During the next year he busied himself with mysterious affairs in the Southwest. He talked and corresponded with prominent men of the region, especially with General James Wilkinson, now governor of Louisiana Territory. Burr was up to something, and Wilkinson was his partner in it, but no one except Burr and Wilkinson themselves knew just what it was, and Burr told different stories. Some people believed (and some historians still believe) that he intended to separate the Southwest from the Union and rule it as an empire of his own. His ultimate aim most probably was the conquest of Spanish territory beyond the boundaries of Louisiana rather than the division of the United States.

In the fall of 1806 the armed followers of Burr, with Blennerhassett's Island as their rendezvous, started by boat down the Ohio River, Burr himself joining them after they were well under way. Wilkinson, suddenly turning against Burr, sent a messenger to tell Jefferson that treason was afoot and that an attack upon New Orleans was expected. Jefferson then issued a proclamation calling for the arrest of Burr and his men as traitors. Eventually Burr was captured and brought to Richmond for trial.

Jefferson, not present in Richmond but managing the prosecution by remote control from Washington, was determined to convict his onetime running mate. The prosecution relied hopefully upon its star witness, General Wilkinson, though Wilkinson was a despicable character who accepted pay as a spy for the Spaniards and who demanded extra money from them on the grounds that, in heading off the Burr expedition, he had saved their territory from attack! But Chief Justice Marshall, presiding over the case on circuit duty, had political as well as judicial reasons for insisting that Burr be given a fair hearing. Marshall issued a subpoena requiring Jefferson to appear as a witness, but the President declined to heed it, thus maintaining the independence of his office. At the trial (1807–1808) Marshall applied quite literally the clause of the Constitution that says no one shall be convicted of treason except upon the testimony of at least two witnesses to the same "overt act." He excluded all evidence not bearing directly upon such an act, and so the jury had little choice but to acquit Burr, since not even one witness had actually seen him waging war against the United States or giving aid and comfort to its enemies.

Though freed, Burr gained lasting notoriety as a traitor; after exiling himself abroad for a few years, he returned and lived long enough to hail the Texas revolution (1836) as the fruition of the same sort of movement that he had hoped to start. The trial had given the Chief Justice another chance to frustrate the President. It had set a precedent that made it almost impossible to convict anyone of treason against the United States. And the loyalty of the Southwestern frontiersmen had been proved beyond a doubt by their patriotic reaction to the cry of treason in their midst.

# Selected Readings

**The Young Republic** J. A. Krout and D. R. Fox, *The Completion of Independence, 1790–1830* (1944); R. B. Nye, *The Cultural Life of the New Nation, 1776–1830°* (1960); C. P. Nettels, *The Emergence of a National Economy, 1775–1815* (1962); J. T. Main, *The Social Structure of Revolutionary America°* (1965); Harry Warfel, *Noah Webster, Schoolmaster to America* (1936);

G. A. Koch, *Republican Religion: The American Revolution and the Cult of Reason* (1938); N. J. Goodman, *Benjamin Rush* (1934); C. M. Green, *Eli Whitney and the Birth of American Technology°* (1956) and *Washington: Village and Capital, 1800–1878* (1962); C. F. Ware, *The Early New England Cotton Manufacture* (1931); P. D. Jordan, *The National Road* (1948); J. A. Durrenburger, *Turnpikes: A Study of the Toll Road Movement in the Middle Atlantic States and Maryland* (1931); J. T. Flexner, *Steamboats Come True* (1944).

**Politics and Administration** Henry Adams, *History of the United States During the Administrations of Jefferson and Madison* (9 vols., 1889–1891), also available in a 2-vol. abridged ed. by Herbert Agar (1947), and *John Randolph°* (1882); Edward Channing, *The Jeffersonian System* (1906); C. G. Bowers, *Jefferson in Power* (1936); L. D. White, *The Jeffersonians: A Study in Administrative History, 1801–1829* (1951); N. E. Cunningham, Jr., *The Jeffersonian Republicans in Power: Party Operations, 1801–1809* (1963); D. H. Fischer, *The Revolution of American Conservatism: The Federalist Party in the Era of Jeffersonian Democracy* (1965); N. K. Risjord, *The Old Republicans: Southern Conservatism in the Age of Jefferson* (1965); Morton Borden, *Parties and Politics in the Early Republic, 1789–1815°* (1967); Russell Kirk, *Randolph of Roanoke: A Study in Conservative Thought* (1951).

**Jefferson and Colleagues** Nathan Schachner, *Thomas Jefferson: A Biography* (2 vols., 1951); Dumas Malone, *Jefferson and the Ordeal of Liberty* (1962); L. W. Levy, *Jefferson and Civil Liberties: The Darker Side* (1963); M. D. Peterson, *The Jefferson Image in the American Mind°* (1960); Adrienne Koch, *The Philosophy of Thomas Jefferson°* (1943) and *Jefferson and Madison: The Great Collaboration* (1950); Irving Brant, *James Madison: Secretary of State, 1800–1809* (1953); Raymond Walters, Jr., *Albert Gallatin: Jeffersonian, Financier, and Diplomat* (1957).

**Territorial Expansion** E. W. Lyon, *Louisiana in French Diplomacy, 1789–1804* (1934) and *The Man Who Sold Louisiana: The Life of François Barbé-Marbois* (1942); R. W. Irwin, *Diplomatic Relations of the United States with the Barbary Powers* (1931); John Bakeless, *Lewis and Clark, Partners in Discovery°* (1947); Bernard De Voto, ed., *The Journals of Lewis and Clark°* (1953); Donald Jackson, ed., *Letters of the Lewis and Clark Expedition* (1963); Nathan Schachner, *Aaron Burr°* (1937), a sympathetic biography; T. P. Abernethy, *The Burr Conspiracy* (1954), an unfriendly account.

---

° Titles available in paperback.

# Chapter 8
# Free Seas and
# Fresh Lands

The European war, renewed in 1803, was both a blessing and a curse for the United States. The continual conflict abroad enabled Americans to develop a profitable trade with the belligerents on both sides and at times to play them off against each other to the diplomatic advantage of this country, as in the cases of the Pinckney Treaty with Spain and the Louisiana treaty with France. Yet the war in Europe jeopardized the policy proclaimed by Washington and endorsed by Jefferson—the policy of neutrality and peace. Twice the United States got involved in the European struggle; the first time in opposition to France (1798), the second time in opposition to Great Britain (1812).

The War of 1812 was anomalous in many ways. Though avowedly waged for free seas and sailors' rights, it was opposed by the group most directly interested in seagoing commerce, the New England merchants, who sneeringly referred to it as "Mr. Madison's war," not theirs. Peace overtures began before the fighting did, and the peace treaty was signed before the last and greatest of the battles had been fought. The treaty did not even mention the most important of the war aims—the conquest of Canada and the elimination of impressment. Indeed, the war was at best a draw, and the United States was lucky to avoid surrendering some of its own territory.

Yet the war had important consequences. It broke the Indian barriers that had stood in the way of the northwestward and southwestward expansion of settlement. It gave a boost to the spirit of nationalism, which discredited the antiwar party and helped to overcome the divisive forces of postwar sectionalism. Perhaps most important of all, it stimulated the growth of manufactures, thus accelerating the progress of the nation toward industrial greatness.

The year the war ended, 1815, marks a turning point in the relations of the United States with the rest of the world. Previously, this country had become involved again and again in the broils of Europe, and much of the time the requirements of diplomacy had dictated domestic policies. Afterward, for almost a century, domestic politics held a clear priority over foreign affairs as the country entered upon a period of comparative "isolation."

## CAUSES OF CONFLICT

The causes of the War of 1812 were debated by politicians at the time and have been disputed by historians ever since. One view emphasizes the question of frontier lands, and another the question of freedom of the seas. Actually, these matters were interrelated, and both must be taken into account.

### Neutral Rights

In the early 1800s the warring nations of Europe found it impossible to take care of their own shipping needs. The merchant ships of France and Spain seldom ventured far upon the ocean, dominated as it was by the seapower of Great

---

**Impressment**
An engraving depicting the seizure of American seamen by the English navy. (The Bettmann Archive)

Britain, and the merchant marine of Britain herself was too busy in the waters of Europe and Asia to devote much attention to those of America. To some degree or other, all the belligerents had to depend upon the neutrals of the world for cargoes essential to effective war-making, and in the size and activity of its merchant marine the United States was the most important of the neutrals. American shipowners prospered as, year after year, they engrossed a larger and larger proportion of the carrying trade between Europe and the West Indies. Farmers shared in the prosperity, for exports from the United States to the West Indies and Europe also increased prodigiously.

In the Battle of Trafalgar (1805) a British fleet practically destroyed what was left of the French navy. Thereafter the supremacy of Great Britain upon the seas was unchallenged, while Napoleon proceeded to extend his domination over the continent of Europe. Powerless to invade the British Isles, Napoleon devised a scheme, known as the Continental System, which he hoped would bring the enemy to terms. The British, he reasoned, were a nation of shopkeepers who depended for their existence upon buying and selling in the rest of the world, especially in Europe. If he could close the continent to their trade, he thought, they ultimately would have to give in. So, in a series of decrees beginning with those of Berlin (1806) and Milan (1807), he proclaimed that British ships and neutral ships touching at British ports were not to land their cargoes at any European port controlled by France or her allies.

The British government replied to Napoleon's decrees with a succession of orders-in-council. These announced an unusual kind of blockade of the European coast. The blockade was intended not to keep goods out of Napoleon's Europe but only to see that the goods were carried either in British vessels or in neutral vessels stopping at a British port and paying for a special license. Thus, while frustrating the Continental System, Britain would compel the neutrals to contribute toward financing her war effort, and she would limit the growth of her maritime rivals, above all the United States.

Caught between Napoleon's decrees and Britain's orders, American vessels sailing directly for Europe took the chance of capture by the British, and those going by way of a British port ran the risk of seizure by the French. Both of the warring powers disregarded American rights and sensibilities, yet to most Americans the British seemed like the worse offender of the two. Possessing effective sea power, they pounced upon Yankee merchantmen all over the wide ocean; the French could do so only in European ports. True, Napoleon's officials sometimes imprisoned and brutally mistreated the crews of confiscated ships, but the British navy far more often infringed upon personal liberty and national sovereignty, stopping American ships on the high seas and taking sailors off the decks as victims of impressment.

## Impressment

The British navy—with its floggings, its low pay, and its dirty and dangerous conditions on shipboard—was a "floating hell" to its sailors. They had to be impressed (forced) into the service and at every good opportunity they deserted, many of them joining the merchant marine of the United States and even its navy. To check this loss of vital manpower, the British claimed the right to stop and search American merchantmen, though not naval vessels, and reimpress deserters. They did not claim the right to take native-born Americans, but they did seize naturalized Americans born on British soil, for according to the laws of England a true-born subject could never give up his allegiance to the King: once an Englishman, always an Englishman. In actual practice the British often impressed native as well as naturalized Americans, and thousands upon thousands of sailors claiming the protection of the Stars and Stripes were thus kidnapped. To these hapless men, impressment was little better than slavery. To their shipowning employers it was at least a serious nuisance. And to millions of proud and patriotic Americans, even those living far from the ocean, it was an intolerable affront to the national honor.

In the summer of 1807, in the *Chesapeake-Leopard* incident, the British went to more outrageous extremes than ever. The *Chesapeake* was a public and not a private vessel, a frigate of the United States navy and not an ordinary mer-

## Seaman's Protection Paper

To protect American sailors from British impressment, Congress authorized the issuance of certificates of American citizenship, which came to be known as "protection" papers. These papers were not always respected by British naval officers. To them a certificate of naturalization was meaningless, for the British government claimed the allegiance of all British subjects for life. A certificate of American birth was not dependable, for it could be obtained by fraud. Some Americans made a business of selling forged documents. One woman, it is said, had an oversized cradle built, for British deserters to climb into, so that she could honestly swear that she had known them from the cradle. (Essex Institute, Salem, Mass.)

chantman. Sailing from Norfolk, with several alleged deserters from the British navy among the crew, the *Chesapeake* was hailed by His Majesty's Ship *Leopard,* which had been lying in wait off Cape Henry, at the entrance to Chesapeake Bay. Commodore James Barron refused to allow the *Chesapeake* to be searched, and so the *Leopard* opened fire and compelled him, unprepared for action as he was, to strike his colors. A boarding party from the *Leopard* dragged four men off the American frigate.

This was an attack upon the United States! When news of the outrage got around the country, most of the people cried for a war of revenge. Not since the days of Lexington and Concord had Americans been so strongly aroused; never again were they to be so solidly united in opposition to Great Britain. Even the "most temperate people and those most attached to England," the British minister reported home, "say that they are bound as a people and that they must assert their honor on the first attack upon it." If Congress had been in session, or if President Jefferson had called a special session, as he was urged to do, the country might have stampeded into war. But, as the French minister in Washington informed Talleyrand, "the President does not want war," and "Mr. Madison dreads it now still more."

Instead of assembling Congress and demanding a war declaration, Jefferson made a determined effort to maintain the national honor with peace. First, he issued an order expelling all British warships from American waters, so as to lessen the likelihood of future incidents. Then he sent instructions to his minister in England, James Monroe, to get satisfaction from the British government and to insist again upon the complete renunciation of impressment. On the whole the British government was conciliatory enough. It disavowed the action of Admiral Berkeley, the officer primarily responsible for the *Chesapeake-Leopard* affair, recalled him, and offered to indemnify the wounded and the families of the killed and to return the captured sailors (only three were left; one had been hanged). But the British cabinet refused to concede anything to Jefferson's main point; instead, the cabinet issued a proclamation reasserting the right of search to recover deserting seamen.

Thus the impressment issue stood between the British and American governments and prevented a compromise that might have led away from war. Though by 1812 the British had made a money settlement, the *Chesapeake* outrage meanwhile remained an open sore in Anglo-American relations. This incident, together with the impressment issue involved in it, was probably the most important single cause of the War of 1812, even though its final effect was delayed for five years.

## "Peaceable Coercion"

Even at the height of the excitement over the *Chesapeake,* Jefferson made no preparations for a possible war. He and Madison believed that, if worse came to worst, the United States could bring Great Britain to terms, and France as well, through the use of economic pressure instead of military or naval force. Dependent as both nations were upon the Yankee carrying trade, they presumably would mend their ways if they were completely deprived of it.

Hence, when Congress met for its regular session, Jefferson hastily drafted an embargo bill, Madison revised it, and both the House and the Senate promptly enacted it into law. The embargo prohibited American ships from leaving this country for any port in the world; if it had specified only British and French ports it could have been evaded by means of false clearance papers. Congress also passed a force act to make the embargo effective.

Though the law was nevertheless evaded in various ways, it was effective enough to be felt in France, much more in Great Britain, and still more in the United States itself. Throughout the United States—except in the frontier areas of Vermont and New York, which soon doubled their overland exports to Canada—the embargo brought on a serious depression. The planters of the South and the farmers of the West, though deprived of foreign markets for their crops, were willing to suffer in comparative silence, devoted Jeffersonian Republicans that most of them were. But the Federalist merchants and shipowners of the Northeast, still harder hit by the depression, made no secret of their rabid discontent.

Though the Northeastern merchants disliked

**Commercial Warfare
[1806–1810]**

**Napoleon's Berlin Decree, 1806**
No vessel coming from or touching at a British port shall be received in any European port of France or her allies.

**British Orders-in-Council, 1807**
All vessels trading to or from enemy ports shall be subject to capture unless they first put in at a British port, pay a fee, and obtain a certificate.

**Napoleon's Milan Decree, 1807**
Any vessel submitting to search by an English ship, or paying any fee to the English government, shall be considered as an English vessel and shall be liable to seizure.

**The U.S. Embargo Act, 1807**
No ship shall clear from the United States for any foreign port. No ship shall depart even for another American port without first giving bond, of twice the value of ship and cargo, that the goods will be relanded within the United States.

**The U.S. Non-Intercourse Law, 1809**
All shipping and trade between the United States and British- or French-controlled ports (but not the rest of the world) are prohibited. If either Great Britain or France ''shall cease to violate the neutral commerce of the United States,'' trade and shipping will be resumed with the nation so doing.

**Macon's Bill No. 2, 1810**
Intercourse with France and Great Britain is renewed, but if either nation ceases its violations of American rights, and the other refuses to do so, the provisions of the Non-Intercourse Law will be reimposed against the nation thus refusing.

every day their ships idled at the wharves. Again, as at the time of the Louisiana Purchase, they concluded that Jefferson had violated the Constitution (as indeed he had—if judged by the principles he had advocated before becoming President).

In the midst of the embargo-induced depression came the election of 1808. The Federalists, with C. C. Pinckney again their candidate, made the most of the embargo's unpopularity and won a far larger proportion of the popular and electoral votes than in 1804, yet Madison was safely elected as Jefferson's successor. The Federalists also gained a number of seats in the House and the Senate, though the Republicans continued to hold a majority in both houses. To Jefferson and Madison the returns indicated plainly enough that the embargo was a growing liability in politics. A few days before going out of office, Jefferson approved a bill terminating his and Madison's first experiment with what he called "peaceable coercion." But Jefferson's succession by Madison meant no basic change in policy, and other experiments with measures short of war were soon to be tried.

By the time he entered upon his presidential duties, James Madison already had a career behind him that would assure him immortality in history books. He was not only experienced in affairs of government; he was also a more profound and original thinker than he was credited with being by his contemporaries and by later generations who have assumed that he was merely Jefferson's echo. Unfortunately for his reputation, he was not an impressive figure of a man, but was small and wizened, with a scholarly frown. Nor was he equipped with the personal charm or politician's skill needed for strong presidential leadership. What he lacked in personality, his wife more than supplied. Dolley Madison, North Carolina born, was as gay and gracious a First Lady as ever adorned the White House.

Just before Madison's inauguration, Congress passed a modified embargo bill known as the Nonintercourse Act. The Nonintercourse Act was soon replaced by another expedient commonly called Macon's Bill No. 2 (1810). This freed commercial relations with the whole world, including Great Britain and France, but

impressment, the orders-in-council, and Napoleon's decrees, they hated Jefferson's embargo much more. Previously, in spite of risks, they had kept up their business with excellent and even fabulous returns; now they lost money authorized the President to prohibit intercourse with either belligerent if it should continue its violations after the other had stopped. The freeing of American trade was more to the advantage of the British than the French, since it fitted in with the efforts of the former to pierce and weaken the Continental System. Napoleon had every incentive to induce the United States to reimpose the embargo against his enemy. He succeeded in doing so by means of a trick, the Cadore letter, which pretended to revoke the Berlin and Milan decrees as far as they interfered with American commerce. Madison accepted the Cadore letter as evidence of Napoleon's change of policy, even though the French continued to confiscate American ships. He announced that early in 1811, an embargo against Great Britain alone would automatically go into effect, in accordance with Macon's Bill, unless Britain meanwhile rescinded her orders-in-council.

In time the new embargo, though less well enforced than the earlier, all-inclusive one had been, hurt the economy of England enough to cause influential Englishmen to petition their government for repeal of the orders-in-council. Eventually the orders were repealed—too late to prevent war, even if they had been the only grievance giving rise to the martial spirit in the United States. But there were other grievances, namely, impressment and a border conflict between the British Empire and the expanding American frontier.

## Red Men and Redcoats

Ever since the days of the Revolution the Indians generally had looked to their old "white father," the King of England, for protection against the relentlessly advancing Americans. And the British in Canada had relied upon Indian friendship to keep up their fur trade, even within the territory of the United States, and to maintain potentially useful allies. At one time, in 1794, this country nearly went to war with Great Britain because of her Indian policy, but Anthony Wayne's victory over the tribes at Fallen Timbers and the conclusion of Jay's Treaty dispelled the war danger and brought on a period of comparative peace. Then, in 1807, the border quiet was disturbed by an event

occurring far away—the British assault upon the *Chesapeake*. The ensuing war crisis had repercussions that, as will be seen, terribly aggravated the frontier conflict between tribesmen and settlers. Much of this conflict of red men and white was personified in the two opposing leaders, Tecumseh and William Henry Harrison.

The Virginia-born Harrison, already a veteran Indian fighter at twenty-six, went to Washington as the congressional delegate from the Northwest Territory in 1799. He was largely responsible for the passage of the Harrison Land Law (1800), which enabled settlers to acquire farms from the public domain on much easier terms than before. Land in the Northwest Territory soon was selling fast. The growth of population led to a division of the area into the state of Ohio and the territories of Indiana, Michigan, and Illinois. By 1812 Ohio contained 250,000 people and was beginning to look like an Eastern state, as paths widened into roads, villages sprang up and in some cases grew into cities, and the forests receded before the spreading cornfields. By 1812 Michigan had few settlers, but Illinois contained a scattered population of about 13,000, and Indiana 25,000.

Receiving from Jefferson an appointment as governor of Indiana Territory, Harrison devoted himself to carrying out Jefferson's policy of Indian removal. According to the Jeffersonian program, the Indians must give up their claims to tribal lands and either convert themselves into settled farmers or migrate to the west of the Mississippi. Playing off one tribe against another, and using whatever tactics suited the occasion—threats, bribes, trickery—Harrison made treaty after treaty with the separate tribes of the Northwest. By 1807 the United States claimed treaty rights to eastern Michigan, southern Indiana, and most of Illinois. Meanwhile, in the Southwest, millions of acres were taken from other tribes in the states of Georgia and Tennessee and in Mississippi Territory. Having been forced off their traditional hunting grounds, the Indians throughout the Mississippi Valley seethed with discontent. But the separate tribes, helpless by themselves against the power of the United States, probably would have quieted down and accepted their fate if two complicating factors had not arisen.

One complication was the policy of the British authorities in Canada. For years they had neglected their Indian friends across the border to the south. Then came the *Chesapeake* incident and the surge of anti-British feeling throughout the United States. Now the Canadian authorities, expecting war and an attempted invasion of Canada, began to take desperate measures for their own defense. "Are the Indians to be employed in case of a rupture with the United States?" asked the lieutenant governor of Upper Canada (December 1, 1807). And Sir James Craig, the governor general of the entire province, replied: "If we do not employ them, there cannot exist a moment's doubt that they will be employed against us." Craig at once took steps to renew friendship with the Indians and provide them with increased supplies. Thus the trouble on the sea over the question of impressment intensified the border conflict hundreds of miles inland.

The second factor intensifying this conflict was the rise of a remarkable native leader, one of the most admirable and heroic in Indian history. Tecumseh, "The Shooting Star," chief of the Shawnees, aimed to unite all the tribes of the Mississippi Valley, resist the advance of white settlement, and recover the whole Northwest, making the Ohio River the boundary between the United States and the Indian country. He maintained that Harrison and others, by negotiating with individual tribes, had obtained no real title to land in the various treaties, since the land belonged to all the tribes and none of them could rightfully cede any of it without the consent of the rest. "The Great Spirit gave this great island to his red children. He placed the whites on the other side of the big water." So Tecumseh eloquently told Harrison. "They were not contented with their own, but came to take ours from us. They have driven us from the sea to the lakes—we can go no farther."

In his plans for a united front, Tecumseh was aided by his brother, a one-eyed, epileptic medicine-man known as the Prophet. The Prophet, visiting the Great Spirit from time to time in trances, inspired a religious revival that spread through numerous tribes and helped bring them together. Few Indians doubted his supernatural powers after, having secretly learned from Cana-

dian traders of a forthcoming eclipse, he commanded the sun to be dark on the appointed day. The Prophet's town, at the confluence of Tippecanoe Creek and the Wabash River, became the sacred place of the new religion as well as the headquarters of Tecumseh's confederacy. Leaving his brother there after instructing him to avoid war for the time being, Tecumseh journeyed down the Mississippi in 1811 to bring the Indians of the South into his alliance. At that time a great earthquake occurred centering at New Madrid, Missouri, and rumbling up and down the Mississippi Valley, causing much of the river to change its course. To many of the Indians, this seemed another awesome sign that a new era was at hand for them.

During Tecumseh's absence, Governor Harrison saw a chance to destroy the growing influence of the two Indian leaders. With 1,000 soldiers he camped near the Prophet's town, provoked an attack (November 7, 1811), and though suffering losses as heavy as those of the enemy, succeeded in driving off the Indians and burning the town. This, the Battle of Tippecanoe, disillusioned many of the Prophet's followers, for they had been led to believe that his magic would protect them from the white man's bullets. Tecumseh returned to find his confederacy shattered, yet there were still plenty of warriors eager for the warpath, and by the spring of 1812 they were busy with hatchet and scalping knife all along the frontier, from Michigan to Mississippi.

Westerners blamed Great Britain for the bloodshed along the border. Her agents in Canada encouraged Tecumseh, used the Prophet as a "vile instrument," as Harrison put it, and provided the guns and supplies that enabled the Indians to attack. To Harrison and to most of the frontiersmen, there seemed only one way to make the West safe for Americans. That was to drive the British out of Canada and annex that province to the United States.

While frontiersmen in the North demanded the conquest of Canada, those in the South looked to the acquisition of Florida. In Spanish hands, that territory was a perpetual nuisance, with slaves escaping across the line in one direction and Indians raiding across it in the other. Through Florida ran rivers like the Alabama, the Apalachicola, and others which in American possession would give access to the Gulf of Mexico and the markets of the world. In 1810 American settlers in West Florida took matters into their own hands, fell upon the Spanish fort at Baton Rouge, and requested that the territory be annexed to the United States. President Madison unhesitatingly proclaimed its annexation, then schemed to get the rest of Florida too. With Madison's connivance, the former Georgia governor George Mathews attempted to foment a revolt in East Florida (1811). Spain protested, and Madison backed down, but the desire of Southern frontiersmen for all of Florida did not abate. Spain was Britain's ally, and a war with Britain would give these frontiersmen an excuse for taking Spanish as well as British territory.

Thus the war fever was raging on both the Northern and the Southern frontiers by 1812. The denizens of these outlying regions were not numerous as compared with the population of the country as a whole, and for the most part they were not directly represented in Congress, except by a few territorial delegates. Nevertheless, they were ably represented at the national capital by a group of determined young congressmen who, with good reason, soon gained the name of "war hawks."

## The War Hawks

Three days before the Battle of Tippecanoe a new Congress met in Washington for the session of 1811–1812. In the congressional elections of 1810, most of the voters had indicated their disgust with such expedients as Macon's Bill No. 2 by defeating large numbers of Republican advocates of measures short of war, as well as Federalist advocates of continued peace. Of the newly elected congressmen and senators, the great majority were warlike Republicans, and after the news of Tippecanoe they became more eager than ever for a showdown with the power that seemed to threaten both the security of the frontier and the freedom of the seas.

A new generation had arrived upon the political scene, a group of daring young men of whom the most influential came from the new states in the West or from the back country of the old states in the South. Two of the natural leaders were Henry Clay and John C. Calhoun, whose

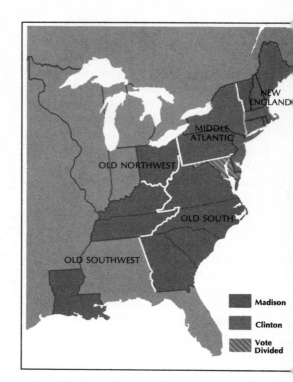

**Election of 1812**

careers were to provide much of the drama of American politics for the next four decades. The tall, magnetic Clay, barely thirty-four, was a Virginian by birth but had made Kentucky his home. Already, while still under the legal age for a senator, he had appeared briefly in the United States Senate. As handsome as Clay though less appealing, the twenty-nine-year-old Calhoun was the son of Scotch-Irish pioneers in the South Carolina hills.

When Congress organized in 1811, the war faction of young Republicans got control of both the House and the Senate. As Speaker of the House, Clay held a position of influence then second only to that of the President himself. Clay filled the committees with the friends of force, appointing Calhoun to the crucial Committee on Foreign Affairs, and launched a drive toward war for the conquest of Canada. This would bring Great Britain to terms and avenge the wrongs that Clay recited eloquently and at length. Or at least he supposed it would, and he further imagined that the conquest would be quick and easy.

# Part One
# The Course of American Art

Colonial painting, architecture, and crafts, like colonial culture in general, were based on European precedents. In response to the conditions of their new environment, colonists modified these traditional forms and gave them a uniquely American character. For example, the early settlers of New England came from provincial areas, where fourteenth- and fifteenth-century structures were the dominant architectural forms. Copying what they remembered of these familiar medieval English buildings, the settlers were forced by the colder New England climate to make modifications, such as the more frequent use of protective weatherboard and moving the chimney from the sides of the house to its center to provide a more efficient heating system. This central

*Plate 1*
**The Whipple House.**
Anonymous. (Cushing)

chimney design, as seen in the Whipple House built at Ipswich, Massachusetts, in 1639 (*Plate 1*) became typical of seventeenth-century New England architecture.

As time passed colonists began to borrow directly from contemporary European sources, such as pattern books imported from England (e.g., James Gibbs' *A Book of Architecture*, London, 1728). The Vassal House in Cambridge, Massachusetts, completed in 1759 (*Plate 2*), has two-story pilasters on the façade and a pediment above the entrance, motifs common in English Georgian buildings. In England this style was used for large and imposing stone houses, but American architects reduced the size and substituted more easily worked wood for stone.

A like modification of contemporary English sources is seen in the interior of the Stamper Blackwell House, built at Philadelphia in 1764 (*Plate 3*). The plain exterior gave no clue to an interior designed to mirror a fashionable English home of the day. A frieze above the mantel depicts a scene from the very popular *Aesop's Fables*. The furniture, though built by Philadelphia craftsmen, is copied from English designs, as illustrated in books like Thomas Chippendale's *The Gentleman's and Cabinet Maker's Director* (London, 1754).

In contrast to the interest in pattern-book models, there flourished in the colonies a more whimsical style, largely restricted to carved wood figureheads and copper weather vanes. Although the basic forms were not indigenous to

*Plate 2*
**The Vassal House.**

Anonymous. (Sandak)

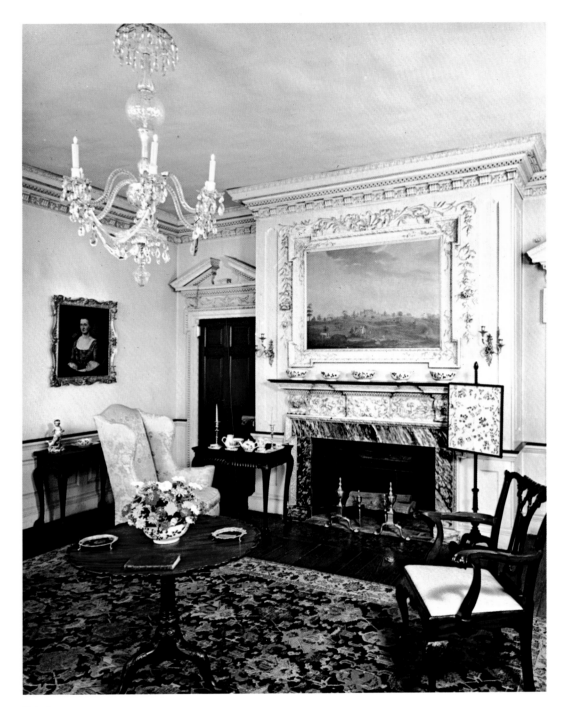

*Plate 3*
**The Stamper Blackwell House.**

Anonymous. (Courtesy, The Henry du Pont Winterthur Museum)

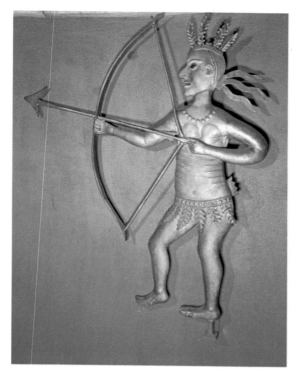

Plate 4
**Indian Weather Vane.**

Shem Drowne. (Massachusetts Historical Society; Cushing)

America, craftsmen were able to exercise great ingenuity in their choice of design. Frequently, native themes were adopted, for example, in Shem Drowne's Indian weather vane (*Plate 4*).

More commonly, lacking either the skill or the confidence of their European contemporaries, colonial craftsmen relied heavily on imported models for inspiration. This was true throughout the colonies, whether settled originally by English, French, or Dutch emigrants. While most craftsmen turned to the countries from which they or their forebears had come, this was not always the case. John Coney, a prominent New England silversmith, based his designs on models found in sixteenth-century Italian pattern books. His sugar box, created in 1690 (*Plate 5*), had a heavy, rounded, baroque form, but Coney

Plate 5
**Silver Sugar Box.**

John Coney. (Courtesy, Museum of Fine Arts, Boston, gift of Mrs. J. R. Churchill)

*Plate 6*

**"John van Cortlandt."**

Anonymous. (In The Brooklyn Museum Collection)

Plate 7
**"Lapowinsa."**

Gustavus Hesselius. (Courtesy, The Historical Society of Pennsylvania)

used less ornament and simpler lines. Naturalistic relief on the lid provided an original touch.

In New York, an anonymous artist was influenced directly by contemporary prints in his portrait of John van Cortlandt, son of a prominent family of Dutch origin (*Plate 6*). Although the work is bolder and simpler than its English models, the artist conformed to tradition by portraying the child in fancy dress and placing him in a parklike setting. Portraiture was the principal form of painting in the colonies. Although his work was derived mainly from English models, the primary aim of the American portrait painter was to leave a lasting pictorial document. With the relaxation of the strict Puritan injunctions against painting, portraiture became one of the few luxuries and decorations in the colonial home. By imitating European models, without regard to the incongruity of using palatial, landscaped settings, the portrait brought American families into closer contact with

Plate 8
**"Isaac Royall Family."**

Robert Feke. (The Fogg Art Museum, Harvard University)

the European cultural mainstream and stimulated their sense of pride and importance.

Many colonial artists were immigrants, born and trained in Europe, who came to this country with already developed styles. Frequently, living in America inspired them to change their points of view and to explore new subject matter. "Lapowinsa," one of the earliest portraits of an Indian, was painted by Gustavus Hesselius, an emigrant from Sweden, in 1735 (*Plate 7*). Hesselius came to America in 1711 and became one of the leading artists of Philadelphia. In contrast to the lavish costumes and setting common to European portraiture (as shown in the Van Cortlandt portrait), Hesselius' portraits presented the realities of American life. His work is plain and forthright and reveals a concern and respect for individual character.

Artists born and trained in America were not as familiar with traditional European painting, but they undoubtedly came in contact with English engravings and mezzotints, which circulated with increasing abundance in the colonies. The work of native-trained artists, such as Robert Feke's 1741 portrait of the "Isaac Royall Family" (*Plate 8*), seems stiff and flat in comparison to the work of contemporary English artists. Yet the simple linear presentation is part of the carefully worked out structure of this group portrait, rather than the result of lack of training.

Linearity, whether seen in the simplified lines of the Whipple House or in the works of American painters, was one of the principal "American" features of colonial art. This quality is apparent in the work of John Singleton Copley, the most important colonial painter of the eighteenth century. Born in Boston, he received his early training from his stepfather, an English engraver. His portrait of Paul Revere (*Plate 9*) is a strong depiction of the silversmith's character, expressed simply and directly. Copley's early work exemplified colonial painting in its most skillful form. The artist, however, was dissatisfied living in provincial New England and traveled to Europe to study. His later works, though more in keeping with the European grand style of the period, lacked the freshness of his earlier, American paintings. Copley settled in England and became a respected member of the British artistic establishment, thus becoming, along with Benjamin West, one of the first native-born Americans to influence art abroad.

*Plate 9*
**"Paul Revere."**

John Singleton Copley. (Courtesy, Museum of Fine Arts, Boston, gift of the Revere Family)

The Federalists in Congress, representing the commercial interests of the Northeast, deprecated the clamor for Canada and war. But they were powerless to stem the drive toward hostilities, even with the aid of dissident Republicans like the eccentric "Quid," John Randolph of Roanoke. Dubbing the Clay men "war hawks," Randolph ridiculed their cry as being like that of the whippoorwill, "one eternal monotonous tone—Canada! Canada! Canada!"

While Congress debated, President Madison moved reluctantly toward the conclusion that war was necessary. In May the war faction took the lead in the caucus of Republican congressmen who renominated him for the Presidency, and on June 1 he sent his war message to Congress.

In his message the President maintained that Great Britain—by impressing American citizens, interfering with American trade, and inciting the Indians along the frontier—was already waging war against the United States. He recommended that Congress declare war in return. Congress responded with a declaration of hostilities on June 18, two days after a new ministry had announced in Parliament that the orders-in-council were to be suspended, but before the news could reach Washington. The close vote on the declaration, 19 to 13 in the Senate and 79 to 49 in the House, showed how badly the American people were divided.

The division of public opinion was again revealed in the election of 1812. Opposing Madison and the war, a peace faction of the Republicans nominated a rival candidate, De Witt Clinton of New York, and the Federalists gave their support to him. Most of the electors in the Northeast voted for Clinton and peace, but all of those in the South and the West sustained Madison and war, the President being re-elected, 128 to 89.

With the people thus divided, the country as a whole was not psychologically prepared for war, nor was it financially or militarily prepared. Congress had adjourned without increasing the army and navy, voting war taxes, or renewing the charter of the government's indispensable financial agency, the Bank of the United States, which expired in 1811. The war hawks, however, were not worried. On to Canada!

# THE WAR OF 1812

At first Great Britain, preoccupied with her mighty struggle against Napoleon, paid little attention to the American war, a mere annoyance to her. Then, in the fall of 1812, Napoleon launched the Russian campaign that, before the winter was over, was to bring him disaster and prepare the way for his ultimate defeat. As the months passed, Great Britain was able to divert more and more of her military and naval power to America. Only for about a year did the United States undertake the offensive; thereafter this country was forced to fight a defensive war, a war to protect its own territory.

## The Course of Battle

The conquest of Canada, supposedly a "mere matter of marching," as Jefferson himself put it, soon proved to be an exercise in frustration. A three-pronged invasion was planned to strike into Canada by way of Detroit, the Niagara River, and Lake Champlain, with the greatest concentration of force at Detroit. At Detroit, however, after marching into Canada, the elderly General William Hull, Governor of Michigan Territory, retreated and surrendered the fort (August 1812). The other invasion efforts also failed, and Fort Dearborn (Chicago) fell before an Indian attack.

During the year of disaster and defeat on land, the Madison administration and its supporters took what consolation they could in the news of successes on the sea. American frigates engaged British warships in a series of duels and won some spectacular victories, one of the most renowned being the victory of the *Constitution* over the *Guerrière*. American privateers destroyed or captured one British merchant ship after another, occasionally braving the coastal waters of the British Isles and burning vessels within sight of the shore. After that first year, however, the score was evened by the British navy, which not only drove the American frigates to cover but also instituted a close blockade of the United States and harried the coastal settlements from Virginia to Maine.

While British seapower dominated the ocean, American fleets arose to control the Great Lakes. First, the Americans took command of Lake

## Victory at Sea

As of 1812, in the Napoleonic Wars, the British navy had fought 200 battles and won 200 victories, in engagements between single ships or whole fleets. Great Britain seemed invincible on the ocean. Then, on August 19, 1812, in the North Atlantic, the U.S. frigate *Constitution* boldly challenged and decisively defeated H.M.S. *Guerrière*. On October 25, 1812, off the Canary Islands, the frigate *United States* met and destroyed H.M.S. *Macedonian*. This engagement is pictured in the engraving by Cornelius Tiebout, reproduced here. Commanding the *United States* was Stephen Decatur, a hero of the naval wars with Tripoli (1803) and Algiers (1815) as well as the War of 1812. Afterward Decatur made the famous toast: "Our country! In her intercourse with foreign nations may she always be in the right; but our country, right or wrong." In 1812 the score, in naval duels on the high seas, was 5 American and 3 British victories; by the end of the war the score was approximately even. (The Granger Collection)

Ontario, enabling troops to cross over to York (Toronto), the capital of Canada. At York (April 27, 1813) the invaders ran upon a cunningly contrived land mine, the explosion of which killed more than fifty, including General Zebulon M. Pike. Some of the enraged survivors, without authorization, set fire to the capital's public buildings, which burned to the ground. After also destroying some ships and military stores, the Americans returned across the lake.

Next, Lake Erie was redeemed for American use, mainly through the work of the youthful Oliver Hazard Perry. Having constructed a fleet at Presqu' Isle (Erie, Pennsylvania), Perry took up a position at Put-in-Bay, near a group of islands off the mouth of the Maumee River. With the banner "Don't Give Up the Ship" flying on his flagship, he awaited the British fleet, whose intentions he had learned from a spy. He smashed the fleet upon its arrival (September 10, 1813) and established American control of the lake.

This made possible, at last, an invasion of Canada by way of Detroit. The post had been hard to reach overland, for supply wagons either had to struggle through the almost impassable Black Swamp of the Maumee Valley or had to make a long detour around it. After Perry's victory at Put-in-Bay, supplies as well as men could be quickly and easily transported by water. William Henry Harrison, who had replaced Hull in the Western command, now pushed up the River Thames into Upper Canada and won a victory (October 5, 1813), notable for the death of Tecumseh, who had been commissioned a brigadier general in the British army. The Battle of the Thames resulted in no lasting occupation of Canadian soil, but it disheartened the Indians of the Northwest and eliminated the worst of the danger they had offered to the frontier.

While Harrison was harrying the tribes of the Northwest, another Indian fighter was striking an even harder blow at the Creeks in the Southwest. The Creeks, aroused by Tecumseh on his Southern visit, were supplied by the Spaniards in Florida. These Indians had fallen upon Fort Mims, on the Alabama River just north of the Florida border, and had massacred the frontier families taking shelter within its stockade. Andrew Jackson, Tennessee planter and militia general, turning from his plans for invading Florida, tracked down the Creeks. In the Battle of Horseshoe Bend (March 27, 1814) Jackson's men took frightful vengeance, slaughtering squaws and children along with warriors. Then Jackson went into Florida and seized the Spanish fort at Pensacola.

After the Battles of the Thames and Horseshoe Bend, the Indians were of little use to the British. But, with the surrender of Napoleon in Europe, the British could send their veterans of the European war to dispose of the "dirty shirts," the unkempt Americans. In 1814 the British prepared to invade the United States by three approaches—Chesapeake Bay, Lake Champlain (the historic route of Burgoyne), and the mouth of the Mississippi.

An armada under Admiral Sir George Cockburn, a hard-bitten old sea-dog, sailed up the Patuxent River from Chesapeake Bay and landed an army which marched a short distance overland to Bladensburg, on the outskirts of the District of Columbia. Hastily drawn up to oppose this army was a much more numerous force of poorly trained militiamen. When the firing started they gave more than they received, but they were unnerved by the repeated assaults of the well-disciplined redcoats and finally broke formation and ran. The British marched on into Washington (August 24, 1814), putting the government to flight. Then they deliberately burned the public buildings, including the White House, in retaliation for the earlier unauthorized incendiarism at York. The sack of Washington marked the low point of American fortunes in the war; better days were coming.

Leaving Washington in partial ruins, the invading army reembarked and proceeded up the bay, toward Baltimore. But Baltimore, guarded by Fort McHenry, was ready. To block the river approach, the garrison had stretched a chain across the Patapsco and had sunk several boats in the river. From a distance the British bombarded the fort (September 12, 1814) while through the night an American, Francis Scott Key, watched from one of the enemy ships where he had gone to secure the release of a prisoner. At the "dawn's early light," as Key wrote the next day, the flag on the fort was still flying "o'er the land of the free and the home of the brave." The British withdrew, and Key's words, set to the tune of an old drinking song, quickly became popular.

Meanwhile another invasion force was descending upon northern New York. On Lake Champlain the British mustered a fleet about the size of the American fleet drawn up to oppose it, and near by they had an army three times as large as the mixed force of regulars and militia facing it. Yet, in the Battle of Plattsburg (September 11, 1814), the defenders destroyed the invading fleet, and the invading army then retreated to Canada. The northern border was safe.

Far to the south the most serious threat of all soon materialized. In December 1814, a formidable array of battle-hardened veterans, fresh from the Duke of Wellington's Peninsular campaign against the French in Spain, landed below New Orleans. On Christmas, Wellington's brother-in-law Sir Edward Pakenham arrived to take command. Neither he nor anyone else in America knew that a treaty of peace between the British and American governments had been signed in faraway Belgium the day before. Awaiting Pakenham's advance up the Mississippi was Andrew Jackson with a motley collection of Tennesseans, Kentuckians, Creoles, Negroes, and pirates drawn up behind breastworks. For all their drill and bravery, the redcoats advancing through the open (January 8, 1815) were no match for Jackson's well-protected men. Making good use of artillery as well as rifles, the Americans held their fire as each wave of attackers approached, then sent out deadly volleys at close range. Finally the British retreated while an American band struck up

"Hail Columbia!" Left behind were 700 dead, including Pakenham himself, 1,400 wounded, and 500 other prisoners. Jackson's losses: 8 killed, 13 wounded.

## New England Objections

With notable exceptions, such as the Battle of New Orleans, the military operations of the United States, 1812–1815, were rather badly bungled. This should cause little surprise. What is surprising is the fact that American arms succeeded as well as they did. After all, the government was woefully unprepared for the war at the outset and faced increasing popular opposition as the contest dragged on. The opposition centered in New England, and it went to remarkable extremes. Some of the Federalists there celebrated British victories, sabotaged their own country's war effort, and even plotted disunion and a separate peace.

Until 1814 the blockade did not extend north of Newport, Rhode Island, the British government deliberately cultivating the New England trade. Goods carried in Yankee ships helped to feed British troops in Canada as well as Spain, and for a time many a shipowner grew rich by trading with the enemy while denouncing Madison and the war, though eventually the business of the shipowners as a whole fell far below the level of the prosperous prewar years.

Though most of the money in the nation was concentrated in New England, only a small part of the government's war bonds could be sold there. One of the Treasury loans, desperately needed to keep soldiers in the field, almost fell through because of the refusal of the New England banks to lend. Secretary of the Treasury Gallatin had to turn to his friend John Jacob Astor of New York and two foreign-born bankers of Philadelphia for the necessary funds. On several occasions the governors of New England states refused to allow the state militia to take orders from the President or to fight outside the country.

In Congress the Republicans had continual trouble with the Federalist opposition. The leadership of the administration party fell to Calhoun, who devoted himself to justifying the war and raising men and money with which to fight it. At every step he ran against the ob-

structionists, foremost among them the young congressman from New Hampshire, Daniel Webster. Introducing resolution after resolution to embarrass the administration, Webster demanded reasons for the war and intimated that Napoleon had tricked the President into antagonizing England, as in fact Napoleon had. Every measure to finance the fighting—by loans, taxes, tariffs, or a national bank—Webster and his Federalist allies vehemently denounced. At a time when volunteering lagged and the army was seriously undermanned, he opposed a bill to encourage enlistments. In its extremity the administration decided to draft men into the regular army from the state militia. Helping to defeat the conscription bill, Webster warned that no such law could be enforced in his part of the country.

As new states in the South and West, strongly Republican, were added to the Union, the Federalists had become more and more hopelessly a minority party in the country as a whole. But they were the majority in New England. If that section were to become a separate confederacy, they could control its destinies and escape the dictation of slaveholders and backwoodsmen. The talk of secession, heard before at the time of the Louisiana Purchase and again at the time of Jefferson's embargo, was revived during the war and reached a climax in the winter of 1814–1815, when the Republic appeared to be on the verge of ruin.

On December 15, 1814, while the British were beginning their invasion by way of New Orleans, delegates from the New England states met in Hartford, Connecticut, to consider the grievances of their section against the Madison administration. The would-be seceders were overruled by the comparatively moderate men who were in the overwhelming majority at the Hartford Convention. The convention's report reasserted the right of nullification but only hinted at secession, observing that "the severance of the Union by one or more States, against the will of the rest, and especially in time of war, can be justified only by absolute necessity." But the report proposed seven essential amendments to the Constitution, presumably as the condition of New England's remaining in the Union. These amendments were intended to protect

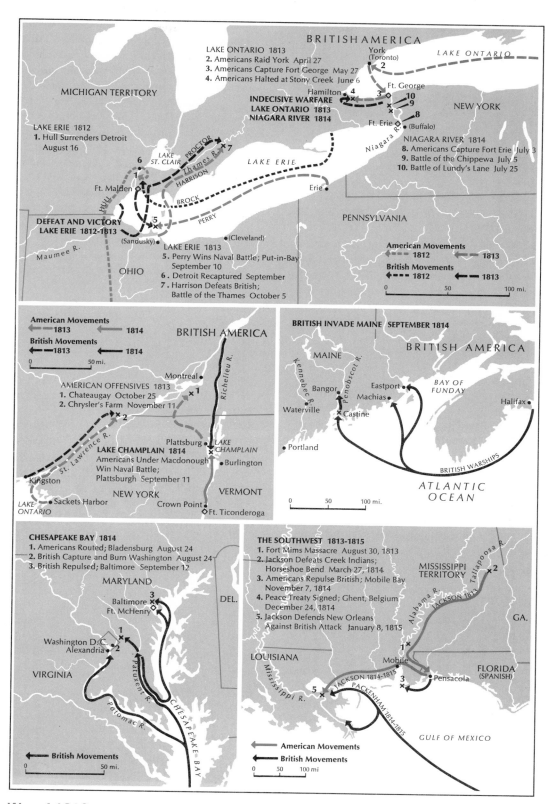

BRITISH AMERICA

LAKE ONTARIO 1813
2. Americans Raid York April 27
3. Americans Capture Fort George May 27
4. Americans Halted at Stony Creek June 6

York
(Toronto)
LAKE ONTARIO

MICHIGAN TERRITORY

**INDECISIVE WARFARE
LAKE ONTARIO 1813
NIAGARA RIVER 1814**

Hamilton
Ft. George
NEW YORK

LAKE ERIE 1812
1. Hull Surrenders Detroit
August 16

Ft. Erie
(Buffalo)

NIAGARA RIVER 1814
8. Americans Capture Fort Erie July 3
9. Battle of the Chippewa July 5
10. Battle of Lundy's Lane July 25

LAKE ST. CLAIR
PROCTOR
Thames R.
HARRISON
BROCK
PERRY

Ft. Malden
HULL

LAKE ERIE

Erie

Niagara R.

**DEFEAT AND VICTORY
LAKE ERIE 1812-1813**

PENNSYLVANIA

(Sandusky)
(Cleveland)

Maumee R.

OHIO

LAKE ERIE 1813
5. Perry Wins Naval Battle; Put-in-Bay
September 10
6. Detroit Recaptured September
7. Harrison Defeats British;
Battle of the Thames October 5

American Movements
1812        1813
British Movements
1812        1813
0        50        100 mi.

American Movements
1813        1814
British Movements
1813        1814
0        50 mi.

BRITISH AMERICA

AMERICAN OFFENSIVES 1813
1. Chateaugay October 25
2. Chrysler's Farm November 11

Montreal
Richelieu R.

BRITISH INVADE MAINE   SEPTEMBER 1814

BRITISH AMERICA

MAINE
Kennebec R.
Penobscot R.
Bangor
Eastport
BAY OF FUNDY
Machias
Halifax
Waterville
Castine

Plattsburg
LAKE CHAMPLAIN

**LAKE CHAMPLAIN 1814**
Americans Under Macdonough
Win Naval Battle;
Plattsburgh September 11

St. Lawrence R.

Burlington

Portland

Kingston

NEW YORK

VERMONT

BRITISH WARSHIPS

LAKE ONTARIO
Sackets Harbor
Crown Point
Ft. Ticonderoga

ATLANTIC OCEAN

0        50        100 mi.

**CHESAPEAKE BAY 1814**
1. Americans Routed; Bladensburg August 24
2. British Capture and Burn Washington August 24
3. British Repulsed; Baltimore September 12

MARYLAND

Baltimore
Ft. McHenry

DEL.

Washington D.C.
Alexandria

VIRGINIA

Patuxent R.

Potomac R.

CHESAPEAKE BAY

British Movements
0        50 mi.

**THE SOUTHWEST 1813-1815**
1. Fort Mims Massacre August 30, 1813
2. Jackson Defeats Creek Indians;
Horseshoe Bend March 27, 1814
3. Americans Repulse British; Mobile Bay
November 7, 1814
4. Peace Treaty Signed; Ghent, Belgium
December 24, 1814
5. Jackson Defends New Orleans
Against British Attack January 8, 1815

MISSISSIPPI TERRITORY

Alabama R.
Tallapoosa R.
JACKSON 1813

GA.

LOUISIANA

Mississippi R.

Mobile

JACKSON 1814-1815
PACKENHAM 1814-1815

FLORIDA
(SPANISH)
Pensacola

GULF OF MEXICO

American Movements
British Movements
0        50        100 mi.

War of 1812

New England from the growing influence of the South and the West.

The Federalists, apparently in a strong bargaining position, assumed that the Republicans would have to give in to the Hartford Convention terms, since the government was in such dire extremity. Soon after the convention adjourned, however, the news of Jackson's smashing victory at New Orleans reached the cities of the Northeast. While most Americans rejoiced, the Federalists were plunged into gloom. A day or two later came tidings from abroad concerning the conclusion of a treaty of peace. Of course, the treaty had been signed before the Battle of New Orleans, but the people heard of the battle first. They got the impression that the United States had won the war. "Peace is signed in the arms of victory!" *Niles's Register* exclaimed. The Hartford Convention and the Federalist party were discredited as not only treasonable but also futile.

## The Peace Settlement

During the War of 1812 peace talks began before the battles did. President Madison, reluctant to ask for a declaration of war and "regretting the necessity which produced it," looked hopefully toward an early end to hostilities. Soon after the declaration the British government, wishing to liquidate a minor war and concentrate upon the major one, against Napoleon, sent an admiral to Washington with armistice proposals, but negotiations failed to develop because of Madison's continued insistence upon the renunciation of impressment. Britain's ally Russia, eager to get supplies from America as well as unhampered military aid from England, twice offered to mediate, the first time on the day before Napoleon's invading forces entered Moscow (September 13, 1812). The British politely declined both of the Czar's offers but finally agreed to meet the Americans in direct negotiations on neutral ground. After prolonged delays the peacemakers got together in Ghent, Belgium, on August 8, 1814.

The American peace delegation at Ghent happened to be composed of men of exceptional ability, men who were more than a match for their opposite numbers around the peace table. The delegation included men of both parties and all sections. At the head of it was John Quincy Adams, a former Federalist who had broken with his party to support Jefferson's embargo, and a diplomat of varied experience who recently had been minister to Russia. One of his colleagues was Henry Clay, once a war hawk, now a peace dove. Another was the Secretary of the Treasury in both Jefferson's and Madison's administrations, Albert Gallatin. A natural diplomat, Gallatin held the delegation together by moderating the disputes of Adams and Clay.

At Ghent the two sets of peacemakers at first presented fantastically extreme demands, then gradually backed down and finally agreed to a compromise. The Americans, in accordance with their instructions, originally demanded the renunciation of impressment as a necessary condition to peace, and they also asked for all or part of Canada and for British aid in acquiring Florida from Spain. The Englishmen, contrary to their instructions, presented an ultimatum requiring the United States to cede territory in the Northwest for the formation of an Indian buffer state. Then, when their home government refused to sustain them in the ultimatum, they withdrew it and proposed that peace be made on the principle of *uti possidetis*. This meant that each of the belligerents should keep the territory it actually held whenever the fighting stopped. Expecting large territorial gains from the invasion of America, the Englishmen at Ghent tried to delay negotiations so as to maximize the gains. But the government in London, becoming more and more alarmed by developments in Europe, decided to hasten the settlement with the United States and recommended peace on the basis of the *status quo ante bellum*, which meant a return to things as they had been before the war began. Already President Madison had advised his delegation that they need no longer make an issue of impressment. A treaty providing for the *status quo*, hastily drawn up, was signed on Christmas Eve 1814.

According to the Treaty of Ghent, the war was to end not immediately, but when the document had been ratified and proclaimed on both sides (hence it is not exactly true, as is sometimes said, that the battle of New Orleans was fought after the war was over). Each of the bel-

## The Hartford Convention [1815]

New England opponents of the war, meeting at Hartford, Connecticut, late in 1814, demanded the following amendments to the federal Constitution in their report, published early in the following year:

1. "Representatives and direct taxes shall be apportioned among the several states . . . according to their respective numbers of free persons. . . ."

2. "No new state shall be admitted into the Union by Congress . . . without the concurrence of two thirds of both houses."

3. "Congress shall not have power to lay any embargo . . . for more than sixty days."

4. "Congress shall not have power, without the concurrence of two thirds of both houses, to interdict the commercial intercourse between the United States and any foreign nation. . . ."

5. "Congress shall not make or declare war, or authorize acts of hostility against any foreign nation, without the concurrence of two thirds of both houses, except such acts of hostility be in defence of the territories of the United States when actually invaded."

6. "No person who shall hereafter be naturalized, shall be eligible as a member of the senate or house of representatives of the United States, nor capable of holding any civil office under the authority of the United States."

7. "The same person shall not be elected president of the United States a second time; nor shall the president be elected from the same state two terms in succession."

ligerents was to restore its wartime conquests to the other. Four commissions with both American and British members were to be appointed to agree upon disputed or undetermined segments of the boundary between Canada and the United States.

The Treaty of Ghent was followed by other settlements that contributed to the improvement of Anglo-American relations. A separate commercial treaty (1815) gave Americans the right to trade freely with England and the British Empire except for the West Indies. A fisheries convention (1818) renewed the privileges of Americans to catch and dry fish at specified places along the shores of British North America. The Rush-Bagot agreement (1817) provided for mutual disarmament on the Great Lakes. Gradually disarmament was extended to the land, and eventually (though not till 1872) the Canadian-American boundary became the longest "unguarded frontier" in the world.

Though the British had not renounced impressment in principle, they ceased to apply it in practice after 1815. With the final end of the Napoleonic wars after the battle of Waterloo, the nations of Europe entered upon a century of comparative peace, broken only by wars of limited scale. So the British no longer had occasion to violate American sovereignty on the high seas, and the government and people of the United States could afford to devote their energies primarily to affairs at home.

## Free Seas Again

No sooner had peace come in 1815 than Congress declared war again, this time against Algiers, which had taken advantage of the War of 1812 to loose its pirates once more against American shipping in the Mediterranean. Two American squadrons now proceeded to North African waters. One of the two, under the command of Stephen Decatur, a naval hero of the late war with England, captured a number of corsair ships, blockaded the coast of Algiers, and forced the Dey to accept a treaty that not only ended the payment of tribute by the United States but required the Dey to pay reparations to this country. Going on to Tunis and Tripoli, Decatur collected additional indemnities in both of those places. This naval action in the Mediterranean brought a more clear-cut victory for the freedom of the seas than had the War of 1812 itself. Of course, the victory was made possible by the growth in naval strength and national spirit which the war with England had occasioned. After 1816, when the Dey of Algiers began to make trouble again, only to have his entire fleet destroyed by combined British and Dutch forces, the United States had no further difficulties with the Barbary pirates.

## POSTWAR EXPANSION

Americans could now give their full attention to domestic problems as the country, during a postwar boom, expanded its economy, its territory, and its population. Suddenly the boom terminated in a bust.

### Banks, Tariffs, Roads

The War of 1812 led to chaos in shipping and banking, as well as stimulating the growth of manufactures, and exposed dramatically the inadequacy of the existing transportation system. Hence arose the postwar issues of reestablishing the Bank of the United States, protecting the new industries, and providing a nationwide network of roads and waterways. On these issues the former war hawks Clay and Calhoun became the leading advocates of the national as opposed to the local or sectional point of view. The party of Jefferson now sponsored measures of a kind once championed by the party of Hamilton. In regard to the Bank and the tariff the new nationalists were completely successful; in regard to internal improvements, only partly so.

The wartime experience seemed to make necessary another national bank. After the first Bank's charter expired (1811), a large number of state banks sprang up. These issued vast quantities of banknotes (promises to pay, which then served much the same purpose as bank checks were later to do) and did not always bother to keep a large enough reserve of gold or silver to redeem the notes on demand. The notes passed from hand to hand more or less as money, but their actual value depended upon the reputation of the bank that issued them, and the variety of issues was so confusing as to make honest business difficult and counterfeiting easy.

This bank money was not legal tender, and it was not issued directly by the state governments, yet its issuance hardly conformed with the clause of the Constitution giving Congress the exclusive power to regulate the currency and forbidding the states to emit bills of credit.

Congress struck at the currency evil not by prohibiting state banknotes but by chartering a second Bank of the United States in 1816. Except that it was allowed a larger capital, this institution was essentially the same as the one founded under Hamilton's leadership in 1791. In return for the charter, the Bank had to pay a "bonus" of $1.5 million to the government. Though its potentialities were not fully realized during the first few years of its existence, this national bank possessed the power of controlling the state banks by presenting their notes from time to time and demanding payment either in cash or in its own notes, which were as good as gold. Once the Bank of the United States began to exercise its power, the state banks had to stay on a specie-paying basis or risk being forced out of business.

The war had a disastrous effect upon American shipping, especially after the British blockade was extended to include the New England coast. Between 1811 and 1814 exports dropped from $61 million to $7 million, and imports from $53 million to $13 million. The total tonnage of American vessels engaged in foreign trade declined from about 950,000 to less than 60,000 tons. Some ships managed to escape the blockade but others were caught and confiscated, altogether about 1,300 of them.

Farmers, unable to get their produce out to the markets of the world, suffered from the ruin of the carrying trade, but manufacturers prospered as foreign competition almost disappeared in consequence of the embargoes and the blockade. Much of the capital and labor formerly employed in commerce and shipbuilding was diverted to manufacturing. Goods were so scarce that, even with comparatively unskilled labor and poor management, new factories could be started with an assurance of quick profits.

The American textile industry had grown rather slowly until English imports were checked by Jefferson's Embargo of 1807 and then by the War of 1812. The first census of manufacturing, in 1810, counted 269 cotton and 24 woolen mills in the country. From 1807 to 1815 the total number of cotton spindles increased from 8,000 to 130,000. Most of the factories were located in New England. Until 1814 they produced only yarn and thread: the weaving of cloth was left to families operating hand looms at home. Then the Boston merchant Francis C. Lowell, after examining textile machinery in England, perfected a power loom that was an improvement on its English counterpart. Lowell organized the Boston Manufacturing Company and founded at Waltham, Massa-

chusetts, the first mill in America to carry on the processes of spinning and weaving under a single roof.

As the war came to an end, the manufacturing prospects of the United States were suddenly dimmed. British ships swarmed alongside American wharves and began to unload their cargoes of manufactured goods at cut prices, even selling below cost. As Lord Brougham explained to Parliament, it was "well worth while to incur a loss upon the first exportation, in order, by the glut, to stifle in the cradle those rising manufactures in the United States, which war had

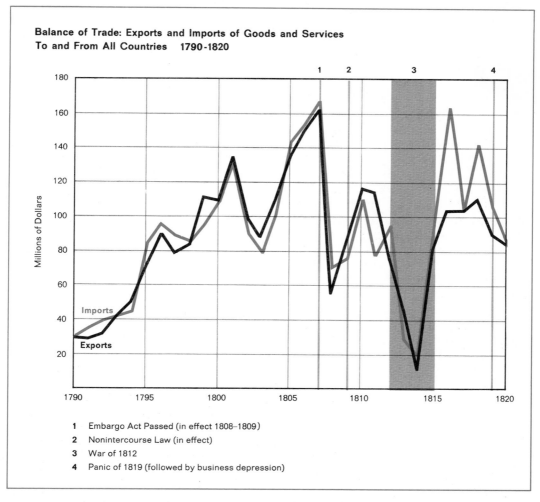

**Balance of Trade: Exports and Imports of Goods and Services To and From All Countries   1790-1820**

Millions of Dollars

1   Embargo Act Passed (in effect 1808–1809)
2   Nonintercourse Law (in effect)
3   War of 1812
4   Panic of 1819 (followed by business depression)

The Embargo Act (1807) reduced trade in 1808 and 1809 to about half of what it had been in the years immediately preceding, when it was stimulated by the war in Europe. The War of 1812 caused trade to shrink still further in

1813 and 1814. During the postwar recovery, imports considerably exceeded exports, creating an "unfavorable balance of trade" and provoking demands for increased tariff protection.

forced into existence, contrary to the natural course of things." Thus, though the war was over, Great Britain persisted in a kind of economic warfare against the United States.

The "infant industries" needed protection if they were to survive and grow strong enough to stand upon their own feet against foreign competition. So the friends of industry maintained, reviving the old arguments of Hamilton. In 1816 the protectionists brought about the passage of a tariff law with rates high enough to be definitely protective, especially on cotton cloth.

The war had delayed the extension of steamboat lines on both eastern and western waters. Not until 1816 did a river steamer, the *Washington,* make a successful voyage upstream as far as Louisville, at the falls of the Ohio. Within a few years steamboats were carrying far more cargo on the Mississippi than all the flatboats, barges, and other primitive craft combined.

When Ohio was admitted as a state (1803) the federal government agreed that part of the proceeds from the sale of public lands there should be used for building roads. In 1807 Jefferson's Secretary of the Treasury, Albert Gallatin, proposed that a national road, financed partly by Ohio land sales, be built from the Potomac to the Ohio, and both Congress and the President approved. The next year Gallatin presented a comprehensive plan of internal improvements,

requiring an appropriation of $20 million, but Jefferson doubted the constitutionality of such an expenditure, and the plan was shelved. Finally, in 1811, construction of the National Road began, at Cumberland, Maryland, on the Potomac. By 1818 this highway, with a crushed stone surface and massive stone bridges, was completed to Wheeling, Virginia, on the Ohio. Meanwhile the state of Pennsylvania contributed $100,000 to a private company which extended the Lancaster pike westward to Pittsburgh.

Over both of these roads moved a heavy traffic of stagecoaches, Conestoga wagons, private carriages, and other vehicles, as well as droves of cattle. Despite the high tolls, freight rates across the mountains now were lower than ever before. They were not low enough to permit the long-distance hauling of bulky loads like wheat or flour. But commodities with a high value in proportion to their weight, especially manufactures, moved from the Atlantic seaboard to the Ohio Valley in unprecedented quantities.

Despite the progress being made with steamboats and turnpikes, there remained serious gaps in the transportation network of the country, as experience during the War of 1812 had shown. Once the coastwise shipping had been cut off by the British blockade, the coastal roads became choked by the unaccustomed volume of north-south traffic. At the river ferries, long

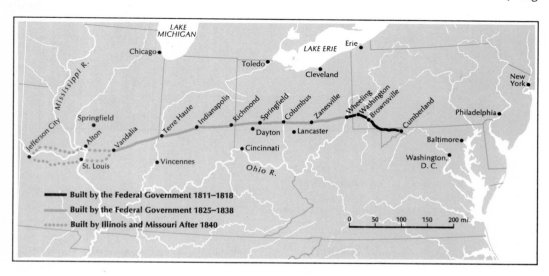

Built by the Federal Government 1811–1818
Built by the Federal Government 1825–1838
Built by Illinois and Missouri After 1840

**The National Road**

lines of wagons waited for a chance to cross. Oxcarts, pressed into emergency service, took six or seven weeks to go from Philadelphia to Charleston. In various localities there appeared serious shortages of goods normally carried by sea, and prices rose to new heights, rice costing three times as much in New York as in Charleston, flour three times as much in Boston as in Richmond. On the northern and western frontiers the military campaigns of the United States were frustrated partly by the absence of good roads.

With this wartime experience in mind, President Madison in 1815 called the attention of Congress to the "great importance of establishing throughout our country the roads and canals which can be best executed under the national authority," and he suggested that a constitutional amendment would resolve any doubts about the authority of Congress to provide for the construction of canals and roads. Representative Calhoun promptly espoused a bill by which the moneys due the government from the Bank of the United States—both the "bonus" and the government's share of the annual profits —would be devoted to internal improvements. "Let us, then, bind the republic together with a perfect system of roads and canals," Calhoun urged. "Let us conquer space."

Congress passed the bonus bill, but President Madison, on his last day in office (March 3, 1817), returned it with his veto. While he approved its purpose, he still believed that a constitutional amendment was necessary. And so, with some exceptions, the tremendous task of internal improvements was left to the state governments and to private enterprise.

## "Era of Good Feelings"

After 1800 the Presidency seemed to have become the special possession of Virginians, who passed it from one to another in unvarying sequence. After two terms in office Jefferson named his Secretary of State, James Madison, to succeed him, and after two more terms Madison secured the nomination of *his* Secretary of State, James Monroe. Many in the North already were muttering against this succession of Virginians, the so-called "Virginia Dynasty," yet the Republicans had no difficulty in electing

their candidate in the remarkably listless campaign of 1816. Monroe received 183 ballots in the electoral college; his opponent, Rufus King of New York, only 34, from the states of Massachusetts, Connecticut, and Delaware.

At the time he became President, Monroe was sixty-one years old. Tall and dignified, he wore the old-fashioned garb of his youthful days, including knee-length pantaloons and white-topped boots. He had reached the peak of a long and varied career as Revolutionary soldier, diplomat, and cabinet officer. Although when young he had been regarded as impulsive and changeable, he now was noted for his caution and patience. He was neither so subtle nor so original as his gifted predecessors from Virginia, Jefferson and Madison, yet he was more able than posterity generally has considered him. He had a mind of his own, and he was the master of his administration, even though he picked a group of exceptionally strong men for his advisers.

In choosing his cabinet, Monroe intended to recognize and harmonize the major interests of the country. For the first and most important position, that of secretary of state, he selected the New Englander and former Federalist, John Quincy Adams. This choice was significant in view of the well-established custom that made the State Department a stepping stone to the Presidency: Monroe appeared to be announcing that he would be the last of the Virginia Dynasty and that the next President (after a second term for Monroe) would be a Massachusetts man. For secretary of war, Monroe chose the forceful South Carolinian, John C. Calhoun, after Henry Clay had declined the office, preferring to continue as Speaker of the House.

Soon after his inauguration Monroe did what no other President since Washington had done: he made a goodwill tour through the country, eastward to New England, westward as far as Detroit. In New England, so recently the scene of rabid Federalist discontent, he was greeted everywhere with enthusiastic demonstrations. The *Columbian Centinel*, a Federalist newspaper of Boston, commenting on the "Presidential Jubilee" in that city, observed that an "era of good feelings" had arrived. This phrase soon became popular; it spread throughout the coun-

**James Monroe**

When Monroe was governor of Virginia (1799–1802) an acquaintance said to him: "To be plain, there is often in his manner an inartificial and even an awkward simplicity, which, while it provokes the smile of a more polished person, forces him to the opinion that Mr. Monroe is a man of most sincere and artless soul." In 1825, when Monroe was in his last year as President, a Virginia lady gave her impression of him after attending a New Year's reception at the White House: "From the frank, honest expression of his eye . . . I think he well deserves the encomium passed upon him by the great Jefferson, who said, 'Monroe is so honest that if you turned his soul inside out there would not be a spot on it.'" The portrait here reproduced was done by **Gilbert Stuart**, who painted portraits of all the men who served as Presidents during his lifetime—Washington, Adams, Jefferson, Madison, Monroe, and John Quincy Adams. (The Pennsylvania Academy of the Fine Arts)

try, and eventually it came to be almost synonymous with the Presidency of Monroe.

There was a good deal of hidden irony in this phrase of 1817, for the "good feelings" did not last long, and the period over which Monroe presided turned into one of very bad feelings indeed. Yet he was reelected in 1820 with the nearest thing to a unanimous electoral vote that any presidential candidate, with the exception of George Washington, has ever had. Indeed, all but one of the electors cast their ballots for Monroe. The lone dissenter, a strong-minded Yankee from New Hampshire who thought Monroe unfit for the Presidency, voted for John Quincy Adams. The Federalists had not even bothered to put up an opposing candidate.

## Florida and the Far West

The first big problem facing John Quincy Adams as Secretary of State was that of Florida. Already the United States had annexed West Florida, but Spain still claimed the whole of the province, East and West, and actually held most of it, though with a grasp too feeble to stop the abuses against which Americans long had complained—the escape of slaves across the border in one direction, the marauding of Indians across it in the other. In 1817 Adams began negotiations with the Spanish minister, Don Luis de Onís, for acquiring all of Florida (or rather for acquiring that part of it which the United States did not already claim). Talks between the cantankerous puritan and the wily don progressed haltingly, then were broken off when the hot-tempered Andrew Jackson took matters forcefully into his own hands.

Jackson, in command of American troops along the Florida frontier, had orders from Secretary of War Calhoun to "adopt the necessary measures" to end the border troubles. Jackson also had an unofficial hint—or so he afterwards claimed—that the administration would not mind if he undertook a punitive expedition into Spanish territory. At any rate he invaded Florida, seized the Spanish forts at St. Marks and Pensacola, and ordered the hanging of two British subjects on the charge of supplying the Indians and inciting them to hostilities. News of these events provoked a sharp discussion behind the scenes in Monroe's cabinet. Calhoun and others insisted that the general should be punished or at least reprimanded for exceeding his authority, but Adams defended Jackson so ably as to prevent any action against him.

Instead of blaming Jackson or disavowing the raid, Adams wished the government to assume complete responsibility for it, for he saw in it a chance to further his Florida diplomacy. Rejecting a Spanish protest, he demanded reparations from Spain to pay the cost of the expedition, though he did not press this demand. He pointed out that Spain had promised in Pinckney's Treaty to restrain the Indians in her territory but had failed to live up to her treaty obligations. The United States, he argued, was justified by international law in taking drastic measures for self-defense. He implied that this country would be justified in going even farther than it had done.

Jackson's raid demonstrated that the United States, if it tried, could easily take Florida by force, unless Spain could get aid from some other power. The only power to which she could look was Great Britain.

Unable to obtain British support, Spain had little choice but to come to terms with the United States, though the resourceful Onís made the most of a bad situation for his country. In the treaty of 1819 it was agreed that the King of Spain should cede "all the territories which belong to him situated to the eastward of the Mississippi and known by the name of East and West Florida." This ambiguous wording was used so as to evade the troublesome question whether Spain was ceding both East and West Florida or whether West Florida already belonged to the United States. In return the United States assumed the claims of its citizens against the Spanish government to the amount of $5 million. This money was to be paid to American citizens, not to the Spanish government: we did not "purchase" Florida, as is sometimes said. The United States also gave up its claims to Texas, and Spain her claims to territory north of the forty-second parallel from the Rockies to the Pacific. Thus a line was drawn from the Gulf of Mexico northwestward across the continent delimiting the Spanish empire and transferring to the United States the Spanish title to the West Coast north of California. Adams and Onís had concluded something more than a Florida agreement: it was a "transcontinental treaty."

President Monroe, with the approval of the Senate, promptly ratified the treaty, but the coming of a revolution delayed ratification by Spain. The treaty finally went into effect in 1821. Thereafter the whole of Florida was, without question, territory belonging to the United States. And for the first time the area of the Louisiana Purchase had a definite southwestern boundary.

At the time of his negotiations with Onís, Adams showed much more interest in the Far West than did most of his fellow countrymen. Few Americans were familiar with the Oregon coast except for New Englanders engaged in Pacific whaling or in the China trade. Only the fur traders and trappers knew intimately any of the land between the Missouri and the Pacific. Before the War of 1812 John Jacob Astor's American Fur Company had established Astoria as a trading post at the mouth of the Columbia River. But when war came Astor sold his interests to the Northwestern Fur Company, a British concern operating from Canada, and after the war he centered his own operations in the Great Lakes area, from which he eventually extended them westward to the Rockies. Manuel Lisa's Missouri Fur Company, founded in 1809, with headquarters in St. Louis, sent traders and supplies up the Missouri and its tributaries and brought back peltries obtained from the Indians. The Rocky Mountain Fur Company, which Andrew Henry and William Henry Ashley organized in 1822, pushed the trade farther north and west and revolutionized the business by sending out white trappers who procured their furs directly and brought them to an annual "rendezvous" in the mountains to be sold to the company's agents.

The trappers or "mountain men," notably Jedediah S. Smith, explored the Far West and gained an intimate knowledge of it, but they did not write books. General information about the region was increased in consequence of the explorations of Major Stephen H. Long. In 1819 and 1820, with instructions from the War Department to find the sources of the Red River, Long with nineteen soldiers ascended the Platte and South Platte rivers, discovered the peak named for him, and returned eastward by way of the Arkansas River, but failed to find the headwaters of the Red. "In regard to this extensive section of country between the Missouri River and the Rocky Mountains," Long said in his report, "we do not hesitate in giving the opinion that it is almost wholly unfit for cultivation, and of course uninhabitable by a people depending upon agriculture for their subsistence." On the published map of his expedition the Great Plains were marked as the "Great

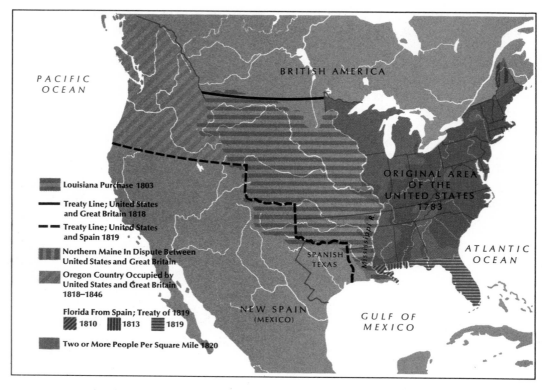

PACIFIC
OCEAN

BRITISH AMERICA

ORIGINAL AREA
OF THE
UNITED STATES
1783

ATLANTIC
OCEAN

SPANISH
TEXAS

NEW SPAIN
(MEXICO)

GULF OF
MEXICO

Louisiana Purchase 1803

Treaty Line; United States
and Great Britain 1818

Treaty Line; United States
and Spain 1819

Northern Maine In Dispute Between
United States and Great Britain

Oregon Country Occupied by
United States and Great Britain
1818–1846

Florida From Spain; Treaty of 1819
1810    1813    1819

Two or More People Per Square Mile 1820

## Boundary Settlements  1818–1819

American Desert." Thus he gave increased currency to the idea earlier put forth by Pike that the farming frontier would run against a great natural barrier beyond the Missouri. Meanwhile the vacant lands to the east, between the Appalachians and the Mississippi, were rapidly being converted into plantations and farms.

### The Great Migration

One of the central themes of American history, for nearly three centuries after the founding of Jamestown, was the movement of population from the Atlantic coast to the interior and ultimately across the continent. This was no steady march, uniform along a broad front. It proceeded in irregular waves, following the lines of greatest attraction and least resistance, and accelerating in times of prosperity and peace. A sudden surge, greater than any preceding it, swept westward during the boom years which followed the War of 1812.

Weakened though it had been, the Indian threat still had to be taken into account. In a

series of treaties forced upon the tribes after 1815, the federal government resumed the policy of compelling the redmen to choose between settling down as civilized farmers and migrating beyond the Mississippi. Along the Great Lakes and the upper Mississippi a chain of stockaded forts was erected to protect the frontier. A "factory" system, by which government factors or agents traded with the Indians, supplying them with goods at cost, was instituted in an effort to drive out of business the Canadian traders who persisted in carrying on their activities on American soil. After several years the government factories were abandoned because of the opposition of American fur companies who objected to government competition with private enterprise. By that time the Canadian traders had retreated across the border, and foreign influence over the American tribes finally came to an end.

The land abandoned by the Indians in the Northwest had been richly favored by nature, though its qualities were not entirely understood by the early pioneers. Over most of the Northwest extended the great primeval forest, but in central Illinois the forest gave way to a grand prairie billowing with wild grass as tall as six feet. The first settlers avoided this treeless stretch, for they saw unfamiliar problems in its tough sod and scarcity of wood, and they little knew the productivity of its black loam.

"Old America seems to be breaking up and moving westward," remarked an Englishman who joined the throng. Some were Kentucky and Tennessee frontiersmen, restless spirits who had begun to feel crowded as their states became increasingly populous. Others were small farmers from the back country of Virginia and the Carolinas who fled the encroachment of slavery and the plantation system. Still others came from the middle states, New England, and foreign countries, but the great majority were Southerners. Whatever the starting point, the Ohio River was for most of the migrants the main route, the "grand track," until the completion of the Erie Canal in 1825. They took the turnpike to Pittsburgh or the National Road to Wheeling and thus reached the river, or they took one of its tributaries such as the Kanawha, the Cumberland, or the Tennessee. Downstream they floated on flatboats bearing all their worldly goods. Then, leaving the Ohio at Cincinnati or at some place farther down, they pressed on overland with wagons, handcarts, packhorses, cattle, and hogs.

Once having arrived at his destination, preferably in the spring or early summer, the settler built a lean-to or cabin for his family, then hewed a clearing out of the forest and put in a crop of corn to supplement the wild game he caught and the domestic animals he had brought with him.

These frontier folk knew loneliness and poverty and dirt, suffered much from the forest fevers and from malnutrition, commonly had a lean and sallow look. Yet they were on the whole remarkably proud, bold, and independent. They were "half wild and wholly free."

To the Southwest moved people from Kentucky, from Tennessee, and from as far away as New England. Most numerous among the settlers on the Southern frontier, however, were farmers and planters from the South Atlantic states, especially from the piedmont of Georgia and the Carolinas. Their motive for migrating was, in a word, cotton. With the spread of cotton cultivation throughout the uplands of the older South, the soil there lost much of its natural fertility from repeated croppings, or washed away as torrential rains gullied the hillsides. Seeking fresh soil with a climate suitable for cotton, the planters naturally looked to the Southwest, around the end of the Appalachian range, where there stretched a broad zone within which cotton could thrive. Included in this zone was the Black Belt of central Alabama and Mississippi, a prairie with a fabulously productive soil of rotted limestone.

The advance of the Southern frontier meant the spread of cotton and slavery. Usually the first arrivals were ordinary frontiersmen like those farther north, small farmers who made rough clearings in the forest. Then came planters who bought up the cleared or partially cleared land, while the original settlers moved on west and started over again. As a rule the planters made the westward journey in a style quite different from that of the other pioneers. Over the alternately dusty and muddy roads came great caravans consisting of herds of livestock, wagonloads of household goods, long lines of slaves, and, bringing up the rear, the planter and his family riding in carriages. Soon the clearings expanded into vast fields white with cotton, and the cabins of the pioneers gave way to more sumptuous log dwellings and ultimately to imposing mansions that demonstrated the rise of a class of the newly rich.

Though by 1819 settlers already were pushing beyond the Mississippi, much of the area to the east of the river, around the Great Lakes and along the Gulf of Mexico, was yet to be occupied. Despite the gaps in settlement, the population of the Mississippi Valley had increased far more rapidly than that of the nation as a whole. The census of 1810 indicated that only one American in seven lived to the west of the Appalachian Mountains; the census of 1820, almost one in four. During the immediate postwar years four new states were created in this region —Indiana (1816), Mississippi (1817), Illinois (1818), and Alabama (1819). Meanwhile Missouri had grown populous enough for statehood,

## From Forest to Farm

First (top left), a clearing is begun and a rude cabin is
built. The stream remains unbridged and has to be forded.
Second (bottom left), the cabin is fenced in (note the
"worm" fence), more trees are cut, stumps are burned,
a small crop is put in, and the stream is spanned by a log
bridge. Third (top right), the cabin is enlarged, a barn is
built, the fencing is improved, fields are widened, and a
bridge is erected. Finally (bottom right), all trace of the
wilderness is gone, an imposing house has replaced the
cabin, a village has grown up nearby, and an arched stone
bridge has been built. These illustrations are from
O. Turner, *Pioneer History of the Holland Land Purchase
of Western New York* (1850).

and the struggle over her admission indicated how important, politically and otherwise, the West was becoming in the eyes of the rest of the nation. For the time being, however, the westward movement was slowed down by the onset of the depression following the Panic of 1819.

## The Panic of 1819

In part the Panic of 1819 was a delayed reaction to the War of 1812 and to the preceding years of warfare in Europe. Since 1793 the continual fighting had drawn manpower from European fields, disrupted business as well as agriculture, and created an abnormal demand for the produce of American plantations and farms. The whole period was one of exceptionally high prices for American producers, and though some prices fell with the decline of trade in 1814, they recovered with the resumption of exports to Europe after the war.

Rising prices for farm products stimulated a land boom in the United States, particularly in the West. After the war the government land offices did a bigger business than ever before; not for twenty years were they to do as good a business again. In 1815 sales totaled about a million acres and in 1819 more than 5 million. Many settlers bought on credit: under the land laws of 1800 and 1804 they could pay as little as $80 down, and they hoped to raise the remaining three installments within four years from the proceeds of their farming. Speculators bought large tracts of choice land, hoping to resell it at a profit to incoming settlers. At the land-office auctions, bidding became so spirited that much of the public land sold for prices far above the minimum of $2 an acre, some in the Black Belt of Alabama and Mississippi going for $100 and more. Still-higher prices sometimes were paid by optimistic real-estate promoters who laid out town sites, even in swamps, and expected to make fortunes through the sale of city lots. Until 1817 neither the settlers nor the speculators needed hard cash to buy government land: they could borrow from the state banks and pay the government with banknotes.

Even after the refounding of the Bank of the United States in 1817, wildcat banks continued to provide easy credit for a few years. Indeed,

### Public Lands: Terms of Sale [1785–1820]

**Ordinance of 1785**
Allowed a minimum purchase of 640 acres and set a minimum price of $1 an acre. Made no provision for credit.

**Act of 1796**
Raised the minimum price to $2 an acre but allowed a year's credit on half of the amount due.

**Act of 1800**
Reduced the minimum purchase from 640 to 320 acres and extended credit to four years, with a down payment of one-fourth of the whole amount and three later installments.

**Act of 1804**
Further reduced the minimum purchase to 160 acres. (Now a man with as little as $80 on hand could obtain a farm from the government, although he would still owe $240 to be paid within four years.)

**Act of 1820**
Reduced the minimum purchase still further, to 80 acres, and the minimum price to $1.25 an acre, but abolished the credit system.
*NOTE:* Under each of these laws, the land was first offered for sale at auction, and much of it sold for more than the minimum price.

the United States Bank itself at first offered easy loans. Then in 1819, under new management, it suddenly began to tighten up. It called in loans and foreclosed mortgages, acquiring thousands of acres of mortgaged land in the West. It gathered up state banknotes and presented them to the state banks for payment in cash. Having little money on hand, many of these banks closed their doors. Most of the rest soon had to follow suit, for they were beset by depositors with notes to be cashed. The panic was on.

Six years of depression followed. Prices rapidly fell. With the prices of farm products so low, those settlers buying land on credit could not hope to keep up their payments. Some stood to lose everything—their land, their improvements on it, their homes. They demanded relief from their congressmen, and Congress responded with the land law of 1820 and the relief act of 1821. By the new land law the credit system was abolished but the minimum price was lowered from $2.00 to $1.25 and the minimum tract from 160 to 80 acres. Hereafter a purchaser would have to buy his farm outright, but he could get one for as little as $100. The relief act allowed a previous buyer to pay off his debt at the reduced price, to accept the reduced acreage and apply the payments to it, and to have an extension of time in meeting his installments.

# Selected Readings

**Backgrounds of Conflict** J. W. Pratt, *Expansionists of 1812* (1925); A. L. Burt, *The United States, Great Britain, and British North America from the Revolution to the Peace After the War of 1812* (1940); Bradford Perkins, *Prologue to War: England and the United States, 1805–1812* (1961); Reginald Horsman, *The Causes of the War of 1812°* (1962); R. H. Brown, *The Republic in Peril: 1812* (1964); J. F. Zimmerman, *Impressment of American Seamen* (1925); L. M. Sears, *Jefferson and the Embargo* (1927).

**War and Peace** F. F. Beirne, *The War of 1812* (1949); H. L. Coles, *The War of 1812°* (1965); William Wood, *The War with the United States* (1915), a Canadian viewpoint; J. R. Jacobs, *The Beginning of the United States Army, 1783–1812* (1947); A. T. Mahan, *Sea Power in Its Relation to the War of 1812* (2 vols., 1919); Fletcher Pratt, *Preble's Boys: Commodore Preble and the Birth of American Sea Power* (1950); F. L. Engelman, *The Peace of Christmas Eve* (1962).

**Postwar Expansion** George Dangerfield, *The Era of Good Feelings°* (1952); F. J. Turner, *Rise of the New West°* (1906); F. S. Philbrick, *The Rise of the West, 1754–1830°* (1965), anti-Turner; T. P. Abernethy, *The South in the New Nation, 1789–1819* (1961); A. L. Kohlmeier, *The Old Northwest as the Keystone of the Arch of the American Federal Union* (1938); R. C. Buley, *The Old Northwest: Pioneer Period, 1815–1840* (2 vols., 1950); Dale Van Every, *The Final Challenge: The American Frontier, 1804–1845°* (1964); E. B. Wesley, *Guarding the Frontier: A Study of Frontier Defense from 1818 to 1825* (1935); H. P. Beers, *The Western Military Frontier, 1815–1846* (1935); R. M. Robbins, *Our Landed Heritage: The Public Domain°* (1942); P. C. Brooks, *Diplomacy and the Borderlands: The Adams-Onís Treaty of 1819* (1939); L. C. Hunter, *Steamboats on the Western Rivers* (1949); M. N. Rothbard, *The Panic of 1819: Reactions and Policies* (1962).

**Biographies** Irving Brant, *James Madison: The President, 1809–1812* (1956) and *James Madison: Commander in Chief, 1812–1836* (1961); C. M. Wiltse, *John C. Calhoun: Nationalist, 1782–1828* (1944); Bernard Mayo, *Henry Clay, Spokesman of the New West* (1937); Freeman Cleves, *Old Tippecanoe* (1939), William Henry Harrison; Marquis James, *Andrew Jackson, Border Captain°* (1933); Glenn Tucker, *Tecumseh: Vision of Glory* (1956); S. F. Bemis, *John Quincy Adams and the Foundations of American Foreign Policy* (1949).

---

° Titles available in paperback.

# Chapter 9
# Sectionalism
# and Patriotism

The westward movement of population led, five years after the end of the War of 1812, to a sectional crisis. The specific question was whether Missouri should be admitted as a slaveholding state, but also involved was the larger question whether the North or the South should control the rising West. Though the Missouri controversy was settled by a compromise, the spirit of sectionalism persisted, awaiting other occasions to flare up.

For the time being, however, there were countervailing forces of nationalism. The ideal of a strong national government was vigorously reasserted in the Supreme Court decisions of Chief Justice John Marshall (though these provoked widespread criticism, especially in the South) and in the foreign policies of President James Monroe. Significantly, both Marshall and Monroe were Southerners. National unity was further strengthened by the revival of the system of two political parties, each of which had members in all parts of the country, so that partisan lines cut across and weakened sectional divisions. Meanwhile, an eventual economic basis for national unity was promised by improvements in transportation—canals and railroads—which began to link the coastal cities with the interior, the East with the West. Business could now be conducted on something approaching a truly nationwide scale.

Still another bond of union was the heritage of patriotism, the heroic memories of the Revolution, annually recalled with fife and drum and flamboyant speechmaking on the Fourth of July. The War of 1812 was too recent for the unpatriotic factionalism it had engendered to be entirely forgotten, but the earlier war with Great Britain, as it receded into the past, was more and more suffused with a haze of heroic legend. When General Lafayette, the French hero of the Revolution, revisited the United States in 1824–1825, the glorious past was revived as never before. Everywhere the beloved general went, crowds without distinction of section or party cheered him in frenzied celebrations.

The Revolutionary heritage was most dramatically brought home to the American people by news of the deaths of Thomas Jefferson and John Adams. Jefferson, the author of the Declaration of Independence, and Adams, "its ablest advocate and defender" (as Jefferson said), who at one time were bitter political rivals, had become friendly correspondents in their old age. They died on the same day, and that day was July 4, 1826, exactly half a century after the adoption of the Declaration. To some, this appeared to be more than a coincidence, perhaps a sign from God instructing the American people to cherish the nationality their ancestors had so dearly won.

**Fourth of July   1819**

Detail from a painting by J. L. Krimmel. (The Historical Society of Pennsylvania)

## THE CANAL AGE

More than ever, with the improvements in transportation and the broadening of business, each part of the country could concentrate on the production of a particular kind of goods, since it could depend upon other parts of the country to buy its surplus and supply its needs. This geographical specialization made the East and the West, the North and the South, increasingly interdependent, though at the same time it also intensified differences of economic interest and thus accounted for much of the persisting sectionalism in politics.

### The People   1820–1840

During the 1820s and 1830s, as during the whole of American history, three trends of population were fairly obvious: rapid increase, migration to the West, and movement to towns and cities.

Americans continued to multiply almost as fast as in the colonial period, the population still doubling every twenty-five years or so. The total figure, lower than 4 million in 1790, approached 10 million by 1820 and rose to nearly 13 in 1830 and to about 17 million in 1840. The United States was growing much more rapidly in population than the British Isles or Europe:

by 1860 it had gone ahead of the United Kingdom and had nearly overtaken Germany and France.

The Negro population increased more slowly than the white. After 1808, when the importation of slaves was made illegal, the proportion of blacks to whites in the nation as a whole steadily declined. In 1820 there was one Negro to every four whites; in 1840, one to every five. The slower increase of Negroes was due to their comparatively high death rate, not to a low birth rate. Slave mothers had large families, but life was shorter for both slaves and free Negroes than for whites.

The mortality rate for whites slowly declined. Public health improved a little, though epidemics continued to take their periodic toll, among them a cholera plague that swept the country in 1832. On the average, people lived somewhat longer than in earlier generations. The population increase, however, was due less to lengthened life than to the maintenance of a high birth rate, which more than offset the death rate.

Immigration accounted for little of the population growth before the 1840s. The long years of war in Europe, from 1793 to 1815, had kept the number of newcomers to America down to

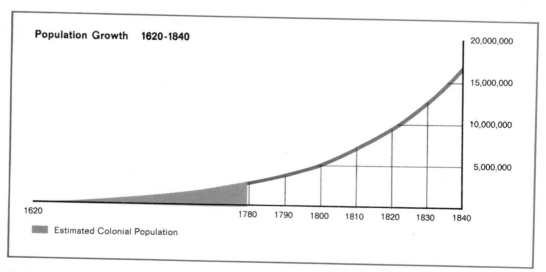

**Population Growth   1620-1840**

20,000,000

15,000,000

10,000,000

5,000,000

1620

1780    1790    1800    1810    1820    1830    1840

▮ Estimated Colonial Population

The United States was the first country to undertake a complete and periodic population count, beginning with the census of 1790. From 1790 to 1840 the American population grew, by actual count, from a little less than 4 million to a little more than 17 million. Meanwhile the

world population grew, according to estimate, from about 700 million to more than 1 billion. During this period the population of the United States was increasing by about 3 per cent a year, that of the United Kingdom less than 1 per cent, and that of France less than one-half of 1 per cent.

not more than a few thousand a year, and then the Panic of 1819 checked the immigrant tide that had risen after Waterloo. During the 1820s arrivals from abroad averaged about 14,000 annually. Of the total population of nearly 13 million in 1830, the foreign-born numbered less than 500,000, mostly naturalized citizens. Soon immigration began to grow, reaching a total of 60,000 for 1832 and nearly 80,000 for 1837.

Since the United States exported more goods than it imported, returning ships often had vacant space and filled it with immigrants as ballast, so to speak. Competition among shipping lines reduced fares so that, by the 1830s, the immigrant could get passage across the Atlantic for as little as $20 or $30. No longer did he need to sell his services to a temporary master in America in order to pay for the voyage. And so the system of indentured servitude, which had dwindled steadily after the Revolution, disappeared entirely after the Panic of 1819.

Until the 1830s most of the new arrivals came from the same sources as had come the bulk of the colonial population—from England and the northern counties of Ireland. In the 1830s, however, the number arriving from the southern counties of Ireland began to grow, anticipating the tremendous influx of Irishmen that was to occur in the next two decades. Generally the newcomers, the Irish as well as others, were welcomed in the United States. They were needed to provide labor for building canals and railroads, manning ships and docks, and performing other heavy work essential to the expanding economic system. But the Irish, as Roman Catholics, excited Protestant prejudices in some communities. In 1834 an anti-Catholic mob set fire to a convent in Charlestown, Massachusetts, and the next year Samuel F. B. Morse (who is better remembered as a portrait painter and as the inventor of the telegraph) published his *Foreign Conspiracy,* which served thereafter as a textbook for nativists crusading against what they imagined was a popish plot to gain control of the United States. Still, the federal government did nothing to check immigration, and shipowners, employers, and some of the states took measures to encourage it.

The West (including both Northwest and Southwest) continued to grow much more rapidly than the rest of the country. By 1830 more than a fourth of the American people lived to the west of the Appalachians; by 1850, nearly a half. Some of the seaboard states suffered serious losses of manpower and womanpower, not to mention the personal property that departing migrants took away. Year after year the Carolinas gave up nearly as much in human resources as they gained by natural increase; their populations remained almost stationary. The same was true of Vermont and New Hampshire. Many a village in these two states was completely depopulated, its houses and barns left to rot, as its people scattered over the country in search of an easier life than the granite hills afforded.

Not all the migrating villagers and farmers sought the unsettled frontier: some moved instead to increasingly crowded population centers. Cities (considered as communities of 8,000 or more) grew faster than the nation as a whole. In 1820 there were more than twice as many cities, and in 1840 more than seven times as many, as there had been in 1790. While the vast majority of Americans continued to reside in the open country or in small towns, the number of city dwellers increased remarkably. In 1790 one person in thirty lived in a community of 8,000 or more; in 1820, one in twenty; and in 1840, one in twelve.

The rise of New York City was phenomenal. By 1810 it had surpassed Philadelphia, which earlier had replaced Boston as the largest city in America. New York steadily increased its lead in both population and trade. Its growth was based on the possession of a superior natural harbor and on several historical developments after the War of 1812. After the war the British chose New York as the chief place to "dump" their manufactured goods and thus helped make it an import center. State laws, which were liberal with regard to auction sales, encouraged inland merchants to do their buying in New York. The first packet line, with regularly scheduled monthly sailings between England and the United States, made New York its American terminus (1816) and hence a more important center of overseas commerce than ever. And the Erie Canal (completed in 1825) gave the city unrivaled access to the interior.

## New York Port 1828

A view of South Street, from the intersection with Maiden Lane, which got its name from the fact that Dutch washermaidens in New Amsterdam used to come here to do their laundry in a brook outside of town. The East River docks lined South Street; there were other docks along the Hudson River on the opposite side of Manhattan Island. Below Maiden Lane, the city by 1828 was almost solidly built up. Above the Lane, there were gardens around the houses, and there were vacant lots which in some cases ran out into open fields. In summer boys swam nude in the East River. The population of the city was approaching 150,000. Note the cobblestone pavement. From a contemporary print. (Courtesy of the New York Public Library, Stokes Collection)

## New Waterways

Despite the road improvements of the turnpike era (1790–1830) Americans continued as in colonial times to depend wherever possible on water routes for travel and transportation. The larger rivers, especially the Mississippi and the Ohio, became increasingly useful as steamboats grew in number and improved in design.

A special kind of steamboat evolved to meet the problems of navigation on the Mississippi and its tributaries. These waters were shallow, with strong and tricky currents, shifting bars of sand and mud, and submerged logs and trees. So the boat had to have a flat bottom, paddle wheels rather than screw propellers, and a powerful, high-pressure engine, which meant a dangerously explosive one. To accommodate as much cargo and as many passengers as possible, the boat was triple-decked, its superstructure rising high in the air. Such a "floating palace" at its best was an impressive sight, elaborately ornamented with gilt and "gingerbread."

River boats carried to New Orleans the corn and other crops of Northwestern farmers, the cotton and tobacco of Southwestern planters. From New Orleans, ships took the cargoes on to Eastern ports. Neither the farmers of the West nor the merchants of the East were completely satisfied with this pattern of trade. Farmers could get better prices for their crops if the alternative existed of sending them directly eastward to market, and merchants could sell larger quantities of their manufactured goods if these could be transported more directly and more economically to the West.

True, the highways across the mountains,

such as the Philadelphia-Pittsburgh turnpike and the National Road, provided a partial solution to the problem. But the costs of hauling goods overland, though lower than before these roads were built, were too high for anything except the most compact and valuable merchandise. New waterways were needed in addition to highways. It was calculated that four horses could pull a wagon weight of one ton twelve miles a day over an ordinary road and one and a half tons eighteen miles a day over a turnpike. On the other hand, four horses could draw a boatload of a hundred tons twenty-four miles a day on a canal.

Sectional jealousies and constitutional scruples stood in the way of action by the federal government, and necessary expenditures were too great for private enterprise. If extensive canals were to be dug, the job would be up to the various states.

New York was the first to act. It had the natural advantage of a comparatively level route between the Hudson River and Lake Erie, through the only break in the entire Appalachian chain. Yet the engineering tasks were imposing. The distance was more than 350 miles, several times as long as any of the existing canals in America, and there were ridges to cross and a wilderness of woods and swamps to penetrate. For many years New Yorkers debated whether the scheme was practical. The canal advocates finally won the debate after De Witt Clinton, a late but ardent convert to the cause, was elected governor. Digging began on the Fourth of July, 1817.

This, the Erie Canal, was by far the greatest

### The Erie Canal

The junction of the Erie and the Northern (or Champlain) canals, near the eastern terminus of the Erie, north of Albany. Note the double set of locks and, at the right, the tandem team of horses on the towpath. From an aquatint by John Hill. (Courtesy of the New-York Historical Society, New York City) construction job that Americans ever had undertaken, and it was the work of self-made engineers. Though one of them made a careful study of English canals, he and his associates did more than merely copy what he saw abroad. They devised ingenious arrangements of cables, pulleys, and gears for bringing down trees and uprooting stumps. Instead of the usual shovels and wheelbarrows, they used specially designed plows and scrapers for moving earth. To make watertight locks they produced an ideal cement from native limestone. The canal itself was simply a big ditch, forty feet wide and four feet deep, with towpaths along the banks for the horses or mules that were to draw the canal boats. (Steamboats were not to be used: the churning of a paddle wheel or propeller would cave in the earthen banks.) Cuts and fills, some

of them enormous, enabled the canal to pass through hills and over valleys; stone aqueducts carried it across streams; and eighty-eight locks, of heavy masonry, with great wooden gates, took care of the necessary ascents and descents.

Not only was the Erie Canal an engineering triumph; it quickly proved a financial success as well. It was opened for through traffic in October 1825, with fitting ceremonies. Governor Clinton at the head of a parade of canal boats made the trip from Buffalo to the Hudson and then downriver to New York City, where he emptied a keg of Erie water into the Atlantic to symbolize the wedding of the lake and the ocean. Soon traffic was so heavy that, within about seven years, the tolls brought in enough to repay the whole construction cost. The prosperity of the Erie encouraged the state to enlarge its canal system

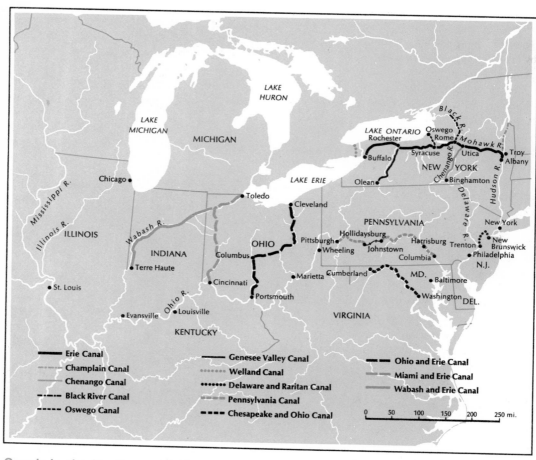

Canals in the Northeast 1840

by building several branches. An important part of the system was the Champlain Canal, begun at about the same time as the Erie and completed in 1822, which connected Lake Champlain with the Hudson River. Though some of the branches did not pay for themselves, they provided useful water connections between New York City and the larger towns of the state. The main line, giving access to Lake Erie as it did, led beyond the state's borders, to the West.

The range of the New York canal system was still further extended when the states of Ohio and Indiana, inspired by the success of the Erie Canal, provided water connections between Lake Erie and the Ohio River. In 1825 Ohio began the building of two canals, one between Portsmouth and Cleveland and the other between Cincinnati and Toledo, both of which were in use by 1833. In 1832 Indiana started the construction of a canal that was to connect Evansville with the Cincinnati-Toledo route. These canals made it possible to ship or to travel by inland waterways all the way from New York to New Orleans, though several changes between canal, lake, and river craft would be necessary. By way of the Great Lakes it was possible to go by water from New York to Chicago. After the opening of the Erie Canal, shipping on the Great Lakes by sail and steam rapidly increased.

The consequences of the development of this transportation network were far-reaching. One of the immediate results was the stimulation of the settlement of the Northwest, not only because it had become easier for migrants to make the westward journey but also, and more important, because it had become easier for them, after taking up their farms, to ship their produce to markets. Towns boomed along the Erie and other canals, New York City benefiting the most of all. Though much of the Western produce, especially corn, continued to go downriver to New Orleans, an increasing proportion of it and most of the wheat of the Northwest went toward New York. And manufactured goods now went in growing volume from New York by the comparatively direct and economical new routes to the West.

Rival cities along the Atlantic seaboard took alarm at the prospect of New York's acquiring so vast a hinterland, largely at their expense. If they were to hold their own, they too must find ways of tapping the Western market. Boston, remote from the West, her way to the Hudson River impeded by the Berkshire Hills, seemed out of the running, at least so far as a canal was concerned. Philadelphia and Baltimore, though they had the still more formidable Allegheny Mountains to contend with, did not give up without an effort at canal building. Beginning in 1834, the commonwealth of Pennsylvania invested in a complicated and costly system of waterways and railways—with an arrangement of "inclined planes," stationary engines, and cable cars to take canal boats over the mountains—intending thus to connect Philadelphia with Pittsburgh. This "Pennsylvania system" proved a failure, financially and otherwise. From Baltimore a canal was projected to ascend the Potomac Valley and tunnel through the mountains, thus achieving essentially the same object as George Washington once had hoped to accomplish. The digging of this grandly conceived Chesapeake and Ohio Canal began in 1828, but it never got farther west than Cumberland. In the South, Richmond and Charleston also aspired to reach the Ohio Valley; Richmond, planning at first to join the James and the Kanawha rivers, eventually saw a canal built as far as Lynchburg.

For none of these rivals of New York did canals provide a satisfactory way to the West. Some cities, however, saw their opportunity in a different and newer means of transportation. Before the canal age had reached its height, the era of the railroad already was beginning.

## The First Railroads

It is hard to date the beginning of railroads, since they resulted from a combination of different elements, each of which had a separate history. One of these was the use of rails, wooden or iron, laid on a prepared roadbed to make a fairly straight and level track. Another was the employment of steam-powered locomotives, and a third was the operation of trains as public carriers of passengers and freight. For nearly two hundred years before the nineteenth century opened, railways with cars pulled by men (and women) or by animals had been used to haul coal from English mines, and in the early 1800s similar railways appeared in the United States. By 1804 both English and American inventors had experimented with steam engines for propelling land vehicles as well as boats. In 1820 John Stevens ran a locomotive and cars around a circular track on his New Jersey estate. Finally, in 1825, the Stockton and Darlington Railroad in England began to operate with steam power over a short length of track and to carry general traffic.

This news quickly aroused the interest of American businessmen, especially in those seaboard cities that sought better communications with the West. First to organize a railroad company was a group of New Yorkers, who in 1826 obtained a charter for the Mohawk and Hudson and five years later began running trains the sixteen miles between Schenectady and Albany. First to begin actual operations was the Baltimore and Ohio; the only living signer of the Declaration of Independence, Charles Carroll of Carrollton, dug a spadeful of earth in the ceremonies to start the work on July 4, 1828, and a thirteen-mile stretch opened for business in 1830. In that same year the Charleston and Hamburg ran trains over a segment of its track in South Carolina; when this line was completed, in 1833, it was the longest in the world (136 miles). The next year the commonwealth of Pennsylvania finished its line from Philadelphia to the Susquehanna River as part of the "Pennsylvania system" of rail and waterways. Meanwhile, in Massachusetts, three companies received charters for routes radiating out from Boston, the most important of these being the Western Railroad, which reached Worcester in 1836. Not only the seaboard but also the Mississippi Valley became the scene of railroad building. By 1836 a total of more than 1,000 miles of track had been laid in eleven states.

There did not yet exist what could be called a railroad system. Even the longest of the lines was comparatively short, and most of them served mainly to connect water routes and supplement water transportation.

During the 1830s the railroad underwent a rapid technological development. At first the track consisted of strap-iron rails laid on wooden

## Traveling by Railroad [1835]

In her widely read work on *Society in America* (1836) the scholarly Englishwoman Harriet Martineau recalled railroad trips she had taken in South Carolina and Pennsylvania:

*My journeys on the Charleston and Augusta railroad were by far the most fatiguing of any I underwent in the country. The motion and the noise are distracting. Whether this is owing to its being on piles in many places, whether the fault is in the ground or the construction, I do not know. Almost all the railroad traveling in America is very fatiguing and noisy. . . .*

*One great inconvenience of the American railroads is that, from wood being used for fuel, there is an incessant shower of large sparks, destructive to dress and comfort, unless all the windows are shut, which is impossible in warm weather. Some serious accidents from fire have happened in this way; and during my last trip on the Columbia and Philadelphia railroad, a lady in the car had a shawl burned to destruction on her shoulders; and I found that my own gown had thirteen holes in it; and my veil, with which I saved my eyes, more than could be counted.*

stringers, which were anchored to granite blocks set in the ground, but this kind of track proved too rigid to absorb the shocks of actual use and was soon replaced by heavier iron rails on wooden ties ballasted with crushed rock. The tracks of different companies varied in width, so that when two different lines connected, the cars and engines of the one might not fit on the tracks of the other. In the early years experiments were made with various forms of motive power—horses, sails, and stationary steam engines with windlasses and cables (for steep grades), as well as steam locomotives. The very first locomotives were imported from England, but as early as 1830 engines of American manufacture like the Charleston and Hamburg's *Best Friend of Charleston* were put into use, and before long only American locomotives were used on American roads; some were even exported. Since railroads in this country were built with sharper curves and steeper grades, the locomotives had to be both more flexible and more powerful than in England. Passenger cars, originally mere stagecoaches adapted to rails, took the form of a large elongated wooden box with two rows of reversible seats and a center aisle soon after 1840. Schedules were erratic and wrecks frequent, most of the roadbeds and bridges being hastily and poorly constructed.

From the outset railroads and canals were bitter competitors. For a time the Chesapeake and Ohio Canal Company blocked the advance of the Baltimore and Ohio Railroad through the narrow gorge of the upper Potomac, and the state of New York prohibited railroads from hauling freight in competition with the Erie Canal and its branches. But railroads had the advantages of speed and year-round operation (canals closed down for the winter freeze) and could be located almost anywhere, regardless of terrain and the availability of water. Where free competition existed, railroads took most of the passenger traffic and the light freight.

The future, in fact, belonged to the towns and cities along the path of the "iron horse," not to those that continued to depend exclusively upon waterways.

## Broadening of Business

While mills and factories multiplied, the household and the workshop slowly declined as producers of manufactured goods. In the textile industry the use of machinery and the dependence on water power (occasionally steam power) made it necessary to bring operations together under a single roof. Yet a good deal of spinning and weaving continued to be done in the home, either for sale or for home use. Though shoes were still made by hand and not by machines, shoe manufacture was increasingly the work of men and women who, in a careful division of labor, specialized in one or another of the various tasks. Mass-produced shoes, in ungraded sizes and without distinction as to rights or lefts,

came in the 1830s chiefly from eastern Massachusetts and were bought mostly by frontier emigrants, sailors, and Southern planters, who used them for their slaves. Other people still made their own shoes or had them made to order by a cobbler. Iron came largely from Pennsylvania, where it was produced in furnaces using local sources of ore, limestone, and charcoal. Other furnaces were scattered over the country, however, and finished iron products were wrought in thousands of local blacksmith shops.

The expansion of business was not simply an automatic result of transportation improvements or other technological changes. It was also the result of daring and imagination on the part of businessmen and their employees. Two industries, one old and one new, illustrate the capacities of Yankee enterprise. One was the whaling industry, which was reaching its heyday in the 1830s. From New Bedford and other New England ports, bold skippers and their crews, having driven most of the whales from the Atlantic, voyaged far into the Pacific in their hazardous tracking of the source of spermaceti for candles, whale oil for lamps, and whalebone for corset stays and other uses. Another example of Yankee enterprise was the ice industry. Though for years Northeastern farmers had harvested winter ice from ponds and stored it for the summer, the large-scale transportation and sale of ice as a commodity began in the 1830s. The New England ice harvest then found a ready market in Northern cities, on Southern plantations, and around the world in India, where it was carried in fast sailing ships; a voyage was considered highly successful if no more than half the cargo melted on the way.

The distribution of goods, whether of foreign or of domestic origin, continued to be rather haphazard by present-day standards, though it was becoming more and more systematic. Stores specializing in groceries, dry goods, hardware, or other lines appeared in the larger cities, but smaller towns and villages depended on the general store, like the one where Abraham Lincoln once clerked in New Salem, Illinois. The storekeeper did much of his business by barter, taking country eggs and other produce in exchange for such things as pins and needles, sugar, and coffee. Many customers, living remote from any store, welcomed the occasional visits of the peddler, who came afoot or by horse, with his pack or with his peddler's wagon equipped with sloping sides which opened to reveal his racks of wares. A special variety of peddler, the Connecticut Yankee, toured the West and the South as a factory agent to sell clocks, at one time made of wood (including the works) but in the 1830s and after usually made of brass.

The organization of business was undergoing a gradual change. Most of it was, and continued to be, operated by individuals or partnerships operating on a small scale. The dominating figure was the great merchant capitalist, who owned and directed much of the big business of the time. He owned his own ships, and he organized certain industries—for example, that of shoe manufacturing—on the putting-out system, according to which he provided the materials, directed the work, and sold the finished product. In the larger enterprises, however, the individual merchant capitalist was giving way before the advance of the corporation. Corporations had the advantage of combining the resources of a large number of shareholders, but their development was long held back by handicapping laws. A corporation had to have a charter, granted by the state, and at first a special act of the legislature was required. By the 1830s the states were beginning to pass general incorporation laws according to which any group meeting certain requirements could secure a charter merely by paying a fee. Moreover, the laws began to grant the privilege of limited liability, which meant that the individual stockholder was liable only to the extent of losing the value of his stock if the corporation should fail.

Corporations made possible the accumulation of larger and larger amounts of capital for manufacturing enterprises as well as for banks, turnpikes, and railroad companies. Some of this capital came from the profits of wealthy merchants who turned from shipping to newer ventures, some from the savings of men of only moderate means, and some from tax collections, since state governments often bought shares in turnpike, canal, and railroad companies. A considerable part was supplied by foreign, especially English, investors. From all these sources too little was derived to meet the demands of promoters with ambitious schemes of personal profit or community improvement. Hence the banks, which should have confined their long-term lending to the limit of their savings deposits, often were induced to issue excessive amounts of bank notes as a means of providing capital for expanding business ventures. As a result of this practice, bank failures were more frequent and bank deposits less secure than they might otherwise have been.

## Workers and Unions

The growth of industry required labor as well as capital. From the colonial beginnings, labor had been scarce in America. At the opening of the nineteenth century nearly ninety of every one hundred Americans still lived and worked on the land: they were farmers. City workers were comparatively few, and many of them were skilled artisans who owned and managed their shops: they were small businessmen, not employees. There were also some unskilled laborers—longshoremen and the like—but there was no sizable reservoir of manpower for new industries to draw upon. In response to the needs of industry a considerable class of wage earners finally began to form. Its members came mostly from the marginal farms of the East (those farms least able to compete with the fertile fields of the West) and somewhat later from the British Isles and Europe.

In the textile mills two different methods of labor recruitment were used. One of these, which prevailed in the middle states and parts of New England, brought whole families to the mill. Father, mother, and children, even those no more than four or five years old, worked together in tending the looms. The second, the Waltham or Lowell system, which was common in Massachusetts, enlisted young women in their late teens and early twenties. These unmarried girls went from farms to factories to work for only a few years and then returned with their savings, to settle down as housewives. They did not form a permanent working class.

Labor conditions in American mills seemed very good in comparison with conditions in English factories and mines. Child labor, indispensable for supplementing the manpower supply, entailed fewer evils in the United States, where

## Cotton Mills, Lowell, Massachusetts

Lowell was incorporated as a town in 1826 and chartered as a city ten years later. It was located near the falls of the Merrimack River, where a drop of 31 feet produced tremendous water power. Canals carried the water to the mills. In the central building of the Boott Cotton Mills, shown here, there were about 900 looms, all tended by girls, one girl to every 4 looms. Altogether about 1,200 "operatives," mostly girls, were employed in the Boott Mills as of 1850. "Visitors," it was said, "will be agreeably surprised with the neat and respectable appearance of the operatives of this industrious city; and equally so with their moral condition. One third of the entire population of this city is connected with the Sunday schools established by the various religious societies; and there is less intemperance and crime than in most other places of its size in New England." (Library of Congress)

the working children remained under the control of their parents, than in England, where asylum authorities hired out orphans to factory employers. The lot of the working woman in mills like those of Lowell appeared idyllic in contrast with the plight of contemporary women who worked in British mines. A parliamentary investigation revealed that some of these unfortunates, naked and filthy, crawled on their hands and knees to pull coal carts through narrow tunnels. No wonder that English visitors considered Lowell a female paradise. The Lowell girls lived in pleasant boarding houses (much like college residence halls) where their morals were carefully supervised. They were well paid by the standards of the period. They found time to write and publish a monthly magazine, the *Lowell Offering*, even though

working hours were long—from sunup to sundown six days a week. In the early days of the factory these hours seemed natural enough to people who were used to the daylong labor of the farm.

Much worse off were the construction gangs who performed the heavy, unskilled work on turnpikes, railroads, and canals. A large and growing number of these men were Irish immigrants. They received low pay and, since their work was seasonal and uncertain, did not make enough in a year to maintain a family at what was generally considered a decent living standard; many of them lived in the most unhealthful of shanties. After about 1840 Irish men and women began to be employed in textile mills. As these newcomers replaced the native farm girls, the earlier paternalistic system broke down and working conditions deteriorated somewhat. Piece rates were paid instead of a daily wage; these and other devices were used to speed up production and exploit the labor force more efficiently.

Neither ditchdiggers nor mill hands, however, were the first to organize and act collectively to improve the conditions of their work. Skilled artisans formed the earliest labor unions and arranged the first strikes (shortly before 1800). From the 1790s on, the printers and cordwainers took the lead. The cordwainers—makers of high-quality boots and shoes, each man fashioning his entire product—suffered from the competition of merchant capitalists who put out work to be performed in separate tasks. These artisans sensed a loss of security and status with the development of mass-production methods, and so did members of other skilled trades, such as carpenters, joiners, masons, plasterers, hatters, and shipbuilders. In cities like Philadelphia, Baltimore, Boston, and New York, the skilled workers of each craft formed societies for mutual aid. During the 1820s and 1830s the craft societies began to combine on a city-wide basis and set up central organizations known as trade unions. Since, with the widening of the market, workers of one city competed with those at a distance, the next step was to federate the trade unions or to establish craft unions of national scope. In 1834 delegates from six cities founded the National Trades' Union, and in 1836 the printers and the cordwainers set up their own national craft unions.

This labor movement soon collapsed. Labor leaders struggled against the handicap of hostile laws and hostile courts. By the common law, as interpreted by judges in the industrial states, a combination among workers was viewed as, in itself, an illegal conspiracy. But adverse court decisions did not halt, though they handicapped, the rising unions. The death blow came from the Panic of 1837 and the ensuing depression.

## SECTIONAL AND NATIONAL TRENDS

While the divisive spirit of sectionalism came to a head in the Missouri controversy, Chief Justice Marshall, in a series of his greatest decisions, was strengthening the national sovereignty against the rights of the states. In 1823, announcing what was later to be known as the Monroe Doctrine, the President appealed to patriotism with an assertion of American leadership in the Western Hemisphere against the pretensions of European powers.

## The Missouri Compromise

When Missouri applied for admission as a state, slavery already was well established there. The French and Spanish inhabitants of the Louisiana Territory (including what became Missouri) had owned slaves, and in the Louisiana Purchase treaty of 1803 the American government promised to maintain and protect the inhabitants in the free enjoyment of their property as well as their liberty and religion. By 1819 approximately 60,000 people resided in Missouri Territory, of whom about 10,000 were slaves. In that year, while Missouri's application for statehood was being considered in Congress, Representative James Tallmadge, Jr., of New York, moved to amend the enabling bill so as to prohibit the further introduction of slaves into Missouri and to provide for the gradual emancipation of those already there. This Tallmadge amendment provoked a controversy that was to rage for the next two years.

Though the issue arose suddenly, waking and terrifying Thomas Jefferson like "a fire bell in the night," as he said, sectional jealousies that produced it had been accumulating for a long time. Already the concept of a balance of power between the Northern and Southern states was well developed. From the beginning, partly by chance and partly by design, new states had come into the Union more or less in pairs, one from the North, another from the South. With the admission of Alabama in 1819, the Union contained an equal number of free and slave states, eleven of each. Thus the free and slave states were evenly balanced in the Senate, though the free states with their more rapidly growing population had a majority in the House. If Missouri should be admitted as a slave state, not only would the existing sectional balance be upset but also a precedent would be established which, in the future, would still further increase the political power of the South.

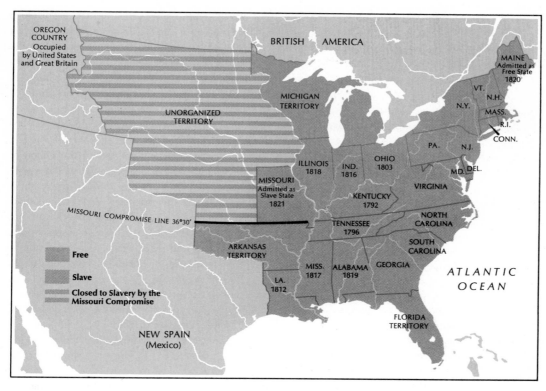

**The Missouri Compromise   1820–1821**

In the North the most active antislavery people were well-to-do philanthropists and reformers who generally supported the Federalist party. They opposed the extension of slavery on both humanitarian and political grounds. On the eve of the dispute over Missouri the Manumission Society of New York was busy with attempts to rescue runaway slaves, and the Quakers were conducting a campaign to strengthen the laws against the African slave trade and to protect free Negroes from kidnappers who sold them into slavery. In the South there were still a large number of critics of slavery and its abuses, but here the humanitarian impulse was not reinforced by political interest as it was in the North. Northerners, in particular the Federalists, never tired in their denunciations of the Virginia Dynasty and the three-fifths clause which, they charged, gave the Southern states a disproportionate weight in national politics.

Once the Missouri controversy had arisen, it provided the opportunity, which Federalist leaders such as Rufus King had awaited, to attempt a revival and reinvigoration of their party. By appealing to the Northern people on the issue of slavery extension, the Federalists could hope to win many of the Northern Republicans away from their allegiance to the Republican party's Southern leadership. In New York the De Witt Clinton faction of the Republicans, who had joined with the Federalists in opposition to the War of 1812 and who were outspoken in their hostility to "Virginia influence" and "Southern rule," were more than willing to cooperate with the Federalists again. The cry against slavery in Missouri, Thomas Jefferson wrote, was "a mere party trick." He explained: "King is ready to risk the union for any chance of restoring his party to power and wriggling himself to the head of it, nor is Clinton without his hopes nor scrupulous as to the means of fulfilling them." Though Jefferson himself took a biased, partisan view of the subject, there seems little reason to doubt that some of the Federalists desired to use the Missouri controversy for creating a new, sectional alignment of parties, the North against the South.

The Missouri question soon was complicated by the application of Maine for admission as a state. Massachusetts had consented to the separation of the northern part of the Commonwealth but only on the condition that Maine be granted statehood before March 4, 1820. The Speaker of the House, Henry Clay, informed Northerners that if they refused to consent to Missouri's becoming a slave state Southerners would deny the application of Maine. In the House the Northern majority nevertheless insisted on the principle of the Tallmadge amendment, but in the Senate a few of the Northerners sided with the Southerners and prevented its passage.

A way out of the impasse opened when the Senate combined the Maine and Missouri bills, without prohibiting slavery in Missouri. Then, to make the package more acceptable to the House, Senator Jesse B. Thomas of Illinois proposed an amendment prohibiting slavery in all the rest of the Louisiana Purchase territory north of the southern boundary of Missouri (latitude 36° 30′). The Senate adopted the Thomas amendment, and Speaker Clay undertook to guide the amended Maine-Missouri bill through the House. Eventually, after the measure had been broken up into three separate bills, he succeeded. A group of Northern Republicans, some of them suspecting the political designs of the Federalists, voted with the Southerners to make the compromise possible.

The first Missouri Compromise (1820) did not end the dispute; a second compromise was necessary. In 1820 Maine was actually admitted as a state, but Missouri was only authorized to form a constitution and a government. When the Missouri constitution was completed, it contained a clause forbidding free Negroes or mulattoes to enter the state. Several of the existing states, denying the right of citizenship to "free persons of color," already had laws against their immigration. Other states, among them New York, recognized colored persons as citizens. According to the federal Constitution, "The citizens of each State shall be entitled to all privileges and immunities of citizens in the

several States." This meant that a citizen of such a state as New York, whether he was white or black, was entitled to all the privileges of a citizen of Missouri, including of course the privilege of traveling or residing in the state. The anti-Negro clause was clearly unconstitutional, and a majority in the House of Representatives threatened to exclude Missouri until it was eliminated. Finally Clay offered a resolution that Missouri should be admitted to the Union on the condition that the clause should never be construed in such a way as to deny to any citizen of any state the privileges and immunities to which he was entitled under the Constitution of the United States. In the circumstances, this resolution was meaningless, yet Clay secured its passage and enhanced his reputation as the "Great Pacificator," a reputation he was again and again to confirm during his long career. Clay's resolution made possible the admission of Missouri as a state in 1821.

Though the Missouri controversy did not unite the North, as some of the Federalists hoped it would, it made at least a beginning toward the creation of a solid South. At that time the most disaffected of the Southern states was Virginia and not, as later on, South Carolina. The Carolinian Calhoun hailed the compromise as a means of preserving the Union. The Virginian Jefferson looked to the fateful day when the South might have to defend itself in a civil war.

In this perspective the subject of education, always one of Jefferson's chief concerns, became even more crucial. He was afraid that Southern youths attending Northern colleges might be indoctrinated with "lessons of anti-Missourianism." Already the University of Virginia, the favorite project of his old age, was under construction. He hoped that this university, devoting itself to sound Southern doctrines, would attract from Virginia and other Southern states a large number of students who otherwise would have pursued their studies in the North. For him, education once had been a means of liberating the human mind; now it became also a means of enabling slaveholders to protect their interests. Henceforth, in the South, the liberal and equalitarian philosophy that we think of as Jeffersonian declined in popularity and respect.

Jefferson himself, in response to the Missouri controversy, had done much toward launching the new conservative trend.

## Marshall and the Court

John Marshall remained as chief justice for almost thirty-five years, from 1801 to 1835. During these years Republican Presidents filled vacancies with Republican justices, one after another, and yet Marshall continued to carry a majority with him in most of the Court's decisions. He was a man of practical and penetrating mind, of persuasive and winning personality, and of strong will. The members of the Court boarded together, without their families, during the winter months when the Court was in session, and Marshall had abundant opportunity to bring his talents to bear upon his younger associates. He not only influenced their ways of thinking; he also molded the development of the Constitution itself. The net effect of the hundreds of opinions delivered by the Marshall Court was to strengthen the judicial branch at the expense of the other two branches of the government; increase the power of the United States and lessen that of the states themselves; and advance the interests of the propertied classes, especially those engaged in commerce.

No state, the Constitution says, shall pass any law "impairing the obligation of contracts." The first Supreme Court case involving this provision was that of *Fletcher* v. *Peck* (1810), which arose out of the notorious Yazoo land frauds. The Court had to decide the question whether the Georgia legislature of 1796 could rightfully repeal the act of the previous legislature granting lands under shady circumstances to the Yazoo Land Companies. In the decision, which was unanimous, Marshall held that a land grant was a contract and therefore, regardless of any corruption involved, the repeal was invalid. This was the first time the Supreme Court had voided a state law on the ground that it conflicted with a provision of the United States Constitution, though the Court previously had declared state laws unconstitutional because they were inconsistent with federal laws or treaties.

*Dartmouth College* v. *Woodward* (1819) was an even more famous case concerning the contract clause. The case had originated in a quarrel between the trustees and the president of the college, and it became a hot political issue in New Hampshire when the Republicans championed the president, and the Federalists took the side of the trustees. Getting control of the state government, the Republicans undertook to revise Dartmouth's charter (granted by King George III in 1769) so as to convert the private college into a state university. Webster, himself a Dartmouth graduate, represented the trustees when the case came before the Supreme Court in Washington. The Court, he reminded the judges, had decided in *Fletcher* v. *Peck* that "a *grant* is a contract." The Dartmouth charter, he went on, "is embraced within the very terms of that decision," since "a grant of corporate powers and privileges is as much a *contract* as a grant of land." Then, according to a later story, he brought tears to the eyes of the justices with an irrelevant peroration concluding: "It is, sir, as I have said, a small college. And yet there are those who love it—" After delaying a year, while some of the justices made up their minds, the Court gave its decision in favor of Webster and the trustees. While the importance of the case often has been exaggerated, it had a significant bearing upon the development of business corporations. It proclaimed the principle that corporation charters were contracts and contracts were inviolable; thereafter the states had to contend against this doctrine in their efforts to control corporate activity.

Did the Supreme Court rightfully have the power to hear appeals from the state courts, as in the Dartmouth College case? The Judiciary Act of 1789 provided that whenever the highest state court decided against a person claiming rights under the federal Constitution, laws, or treaties, the judgment could be reviewed and possibly reversed by the Supreme Court. But Virginia state-rightists denied the constitutionality of the Judiciary Act. They insisted that the federal government, of which the Supreme Court was a branch, could not be the final judge of its own powers, for, they said, it would then be a consolidated government instead of a true federal one such as the Constitution had intended. In the case of *Cohens* v. *Virginia* (1821) Marshall gave the Court's reply to the dissident Virginians. A Virginia court had convicted the

## McCulloch v. Maryland [1819]

Chief Justice Marshall used the following argument in his decision that a state, such as Maryland, could not constitutionally tax a branch of the United States Bank:

*That the power to tax involves the power to destroy; that the power to destroy may defeat and render useless the power to create; that there is a plain repugnance in conferring on one government a power to control the constitutional measures of another, which other, with respect to those very measures, is declared to be supreme over that which exerts the control, are propositions not to be denied. . . .*

*If the States may tax one instrument, employed by the [federal] government in the execution of its powers, they may tax any and every other instrument. They may tax the mail; they may tax the mint; they may tax patent rights; they may tax the papers of the customhouse; they may tax judicial processes; they may tax all the means employed by the government, to an excess which would defeat all the ends of government. This was not intended by the American people. They did not design to make their government dependent on the States.*

Cohens of selling lottery tickets in violation of a state law, and the Cohens had appealed their case under the disputed provision of the Judiciary Act. Though Marshall decided against the Cohens, he did not satisfy the state of Virginia. He affirmed the constitutionality of the Judiciary Act, explaining that the states no longer were sovereign in all respects, since they had given up part of their sovereignty in ratifying the Constitution. The state courts, he insisted, must submit to federal jurisdiction; otherwise the government would be prostrated "at the feet of every state in the Union."

Meanwhile, in *McCulloch* v. *Maryland* (1819), Marshall had confirmed the "implied powers" of Congress by upholding the constitutionality of the Bank of the United States. The Bank, with headquarters in Philadelphia and branches in various cities throughout the country, became so unpopular in the South and the West that several of the states tried to drive the branches out of business by outright prohibition or by prohibitory taxes. Maryland, for one, laid a heavy tax on the Baltimore branch of the Bank. This case presented two constitutional questions to the Supreme Court: could Congress charter a bank and, if so, could one of the states thus tax it? As one of the Bank's attorneys, Webster first repeated the arguments used originally by Hamilton to prove that the establishment of such an institution came within the "necessary and proper" clause. Then, to dispose of the tax issue, Webster added an ingenious argument of his own. The power to tax, he said, involved a "power to destroy," and if the states could tax the Bank at all, they could tax it to death. But the Bank with its branches was an agency of the federal government: no state could take an action tending to destroy the United States itself. Marshall adopted Webster's words in deciding for the Bank.

The case of *Gibbons* v. *Ogden* (1824) brought up the question of the powers of Congress, as against the powers of the states, in regulating interstate commerce. The state of New York had granted Robert Fulton's and Robert Livingston's steamboat company the exclusive right to carry passengers on the Hudson River to New York City. From this monopoly Aaron Ogden obtained the business of navigation across the river between New York and New Jersey. Thomas Gibbons, with a license granted under an act of Congress, went into competition with Ogden, who bought suit against him and was sustained by the New York courts. When Gibbons appealed to the Supreme Court, the justices faced the twofold question whether "commerce" included navigation and whether Congress alone or Congress and the states together could regulate interstate commerce. Marshall replied that "commerce" was a broad term embracing navigation as well as the buying and selling of goods. Though he did not exactly say that the states had no authority whatever regarding interstate commerce, he asserted that the power of Congress in regard thereto was "complete in itself" and might be "exercised to its utmost extent." He concluded that the state-granted monopoly was void.

Here was a grant that neither Marshall nor Webster, Gibbons' attorney, considered sacred. The decision, the last of Marshall's great pronouncements, was the first conspicuous one in which the Marshall Court appeared to be on the popular side. Most people, then as always, hated monopolies and he had declared a monopoly unconstitutional! The lasting significance of *Gibbons* v. *Ogden* was that it freed internal transportation from restraints by the states, and thus prepared the way for the unfettered economic development of the nation. More immediately, it had the effect of helping to head off a movement that was under way for hamstringing the Supreme Court.

For some time Virginia Republicans like Thomas Jefferson, Spencer Roane, and John Taylor of Caroline (a Virginia county) had protested against the views of their fellow Virginian John Marshall. In *Construction Construed and Constitutions Vindicated* (1820) Taylor argued that Marshall and his colleagues were not merely interpreting but were actually changing the nature of the Constitution, which should properly be changed only by the amending process, requiring the approval of three-fourths of the states. In Congress some critics of the Court, mostly from the South and the West, proposed various means of curbing what they called judicial tyranny. A Kentucky senator suggested making the Senate, not the Court, the agency to decide the constitutionality of state laws and to settle interstate disputes. Other senators and congressmen introduced bills to increase the membership of the Court (from seven to ten) and to require more than a mere majority to declare a state law unconstitutional. The Court reformers did not succeed, however, in passing any of their various panaceas, and after the *Gibbons* v. *Ogden* decision the hostility to the judicial branch of the government gradually died down, to be revived in later years.

## Latin American Independence

To most people in the United States, South and Central America had been "dark continents" before the War of 1812. Suddenly they emerged into the light, and Americans looking southward beheld a gigantic spectacle: the Spanish empire struggling in its death throes, a whole continent in revolt, new nations in the making with a future no man could foresee.

Already a profitable trade had developed between the ports of the United States and those of the Río de la Plata in South America, of Chile, and above all of Cuba, with flour and other staples being exported in return for sugar and coins. This trade was small in comparison with that of Great Britain, whose exports to Latin America were several times as large as those of the United States, but the trade was growing steadily, and during the depression after 1819 it held up better than business in general did. Presumably the trade would increase much faster once the United States had established regular diplomatic and commercial relations with the countries in revolt.

In 1815 the United States proclaimed its neutrality in the wars then raging between Spain and her rebellious colonies. This neutrality in itself was advantageous to the rebels, since it implied a recognition of them as belligerents, as nations for the purposes of waging war, though not as nations for all purposes. It meant, for example, that their warships would be treated as bona-fide belligerent vessels, not as pirate ships. Moreover, even though the neutrality law was revised and strengthened in 1817 and 1818, it still permitted the revolutionists to obtain unarmed ships and supplies from the United States. It prohibited the purchase of arms or armed vessels and the enlistment of men in this country, but these prohibitions could be evaded and often were. In short, the United States was not a strict and impartial neutral but a non-belligerent whose policy, though cautious, was intended to help the insurgents and actually did.

Secretary Adams and President Monroe hesitated to take the risky step of recognition unless Great Britain would agree to do so at the same time. In 1818 and 1819 the United States made two bids for British cooperation, and both were rejected. Finally, in 1822, President Monroe informed Congress that five nations—La Plata (Argentina), Chile, Peru, Colombia, and Mexico —were ready for recognition, and he requested an appropriation for sending ministers to them. This was a bold stroke: the United States was going ahead alone as the first country to recognize the new governments, in defiance of the rest of the world.

## Origin of the Monroe Doctrine

In 1823 President Monroe stood forth as an even bolder champion of America against Europe. Presenting to Congress his annual message on the state of the Union, he announced a policy which afterwards—though not for thirty years —was to be known as the "Monroe Doctrine." One phase of this policy had to do with the relationship of Europe to America. "The American continents," Monroe declared, ". . . are henceforth not to be considered as subjects for future colonization by any European powers." Furthermore, "we should consider any attempt on their part to extend their system to any portion of this hemisphere as dangerous to our peace and safety." And we should consider any "interposition" against the sovereignty of existing American nations as an unfriendly act. A second aspect of the President's pronouncement had to do with the relationship of the United States to Europe. "Our policy in regard to Europe," said Monroe, ". . . is not to interfere in the internal concerns of any of its powers."

How did the President happen to make these statements at the time he did? What specific dangers, if any, did he have in mind? Against what powers in particular was his warning directed? To answer these questions, it may be well to consider first the relations of the United States with the European powers as of 1823, and then the main steps in the decision of the Monroe administration to make an announcement to Congress and the world.

After Napoleon's defeat the powers of Europe combined in a "concert" to uphold the principle of "legitimacy" in government and to prevent the overthrow of existing regimes from within or without. When Great Britain withdrew from the concert, it became a quadruple

**Monroe Doctrine [1823]**

". . . The American continents, by the free and independent condition which they have assumed and maintain, are henceforth not to be considered as subjects for future colonization by any European powers. . . .

"In the wars of the European powers in matters relating to themselves we have never taken any part, nor does it comport with our policy to do so. . . . We should consider any attempt on their part to extend their system to any portion of this hemisphere as dangerous to our peace and safety. With the existing colonies or dependencies of the European powers we have not interfered and shall not interfere. But with the Governments who have declared their independence and maintained it, and whose independence we have, on great consideration and on just principles, acknowledged, we could not view any interposition for the purpose of oppressing them, or controlling in any other manner their destiny, by any European power, in any other light than as the manifestation of an unfriendly disposition toward the United States."

alliance with Russia and France as the strongest of its four members. Tsar Alexander I of Russia also sponsored the "Holy Alliance," which eventually was joined by all the European sovereigns except the Pope and the King of England, and which was supposed to put into practice the Tsar's rather fuzzy ideal of peace and justice based upon Christian principles. Though the quadruple alliance and the Holy Alliance were separate, most Americans made no distinction between them, commonly referring to the European concert as the "Holy Alliance." In 1823, after assisting in the suppression of other revolts in Europe, the European allies authorized France to intervene in Spain to restore the Bourbon dynasty that revolutionists had overthrown. Some observers in England and the Americas wondered whether the allies next would back France in an attempt to retake by force the lost Spanish empire in America.

Actually, France was still a relatively weak power, not yet recovered from the long and exhausting Napoleonic wars. Though France disliked Latin American independence, she was willing to accept it as one of the realities of the world, especially if it should result in the creation of monarchies instead of republics. France endeavored to bring about the establishment of pro-French kingdoms in Latin America by means of intrigue, but dared not challenge British seapower with an expedition to subvert the new governments by force.

Russia, the great land power of Europe, lacked naval strength. She desired the friendship of the United States because of her worldwide conflicts with Great Britain. When the Tsar expressed his wish that the United States become a member of the Holy Alliance, Secretary Adams politely let him know that this country could best serve the exalted purpose of the alliance by remaining apart from it. While American pacifists admired the Tsar as a friend of brotherhood and peace, Adams grew sarcastic about the supposedly peace-loving Tsar who sold warships to Spain to assist her war against her revolting colonies. Besides the vague threat Russia offered to Latin American independence, there were other causes of friction between her and the United States. Russia owned Alaska, and Russian fur traders ranged as far south as California. In 1821 the Tsar issued a ukase (imperial order) requiring foreign ships to keep approximately one hundred miles from the Northwest coast above the 51st parallel. This order perturbed Adams not only because it interfered with the activities of American traders and whalers in the North Pacific but also because it implied a Russian territorial claim that would enlarge the area of Russian America. Adams protested strongly to the Russians. Instead of taking offense, they agreed to negotiate regarding the southern boundary of their possessions. The settlement was not completed until 1824, when the Russians abandoned their claim south of 54° 40′. But in 1823 the negotiations were already under way and, for the time being,

Russian-American relations were reasonably good.

In the minds of most Americans, certainly in the mind of their secretary of state, Great Britain at that time seemed a serious threat to American interests. Adams was much concerned about supposed British designs upon Cuba. Like Jefferson and others before him, Adams opposed the transfer of Cuba from a weak power like Spain, its owner, to a strong power like Great Britain. He thought Cuba eventually should belong to the United States, for the "Pearl of the Antilles" had great economic and strategic value and, because of its location, was virtually a part of the American coastline. Adams did not desire to seize the island; he wanted only to keep it in Spanish hands until, by a kind of political gravitation, it should fall naturally to the United States. Despite his worries over the supposed British threat to Cuba, he and other American leaders were pleased to see the rift between Great Britain and the concert of Europe. He was willing to cooperate with her, but only to the extent that her policies and his own coincided in regard to this hemisphere.

These policies did not exactly coincide, however, as was shown by the British rejection of the American overtures for joint recognition of Latin American independence in 1818 and 1819, and as was shown again by the American reaction to a British proposal for a joint statement in 1823. That summer, the British Secretary for Foreign Affairs, George Canning, suggested to the American minister in London, Richard Rush, that Great Britain and the United States should combine in announcing to the world their opposition to any European movement against Latin America. Though Rush lacked instructions to act, he was ready to go ahead with Canning on one condition—that Great Britain agree to recognize the Latin American nations as the United States already had done. When Canning declined to promise recognition, Rush wrote home for instructions. During the summer Canning remained eager for Rush's cooperation, but in the fall, having been assured by the French minister that France had no intention of "acting against the colonies by force of arms," Canning suddenly lost interest in his idea of a joint statement with the United States.

Meanwhile the Monroe administration was considering the proposal that Canning had made earlier. Monroe sent the Rush correspondence to former Presidents Madison and Jefferson for their advice, and both of them recommended that Rush be authorized to sign a joint statement with Canning. Adams objected. For one thing, he did not like the statement that Canning had proposed: it included a pledge by Great Britain and the United States that neither of the two would seek further territory in this hemisphere, and Adams did not wish to stop this country from future territorial acquisitions. For another thing, he believed it would be more honorable for the American government to speak out on its own instead of following along like a "cockboat in the wake of the British man-of-war." Actually, when the time arrived for Monroe's message to Congress, the President no longer faced a question of acting with Great Britain or alone. He had the choice of acting alone or not at all, since Canning had changed his mind about cooperation with the United States.

Though Canning's overture led to Monroe's announcement, the message was directed against all the powers of Europe, including Great Britain, which seemed at least as likely as Russia to undertake further colonizing ventures in America. The message was intended to head off the threat of European schemes against Latin American independence, but the most serious threat was one of undermining that independence by subtle influences rather than overt military action. The message aimed to rally the people of Latin America to look to their own security. It also aimed to stir the people of the United States. In issuing his challenge to Europe, Monroe had in mind the domestic situation as well as the international scene. At home the people were bogged down in a business depression, divided by sectional politics, and apathetic toward the rather lackluster administration of Monroe. In the rumors of European aggression against this hemisphere lay an opportunity for him to arouse and unite the people with an appeal to national pride.

## THE TWO-PARTY SYSTEM REVIVED

After 1816 the Federalist party offered no presidential candidate and soon ceased to exist as a national organization. Presidential politics was carried on within the Republican party alone until the campaign of 1828, when the Republicans divided into two groups and thus set going a party system comparable to the one that had operated before 1820.

### "Corrupt Bargain!"

From 1796 to 1816, presidential candidates had been nominated by caucuses of the members of each of the two parties in Congress. In 1820, when the Federalists declined to oppose his candidacy, Monroe ran as the Republican nominee without the necessity of a caucus nomination. If the caucus system were revived and followed in 1824, this would mean that the nominee of the Republicans in Congress would run unopposed, as Monroe had done. Several men aspired to the Presidency, however, and they and their followers were unwilling to let a small group of congressmen and senators determine which one was to win the prize.

In 1824 "King Caucus" was overthrown. Fewer than a third of the Republicans in Congress bothered to attend the gathering that went through the motions of nominating a candidate (William H. Crawford) and he found the caucus nomination as much a handicap as a help in the campaign. The rest of the candidates received nominations from state legislatures and endorsements from irregular mass meetings throughout the country.

John Quincy Adams, secretary of state for two terms, had made a distinguished record in the conduct of foreign affairs, and he held the office that had become traditionally the stepping stone to the Presidency. But, as he himself ruefully realized, he was a man of cold and forbidding manners, not a candidate with strong popular appeal. Contending against Adams was the Secretary of the Treasury, William H. Crawford of Georgia, an impressive giant of a man who seemed to have a promising future in national politics. The caucus candidate, Crawford had the backing of the extreme state-rights faction of the Republican party. In mid-campaign, however, he was stricken by a paralyzing illness.

Challenging the cabinet contenders was Henry Clay, the Speaker of the House. This tall, black-haired Kentuckian, with his broad smile and his ready handshake, had a personality that gained him a devoted following. He also stood for a definite and coherent program, which he called the "American System." His plan, a familiar one but attractive to citizens just recovering from a business depression, was to create a great home market for factory and farm producers by means of raising the tariff to stimulate industry, maintaining the national bank to facilitate credit and exchange, and spending federal funds on internal improvements to provide transportation between the cities and the farms.

Andrew Jackson offered no such clearcut program as did Clay. Though Jackson had served briefly as a representative in Congress and was a member of the United States Senate, he had no legislative record to run on. Nevertheless, he had the inestimable advantages of a military hero's reputation and a campaign shrewdly managed by the Tennessee politician friends who had put him forward as a candidate. To some of his contemporaries he seemed a crude, hot-tempered frontiersman and Indian-fighter. Actually, though arising from a humble background as an orphan in the Carolinas, he had become a well-to-do planter who lived in an elegant mansion ("The Hermitage") near Nashville and was a gentleman, at least by the standards of the West.

Once the returns were counted, there was no doubt that the next Vice President was to be Calhoun, who ran on both the Adams and the Jackson tickets. But there was considerable doubt as to who the next President would be. In those states where the people chose the presidential electors, Jackson led all the rest at the polls. In the electoral college also he came out ahead, with 99 votes to Adams' 84, Crawford's 41, and Clay's 37. He lacked the necessary majority, however. So, in accordance with the Twelfth Amendment, the final decision was left to the House of Representatives, which was to choose among the three candidates with the

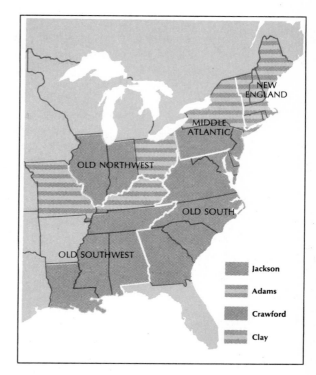

**Election of 1824**

highest electoral vote. Clay, for all his charm, was out of the running.

If Clay, in 1825, could not be President, he could at least be President-maker, and perhaps he could lay the ground for his own election later on. As speaker, he was in a strategic position for influencing the decision of the House of Representatives. In deciding among the three leading candidates, the House was to vote by states, the delegation from each state casting one vote. Clay, as the winner of the recent election in Kentucky, Ohio, and Missouri, could swing the congressional delegations of those three states at least.

Before Congress got around to making the decision, the friends of Jackson, Crawford, and Adams approached Clay in behalf of their respective candidates. To which of the three should he give his support? Jackson's followers insisted that Jackson, with his popular and electoral pluralities, was really the people's choice and that Congress had no rightful alternative but to ratify the people's will. But Jackson was Clay's most dangerous rival for the political affections of the West, and he could not be depended upon to champion Clay's legislative program. Crawford was out of the question, for he was now a paralytic, incapable of discharging the duties of the Presidency. Only Adams was left. Personally, he was no friend of Clay and had clashed with him repeatedly when both were peace delegates at Ghent and afterward. Politically, however, Adams was similar to Clay in cherishing nationalistic principles such as those of the "American System." Finally Clay gave his support to Adams, and the House elected him.

The Jacksonians were angry enough at this, but they became far angrier when the new President made known his appointments. Clay was to be the secretary of state! The State Department being the well-established route to the Presidency, Adams thus appeared to be naming Clay as his own successor. The two must have agreed to make each other President —Adams now, Clay next—or so the Jacksonians exclaimed, and they pretended to be horrified by this "corrupt bargain." Very likely there had been some sort of understanding, and though there was nothing improper in it, it proved to be politically unwise for both Adams and Clay.

Soon after Adams' inauguration as President, Jackson resigned from the Senate to accept a renomination for the Presidency from the Tennessee legislature and to begin a three-year campaign for election in 1828. Politics now overshadowed everything else. Throughout his term in the White House, Adams and his policies were to be thoroughly frustrated by the political bitterness arising from the "corrupt bargain."

## The Second President Adams

The career of John Quincy Adams divides naturally into three parts. In the first part, as befitted the son of John Adams, he made a brilliant record in diplomacy, serving as the American minister in one foreign capital after another and then as one of the most successful of all secretaries of state. In the second phase of his career, as President (1825–1829), he endured four ineffectual years that amounted to a mere interlude between the periods of his greatness. In the third, as a congressman from

**John Quincy Adams**

When this photograph was taken, shortly before his death in 1848, Adams was more than eighty years old and was a congressman from Massachusetts. He had left the Presidency almost twenty years earlier. During his White House days, as always, he was a hard, conscientious worker. He rose at four in the morning and built a fire before the servants were up. Then he made a long entry in his diary for the previous day. He wrote so much that his right hand sometimes became paralyzed with writer's cramps, so he taught himself to use his left hand also. Occasionally, in the early morning, he swam nude in the Potomac River. Once his boat overturned with his clothes, and he hid in the shrubbery along the bank while his servant fetched a dry outfit. (Brown Brothers)

Massachusetts, he served his constituents and the nation with high distinction, gaining fame as "Old Man Eloquent," the foremost congressional champion of free speech. His frustration in the White House shows that the Presidency demands more than exceptional ability and high-mindedness, for John Quincy Adams possessed both. The Presidency also requires political skill and political luck, and these he did not have.

In his inaugural address and in his first message to Congress he boldly stated a broad conception of the powers and duties of the federal government. He recommended "laws promoting the improvement of agriculture, commerce, and manufactures, the cultivation of the mechanic and of the elegant arts, the advancement of literature, and the progress of the sciences, ornamental and profound." He had no chance of getting an appropriation from Congress to improve the minds of his countrymen. The most he could get was a few million dollars for improving rivers and harbors and for extending the National Road westward from Wheeling. This amount was more than Congress had appropriated for internal improvements under all his predecessors together, but it was far less than he hoped for.

Even in the field of diplomacy, where Adams had more experience than any other President before or since, he failed in the major efforts of his administration. Yielding to Secretary of State Clay's wish for cooperation with the Latin American governments, Adams appointed two delegates to attend an international conference which the Venezuelan liberator, Simon Bolívar, had called to meet at Panama in 1826. Objections arose in Congress for two reasons. One was that Southerners hated to think of white Americans mingling in Panama with colored delegates from Haiti, the independence of which the United States refused to recognize. The other reason for obstruction was simply politics—the determination of Jacksonians to discredit the administration. They charged that Adams aimed to sacrifice American interests and involve the nation in an entangling alliance. While the Jacksonians filibustered, Congress delayed the Panama mission so long that it became futile. One of the American delegates died on the way to the conference, and the other arrived after it was over. The United States had accomplished nothing to offset British influence, which prevailed in Latin America.

Adams was worsted also in a contest with the state of Georgia. That state attempted to remove the remaining Creek and Cherokee Indians so as to gain additional soil for cotton planters. The Creeks, however, had a treaty with the United States (1791) that guaranteed them the possession of the land they occupied. A new treaty (1825) ceded the land to the state,

but Adams refused to enforce this treaty, believing that it had been obtained by fraud. The Georgia governor defied the President of the United States and went ahead with plans for Indian removal. At last the Creeks agreed to still another treaty (1827) in which they yielded their claims. Adams' stand had been honorable but unpopular. Southerners condemned him for encroaching upon state rights, and Westerners as well as Southerners disapproved of his interfering with efforts to get rid of the Indians.

Southerners again denounced the administration and its supporters on account of the tariff of 1828. This measure originated in the demands of Massachusetts and Rhode Island woolen manufacturers, who complained that the British were dumping woolens on the American market at prices with which the domestic mill owners could not compete. Petitioning Congress, the distressed mill owners expected relief from the Woolens Bill of 1827. It passed the House but was defeated in the Senate when Vice President Calhoun cast his negative vote to break a tie. Thus frustrated, the protectionists of New England combined with those of the middle and Western states to bring further pressure upon Congress, after getting together in a grand tariff convention at Harrisburg, Pennsylvania.

The bill of 1828 contained high duties not only on woolens but also on a number of other items, such as flax, hemp, iron, lead, molasses, and raw wool. Thus it displeased New England manufacturers, for it would raise the cost of their raw materials as well as the price of their manufactured goods. A story arose that the bill had taken its shape from a Jacksonian plot to embarrass New Englanders and discredit Adams. The bill related to "manufactures of no sort or kind but the manufacture of a President of the United States," John Randolph said. Supposedly it was intended to put Adams in a dilemma that would lose him friends whether he signed or vetoed it. While some politicians did see the measure as an electioneering device, others intended it seriously as a means of benefiting the farmers and manufacturers of the middle states and the West.

When the bill was considered item by item, Southerners voted against reductions in the hope that some of its outrageous duties would so antagonize New Englanders that they would help defeat it. But when it came to a final test, Daniel Webster voted for it despite its duties on raw materials, and he carried with him enough New England votes to enable it to pass. Adams signed it. The Southerners, whose tactics had backfired, cursed it as the "tariff of abominations."

## Jackson Vindicated

By 1828, the Republican party having split completely, there were again two parties in the campaign—the Adamsites, who called themselves National Republicans, and the Jacksonians, who took the name of Democratic Republicans. Adams himself once had been a Federalist, and most of the old Federalists joined his party, though some became followers of Jackson.

Issues figured little in the campaign of 1828, though much was said about the "corrupt bargain" and something was said about the West Indian trade and the "tariff of abominations." Regarding the tariff, Adams was on record, having signed the abominations bill, but nobody knew exactly where Jackson stood. Again, as in 1824, more was made of personalities than of policies, and this time there was far worse mudslinging than ever before. Indeed, one would have thought that two criminals were running for the highest office in the land.

As for Adams, the Jacksonians charged that as President he had been guilty of gross waste and extravagance, using public funds to buy gambling devices (a chess set and a billiard table) for the White House. But that was not the worst of Adams' alleged crimes. Once, as minister to Russia, he had tried to procure a beautiful American girl for the sinful pleasures of the Tsar, or so the Jacksonians said. Of course, these charges were wholly false. Indeed, they were fantastic things to say about a man as conscientious and puritanical as John Quincy Adams.

As for Jackson, the Adamsites had accusations even worse. He was a murderer and an adulterer, according to the speeches, handbills, and pamphlets of his party foes. A "coffin handbill" listed within coffin-shaped outlines the

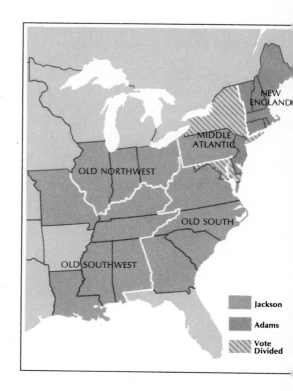

names of militiamen whom Jackson was said to have shot in cold blood during the War of 1812. Actually, these men had been deserters who were executed after due sentence by a court martial. It was also rumored that Jackson knowingly had lived in sin with the wife of another man. Actually, he had married the woman, his beloved Rachel, at a time when the pair honestly though mistakenly supposed her first husband had divorced her.

Though the majority voted for Jackson, a large minority (44 per cent) favored Adams, who received all but one of the electoral votes from New England, all from New Jersey and Delaware, and some from New York and Maryland. These totaled only 83, however, as compared with 178 for Jackson, who carried the rest of the country. His victory was decisive enough, even though not quite so sweeping as it seemed. In the eyes of his followers, he—and they—were vindicated in their claim that he had been wrongfully deprived of the Presidency in 1825.

# Selected Readings

**Canals and Railroads** G. R. Taylor, *The Transportation Revolution, 1815–1860* (1951); R. E. Shaw, *Erie Water West: A History of the Erie Canal, 1792–1854* (1966); Nathan Miller, *The Enterprise of a Free People: Aspects of Economic Development in New York State During the Canal Period, 1792–1828* (1962); Carter Goodrich and others, *Canals and American Economic Development* (1961); W. S. Sanderlin, *The Great National Project* (1947), the Chesapeake and Ohio Canal; A. D. Trumbull, *John Stevens: An American Record* (1928); F. W. Stevens, *The Beginnings of the New York Central Railroad* (1926); Edward Hungerford, *The Story of the Baltimore and Ohio Railroad, 1827–1927* (2 vols., 1928); S. M. Derrick, *Centennial History of the South Carolina Railroad* (1930).

**Industry and Trade** A. H. Cole, *The American Wool Manufacture* (2 vols., 1926); C. A. Ware, *The Early New England Cotton Manufacture* (1931); S. E. Morison, *The Maritime History of Massachusetts, 1783–1860°* (1921); F. R. Dulles, *The Old China Trade* (1930).

**Urban Development** R. G. Albion, *The Rise of New York Port, 1815–1860* (1939); Blake McKelvey, *Rochester, the Water-Power City, 1812–1854* (1945); L. D. Baldwin, *Pittsburgh: The Story of a City* (1938); J. W. Livingood, *The Philadelphia-Baltimore Trade Rivalry, 1780–1860* (1947); R. C. Wade, *The Urban Frontier: The Rise of Western Cities, 1790–1830°* (1959); N. M. Blake, *Water for the Cities* (1956).

**Nationalism and Sectionalism** George Dangerfield, *The Awakening of American Nationalism, 1815–1828°* (1965); Merle Curti, *The Roots of American Loyalty* (1946); W. E. Davies, *Patriotism on Parade: The Story of Veterans' and Hereditary Organizations in America, 1783–1900* (1955); W. F. Craven, *The Legend of the Founding Fathers°* (1956); P. C. Nagel, *One Nation Indivisible: The Union in American Thought, 1776–1861* (1964); Glover Moore, *The Missouri Controversy, 1819–1821* (1953).

**The Marshall Court** A. J. Beveridge, *The Life of John Marshall* (4 vols., 1916–1919); R. K. Faulkner, *The Jurisprudence of John Marshall* (1968); M. G. Baxter, *Daniel Webster and the Supreme Court* (1966).

**The Monroe Doctrine** A. P. Whitaker, *The United States and the Independence of Latin America, 1800–1830°* (1941); E. H. Tatum, *The United States and Europe, 1815–1823* (1936); Dexter Perkins, *The Monroe Doctrine, 1823–1826* (1927); C. C. Griffin, *The United States and the Disruption of the Spanish Empire* (1937); Bradford Perkins, *Castlereagh and Adams: England and the United States, 1812–1823* (1964); J. H. Powell, *Richard Rush, Republican Diplomat, 1780–1859* (1942); Frank Thistlethwaite, *The Anglo-American Connection in the Early Nineteenth Century* (1959).

**Party Politics** S. F. Bemis, *John Quincy Adams and the Union* (1956); R. V. Remini, *The Election of Andrew Jackson°* (1964); Shaw Livermore, Jr., *The Twilight of Federalism: The Disintegration of the Federalist Party, 1815–1830* (1962).

---

° Titles available in paperback.

OF VETO MEMORY.

KING ANDREW THE FIRST.

# Chapter 10
# Jacksonian Democracy

In 1831–1832 a twenty-six-year-old French nobleman, Alexis de Tocqueville, made a tour of the United States, talking with people of all kinds, from President Jackson in the White House to Negro slaves in the cotton fields of the South. Tocqueville's aim was to study the workings of democracy—or, more specifically, the idea of equality—in what he considered the most democratic country on earth. He believed that democracy was the way of the future, that it was bound to come sooner or later to France. He wanted to find its good and bad and its essential and unessential features so that his own country could be prepared to adopt the best and avoid the worst. His two-volume study of *Democracy in America* (1835–1840) still stands as the most perspicacious general account of American institutions ever to be written by a foreigner.

"The government of democracy," Tocqueville wrote, "brings the notion of political rights to the level of the humblest citizens, just as the dissemination of wealth brings the notion of property within the reach of all the members of the community; and I confess that, to my mind, this is one of its greatest advantages." But he feared that, with the continued growth of factories, there might eventually arise in the United States a large group of dependent workingmen and a small group of new aristocrats, an industrial plutocracy. For "at the very moment at which the science of manufactures lowers the class of workmen, it raises the class of masters."

With this prospect of widening class differences, some Americans wondered about the wisdom of extending political rights to larger and larger numbers. President Jackson and his followers, however, generally endorsed and aided the extensions of democratic thought and practice that preceded, accompanied, and followed his rise to power. Viewing himself as the real representative of the people, Jackson dominated American politics for a time. Like a powerful magnet, he attracted a majority of the voters to him, and he polarized the others into a pattern of opposition—anti-Jacksonians against Jacksonians or, as they came to be known, Whigs against Democrats. He took a decisive part in the major controversies that arose. These concerned not only the role of the common man in government but also the rights of the states and the rights of the Indians, the nullification threat from South Carolina, and the alleged danger to democracy arising from a great financial monopoly, the Bank of the United States.

The Jacksonians made strenuous efforts to arouse and organize the citizens and bring them out to vote. Then, stealing the Jacksonians' thunder, the Whigs came into office in 1840 by stirring up the electorate as not even Jackson had been able to do. This, rather than 1828, was the year of a "mighty democratic uprising." Politicians now developed new techniques of mass manipulation, and politics took on a modern look.

---

**King Andrew the First**

This Whig cartoon of the 1830s presents President Jackson as a tyrant with a scepter in one hand and a veto in the other; he is trampling upon the Constitution, the judiciary, internal improvements, and the Bank of the United States. (Library of Congress)

## ADVENT OF MASS POLITICS

On March 4, 1829, unprecedented thousands of Americans attended the inaugural ceremonies at the Capitol, and then the noisy crowd followed their hero to the White House, where at a public reception they trampled one another and even the elegantly upholstered sofas and chairs in their eagerness to shake his hand. "It was a proud day for the people," one of the Jacksonians, Amos Kendall, reported to his newspaper in Kentucky. "General Jackson is *their own* president." But most old Federalists and all lovers of political decorum were horrified. John Marshall's friend and colleague Justice Joseph Story disgustedly remarked: "The reign of King 'Mob' seemed triumphant."

### The Common Man's President

Though the new President was no democratic philosopher like Jefferson, he nevertheless held certain democratic convictions, notably the conviction that government should offer "equal protection and equal benefits" to all the people. His enemies denied that he ever really championed the people's cause, but they could not deny that he became a living symbol of democracy or that, far more than any of his predecessors, he gave a sense of participation in government to the common man.

As President, Jackson promptly set about to "reform" the personnel procedures of the federal government. For a generation, ever since the downfall of the Federalists in 1800, there had been no complete party turnover in Washington. Officeholders accordingly stayed on year after year and election after election, many of them growing gray and some of them growing corrupt in office. "Office is considered as a species of property," Jackson told Congress, "and government rather as a means of promoting individual interests than as an instrument created solely for the service of the people." He believed that official duties could be made "so plain and simple that men of intelligence may readily qualify themselves for their performance." According to him, offices belonged to the people, not to the entrenched officeholders. Or, as one of his henchmen, William L. Marcy of

---

### Jackson's Inaugural Reception [1829]

Andrew Jackson's inauguration impressed a Washington society woman, Mrs. Samuel H. Smith, as a solemn and sublime event. Afterward Mrs. Smith went with a party of friends to the inaugural reception at the White House. "But what a scene did we witness!" she wrote a few days later, in a letter to an out-of-town relative.

*The* Majesty of the People *had disappeared, & a rabble, a mob, of boys, negros, women, children, scrambling, fighting, romping. What a pity, what a pity! No arrangements had been made, no police officers placed on duty & the whole house had been inundated by the rabble mob. We came too late. The President, after having been* literally *nearly pressed to death & almost suffocated & torn to pieces by the people in their eagerness to shake hands with Old Hickory, had retreated through the back way or south front & had escaped to his lodgings at Gadsby's. Cut glass & china to the amount of several thousand dollars had been broken in the struggle to get the refreshments, punch & other articles had been carried out in tubs & buckets, but had it been in hogsheads it would have been insufficient, ice-cream, & cake & lemonade, for 20,000 people, for it is said that number were there, tho' I think the estimate exaggerated. Ladies fainted, men were seen with bloody noses & such a scene of confusion took place as is impossible to describe,—those who got in could not get out by the door again, but had to scramble out of windows.*

---

New York, more cynically put it, "To the victors belong the spoils."

A corollary to the spoils system was the doctrine of rotation in office. Since ordinary men ("of intelligence") presumably were fit or could easily be fitted for government service, and since loyal members of the victorious party deserved government jobs, a particular position should not be held too long by any one person but should be passed around, or rotated, among several deserving applicants.

In actual practice, Jackson did not make such drastic removals as his partisan critics then and afterward asserted. During the entire eight years of his Presidency he removed a total of no more than one-fifth of the federal officeholders, and many of these he removed for cause, such as misuse of government funds. Proportionally, Jackson dismissed no more of the jobholders than Jefferson had done. Nor did he appoint illiterate coon-hunters or the like to positions requiring special training or skill. The fact remains, nevertheless, that the Jackson administration, adapting the spoils system from some of the states, fixed it firmly upon national politics.

Eventually the Jacksonians adopted another instrument of democratic politics—the national nominating convention—which was originated by the earliest of the third parties in American history, the Anti-Masonic party. This party was a response to widespread resentment against the secret and exclusive, hence supposedly undemocratic, Society of Freemasons. Feeling rose to new heights when, in 1826, a man named William Morgan mysteriously disappeared from his home in Batavia, New York. Since Morgan had been about to publish a book purporting to expose the secrets of freemasonry, his friends believed that vengeful Masons had done away with him. The excitement spread, and politicians in New York, Pennsylvania, and several other states seized upon it to organize a party with popular appeal. The party was anti-Jackson as well as Anti-Mason, Jackson being a high-ranking member of the lodge. In 1831 the Anti-Masons held a national convention in Harrisburg, Pennsylvania, to nominate a candidate for the next year's presidential campaign.

## More and More Voters

When Ohio and other new states in the West joined the Union, they adopted constitutions that gave the vote to all adult white males and allowed all voters the right to hold public office. Thus the new states set an example for the older

ones. These older states became concerned about the loss of their population to the West, and they began slowly and haltingly to grant additional political rights to their people so as to encourage them to stay at home. Even before the War of 1812 a few of the Eastern states permitted white men to vote whether or not they owned property or paid a tax. After 1815 the states began to revise their constitutions by calling conventions that served as grand committees of the people to draw up new documents and submit them for public approval. Eventually all the states (some of them not till after the Civil War) changed their constitutions in the direction of increased democracy.

Change was resisted, and at times the democratic trend was stopped short of the aims of the more radical reformers, as, for example, when Massachusetts held its convention in 1820. The reform-minded delegates complained that in the Massachusetts government the rich were better represented than the poor, both because of the restrictions on voting and office-holding and because of the peculiar system of property representation in the state senate. The number of senators from each district of the state depended not upon the number of people in the district but upon the amount of its taxable wealth. The reformers urged an amendment apportioning senators according to population alone. Daniel Webster, one of the conservative delegates, opposed the change on the grounds that "power *naturally* and *necessarily* follows property" and that "property as such should have its weight and influence in political arrangement." Webster and the rest of the conservatives could not prevent the reform of senate representation, nor could they prevent elimination of the property requirement for voting. But, to the disgust of the radicals, the new constitution required that every voter be a taxpayer and that the governor be the owner of considerable real estate.

In the New York convention of 1821 the conservatives, led by Chancellor James Kent, insisted that a taxpaying requirement for suffrage was not enough and that, at least in the election of state senators, the property qualification should be retained. Kent argued that society "is an association for the protection of property as

## An Argument Against Universal Suffrage [1821]

According to the original constitution of New York, the state senate was elected by owners of land worth at least $250 and the assembly by owners of land worth at least $50. At the constitutional convention of 1821 the radicals proposed to abolish all property qualifications for voting. A conservative delegate, James Kent, objected. Then chancellor of the state chancery court, Kent was one of the nation's foremost legal authorities. Later he wrote a classic four-volume work entitled *Commentaries on American Law* (1826–1830). In 1821 he was willing to abolish the property qualification for assembly elections, but he wished to "preserve our Senate as the representative of the landed interest." He told his fellow delegates:

*By the report before us, we propose to annihilate, at one stroke, all those property distinctions and to bow before the idol of universal suffrage. That extreme democratic principle, when applied to the legislative and executive departments of the government, has been regarded with terror, by the wise men of every age, because in every European republic, ancient and modern, in which it has been tried, it has terminated disastrously, and been productive of corruption, injustice, violence, and tyranny. . . .*

*The apprehended danger from the experiment of universal suffrage applied to the whole legislative department, is no dream of the imagination. It is too mighty an excitement for the moral constitution of men to endure. The tendency of universal suffrage is to jeopardize the rights of property and the principles of liberty. There is a constant tendency . . . in the poor to covet a share in the plunder of the rich; in the debtor to relax or avoid the obligation of contracts; in the majority to tyrannize over the minority, and trample down their rights; in the indolent and profligate to cast the whole burthens of society upon the industrious and the virtuous; and there is a tendency in ambitious and wicked men to inflame these combustible materials.*

well as of life" and that "the individual who contributes only one cent to the common stock ought not to have the same power and influence in directing the property concerns of the partnership as he who contributes his thousands." The reformers, appealing to the Declaration of Independence, maintained that life, liberty, and the pursuit of happiness, not property, were the main concerns of society and government. The property qualification was abolished in New York.

Other states proceeded more slowly in the broadening of democracy, none of them going to radical extremes. Progress was peaceful, except in Rhode Island. There the constitution was the old colonial charter, little changed, and it disqualified as voters more than half of the adult males of the state. Thomas L. Dorr and his suffragist followers, despairing of reform by legal processes, held a convention of their own, drew up a new constitution, and tried to set up an administration with Dorr as governor. When the existing state government began to imprison his followers he led a band of his men in an attack upon the Providence arsenal (1842). The Dorr Rebellion was quickly put down, yet it hastened the reforms that came afterward in Rhode Island.

In the South reformers criticized the over-representation of the tidewater areas and the underrepresentation of the back country in the legislatures. When the Virginia constitutional convention met, in 1829, the delegates from the western counties gained some slight concessions but not enough to satisfy them. Elsewhere in the Southeast the planters and politicians of the older counties continued to dominate the state governments.

With few exceptions, free Negroes could not vote anywhere in the South, nor could they vote in most of the Northern states. Pennsylvania at one time allowed Negro suffrage but eventually (1838) amended the constitution so as to prohibit it. In North and South, women continued to be denied the vote, regardless of the amount of property they might own. Everywhere the ballot was open, not secret, and often it was cast as a spoken vote rather than a written one. The lack of secrecy meant that voters could be, and sometimes were, bribed or intimidated.

In most of the states there was at first no popular vote for President. As late as 1800, the legislature chose presidential electors in ten of the states, and the people in only six. The trend was toward popular election, however, and after 1828 the legislature made the choice in only one state, South Carolina. There the people had no chance to vote in presidential elections till after the Civil War.

Despite the persisting limitations, the number of voters increased far more rapidly than did the population as a whole. In the presidential election of 1824 fewer than twenty-seven in one hundred of adult white males voted (though previously, in some of the states, more than fifty had done so). In the election of 1828 the proportion rose to about fifty-five in one hundred— more than twice the figure for 1824—and in the elections of 1832 and 1836 the proportion remained approximately the same as in 1828. Then, in 1840, people flocked to the polls as never before, seventy-eight in one hundred white men casting their ballots. The multiplication of voters was due only in part to the widening of the electorate. It was due in greater measure to a heightening of interest in politics and a strengthening of party organization. Citizens now were aroused and brought out to vote who in former times had seldom bothered with elections.

Not only did the number of voters increase; so did the number of elective offices in the states. The first state constitutions had provided for the appointment of high state officials by the governor or by the legislature. The newer constitutions put the election of these officials, including judges in some cases, into the hands of the people. Supposedly the people thus were to have increased control over government. Actually, with authority so divided and diffused, it was harder than ever for the people to locate and hold to account the officials responsible for particular policies.

Political parties became more important as both the electorate and the elections grew in number and complexity. Parties were necessary for bringing together voters of diverse interests and providing common goals so that the will of the people could express itself in a united and meaningful way. Parties were also necessary to give central direction to governments made up of independently elected officials. Hence, as the states became more democratic, political organizations within them became more tightly knit. Political machines and party bosses appeared in states like New York and Pennsylvania which had large and heterogeneous electorates with a variety of conflicting interests. In New York and Pennsylvania the spoils system was introduced before it was transplanted to the federal government. State jobs were awarded to loyal workers of the victorious party, and job-seeking came to be the motive that held together and inspirited the core of the party membership.

## "OUR *FEDERAL* UNION"

President Jackson had taken office with no clearly announced program to carry out. His followers—who soon began to call themselves simply Democrats—had interests so diverse that a statement of definite aims would have alienated many of the party at the outset. This is not to say that Jackson himself was wishy-washy or lacking in convictions. Far from it. Besides believing in government by and for the common man, he stood for strong presidential leadership and, while respecting what he considered the legitimate rights of the states, he was devoted to the national Union. He did not hesitate to assert his principles when South Carolina tried to put into effect the nullification (or interposition) theory of John C. Calhoun.

## Calhoun: His Theory

At the age of forty-six (in 1828) Calhoun had a promising future as well as a distinguished past. A congressional leader during the War of 1812, afterward head of the War Department for eight years (making a record that entitles him to rank as one of the few truly great secretaries of war), then Vice President in John Quincy Adams' administration, he now was running as the vice-presidential candidate on the Jackson ticket. And he could look forward to the Presidency itself after a term or two for Jackson—if all went well.

But the tariff question placed Calhoun in a dilemma. Once he had been a forthright protectionist, coming out strongly for the tariff of 1816, but since that time many South Carolinians had changed their minds on the subject, and so had he. Carolina cotton planters were disturbed because their plantations did not pay, or at least were less profitable than it seemed they should have been. The whole state appeared to be stagnating, its population remaining almost stationary, its countryside showing signs of ruin and decay. One reason was the exhaustion of the South Carolina soil, which could not well compete with the newly opened, fertile lands of the Southwest. But the Carolinians blamed their trouble on quite another cause—the tariff, in particular the "tariff of abominations," the law of 1828. They reasoned that protective duties raised the prices of the things they had to buy, whether they bought them at home or from abroad, and lowered the price of the cotton they sold, most of which was exported. They had a point: in order to export, a nation has to import, and to the extent that the tariff kept foreign goods out of the United States it also reduced the foreign market for American cotton. Some exasperated Carolinians were ready to seek escape from the hated law through revolution—that is, through secession. Here was a challenge Calhoun had to meet in order to maintain his leadership in the state and make a future for himself in national politics.

Quietly he worked out a theory to justify state action in resisting the tariff law. He intended for this action, if and when it became necessary, to be strictly legal and constitutional, not revolutionary. So he had to find a basis for his plan in the Constitution itself. In his earlier career, as a nationalist, he had said the Constitution was not a thing for logicians to exercise their ingenuity upon, but should be construed with plain good sense. Now he himself resorted to subtle and ingenious logic, discovering implications in the Constitution that were not obvious to everybody—not even to the "father of the Constitution," James Madison, who denounced the Calhoun theory when he heard of it. Calhoun believed, however, that he was following the lines laid down by Madison and Jefferson in their Virginia and Kentucky resolutions of 1798–1799. Indeed, his reasoning was quite similar to theirs, but he carried it farther than they had done, and he provided a definite procedure for state action, which they had not.

Calhoun started his reasoning with the assumption that sovereignty, the ultimate source of power, lay in the states considered as separate political communities. He went on to assume that these separate peoples had created the federal government, through their conventions that ratified the Constitution after it had been drawn up. Putting this in legal terminology, he described the states (meaning their peoples, not their governments) as the "principals," the federal government as their "agent," and the Constitution as a "compact" containing instructions within which the agent was to operate.

From these assumptions the rest of his theory followed logically enough. The Supreme Court was not competent to judge whether acts of Congress were constitutional, since the Court, like the Congress, was only a branch of an agency created by the states. No, Calhoun reasoned, the principals must decide, each for itself, whether their instructions were violated. If Congress enacted a law of doubtful constitutionality—say, a protective tariff—a state could "interpose" to frustrate the law. That is, the people of the state could hold a convention, and if (through their elected delegates) they decided that Congress had gone too far, they could declare the federal law null and void within their state. In that state the law would remain inoperative until three-fourths of the whole number of states should ratify an amendment to the Constitution specifically assigning Congress the

# Where Historians Disagree

## Jacksonian Democracy

Many of the early biographers of Andrew Jackson and historians of the Jackson period were upper-middle-class Easterners who sympathized with his opponents, the Whigs. These unfriendly, Whiggish authors described him as a "barbarian" whose election was a "mistake" and whose policies on the whole were "deplorable." Such views prevailed until the end of the nineteenth century.

Then a new generation of scholars, nearly all of them from the West or the South, began to rewrite history in a manner highly favorable to Jackson. They saw him as a true democrat who, much like the progressives of their own time, strove to make government responsive to the will of the people rather than the desires of the special interests. The most influential of the newer historians, Frederick Jackson Turner, in his famous essay "The Significance of the Frontier in American History" (1893) and in later writings, maintained that Jacksonian Democracy had originated in the "frontier democratic society" of the West. Turner's "frontier interpretation" soon became predominant, though one authority on early Tennessee politics (Thomas P. Abernethy) insisted that Jackson actually had been a frontier aristocrat and had opposed the democratic trend in his own state.

In recent years historians have emphasized social classes rather than geographical sections in seeking to explain Jackson and his program, but they have disagreed about which class he represented. Arthur M. Schlesinger, Jr., contended in *The Age of Jackson* (1945) that Jacksonian Democracy was an effort "to control the power of the capitalistic groups, mainly Eastern, for the benefit of noncapitalist groups, farmers and laboring men, East, West, and South." Critics of Schlesinger, however, argued that Jackson was antilabor rather than pro-labor and that he really reflected the interests of the rising businessmen. In *The American Political Tradition and the Men Who Made It* (1948) Richard Hofstadter characterized the Jackson movement as "a phase in the expansion of liberated capitalism" and as "closely linked to the ambitions of the small capitalists."

The truth seems to be that the movement was everything it has been called—and more. Different historians have caught different aspects of it, but none has yet grasped the whole in all its complexity.

power in question. And if the other states should ever get around to doing this, the nullifying state would then submit—or it could secede.

The legislature of South Carolina published Calhoun's first statement of his theory, anonymously, in a document entitled *The South Carolina Exposition and Protest* (1828). This condemned the recent tariff as unconstitutional, unfair, and unendurable—a law fit to be nullified. Calhoun had good reason for not wishing to be identified publicly as the author of the document. It was bound to arouse a certain amount of opposition in parts of the country, and of course he hoped to be reelected Vice President and later to be elected President.

After the Jackson-Calhoun ticket had won its victory at the polls, Calhoun was no more eager than before to see nullification put into effect. He waited, hoping that Jackson as President would persuade Congress to make drastic reductions in tariff rates and thus mollify the outraged Carolina planters. It remained to be seen what chance Calhoun would have for the Presidency as Jackson's friend and successor. As soon as the major appointments had been made, he gained an inkling of his importance, or unimportance, in the new administration. He then realized he had a powerful rival for Jackson's favor in the person of Martin Van Buren.

## Van-Buren to the Fore

Van Buren, about the same age as Calhoun and equally ambitious, was quite different in background and personality. Born of Dutch ancestry in the village of Kinderhook near Albany, New York, he advanced himself through skillful maneuvering to the position of United States senator (1820–1828). He also made himself the party boss of his state by organizing and leading the Albany Regency, the Democratic machine of New York. Though he supported Crawford for President in 1824, he afterwards became one of the most ardent of Jacksonians, doing much to carry his state for Jackson in 1828 while getting himself elected as governor. By this time he had a reputation as a political wizard. Short and slight, with reddish gold sideburns and a quiet manner, he gained a variety of revealing nicknames, such as "the Sage of Kinderhook," "the Little Magician," and "the Red Fox." Never

giving or taking offense, he was in temperament just the opposite of the choleric Jackson, yet the two were about to become the closest of friends. Van Buren promptly resigned the governorship and went to Washington when Jackson called him to head the new cabinet as secretary of state.

Except for Van Buren, this cabinet contained no one of more than ordinary talent. It was intended (as cabinets usually are) to represent and harmonize the sectional and factional interests within the party. No Virginian was included: for the first time since 1789 Virginia provided neither the President nor any of the secretaries. Friends of both Van Buren and Calhoun were given places. This cabinet was not intended to form a council of advisers: Jackson did not even call cabinet meetings.

Instead, he relied on an unofficial circle of political cronies who came to be known as the "Kitchen Cabinet." Noteworthy in this group were several newspaper editors, among them Isaac Hill, a hunchbacked master of invective from New Hampshire, and Amos Kendall and Francis P. Blair from Kentucky. After 1830 Blair edited the administration's official organ, the Washington *Globe*. The close-mouthed, asthmatic, "invisible" Kendall was said to be the genius who, behind the scenes, really ran the administration. While doubtless influential, he was no more so than several others, especially Jackson's old Tennessee friend and political manager William B. Lewis, who roomed at the White House and had ready access to the President. Soon to be the most important of all was Van Buren, a member of both the official and the unofficial cabinet.

Vice President Calhoun, to his dismay, saw signs of Van Buren's growing influence when he viewed the division of the spoils. Not only did Van Buren get cabinet places for himself and his friends; he also secured the appointment of his followers to most of the lesser offices. Already, beneath the surface, there was the beginning of a rift between the Vice President and the President. Then Calhoun and Jackson were further estranged, and at the same time Jackson and Van Buren were brought closer together, in consequence of a curious quarrel over a woman and etiquette.

Peggy O'Neil, the bright-eyed, vivacious daughter of a Washington tavern-keeper, was the kind of woman whom men admire and women dislike. Jackson's Tennessee friend Senator John H. Eaton took the young widow as his wife, with Jackson's blessing. Washington gossips told and retold scandalous stories about her relationship with Eaton while her former husband had been still alive. All the talk would have amounted to little if Jackson had not appointed Eaton as his secretary of war and thus made Mrs. Eaton a cabinet wife. The rest of the administration wives, led by Mrs. Calhoun, snubbed Mrs. Eaton. Jackson was furious. His own wife, the dead Rachel, had been slandered by his political enemies, and he was confident that Peggy too was virtuous, an innocent victim of dirty politics. He not only defended her virtue: he demanded that his secretaries and associates concede it and treat her with respect. But they had their wives to contend with. Calhoun, for one, had no choice but to take sides against Mrs. Eaton, which meant taking sides against her champion, Jackson. With Van Buren the case was different. A widower, without daughters, he had no womenfolk to worry about. From the outset he befriended the Eatons and thus ingratiated himself with the President.

The Eaton affair dragged on, and finally Jackson decided to get rid of his uncooperative secretaries and reorganize his cabinet (1831). Van Buren resigned and so did two of his friends; the others took the hint and submitted their resignations too. Jackson appointed a new cabinet which on the whole was considerably stronger than the first one. Thereafter he relied more on his official advisers, less on the Kitchen Cabinet. As for Van Buren, he was sent to England as American minister, the appointment being made while the Senate was not in session. When the Senate met, there was a tie vote on the question of confirming the appointment, and Calhoun as the presiding officer broke the tie by casting his own ballot against Van Buren. This brought Van Buren home but gave no advantage to Calhoun.

Already Jackson had picked Van Buren for the presidential succession and had marked Calhoun as the worst of foes. The final break came when Jackson learned the inside story of a Monroe cabinet meeting years earlier. At the time of Jackson's Florida raid (1817) and for a long time afterward he supposed that Calhoun, as Monroe's secretary of war, had stood up for him when others in the administration proposed to punish him for his action. The truth, as Calhoun's enemies at last convinced Jackson, was quite otherwise.

## The Webster-Hayne Debate

If there had been only personal differences between Jackson and Calhoun, their parting would have been less significant than it actually was. But there were also differences of principle. At the height of the Eaton affair the opposing views of the two men were dramatically revealed in consequence of a great debate on the nature of the Constitution.

The Webster-Hayne debate, in January 1830, grew out of a Senate discussion of public lands, a discussion provoked when a senator from Connecticut suggested that all land sales and surveys be discontinued for the time being. This suggestion immediately aroused Senator Thomas Hart Benton of Missouri, once Jackson's antagonist in a wild frontier brawl, now the Jacksonian leader in the Senate and a sturdy defender of the West. Always suspicious of New England, he charged that the proposal to stop land sales was intended to keep New England workers from going West and thus to choke off the growth and prosperity of the frontier.

A young, debonair senator from South Carolina, Robert Y. Hayne, took up the argument after Benton. Hayne and other Southerners hoped to get Western support for their drive to lower the tariff, and at the moment they were willing to grant abundant and cheap lands to the Westerners in exchange for such support. He hinted that the South and the West might well combine in self-defense against the Northeast.

Daniel Webster, now a senator from Massachusetts, once had been a state-rights and anti-tariff man but, like Calhoun, only in reverse, he had changed his position with the changing interests of his section. The day after Hayne's speech he took the floor in an effort to head off the threatened rapprochement of the West and the South and thus to protect the interests of New England, including the tariff interest. Ignoring Benton, he directed his remarks to Hayne and, through him, to Calhoun in the Vice President's chair. He reviewed much of the history of the republic, with occasional disregard for historical facts, to prove that New England always had been the friend of the West. Referring to the tariff of 1816 he said that New England was not responsible for beginning the protectionist policy but had accepted it after other sections had fixed it upon the nation. Then, changing the subject, he spoke gravely of disunionists and disunionism in South Carolina.

Thus he challenged Hayne to meet him, not on the original grounds of the public lands and the tariff, but on the issue of state rights versus national power, an issue that could be made to seem one of treason versus patriotism. And in due time Hayne, coached by Calhoun, came back with a flashing defense of the nullification theory. It took Webster two afternoons to deliver what schoolboys were afterward to know as the second reply to Hayne. "I go for the Constitution as it is, and for the Union as it is," he declaimed, as he turned to an exposition of the "true principles" of the Constitution. "It is, Sir, the people's Constitution, the people's government, made for the people, made by the people, and answerable to the people." And he meant one people, the whole nation. He concluded with the ringing appeal: "Liberty *and* Union, now and for ever, one and inseparable!"

Calhoun's followers were sure that Hayne had the better of the argument. The important question at the moment, however, was what President Jackson thought and what side, if any, he would take.

An answer soon was given at a Democratic banquet that was supposed to honor Thomas Jefferson as the founder of the party. At the banquet the friends of Calhoun hoped to build up the alliance of South and West and strengthen his presidential prospects by identifying his principles with those of Jefferson. As was customary at such affairs, the guests settled down after

### Webster Replying to Hayne

Hayne is sitting in the front center, with his hands together. Calhoun, presiding as Vice President, leans intently on his desk, in the shadow at the extreme left. Note the bonneted ladies in the gallery and the page in the left foreground. From G. P. A. Healy's painting, which hangs in Faneuil Hall, Boston. (Frick Art Reference Library) dinner to an evening of drinking toasts. The President, forewarned by Van Buren, was ready with a toast of his own, which he had written down, underscoring certain words. When his turn came, he stood up and proclaimed: "Our *Federal* Union—*It must be preserved.*" While he spoke he looked sternly at Calhoun. Van Buren, who stood on his chair to see better from the far end of the table, thought he saw Calhoun's hand shake and a trickle of wine run down the outside of his glass. Calhoun responded to Jackson's toast with his own: "The Union—next to our liberty most dear. May we always remember that it can only be preserved by distributing evenly the benefits and the burthens of the Union."

## State Rights, Indians, Georgia

Jackson's pro-Union and antinullification feelings, as expressed in his Jefferson's birthday toast, did not mean that he was opposed to state rights as such. On the contrary, as he had declared in his inaugural address, he believed in none but "constitutional" undertakings by the federal government. During his administration he readily vetoed laws that he thought exceeded the powers originally granted to Congress by the states; in fact, he used the veto more freely than any President before him. And he stood up for state rights when Georgia defied the Supreme Court in dealing with the Indians within its borders.

The Maysville Road Bill (1830) brought on the most significant of Jackson's vetoes. This bill, by authorizing the government to buy stock in a private company, would have given a federal subsidy for the construction of a turnpike from Maysville to Lexington, within the state of Kentucky. The Maysville pike was a segment of a projected highway that was to form a great Southwestern branch of the National Road. Nevertheless, since the pike itself was an intrastate and not an interstate project, Jackson doubted whether Congress constitutionally could give aid to it. Earlier (in 1822) President Monroe, vetoing the Cumberland Road Bill, had declared that the federal government should support only those improvements that were of general rather than local importance, and Jackson then had agreed with Monroe. Now, with

Van Buren's assistance, Jackson prepared a veto message based on similar grounds. He also urged economy, denounced the selfish "scramble for appropriations," and stressed the desirability of paying off the national debt. Though Jackson also refused to sign other appropriation bills, he did not object to every proposal for federal spending to build roads or improve rivers and harbors. During his two terms such expenditures continued to mount, far exceeding even those of the John Quincy Adams administration.

The Maysville veto was not popular in the West, where better transportation was a never-ending demand, but Jackson's Indian policy was wholeheartedly approved in both the West and the South. As an old Indian-fighter, Jackson was no lover of the red man, and he desired to continue and expedite the program, which Jefferson had begun, of removing all the tribes to the west of the Mississippi. The land between the Missouri and the Rockies, according to such explorers as Lewis and Clark and Stephen H. Long, was supposed to be a vast desert, unfit for white habitation. Why not leave that land for the Indians? By the Indian Removal Act of 1830 Congress proposed to exchange tribal lands within the states for new homes in the West, and by the Indian Intercourse Act of 1834 Congress marked off an Indian country and provided for a string of forts to keep the Indians inside it and the whites outside. Meanwhile the President saw that treaties, nearly a hundred in all, were negotiated with the various tribes and that reluctant tribesmen along with their women and children were moved west, with the prodding of the army.

In the process of Indian removal there was much tragedy and a certain amount of violence. When (in 1832) Chief Black Hawk with a thousand of his hungry Sac and Fox followers—men, women, and children—recrossed the Mississippi into Illinois to grow corn, the frontiersmen feared an invasion. Militiamen and regular troops soon drove the unfortunate Indians into Wisconsin and then slaughtered most of them as they tried to escape down the Wisconsin River. Such was the Black Hawk War, in which Abraham Lincoln was a captain of militia (he saw no action) and Jefferson Davis a lieutenant in the regular army. More serious was the Seminole War. It began when Chief Osceola led an uprising of his tribesmen (including runaway Negroes), who refused to move west in accordance with a treaty of 1833, and the fighting lasted off and on for several years. Jackson sent troops to Florida, but the Seminoles with their Negro associates were masters of guerrilla warfare in the jungly Everglades. Even after Osceola had been treacherously captured under a flag of truce and had died in prison, the red and black rebels continued to resist.

Unlike the Sacs and Foxes or the Seminoles, the Cherokees in Georgia were a civilized people, with a written language of their own (invented by the half-breed Sequoyah in 1821) and with a settled way of life as farmers. Yet the state of Georgia, after getting rid of the Creeks, was eager to remove the Cherokees also and open their millions of acres to white occupation. In 1827 these Indians adopted a constitution and declared their independence as the Cherokee Nation. Promptly the Georgia legislature extended its laws over them and directed the seizure of their territory. Hiring a prominent lawyer, the Cherokees appealed to the Supreme Court. In the case of *Cherokee Nation* v. *Georgia* (1831) Chief Justice Marshall gave the majority opinion that the Indians were "domestic dependent nations" and had a right to the land they occupied until they voluntarily ceded it to the United States. In another case, *Worcester* v. *Georgia* (1832), Marshall and the Court held that the Cherokee Nation was a definite political community with territory over which the laws of Georgia had no force and into which Georgians could not enter without permission.

President Jackson did not sympathize with the Cherokees as President Adams had done with the Creeks. Vigorously supporting Georgia's position, Jackson did nothing to aid the Indians or to see that the rulings of the Supreme Court were carried out. The Chief Justice had implied that it was the President's duty to uphold the rights of the Indians. Jackson's attitude is well expressed in the comment attributed to him: "John Marshall has made his decision; now let him enforce it." The decision was never enforced. After a few years the Cherokees signed a treaty and most of them migrated, some at the point of a bayonet, to what afterwards

became Oklahoma. About a thousand fled across the state line to North Carolina, where eventually the federal government provided a reservation for them.

In a sense Georgia nullified federal authority when, proclaiming state rights, she flouted the rulings of the highest court of the United States. In doing so, nevertheless, the state had the backing of the President. But when, in the midst of the Georgia controversy, another state attempted out-and-out nullification of an act of Congress, Jackson reacted quite differently.

## South Carolina Interposes

After waiting four years for Congress to undo the "tariff of abominations," the South Carolina followers of Calhoun had little patience left, and they lost that when Congress denied them any real relief in the tariff of 1832. Though making certain changes in individual rates, the new law did not lower the tariff as a whole, enough to satisfy the cotton planters of the state. And the rice growers, though not concerned about the tariff, were apprehensive that slavery might be threatened if federal power remained unchecked.

Some of the South Carolinians now were ready for revolt, and had it not been for Calhoun's program and leadership, they might have taken even more drastic action than they did. Having ceased to be Jackson's friend and prospective successor, Calhoun had come out openly for nullification, elaborated the doctrine further, and induced the extremists to adopt it as their remedy. To nullify or not to nullify— that was the question in the state election of 1832. The nullifiers proved to be the majority, but their opponents (who called themselves Unionists) made up a large minority, the vote being approximately 23,000 to 17,000. Without delay the newly elected legislature called for the election of delegates to a state convention. The convention adopted an ordinance of nullification that declared null and void the tariffs of 1828 and 1832 and forbade the collection of duties, within the state. The legislature then passed laws to enforce the ordinance and make preparations for military defense. Needing a strong man to take command at home, and another to present the South Carolina case ably in Washington, the

## Nullification Ordinance [1832]

Having failed to obtain relief from what most planters considered an oppressive and unfair tariff, South Carolina put Calhoun's theory into practice with the following resolutions:

*Whereas the Congress of the United States, by various acts, purporting to be acts laying duties and imports on foreign imports, but in reality intended for the protection of domestic manufactures, and the giving of bounties to classes and individuals engaged in particular employment, at the expense and to the injury and oppression of other classes and individuals, . . . hath exceeded its just powers under the Constitution, which confers on it no authority to afford such protection, and hath violated the true meaning and intent of the Constitution, which provides for equality in imposing the burthens of taxation upon the several States and portions of the Confederacy. . . .*

*We, therefore, the people of the State of South Carolina, in Convention assembled, do declare and ordain . . . That the several acts and parts of acts of the Congress of the United States, purporting to be laws for the imposing of duties and imposts on the importation of foreign commodities . . . [especially the tariff acts of 1828 and 1832] . . . are unauthorized by the Constitution of the United States, and violate the true meaning and intent thereof, and are null, void, and no law, nor binding upon this State. . . .*

nullifiers arranged for Hayne to become governor and for Calhoun to replace Hayne as senator. So Calhoun resigned as Vice President.

While the nullifiers prepared for war they hoped for peace. According to the Calhoun theory the federal government had no rightful recourse, and the rest of the states could do nothing except to amend the Constitution. When the theory was put to the test, however, not a single state came to South Carolina's support.

Unofficially the President threatened to hang Calhoun. Officially he proclaimed that nullification was treason and its adherents traitors. Jackson did not confine himself to mere words. Co-operating closely with the Unionists of South Carolina, he also took steps to strengthen the federal forts in the state, ordering General Winfield Scott and a warship and several revenue cutters to Charleston.

When Congress met, the President asked for specific authority with which to handle the crisis. His followers introduced a "force bill" authorizing him to use the army and navy to see that acts of Congress were obeyed. The force bill, like Jackson's proclamation, further antagonized the South Carolina extremists. Violence seemed a real possibility early in 1833, as Calhoun took his place in the Senate to defend his theory and its practice. He introduced a set of resolutions on the "constitutional compact" and then made a speech against the force bill.

Webster's reply to Calhoun (February 16, 1833), if less colorful than his reply to Hayne three years earlier, dwelt more fully and more cogently upon the constitutional issues at stake. The Constitution, Webster argued, was no mere compact among sovereign states that might secede at will. It was an "executed contract," an agreement to set up a permanent government, supreme within its allotted sphere and acting directly upon the people as a whole. Webster dismissed secession as a revolutionary but not a constitutional right, then denounced nullification as no right at all. The nullifiers, he said, rejected "the first great principle of all republican liberty; that is, that the majority must govern." They pretended to be concerned about minority rights, but did they practice what they preached? "Look to South Carolina, at the present moment. How far are the rights of minorities there respected?" Obviously the nullificationist majority was proceeding with a "relentless disregard" for the rights of the Unionist minority—"a minority embracing, as the gentleman himself will admit, a large portion of the worth and respectability of the state."

At the moment Calhoun was in a predicament. South Carolina, standing alone, itself divided, could not hope to prevail if a showdown

## Jackson's Proclamation [1832]

*Our present Constitution was formed . . . in vain if this fatal doctrine [nullification] prevails. It was formed for important objects that are announced in the preamble, made in the name and by the authority of the people of the United States, whose delegates framed and whose conventions approved it. The most important among these objects—that which is placed first in rank, on which all the others rest—is "to form a more perfect union." Now, is it possible that even if there were no express provision giving supremacy to the Constitution and laws of the United States over those of the States, can it be conceived that an instrument made for the purpose of "forming a more perfect union" than that of the Confederation could be so constructed by the assembled wisdom of our country as to substitute for that Confederation a form of government dependent for its existence on the local interest, the party spirit, of a State? Every man of plain, unsophisticated understanding who hears the question will give such an answer as will preserve the Union. Metaphysical subtlety, in pursuit of an impracticable theory, could alone have devised one that is calculated to destroy it. . . .*

*The laws of the United States must be executed. I have no discretionary power on the subject; my duty is emphatically pronounced in the Constitution.*

with the federal government should come. If the nullifiers meekly yielded, however, they would lose face and their leader would be politically ruined. Calhoun was saved by the timely intervention of the Great Pacificator, Henry Clay. Newly elected to the Senate, Clay in consultation with Calhoun devised a compromise scheme by which the tariff would be lowered year after year, reaching in 1842 approximately the same

level as in 1816. Finally Clay's compromise and the force bill were passed on the same day (March 1, 1833). Webster consistently opposed any concessions to the nullifiers, but Jackson was satisfied: he signed the new tariff measure as well as the force bill.

In South Carolina the convention reassembled and repealed its ordinance of nullification as applied to the tariffs of 1828 and 1832. Then, as if to have the last word, the convention adopted a new ordinance nullifying the force act. This proceeding meant little, since the force act would not go into effect anyhow, the original ordinance (against which it was directed) having been withdrawn. The second nullification was intended to reinforce the impression that Calhoun's program was a success and was still to be reckoned with. Though Calhoun and his followers, having brought about tariff reduction, claimed a victory for nullification, the system had not worked out in the way its sponsors had intended. Calhoun had learned a lesson: no state could assert and maintain its rights by independent action. Thereafter, while continuing to talk of state rights and nullification, he devoted himself to building up a sense of Southern solidarity so that, when another trial should come, the whole section might be prepared to act as a unit in resisting federal authority.

## JACKSON AND THE BANK

The Bank of the United States was a private corporation with a charter from the federal government, which owned one-fifth of the stock. It was a monopoly, having an exclusive right to hold the government's deposits. With its headquarters in Philadelphia and its branches in twenty-nine other cities, it also did a tremendous business in general banking, totaling about $70 million a year. Its services were important to the national economy because of the credit it provided for profit-making enterprises, because of its banknotes that circulated throughout the country as a dependable medium of exchange, and because of the restraining effect that its policies had upon the less well-managed banks chartered by the various states.

## Biddle's Institution

Nicholas Biddle, president of the Bank from 1823 on, had done much to put the company on a sound and prosperous basis. A member of an aristocratic Philadelphia family, Biddle was educated at the University of Pennsylvania and thereafter devoted himself to a number of intellectual interests, including poetry. He personally owned a large proportion of the Bank's stock, so much of it that together with two other large stockholders he controlled the Bank. He could and did choose the officials of the branches, decide what loans were to be made, and set the interest rates. For several years after he took charge he made these decisions according to financial considerations. A banker, not a politician, he had no desire to mix in politics.

But he finally concluded it was necessary to do so in self-defense when, with the encouragement of Jackson, popular opposition to the Bank rose to a threatening pitch.

Opposition came from two very different groups, the "soft-money" and the "hard-money" men. The former, consisting largely of state bankers and their friends, objected to the Bank of the United States because it restrained the state banks from issuing notes as freely as some of them would have liked, through its policy of collecting such notes and presenting them for payment in cash. These critics of the Bank desired more paper money (that is, banknotes circulating as money), not less. The other set of critics, the hard-money people, had the opposite complaint. Believing in coin as the only safe currency, these people condemned all banks

### The Second Bank of the United States

Architecturally, the home office of the bank, in Philadelphia, was an excellent example of the Greek Revival style. In 1818 architects were invited to submit competitive plans for "a chaste imitation of Grecian architecture." **William Strickland** won the competition with a design modeled on that of the Parthenon of ancient Athens.

**Benjamin H. Latrobe,** who had submitted a similar plan, charged that Strickland had stolen the Latrobe design. After the expiration of the bank's charter, the building became the Philadelphia Custom House. (The Granger Collection)

## The Bank Cartooned 1833

President Jackson, who says he has read the *American Family Physician*, looks in the sickroom window to see the results of the medicines he has prescribed for the Bank of the United States—veto of the recharter bill and removal of the deposits—represented by the broken bottles on the floor. Clay, Webster, and Calhoun discuss the case, proposing as cures the American System, common sense, and nullification respectively. Biddle holds the head of "Mother U. S. Bank" while she spews money into other banks, represented by the basins. "D——n that Doctor Jackson," says Biddle. "This is the effect of that last prescription." (Brown Brothers)

of issue—all banks issuing banknotes—whether chartered by the states, as all but one of them were, or by the federal government, as the Bank alone was.

Jackson himself was a hard-money man. At one time in his life he had dealt in grandiose land and mercantile speculations based on paper credit. Then a financial panic (1797) ruined his business and put him deeply into debt. Thereafter he was suspicious of all banks. After he became President he raised the question, in his inaugural address and in other statements, whether the charter of the Bank of the United States should be renewed. Unless renewed, it would expire in 1836.

To preserve the institution, Biddle began to grant banking favors to influential men in the hope of winning them to his side. At first he sought to cultivate Jackson's friends, with some success in a few instances. Then he turned more and more to Jackson's opponents. He extended loans on easy terms to several prominent newspaper editors, to a number of important state politicians, and to more than fifty congressmen and senators. In particular, he relied upon Senators Clay and Webster, the latter of whom was connected with the Bank in various ways— as legal counsel, director of the Boston branch, frequent and heavy borrower, and Biddle's personal friend.

Clay, Webster, and other advisers persuaded Biddle to apply to Congress for a recharter bill in 1832, four years ahead of the expiration date. After investigating the Bank and its business, Congress passed the recharter bill. At once Jackson vetoed it, sending it back to Congress with a stirring message in which he denounced the Bank as unconstitutional, undemocratic, and un-American. The veto stood, for the Bank's friends in Congress failed to obtain the two-thirds majority necessary for overriding it. And so the Bank question emerged as the paramount issue of the coming election, just as Clay had fondly hoped it would.

In 1832 Clay ran as the unanimous choice of the National Republicans, who had held a nominating convention in Baltimore late in the previous year. Jackson, with Van Buren as his running mate, sought reelection as the candidate of the Democratic Republicans, or Democrats. Still another candidate was in the field, representing a third party for the first time in American history. He was William Wirt, a prominent Baltimore lawyer and man of letters, the nominee of the Anti-Masonic party. Though he preferred Clay to Jackson, Wirt drew more votes away from the former than from the latter, though he did not draw a great many from any source, carrying only the state of Vermont. The legislature of South Carolina gave that state's electoral vote in protest to a man who was not even a candidate, John Floyd, one of Calhoun's Virginia followers. Of the remaining electoral votes, Jackson received more than five times as many as Clay.

## The "Monster" Destroyed

Jackson took his decisive reelection as a sign that the people endorsed his views on the Bank of the United States. As soon as the nullification crisis had been disposed of, he determined to strike a blow at this banking "monster," this dangerous money power, as he saw it. He could not put an end to the Bank before the expiration of its charter, but at least he could lessen its power by seeing to the removal of the government's deposits. By the law establishing the Bank, the secretary of the treasury had to give the actual order for removing them. When the incumbent secretary refused to give the order, Jackson appointed a new one, and when this man procrastinated, Jackson named a third, Roger B. Taney, previously the attorney general and a member of the Kitchen Cabinet. Taney was more than willing to cooperate.

With Taney at the head of the Treasury Department, the process of removing the government's deposits was immediately begun. The government stopped putting new funds in the Bank, but continued paying its bills by drawing on its existing deposits, which steadily dwindled. Meanwhile the government opened accounts with a number of state banks, depositing its incoming receipts with them. These banks, including one in Baltimore with which Taney himself was associated, were chosen presumably on the basis of their financial soundness but not always without consideration of their political leanings. Jackson's enemies called them his "pet banks." By 1836 there were 89 of them.

The proud and poetic Biddle, "Czar Nicholas" to Jacksonians, was not the man to give in without a fight. "This worthy President," he wrote sarcastically, "thinks that because he has scalped Indians and imprisoned Judges, he is to have his way with the Bank. He is mistaken." Biddle struck back when the Jackson administration began to transfer funds directly from the Bank of the United States to the pet banks. He felt that the loss of government deposits, amounting to several millions, made it necessary for him to call in loans and raise interest rates, since the government deposits had served as the basis for much of the Bank's credit. He realized that, by making borrowing more difficult, he was bound to hurt business and cause unemployment, but he consoled himself with the belief that a short depression would help to bring about a recharter of the Bank. "Nothing but the evidence of suffering," he told the head of the Boston branch, would "produce any effect in Congress."

During the winter of 1833–1834, with interest high and money scarce, there was suffering indeed, as many businessmen failed and thousands of workers lost their jobs. All over the country, friends of the Bank organized meetings to adopt petitions begging for relief from Congress, petitions which delegates then brought in person to Washington, and which pro-Bank senators or representatives introduced with appropriately lugubrious speeches. But Jackson and the Jacksonians denied responsibility. When distressed citizens appealed to the President he answered, "Go to Biddle."

The banker finally carried his contraction of credit too far to suit his own friends among the anti-Jackson businessmen of the Northeast, and some of them did go to Biddle. A group of New York and Boston merchants protested (as one of them reported) that the business community "ought not and would not sustain him in further pressure, which he very well knew was not necessary for the safety of the bank, and in which his whole object was to coerce a charter." To appease the business community he at last reversed himself and began to grant credit in abundance and on reasonable terms.

The "Bank War" was over, and Jackson had won it. But, with the passing of the Bank of the United States (in 1836), the country lost an indispensable financial institution. Economic troubles lay ahead.

## WHIGS AGAINST DEMOCRATS

During the bank war the opponents of Jackson not only formally censured him in the Senate but also denounced him throughout the country for his allegedly high-handed and arbitrary actions. His opponents often referred to him as a tyrant, "King Andrew I," and they began to call themselves "Whigs," after the party which in England stood traditionally for limiting the power of the King. At the end of a single term for Jackson's hand-picked successor, who had the misfortune to preside over the worst business depression yet, the Whigs outdid the Democrats in demagoguery and turned them out of office.

### Party Principles

The Whig party, organized in time for the congressional elections of 1834 and the presidential election of 1836, was an aggregation of dissimilar groups. It included the National Republicans who had opposed Jackson in 1828 (some of these were old Federalists, others former Jeffersonian Republicans), and it also included many people who had supported Jackson in 1828 but had turned against him afterward because of his stand on internal improvements, nullification, or the Bank. Some of the Whigs, as in Virginia, were really state-rights Democrats who had broken with the President when he threatened to use force against a sister state, South Carolina. On the whole the new party was strongest among the merchants and manufacturers of the Northeast, the wealthier planters of the South, and the farmers most eager for internal improvements in the West. But the party as a rule did not appeal very strongly to the mass of voters. Throughout its existence of twenty years or so the party was able to win only two presidential elections (1840 and 1848), both of them with military heros as its candidates.

In Jackson the Democrats had a military hero and popular leader whom no Whig could match. True, each of the two foremost Whigs, Clay and Webster, had a devoted following. The glamorous Clay, "Harry of the West," won friends throughout the country—but not enough friends ever to elect him President, though he was a candidate three times. The eloquent Webster gained fame and respect for his speeches expounding the Constitution and upholding the Union, and some of his businessman admirers thought him a greater man than any President. But his close connection with the unpopular Bank of the United States and his dependence on rich men for his financial support disqualified him in the minds of many voters. He and Clay were bitter rivals, and their rivalry weakened the party, though at times they cooperated in politics. Sometimes associated with them and sometimes opposing them was Calhoun, the third member of what came to be known as the Great Triumvirate. Calhoun did not consider himself a Whig: after his break with Jackson he thought of himself as a no-party man. Nevertheless he joined with Webster and Clay on the Bank issue. One thing the three men and all Whigs had in common was their opposition to Jackson and most of what he stood for.

Jackson and his party, in the course of his two presidential terms, developed a fairly definite and coherent political philosophy. The Jacksonians believed in laissez faire. That is, they believed that the government should let economic activities pretty much alone. They proposed the elimination of governmental favors to private enterprise, the destruction of government-granted monopolies and other corporate privileges. Then in theory the people through free and fair competition would be able to take care of themselves, each prospering in accordance with his own labor and skill. The worst of poverty and of social inequality would thus be done away with when the government ceased to help the rich and hinder the poor. While the Democrats did not advocate social revolution, the more radical of them (known as "Loco Focos") maintained that revolutionary violence might unfortunately appear unless economic inequalities were removed.

Calhoun agreed with the Loco Focos that the dangers of class struggle were very real, and he explored the nature and prospects of the struggle more thoroughly than anyone else of his time. Long before Karl Marx and Friedrich Engels published their *Communist Manifesto* (1848) he elaborated a similar view, though he hoped to prevent revolution whereas they intended to hasten it. In his *South Carolina Exposition and Protest* (1828) and in later writings he predicted that capitalist society would tend to divide into only two classes, "capitalists" and "operatives," that the former would expropriate and impoverish the latter, and that a revolutionary crisis would eventuate. "There is and always has been in an advanced stage of wealth and civilization," he insisted (1837), "a conflict between labor and capital." He hoped that the revolutionary danger would cause Northern businessmen to join with Southern planters in self-defense.

Webster, the leading Whig philosopher, stoutly denied the contentions of Calhoun and the radical Democrats. "In the old countries of Europe there is a clear and well-defined line between capital and labor," Webster conceded, but he declared there was no line so "broad, marked, and visible" in the United States. If there was any revolutionary discontent among the American people, he charged, it was due to the policies of the Jackson administration and the clamor of Democratic agitators. He maintained that the people had common interests rather than conflicting ones, at least so long as the government pursued the correct policies. He believed that a wise and active federal government, by stimulating and regulating economic activity through a national banking system, a protective tariff, and expenditures for internal improvements, could assure the economic well-being of all the people and thereby harmonize the interests of every section and class.

Thus both parties thought of themselves as representing the best interests of the whole country, though they differed in their notions of the appropriate means of achieving the general welfare. For the time being the Democrats were in power and their policies prevailed.

Party feeling affected opinions on foreign as well as domestic affairs. The Whigs opposed Jackson on an issue of foreign policy when he became involved in a dispute with France. A number of American citizens held claims against the French government on account of ships seized or destroyed under Napoleon's decrees before the War of 1812. In 1831 the French government agreed to pay 25 million francs in partial satisfaction of these so-called spoliation claims. The French Chamber of Deputies, however, failed to appropriate money for making the payment. Demanding that France make good its acknowledged debt, Jackson recommended to Congress the confiscation of French property in this country. The French took this as an insult to their national honor and insisted upon an apology. Though he refused to apologize, Jackson explained that he had meant no insult. As if expecting war he asked Congress (1835) for appropriations to build up the navy and the fortifications along the coast. The Whigs, denouncing him as a warmonger, voted against such appropriations. Despite political opposition at home, he won a diplomatic victory when the Chamber of Deputies at last provided funds and the debt was paid.

## Three Against One   1836

At stake in the party contests of the time were not only issues of foreign and domestic policy but also questions of federal jobholding and other prerequisites of political power. The Democrats had the power and the jobs; the Whigs wanted them. As the presidential election of 1836 approached, the Democrats had the advantages of patronage, Jackson's prestige, and a superior party organization. Jackson, not desiring a third term for himself, was able to choose the President to succeed him. The Democratic convention readily nominated his favorite, Van Buren.

The Whigs in 1836 could boast no such unity and discipline. Indeed, they could not even agree upon a single candidate. Their strategy, master-minded by Biddle, was to run several candidates, each of them supposedly strong in part of the country. Webster was the man for New England, and Hugh Lawson White of Tennessee was to seek the votes of the South. The former Indian fighter and hero of the War of 1812 from Ohio, William Henry Harrison, was counted upon in the middle states and the West. As Biddle advised: "This disease is to be treated as a local disorder—apply local remedies —if General Harrison will run better than anybody else in Pennsylvania, by all means unite upon him." None of the three candidates could expect to get a majority in the electoral college, but separately they might draw enough votes from Van Buren to prevent his getting a majority. The election would then devolve, as in 1824–1825, upon the House of Representatives, where conceivably the Whigs might be able to elect one of their men.

The three Whigs proved to be no match for the one Democrat. When the returns were in, Van Buren had 170 electoral votes to 124 for all his opponents. Again the South Carolina legislature gave that state's 11 electoral votes to a man who was not a regular candidate—Willie P. Mangum, of North Carolina. One of the Whig leaders of New York, William H. Seward, explained the victory of Van Buren thus: "The people are for him. Not so much for him as for the principle they suppose he represents. That principle is Democracy."

## The Panic of 1837

At the time of the election of 1836 a nationwide boom was reaching its height. Canal enterprisers and railroad builders were busy digging ditches and laying tracks here, there, and everywhere. Prices were high and going higher, as people indulged in an orgy of spending and speculating. Money was plentiful. Much of it came from abroad, English investors buying large amounts of American corporation securities and state bonds. Most of it was manufactured by the banks, which multiplied their loans and notes with little regard to their reserves of cash, until, by 1837, bank loans outstanding amounted to five times as much as in 1830. Never had the nation seemed so prosperous.

Land as usual was a favorite speculation,

**Election of 1836**

especially the land sold by the federal government. After the act of 1821 had abolished installment buying and set the minimum price at $1.25 an acre, sales of public lands reached an average of 300,000 to 400,000 acres a year in the late 1820s and early 1830s. Then the business suddenly boomed. Between 1835 and 1837 nearly 40 million acres were disposed of, and the expression "doing a land-office business" came into use to describe fast selling of any kind. Nearly three-fourths of the land being sold went to speculators—men acquiring large tracts in the hope of reselling at a profit—and only about a fourth of it to actual settlers. Speculators generally borrowed from the banks to make payment at the land offices.

For the time being the government profited. Receipts from land sales, which had averaged less than $2.4 million annually for the ten years preceding 1835, rose to more than $24 million in 1836. This was the government's largest source of revenue, but customs duties under the compromise tariff of 1833 added considerably to total income. The government received more money than it paid out. Steadily the national debt was reduced, as Jackson insisted it should be, and finally from 1835 to 1837 the government for the first and only time in its history was out of debt. Not only that: there was also a large and growing surplus in the federal treasury.

The question for Congress and the administration was how to get rid of the treasury surplus. Tampering with the tariff was not to be considered, since the recent compromise had put to rest that touchy subject and few wanted to reopen it.

Why not give the federal surplus to the states? This would be an effective way of getting rid of it, and the idea appealed to Congress. In 1836 Congress passed and Jackson signed a distribution act providing that the surplus accumulated by the end of the year (estimated at $40 million) be paid to the states in four quarterly installments as a loan without security or interest, each state getting a share proportional to its representation in Congress. No one seriously expected the "loan" to be repaid. As the states began to receive their shares they promptly spent the money, mainly to encourage the construction of highways, railroads, and canals. The distribution of the surplus thus gave further

stimulus to the speculative boom. At the same time the withdrawal of federal funds strained the "pet banks," for they had to call in a large part of their own loans in order to make the transfer of funds to the state governments.

Congress did nothing to check the speculative fever, with which many congressmen themselves were badly infected, Webster for one buying up thousands of acres in the West. But the President was much concerned. Though money continued to pour into the treasury from the land offices, most of it was money of dubious value. The government was selling good land and was receiving in return a miscellaneous collection of state banknotes, none of them worth any more than the credit of the issuing bank. Jackson finally decided to act. He issued his Specie Circular (1836) announcing that in the future only hard money or the notes of specie-paying banks would be accepted in payment for public lands. This was but one sign of trouble ahead for prosperity-crazed Americans. There were also other signs, for those who cared to see them.

As Jackson reached the end of his second term the nation was still seemingly prosperous. On his last full day in office, March 3, 1837, he recognized the independence of Texas (this sub-

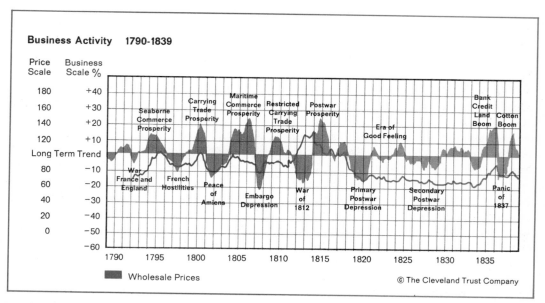

**Business Activity   1790-1839**

For the years 1790 to 1839 the index of business activity was computed on the basis of the following ten measures: blast furnace activity; cotton and pig iron consumption; canal and railroad freight ton miles; new railroad and ship construction; coal, locomotive and rail production.

### The Panic of 1837

The banner beneath the flag reads: "July 4th 1837. 61st Anniversary of Our Independence." Militiamen parade to observe the occasion, but the people, instead of watching, are preoccupied with their troubles. Mechanics stand idle with their tools. The only busy places are the shop of "Shylock Graspall, Licensed Pawnbroker," where the unemployed seek loans with which to buy liquor; the "Mechanics' Bank," where depositors try to get cash for their worthless bank notes; and the "Sheriff's Office," where property is being sold for unpaid taxes. From a contemporary lithograph. (Courtesy of the New-York Historical Society, New York City)

ject will be treated in Chapter 13) and on the following day he saw his hand-picked successor, Van Buren, inaugurated as President. Soon Jackson, justifiably proud of the success of his two administrations, left for the peace and quiet of his beloved home.

Van Buren had been in office less than three months when the panic broke. The banks of New York, followed by those of the rest of the country, suddenly suspended specie payments (that is, they stopped paying cash on demand for their banknotes and other obligations). During the next few years hundreds of banks failed, and so did hundreds of other business firms. As unemployment grew, bread riots occurred in some of the larger cities. Prices fell, especially the price of land, which now became a burden to the recently optimistic speculators, Webster being only one of a great many who all at once found themselves "land-poor." Many railroad and canal schemes were abandoned; several of the debt-burdened state governments ceased to pay interest on their bonds and a few repudiated their debts, at least temporarily. The depression, the worst the American people ever had experienced, lasted for about five years.

The Whigs blamed Jackson for the depression. It had come, they said, because of his destruction of the national bank and his mismanagement of public finance. But they were also in part to blame. The distribution of the treasury surplus was a Whig measure, though Jackson signed it (with the onset of the panic, the distribution was halted before the entire surplus had been transferred to the states). This step, by weakening the .pet banks, helped to bring on the crash. So did Jackson's Specie Circular, which started a general run on the banks as land buyers rushed to get cash in return for banknotes to make land-office payments. Distribution of the surplus and the Specie Circular only precipitated the depression, however; they did not cause it.

While the Bank of the United States, if continued, could have lessened the overexpansion of credit, a period of financial stringency doubtless would have come anyhow, sooner or later. For the depression was international, affecting England and Western Europe as well as the United States. As English investors faced a financial crisis at home, they began to withdraw funds from America, thus accounting for part of the strain on American banks. A succession of crop failures on American farms not only reduced the purchasing power of farmers but also necessitated imports of foodstuffs; to pay for these imports, additional money was drawn out of the country.

Besides its economic consequences, the Panic of 1837 had other significant results. Hard times increased social, sectional, and economic tensions. Want in the cities heightened the feeling that there existed even in America a real and dangerous class conflict—a struggle between the poor and the rich. Heavy losses suffered by Southern planters confirmed them in their conviction that national policies worked to their disadvantage, while the decline of business profits in the North intensified the belief of manufacturers that the compromise of 1833 must be undone and the tariff raised. Defaults on interest payments and outright repudiation of state bonds, many of them held by Englishmen, added to difficulties in the relations between the United States and Great Britain. Distress among the people was turned into dissatisfaction with the administration, so that the predominance of the Democrats was brought temporarily to an end after Van Buren had served but a single term.

## The Van Buren Program

The modern concept that government can successfully fight depressions, and has an obligation to do so, simply did not exist in President Van Buren's time. The only tradition of government intervention in economic matters was the Federalist-National Republican-Whig program of aid to business, to which Democrats were fiercely opposed. Consequently Van Buren

recommended but few direct antidepression measures. He advised Congress to authorize the borrowing of $10 million to meet expenses during the emergency, and Congress did so. He also urged that the government should accept only specie for taxes and other due payments, a policy that would not raise either prices or confidence in the banking system.

In formulating a program of permanent legislation, the administration clearly reflected the wishes of the dominant farmer-labor segment of the party. The President urged Congress to reduce the price of public lands, and he recommended passage of a general preemption bill giving settlers the right to buy 160 acres at a set minimum price before land in any particular area was opened for public sale. A bill graduating land prices downward passed the Senate three times but was blocked in the House. A similar fate befell the preemption bill. His program of agrarian reform foiled by legislative opposition, Van Buren had to resort to executive action to please his urban followers. By presidential order he established a ten-hour work day on all federal works. For the first time in the nation's history the government thus took direct action to aid the rising labor class.

The most important measure in the President's program, and the most controversial, was his proposal for a new fiscal system. With the Bank of the United States destroyed and with Jackson's expedient of "pet banks" discredited, some kind of new system was urgently needed. Van Buren's fiscal ideas demonstrate both his mental ingenuity and his sincere devotion to Democratic principles. The plan he suggested, known as the "Independent Treasury" or "Subtreasury" system, was simplicity itself. Government funds would be placed in an independent treasury at Washington and in subtreasuries in specified cities throughout the country. Whenever the government had to pay out money, its own agents would handle the funds. No bank or banks would have the government's money or name to use as a basis for speculation. The government and the banks would be "divorced."

Van Buren placed the Independent Treasury proposal before Congress in a special session he called in 1837. It encountered the immediate and bitter opposition of most Whigs and of

## Whig Broadside of 1840

This Whig campaign document depicts the principal episodes in the career of General Harrison—from his humble log cabin beginnings to fame as soldier and statesman. (Library of Congress)

many conservative Democrats. Twice a bill to establish an independent treasury passed the Senate only to fail in the House. Not until 1840, the last year of Van Buren's Presidency, did the administration succeed in driving the measure through both houses of Congress.

## The Log Cabin Campaign

As the campaign year of 1840 approached, the Whigs scented victory. The effects of the depression still gripped the country, and the Democrats, the party in power, could be blamed for the depression. So reasoned the Whigs, who now realized that a party representing the upper income groups must, if it expected to win, pose as a party of the people.

The Whigs also realized that they would have to achieve more unity and a stronger organization than they had demonstrated in 1836. They would have to settle on one candidate who could appeal to all segments of the party and to all sections of the country. Obviously the easiest way to coordinate the party was through the new mechanism of the national nominating convention, already used by the Democrats. Accordingly the Whigs held their first convention in Harrisburg, Pennsylvania, in December 1839. Their veteran leader, Henry Clay, "Mr. Whig," expected the nomination, but the party bosses decided otherwise. Clay had too definite a record; he had been defeated too many times; he had too many enemies. Passing him over, the convention nominated William Henry Harrison of Ohio, and for Vice President, John Tyler of Virginia.

William Henry Harrison was a descendant of the Virginia aristocracy, but all of his adult life had been spent in the Northwest, where he first went as a young army officer in General Wayne's campaign against the Indians. His governmental experience was limited, but he was a renowned Indian fighter (like Jackson) and a popular national figure.

The Democrats, meeting in national convention at Baltimore, nominated Van Buren, pointed proudly to their record, especially the Independent Treasury, and condemned all the works of Whigs, especially the Bank of the United States. Demonstrating that their party was, in some respects, no more united than the Whigs, the Democrats failed to nominate a vice-presidential candidate, declaring vaguely that they would leave the choice of that office to the wisdom of the voters.

The campaign of 1840 set a new pattern in American politics. It inaugurated the circus-carnival atmosphere that would mark presidential elections for years in the future and that would awe or amuse European beholders—vast meetings, shouting parades, party badges and other insignia, and campaign songs.

Throughout the campaign the eager Whigs

were on the offensive. They depicted themselves as the party of the people and the party that could save the nation from depression. They said Van Buren was an aristocrat who used cologne, drank champagne, and engaged in other undemocratic and un-American practices. A Democratic newspaper unwisely sneered that Harrison was a simple soul who would be glad to retire to a log cabin if provided with a pension and plenty of hard cider. In a country where many people lived or had lived in log cabins, this was almost handing the election to the Whigs, and they took the cue. Yes, their candidate was a simple man of the people, they proclaimed, and he loved log cabins and cider (actually he was a man of substance and lived in a large and well-appointed house).

Thereafter the log cabin was an established symbol at every Whig meeting, and hard cider an established beverage. Hundreds of Whig orators bragged that they had been born in log cabins or apologized for having been brought into the world in more sumptuous edifices. Thousands of Whig auditors listened to these effusions and happily chanted the songs that turned every Whig gathering into a frenzy of enthusiasm: "Tippecanoe and Tyler too" and "Van, Van is a used-up man." Against such techniques and the lingering effects of the depression the Democrats could not avail. When the votes were counted in November, Harrison had 234 electoral votes to 60 for Van Buren. The Whig victory was not as sweeping as it seemed; of the popular vote, Harrison had 1,275,000 to Van Buren's 1,129,000, a majority of less than 150,000.

## The Taney Court

Though the Democrats had lost control of the executive branch, they kept their hold on the Supreme Court. Jackson had been able to appoint seven new justices; and so, of the nine members, seven were Democrats. And the Chief Justice after 1835, Roger B. Taney, was a Jacksonian of the Jacksonians.

Between the Marshall-dominated Court and the Taney-dominated Court there was no sharp break in constitutional interpretation. But there was a marked change in emphasis. Taney and the majority of his colleagues were moderate agrarian liberals. In general they tended to recognize the right of popular majorities, acting through state legislatures, to regulate private property rights and the activities of corporations. In general, without adhering at all to the doctrines of Calhoun, they were inclined to modify the nationalism of the Marshall Court.

The attitude of the Court was revealed in the case of *Charles River Bridge* v. *Warren Bridge* (1837). In briefest essence, the background of this case was as follows: one company had a charter from Massachusetts to operate a toll bridge for a specified period of years; the legislature authorized another corporation to erect a bridge that would be toll-free; the first company contended that the state's action was invalid because it was a breach of contract. It was the old question—Could a state alter an agreement with a corporation?—which in the Dartmouth College case Marshall had decided against the state. But now Taney, speaking for the Democratic majority, supported Massachusetts. Though he advanced legal precedents to justify the decision, Taney based his position broadly on Jacksonian social doctrine. The object of government, he said, was to promote happiness, and this purpose was superior to property rights: a state had power to regulate corporations if such action was necessary to achieve the well-being of the community. Although the decision opened the way to increased state control and was wildly denounced by conservatives, it really aided the development of business. Industry was not going to grow if older corporations could maintain monopolies and choke off the competition of newer companies.

Another Taney case that enlarged state powers was *Bank of Augusta* v. *Earle* (1839). The question here was whether a corporation chartered in one state could do business in another that wished to exclude it. The Court held that under interstate comity a corporation had a general right to operate in other states, but that a state could, if it wished, exclude a foreign corporation or establish regulations for its entrance. This decision led many states to enact regulatory laws for outside corporations. In the absence of any federal regulation of interstate commerce, these measures were the only restrictions on companies engaged in business on a regional or on a national scale.

# Selected Readings

**Democratic Trends** Alexis de Tocqueville, *Democracy in America°* (2 vols., 1945); M. Ostrogorski, *Democracy and the Organization of Political Parties°* (2 vols., 1902); Chilton Williamson, *American Suffrage from Property to Democracy, 1760–1860* (1960); C. R. Fish, *The Civil Service and the Patronage* (1905); Louis Hartz, *The Liberal Tradition in America°* (1955).

**Jacksonian Democracy** G. G. Van Deusen, *The Jacksonian Era, 1828–1848°* (1959); A. M. Schlesinger, Jr., *The Age of Jackson°* (1945); R. P. McCormick, *The Second American Party System: Party Formation in the Jacksonian Era* (1966); C. G. Bowers, *The Party Battles of the Jackson Period* (1922); L. D. White, *The Jacksonians: A Study in Administrative History, 1829–1861* (1954); R. V. Remini, *Andrew Jackson* (1966); H. C. Syrett, *Andrew Jackson: His Contribution to the American Tradition* (1953); J. W. Ward, *Andrew Jackson: Symbol for an Age°* (1955).

**Leading Jacksonians** W. N. Chambers, *Old Bullion Benton, Senator from the New West* (1956); E. B. Smith, *Magnificent Missourian: The Life of Thomas Hart Benton* (1958); I. D. Spencer, *The Victor and the Spoils: A Life of William L. Marcy* (1959); C. G. Sellers, Jr., *James K. Polk, Jacksonian, 1795–1843* (1957); C. B. Swisher, *Roger B. Taney* (1936); R. V. Remini, *Martin Van Buren and the Making of the Democratic Party* (1959); J. A. Garraty, *Silas Wright* (1949).

**Indian Policy** F. P. Prucha, *American Indian Policy in the Formative Years* (1962); Grant Foreman, *Indian Removal: The Emigration of* the Five Civilized Tribes (1923); A. H. Abel, *A History of Events Resulting in Indian Consolidation West of the Mississippi* (1908); U. B. Phillips, *Georgia and State Rights* (1902); Donald Jackson, ed., *Black Hawk: An Autobiography* (1955).

**Nullification** C. S. Sydnor, *The Development of Southern Sectionalism* (1948); W. W. Freehling, *Prelude to Civil War: The Nullification Controversy in South Carolina, 1816–1836* (1966); Frederick Bancroft, *Calhoun and the South Carolina Nullification Movement* (1928); C. M. Wiltse, *John C. Calhoun, Nullifier, 1829–1839* (1949); M. L. Coit, *John C. Calhoun: American Portrait*° (1950); G. M. Capers, *John C. Calhoun —Opportunist: A Reappraisal*° (1960); R. N. Current, *John C. Calhoun*° (1963).

**The Bank and the Panic** Bray Hammond, *Banks and Politics in America from the Revolution to the Civil War* (1957); W. B. Smith, *Economic Aspects of the Second Bank of the United States* (1953); T. P. Govan, *Nicholas Biddle, Nationalist and Public Banker, 1786–1844* (1959); R. C. McGrane, *The Panic of 1837*° (1924); W. B. Smith and A. H. Cole, *Fluctuations in American Business, 1790–1860* (1935).

**The Whigs** E. M. Carroll, *Origins of the Whig Party* (1925); A. C. Cole, *The Whig Party in the South* (1913); C. M. Fuess, *Daniel Webster* (2 vols., 1930); R. N. Current, *Daniel Webster and the Rise of National Conservatism*° (1955); G. R. Poage, *Henry Clay and the Whig Party* (1936); G. G. Van Deusen, *The Life of Henry Clay*° (1937); R. G. Gunderson, *The Log Cabin Campaign* (1957).

**State Studies** T. P. Abernethy, *From Frontier to Plantation in Tennessee* (1932); D. R. Fox, *The Decline of Aristocracy in the Politics of New York*° (1919); Walter Hugins, *Jacksonian Democracy and the Working Class: A Study of the New York Workingmen's Movement, 1829–1837* (1960); Lee Benson, *The Concept of Jacksonian Democracy: New York as a Test Case*° (1961); D. T. Miller, *Jacksonian Aristocracy: Class and Democracy in New York, 1830–1860* (1967); R. P. McCormick, *The History of Voting in New Jersey* (1953); A. B. Darling, *Political Changes in Massachusetts, 1824–1848* (1925).

---

° Titles available in paperback.

# Chapter 11
# The North and
# National Unity

Sectionalism—the rivalry of one part of the country against another—had its origins early in American history. Even in colonial times there were three great areas (New England, the middle colonies, and the South) that developed characteristics different enough to set them apart as distinct sections. As the country grew after independence, the composition of the sections changed, and sectional feelings were intensified. By the 1840s and 1850s three sections that could be distinguished were the Northeast, the Northwest, and the South. These were gradually reduced to two—the North and the South—and the antagonism between them increasingly threatened to disrupt the nation.

If the sectional division had been a mere matter of geography, the dividing line might have run in a different direction. The Appalachian range, a great natural barrier, separated the East from the West, and beyond it the Mississippi Valley formed a vast geographic unit. In the minds of statesmen of the early republic, these geographical facts seemed to indicate that a new trans-Appalachian nation might someday arise and declare its independence.

With the elimination of slavery in New England and the middle states, however, all these states came to constitute a single, more or less homogeneous area, the Northeast. The new states of the Northwest, where the Northwest Ordinance prohibited slavery, developed a somewhat similar free-labor economy, and these states were connected with the Northeast through the construction of canals and railroads. Those of the original states where slavery persisted comprised an increasingly distinctive South, and this section, with the westward spread of slavery, included the newer states of the Southwest. Thus the slave boundary cut across both the Appalachian Mountains and the Mississippi Valley. So terribly potent was the slavery issue that it distorted the natural lines of separation and cohesion.

There nevertheless remained strong forces tending to hold the North and the South together. Groups within each section had conflicting interests, which weakened sectional loyalties, and groups in both sections had common interests, which led to intersectional cooperation. Improvements in transportation and communication provided a better and better technological basis for national unity. And cultural nationalism persisted. Many people, especially in the North, while priding themselves on the intellectual attainments of the United States, continued to call for a civilization no longer imitative of Europe but distinctively American.

## Two Views of Immigration

These two pictures show the sometimes antithetical attitudes that Americans had about immigrants. The illustration above by an unknown artist glorifies the lure of the land of plenty and liberty to English immigrants and depicts the immigrants as essentially good people. (Museum of the City of New York) The picture below shows political workers operating at the naturalization office before an election. They are ready to testify that an immigrant has been in the United States for five years —provided the immigrant will promise his vote. Note that the immigrants are represented as beings of a low social order. From *Harper's Weekly* (1857).

## THE NORTHERN ECONOMY

Even without the moral question of slavery, the political and economic issues involved in the sectional controversy would have strained the national fabric. Many of the political questions of the 1840s and 1850s were economic in origin, and the economy of each section had much to do with determining its social and cultural as well as political views. In each section a particular economic activity predominated, and hence a particular class tended to control the wealth and lead the other classes in politics. In the Northeast, where industry and overseas commerce predominated, the manufacturers and bankers were the leaders. In the Northwest, where most of the people were small farmers, they themselves were uppermost in both economic and political life. In the South, by contrast, though small farmers were the most numerous group, they yielded to the large planters, who exercised a controlling influence.

### The Northeast: Business

Between 1840 and 1860 American industry experienced a steady and, in some fields, a spectacular growth. In 1840 the total value of manufactured goods produced in the United States stood at $483 million; ten years later the figure had climbed to over $1 billion; and in 1860 it reached close to $2 billion. For the first time the value of manufactured goods was approximately equal to that of agricultural products. In the cotton textile industry the number of spindles in operation doubled during this twenty-year period.

Industrial growth was greatest in the states of the Northeast. Most conspicuous in this part of the country were the change from domestic or household manufactures to the factory system, the shift of economic power from merchant capitalism to industrial capitalism, the spread of the corporate organization in business, and other innovations that heralded the coming of modern America. A few figures will illustrate the industrial predominance of the Northeast. Of the approximately 140,000 manufacturing establishments in the country in 1860, 74,000 were located in this section; they represented well over half the total national investment in manufactures, and the annual value of their products was two-thirds of the national figure. Of the 1,311,000 workers in the entire country, about 938,000 were employed in the mills and factories of New England and the middle states.

Even the most highly developed industries still showed qualities of immaturity and were still far away from the production goals they would attain after 1865. The cotton manufacturers, for example, concentrated on producing goods of coarse grade, making little attempt to turn out fine items, which continued to be imported from England. A similar situation existed in the woolens industry, which because of a short American supply of raw wool could not even meet the domestic demand for coarse goods. As yet, American industry, which exported very little, was unable to satisfy fully the wants of American consumers.

Technology and industrial ingenuity were, however, preparing the way for future American industrial supremacy. The machine tools used in the factories of the Northeast, such as the turret lathe, the grinding machine, and the universal milling machine, were better than those in European factories. The principle of interchangeable parts, applied earlier in gun factories by Eli Whitney and Simeon North, was being introduced into other lines of manufacturing. Coal was replacing wood as an industrial fuel, particularly in the smelting of iron. Coal was also being used in increasing amounts to generate power in the steam engines that were replacing the water power that had driven most of the factory machinery in the Northeast. The production of coal, most of it mined in the Pittsburgh area of western Pennsylvania, leaped from 50,000 tons in 1820 to 14 million tons in 1860.

The great technical advances in American industry owed much to American inventors. The patent records reveal the growth of Yankee ingenuity. In 1830 the number of inventions patented was 544; in 1850 the figure rose to 993; and in 1860 it stood at 4,778. In 1839 Charles Goodyear, a New England hardware merchant, discovered a method of vulcanizing rubber; his process had been put to 500 uses by 1860, and the rubber industry was firmly established. In 1846 Elias Howe of Massachusetts

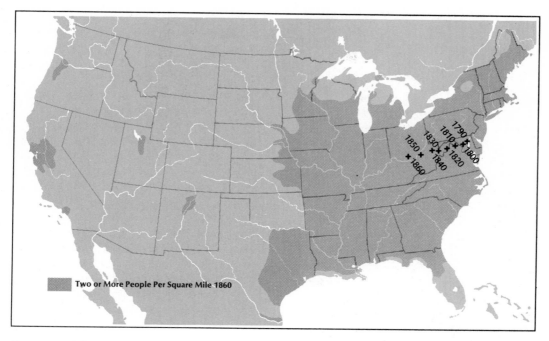

Two or More People Per Square Mile 1860

**Centers of Population    1790–1860**

constructed a sewing machine, upon which improvements were soon made by Isaac Singer.
The Howe-Singer machine was soon employed
in manufacturing ready-to-wear clothing. A little
later, during the Civil War, it would supply the
Northern troops with uniforms.

In an earlier period the dominant economic
figure in the Northeast had been the merchant
capitalist—the man who engaged in foreign or
domestic trade, who invested his surplus capital
in banks, and who sometimes financed small-
scale domestic manufacturers. By 1840 merchant capitalism was in a state of decline, though
the merchant by no means disappeared. In
cities like New York, Philadelphia, and Boston,
there were important and influential mercantile
groups that operated shipping lines to Southern
ports—carrying away cotton, rice, and sugar—
or dispatched fleets of trading vessels to the
ports of Europe and the Orient. Many of these
vessels were the famous clippers, the most beautiful and the fastest sailing ships afloat. In their
heyday in the late forties and early fifties, the
clippers were capable of averaging 300 miles a
day, which compared favorably with the best
time then being made by steamships. Though

the value of American exports, almost entirely
agricultural in nature, increased from $124 mil-
lion in 1840 to $334 million in 1860, American
merchants in the 1850s saw much of their carrying trade fall into the hands of British competitors, who enjoyed the advantages of steam-
driven iron ships and government subsidies.

It was not foreign rivalry, however, that
caused the decline of the merchant capitalist,
but rather the rise of the factory system in the
United States. The merchants saw greater opportunities for profit in manufactures than in
trade. They shifted their capital from mercantile
investments to industry, becoming owners and
operators of factories or placing their money
in companies operated by others. Indeed, one
reason why industries developed soonest in the
East was that the merchant class had the money
and the will to finance them.

Many business concerns were owned by one
man, by a family, or by partners. But, particularly in the textile industry, the corporation
form of organization spread rapidly. In their
overseas ventures the merchants had been accustomed to diversifying their risks by buying
shares in a number of vessels and voyages. They

## John Murray Forbes

The migration of New England capital from overseas trade to manufacturing is mirrored in the career of John Murray Forbes (1813–1898). This cultured and charming merchant made a fortune in the China trade while still a young man. Returning to the United States, he continued his mercantile activities, but began to shift his interest and eventually his investments into textiles and other industries. In 1846 he turned his attention to railroads in the Mississippi Valley. He was the leading figure in the group of Eastern merchants who purchased and completed the Michigan Central Railroad from Detroit to Chicago. Forbes was also allied with New York capitalists who controlled the Illinois Central, the north-south route in Illinois that by 1858 linked Chicago and Cairo. At the same time Forbes and his associates took over and combined several lines into the Chicago, Burlington and Quincy Railroad; the first line to enter Iowa from the east. Still another road that came under his guiding hand was the Hannibal and St. Joseph. In the Civil War and postwar period Forbes devoted his major energies to public service, but railroads continued to be his dominating economic interest. The railroad king had permanently replaced the merchant prince.

employed the same device when they moved their capital from trade to manufacturing, purchasing shares in several textile companies.

Regardless of the forms of business organization, the industrial capitalists became the ruling class, the aristocrats of the Northeast. As they had sought and secured economic dominance, they reached for and grasped political influence. In politics, local or national, they liked to be represented by highly literate lawyers who could articulate their prejudices and philosophy. Their ideal of a representative was Daniel Webster of Massachusetts, whom the businessmen

of the section, at considerable financial cost to themselves, supported for years in the United States Senate.

## The Northeast: Farms and Labor

The story of agriculture in the Northeast after 1840 is largely one of economic deterioration. The reason for the worsening situation is simple: the farmers of this section could not produce goods in competition with the new and richer soil of the Northwest. Eastern farmers turned to a system of production that aimed at a rude self-sufficiency or to the cultivation of products that would not suffer from Western competition. Many went West and took up new farms, or moved to the mill towns and became laborers. As a result, the rural population in many parts of the Northeast continued to decline.

The centers of production shifted westward for wheat, corn, grapes, cattle, sheep, and hogs. In 1840 the leading wheat-growing states were New York, Pennsylvania, Ohio, and Virginia; in 1860 they were Illinois, Indiana, Wisconsin, Ohio, and Michigan. In the case of corn, Illinois, Ohio, and Missouri supplanted New York, Pennsylvania, and Virginia. In 1840 the most important cattle-raising areas in the country were in New York, Pennsylvania, and New England, but by the 1850s the leading cattle states were Illinois, Indiana, Ohio, and Iowa, in the West, and Texas in the South.

In some lines of agriculture the Northeast held its own or even surpassed the Northwest. As the Eastern urban centers increased in population, many farmers turned profitably to the task of supplying foods to the city masses, engaging in truck gardening (vegetables) or fruit raising. New York led all other states in apple production. Also stimulated by the rise of cities was dairy farming. The profits to be derived from supplying milk, butter, and cheese to local markets attracted many farmers in central New York, southeastern Pennsylvania, and various parts of New England. Approximately half of the dairy products of the country were produced in the East; the other half came from the West, with Ohio being the dairy center of that section. Partly because of the expansion of the dairy industry, the Northeast led other sections in the production of hay. New York was the leading hay state in the nation, and large crops were grown in Pennsylvania and New England. The Northeast also exceeded other areas in producing potatoes.

Most of the workers in Northeastern factories during the decade of the forties came from the native population of the section—from the farming classes that were being pinched off the land by Western competition. Almost half of the laborers were women and children, and in some industries, notably textiles, the percentage was much higher. The rural people who flocked to the mill towns in the hope of finding a better life soon discovered that their situation there was little if any better than it had been back on the farms. Most mill towns were cheerless, ugly places in which to live, and most factories were unsanitary, unhealthful buildings in which to work. The average workday was twelve to fourteen hours. The wages of skilled workers ranged from $4 to $10 a week; unskilled workers and women and children received $1 to $6 per week.

Workers attempted, with little success, to persuade state legislatures to pass laws setting a maximum workday. New Hampshire, in 1847, enacted a statute providing that no person be required to work more than ten hours in one day unless he agreed to an "express contract" calling for greater time; in the following year Pennsylvania adopted a similar law for the textile and paper industries. These measures were largely inoperative because many employers forced prospective employees to sign agreements for longer hours. Three states—Massachusetts, New Hampshire, and Pennsylvania—passed laws regulating child labor, but the statutes merely forbade the employment of minors for more than ten hours in a day without the consent of their parents. Probably the greatest legal victory achieved by labor was in a judicial case in Massachusetts. The supreme court of that state, in *Commonwealth* v. *Hunt* (1842), declared that unions were lawful organizations and that the strike was a lawful weapon. Other state courts gradually accepted the principles of the Massachusetts decision.

During the 1840s the factory labor supply of the Northeast was augmented by immigrants from Europe. The immigrant flood helped to delay the development of the labor organizations that had experienced a vigorous growth in the thirties but had been hard hit by the depression after 1837. Generally the newcomers were willing to work for less than the wages demanded by native workers. Labor never recovered, before 1860, the ground it had lost in the lean depression years. By the 1850s several national craft unions had been formed by such groups as machinists, hat workers, printers, molders, stone cutters, and a few others. But these were organizations of skilled workers, representing only a tiny minority of labor and manifesting almost no class awareness. The mass of laborers remained unorganized.

## The Northwest

There was some industry in the Northwest, more than in the South, and in the two decades before the Civil War the section experienced a steady industrial growth. By 1860 it had 36,785 manufacturing establishments employing 209,909 workers. Along the southern shore of Lake Erie was a flourishing industrial and commercial area of which Cleveland was the center. Another manufacturing locality was in the Ohio River Valley, with the meat-packing city of Cincinnati as its nucleus. Farther west, the rising city of Chicago, destined to be the great metropolis of the section, was emerging as the national center of the agricultural machinery and meat-packing industries. The most important industrial products of the West were farm machines, flour, meats, distilled whiskey, and leather and wooden goods.

But the West predominantly was a land of family farms and small farmers. The average size of Western farms was 200 acres, and the great majority of the farmers owned their own land.

In concentrating on corn, wheat, cattle, sheep, and hogs, the Western farmer was motivated by sound economic reasons. As the Northeast became more industrial and urban, it enlarged the domestic market for farm goods. At the same time England and certain European nations, undergoing the same process, started to import larger amounts of food from the outside. This steadily increasing world-wide demand for farm products resulted in steadily rising farm prices. For the farmers, the forties and early fifties were years of prosperity.

The expansion of agricultural markets had profound effects on sectional alignments in the United States. Of the Northwest's total output, by far the greatest part was disposed of in the Northeast; only the surplus remaining after domestic needs were satisfied was exported abroad. The new well-being of Western farmers, then, was in part sustained by Eastern purchasing power. Eastern industry, in turn, found an augmenting market for its products in the prospering West. Between the two sections there was being forged a fundamental economic relationship that was profitable to both.

To meet the increasing demands for its products, the Northwest had to enlarge its productive capacities. The presence of large blocks of still unoccupied land made it possible to enlarge the area under cultivation during the 1840s. By 1850 the growing Western population had settled the prairie regions east of the Mississippi and was pushing beyond the river. Stimulated to greater production by rising prices and conscious of the richness of his soil, the average Western farmer engaged in wasteful, exploitative methods of farming that often resulted in rapid soil exhaustion.

Some improvements in farming methods did, however, find their way into use. New varieties of seed, notably Mediterranean wheat, which was hardier than the native type, were introduced in some areas; better breeds of animals, such as hogs and sheep from England and Spain, were imported to take the place of native stock. In nearly every case these and similar innovations were first tried out on Eastern farms, and later won whole or partial acceptance in the West.

Of greater importance were the improvements that Americans continued to introduce in farm machines and tools. During the forties more

### St. Louis in the 1850s

As the West grew in population and expanded its economy, its cities became larger. They began to assume the form and to exercise the functions of metropolitan centers in the East. This print shows one of the principal Western cities, St. Louis, as it appeared in the 1850s. Of the three major cities of the West, St. Louis and Cincinnati were older than Chicago and for years were more populous. But by 1860 the Lake Michigan city, experiencing a spectacular growth, was hard on their heels, and after the Civil War it would emerge as the metropolis of the section. (Courtesy Chicago Historical Society) efficient grain drills, harrows, mowers, and hay rakes were placed in wide use. The cast-iron plow, devised earlier, continued to be popular because its parts could be replaced when broken. An even better implement appeared in 1847 when John Deere established at Moline, Illinois, a factory to manufacture plows with steel moldboards, which were more durable than those made of iron and were also self-scouring.

Two new machines heralded a coming revolution in grain production. The most important was the automatic reaper, invented by Cyrus H. McCormick of Virginia. The reaper, taking the place of sickle, cradle, and hand labor, enabled a crew of six or seven men to harvest in a day as much wheat (or any other small grain) as fifteen men could harvest using the older methods. McCormick, who had patented his device in 1834, established in 1847 a factory at Chicago in the heart of the grain belt. By 1850 he was turning out 3,000 reapers a year; by 1860, over 100,000 were in use on Western farms. Almost as helpful an aid to the grain grower was the thresher, which appeared in large numbers after 1840. Before that time, grain was flailed out by hand (seven bushels a day was a good average) or trodden out by farm animals (twenty bushels a day on the average). The threshing machines could thresh twenty-five bushels or more in an hour. Most of the threshers were manufactured at the Jerome I. Case factory in Racine, Wisconsin.

The Northwest was the most democratic of the three sections in the sense that the farmers, the majority, were the dominant economic class and generally had their way in politics. Theirs was a capitalistic, property-conscious, middle-class kind of democracy. Abraham Lincoln, an Illinois Whig, voiced the economic opinions of many of the people of his section. "I take it that it is best for all to leave each man free to acquire property as fast as he can," said Lincoln. "Some will get wealthy. I don't believe in a law to prevent a man from getting rich; it would do more harm than good. . . . When one starts poor, as most do in the race of life, free society is such that he knows he can better his condition; he knows that there is no fixed condition of labor for his whole life."

**Cyrus H. McCormick and the Evolution of Farm Machinery**

The above print illustrates the rather rapid developments in farm machinery that occurred after McCormick introduced the first successful reaper in 1831. In the lower right-hand corner men are shown mowing grain by hand. Next, to the left, is shown an early mower; it cut the grain, which was raked and bundled by men who followed it. Then came the reaper, which deposited the cut grain on an attached platform; from here it was dumped to the ground and bundled by workers. Last came the self-binding harvester, which combined all the harvesting operations. McCormick, who was from Virginia, with great foresight located his manufacturing plant in Chicago in the growing Northwest. (Culver)

The democratic conservatism of the West was apparent in the program it advocated in national politics: internal improvements, cheap or preferably free lands, and territorial expansion.

## UNIFYING AND DIVISIVE FORCES

Between 1850 and 1860 the population of the United States rose by more than third, from 23 million to over 31 million, as the nation continued its phenomenal human as well as material growth. Much of this increase was due to immigration. On the one hand, the immigrants stimulated a sense of nationalism, both because of their attachment to their new homeland as a

## Urban Growth [1840–1860]

In 1840 the largest cities in the country were in the Northeast and the South. But in the next two decades, as the East became increasingly industrialized, cities there shot ahead of their Southern rivals. The following figures show the comparative rates of growth:

The most spectacular population gains were scored by the new Western cities. From 40,000 in the 1830s, Cincinnati climbed to 161,000 in 1860. In the same period St. Louis went from 10,000 to 160,000, and Chicago, astonishing everybody but itself, from 250 to 109,000.

|  | 1840 | 1850 | 1860 |
|---|---|---|---|
| New York | 312,000 | 515,000 | 805,000* |
| Philadelphia | 220,000 | 340,000 | 565,000 |
| Boston | 93,000 | 136,000 | 177,000 |
| Baltimore | 102,000 | 169,000 | 212,000 |
| New Orleans | 100,000 | 116,000 | 165,000 |

* Or 1,200,000 including Brooklyn.

whole (they had no inherited loyalty to any of the particular states) and because of the antiforeigner and self-consciously "American" feeling that some of them aroused on the part of many of the native Americans. On the other hand, the new arrivals contributed to social differentiation between North and South, since they did not distribute themselves evenly throughout the country but settled in much the larger numbers in the North.

A more positive unifying force was to be found, at least potentially, in the development of railroads and the introduction of the telegraph. "The fifties," writes the historian A. C. Cole, "saw the emerging outlines of a genuinely national system of transportation and communication."

## Rising Immigration

Between 1830 and 1840 only about 500,000 immigrants had entered the country, with the highest yearly figure, 84,000, being reached in 1840. Then the floodgates opened. From 1840 to 1850 over 1.5 million Europeans moved to America; in the last years of the decade the average number arriving yearly was almost 300,000. Of the 23 million people in the United States in 1850, 2,210,000 were foreign-born; of these almost 1 million were Irish and over 500,000 were German. Special reasons explained the prevalence of immigrants from Ireland and Germany: widespread poverty caused by the economic dislocations of the Industrial Revolution; famines resulting from the failure of the potato and other crops; dislike of English rule by the Irish; and the collapse of the liberal revolutions of 1848 in Germany. The great majority of the Irish settled in the Eastern cities where they swelled the ranks of unskilled labor. Not until after 1850, however, when the tide of immigration reached even greater heights, did foreigners outnumber the native-born in the labor population. Most of the Germans, having a little more money than the Irish, who had practically none, moved on to the Northwest, where they became farmers or went into business in the Western towns.

The number of immigrants who came in the fifties exceeded even that of the previous decade, reaching an estimated aggregate of over 2.5 million. As before, the overwhelming majority of the newcomers hailed from Ireland and Germany. By 1860 more than 1.5 million Irishmen had migrated to the United States, and approximately 1 million Germans. Other nationalities represented in the immigrant tide were Englishmen, Frenchmen, Italians, Scandinavians, Poles, and Hollanders. Most of the foreigners collected in the urban centers of the Northern states. Almost half of the population of New York City consisted of aliens, and in St. Louis, Chicago, and Milwaukee the foreign-born outnumbered those of native birth. Few immigrants settled in the South. Only 500,000 lived in the slave states in 1860, and a third of these were concentrated in Missouri; of the Southern cities, only New Orleans contained a large number of foreign-born residents. Immigrants avoided the South partly because of the climate, partly because most of them were opposed to slavery or feared the competition of slave labor, but mostly because the bulk of them landed at Northern ports and from these points gravitated easily to areas in the North that attracted them.

In some cities and states the foreign vote assumed pivotal importance. Existing laws in many states permitted aliens to vote if they had been in the country for a year and had declared intention to seek citizenship. Particularly in the large cities, the politicians courted the immigrant voters with material favors, including outright money payments, and in some places it became common to buy votes in blocks. In general, the immigrants tended to affiliate with the Democrats, whose party they regarded as the representative of the common man.

## The Nativist Movement

The presence of huge numbers of aliens occasioned the first important organized nativist movement in American history. While some natives recognized the contribution that the newcomers were making to the cultural and material development of their adopted land, many others disliked their ways and feared their influence. These critics contended that many of the immigrants were mentally and physically defective, that they created slums, and that they corrupted politics by selling their votes. Laborers complained that the aliens, willing to work for low wages, were stealing their jobs. Protestants, impressed by the aptitude that the Catholic Irish demonstrated for politics, believed, or affected to believe, that the Church of Rome was attaining an undue power in American government. Many Americans of older stock were honestly concerned that the immigrants would not assimilate into national life or would inject new and radical philosophies into national thought.

Out of these tensions and prejudices emerged

a number of secret societies to combat the "alien menace." Originating in the East and later spreading to the West and South, these groups combined in 1850 to form the Supreme Order of the Star-Spangled Banner. Included in the official program of the order were opposition to Catholics or aliens holding public office and support of stricter naturalization laws and literacy tests for voting. When members were asked to define their platform, they replied, because of the secrecy rule, "I know nothing," and hence were dubbed "Know-Nothings."

Soon the leaders, deciding to seek their objectives by political methods, formed the so-called American party. In the East the new organization scored an immediate and astonishing success in the elections of 1854, casting a large vote in Pennsylvania and New York and winning control of the state government in Massachusetts. Elsewhere the progress of the Know-Nothings was more modest and tempered by local conditions. Western members of the party, because of the presence of many German voters in the area, found it expedient to proclaim that they were not opposed to naturalized Protestants. In the South, where Catholics were few, the leaders disavowed any religious bias, and Catholics participated in the movement. The party's spectacular growth would soon be interrupted by the rise of the larger issue of slavery.

## Development of Railroads

The swelling domestic trade between East and West could not have developed without an adequate transportation system. In the 1830s most of the goods exchanged between the two sections were carried on the Erie Canal. After 1840 railroads gradually supplanted canals and all other modes of transport. In 1840 the total railroad trackage of the country was only 2,818 miles. There was a speed-up of construction in the forties, and by the end of the decade the trackage figure had risen to 9,021 miles. Most of the new lines ran east and west and several of them crossed New York State. The railroads enabled the Western farmers to ship their products cheaply and quickly to Eastern markets and thus helped to force many Eastern farmers out of business.

An outburst of railroad construction without

previous parallel occurred in the fifties. The amount of trackage tripled between 1850 and 1860. The Northeast had the most efficient system, with twice as much trackage per square mile of land as the West and four times as much as the South. Railroads were reaching even west of the Mississippi, which at several points was spanned by iron bridges. One line ran from Hannibal to St. Joseph on the Missouri River, and another was being built from St. Louis to Kansas City. As for the South, many of its lines were short ones, and there were few through lines. Nevertheless, such towns as Charleston, Atlanta, Savannah, and Norfolk had direct connections with Memphis, and thus with the Northwest; and Richmond was connected, via the Virginia Central, with the Memphis and Charleston rail-

road. In addition, several independent lines furnished a continuous connection between the Ohio River and New Orleans.

A new feature in railroad development—and one that would profoundly affect the nature of sectional alignments—was the trend toward the consolidation of short lines into trunk lines. By 1853 four roads had surmounted the Appalachian barrier to connect the Northeast with the Northwest. Two, the New York Central and the New York and Erie, gave New York City access to the Lake Erie ports. The Pennsylvania road linked Philadelphia and Pittsburgh, and the Baltimore and Ohio connected the Maryland metropolis with the Ohio River at Wheeling. From the terminals of these lines, other railroads into the interior touched the Mississippi River at

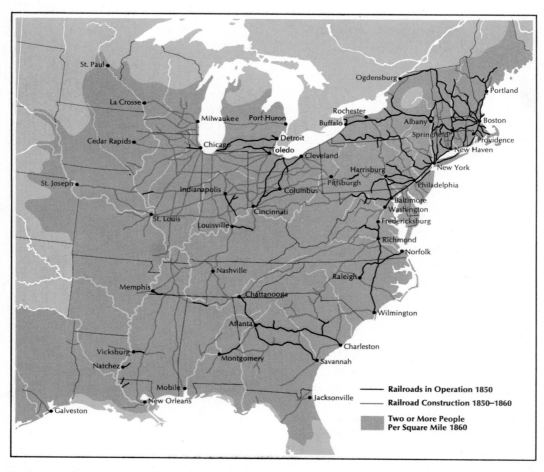

**Railroads in Operation 1850;  Railroads Under Construction 1850–1860**

## Niagara Suspension Bridge

As the railroads penetrated to all parts of the country, the builders of the roads had to surmount the problem of flinging their lines across large rivers or deep gorges. There appeared to aid them great bridge builders. One of these was John A. Roebling, who believed that for spanning the greatest distances the suspension bridge, with a roadway hung from huge cables, was the best type. Roebling demonstrated his theory by constructing such a bridge over the Niagara gorge in 1855. (Photo by William England. Collection, The Museum of Modern Art, New York)

eight points. Other important trunk routes were the Michigan Central and the Michigan Southern, which entered Chicago from the East, and the Rock Island and Chicago, which connected the Great Lakes and the Mississippi. Chicago became the rail center of the West, served by fifteen lines and over a hundred daily trains. The appearance of the great trunk lines tended to divert traffic from the water routes—the Erie Canal and the Mississippi River. By lessening the dependence of the West upon the Mississippi, the railroads helped to weaken the connection between the Northwest and the South.

By binding more closely the East and West, they prepared the way for a coalition of those sections.

At the opening of the century the average freight rate by wagon had been 33 cents per ton mile; the average passenger rate was 6 cents per mile. In the stagecoach era of the 1830s a trip from Boston to New York consumed forty-one hours; from New York to St. Louis, a distance of 1,600 miles, over three weeks were required. The average coach fare for 300 miles was $15. The principal result of the advent of water transportation was to reduce freight

**Speed by Water and by Rail [1850s]**

The following table indicates the rapidity of rail as compared with water travel and transportation between New York City and Western cities:

| From New York To | Distance in Miles | Time by Water | Time by Railroads |
|---|---|---|---|
| Cleveland | 700 | 9 days | 3 days |
| Detroit | 825 | 10 days | 4 days |
| Chicago | 1,500 | 14½ days | 6½ days |
| St. Louis | 1,600 | | 12½ days |

charges. According to one estimate, the costs of traffic on the various means of transportation in 1840 were as follows: roads, 10 to 20 cents per mile; canals, 1½ cents; lake steamers, 2 to 4 cents; river steamers, 1½ cents; railroads, 2½ cents. Water transportation continued to be cheaper than railroad transportation, but the railroads could move goods in about half the time required on water. Railroad freight rates continued to decrease, reaching by the decade of the 1860s an average of slightly less than 2 cents per ton mile.

Capital to finance the railroad boom came from various sources. Part of it was provided by American investors, and large sums were borrowed abroad. Substantial aid was provided by local governmental units—states, cities, towns, counties—eager to have a road to serve their needs. This support took the form of loans, stock subscriptions, subsidies, and donations of land for rights of way. The railroads also obtained assistance from the federal government in the shape of public land grants. In 1850 Senator Stephen A. Douglas and other railroad-minded politicians persuaded Congress to grant lands to the state of Illinois to aid the Illinois Central, then building toward the Gulf of Mexico; Illinois was to transfer the land to the Central as it carried its construction forward. Other states and their railroad promoters demanded the same privileges, and by 1860 Congress had allotted over 30 million acres to eleven states.

The operation of railroads was facilitated by the magnetic telegraph, the lines of which were extended along the tracks to connect one station with another.

## The Telegraph

Culminating several years of experimentation with an electric (magnetic) telegraph, Samuel F. B. Morse in 1844 transmitted from Baltimore to Washington the news of James K. Polk's nomination for the Presidency. The Morse telegraph seemed, because of the relatively low cost of constructing wire systems, the ideal answer to the problems of long-distance communication. By 1860 over 50,000 miles of wire connected most parts of the country, and a year later the Pacific telegraph, with 3,595 miles of wire, was open between New York and San Francisco. Nearly all of the independent lines had been absorbed into one organization, the Western Union Telegraph Company. American enthusiasm for wire communication was not limited to the confines of the nation. Cyrus W. Field, a New York businessman, conceived the project of laying an Atlantic cable between Newfoundland and Ireland. With financial aid from associates and encouragement from the British and American governments, he completed a cable in 1858. Messages between Great Britain and the United States were exchanged, and man seemed to have accomplished another conquest of distance. But within a few weeks the cable went dead, nor could Field, who continued to believe in his idea, get it to work again. (After the Civil War, Field returned to his labors, and in 1866 succeeded in laying a permanent cable.)

## The New Journalism

In 1846 Richard Hoe invented the steam cylinder rotary press, making it possible to print newspapers at a much faster rate and a much lower cost. The development of the telegraph, together with the introduction of the rotary press, made possible much speedier collection and distribution of news than ever before. In 1846 the Associated Press was organized for the purpose of cooperative news gathering by wire; no longer did publishers have to depend on exchanges of newspapers for out-of-town reports.

Other changes in journalism also occurred. Originally Washington had been the national news center, and the papers published there had been government or party organs that filled their columns with dull documents and speeches. With the advent of the telegraph and the railroad and with the government's assumption of the function of public printing, the center of news transmission shifted to New York. A new type of newspaper appeared, one that was more attuned to the spirit and the needs of the new America. Although newspapers continued to concentrate on politics, they came to report more human interest stories and to record the most recent news, the happenings of yesterday, which they could not have done before the telegraph. The New York papers, and to a lesser degree those of other Northern cities, maintained corps of special correspondents to go into all parts of the country to cover any event that seemed newsworthy.

Most of the metropolitan journals were owned in whole or in part by their editors, who were also in many cases their founders; unlike modern newspapers they bore the imprint of a single personality and are often referred to as "personal" organs. The leading Northern papers were Horace Greeley's *Tribune,* James Gordon Bennett's *Herald,* and Henry J. Raymond's *Times,* all of New York. The *Herald* specialized in scandal and crime, the *Tribune* in self-improvement and social uplift. With a separate weekly edition, the *Tribune* served as a national or at least

a sectional paper, having mail subscribers scattered throughout the Northeast and Northwest. Southern papers, with smaller budgets, tended to follow the older pattern of reporting mainly rather stale political news. The combined circulation of the New York *Tribune* and *Herald* exceeded that of all the dailies published in the South. In the country as a whole, there were more than 3,000 newspapers by 1860.

During the fifties Americans experienced the impact of a new kind of magazine journalism. In increasing numbers the upper and middle classes were reading monthly magazines that featured fiction and news articles by some of the country's outstanding writers. Easily the leader in this field was *Harper's New Monthly Magazine,* with 170,000 subscribers, but competition was furnished by *Putnam's Magazine* and the *Atlantic Monthly,* both founded in the fifties. Another organ that appealed to the more literate groups was the New York religious-political weekly, the *Independent,* with a circulation of nearly 100,000. For the edification of the masses there appeared the pictorial weeklies, lavishly illustrated with drawings by America's best popular artists. The pioneer among the picture journals was the *National Police Gazette,* established in 1845 by George Wilkes. It was also the most sensational, reporting "horrid murders, outrageous robberies, bold forgeries, astounding burglaries, hideous rapes, vulgar seductions." Other picture magazines reaching huge audiences were *Leslie's Illustrated Newspaper* (1855) and *Harper's Weekly* (1857).

In one sense, the new journalism helped to feed the fires of sectional discord. The rapid reporting of detailed information regarding differences between the sections prompted men to anger more quickly and more often than otherwise would have been the case. But viewed in a longer perspective, the revolution in news was a unifying factor in American life. As one historian of journalism (L. M. Starr) has pointed out, the ultimate result of the news revolution was to endow the American people with that mystic sense of common destiny that is conveyed only by news of great events being reported everywhere simultaneously and soon after their occurrence.

## PERSISTING CULTURAL NATIONALISM

"In the four quarters of the globe, who reads an American book? or goes to an American play? or looks at an American picture or statue?" So asked the English wit Sydney Smith in the *Edinburgh Review* (1820), and he assumed that the answer was obvious—nobody. Like him, many cultivated Europeans believed that the American democracy was a cultural vacuum.

### Democracy and Civilization

On the whole, British travelers in the United States confirmed Smith's impression of American culture. Occasionally these book-writing tourists had a kind word about the American and his habits. One of the most sympathetic, Harriet Martineau, author of *Society in America* (1837), admitted that the American people already had realized many ideals for which the rest of the world still strove. Though Americans had their faults, she added, they could not be discouraged by them, for they "are in possession of the glorious certainty that time and exertion will infallibly secure all wisely desired objects." Even when the British were complimentary, however, they were inclined to be condescending. Much of the time they were highly critical. To them the typical Yankee seemed filthy, rude, ignorant, quarrelsome, boastful, and greedy, as well as sickly and sallow. The Southerner seemed even worse, tyrannical and brutal, a beater of slaves. North, South, and West, the American male according to the British visitors

### Dancing the Quadrille

This ballroom scene of the 1840s, in the Tremont Hotel, Boston, indicates that American society did not consist entirely of tobacco-spitting backwoodsmen, though it was perhaps a little behind the times. The quadrille was a square dance that had originated in France and had become fashionable in England as early as about 1815. From an illustration for the cover of a piece of sheet music.

was an inveterate tobacco chewer and spitter, with an aim that was none too good.

What these writers saw in America reflected their own prejudices as well as the objective facts. English authors, including Charles Dickens, were personally aggrieved because American publishers "pirated" their works, that is, reprinted them without paying royalties. Along with other Englishmen, men of letters also lost money by investing in state bonds that proved worthless or nearly so with the defaults and repudiations following the Panic of 1837. Quite often the interpreters of the United States to the English public were Tories who feared democracy at home and therefore wished to discredit it abroad. They were fighting against the campaign to widen the suffrage in England, a campaign that culminated in the Reform Bill of 1832 and in the Chartist movement of 1848. Reviewers of the travel books in British quarterlies gave much attention to the criticisms of American democracy and pointed out the seemingly obvious conclusion: true morality and real culture could have no place in a country where the will of the majority prevailed.

Quite different was the attitude of the young French visitor Alexis de Tocqueville, who welcomed political equality as the way of the future for France and the world. Even though he disapproved of much that he saw, he sought to understand American behavior, not to denounce it. Like the British observers, he concluded that Americans were backward in respect to science, literature, and the arts, but he did not blame their backwardness upon democracy. He wrote: "Their strictly Puritanical origin—their exclusively commercial habits—even the country they inhabit, which seems to divert their minds from the pursuit of science, literature and the arts—the proximity of Europe, which allows them to neglect these pursuits without relapsing into barbarism—a thousand special causes, of which I have only been able to point out the most important—have singularly concurred to fix the mind of the American upon purely practical objects."

Colonial attitudes persisted in America so far as things of the mind were concerned. Seldom was an American author appreciated at home until he had been praised by critics abroad, and

sometimes not even then. In 1830, it has been estimated, 70 per cent of the books sold in America were published in England. By 1840 this percentage had been drastically reduced, to only about 30. In the space of one decade the American book industry had grown tremendously, though most of the books had to be subsidized or else produced for advance orders secured by subscriptions. Despite the rise of book publishing in several American cities, especially in New York, the great majority of books published and sold were written, as before, by English authors. The romantic novels of Charles Dickens and Sir Walter Scott were as much the rage in the United States as in the British Isles. Scott was a special favorite among Southerners, who often applied Scott's word "Southron" to themselves, and who viewed their own section as the contemporary land of chivalry and romance.

American writers had other outlets for their wares in the hundreds of magazines that appeared and disappeared, their average life being about two years. In the best of these magazines some of the greatest of native authors found a market for their works. In many other magazines, however, neither the writers nor their stories were great by any standard except popular appeal. The taste of most readers, especially women, was little different from that of their descendants who a century later were to listen to soap operas on radio or television. Sentimental tales of struggling womanhood were as popular a hundred years ago as now.

As in the Revolutionary era, the question of literary independence continued to draw much discussion from American writers. Some responded to British criticisms by declaring war again—the so-called "war of the quarterlies"— in which magazine replied to magazine, the Americans defending life in the United States and denouncing the customs of England. Instead of joining in such recriminations, a few thoughtful Americans called upon their countrymen for increased originality and creative effort. "The more we receive from other countries, the greater the need of an original literature," said William Ellery Channing (1830). He went on to contend: "A people into whose minds the thoughts of foreigners are poured perpetually, needs an energy within itself to resist, to modify this mighty influence, and without it will inevitably sink under the worst bondage, will become intellectually tame and enslaved." And Ralph Waldo Emerson, in his notable Phi Beta Kappa address at Harvard (1837), urged scholars, philosophers, and men of letters to do all they could toward developing a self-reliant nationhood. But there were also arguments on the other side. Confessing that American literature was largely derivative, James Russell Lowell said (1849), "There is no degradation in such indebtedness"; and he suggested, "It may not be our destiny to produce a great literature."

## Literature: A Golden Age

Foreign critics were too severe and native commentators too modest in their appraisals of American letters. In retrospect the period from the 1820s to the 1850s has seemed, indeed, a kind of golden age of literature in the United States. It was the time of Washington Irving, James Fenimore Cooper, Herman Melville, and Walt Whitman (all New Yorkers); Edgar Allan Poe (a Southerner by affirmation though not by birth); and Ralph Waldo Emerson, Henry David Thoreau, and Nathaniel Hawthorne (New Englanders). All these writers contributed to world literature: sooner or later they won lasting renown abroad as well as at home. Besides them, a number of others gained the esteem at least of their own countrymen and their own generation.

Irving, author of the earliest American literary "classics," was the first to achieve foreign recognition. His *History of New York* (1809) aimed, in his words, "to embody the traditions of the city in an amusing form," and did so in the stories of an imaginary historian of Dutch descent, Diedrich Knickerbocker. Irving's most famous work, *The Sketch Book* (1819–1820), containing "Rip Van Winkle" and "The Legend of Sleepy Hollow," made further use of the Dutch folklore of New York. Afterward Irving lived for a number of years in Spain and found story materials there, and still later he wrote historical works about the American West. A conservative in politics, he avoided contemporary political and social problems as literary themes. He did not disturb his readers with

philosophical challenges but charmed them with his easy style and graceful art.

Cooper, a less polished but more prolific writer, turned out more than thirty novels in thirty years (1820–1850). Born into a well-to-do family, Cooper grew up in Cooperstown, New York, at a time when the frontier was not far away. He served for several years in the navy. Thus he knew the forest and the sea, the settings of his adventure stories. Among the most successful were *The Spy* (1821), a novel of the Revolutionary War, and several "Leatherstocking" tales, including *The Last of the Mohicans* (1826) and *The Deerslayer* (1841). Over and over Cooper used the same formula of heroic action, breathless pursuit, and narrow escape. A born storyteller, he held his readers' attention despite the stilted dialogue of his stylized characters—the noble red man, the resourceful pioneer, the virtuous maid, and the enemy villain. He created a enduring character in the frontiersman Natty Bumppo ("Leatherstocking"). In some of his novels and also in his essays Cooper turned to social criticism. As a Democrat with aristocratic ideals, he condemned the pushing, go-getting spirit of his fellow Americans.

Melville, once a sailor and a resident of the South Seas, had a background even more adventurous than Cooper's, and he too wrote narratives of adventure. But Melville was vastly more subtle and sophisticated in his writing, and he filled his stories with discursive philosophizing and extraordinary symbolism. The greatest of his books, *Moby Dick* (1851), is both an epic of man's industry and courage and a tragedy brought on by overweening pride. A great hero, Captain Ahab, destroys his ship, his crew, and himself in a mad attempt to get revenge on the white whale, Moby Dick, which has maimed him and has thus become for him the embodiment of universal evil. For all the vividness of Melville's scenes, the depth and complexity of his characters, and the richness of his style, his plots move too slowly and his meaning was too obscure for the reading public of his time. A century later he was recognized as one of the greatest novelists ever to write in the English language.

Whitman, the self-proclaimed poet of Amer-

**Walt Whitman**

This picture of the youthful, jaunty, bearded poet
appeared as the frontispiece in the first edition of
*Leaves of Grass* (1855). It is an engraving made from
a painting by **Francis B. Carpenter**. Born in Homer,
New York, and largely self-taught, Carpenter became
one of the most successful portrait painters of the
second half of the nineteenth century. He lived in the
White House from February to July 1864 while doing
a canvas of Lincoln reading his emancipation
proclamation to the cabinet. He afterward wrote
*Six Months at the White House* (1866), giving an
inside view of Lincoln at home.
(New York Public Library)

*I celebrate myself, and sing myself,*
*And what I assume you shall assume,*
*For every atom belonging to me as good be-*
*longs to you.*

Five more editions of *Leaves of Grass*, with
added poems, appeared before Whitman's death
(1892), and so did other volumes of poetry and
essays, the most notable of which was *Demo-*
*cratic Vistas* (1871). His work eventually was
translated into many languages. Today he is
looked upon as a forerunner of twentieth-century poetry, a bold experimenter who liberated
verse from restrictive conventions of form and
content on the assumption that the "old forms
must be fitted to the new age."

Poe, in a short and unhappy life that ended in
1849, made himself an even more controversial
figure than Whitman. After briefly attending
the University of Virginia and the United States
Military Academy, Poe made a living as best he
could by editing literary magazines and selling
an occasional bit of writing. He devised a theory
of esthetics—supposedly based on music and
mathematics—which he put into practice in
his haunting onomatopoetic verse, his macabre,
personality-probing tales (he invented the detective story), and his sharp literary criticism. His
first book, *Tamerlane and Other Poems* (1827),
published anonymously, brought him little
money and no fame, but he gained a national
reputation with "The Raven" when it appeared
in a newspaper in 1845. Some critics were con-
temptuous of his musical effects, and Emerson
referred to him sneeringly as the "jingle man."
In England, however, Alfred Lord Tennyson
hailed Poe as a true, original poet, and in France
Charles Baudelaire took him as an inspiration
and a model. Indeed, Poe's writings influenced
European literature far more than did those
of any other nineteenth-century American.

## The Flowering of New England

New York, where Poe spent his last years, had
become the literary capital of the nation after
1820. Then during the 1840s and 1850s New
York, as a center of authorship, was largely
eclipsed by New England, if not by the one
village of Concord, Massachusetts. Why there
should have been such a literary "flowering" in

ican democracy, likewise was more widely appreciated by posterity than by his contemporaries, though some of them hailed him as
the most original and authentic voice of the
United States. The son of a Long Island carpenter, Whitman roamed the country and supported himself by odd jobs while composing his
first poems. When he hired a printer to put out
a thin volume of his work, *Leaves of Grass*
(1855), he could find few buyers or readers, and
he scandalized most of them. His verse, uncon-
fined by rhyme, praised democracy and sang
exuberantly of the flesh as well as the spirit.
Whitman identified himself with the American
people. He wrote:

New England is hard to explain. Of course, there was a long tradition of literacy and scholarship in the region. Ships returning from exotic ports throughout the world, including the Far East, brought in stimulating ideas along with profitable cargoes. Travelers, among them students attending German universities, returned with the stimulus of European romanticism. And the rise of industry altered society and the countryside, unsettling old habits and beliefs and, perhaps, provoking the imagination.

Emerson, leader of the Concord literary circle, began his career as a Unitarian minister, then resigned (1832) and devoted himself to the exposition of a transcendental philosophy. He derived his ideas partly from wide reading in the works of Plato, Plotinus, seventeenth-century Neoplatonists, and writers of China, Persia, and India. He was inspired even more by European travel and by conversation with English romantic authors such as Samuel Taylor Coleridge and Thomas Carlyle. From various sources Emerson put together a distinctively American philosophy of optimism, which saw reality as essentially good, and individualism, which stressed the capability of self-reliant man. Though he also wrote poetry, Emerson was most noted for his platform lectures, some of which were condensed and revised for publication under the title *Essays* (1841–1844). Through both the printed and the spoken word, he reached and influenced a wide audience, though he did not convince all who read or heard him, not even all his friends. One admirer, Melville, thought him full of "oracular gibberish" at times.

Thoreau, a friend and disciple of Emerson's, built a shack in the woods on Emerson's property and lived there, beside Walden Pond, for two years. Afterward he explained: "I went to the woods because I wished to live deliberately, to front only the essential facts of life, and see if I could not learn what it had to teach, and not, when I came to die, discover that I had not lived." He was delayed five years in finding a publisher for his account of the experience, which finally appeared as *Walden* (1854). A man of ruggedly honest principles as well as ruggedly honest prose, Thoreau meanwhile spent a night in jail for refusing to pay taxes for

the support of what he considered an unjust government (the United States then being at war with Mexico). He justified his stand in *Resistance to Civil Government* (1849), an essay on "civil disobedience" or "passive resistance" that afterward influenced a number of revolutionaries abroad, among them Mahatma Gandhi in India.

Hawthorne, at different times a friend and neighbor of Emerson's and of Melville's, had an outlook more like Melville's than Emerson's. A latter-day Puritan, Hawthorne dwelt upon somber themes from the Puritan past, with a conviction that evil was a grim reality. In a series of magazine stories, collected in *Twice-Told Tales* (1837), he probed the psychology of sin, much as Jonathan Edwards might have done if Edwards had written fiction instead of theological treatises. Hawthorne's greatest success was *The Scarlet Letter* (1850), which is still regarded as one of the most nearly perfect of American novels. Treating the familiar triangle in an unfamiliar way, this psychological novel tells of the beautiful Hester Prynne, her husband, and her lover, and their very different responses to the evil in their lives.

Besides Emerson, Thoreau, and Hawthorne, there were other New England authors who, in their own time, enjoyed reputations as high or higher than any of those three. William Cullen Bryant, as a young man in the Berkshire Hills, wrote "Thanatopsis" and other poems that brought him a reputation as America's foremost poet by 1832, after he had moved to New York to edit a newspaper, the *Evening Post*. Henry Wadsworth Longfellow, a sedate Harvard professor, appealed to popular tastes with his short poems on familiar subjects, like the village blacksmith, and his long poems elaborating historic traditions, such as *Evangeline* (1847), *The Song of Hiawatha* (1855), and *The Courtship of Miles Standish* (1858). His books sold well—a total of 300,000 copies by 1857. Oliver Wendell Holmes, another Harvard professor, a physician who taught in the Medical School, had time to write light verse and witty essays. James Russell Lowell, the first editor of the *Atlantic Monthly*, was a leading critic, essayist, and versifier. John Greenleaf Whittier, the "Quaker Poet," composed gentle, homespun verse about rural life in New England—and not so gentle verse attacking slavery in the South.

Though each section had its historians, New England had the ablest. George Bancroft celebrated the successes of what he considered God's chosen people in his ten-volume *History of the United States* (1834–1882). Like many of the intellectuals of the time, Bancroft was a Jacksonian, and his political feelings were apparent when the first volume came out, though it dealt with the colonial beginnings and not with contemporary events. The book, critics said, voted for Jackson. Works of more enduring value, because of their literary quality and their critical use of evidence, were written by William H. Prescott, Francis Parkman, and John Lothrop Motley. These writers looked outside the United States for their subject matter—to Mexico and Peru, New France, and the Dutch republic.

## Arts and Sciences

In the arts of drama, painting, sculpture, and music, and in the sciences, Americans produced much less of originality and lasting value than in literature. Yet, even in these fields, Americans were not always wholly imitative during the four decades from 1820 to 1860.

The theater became increasingly popular, though not entirely respectable, despite its efforts to appear on the side of morality through the presentation of temperance dramas like *The Drunkard* and *Ten Nights in a Bar-room*. Regular stock companies, English and American, toured the cities and larger towns. The companies depended on their stars to attract audiences. Fanny Kemble and William Charles Macready, both English, were outstanding attractions. So were the Americans Joseph Jefferson, who played the role of Rip Van Winkle before countless applauding audiences after 1859, and Edwin Forrest, famous for Shakespearean parts. Intense rivalries developed between celebrities and between their respective fans. In 1849 a mob of Forrest's admirers marched upon a New York theater where Macready was playing, and in the ensuing riot twenty-two persons were killed and many more injured. The legitimate stage often resorted to cheap showmanship to compete with such spectacles as circuses, minstrel shows, and "mu-

seums," containing freaks and oddities like the midget Tom Thumb. In the 1840s P. T. Barnum rose to become the leading promoter of these kinds of mass amusement.

Painters generally conformed to the sentimental taste of their customers, who demanded soft landscapes, flattering portraits, and storytelling pictures. Among the better artists, Asher B. Durand and others of the "Hudson School" concentrated upon natural scenery, William Sidney Mount portrayed his fellow Long Islanders at work and play, and George Caleb Bingham recorded everyday scenes of life in Missouri. The most successful sculptor was Hiram Powers, whose statue of a naked woman, entitled "The Greek Slave," attracted attention and provoked controversy on moral rather than esthetic grounds.

By the 1840s New York, Philadelphia, and Boston possessed orchestras of their own, and Americans flocked to the performances of such foreign celebrities as the Norwegian violinist Ole Bull and the "Swedish Nightingale" Jenny Lind. But American composers were rare, the most successful (judged by their enduring popularity) being John Howard Payne, Lowell Mason, and Stephen C. Foster. Payne, an actor and playwright, wrote "Home, Sweet Home" for an opera (1823). Mason, a Boston music teacher, composed the tunes for "Nearer, My God, to Thee," "From Greenland's Icy Mountains," and other stately hymns. Foster wrote "Oh! Susanna," "Old Black Joe," and more than 200 other melodies, most of them to accompany his own verse. Many of these songs, written for blackface minstrel bands, convey a sense of genuine nostalgia for the plantation, though Foster was born in Pennsylvania and spent his brief and tragic life (1826–1864) in the Northeast.

Americans were more noted for applied science than for scientific theory. Nevertheless, from observation and experiment, some of them made significant contributions to scientific knowledge. John J. Audubon, pioneer ornithologist, published his exquisite sketches in *Birds of America* (1827–1838). Joseph Henry, the most original American scientist since Benjamin Franklin, made important discoveries in electromagnetism (thus preparing the way for Morse's invention of the telegraph). A Georgia physician, Crawford W. Long, demonstrated the practicability of ether as an anesthetic (1842).

The federal government sponsored some kinds of scientific work, though not as generously as it might have done had congressmen not opposed expenditures on grounds of thrift and state rights. Geographical knowledge was increased by the United States Coast Survey, begun in 1832, and by the United States Exploring Expedition, which between 1838 and 1842 surveyed extensive areas of the Pacific Ocean, under the leadership of Lieutenant Charles Wilkes. In the 1840s Congress voted funds to support the Naval Observatory and Hydrographical Office, an agency to study and report on nautical and astronomical subjects. Matthew Fontaine Maury became its director and began a monumental investigation of oceanography. In 1846 the Smithsonian Institution was founded in Washington, after an Englishman had willed his fortune of $500,000 to the United States "for the increase and diffusion of knowledge." Appropriately the noted physicist

Joseph Henry became the first head of the institution.

The leading colleges, Yale and Harvard, also served as important patrons of science. At Yale Benjamin Silliman taught chemistry and mineralogy for a half-century after his appointment in 1802, and for many years he edited the *American Journal of Science and Art*, after founding it in 1818. Though not a notable researcher, Silliman was an outstanding teacher who kept American students and scholars informed of scientific developments throughout the world. At Harvard the zoologist and geologist Louis Agassiz and the botanist Asa Gray not only taught but also carried on important research in their respective fields. Through his studies of plant distribution Gray assisted the English scholar Charles Darwin in formulating the theory of evolution. When Darwin's epoch-making book *On the Origin of Species* appeared (1859), Gray endorsed and Agassiz rejected the idea that plants and animals, instead of remaining unchanged since God created them, had developed through a process of natural selection.

# Selected Readings

**The Economy in General** D. C. North, *The Economic Growth of the United States, 1790–1860*° (1961); Stuart Bruchey, *The Roots of American Economic Growth*° (1965); T. C. Cochran and William Miller, *The Age of Enterprise*° (1942); L. M. Hacker, *The Triumph of American Capitalism*° (1940); Roger Burlingame, *The March of the Iron Men*° (1938); E. W. Martin, *The Standard of Living in the United States in 1860* (1942).

**Agriculture, Industry, Trade** P. W. Gates, *The Farmer's Age* (1960); P. W. Bidwell and J. I. Falconer, *History of Agriculture in the Northern United States, 1620–1860* (1925); V. S. Clark, *History of Manufactures in the United States* (3 vols., 1928); Allan Nevins, *Abram S. Hewitt, With Some Account of Peter Cooper* (1935); J. R. Commons and others, *History of Labour in the United States* (4 vols., 1918–1935); Norman

Ware, *The Industrial Worker, 1840–1860* (1924); E. R. Johnson and others, *History of the Domestic and Foreign Commerce of the United States* (2 vols., 1915).

**Transportation and Communication** Seymour Dunbar, *A History of American Travel* (4 vols., 1915; 1-vol. edition, 1937); G. R. Taylor, *The Transportation Revolution, 1815–1860* (1951); J. F. Stover, *American Railroads*° (1961); T. C. Cochran, *Railroad Leaders, 1845–1890* (1953); E. C. Kirkland, *Men, Cities, and Transportation, 1820–1900* (2 vols., 1948), on New England; U. B. Phillips, *A History of Transportation in the Eastern Cotton Belt to 1860* (1908); P. W. Gates, *The Illinois Central Railroad and Its Colonization Work* (1934); R. W. Fogel, *Railroads and American Economic Growth* (1964); Albert Fishlow, *American Railroads and the Transformation of the Ante-Bellum Economy* (1965); C. C.

Cutler, *The Story of the American Clipper* (1930); R. L. Thompson, *Wiring a Continent* (1947).

**Immigration and Nativism** M. L. Hansen, *The Immigrant in American History* ° (1940) and *The Atlantic Migration, 1607–1860* ° (1940); Carl Wittke, *Refugees of Revolution: The German Forty-Eighters in America* (1952) and *The Irish in America* (1956); Oscar Handlin, *Boston's Immigrants* ° (1941); Robert Ernst, *Immigrant Life in New York City, 1825–1863* (1949); R. A. Billington, *The Protestant Crusade, 1800–1860* ° (1938); Sister M. E. Thomas, *Nativism in the Old Northwest, 1850–1860* (1936); W. D. Overdyke, *The Know-Nothing Party in the South* (1950).

**Journalism** F. L. Mott, *American Journalism* (1950) and *A History of American Magazines*, vol. 1, *1741–1850* (1930), vol. 2, *1850–1865* (1938); E. F. Brown, *Raymond of the Times* (1951); D. C. Seitz, *The James Gordon Bennetts* (1928); G. G. Van Deusen, *Horace Greeley* (1953).

**Cultural Trends** Max Berger, *The British Traveller in America, 1836–1860* (1943); Van Wyck Brooks, *The Flowering of New England, 1815–1865* ° (1936); F. O. Matthiessen, *American Renaissance* (1941); Lewis Mumford, *The Golden Day* ° (1926); R. L. Rusk, *The Life of Ralph Waldo Emerson* (1949); Neil Harris, *The Artist in American Society: The Formative Years, 1790–1860* (1966); Carleton Mabee, *The American Leonardo: A Life of Samuel F. B. Morse* (1943); Carl Bode, *The Anatomy of American Popular Culture, 1840–1861* (1959).

---

°Titles available in paperback.

# Chapter 12
# Slavery and the South

America, the scene of Thomas More's sixteenth-century book *Utopia*, still seemed in the nineteenth century a land of utopian possibilities, at least to a great many Americans. To them, progress was a profound faith. As invention followed invention, they were confirmed in the belief that they lived in a wondrous age of increasing ease and plenty. Some assumed that progress in material things led automatically to progress in government and society as well. Others came to the conclusion that active effort would be needed to keep social improvement abreast of technological advance.

These progress-minded Americans were convinced that their country led the rest of the world in moral as well as material development. They sprang to the defense whenever foreigners criticized American ways, as foreigners often did. The Americans themselves, however, readily found fault with conditions in their own country when these conditions seemed to hinder the perfecting of society and man. There resulted a tumultuous and many-sided movement for social reform, which picked up momentum in the 1830s and continued through the 1850s.

From the reformers' point of view, one social evil came to stand out above all others. This was the plight of the more than 4 million Americans of African descent, most of whom were slaves, and the rest of whom were less than wholly free. Eventually the reform drive concentrated its main force on a single goal, the elimination of slavery.

Since all the slaves and nearly all the Negroes were concentrated in one section, the reform movement took on a sectional aspect. The economy and society of the South were based largely on the enslavement of the blacks, and most Southern whites feared the economic and social consequences of the slaves' liberation. The reform spirit—a ''freedom's ferment''—had never stirred the South so much as it had the North, and with the development of an antislavery crusade white Southerners resisted more strongly than ever the radical ''isms'' of the day as they rallied to a defense of their ''peculiar institution.'' Thus the nation began increasingly to divide on moral as well as economic and political grounds.

## FREEDOM'S FERMENT

"In no country in the world has the principle of association been more successfully used, or more unsparingly applied to a multitude of different objects, than in America," Tocqueville observed. "Societies are formed to resist enemies which are exclusively of a moral nature, and to diminish the vice of intemperance: in the United States associations are established to promote public order, commerce, industry, morality, and religion; for there is no end which the human will, seconded by the collective exertions of individuals, despairs of attaining."

Indeed, Americans organized reform societies of all kinds, not only for temperance but also for education, world peace, the care of the poor and

### Plantation Life on the Mississippi
*Detail.* A nineteenth-century American newspaper engraving. (The Granger Collection)

the handicapped, the improvement of prisons, women's rights, the abolition of slavery, and dozens of other idealistic purposes.

## Spirit of Social Reform

This reform spirit derived from a variety of sources, religious and rational, domestic and foreign. The Christian doctrine of human worth, the Revolutionary philosophy of the equality of man—these were part of the general background. More immediately, the rise of industrialism in the British Isles and Western Europe as well as the United States produced social dislocations and suffering but at the same time gave promise of a more abundant life for all. No doubt, with some people, a determination to improve human welfare was stimulated by the contrast between what actually was and what apparently might be. The humanitarian stirrings of the time were to be found in many lands at once, and most conspicuously in those countries that were being most rapidly industrialized.

In Europe the agitation was in some ways quite different from that in this country. There, it led to violent outbreaks, to the revolutionary attempts of 1830 and 1848. In America, where (except in the Southern states) there was no repressive government to contend with, the reformers had to fear violence only at the hands of unsympathetic mobs: reform did not mean revolt, though it culminated in the Civil War. Despite the differences in the American and European movements, American reformers often consulted and cooperated with their European counterparts, particularly with Englishmen. When it came to human betterment, cultural nationalism gave way to cosmopolitanism.

In Protestant countries the reform ethic was stronger than in Roman Catholic countries, which for the most part were less highly industrialized. Protestantism and reformism were closely related. In the United States the stimulus to reform came largely from two quite different Protestant trends—from the revivalistic, hellfire teachings of "New Light" Calvinists, on the one hand, and on the other hand from optimistic, salvation-for-all ideas of Universalists, Unitarians, and others who completely repudiated the tenets of Calvinism.

### Transcendentalism and Reform [1837]

In his Phi Beta Kappa address, "The American Scholar," which he delivered at Harvard College on August 31, 1837, Ralph Waldo Emerson presented a kind of intellectual declaration of independence for the United States. He also adumbrated his transcendentalist philosophy, speaking of the "human mind" as "one central fire," "one light which beams out of a thousand stars," and "one soul which animates all men." He suggested a relationship between transcendentalism and reform in the following passage:

*It is a mischievous notion that we are come late into nature; that the world was finished a long time ago. As the world was plastic and fluid in the hands of God, so it is ever to so much of his attributes as we bring to it. To ignorance and sin, it is flint. They adapt themselves to it as they may; but in proportion as a man has any thing in him divine, the firmament flows before him and takes his signet and form. Not he is great who can alter matter, but he who can alter my state of mind. They are the kings of the world who give the color of their present thought to all nature and art, and persuade men by the cheerful serenity of their carrying the matter, that this thing which they do is the apple which the ages have desired to pluck, now at last ripe, and inviting nations to the harvest. The great man makes the great thing.*

Emerson's philosophy of transcendentalism contributed to the reform spirit. Emerson evolved the doctrine of the Oversoul or spiritual essence from which all things derived, including the soul of man. Since all humanity shared in this essential Being, this all-in-all, there existed a very real brotherhood of mankind. And since the Oversoul was good there could be no such thing, in the last analysis, as evil. (The later teachings of Mary Baker G. Eddy, founder of Christian Science, were in some respects similar to those of Emerson.) This philosophy, for all its obscurities and inconsistencies, had practical consequences for its believers. It made them optimistic. It taught them that they were potentially divine and could increase their divinity by identifying themselves more and more fully with the Oversoul, with Being, with Truth. It led them to believe in the perfectibility of man.

Still more important as a call to reform were the preachings of the revivalist Charles G. Finney, who was at first a Presbyterian and later a Congregationalist. In upstate New York and in Ohio, beginning in the 1820s, Finney delivered many a memorable sermon on the dangers of damnation and the possibilities of salvation—through good works as well as faith. "The church," he maintained, "must take right ground on the subject of Temperance, and Moral Reform, and all the subjects of practical morality which come up for decision from time to time." Not all the churches did so, and some reformers (known as "come-outers") left the fold and even turned against organized religion, denouncing it as a bulwark to the status quo. Yet many churches heeded Finney's call, especially Presbyterian and Congregational churches, which provided more reform leaders than did any of the other Protestant sects, even the Quakers.

These leaders implied by their activities that they believed in a sort of earthly millennium as well as a heavenly one. Going a step further, one religious prophet together with his thousands of followers expected and awaited the actual second coming of Christ. From his studies of the Bible and from other signs and calculations, William Miller of Low Hampton, New York, predicted that on a certain day in 1843 Christ would appear and all true believers would ascend bodily to heaven. After new predictions and repeated disappointments he made the date indefinite. His followers formed a lasting sect, the Seventh-Day Adventists.

Miller and other prophets of the time, such as Finney and also Joseph Smith, the founder of Mormonism, were New Englanders by birth and residents of upstate New York at some stage

in their careers. So, too, the great majority of reform leaders were New England-born, and a large number of them lived at least temporarily in New York State. Most were descended from substantial New England families, neither rich nor poor, whose heads once had been highly respected as preachers, doctors, teachers, and farmers. With the rise of commerce and industry these families lost status in comparison with the upcoming merchants and manufacturers. The families who migrated to New York settled in counties that at first were economically dominant but that by the 1830s had fallen behind the rest of the state. These family backgrounds suggest that the typical reformer was unconsciously a product of social changes under way in the North.

The reform spirit was far more prevalent among Whigs than among Democrats. Though it affected some of the latter too, it cannot be considered as essentially an extension of Jacksonian Democracy. The Jacksonians advocated political and economic reforms, such as the widening of the suffrage and the destruction of monopoly, but were far from unanimous in supporting social reforms, such as the abolition of slavery. Nor can the reform spirit be viewed as an outgrowth of the labor movement, except in certain cases, notably the drive for free public schools. Most reform leaders disbelieved in unions, opposed strikes, and were indifferent to the plight of the unemployed. William Lloyd Garrison, the abolitionist, denounced labor agitators for trying "to inflame the minds of our working classes against the more opulent, and to persuade men that they are contemned and oppressed by a wealthy aristocracy." A few of the "more opulent," such as the merchants Arthur and Lewis Tappan of New York and Amos and Abbott Lawrence of Boston, contributed vast sums to finance various reforms. This is not to say, however, that big business in general was favorable to the reform movement. More often than not, reform was resisted by both the laborer and the capitalist. It was essentially a middle-class movement, receiving its greatest support from the reasonably well-to-do farmers, shopkeepers, and professional people of the North and the West.

## Free Public Schools

As of 1830 no state could yet boast a general system of free public education in the modern sense —with full tax support, compulsory attendance, and enforced maintenance of schools—though Massachusetts, as in earlier times, came fairly close to it. A very high proportion of American children had the benefit of the three R's, but most of them still got their learning from church schools, proprietary institutions, private tutors, or members of their own families.

Then, during the 1830s, a widespread demand for state-supported primary education arose. This demand came from reformers who feared the consequences of allowing every man to vote, including in many cases even the newly arrived immigrant, without making public provision for his literacy at least. The demand came also from workingmen who hoped that book learning would enable their children to rise in the world. Opposition was forthcoming, however, from taxpayers (especially childless ones) who objected to paying for the education of other people's families, and from Lutherans, Roman Catholics, and other religious groups who already supported their own church schools and did not wish to be taxed for public education besides.

Educational reformers made considerable headway against such opposition in several of the states. The greatest of these leaders was Horace Mann, the first secretary of the Massachusetts board of education, which was established in 1837. He reorganized the state's school system, lengthened the school year (to six months), doubled teachers' salaries, enriched the curriculum, and improved teacher training and teaching methods. Henry Barnard led the way to better schools in Connecticut and Rhode Island. In Pennsylvania a school law was passed in 1835, making state funds available for the education of all children and not merely the children of paupers, as formerly; but only the exertions of Thaddeus Stevens in the legislature saved the law from an early repeal. In New York, after William H. Seward became governor in 1839, the upstate system of school districts supporting their own schools was extended to the metropolis. This step aroused much opposition, since it

### Horace Mann on Education [1848]

*Now surely nothing but universal education can counterwork this tendency to the domination of capital and the servility of labor. If one class possesses all the wealth and the education, while the residue of society is ignorant and poor, it matters not by what name the relation between them may be called: the latter, in fact and in truth, will be the servile dependents and subjects to the former. But, if education be equally diffused, it will draw property after it by the strongest of attractions; for such a thing never did happen, and never can happen, as that an intelligent and practical body of men should be permanently poor. Property and labor in different classes are essentially antagonistic; but property and labor in the same class are essentially fraternal.*

gave control of some new districts to the local Roman Catholic majorities.

By the 1850s the principle of tax-supported elementary schools was accepted in all the states, and all of them were making at least a start toward putting the principle into practice. Still, there were vast differences in the quantity and quality of public schools from place to place, the poorest performances and the lowest literacy rates being found in the newly settled areas of the West and in the more sparsely populated parts of the South. In the country as a whole, only a small proportion of children of school age were actually going to school—one white child out of every seven in the South and one out of every six elsewhere (1860).

Most teachers were poorly paid and poorly prepared, and many of them were scarcely able to read, write, and cipher. In rural district schools, containing husky youths along with tender tots, what the schoolmaster needed was a strong arm rather than a well-stocked mind. If he could not thrash the most obstreperous of his pupils, he could get nowhere with his lessons. Reformers like Mann and Barnard, believing that human nature was essentially good, advocated gentleness and understanding as practiced by progressive educators in Switzerland (notably Johann Pestalozzi). Most teachers—and parents too—subscribed to the old Calvinist doctrine of inborn wickedness: they did not wish to spare the rod.

Under the circumstances the majority of teaching positions continued to be filled by men, even in the elementary schools. Seldom did these men look upon teaching as a career; often they were aspiring lawyers or preachers who worked their way through college by doubling as schoolmasters in vacation periods. Nevertheless, teaching was beginning to be looked upon as a profession, and an increasing number of young women were going into it. With Mann taking the lead, Massachusetts in 1839 established the first American state-supported teacher-training or "normal" school, at Lexington. In 1845 he organized a state association of teachers.

Since so many teachers were poorly prepared, both they and their pupils had to rely heavily upon textbooks. Noah Webster's spellers and grammars continued to be widely used. Supplementing them and rivaling them in popularity were the six graded *Eclectic Readers* (1835–1857) prepared by William Holmes McGuffey, who was an Ohio professor and college president and then for many years a professor at the University of Virginia. The McGuffey readers were filled with moral lessons, patriotic declamations, sentimental verse, and fascinating facts. A favorite recitation piece was the following:

> *Woodman, spare that tree;*
> *Touch not a single bough.*
> *In youth it sheltered me,*
> *And I'll protect it now.*

Eventually adopted in thirty-seven states, the McGuffey books gave thousands of schoolchildren a shared background of popular culture and helped to mold the literary tastes of the reading public.

The principle of state support was applied later to secondary than to elementary schools. By 1860 there were 22 tax-supported "free academies" in New York, more than 100 public high schools in Massachusetts, and a total of about 300 such institutions in the nation as a whole. At the same time there were approximately 6,000 private academies. Most of them were open to boys only, a few were coeducational, and a growing number were female seminaries.

## Higher Education

While the private academies were multiplying, so were the private colleges, though at a slower rate, about eighty being founded between 1830 and 1850. Almost all of these were denominational colleges, with close church connections, and their chief though not their only purpose was to prepare a learned clergy. These institutions became too numerous for their own good. Their enrollments were small, in many cases fewer than 100 in the 1850s (even Harvard and Yale had only 400 or 500 students apiece, though the College of William and Mary had nearly 1,000). Generally endowments were scanty, facilities poor, salaries low, and professors unscholarly, though self-sacrificing and sincere.

None of these institutions admitted women until, in 1837, Oberlin accepted four girls as regular students and thus became the first coeducational college. Some outsiders feared that coeducation was a rash experiment approximating free love, but the Oberlin authorities were confident that "the mutual influence of the sexes upon each other is decidedly happy in the cultivation of both mind & manners." Only a few other institutions copied Oberlin's example before the Civil War. Some of the young ladies' seminaries—notably Mount Holyoke, which the most famous of all women educators, Mary Lyon, founded in Massachusetts in 1837—eventually became full-fledged women's colleges.

The idea of state support for higher education had to contend against the prevailing concept of private, denominational control. Besides the older states with public universities (Vermont, North Carolina, Georgia, Ohio, Virginia) many of the newer states of the Northwest and Southwest committed themselves to the support of higher learning. State universities were established in Indiana, Michigan, Kentucky, Missouri, Mississippi, Iowa, Wisconsin, Minnesota, and Louisiana before the Civil War. None of these, whether old or new, was a true university in the European sense of an institution devoted to high-level, graduate training.

The standard curriculum, whether in the private college or the state university, still emphasized the old-fashioned liberal arts. A young man who desired training for a professional career (other than the ministry) had few institutions to choose from. He could study engineering at the United States Military Academy, Rensselaer Polytechnic Institute (1824), or at Yale or Harvard, which set up engineering schools in 1846 and 1847. He could study law or medicine at one of several institutions, but no American medical school compared with the best ones abroad. In most cases, as in earlier times, he apprenticed himself to a practicing physician, learned engineering on the job (the Erie Canal was a most productive "school" for engineers), or "read law" in the office of some successful lawyer.

Adult education was furthered by the founding of numerous libraries, study clubs, and self-improvement societies of various kinds. Noteworthy was the Lyceum, which was started by Josiah Holbrook in Massachusetts (1826) and spread rapidly throughout the North. "The first step to form a Lyceum," Holbrook explained, "is for a few neighbors or citizens to agree to hold meetings for their mutual improvement." Next, they could acquire books, scientific apparatus, specimens of rocks and plants, and the like. Then they could conduct experiments, carry on discussions among themselves, and sponsor public lectures. The sponsorship of lectures soon became their principal activity. Through the Lyceum many thousands of Americans were able to hear scientists like Agassiz, foreign authors like Dickens, exemplars of self-culture like the "learned Blacksmith" Elihu Burritt, popular philosophers like Emerson, and social reformers like the abolitionist Garrison or the repentant drunkard John B. Gough.

## Model Communities

While many reformers hoped to make possible a better life by creating opportunities through education or by eliminating specific social evils, some of the more advanced thinkers aspired to start afresh and remake society by founding ideal, cooperative communities. America still seemed a spacious and unencumbered country where models of a perfect society could be set up with a good chance to succeed. Presumably success would lead to imitation, until communities free of crime, poverty, and other evils

**A Lyceum Lecture**

James Pollard Espy, author of *Philosophy of Storms* (1841), is known as the father of American meteorology. Espy, his paraphernalia, and his audience—in New York about 1838 —are caricatured by an unknown artist. The lecture has to do with weather, and the chart on the wall is headed: "Probability of Rain after Sunshine." (Museum the City of New York) would cover the land. A number of religious groups, notably the Shakers, practiced a kind of socialism as a means of realizing what they considered a truly Christian life. But the impetus to communitarianism as a way of perfecting earthly society came chiefly from non-religious, rationalistic thinkers.

Among the communitarian philosophers, three of the most influential were Robert Owen, Charles Fourier, and John Humphrey Noyes. Owen, famous for his humanitarian policies as owner of prosperous textile mills in Scotland, reached the conclusion that faulty environment was to blame for human failings, and hence that poverty and crime would not appear in a rationally planned society. In 1825 he put his principles into practice at New Harmony, on the banks of the Wabash in Indiana. Within a few years New Harmony failed as an economic enterprise, though in other respects it was a success. Fourier, a mere commercial employee in France, never visited the United States. His theories of cooperative living, however, influenced many Americans through the writings of Albert Brisbane, whose *Social Destiny of Man* (1840) explained the principles of Fourierism with its self-sufficient associations, or "phalanxes." One or more of these phalanxes was organized in every Northern state, the most famous of them being Brook Farm, a community of intellectuals including Hawthorne, near Boston. Noyes, a native Vermonter and a former Yale divinity student, founded the most bizarre and most enduring of all the utopian colonies, the Oneida Community in upstate New York (1848), where his followers carried out his unorthodox sexual theories, old men mating with young women and vice versa, all changing partners at his direction, supposedly in the interest of scientific breeding. Needless to say, none of these experiments set a pattern for American life.

## Remedying Social Ills

Less thoroughgoing reforms, however, did much to alleviate the ills of society as it actually was. No evil was more glaring than the treatment of social offenders and unfortunates. Criminals of all kinds, debtors unable to pay their debts, senile paupers, and the mentally ill were crowded indiscriminately into prisons and jails which in many cases were literally holes, one jail in Connecticut being an abandoned mine shaft.

From the 1820s on, the states one by one abolished imprisonment for debt, and some of them greatly improved their handling of the criminal and the insane. New York, with the erection of its new prison at Auburn (1821), introduced a system of solitary confinement by night and group work with absolute silence by day; Pennsylvania tried solitary confinement for both day and night. Though both of these systems now seem harsh, they were then hailed as progressive steps, since they gave each prisoner an opportunity to meditate upon his wrongdoing and also checked the tendency for old convicts to corrupt the young. Public hangings, supposedly a deterrent to crime, used to attract spectators by the thousands, including thieves and pickpockets busily plying their trade. In the 1830s several states began to hold executions within the privacy of prison walls, and a few states did away with capital punishment entirely. While a few mental hospitals already existed, the insane (unless cared for at home) generally were kept in jail and treated brutally. The Boston schoolmistress, Dorothea Dix, shocked by her chance visit to the Cambridge jail (1841), devoted her life to securing the establishment of insane asylums in Massachusetts and other states.

In looking for causes of insanity, pauperism, and crime, many reformers concluded that these evils could be traced largely to strong drink. Americans of earlier generations had been an alcoholically convivial people, with a remarkable per capita consumption of whiskey, hard cider, and rum. The Puritans had been hard drinkers and many respectable preachers continued to resort to stimulants. Few Americans supposed that a birth, a wedding, or a funeral could be properly observed without plenty of liquor—the story is told of drunken pallbearers who lost their way to the grave. From colonial times on, however, a few men like Cotton Mather and Dr. Benjamin Rush had spoken out against intemperance.

In the early 1800s an organized temperance movement began with the formation of local societies in New England, and in 1826 the American Society for the Promotion of Temperance appeared as a coordinating agency for the various groups. The movement gained in sensationalism when six reformed drunkards of Baltimore organized the Washington Temperance Society in 1840 and began to draw crowds to hear their intriguing confessions. As the temperance forces grew and spread over the country, the crusaders diverged, some advocating total abstinence and others seeing no harm in wine or beer; some favoring prohibition laws and others relying on the individual conscience. Massachusetts and other states experimented with legislation for local option, allowing communities to regulate or prohibit liquor sales, and Maine passed a statewide prohibition law in 1851. Prohibitionists in a few other states gained similar victories, but the laws were unpopular and soon were repealed except in Maine.

To some it seemed that not only alcoholic beverages but also tobacco, coffee, and unnatural foods hindered the full realization of man's perfectionist possibilities. A leading health faddist, Dr. Sylvester Graham, believed that one way to social happiness was through the eating of coarse, whole wheat bread (the "Graham cracker" is a faint reminder of him). Other health reformers relied on hydropathy with its regimen of bathing and water-drinking; spas like the Hot Springs in Virginia became fashionable places for taking the "water cure." Orson Fow-

### The "Cold Water" Pledge

Members of the Washington Temperance Society—themselves reformed drunkards—urged drinkers to join them in signing a pledge of total abstinence. This lithograph of 1846, which associates poverty with drink, is dedicated to "the Washingtonians of the United States" and is "commemorative of their Declaration of Independence from the dominion of King Alcohol." (Library of Congress) ler, the foremost exponent of phrenology (a "science" based on the notion that character and personality are revealed in the contour of the cranium), expected to bring about a "renovating of mankind" through the self-understanding that was supposed to result from the examination of bumps on the head. This science gained such popularity that practically everyone turned into an amateur phrenologist.

Whatever the social handicaps that beset man as man, those that a woman had to face were considerably worse. In America she enjoyed a freer life and greater respect than in England or Europe, yet in this country too she was legally an inferior. According to the Anglo-American common law a husband had almost absolute authority over the person and property of his wife: what was his was his, and what was hers was his also. In case of divorce he was far more likely than she to get custody of the children. Though women worked in household and mill, they could not look forward to careers in medicine, the ministry, politics, or law. By custom they were forbidden to speak in public to a mixed audience, lest they "unsex" themselves and lose their feminine charm.

Though women were active in the reform movements, especially temperance and abolition, male reformers usually compelled them to take a back seat. This discrimination intensified an already growing demand for women's rights. In 1848 Lucretia Mott and Elizabeth Cady Stanton called a convention of women; it met in Seneca Falls, New York, and adopted resolutions (patterned on the Declaration of Independence) to the effect that all men *and women* are created equal and endowed with certain inalienable rights. While the feminists failed to obtain the right to vote or hold office, they made noticeable gains before the Civil War. As early as 1839, Mississippi had recognized the right of married women to control their own property; during the next two decades several other states did the same. At least one woman, Dr. Elizabeth Blackwell, gained acceptance and fame as a physician; several women, prominent among them Lucy Stone (who with her husband's approval retained her maiden name), became successful lecturers; a still larger number, including Emma Willard and Catherine Beecher, made

### The Bloomer Costume

An enterprising Philadelphia music publisher, taking advantage of a timely topic, brought out "The New Costume Polka" and dedicated it to Mrs. Amelia Bloomer. The cover of the sheet music was adorned with this picture of a demure yet stylish young lady wearing the clothes that Mrs. Bloomer recommended. (Library of Congress)

great contributions to progressive education, especially for women. Some of the feminists, apparently thinking equality with men meant similarity to them, cut their hair short and wore more or less mannish clothes. Mrs. Amelia Bloomer, for example, attempted to popularize the skirt-and-pantalettes costume that was named for her.

Recalling the Napoleonic Wars and the War of 1812, many reformers agreed with the Quakers that one of the worst ills of the world was war. By 1819 more than a dozen local peace societies had sprung up in various parts of the United States, and in 1828 the Maine merchant William Ladd undertook to coordinate the movement by founding the American Peace Society with headquarters in New York. Later (1840) Ladd devised a peace plan embracing a

Congress of Nations and a Court of Nations whose decisions were to be enforced by public opinion rather than economic or military sanctions. Meanwhile the pacifists disagreed, some approving defensive but not offensive wars, others taking a pledge of complete nonresistance. To most of the peace workers in New England, the Mexican War (1846–1848) seemed an act of proslavery aggression on the part of the United States, and they took their stand against it, Henry David Thoreau refusing to pay taxes for its support, and James Russell Lowell writing in the *Bigelow Papers*: "Ez fer war, I call it murder,—there you hev it plain an' flat." But the Civil War put the pacifists in a dilemma, at least momentarily, since most of them were also abolitionists. Finally the antislavery cause took precedence over the antiwar cause, as it already had taken precedence over the rest of the reform crusades.

## THE ANTISLAVERY CRUSADE

Mid-nineteenth-century Americans would have had some justification for boasting of their democratic society if they could have ignored the Negro—the freeman as well as the slave. But they could not ignore him. Reformers black and white would not let them.

### The Negro in the North

In the 1850s there were more than 4 million black Americans, of whom about 95 per cent were confined to the South. That left nearly a quarter of a million of them living in the North. These people were concentrated mainly in the cities, about 22,000 in Philadelphia and about 12,000 in New York. Many were fugitives from slavery.

In some respects the free Negroes of the North were little if any better off than the free Negroes or even the slaves of the South. An English traveler, who was acquainted with the treatment of the black man in both sections, reported in 1854 that he was "utterly at a loss to imagine the source of that prejudice which subsists against him in the Northern states, a prejudice unknown in the South, where the relations between the African and the European [white

American] are so much more intimate." This confirmed an earlier observation of Tocqueville's: "the prejudice which repels the Negroes seems to increase in proportion as they are emancipated."

Certainly the Northern Negro faced severe handicaps in even managing to exist. He had little or no political influence: he could vote only in New England (not including Connecticut), and in New York only if he owned a certain amount of property, which was not required of white voters. In most places he was excluded from the public schools that whites attended. He faced the constant danger of being attacked by white mobs or kidnapped by slave dealers and sold, or resold, into slavery. Usually he had no choice but to take a low-paid job as a domestic servant or unskilled laborer. Seafaring offered him one of his best opportunities; in the 1850s, when the American merchant marine was at its height, nearly half of the sailors in it were blacks. The typical city Negro lived in squalor in a segregated neighborhood. He was eleven times as likely as a white man to be jailed on a charge of theft, robbery, or other crime.

Despite the almost hopeless odds, a number of Northern Negroes managed to succeed in business or the professions. James Forten, for example, started out as an errand boy around the Philadelphia docks, became a sailmaker, and accumulated a small fortune. The Negroes of New York City, as early as 1837, owned $1.4 million worth of taxable real estate and had $600,000 on deposit in savings banks. But what most distinguished the free Negroes of the North from those of the South (some of whom also acquired property) was the opportunity to speak out, to protest the plight of black people both free and slave, and to try and do something about it.

In the early 1800s a Massachusetts free Negro, Paul Cuffe, tried to begin a back-to-Africa movement so as to give his people a new life in their ancestral homeland. Cuffe had spent $4,000 on the project, without success, when he died in 1817. That same year a group of prominent white Virginians organized the American Colonization Society to "colonize" freed slaves in Africa. Some Northern Negroes feared this was a scheme to get rid of them, and James

# Where Historians Disagree

## The Abolitionists

On both the leadership and the motivation of the antislavery movement, historians have long disagreed.

According to older historians such as James Ford Rhodes, who wrote in the 1890s, the outstanding leader and indeed the virtual personification of abolitionism was William Lloyd Garrison, whose main support and whose base of operations lay in New England. But Gilbert H. Barnes sharply challenged that interpretation in his book *The Antislavery Impulse, 1830–1844* (1933). Barnes insisted that Garrison's influence had been severely limited because of his extremism, as seen especially in his denunciation of those churches that refused to declare themselves unequivocally in favor of immediate abolition. Barnes argued that, instead of Garrison, the most influential figure was Theodore Weld, who centered his activities in New York, Pennsylvania, and Ohio, and who worked with rather than against the churches.

A recent writer, John L. Thomas, in *The Liberator: A Biography of William Lloyd Garrison* (1963), has presented a more balanced view, recognizing the contributions of both Garrison and Weld. Thomas contends, however, that Garrison was responsible for Weld's conversion to the principle of immediate emancipation and that New England was the geographical core of the movement, most of the Western abolitionists being "transplanted New Englanders."

The earlier authorities—and some of the later ones, such as Barnes and Dwight L. Dumond —believed that the abolitionists had been motivated simply by Christian and democratic ideals, particularly as expressed in the Sermon on the Mount and the Declaration of Independence. But "revisionist" historians, notably Avery Craven, began in the 1930s to emphasize psychological considerations. The abolitionists, these writers indicated, were mere fanatics who were impelled by their neuroses and who made the slaveholder a scapegoat for their own unhappiness. "To him," Craven said, "were transferred resentments and fears born out of local conditions." Later David Donald offered a similar interpretation in a more refined and explicit form. Donald analyzed the backgrounds of a number of antislavery leaders and concluded that these men were products of a status revolution. They belonged, he wrote, to a former "social elite," to prominent families that had lost their social standing with the industrialization of New England and the rise of a new business class. "Reform gave meaning to the lives of this displaced social elite."

Rejecting such interpretations, Martin Duberman has recently pointed out that the antislavery movement actually included men of widely differing backgrounds and personalities. Duberman cautions: "We know far too little about why men do anything—let alone why they do something as specific as joining a reform movement—to assert as confidently as historians have, the motives of whole groups of men."

**Negro Leader**

The most prominent American Negro of the pre-Civil War era, and indeed of the nineteenth century, was Frederick Douglass. He was born in Maryland, of an unknown white father and a slave mother. In 1838 he escaped from slavery and went to the Northeast. There he shortly became a leader in the abolitionist movement, appearing on the lecture platform, editing a newspaper, the *North Star,* and publishing his auto-biography, *Narrative of the Life of Frederick Douglass* (1845). Douglass demanded not only emancipation for his race but also social and economic equality. (United Press International)

Forten called a mass meeting of Philadelphia blacks to object to it. Many well-meaning North-ern whites favored it as a step toward emancipa-tion; they thought it would encourage slave-owners to free at least some of their slaves. The American Colonization Society received private contributions and appropriations from Congress and the Virginia and Maryland legislatures to carry on the work. Though shipping out of the country fewer Negroes in a decade than were being born in it each month, the society succeeded in founding and governing on the west coast of Africa the colony of Liberia, which it converted into an independent black republic in 1846.

Meanwhile, in Massachusetts, a new note of black militancy had been struck. David Walker, born free in North Carolina, made his living by selling second-hand clothes in Boston. There, in 1829, he published a pamphlet entitled *Walker's Appeal . . . to the Colored Citizens*. In it he de-clared: "America is more our country that it is the whites'—we have enriched it with our *blood and tears.*" He warned: "The whites want slaves, and want us for their slaves, but some of them will curse the day they ever saw us." He ridi-culed the "Christian" pretensions of the slave-holders and urged slaves to cut their masters' throats. "Kill, or be killed!"

A number of other black critics of slavery, most of them less bitterly outspoken than Walker, appeared in the North. The greatest of all—and one of the most electrifying orators of his time, black or white—was Frederick Doug-lass. Born a slave in Maryland, Douglass ran off to Massachusetts in 1838, made a name for himself as an antislavery leader, and lectured for two years in England, where he was lionized. (More than a dozen other black abolitionists also visited the British Isles and made a strong impression there.) After returning to the United States in 1847, Douglass purchased his freedom from his Maryland owner and founded an anti-slavery newspaper, the *North Star,* in Rochester, New York.

As early as 1830, black abolitionists had held their first national convention. They were ready to cooperate with white reformers when some of these launched an aggressive antislavery movement.

## The White Abolitionists

During the 1820s the most active white crusader against slavery was the New Jersey Quaker Benjamin Lundy, who published the leading antislavery newspaper of the time, the *Genius of Universal Emancipation,* in Baltimore. Lundy used moderate language and advocated a mild and gradual program.

In 1831 his helper, the young Massachusetts-born printer William Lloyd Garrison, sounded a much more strident note when he presented the first issue of his own weekly, *The Liberator,* in Boston. From the outset Garrison condemned the thought of gradual, compensated emancipa-tion and demanded immediate abolition, without reimbursement for slaveholders. He denounced the American Colonization Society as no emancipationist agency but the reverse, a group whose real aim was to strengthen slavery by ridding the country of Negroes already free. He got support from free Negroes, who bought most of the subscriptions to *The Liberator*. Despite his strong language, he was no advocate of slave rebellions, and he criticized *Walker's Appeal* as a "most injudicious publication."

Under the leadership of Garrison the New England Antislavery Society was founded in 1832 and the American Antislavery Society the following year. But he shocked many friends of freedom, including Frederick Douglass, by the extremes to which he went. He opposed the government, characterizing the Constitution as "a covenant with death and an agreement with hell," and he opposed the churches on the grounds that they were bulwarks of slavery. In 1840 he split the American Antislavery Society by insisting upon the right of women to participate fully in its activities, even to speak before audiences that included men as well as women.

By that time there were in existence nearly 2,000 local societies with a total of almost 200,000 members. These societies remained alive, active, and growing after the disruption of the national organization.

Another outstanding leader, busy in New York and the Northwest, was Theodore Weld. Converted to reform by Charles G. Finney's preaching, Weld worked within the churches, especially the Presbyterian and Congregational. He married Angelina Grimké, a South Carolina planter's daughter who, with a sister, had turned against slavery. With the aid of his wife, Weld compiled an overwhelming factual indictment of the institution in the book *American Slavery As It Is: Testimony of a Thousand Witnesses* (1839).

But the most powerful of all abolitionist propaganda was a work of fiction, Harriet Beecher Stowe's novel *Uncle Tom's Cabin*. This first appeared as a serial in an antislavery weekly (1851–1852). It was then published as a book, which sold more than 300,000 copies in the year of its publication and was later reissued again and again, to become one of the most remarkable best sellers in American publishing history. Dramatized in various versions, and presented by

**The Liberator: First Issue [1831]**

William Lloyd Garrison made clear his fiery spirit and his uncompromising aim in the very first number of his abolitionist newspaper, *The Liberator*. He told his readers:

*I am aware that many object to the severity of my language; but is there not cause for severity? I will be as harsh as truth, and as uncompromising as justice. On this subject, I do not wish to think, or speak, or write with moderation. No! No! Tell a man whose house is on fire, to give a moderate alarm; tell him to moderately rescue his wife from the hands of the ravisher; tell the mother to gradually extricate her babe from the fire into which it has fallen;—but urge me not to use moderation in a cause like the present. I am in earnest—I will not equivocate—I will not excuse—I will not retreat a single inch—AND I WILL BE HEARD.*

countless theatrical companies throughout the North, the story brought its emotional message to many thousands besides those who read it. Mrs. Stowe belonged to a famous New England ministerial family (her father and seven brothers were preachers). While living in Cincinnati she had made several excursions into Kentucky to view slavery and plantation life. In her novel she intended no personal attack upon Southern whites, and she made the worst of her villains a New England native, Simon Legree. Her aim was to show the brutalizing effect that slavery had upon all who were connected with it.

Through *Uncle Tom's Cabin* and other antislavery writings and speeches, a great many Northerners who never joined an abolitionist society came to disapprove strongly of slavery. Hence it is hard to say how many antislavery people there were at any given time, especially since "antislavery" was a term broad enough to include all kinds and degrees of opposition.

## The Campaign for Liberation

Most of the active members of organized societies were "abolitionists" in the sense that they
favored immediate abolition. But this did not
mean precisely what it seemed to mean. The
abolitionists aimed at what they called "immediate abolition gradually accomplished." That is,
they hoped to bring about a sudden and not a
gradual end to slavery, but they did not expect
to achieve this for some time. At first, they
counted on "moral suasion": they were going to
appeal to the conscience of the slaveholder and
convince him that slaveholding was a sin. Later
they turned more and more to political action,
seeking to induce the Northern states and the
federal government to aid the cause where
possible. They helped runaway slaves find refuge
in the North or in Canada, though in doing so
they did not set up any such highly organized
system as the term "Underground Railroad" implies. After the Supreme Court (in *Prigg* v. *Pennsylvania*, 1842) held that the states need not aid
in enforcing the federal fugitive-slave law of
1793, abolitionists secured the passage of "personal liberty laws" in several of the Northern
states. These laws forbade state officials to assist
in the capture and return of runaways. Above
all, the antislavery societies petitioned Congress
to abolish slavery in places where the federal
government had jurisdiction—in the territories
and the District of Columbia—and to prohibit
the interstate slave trade. Only a very few of
the abolitionists supposed that Congress constitutionally could interfere with a "domestic"
institution like slavery within the Southern states
themselves.

While the abolitionists engaged in pressure
politics, they never formed a political party with
an abolition platform. In 1840 the Liberty party
was launched, with the Kentucky antislavery
leader James G. Birney as its presidential candidate, but this party and its successors did not
campaign for outright abolition: they stood for
"free soil," that is, for keeping slavery out of the
territories. Some free-soilers were friends of the
slave; others were Negrophobes who cared
nothing about slavery but desired to make the
West a white man's country. Garrison said free-
soil-ism was really "white-man-ism."

The real friends of the Negro were quite
aware that, to be consistent, they would have to
help the free as well as the enslaved, since so-
called freedom was "but an empty name—but
the debasing mockery of true freedom." Garrison assured his "free colored brethren" that
the attainment of equal rights for them was "a
leading object." He and other abolitionists did
try to open new opportunities for them. They
had little success in appealing to employers to
hire additional Negroes and give them training
as apprentices. But the reformers made other
rather modest gains. They established schools
for Negroes (by 1837 there were a hundred
young white women teaching black children in
Ohio) and even colleges (Wilberforce in Ohio,
Avery in Pennsylvania). They opened Oberlin
College to black students. They brought about
the desegregation of all Massachusetts public
schools in 1855, six years after Charles Sumner
had argued in a Boston lawsuit (as opponents of
segregation elsewhere were to do a century
later) that, no matter how good the facilities
provided for Negro pupils, "the separate school
is not an equivalent." The reformers also secured the repeal of Massachusetts and Ohio
laws requiring separate Negro cars on railroads.

The abolitionists might have accomplished
more reforms in the North if it had not been for
the widespread anti-Negro if not proslavery feeling there. Prejudice was reinforced by the desire
of many Northern businessmen to keep on good
terms with Southern customers or suppliers, and
by the fear on the part of wage-earning Northern whites that Negroes, if freed and given equal
opportunities, would be dangerous competitors
for jobs. The antislavery movement provoked
much hostility in the North, especially during
the early years. When Prudence Crandall undertook to admit Negro girls to her private school
in Connecticut, local citizens had her arrested
and threw filth into her well, forcing her to close
the school. A mob burned the Philadelphia abolitionists' "temple of liberty" and started a bloody
race riot (1834). Another mob seized Garrison on
the streets of Boston and threatened to hang
him, and a member of still another group shot
and killed the antislavery editor Elijah Lovejoy
in Alton, Illinois (1837). Throughout the North
antislavery lecturers, risking their health if not

their lives, time and again were attacked with rotten eggs or stones.

In the South the reaction was far stronger, and if no abolitionists were killed there, it was only because (from the 1830s on) very few of them dared even venture into that part of the country.

## THE SOUTHERN WAY OF LIFE

Of the three great sections of the country, the South was the one that possessed the highest degree of cultural unity, the one that presented the strongest appearance of solidarity to the outside world. The South (defined as the area of the slave states) was an entity even though within its vast expanse it exhibited immense differences in climate, soil, and people—more perhaps than were to be found in any other region.

### Elements of Southernism

The qualities that gave the South its distinctive flavor are not easy to define. Generally, the climate is warm and mild; on the lower Gulf coast, it is subtropical. The growing seasons are longer than in the North, varying from six months in the upper South to nine months in the Gulf states. The economy, predominantly agricultural, was characterized by the presence of the large plantation as well as the small farm. Farming was largely commercial, concentrating on producing certain staple crops—cotton, tobacco, sugar, and rice—for sale to outside areas. Unlike the West, the South disposed of the bulk of its products in England and Europe rather than the domestic market; it felt closer economic ties with England than with the Northeast. The South was a rural land, with fewer cities, towns, and villages than there were in the Northern states, and its population was more diffused (about thirteen persons per square mile in 1860 as compared with twenty in the North). The great majority of the Southern white people were Anglo-Saxon in origin and in cultural ideals and Protestant in religion.

The South was the only area in the United States (indeed in all the Western world except for Brazil and Cuba) where slavery existed. It was the only section that contained vast numbers of a race other than white. Southerners might differ among themselves on political and economic questions, but by the 1850s they had closed ranks on the issue of race. They were determined to keep the South a white man's country, and they viewed slavery as the best means to that end. Thus slavery was more than a labor system. It was also a white-supremacy device, and as such it finally enlisted the support of the Southern white masses, including the great majority who did not own slaves. Race consciousness, then, helped to account for the oneness of the South.

An ever mounting condemnation of slavery came not only from the Northern states but also from the Latin Amernean countries that had outlawed it, and from Great Britain, whose government had abolished it throughout the British Empire in 1833. The South was an area of Western civilization—not a nation but a section of a nation (and in point of population a minority section)—that cherished an institution at variance with the culture of the civilization of which it was a part.

Thoughtful Southerners realized that slavery isolated them from most of the rest of mankind. Said William Harper of South Carolina: "The judgment is made up. We can have no hearing before the tribunal of the civilized world. Yet, on this very account, it is more important that we, the inhabitants of the slaveholding States, insulated as we are by this institution, and cut off, in some degree, from the communion and sympathies of the world by which we are surrounded, . . . and exposed continually to their animadversions and attacks, should thoroughly understand this subject, and our strength and weakness in relation to it."

Was slavery profitable? On the whole, the planters themselves believed they were making very satisfactory profits, which is the important thing. At the same time there can be no doubt that the slave system, or rather the economic system of which slavery was a part, retarded Southern development and posed some grave problems for the section. Because of the concentration on agriculture, the South had to purchase its finished goods from the outside. Thoughtful Southerners realized the economic subordination of their region. "From the rattle with which the nurse tickles the ear of the child born in the South to the shroud that covers the cold form of the dead, everything comes to us from the North," exclaimed Albert Pike. Said a writer in *De Bow's Review:* "I think it would be safe to estimate the amount which is lost to us annually by our vassalage to the North at $100,000,000. Great God!" The antebellum South had a colonial economy.

The white Southerners' sense of being exploited by the North, together with their race consciousness and their minority status in the nation and in the world, intensified their feeling of sectional unity.

## Gradations of White Society

Only a minority of Southern whites owned slaves. In 1850, when the total white population of the South was over 6 million, the number of slaveholders was 347,525. In 1860, when the white population was just above 8 million (the slave population was 3,950,513), the number of

slaveholders had risen to only 383,637. These figures, taken in themselves, give a somewhat misleading impression. Each slaveholder was normally the head of a family averaging five members. To arrive at the number of whites having a proprietary interest in slavery, it is necessary to multiply by five the number of slaveholders. This formula shows 1,737,625 whites connected with slave ownership in 1850, and 1,937,625 in 1860. Broadly speaking, one family in four owned slaves. Of the minority of whites holding slaves, only a small proportion owned substantial numbers.

At the apex of society stood the large planters —the cotton magnates and the sugar, rice, and tobacco nabobs—who owned at least forty or fifty slaves and 800 or more acres. Next came the small and medium planters, with ten to forty slaves apiece. Farmers with from one to nine slaves outranked those more numerous farmers who owned none at all.

The total number of planters—large, medium,

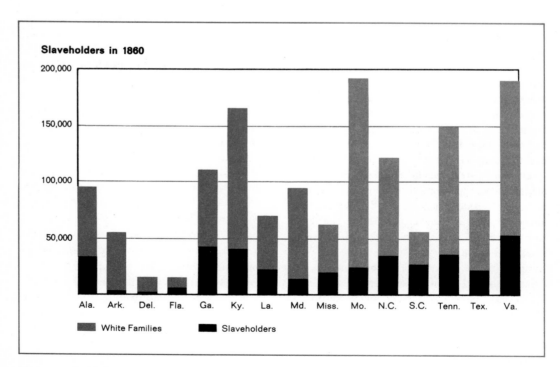

**Slaveholders in 1860**

White Families   Slaveholders

The proportion of slaveholding families in relation to the total white families tended to be higher in the cotton states of the Deep South than in the border states. For example, the number of slaveholders in Georgia and Kentucky was approximately the same, yet in Georgia they constituted almost half of the white population while in Kentucky they represented less than one-third.

and small—was 92,257 in 1850. The large planters represented the social ideal of the South. Enriched by vast annual incomes, dwelling in palatial homes, surrounded by broad acres and many black servants, they were the class to which all others paid a certain deference. Enabled by their wealth to practice the leisured arts, they cultivated gracious living, good manners, learning, and politics. Their social pattern determined to a considerable degree the tone of all Southern society.

The Southern planters constituted the closest approach to an aristocracy to be found in the United States. They enjoyed in their section a higher social position, a greater political power, a more unquestioned leadership than did the factory owners of the Northeast.

Class distinctions were more sharply drawn in the South than in other sections. Some Southerners spoke scornfully of democracy. Yet, particularly in the newer states, an ambitious person could move from one class to another. Farmers nursed the hope of becoming small slaveholders, and small planters aimed to become large ones. Many achieved their goal. In fact, the great majority of the cotton lords of the Mississippi Valley states had come from the ranks of the obscure and the ordinary. Planters who wished to exercise political influence, whether or not they believed in majority rule, had to affect democratic manners and mouth principles that would please the multitudes.

The farmers, those who owned a few slaves and the greater number who owned none, lived lives of rude plenty, devoting more attention to subsistence farming than did the planters. Most of them owned their land. During the 1850s the number of nonslaveholding landowners increased much faster than the number of slaveholding landowners.

In Southern society the business classes—the manufacturers and merchants—were of considerable importance, though comparatively few. Flour milling and textile and iron manufacturing were the main Southern industries, with the principal mill areas being located in Virginia, the Carolinas, and Georgia. The Tredegar Iron Works in Richmond compared favorably with the best iron mills in the Northeast. The value of Southern textile goods increased from $1.5 million in 1840 to $4.5 million in 1860. Despite some promising beginnings, however, Southern industry before 1860 remained largely in a formative stage. Most Southerners showed a distaste for industrialism, and those with surplus capital usually preferred to invest it in slaves and land.

More important than the budding manufacturers were the merchants, particularly the brokers or factors who marketed the planters' crops. These individuals, in towns like New Orleans, Charleston, Mobile, and Savannah, acted as selling agents for the planters, and sometimes also as purchasing agents. Frequently the broker became a banker to the planter, furnishing money or goods on credit. In such cases the planter might be in debt to his factor for a long period, during which time he would have to consign his entire crop to the broker. The merchant-broker, dominating as he did the credit facilities of the rural South, was in a position to exert great economic pressure on the planter.

Closely linked economically with the planters were the professional classes—lawyers, editors, doctors, and others. Because their well-being largely depended on planter prosperity, the professional groups usually agreed with and voiced the ideals of the dominant class.

In the Southern mountains—the Appalachian ranges east of the Mississippi and the Ozarks west of the river—lived the Southern highlanders, the white groups set most apart from the mainstream of Southern life. These mountaineers practiced a crude form of subsistence agriculture, with practically no slaves. They had a proud sense of seclusion, and they held to old ways and old ideals, which included the ideal of loyalty to the nation as a whole. The mountain region was the only part of the South that defied the trend toward sectional conformity.

Occupying the lowest position in Southern white society was that tragic and degraded class known as the poor whites, who in 1850 totaled perhaps half a million. The poor whites were distinct from the ordinary farmers and from the highlanders. The "crackers," "sand hillers," or "white trash" occupied the infertile lands of the pine barrens, the red hills, and the swamps.

Here they lived in miserable cabins surrounded by almost unbelievable squalor. Their degradation resulted partly from dietary deficiencies and disease. Afflicted by pellagra, hookworm, and malaria, the poor whites resorted to eating clay, a practice which in itself indicated a serious shortcoming in their diet.

## King Cotton

The Southern agricultural system was organized around the great staples: tobacco, rice, sugar, and above all cotton. These were the section's money crops, but they did not constitute by any means its only forms of agricultural effort. What might be termed general or diversified farming was carried on in many areas, notably in the Shenandoah Valley of Virginia and the Bluegrass region of central Kentucky. Most planters aimed to produce on the plantation the foodstuffs needed by the family and the slaves. On some large plantations, more acres were planted in corn than in cotton, and in 1850 half the corn crop of the country was raised in the South. The section produced 87 per cent of the nation's hemp supply (in Kentucky and Missouri) and 80 per cent of its peas and beans. Other important products of Southern husbandry were apples, peaches, peanuts, sweet potatoes, hogs, and mules. Despite the planters' efforts to achieve self-sufficiency, they could not supply all the needs of their slaves, and large amounts of corn and pork had to be imported annually from the Northwest.

But the staples dominated the economic life of the section and absorbed the attention of the majority of the people. Climatic and geographical conditions dictated the areas where each was produced. Tobacco, which needed only a fairly short growing season (six months), was grown in tidewater Maryland west of the Chesapeake, in piedmont Virginia and adjacent North Carolina, in northern and western Kentucky, in northwestern Tennessee, and in the Missouri River Valley of Missouri. Rice demanded a growing season of nine months and irrigation, and hence was restricted to the coastal region of South Carolina and Georgia. Sugar, with a similar period necessary for maturation, was concentrated in southern Louisiana and a small area in eastern Texas (around Galveston). Cotton, which required a growing season of seven to nine months and could be produced in a variety of soil formations, occupied the largest zone of production. The Cotton Kingdom stretched from North Carolina to Texas.

From the sale of the great staples, the South derived its chief sources of revenue. Into the markets of the world in the 1850s the section poured annually over 400,000 pounds of tobacco, over 360,000 hogsheads of sugar, and over 240,000 pounds of rice. But the big money crop was cotton. From 1 million bales in 1830, Southern production of cotton steadily increased until it reached 4 million bales in 1860. In that year Southern cotton brought $191 million in the European markets and constituted almost two-thirds of the total export trade of the United States. (By way of contrast, the annual value of the rice crop was $2 million.) No wonder that Southerners said smugly, "Cotton is King."

As cotton culture expanded, the centers of production moved westward into the fresher lands of Alabama, Mississippi, Arkansas, Louisiana, and Texas. The extension of the Cotton Kingdom into this area bore certain resemblances to the rush of gold seekers into a new frontier. The prospect of tremendous profits quickly drew settlers by the thousands. Some who came were wealthy planters from the older states who transferred their assets and slaves to a cotton plantation. Most were small slaveholders or slaveless farmers who intended to become planters.

A similar shift occurred in slave population. The number of slaves in Alabama leaped from 41,000 in 1820 to 435,000 in 1860, and in Mississippi from 32,000 to 436,000. In the same period in Virginia, the increase was only from 425,000 to 490,000. It has been estimated that between 1840 and 1860, 410,000 slaves were moved from the upper South to the cotton states.

Like the farmers of the Northwest, those of the South employed methods that exhausted the soil. They gave little attention to crop rotation, the use of fertilizers, or deep plowing. Like other Americans, they considered it easier to migrate to new lands than to restore old ones. Still, there were agricultural societies and journals in the South, as in the other sections,

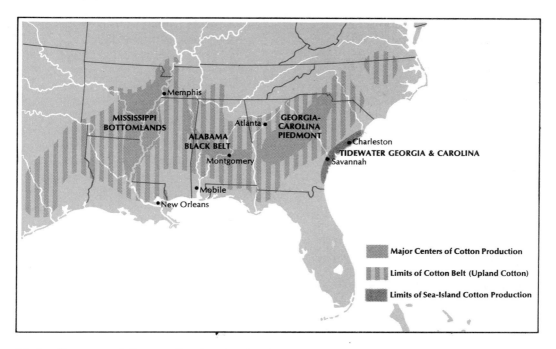

**Major Centers of Cotton Production in the Antebellum South**

and there were dedicated individuals who labored to improve farm techniques. Such a man was the famous Edmund Ruffin of Virginia, advocate of fertilization, rotation, and deep plowing. The author of a work on calcareous manures and the founder of the excellent *Farmers' Register*, Ruffin was one of the best agricultural experts in the country during the 1850s. Through his efforts and those of others, some progress in checking soil depletion was made in the older states.

## The Mind of the South

Most Southerners took their literary cues from English or New York sources. Though the planters bought books in large numbers, they usually chose the works of English and Northern writers, almost ignoring the authors of their own section. They showed the same lack of appreciation for Southern magazines. Of the one hundred magazines founded in the South, only nine survived for any length of time. And of the nine, only three attained much vogue: the excellent literary journals, *The Southern Literary Messenger* (Richmond, 1834–1864) and *The Southern Quarterly Review* (New Orleans

and Charleston, 1842–1857), and the magazine of Southern commercial and agricultural expansion, *De Bow's Review* (New Orleans, 1846–1880). Even these periodicals had to take second place to Northern productions. In that hotbed of Southern sentiment, Charleston, *De Bow's Review* sold an average of 173 copies, while *Harper's Magazine* was regularly purchased by 1,500 Carolinians.

Considering the bleak reception accorded local authors, it is surprising that the section contained as many fine writers as it did. In the 1830s most of the outstanding authors had been from the Virginia-Maryland area: Nathaniel Beverly Tucker (*The Partisan Leader*), William Alexander Caruthers (*The Cavaliers of Virginia*), and John Pendleton Kennedy (*Swallow Barn* and *Horseshoe Robinson*). They were novelists who wrote historical romances or romantic eulogies of the plantation system in the upper South. After 1840 the Southern literary capital shifted to Charleston. Here lived and wrote the antebellum South's most distinguished man of letters, William Gilmore Simms. Primarily a novelist, although he composed some tolerable poetry, Simms wrote over thirty works of fiction, some of them novels (such as *The Yemassee*) glorifying Charleston and South Carolina, others historical romances of the Revolution. He had a rare talent for earthy description of common folk, and his better work compares favorably with that of James Fenimore Cooper. Other Charlestonians were Hugh Sinton Legaré, perhaps the best linguist in America and an authority on the history of law, and the young poets Henry Timrod and Paul Hamilton Hayne, who would achieve their chief renown after the Civil War.

Producing works more distinctively American were the writers of the Southern frontier. These men depicted the society of the backwoods rural areas; they described ordinary people and poor whites instead of aristocratic cavaliers; they were deliberately and sometimes painfully realistic; and they seasoned their sketches with a robust, vulgar humor that was something new in American literature. The leading frontier writer was Augustus B. Longstreet of Georgia (*Georgia Scenes*). Others who wrote in the same vein were Joseph G. Baldwin (*Flush Times of Alabama and Mississippi*) and Johnson J. Hooper (*Some Adventures of Captain Simon Suggs*). Together, these Southern realists established a tradition of humor that was uniquely American and that was ultimately to find a supreme exponent in Mark Twain.

It has been said (by H. C. Nixon) that in the South there were more people who could read Latin and fewer who could read English than in any other part of the country. The educational system of the section reflected the aristocratic ideals of the plantation regime. In 1860 there were 260 Southern colleges and universities, public and private, with 25,000 students enrolled in them, or more than half the total number of students in the United States. The South had twice as many students per 1,000 of white population in college as any other section. The lower South had 11,000 students in its institutions of higher learning, while New England, with approximately the same population, could boast of only 3,748. Below the college level, the schools of the South were not only fewer but also inferior to those of the East, but about as good as those of the West. Libraries where an enterprising individual might educate himself also were fewer in the South. In Louisiana there were only one hundred books to each 1,218 white people, while in Massachusetts there were one hundred to each 118 persons. The South had over 500,000 white illiterates, or more than half of the country's total.

In the fields of belles-lettres and science, the South was primarily a section of consumers rather than producers. The section did not produce a literature or a body of scientific findings to compare with those of the Northeast. Among the reasons for the relative backwardness of the South was the rural character of the region. There were few cities, and not one like New York or Boston that could act as a focal point of culture, and there were few publishing facilities. The high illiteracy rate among white adults decreased the potential reading audience. In the simple nature of Southern society there were few complexities to intrigue the writer and impel him to find an explanation. The planters, the class that might have patronized a Southern literature, considered oratory and statesmanship to be much more significant activities. At a time when writing was becoming a recognized and respected profession in the North, Southern authors, as so many of them bitterly testified, were regarded as amusing fellows who had little to offer their society.

Furthermore, after 1830 much of the creative energy of the South was channeled into the defense of slavery. Under criticism from the outside, the section felt a compulsion to glorify its image of itself and to enforce conformity to that image. Freedom of thought, which was largely accepted in the North and which Jefferson and other former Southern leaders had said was necessary in a good society, was stifled in the South.

## THE "PECULIAR INSTITUTION"

When slaveowners referred to the "peculiar institution" of the South, they did not mean to imply that slavery was somehow odd or queer. Rather, they indicated their belief that it was special and distinctive.

## The Regimen of Slavery

Slavery was an institution established by law and regulated in detail by law. The slave codes of the Southern states forbade a slave to hold property, to leave his master's premises without permission, to be out after dark, to congregate with other slaves except at church, to carry firearms, to strike a white man even in self-defense. The codes prohibited teaching a slave to read or write, and denied the right of a slave to testify in court against a white person. They contained no provisions to legalize slave marriages or divorces. Any person showing a strain of African ancestry was presumed to be a slave unless he could prove otherwise. If an owner killed a slave while punishing him, the act was not considered a crime.

These and dozens of other restrictions and impositions indicate that the slaves lived under a harsh and dismal regime, which would have been unrelieved had the laws been drastically enforced. In fact, they were applied unevenly. Sometimes slaves did acquire property, were taught to read and write, and assembled with other slaves, the laws to the contrary notwithstanding. Most slave offenses were tried by the master, who might inflict punishments ranging from some mild disciplinary action to flogging or branding for running away. Major offenses, including crimes, were generally referred to the courts. Slaves faced the death penalty for the following offenses: killing or even resisting a white person and inciting to revolt or even participating in what was suspected to be an insurrectionary plot.

The routine of plantation life was governed by a system of rules created by custom and the planters. A small planter directly supervised the work on his place. A medium or large planter hired an overseer and perhaps an assistant overseer to represent him. The "head driver," a trusted and responsible slave, acted under the overseer as a kind of foreman. Under him might be several subdrivers. Two methods or systems of assigning slave labor were employed. One was the task system, most widely used in rice culture. Here a slave was allotted a particular task in the morning, say to hoe one acre; when he completed his job he was free for the rest of the day. The other was the gang system, employed on the cotton, sugar, and tobacco plantations. Here the slaves were simply divided into groups, each of which was directed by a driver, and were worked for as many hours as the overseer considered a reasonable work day.

Slaves were provided with enough necessities to enable them to live and work. They were furnished with an adequate if rough diet, consisting mainly of corn meal, salt pork, and molasses; many were allowed to raise gardens for their own use, and were issued fresh meats on special occasions. They received issues of cheap clothes and shoes. They lived in rude cabins, called the slave quarters. Medical care was provided by the plantation mistress or a doctor retained by the owner. The slave worked hard, beginning with light tasks as a child, and his work day was longest at harvest time. He sometimes had time off to hunt and fish, and he attended the church services and some of the social festivities of his white family.

The master had an economic interest in taking reasonably good care of his slaves. He was likely to use hired labor, when available, for the most unhealthful or dangerous tasks. A traveler in Louisiana noted, for example, that Irishmen were employed to clear malarial swamps and to handle cotton bales at the bottom of chutes extending from the river bluff down to a boat landing. If an Irishman died of disease or was killed in an accident, the master could hire another for a dollar a day or less. But he would be out perhaps a thousand dollars or more if he lost a prime field hand. Still, a cruel master might forget his pocketbook in the heat of momentary anger. And slaves were often left to the discipline of an overseer, who had no pecuniary stake in their well-being; he was paid in proportion to the amount of work he could get out of them.

Household servants had a somewhat easier life than did field hands. On a small plantation the same persons might serve in both capacities, but on a large one there would be a separate staff of nursemaids, housemaids, cooks, butlers, coachmen, and the like. These people lived close to the master and his family, eating the leftovers from the family table, and in some cases even sleeping in the "big house." Between the blacks and whites of such a household, there might develop an affectionate, almost familial relationship.

Slavery in the cities differed significantly from slavery in the country. On the more or less isolated plantation the slaves were kept apart from free Negroes and lower-class whites. The master, his family, and his overseers maintained a fairly direct and effective control. A deep and unbridgeable chasm yawned between slavery and freedom. In the city, however, the master often could not supervise his slaves closely and at the same time use them profitably. Even if they slept at night in carefully watched backyard barracks, they went about by day on errands of various kinds. Others were hired out, and after hours they fended for themselves, neither the owner nor the employer caring to look after them. Thus the urban slaves gained numerous opportunities to mingle with free Negroes and with whites, including fair-complexioned prostitutes. A line between slavery and freedom remained, but it became less and less distinct.

Indeed, slavery was basically incompatible with city life, and as Southern cities grew, the number of slaves in them dropped, relatively if not absolutely. The reasons were social rather than economic. Fearing conspiracies and insurrections, urban slaveowners sold off much of their male property to the countryside. The cities were left with an excess of Negro women while continuing to have an excess of white men (a circumstance that helped to account for the birth of many mulattoes). While slavery in the cities declined, segregation of Negroes both free and slave increased. Segregation was a means of social control intended to make up for the loosening of the discipline of slavery itself.

The transfer of slaves from one part of the South to another (when the slaves were not carried by their migrating owners) was accomplished through the medium of professional slave traders. In long-distance traffic the slaves were moved on trains or on river or ocean steamers. Or they were moved on foot, trudging in coffles of hundreds along the dusty highways. Eventually they arrived at some central market like Natchez, New Orleans, Mobile or Galveston, where purchasers collected to bid for them. At the auction the bidders checked the slaves like livestock, watching them as they were made to walk or trot, inspecting their teeth, feeling their arms and legs, looking for signs of infirmity or age. It paid to be careful, for traders were known to deceive buyers by blacking gray hair, oiling withered skin, and concealing physical defects in other ways. A sound young field hand would fetch a price that, during the 1840s and 1850s, varied from $500 to $1,700, depending mainly on fluctuations in the price of cotton. The average figure was about $800. A good-looking "fancy girl," desirable as a concubine, might bring several times that much.

The domestic slave trade, while essential to the growth and prosperity of the whole system, was one of the least defensible aspects of it. Not only did the trade dehumanize all who were involved in it; it also separated children from parents, and parents from one another. Even in the case of a kindly master who had kept families together, they might be broken up in the division of his estate after his death. Planters condoned the trade and eased their consciences by holding the traders in contempt and assigning them a low social position—except those who invested their profits in plantations (like Nathan Bedford Forrest, a slave trader and then a planter and eventually a war hero of the Confederacy).

The foreign slave trade was as bad or worse. Though federal law had prohibited the importation of slaves from 1808 on, they continued to be smuggled in as late as the 1850s. The numbers can only be guessed at. They were not

## Slave Scenes

Photographs of slaves at work or performing any function are almost impossible to obtain. But during the Civil War and after it photographs of Negroes on plantations were taken, and these often reproduce the conditions of labor and life under slavery. Thus the picture of the cotton pickers

(top right) is postwar, but the harvesting techniques were the same as those used before the war. The other picture (bottom right) shows Negro, or slave, quarters on a South Carolina plantation. (Courtesy of the New-York Historical Society, New York City)

large enough to satisfy all planters, and the Southern commercial conventions, which met annually to consider means of making the South economically independent, began to discuss the legal reopening of the trade. "If it is right to buy slaves in Virginia and carry them to New Orleans ," William L. Yancey of Alabama asked his fellow delegates at the 1858 meeting, "why is it not right to buy them in Cuba, Brazil, or Africa and carry them there?" The convention that year voted to recommend the repeal of all laws against slave imports. Only the delegates from the states of the upper South, which profited from the domestic trade, opposed the opening of foreign competition.

## The Slave's Response

Slavery in essence meant absolute power on the one hand and total subjection on the other. The slaves were subject to the whim of the master. He was the father image for all, including the slave fathers themselves, who had no real authority over their own families. The slaves also had to depend upon him and his kind for most of what they knew: their language, religion, and practical knowledge and skills.

By the 1850s few slaves in America could do more than dimly recall the lore of their ancestors in Africa. The Africans had developed a variety of complex cultures, but much of the tribal custom and language was lost in the transition to slavery. Some African ways survived in the United States—for instance, shouting and hand-clapping at religious exercises, women carrying burdens on their heads, the Gullah dialect along the South Carolina coast—and these affected the slaves' adaptations of white culture. They also influenced the white man's civilization itself, enriching his speech with words of African origin (such as *goober* and *banjo*), possibly setting a pattern for the emotionalism of his religious camp meetings, and no doubt contributing to the formation of his Southern accent.

Nevertheless, the slaves no longer possessed a tribal or cultural identity of a kind that would help them much to offset the depersonalizing effects of slavery. They were left to respond to their lot, individually, as best they could, and they responded in a variety of ways. Some, es-

pecially among favored domestic servants, identified with the master and accepted their subservient position with little difficulty, perhaps with real contentment. Others learned to adjust to necessity by acting out, in the white man's presence, the expected role of shuffling, grinning, head-scratching deference. Still others could never quite bring themselves to either acceptance or accommodation. They harbored an unquenchable spirit of rebelliousness, and from the frustration it brought them they sometimes developed personality disorders (signs of these were seen in newspaper advertisements for runaways who were described as having a stutter or other behavioral quirks).

For the vast majority, there was no way out of their predicament. A few were allowed to earn money with which they managed to buy their own and their families' freedom. Some had the good luck to be set free by their master's will after his death—like the more than 400 slaves belonging to John Randolph of Roanoke (1833). From the 1830s on, however, state laws made it more and more difficult, and in some cases practically impossible, for an owner to manumit his slaves. The laws, when permitting manumission, often required the removal of the freed slaves from the state. The masters objected to the very presence of free Negroes, who by their existence set a disturbing example for the slaves.

By 1860 there nevertheless were about 250,-000 free Negroes in the slaveholding states, more than half of them in Virginia and Maryland. A few, as in the North, attained wealth and prominence. A few themselves owned slaves, usually relatives whom they had bought in order to assure their ultimate emancipation. Most lived in abject poverty, even worse than in the North. Law or custom closed many occupations to them, forbade them to assemble without white supervision, and placed numerous other restraints upon them. They were only quasi-free, and yet they had all the burdens of freedom, including the obligation of paying taxes.

Great as were the hardships of freedom, Negroes generally preferred them to the hardships of slavery. Occasionally slaves sought freedom through flight. They might succeed in hiding out for a time, but the chance of escaping to the North or to Canada was exceedingly slim except for those who lived fairly close to the free-state border and who got help from free Negroes and friendly whites on the so-called Underground Railroad. For fugitives from the deep South, the hazards of distance and geographical ignorance, of white patrols and bloodhounds, were hard if not impossible to overcome, especially since every Negro at large was presumed to be a runaway slave unless he carried documentary proof to the contrary.

The discontented slave could express his feelings through individual acts of resistance. He might be deliberately careless with his master's property, losing or breaking tools, setting fire to houses or barns. He might make himself useless by cutting off his fingers or even committing suicide. Or, despite the terrible consequences, he might turn upon the master and kill him.

The idea of combining with other blacks, rising up, and overthrowing the masters occurred to slaves and free Negroes from time to time. In 1800 Gabriel Prosser gathered a thousand rebellious slaves outside of Richmond, but two blacks gave the plot away, and the Virginia militia were called out in time to head it off. Gabriel and thirty-five others were executed. In 1822 the Charleston free Negro Denmark Vesey and his followers—rumored to total 9,000—made preparations for revolt, but again the word leaked out and retribution followed. In 1831 Nat Turner, a slave preacher, led a band of Negroes who armed themselves with guns and axes and, on a summer night, went from house to house in Southampton County, Virginia. They slaughtered sixty white men, women, and children before being overpowered by state and federal troops. More than a hundred Negroes were put to death in the aftermath. Nat Turner's was the only actual slave insurrection in the nineteenth-century South, but slave conspiracies and threats of renewed violence continued throughout the section as long as slavery lasted.

## The Proslavery Reaction

By the 1830s slavery was being threatened from three directions—from the slaves themselves, from Northern abolitionists, and from Southern slaveless farmers. There were still antislavery so-

cieties in the South, and as late as 1827 there had been a larger number than in the North. They were most numerous in the border slave states, where a few antislavery men, notably Cassius M. Clay of Kentucky, kept up their campaign through the 1850s. Between 1829 and 1832 a Virginia constitutional convention and then the state legislature, responding to demands from non-slaveholders in the western part of the state, seriously considered ending slavery through compensated emancipation but were discouraged by the tremendous expense it would have required.

Meanwhile the news of the Turner insurrection terrified whites in Virginia and all over the South. They had always been uneasy, always mindful of the horrors of the successful slave uprising in Santo Domingo (in the 1790s). Now they were reminded of their insecurity, and they were especially horrified because there had been long trusted house servants among Nat's followers who, axe in hand, had suddenly confronted their masters' sleeping families. Who among the blacks could the whites really depend upon? Many of the master class now blamed Garrison and the abolitionists for the slaves' defection. Planters were determined to make slavery secure against all dangers.

While the Southern states strengthened their slave codes, controlling the movement of slaves and prohibiting their being taught to read, Southern leaders proceeded to elaborate an intellectual defense of slavery. In 1832 Professor Thomas R. Dew of the College of William and Mary published a pamphlet outlining the slavery case. In subsequent years many others added their contributions to the cause, and in 1852 the defense was summed up in an anthology, *The Pro-Slavery Argument.*

As early as 1837 John C. Calhoun boasted that Southerners had ceased to apologize for slavery as a necessary evil and had been convinced that it was "a good—a positive good." According to the proslavery argument it was good for the slave because he was an inferior creature who needed the master's guidance and who was better off—better fed, clothed, and housed, and more secure—than the Northern factory worker. It was good for Southern society because it was the only way two races so

## Calhoun on Slavery [1837]

*I hold that in the present state of civilization, where two races of different origin, and distinguished by color, and other physical differences, as well as intellectual, are brought together, the relation now existing in the slave-holding States between the two is, instead of an evil, a good—a positive good. I feel myself called upon to speak freely upon the subject where the honor and interests of those I represent are involved. I hold then, that there never has yet existed a wealthy and civilized society in which one portion of the community did not, in point of fact, live on the labor of the other. . . . I may say with truth that in few countries so much is left to the share of the laborer, and so little exacted from him, or where there is more kind attention paid to him in sickness or infirmities of age. Compare his condition with the tenants of the poor houses in the more civilized portions of Europe—look at the sick and the old and infirm slave, on one hand, in the midst of his family and friends, under the kind superintending care of his master and mistress, and compare it with the forlorn and wretched condition of the pauper in the poor house.*

different as the black and the white could live together in peace. It was good for the nation as a whole because the entire Southern economy depended on it, and the prosperity of the nation depended on the prosperity of the South. It was good in itself because the Bible sanctioned it— did not the Hebrews of the Old Testament own bondsmen, and did not the New Testament apostle Paul advise, "Servants, obey your masters"? These and other arguments convinced most Southerners, even those (the great majority) who owned no slaves and had no direct interest in the peculiar institution.

Some proslavery propagandists concluded that slavery was such a good thing it should be extended to include white workers in the North as well as black laborers in the South. In *Sociology for the South, or the Failure of Free Society* (1854) George Fitzhugh, of Virginia, praised slavery as the only workable form of socialism and urged the whole world to adopt it, at once, as the sole cure for class conflict and the other ills of competitive society.

While spreading proslavery propaganda, Southern leaders tried to silence the advocates of freedom. Southern critics of slavery found it healthful to leave home, among them Hinton Rowan Helper of North Carolina, whose *Impending Crisis of the South* (1857) contended that slavery hurt the welfare of the nonslaveholder and made the whole region backward. In 1835 a mob destroyed sacks containing abolition literature in the Charleston post office, and thereafter Southern postmasters generally refused to deliver antislavery mail. Southern state legislatures passed resolutions demanding that Northern states suppress the "incendiary" agitation of the abolitionists. In Congress, Southern representatives with the cooperation of Northerners secured the adoption of the "gag rule" (1836) according to which antislavery petitions were automatically laid on the table without being read.

As a champion of freedom of speech and petition, John Quincy Adams led a struggle against the gag rule, finally (1844) securing its repeal. Throughout the North many people who were not abolitionists began to feel that civil liberties were endangered in the entire country, not just the South. These people were inclined to sympathize with the abolitionist as a martyr for freedom in the broadest sense. They came to suspect that there really existed, as the abolitionist claimed, a kind of "Slave Power Conspiracy" to destroy the liberties of the country as a whole. They began to wonder, as Abraham Lincoln did, whether the nation could long continue to be half slave and half free—whether the nation might not become all slave. Thus the majority of Northerners, though not necessarily for love of the Negro, eventually came to sympathize in varying degrees with the antislavery cause, while an even larger and more determined majority of Southerners rallied to the defense of the peculiar institution, thereby laying the foundation for a "solid South."

# Selected Readings

**The Reform Spirit** A. M. Schlesinger, *The American as Reformer* (1950); W. R. Cross, *The Burned-Over District°* (1950); A. A. Ekirch, *The Idea of Progress in America, 1815–1860* (1944); C. C. Cole, Jr., *The Social Ideals of the Northern Evangelists, 1826–1860* (1954); T. L. Smith, *Revivalism and Social Reform in Mid-Nineteenth-Century America* (1957); C. S. Griffin, *Their Brothers' Keepers: Moral Stewardship in the United States, 1800–1865* (1960).

**Miscellaneous Reforms** A. F. Tyler, *Freedom's Ferment: Phases of American Social History to 1860°* (1940); M. E. Curti, *The American Peace Crusade* (1929); Paul Monroe, *The Founding of the American Public School System* (1949); Arthur Bestor, *Backwoods Utopias: The Sectarian and Owenite Phases of Communitarian Socialism in America, 1663–1829°* (1950); Carl Bode, *The American Lyceum* (1956); N. K. Teeters and J. D. Shearer, *The Prison at Philadelphia* (1957); J. D. Davies, *Phrenology: Fad and Science* (1955); H. S. Commager, *Theodore Parker, Yankee Crusader°* (1936); H. E. Marshall, *Dorothea Dix, Forgotten Samaritan* (1937); Otelia Cromwell, *Lucretia Mott* (1958); F. O. Gatell, *John Gorham Palfrey and the New England Conscience* (1963); I. H. Bartlett, *Wendell Phillips, Brahmin Rebel* (1961); R. V. Harlow, *Gerrit Smith, Philanthropist and Reformer* (1939).

**The Negro in the North** L. F. Litwack, *North of Slavery: The Negro in the Free States, 1790–1860* (1961); Benjamin Quarles, *Black Abolitionists* (1969); William Stanton, *The Leopard's Spots: Scientific Attitudes Toward Race in America, 1815–59* (1960).

**The Antislavery Movement** Louis Filler, *The Crusade Against Slavery, 1830–1860°* (1960); F. L. Dumond, *Antislavery: The Crusade for Freedom in America* (1961); G. H. Barnes, *The Antislavery Impulse, 1833–1844°* (1933); D. B. Davis, *The Problem of Slavery in Western Culture°* (1966); Bertram Wyatt-Brown, *Lewis Tappan and the Evangelical War Against Slavery* (1969); Martin Duberman, ed., *The Antislavery Vanguard* (1965); Larry Gara, *The Liberty Line: The Legend of the Underground Railroad* (1961); R. B. Nye, *Fettered Freedom: Civil Liberties and the Slavery Controversy, 1830–1860* (1949) and *William Lloyd Garrison and the Humanitarian Reformers°* (1955); W. M. Merrill, *Against Wind and Tide: A Biography of Wm. Lloyd Garrison* (1963); J. L. Thomas, *The Liberator: William Lloyd Garrison* (1963); A. S. Kraditor, *Means and Ends in American Abolitionism: Garrison and His Critics on Strategy and Tactics, 1834–1850* (1969); B. P. Thomas, *Theodore Weld, Crusader for Freedom* (1950); M. L. Dillon, *Benjamin Lundy and the Struggle for Negro Freedom* (1966); Betty Fladeland, *James Gillespie Birney: Slaveholder to Abolitionist* (1955); D. L. Smiley, *Lion of White Hall: The Life of Cassius M. Clay* (1962).

**The Southern Economy** L. C. Gray, *History of Agriculture in the Southern United States to 1860* (2 vols., 1933); U. B. Phillips, *Life and Labor in the Old South°* (1929); F. L. Olmsted, *The Cotton Kingdom*, ed. by A. M. Schlesinger (1953); R. R. Russel, *Economic Aspects of Southern Sectionalism, 1840–1861* (1924); F. L. Owsley, *Plain Folk of the Old South°* (1949).

**Southern Thought** Clement Eaton, *Freedom of Thought in the Old South°* (1940), *The Growth of Southern Civilization, 1790–1860°* (1961), and *The Mind of the Old South°* (1964); W. J. Cash, *The Mind of the South°* (1941); W. R. Taylor, *Cavalier and Yankee: The Old South and American National Character°* (1961); J. H. Franklin, *The Militant South* (1956); R. G. Osterweis, *Romanticism and Nationalism in the Old South°* (1949); J. B. Hubbell, *The South in American Literature, 1607–1900* (1954); Frank Freidel, *Francis Lieber* (1947); Harvey Wish, *George Fitzhugh, Propagandist of the Old South* (1943); W. S. Jenkins, *Pro-Slavery Thought in the Old South* (1935).

**Slavery** U. B. Phillips, *American Negro Slavery°* (1918); K. M. Stampp, *The Peculiar Institution: Slavery in the Ante-Bellum South°* (1956); S. M. Elkins, *Slavery: A Problem in American Institutional and Intellectual Life°* (1959); E. D. Genovese, *The Political Economy of Slavery°* (1965); R. C. Wade, *Slavery in the Cities°* (1964); Frederic Bancroft, *Slave-Trading in the Old South* (1931); W. K. Scarborough, *The Overseer: Plantation Management in the Old South* (1966).

---

° Titles available in paperback.

# Chapter 13
# Fruits of Manifest Destiny

In the time of James K. Polk the egalitarian spirit of Jacksonian Democracy broadened into a nationalistic demand for military conquest. Expansionism seemed a corollary of egalitarianism to Democratic party intellectuals who rationalized the demand. Conquest was "Manifest Destiny," a phrase coined by a party journalist who, in 1845, prophesied "the fulfillment of our manifest destiny to overspread the continent allotted by Providence for the free development of our yearly multiplying millions." In other words, the United States had a divine mission to take the whole of North America, by force if necessary, and thus make room for its own rapidly growing people while carrying the blessings of democracy to less favored peoples who happened to occupy attractive lands nearby.

Not all Americans of the time agreed with that. Many, especially among the Whigs, believed their country had a mission to encourage the American brand of democracy and civilization throughout the continent and, indeed, the entire world—but only by peaceful means. "I have always wished," said Daniel Webster, for one, "that this country should exhibit to the nations of the earth the example of a great, rich, and powerful republic which is not possessed by a spirit of aggrandizement."

Even the forceful expansionists were not motivated merely by the grandiose notion of Manifest Destiny. They usually had fairly specific goals in mind. Polk himself focused his attention on the two great natural harbor areas of the Pacific Coast: Puget Sound and San Francisco Bay. Nor did the expansionists press their conquests to try and include the entire North American continent. During the expansionist flurry of the 1840s and 1850s the United States attained essentially the size and shape that it still has (so far as the forty-eight contiguous states are concerned). It might have added other territories—including overseas possessions such as Cuba and the Hawaiian Islands—if the expansionists had remained sufficiently united in their aims. But they came to be divided on the question of slavery in the new acquisitions.

Expansion arose from nationalism and ultimately was to strengthen it. But the immediate result was to endanger national unity, for expansion provoked and intensified sectional conflict. And because of this conflict the acquisition of an overseas empire was to be postponed for half a century.

---

**Migrants Crossing the Plains**

Migrants of the Western trails traveled in canvas covered wagons. Some of the heaviest wagons weighed from 3,000 to 7,000 pounds and required the pulling service of ten or twelve horses or oxen. A wagon train of migrants operated under the direction of a captain who assigned each wagon a position. An average day's trip for a train was from 15 to 20 miles. (Top left, Library of Congress; bottom left, Brown Brothers)

## THE TYLER ADMINISTRATION

The fruition of Manifest Destiny was not to come until after the election of 1844 had brought the Democrats back into power. Meanwhile, the Whigs found themselves divided and frustrated despite their overwhelming victory in the "log cabin" campaign of 1840, which had brought into office their appealing ticket of "Tippecanoe and Tyler too."

"Old Tippecanoe," William Henry Harrison, was never to have a chance to demonstrate what sort of President he would have made. Though he seemed to be in good health, he was sixty-eight years old in 1841, and the strain of the campaign and the inauguration and the pressing demands of his office-seeking supporters were apparently too much for him. He contracted a cold which turned into pneumonia, and he died on April 4, 1841, exactly one month after he had been inaugurated—the first President to die in office. In his brief presidential tenure he had looked for advice to the accepted leaders of the party, particularly to Clay and Webster. Webster became secretary of state, and four of Clay's friends went into the cabinet. Clay and Webster had expected to guide the old soldier through the political jungle, but now Tippecanoe was dead. "Tyler too," a practicing politician and a Southern Whig, was in the White House.

### Frustration of the Whigs

Vice President John Tyler, though some contended he was merely the second officer acting as the first, immediately assumed the title as well as the powers of the Presidency. For the time being, he kept Harrison's cabinet. A member of an aristocratic Virginia family, Tyler had left the Democratic party in protest against Jackson's overly equalitarian program and imperious methods. One reason the Whigs had put him on the ticket with Harrison was the hope that he would attract the votes of similar conservative former Democrats. Nevertheless, Clay apparently had the impression that the new President would support a national bank and other Whig projects, but Tyler soon broke with Clay.

A part of Clay's program was enacted without causing serious division in the party. With near unanimity the Whigs passed a measure, which Tyler signed, abolishing the Independent Treasury system. They also agreed on a bill, the Tariff of 1842, which raised the rates to approximately the same level as in 1832. Tyler accepted this bill, too, but with no great show of enthusiasm.

Part of the Whig legislative program made a bid for the approval of Western settlers and farmers. The frontier was continuing its steady expansion. Arkansas became a state in 1836, Michigan in 1837, and Florida in 1845. The greatest rush of settlers was into the future states of Wisconsin, Iowa, and Minnesota. To attract Western voters the Whig leadership put through the Preemption Act of 1841, which made it possible for a man to claim 160 acres of land before they were offered publicly for sale and to pay for them later at $1.25 an acre. This "log cabin bill" was hailed by the Whigs as a relief measure for sufferers from the depression and as a proof of their party's devotion to the welfare of the common man.

The Whig leadership was committed to restoring a financial system similar to the Bank of the United States. But Tyler desired a kind of "state-rights national bank," one that would confine its operations to the District of Columbia and establish branches in the states only with their consent. He twice vetoed bills for setting up what the Whigs tried to disguise as a "Fiscal Corporation."

Lacking a sufficient majority to override the veto, the Whigs fumed with rage at the President, who added to their anger by vetoing a number of internal improvement bills. In an unprecedented action, a conference of congressional Whigs read Tyler out of the party. All the cabinet members resigned except Webster, who had some diplomatic business with Great Britain that he wished to settle. To fill their places, the President appointed five men of his own stripe—former Democrats.

A portentous new political alignment was taking shape. Tyler and a small band of conservative Southern Whigs who followed him were getting ready to rejoin the Democrats. When the office of secretary of state became vacant in 1844, Tyler appointed John C. Calhoun—who had left the Democratic party in the 1830s and had since rejoined it. Into the common man's party of Jackson and Van Buren came a group of men who had aristocratic ideas about government, who thought that government had an obligation to protect and even expand the institution of slavery, and who believed in state rights with a single-minded, almost fanatical devotion.

## Webster's Diplomacy

Starting in the late 1830s a series of incidents brought Great Britain and the United States close to actual war. In 1837 rebellion broke out in the eastern provinces of Canada, and many Americans applauded the rebels and furnished them with material aid. The rebels chartered a small American steamship, the *Caroline*, to carry supplies across the Niagara River from New York. One night while the ship was moored at a wharf on the American side, the Canadian authorities sent over a force that took possession of the *Caroline* and burned her; in the melee one American was killed. Excitement flared on both sides of the border. President Van Buren issued a proclamation asking Americans to abide by the neutrality laws, and he sent General Winfield Scott to the border to act as a pacifier. The State Department demanded an apology and reparations from Great Britain, but the British government neither disavowed the attack nor offered compensation for it.

While the *Caroline* affair simmered, the troublesome issue of the Maine boundary came up. As defined by the Treaty of 1783, this line was impossible to locate. Previous attempts to fix it by mutual agreement and by arbitration had failed. In 1838 Americans and Canadians, mostly lumberjacks, began to move into the Aroostook River region in the disputed area. A head-smashing brawl between the two parties—the "Aroostook War"—threatened more trouble between England and America.

Soon a Canadian named Alexander McLeod was arrested in New York and charged with the murder of the American who had died in the *Caroline* incident. The British government reacted with majestic rage, contending that McLeod could not be accused of murder because

he had acted under official orders. The foreign secretary, the bellicose Lord Palmerston, demanded McLeod's release and threatened that his execution would bring "immediate and frightful" war. Webster as secretary of state did not think McLeod was worth a war, but could do nothing to release him. The prisoner was under New York jurisdiction and had to be tried in the state courts, a peculiarity of American jurisprudence that the British did not seem to understand. Fortunately for the cause of peace—and for himself—McLeod was able to establish an alibi and was acquitted.

Festering points of disagreement still remained. In an attempt to stamp out the African slave trade, Great Britain was asking for the right to search American merchant ships suspected of carrying black cargoes. Since the American government, sensitive on the matter of search, had always refused the British request, slavers of other nations frequently sought to avoid capture by hoisting the American flag. Complicating the issue was the domestic slave trade, in which slaves were carried by sea from one American port to another. Sometimes the ships in this trade were blown off their course to the British West Indies, where the authorities, acting under English law, freed the slaves. In 1841 an American brig, the *Creole*, sailed from Virginia for New Orleans with over a hundred slaves aboard. En route the slaves mutinied, took possession of the ship, and took it to the Bahamas. Here British officials declared the bondsmen free. Although Webster protested, England refused to return the slaves. Many Americans, especially Southerners, were infuriated.

At this critical juncture a new government came to power in Great Britain, one that was more disposed to conciliate the United States and to settle the outstanding differences between the two countries. The new ministry sent to America an emissary, Lord Ashburton, to negotiate an agreement on the Maine boundary and other matters. Ashburton liked Americans, and Webster admired the English. To avoid war, both were willing to compromise. The result of their deliberations was the Webster-Ashburton Treaty of August 9, 1842.

By the terms of this arrangement, the United States received about seven-twelfths of the disputed area, which was about as much as it could expect. Minor rectifications in the boundary were made in the Lake Champlain area and from Lake Superior to the Lake of the Woods. The boundary was now established as far west as the Rocky Mountains. Other issues disposed of were the extradition of criminals and the slave trade. Seven crimes were listed for which the United States and Canada would extradite accused citizens of the other country. It was agreed that both Great Britain and the United States would maintain naval squadrons off the African coast, the American ships being charged with chasing slavers using the American flag.

Through exchanges of notes that were not part of the treaty, Webster and Ashburton also eased the memory of the *Caroline* and *Creole* affairs. Ashburton expressed "regret" for the raid on the *Caroline,* and he pledged that in the future there would be no "officious interference" with American ships forced by "violence or accident" to enter British ports—presumably meaning there would be no repetition of the *Creole* episode.

Webster used secret funds to inspire newspaper propaganda favorable to his arrangements with Ashburton, and the treaty proved quite popular. War talk was forgotten for the time being, as Anglo-American relations suddenly looked better than they had for many years.

During the Tyler administration the United States established diplomatic relations with China. In 1842 Britain forced China to open certain ports to foreign trade. Eager to share the new privileges, American mercantile interests persuaded Tyler and Congress to send a commissioner to China to negotiate a trade treaty. Webster wrote the instructions for the first commissioner, Caleb Cushing. In the Treaty of Wanghia, concluded in 1844, Cushing secured most-favored-nation provisions giving Americans the same privileges as Englishmen. He also persuaded the Chinese to grant Americans the right of extraterritoriality—the right, if accused of crimes, to be tried by American officials rather than by Chinese judges. In the next ten years American trade with China steadily increased.

## POLK AND EXPANSION

During the James K. Polk administration (1845–1849) over 1 million square miles of new territory came under American control, and the western boundary of the United States advanced from the Louisiana Purchase line to the Pacific Ocean. Well might the ordinary-looking little man from Tennessee feel proud of his work. No other President except Jefferson had acquired so much for his country.

### Election of 1844

In 1844 Henry Clay expected to be the Whig candidate, and Van Buren the Democratic nominee. Both wanted to avoid taking a stand on the annexation of Texas, because a stand, no matter on which side, was certain to lose some votes. Consequently, they issued separate statements, so similar in tone as to indicate previous consultation between the authors. They both favored annexation, but only with the consent of Mexico. Since this consent was most unlikely to be forthcoming, the statements had little or no meaning.

Clay's action did not harm his candidacy. The Whig convention nominated him unanimously, although the platform discreetly omitted any reference to Texas. But Van Buren had destroyed his chances with the Democrats, particularly with those from the South, who were enraged by his equivocal stand on annexation. The Democratic convention threw him aside, and nominated James K. Polk, a champion of expansion. The platform caught the prevailing mood in its key resolution: "that the re-occupation of Oregon and the re-annexation of Texas at the earliest practicable period are great American measures." The words "*re*-occupation" and "*re*-annexation" were intended to imply that, in taking Oregon and Texas, the United States would only be confirming its claim to territories that had already belonged to it. By combining Oregon and Texas, the Democrats hoped to appeal to both Northern and Southern expansionists.

Too late Clay realized that he had muffed the expansion issue. In mid-campaign he announced that under certain circumstances he might be for the acquisition of Texas. His tardy straddling

# Part Two
# The Course of American Art

Once American independence was achieved, it became necessary to find an architectural style expressive of the ideals and achievements of the new republic. Most influential in determining this style was Thomas Jefferson, who saw in Classical Roman forms the appropriate mixture of monumentality with the concepts of justice and liberty connoted by Roman republican government. For the state capital at Richmond, Virginia (*Plate 1*), he chose as his model the Maison Carrée, a Roman temple at Nîmes, France. Jefferson's adaptations allowed for a complex interior, several stories, and windows, all of which were lacking in the model. The Virginia capital was the first public building in America

*Plate 1*
**State Capital, Richmond, Virginia.**

Thomas Jefferson. (Virginia Department of Conservation and Economic Development)

*Plate 2*
**The Octagon House.**
William Thornton. (Sandak)

to use the temple form and led to a long succession of buildings in this ancient style.

Among those influenced by Jefferson was another amateur, William Thornton, a physician whose classical design was chosen for the United States Capitol in 1793. But in his designs for private houses, such as the Octagon House in Washington, D.C. (*Plate 2*), Thornton combined classical motifs—limited to the colonnaded portico—with the red brick architecture found in contemporary English "Regency" buildings.

Though Jefferson and Thornton were amateurs, they were members of the American aristocracy, conscious of the ideological value of their designs. At the same time, there were many other un-tutored artists who chose to work on a more modest and intimate scale. Primitive watercolors, with their feeling of spontaneity and delicacy, were executed by anonymous folk artists, who learned their techniques from contemporary English instruction books. The subjects of these watercolors varied greatly, ranging from portraits to imaginative renderings of Biblical or Classical themes (e.g., "Venus Drawn by Doves," 1815, *Plate 3*). These primitive works marked the emergence of a new attitude toward art in America. No longer considered appropriate only for the wealthy, an art was developing produced by the people and for them.

During the early nineteenth century, a great number of immigrants from different parts of Europe began to settle in America, bringing new art to their new land. In spite of a growing sense of unity among the American people, strong regional differences continued to exist. Such groups as the Pennsylvania Dutch evolved their own distinctive crafts. Their pottery was especially important and featured stylized motifs of leaves, fruits, and flowers which had derived from the peasant art of their German homeland. Each potter gave his work a touch of originality, as did Benjamin Bergey in the dinner plate he created around 1830 (*Plate 4*).

*Plate 4*
**Dinner Plate**.

Benjamin Bergey. (Collection of the Philadelphia Museum of Art; Photo by A. J. Wyatt)

*Plate 3*
**"Venus Drawn by Doves."**

Anonymous. (Abby Aldrich Rockefeller Folk Art Collection)

Plate 5
**"Bargaining for Horses. "**
William S. Mount. (Courtesy of The New-York Historical
Society, New York City)

Between 1830 and the Civil War, a
new type of painting, stimulated by a
concern for the common man, rivaled the
established schools of landscape painting
in America. Whereas the Hudson Valley
landscape painters glorified the natural
environment, genre painting depicted
familiar scenes of daily life in a realistic
technique. These works were painted for
middle-class Americans who no longer
considered the portrait the only appropriate subject for painting. One of the
most able and popular genre painters
was William S. Mount. Living on Long
Island, he reproduced anecdotal scenes,

including "Bargaining for Horses,"
painted in 1835 (*Plate 5*). Mount combined technical skill—seen in such details as the horse's coat and the wooden
fence—with a quality of warmth and
humor.

Genre painting, while expressive of the
life of the common man, through the
warmth and innocence of its character-
ization also depicted the ideal American
life. One of the greatest genre painters
who chose to represent this ideal was
George Caleb Bingham. Born in Virginia,
Bingham moved with his family to the
Missouri frontier when he was eight.

There he was first trained by Chester Harding, a noted painter who was searching for Daniel Boone so that he could paint his portrait. Later, Bingham studied at the Pennsylvania Academy of Fine Arts where he became acquainted with the work of earlier American artists. In "The Verdict of the People," painted around 1854 (*Plate 6*), he portrayed with simple directness the drama of frontier democracy. The crowd is made up of carefully individualized figures, and the whole conveys a feeling of liveliness and joy.

The desire to glorify the American ideal continued to be an important theme in nineteenth-century American art. In 1876, a great exposition was set up at Philadelphia to commemorate the nation's founding 100 years earlier. The Philadelphia Centenial provided the impetus for a great many artists to express their patriotic fervor. Among them was Erastus Salisbury Field, a folk artist, who produced "The Historical Monument of the American Republic" (*Plate 7*). His work, though primitive in execution, was massive in conception, utilizing elabor-

*Plate 6*
**"The Verdict of the People."**

George Caleb Bingham. (Boatman's National Bank, St. Louis)

*Plate 7*

**"The Historical Monument of the American Republic."**

Erastus Salisbury Field. (Museum of Fine Arts, Springfield, Massachusetts)

*Plate 8*

**The New York Crystal Palace.**

Cartensen and Gildenmeister. (The Granger Collection)

*Plate 9*
**The Moorish Room, John D. Rockefeller House.**
Anonymous. (In The Brooklyn Museum Collection)

ate architectural forms on which were portrayed important episodes of our nation's history.

While genre painting and works by such artists as Field were, in a sense, fantasies, harking back to the traditions and pleasures of the past, other artists concerned themselves with expressing the excitement of contemporary American life. The Industrial Revolution, with its technological achievements, stimulated a great variety of inventive architectural designs. In 1853, the New York Crystal Palace (*Plate 8*), reflected these advances. Based on an English prototype, the building was constructed entirely of cast-iron ribs and glass, creating a large, unobstructed interior space which was used for exhibitions. In spite of the advanced construction, the architects felt compelled to coat the structure with Gothic details and to place Moorish minarets on the edges of the octagonal base.

For the Industrial Revolution, at the same time as it evoked pride in our nation's progress, also fostered a desire to escape from the sometimes harsh and unattractive realities of an increasingly mechanized world. By the end of the nineteenth-century, the vogue for "Turkish corners" testified to the intesity of this desire. Throughout the nation, homes of the middle class and wealthy featured an area filled with cushions, Oriental rugs, and overstuffed, fringed chairs. The Moorish Room of the John D. Rockefeller House (*Plate 9*) is only one of a great many such escapist "corners."

Only at the end of the century did there develop any real concern with accurately depicting American middle-class life. Naturalism, combining the older genre tradition with a scientific respect for reality, appeared in the works of Winslow Homer and Thomas Eakins. Eakins, in paintings such as the "Agnew Clinic" (*Plate 10*), goes beyond the anecdotal to minutely scrutinize with almost photographic realism, the details of the scene. Eakins' psychological insight, evident in his portrayal of individual character, communicates the uncompromising honesty of his approach. This combines with a strong feeling for drama, seen in the spotlighting of the figures in the foreground. Eakins offers a pictorial record of America in his period, much as Copley, the first exponent of the native, realistic tradition, had earlier achieved.

*Plate 10*
**"Agnew Clinic."**

Thomas Eakins. The School of Medicine, University of Pennsylvania)

## "Manifest Destiny" [1845]

The phrase "manifest destiny" was put into circulation by a Jacksonian journalist, John L. O'Sullivan (1813–1895), writing in the *Democratic Review*, of New York, in July 1845, and again in the New York *Morning News* in December of the same year. The essence of his idea is suggested by the following passages from his *Morning News* editorial:

*Texas has been absorbed into the Union in the inevitable fulfillment of the general law which is rolling our population westward; the con-nexion of which with that ratio of growth in population which is destined within a hundred years to swell our numbers to the enormous population of two hundred and fifty millions (if not more), is too evident to leave us in doubt of the manifest design of Providence in regard to the occupation of this continent. . . .*

*A population will soon be in actual occupation of California, over which it will be idle for Mexico to dream of dominion. They will neces-sarily become independent. All this without agency of our govern-ment, without responsibility of our people—in the natural flow of events, the spontaneous working of principles, and the adaptation of the tendencies and wants of the human race to the elemental circum-stances in the midst of which they find themselves placed.*

he was not so obscure as all that. Born in North Carolina, he had moved, when in his mid-twenties, to Tennessee, thus following the pattern of the man who became his political mentor, Andrew Jackson. Elected to the national House of Representatives, he held his seat for fourteen consecutive years, serving for four of them as speaker. He was thin, worn, even grim-looking, and his public manners comported with his appearance. But he had a good mind, he worked hard at his job, and above all he had an iron, implacable will. Probably no other President entered office with so clearly defined a program and accomplished so much of it as did Polk.

### Partitioning of Oregon

The ownership of Oregon was long in dispute, but its boundaries were clearly defined—on the north the latitude line of 54° 40', on the east the crest of the Rocky Mountains, on the south the 42nd parallel, and on the west the Pacific Ocean. Included in its half-million square miles were the present states of Oregon, Washington, and Idaho, parts of Montana and Wyoming, and half of British Columbia.

At various times in the past the Oregon country had been claimed by Spain, Russia, France, England, and the United States. By the 1820s only the last two nations remained in contention. The others had withdrawn and surrendered their rights to Britain or to the United States or to both. The American and British claims were equally valid—or invalid. Both countries could assert title on the basis of the activities of their explorers, maritime traders, and fur traders. The English had one solid advantage: they were in actual possession of a part of the area. In 1821 the powerful British fur trading organization, the Hudson's Bay Company, under the leadership of its factor, John McLoughlin, established a post at Fort Vancouver, north of the Columbia River.

Several times the English government proposed the Columbia as a suitable line of division. The United States, also showing a desire to compromise, countered by suggesting the 49th parallel. This difference in official views prevented a settlement of the Oregon question in the Treaty of 1818. Unable to agree on a demarcation line, the diplomats of the two powers negotiated a

probably cost him more votes than it gained. Polk carried the election by 170 electoral votes to 105, though his popular majority was less than 40,000. The Liberty party, running James G. Birney a second time, polled 62,000 votes (as compared with 7,000 in 1840), most of which were cast by Whigs who turned against Clay.

"Who is James K. Polk?" the Whigs had sarcastically asked during the campaign. Actually, compact whereby the citizens of each were to have equal access to Oregon for ten years. This arrangement, called joint occupation, was renewed in 1827 for an indefinite period, with either nation empowered to end it on a year's notice.

The first real American interest in Oregon came as a result of the activities of missionaries, notably Jason Lee, Marcus Whitman, and Father Pierre Jean de Smet. All the missionaries located their posts south of the Columbia River, mostly in the fertile Willamette Valley. They described their work in reports and letters that were published in influential religious journals and widely reprinted in secular newspapers. These reports dwelt as much on the rich soil and lovely climate of Oregon as on the spiritual condition of the Indians.

Beginning in 1841, thousands of pioneers set out for Oregon. Amazed observers remarked upon the "Oregon fever." Two thousand miles in length, the Oregon Trail penetrated Indian country and crossed mountains and semidesert regions. To the emigrants, traveling in caravans of covered wagons and accompanied by huge herds of cattle, it presented enormous problems in transportation. The average period required for the journey was from May to November. Some never lived to complete it. But the great majority got through. By 1845, 5,000 Americans were living south of the Columbia—and demanding that their government take possession of Oregon.

When Polk assumed office, though in his inaugural address he seemed to reassert American title to all of Oregon, he was in reality willing to compromise—to effect a division on the line of the 49th parallel. The British minister in Washington rejected Polk's offer without referring it to London.

Abruptly Polk took a more militant attitude. Saying America should look John Bull "straight in the eye" and hinting at war, he asserted claim to all of Oregon. In his annual message to Congress, in December 1845, he asked leave to give notice to England that joint occupation would end in a year. The United States, he said, would not permit further European colonization. This was a restatement of the Monroe Doctrine, which had been largely forgotten since 1823.

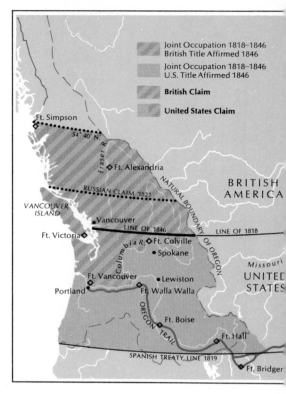

**American Expansion in Oregon**

Congress, with some Whigs dissenting, complied with the President's request.

Though there was loose talk of war on both sides of the Atlantic, neither nation really wished to resort to force. The British government now offered to divide Oregon at the 49th parallel—that is, to accept Polk's original proposal. The President affected to believe the offer should be rejected, but he was easily persuaded by his cabinet to submit it to the Senate for advice. Probably he was relieved to shift the responsibility for making a decision to the senators. They accepted the proposed agreement, and on June 15, 1846, a treaty was signed fixing the boundary at the 49th parallel. The United States had secured the larger and better part of the Oregon country and certainly all that it could have legitimately expected to get.

## Annexation of Texas

Southwest of the United States stretched the northern provinces of Mexico—Texas, New Mexico, and Upper California—once parts of

Spain's colonial empire in North America but, since 1822, states in the independent republic of Mexico. Under Spanish rule the provinces had been subject to only the lightest supervision from the government of the vice-royalty in Mexico, and only a few thousand white men had settled in them. The same conditions prevailed under the republic, which lacked the power and the population to govern and settle such distant areas. At one time the United States had advanced a claim to Texas as a part of the Louisiana Purchase, but had renounced the claim in 1819. Twice thereafter, however, in the Presidencies of John Quincy Adams and Jackson, the United States had offered to buy Texas, only to meet with indignant Mexican refusals.

The Mexican government invited the inevitable in Texas. In the early 1820s it encouraged American immigration by offering land grants to men like Stephen Austin who promised to colonize the land. Probably the motive of the government was to build up the economy of Texas, and hence its tax revenues, by increasing the population with foreigners, but the experiment was to result in the loss of Texas to the United States. Thousands of Americans, attracted by reports of the rich soil in Texas, took advantage of Mexico's welcome. The great majority, by the very fact of geography, came from the Southern states, sometimes bringing with them slaves, although slavery was forbidden in Mexico after 1829. By 1835 approximately 35,-000 Americans were living in Texas.

Almost from the beginning there was friction between the settlers and both the Mexicans and the Mexican government. Finally the Mexican government, realizing that its power over Texas was being challenged by the settlers, moved to exert control. A new law reduced the powers of the various states of the republic, a measure that the Texans took to be aimed specifically at them. In 1836 the Texans proclaimed their independence.

The Mexican dictator, Santa Anna, advanced into Texas with a large army. Even with the aid of volunteers, money, and supplies from private groups in the United States, the Texans were having difficulty in organizing a resistance. Their garrison at the Alamo mission in San Antonio was exterminated; another at Goliad suffered substantially the same fate when the Mexicans murdered most of the force after it surrendered. But General Sam Houston, emerging as the national hero of Texas, kept a small army together, and at the battle of San Jacinto (April 21, 1836, near present-day Houston) he defeated the Mexican army and took Santa Anna prisoner. Although the Mexican government refused to recognize the captured dictator's vague promises to withdraw Mexican authority from Texas, it made no further attempts to subdue the province. Texas had won its independence.

The new republic desired to join the United States and through its president, Sam Houston, asked for recognition, to be followed by annexation. Though President Andrew Jackson favored annexation, he proceeded cautiously.

Abolitionism was beginning to make its influence felt in politics. Many Northerners expressed a conviction that it would be immoral to extend the dominion of slavery. Others were opposed to incorporating a region that would add to Southern votes in Congress and in the electoral college. Jackson feared that annexation might cause an ugly sectional controversy and bring on a war with Mexico. He did not, therefore, propose annexation and did not even extend recognition to Texas until just before he left office in 1837. His successor, Van Buren, also refrained, for similar reasons, from pressing the issue.

Refused by the United States, Texas sought recognition, support, and money in Europe. Her leaders talked about creating a vast southwestern nation, stretching to the Pacific, which would be a rival to the United States. It was the kind of talk that Europe, particularly England, was charmed to hear. An independent Texas would be a counterbalance to the United States and a barrier to further American expansion; it would supply cotton for European industry and provide a market for European exports. England and France hastened to recognize Texas and to conclude trade treaties with her. The English government played with the idea of guaranteeing Texan independence. President Tyler, eager to increase Southern power, persuaded Texas to apply again, and Secretary of State Calhoun submitted an annexation treaty to the Senate in April 1844. Unfortunately for Texas, Calhoun

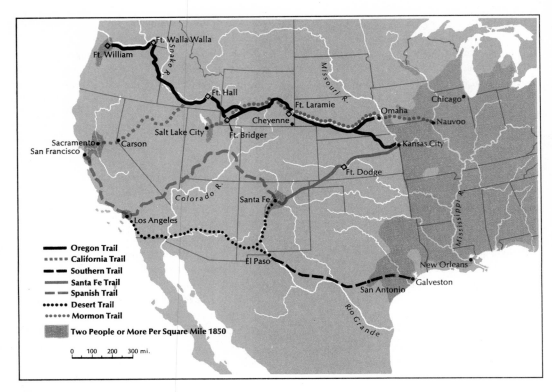

**Western Trails**

presented annexation as if its only purpose were to extend and protect slavery. The treaty was soundly defeated.

President Tyler, who remained in office until March 1845, viewed the election returns of 1844 as a mandate to carry annexation through. He proposed to Congress that Texas be annexed by a joint resolution of both houses, a device that would get around the necessity of obtaining a two-thirds majority in the Senate for a treaty. In February 1845, Congress voted to admit Texas to the Union. Conditions were affixed: Texas could be subdivided into not more than four additional states; it had to pay its own public debts but was to retain its public lands; and it had to submit to the United States any boundary disputes in which it became involved. After Polk's inauguration Texas accepted the conditions. It became a state in December 1845.

Promptly, the Mexican government broke diplomatic relations with the United States. To make matters worse, a dispute over Texas'

boundary with Mexico now developed. The Texans claimed that the Rio Grande constituted the western and southern border, an assertion that would place much of what is now New Mexico in Texas. Mexico, while not formally conceding the loss of Texas, replied that the border had always been the Nueces River. Polk recognized the Texan claim, and in the summer of 1845 he sent a small army under General Zachary Taylor to the Nueces line to protect Texas, he said, against the Mexicans.

## Lands Beyond Texas

New Mexico, another of Mexico's frontier provinces, supported a scanty population on a semi-primitive economy. Its small metropolis and trade center, Sante Fe, was 300 miles from the most northern settlements in Mexico. Under Spanish rule the New Mexicans had to export their few products over 1,000 miles to Mexico City and Vera Cruz and from these economic centers import their meager finished goods.

When Mexico became independent, she let it be known that traders from the United States would be welcome in New Mexico.

An American, William Becknell, wagoned a load of merchandise to Santa Fe in 1821 and sold it at a high profit. Out of his success arose the famous and colorful "Santa Fe trade." Every year traders with a stock of manufactured goods gathered at Independence, Missouri, and traveled in an organized caravan over the Sante Fe Trail, more than 800 miles long. The merchants brought back gold, silver, furs, and mules. The Santa Fe trade opened up another route to the West and pointed another direction for expansion.

Even more distant from Mexico City and even freer from Mexican supervision was the third of the northern provinces, California. In this vast, rich region lived perhaps 7,000 Mexicans, descendants of Spanish colonists, who engaged in agricultural pursuits, chiefly ranching, lived lives of primitive plenty, and carried on a skimpy trade with the outside world.

The first Americans to enter California were maritime traders and captains of the Pacific whaling ships, who stopped to barter goods or acquire supplies. Following them came merchants, who established stores, imported merchandise, and conducted a profitable trade with the Mexicans and Indians. Thomas O. Larkin, who set up business in Monterey in 1832, soon attained the status of a leading citizen. Although Larkin maintained close and friendly relations with the Mexican authorities, he secretly longed for the day when California would become an American possession. In 1844–1845 he accepted

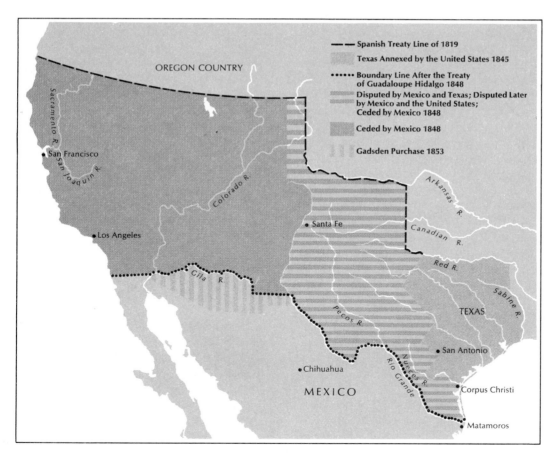

**American Expansion Into the Southwest**

an appointment as United States consul, with instructions to arouse sentiment among the Californians for annexation.

As reports spread of the rich soil and mild climate, immigrants began to enter California from the east by land. These were pioneering farmers, men of the type who were penetrating Texas and Oregon in search of greener pastures. By 1845 there were 700 Americans in California, most of them concentrated in the valley of the Sacramento River. The overlord of this region was John A. Sutter, once of Germany and Switzerland, who had moved to California in 1839 and had become a Mexican citizen. His headquarters at Sutter's Fort was the center of a magnificent domain where the owner ranched thousands of cattle and horses and maintained a network of small manufacturing shops to supply his armed retainers.

President Polk feared that Great Britain wanted to acquire or dominate California as well as Texas—a suspicion that was given credence by the activities of British diplomatic agents in the province. His dreams of expansion went beyond the Democratic platform. He was determined to acquire for his country New Mexico and California and possibly other parts of northern Mexico.

At the same time that he sent Taylor to the Nueces, Polk also sent secret instructions to the commander of the Pacific naval squadron to seize the California ports if he heard that Mexico had declared war. A little later Consul Larkin was informed that, if the people wanted to revolt and join the United States, they would be received as brethren. Still later an exploring expedition led by Captain John C. Frémont, of the army's corps of topographical engineers, entered California. The Mexican authorities, alarmed by the size of the party and its military aspects, ordered Frémont to leave. He complied, but moved only over the Oregon border.

After preparing measures that looked like war, Polk resolved on a last effort to achieve his objectives by diplomacy. He dispatched to Mexico a special minister, John Slidell, a Louisiana politician, with instructions to settle with American money all the questions in dispute between the two nations. If Mexico would acknowledge the Rio Grande boundary for Texas,

the United States would assume the damage claims, amounting to several millions, which Americans held against Mexico. If she would cede New Mexico, the United States would pay $5 million. And for California, the United States would pay up to $25 million. Slidell soon notified his government that his mission had failed. Immediately after receiving Slidell's information, on January 13, 1846, Polk ordered Taylor's army to move across the Nueces to the Rio Grande.

If Polk was hoping for trouble, he was disappointed for months. Finally, in May, he decided to ask Congress to declare war on the grounds that Mexico had refused to honor its financial obligations and had insulted the United States by rejecting the Slidell mission. While Polk was working on a war message, the news arrived from Taylor that Mexican troops had crossed the Rio Grande and attacked a unit of American soldiers. Polk now revised his message. He declared: "Mexico has passed the boundary of the United States . . . and shed American blood upon the American soil"—"war exists by the act of Mexico herself." Congress accepted Polk's interpretation of events and on May 13, 1846, declared war by votes of 40 to 2 in the Senate and 174 to 14 in the House.

Although Congress had accepted war with near-unanimity, there was more opposition than appeared on the surface. Opposition increased and intensified as the war continued and costs and casualties came home to the people. The Whigs in Congress supported the military appropriation bills, but they became ever bolder and more bitter in denouncing "Mr. Polk's war" as aggressive in origin and objectives.

## War With Mexico

In the opening phases of the war President Polk assumed the planning of grand strategy, a practice that he continued almost to the end of the war. His basic idea was to seize key areas on the Mexican frontier and then force the Mexicans to make peace on American terms. Accordingly, he ordered Taylor to cross the Rio Grande and occupy northeastern Mexico, taking as his first objective the city of Monterrey. Polk seems to have had a vague idea that from Monterrey Taylor could advance southward, if necessary, and menace Mexico City. Taylor, "Old Rough and

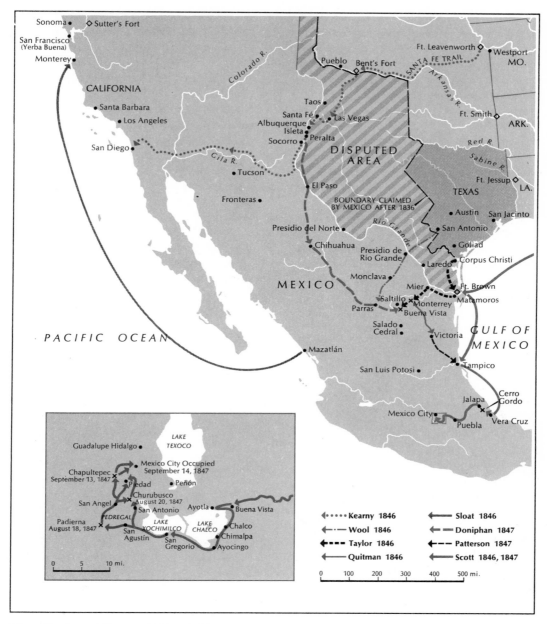

**The Mexican War    1846–1848**

Legend:
- ◄·····  Kearny 1846
- ◄—·—  Wool 1846
- ◄- - -  Taylor 1846
- ◄——  Quitman 1846
- ◄——  Sloat 1846
- ◄— —  Doniphan 1847
- ◄—-—  Patterson 1847
- ◄——  Scott 1846, 1847

Ready," beloved by his soldiers for his courage and easy informality but ignorant of many technical aspects of war, attacked Monterrey in September 1846. After a hard fight he captured it, but at the price of agreeing to let the garrison evacuate without pursuit. Although the country hailed Taylor as a hero, Polk concluded that he did not possess the ability to lead an offensive against Mexico City. Also, Polk began to realize that an advance south through the mountains would involve impossible problems of supply.

Two other offensives planned by Polk were aimed at New Mexico and California. In the summer of 1846 a small army under Colonel

Stephen W. Kearny made the long march to Santa Fe and occupied the town with no opposition. Kearny sent part of his army (Missouri volunteers under Colonel A. W. Doniphan) south to join Taylor, and disposed other parts to garrison the province. Then, acting under instructions from Polk, Kearny proceeded with a few hundred troopers to California to take charge of operations there. In California a combined revolt and war was being staged by the settlers, Frémont's exploring party, and the American navy. The settlers had proclaimed California an independent state in the "Bear Flag Revolution." Frémont had returned from Oregon to lead the rebels, and the navy had landed forces and annexed California to the United States. When Kearny arrived, the Americans were fighting under the direction of Commodore R. F. Stockton of the navy. With some

difficulty, Kearny brought the disparate American elements under his command, and by the autumn of 1846 completed the conquest of California.

In addition to northeastern Mexico, the United States now had possession of the two provinces for which it had gone to war. In a sense, the objectives of the war had been achieved. The only trouble was that Mexico refused to recognize realities; she would not agree to a peace and cede the desired territory. At this point Polk turned to General Scott, the commanding general of the army and its finest soldier, for help.

Together Polk and Scott devised a plan to force the Mexicans to accept peace. Scott would assemble at Tampico an army to be made up partly of troops from Taylor's army and partly of forces from other areas. The navy would

**Taylor at Buena Vista**

This sketch shows "Old Rough and Ready" as he appeared to his soldiers on the field and to the public at home, calm and unhurried in the shock of battle. (Culver)

transport this army down the coast to Vera Cruz, which would be seized and made into a base. From Vera Cruz, Scott would move west along the National Highway to Mexico City. Late in 1846 Scott went to Mexico to organize his forces. Taylor, who lost about half of his army to Scott, was instructed to stand on the defensive.

While Scott was assembling his army off the coast, General Santa Anna, the Mexican dictator, decided to take advantage of the division of American forces by marching northward and crushing Taylor and then returning to deal with Scott. With an army much larger than Taylor's, Santa Anna attacked the Americans at Buena Vista (February 1847). Santa Anna could not break the American line and had to return to defend Mexico City.

In the meantime Scott had taken Vera Cruz by siege and was moving inland, in one of the most brilliant campaigns in American military annals. With an army that never numbered more than 14,000, he advanced 260 miles into enemy territory, conserved the lives of his soldiers by using flanking movements instead of frontal assaults, and finally achieved his objective without losing a battle. At Cerro Gordo, in the mountains, he inflicted a smashing reverse on the Mexicans. He met no further resistance until he was within a few miles of Mexico City. After capturing the fortress of Chapultepec in a hard fight, the Americans occupied the enemy capital. A new Mexican government came into power, one that recognized the fact of defeat and that was willing to make a peace treaty.

Polk, in his growing anxiety to get the war finished, had sent with the invading army a presidential agent who was authorized to negotiate an agreement. On February 2, 1848, the agent concluded the Treaty of Guadalupe Hidalgo. Mexico agreed to cede California and New Mexico and to acknowledge the Rio Grande boundary of Texas. In return, the United States contracted to assume the claims of its citizens against Mexico and to pay $15 million to Mexico.

Some expansionists in the United States were demanding that the government hold out for the annexation of *all* Mexico. This permitted the antislavery leaders to charge that Southern slaveholders were running the government for their own ends. (Actually, some antislavery men, convinced that slavery could never thrive in Mexico, favored taking the whole country.) Polk acted quickly to silence the extremists on both sides. He submitted the treaty to the Senate, and by a vote of 38 to 14, it was approved.

## A NEW SECTIONAL CRISIS

The Mexican War, with the vast territory it yielded, led directly to the most serious threat of disunion yet to confront the United States.

### Settlers in the Far West

When the war ended, a portion of the territory acquired from Mexico was already settled by Americans who, oddly enough, had left their country because they were unhappy there. These people were adherents of a religious sect formally known as the "Church of Jesus Christ of Latter Day Saints" and more commonly known as Mormons. The Mormon faith, one of the numerous new religions that flowered in America in the 1820s and 1830s, had originated in western New York. The Mormons believed in a tightly knit and disciplined community life directed by the church elders. Seeking a more congenial environment, under the leadership of their prophet, Joseph Smith, they moved to Ohio, then to Missouri, and finally to Nauvoo, Illinois. Everywhere they met with resentment, largely caused by their economic and community organization. At Nauvoo they particularly outraged the opinions of their neighbors by introducing polygamy. Their troubles came to a climax when a mob lynched Smith.

Smith's successor, Brigham Young, now decided that if the Mormons were to escape further persecution they would have to move outside the United States. In 1846 almost the entire Mormon community left Nauvoo. Their destination, picked out by Young, was the Great Salt Lake basin in Utah, so arid that no other people would have the courage to live there. By 1850 over 11,000 people were settled in and around the Mormon metropolis of Salt Lake City. With the aid of irrigation they made the desert bloom. They established thriving home industries, and

**Mormon Leader**

Brigham Young was born in Vermont and grew up in western New York in an area known, because of the fiery religious revivals that swept across it, as the "burnt-over district." Here the Mormon faith originated, and here Young was converted to it. He quickly became a leader in the church and became its president on Smith's death in 1844. He led his people to Utah and on seeing the grim and forbidding Great Salt Lake basin, he exclaimed: "This is the place." (United Press International)

they built up a profitable trade with emigrants on the way to California.

In January 1848, gold was accidentally discovered in the Sacramento Valley in California. As word of the strike spread, inhabitants of California and the whole Far West, fired by hopes of becoming immediate millionaires, stampeded to the area to stake out claims. By the end of summer the news had reached the Eastern states and Europe. Then the gold rush really started. From the United States and all the world, thousands of "Forty-Niners" poured into California. Those who left from the older states could choose between three routes of travel: overland by covered wagon, inexpensive but involving a long journey over the Great Plains and across the Rockies; by ship around Cape Horn, quicker but more expensive; or the dangerous, difficult shortcut across the Isthmus of Panama. By all

three routes, disdaining hunger, thirst, disease, and even death, the seekers after gold came—more than 80,000 of them in 1849. By the end of that year, California had a population of approximately 100,000, more than enough to entitle her to statehood.

## Wartime and Postwar Politics

In domestic politics President Polk was as aggressive—and successful—as he was in foreign policy. At his insistence Congress reestablished the Independent Treasury system, thus pleasing all sections of the Democratic party and redeeming one of its platform promises. Again at his demand, Congress fulfilled another platform pledge by lowering the tariff. The Tariff of 1846 reduced the average rates enough to delight the South, but it could not have been passed without the votes of Northwestern Democrats.

Naturally, the Westerners expected something in return, and specifically they expected Southern support for internal improvements. Two internal improvements bills passed Congress, but Polk, who sincerely believed that the national government had no legal power to finance such projects, vetoed both of them. The Westerners were disappointed and angered. As in the case of Oregon, they thought that Polk was sacrificing their interests to those of the South.

Before Polk left office, a much more dangerous issue emerged. In August 1846, while the war was in progress, he had asked Congress to provide him with $2 million that he could use to purchase peace with Mexico. When the appropriation was introduced in the House, David Wilmot of Pennsylvania, an antislavery Democrat from a high-tariff state, moved an amendment that slavery should be prohibited in any territory secured from Mexico. The so-called Wilmot Proviso passed the House, but failed in the Senate. It would be called up again and be debated and voted on for years.

Diametrically opposed to the Wilmot Proviso was the formula of the Southern extremists. They contended that the states jointly owned the territories and that the citizens of each state possessed equal rights in them, including the right to move to them with their property, particularly slave property. According to this view,

Congress, which was the only agent for the joint owners, had no power to prohibit the movement of slavery into the public domain or to regulate it in any way except by extending protection. Neither could a territorial legislature, which was a creature of Congress, take any action to ban slavery.

Two compromise plans were presented. One, which numbered President Polk among its advocates, proposed to run the Missouri Compromise line of 36° 30′ through the new territories to the Pacific coast, banning slavery north of the line and permitting it south. The other, first prominently espoused by Lewis Cass, Democratic senator from Michigan, was originally called "squatter sovereignty." Later, when taken up by Stephen A. Douglas, an Illinois senator of the same party, it was given the more dignified title of "popular sovereignty." According to this formula, the question of slavery in each territory should be left to the people there, acting through the medium of their territorial legislature.

Congress and the country debated the various formulas, but at the end of Polk's administration a decision had still not been reached. No territorial government had been provided for California or New Mexico (New Mexico included most of present New Mexico and Arizona, all of Utah and Nevada, and parts of Colorado and Wyoming). Even the organization of Oregon, so far north that obviously slavery would never enter it, was held up by the controversy. Southern members of Congress, hoping to gain some advantage in the regions farther south, blocked a territorial bill for Oregon until August 1848, when a free-soil government was finally authorized.

The debate was partially stilled by the presidential campaign of 1848. Both the Democrats and the Whigs tried to avoid definite and provocative references to the slavery question. The Democrats nominated as their candidate Lewis Cass of Michigan, an elderly, honest, dull wheel horse of the party. Although the platform was purposely vague, it was capable of being interpreted as an endorsement of squatter sovereignty. The Whigs adopted no platform and presented as their candidate a military hero with no political record—General Zachary Taylor of Louisiana.

Ardent abolitionists and even moderates who merely opposed the expansion of slavery found it difficult to swallow either Cass or Taylor. The situation was ripe for the appearance of a third party. The potential sources for such a group were the existing Liberty party and the antislavery members of the old organizations. Late in the campaign, third-party promoters held a national convention, adopted a platform endorsing the Wilmot Proviso, free homesteads, and a higher tariff, and nominated former President Van Buren for the Presidency. Thus was launched the Free-Soil party.

Taylor won a narrow victory. Though Van Buren failed to carry a single state, he polled an impressive 291,000 votes, and the Free-Soilers elected ten members to Congress. It is probable that Van Buren pulled enough Democratic votes away from Cass, particularly in New York, to throw the election to Taylor.

## Taylor and the Territories

Zachary Taylor was the first man to be elected President with no previous political training or experience. He was also the first professional soldier to sit in the White House. Though a Southerner and a slaveholder, he had acquired a national outlook from his long years in the army.

Since Congress had failed to provide civil government for the area annexed from Mexico, those regions were being administered by military officials who were responsible to the President. The situation was unsatisfactory to everybody concerned with it. To President Taylor, statehood seemed to be the solution to California's problem and to the controversy over slavery in the territories. Let California and also New Mexico frame state constitutions and apply for admission to the Union. Once they had become states, nobody could deny their right to dispose of slavery as they wished. So Taylor directed military officials in the territories to expedite statehood movements.

California promptly ratified a constitution in which slavery was prohibited. When Congress assembled in December 1849, Taylor rather proudly described his efforts. He recommended that California be admitted as a free state and that New Mexico, when it was ready, be per-

**Washing for Gold**

These miners in a Western gold camp are engaging in placer mining. The gold found in the first strikes was located in the form of particles along stream beds. Prospec-tors separated the gold from sand or gravel by washing the deposit in a swirl of water. Washing was done in pans or boxes. From Samuel Bowles, *Our New West.*

mitted to come in with complete freedom to decide the status of slavery as it wished. But Congress was not about to accept the President's program.

Complicating the situation was the emergence of side issues generated by the conflict over slavery in the territories. One such issue concerned slavery in the District of Columbia. Antislavery people, charging that human servitude in the capital was a national disgrace, demanded that it be abolished there. Southerners angrily replied that the institution could not be touched without the consent of Maryland, which had originally donated the land, and that to abolish it would place a stigma on the entire South.

Another disturbing question concerned the rendition of fugitive slaves. Northern "personal liberty laws," forbidding courts and police officers to assist in the return of runaways, provoked Southerners to call for a new, more stringent *national* fugitive slave law.

A third issue related to the boundary between Texas and New Mexico. Texas claimed the portion of New Mexico east of the Rio Grande, although the national government during the Mexican War had assigned this region to New Mexico. To Texans it seemed that Washington was trying to steal part of their territory. They also resented the government's refusal to assume the Texas war debt. Southern extremists supported the pretensions of Texas, while Northerners, eager to cut down the size of a slave state, upheld New Mexico.

But the biggest obstacle in the way of the President's program was the South—angered and frightened by the possibility that two new free states would be added to the Northern majority. Only in the Senate did the South still maintain equality. The number of free and slave states was equal in 1849—fifteen of each. But now the admission of California would upset the balance, and New Mexico, Oregon, and Utah were yet to come.

Responsible Southern leaders declared that if California was to be admitted, and if slavery was to be prohibited in the territories, the time had come for the South to secede from the Union. At the suggestion of Mississippi, a call went out for a Southern-rights convention to meet in June 1850 at Nashville, Tennessee, to consider whether the South should resort to the ultimate act of secession. In the North excitement ran equally high. Every Northern state legislature but one adopted resolutions demanding that slavery be barred from the territories. Public meetings all through the free states called for the passage of the Wilmot Proviso and the abolition of slavery in the District of Columbia. Such was the crisis that confronted Congress and the country as the tense year of 1850 opened.

## The Compromise of 1850

Moderate men and lovers of the Union turned their thoughts, during the winter of 1849–1850, to the framing of a great congressional compromise that would satisfy both sections and restore tranquillity. The venerable statesman from Kentucky, Henry Clay, headed the forces of conciliation. To Clay's way of thinking, no compromise would have any lasting effect unless it settled all the issues in dispute between the sections. Accordingly, he took a number of separate measures, which had been proposed before, combined them into one set of resolutions, and on January 29, 1850, presented these to the Senate. He recommended (a) that California be admitted as a free state; (b) that, in the rest of the Mexican cession, territorial governments be formed without restrictions as to slavery; (c) that Texas yield in her boundary dispute with New Mexico and be compensated by the federal government's taking over her public debt; (d) that the slave trade, but not slavery itself, be abolished in the District of Columbia; and (e) that a new and more effective fugitive-slave law be passed.

These resolutions started a debate that raged for months in Congress and throughout the country. Clay himself opened the oratorical tournament with a defense of his measures and a plea to North and South to be mutually conciliatory and forebearing.

Early in March, Calhoun, who had less than a month to live, presented the views of the

Southern extremists. Too ill to speak, he sat grimly in his seat while a colleague read his speech. Almost ignoring Clay's proposals, he devoted his argument to what to him was the larger and the only subject—the minority South—and he asked more for his section than could be given. Because of Northern aggressions, the cords that bound the Union were snapping, he said. What would save the Union? The North must admit that the South possessed equal rights in the territories, must agree to observe the laws concerning fugitive slaves, must cease attacking slavery, and must accept an amendment to the Constitution guaranteeing a balance of power between the sections. The amendment he had in mind provided for the election of dual Presidents, one from the North and one from the South, each possessing a veto power. In short,

## An Extreme Southern View on Compromise in 1850

In his last speech Calhoun insisted that the North should either agree to everything that the South demanded as its rights or permit the minority section to depart the Union:

*It is time, Senators, that there should be an open and manly avowal on all sides, as to what is intended to be done. If the question is not now settled, it is uncertain whether it ever can hereafter be; and we, as the representatives of the States of this Union, regarded as governments, should come to a distinct understanding as to our respective views, in order to ascertain whether the great questions at issue can be settled or not. If you, who represent the stronger portion, cannot agree to settle them on the broad principle of justice and duty, say so; and let the States we both represent agree to separate and part in peace, tell us so; and we shall know what to do, when you reduce the question to submission or resistance. If you remain silent, you will compel us to infer by your acts what you intend.*

nothing would satisfy Calhoun except abject surrender by the North.

After Calhoun came the third of the elder statesmen, Webster. His "Seventh of March address" was probably the greatest forensic effort of his long oratorical career. Still nourishing White House ambitions, he now sought to calm angry passions and to rally Northern moderates to support Clay's compromise. The voice of the Northern extremists was the New York Whig William H. Seward, who maintained extremely cordial personal relations with President Taylor. There was a higher law than the Constitution, Seward proclaimed, the law of God, which required men to oppose slavery.

Popular sentiment in all sections was slowly swinging in favor of some kind of compromise. The country was entering upon a period of prosperity—the result of an expanding foreign trade, the flow of gold from California, and a boom in railroad construction—reminiscent of the flush days of the 1830s. Conservative economic interests everywhere wanted to terminate the sectional dispute and concentrate the attention of the nation upon internal expansion. Even in the South excitement seemed to be abating. The Nashville convention met in June, and after adopting some tame resolutions, adjourned to await final action by Congress.

For a time, however, it seemed that Congress was not going to act. One reason was the opposition of Taylor. The President persisted in his stand that the admission of California, and possibly New Mexico, must come first. After that, it might be possible to discuss other measures. In the meantime, if the South wanted to try anything like secession, "Old Zack" was ready to use force against his native section and to lead the armed forces in person.

On July 9, President Taylor suddenly died, the victim of a violent stomach disorder following an attack of heat prostration. He was succeeded by the Vice President, Millard Fillmore of New York. The new chief executive was a handsome, dignified man of no great abilities, but he was also a practical politician who understood the importance of give and take. He ranged himself on the side of the Compromise, using his powers of persuasion and patronage to swing Northern Whigs into line. Clay, exhausted

> ### An Extreme Northern View on Compromise in 1850
>
> William H. Seward, Senator from New York, expressed the feelings of those Northerners who refused to make any further concessions to the South in 1850:
>
> I AM OPPOSED TO ANY SUCH COMPROMISE, IN ANY AND ALL THE FORMS IN WHICH IT HAS BEEN PROPOSED. *Because, while admitting the purity and the patriotism of all from whom it is my misfortune to differ, I think all legislative compromises radically wrong and essentially vicious. They involve the surrender of the exercise of judgment and conscience on distinct and separate questions, at distinct and separate times, with the indispensable advantages it affords for ascertaining truth. They involve a relinquishment of the right to reconsider in future the decisions of the present, on questions prematurely anticipated. And they are a usurpation as to future questions of the province of future legislators.*

by his labors, temporarily left Congress, and Stephen A. Douglas took over the leadership of the Compromise forces. Douglas broke up Clay's "omnibus bill" into separate measures and presented them one by one. By mid-September, all had been enacted by both houses of Congress and signed by the President.

It was one thing to pass the Compromise through Congress and another to persuade the country to accept it. In the North the most objectionable of the measures was the Fugitive Slave Act. By this law, a Negro accused of being a runaway was denied trial by jury and the right to testify in his own behalf. His status was to be decided by a federal judge or by a special commissioner appointed by the federal circuit courts. He could be remanded to slavery on the bare evidence of an affidavit presented by the man who claimed to be his owner.

But the Fugitive Slave Act was the only part of the Compromise that most Southerners could approve. The adjourned session of the Nashville convention met in November 1850 (with only about a third of the original delegates present) and condemned the Compromise. Eventually, the South brought itself to accept the settlement, but only after much agonizing, and then only conditionally. Epitomizing the feelings of its people was the "Georgia Platform." This declared that Georgia would acquiesce in the Compromise—but if the North disregarded the Fugitive Slave Act, or attempted to abolish slavery in the District of Columbia, or denied admission to a state because it wished to have slavery, then Georgia would consider the compact broken and would protect its rights even to the length of seceding.

## AN UNEASY TRUCE

The Compromise of 1850 proved to be only a truce, and a short and uneasy one at that. During the next few years the sectional conflict continued to smolder. It was reflected in both domestic politics and foreign policy.

### Renewed Agitation

At their national convention in 1852 the Democrats adopted a platform pledging their unswerving devotion to the Compromise of 1850 and their united opposition to all attempts in any "shape or color" to renew the agitation of the slavery question. Not so unanimous when it came to choosing a candidate, they wrangled through forty-nine ballots, with no one of the leading contenders—Cass, Douglas, or James Buchanan of Pennsylvania—being able to secure a two-thirds majority. Finally, the prize went to one of the more obscure aspirants, a "dark horse," Franklin Pierce of New Hampshire. The Whigs likewise endorsed the Compromise but in much milder terms and over the opposition of many antislavery, or "Conscience," Whigs. Instead of nominating a man connected with and committed to the Compromise, they named, after fifty-three ballots, General Winfield Scott, whose views were unknown and whose support by Northern delegates made him suspect to Southerners even though he was a Virginian. He was to be the last Whig candidate. Only the Free-Soilers, with John P. Hale of New Hampshire as their candidate, repudiated the Compromise.

Probably because the Democrats had taken the strongest stand in favor of the Compromise, they won at the polls. When Franklin Pierce was inaugurated in 1853, he was, at the age of forty-nine, the youngest man up to that time to become President. Amiable and charming, he had been selected as the Democratic nominee largely for reasons of party harmony. In his short political career he had upheld few opinions and made few enemies. As President, he was dominated by the strong men of his cabinet, especially Secretary of State William L. Marcy of New York and Secretary of War Jefferson Davis of Mississippi.

The Compromise did not dissolve the abolitionist organizations nor stop their crusade to convince the Northern masses that slavery was a sin. In the 1850s the abolitionists found new allies and more effective media of expression. Several Free-Soilers now sat in Congress, and these men—such as Charles Sumner of Massachusetts in the Senate and Joshua R. Giddings of Ohio in the House—could denounce slavery from the vantage point of the national forum.

Northern hostility to the new Fugitive Slave Act was intensified when Southerners appeared in the Northern states to pursue fugitives or to claim as slaves Negroes who had been living for years in Northern communities. Mobs attempted to impede enforcement of the law. In 1851 a crowd in Boston took from a federal marshal a runaway named Shadrach and sent him on his way to Canada. Later in the same year at Syracuse, New York, there was a similar rescue of a slave named Jerry McHenry. In 1854 a Boston mob led by respectable and prominent men tried unsuccessfully to take Anthony Burns from the custody of federal officers.

These displays of violence alarmed the South, and so did the new personal-liberty laws passed by several Northern legislatures. The frank purpose of the statutes was to render the Fugitive Slave Act a nullity. They interposed state power

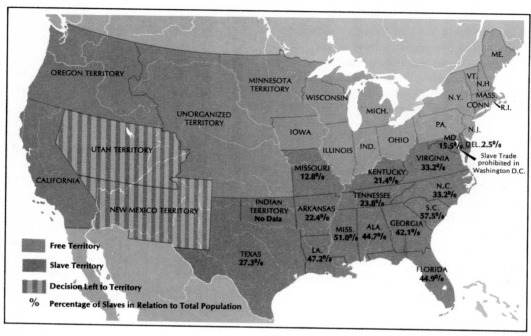

**Slave and Free Territory   1850**

between the accused fugitive and the federal authority. In Wisconsin and Massachusetts, state courts were instructed to issue writs of habeas corpus (requiring an appearance before a judge) against any person detaining a fugitive and to grant the fugitive a judicial hearing in which the burden of proof was placed on the pursuer. The supreme court of Wisconsin, in the case of *Ableman* v. *Booth* (1857), declared the national law void. When the Supreme Court of the nation decided against the state, the Wisconsin court ignored the decision. Thus legal and judicial barriers were being thrown in the way of the one provision of the Compromise that the South considered a positive victory, and Southerners were deeply angered.

## "Young America"

In Europe the great liberal and nationalist revolutions of 1848 were running their course, some succeeding, others petering out in failure. A vision of a republican Europe, with governments to be based on the model of the United States, stirred the American imagination. A group of Democrats started a "Young America" movement with vague ideas of aiding revolutionaries

abroad. These adventurous Democrats also aimed to promote American commerce in the Pacific and elsewhere and to extend the sweep of Manifest Destiny with new acquisitions in this hemisphere. Other politicians in both parties caught the "Young America" spirit, and it influenced the foreign policies of both the Fillmore and the Pierce administrations. At first these aggressive policies abroad were intended to offset the divisive, sectional feelings at home. Before long, however, the interest in additional territories complicated the relations between the sections as well as the relations between the United States and foreign governments.

The Whig Daniel Webster, secretary of state a second time, under Fillmore, saw a chance to play upon the national pride when the Austrian representative in Washington protested against the apparent readiness of the United States to recognize the independence of the Hungarians, who were revolting against Austrian rule. In reply, Webster dismissed the protest and added the gratuitous observation that, in comparison with the vast extent of the United States, the domain of Austria was "but as a patch on the earth's surface." And when (after the collapse of the Hungarian revolt) the rebel leader Louis Kossuth visited the United States, Webster joined in Kossuth's enthusiastic reception by speaking at a banquet in his honor.

Showing concern for Pacific commerce, the Fillmore administration sent out an expedition under Commodore Matthew C. Perry to open trade relations with Japan, which for two centuries had been a hermit nation. Perry touched at Japan in 1853 and reappeared there the following year with an impressive display of naval might. He obtained a treaty opening two ports and providing for the residence of an American consul in one of them. The first consul, Townsend Harris, after years of patient labor, secured a new treaty (1858) with additional trading rights.

The Fillmore administration was cautious about American schemes for taking Cuba, the rich "pearl of the Antilles," which Polk once had tried to purchase from Spain. Later a Venezuelan adventurer, General Narciso López, proposed to conquer the island with a force of American volunteers and present it to the United States. On his third attempt, in 1851, López landed in Cuba with about 400 men, mostly Americans, but ran into a much stronger army of Spaniards. They defeated and captured him and most of his followers, then executed him and more than fifty others. While a retaliating mob wrecked the Spanish consulate in New Orleans, the governments of Great Britain and France took alarm at the American filibustering. They proposed that the United States join them in a tripartite agreement guaranteeing Cuba to Spain. Edward Everett, Webster's successor as secretary of state, declined the proposal. He explained that his government could make no pledge never to acquire Cuba, since the island, so close by, was of immense strategic importance to the United States and someday "might be almost essential to our safety."

The Pierce administration, though more aggressive, was frustrated in its expansionist hopes because of sectional jealousies. Schemes to get new slave territories aroused opposition in the North, and the acquisition of lands unsuited to slavery was unpopular in the South. Though the kingdom of Hawaii agreed to join the United States (1854), the annexation treaty had no chance for Senate approval, since it contained a clause prohibiting slavery.

The old idea of adding Canada to the United States had never died out among Americans, and it was beginning to appeal to more and more Canadians. Some of them saw a union as the only way out of their economic difficulties. As a result of British free-trade policy (after 1846) and the American tariff, Canadians had lost much of their export trade. Annexation would open the American market to them. To deal with Canada's economic problem, and to settle a revived quarrel over American fishing rights along the Newfoundland and Labrador coasts, the British government sent Lord Elgin on a special mission to Washington in 1854. Lord Elgin and Secretary of State William L. Marcy negotiated a treaty specifying fishing rights and providing for tariff reciprocity. Canada was to accept certain American commodities, and the United States certain Canadian commodities, duty free. Thus Canadians, without annexation, would have access to American markets. The Elgin Treaty was promptly ratified. A Vermont senator explained that many of his fellow senators, those from the South, had been in a hurry to head off the union movement.

Central America had attracted attention for several years, ever since the California gold rush, when many gold-seekers crossed the isthmus on their way to the West Coast. With the rapid settlement of California, some Americans began to think of improving communications by constructing a canal somewhere across Central America. But Great Britain also had strong interests in that part of the world. A possible clash was averted by the Clayton-Bulwer Treaty (1850), in which Great Britain and the United States agreed that, if and when a canal were ever built, it would be a joint Anglo-American project.

New trouble with Britain in Central America arose from the filibustering activities of William Walker, the "gray-eyed man of destiny," an American of tremendous drive in a tiny body (he weighed just 100 pounds). With a band of American soldiers of fortune, most of them veterans of the war with Mexico, Walker made himself dictator of Nicaragua (1855) and had visions of heading a federation of Central American states. The British government, along with antislavery Americans, supposed that he was acting as an agent for President Pierce and was preparing the way for American annexation. This suspicion, though unfounded, seemed to be confirmed when Pierce recognized Walker's government. When Walker, after having been driven out of Nicaragua, attempted to return by way of Honduras, a British naval officer seized him and turned him over to the Honduran authorities. They disposed of him with a firing squad.

Meanwhile the Pierce administration had made all too clear its determination to obtain Cuba. In 1854 Secretary Marcy instructed the minister to Spain, Pierre Soulé of Louisiana, to make a new offer to buy the island. If this was refused he was to try to "detach" Cuba from Spain. Soulé was plotting with Spanish revolu-tionaries to overthrow the Spanish monarchy when he received new instructions: he was to consult with the ministers to England and France, James Buchanan and John Y. Mason. The three embodied their recommendations in a diplomatic dispatch that shortly found its way into the newspapers and became notorious as the Ostend Manifesto. This remarkable document stated that if Spain should persist in refusing to sell Cuba, and if disturbances there should threaten American security, the United States would be justified in "wresting" the island from Spain.

Antislavery Northerners now charged the administration with violating the spirit of the Compromise of 1850. They said that Pierce, acting as the tool of the South, was conspiring to bring in a new slave state even at the risk of war with Spain and other European powers.

### The Technique of Ostend

This anti-Democratic cartoon mocks the method proposed by James Buchanan and the other American ministers to acquire Cuba. A gang of thugs is threatening to use the same method on Buchanan. (New York Public Library)

# Selected Readings

**From Harrison to Polk** J. A. Green, *William Henry Harrison* (1941); O. P. Chitwood, *John Tyler* (1939); Robert Seager II, *And Tyler Too: A Biography of John and Julia Gardiner Tyler* (1963); O. D. Lambert, *Presidential Politics in the United States, 1841–1844* (1936); C. G. Sellers, *James K. Polk, Continentalist, 1843–1846* (1966).

**The Expansionist Urge** R. A. Billington, *The Far Western Frontier, 1830–1860°* (1956); N. A. Graebner, *Empire on the Pacific* (1955); A. K. Weinberg, *Manifest Destiny°* (1935); Frederick Merk, *Manifest Destiny and Mission in American History: A Reinterpretation* (1963) and, with L. B. Merk, *The Monroe Doctrine and American Expansion, 1843–1849* (1966); Bernard De Voto, *The Year of Decision, 1846°* (1943).

**Far Western Trade and Exploration** P. C. Phillips, *The Fur Trade* (2 vols., 1961); R. G. Cleland, *This Reckless Breed of Men: The Trappers and Fur Traders of the Southwest* (1950); G. G. Cline, *Exploring the Great Basin* (1963); Allan Nevins, *Frémont, Pathmarker of the West* (1955); Donald Jackson and M. L. Spence, eds., *The Expeditions of John Charles Frémont* (3 vols., 1970); R. L. Duffus, *The Santa Fe Trail* (1930).

**Texas** E. C. Barker, *Mexico and Texas, 1821–1835* (1928); W. C. Binkley, *The Texas Revolution* (1952); W. R. Hogan, *The Texas Republic* (1946); J. W. Schmitz, *Texan Statecraft, 1836–1845* (1945).

**Oregon and California** Francis Parkman, *The Oregon Trail°* (1849 and later editions); C. M. Drury, *Marcus Whitman, M.D., Pioneer and Martyr* (1937); W. J. Ghent, *The Road to Oregon* (1929); Jay Monaghan, *The Overland Trail* (1937); R. G. Cleland, *From Wilderness to Empire: A History of California, 1542–1900* (1944); R. W. Paul, *California Gold: The Beginning of Mining in the Far West°* (1947); J. W. Caughey, *Gold Is the Cornerstone* (1948).

**The Mormons** F. M. Brodie, *No Man Knows My History: The Life of Joseph Smith* (1945); Preston Nibley, *Brigham Young: The Man and His Work* (1936); Wallace Stegner, *The Gathering of Zion: The Story of the Mormon Trail* (1964); Nels Anderson, *Desert Saints: The Mormon Frontier in Utah°* (1942); N. F. Furniss, *The Mormon Conflict, 1850–1859* (1960).

**The Mexican War** J. S. Reeves, *American Diplomacy under Tyler and Polk* (1907); J. H. Smith, *The War with Mexico* (2 vols., 1919); A. H. Bill, *Rehearsal for Conflict: The War with Mexico, 1846–1848* (1947); O. A. Singletary, *The Mexican War°* (1960); Holman Hamilton, *Zachary Taylor, Soldier of the Republic* (1941); C. W. Elliott, *Winfield Scott* (1937).

**Crisis and Compromise** Holman Hamilton, *Prologue to Conflict: The Crisis and Compromise of 1850°* (1964) and *Zachary Taylor, Soldier in the White House* (1951); Allan Nevins, *Ordeal of the Union* (2 vols., 1947); R. H. Shryock, *Georgia and the Union in 1850* (1926); C. M. Wiltse, *John C. Calhoun, Sectionalist, 1840–1850* (1951); F. B. Woodford, *Lewis Cass* (1950); Clement Eaton, *Henry Clay and the Art of American Politics°* (1957); G. F. Milton, *The Eve of Conflict: Stephen A. Douglas and the Needless War* (1934); G. M. Capers, *Stephen A. Douglas, Defender of the Union* (1959); R. J. Rayback, *Millard Fillmore* (1959).

**Postwar Diplomacy** S. F. Bemis, ed., *American Secretaries of State*, vols. 5 and 6 (1928); A. A. Ettinger, *The Mission to Spain of Pierre Soulé* (1932); Basil Rauch, *American Interest in Cuba, 1848–1855* (1948); M. W. Williams, *Anglo-American Isthmian Diplomacy, 1815–1915* (1916); J. B. Brebner, *North Atlantic Triangle* (1945).

---

° Titles available in paperback.

# Chapter 14
# The Breaking
# of the Union

George Washington on leaving the Presidency had cautioned his fellow citizens that it might "disturb our Union" if political parties should ever be organized on a geographical basis—Eastern against Western or Northern against Southern—"whence designing men may endeavour to excite a belief that there is a real difference of local interests and views." He explained: "One of the expedients of party to acquire influence, within particular districts, is to misrepresent the opinions and aims of other districts."

From the beginning the parties had been national, not sectional. From the 1830s on, Whigs from North and South cooperated against Democrats from North and South. Partisan loyalties cut across geographical lines and served as bonds of union. So did denominational loyalties at a time when Northerners and Southerners belonged to the same national churches.

But bonds of union began to break. In the 1840s the Methodists and Baptists divided, because of the slavery question, into separate Northern and Southern organizations, and thereafter other churches were torn by sectional quarrels. Then, during the 1850s, the Whig party disintegrated. In the North it was replaced by a new party, the Republican, which had no members in the South. For a while the Democratic party continued to have a nationwide membership, but the party was weakened by sectional strains, and in 1860 it split into Northern and Southern wings. The time was at hand against which George Washington had warned.

No doubt some of the politicians of each section had misinterpreted the "opinions and aims" of the other. Still, the sectionalization of parties was due not merely to the influence of "designing men" but also to a "real difference of local interests and views." The breaking of the bonds of union and of the Union itself could hardly have occurred without real and substantial causes—the rise of opposition to slavery on moral grounds, the rapid industrialization of the North, the westward movement of population. The political disputes that led to national disruption centered on the question of future slavery in the West, not present slavery in the South, but that was largely due to the nature of the American Constitution. Opponents of slavery could hardly contend that the Constitution gave the federal government power to abolish it in the states where it already existed. These people did maintain—though defenders of slavery denied—that the federal government could, and should, prevent its spread to new territories.

---

**A Union Army Camp**

This photograph of an encampment of the Army of the Potomac gives an impression of the huge, sprawling expanse of a Civil War army at rest—the array of tents, artillery, and wagons. This particular camp occupied a space of 20 square miles. (Top left, Library of Congress)

**A Recruiting Poster for Negro Soldiers**

This poster was typical of many put out by organizations in the North to induce Negroes to join the Union armies. Negro units were nearly always commanded by white officers. (Bottom left, Library of Congress)

## NEW TERRITORIAL CONTROVERSY

By the 1850s the line of frontier settlement had reached the great bend of the Missouri. Beyond the western boundaries of Minnesota, Iowa, and Missouri stretched the vast expanse of plains earlier called the Great American Desert and designated as an Indian reserve. Now it was known that large sections of this region were suited to farming, and in the Northwest people were saying that the national government should open the area to settlement, provide it with territorial government, and remove the Indians. The problem of communication between the older states and the trans-Mississippi West had become urgent.

### The Kansas-Nebraska Act

The idea of a transcontinental railroad had been discussed in and out of Congress for years. Disagreement arose when people talked about the eastern terminus of the road and its specific route. Several cities pressed their claims, but the leading contenders were Chicago, St. Louis, Memphis, and New Orleans. The transcontinental railroad, like nearly everything else in the fifties, became entangled in sectionalism. It became a prize that the North and South struggled to secure.

One argument against a southern route had been removed through the foresight of Secretary of War Jefferson Davis. Surveys had indicated that a road from a southern terminus would probably have to pass through an area south of the Gila River, in Mexican territory. At Davis' suggestion, Pierce appointed James Gadsden, a Southern railroad builder, to negotiate with Mexico for the sale of this region. Gadsden persuaded the Mexican government to dispose of a strip of land that today comprises a part of Arizona and New Mexico, the so-called Gadsden Purchase (1853), which cost the United States $10 million.

Particularly interested in a transcontinental railroad was Senator Stephen A. Douglas, and his interest influenced him to introduce in Congress a fateful legislative act, one that accomplished the final destruction of the Compromise of 1850. As a senator from Illinois and a resident

of Chicago and, above all, as the acknowledged leader of the Northwestern Democrats, Douglas naturally wanted the transcontinental railroad for his own city and section. He realized too the potency of the principal argument urged against the northern route: that west of the Mississippi it would run largely through unsettled Indian country. In January 1854, as chairman of the Committee on Territories, he acted to forestall this argument. He introduced a bill to organize a huge new territory, to be known as Nebraska, west of Iowa and Missouri.

Douglas seemed to realize that his bill would encounter the opposition of the South, partly because it would prepare the way for a new free state, the proposed territory being in the Louisiana Purchase area north of the 36° 30' line of the Missouri Compromise and hence closed to slavery. In an effort to make the measure acceptable to Southerners, Douglas inserted a provision that the status of slavery in the territory would be determined by the territorial legislature, that is, according to popular sovereignty. Theoretically at least, this would open the region to slavery. The concession was not enough to satisfy extreme Southern Democrats, particularly those from Missouri who feared that their state would be surrounded by free territory. They demanded more, and Douglas had to give more to get their support. He agreed to two additions to his bill: a clause specifically repealing the antislavery provision of the Missouri Compromise, and another creating two territories, Nebraska and Kansas, instead of one. Presumably Kansas would become a slave state. In its final form the measure was known as the Kansas-Nebraska Act.

Douglas induced President Pierce to endorse his bill, and so it became an official Democratic measure. But even with the backing of the administration, it encountered stiff opposition and did not become a law until May 1854. Nearly all the Southern members of Congress, whether Whigs or Democrats, supported the bill, and nearly all the Northern Whigs opposed it. The Northern Democrats split, with half of their votes in the House going for the act and half against it.

Of greater importance than the opposition to the Kansas-Nebraska Act in Congress was the reaction against it in the Northern states. The whole North seemed to blaze with fury at this latest demonstration of the power of the slavocracy, and much of the fury was directed at Douglas, who, in the eyes of many Northerners, had acted as a tool of the slaveholders. No other piece of legislation in congressional history produced as many immediate, sweeping, and ominous changes as the Kansas-Nebraska Act. It destroyed the Whig party in the South except in the border states. At the same time, as many Southern Whigs became Democrats, it increased Southern influence in the Democratic party. It destroyed the popular basis of Whiggery in the North, with the result that by 1856 the national Whig party had disappeared and a conservative influence in American politics had been removed. It divided the Northern Democrats and drove many of them from the party. Most important of all, it called into being a new party that was frankly sectional in composition and creed.

Men in both the major parties who opposed Douglas' bill took to calling themselves Anti-Nebraska Democrats and Anti-Nebraska Whigs. In 1854 these men formed a new party and began to call themselves "Republicans." Originating in a series of spontaneous popular meetings throughout the Northwest, the Republican movement soon spread to the East. In the elections of 1854 the Republicans, often acting in concert with the Know-Nothings, elected a majority to the House and won control of a number of Northern state governments. For the moment the new party was a one-idea organization: its only platform was opposition to the expansion of slavery into the territories. Composed mainly of former Whigs and Free-Soilers but also including a substantial number of former Democrats, it represented in large part the democratic idealism of the North. But it contained, in addition, Northern power groups who felt that the South—the champion of a low tariff, the enemy of homesteads and internal improvements—was blocking their legitimate economic aspirations.

## "Bleeding Kansas"

The pulsing popular excitement aroused in the North by the Kansas-Nebraska Act was sustained by events occurring during the next two years in Kansas. Almost immediately settlers moved into this territory. Some went as dedicated men who were determined to make Kansas free—or slave. Those from the North were encouraged by press and pulpit and the powerful organs of abolitionist propaganda. Often they received financial help from organizations like the New England Emigrant Aid Company, which had been created to render such assistance. Those from the South often received financial contributions from the communities they left.

In the spring of 1855 elections were held for a territorial legislature. Thousands of Missourians, some traveling in armed bands, moved into Kansas and voted. Although there were probably only some 1,500 legal votes in the territory, over 6,000 votes were counted. With such conditions prevailing, the proslavery forces elected a majority to the legislature, which proceeded immediately to enact a series of laws legalizing slavery. The outraged free-staters, convinced that they could not get a fair deal from the Pierce administration, resolved on extralegal action. Without asking permission from Congress or the territorial governor, they elected delegates to a constitutional convention which met at Topeka and adopted a constitution excluding slavery. They then chose a governor and legislature, and petitioned Congress for statehood. Pierce stigmatized their movement as unlawful and akin to treason. The full weight of the government, he announced, would be thrown behind the proslavery territorial legislature.

A few months later a proslavery federal marshal assembled a huge posse, consisting mostly of Missourians, to arrest the free-state leaders in Lawrence. The posse not only made the arrests but sacked the town. Retribution came immediately. Among the more extreme antislavery men was a fierce, fanatical old man named John Brown who considered himself an instrument of God's will to destroy slavery. Estimating that five antislavery men had been murdered, he decided that it was his sacred duty to take revenge. He gathered six followers, and in one night murdered five proslavery settlers (the "Pottawatomie massacre"). The result was to touch off civil war in Kansas—irregular, guerrilla war conducted by armed bands, some of them more interested in land claims or loot than in ideologies.

People in the North and the South believed (and whether or not their beliefs were completely correct is historically unimportant) that the aggressive designs of the other section were epitomized by what was happening in Kansas. Thus "Bleeding Kansas" became a symbol of the sectional controversy.

In May 1856 Charles Sumner of Massachusetts arose in the Senate to discuss affairs in the strife-torn territory. He entitled his speech "The Crime against Kansas." Handsome, humorless, sincere, doctrinaire, Sumner embodied the extreme element of the political antislavery movement. In his address he fiercely denounced the Pierce administration, the South, and slavery; and he singled out for particular attention as a champion of slavery Senator Andrew P. Butler of South Carolina. It was an age when orators were wont to indulge freely in personal invec-

tive, but in his allusions to Butler and others, Sumner went farther than most.

Particularly enraged by the attack was Butler's nephew, Preston Brooks, a member of the House from South Carolina. He resolved to punish Sumner by a method approved by the Southern code—by publicly and physically chastising him. Approaching him at his desk when the Senate was not in session, Brooks proceeded to beat him with a cane until Sumner fell to the floor in bloody unconsciousness. The injured senator stayed out of the Senate four years, and during his absence his state refused to elect a successor. Brooks, censured by the House, resigned and stood for reelection. He was returned by an almost unanimous vote.

The violence in Congress, like that in Kansas, was a symbol. It showed that Americans were becoming so agitated by their differences that they could not settle them by the normal political processes of debate and the ballot.

**Violence in Congress**

This print from a Northern source shows Preston Brooks attacking Charles Sumner. The laughing onlookers are Southern senators, some of whom did admit that they approved Brooks' action. (Culver)

## Buchanan and Depression.

The presidential campaign of 1856 got under way with the country convulsed by the Brooks assault and the continuing violence in Kansas. The Democrats adopted a platform that endorsed the Kansas-Nebraska Act and defended popular sovereignty. The leaders wanted a candidate who had not made many enemies and who was not closely associated with the explosive question of "Bleeding Kansas." So the nomination went to James Buchanan of Pennsylvania, a reliable party stalwart who as minister to England had been safely out of the country during the recent troubles, though he was a signer of the highly controversial Ostend Manifesto.

The Republicans, engaging in their first presidential contest, faced the campaign with confidence. They denounced the Kansas-Nebraska Act and the expansion of slavery but also approved a program of internal improvements, thus beginning to combine the idealism of antislavery with the economic aspirations of the North. Just as eager as the Democrats to present a safe candidate, the Republicans nominated John C. Frémont, who had made a national reputation as an explorer of the Far West. Although a sincere Republican, the glamorous "Pathfinder" was selected because he had no political record and hence was highly available.

The Native American or Know-Nothing party was beginning to break apart on the inevitable rock of sectionalism. At its convention, many Northern delegates withdrew because the platform was not sufficiently firm in opposing the expansion of slavery. The remaining delegates nominated former President Millard Fillmore. His candidacy was endorsed by the sad remnant of another party, the few remaining Whigs who could not bring themselves to support either Buchanan or Frémont.

The campaign was the most exciting since 1840. Its frenzied enthusiasm was due largely to the Republicans. They shouted for "Free Soil, Free Speech, Free Men, and Frémont," depicted "Bleeding Kansas" as a sacrifice to the evil ambitions of the slavocracy, and charged that the South, using Northern dupes like Buchanan as its tools, was plotting to extend slavery into every part of the country.

The returns seemed to indicate that the prevailing mood of the country was conservative. Buchanan, the winning candidate, polled 1,838,000 popular votes to 1,341,000 for Frémont, and 874,000 for Fillmore. A slight shift of votes in Pennsylvania and Illinois would have thrown those states into the Republican column and elected Frémont.

James Buchanan had been in public office almost continuously since the age of twenty-three. Nearly sixty-six at the time of his inauguration he was, except for William Henry Harrison, the oldest President ever to take office. Undoubtedly his age and his physical infirmities had much to do with the indecision he was often to display.

In the year Buchanan took over, a financial panic struck the country, followed by several years of stringent depression. Europe had shown an unusual demand for American food during the Crimean War (1854–1856) and when the demand fell off, agricultural prices were seriously depressed. The depression sharpened sectional differences. The South was not hit as hard as the North. Southern leaders now found confirmation for their claim that their economic system was superior to that of the free states. Smarting under previous Northern criticisms of Southern society, they loudly boasted of their superiority to the North.

In the North the depression strengthened the Republican party and weakened the Democratic. Distressed economic groups—manufacturers and farmers—came to believe that the hard times had been caused by unsound policies of Southern-controlled Democratic administrations. These groups thought that prosperity could be restored by a high tariff (the tariff was lowered again in 1857), a homestead act, and internal improvements—all measures to which the South was opposed. In short, the frustrated economic interests of the North were being drawn into an alliance with the antislavery elements as represented by the Republican party.

## The Dred Scott Case

The Supreme Court of the United States projected itself into the sectional controversy with its decision in the case of *Dred Scott* v. *Sanford,* handed down two days after Buchanan was inaugurated.

Dred Scott was a Missouri slave, once the property of an army surgeon who on his military pilgrimages had carried him to Illinois, a free state, and to Minnesota Territory, where slavery was forbidden by the Missouri Compromise. Scott was persuaded by some abolitionists to bring suit in the Missouri courts for his freedom on the ground that residence in a free territory had made him a free man. The state supreme court decided against him. Meanwhile, the surgeon having died and his widow having married an abolitionist, ownership of Scott was transferred to her brother, J. F. A. Sanford, who lived in New York. Now Scott's lawyers could get the case into the federal courts on the ground that the suit lay between citizens of different states. Regardless of the final decision, Scott would be freed, as his abolitionist owners would not keep him a slave. The case was intended to secure a federal decision on the status of slavery in the territories.

Of the nine justices, seven were Democrats (five of them from the South), one was a Whig, and one was a Republican. Chief Justice Taney, in the majority opinion, declared that Scott was not a citizen of Missouri and hence could not bring a suit in the federal courts. According to Taney, no Negro could qualify as a citizen. So far as the Constitution was concerned, he added, Negroes had no rights that white men were bound to respect. Having said this, Taney could simply have declined jurisdiction over the case. Instead, he went on to argue that Scott's sojourn in Minnesota had not affected his status as a slave. Slaves were property, said Taney, and the Fifth Amendment prohibited Congress from taking property without "due process of law." Consequently, Congress possessed no authority to pass a law depriving persons of their slave property in the territories. The Missouri Compromise, therefore, had always been null and void.

Few judicial opinions have stirred as much popular excitement as this one did. Southern whites were elated: the highest tribunal in the land had invested with legal sanction the extreme Southern argument. On behalf of abolitionists black and white, Frederick Douglass

declared: "This very attempt to blot out forever the hopes of an enslaved people may be one necessary link in the chain of events preparatory to the complete overthrow of the whole slave system." Republicans denounced the decision. They said it deserved as much consideration as any pronouncement by a group of political hacks. They threatened that when they secured control of the national government, they would reverse the decision—by altering the personnel of the Court and "packing" it with new members.

## Deadlock Over Kansas

Endorsing the decision, President Buchanan concluded that the best solution for the Kansas troubles was to force the admission of that territory as a slave state. The existing proslavery territorial legislature called an election for delegates to a constitutional convention. The free-state people refused to participate. As a result, the proslavery forces won control of the convention, which met in 1857 at Lecompton and framed a constitution establishing slavery. When an election for a new territorial legislature was called, the antislavery groups turned out to vote and won a majority. Promptly the legislature moved to submit the Lecompton constitution to the voters. The document was rejected by more than 10,000 votes.

Although both sides had resorted to fraud and violence, the Kansas picture was clear enough. The majority of the people did not want to see slavery established. Unfortunately Buchanan could not see, or did not want to see, the true picture. He urged Congress to admit Kansas under the Lecompton constitution, and he tried to force the party to back his proposal. Stephen A. Douglas and other Western Democrats refused to accept this perversion of popular sovereignty. Openly breaking with the administration, Douglas denounced the Lecompton proposition. And although Buchanan's plan passed the Senate, Western Democrats helped to block it in the House. Partly to avert further division in the party, a compromise measure, the English bill, was now offered (1858) and passed. It provided that the Lecompton constitution should be submitted to the people of Kansas for the third time. If the document was approved,

Kansas was to be admitted and given a federal land grant; if it was disapproved, statehood would be postponed until the population reached 93,600, the legal ratio for a representative in Congress. Again, and for the last time, the Kansas voters decisively rejected the Lecompton constitution. Not until the closing months of Buchanan's administration, in 1861, when a number of Southern states had withdrawn from the Union, would Kansas enter the Union—as a free state.

## Lincoln Against Douglas

The congressional elections of 1858 were of greater interest and importance than is usually true of such mid-term contests. Not only did they have an immediate and powerful influence on the course of the sectional controversy, but they projected into the national spotlight the man who was to be the dominating figure in the tragic years just ahead.

The widest public attention was attracted by the senatorial election in Illinois. There Stephen A. Douglas, the most prominent Northern Democrat, was a candidate for reelection, and

he was fighting for his political life. Since Douglas, or his successor, would be chosen by a legislature that was yet to be elected, the control of that body became a matter of paramount importance. To punish Douglas for his resistance to the Lecompton constitution, the Buchanan administration entered Democratic candidates opposed to him in many legislative districts. But Douglas' greatest worry was that he faced Abraham Lincoln, the ablest campaigner in the Republican party.

Lincoln had been the leading Whig in Illinois. He was now the leading Republican in the state, though hardly a national figure—his reputation could not compare with that of the famous Douglas. Lincoln challenged the senator to a series of seven joint debates. Douglas accepted, and the two candidates argued their cases before huge crowds. The Lincoln-Douglas debates were widely reported by the nation's press, and before their termination the Republican who had dared to challenge the "Little Giant" of the Democracy was a man of national prominence.

Douglas, while defending popular sovereignty, accused the Republicans of promoting

### Lincoln and Douglas in Debate

This is a depiction by a later artist, R. M. Root, of the debate between Lincoln and Douglas at Charleston. Lincoln, who was beardless until 1861, is speaking, and Douglas sits at his right. Various dignitaries of both parties are on the platform. The man behind Lincoln and to the left taking notes is probably a reporter. In the 1850s speeches were frequently recorded by men known as "stenographic reporters." They used a system of shorthand devised by Isaac Pitman and described by him in a book published in 1837, *Stenographic Sound Hand.* (Illinois State Historical Library) a war of sections, of wishing to interfere with slavery in the South, and of advocating social equality of the races. Lincoln, denying these charges (which were untrue), accused the Democrats and Douglas of conspiring to extend slavery into the territories and possibly, by means of another Supreme Court decision, into the free states as well (a charge which also was untrue). Lincoln was particularly effective in making it appear that Douglas did not regard slavery as morally wrong. He quoted Douglas as saying he did not care whether slavery was "voted up, or voted down."

Lincoln was opposed to slavery—on moral, political, and economic grounds. He believed that it contradicted the American ideal of democracy. Let the idea be established that Negroes were not created with an equal right to earn their bread, he said, and the next step would be to deny the right to certain groups of whites, such as day laborers. His solicitude for the economic well-being of the white masses impelled Lincoln to oppose the introduction of slavery into the territories. He maintained that the national lands should be preserved as places for poor white people to go to better their condition.

Yet Lincoln was opposed to the abolitionists. The physical fact of slavery, he believed, must be taken into account. "We have a due regard to the actual presence of it amongst us and the difficulties of getting rid of it in any satisfactory way and all the constitutional obligations thrown about it." He and his party would "arrest the further spread of it," that is, prevent its expansion into the territories, and thus prepare for its "ultimate extinction." His plan, then, was to pen up slavery in the South, where he hoped it would eventually die a natural death.

In the debate at Freeport, Lincoln asked Douglas: Can the people of a territory exclude slavery from its limits prior to the formation of a state constitution? Or in other words, is popular sovereignty still a legal formula despite the Dred Scott decision? The question was a deadly trap, for no matter how Douglas answered it, he would lose something. If he disavowed popular sovereignty he would undoubtedly be defeated for reelection and his political career would be ended. But if he reaffirmed his formula, Southern

Democrats would be offended, the party split deepened, and his chances of securing the Democratic nomination in 1860 damaged if not destroyed.

Boldly Douglas met the issue. The people of a territory, he said, could, by lawful means, shut out slavery prior to the formation of a state constitution. Slavery could not exist a day without the support of "local police regulations": territorial laws recognizing the right of slave ownership. The mere failure of a legislature to enact such laws would have the practical effect of keeping slaveholders out. Thus, despite the Dred Scott decision, a territory could exclude slavery. Douglas' reply became known as the Freeport Doctrine or, in the South, as the Freeport Heresy. It satisfied his followers sufficiently to win him a return to the Senate, but throughout the North it aroused little enthusiasm.

The elections went heavily against the Democrats, who lost ground in almost every Northern state. The administration retained control of the Senate but lost its majority in the House, where the Republicans gained a plurality. In the holdover or short session of 1858–1859, in which the Democrats were in the majority, and in the regular session of 1859 (elected in 1858), every demand of the Republicans and Northern Democrats was blocked by Southern votes or by presidential vetoes. These defeated measures included a tariff increase, a homestead bill, a Pacific railroad, and federal land grants to states for the endowment of agricultural colleges. The 1859 session was also marked by an uproarious struggle over the election of a speaker of the House.

## THE SEPARATION OF THE SECTIONS

During the 1850s the nation seemed at first to drift and then to rush toward disunion. The fateful goal was reached during the winter of 1860–1861. Thereafter, for more than four years, Americans were divided into what, in effect, amounted to two separate and hostile countries.

## John Brown's Raid

Hastening the trend toward disunion was a grim event of 1859. John Brown, the antislavery fanatic from Kansas, now made a spectacular appearance on the national scene. Still convinced that he was God's instrument to destroy slavery, he decided to transfer his activities from Kansas to the South itself. With encouragement and financial aid from some Eastern abolitionists, he devised a wild scheme for putting an end to slavery. His plan was to seize a mountain fortress in Virginia from which he could make raids to liberate slaves. He would arm the freedmen, set up a Negro republic, and eventually force the South to concede emancipation. He was out to lead a slave insurrection. Because he needed guns, he chose Harpers Ferry, where a United States arsenal was located, as his base of operations. In October, at the head of eighteen followers, he descended on the town and captured the arsenal. Almost immediately he was attacked by citizens and local militia companies, who were shortly reinforced by a detachment of United States marines sent to the scene by the national government. With ten of his men killed, Brown had to surrender. He was promptly tried in a Virginia court for treason against the state, found guilty, and sentenced to death by hanging. Six of his followers met a similar fate.

Probably no other event had so much influence as the Brown raid in convincing Southerners that their section was unsafe in the Union. Despite all their eulogies of slavery, one great fear always secretly gnawed at their hearts: the possibility of a general slave insurrection. Southerners now jumped to the conclusion that the Republicans were responsible for

### The Hanging of John Brown

This print from a New York weekly magazine shows with essential accuracy the scene of Brown's death. The troops were Virginia militia who were present to prevent a feared attempt to rescue Brown. Curiously, one of the soldiers was John Wilkes Booth, who later would assassinate Abraham Lincoln. (Library of Congress)

Brown. This was, of course, untrue; prominent Republicans like Lincoln and Seward condemned Brown as a criminal. But Southerners were more impressed by the words of such abolitionists as Wendell Phillips and Ralph Waldo Emerson, who now glorified Brown as a new saint. His execution made him a martyr to thousands of Northerners.

## Election of Lincoln

The election of 1860, judged by its consequences, was the most momentous in our history.

As the Democrats gathered in convention at Charleston, South Carolina, in April, most of the Southern delegates came with the determination to adopt a platform providing for federal protection of slavery in the territories: that is, an official endorsement of the principles of the Dred Scott decision. The Western Democrats, arriving with bitter recollections of how Southern influence had blocked their legislative demands in the recent Congress, were angered at the rule-or-ruin attitude of the Southerners. The Westerners hoped, however, to negotiate a face-saving statement on slavery so as to hold the party together. They vaguely endorsed popular sovereignty and proposed that all questions involving slavery in the territories be left up to the Supreme Court. When the convention adopted the Western platform, the delegations from eight lower South states withdrew from the hall. The remaining delegates then proceeded to the selection of a candidate. Stephen A. Douglas led on every ballot, but he could not muster the two-thirds majority (of the original number of delegates) required by party rules. Finally the managers adjourned the convention to meet again in Baltimore in June. At the Baltimore session, most of the Southerners reappeared, only to walk out again. The rest of the Southerners had assembled at Richmond. The rump convention at Baltimore nominated Douglas. The Southern bolters at Baltimore and the men in Richmond nominated John C. Breckinridge of Kentucky.

Sectionalism had at last divided the historic Democratic party. There were now two Democratic candidates in the field, and, although Douglas had supporters in the South and Breck-

inridge in the North, one was the nominee of the Northern Democrats and the other of the Southern Democrats.

The Republicans held their convention in Chicago in May. Although the divisions developing in the Democratic ranks seemed to spell a Republican triumph, the party managers were taking no chances on a slip-up. They were determined that the party, in both its platform and its candidate, should appear to the voters as representing conservatism, stability, and moderation rather than radical idealism. No longer was the Republican party a one-idea organization composed of crusaders against slavery. It now embraced, or hoped to embrace, every major interest group in the North that believed that the South, the champion of slavery, was blocking its legitimate economic aspirations.

The platform endorsed such measures as a high tariff, internal improvements, a homestead bill, and a Pacific railroad to be built with federal financial assistance. On the slavery issue, the platform affirmed the right of each state to control its own institutions, which was the Republicans' way of saying that they did not intend to interfere with slavery in the South. But they also denied the authority of Congress or of a territorial legislature to legalize slavery in the territories, which was equivalent to saying that they still would oppose the expansion of slavery.

The leading contender for the nomination was William H. Seward, who faced the competition of a number of favorite-son candidates. His prominence and his long political record damaged his chances. Passing him and other aspirants over, the convention nominated on the third ballot Abraham Lincoln—who was prominent enough to be respectable but obscure enough to have few foes, and who was radical enough to please the antislavery faction in the party but conservative enough to satisfy the ex-Whigs. To complete the strategy of availability, the vice-presidential nomination went to Hannibal Hamlin of Maine, a former Democrat.

As if three parties were not enough, a fourth entered the lists—the Constitutional Union party. Although posing as a new organization, it was really the last surviving remnant of the oldest conservative tradition in the country; its leaders were elder statesmen and most of its

# Where Historians Disagree

## The Causes of the Civil War

On the causation of the Civil War, historians' views have changed with changing times, thus illustrating the fact that history reflects the period *in* which it is written as well as the period *about* which it is written. In the 1890s, when the United States was emerging as a world power, the Civil War seemed to have been concerned with fundamental issues, for it had not only destroyed slavery but also preserved the Union, thus making possible the nation's rise to greatness. Such was the implied theme of the leading authority of the time, James Ford Rhodes. In his *History of the United States from the Compromise of 1850 . . .* (7 vols., 1893–1900) Rhodes saw the war as originating in the conflict between Northern opponents and Southern defenders of slavery.

This view prevailed until the 1920s, when Charles and Mary Beard challenged it in *The Rise of American Civilization* (2 vols., 1927). The Beards believed that in politics the most powerful of human motivations were economic. Like many of their contemporaries among the intellectuals, these authors were disillusioned with the efforts of progressives to curb business monopolies. The Beards maintained that the basic causes of the Civil War were economic. According to them, the war arose out of a clash between Northern industrialists and Southern planters, each group seeking to control the federal government in its own interest, and both groups using arguments about slavery and state rights only as smoke screens. The Beards had doubts about the results of the "Second American Revolution," as they called the war, for it brought on the evils associated with the rise of big business.

In the 1930s the Beardian interpretation began to be superseded by the views of the "revisionists." While these men were writing, the American revulsion against war was at its height. The recent war to "end war" and "make the world safe for democracy" had obviously done neither, and American participation in it seemed now like a great mistake. The Civil War, too, had been unfortunate and useless according to the revisionists, such as Avery Craven and James G. Randall, who blamed it on the fanaticism and political ineptitude of a "blundering generation."

After World War II, which appeared to have saved democracy from the threat of Hitlerism, historians took a new look at the Civil War and concluded, once again, that it had been necessary and worthwhile. Arthur Schlesinger, Jr., explained that violence was sometimes indispensable for clearing away obstacles to social progress and that slavery had been such an obstacle. Allan Nevins, beginning a multi-volume restudy of the period 1850–1877 in *The Ordeal of the Union* and *The Emergence of Lincoln* (4 vols., 1947–1950), characterized the Civil War as "a war over slavery *and* the future position of the Negro race in North America." As the civil rights movement gained momentum in the 1950s and 1960s, historians gave more and more attention to slavery and race relations as central issues in the sectional conflict of the 1850s and 1860s. Eugene Genovese, for one, saw the war as growing out of the Southern planters' efforts to protect and expand the slave system.

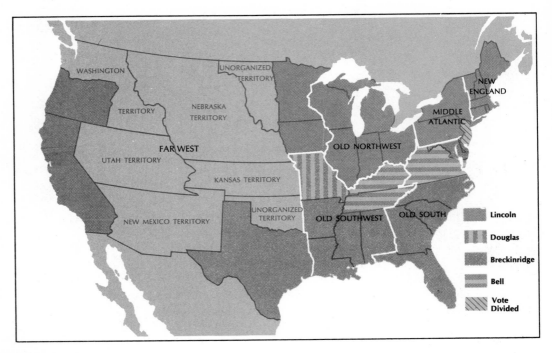

**Election of 1860**

members were former Whigs. Meeting in Baltimore in May, this party nominated John Bell of Tennessee and Edward Everett of Massachusetts. Its platform favored the Constitution, the Union, and enforcement of the laws.

In the North the Republicans conducted a campaign reminiscent of the exciting contest of 1840, with parades, symbols, and mass meetings. For the most part, they stressed the economic promises in their platform and subordinated the slavery issue. Lincoln, following the customary practice of candidates, made no speeches, leaving this work to lesser party luminaries. Unlike previous candidates, he refused to issue any written statements of his views, claiming that anything he said would be seized on by Southerners and misrepresented.

In the November election Lincoln won a majority of the electoral votes and the Presidency, though only about two-fifths of the popular votes. The Republicans had elected a President, but they had failed to secure a majority in Congress; and of course they did not control the Supreme Court.

## Secession of the South

During the campaign various Southern leaders had threatened that if the Republicans won the election the South would secede from the Union. Southerners had voiced secession threats at intervals since 1850, and Northerners had come to believe that the Southerners were bluffing. This time, however, some of them were in earnest.

The concept of secession was rooted in the political philosophy that the South had developed to protect its minority status. According to this doctrine, the Union was an association of sovereign states. The individual states had once joined the Union; they could, whenever they wished, dissolve their connections with it and resume their status as separate sovereignties. For a state to leave the Union was a momentous act but a lawful one, from the Southern point of view. The governor and the legislature could call an election for a special state convention and this body could pass an ordinance of secession.

South Carolina, long the hotbed of Southern

separatism, led off the secession parade, its convention taking the state out of the Union on December 20, 1860, by a unanimous vote. Before Lincoln ever assumed the Presidency, six other Southern states had left the Union. Not only that, but in February 1861 representatives of the seceded states met at Montgomery, Alabama, and formed a new, Southern nation—the Confederate States of America.

Something of the indecision in Northern attitudes was reflected in the thinking of President Buchanan. In his message to Congress of December 1860, he denied the right of a state to secede but did not think the federal government possessed the power to force a state back into the Union. He intended to avoid a collision of arms and to maintain the symbolic authority of the national government until his successor could take office.

As the various states seceded, they took possession of federal property within their boundaries, but they lacked the strength to seize certain offshore forts, notably Fort Sumter in the harbor of Charleston, South Carolina, and Fort Pickens in the harbor of Pensacola, Florida. South Carolina sent commissioners to Washington to ask for the surrender of Sumter, garrisoned by a small force under Major Robert Anderson. Buchanan, fearful though he was of provoking a clash, refused to yield the fort. In January 1861 he decided to reinforce it. By his direction an unarmed merchant ship, the *Star of the West,* proceeded to Fort Sumter with troops and supplies. When the vessel attempted to enter the harbor, it encountered the fire of shore batteries and turned back.

Meanwhile Buchanan recommended to Congress that it frame compromise measures to hold the Union together. The Senate and the House appointed committees to study plans of adjustment. The Senate committee concentrated on a proposal submitted by Senator John J. Crittenden of Kentucky. The Crittenden Compromise called for a series of constitutional amendments: one would have guaranteed the permanence of slavery in the states; others were designed to satisfy Southern demands on such matters as fugitive slaves and slavery in the District of Columbia. But the heart of Crittenden's plan dealt with slavery in the territories. He proposed to reestablish the Missouri Compromise line of 36° 30′ in all the territory of the United States then held or *thereafter acquired.* Slavery was to be prohibited north of the line and permitted

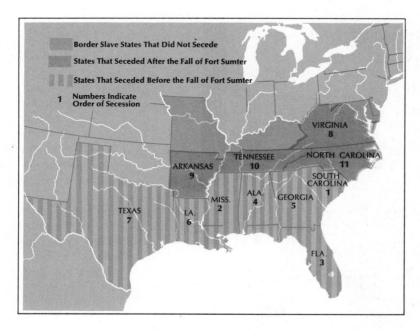

**The Process of Secession**

south of it. The Southern members of the committee indicated they would accept this territorial division if the Republicans also would. The Republicans, after sounding out President-elect Lincoln in Illinois, voted against the proposal. Lincoln took the position that the restoration of the Missouri Compromise line would encourage the South to embark on imperialist adventures in Latin America.

## The Aggressor, According to Lincoln

In his July 4, 1861, message to Congress, President Lincoln said with regard to Fort Sumter:

*As had been intended, in this contingency, it was also resolved to notify the Governor of South Carolina, that he might expect an attempt would be made to provision the Fort; and that, if the attempt should not be resisted, there would be no effort to throw in men, arms, or ammunition, without further notice, or in case of an attack upon the Fort. This notice was accordingly given; whereupon the Fort was attacked, and bombarded to its fall, without even awaiting the arrival of the provisioning expedition.*

*It is thus seen that the assault upon and reduction of Fort Sumter was, in no sense, a matter of self defence on the part of the assailants. They well knew that the garrison in the Fort could, by no possibility, commit aggression upon them. They knew—they were expressly notified—that the giving of bread to the few brave and hungry men of the garrison was all which would on that occasion be attempted, unless themselves, by resisting so much, should provoke more. They knew that this Government desired to keep the garrison in the Fort, not to assail them, but merely to maintain visible possession, and thus to preserve the Union from actual and immediate dissolution. . . .*

One notable attempt to effect a compromise was made outside Congress. The legislature of Virginia invited the other states to send delegates to a peace conference at Washington. Representatives from twenty-one states assembled early in February, and spent most of the month framing compromise proposals. The plan of this Peace Convention followed closely the Crittenden scheme. The convention submitted the plan to the Senate, but it received almost no support.

And so nothing had been resolved when Abraham Lincoln was inaugurated President on March 4, 1861. In his inaugural address he laid down the following basic principles: the Union was older than the Constitution, no state could of its own volition leave the Union, the ordinances of secession were illegal, and acts of violence to support secession were insurrectionary or revolutionary. He declared that he meant to execute the laws in all the states and to "hold, occupy, and possess" the federal property in the seceded states (Forts Sumter and Pickens).

Lincoln soon found an opportunity to apply his policy in the case of Fort Sumter. Major Anderson was running short of supplies; unless he received fresh provisions the fort would have to be evacuated. If Lincoln permitted the loss of Sumter, the South and perhaps the North would never believe that he meant to sustain the Union. After much deliberation he decided to dispatch a naval relief expedition to the fort. Carefully he informed the South Carolina authorities, who, of course, would have to notify the Confederate government, that ships were on the way to bring supplies but not to land troops or munitions unless resistance was offered. His move placed the Confederates in a dilemma. If they permitted the expedition to land, they would be bowing tamely to federal authority; their people would not believe that they meant to sustain secession. But the only alternative was to reduce the fort before the ships arrived. After hours of anguished discussion, the government in Montgomery ordered General P. G. T. Beauregard, in charge of Confederate forces at Charleston, to demand Anderson's surrender and, if the demand was refused, to reduce the fort. Beauregard made the demand and Anderson rejected it. The Confederates then bombarded the fort for two days, April 12–13, 1861. On April 14, Anderson surrendered.

War had come. Lincoln moved to increase the army and called on the states to furnish troops to restore the Union. Now four more slave states seceded and joined the Confederacy: Virginia (April 17); Arkansas (May 6); Tennessee (May 7); and North Carolina (May 20). The mountain counties in northwestern Virginia re-fused to accept the decision of their state, established their own "loyal" government, and in 1863 secured admission to the Union as the new state of West Virginia. The four remaining slave states, Maryland, Delaware, Kentucky, and Missouri cast their lot with the Union. Lincoln kept a keen watch on their actions, and in two, Maryland and Missouri, helped to ensure their decision by employing military force.

## The Opposing Sides

A comparison of the combatants on the eve of war reveals that all the great material factors were on the side of the North. And these advantages became more significant as the conflict continued and the superior economy of the North became geared for war production. The North had a larger manpower reservoir from which to draw its armed forces. In the North, or the United States, were twenty-three states with a population of approximately 22 million. In the South, or the Confederate States, were eleven states with a population of about 9 million. Of these, approximately 3.5 million were slaves, leaving a white population of something under 6 million.

The North's greater economic potential was most formidably apparent in industrial production. Almost any set of comparative figures can be chosen to illustrate the overwhelming nature of Northern superiority. These statistics, translated into material terms, meant that the Northern armies, once the economic system had been converted to war production, would have more of everything than the Southern forces. This was not true, of course, in the first year of the war, when both sides purchased large amounts of supplies, particularly arms, from Europe. After 1862 the North was able to manufacture practically all of its war materials; its dependence on Europe ceased. The South, on the other hand, had to rely on Europe all during the war. It also tried desperately to expand its own industrial facilities. The brilliant Confederate chief of ordnance, Josiah Gorgas, accomplished wonders in building arsenals and in supplying the armies with weapons and munitions. Nevertheless, both the quantity and the quality of Confederate firearms were inferior. The Southern economic system was unable to provide its soldiers and

### The Aggressor, According to Stephens

President Davis, Vice President Stephens, and indeed all good Confederates maintained that "the war was inaugurated" by Lincoln himself. Stephens expressed the Confederate view in the first volume of his postwar work entitled *A Constitutional View of the Late War Between the States* (1868):

It is a fact that the first gun *was fired by the Confederates. . . . But did the firing of the first gun or the reduction of Fort Sumter inaugurate or begin the war? . . . Hallam [an authority on international law] has well said that "the aggressor in a war (that is, he who begins it) is not the first who uses force, but the first who renders force* necessary."

*Which side, according to this high authority (that only announces the common sentiments of mankind), was the aggressor in this instance? Which side was it that provoked and rendered the first blow necessary? The true answer to that question will settle the fact as to which side began the war.*

*I maintain that it was inaugurated and begun, though no blow had been struck, when the hostile fleet, styled the "Relief Squadron," with eleven ships, carrying two hundred and eighty-five guns and two thousand four hundred men, was sent out from New York and Norfolk with orders from the authorities at Washington to re-enforce Fort Sumter peaceably, if permitted—"but forcibly if they must."*

civilians with the other matériel of modern war: clothes, boots, blankets, stockings, medical supplies, and the like. Its failure in this respect was one reason why Southern morale dropped badly after 1863.

In every respect the transportation system of the North was superior to that of the South. The North had more and better inland water transport (steamboats, barges), more surfaced roads, and more wagons and animals. The North had approximately 20,000 miles of railroads, while the South, containing at least as large a land area, had only 10,000 miles. The trackage figures, however, do not tell the whole story of Southern inferiority. There were important gaps between key points in the South, which meant that supplies had to be detoured long distances or carried between railheads by wagons. As the war wore on, the Confederate railroad system steadily deteriorated, and by the last year and a half of the struggle it had almost collapsed.

When the material factors are analyzed and weighed, the impression emerges that the South had absolutely no chance to win the war. Actually, the material odds were not so great as they appear at first glance. The South might have won a decision on the battlefield up to 1863. Southern inferiority in manpower and materials was partially offset by other factors. The South, for the most part, fought on the defensive in its own country and commanded interior lines. The Northern invaders had to maintain long lines of communication, to supply themselves in areas where transportation was defective, and to garrison occupied regions. Furthermore, the North had to do more than capture the enemy capital or defeat enemy armies. It had to convince the Southern civilian population that the war was hopeless by seizing and holding most of the Confederacy. The South was fighting for something very concrete, very easy for its people to understand. It simply wanted to be independent, to be let alone; it had no aggressive designs on the North. If the South could have convinced the North that it could

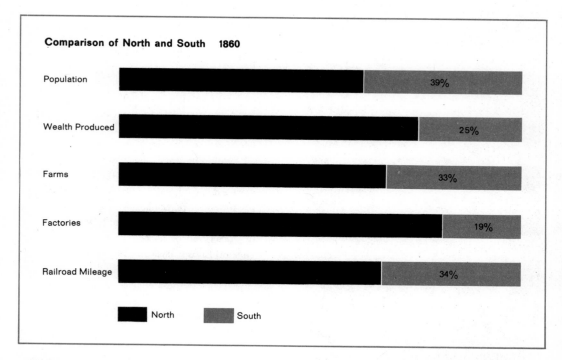

**Comparison of North and South   1860**

| | |
|---|---|
| Population | 39% |
| Wealth Produced | 25% |
| Farms | 33% |
| Factories | 19% |
| Railroad Mileage | 34% |

North   South

If the slaves were not included in the South's total population, the North's manpower advantage would appear greater than shown above. Because many of the South's so-called factories were small, the superiority of the North's industrial production was actually greater than this chart indicates.

not be conquered or that the result would not be worth the sacrifices, it might, even after 1863, have won its independence.

Southerners thought that even if the Southern human resources could not make up for Northern material advantages, there was still an almost certain guarantee of Confederate victory: Europe would intervene in the war on the side of the South. England and France had to have Southern cotton, and they would force the North to recognize the Confederacy.

## THE NORTH MOBILIZES

For the North the wartime years became a period of prosperity and expansion. Both industry and agriculture increased their productive facilities and, at the end of the war, were turning out more products than at the beginning.

### Economic Measures

A powerful stimulant to the expanding economy was provided by the economic legislation enacted by the Republican party during the war. The Republicans represented Northern industry and agriculture, and, now that the war had removed Southern opposition, they proceeded to put into effect the kind of program their supporters expected.

The Homestead Act (1862) and the Morrill Land Grant Act (1862) were measures that the West had long sought. The first provided that any citizen or any alien who had declared his intention to become a citizen could register claim to a quarter section of public land (160 acres), and, after giving proof that he had lived on it for five years, receive title on payment of a small fee. The Morrill Law gave every state 30,000 acres of public land for each of its congressional representatives, the proceeds from the donation to be used for education in agriculture, engineering, and military science. This provided a basis for the development of the so-called "land-grant" colleges and universities.

Industry scored its first gain a few days before President Buchanan left office. Congress passed the Morrill Tariff Act, which provided a moderate increase in duties, bringing the rates up to approximately what they had been before 1846.

Later measures enacted in 1862 and 1864 were frankly protective. By the end of the war the average of duties was 47 per cent, the highest in the nation's history, and more than double the prewar rate.

Other legislative victories for business were achieved in connection with railroad and immigration. Two laws, passed in 1862 and 1864, created two federal corporations: the Union Pacific Railroad Company, which was to build westward from Omaha, and the Central Pacific, which was to build eastward from California. The government would aid the companies by donating public lands and advancing government loans. Immigration from Europe fell off in the first years of the war, partly because of the unsettled conditions. The decrease, coupled with the military demands for manpower, threatened to cause a labor shortage, and President Lincoln and business leaders asked Congress for governmental encouragement of immigration. In 1864 Congress passed a contract labor law authorizing employers to import laborers and collect the costs of transportation from future wages.

Perhaps the most important measure affecting the business-financial community was the National Bank Act, enacted in 1863 and amended in 1864. The act created the National Banking System, which lasted without serious modification until 1913. Its architects, including Secretary of the Treasury Salmon P. Chase, argued that, both for the military present and the economic future, the country needed a uniform and standard bank-note currency. At the outbreak of the war 1,500 banks chartered by twenty-nine states were empowered to issue notes. Furthermore, Chase and his supporters claimed, national supervision of the banking system would enable the government to market its bonds more economically, thus aiding war finance.

An existing state bank or a newly formed corporation could secure a federal charter and become a national bank. Each association was required to possess a minimum amount of capital and to invest one-third of its capital in government securities. Upon depositing the securities with the national Treasury, it would receive, and could issue as bank notes, United States Treasury notes up to 90 per cent of the

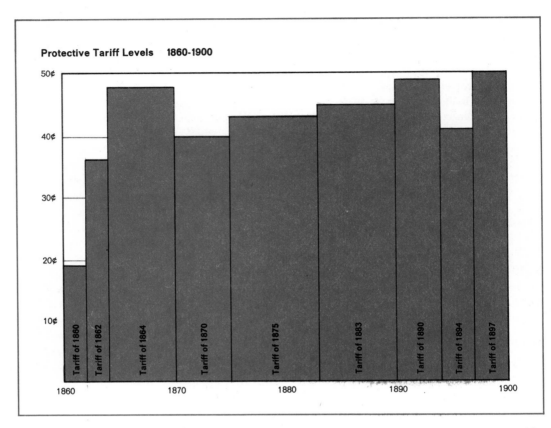

**Protective Tariff Levels   1860-1900**

The chart indicates the average duties paid per dollar's worth of imports on dutiable goods only. Average duties were 19 cents in 1860 and rose during the Civil War to 48 cents. They were lowered slightly after the war but during the 1890s rose again, and after the passage of the Dingley Tariff in 1897 they reached 50 cents, the highest level yet achieved in tariff history.

current value of the bonds. Congress (in 1865) placed a tax on all state bank notes. This forced state notes out of existence and induced reluctant state banks to seek federal charters.

The North financed the war from three principal sources: taxation, loans, and paper money issues. From taxes, including the tariff, the government received approximately $667 million; loans, including Treasury notes, accounted for $2.6 billion; and $450 million of paper currency ("greenbacks") was issued.

Since the greenbacks bore no interest, were not supported by a specie reserve, and depended for redemption on the good faith of the government (and its ability to win the war), they fluctuated in value. In 1864 a greenback dollar, in relation to a gold dollar, was worth only 39 cents, and even at the close of the war its value had advanced to but 67 cents.

In America's previous wars, bonds had been sold only to banks and to a few wealthy investors. Through the agency of Jay Cooke, a Philadelphia banker, the Treasury now launched a campaign to persuade the ordinary man (and woman) to buy a bond. By high-pressure propaganda techniques, Cooke disposed of $400 million of bonds—the first example of mass financing of a war in our history.

Not until 1862, when mounting war expenses forced the country to face realities, did Congress adopt an adequate tax program. Then it passed the Internal Revenue Act, which placed duties on practically all goods and most occupations. For the first time, in 1861, the government levied an income tax: a duty of 3 per cent on incomes above $800. Later the rates were increased to 5 per cent on incomes between $600 and $5,000, and to 10 per cent on incomes above the latter figure. Through the medium of the various war taxes, the hand of the government was coming to rest upon most individuals in the country. The United States was in the process of acquiring a national internal revenue system —in fact, a national tax system—one of the many nationalizing effects of the war.

## Raising the Union Armies

When hostilities started, the regular army numbered only about 16,000 troops, and many of its units were scattered throughout the West. President Lincoln, in his first call for troops to repress the "rebellion," summoned 75,000 militia for three months, the usual period of service set for

state troops by existing militia law. Lincoln soon realized that the war would be of longer duration. Without constitutional sanction, he called for 42,000 volunteers for national service for three years and authorized an increase of 23,000 in the regular army. When Congress met in July 1861, it legalized the President's acts, and, at his recommendation, provided for enlisting 500,000 volunteers to serve for three years.

For a time the volunteering system served to bring out enough men to fill the armies, but not after the first flush of enthusiasm had worn off. Finally, in March 1863, Congress enacted the first national draft law in American history (the South had employed conscription almost a year earlier). Few exemptions were permitted: only

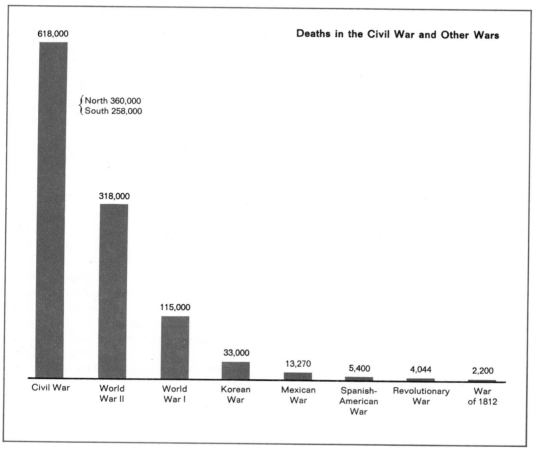

**Deaths in the Civil War and Other Wars**

618,000 — Civil War { North 360,000 / South 258,000 }
318,000 — World War II
115,000 — World War I
33,000 — Korean War
13,270 — Mexican War
5,400 — Spanish-American War
4,044 — Revolutionary War
2,200 — War of 1812

The number of service deaths in the Civil War exceeded the total in all our other wars combined. As of May 8, 1970 there have been 41,733 American service deaths in the Vietnam War.

high national and state officials, preachers, and men who were the sole support of a dependent family. But a drafted man could escape service by hiring a substitute to go in his place or by paying the government a fee of $300.

The purpose of the law was to spur enlistments by threatening to invoke conscription. Each state was divided into enrollment districts and was assigned a quota of men to be raised. If a state could fill the quota, it would escape the draft completely; if certain districts failed to meet their quota, a sufficient number of men were drafted to make up the difference. Some states and many districts never experienced conscription. Although the draft directly inducted only 46,000 men, it stimulated enlistments enormously. These totaled 2.9 million, but that figure includes many who enlisted several times or served short terms. Probably 1.5 million men, all together, served in the Union armies (as contrasted with 900,000 in the Confederate forces).

The casualty rate was tremendous. Not until World War I would military medicine reach a point where fewer men died from sickness than from bullets. Doubtless the death rate in camp and hospital would have been even greater but for the work of a number of private relief organizations, the largest being the United States Sanitary Commission, which provided medical care, medical supplies, and food to the armed forces.

To a people accustomed to a government that had hardly touched their daily lives, conscription seemed a strange and ominous thing. Opposition to the law was widespread, particularly from laborers, immigrants, and Peace Democrats. In places it erupted into violence. Demonstrators against the draft rioted in New York City for four days in July 1863, killed several hundred people, mostly Negroes, and burned down Negro homes and businesses. Federal troops had to be brought in to subdue the rioters. Some Democratic governors who supported the war (like Horatio Seymour of New York) contended that the national government had no constitutional power to conscript, and they openly challenged the Lincoln administration on the issue.

## Politics and Emancipation

When Lincoln first took over the Presidency, he was widely considered a small-time prairie politician, unfit for his job. He strengthened this impression by his unpretentious air. Actually, he was well aware of his great abilities and of his superiority over other Northern leaders. His supreme confidence in himself was demonstrated by his choice of a cabinet. Representing every faction of the Republican party and every segment of Northern opinion, it was an extraordinary assemblage of advisers and a difficult set of prima donnas to manage. Three of the secretaries, Seward, Chase, and Stanton, were first-rate men. Seward and Chase thought that they were abler than Lincoln and should be in his place. At the very beginning of the administration, Seward made an attempt to dominate Lincoln, failed, and became his loyal supporter. Chase never learned that the President was a bigger man than he.

Lincoln's confidence in his inner strength was revealed by his bold exercise of the war powers of his office. In order to accomplish his purposes, he was ready to violate parts of the Constitution, explaining that he would not lose the whole by being afraid to disregard a part. In this spirit he called for troops to repress the rebellion (an act that was equivalent to a declaration of war), illegally increased the size of the regular army, and proclaimed a naval blockade of the South.

Opposition to the war came from two sources: from Southern sympathizers in the Union slave states and from the peace wing of the Democratic party. War Democrats were willing to support the war and even to accept offices from the administration. Peace Democrats or, as their enemies called them, "Copperheads," feared that agriculture and the West were being subordinated to industry and the East and that state rights were going down before nationalism. These Democrats proposed to call a truce in the fighting, invite the South to attend a national convention, and amend the Constitution to preserve both the Union and state rights. Some advocated the formation of a Western confederacy, and some joined secret societies (Knights of the Golden Circle, Sons of Liberty) which allegedly conspired to aid the Southern rebels.

To deal with opponents of the war, Lincoln resorted to military arrests. He suspended the right of habeas corpus, so that an alleged offender could be arrested and held without trial or, if tried, had to appear before a military court. At first Lincoln denied the civil process only in specified areas, but in 1862 he proclaimed that all persons who discouraged enlistments or engaged in disloyal practices would come under martial law. In all, over 13,000 persons were arrested and imprisoned for varying periods. Among those placed in custody was a Maryland secessionist leader whom Lincoln refused to release, even under a writ from Chief Justice Taney (*Ex parte Merryman*). The most prominent Copperhead in the country, Clement L. Vallandigham of Ohio, was seized by military authorities, and Lincoln exiled him to the Confederacy. (After the war, in 1866, the Supreme Court held, in *Ex parte Milligan,* that military trials in areas where the civil courts were capable of functioning were unconstitutional.)

In the Republican as well as the Democratic party there were factions—the Radicals and the Conservatives. On most questions, including economic matters, the two groups were in fundamental agreement, but they differed violently, on slavery. Leaders of the Radicals were Thaddeus Stevens of Pennsylvania, master of the party machine in the House, and Senators Charles Sumner of Massachusetts and Benjamin F. Wade of Ohio. Heading the Conservatives was President Lincoln. The Radicals wanted to seize the opportunity of the war to strike slavery down—abolish it suddenly and violently. The Conservatives, who were also antislavery, wanted to accomplish the same result in a different way—easily and gradually. Lincoln made several notable although unsuccessful attempts to persuade the loyal slave states to agree to a program of compensated gradual emancipation. He feared, at first, that the introduction of abolition as a war aim would divide Northern opinion and alienate the border slave states.

**A Northern View of Emancipation**

This drawing originally appeared in *Harper's Weekly* and later was circulated widely as a broadside. It was, of course, a frankly Northern depiction of the significance of emancipation. (Library of Congress)

A Confiscation Act, passed in August 1861, declared free all slaves used for "insurrectionary" purposes. Subsequent laws abolished slavery in the District of Columbia, with compensation to owners (April 1862), and in the national territories (June 1862). In the summer of 1862 the Radicals decided that Northern opinion had reached a point where they could move against slavery in the states. In July they pushed through Congress the second Confiscation Act, which was in essence a bold attempt to accomplish emancipation by legislative action. It declared the property of persons supporting the "rebellion" subject to forfeiture to the United States government; declared free the slaves of persons aiding and supporting the insurrection; and authorized the President to employ Negroes, including freed slaves, as soldiers.

The Republican party was coming under Radical control, and the country was beginning to accept emancipation as an aim of the war. The signs were not lost on the astute master of politics in the White House. Lincoln saw that in order to achieve his larger purpose of saving the Union he would have to yield his lesser goal of preventing the sudden destruction of slavery. To preserve the nation he had to have the support of his own party and particularly of the Radicals, who were the last-ditch Unionists, the men who would never give up the war. And if a majority of the Northern people wanted slavery destroyed, as seemed the case, he could not afford to divide popular opinion by opposing their will. In July 1862 he decided to take the leadership of the antislavery impulse away from the Radicals by putting himself at the head of it.

On September 22, 1862, after the Battle of Antietam, the President issued his preliminary Emancipation Proclamation, and on the first day of 1863 his final Emancipation Proclamation. This declared forever free the slaves in designated areas of the Confederacy. Excepted from the edict was the whole state of Tennessee, most of which was under Union control, and western Virginia and southern Louisiana, which were occupied by Federal troops. Presumably these areas were omitted because they were not enemy territory and hence were not subject to the President's war powers. For a similar reason

the Proclamation did not apply to the border slave states.

The Proclamation freed immediately only a few slaves. But it indicated that henceforth there was to be a war for the emancipation of the slaves as well as for the preservation of the Union. Eventually as Federal armies occupied large areas of the South, the Proclamation became a practical reality, and hundreds of thousands of slaves were freed by its operation. Equally important in the process of emancipation was the induction of many former slaves into the armed forces: some 186,000 served as soldiers, sailors, and laborers, thereby making a substantial contribution to the freeing of their race. Furthermore, the impulse to abolition which the Proclamation symbolized increased in intensity throughout the country, affecting even the border states. Before the end of the war, slavery had been abolished in two Union slave states, Maryland and Missouri, and in three "reconstructed" or occupied Confederate states, Tennessee, Arkansas, and Louisiana. The final and inevitable action was taken early in 1865 when Congress approved the Thirteenth Amendment (ratified by the required number of states several months after the war closed), which freed all slaves everywhere and abolished slavery as an institution.

Early in the war, and particularly after the election of 1862, in which the Republicans suffered heavy losses, the party leaders proceeded to form a broad coalition of all groups who supported the war, trying particularly to attract the War Democrats. The new organization, which was composed of a Republican core with a fringe of War Democrats, was known as the Union party. It encountered its major political test in the presidential election of 1864, which was the first national election held in the midst of a great war.

When the Union convention met in June, it nominated Lincoln, with the chilly assent of the Radicals, and, for Vice President, Andrew Johnson of Tennessee, a War Democrat who had refused to follow his state into secession. In August the Democratic convention nominated George B. McClellan, former Union general and an object of hatred to all good Radicals. The peace faction got a plank into the platform denouncing the war as a failure and calling for a truce to be followed by an invitation to the South to enter a national convention. Although McClellan repudiated the plank, the Democrats stood before the country as the peace party. At the same time several Northern military victories, particularly the capture of Atlanta, Georgia, early in September, rejuvenated Northern morale and gave promise of Republican success in November.

The outcome of the election was a smashing electoral triumph for Lincoln, who got 212 votes to McClellan's 21 and carried every state except Kentucky, New Jersey, and Delaware. Lincoln's popular majority, however, was uncomfortably small, 2,213,000 to 1,805,000 or an advantage of only 400,000. A slight shift of popular votes in some of the more populous states would have changed the result.

## THE SOUTH MOBILIZES

Although the first seven Southern states to secede had left the Union as individual sovereignties, they intended from the first to come together in a common confederation, which they hoped the states of the upper South would eventually join. Accordingly, representatives of the seceded states assembled at Montgomery, Alabama, early in February 1861, to create a Southern nation. After Virginia seceded, the government moved to Richmond, partly out of deference to Virginia, partly because Richmond was one of the few Southern cities large enough to house the government.

### The Confederate Government

In the Confederate constitution, state sovereignty was expressly recognized, but not the right of secession. A few governmental reforms were introduced, such as the "item veto"—the President's power to veto part of a bill without rejecting the whole thing. Slavery was mentioned by name, and various provisions made its abolition (even by one of the states) practically impossible. In most other respects the constitution of the Confederate States was identical with that of the United States.

**An English View of Jefferson Davis**

William Howard Russell, war correspondent for the *Times* of London, visited the Confederate President at Montgomery, Alabama, in 1861. Although the Britisher had some reservations about Davis, he was favorably impressed with his freedom from the almost universal American habit of chewing tobacco:

*I had an opportunity of observing the President very closely: he did not impress me as favorably as I had expected, though he is certainly a very different looking man from Mr. Lincoln. He is like a gentleman—has a slight, light figure, little exceeding middle height, and holds himself erect and straight. He was dressed in a rustic suit of slate-colored stuff, with a black silk handkerchief round his neck; his manner is plain, and rather reserved and drastic; his head is well formed, with a fine full forehead, square and high, covered with innumerable fine lines and wrinkles, features regular, though the cheekbones are too high, and the jaws too hollow to be handsome; the lips are thin, flexible, and curved, the chin square, well defined; the nose very regular, with wide nostrils; and the eyes deep-set, large and full—one seems nearly blind, and is partly covered with a film, owing to excruciating attacks of neuralgia and tic. Wonderful to relate, he does not chew, and is neat and clean-looking, with hair trimmed, and boots brushed.*

Besides framing a constitution and passing temporary laws, the Montgomery convention named a provisional President and a provisional Vice President, Jefferson Davis of Mississippi and Alexander H. Stephens of Georgia. Afterward, in a general election, the same two men were chosen, without opposition, for regular six-year terms. Davis had been a firm but not extreme advocate of Southern rights in the former Union; he was a moderate but not an extreme secessionist. Stephens had been the chief among those who had contended that secession was unnecessary.

Jefferson Davis embodied the spirit of the nation he had been called to lead. His family, which was of Southern yeoman stock, had moved from Kentucky, where he was born, to the new lush cotton lands of Mississippi, where they became rich planters almost overnight. Davis was a first-generation aristocrat. So also were most of the members of his government. The Confederacy was run by the cotton nabobs of the newer "Western" South, not by the old aristocracy of the seaboard states.

Whereas Lincoln's task was to preserve a nation, Davis' was to make one. Lincoln succeeded; Davis failed. He spent too much time on routine items, on what one observer called "little trash." A good administrator, he was his own secretary of war, but he rarely rose above the secretarial level. Moreover, he proceeded on the assumption that the Confederacy was a legal and permanent organization that could fight a war in the normal fashion of older countries. The situation demanded ruthless efficiency, yet he tried to observe every constitutional punctilio. Lincoln, without clear constitutional sanction, suspended habeas corpus; Davis asked his Congress to let him suspend it and received only partial permission. One shrewd Confederate official (R. G. H. Kean) wrote: "All the revolutionary vigor is with the enemy. . . . With us timidity—hair splitting."

The Confederate cabinet displayed, at best, only average ability. The personnel changed rapidly and frequently. There were three secretaries of state, two secretaries of the treasury, four attorney generals, and five secretaries of war. Not one of them ever dared to oppose the will of President Davis.

## Money and Men

In contrast to the burgeoning prosperity of the wartime North, the South in the war years underwent shortages, suffering, and sacrifice. The Southern economy, despite a frantic expansion of industrial facilities, was unable to supply the needs of its armies and civilian population.

The men seeking to devise measures for financing the Confederacy's war effort, Secretary of the Treasury Christopher G. Memminger and the congressional leaders, had to reckon with a number of hard facts. A national revenue system had to be created to collect money from a people unaccustomed to bearing large tax burdens. Southern banking houses, except in New Orleans, were fewer and smaller than those of the North. Because excess capital in the South was usually invested in slaves and land, the sum of liquid assets on deposit in banks or in individual hands was relatively small. The only specie possessed by the government was that seized in United States mints located in the South (amounting to about $1 million). In an attempt to secure more specie, the government dispatched an army column into New Mexico, but this force, after some initial success, was repelled.

The Confederate Congress, like its counterpart in the North, showed some reluctance to enact rigorous wartime taxes. In 1861 the legislators provided for a direct tax on property to be levied through the medium of the states. If a state preferred, it could meet its quota by paying as a state. Most of the states, instead of taxing their people, assumed the tax, which they paid by issuing bonds or their own notes. Moving more boldly in 1863, Congress passed a bill that included license levies and an income tax. A unique feature was "the tax in kind." Every farmer and planter had to contribute one-tenth of his produce to the government. All together, the revenue realized from taxation was relatively small—only about 1 per cent of total income.

The borrowing record of the Confederacy was little better than its tax program. Eventually the government issued bonds in such large amounts that the people suspected its ability to redeem them. Congress authorized a $100 million loan to be paid in specie, paper money, or produce. The expectation was that the bulk of the proceeds would be in the form of products—"the loan in kind." The loan was subscribed, partly in paper currency and mostly in produce or pledges of produce. But many of the pledges were not redeemed, and often the promised products were destroyed by the enemy. The Confederacy also attempted to borrow money in Europe by pledging cotton stored in the South for future delivery. Its most notable venture in foreign finance was the famous Erlanger loan, which was supposed to net $15 million. Actually, Erlanger, a French financier, was interested in conducting a huge cotton speculation. The Confederate government received only $2.5 million from the loan.

Since ready revenue was needed and since cash was scarce, the government resorted to the issuance of paper money and treasury notes in 1861. Once it started, it could not stop. By 1864 the staggering total of $1 billion had been issued. In addition, states and cities issued their own notes. The inevitable result was to depreciate the value of the money. Prices skyrocketed to astronomical heights. Many people, particularly those who lived in towns or who had fixed incomes, could not pay these prices. Such people often lost some of their will to fight.

Like the United States, the Confederate States first raised armies by calling for volunteers. By the latter part of 1861 volunteering had dropped off badly. As the year 1862 opened, the Confederacy was threatened by a manpower crisis.

The government met the situation boldly. At Davis' recommendation, Congress in April enacted the First Conscription Act, which declared that all able-bodied white males between the ages of eighteen and thirty-five were liable to military service for three years. A man who was drafted could escape his summons if he furnished a substitute to go in his place. The prices for substitutes eventually went up to as high as $10,000 in Confederate currency. The purpose of this provision was to exempt men in charge of agricultural and industrial production, but to people who could not afford substitutes it seemed like a special privilege to the rich. It was repealed late in 1863 after arousing bitter class discontent.

The first draft act and later measures provided for other exemptions, mostly on an occupational basis. The government realized that conscription had to be selective, that some men had to be left on the home front to perform the functions of production. It erred in excusing men who were not doing any vital services and in permitting too many group exemptions. The provision most bitterly criticized was that exempting one white man on each plantation with twenty or more slaves. Angrily denounced as the "twenty-nigger law," it caused ordinary men to say: "It's a rich man's war but a poor man's fight."

In September 1862 Congress adopted a second conscription measure, which raised the upper age limit to forty-five. At the end of the year, an estimated 500,000 soldiers were in the Confederate armies. Thereafter conscription provided fewer and fewer men, and the armed forces steadily decreased in size. Federal armies seized large areas in the South, depriving the Confederacy of manpower in the occupied regions. Military reverses in the summer of 1863 convinced many Southerners that the war was lost, causing a kind of passive resistance to the draft as men sought to avoid it by hiding in the hills and woods, and desertions began to increase.

As 1864 opened, the situation was critical. In a desperate move, Congress lowered the age limits for drafted men to seventeen and raised them to fifty, reaching out, it was said, toward the cradle and the grave. Few men were obtained. War weariness and the certainty of defeat were making their influence felt. In 1864–1865 there were 100,000 desertions. An observant Confederate diarist (Mrs. Mary B. Chesnut) wrote in her journal in March 1865: "I am sure our army is silently dispersing. Men are moving the wrong way, all the time. They slip by with no songs and no shouts now. They have given the thing up." In a frantic final attempt to raise men, Congress in 1865 authorized the drafting of 300,000 slaves. The war ended before this incongruous experiment could be tried out.

## State Rights in the Confederacy

In overwhelming numbers the Southern people were ready to support the war for Southern independence. The only important organized opposition to the war came from the inhabitants of the mountain areas, whose population was less than 10 per cent of the Southern total. Here supporters of the national cause carried on a kind of guerrilla warfare against the occupying Confederate forces until liberated by the Federals late in 1863.

Though united in their desire to sustain the war, Southerners were bitterly divided on how it should be conducted. The differences that emerged did not take the form of party issues: the Confederacy did not last long enough for distinct parties to develop.

The great dividing force was, ironically enough, the principle of state rights—the foundation of Southern political philosophy—for whose conservation and consecration the South had left the old Union. State rights had become such a cult with Southerners that they reacted against all central controls, even those necessary to win the war. If there was an organized faction of opposition to the government, it was that group of quixotic men who counted Vice President Stephens as their leader. They had one simple, basic idea. They wanted the Confederacy to win its independence, but they would not

agree to sacrificing one iota of state sovereignty to achieve that goal. If victory had to be gained at the expense of state rights, they preferred defeat. The state-righters concentrated their criticisms upon two powers that the central government sought to exercise: the suspension of habeas corpus, and conscription. Recalcitrant governors, like Joseph Brown of Georgia and Zebulon M. Vance of North Carolina, contending that the central government had no right to draft troops, tried in every way to obstruct the enforcement of conscription.

The idea of a negotiated peace fascinated the state-righters, especially Vice President Stephens. They never made it clear whether they were thinking of reunion or of Southern independence. As early as 1863 they urged a peace based on recognition of state sovereignty and the right of each state to control its domestic institutions—which implied a restored Union. At times, however, they proposed negotiations based on the independence of the Confederacy.

# Selected Readings

**Increasing Sectionalism** A. O. Craven, *The Coming of the Civil War* (1942); Allan Nevins, *The Emergence of Lincoln* (2 vols., 1950); A. W. Crandall, *The Early History of the Republican Party, 1854–1856* (1930); D. E. Fehrenbacher, *Prelude to Greatness: Lincoln in the 1850s*° (1962); H. V. Jaffa, *Crisis of the House Divided* (1959), on the Lincoln-Douglas debates; J. A. Isely, *Horace Greeley and the Republican Party, 1853–1861* (1947); M. B. Duberman, *Charles Francis Adams* (1961); David Donald, *Charles Sumner and the Coming of the Civil War* (1960); Vincent Hopkins, *Dred Scott's Case*° (1951); G. W. Van Vleck, *The Panic of 1857: An Analytical Study* (1943); R. F. Nichols, *The Disruption of the American Democracy*° (1948); P. S. Klein, *President James Buchanan* (1962).

**Kansas and John Brown** J. C. Malin, *The Nebraska Question, 1852–1854* (1953) and *John*

*Brown and the Legend of Fifty-Six* (1942); O. G. Villard, *John Brown, 1800–1859* (1910); P. W. Gates, *Fifty Million Acres: Conflicts over Kansas Land Policy, 1854–1890*° (1954); J. C. Furnas, *The Road to Harpers Ferry* (1959).

**The Crisis of 1860–1861** W. T. Baringer, *Lincoln's Rise to Power* (1937) and *A House Dividing* (1945); R. H. Luthin, *The First Lincoln Campaign* (1944); D. L. Dumond, *The Secession Movement, 1860–1861* (1931); R. A. Wooster, *The Secession Conventions of the South* (1962); L. A. White, *Robert Barnwell Rhett* (1931); P. S. Foner, *Business and Slavery: The New York Merchants and the Irrepressible Conflict* (1941); T. H. O'Connor, *Lords of the Loom: The Cotton Whigs and the Coming of the Civil War* (1968); R. G. Gunderson, *Old Gentlemen's Convention: The Washington Peace Conference of 1861* (1961); A. D. Kirwan, *John Jordan Crittenden* (1962); D. M. Potter, *Lincoln and His Party in* *the Secession Crisis, 1860–1861°* (1942); K. M. Stampp, *And the War Came: The North and the Secession Crisis, 1860–1861°* (1950); R. N. Current, *Lincoln and the First Shot°* (1963).

**President Lincoln** B. P. Thomas, *Abraham Lincoln* (1952); J. G. Randall, *Lincoln the President* (4 vols., 1945–1955); Carl Sandburg, *Abraham Lincoln: The War Years°* (4 vols., 1939); David Donald, *Lincoln Reconsidered°* (1956); R. N. Current, *The Lincoln Nobody Knows°* (1958).

**Union Mobilization** Allan Nevins, *The War for the Union* (2 vols., 1959–1960); F. A. Shannon, *Organization and Administration of the Union Army* (2 vols., 1928); E. P. Oberholtzer, *Jay Cooke, Financier of the Civil War* (2 vols., 1907).

**Wartime Politics and Emancipation** T. H. Williams, *Lincoln and the Radicals°* (1941); W. B. Hesseltine, *Lincoln and the War Governors* (1948); Wood Gray, *The Hidden Civil War: The Story of the Copperheads°* (1942); Frank Klement, *The Copperheads in the Middle West* (1960); J. H. Franklin, *The Emancipation Proclamation* (1963); V. J. Voegeli, *Free but Not Equal* (1967); J. G. Randall, *Constitutional Problems under Lincoln* (1926); H. D. Hunt, *Hannibal Hamlin of Maine: Lincoln's First Vice President* (1969).

**The Confederacy** E. M. Coulter, *The Confederate States of America, 1861–1865* (1950); Clement Eaton, *A History of the Southern Confederacy°* (1954); C. P. Roland, *The Confederacy°* (1960); W. B. Yearns, *The Confederate Congress* (1960); Hudson Strode, *Jefferson Davis, Confederate President* (1959) and *Jefferson Davis, Tragic Hero* (1964); R. R. Von Abele, *Alexander H. Stephens: A Biography* (1946); B. J. Hendrick, *Statesmen of the Lost Cause* (1939); R. W. Patrick, *Jefferson Davis and His Cabinet* (1944): R. D. Meade, *Judah P. Benjamin* (1943); A. B. Moore, *Conscription and Conflict in the Confederacy* (1924); F. L. Owsley, *State Rights in the Confederacy* (1925); B. I. Wiley, *Plain People of the Confederacy°* (1943); C. W. Ramsdell, *Behind the Lines in the Southern Confederacy* (1944).

---

° Titles available in paperback.

# Chapter 15
# The War of
# the Rebellion

From the seceders' point of view, the Civil War was a war for Southern independence. Afterwards (but not at the time) Southerners were to call it "the War between the States," thus implying that secession and resistance to federal authority had been legitimate, constitutional exercises of state rights. Yet the Southerners both during and after the fighting were proud to call themselves "rebels," and from the Northern point of view they were certainly engaging in rebellion as well as war. The official name that the Union government gave the conflict was "the War of the Rebellion."

This was the first great military experience of the American people. Compared to it the earlier wars—the one with Mexico, the War of 1812, even the Revolutionary struggle itself—were minor and episodic. It has been called the first of modern wars. It involved masses of men and new kinds of technology: railroads and railroad artillery, the telegraph, armored ships, balloons, the Gatling gun (precursor of the machine gun), repeating rifles, trenches, wire entanglements, water and land mines (including what then were called "infernal machines" and now would be known as "booby traps"), torpedo boats, even submarines. It compelled both sides to concentrate a high proportion of their resources on the pursuit of total victory.

For the American people, Northern and Southern, of both the wartime generation and later generations, the Civil War was the most dramatic and traumatic event in their history. More than most wars, it settled some things and settled them permanently. It brought about the destruction of slavery and the preservation of the Union. After the Union victory no class or faction or section could seriously consider secession as a feasible step.

In the war's aftermath, however, difficult problems emerged to test the statesmanship of both the victors and the vanquished. What should be the status of the 4 million emancipated slaves? Upon what terms and by what process should the states of the defeated Confederacy be restored to the Union?

Thus, while the victory had decided that no state could secede and that no man could own another as his slave, it had not settled the question of the precise relationship of the states to the Union or of the blacks to the whites. These questions remained, and in one form or another they still remain, the most perplexing and tormenting issues of American life more than a century after the end of the Civil War.

## The North's Greatest General

One observer of Ulysses S. Grant said: "He habitually wears an expression as if he had determined to drive his head through a brick wall, and was about to do it." Of average height and small stature, slouchy in dress and manner, Grant did not look like a great general, but he was, as C. F. Adams, Jr., noted, the kind of man that all would instinctively turn to in a moment of crisis.
(Left, Library of Congress)

## The South's Greatest General

Robert E. Lee was a magnificent physical figure. Five feet eleven inches tall and 175 pounds in weight, he seemed larger than he was because of his massive head and wide shoulders. He was grave and reserved in manner like George Washington, his hero and model. And like Washington, he lived by a self-imposed code of high conduct. "Duty is the sublimest word in our language," he once wrote.
(Right, National Archives)

## STRATEGY AND DIPLOMACY

So far as strategic planning was concerned, the objectives of the Union were positive and those of the Confederacy negative. To achieve a victory, the Union had to conquer the rebels and reduce them to subjection, to obedience to federal law. The Confederacy had only to stave off defeat.

In diplomacy—in relations with European powers—it was the other way around. The objectives of the Confederacy were positive and those of the Union negative. The Confederacy hoped to persuade foreign governments to recognize its independence and to step into the war and help make that independence a reality. The Union aimed to prevent recognition and intervention.

### The Commanders in Chief

It was the responsibility of the President as commander in chief of the army and navy—of Abraham Lincoln for the Union and Jefferson Davis for the Confederacy—to see to the making and carrying out of an overall strategy for winning the war. Lincoln, a civilian all his life, had had no military education and no military experience except for a brief militia interlude. Yet he became a great war President, and a great commander in chief, superior to Davis, who was a trained soldier. By the power of his mind, Lincoln made himself a fine strategist, often showing keener insight than his generals. He recognized that numbers and matériel were on his side, and immediately he moved to mobilize the maximum strength of Northern resources. He urged his generals to keep up a constant pressure on the whole defensive line of the Confederacy until a weak spot was found, and a breakthrough could be made. At an early date he realized that the proper objective of his armies was the destruction of the Confederate armies and not the occupation of Southern territory.

During the first three years of the war, Lincoln performed many of the functions that in a modern command system would be done by the chief of the general staff or the joint chiefs of staff. He formulated policy, devised strategic plans, and even directed tactical movements. Some of his decisions were wise, some wrong, but the general effect of his so-called "interfering" with the military machine was fortunate for the North.

At the beginning, Lincoln was inclined to take the advice of General Winfield Scott. The old general, however, was unable to adjust his thinking to the requirements of mass war. He retired from service on November 1, 1861, and as general in chief, Lincoln replaced Scott with young George B. McClellan, who was also the commander of the Federal field army in the East, the Army of the Potomac. McClellan lacked the abilities to formulate strategy for all theaters of the war. The one grand strategic design he submitted was defective because it envisioned operations in only one theater, his own, and because it made places instead of enemy armies his objective. When McClellan took the field in March 1862, Lincoln removed him as general in chief. In July Lincoln designated General Henry W. Halleck to direct the armies. The foremost American student of the art of war, Halleck had won an undeserved reputation as a successful general in the West. Now he cast himself in the role of an adviser instead of a maker of decisions. Again Lincoln himself was forced to take up the function of forming and directing strategy, a task that he performed until March 1864, when the nation finally achieved a modern command system.

In the system arrived at in 1864, Ulysses S. Grant, who had emerged as the North's greatest general, was named general in chief. Charged with directing the movements of all Union armies, Grant, because he disliked the political atmosphere of Washington, established his headquarters with the Army of the Potomac but did not technically become commander of that army. As director of the armies, Grant proved to be the man for whom Lincoln had been searching. He possessed in superb degree the ability to think of the war in overall terms and to devise strategy for the war as a whole. Because Lincoln trusted Grant, he gave the general a relatively free hand. Grant, however, always submitted the broad outlines of his plans to the President for approval before putting them in motion. Under the new arrangement, Halleck became "chief of staff," a post in which he acted as a channel of communication between Lincoln and Grant and between Grant and the departmental commanders.

Lincoln's active command role underlines one of the most important changes occurring in modern warfare: the emergence of the civilian in strategic planning. As war became more technological and total, strategy became a problem of directing the whole resources of a nation. It was too vast a problem for any one set of leaders, especially for the military.

The most dramatic example of civilian intervention in military affairs was the Committee on the Conduct of the War, a joint investigative committee of both houses of Congress and the most powerful agency that the legislative branch has ever created to secure for itself a voice in formulating war policies. Established in December 1861, under the chairmanship of Senator Benjamin F. Wade of Ohio, it became the spearhead of the Radical attack on Lincoln's war program. The Radicals sensed that many of the Northern generals were not animated by a driving, ruthless desire for victory. The generals at first were influenced by the eighteenth-century concept of war as a kind of game—as chessboard maneuvers conducted in leisurely fashion and without heavy casualties. The Radicals ascribed the generals' hesitancy to a secret sympathy for slavery, which the professionals were supposed to have imbibed at West Point. The generals whom the committee favored—most of them incompetent amateurs—would have been no improvement, but the spirit represented by the committee helped to infuse a hard, relentless purpose into the conduct of the war.

Southern command arrangements consisted mainly of President Davis. The Confederacy failed to achieve a modern command system. Early in 1862 Davis assigned General Robert E. Lee to duty at Richmond, where, "under the direction of the President," he was "charged" with the conduct of the Confederate armies. Despite the fine words, this meant only that Lee, who had a brilliant military mind, was to act as Davis' adviser, furnishing counsel when called on. After serving a few months, Lee went

to the field, and Davis did not appoint another adviser until February 1864. Then he selected Braxton Bragg, whom he had been forced to remove from field command after Bragg was defeated in the West. Bragg had real strategic ability, but he understood his position and restricted his function to providing technical advice. In February 1865 the Confederate Congress, in a move directed at Davis, created the position of general in chief, which was intended for Lee. Davis named Lee to the post but took care to announce that legally he himself was still commander in chief. Lee accepted the job on the basis offered by the President: as a loyal subordinate instead of the dictator some people wanted him to be. The war ended before the new command experiment could be fully tested.

## The Role of Sea Power

The Union had the advantage of overwhelmingly preponderant sea power, and President Lincoln made the most of it. It served two main functions. One was to enforce the blockade of the Southern coast that he proclaimed at the start of the war (April 19, 1861). The other was to assist the Union armies in combined land-and-water operations.

In the Western theater of war, the vast region between the Appalachian Mountains and the Mississippi River, the larger rivers were navigable by vessels of considerable size. The Union navy helped the armies to conquer this area by transporting supplies and troops for them and joining them in attacking Confederate strong points. In defending themselves against the Union gunboats on the rivers, the Confederates had to depend mainly on land fortifications because of their lack of naval power. These fixed defenses proved no match for the mobile land-and-water forces of the Union.

At first, the blockade was too large a task for the Union navy. Even after the navy had grown to its maximum size, it was unable to seal off completely the long shoreline of the Confederacy. Though ocean-going ships were kept away, small blockade runners continued to carry goods into and out of some of the Southern ports. Gradually the Federal forces tightened the blockade by occupying stretches of the

## First Battle of Ironclads

This print depicts, with some exaggeration, the fight between the *Monitor* and the *Merrimack*. The two contestants, in the foreground, the *Monitor* on the left and the *Merrimack* on the right, are represented with reasonable accuracy, but the damaged Union ships were not in the battle. (Library of Congress)

coast and seizing one port after another, the last remaining important one (Wilmington, North Carolina) early in 1865. Fewer and fewer blockade runners got through, and the blockade increasingly hurt the South.

In bold and ingenious attempts to break the blockade, the Confederates introduced some new weapons, among them an ironclad warship. They constructed this by plating with iron a former United States frigate, the *Merrimack*, which the Yankees had scuttled in Norfolk harbor when Virginia seceded. On March 8, 1862, the *Merrimack* steamed out from Norfolk to attack the blockading squadron of wooden ships in Hampton Roads. She destroyed two of the ships and scattered the rest. Jubilation reigned in Richmond, and consternation in Washington. But the federal government had already placed orders for the construction of several ironclads of its own, which had been designed by John Ericsson. One of these, the

*Monitor,* arrived at Hampton Roads on the night of March 8. When the *Merrimack* emerged on the following day to hunt for more victims, the *Monitor* met her and engaged her in the first battle between ironclad ships. Neither vessel was able to penetrate the other's armor, but the *Monitor* put an end to the depredations of the *Merrimack*.

The Confederates later experimented with other new kinds of craft in the effort to pierce the blockade. One of these was a torpedo boat, which carried the torpedo (mine) on a long pole projecting out in front. Another was a small, cigar-shaped, hand-powered submarine. In 1864, in Charleston harbor, such a submarine, pulling its mine behind it on a cable, dived under a blockading vessel, exploded the mine against the hull, and then was dragged to the bottom by the sinking ship. For the first time in the history of warfare, a submarine had made a successful strike. This and other ingenious efforts, however, fell far short of breaking or even weakening the blockade.

To weaken it, the Confederates had meanwhile decided to build or buy fast ships to prey on the Northern merchant marine on the high seas. The hope was that the Union would detach ships from the blockade to pursue the commerce raiders. The Confederates also hoped to get, from abroad, a specially built "ram" with which to smash the wooden blockading ships. As a result of these efforts, the naval war became an important element in the relations of the Union with the Confederacy, on the one hand, and with the powers of Europe on the other.

## Europe and the Disunited States

Judah P. Benjamin, who occupied the Confederate foreign office for the greater part of the war, was a clever and intelligent man, but he lacked strong convictions and confined most of his energy to administrative routine. Seward, on the other hand, after some initial blunders, learned his job well and went on to become one of the outstanding American secretaries of state. In the key diplomatic post at London, the North was represented by a distinguished minister, Charles Francis Adams, who seemed to have inherited the diplomatic abilities of his father (John Quincy Adams) and grandfather (John Adams).

In the relationship of Europe to the Civil War, the key nations were Great Britain and France. These two had acted together against Russia in the Crimean War and were united by an entente, one of the understandings of which was that questions concerning the United States fell within the sphere of British influence. Napoleon III, therefore, would not act in American affairs without the concurrence of Britain. Russia, the third power of Europe, was, like the United States, an up-and-coming nation that thought its aspirations were being blocked by England. Feeling a community of interest with democratic America, autocratic Russia openly expressed sympathy for the Northern cause. In 1863, when war threatened to break out between Russia and England over Poland, Russia, in order to get her navy into position to attack British commerce, dispatched two fleets to American waters. One turned up at New

York and the other at San Francisco, thereby creating a legend that they had come to support the United States if England and France should attempt to break the blockade.

At the beginning of the war the sympathies of the ruling classes of England and France were with the Confederacy. But English liberals like John Bright and Richard Cobden saw the war as a struggle between free and slave labor, and they presented it in these terms to their followers. The politically conscious but unenfranchised workers in Britain expressed their sympathy for the Northern cause frequently and unmistakably—in mass meetings, in resolutions, and, through the medium of Bright and other leaders, in Parliament itself. After the issuance of the Emancipation Proclamation, these groups intensified their activities on behalf of the Union cause.

In the minds of Southern leaders, cotton was their best diplomatic weapon. Their analysis was as follows: the textile industry was basic to the economies of England and France, which depended on the South for the bulk of their cotton supply; deprived of Southern cotton, these countries would face economic collapse. Therefore they would have to intervene on the side of the Confederacy.

But this diplomacy based on King Cotton never worked as its champions envisioned. In 1861 English manufacturers had a surplus of cotton on hand. The immediate effect of the blockade was to enable the textile operators to dispose of their remaining finished goods at high prices. Thereafter the supply became increasingly short, and many mills were forced to close. Both England and France, however, managed to avoid a complete shutdown of their textile industries by importing supplies from new sources, notably Egypt and India. Most important of all, the workers, the people most seriously affected by the shortage, did not clamor to have the blockade broken. Even the 500,000 English textile workers thrown out of jobs continued to support the North.

No European nation extended diplomatic recognition to the Confederacy. Though several times England and France considered offering mediation, they never moved to intervene in the war. Neither could afford to do so unless the

Confederacy seemed on the point of winning, and the South never attained a prospect of certain victory.

Immediately after the outbreak of hostilities, Great Britain issued a proclamation of neutrality, thus attributing to the Confederacy the status of a belligerent. France and other nations followed suit. Although the Northern government, which officially insisted that the war was not a war but a domestic insurrection, furiously resented England's action, the British government had proceeded in conformity with accepted rules of neutrality and in accordance with the realities of the situation. The United States was fighting a *war*, a fact that Lincoln himself had recognized in his proclamation establishing a blockade. Thereafter three crises or near-crises between England and the United States developed, any one of which could have resulted in war between the two countries.

The first crisis, and the most dangerous one—the so-called *Trent* affair—occurred late in 1861. The Confederate commissioners to England and France, James M. Mason and John Slidell, had slipped through the then ineffective blockade to Havana, Cuba, where they boarded an English steamer, the *Trent*, for England. Hovering in Cuban waters was an American frigate, the *San Jacinto*, commanded by Captain Charles Wilkes, an impetuous officer who knew that the Southern diplomats were on the *Trent*. Acting without authorization from his government, Wilkes stopped the British vessel, arrested the commissioners, and bore them off in triumph to Boston. The British government drafted a demand for the release of the prisoners, reparation, and an apology. Lincoln and Seward, well aware that war with England would be suicidal, spun out the negotiations until American opinion had cooled off, then returned the commissioners with an indirect apology.

The second issue—the case of the Confederate commerce destroyers—generated a long-lasting diplomatic problem. Lacking the resources to construct the vessels, the Confederacy contracted to have them built and equipped in British shipyards. Six cruisers, of which the most famous were the *Alabama*, the *Florida*, and the *Shenandoah*, were sold to the Confederacy. The British government knew what was going on, being regularly and indig-

nantly informed by Minister Adams, but winked at the practice. The United States protested that it was in violation of the laws of neutrality. The protests formed the basis, after the war, for damage claims which the United States served on Great Britain.

The third incident—the affair of the Laird rams—could have developed into a crisis, but did not because the British government suddenly decided to mend its ways. In 1863 the Confederacy placed an order from the Laird shipyards for two powerful ironclads with pointed prows for ramming and sinking Union vessels and thus breaking the blockade. Adams was instructed to inform the British that if the rams, or any other ships destined for the Confederacy, left port, then there would be danger of war. Even before Adams delivered his message, the British government acted to detain the rams and to prevent the Confederacy from obtaining any other ships.

If Napoleon III had had his way, France and England would have intervened at an early date. Unable to persuade Britain to act, he had to content himself with expressing sympathy for the Southern cause and permitting the Confederates to order commerce destroyers from French shipyards. The Emperor's primary motive for desiring an independent South was his ambition to establish French colonial power in the Western hemisphere: a divided America could not block his plans. He seized the opportunity of the war to set up a French-dominated empire in Mexico.

Napoleon's Mexican venture was a clear violation of the Monroe Doctrine, perhaps the greatest one that had ever occurred. The United States viewed it in such a light, but for fear of provoking France into recognizing the Confederacy, it could do no more than register a protest. Only after the Civil War was ended did the United States feel strong enough to put pressure on France to get out of Mexico.

## CAMPAIGNS AND BATTLES

Since the powers of Europe refrained from direct intervention in the war, the two contestants in America were left to fight it out on their own.

## The Opening Clashes   1861

The year 1861 witnessed several small battles that accomplished large results and one big battle that had no important outcome. The small engagements occurred in Missouri and in western Virginia, the mountainous region that shortly would become the state of West Virginia.

In Missouri the contending forces were headed on the one hand by Governor Claiborne Jackson and other state officials, who wanted to take the state out of the Union, and on the other by Captain (later General) Nathaniel Lyon, commanding a small regular army force at St. Louis. Lyon led his column into southern Missouri, where he was defeated and killed by a superior Confederate force at the Battle of Wilson's Creek (August 10). He had, however, seriously blunted the striking power of the Confederates, and Union forces were able to hold most of the state.

Into western Virginia came a Federal force that had been assembled in Ohio under the command of George B. McClellan. Crossing the Ohio River, the invaders succeeded by the end of the year in "liberating" the mountain people. Although possession of the region placed the Federals on the flank of Virginia, they could not, because of the transportation obstacles presented by the mountains, use it as a base from which to move eastward. The occupation of western Virginia was, however, an important propaganda victory for the North: a Union-sympathizing area in the Confederacy had been wrenched from Southern control.

The one big battle of the year was fought in Virginia in the area between the two capitals. On the Virginia front the Federals occupied three positions. A small force held Fort Monroe on the coast between the York and James rivers. Just south of Washington was an army of over 30,000 under the command of General Irvin McDowell. In the northern end of the Shenandoah Valley (usually called in Civil War literature simply the Valley) were 14,000 Federals commanded by General Robert Patterson, a venerable veteran of the War of 1812 and the Mexican War. Confronting the semicircle of Union armies were three Confederate armies: a small force opposite Fort Monroe; an army of over 20,000 under P. G. T. Beauregard based at Manassas in northern Virginia about thirty miles southwest of Washington; and 9,000 troops in the Valley, commanded by Joseph E. Johnston.

The Federals had larger forces in Virginia than the Confederates, and if McDowell's army could knock out Beauregard's (the principle Confederate force), the war might be ended immediately. The problem was to prevent other Confederate forces from coming to Beauregard's aid. The plan, as worked out, called for Patterson to contain Johnston so that McDowell could deal with Beauregard alone. But Patterson failed.

In mid-July McDowell marched his inexperienced troops toward Manassas, his movement well advertised to the Confederates by Northern newspapers and Southern spies. Beauregard retired behind Bull Run, a small stream north of Manassas, and called on the government to order Johnston to join him. Most of Johnston's army reached Beauregard the day before the battle, making the Northern and Southern armies approximately equal in size, each numbering something over 30,000.

The Battle of Bull Run, or Manassas (July 21), might be summarized by saying that Beauregard never got his offensive into motion and that McDowell's attack almost succeeded. The Confederates stopped a last strong Union assault. Beauregard then ordered a counterattack. As the Confederates slashed forward, a sudden wave of panic struck through the Union troops, wearied after hours of hot, hard fighting and demoralized by the abrupt change of events. They gave way and crossed Bull Run in a rout. Unable to get them in hand north of the stream, McDowell had to order a retreat to Washington.

The Confederates, as disorganized by victory as the Federals were by defeat, and lacking supplies and transport, were in no condition to undertake a forward movement. Lincoln replaced McDowell with General McClellan, the victor of the fighting in western Virginia, and took measures to increase the army. Both sides girded themselves for real war.

## The Western Theater   1862

The first decisive operations in 1862 were in the Western theater. Here the Federals were trying to secure control of the Mississippi line by moving on the river itself or parallel to it. Most of their offensives were combined land-and-naval operations. To achieve their objective, the Federals advanced on the Mississippi from the north and south, moving down from Kentucky and up from the Gulf of Mexico toward New Orleans.

In April a Union squadron of ironclads and wooden vessels commanded by David G. Farragut, destined to be the first American admiral, appeared in the Gulf. Smashing by the weak forts near the mouth of the river, Farragut ran up to New Orleans, defenseless because the Confederate high command had expected the attack to come from above, and forced the civil authorities to surrender the city (April 28–May 1). For the rest of the war the Federals held New Orleans and the southern part of Louisiana. They closed off the mouth of the great river to Confederate trade, grasped the South's largest city and greatest banking center, and secured a base for future operations.

Federal land forces in the West, meanwhile, were under the direction of two departmental commanders. One army, with its base at Louisville, was led by General Don Carlos Buell.

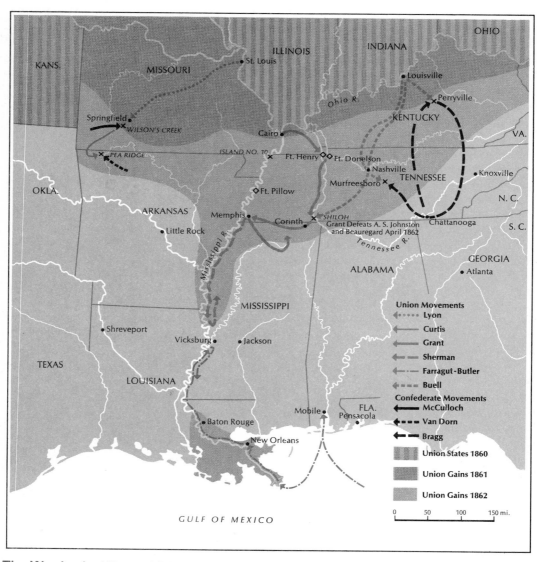

**The War in the West   1861–1862**

West of the Mississippi, Henry W. Halleck, with headquarters in St. Louis, was in command. An army subject to Halleck's control was stationed in western Kentucky under Ulysses S. Grant. All Confederate troops in the West were under the command of one general, Albert Sidney Johnston. A fatal weakness marked the Confederate line in Kentucky. The center, through which flowed the Tennessee and Cumberland rivers, was thrown back (southward) from the flanks, and was defended by two forts, Henry on the Tennessee and Donelson on the Cumberland. The forts had been built when Kentucky was trying to maintain a position of neutrality, and were located just over the Tennessee line. If the Federals, with the aid of naval power, could pierce the center, they would be between the two Confederate flanks and in position to destroy either.

This was exactly what the Federals did in February. Grant secured permission from Halleck to attack Fort Henry, whose defenders, awed by the ironclad river boats accompanying the Union army, surrendered with almost no resistance (February 6). Grant then marched to Donelson while his naval auxiliary moved to the Cumberland River. At Donelson the Confederates put up a scrap, but eventually the garrison of 20,000 had to capitulate (February 16). Grant, by the simple process of cracking the Confederate center and placing himself astride the river communications, had inflicted a near-disaster on the Confederacy. As a result of his movement, the Confederates were forced out of Kentucky and had to yield half of Tennessee.

Halleck now ordered Grant, with about 40,000 troops, to proceed up the Tennessee (southward), and directed Buell, who had occupied Nashville, to march to join Grant. The immediate objective was to destroy Confederate railroad communications in the Corinth, Mississippi, area. Grant debarked his army at Pittsburg Landing, about thirty miles from Corinth. At the latter place, Johnston and Beauregard decided that their only chance to retrieve the recent reverses was to smash Grant before he was joined by Buell. Early in April they moved, 40,000 strong, toward Pittsburg Landing to attack the Federals, who were encamped between two streams flowing into the Tennessee. The

battle that ensued (April 6–7) is usually known as Shiloh. The Confederates caught Grant by surprise, and by the end of the first day's fighting drove him back to the river, but here the attack was halted. At the height of the battle Johnston was killed, and Beauregard assumed command. The next day Grant, reinforced by 25,000 of Buell's troops, went over to the offensive, and regained his original lines. Beauregard then disengaged, and withdrew to Corinth. In the tactical sense, Shiloh was an extremely narrow Union victory. The most important result was strategic in nature: the Confederates had failed to prevent a concentration of the Federal armies.

After Shiloh, Halleck, bringing reinforcements with him, came to Pittsburg Landing to personally direct the advance on Corinth. Moving with excessive caution, he took almost a month to reach the town and to place his army in position to take it by siege. Beauregard, rather than risk the certain entrapment of his forces, wisely evacuated his lines. The Federals now had Corinth and the railroads of which it was the hub. Furthermore, by seizing areas parallel to the Mississippi, they flanked the Confederates out of their positions on the river. By early June the Federals had occupied the river line down as far as Memphis.

At this point Halleck was called to Washington to become general in chief. Before he left, he had assigned missions to Grant and Buell, who again became departmental commanders. To Grant, the best fighting Union general yet to appear, he gave the relatively unimportant task of guarding communications in western Tennessee and northern Mississippi. To Buell, who had done practically no fighting, he assigned the vital objective of seizing Chattanooga on the Tennessee line. For the next few months Grant did little except to repel a Confederate attempt to recover Corinth. Buell took his army to Nashville to prepare his offensive. The Confederate field army in Mississippi now commanded by Braxton Bragg (Davis had relieved Beauregard after the loss of Corinth), moved to Chattanooga, where it would be in position to undertake an offensive.

The Confederates held approximately the eastern half of Tennessee. Bragg's problem was to recover the rest of the state and, if possible, return the war to Kentucky. He was a brilliant strategist with a fatal weakness—he lacked the iron resolution to complete his plans. He now conceived a brilliant scheme. Instead of risking battle with Buell between Chattanooga and Nashville, he would rapidly invade Kentucky, forcing Buell to follow him out of Tennessee. If he could reach Kentucky first, he could place himself between Buell and Louisville and force the Federals to fight on grounds of his own choosing. With Buell smashed, success would be at hand—Kentucky redeemed and the Western states open to invasion. Bragg did get to Kentucky first, he did stand between Buell and Louisville. But instead of fighting he withdrew. Buell went into the city and, reinforced, came out looking for Bragg. The two armies met at the indecisive Battle of Perryville (October 8), after which Bragg retired to Tennessee. Buell followed cautiously, and shortly the President relieved him. His successor was William S. Rosecrans. Toward the end of the year Bragg and Rosecrans, moving forward in simultaneous advances, came together in the hard-fought Battle of Murfreesboro or Stone's River (December 31–January 2). Again Bragg had to retire.

## The Virginia Front   1862

In the Eastern theater in 1862 Union operations were directed by young George B. McClellan, commander of the Army of the Potomac and the most controversial general of the war. McClellan was a superb trainer of men but lacked the fighting instinct, necessary in a great captain, to commit his men to decisive battle.

During the winter of 1861–1862 McClellan had remained inactive, training his army of 150,000 men near Washington. He finally settled on a plan of operations for the spring campaign. Instead of striking for Richmond by moving southward from Washington, he would have the navy transport his army to Fort Monroe on the Virginia coast in the region between the York and James rivers known as the Peninsula. Late in March McClellan started putting his troops on transports to begin his Peninsula campaign. After the general himself had departed for Virginia, Lincoln decided, on the basis of

good evidence, that McClellan had not complied with the directive to leave enough men to protect Washington. Accordingly, he ordered McDowell's corps of over 30,000 men, about to embark to join McClellan, to remain south of Washington.

McClellan was thus deprived of a substantial part of his army, leaving him with something over 100,000. He had, nevertheless, a decisive numerical superiority over the Confederates when he landed at Fort Monroe. By mid-May he was within twenty miles of Richmond, and by the latter part of the month he was approaching the gates of the city. He continued to press Lincoln to send McDowell to him, and finally the President agreed.

The Confederate high command (Davis and Lee) had misgivings about General Joseph E. Johnston's strategy of drawing McClellan closer to Richmond before fighting and they were worried by the possibility that reinforcements, particularly McDowell's corps, might join McClellan. To prevent this, Lee devised a scheme which Davis approved. The commander of the Confederate forces in the Shenandoah Valley, Thomas J. ("Stonewall") Jackson, was directed to move northward, giving the impression that he meant to cross the Potomac. In the brilliant Valley campaign (May 4–June 9) Jackson attacked and defeated two separate Federal armies, then drove toward the northern end of the Valley. Partly to defend the approaches to Washington and partly to trap Jackson, Lincoln rushed forces to the Valley, including McDowell's corps. Jackson slipped back to safety before the various Union forces could converge on him. McDowell's troops were so fatigued by their long march that their movement to McClellan had to be suspended.

While these events were unfolding in the Valley, Johnston at last attacked McClellan at Fair Oaks or Seven Pines (May 31–June 1). The attack failed to budge McClellan, and Johnston was so seriously wounded that he had to relinquish the command. To replace him Davis named the man who would lead the Army of Northern Virginia for the rest of the war, Robert E. Lee.

Lee, a brilliant field commander, realized that the Confederacy could not win its independence

## Union Dead at Gettysburg

Photography was a well-developed art in America at the time of the Civil War. Photographers followed the armies and took many pictures of camp and field scenes, like the one shown here. Although these men were good artists, they labored under handicaps that prevented them from recording the war fully. The size and weight of their cameras and tripods restricted their freedom of movement. More important, the early cameras required a long exposure, which made it almost impossible to photograph any subject in motion. (Library of Congress)

merely by repelling offensives. It would have to destroy a Union army, and to achieve this purpose Lee was ready to risk something. Informed by his cavalry leader, J. E. B. Stuart, that one-third of McClellan's army was north of the Chickahominy and two-thirds south, Lee devised a daring plan. He would call Jackson from the Valley, bringing his army up to 85,000 (as compared to McClellan's 100,000), mass his forces north of the Chickahominy, and fall on the exposed Union right and destroy it. Lee's thought was that then McClellan would retreat to the York River and that he could follow and smash him before he reached his base. The risk in the plan was that McClellan would discover he confronted only a small enemy force on his left and would move into Richmond.

The operation that followed, which involved several engagements, is known as the Battle of the Seven Days (June 25–July 1). It did not pro-ceed as Lee expected. He drove back the Union right wing but was unable to destroy it. Then McClellan, instead of retiring to the York, abandoned his base there and headed southward for the James, where he had asked the navy to set up a new base. Lee followed, trying desperately to destroy the Federals, but McClellan extricated his army, even inflicting a bloody repulse on Lee at Malvern Hill. He reached Harrison's Landing on the James, where with naval support, he was safe from any attack Lee could launch.

At Harrison's Landing the Federal army was only twenty-five miles from Richmond, and it had a secure line of water communications. But Lincoln, instead of replacing McClellan with a more aggressive commander, decided to evacuate the army to northern Virginia where it would be combined with a smaller force under John Pope—in short, to begin a new operation on the Washington-to-Richmond "overland" route.

As the Army of the Potomac left the Peninsula by water, Lee, understanding what was happening, moved his army northward with the purpose of striking Pope before he was joined by McClellan. As Lee approached, Pope retired north of the Rappahannock River. Some units of McClellan's army had reached him, and, as it developed that he might be forced into a battle, others were sent on as soon as they arrived. By a brilliant stratagem, Lee passed part of his army to Pope's rear, drawing the Federals north, and then followed with the remainder of his force. Pope, who was rash where McClellan was timid, was under the delusion that he faced only Jackson's corps. Although not all of McClellan's troops had joined him, he attacked the Confederates near Manassas: the Battle of Second Manassas or Second Bull Run (August 29–30). Lee easily halted the assault, and in a powerful counterstroke swept Pope from the field. The beaten Federals retired to the Washington defenses, where Lincoln relieved Pope and placed all the troops around the city under McClellan's command.

Lee gave the Federals no respite. Early in September he went over to the offensive, invading western Maryland. With some misgivings, Lincoln let McClellan go to meet Lee. As McClellan advanced, he had a wonderful piece of luck. He captured an order by Lee showing that the Confederate army was divided, a part of it under Jackson having gone to capture Harpers Ferry. McClellan's move was to advance rapidly and attack before the enemy could concentrate. But Lee had time to pull most of his army together behind Antietam Creek near the town of Sharpsburg. Here, on September 17, McClellan, with 87,000 men, threw a series of powerful attacks at Lee's 50,000. Late in the day it seemed that the Confederate line would break, but at this moment the rest of Jackson's troops arrived from Harpers Ferry to plug the hole. Even then McClellan might have won with one more assault. But his caution asserted itself, and he called off the battle. Lee retired to Virginia, and after an interval of reorganization McClellan followed. Lincoln, disgusted by McClellan's failure to exploit his victory, removed him from command in November. It was Mc-

Clellan's last military appearance in the war.

As McClellan's successor Lincoln appointed Ambrose E. Burnside, a modest mediocrity. Burnside thought that the government desired him to fight, and fight he would. He planned to drive at Richmond by crossing the Rappahannock at Fredericksburg, the strongest defensive point on that river. On December 13 he flung his army at Lee's defenses in a hopeless, bloody attack. At the end of a day of bitter failure and after suffering 12,000 casualties, he withdrew to the north side of the Rappahannock. Soon he was relieved at his own request.

## Year of Decision   1863

As 1863 opened, the Union army in the East was commanded by Burnside's successor, Joseph Hooker—"Fighting Joe," as the newspapers called him. His army, which numbered 120,000, lay north of the Rappahannock opposite Fredericksburg. Hooker maneuvered opposite the town to hold Lee's attention, and crossed part of his army far up the Rappahannock. This flanking force came down on the south side, threatening to turn Lee's left. To complete his brilliant movement Hooker had only to push on to the open country around Fredericksburg—and he would have Lee in a vise. But Hooker lost his nerve. Now he hesitated, and fell back to a defensive position at Chancellorsville in the desolate area of scrub trees and brush known in Virginia as the Wilderness. Here Lee came up to attack him.

The Battle of Chancellorsville (May 1–5) was one of Lee's most brilliant exploits. With an army of only 60,000 (part of his force had been detached for other service), he took great but justified risks. Leaving a small force at Fredericksburg to contain the Federals at that point, he moved to confront Hooker. He divided his army and sent Jackson to hit the Union right, which was exposed, while he struck from in front. Finally Hooker, aided by a diversion from his troops at Fredericksburg, extricated his forces to the north side of the river. Again Lee had won, but not the decisive victory he had hoped for. And he had lost his ablest lieutenant. Jackson, wounded in the fighting, died soon afterward.

While the Federals were failing in the East,

**Vicksburg Campaign  1863**

a different story was unfolding in the West, one that would influence future operations in the Eastern theater. U. S. Grant was driving at Vicksburg, the most strongly fortified Confederate point on the Mississippi River. Coming down the river with naval support, he debarked his army on the Louisiana side above the city. From here he crossed to the east bank, and struck at the Confederate defenses, which were commanded by John C. Pemberton. He struck several blows, and each one failed. The terrain he was operating in north of Vicksburg was low, marshy, and laced by numerous streams and bayous, and it baffled every attempt of the army and navy to traverse it. Grant had little confidence that any of his moves would succeed; he was keeping his forces busy until the spring, when he intended to try another route to the city.

In May he unveiled his plan. The navy ran transports past the river batteries to a point below Vicksburg. The army marched down the west side, where it was met by the navy and transported to the east side. Now Grant was south of Vicksburg on relatively high and dry ground. Moving rapidly, he defeated enemy forces barring his way at Champion's Hill and the Big Black River, and closed in on Vicksburg itself. After failing to storm the strong works, he settled down to a siege, which endured for six weeks. Pemberton, realizing that his government could not break Grant's hold and that his garrison of 30,000 was exhausted by constant fighting, surrendered on July 4. Immediately thereafter the other Confederate strong point on the river, Port Hudson (Louisiana) surrendered to a Federal force that had come up from New Orleans under N. P. Banks.

At last the Federals had achieved one of their principal strategic aims; they had gained control of the Mississippi line. The Confederacy was split into two parts, and the trans-Mississippi area was isolated from the main section. A great turning point in the war had been reached.

When the siege of Vicksburg began, the Confederate high command in Richmond was dismayed at the prospect of losing the great river fortress. Various plans to relieve the city were discussed, the principal one being a proposal to send part of Lee's army to Tennessee, possibly with Lee himself in command, to launch an offensive. But Lee demurred; he did not want to leave Virginia. He put forward a counterscheme: he would invade Pennsylvania. If he could win a victory on Northern soil, he said, great results would follow. The North might abandon the war, England and France might intervene, and the pressure on Vicksburg and other fronts would be broken. The government assented, and in June Lee started his movement, swinging his army west toward the Valley and then north through Maryland into Pennsylvania.

As Lee advanced, Hooker moved back to confront him, marching parallel to the line of Lee's route. But Hooker evidently had been unnerved by his experience at Chancellorsville. He seemed to be looking for a chance to escape his responsibility, and he soon found an excuse to ask to be relieved. To replace him Lincoln appointed an army corps commander, George G. Meade, a solid if unimaginative soldier. Meade followed Lee, and approached what might be called the strategic rear of the Confederate army in southern Pennsylvania. Lee, who had not expected the Federals to move so rapidly, was astounded when he learned of their nearness. With his army marching in three columns, he was in a dangerous position; hurriedly he had to concentrate his forces. Meade, realizing that Lee in enemy country had to attack or retreat, selected a strong defensive site at the little town of Gettysburg, a road hub in the region, and Lee, seeking contact with the Federals, moved toward the same spot. Here on July 1–3 was fought the most celebrated battle of the war.

The Union army occupied a formidable position on the heights south of the town. Their line resembled an inverted fishhook, the right resting on Culp's Hill and Cemetery Hill and the front stretching along Cemetery Ridge for three miles. On the first day (July 1) the two armies jockeyed for position around Gettysburg; the tough fighting started the following day. Lee, confident of the prowess of his troops and combative by nature, decided to attack even though he was outnumbered 90,000 to 75,000. On July 2 he threw an assault at the Union left on Cemetery Ridge which crumpled up an advanced Federal corps but failed to reach the main line. On July 3 he mounted a greater effort: 15,000

men were to hit the center of the ridge and crack the Federal line wide open. The attacking force advanced over almost a mile of open space swept by enemy fire (the famous Pickett's charge). Only about 5,000 men reached the ridge, and these had to surrender or retreat. After a day of sullen waiting by both armies, Lee withdrew his shattered forces to Virginia. Meade, who had little aggressive instinct, made but a feeble pursuit. Although Meade had thrown away an opportunity to end the war, Gettysburg was another turning point. The total Confederate losses in the campaign were close to 25,000. Never again would Lee feel strong enough to fight offensively.

A third turning point against the Confederacy was reached in Tennessee. In the autumn Rosecrans moved toward Chattanooga. Bragg, in order to secure room to maneuver, evacuated the town, which was occupied by the Federals on September 9. Rosecrans, forgetting that he had not defeated Bragg, rashly plunged over the Georgia line in pursuit, where Bragg, reinforced by troops from Lee's army, was lying in wait to attack. Rosecrans barely got his scattered forces in hand before Bragg delivered his assault at Chickamauga (September 19–20). This was one of the few battles in which the Confederates enjoyed a numerical superiority (70,000 to 56,000). On the second day Bragg smashed the Union right wide open. Rosecrans and his corps generals on that flank fled to Chattanooga even though his left continued to fight under the command of George H. Thomas, who here won the nickname of "the Rock of Chickamauga." Shortly Thomas too had to retire, and the beaten army fell back into the Chattanooga defenses.

Bragg did not move rapidly to exploit his victory, partly because of his heavy casualties (17,000), but eventually he advanced and occupied the heights south of Chattanooga. Mounting batteries on these points, he commanded the roads leading into the city and virtually shut off its supplies. The Union high command, however, had ample resources to break the siege. Grant was named departmental commander of the West. Immediately he replaced Rosecrans with Thomas, and came with part of his own army to Chattanooga. The reinforced Federal army numbered 60,000, while Bragg's army was

**Gettysburg Campaign 1863**

weakened by the detachment of a force for a fruitless operation against Knoxville. At the Battle of Chattanooga (November 23–25) the Federals hurled Bragg from his lines on Missionary Ridge and Lookout Mountain and back into northern Georgia. They then proceeded to occupy most of east Tennessee.

A second objective of Northern strategy had been achieved: possession of the Tennessee River line. From the Chattanooga base the Federals were in position to split the Confederacy again—what was left of it. Chattanooga deserves to be ranked with Vicksburg and Gettysburg. After 1863 the Confederacy had no chance on any front to win its independence by a military decision. Now it could hope to triumph only by exhausting the Northern will to fight.

## The Ending   1864–1865

Grant's plans for 1864 called for two great offensives. The Army of the Potomac, commanded by Meade but accompanied and directed by Grant, was to seek to bring Lee to decisive battle in northern Virginia. From near Chattanooga the Western army, commanded by William T. Sherman, was to advance into northern Georgia, destroy the Confederate army, now commanded by Joseph E. Johnston, and wreck the economic resources of Atlanta.

The two offensives started in May. From its position in northern Virginia the Army of the Potomac, 115,000 strong, crossed the Rappahannock and Rapidan rivers, and plunged into the Wilderness area. Grant's plan was to envelop Lee's right and force him to a showdown battle. Lee, whose army numbered about 75,000 at the beginning of the campaign, was determined to avoid a showdown unless he saw a chance to deal a decisive blow. In the Battle of the Wilderness (May 5–7) each commander struck savagely at the other. Demonstrating superb defensive skill, Lee prevented Grant from turning his right. But the Federal commander, instead of retiring to reorganize as his predecessors had done after a reverse, slid off to his left

**Military Engagements**
1 Wilderness May 5–7, 1864
2 Spotsylvania May 8–19, 1864
3 North Anna May 23–26, 1864
4 Cold Harbor June 1–3, 1864
5 Petersburg Campaign June 1864–April 1865
6 Five Forks April 1, 1865
7 Saylor's Creek April 6, 1865
8 Appomattox Court House
   Lee Surrenders to Grant April 9, 1865

Union Movements
Confederate Movements
Confederate Defense Line

0   10   20   30 mi.

**Virginia Campaigns   1864–1865**

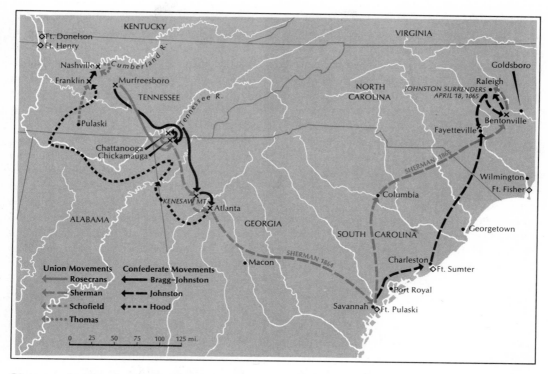

**Sherman's March Through the Confederacy    1864–1865**

and to the southeast. He turned up at Spotsylvania Court House, where Lee moved to meet him. Here another bloody, indecisive engagement was fought (May 8–19). Again Grant sidled to his left, and again Lee slid with him. In this manner, without fighting another major clash, the two armies moved until they reached Cold Harbor, a few miles north of Richmond. At this point Grant made a last attempt to destroy Lee north of Richmond (June 1–3) and was bloodily repulsed. In a month of fighting Grant had lost in total casualties 55,000 men, and Lee, 31,000.

Now Grant had to alter his strategy. If he remained where he was, Lee would retire into the Richmond defenses to stand a siege, something Grant wanted to avoid. Masking his movements from his adversary, Grant moved southward across the James heading for Petersburg, directly south of Richmond. Petersburg was the hub of all the railroads feeding into the capital; if Grant could secure it he could force Lee to come into the open to fight for his communica-

tions. He almost succeeded. Petersburg was defended only by a small force under Beauregard, who managed, however, to hold Grant off until Lee's army could arrive. Grant now realized that he would have to resort to siege operations. He dug in, and so did Lee. The trench lines of the two armies stretched for miles above and below Petersburg. Always Grant strove to extend his left around Lee's right so as to get on the railroads that were the lifeline of the Southern army. It would be nine months until he reached his objective.

In May, Sherman, with an army of over 90,-000, moved against Johnston's army at Atlanta, which numbered 60,000 at the beginning. Johnston's plan was to delay Sherman, to fight for time, and not to commit his forces unless the conditions were exceptionally favorable. The Atlanta campaign developed primarily into a game of maneuver in which Sherman tried to trap his rival, who avoided being caught. The two armies skirmished and fought almost constantly, but the only set battle was at Kennesaw

Mountain (June 27). As Sherman was approaching Atlanta, President Davis replaced Johnston with John B. Hood. Combative by nature, Hood threw two successive attacks at Sherman, both of which failed. The Union army occupied Atlanta on September 2.

Sherman had not destroyed the enemy army. Eager to strike deeper into Georgia, he sent 30,000 of his army to Tennessee under Thomas, and prepared to move for Savannah on the coast. At the same time Hood decided to invade Tennessee, hoping to force Sherman to follow him.

Confronting Hood, and seeking to delay him, was a Union force of about 30,000 under John M. Schofield. Hood caught up with Schofield at Franklin, Tennessee, on November 30. With no artillery support, Hood resolved to attack across two miles of open space, though the Federals were entrenched in a strong position. In six fruitless charges he lost 6,000 men; eleven of his generals were killed or wounded. After that he might as well have gone back to Georgia. But he moved forward and took up a position south of Nashville. In the city Thomas was gathering an army that would eventually number over 60,000. When he was ready, he came out looking for Hood. At the Battle of Nashville (December 15–16) he smashed Hood from the field. As the Confederates retreated toward Mississippi, they were harried by the most merciless cavalry pursuit of the war. Only a few units reached Mississippi intact. The Confederate Army of Tennessee had, in effect, ceased to exist.

In the meantime Sherman was marching almost unopposed across Georgia, inaugurating a new kind of warfare. He was the prophet of modern total war—war against the civilian population of the enemy, war intended to break the enemy people's will to resist. His army marched on a sixty-mile front, destroying property and supplies that might be used by the Confederate forces and committing many individual depredations as well. But the greatest result of Sher-

man's march was psychological rather than economic. What Southerner who heard of a Union army moving at will through the heart of the South could ever believe again that the Confederacy could win the war? In Virginia soldiers in Lee's army deserted to go home to take care of their families. By December 20 Sherman was at Savannah.

Sherman then turned into South Carolina, still facing slight opposition and still ripping up enemy property. He was accomplishing two objectives: destroying both Confederate resources and the railroads that brought supplies from the lower South to Lee's army. When he advanced into North Carolina, the Confederate government got together an army of 30,000 under Johnston to oppose him, but this small force could do little more than delay his march. Nor could Lee move against him, for he was pinned down at Petersburg by Grant.

In April 1865, Grant finally passed a part of his army around Lee's right to the vital railroads. The Confederates evacuated Petersburg and Richmond, and Lee moved westward with his army, now shrunk to about 25,000. His one forlorn hope was to reach a rail line to North Carolina and unite with Johnston. But the pursuing Federal army barred his escape route. At last he realized that further fighting was hopeless, and on April 9 he met Grant at Appomattox and surrendered the Army of Northern Virginia. In North Carolina Joe Johnston reached the same conclusion, and on April 18 he surrendered to Sherman near Durham. Jefferson Davis, defiant to the last and unable to recognize defeat, fled southward, and was captured in Georgia. The war was soon over.

## THE PROBLEM OF PEACEMAKING

The Constitution provides for peacemaking at the end of a foreign war. The President, with the advice and consent of the Senate, ratifies a

### The Impact of War on the South

Because most of the fighting in the Civil War occurred in the South, that section suffered widespread destruction of its physical resources. At the top is Fredericksburg, Virginia, the site of a battle in 1862, and below is Columbia, South Carolina, much of which was burned when occupied by Sherman's army in 1864. (Library of Congress)

treaty of peace. But the Constitution naturally makes no provision for ending a civil war. And Lincoln could not negotiate a treaty with Confederate leaders, for that would mean recognizing the legal existence of the Confederacy. Yet, once the armies had stopped fighting, a peace arrangement somehow had to be made.

## The War's Aftermath

In the North, the wartime prosperity continued into the postwar years, but Northerners who visited the South were appalled when they gazed upon the desolation left in the wake of the war—gutted towns, wrecked plantations, neglected fields, collapsed bridges, and ruined railroads. Much of the personal property of Southerners had been lost with the lost cause. Confederate bonds and currency were now worthless, and capital that had been invested in them was gone forever. And with the emancipation of the slaves, Southern whites would be deprived of property worth an estimated $2 billion.

Matching the shattered economy of the South was the disorganization of its social system. In the months that followed the end of the war, when thousands of soldiers were drifting back to their homes—258,000 never returned and other thousands went back wounded or sick— life was seriously deranged. To many people the problem of keeping alive, of securing food and shelter, seemed the only thing that mattered.

If conditions were bad for Southern whites, they were generally worse for Southern blacks —the 4 million who were emerging from the bondage that had held them and their ancestors for two and a half centuries. Many of these people, too, had seen service of one kind or another during the war. Some had served as body servants for Confederate officers or as teamsters and laborers for the Confederate armies. Tens of thousands had fought as combat troops in the Union ranks, and more than 38,000 had given their lives for the Union cause. Among the black soldiers the death rate was much higher than among the whites, partly because of the haste and poor preparation with which Negroes were sometimes sent into action, partly because of the usual Confederate practice of granting them

no quarter in battle. Countless other Negroes, who never wore a uniform or drew army pay, assisted the Union forces as spies or scouts. Still others ran off from the plantations, thus depriving the South of labor, and flocked into the Union lines, often to be put to work for the Union armies. Certainly the blacks contributed a great deal of effort and sacrifice to the winning of their own freedom.

As the war ended, freedom appeared to be on the way, but its arrival was uncertain. The Thirteenth Amendment, which would make slavery unconstitutional, had yet to be ratified by the requisite number of states (it had passed Congress on February 1, 1865, and was to be proclaimed in effect on December 18, 1865). On many plantations the blacks were still being detained and forced to work. Most planters agreed with a former Confederate leader who was saying (in June 1865) that slavery had been "the best system of labor that could be devised for the Negro race" and that the wise thing to do now would be to "provide a substitute for it."

To get away from their old masters, thousands of Negroes continued to leave the plantations. Old and young, many of them feeble and ill, they trudged to the nearest town or city or they roamed the countryside, camping at night on the bare ground. Few had any possessions except the rags on their backs. Somehow they managed to stay alive.

What the Negroes wanted was, first of all, to be assured of their freedom—to feel it, to exercise it, and to know it was not going to be taken from them. Next, they needed immediate relief from the threat of starvation. Then, looking ahead, they desired land, farms of their own, a bit of economic independence. A few of the freed slaves had already settled on abandoned plantations, notably on the Sea Islands along the South Carolina coast and on land in Mississippi that had belonged to the Davis family. The Negroes also longed for schooling for their children if not for themselves. In some places, above all in New Orleans, there were well educated and highly cultured communities of blacks who had been free for generations. But education was a rare and precious thing to the new freedmen, most of whom were as illiterate as the slave codes had intended them to be. Finally, a num-

## The Black Code of Louisiana

The sections in the Black Codes regulating Negro labor angered Northern opinion and turned many people in favor of Radical Reconstruction. The Louisiana Code had this to say:

*Sec. 1. Be it enacted by the Senate and House of Representatives of the State of Louisiana in general assembly convened, That all persons employed as laborers in agricultural pursuits shall be required, during the first ten days of the month of January of each year, to make contracts for labor for the then ensuing year, or for the year next ensuing the termination of their present contracts. All contracts for labor for agricultural purposes shall be made in writing, signed by the employer, and shall be made in the presence of a Justice of the Peace and two disinterested witnesses, in whose presence the contract shall be read to the laborer, and when assented to and signed by the latter, shall be considered as binding for the time prescribed. . . .*

*Sec. 2. Every laborer shall have full and perfect liberty to choose his employer, but, when once chosen, he shall not be allowed to leave his place of employment until the fulfillment of his contract . . . and if they do so leave, without cause or permission, they shall forfeit all wages earned to the time of abandonment. . . .*

ber of the Negroes were beginning to demand political rights. "The only salvation for us besides the power of the Government is in the *possession of the ballot*," a convention of the colored people of Virginia resolved in the summer of 1865. "All we ask is an *equal chance.*"

The federal government, besides keeping troops (many of them black) in the South to preserve order and protect the Negroes, was doing something to assist them in the transition from slavery to freedom. Congress had set up (in March 1865) the Bureau of Freedmen, Refugees, and Abandoned Lands as an agency of the army. This Freedmen's Bureau was empowered to provide food, transportation, assistance in getting jobs and fair wages, and schools for former slaves, and also to settle them on abandoned or confiscated lands. Under the able direction of General Oliver O. Howard, the bureau undertook to perform its allotted functions, and more. Its agents soon distributed 20 million rations in the South, to hungry whites as well as blacks. Cooperating with the bureau, especially in its educational work, were missionaries and teachers who had been sent to the South by Freedmen's Aid Societies and other private and church groups in the North.

Nevertheless, the future of the blacks remained in doubt. The Freedmen's Bureau, according to the law creating it, was to last for only one year after the end of the war. Meanwhile, the majority of Southern whites resented the activities of the bureau and its agents. These outsiders stood in the way of the desire to set up a substitute for slavery, a substitute that would serve both as a cheap-labor system and as a white-supremacy device.

## Reconstruction: The Issues

The word "Reconstruction," as contemporaries used it, referred to the process by which peace was to be made, that is, the process by which the states of the defeated Confederacy were to be brought back to their former places in the Union. One possibility would be to grant easy terms, permitting the states to return promptly and with little internal change except for the elimination of slavery. Another possibility would be to make a harsh peace, delaying the readmission of the states until they had been reconstructed in such a way as to reduce the power of the rebel leaders.

A quick and easy restoration of the Union would be to the advantage of the former Confederates and the Democratic party North and South. Ironically, the abolition of slavery would increase the power of the Southern states in national politics. In the past, under the "three-fifths clause" of the Constitution, only three-fifths of the slaves had been counted in determining a state's representation in Congress and its electoral votes in presidential elections. In the future, *all* the former slaves would be counted, whether or not they themselves were given political rights. A state such as South Carolina, where about half of the population was black, would have its congressional representation increased, for example, by approximately 20 per cent. With this added strength the Southern Democrats could rejoin the Northern Democrats and get control of both Congress and the Presidency.

The consequences of an easy peace, by the same token, could be disastrous for the Republican party. The Republicans had gained control of the federal government in 1860–1861 only because of the split in the Democratic party and the secession of the Southern states. Once these had been restored and the Democratic party had been reunited, the Republicans would face the uncomfortable prospect of being reduced to a minority group once again. The outlook was disturbing also for Northern businessmen who during the war had obtained favors from the federal government—a high tariff, railroad subsidies, the national banking system —which might be ended once the Democrats were back in power.

For the Negroes emerging from slavery, a quick restoration of the Southern states would be catastrophic. The master class, which had dominated the state governments before and during the war, would continue to do so. The Negroes then could expect to be kept in a position that, at best, would be somewhere between slavery and freedom.

Thus the issues of Reconstruction were very similar to those of the war itself. So far as the Southern leaders were concerned, the war had been fought for the independence of the South and for the preservation of slavery (in 1861 the Confederate Vice President, Alexander H. Stephens, had frankly proclaimed that slavery was the "cornerstone" of the Confederacy). After the war these leaders hoped to maintain a considerable degree of Southern autonomy through

the assertion of state rights, and they hoped to retain much of the essence of slavery by finding some substitute for it. If they should have their way in Reconstruction, the "lost cause" they had fought for would not be completely lost.

The issues were often obscured and complicated by the emotionalism of the controversy over Reconstruction. On both sides people approached the question in a spirit of hatred left over from the four years of bloodshed. In the North there was the memory of sacrifice, suffering, and personal loss; in the South there was even more of that, plus the added bitterness of defeat. In the North there was a widespread feeling that Southerners ought to be required to acknowledge their defeat by some gesture of submission, and that at least a few of them ought to be punished for their guilt in bringing on the war and also for the atrocities which, according to Northern wartime propaganda, they had committed in the course of it. Moreover, there was a general conviction that the former slaves ought to be protected in their freedom and assured of justice. And there was a growing belief that Reconstruction offered a heaven-sent opportunity to recast the South in the image of the North—to take that supposedly backward, feudal, undemocratic section and civilize and modernize it.

The Reconstruction question was further complicated by disputes over the respective roles that the President and Congress were to play. Presumably, the task should have been one for the executive and the legislative branches, the two acting in cooperation. As it happened, however, the President and the congressional majority differed on the policy to be followed. Hence arose the issue of presidential as opposed to congressional powers.

Even among the majority in Congress—the Republicans—there was disagreement as to the kind of peace that should be imposed upon the South. The same factions of the party (the Conservatives and the Radicals) that had clashed on wartime emancipation now confronted each other on the issue of Reconstruction. The Conservatives advocated a mild peace and the rapid restoration of the defeated states to the Union; beyond insisting that the South accept the abolition of slavery, they would not interfere with

## Thaddeus Stevens on Reconstruction [1865]

Bitterly frank in speech, Stevens announced his purposes in Reconstruction in a speech delivered in 1865:

*The whole fabric of southern society must be changed and never can it be done if this opportunity is lost. Without this, this Government can never be, as it never has been, a true republic. Heretofore, it had more the features of aristocracy than of democracy.—The southern States have been despotisms, not governments of the people. It is impossible that any practical equality of rights can exist where a few thousand men monopolize the whole landed property. The larger the number of small proprietors the more safe and stable the government. If the South is ever to be made a safe republic let her lands be cultivated by the toil of the owners or the free labor of intelligent citizens. This must be done though it drive her nobility into exile. If they go, all the better.*

race relations or attempt to alter the social system of the South. The Radicals, directed by leaders like Thaddeus Stevens of Pennsylvania and Charles Sumner of Massachusetts, stood for a hard peace; they urged that the civil and military chieftains of the late Confederacy be subjected to severe punishment, that large numbers of Southern whites be disfranchised, and that the property of rich Southerners who had aided the Confederacy be confiscated and distributed among the freedmen. From the first, some Radicals favored granting suffrage to the former slaves, as a matter of right or as a means of creating a Republican electorate in the South. Other Radicals agreed with them, but hesitated to state a position for fear of public opinion— not all Northern states permitted Negroes to vote.

Between the Radicals and the Conservatives stood a faction of uncommitted Republicans who may be termed the Moderates. They would go further than the Conservatives in demanding concessions of the South, particularly in regard to rights for Negroes, but they rejected the punitive goals of the Radicals. As the Reconstruction controversy developed, the pressure of events would inexorably force the Moderates into the Radical camp.

The various proponents of a Reconstruction policy, following an honored American tradition, attempted to buttress their position with constitutional sanction. The Conservatives, claiming that secession was illegal, contended that the seceded states had never legally been out of the Union, were still in it, and had all the rights of states. The Radicals, the uncompromising nationalists of the war, now insisted that the Southern states had in fact withdrawn from the nation and had therefore forfeited their rights as states. Sumner argued that by seceding they had committed "state suicide," and Stevens bluntly referred to them as "conquered provinces." On the other hand, Southerners who had fought to uphold the right of secession now demanded all the privileges they had previously enjoyed in the Union they had tried to dissolve.

## Lincoln's Plan

The process of Reconstruction was put into motion while the war was still going on, and the first plan was presented by President Lincoln. He believed there were a considerable number of actual or potential Unionists in the South. These people, most of them former Whigs, could possibly be encouraged to rejoin the old Whigs of the North and thus strengthen the Republican party, once the Union had been restored. More immediately, these men could serve as the nucleus for setting up new and loyal states in the South and thereby hastening reunion. All along, Lincoln was concerned with principle as well as politics: the principle of the inviolability of the Union. He wanted to restore the American experiment in democracy as soon as possible. Consequently, he proposed an easy mode of Reconstruction. He would subordinate to his larger goal such questions as punishment of the defeated side or determination of the status of the freedmen. The question of whether the defeated states were in or out of the Union he dismissed as a "merely pernicious abstraction." They were only out of their proper, practical relationship to the Union, he said, and they should be restored to that relationship as soon as possible.

Specifically, Lincoln's plan, which he announced to the public in a proclamation of December 1863, offered a general amnesty to all who would take an oath pledging future loyalty to the government. Temporarily excluded from the right to swear the oath were high civil and military officials of the Confederacy. Whenever in any state 10 per cent of the number of voters in 1860 took the oath, they could proceed to set up a state government. The oath required acceptance of the wartime acts and proclamations of Congress and the President concerning slavery. This was the only provision in the plan that imposed on the South a condition for readmission and the only part of the plan that dealt with national supervision of race relations. Instead of demanding outright abolition (the Thirteenth Amendment had not yet been passed, and the postwar effect of the Emancipation Proclamation was uncertain, since it was a war measure), Lincoln told Southern leaders that he hoped they would provide for permanent freedom. He also urged them to give the ballot to at least a few Negroes—to those who were educated, owned property, and had served in the Union army. In three Southern states—Louisiana, Arkansas, and Tennessee—loyal governments were reestablished under the Lincoln formula in 1864.

The Radical Republicans were angered and astonished at the mildness of Lincoln's program, and they were able to induce Congress to repudiate his governments. Representatives from the Lincoln states were not admitted to Congress, and the electoral vote of those states was not counted in the election of 1864. In defeating Lincoln's plan, the Radicals were aided by a number of Moderate Republicans who thought that the President's scheme did not provide adequate protection for the freedmen. The Radicals could not stop, however, with a rejection of Lincoln's plan. The requirements of politics dictated that they produce a plan of their own. But at the moment the Radicals had not thought the Reconstruction problem through. They were not agreed as to how "hard" a peace they should enforce on the South, and they were not certain that Northern opinion would support the ideas of their more extreme leaders.

Under pressure, they prepared and passed (in July 1864) the Wade-Davis Bill, which may be considered the first Radical plan of Reconstruction. By its provisions, the President was to appoint for each conquered state a provisional governor who would take a census of all adult white males. If a majority of those enrolled—instead of Lincoln's 10 per cent—swore an oath of allegiance, the governor was to call an election for a state constitutional convention. The privilege of voting for delegates to this meeting was limited to those who could swear that they had never borne arms against the United States, the so-called "iron-clad oath." The convention was required to put provisions into the new constitution abolishing slavery, disfranchising Confederate civil and military leaders, and repudiating the Confederate and state war debts. After these conditions had been met, Congress would readmit the state to the Union. The Wade-Davis Bill was more drastic in almost every respect than the Lincoln plan, and it assumed that the seceded states were out of the Union and hence under the dictation of Congress. But the bill, like the President's proposal, left up to the states the question of political rights for Negroes.

The Wade-Davis Bill was passed a few days before Congress adjourned, which enabled Lincoln to dispose of it with a pocket veto. His action enraged the authors of the measure, Benjamin F. Wade and Henry Winter Davis, who issued a blistering denunciation of the veto, the Wade-Davis Manifesto, warning the President not to interfere with the powers of Congress to control Reconstruction. Lincoln could not ignore the bitterness and the strength of the Radical opposition. Practical as always, he realized that he would have to accept some of the objections of the Radicals. He began to move toward a new approach to Reconstruction, possibly one that included greater national supervision of the freedmen.

What plan he would have come up with nobody can say. On April 14, 1865, a crazed actor, John Wilkes Booth, under the delusion that he was helping the South, shot the President in a Washington theater. Lincoln died early the following morning, and because of the circumstances of his death—the heroic leader, the Great Emancipator struck down in the hour of victory by an assassin—he achieved immediate martyrdom. In the wild excitement of the hour, it was widely assumed that Booth had been instigated to his mad act by men in the South, and the Radicals played on this theme with reckless charges implicating high Confederates. Ironically, Lincoln's death helped to kill his policy of a generous peace.

## Johnson and "Restoration"

The conservative leadership in the controversy over Reconstruction fell upon Lincoln's successor, Andrew Johnson. Of all the men who accidentally inherited the Presidency, Johnson was undoubtedly the most unfortunate. A Southerner and former slaveholder, he became President as a bloody war against the South was drawing to a close. A Democrat before he had been placed on the Union ticket with Lincoln in 1864, he became the head of a Republican administration at a time when partisan passions, held in some restraint during the war, were about to rule the government. As if these handicaps of background were not enough, Johnson was intemperate in language and tactless in manner, and he lacked Lincoln's skill in handling people. Unlike Lincoln, he was theoretical rather than practical, dogmatic rather than pragmatic. In dealing with Reconstruction, he stood righteously by the Constitution, even though that document obviously did not envision the unprecedented constitutional situation that existed after the war.

Johnson revealed his plan of Reconstruction —or "Restoration," as he preferred to call it— soon after he took office, and he proceeded to execute it during the summer of 1865 when Congress was not in session. He applied it to the eight states of the late Confederacy that had not come under the Lincoln plan; he recognized as legal organizations the Lincoln governments in Louisiana, Arkansas, Tennessee, and Virginia.

In some ways Johnson's scheme resembled Lincoln's; in others it was similar to the Wade-

**Andrew Johnson**

Johnson, who was a tailor before going into politics, was of medium height and size. He had a dark complexion and piercing black eyes. A powerful orator on the stump, he easily lost his temper when heckled and used crude and intemperate language. Sincerely devoted to his principles, he was sometimes too theoretical in upholding them. (Library of Congress)

Davis Bill. Like his predecessor, Johnson assumed that the seceded states were still in the Union, and, also like Lincoln, he announced his design in a proclamation of amnesty that extended pardon for past conduct to all who would take an oath of allegiance. Denied the privilege of taking the oath until they received individual pardons from the President were high-ranking Confederate officials and also men with land worth $20,000 or more; Johnson excluded a larger number of leaders than Lincoln had. For each state the President appointed a provisional governor who was to invite the qualified voters to elect delegates to a constitutional convention. Johnson did not specify that a minimum number of voters had to take the oath, as had the Lincoln and Wade-Davis proposals, but the implication was plain that he would require a majority. As conditions of readmittance, the state had to revoke the ordinance of secession, abolish slavery and ratify the Thirteenth Amendment, and repudiate the Confederate and state war debts—essentially the same stipulations that had been laid down in the Wade-Davis Bill. The final procedure before restoration was for a state to elect a state government and send representatives to Congress.

By the end of 1865 the states affected by Johnson's plan had complied with its requirements. Indeed, if the Lincoln governments are included, all of the seceded states had been reconstructed and were ready to resume their places in the Union—if Congress chose to recognize them when it met in December 1865.

Recognition of the Johnson governments was exactly what the Radicals were determined to prevent. And many people in the North agreed with them that Reconstruction was being rushed too fast and was being accomplished too easily.

Northerners were disturbed by the seeming reluctance of some members of the Southern conventions to abolish slavery and by the refusal of all the conventions to grant suffrage to even a few Negroes. They were astounded that states claiming to be "loyal" should elect as state officials and representatives to Congress prominent leaders of the recent Confederacy. Particularly hard to understand was Georgia's choice of Alexander H. Stephens, former Vice President of the Confederacy, as a United States Senator.

# Selected Readings

**Wartime Diplomacy** E. D. Adams, *Great Britain and the American Civil War* (2 vols., 1925); Donaldson Jordan and E. J. Pratt, *Europe and the American Civil War* (1931); F. L. Owsley, *King Cotton Diplomacy* (1931, 1959); G. G. Van Deusen, *William H. Seward* (1967); M. B. Duberman, *Charles Francis Adams, 1807–1886* (1961).

**The War in General** Bruce Catton, *Mr. Lincoln's Army*° (1951), *Glory Road*° (1952), and *A Stillness at Appomattox*° (1954); J. B. Mitchell, *Decisive Battles of the Civil War*° (1955); Jay Monaghan, *Civil War on the Western Border, 1854–1865* (1955); B. I. Wiley, *The Life of Johnny Reb*° (1943), *The Life of Billy Yank*° (1952), and *The Road to Appomattox*° (1956); Benjamin Quarles, *The Negro in the Civil War* (1953); D. T. Cornish, *The Sable Arm*° (1956), an account of the black troops; David Donald, ed., *Why the North Won the Civil War*° (1960); H. S. Commager, ed., *The Blue and the Gray: The Story of the Civil War as Told by Participants* (2 vols., 1950); David Donald, ed., *Divided We Fought: A Pictorial History of the Civil War* (1952); R. M. Ketchum, *The American Heritage Picture History of the Civil War* (1960).

**The Union Side** T. H. Williams, *Lincoln and His Generals* (1952) and *McClellan, Sherman,*

*and Grant* (1962); K. P. Williams, *Lincoln Finds a General: A Military History of the Civil War* (4 vols., 1949–1956); R. V. Bruce, *Lincoln and the Tools of War* (1956); Lloyd Lewis, *Sherman, Fighting Prophet* (1932); W. W. Hassler, Jr., *General George B. McClellan: Shield of the Union* (1957).

**The Confederate Side** D. S. Freeman, *R. E. Lee: A Biography* (4 vols., 1934–1935) and *Lee's Lieutenants* (3 vols., 1942–1944); F. E. Vandiver, *Rebel Brass* (1956); Archer Jones, *Confederate Strategy from Shiloh to Vicksburg* (1961); T. L. Connelly, *Army of the Heartland* (1967); F. E. Vandiver, *Mighty Stonewall* (1957); T. H. Williams, *Beauregard, Napoleon in Gray*° (1955); Gilbert Govan and J. W. Livingood, *A Different Valor* (1956), on J. E. Johnston.

**The Naval War** V. C. Jones, *The Civil War at Sea* (3 vols., 1960–1962); C. E. Macartney, *Mr. Lincoln's Admirals* (1956); R. S. West, Jr., *Mr. Lincoln's Navy* (1957); J. P. Baxter III, *The Introduction of the Ironclad Warship* (1933); R. W. Daly, *How the Merrimack Won* (1957); T. C. and Ruth White, *Tin Can on a Shingle* (1957), on the *Monitor-Merrimack* duel.

**The Reconstruction Problem** Herman Belz, *Reconstructing the Union: Theory and Policy During the Civil War* (1969); W. B. Hesseltine,

*Lincoln's Plan of Reconstruction*° (1960); W. L. Rose, *Rehearsal for Reconstruction: The Port Royal Experiment*° (1964); G. R. Bentley, *A History of the Freedmen's Bureau* (1955); Sidney Andrews, *The South Since the War* (1866); J. H. Trowbridge, *A Picture of the Desolated States* (1866; abridgment with title *The Desolate South*, ed. by Gordon Carroll, 1956); F. W. Klingberg, *The Southern Claims Commission* (1955).

**Johnson and the Radicals** David Donald, *The Politics of Reconstruction, 1863–1867*° (1965);

H. K. Beale, *The Critical Year: A Study of Andrew Johnson and Reconstruction* (1930); E. L. McKitrick, *Andrew Johnson and Reconstruction* (1960); La Wanda and J. H. Cox, *Politics, Principles, and Prejudice, 1865–1867* (1963); R. N. Current, *Old Thad Stevens: A Story of Ambition* (1942); F. N. Brodie, *Thaddeus Stevens, Scourge of the South* (1959).

————————

°Titles available in paperback.

HERE
LIES
THE
DEMOCRATIC
TIGER.
GREATLY MOURNED
BY THE BEREAVED
FILIBUSTERS.

# Chapter 16
# Reconstructing the Nation

When Americans of a later generation looked back on the 1860s and 1870s, it seemed to many of them that there had been a sharp break between the Civil War and the ensuing period of Reconstruction. The war itself, for all its suffering and sacrifice, was remembered on the whole as an ennobling experience, one of high purpose and gallantry on both sides. The postwar years, by contrast, appeared to have been a time of low, unscrupulous politics, a time when vengeful men among the victors disgraced the country while unnecessarily delaying a real, heartfelt reunion of the North and the South.

That view contains elements of historical reality, but it misses an essential truth about the troubled postwar period. The struggle over Reconstruction was, in part, a continuation of the Civil War. It was a struggle, as the war had been, that involved (among other things) the question of both state rights and human rights. The victory for Union and emancipation had not been completely won at Appomattox. In the postwar years an effort was made to confirm the supremacy of the national government over the Southern states and to assure the benefits of freedom to the millions of emancipated slaves. This effort, provoking resistance as it did, had the effect of keeping the country psychologically divided.

Politicians on both sides added to the divisive effect by playing upon the hatreds left over from the war. Republicans implied that all Democrats, Northern as well as Southern, had been traitors. "Every man that shot Union soldiers was a Democrat," a typical Republican orator declaimed. "The man that assassinated Abraham Lincoln was a Democrat." This technique of reviving wartime emotions in order to win postwar elections came to be known, among Democrats, as "waving the bloody shirt." But in the South the Democrats waved a bloody shirt of their own. They denounced their opponents, black and white, as desecrators of the Confederate cause. The Ku Klux Klan, an anti-Republican terrorist group, pretended that its members were ghosts of the Confederate army.

The struggle over Reconstruction ended in the Compromise of 1877. This arrangement, a combination of "reunion and reaction," brought the sections together at the expense of the Negro. The federal government gave up the attempt to enforce the Negro's rights and left the Southern states in the hands of the Democrats. Yet two great charters of human liberty still stood as documents of the Reconstruction era—the Fourteenth and Fifteenth amendments to the federal Constitution—which had been intended to assure citizenship and the suffrage to the former slaves. For the time being, these documents were disregarded, but a day was to come, several decades later, when they would provide the legal basis for a renewed drive to bring true freedom and equality to all Americans.

---

## A Damaging Victory

Cartoonist Thomas Nast depicted the effects of the disputed election of 1876 on the Republican party. The triumphant but battered elephant sits at the grave of the Democrats saying "Another such victory, and I am undone." Nast created the elephant as the symbol of the Republican party and the donkey as the symbol of the Democratic party. From *Harper's Weekly* (1877).

## RADICAL RECONSTRUCTION

When Congress met in December 1865, it denied admission to the senators and representatives from the states that Johnson had "restored." The Radical leaders explained that the Southerners should be excluded until Congress knew more about conditions in the South. Congress must first be assured that the former Confederates had accepted the results of the war and that Southern Negroes and loyal whites were safe. Accordingly, Congress set up the Joint Committee on Reconstruction to investigate opinions in the South and to advise Congress in laying down a Reconstruction policy.

### Congress Takes Over

During the next few months the Radicals, though disagreeing among themselves, advanced toward a more severe program than their first plan, the Wade-Davis Bill of 1864. The Radicals gained the support of moderate Republicans because of Johnson's intransigent attitude. Johnson insisted that Congress had no right even to consider a policy for the South until his own plan had been accepted and the Southern congressmen and senators had been admitted.

Northern opinion was aroused by the so-called Black Codes, which the Southern legislatures adopted during the sessions of 1865–1866. These measures were the South's solution for the problem of the free Negro laborer, and they were also the South's substitute for slavery as a white-supremacy device. Economically, the codes were intended to regulate the labor of a race that, in the opinion of the whites, would not work except under some kind of compulsion. Although the economic provisions varied in stringency from state to state, they all authorized local officials to apprehend unemployed Negroes, fine them for vagrancy, and hire them out to private employers to satisfy the fine. Some of the codes tried to force Negroes to work on the plantations by forbidding them to own or lease farms or to take other jobs except as domestic servants. Socially, the codes were designed to govern relations between the races and to invest the Negroes with a legal although subordinate status. The acts conferred certain civil rights upon blacks, but they also placed special restrictions on Negroes that did not apply to whites. To the South, the Black Codes were a realistic approach to a great social problem. To the North, they seemed to herald a return to slavery.

An appropriate agency for offsetting the Black Codes was the Freedmen's Bureau, but its scheduled year of existence was about to end. It had been losing some of its original functions. With the passing of the immediate postwar emergency, there was decreasing need for the bureau's relief activities. And President Johnson had been pardoning so many former rebels—thus restoring to them their confiscated plantations—that there was less and less land available for resettling former slaves.

In February 1866 Congress passed a bill to prolong the life of the bureau and to widen its powers by authorizing special courts for settling labor disputes. Thus the bureau could set aside work agreements that might be forced upon Negroes under the Black Codes. Johnson vetoed the bill, denouncing it as unconstitutional.

In April Congress again struck at the Black Codes by passing the Civil Rights Bill, which made United States citizens of Negroes and empowered the federal government to intervene in state affairs when necessary for protecting the rights of citizens. Johnson vetoed this bill, too. With moderates and Radicals acting together, Congress had the necessary two-thirds majority, and it promptly overrode the veto. Then, despite another veto, Congress repassed the Freedmen's Bureau Bill.

Emboldened by their evident support in Congress, the Radicals now struck again, and harder. The Joint Committee on Reconstruction submitted to Congress in April 1866 a proposed amendment to the Constitution, the Fourteenth, which constituted the second Radical plan of Reconstruction.

The Fourteenth Amendment, which was adopted by Congress and sent to the states for approval in the early summer, is so important, both in its immediate bearing upon Reconstruction and in its future influence upon federal-state relationships, as to deserve particular analysis.

Section 1 declared that all persons born or naturalized in the United States were citizens of the United States and of the state of their residence. This clause, which set up for the first time a national definition of citizenship, was followed by a statement that no state could abridge the rights of citizens of the United States or deprive any person of life, liberty, or property without due process of law or deny to any person within its jurisdiction the equal protection of the laws.

Section 2 provided that if a state denied the suffrage to any of its adult male inhabitants, its representation in the House of Representatives and the Electoral College should suffer a proportionate reduction. This clause was intended to be a corrective to the curious effect of emancipation upon the basis of representation, by which every Southern state stood to increase its influence in the national government.

Section 3 disqualified from any state or federal office persons who had previously taken an oath to support the Constitution and later had aided the Confederacy—until Congress by a two-thirds vote of each house should remove their disability.

The Southern legislatures knew that if they ratified the amendment their states would be readmitted and Reconstruction probably would be ended. But they could not bring themselves to approve the measure, mainly because of Section 3, which put a stigma on their late leaders. Johnson himself advised Southerners to defeat the amendment. Only Tennessee, of the former Confederate states, ratified it, thus winning readmittance. The other ten, joined by Kentucky and Delaware, voted it down.

The amendment thus failed to receive the required approval of three-fourths of the states and was defeated—but only temporarily. When the time was more propitious, the Radicals would bring it up again. Meanwhile, its rejection by the South strengthened the Radical cause. To many people in the North, the amendment had seemed to be a reasonable and moderate proposal.

Public acceptance of the Radical program was strikingly manifested in the elections of 1866. This was essentially a contest for popular support between Johnson and the Radicals. The Radicals could point to recent events in the South—bloody race riots in which Negroes were the victims—as further evidence of the in-

adequacy of Johnson's policy. Johnson did his own cause no good by the intemperate, brawling speeches he made on a stumping tour from Washington to Chicago and back. The voters returned to Congress an overwhelming majority of Republicans, most of them of the Radical variety. In the Senate the line-up of the parties was 42 Republicans to 11 Democrats; in the House, 143 Republicans to 49 Democrats. Now the Republicans could enact any kind of Reconstruction plan they could themselves agree on. Confidently they looked forward to the struggle with Johnson that would ensue when Congress assembled in December 1866—and to their final victory over the President.

## The Congressional Plan

After compromising differences among themselves and with the Moderates, the Radicals formulated their third plan of Reconstruction in three bills that passed Congress in the early months of 1867. All three were vetoed by Johnson and repassed. As these Reconstruction Acts were really parts of one piece, their provisions may be studied as a unit.

This plan was based squarely on the principle that the seceded states had lost their political identity. The Lincoln-Johnson governments were declared to have no legal standing, and the ten seceded states (Tennessee was now out of the Reconstruction process) were combined into five military districts. Each district was to be put in the charge of a military commander, supported by troops, who was to prepare his provinces for readmission as states. To this end, he was to have made a registration of voters, which was to include all adult Negro males and white males who were not disqualified for participation in rebellion. The whites who were excluded were those coming under the disability of the Fourteenth Amendment; but each voter had to swear a complicated loyalty oath, and the registrars were empowered to reject white men on the suspicion that they were not acting in good faith.

After the registration was completed in each province, the commanding general was to call on the voters to elect a convention to prepare a new state constitution that had to provide for Negro suffrage. If this document were ratified by the voters, elections for a state government could be held. Finally, if Congress approved the constitution, if the state legislature ratified the Fourteenth Amendment, and if this amendment were adopted by the required number of states and became a part of the Constitution—then the state was to be restored to the Union.

By 1868 six of the former Confederate states —Arkansas, North Carolina, South Carolina, Louisiana, Alabama, and Florida—had complied with the process of restoration outlined in the Reconstruction Acts and were readmitted to the Union. Delaying tactics by the whites held up the return of Mississippi, Virginia, Georgia, and Texas until 1870. These four laggard states had to meet an additional requirement, which with the existing requirements constituted the fourth and final congressional plan of Reconstruction. They had to ratify another constitutional amendment, the Fifteenth, which forbade the states and the federal government to deny the suffrage to any citizen on account of "race, color, or previous condition of servitude."

The great majority of the Northern states still denied the suffrage to Negroes at the time when the Reconstruction Acts granted it to Negroes in the Southern states. Recent attempts to give the vote to Northern blacks by amending the state constitutions had met with practically no success. Hence an amendment to the federal Constitution seemed necessary. Its sponsors were motivated by both idealistic and practical considerations. They would be consistent in extending to the Negro in the North a right they had already given to him elsewhere. At the same time they would be putting into the Constitution, where it would be safe from congressional repeal, the basis of Republican strength in the South. They were also concerned with the party's future in the North. A warning of trouble ahead had appeared in the state elections of 1867 in Pennsylvania, Ohio, and Indiana, all of which went Democratic that year. "We must establish the doctrine of national jurisdiction over all the states in state matters of the franchise," the Radical leader Thaddeus Stevens now concluded. "We must thus bridle Pennsylvania, Ohio, Indiana et cetera, or the South *being in*, we shall drift into Democracy." In several of the Northern states the Negro vote, though small,

would be large enough to decide close elections in favor of the Republicans.

A number of the Northern and border states refused to approve the Fifteenth Amendment, and it was adopted only with the support of the four Southern states that had to ratify it in order to be readmitted to the Union. In the case of both the Fourteenth and Fifteenth amendments, the Southern states were deemed capable of ratifying even while they were not otherwise recognized as states and had no representation in Congress.

## Congressional Supremacy

The Radicals thought of themselves as architects of a revolution, and they did not intend to let either the executive or the judiciary get in their way. They were prepared, if necessary, to establish a kind of congressional dictatorship.

To curb the President, and also to facilitate Radical administration of the acts of 1867, Congress passed two remarkable laws. One, the Tenure of Office Act (1867), forbade the President to remove civil officials, including members of his cabinet, without the consent of the Senate. Its principal purpose was to protect the job of Secretary of War Edwin M. Stanton, who was cooperating with the Radicals. The other law, the Command of the Army Act (1867), prohibited the President from issuing military orders except through the commanding general of the army (General Grant), whose headquarters were to be in Washington and who could not be relieved or assigned elsewhere without the consent of the Senate.

The Supreme Court, under Chief Justice Salmon P. Chase, declared in *Ex parte Milligan* (1866) that military tribunals were unconstitutional in places where civil courts were functioning. Although the decision was applied to a case originating in the war, it seemed to threaten the system of military government that the Radicals were planning for the South. Radical anger at the Court was instant and intense. In Congress proposals were made to require a two-thirds majority of the justices for overruling a law of Congress, to deny the Court jurisdiction in Reconstruction cases, to reduce its membership to three, and even to abolish it. The judges apparently took the hint. When the state of

# Where Historians Disagree

## The Nature of Reconstruction

Historical writing on Reconstruction, even more controversial than that on the Civil War, similarly reflects the patterns of thought that have prevailed from time to time. The first professional historian of Reconstruction, William A. Dunning, who taught at Columbia University from the 1880s to the 1920s, carried on his work during a period when scholars generally held that certain racial and ethnic groups were inherently superior to others. Dunning assumed that Negroes were inferior and hence unfit to receive the vote. Many of his students wrote books dealing with Reconstruction in particular states, and he himself provided a general account, *Reconstruction, Political and Economic* (1907), which for many years was accepted as authoritative. According to Dunning and the members of the "Dunning school," the Republicans imposed their Radical program upon the South mainly to keep their party in power. (Some later writers, notably Howard K. Beale, added an economic motive—to protect Northern business interests.) Under the Radical plan, the Southern states suffered the agonies of "bayonet rule" and "Negro rule," when with army support the blacks and their unscrupulous white accomplices plundered the people in an unbelievable orgy of corruption, ruinous taxation, and astronomical increases in the public debt.

The first historian seriously to challenge the Dunning interpretation was the Negro scholar William E. B. Du Bois. In an article in the *American Historical Review* (1910) Du Bois pointed out that the misdeeds of the Reconstruction state governments had been exaggerated and their achievements overlooked. These governments were expensive, he explained, because they undertook to provide public education and other public services on a scale never before attempted in the South. In a long book, *Black Reconstruction* (1935), Du Bois described Reconstruction politics in the Southern states as an effort on the part of the masses, black and white, to create a true democratic society. Writing under the influence of Marxism, he assumed a class consciousness for which few other historians could find much evidence.

By the 1940s the attitudes toward race, on the part of scholars at least, had drastically changed. Since that time a new generation of historians has arisen—among them C. Vann Woodward, John Hope Franklin, Eric McKitrick, and John and La Wanda Cox—who assume that the freedmen of the 1860s and 1870s, despite the handicaps of their previous servitude, were by nature quite capable of participating in self-government. According to the new historians, the Radical Republicans were motivated less by partisan or economic interests than by a determination to guarantee basic rights to the former slaves and thus to secure the war aims of reunion and freedom. There was little if anything in the South that could properly be called either military rule or Negro rule, and the Negro, carpetbagger, and scalawag politicians were at least as honest and capable as others of their time. The mistake in Reconstruction was not the attempt to confer civil and political rights upon blacks, but the failure to provide an adequate economic and educational basis and sufficient governmental protection for the assurance of those rights. The recent views are ably synthesized in Kenneth M. Stampp, *The Era of Reconstruction* (1965).

Mississippi in 1867 asked for an injunction restraining Johnson from enforcing the Reconstruction Acts, the Court refused to accept jurisdiction (*Mississippi* v. *Johnson*). But the next year the Court agreed to hear arguments, on a writ of habeas corpus, in a case involving military courts in Mississippi (*Ex parte McCardle*) and by implication involving the legality of the Reconstruction Acts. The Radicals rushed through Congress a law denying the Court appellate jurisdiction in cases concerning habeas corpus. The Court bowed by refusing to hear the case. It bowed again in *Texas* v. *White* (1869), in which Chase, while accepting the Lincoln-Johnson theory that the seceded states were still in the Union, conceded that Congress possessed the power to determine permanent conditions of Reconstruction.

Although the Supreme Court evaded the Reconstruction issue, it was not an ineffective agency during this period. In the entire history of the country before 1864 the Court had declared only two acts of Congress unconstitutional. During Chase's tenure (1864–1873), it voided ten of them.

The most aggressive move of the legislative against another branch of the government occurred when the Radicals attempted to remove the President from office. They wanted to get rid of him because of his opposition to their Reconstruction program. Early in 1867 they began searching for evidence that Johnson had committed crimes or misdemeanors in office, the only legal grounds for impeachment, but they could find nothing upon which to base charges. Then he gave them a plausible reason for action by deliberately violating the Tenure of Office Act. He suspended Secretary of War Stanton,

### The Impeachment of Andrew Johnson

In this print the Senate is voting on the charges against the President. Chief Justice Chase, the presiding officer, stands at the right. At the left Senator Ross of Kansas announces he votes "Not Guilty." From *Frank Leslie's Illustrated Newspaper* (1868).

who had worked with the Radicals against Johnson, and named General Grant as his successor. Johnson hoped in this manner to secure a Court test case of the tenure law, which he believed to be unconstitutional. But when the Senate refused to concur in the suspension, Grant relinquished the office to Stanton. Johnson then dismissed Stanton.

In the House of Representatives the elated Radicals framed and presented to the Senate eleven charges against the President. The first nine accusations dealt with the violation of the Tenure of Office Act. The tenth and eleventh charged Johnson with making speeches calculated to bring Congress into disrespect and of not faithfully enforcing the various Reconstruction Acts. In the trial before the Senate (March 25 to May 26, 1868) Johnson's lawyers maintained that he was justified in technically violating a law in order to force a test case and that the measure did not apply to Stanton anyway: it gave tenure to cabinet members for the term of the President by whom they had been appointed, and Stanton had been appointed by Lincoln. The House managers of the impeachment stressed the theme that Johnson had opposed the will of Congress. They implied that in doing so he was guilty of crimes and misdemeanors. They brought terrific pressure upon all the Republican senators, but seven Republicans joined the twelve Democrats to vote for acquittal. On three of the charges the vote was identical, 35 to 19, one short of the required two-thirds majority. Thereupon the Radicals called off the proceedings.

## The Reconstructed States

In the ten states of the South that were reorganized under the congressional plan, approximately one-fourth of the white men were at first excluded from voting or holding office. The voter registration of 1867 enrolled a total of 703,000 black and 627,000 white voters. The Negro voters constituted a majority in half of the states—Alabama, Florida, South Carolina, Mississippi, and Louisiana—though only in the last three of these states did the blacks outnumber the whites in the population as a whole. However, once new constitutions had been made and new governments launched, most of these

permitted nearly all whites to vote (though for several years the Fourteenth Amendment continued to keep the leading ex-Confederates from holding office). This meant that in most of the Southern states the Republicans could maintain control only with the support of a great many Southern whites.

These Southern white Republicans, whom their opponents derisively called "scalawags," consisted in part of former Whigs who, after the break-up of the Whig organization in the 1850s, had acted with the Southern Democrats but had never felt completely at home with them. Some of the scalawag leaders were wealthy (or once wealthy) planters or businessmen. James L. Alcorn, for example, had been one of the largest slaveholders in Mississippi, a Whig leader of the state, and an opponent of secession. Such men, having long controlled the Negroes as slaves, expected to control them also as voters. Many other Southern whites who joined the Republican party were farmers living in areas where slavery had been unimportant or nonexistent. These men, many of whom had been wartime Unionists, favored the Republican program of internal improvements, which would help them get their crops to market.

White men from the North also served as Republican leaders in the South. Opponents of Reconstruction referred to them as "carpetbaggers," thus giving the impression that they were penniless adventurers who had arrived with all their possessions in a carpetbag (a then common kind of valise covered with carpeting material) in order to take advantage of the Negro vote for their own power and profit. In fact, the majority of the so-called carpetbaggers were veterans of the Union army who had looked upon the South as a new frontier, more promising than the West, and at the war's end had settled in it as hopeful planters or business or professional men. They had brought with them money to invest, but many of them lost it because of their own inexperience and the hostility of their Southern white neighbors.

The most numerous Republicans in the South were the freedmen, the vast majority of whom had no formal education and no previous experience in the management of affairs. Among the Negro leaders, however, were well-educated,

**Hiram R. Revels**

Revels was one of the few Negroes to attain high
office during Reconstruction, acting as United States
Senator from Mississippi from 1870–1871. Born in
North Carolina of free parents, Revels became a
Methodist minister and during the Civil War served as
an army chaplain in Mississippi. Returning to the state
after the war, he resumed his ministerial duties but
entered politics. He was a moderate Republican and
in 1875 joined with the Democrats to overthrow the
Republican state regime. For years he was president
of Alcorn College, a Negro institution. (Culver)

highly intelligent and even brilliant men, most
of whom had never been slaves and many of
whom had been brought up in the North or
abroad. The blacks quickly became politically
self-conscious. In various states they held their
own "colored conventions," the one in Alabama
announcing (1867): "We claim exactly *the same
rights, privileges and immunities as are enjoyed
by white men*—we ask nothing more and will be
content with nothing less." Negroes were organized, often with the assistance of Freedmen's
Bureau agents and other Northern whites, in
chapters of the Union League, which had been
founded originally as a Republican electioneering agency in the North during the war. At
secret night meetings, with mysterious ritual,
the new members of the Union League in the
South received instruction in political rights
and political techniques. Another organization
that gave unity and self-confidence to black people was the Negro church. Once they were
emancipated, they had begun to withdraw from

the white churches and form their own. "The
colored preachers are *the great power* in controlling and uniting the colored vote," a carpetbagger observed in 1868.

Negroes served as delegates to the conventions that, under the congressional plan, drew up
new state constitutions in the South. Then, in
the reconstructed states, Negroes were elected
to public offices of practically every kind. All
together (between 1869 and 1901) twenty of
them were sent to the House of Representatives
in Washington. Two went to the United States
Senate, both of them from Mississippi. Hiram
R. Revels—an ordained minister of the African
Methodist Episcopal Church and a former North
Carolina free Negro who had been educated at
Knox College in Illinois—took the Senate seat
(1870) that Jefferson Davis once had occupied.
Blanche K. Bruce, who had escaped from slavery
in Virginia and studied in the North, was made
a senator in 1874 (he was the only Negro to be
elected to a full term in the Senate until the
election of Edward Brooke, of Massachusetts,
in 1966).

Yet no such thing as "Negro rule" ever existed
in any of the states. No Negro was elected governor, though Lieutenant-Governor P. B. S.
Pinchback briefly occupied the governor's chair
in Louisiana. Negroes never controlled any of
the state legislatures, though they held a majority in the lower house of South Carolina. In
the South as a whole the number of Negro
officeholders was less than proportionate to the
number of Negroes in the population. Nor did
the state governments show much if any favoritism toward blacks as a group. Constitutions or
statutes prohibited, on paper, discrimination on
the basis of color, but segregation remained the
common practice. Only in New Orleans were
there, for a time, a few integrated schools.

The record of the Reconstruction governments is many-sided. As some of the leaders in
the convention that framed the new state constitutions were Northerners, they put into these
documents the most advanced provisions in
those of the most progressive Northern states—
provisions embodying the latest advances in
local government, judicial organization, public
finance, and poor relief. Generally, these

changes had the effect of modernizing Southern state government and placing it in step with governmental trends in the rest of the country. But some of the provisions, which looked excellent on paper, were not suited to the peculiar environment of the rural South.

The financial program of the Republican governments was a compound of blatant corruption and well-designed, if sometimes impractical, social legislation. The corruption and extravagance are familiar aspects of the Reconstruction story. State budgets expanded to hitherto unknown totals, and state debts soared to previously undreamed of heights. In South Carolina, for example, the public debt increased from $7 million to $29 million in eight years.

In large measure, the corruption in the South was a phase of a national phenomenon, with the same social force—an expanding capitalism eager to secure quick results—acting as the corrupting agent. Included in the spending programs of the Reconstruction governments were subsidies for railroads and other internal improvements, some of which materialized and some of which did not—because the promoters and the politicians pocketed the subsidies. That much of the alleged corruption was a product of deep forces in contemporary society is demonstrated by the continuance of dishonesty in state government after Republican rule was overthrown.

The state expenditures of the Reconstruction years seem huge only in comparison with the niggardly budgets of the conservative governments of the prewar era; they do not appear large when measured against the sums appropriated by later legislatures. The reconstructed governments represented the poor Negroes, and these people had a concept, albeit a vague one, of what today would be called the welfare state. They demanded public education, public-works programs, poor relief, and other services that cost money. If there were thieving and foolish spending there were also positive and permanent accomplishments, particularly in education. One example is offered by South Carolina, which in 1860 had only 20,000 children in public schools; by 1873 some 50,000 white and 70,000 Negro students were enrolled.

# THE GRANT ADMINISTRATION

The voters looked trustingly to General Ulysses S. Grant, the conquering hero of the war, to guide them through the troubled postwar years. He was President during a time (1869–1877) that would have taxed the abilities of a master of statecraft. Only a superb politician with profound spiritual insight—some rare leader like Lincoln—could have held the Presidency at that time and escaped with an unblemished reputation. Grant, for all his fine qualities, proved to be no such political leader.

## A Soldier President

At the end of the war both parties had angled to make Grant their candidate, and he could have had the nomination of either party. As he watched the congressional Radicals triumph over President Johnson, he concluded that the Radical Reconstruction policy expressed the real wishes of the people. He was receptive when the Radical leaders approached him with offers of the Republican nomination.

The Republicans placed candidate Grant on an ambiguous platform. They endorsed Radical Reconstruction and Negro suffrage for the South, but declared that in the North the question of Negro voting should be determined by each state. (Thus during the campaign the Republicans opposed the suffrage amendment, the Fifteenth, which they were to pass soon after the election.) Reflecting the influence of business, the platform called for the payment of the national debt in "the spirit of the laws" under which it had been contracted, which meant in gold instead of greenbacks; on the tariff issue, the platform was discreetly silent. Obviously the Republicans meant to make Reconstruction the big issue while subordinating economic questions that might divide the party.

Unwisely the Democrats decided to meet the Republican challenge. Their platform also emphasized Reconstruction, denouncing in extravagant terms the Radical program and demanding restoration of "home rule" in the South. Thus the Democrats chose to fight the campaign on an issue that was related to the war and its emotions—an issue that enabled their

**The "Strong" Government  1869–1877**
President Grant's Reconstruction policies are presented in
this cartoon from *Puck* (1880). (The Granger Collection)

opponents to associate them with rebellion.
They did, however, attempt to inject a new
question of an economic nature into the contest.
In 1868 approximately $356 million of the Civil
War greenbacks were in circulation, and Middle
Western Democrats, led by George Pendleton

of Ohio, wanted to keep the paper currency and
use it when legally possible to pay off the national debt. Behind this so-called "Ohio idea"
was the larger question of retaining the greenbacks as a permanent part of the money supply.
This proposal appealed to the debtor farmers of

the West and also to many hard-pressed businessmen of the East. The Westerners succeeded in writing the Ohio idea into the platform, but the party nominated Horatio Seymour of New York, a gold or "sound money" man, who repudiated the currency plank.

After a bitter campaign revolving around Reconstruction and Seymour's war record as governor of New York (he had been a Peace Democrat), Grant carried twenty-six states and Seymour only eight. But Grant got only 3,012,000 popular votes to Seymour's 2,703,000, a scant majority of 310,000, and this majority was due to Negro votes in the reconstructed states of the South.

Ulysses S. Grant was the second professional soldier to be elected to the Presidency (Zachary Taylor having been the first), and the last to be chosen until Dwight D. Eisenhower was selected in 1952. After graduating from West Point with no particular distinction, Grant had entered the regular army, from which after years of service he resigned under something of a cloud. In civilian life he undertook several dismal ventures that barely yielded him a living. His career before 1861 could be characterized as forty years of failure. Then came the Civil War, and Grant found at last the one setting, the one vocation for which he was supremely equipped—war.

His political naïveté as President was displayed in many of his appointments. For the important office of secretary of state he chose an old friend, the former Illinois Congressman Elihu B. Washburne. By agreement, Washburne was to hold the position only a week before resigning to become minister to France, the purpose being to enable him to brag in Paris that he had headed the foreign office. After offering the appointment to another man, who declined it on the grounds of expense, Grant named Hamilton Fish of New York. Like other Americans of the time, Grant inordinately admired millionaires, and he appointed A. T. Stewart, a wealthy merchant, secretary of the treasury. Stewart, however, was ineligible because of a law barring from the office any person in "trade or commerce."

In choosing his official family, Grant proceeded as if he were creating a military staff. He sent several appointments to the Senate for confirmation without asking the recipients if they would serve; they first heard the news in the papers. Fish, who had been out of politics for twenty years, wired Grant that he could not accept, but his name was already being acted on in the Senate and he was persuaded to let it go through. During his two administrations, Grant named a total of twenty-five men to the cabinet. Most of his later appointments went to men who were, at best, average, and some to men who were incompetent or corrupt, or both. Increasingly, in dispensing cabinet and executive patronage, Grant came to rely on the machine leaders in the party, on the groups most ardently devoted to the spoils system.

## Successes in Foreign Affairs

In foreign affairs the Grant administration achieved its most brilliant successes, as the Johnson administration also had done. These were the accomplishments of two outstanding Secretaries of State: William H. Seward (1861–1869) and Hamilton Fish (1869–1877).

An ardent expansionist and advocate of a vigorous foreign policy, Seward acted with as much daring as the demands of Reconstruction politics and the Republican hatred of President Johnson would permit. By exercising firm but patient pressure, he persuaded Napoleon III of France to abandon his Mexican empire, which was established during the war when the United States was in no position to protest. Napoleon withdrew his troops in 1867, his puppet Emperor Maximilian was executed by the Mexicans, and the validity of the Monroe Doctrine was strikingly reaffirmed.

When Russia let it be known that she would like to sell Alaska to the United States, the two nations long having been on friendly terms, Seward readily agreed to pay the asking price of $7.2 million. Only by strenuous efforts was he able to induce the Senate to ratify the treaty and the House to appropriate the money (1867–1868). Critics jeered that the secretary had bought a useless frozen wasteland—"Seward's Icebox" and "Walrussia" were some of the terms employed to describe it—but Alaska, a center for the fishing industry in the North Pacific and potentially rich in such resources as gold, was a distinct bargain. Seward was not content with expansion in continental North America. In 1867 he engineered the annexation of the tiny Midway Islands west of Hawaii.

In contrast with its sometimes shambling course in domestic politics, the performance of the Grant administration in the area of foreign affairs was generally decisive and firm, yet showing a wise moderation. For this, Secretary Fish, to whom President Grant gave almost a free hand, deserves the major credit. A number of delicate and potentially dangerous situations confronted Fish from the beginning, but the most serious one arose out of strained relations with Great Britain.

The United States had a burning grievance against England which had originated during the Civil War. At that time the British government, according to the American interpretation, had violated the laws of neutrality by permitting Confederate cruisers, the *Alabama* and others, to be built and armed in English shipyards and let loose to prey on Northern commerce. American demands that England pay for the damages committed by these vessels became known as the "Alabama claims." Although the British government realized its diplomatic error in condoning construction of the cruisers (in a future war American-built *Alabamas* might operate against Britain), it at first hesitated to submit the issue to arbitration.

Other differences clouded Anglo-American relations. England contended that the United States should compensate British subjects who had suffered property losses in the way of cotton and ships during the war. The ancient controversy of the North Atlantic fisheries and American rights off Canadian shores had flared up again. Another dispute involved the location of the boundary between the United States and British Columbia in Puget Sound. And finally there were the Fenians—the Irish-American crusaders who thought they could free Ireland of British rule by conquering Canada. Several times during the Johnson-Grant period Fenian "armies" harassed the Canadian border. Although the American government tried to restrain these outbreaks, it refused British suggestions that it should pay for the damages committed by the Fenians.

Seward tried earnestly to settle the Alabama claims before leaving office. The American minister to England, Reverdy Johnson, negotiated an agreement, the Johnson-Clarendon Convention (1869), providing that all claims on both sides since 1853 be submitted to arbitration. The pact was distasteful to Americans because it embraced so many issues and contained no expression of British regret for the escape of the *Alabama*. Coming before the Senate immediately after Grant took office, it was rejected 54 to 1. The debate featured a speech by Charles Sumner, chairman of the Committee on Foreign Relations, denouncing Britain for her course in the Civil War and arguing that her conduct had prolonged the war by two years. Therefore, said Sumner, England owed the United States for "direct damages" committed by the cruisers and "indirect damages" for the cost of the war for two years—which would have reached the staggering total of some $2 billion. Americans who supported Sumner's position, and they were undoubtedly a majority, professed themselves willing to accept the cession of Canada as a substitute for a cash payment.

England naturally would have nothing to do with any arrangement involving indirect claims, and settlement of the problem was temporarily stalled. Secretary Fish, however, continued to work for a solution, and finally in 1871 the two countries agreed to the Treaty of Washington, one of the great landmarks in international pacification, providing for arbitration of the cruiser issue and other pending controversies. The Alabama claims were to be laid before a five-member tribunal appointed by the governments of the United States, England, Italy, Switzerland, and Brazil. In the covenant Britain expressed regret for the escape of the *Alabama* and agreed to a set of rules governing neutral obligations that virtually gave the British case away. In effect, this meant that the tribunal would have only to fix the sum to be paid by Britain. Convening at Geneva in Switzerland, the arbitrators awarded $15.5 million to the United States.

The other disputes covered by the treaty were compromised just as pacifically. The question of the Puget Sound boundary was submitted to the German Emperor, who ruled in favor of the United States title to the contested San Juan Is-

**Hamilton Fish**

Fish, a member of a distinguished New York family, had been out of politics for years when Grant offered him the position of Secretary of State. Accepting it reluctantly, he served for both of Grant's terms, and left a record of solid accomplishments. Fish represented the older tradition of cultivated gentlemen in politics. This sketch, almost a caricature, exaggerates some of his features but still conveys his aura of dignity. (Culver)

lands. An arbitration commission awarded nearly $2 million to England for damages suffered by her citizens during the Civil War. Because the treaty had extended American fishing privileges, England claimed a payment for the concessions, and a special commission, after some wrangling, decided in 1877 that the United States should compensate Britain with $5.5 million. If the value of the arbitrations were computed in money, which of course it really could not be, the United States thus netted approximately $8 million from the awards. The real and enduring significance of the procedure was that

again the two countries—as they had been doing since 1818—adjusted serious differences without resorting to force.

## The Liberals Defect

Through both his foreign and his domestic policies, President Grant antagonized and alienated a number of prominent Republicans, among them the famous Radical, Charles Sumner. Senator Sumner's extravagant demand for damages from Great Britain embarrassed Secretary Fish in the latter's diplomacy. Still worse, from the President's point of view, Sumner blocked a treaty for the annexation of Santo Domingo, a project in which Grant took a deep personal interest—indeed, it was a kind of monomania with him. The angry President got revenge by inducing his Senate friends to remove Sumner from the chairmanship of the Committee on Foreign Relations.

Sumner and other Republican leaders joined with civil-service reformers to criticize Grant for his use of the spoils system, his reliance on ruthless machine politicians. Scholarly journalists like E. L. Godkin of the *Nation* and George William Curtis of *Harper's Weekly* were arguing that the government ought to base its appointments not on services to the party but on fitness for office as determined by competitive examinations, as the British government already was doing. Grant yielded to the extent of recommending the establishment of a Civil Service Commission, which Congress authorized in 1871, to devise a system of hiring based on merit. This agency, under the headship of Curtis, proposed a set of rules that seemed to meet Grant's approval. But Grant was not really much interested in reform, and even if he had been he could not have persuaded his followers to accept a new system that would undermine the very basis of party loyalty—the patronage. Congress, by neglecting to renew the commission's appropriation, soon ended its existence.

Republican critics of the President also denounced him for his support of Radical Reconstruction. He continued to station federal troops in the South, and on numerous occasions he sent them to the support of Negro-and-carpetbag governments that were on the point of collapsing. To growing numbers in the North this

**FRANK LESLIE'S ILLUSTRATED NEWSPAPER.**

**A REMARKABLE SACRIFICE.**

U. S. G.—*"I don't want to go to Washington; I want to go to the races with Tom Murp'y."*
R. C——G.—*" Oh, but you must make a sacrifice now, and after election you can go to as many races as you like."*

### Grant Wants to Go to the Horse Races

This print depicts a widely held impression of Grant. Because the President admired fine horses, it was believed that he liked racing and gambling. Grant, shown here as an obvious weakling, is saying that he does not want to go to the White House but to the races. Two party bosses, Roscoe C. Conkling and Oliver P. Morton, are forcing him to shoulder his political responsibilities. From *Frank Leslie's Illustrated Newspaper* (1872).

seemed like dangerous militarism, and they were more and more disgusted by the stories of governmental corruption and extravagance that came up from the South. Some Republicans were beginning to suspect that there was corruption not only in the Southern state governments but also in the federal government itself. Still others criticized Grant because he had declined to speak out in favor of a reduction of the tariff. The high wartime duties remained substantially unchanged even though the wartime justification for them was past.

Thus, before the end of Grant's first term, members of his own party had begun to oppose him for a variety of reasons—his foreign policies, his use of the patronage, his resort to military force in the South, his high-tariff stand, and his suspected taint of corruption—all of which added up to what the critics called "Grantism." In 1872, hoping to prevent Grant's reelection, his opponents bolted the party. Referring to themselves as Liberal Republicans, they proceeded to set up their own organization for running presidential and vice-presidential candidates.

The greatest weakness of the Liberal movement lay in its diversity and disunity. This was cruelly exposed when the Liberals held their national convention and began to consider a platform. They were able to agree on resolutions that approved of civil-service reform and endorsed the basic policy of Reconstruction, but called for universal amnesty (with the restoration of full political rights to former Confederates) and the withdrawal of troops from the South. When the tariff question came up, however, the convention found itself hopelessly divided. The delegates finally compromised on an evasive plank referring the issue to the people and Congress. This evasion lessened the Liberals' chances of gaining Democratic endorsement and Southern support. They compounded their blunder in choosing a nominee. Passing over Charles Francis Adams and other able and available men, they named Horace Greeley, veteran editor and publisher of the New York *Tribune*.

Greeley over a course of thirty years had stated his position on practically every issue before the country. He had been a Whig and a Republican, a proponent of antislavery and a high tariff, an economic and political nationalist. Impulsive and erratic, he had crusaded for most of the fads that had at one time or another intrigued popular attention—spiritualism, vegetarianism, and others—and he cultivated an idiosyncratic dress and manner. With his record and personality, he was hardly the strongest

candidate the Liberals could have put forward to attract the Democratic, Southern, and independent vote. The Democratic convention, seeing in his candidacy the only chance to unseat the Republicans, endorsed him with no great enthusiasm. Despite his recent attacks on Radical Reconstruction, many Southerners, remembering Greeley's own Radical past, prepared to stay at home on election day. The Republicans, with Grant as their standard-bearer and a platform justifying Reconstruction and calling for a high tariff, moved into the campaign with confidence.

To everybody's surprise, Greeley turned out to be a vigorous and hard-hitting campaigner. Breaking with precedent, he stumped the country advocating the Liberal cause. But the factors surrounding his candidacy made the odds against him impossible. In November Grant polled 286 electoral votes and 3,597,000 popular votes to Greeley's 62 and 2,834,000. The optimistic editor carried only two Southern and four border states. Three weeks later Greeley, apparently crushed by his defeat, died.

During the campaign the first of a series of political scandals had come to light. Although the wrongdoing had occurred before Grant took office, it involved his party and the onus for it fell on his administration. This scandal originated with the Crédit Mobilier construction company that helped build the Union Pacific Railroad. In reality, the Crédit Mobilier was controlled by a few Union Pacific stockholders who awarded huge and fraudulent contracts to the construction company, thus milking the Union Pacific, a company of which they owned a minor share, of money which in part came from government subsidies. To avert a congressional inquiry into the deal, the directors, using Oakes Ames, a Massachusetts representative, as their agent, sold at a discount (in effect gave) Crédit Mobilier stock to key members of Congress. A congressional investigation was held, and it revealed that some high-placed Republicans had accepted stock, including Schuyler Colfax, now Grant's Vice President.

One dreary episode followed another in Grant's second term. Benjamin H. Bristow, Grant's third secretary of the treasury, discovered that some of his officials and a group of distillers operating as a "Whiskey Ring" were cheating the government out of taxes by means of false reports. Among the prominent Republicans involved was the President's private secretary, Orville E. Babcock. Grant defended Babcock, appointed him to another office, and eased Bristow out of the cabinet. A House investigation revealed that William W. Belknap, secretary of war, had accepted bribes to retain an Indian-post trader in office. Belknap resigned with Grant's blessing before the Senate could act on impeachment charges brought by the House. Lesser scandals involved the Navy Department, which was suspected of selling business to contractors, and the Treasury, where John D. Sanborn, a special agent appointed to handle overdue taxes, collected $427,000 and retained a 50-per-cent commission for himself and the Republican bigwigs who had placed him in the job. Not to be left out of the picture, Congress passed an act doubling the annual salary of the President from $25,000 to $50,000 (the first increase since George Washington's time), and raising the salaries of members of Congress from $5,000 to $7,500 a year. The increases were justifiable, but the country was enraged to learn that its representatives had also voted themselves two years of back pay. Bowing before a storm of denunciation, the next Congress hastened to repeal the so-called "Salary Grab."

## The Greenback Question

Meanwhile the Grant administration along with the country as a whole had suffered another blow when the Panic of 1873 struck. It was touched off by the failure of a leading investment banking firm, Jay Cooke and Company, the "financier of the Civil War," which had done well in the handling of government war bonds but had sunk excessive amounts in postwar railroad building. Depressions had come before with almost rhythmic regularity—in 1819, 1837, and 1857—but this was the worst one yet. It lasted four years, during which unemployment rose to 3 million, and agricultural prices fell so far that thousands of farmers, unable to meet mortgage payments, went more deeply into debt or lost their farms.

Debtors hoped the government would follow an inflationary, easy-money policy, which would have made it easier for them to pay their debts and would have helped to stimulate recovery from the depression. But President Grant and most Republicans preferred what they called a "sound" currency, which was to the advantage of the banks, money-lenders, and other creditors.

The money question, after figuring in the election of 1868, had confronted Grant and the Republicans in Congress from the beginning of his administration. The question was twofold: How should interest and principal of the war bonds be paid, and what should be the permanent place of the greenbacks in the national currency? Supporters of the Ohio idea, representing debtor interests, argued that the bonds had been purchased in greenbacks of depreciated value and should, unless stipulated otherwise by law, be redeemed in the same currency. The President favored payment in gold, and the Republican Congress moved speedily to promise redemption in "coin or its equivalent" and to enact a refunding act providing for long-term refinancing of the debt (1869–1870).

Approximately $450 million in greenbacks had been issued during the Civil War, and $400 million of them were still in circulation at the end of the conflict. In the Johnson administration, Congress had authorized the Treasury to reduce their quantity, but the protests of farmers and some business groups had halted further action. When Grant entered the White House, the greenback circulation was some $356 million, and the gold value of a greenback dollar was 73 cents.

Before Congress could make any disposition of the problem, the Supreme Court intervened with a decision concerning the legality of the greenbacks as legal tender. In *Hepburn* v. *Griswold* (1870), Chief Justice Chase, speaking for a divided 4-to-3 Court, declared that greenbacks were not legal tender for debts contracted prior to their issuance. This pronouncement angered agrarians and alarmed businessmen who had incurred obligations that they would now have to pay with a more valuable dollar. Demands for a reversal of the Court's decision were insistent. It so happened that Congress was about to raise the number of justices (recently reduced to seven) back to nine, and Grant appointed two men who were known to oppose the decision. It was charged that he had ascertained their opinions and was in effect packing the Court, but no proof of this exists. The government did, however, move immediately for a rehearing, and in *Knox* v. *Lee* (1871) the Court by a 5-to-4 vote reversed the previous decision.

With the legality of greenbacks established, the Treasury, as a relief measure after the Panic of 1873, increased the amount in circulation. For the same reason Congress, in the following year, voted to raise the total to $400 million. Grant, responding to pressures from the financial interests, vetoed the measure. In 1875 the Republican Congress enacted the Resumption Act, providing that after January 1, 1879, the government would exchange gold dollars for greenbacks and directing the government to acquire a gold reserve for redemption purposes. The law had its intended result: with the specie value of greenbacks assured, they were equal in worth to gold. The interests of the creditor classes were adequately protected, but at the same time, the debtor groups could take some comfort in the retention of the greenbacks. (Subsequently, in 1878, Congress decided that some $346 million of greenbacks should form a permanent part of the money supply.) Not all the agrarian-debtor groups accepted resumption as a satisfactory conclusion. Some dissident elements created the National Greenback party in 1875, which was active in the next three presidential elections. It failed, however, to attract wide support. After 1879 those interests favoring inflation would turn to forms of currency other than paper.

## A RETURN TO WHITE SUPREMACY

The period of Republican control in the South varied from state to state. In a few states the Democrats (or Conservatives) got into power as soon or almost as soon as restoration occurred. The longest that Republican rule lasted in any of the states was about ten years. It was ended in Virginia, North Carolina, and Georgia in 1870; in Texas in 1873; in Alabama and Arkansas in 1874; in Mississippi in 1875; and in South Carolina, Louisiana, and Florida in 1877.

### The Ku Klux Klan: A Southern View

This Klan broadside depicts the organization as most Southerners saw it. The figure with the flag and sword epitomizes white culture and has overthrown the Negro enemy. Note the incendiary torch in the hand of the Negro and the broken chains symbolizing his former slave status. (Rutherford B. Hayes Library)

## Southern Republicans Lose

In the states where the whites constituted a majority—the upper South states—overthrow of Republican control was a relatively simple matter. The whites had only to organize and win the elections. Their success was facilitated by the early restoration of the suffrage to those whites who had been deprived of it by national or state action. Presidential and congressional pardons returned the privilege to numerous individuals, and in 1872 Congress, responding to public demands to forgive the penalties of the war, enacted the Amnesty Act, which restored political rights to 150,000 ex-Confederates and left only 500 excluded from political life.

In other states, where the Negroes were in the majority or the population difference between the races was small, the whites resorted to intimidation and violence. Frankly terroristic were the secret societies that appeared in many parts of the South—the Ku Klux Klan, the Knights of the White Camellia, and others—which attempted to frighten or physically prevent Negroes from voting. Although the societies were effective, their influence has been exaggerated by writers intrigued by their romantic hooded and robed apparel and their elaborate ritual. Moving quickly to stamp out these societies, Congress passed two Force Acts (1870-1871) and the Ku Klux Klan Act (1871) which authorized the President to use military force and martial law in areas where the orders were active.

More potent than the secret orders were the open semimilitary organizations that operated under such names as Rifle clubs, Red Shirts, and White Leagues. After the first such society was founded in Mississippi, the idea spread to other states, and the procedure employed by the clubs was called the Mississippi Plan. Briefly stated, the plan called for the whites in each community to organize and arm, and to be prepared, if necessary, to resort to force to win elections. But the heart of the scheme was in the phrase "drawing the color line." By one method or another, legal or illegal, every white man was to be forced to join the Democratic party or leave the community. By similar methods, every

### The Ku Klux Klan: A Northern View

This drawing in a Northern illustrated paper shows a group of Klansmen about to murder a carpetbagger whom they have abducted. (Library of Congress)

Negro male was to be excluded from political action; in a few states he was permitted to vote —if he voted Democratic.

Perhaps an even stronger influence than the techniques practiced by the armed bands was the simple and unromantic weapon of economic pressure. The war had freed the Negro, but he was still a laborer—a hired worker or a tenant— dependent upon the whites for his livelihood. The whites readily discovered that this dependence placed the Negro in their power. Planters refused to rent land to Republican Negroes, storekeepers refused to extend them credit, employers refused to give them work. Economic pressure was a force that the Negro could not fight. If the Radicals, in bringing the Negro to political power, had accomplished a revolution, it was a superficial one. They failed to provide the Negro with economic power, as they might have done by giving him possession of confiscated land. Hence, his political rights had no lasting basis.

Certainly the Negro's political position was hopeless without the continued backing of the Republican party and the federal government. But he was losing the support of people in the North, even of many humanitarian reformers who had worked for emancipation and Negro rights. After the adoption of the Fifteenth Amendment (1870), most of the reformers convinced themselves that their long campaign in his behalf at last was over, that with the vote he ought to be able to take care of himself. Republican disillusionment with the corruption and disorders in the Southern states helped to bring about the party split of 1872, which in turn weakened the Republicans in the South still further. They beheld the discouraging spectacle of former Radical leaders like Charles Sumner and Horace Greeley now calling themselves Liberals, cooperating with the Democrats, and outdoing even them in denunciations of what they viewed as Negro-and-carpetbag misgovernment. Most of the white Republicans of the South, including some of those who had come from the North, joined the Liberal movement and went over to the Democrats. Friction between the remaining carpetbaggers and the black Republicans grew because of a well-justified feeling on the part of the blacks that they

were not receiving a fair share of the power and the jobs.

When the depression came in 1873, the hard times aggravated political discontent both North and South. In the congressional elections of 1874 the Democrats gained a majority of the seats in the national House of Representatives. After 1875, when the new House met, the Republicans no longer controlled the whole Congress, as they had done since the beginning of the war. And President Grant, in view of the changing temper of the North, no longer was willing to use military force to save from violent overthrow the Republican regimes that were still standing in the South. In 1875, when the Mississippi governor, Adelbert Ames (originally from Maine), appealed to Washington for troops to protect the Negroes from the terrorism of the Democrats, he received in reply a telegram that quoted Grant as saying: "The whole public are tired out with these annual autumnal outbreaks in the South, and the great majority are now ready to condemn any interference on the part of the government."

After the Democrats had taken Mississippi, only three states were left in the hands of the Republicans—South Carolina, Louisiana, and Florida. In the elections of 1876, again using terrorist tactics, the Democrats claimed victory in all three. But the Republicans maintained that they themselves had won, and they were able to continue holding office because federal troops happened to be on the scene. If the troops should be withdrawn, the last of the Republican regimes would fall. The future was to depend on the settlement of the presidential election of 1876, which was disputed in consequence of the electoral disputes in the South.

## The Compromise of 1877

U.S. Grant was eager to run for another term in 1876, and his friends among the Republican bosses tried to secure the nomination for him. But the majority of the Republican leaders ruled Grant out. Impressed by the recent upsurge of Democratic strength, which had delivered the House of Representatives and a number of state governments to the opposition party, and fearful of the third-term issue, they searched for a candidate who was not associated with the scan-

## Ingersoll's Speech Nominating Blaine [1876]

At the Republican convention in 1876 Robert G. Ingersoll nominated Blaine in a speech typical of the extravagant rhetoric of the time. Like all Republican orators, Ingersoll seized the opportunity to recall the emotions of the Civil War and to equate Democrats with traitors. After this speech Blaine was known to his admirers as "the plumed knight":

*This is a grand year—a year filled with recollections of the Revolution; filled with the proud and tender memories of the past; with sacred legends of liberty; a year in which the sons of freedom will drink from the fountains of enthusiasm; a year in which the people call for a man who has preserved in Congress what our soldiers won upon the field; a year in which they call for the man who has torn from the throat of treason the tongue of slander—for the man who has snatched the mask of Democracy from the hideous face of rebellion; for this man who, like an intellectual athlete, has stood in the arena of debate and challenged all comers, and who is still a total stranger to defeat. Like an armed warrior, like a plumed knight, James G. Blaine marched down the halls of the American Congress and threw his shining lance full and fair against the brazen foreheads of the defamers of his country and the maligners of her honor.*

were supposed to incriminate him. Actually, he had carefully selected innocent portions of the correspondence, and many people were unconvinced. The so-called "Mulligan letters" hurt his chances in 1876 and would impede his career in the future.

The Republican convention passed over Blaine and other hopefuls and named as the standard-bearer Rutherford B. Hayes, a former Union army officer and congressman, three times governor of Ohio, and a champion of civil-service reform. The platform included the usual endorsements of Reconstruction and Republican economic legislation.

No personal rivalries divided the Democrats. Only one aspirant commanded serious attention, and with him as their candidate the Democrats were confident of returning to power. The bearer of the party's hopes was Governor Samuel J. Tilden of New York, whose name had become synonymous with governmental reform. A corporation lawyer and a millionaire, Tilden had long been a power in the Democratic organization of his state, but he had not hesitated to turn against Tammany's corrupt Tweed Ring and aid in its overthrow. His fight against Tweed brought him national fame and the governorship, in which position he increased his reputation for honest administration. The Democratic platform contained some general references to the tariff and currency problems, but its emphasis was upon reform in government. It called for an end to Reconstruction and the establishment of civil service, and declared that the primary issue of the campaign was the ejection of rascals from government and the installation in their place of "honest men."

Despite the fury of the charges flung at each other by the parties in the canvass, there were almost no differences of principle between the candidates. Hayes was on record as favoring withdrawal of troops from the South, he advocated civil service, and his record for probity was equal to Tilden's. Although the New York governor, reflecting Eastern importing interests, was amenable to some kind of tariff reduction, on other economic issues he was at least as conservative as his rival. He was a gold or "sound-money" man, and he believed that government had no business interfering with economic proc-

dals of the last eight years and who could entice the Liberals back into the fold and unite the party until after the election.

Senator James G. Blaine of Maine offered himself, but he had recently been involved in an allegedly crooked railroad deal. In a remarkable display of oratory and effrontery, Blaine defended himself against the charge of corruption by reading to Congress some private letters that esses. He looked on himself as a modern counterpart of Thomas Jefferson.

The November election revealed an apparent Democratic victory. In addition to the South, Tilden carried several large Northern states, and his popular vote was 4,300,000 to 4,036,000 for Hayes. But the situation was complicated by the disputed returns from Louisiana, South Carolina, and Florida, whose total electoral vote was 19. Both parties claimed to have won these states, and double sets of returns were presented to Congress. Adding to the confusion was a contested vote in Oregon, where one of the three successful Republican electors was declared ineligible because he held a federal office. The Democrats contended that the place should go to the highest Democratic elector, but the Republicans insisted that according to state law the remaining electors were to fill the vacancy. The dual and disputed returns threw the outcome of the election into doubt. As tension and excitement gripped the country, two clear facts emerged from the welter of conflicting claims. Tilden had for certain 184 electoral votes, only one short of a majority. The 20 votes in controversy would determine who would be President, and Hayes needed all of them to secure the prize.

With surprise and consternation, the nation now learned that no measure or method existed to determine the validity of disputed returns. The Constitution stated: "The President of the Senate shall, in the presence of the Senate and House of Representatives, open all the certificates and the votes shall then be counted." The question was, how and by whom? The Senate was Republican and so, of course, was its president, and the House was Democratic. Constitutional ambiguity and congressional division rendered a fair and satisfactory solution of the crisis impossible. If the president of the Senate counted the votes, Hayes would be the victor. If the Senate and House judged the returns separately, they would reach opposite decisions and checkmate each other. And if the houses voted jointly, the Democrats, with a numerical majority, would decide the result. Resort to any one of these lines of action promised to divide the country and possibly result in chaos.

Not until the last days of January 1877 did Congress act to break the deadlock. Then it created a special Electoral Commission to pass on all the disputed votes. The commission was to be composed of five senators, five representatives, and five justices of the Supreme Court. Because of the party lineup, the congressional delegation would consist of five Republicans and five Democrats. The creating law named four of the judicial commissioners, two Republicans and two Democrats. The four were to select their fifth colleague, and it was understood that they would choose David Davis, an independent Republican, thus ensuring that the deciding vote would be wielded by a relatively unbiased judge. But at this stage Davis was elected to the Senate from Illinois and suddenly resigned his seat. His place on the commission fell to a Republican. Sitting throughout February, the commission by a partisan vote of 8 to 7 decided every disputed vote for Hayes. Congress accepted the final verdict of the agency on March 2, only two days before the inauguration of the new President.

Ratification of the commission's findings was not accomplished, however, without some complicated compromising among the politicians. Behind the dealing, and partially directing it, were certain powerful economic forces with a stake in the outcome. A decision by the commission was not final until approved by Congress, and the Democrats could have prevented action by filibustering. The success of a filibuster, however, depended on concert between Northern and Southern Democrats, and this the Republicans disrupted by offering the Southerners sufficient inducement to accept the commission's findings. According to the traditional account, certain Republicans and Southern Democrats met at Washington's Wormley Hotel, and the Republicans pledged that Hayes, after becoming President, would withdraw the troops from the South. As withdrawal would mean the downfall of the last carpetbag governments, the Southerners, convinced they were getting as much from Hayes as they could get from Tilden, abandoned the filibuster.

Actually, the story behind the "Compromise of 1877" is somewhat more complex. Hayes was on record before the election as favoring withdrawal of the troops, and in any event the Democrats in the House could have forced withdrawal simply by cutting out appropriations for the army in the Reconstruction process. The real agreement, the one that brought the Southern Democrats over, was reached before the Wormley meeting. As the price for their cooperation the Southern Democrats (among them some old Whigs) exacted from the Republicans the following pledges: the appointment of at least one Southerner to the Hayes cabinet, control of federal patronage in their sections, generous internal improvements, national aid for the Texas and Pacific Railroad, and, finally, withdrawal of the troops. The Conservatives who were running the redeemed Southern states were primarily interested in economics—in industrializing the South—and they believed that the Republican program of federal aid to business would be more beneficial for their region than the archaic state-rights policy of the Democrats.

## Discrimination Made Legal

In his inaugural address Hayes stressed the Southern problem. While he took care to say that the rights of the Negroes must be preserved, he announced that the most pressing need of the South was the restoration of "wise, honest, and peaceful local self-government"—which meant that he was going to withdraw the troops and let the whites take over control of the state governments. Hayes laid down this policy knowing that his action would lend weight to current charges that he was paying off the South for acquiescing in his election and would strengthen those critics who referred to him as "His Fraudulency."

The President hoped to build up a "new Republican" party in the South composed of whatever conservative white groups could be weaned away from the Democrats and committed to some acceptance of Negro rights. But his efforts, which included a tour of Southern cities, failed to produce any positive results. Although many Southern leaders sympathized with the economic credo of the Republicans, they could not advise their people to support the party that had imposed Reconstruction. Nor were Southerners pleased by Hayes' bestowal of offices on carpetbaggers who now had to leave the section or by his vetoes of Democratic attempts to repeal the Force Acts. The "solid South" had come into existence, and there was nothing Hayes or any Republican could do to crack it.

The withdrawal of the troops was a symbol that the national government was giving up its attempt to control Southern politics and to determine the place of the Negro in Southern society. The surrender, it is to be noted, was made by the Republicans. They could yield with good grace because after 1877 they had no particular need for the support of the reconstructed South. The economic legislation of the war and postwar years was safe from repeal; industry was securely entrenched in the national economy; and Republican dominance could be maintained without Southern votes.

Another symbol of retreat was furnished by the Supreme Court, which in a series of decisions emasculated the Fourteenth and Fifteenth amendments of much of their significance. In the Civil Rights Cases (1883) the Court took the position that the Fourteenth Amendment prohibited states from discriminating against people on account of color but did not restrict private individuals or organizations. That is, railroads, hotels, theaters, and the like could legally practice segregation. Eventually the Court validated state legislation that discriminated against Negroes. In *Plessy* v. *Ferguson* (1896), a case involving a law that required separate seating arrangements for the races on railroads, the Court held that separate accommodations did not deprive the Negro of equal rights if the accommodations were equal. And in *Cumming* v. *County Board of Education* (1899) the Court held that laws establishing separate schools for whites and Negroes were valid if the facilities were equal for both.

The men who came to power in the South after 1877 were not in the old agrarian planter tradition. Known as "Bourbons" or "Redeemers," they were industrialists or would-be industrialists. They preached the industrialization of the South through the importation of Northern capital, a policy of low taxes to attract business, and a political alliance with the Northeast instead of with the South's traditional ally, the West. Controlling state governments through the medium of the Democratic party, which as

## Plessy v. Ferguson [1896]

In this famous case the Supreme Court held that enforced separate facilities for Negroes did not imply that Negro people were inferior and did not violate the Fourteenth Amendment:

*The object of the amendment was undoubtedly to enforce the absolute equality of the two races before the law, but in the nature of things it could not have been intended to abolish distinctions based upon color, or to enforce social, as distinguished from political, equality, or a commingling of the two races upon terms unsatisfactory to either. Laws permitting, and even requiring their separation in places where they are liable to be brought into contact do not necessarily imply the inferiority of either race to the other, and have been generally, if not universally, recognized as within the competency of the state legislatures in the exercise of their police power. The most common instance of this is connected with the establishment of separate schools for white and colored children, which have been held to be a valid exercise of the legislative power even by courts of states where the political rights of the colored race have been longest and most earnestly enforced. . . .*

a result of Reconstruction was the only party in the section, they practiced a program marked by economy in government, reduced taxes, and few social services. They did not attempt to abolish Negro suffrage but instead used the Negro vote to maintain white power, as men of their class had tried to use it during Reconstruction. Negroes continued to vote after the return of white supremacy, but in reduced numbers. In some states they were prevented from voting by an implied threat of force; in others, their influence was nullified by tricky devices—tissue ballots and a complicated arrangement of ballot boxes—that disqualified their votes. But in many areas the black vote was a purchased and directed vote, paid for by the Bourbons and used by them to beat down attempts of the farmers to take over control of the Democratic party.

Not until the 1890s did the Southern states pass laws to disfranchise the Negroes, and the impetus for the attempt was furnished by the white farmers. The farmers demanded disfranchisement because they were opposed for racial reasons to Negro voting and because they objected to the Negro vote being employed against them. The rich whites acquiesced, partly out of a desire to placate the white masses and partly because in the agrarian unrest that characterized the nineties the farmers in some states had sought to get the Negro vote on their side. The threat of competition for the Negro vote frightened all whites, and there was a general feeling that the time had come to close ranks if white supremacy was to be maintained.

In devising laws to disfranchise the Negroes, the Southern states had to take care to evade the intent of the Fifteenth Amendment. That measure did not confer suffrage upon the Negroes, but merely prohibited states from denying it because of color. The Southern problem, then, was to exclude Negroes from the franchise without seeming to base the exclusion on race. Two devices were widely employed before 1900. One was the poll tax or some form of property qualification. The other was the literacy and understanding test, which required a voter to demonstrate an ability to read and to interpret the Constitution. The reasoning behind the latter law was that local registrars could administer an impossible reading test to Negroes or rule that their interpretation of the Constitution was inadequate. Both of these devices could be used, and were used, to deny the franchise to poor white men, who protested against tests being applied to them. So, many states passed so-called "grandfather laws," which permitted men who could not meet the literacy and property qualifications to be admitted to the suffrage if their ancestors had voted before 1867 or some date before Reconstruction began.

The Supreme Court proved as compliant in ruling on the disfranchising laws as it was in dealing with the civil rights cases. Although the

Court eventually voided the grandfather laws, it validated the literacy tests (*Williams* v. *Mississippi*, 1898) and manifested a general willingness to let the Southern states define suffrage standards—provided the evasions of the Fifteenth Amendment were not too glaring.

One Negro leader believed that his race would have to acquire economic independence before it could ask for complete social acceptance. This was Booker T. Washington, who became the head of the Tuskegee Institute in Alabama, an industrial school for Negroes, and eventually the spokesman for a large segment of his people. Washington feared that in what he called "the great leap from slavery to freedom" the Negroes had forgotten that they would have to live by the work of their hands. Therefore, he preached that education for Negroes should stress industrial and practical aspects rather than classical matters. Eventually, Washington evolved a whole new concept of race relations. He set it forth in a speech at Atlanta in 1895. Known as the Atlanta Compromise, it proposed that for the time the Negro eschew agitation for social equality and devote his efforts to achieving economic security. Upper-class whites approved

Washington's philosophy and supported his endeavors, as did some wealthy whites in the North. Most Negroes also accepted the Atlanta strategy, but some were soon to reject it as too passive.

As the turn of the century approached, Southern whites seemed to have won a complete victory over the outside influences that had sought to disturb their way of life, and Reconstruction seemed to these people like a bad dream receding into the past. But the deep and turbulent forces generated in the years between 1865 and 1877 were only temporarily exhausted. They would appear again as Americans continued to search for solutions to the problems left by the Civil War and its troubled aftermath.

## The "New South"

With relative rapidity, the South recovered from the effects of war and restored its economic life. Since it was an agricultural society, its productive powers rested on the basis of land, and the land had survived the war. The chief problem was to get the plantations and farms under cultivation again. Work began at once (crops were harvested in 1865), and progress was steady. By

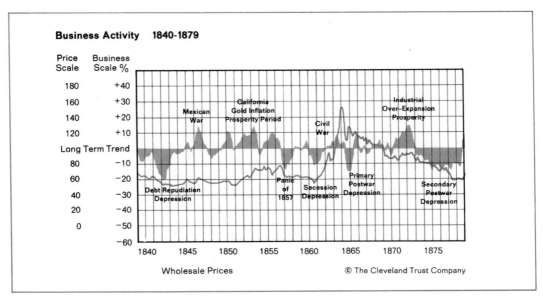

For the years 1840 to 1879 the index of business activity was computed on the basis of the following ten measures: blast furnace activity; cotton and pig iron consumption; canal and railroad freight ton miles; new railroad and ship construction; coal, locomotive, and rail production.

1879 the cotton crop exceeded that of 1860, part of the increase resulting from the opening of new growing areas west of the Mississippi, in Texas and Arkansas.

The rehabilitation of the South's economy was accomplished with relatively few changes in its agriculture. There was something of a shift in the distribution of land ownership, resulting in an increase in the number of small holders. In the economic travail following the war, many planters were unable to hold on to their property and were forced to offer their land for sale at low prices. In many cases the purchasers were white yeomen. According to the census, the number of farms in Mississippi increased from 43,000 in 1860 to 68,000 by 1870; in South Carolina from 33,000 to 52,000; and in Louisiana from 17,000 to 28,000. Actually, these figures are somewhat deceptive because some of the farms listed were under ten or twenty acres in area and were really units in a plantation, worked by tenants who were sometimes white but usually Negro.

The plantation system was modified, but it did not disappear. In the ownership of the system, however, an important change took place. The old planter (or the old type of planter who lived on the plantation) tended to disappear. More and more, the large land units were owned and administered by merchants, banks, and corporations—or by planters who lived in towns or cities where they could devote themselves to business as well as agricultural pursuits.

During the Reconstruction period, perhaps a third or more of the farmers in the South were tenants; by 1900 the figure had increased to 70 per cent. Several factors accounted for the trend toward tenancy. The Negroes, when they became freedmen, had, of course, no property. They were forced, as a simple matter of survival, to become laborers or tenants, and most of them were unable to accumulate enough resources to rise above this status. As late as 1890 there were only 121,000 Negro landowners in the South. Probably the strongest influence promoting tenancy among both races was the lack of an adequate credit system, with a resulting scarcity of money. The National Bank System was slow to establish itself in the Southern states, and state banks were slow to recover from the effects of

the war. Landlords did not have enough cash to hire laborers to work their land, and laborers could not secure loans to buy land or even raise sufficient currency to rent land on a cash basis.

Out of this situation developed an economic arrangement peculiar to the South, the share-crop and crop-lien system, in which produce and labor took the place of money. There were share tenants and sharecroppers, and there was a difference between the two groups. The share tenants, most of whom were whites, worked strips of land on a large unit, and paid as rent to the landlord one-fourth to one-third of their crop; they provided their own tools, seed, stock, and other supplies. The sharecroppers, most of whom were Negroes, provided nothing but their own labor. For the average cropper, the landlord would furnish all the above materials, and a horse or mule and a house as well. In addition, until the crop was harvested he would arrange credit facilities for the cropper and his family at a local country store owned by himself or a merchant. The cropper, for his part, agreed to consign from one-third to one-half of his crop to the landlord. Moreover, the storekeeper, the source of credit, protected his interest by taking a mortgage or lien on the tenant's share of the crop. (As time passed, the landlord and the merchant tended to become one person, and the planter-storekeeper became a major figure in the Southern credit complex.)

The lien system was a necessary credit device in the postwar years; but when it was continued and expanded after that period, it had a harmful influence upon Southern agriculture. The merchant or landlord pressed the cropper to produce a single money crop, cotton, to the neglect of diversified farming and scientific farming methods. More serious were the social results of the system. The typical sharecropper was an unlettered person who did not know how to handle his own money carefully and who did not understand the mechanics of credit. Frequently, after harvesting his crop, he found himself owing money to the storekeeper and hence forced to pledge his labor to the same source for another year. Not only did the lien system prevent tenants from rising to the owning class; it also operated to bind them to particular pieces of land, to create a state of peonage. The Negro sharecropper was not a slave, but he was not completely free.

The Reconstruction period witnessed a restoration of Southern industrial facilities damaged or destroyed during the war, as well as some promising beginnings in new industrial activities. Most of the rehabilitation and expansion was financed with local, Southern capital, which was subscribed by the people of a town who wanted to improve their community by locating a factory in it. The only Southern enterprise that attracted Northern and European investors was the railroads. With outside aid, the war-weakened rail system was soon put in running order again, and by 1873 over 4,000 miles of new track had been constructed. Modest but noteworthy progress was recorded in tobacco manufacturing, in the lumber industry, and in iron making; in 1880 the South produced 212,000 tons of iron.

The most substantial growth occurred in tex-

tiles, which had a prewar basis to build on. Southern leaders during Reconstruction preached the economic advantage of building cotton mills where the raw material was produced, and the Southern people took this logic to heart. Practically all the mills that began to appear in Southern towns were financed by local investors. By 1880 the South could boast of 161 textile factories housing 524,000 spindles and employing 16,000 workers.

But the great industrial development of the section, the development that created the "New South," would not come until later. And even that forward economic surge would not greatly change the nature of Southern life, would not make the South very "new." As late as 1910 only 15 per cent of all the people in the region were connected with manufacturing. For many years the South would remain, as it was in the Reconstruction era, a rural and a traditional land.

# Selected Readings

**Interpretations of Reconstruction** W. A. Dunning, *Reconstruction, Political and Economic, 1865–1877°* (1907); W. E. B. DuBois, *Black Reconstruction°* (1935); J. S. Allen, *Reconstruction: The Battle for Democracy, 1865–1876°* (1937); E. M. Coulter, *The South During Reconstruction, 1865–1877* (1947); J. H. Franklin, *Reconstruction After the Civil War°* (1962); W. R. Brock, *An American Crisis°* (1963); K. M. Stampp, *The Era of Reconstruction* (1965); R. W. Patrick, *The Reconstruction of the Nation°* (1967); J. E. Sefton, *The United States Army and Reconstruction* (1967); S. I. Kutler, *Judicial Power and Reconstruction Politics* (1968).

**Grant and the Republicans** L. D. White, *The Republican Era°* (1958); M. R. Dearing, *Veterans in Politics* (1952); C. H. Coleman, *The Election of 1868* (1933); W. B. Hesseltine, *U. S. Grant, Politician* (1935); Allan Nevins, *Hamilton Fish: The Inner History of the Grant Administration* (1936); Goldwin Smith, *The Treaty of Washington, 1871* (1941); Sumner Welles, *Na-*

*both's Vineyard* (2 vols., 1928), on the U. S. and Santo Domingo; A. B. Callow, Jr., *The Tweed Ring* (1966); E. D. Ross, *The Liberal Republican Movement* (1919); C. M. Fuess, *Carl Schurz, Reformer* (1932); Ari Hogenboom, *Outlawing the Spoils* (1961); R. P. Sharkey, *Money, Class, and Party°* (1959); Irwin Unger, *The Greenback Era* (1964); W. T. K. Nugent, *Money and American Society, 1865–1880* (1968).

**The Democratic Opposition** Stewart Mitchell, *Horatio Seymour* (1938); A. C. Flick, *Samuel Jones Tilden* (1939); Irving Katz, *August Belmont: A Political Biography* (1968).

**The New South** C. V. Woodward, *Origins of the New South, 1877–1913°* (1951) and *Reunion and Reaction: The Compromise of 1877 and the End of Reconstruction°* (1951); V. P. De Santis, *Republicans Face the Southern Question: The New Departure Years, 1877–1897* (1959); S. P. Hirshson, *Farewell to the Bloody Shirt: Northern Republicans and the Southern Negro, 1877–1893* (1962); Harry Barnard, *Rutherford B. Hayes and His America* (1964); R. B. Nixon,

*Henry W. Grady, Spokesman of the New South* (1943); Broadus Mitchell, *The Rise of Cotton Mills in the South* (1921); P. H. Buck, *The Road to Reunion, 1865–1900°* (1937).

**The Negro After 1865** William Gillette, *The Right to Vote: Politics and the Passage of the Fifteenth Amendment°* (1967); R. W. Logan, *The Negro in American Life and Thought: The Nadir, 1877–1901* (1954); Paul Lewinson, *Race, Class, and Party: A History of Negro Suffrage and White Politics in the South°* (1932); August Meier, *Negro Thought in America, 1880–1915°* (1963); B. T. Washington, *Up from Slavery°* (1901); S. R. Spencer, Jr., *Booker T. Washington and the Negro's Place in American Life°* (1955); C. V. Woodward, *The Strange Career of Jim Crow°* (1966); V. L. Wharton, *The Negro in Mississippi, 1865–1900°* (1947); G. B. Tindall, *South Carolina Negroes, 1877–1900°* (1952); J. R. Williamson, *After Slavery: The Negro in South Carolina During Reconstruction* (1966).

---

° Titles available in paperback.

# Chapter 17
# Industrialization
# and Urbanization

"With a stride that astonished statisticians, the conquering hosts of business enterprise swept over the continent; twenty-five years after the death of Lincoln, America had become, in the quantity and value of her products, the first manufacturing nation of the world," the historians Charles and Mary Beard have written. "What England had accomplished in a hundred years, the United States had achieved in half the time."

This rise to industrial supremacy during the last decades of the nineteenth century was due to a combination of factors. The United States was not necessarily superior in every one of them but certainly had an advantage in respect to all of them taken together.

First, this nation had an abundance of basic raw materials and sources of energy: coal, iron and other ores, timber, petroleum, water power. Second, there was a large and growing supply of willing labor, consisting in the main of American farmers and European peasants who flocked from the countryside of two continents to the rising industrial centers of the United States. Third, Americans had inherited a good deal of technological ingenuity—the "Yankee inventiveness" that had become a mark of the American character—which was capable of devising or adapting the necessary machines. Fourth, a number of remarkable business organizers, "captains of industry," had the skill to bring together raw materials, workers, and machines, to use them efficiently in the processes of production, and to distribute the resulting goods profitably in the national market. Fifth, this market itself, which was being enlarged by the growth of population and the extension of the rail network, made possible the mass consumption that is a prerequisite to mass production. Finally, the federal government, while refraining from interference with business enterprise, encouraged and assisted it by turning over public resources for private exploitation, by giving tariff protection against foreign competition, by setting up a helpful banking and monetary system, and by providing direct subsidies of land and money.

In the United States, large-scale industry had received a start before the Civil War. The war, while temporarily setting back some industrial activities, stimulated others and—most important—removed the Southern planters as a political obstacle to governmental policies favoring Northern capitalists. The rate of industrial growth increased so rapidly in the postwar decades that these came to constitute a new age of industrialization. It was also an age of urbanization, in which cities assumed a greater and greater importance. The tremendous increase in the output of goods—and the multiplication of conveniences that city life afforded—made possible a higher and higher average level of living. But all the people did not share equally in the benefits of the industrial system. There were gross inequalities, and these provoked severe criticisms of the system and led to determined and sometimes violent attempts to bring about a redistribution of income.

**Tenement Street**

The teeming life of a tenement district and something of its squalor are suggested in this view of Mulberry Street in New York City. (Library of Congress)

## THE RISE OF BIG BUSINESS

Between 1865 and 1900 American business moved in the direction of monopoly. Fewer and fewer firms produced more and more of the nation's goods. Small corporations were merged to create large ones. These often were brought together to form still larger combinations: *pools*, the members of which agreed to avoid competition and divide profits; *trusts*, in which a board of trustees controlled several corporations; or *holding companies*, which held stock in other companies and thus directed them. Regardless of their specific nature, the various combinations were popularly known as "trusts." By 1900 there were more than 300 of these trusts, and the largest ones, comprising fewer than 2 per cent of the manufacturing firms, turned out almost 50 per cent of all the manufactured goods in the country.

### Some Basic Inventions

This economic transformation was accompanied by a flood of inventions and technological innovations. In the entire history of the country up to 1860 only 36,000 patents had been granted, but for the period from 1860 to 1890 the figure was 440,000.

Many of the postwar inventions and discoveries were in the field of communication. In 1866 Cyrus W. Field succeeded in his project of laying a trans-Atlantic cable to Europe. During the next decade Alexander Graham Bell developed the first practicable telephone, and by the 1890s the American Telephone and Telegraph Company, which handled his interests, had installed nearly half a million instruments in American cities. Other inventions that speeded the pace of business organization were the typewriter (by Christopher L. Sholes in 1868), the cash register (by James Ritty in 1879), and the calculating or adding machine (by William S. Burroughs in 1891).

Undoubtedly the technological innovation that had the most revolutionary effect upon industry and upon lives of the urban masses in the industrial centers was the introduction in the 1870s of electricity as a source of light and

**An Early Typewriter**

The first practical typewriter was developed in Milwaukee between 1867 and 1873, by Christopher L. Sholes and several associates. In 1873, the patent owners made an arrangement with the Remington Gun Company for the manufacture of typewriters on a commercial scale, and by the next decade the machine had become standard equipment in business offices. This picture shows Sholes' daughter at one of his first machines. (Culver)

power. Among the several men who pioneered in developing a commercially practical dynamo were Charles F. Brush, who devised the arc lamp for street illumination, and Thomas A. Edison, who invented, among many other electrical contrivances, the incandescent lamp, which could be used for both street and home lighting. Edison and others designed improved generators and built central power plants to furnish electricity to office buildings, factories, and dwellings. Before the turn of the century 2,774 power stations were in operation, and some 2 million electric lights were in use in the country. Already electric power was being employed in street railway systems and in electric elevators in urban skyscrapers, as well as for driving the machines of factories. The electric power industry was dominated by two large corporations: the General Electric Company, which took over the Edison interests, and the Westinghouse Electric and Manufacturing Company.

## Steel and Oil

The Age of Steel began in 1865. A process by which iron could be transformed into steel had been discovered simultaneously in the 1850s by an Englishman, Henry Bessemer, and an American, William Kelly (it consisted of blowing air through the molten iron to burn out the impurities), but it was not put into use until after the Civil War. In 1868 another method of making steel, the open-hearth process, was introduced from Europe by Abram S. Hewitt, a New Jersey ironmaster. Both techniques were employed in the many steel mills that began to appear—and with revolutionary effects. Hitherto steel had been used only in the manufacture of small and very expensive articles, tools and cutlery, but now it was possible to produce bulky items like locomotives and rails from steel instead of iron.

The steel industry was first concentrated where the iron industry had existed, in western Pennsylvania and eastern Ohio. Here, in a region where iron ore and coal were found in abundance, Pittsburgh reigned as the center of the steel world. But as the industry expanded, new sources of ore had to be tapped, and by the 1870s the mines of the upper peninsula of Michigan were furnishing over half of the supply. Then in the 1890s the Eastern steelmasters began to exploit the extensive Mesabi range in Minnesota, which developed into the greatest ore-producing region in the world. Another rich source was discovered around Birmingham, Alabama. Although the Michigan and Minnesota fields were located at a great distance from the Eastern plants, the ore could be transported easily and cheaply by means of railroads and Great Lakes steamers. Eventually new centers of production with ready access to ore and coal arose: Cleveland and Lorain in Ohio, Detroit, Chicago, and Birmingham.

Inevitably the high profits to be made in steel tempted consolidation, and there appeared men who had a genius for organization. The central figure in steel was Andrew Carnegie, a Scottish immigrant boy who had worked his way up in the railroad industry. Adopting the Bessemer process, he opened in 1873 the J. Edgar Thompson Steel Works in western Pennsylvania, named in honor of his former railroad employer, the head of the Pennsylvania Railroad. Soon Carnegie had built up his company to a place of dominance in the industry.

His methods were those commonly employed by other great consolidationists of the times. He obtained rebates from railroads on his shipments, so that he could cut his costs and hence his prices, and he bought out rival concerns that could not meet his competition. In collaboration with his ablest associate, Henry Clay Frick, he set up a policy of integration designed to control the processing of steel from mine to market. His company operated a fleet of ore ships on the Great Lakes, acquired railroads and coal mines, and leased part of the Mesabi range.

The machines of the Age of Steel could not run without lubrication, and so another vast enterprise came into being in the postwar era, the petroleum industry. For years before the Civil War the existence of petroleum had been known, particularly in western Pennsylvania where it often seeped to the surface of streams and springs. No one was quite sure what it was or what to do with it. Some enterprising individuals peddled it in bottles as a patent medicine. The first person to glimpse its commercial possibilities as an illuminant was George H. Bissell, who sent a sample of oil to Professor Benjamin Silliman of Yale for analysis. Silliman reported in 1855 that the substance could be used for lighting purposes, and that it would also yield such products as paraffin, naphtha, and lubricating oil. Bissell then raised enough money to begin drilling operations, and in 1859 Edwin L. Drake, employed by Bissell, put down the first oil well near Titusville, Pennsylvania. Labeled "Drake's folly" by the skeptical, it was soon producing oil at the rate of 500 barrels a month.

It also started an oil rush, as promoters searched for and found other fields, not only in Pennsylvania but in Ohio and West Virginia as well. By the 1870s nearly 40 million barrels of petroleum had been produced, oil had advanced to fourth place among the nation's exports, and the annual production was approaching 20 million barrels. Because relatively little capital was required for a man to make a start in the oil business, either as a producer or a refiner, competition at first ran wild. Refineries, which were even more profitable than wells, dotted the Pennsylvania-Ohio region, with Pittsburgh and Cleveland constituting the two principal refining centers. Then the greatest consolidationist of the time stepped into the picture to bring order to the industry.

John D. Rockefeller was a successful businessman at an age when most boys of today would be in college. When only nineteen, he became a partner in a produce commission company in Cleveland that took solid profits selling goods to the government during the Civil War. Farsighted, highly acquisitive, and possessing abundant talents for organization, he decided that his economic future lay with oil. He also concluded that Cleveland, connected by rail and water with the Eastern and Western markets, was destined to surpass Pittsburgh, which had access only to the East through the Pennsylvania Railroad, as the oil-refining center of the country. At the end of the war he and Sidney Andrews, a Cleveland refiner, launched their own business. From the beginning Rockefeller sought to eliminate the competition and the

small-scale companies that in his opinion were ruining the petroleum industry. He and Andrews enlarged their operations, took in H. M. Flagler and S. V. Harkness as allies, and proceeded methodically to buy out other refineries. In 1870 the associates formed the Standard Oil Company of Ohio, which in a few years had acquired twenty of the twenty-five refineries in Cleveland, in addition to plants in Pittsburgh, Philadelphia, New York, and Baltimore.

In its rise to dominance Standard Oil employed the familiar consolidating devices of the period, plus a few which were its own invention. The company emphasized efficient and economic operation, research, and sound financial practices. At Rockefeller's insistence, a large cash reserve was maintained to avoid reliance on banks and to purchase competitors. The company obtained rebates from railroads, and even, for a brief time, forced three of the Eastern roads to pay rebates to it on oil shipped by competing companies. Rockefeller waged price wars to drive competitors out of business and, always victorious, took over the defeated concerns.

Like Carnegie in steel, Rockefeller set up an

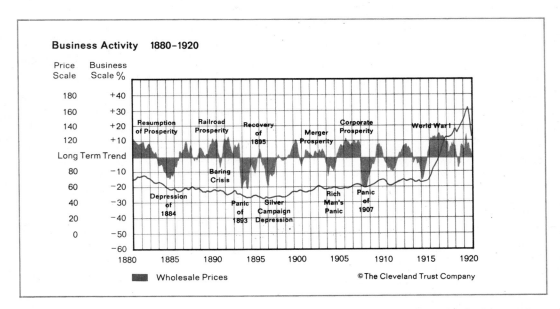

For the years 1880–1920, the index of business activity was computed on the basis of the following ten measures: commodity prices; imports; imports retained for consumption; government receipts; ship construc-tion; government expenditures; coal production; exports; iron exports; and tons of registered shipping in service.

# Where Historians Disagree

## The Motivation and Methods of Business

Historians have written much about the rise of big business in America. They have generally agreed as to what happened, but they have not always agreed as to why it happened. They have clashed, specifically, on the motives of the businessmen and the methods used by these men to build their empires.

The first general study of the magnates of the new industrial order appeared in 1907, when Gustavus Myers published *The History of the Great American Fortunes*. It was written at a time when many intellectuals were repelled by the power and practices of business, and it stated a dogmatic thesis. In essence, it said that the big businessmen had not, as was commonly assumed, amassed their wealth by adhering to the traditional American values of thrift and hard work. Rather, they had prospered because they had been unscrupulous, ruthless, bold. They had secured their ends by crushing competitors and corrupting politicians.

The Myers thesis had a subtle influence on the thinking of historians about business. But it did not become really prevalent until the depression decade of the 1930s, when business fell under public disfavor. A host of writers took up Myers' views and expanded and popularized them. Leading such writers was Matthew Josephson, who, in a book published in 1934, applied to the tycoons of business a label that would stick: *The Robber Barons*. Most historians accepted the title as being a reasonably accurate indicator of the character of businessmen, at least those of the Gilded Age.

The robber baron concept was challenged almost immediately. In 1940 Allan Nevins published *John D. Rockefeller: The Heroic Age of American Enterprise*. (The book was reissued thirteen years later, revised and with a somewhat different title.) Nevins depicted Rockefeller, and by implication other magnates, in a different, more favorable light; they were, he maintained, men of heroic mold engaged in heroic endeavors. Younger scholars, among them T. C. Cochran and William Miller, followed Nevins' lead and wrote more general studies, and E. C. Kirkland summarized many of their findings in *Dream and Thought in the Business Community* (1956). Significantly, these historians did their work in the World War II and cold war eras, when intellectuals were beginning to have a new appreciation of the values of an industrial America.

The later historians are not overly concerned with the charges leveled against business by earlier writers. They point out that the small companies crushed by bigger ones were themselves often ruthless and usually inefficient. And if business sometimes corrupted politics, it had to deal with scheming politicians who were not above blackmailing it on occasion. Present-day writers concentrate on what they consider the accomplishments of the big businessmen: the stimulation of economic growth and the creation of a basis for a greater economy with a higher standard of living for all people.

Critics of these historians have contended that they lean over backward to excuse the excesses of business. Their viewpoint is, however, accepted by most historians and has entered into modern writing about business. But like some of the views of the past, it may be challenged in the future.

integrated system of production. He built his own terminal warehouses and barrel factories and a network of pipelines that gave him control over most of the facilities for transporting petroleum. Standard also owned its own marketing organization, thus escaping commissions to middlemen. For sales purposes the United States was divided into districts, each of which

was administered by a company executive who was assisted by a corps of agents. The salesmen were under orders to sell Standard products by almost any method, and almost always they succeeded. When the Standard Oil Trust was formed in 1882, it was only a formal recognition of the near-monopoly that Rockefeller and his associates had already established.

PUBLISHED BY CURRIER & IVES

The Bridge is to cross the river by a single span of 1600 feet to start on the New York side from the City Hall rising by a gradual approach of 2361 feet in length, and on the Brooklyn side by an approach of 1861 feet; its elevation above the river in the

## THE GREAT EAST RIVER BRIDGE.
To Connect the Cities of New York & Brooklyn.

centre of the bridge will be 130 feet, its floor is to be 80 feet wide with tracks for steam cars, roadway for carriages, and walks for foot passengers; it is to have an elevated promenade commanding a view of extraordinary beauty and extent, and its cost is to be about $8,000,000.

### Brooklyn Bridge

As a story of persevering courage, the erection of Brooklyn Bridge by John A. and Washington Roebling can match anything in American military history. In 1866 Manhattan Island was connected with Brooklyn and the rest of Long Island only by ferries. When the East River froze, the tie was sundered. A bridge was needed. John Roebling, engineer and manufacturer of wire cables, proposed a suspension bridge with a central span of 1,600 feet—longer than had been built anywhere in the world. Other great engineers said it could not be done. But Roebling's prestige and forcefulness got approval for the idea, and he designed the bridge. Then he unexpectedly died. His son Washington Roebling was stricken by caisson

bends. An invalid, he was confined to his bed at Columbia Heights. His wife watched the construction by telescope, and he supervised every detail by letter. In 1883 twelve years after work began, the bridge opened, an object of practical use which also was a thing of beauty. Here was the austere art of the Age of Steel: the massive granite towers were united in tension with the spidery cables of nineteen wire strands, and the tension held the bridge aloft. The father was dead; the son, paralyzed, growing deaf and blind; but they had shown how straightforward statement of fact could unify industrialism with aesthetics. (Currier & Ives)

## Other Industries

Three developments brought significant changes to the meat-packing business. They were the appearance of the range-cattle industry in Texas and the Great Plains, the extension of railroad lines across the Mississippi into the plains country, and the introduction of the refrigerated freight car. Chicago, situated close to the cattle supply of the trans-Mississippi area and the hog supply of the Middle West, and elaborately connected by railroads with both the producing areas and the urban markets, became the undisputed capital of the meat-packing industry. Imaginative and aggressive leaders, the counterparts of Rockefeller and Carnegie, appeared to form the inevitable combinations: Philip D. Armour, Nelson Morris, and Gustavus F. Swift. Swift sponsored the most important technological development in the industry, the refrigerator car cooled by artificial ice.

Like the meat business, flour milling was originally a localized enterprise, carried on in thousands of small mills in all parts of the country. And like meat packing, the milling industry moved west to be nearer the source of the wheat supply, adopted new technological processes, and originated large-scale organizations which turned out standardized products. By the close of the Civil War the center of wheat production had shifted to the upper Mississippi Valley, and Minneapolis, Minnesota, became the center of the milling industry. The leading millers were Cadwallader C. Washburn, Charles A. Pillsbury, and George M. Christian, the last of whom eventually merged his interests with Washburn. Two manufacturing methods introduced from Europe resulted in a greatly improved product. The first, called the "middlings-purifier" or "gradual-reduction" process, preserved a higher content of gluten in finished flour than previously had been the case. The second was a process of passing wheat slowly through chilled iron rollers to achieve a flour of superior quality and unusual whiteness. By 1880 flour milling had become one of the country's largest businesses and was supplying its product to European as well as to American markets.

Many other industries, some of them antedating the war and some emerging after it, also underwent the common process of expansion and concentration. The coal industry, which supplied the bulk of the fuel used by the nation's industries, increased its output from approximately 20 million tons in 1860 to 270 million by 1900. In 1890 a near monopoly was created in tobacco manufacturing when James B. Duke fused five large corporations into the American Tobacco Company.

The prepared-foods business, concentrating on the canning of vegetables, became a major industry and in the process helped to alter the eating habits of the American people. A leader in this industry was Gail Borden. Born in rural New York, Borden had less than two years of formal schooling. After a business career in Texas, he interested himself in the possibilities of concentrated foods. He developed a process for condensing milk by evaporation and set up his first large condensary in New York State in 1861. His condensed milk was used by the Northern armies in the Civil War and thus became known to the general public. After the war he founded the town of Borden in Texas and established a plant there for concentrating fruit juices, cocoa, tea, and coffee.

Industries of a prewar origin which continued to experience growth after 1865 were boots and shoes, ready-made clothing, textiles, firearms, distilled liquors, and agricultural machinery.

## Railroad Expansion

In 1860 the railroads constituted the biggest business and the most important single economic interest in the United States. Their total mileage was approximately 30,000, and in rolling stock they counted 100,000 freight and passenger cars and 1,000 locomotives. Every decade the trackage figure increased: 52,000 miles in 1870, 93,000 in 1880, 163,000 in 1890, and 193,000 in 1900. The railroads made it possible for industry to secure its raw materials from a national producing area and to distribute its products in a national market.

Accompanying the expansion of railroad facilities was a host of technological improvements that made rail travel and transportation more efficient, convenient, and safe. Among the innovations were steel rails, heavier locomotives and cars, a uniform gauge (4 feet, 8½ inches), and

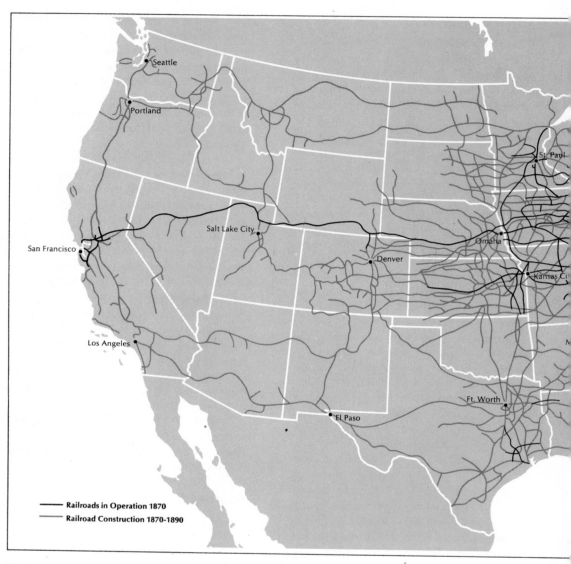

Railroads in Operation 1870; Railroad Construction 1870–1890

wider roadbeds. Perhaps the most important invention affecting railroads was the Westinghouse air brake, developed by George Westinghouse in 1869. In 1874 interlocking block signals were introduced from England. George Pullman had produced in 1864 the first sleeping car, and within a few years dining, parlor, and drawing-room cars appeared.

The major Eastern railroads were the New York Central, the Pennsylvania, the Erie, and the Baltimore and Ohio. By 1874 all of them had consolidated lesser lines into their systems and established connections with the Western market at Chicago. The creator of the New York Central system was Cornelius Vanderbilt, a salty, colorful character who had previously operated a steamship line and was endearingly known as "Commodore." A ruthless competitor but a sound railroad man, Vanderbilt improved facilities on the Central and bought up smaller roads to complete his empire. Second only to the Central in facilities was the Pennsylvania it was controlled during the seventies by Daniel Drew, Jay Gould, and James Fisk, three of the most unscrupulous speculators of the era, who were more interested in milking it of profits than in making it into a railroad. The Baltimore and Ohio had built lines from Baltimore as far as Wheeling on the Ohio River before the Civil War. After the war John W. Garrett, its president, extended its lines to Chicago, Cincinnati, St. Louis, and Philadelphia; it was not able, however, to obtain access to New York.

In the South the first railroad activity in the years immediately after 1865 was the rehabilitation of facilities damaged in the war. Then an outburst of construction, financed by Northern and European capital, got under way, and by 1890 the South had increased its trackage from 9,000 to 50,000 miles. In 1893 the Southern Railway was organized, with lines extending from Washington to New Orleans and connecting with the Middle West at St. Louis and Cincinnati. Chief rival to the Southern was the Atlantic Coast Line Railroad, which consolidated dozens of small roads to monopolize transportation from Richmond to Florida. The third big system in the South, the Illinois Central, was really a Middle Western road with a Southern terminal. Shortly before the Civil War it had built as far as Cairo, Illinois, at the confluence of the Ohio and the Mississippi. In the postwar era the Central achieved its original purpose of reaching the Gulf of Mexico. By gobbling up smaller lines in the South, it increased its trackage from approximately 1,000 to 9,000 miles, reached New Orleans on the Gulf, and eventually touched the Atlantic at Savannah, Georgia.

From 1865 to 1873 there was more railroad construction in the Mississippi Valley than in any other part of the country. The Chicago and Northwestern stretched its lines to Omaha; the Chicago, Burlington and Quincy drove through to Kearney, Nebraska; the Missouri Pacific built from Kansas City to St. Louis; and the Kansas Pacific moved from Kansas City to Denver and then on to Cheyenne in Wyoming Territory.

## The Transcontinental Lines

Of all the stupendous railroad projects of the era between 1865 and 1900, none so gripped the popular imagination as the great "transcon-

Railroad, whose original route ran between Philadelphia and Pittsburgh. Under the leadership of J. Edgar Thompson, the Pennsylvania established connections with Chicago, St. Louis, Baltimore, and Richmond, and in 1899, by tunneling under the Hudson River, entered New York City to compete directly with the Central. The Erie, chartered in the 1850s to link New York City and Lake Erie, in the postwar years stretched its connections to Cleveland, Cincinnati, and St. Louis. Unfortunately for the Erie, tinental" lines. An act of Congress passed in 1862 and amended in 1864 chartered two railroad corporations, the Union Pacific and the Central Pacific. The Union Pacific was to build westward from Omaha, Nebraska, and the Central Pacific eastward from Sacramento, California, until they met.

To provide the financial aid deemed necessary to initiate the roads, Congress donated a right of way across the public domain and offered the companies special benefits: for each mile of track a company laid, it would receive twenty square miles of land in alternate sections along the right of way and a thirty-year loan of $16,000, $32,000, or $48,000, depending on whether the construction was in plains, foothill, or mountain country.

Because of a scarcity of labor, the Union Pacific resorted to hiring thousands of Irish immigrants, while the Central Pacific imported several thousand Chinese workers. The builders had to cross deserts, penetrate mountain ranges, and fight off Indians. In the spring of 1869, engines of the two lines met at Promontory Point in Utah Territory, and the nation was linked by rail from the Atlantic to the Pacific.

By the end of the century five transcontinental systems were in operation: (1) the Union Pacific–Central Pacific, joining Omaha to Sacramento and San Francisco; (2) the Southern Pacific, extending from San Francisco to St. Louis and New Orleans; (3) the Northern Pacific, linking St. Paul and Minneapolis to Portland, Oregon; (4) the Atchison, Topeka and Santa Fé, running from Atchison, Kansas, to San Diego, California; and (5) the Great Northern, stretching from Duluth and St. Paul to Seattle and Tacoma, Washington. All except the Great Northern were built with some form of assistance from the national government or from state governments.

State governments put up an estimated $228 million to entice promoters into their boundaries, and in addition placed their credit at the disposal of railroads, subscribed to stock, and donated 50 million acres of land. The federal government granted over 130 million acres and provided over $60 million in loans to various Western roads. In a number of cases, the aid supplied by the government more than paid for the cost of construction. It was small wonder that many people regarded the railroads, although operated by private enterprise, as essentially public projects.

As the network of rails covered the country, it became evident that the railroad industry was being overbuilt and overextended; many railroad corporations, including some of the largest ones, were overexpanded, overcapitalized, and afflicted with impossible debt burdens. Moreover, many roads were looted and wrecked by their own directors or subjected to harassing competition by speculators like Jay Gould. In some areas of the country certain railroads enjoyed monopolies, but wherever competition existed it was savage and sustained. Competing roads fought ferocious rate wars and struggled for business by offering rebates to big shippers. The inevitable effects of overexpansion, fraudulent management, and cutthroat competition were apparent in the depression of the seventies, when 450 roads went into bankruptcy. Twenty years later, in the hard times of the nineties, 318 companies controlling 67,000 miles fell into the hands of receivers.

After the economic crisis of 1893 railroad capitalists moved to curb competition by creating larger systems. Reorganizing the railroads required huge sums of cash and credit, which could be supplied only by the big New York investment banking houses. The investment bankers, led by J. P. Morgan, were eager to finance consolidation in order to stop the railroads, with their wild financing and frenzied speculating, from ruining the investment business. But the bankers, as the price for their aid, insisted on being given a voice in the management of the roads, a condition which the railroad promoters had to accept. By the end of the century a few major railroad systems controlled over half the mileage in the country, and these systems were wholly or partially controlled by two banking houses.

## GROWTH OF CITIES

Society was being transformed along with the economy: a rural nation was being reshaped in an urban mold as cities grew with the growth of industry. The urban areas were the seats of the developing economic system, the places where most of the factories and corporate offices were located. Cities had existed from colonial times, of course, but now they assumed a new character, size, and significance.

The movement to cities was a contemporary phenomenon of much of the Western world. From countries—or parts of countries—that were industrializing slowly if at all, people moved to other countries—or to other parts of their own country—that were industrializing rapidly. Rural folk from both America and Europe made their way to the business and industrial centers of the United States.

## The City's Lure

"We cannot all live in cities, yet nearly all seem determined to do so," Horace Greeley wrote soon after the Civil War. " 'Hot and cold water,' baker's bread, gas, the theatre, and the streetcars . . . indicate the tendency of modern taste." The city lured people because of its many conveniences, among them the telephone and the electric light, which it enjoyed for years before such things reached the village or the farm. It drew people because of its institutions of entertainment and culture, not only its theaters and other amusements but also its libraries and museums, its superior colleges and schools. It attracted people because, above all, it offered opportunities for employment at higher pay than the countryside afforded. The lure of the city persisted even though many who came were disappointed and urban life acquired some very unpleasant characteristics.

In the half century from 1860 to 1910 the rural population almost doubled, but the urban population increased seven times. In 1860 approximately one-sixth of the people lived in towns of 8,000 or larger; by 1900, one-third of the people. The number of cities with more than 50,000 inhabitants was 16 in 1860 and 109 in 1910. The population of the New York urban area (the city and its environs) grew from less than 1 million in 1860 to more than 3 million in 1900. Even more spectacular was the growth of Chicago, which had 100,000 inhabitants in 1860 and more than a million at the end of the century. Towns and cities were getting bigger and

more numerous in all sections of the country. And this vast industrial-urban complex that was taking shape was linked in all its parts by rapid railroad transportation and instantaneous telegraphic communication.

While the cities gained, some rural parts of the country were actually losing population (as had happened to a much smaller extent in the early nineteenth century). During the 1880s, for instance, the number of inhabitants was decreasing in two-fifths of Pennsylvania's total area, three-fifths of Connecticut's, more than half of Ohio's and Illinois', and five-sixths of New York's. People seldom moved directly to a city from the farms. As the historian A. M. Schlesinger has observed, "the tendency was to move from the countryside to the nearest hamlet, from the hamlet to the town, and from the town to the city." So for a time the country town retained some importance as a market and a cultural center, but more and more the city overshadowed it. The city was the ultimate goal of restless farm and village folk. They and the immigrants, most of whom also came from rural areas, made up the great majority of urban dwellers.

## The Newer Immigrants

Between 1860 and 1900 the total population of the United States more than doubled, rising from about 31 million to almost 76 million. Immigration accounted for a substantial portion of the increase; in this forty-year period some 14 million aliens entered the country. This was almost three times the 5 million who had come in the four decades preceding 1860, but in relation to the total population the immigrant tide was no greater after the Civil War than before. The percentage of foreign-born was about the same. In 1880 the ethnic composition of the population was substantially what it had been fifty years before. Up to that year the great majority of the immigrants had originated in the countries of Western and Northern Europe: England, Ireland, Germany, and the Scandinavian countries. Although there had been friction between these people and "native" Americans and some resistance to their presence, especially to the Irish, they were in culture and outlook essentially like those among whom they settled, and they were

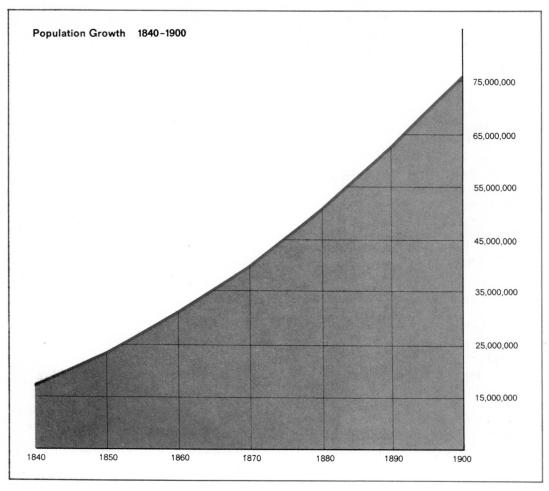

Population Growth    1840–1900

| | |
|---|---|
| | 75,000,000 |
| | 65,000,000 |
| | 55,000,000 |
| | 45,000,000 |
| | 35,000,000 |
| | 25,000,000 |
| | 15,000,000 |

1840    1850    1860    1870    1880    1890    1900

The total population of the country increased significantly every decade between 1840 and 1900. At the close of the century the number of Americans was over four times the figure in 1840 and over twice that at the beginning of the Civil War.

assimilated without too much difficulty into the national structure.

But in the eighties the immigrant stream began to flow from another source—Southern and Eastern Europe. By the 1890s about fifty-two in one hundred immigrants were coming from this part of the world (in the 1860s it had been fewer than two in one hundred). Among the new ethnic stocks were Austrians, Hungarians, Bohemians, Poles, Serbs, Italians, Russians, and Jews from Poland and Russia. These people came for essentially the same reasons as earlier immigrants: the desire to escape unfavorable economic and political conditions at home. Now

railroads, in order to dispose of landholdings, painted an alluring picture of America in advertisements. Industrial employers demanded cheap labor and until 1885 could import workers under the labor contract law.

Of the earlier immigrants only the Irish had tended to congregate in the Eastern cities. Most of the Germans went West to become farmers, while those that had a proclivity for urban life settled in such Middle Western centers as Milwaukee, St. Louis, and Cincinnati. Nearly all of the Scandinavians took up land in the Middle West or the Great Plains. Those earlier arrivals who became urban dwellers were, with exception of the Irish, businessmen, professional men, or skilled laborers; and the Irish, who at first were laborers, rapidly achieved economic independence and raised their social status. In direct contrast, the later immigrants flocked in preponderant numbers to the industrial cities and became unskilled laborers. They did not have the capital to begin farming operations in the West. They had to have immediate employment, and this was offered them by the meat packers, railroads, coal producers, and steel manufacturers, hungry for cheap labor. Besides, in a strange land the newcomers felt the need of that association with their fellows that only city life could give.

The later immigrants provoked more fear and resentment among native Americans than had the earlier arrivals, most of whom, or their offspring, were now assimilated and thoroughly suspicious of new foreigners. The recent arrivals had different cultural and economic standards and spoke diverse languages (the British and Irish who composed the bulk of the previous immigration had presented no language dissimilarity). They were in overwhelming numbers Catholics in a predominantly Protestant country, and their influx called into existence a short-lived nativist organization, the American Protective Association, which was vaguely but bitterly antialien and anti-Catholic. Some people reacted against the immigrants out of plain prejudice, others honestly wondered if they could be absorbed into national life. Laborers, fighting to raise their incomes and improve their working conditions, were incensed by the willingness of the immigrants to accept lower wages and to take over jobs of strikers.

With the mounting of the alien tide, the first demands for immigration restrictions rose in the land. Congress acted in 1882 to exclude the Chinese. In the same year it passed a general immigration law denying entry to certain undesirables—convicts, paupers, idiots—and placed a tax of 50 cents on every person admitted. Later legislation of the nineties enlarged the proscriptive list and increased the tax. These measures reflected a rising fear that continuing unlimited immigration would exhaust the resources of the nation and endanger its social institutions. They kept out only a small number of aliens, however,

and were far from fulfilling the purposes of the extreme exclusionists. The latter group worked for a literacy test, a device intended to exclude immigrants from Eastern and Southern Europe. Congress passed a literacy law in 1897, but President Grover Cleveland vetoed it. Powerful business interests, the employers of cheap labor, continued to oppose restrictions.

## The Urban Scene

The city was a place of unbelievable contrasts, with the most palatial homes and the most wretched hovels, the greatest of conveniences and the worst of problems—misgovernment, poverty, overcrowding, traffic jams, filth, epidemics, and conflagrations. The basic trouble was that the city was growing too fast for planning and building to keep pace. "The problem in America," as one municipal reformer said, "has been to make a great city in a few years out of nothing."

Most city people rented the places they lived in. Landowners, to maximize the rent, encouraged as many as possible to crowd into a given space. New York was not only the largest but also the most congested city. On Manhattan Island, by 1894, the average population density had reached 143 per acre, as compared with 127 for Paris and 101 for Berlin. More than a million poor New Yorkers were jammed in tenements. (Originally the word *tenement* meant simply a multiple-family rented building; eventually the term was applied only to slum dwellings.) When the first tenement was put up (in 1850) it was hailed as a great improvement in housing for the poor. "It is built with the design of supplying the laboring people with cheap lodgings," a local newspaper commented, "and will have many advantages over the cellars and other miserable abodes, which too many are forced to inhabit." But tenements themselves became miserable abodes, three to five stories high, with many windowless rooms, little or no provision for plumbing or for central heating, and perhaps a row of privies in the basement. A New York state law of 1879 required a window in every bedroom of tenements built thereafter. Still, in 1890, the Danish immigrant and New York newspaper reporter Jacob Riis found deplorable conditions, which he described in his book *How the Other Half Lives.* A typical building was sunless and practically airless and "poisoned" by "summer stenches." "The hall is dark and you might stumble over the children pitching pennies back there."

Some of the wealthy lived in downtown mansions. Many of the rich or the reasonably well-to-do tried to combine the advantages of city and country living by moving to the city's outskirts. In the 1870s Chicago boasted of nearly one hundred residential suburbs connected with the city by railroad and offering the joys of "pure air, peacefulness, quietude, and natural scenery." The growth of the city and its suburbs —and indeed the maintenance of the very life of the city—depended on improvements in urban transportation.

Old city streets were in many cases too narrow for the heavy traffic that was beginning to move over them. A few were paved with cobblestones, but most of them lacked a hard surface and were filled alternately with mud and dust. In the last decades of the century, more and more streets were paved, usually with wooden blocks, bricks, or asphalt, but paving could not even keep up with the laying out of new thoroughfares. By 1890 Chicago had surfaced only about 600 of more than 2,000 miles of streets.

Up and down the streets of every city a variety of horse-drawn vehicles clattered—wagons and drays, hacks and omnibuses, and private carriages of many kinds—littering the ground with horse droppings that attracted flies in summer. The great cities of the time could hardly have existed without the horse, and many of them were nearly paralyzed when an epidemic of the epizootic, a horse disease, swept through the Northeast and the Midwest in the 1870s. In normal times the vehicles could scarcely move at the busiest hours of the day. As early as the 1850s New York visitors had been amazed by the frequency with which the "whole traffic of the city" came to a "deadlock."

Already streetcars drawn by horses were operating on rails laid down in many city streets; by 1866 New York had 16 lines using 800 cars and nearly 8,000 horses. Passengers found the horsecars smoother and a little faster than omnibuses, but not fast enough. In 1870 New York

opened its first elevated railway, with cars pulled by steam locomotives, which were noisy and often scattered hot ashes on pedestrians below. New York, Chicago, San Francisco, and other cities experimented with cable cars, which were towed by an endless cable that moved underground and was powered by a stationary steam engine. A better solution came with the development of the electrified railway, which first appeared in Richmond, Virginia, in 1888, when 40 trolley cars began to run over a 12-mile line. Trolley systems spread rapidly, and by 1895 they were operating in 850 towns and cities, with a total of 10,000 miles of track. Interurban lines were beginning to be extended through the countryside. In 1897, putting streetcars below ground, Boston opened the first American subway, a mile and a half long.

The horsecar and then the trolley enabled cities to expand and suburbs to grow. As a rule, cities spread fastest along the radiating lines of transportation, in a kind of star-shaped pattern. They grew upward as well as outward. The technique of constructing skyscrapers, with cast-iron and then steel frames, was first perfected in Chicago, where a ten-story office building rose in 1884. By that time the electric elevator was replacing the steam-powered hoist and making possible safe and rapid vertical movement. As tall buildings became more numerous, traffic congestion increased on city streets.

Chicago had been forced to rebuild after a conflagration in 1871, and Boston suffered a disastrous fire the same year. While more fireproof structures were appearing, wooden buildings continued to predominate in every city, and these were always in danger of going up in flames. To meet the hazard, volunteer fire-fighters were beginning to give way to professional fire departments.

An even greater hazard was disease, especially in the slums, whence it often spread to the better areas of a city. Even though the germ theory was known to public-health experts, few people appreciated the relationship of sewage disposal and water contamination to such epidemic diseases as typhoid fever and cholera. To the end of the nineteenth century, most city dwellers relied on private vaults and cesspools for the disposal of human wastes. The water closet (flush

**New York's Elevated Railroad**

With the rise of the city in America there emerged the problem of urban rapid transit—how to transport huge numbers of people, particularly workers who went to their jobs or left them at the same hours of the day. New York was the first to experiment with an elevated railroad. A short line was opened in 1870, and a longer one, the Sixth Avenue Elevated, shown here, in 1878. Other cities to follow suit were Brooklyn, Kansas City, Chicago, and Boston. Steam locomotives furnished the power on the "Els." Transit on streets in New York, as in many other cities, was provided by horse-drawn cars, also depicted in the print. (Library of Congress)

toilet) had been perfected in the 1870s, and a number of cities had begun to extend their sewerage systems, but these seldom kept up with population growth. Besides, the sewer commonly emptied into an open ditch within the city limits or into a stream nearby, from which the city itself or some other city derived its drinking water. Philadelphia, for example, polluted its own water supply by pouring raw sewage into the Delaware River. By 1900 a few cities had fairly adequate sewage disposal, regular garbage collections, and water-purification systems.

Urbanization brought more than new conveniences and new insecurities. "The complex interrelationship of life in the modern city called for unprecedented precision," as the historian Oscar Handlin has written. "The arrival of all those integers who worked together, from whatever part of the city they inhabited, had to be coordinated to the moment. There was no natural span for such labor; arbitrary beginnings and ends had to be set and adhered to. The dictatorship of the clock and the schedule became absolute." Thus the modern city brought a new concept of time, which to rural Americans had been a matter of human whims and natural phenomena such as sunrises and sunsets. Rural Americans, still the great majority, had an ambivalent attitude toward the city. While a place of strong allure, it was also to them a place of poverty and sin, and of foreigners with their strange customs. However country people felt toward it, the city imposed its ways upon them as well as its own inhabitants. More and more, it set the pattern for American character and culture.

## CAPITALISM AND ITS CRITICS

With the rise of big business, a varied rationale was developed to justify its methods and its consequences. There also appeared a variety of criticisms. Still, the philosophy of business prevailed not only among the captains of industry themselves but also among the majority of the American people.

### Self-Made Men

The economic revolution raised up a new ruling class in America. The industrialists and the investment bankers now sat in the seats of power formerly held by Southern planters and Northeastern merchants, by members of the old aristocracy of inherited wealth and the old middle class, by politicians and statesmen of the antebellum Webster-Clay model.

Before the Civil War there had been few millionaires in America; by 1892 there were more than 4,000 of them. Most of the new business tycoons had begun their careers from comfortable and privileged positions in the economic scale. But some—enough to invest the entire group with the aura of the American success story—had emerged from obscurity to riches. Andrew Carnegie had worked as a bobbin boy in a Pittsburgh cotton mill, James J. Hill had been a frontier clerk, John D. Rockefeller had started out as a clerk in a Cleveland commission house, and E. H. Harriman had begun as a broker's office boy. Regardless of economic background, the new millionaires were—or considered themselves to be—self-made men.

Many had gotten ahead through a ruthless disregard for the public welfare. Their attitude was epitomized by Commodore Vanderbilt's belligerent question: "Can't I do what I want with my own?" and by the much-quoted statement of his son William: "The public be damned." Once, when the Commodore's lawyers warned him that a move he contemplated was illegal, he

bellowed: "What do I care about the law? Hain't I got the power?" Men like Vanderbilt had the power, indeed. Through their financial contributions to politicians and to parties, by gifts of stock and outright bribes to political personages, they generally managed to get what they wanted from the national and the state governments. It was said that Standard Oil did everything to the Ohio legislature except to refine it. On one occasion a member of the Pennsylvania legislature was reported to have said: "Mr. Speaker, I move we adjourn unless the Pennsylvania Railroad has some more business for us to transact."

Wholesale bribery was a weapon in the notorious "Erie war" fought by Commodore Vanderbilt against Jay Gould and Jim Fisk for control of the Erie Railroad. Vanderbilt attempted to take over the Erie by buying stock, a move which his antagonists blocked by the simple expedient of printing more stock than he could purchase. When a bill to legalize the issue of the new stock was introduced in the New York legislature, Gould was present with $500,000, and also on hand was a Vanderbilt agent. Exactly how much money was paid out by both parties before the Commodore admitted defeat is not known. The market price of legislators during the fight was $15,000 a head. One influential and imaginative leader collected $75,000 from Vanderbilt and $100,000 from Gould.

Before passing judgment on the relation of business to government, however, it should be noted that in many cases the politicians deliberately created situations where they had to be bought—in effect, they blackmailed businessmen. And whatever indictments may be brought against the lords of business, these men were emphatically products of their environment; even the most crude and crass of their activities reflected prevailing mores in American society. The big corporations did a quick, if sometimes wasteful and ruthless, job of developing the country's potential economic resources. And the businessmen who headed the corporations ran various risks in whatever they did—the risk of overexpansion, the risk of unscrupulous competition. Not every businessman became a Rockefeller or a Gould.

Even the most ruthless of the tycoons were

builders rather than wreckers. They were building, perhaps without realizing what they were doing, the basis of a great economic society. By integrating operations and cutting costs, they were, says Frederick Lewis Allen, opening the way to economical mass production: "In the process of playing remunerative games with the tokens that represented capital, the bankers and the steel men had introduced into America something new: twentieth-century industry, undisciplined still, but full of promise."

## Survival of the Fittest

Most tycoons believed that they had attained their wealth by exercising the old American and Protestant virtues of hard work, acquisitiveness, and thrift. They had gotten where they were because they deserved it; people who were not so fortunate were lazy, unintelligent, or profligate. In some way it was all connected with the moral law and with divine will. "God gave me my money," explained John D. Rockefeller.

To many businessmen, the formula of social Darwinism seemed to explain both their own success and the nature of the society in which they operated. Social Darwinism was Charles Darwin's law of evolution applied to social organization. As expounded by the Englishman Herbert Spencer, it taught that struggle was a normal human activity, especially in economic life. The weak went down, the strong endured and became stronger, and society was benefited because the unfit were eliminated and the fit survived.

Men who had risen to dominance by crushing their competitors were intrigued and comforted by a doctrine that justified any method that succeeded, and they proclaimed that wealth was a reward of competence. Carnegie, who made himself the leading disciple of Spencer in the United States, contended that the natural law of competition was responsible for the great material growth of the country: "It is here; we can not evade it; no substitutes for it have been found; and while the law may be sometimes hard on the individual, it is best for the race, because it insures the survival of the fittest in every department."

According to social Darwinism, all attempts by labor to raise its wages by forming unions and all endeavors by government to regulate economic activities would fail, because economic life was controlled by a natural law, the law of competition. This coincided with another supposed "law" that seemed to justify business practices and business dominance: the law of supply and demand as defined by Adam Smith and the classical economists. According to them, the economic system was like a great and delicate machine functioning by natural and automatic rules. The greatest among these rules, the law of supply and demand, determined all economic values—prices, wages, rents, interest rates—at a level that was just to all concerned. Supply and demand worked because man was essentially an economic creature who understood and followed his own interests, and because he operated in a free market where competition was open to all.

Businessmen mouthed the clichés of classical economics even though the combinations they were creating were undermining the foundations of the free competitive market and modifying, if not destroying, the validity of the law of supply and demand. Samuel C. T. Dodd, the lawyer who devised the trust organization for Standard Oil, spoke glowingly of the unrestrained right of competition and the unrestrained right of combination. What would happen to competition if combination triumphed, Dodd did not explain.

Tempering the principle of the survival of the fittest was the "gospel of wealth." If rich men held economic power, they also had responsibilities to exercise their power with Christian magnanimity. If God gave the tycoons their money, as John D. Rockefeller believed, it behooved them to use the money for social purposes.

Carnegie himself elaborated on the idea in his book *The Gospel of Wealth* (1901). The man of wealth, he wrote, ought to consider all revenues in excess of his own needs as "trust funds" that he should administer for the good of the community, "thus becoming the mere trustee and agent for his poorer brethren." Carnegie did not believe in giving directly to the poor, for he feared that such charity would have a pauperizing effect. He preferred to contribute to institutions, notably libraries, that presumably would

**The Modern Robber Barons**

In this cartoon the millionaires of business are likened to the "robber barons" of the Middle Ages. As the serfs brought tribute to the feudal lords, so farmers, laborers, and small businessmen had to pay tribute in the form of wages and interest to the masters of the trusts. The term "robber baron" as a descriptive tag for the big businessmen of the period became popular and even passed into historical usage. From *Puck* (1889).

help the poor to help themselves. He and other men of wealth devoted part of their fortunes to philanthropic works.

The notion of private wealth as a public blessing was spread by numerous popularizers. One of the most persistent was Russell H. Conwell, a Baptist minister, who delivered one lecture on the subject, *Acres of Diamonds*, over 6,000 times. "We ought to get rich if we can by honorable and Christian methods," cried Conwell (who got rich by lecturing), "and those are the only methods that sweep us quickly toward the goal of riches."

Conwell was a champion of another concept that was becoming a part of the American myth: the success story, the notion that any poor boy who was industrious and thrifty could succeed in business. Most of the millionaires in the country, Conwell claimed, had begun on the lowest rung of the economic ladder. Another promoter of the success story was Horatio Alger, a New York minister who wrote over a hundred novels of which, all together, more than 20 million copies were sold. These books rejoiced in such titles as *Andy Grant's Pluck, Tom the Bootblack,* and *Sink or Swim.* In every volume a poor boy from a small town went to the big city to seek his fortune, and by work, perseverance, and luck he became rich.

## Doubt and Dissent

Most people, poor as well as rich, accepted the rationalizations that were made by and for big business, but there were many who listened to voices of doubt and dissent. Thoughtful Americans did not agree among themselves on the lessons to be derived from Darwin's theory of evolution.

It was, perhaps, characteristic of optimistic Americans to combine the Darwinian method with the older idea of progress and come up with a hopeful prognostication. Such an analysis was attempted by Lewis H. Morgan, a pioneer anthropologist, in his *Ancient Society* (1878), in which he traced human development from its first simple beginnings to the complex but beneficent industrial order of the nineteenth century. The works of men like Morgan stressed that change was gradual and cumulative in character and that present society was safely linked with the past. Although such writers foresaw a hopeful future, they rejected the concept of unlimited progress that had marked earlier American thought. They also departed from former notions in insisting that change was evolutionary instead of revolutionary and that American development was a phase of a larger European or world scheme and not a unique experiment in a specially favored land. Opposing directions taken by American Darwinians are illustrated by the writings of two pioneers in sociology: William Graham Sumner and Lester F. Ward.

Sumner, a scholar with a tough mind and a sharp tongue, elaborated his theories in lectures at Yale, in magazine articles, and finally in a famous book, *Folkways* (1906). In contradiction to earlier thinkers who had held that man was a free agent actuated by rational powers, Sumner contended that the human mind was molded by circumstances beyond its control and that men's activities consisted of routine behavior determined by mechanistic forces. In short, man had no innate ideas and no power to reform his environment. His freedom was limited to certain narrow areas in which tradition permitted him to operate. But within these areas, Sumner insisted, man must have absolute freedom to struggle, to compete, to gratify his instinct for self-interest. The struggle for survival should be allowed to work itself out, and should not be delimited by laws or the state. Sumner's devotion to the principle of the survival of the fittest caused him to be known as the foremost champion of social Darwinism. Yet his insistence on the freedom to compete caused him to oppose protective tariffs and thus made him a critic of business policy. Essentially, he was trying to preserve the older America of truly free enterprise by employing the new insights of Darwinism.

Standing in direct opposition to Sumner was Lester Ward, though he was just as much a Darwinian as the Yale sage. Ward expressed his concepts in a number of notable books, beginning with *Dynamic Sociology* (1883). He argued that various forces altered the Darwinian process when applied to complex societies. Desire became subordinated to and controlled by intelligence. Mind thus became the master of nature, and man became capable of devising instruments to direct and improve his evolutionary future. The chief goal of modern society, Ward said, was the greatest good of all its members, and the best instrument to attain the goal was government. In contrast to Sumner, who believed that state intervention to remodel the environment was futile, Ward thought that a positive, planning government was man's only hope.

There came to be widespread acceptance of the principle that institutions should meet social needs and thus be "functional." Even in the churches there was an effort to accommodate functional concepts. Noted ministers and theologians like Washington Gladden, Walter Rauschenbusch, and Shailer Mathews proclaimed that religion had to concern itself with the material conditions in which Christ's children lived, and these men advocated such causes as industrial peace, better working conditions, slum clearance, and temperance.

## Socialists and Single-Taxers

While some Americans questioned the beneficence of capitalism, others proposed more or less drastic changes in the system, and at least a few thought it should be thrown out entirely.

Americans were less inclined than Europeans to adopt extremely radical programs such as the "scientific socialism" of Karl Marx (whose *Capital*, the first volume of which appeared in 1867, was one of the most influential books ever written) or the violent anarchism of Mikhail Bakunin. But Marxism and anarchism had some following in America, especially among recent immigrants.

The Socialist Labor party, founded in the seventies, fell under the leadership of Daniel De Leon, an immigrant from the West Indies; other party chiefs hailed from Eastern Europe. Although De Leon aroused something of a following in the industrial cities, the party never succeeded in polling over 82,000 votes. De Leon's somewhat theoretical and dogmatic approach pleased intellectuals but evoked no warmth among workers and seemed ill-suited to the American scene. A right-wing faction of the party sensed the fault in its approach and, seeking a more American approach, split away in 1900 to form the Socialist party.

Native radicals, with less extreme programs, gained a wider following. One of the most influential was Henry George. His angrily eloquent *Progress and Poverty*, published in 1879, was an immediate success; reprinted in successive editions, it became one of the ten best-selling nonfiction works in American publishing history. George addressed himself to the question of why poverty existed amidst the wealth created by modern industry. "This association of poverty with progress is the great enigma of our times," he wrote. "So long as all the increased wealth which modern progress brings goes but to build up great fortunes, to increase luxury and make sharper the contrast between the House of Have and the House of Want, progress in not real and cannot be permanent."

George blamed all this on monopoly, and he proposed a remedy, a "single tax" on the "unearned increment" in the value of land. An increase in the value of land resulted from the growth of society around it. Hence, George argued, the private owner had not earned the increment, and the community should receive it. A tax taking the whole of this increase would supposedly destroy monopolies, distribute wealth more equally, and eliminate poverty. Single-tax societies sprang up in many cities, and in 1886 George, backed by labor and the Socialists, narrowly missed being elected mayor of New York.

Rivaling George in popularity was Edward Bellamy, whose *Looking Backward*, published in 1888, became a best seller within a few years and eventually topped the million mark. Bellamy's book was a novel, a romance of a socialist utopia. It described the experiences of a young Bostonian who in 1887 went into a hypnotic sleep from which he awakened in the year 2000. He found a new social order, based on collective ownership of property, where want, politics, and vice were unknown, and where people were incredibly happy. All this had come about through a peaceful and evolu-

tionary process: trusts had gone on combining with one another until they formed one big trust, and the government had taken this over. Shortly, over 160 "Nationalist Clubs" sprang up to propagate Bellamy's ideas, and the author devoted the remainder of his life to championing his brand of socialism.

Thirty-eight similar novels appeared in the nineties, though none of them approached Bellamy's in success. It is not to be thought that the hundreds of thousands of Americans who read Bellamy and the other utopian authors wished to see a socialist system established in the United States. Nor were they merely seeking in literary fantasies an escape from the real problems of their times. The great majority were intrigued by the descriptions of societies that were prosperous and stable because government played a large role, and in their own troubled society they saw the need, not for a collective state, but for a larger place for government.

More realistic was the philosophy in Henry Demarest Lloyd's *Wealth Against Commonwealth*. Published in 1894, this book was a tremendous, although not always accurate, attack on the Standard Oil trust and the methods by which it had risen to dominance. Lloyd advocated strict governmental regulation of such monopolies.

## INDUSTRIAL CONFLICT

Very few industrial workers or labor leaders in late nineteenth-century America aimed to overthrow capitalism itself. What most of them wanted was a larger share of its benefits. Their efforts to get a larger share led to industrial conflicts that were often bitter and sometimes bloody.

### Labor Organizes

As business became big, consolidated, and national, inevitably labor attempted to create its own organizations that would match the power of capital. The economic revolution changed the worker from an artisan who owned his own tools to a factory laborer who operated machines owned by his employer; it placed his wages, his tenure, his working environment at the pleasure of an impersonal corporation too powerful for the individual worker to bargain with. Between 1865 and 1897—a period of falling prices and a consequent decline in the cost of living—real wages increased, except for those workers who lost their jobs because of technological or cyclical unemployment. Nevertheless, at the turn of the century the income of the average worker was pitifully small: $400–500 a year. Students of the standard of living estimated that, to maintain a decent level of comfort, a yearly income of $600 was the absolute minimum. According to one survey, 10 million Americans lived in poverty. The average workday in 1900 was ten hours, for a six-day week. Because employers paid little attention to safety devices or programs, the accident rate was appalling: 1 in every 26 railroad workers was injured, 1 in every 399 killed per year.

Against such conditions, labor fought back by forming unions to bargain collectively with employers. During the Civil War, twenty craft unions were formed, and by 1870 the industrial states counted thirty such organizations, nearly every one of which represented skilled workers. The first attempt to federate separate unions into a single national organization came in 1866, when, under the leadership of William H. Sylvis, the National Labor Union was founded. Claiming a membership of 640,000, it was a polyglot association that included, in addition to a number of unions, a variety of reform groups having little direct relationship with labor. After the Panic of 1873 the National Labor Union disintegrated and disappeared.

The trade unions experienced stormy times during the hard years of the 1870s. Their bargaining power weakened by depression conditions, they faced antagonistic employers eager to destroy them, and a hostile public that rejected labor's claim to job security. Several of the disputes with capital were unusually bitter and were marked by violence, some of it labor's fault and some not, but for all of which labor received the blame. Startling to most Americans was the exposure of the activities of the "Molly Maguires" in the anthracite coal region of Pennsylvania. A terrorist group, the "Mollies" operated within the Ancient Order of Hibernians

(that is, Irishmen) and intimidated the coal operators with such direct methods as murder. But excitement over this was nothing compared to the near-hysteria that gripped the country during the railroad strikes of 1877. The trouble started when the principal Eastern railroads announced a 10-per-cent slash in wages. Immediately railroad workers, whether organized or not, went out on strike. Rail service was disrupted from Baltimore to St. Louis, equipment was destroyed, and rioting mobs roamed the streets of Pittsburgh and other cities.

The strikes were America's first big labor conflict and a flaming illustration of a new reality in the American economic system: with business becoming nationalized, disputes between labor and capital could no longer be localized but would affect the entire nation. State militia were employed against the strikers, and finally, and significantly, federal troops were called on to suppress the disorders. The power of the various railroad unions was seriously sapped by the failure of the strikes, and the prestige of unions in other industries was weakened by similar setbacks.

## The Knights and the AFL

Meanwhile, another national labor organization appeared on the scene, the Noble Order of the Knights of Labor, founded in 1869 under the leadership of Uriah S. Stephens. Instead of attempting to federate unions, as the National Labor Union had done, the Knights organized their association on the basis of the individual. Membership was open to all who "toiled," and the definition of a toiler was extremely liberal: the only excluded groups were lawyers, bankers, liquor dealers, and professional gamblers. The amorphous masses of members were arranged in local "assemblies" that might consist of the workers in a particular trade or a local union or simply all the members of the Knights in a city or district. Presiding laxly over the entire order was an agency known as the general assembly. Much of the program of the Knights was as vague as the organization. Although they championed an eight-hour day and the abolition of child labor, the leaders were more interested in the long-range reform of the economy than in the immediate objectives of wages and hours which appealed to the trade unions.

Under the leadership of Terence V. Powderly, the order entered upon a spectacular period of expansion that culminated in 1886 with the total membership reaching 700,000. Important factors contributing to the increase in numerical strength were a business recession in 1884 that threw many workers out of jobs, and a renewal of industrial strife that impelled unorganized laborers as well as some trade unions to affiliate with the Knights. Not only was the membership enlarged, but the order now included many militant elements that could not always be controlled by the moderate leadership. Against Powderly's wishes, local unions or assemblies associated with the Knights proceeded to inaugurate a series of strikes. In 1885 striking railway workers forced the Missouri Pacific, a link in the Gould system, to restore wage cuts and recognize their union. Although this victory redounded to the credit of the Knights, it was an ephemeral triumph. In the following year a strike on another Gould road, the Texas and Pacific, was crushed and the power of the unions in the Gould system was broken. By 1890 the membership of the Knights had shrunk to 100,-000, and within a few years the order would be a thing of the past.

Even before the Knights had entered on their period of decline, a rival organization, based on an entirely different organizational concept, had appeared. In 1881 representatives of a number of craft unions formed the Federation of Organized Trade and Labor Unions of the United States and Canada. Five years later this body took the name which it has borne ever since, the American Federation of Labor (AFL). Under the direction of its president and guiding spirit, Samuel Gompers, the Federation soon became the most important labor group in the country. As its name implies, it was a federation or association of national trade unions, each of which enjoyed essential autonomy within the larger organization. Rejecting completely the idea of individual membership and the corollary of one big union for everybody, the Federation was built on the principle of the organization of skilled workers into craft unions.

The program of the Federation differed as

markedly from that of the Knights as did its organizational arrangements. Gompers and his associates accepted the basic concepts of capitalism; their purpose was to secure for labor a greater share of capitalism's material rewards. Repudiating all notions of fundamental alteration of the existing system or long-range reform measures or a separate labor party, the AFL concentrated on labor's immediate objectives: wages, hours, and working conditions. While it hoped to attain it ends by collective bargaining, the Federation was ready to employ the strike if necessary.

As one of its first objectives, the Federation called for a national eight-hour day, to be attained by May 1, 1886, and to be obtained, if necessary, by a general strike. On the target day, strikes and demonstrations for a shorter workday took place all over the country. Although the national officers of the Knights had refused to cooperate in the movement, some local units joined in the demonstrations. So did a few unions that were dominated by anarchists—European radicals who wanted to destroy "class government" by terroristic methods—and that were affiliated with the so-called Black International. The most sensational demonstrations occurred in Chicago, which was a labor stronghold and an anarchist center.

At the time, a strike was in progress at the McCormick Harvester Company; and when the police harassed the strikers, labor and anarchist leaders called a protest meeting at the Haymarket Square. During the meeting, the police appeared and commanded those present to disperse. Someone—his identity was never determined—threw a bomb that resulted in the death of seven policemen and injury to sixty-seven others. The police, who on the previous day had killed four strikers, fired into the crowd and killed four more people. The score was about even. News of the Haymarket affair struck cold fear into Chicago and the business community of the nation. Blinded by hysteria, conservative, property-conscious Americans demanded a victim or victims—to demonstrate to labor that it must cease its course of violence. Chicago officials finally rounded up eight anarchists and charged them with the murder of the policemen on the grounds that they had

**The Haymarket Tragedy**

This is a contemporary artist's conception of the bomb
exploding among the police. (Library of Congress)

incited the individual who hurled the bomb. In
one of the most injudicious trials in the record
of American juridical history, all were found
guilty. One was sentenced to prison and seven
to death. Of the seven, one cheated his sentence
by committing suicide, four were executed, and
two had their penalty commuted to life imprisonment.

Although some of the blame for the Haymarket tragedy was unloaded on the AFL, at
least as much fell on the Knights, who had had
almost nothing to do with the May demonstrations. In the public mind the Knights were
dominated by anarchists and Socialists. The
Knights never managed to free themselves from
the stigma of radicalism as the AFL did.

## The Homestead Strike

Some of the most violent strikes in American
labor history occurred in the nineties. Two of
the strikes, the one at the Homestead plant of

the Carnegie Steel Company in Pennsylvania
and the one against the Pullman Palace Car
Company in the Chicago area, took place in
companies controlled by men who prided themselves on being among the most advanced of
American employers: Andrew Carnegie, who
had written magazine articles defending the
rights of labor, and George M. Pullman, who had
built a "model town" to house his employees.

The Amalgamated Association of Iron and
Steel Workers, which was affiliated with the
American Federation of Labor, was the most
powerful trade union in the country. It had
never been able, however, to organize all the
plants of the Carnegie Steel Company, the
largest corporation in the industry; of the three
major steel mills in the Carnegie system, the
union was a force only in one, the Homestead
plant. In 1892, when the strike occurred,
Carnegie was in Scotland, visiting at a castle
that he maintained as a gesture of ancestral

pride, and the direction of the company was in the hands of Henry Clay Frick, manager of Homestead and chairman of the Carnegie firm. Carnegie was, nevertheless, responsible for the company's course. Despite his earlier fine words about labor, he had decided with Frick before leaving to operate Homestead on a nonunion basis, even if this meant precipitating a clash with the union.

The trouble began when the management announced a new wage scale that would have meant cuts for a small minority of the workers. Frick abruptly shut down the plant, and asked the Pinkerton Detective Agency to furnish 300 guards to enable the company to resume operations on its own terms. (The Pinkerton Agency was really a strikebreaking concern.)

The hated Pinkertons, whose mere presence was enough to incite the workers to violence, approached the plant on barges in an adjacent river. Warned of their coming, the strikers met them at the docks with guns and dynamite, and a pitched battle ensued on July 6, 1892. After several hours of fighting, which brought death to three guards and ten strikers and severe injuries to many participants on both sides, the Pinkertons surrendered and were escorted roughly out of town. The company and local law officials then asked for militia protection from the Pennsylvania governor, who responded by sending the entire National Guard contingent, some 8,000 troops, to Homestead. Public opinion, at first sympathetic to the strikers, turned abruptly against them when an anarchist made an unsuccessful attempt to assassinate Frick. Slowly workers drifted back to their jobs.

## The Pullman Strike

A dispute of greater magnitude and equal bitterness, although involving less loss of life, was the Pullman strike in 1894, a depression year that saw over 700,000 workers throughout the country out on strike. Near Chicago were the works of the Pullman Palace Car Company, a corporation that leased sleeping and parlor cars to most of the nation's railroads and that manufactured and repaired its own cars and also freight and passenger cars; over 5,000 workers were employed in the various shops and factories of the company. At the instigation of George

> ### Contrasting Opinions on the Pullman Strike [1894]
>
> Eugene Debs issued this appeal for support of the boycott of Pullman cars:
>
> *To the Railway Employes of America: The struggle with the Pullman Company has developed into a contest between the producing classes and the money power of the country. We stand upon the ground that the workingmen are entitled to a just proportion of the proceeds of their labor. This the Pullman Company denied them. Reductions had been made from time to time until the employees earned barely sufficient wages to live, not enough to prevent them from sinking deeper and deeper into Pullman's debt, thereby mortgaging their bodies and souls, as well as their children's, to that heartless corporation.*
>
> One editor thus denounced the boycott:
>
> *The brigand who demands ransom for his prisoner, with mutilation or death as the alternative; the police captain who sells for money his power to arrest the dealers in vice and crime; the newsmonger who gathers scandal in order that he may be paid for suppressing it—these are the types of blackmailers whom all the world loathes. The boycott ordered by the railway union is morally no better than any of these acts. It is an attempt at blackmail on the largest scale.*

M. Pullman, inventor of the car that bore his name and president of the firm, the company had built the 600-acre town of Pullman, containing dwellings that were rented to the employees, and churches and schools, parks and playgrounds, a bank and a library—all owned and operated by the company. Pullman liked to exhibit his town as a model solution of the industrial problem and to refer to the workers as his "children"; his attitude was completely feudalistic and patronizing.

Nearly all of the workers were members of a union, a very militant one, the American Railway Union; this association had recently been organized by Eugene V. Debs, a sincere and idealistic labor leader formerly active in the Railroad Brotherhoods. Becoming disgusted with the Brotherhoods' lack of interest in the lot of the unskilled workers, he had formed his own union, which soon attained a membership of 150,000, mainly in the Middle West.

The strike at Pullman began when the company during the winter of 1893–1894 slashed wages by an average of 25 per cent. With revenues reduced by depression conditions, there was some reason for the company's action, but the cut was drastic, and several workers who served on a committee to protest to the management were discharged. At the same time, Pullman refused to reduce rentals in the model town, even though the charges were 20 to 25 per cent higher than for comparable accommodations in surrounding areas. The strikers appealed to the Railway Union for support, and that organization voted to refuse to handle Pullman cars and equipment.

The General Managers' Association, representing twenty-four Chicago railroads, prepared to fight the boycott. Switchmen who refused to handle Pullman cars were summarily discharged. Whenever this happened, the union instructed its members to quit work. Within a few days thousands of railroad workers in twenty-seven states and territories were on strike, and transportation from Chicago to the Pacific coast was paralyzed.

Ordinarily, state governors responded readily to appeals from strike-threatened business, but the governor of Illinois was different. John P. Altgeld was a courageous and committed liberal and a somewhat visionary champion of lost causes. He had pardoned the Haymarket anarchists remaining in prison. Business was not likely to appeal to such an executive for aid, and Altgeld was not the man to employ militia to smash a strike.

Bypassing Altgeld, the railroad operators besought the national government to send regular army troops to Illinois. At the same time federal postal officials and marshals were bombarding Washington with information that the strike was preventing the movement of mail on the trains. President Cleveland was inclined to gratify the companies, and so was his Attorney

**Troops Guarding a Train During the Pullman Strike**
(Library of Congress)

General, Richard Olney, a former railroad lawyer and a bitter foe of labor. Cleveland and Olney decided that the government could employ the army to keep the mails moving, and in July 1894 the President, over Altgeld's strident protest, ordered 2,000 troops to the Chicago area.

At Olney's suggestion, government lawyers obtained from a federal court an order restraining Debs and other union officials from interfering with the interstate transportation of the mails. This "blanket injunction" was so broad in scope that it practically forbade Debs and his associates to continue the strike. They ignored the injunction and were arrested, tried for contempt of court (without a jury trial), and sentenced to six months in prison. With federal troops protecting the hiring of new workers and with the union leaders in a federal jail, the strike quickly collapsed.

It left a bitter heritage. Labor was convinced that the government was not a neutral arbiter representing the common interest, but a supporter of one side alone. Debs emerged from prison a martyr in the eyes of workingmen, a convert to Marxian socialism, and a dedicated enemy of capital.

Despite all the organizations that were formed and all the strikes and demonstrations that were so hopefully launched, labor accomplished relatively little for its cause in the years between 1865 and 1900. Its leaders could point to a few legislative victories: the abolition by Congress in 1885 of the Contract Labor law; the establishment by Congress in 1868 of an eight-hour day on public works and in 1892 of the same work period for government employees; and a host of state laws governing hours of labor and safety standards, most of which were not enforced. But an overwhelming majority of employers still regarded labor as a force to be disregarded when possible and to be crushed when practicable, and the American public in overwhelming numbers considered unions to be alien and dangerous elements in the national economy.

Labor's greatest weakness was that only a small part of its vast strength was organized. The AFL with its half million members, and the Railroad Brotherhoods (engineers, conductors, firemen, trainmen) represented the skilled workers, but the mass of laborers were not enrolled in any union. All told, only 868,500 workers were union members at the turn of the century. Big Business was firmly entrenched; Big Labor awaited the future.

# Selected Readings

**General Accounts** I. M. Tarbell, *The Nationalizing of Business, 1878–1898* (1936); S. P. Hays, *The Response to Industrialism, 1885–1914*° (1957); E. C. Kirkland, *Industry Comes of Age: Business, Labor, and Public Policy, 1860–1897* (1961); Rendig Fels, *American Business Cycles, 1865–1897* (1959).

**Inventions and Industries** Roger Burlingame, *Engines of Democracy: Inventions and Society in Mature America* (1940); Matthew Josephson, *Edison*° (1959); R. N. Current, *The Typewriter and the Men Who Made It* (1954); H. C. Passer, *The Electrical Manufacturers, 1875–1900* (1953); R. A. Clemens, *The American Livestock and Meat Industry* (1932); C. B. Kuhlmann,

*The Development of the Flour-Milling Industry in the United States* (1929).

**The Railroads** G. R. Taylor and I. D. Neu, *The American Railroad Network, 1861–1900* (1956); E. G. Campbell, *The Reorganization of the American Railroad System, 1893–1900* (1938); J. F. Stover, *Railroads of the South, 1865–1900* (1955); R. E. Overton, *Burlington West: A Colonization History of the Burlington Railroad* (1941) and *Gulf to Rockies* (1953); James McCague, *Moguls and Iron Men* (1964), on the transcontinental lines.

**Business Leaders** Matthew Josephson, *The Robber Barons*° (1934); T. C. Cochran, *Railroad Leaders, 1845–1900* (1953); Allan Nevins,

*Study in Power: John D. Rockefeller* (2 vols., 1953); J. K. Winkler, *Incredible Carnegie* (1931); B. J. Hendrick, *Andrew Carnegie* (2 vols., 1932). **Capitalism, Pro and Con** E. C. Kirkland, *Dream and Thought in the Business Community, 1860–1900°* (1956); Sidney Fine, *Laissez Faire and the General Welfare State: A Study of Conflict in American Thought, 1865–1901°* (1956); Richard Hofstadter, *Social Darwinism in American Thought°* (1944); I. G. Wyllie, *The Self-Made Man in America°* (1954); A. E. Morgan, *Edward Bellamy* (1944); C. A. Barker, *Henry George* (1955); Samuel Churgerman, *Lester F. Ward, the American Aristotle* (1939); C. M. Destler, *Henry Demarest Lloyd and the Empire of Reform* (1963); H. H. Quint, *The Forging of American Socialism* (1953). **Immigration and Poverty** Oscar Handlin, *The Uprooted* (1951); John Higham, *Strangers in the Land* (1955); Barbara Solomon, *Ancestors and Immigrants°* (1956); M. A. Jones, *American Immigration°* (1960); R. H. Bremner, *From the Depths: The Discovery of Poverty in the United States* (1956); Jacob Riis, *How the Other Half Lives°* (1890); C. D. Long, *Wages and Earnings in the United States, 1860–1890* (1960).

**The Labor Movement** Henry Pelling, *American Labor°* (1960); N. J. Ware, *The Labor Movement in the United States, 1860–1893°* (1929); Philip Taft, *The A. F. of L. in the Time of Gompers* (1957); Bernard Mandel, *Samuel Gompers* (1963); R. V. Bruce, *1877: Year of Violence* (1959); Henry David, *History of the Haymarket Affair* (1936); A. L. Lindsay, *The Pullman Strike°* (1942); Harry Barnard, *"Eagle Forgotten": The Life of John Peter Altgeld°* (1938); Ray Ginger, *Altgeld's America—Lincoln Ideal Versus Changing Realities°* (1958). **Urban Development** A. M. Schlesinger, *The Rise of the City, 1878–1898* (1933); Blake McKelvey, *The Urbanization of America, 1860–1915* (1963); C. M. Green, *The Rise of Urban America* (1965); C. N. Glaab and A. T. Brown, *A History of Urban America°* (1967); S. B. Warner, Jr., *Streetcar Suburbs: The Process of Growth in Boston, 1870–1900°* (1962); C. W. Patton, *The Battle for Municipal Reform: Mobilization and Attack, 1875–1900* (1940).

° Titles available in paperback.

# Chapter 18
# The End of the Old Frontier

The census report for 1890 noted that the unsettled area of the West had been "so broken into by isolated bodies of settlement" that a continuous frontier line could no longer be drawn. Three years later a young historian from the University of Wisconsin, Frederick Jackson Turner, startled the American Historical Association with a memorable paper, "The Significance of the Frontier in American History." The roots of the national character, Turner asserted, lay not so much in the East or in Europe as in the West. As he saw it, "the existence of an area of free land, its continuous recession, and the advance of settlement westward, explain American development." This experience, by stimulating individualism, nationalism, and democracy, had made Americans the distinctive people that they were. "Now," Turner concluded ominously, "four centuries from the discovery of America, at the end of a hundred years of life under the Constitution, the frontier has gone, and with its going has closed the first period of American history."

The foreboding of Professor Turner was, in one respect, a bit premature. A vast public domain still existed in 1890, and during the forty years thereafter the government was to give away many more acres than it had given free before that time. Nevertheless, most of the best farming land had already been taken up. Gone was the chance of acquiring a farm for little or nothing, of cultivating it at a relatively low cost, of selling it at a profit and moving on west to start all over again.

In the passing of the frontier, perhaps the greatest loss to the American people was a psychological one. So long as the country had remained open at one end, there had seemed to be constantly revitalizing opportunities in American life. Now there was a vague, premonitory sense of being hemmed in. The psychological loss was all the greater because of what Henry Nash Smith in *Virgin Land* (1950) has called the "myth of the garden," the once widely held belief (to be found in many poems, novels, and other writings) that the West was a kind of potential Garden of Eden where life could be begun anew and all the ideals of democracy realized. The setting for utopia, once the New World as a whole, had shrunk to the West of the United States. To some extent Professor Turner himself reflected the myth in his "frontier interpretation" of American history.

Actually, long before 1890, the city had come to replace the "virgin land" as the symbol of opportunity in America. The great folk movement of the time was from the country to the city, not the other way around. But American values had long been shaped by the rural background in which most of the people were brought up. Only slowly and with considerable stress did these values change in response to the more and more pervasive influence of the urban environment. Change they nevertheless did, and in the last decades of the nineteenth century the culture of the city came to predominate in American civilization.

---

**Mining in Colorado**

If miners thought that gold or silver was present in an area, they would turn the surface over and over in their search. Thus they literally honeycombed mountains with tunnels. (Culver)

## THE LAST WEST

In 1860 the frontier line, the western rim of settlement, conformed roughly to the western boundaries of the tier of states immediately beyond the Mississippi—Minnesota, Iowa, Missouri, Arkansas—jutting outward to include the eastern parts of Nebraska and Kansas and cutting across central Texas. West of this line was a huge expanse inhabited by roving Indians and wild animals, and peopled only thinly by whites until the settled districts of California and Oregon on the Pacific coast were reached. Within the confines of this vast West are three distinct natural, or physiographic, regions: the Great Plains, the Rocky Mountains, and the Basin and Plateau region between the Rockies on the east

and the Sierra Nevada–Cascade mountain chain on the west.

### Delayed Settlement

When the westward-pushing pioneers entered upon the Great Plains, they saw a strange and even alien environment, utterly different from the fertile prairie lands behind them or the wooded areas of the Ohio Valley and the East. The physical features that in combination distinguish the Great Plains from earlier frontiers are a level surface, a dearth of timber, and a deficiency in rainfall. Early explorers had dubbed this region "the Great American Desert," and in the 1840s settlers had hastened through it on their way to California and Oregon. Its forbidding reputation was largely re-

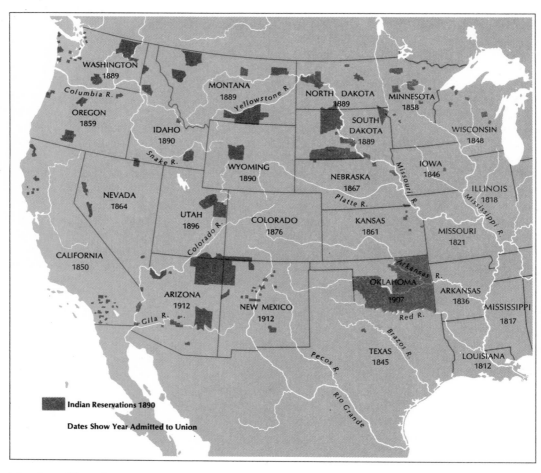

**The Last Frontier**

sponsible for the curious fact that the frontier, after crossing the Mississippi, had jumped 1,500 miles to the Pacific coast.

By the 1860s, however, people had begun to head for the unsettled parts of the West. They were attracted by gold and silver deposits, by the short-grass pasture for cattle and sheep, and finally by the plains' sod and the mountain meadowland that seemed suitable for farming or ranching.

Settlement was encouraged by the great transcontinental railroad lines. These roads and their feeders moved settlers and supplies into the vast interior spaces and furnished access to outside markets; they provided what the region could not have had without them—the basis for a permanent population and a durable economy. In addition, they directly excited migration by disposing of their lands to settlers. All told, in national and state land grants, the railroads owned over 183 million acres. Although some companies attempted to reserve their lands or sell them at fancy prices, most of the lines realized that an increased population meant larger freight and passenger revenues. Consequently, they offered land for as little as $2.50 an acre, advertised the glories of the West in the East and in Europe, and transported prospective buyers at reduced rates.

Settlement was also encouraged by the land policy of the federal government, though this had less effect than had been intended. According to the Homestead Act of 1862, for a small fee a settler could obtain a plot of 160 acres if he occupied and improved it for five years. (A similar acreage could be secured, ordinarily for $1.25 per acre, by the terms of the Preemption Act of 1841.) A good deal of idealism had gone into the framing of the Homestead Act. It was intended to be a democratic measure, the bestowal of a free farm on any American who needed one, a form of government relief to raise the living standards of the masses. But in practice the act proved a disappointment. Some 400,000 homesteaders became landowners, but a much larger number abandoned the attempt to stake out a farm on the windswept plains.

The Homestead Act was defective. It assumed that mere possession of land was enough to sustain farm life, but this ignored the increasing mechanization of agriculture and the rising costs of operation. Even worse, it was based on Eastern agricultural experiences that were inapplicable to the region west of the Mississippi. A unit of 160 acres was too small for the grazing and grain farming that came to be carried on in the Great Plains.

Responding to Western pressures, Congress acted to increase allotments. The Timber Culture Act (1873) permitted a homesteader to receive a grant of 160 additional acres if he planted on it 40 acres of trees. The Desert Land Act (1877) provided that a claimant could buy 640 acres at $1.25 an acre provided he irrigated part of his holding within three years. The Timber and Stone Act (1878), presumably applying to nonarable land, authorized sales of quartersections at $2.50 an acre.

Through the operation of the various laws, it was possible for an individual to acquire at little cost 1,280 acres. Some enterprising persons got much more. Fraud ran rampant in the administration of the acts. Lumber, mining, and cattle companies, by employing "dummy" registrants and using other tricky devices, grasped millions of acres of the public domain.

Settlement was made possible by the readiness of the federal government to police the vast and desolate region and to subdue the red men who resisted the white advance.

Political organization followed on the heels of settlement. After the admission of Kansas as a state in 1861, the remaining territories of Washington, New Mexico, Utah, and Nebraska were divided into smaller and more convenient units. By the close of the sixties territorial governments were in operation in the new provinces of Nevada, Colorado, Dakota, Arizona, Idaho, Montana, and Wyoming. Statehood rapidly followed. Nevada became a state in 1864, Nebraska in 1867, and Colorado, attracting attention as the centennial state, in 1876. In 1889 the "omnibus states," North and South Dakota, Montana, and Washington, won admission; Wyoming and Idaho entered the next year. Utah was denied statehood until its Mormon leaders convinced the government in 1896 that polygamy had been abandoned. At the turn of the century only three territories remained outside the fold: Arizona

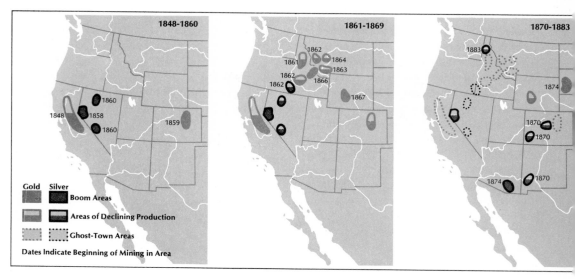

**Mining Towns**

and New Mexico, excluded because of their scanty population and wrong politics (they were predominantly Democratic) and their refusal to accept admission as a single state, and Oklahoma, which was opened to white settlement and granted territorial status in 1889–1890.

## The Miners Arrive

The first colonists of the last frontier were miners, and the first part of the area to be settled was the mineral-rich region of mountains and plateaus. The life span of the mining frontier was brief. It burst into being around 1860, flourished brilliantly until the 1890s, and then abruptly declined.

News of a gold or silver strike would start a stampede reminiscent of the California gold rush of 1849. Settlement usually followed a pattern of successive stages: (1) individual prospectors exploited the first ores with pan and placer mining; (2) after the shallower deposits were depleted, corporations moved in to engage in lode or quartz mining; (3) commercial mining either disappeared eventually or continued on a restricted basis, and ranchers and farmers appeared on the scene to establish a more permanent economy.

The first great strikes occurred just before the Civil War. In 1858 gold was discovered in the Pike's Peak district of what would soon be the territory of Colorado, and the following year a mob of 50,000 prospectors stormed in from California and the Mississippi Valley and the East. Denver and other mining camps blossomed into "cities" overnight. Almost as rapidly as it developed, the boom ended. Eventually corporations, notably the Guggenheim interests, revived some of the glories and profits of the gold boom, and the discovery of silver near Leadville supplied a new source of mineral wealth.

While the Colorado rush of 1859 was in progress, news of another strike drew miners to Nevada, then a part of Utah Territory. Gold had been found in the Washoe district, but the most valuable ore in the great Comstock Lode and other veins was silver. The first prospectors to reach the Washoe fields came from California (here the frontier movement was from west to east), and from the beginning Californians dominated the settlement and development of Nevada. In a remote desert without railroad transportation, the territory produced no supplies of its own, and everything, from food and machinery to whiskey and prostitutes, had to be freighted in from California to Virginia City, Carson City, and other roaring camp towns. When the placer deposits ran out, California capital bought the claims of the pioneer prospectors and installed quartz mining. For a brief span the outside owners reaped tremendous profits; from 1860 to 1880 the Nevada lodes yielded bullion worth $306 million.

No new discoveries agitated the mining frontier until 1874, when gold was found in the Black Hills of southwestern Dakota Territory. Prospectors swarmed into the area, which was then and for years later served only by stagecoach transportation. Deadwood burst into life as a center of supplies and sin for other camps. For a short time the boom flared, and then came the inevitable fading of resources. Corporations took over from the miners, and one gigantic company, the Homestake, came to dominate the fields. The population declined, and the Dakotas, like other boom areas of the mineral empire, waited for the approach of the agricultural frontier.

Life in the camp towns of the mineral empire had a hectic tempo and a gaudy flavor not to be found in any other part of the last frontier. The speculative spirit, a mood of incredible optimism, a get-rich-quick philosophy gripped everybody and dominated every phase of community activity. The conditions of mine life—

the presence of precious minerals, the vagueness of claim boundaries, the cargoes of gold being shipped out—tempted outlaws and "bad men," operating as individuals or gangs, to ply their trade. When the situation became intolerable in a community, those members interested in order set up their own law and enforced it through a vigilance committee, an agency used earlier in California. Sometimes criminals themselves secured control of the committee and sometimes the vigilantes continued to operate as private "law" enforcers after the creation of regular governments.

## The Day of the Cowboy

The open range—that is, the unclaimed grasslands of the public domain—provided a huge area on the Great Plains where cattlemen could graze their herds free of charge and unrestricted by the boundaries that would have existed in a farming economy. The railroads gave the range-cattle industry access to markets and thus brought it into being; then they destroyed it by bringing the farmers' frontier to the plains.

**A Sod House on the Plains**

Settlers on the treeless Great Plains frequently lived their first years in sod houses. A sod house was constructed by plowing up long strips of the tough turf and cutting these into smaller pieces in the shape of bricks. The pieces were then laid on top of each other to make a wall. The roof consisted of a support of poles or canvas covered by earth. Damp, dark, and poorly ventilated, the sod house was used until its owner could import enough wood to build a frame house. (The Kansas State Historical Society, Topeka)

In ancestry the cattle industry was Mexican and Texan. Long before the Americans invaded the Southwest, Mexican ranchers and vaqueros had developed the techniques and tools employed later by the cattlemen and cowboys of the Great Plains: branding (a device known in all frontier areas where stock was common), roundups, roping, and the equipment of the herder—his lariat, saddle, leather chaps, and spurs. All these things and others were taken over by the Americans in Texas and by them transmitted to the the northernmost ranges of the cattle kingdom. Also in Texas were found the largest herds of cattle in the country, the animals descended from imported Spanish stock —the famous wiry, hardy long-horns—and allowed to run wild or semiwild. Here too were the horses that enabled the caretakers of the herds to control them—the small, muscular broncos or mustangs—sprung from blooded progenitors brought in by the Spanish and ideally adapted to the requirements of the cow country.

At the end of the Civil War an estimated 5 million cattle roamed the Texas ranges, and Northern markets were offering fat prices for steers in any condition. Early in 1866 some Texas cattlemen started their combined herds, some 260,000 head, north for Sedalia, Missouri, on the Missouri Pacific Railroad. Traveling over rough country and beset by outlaws, Indians, and property-conscious farmers, the caravan suffered heavy losses, and only a fraction of the animals were delivered to the railroad. But a great experiment had been successfully tested—cattle could be driven to distant markets and pastured along the trail and would gain weight during the journey. The first of the "long drives" prepared the way for the cattle kingdom.

With the precedent established, the next step was to find an easier route leading through more accessible country. Special market facilities were provided at Abilene, Kansas, on the Kansas Pacific Railroad, and for years this town reigned as the railhead of the cattle kingdom. Between 1867 and 1871, 1,460,000 cattle were moved up the Chisholm Trail to Abilene, a town that, filled with rampaging cowboys at the end of a drive, rivaled the mining towns in robust wickedness. But as the farming frontier pushed farther west in Kansas and as the supply of ani-

mals increased, the cattlemen had to develop other market outlets and trails. Railroad towns that flourished after Abilene were Dodge City and Witchita in Kansas, Ogallala and Sidney in Nebraska, Cheyenne and Laramie in Wyoming, and Miles City and Glendive in Montana.

From first to last, a long drive was a spectacular episode. It began with the spring, or calf, roundup. The cattlemen of a district met with their cowboys at a specified place to round up the stock of the owners from the open range. As the cattle were driven in, the calves were branded with the marks of their mothers. Stray calves with no identifying symbols, "mavericks," were divided on a pro-rata basis. Then the cows and calves were turned loose to pasture, while the yearling steers were readied for the drive to the north. The combined herds, usually numbering from 2,000 to 5,000 head, moved out, attended by the cowboys of each outfit.

Among the cowboys the majority (in the early years) were veterans of the Confederate army. Outnumbering all the rest—white Northerners, Mexicans, and other foreigners—were the Negroes, who usually were assigned the humbler jobs on the trail crew, such as those of wrangler or cook. (In the Wild West black men played a role not only as cowboys but also as explorers, trappers, miners, outlaws, and cavalrymen.) The cowboy was glorified as a Nordic superman in Owen Wister's novel *The Virginian* (1902) and in countless later "Westerns" that followed the Wister pattern. Actually the life of the cowboy, whatever his color, was dull, dirty, and rather brutish. He was at best only a hired hand, who made little money and kept still less. The big profits went to his employer, the cattleman.

All cattlemen had to have a permanent base from which to operate, and so the ranch emerged. A ranch consisted of the employer's dwelling, quarters for employees, and a tract of grazing land. It might be fenced in or open, owned or leased or held by some quasi-legal claim, but it was definite and durable. Possession of a ranch meant unquestioned access to precious water. As farmers and sheepmen encroached on the open plains, the ranch began to replace the range.

There had always been an element of risk and speculation in the open-range cattle business.

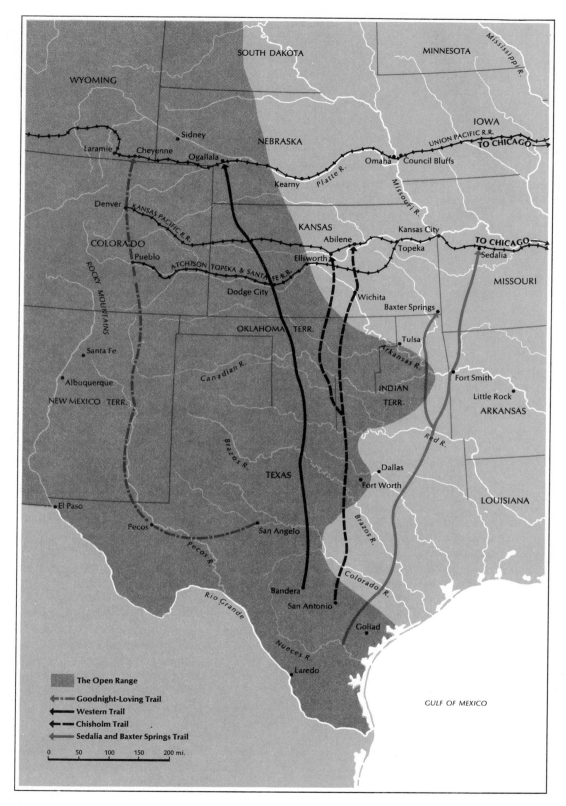

**The Cattle Kingdom**

At any time the "Texas fever," transmitted by a parasite carried by ticks, might decimate a herd. Rustlers and Indians frequently drove off large numbers of animals. Sheepmen from California and Oregon brought their flocks onto the range to compete for grass and force cattle out (cattle will not graze after sheep); bitter "wars" followed between cattlemen and sheepherders in which men and stock were killed and equipment destroyed. Farmers, "nesters," threw fences around their claims, blocking trails and breaking up the open range. More wars were fought bringing losses to both sides.

Accounts of the lofty profits to be made in the cattle business—it was said that an investment of $5,000 would return $45,000 in four years—tempted Eastern, English, and Scottish capital to the plains. Increasingly the structure of the cattle economy became corporate in form; in one year twenty corporations with a combined capital of $12 million were chartered in Wyoming. The inevitable result of this frenzied extension was that the ranges, already severed and shrunk by the railroads and the farmers, were overstocked. There was not enough grass to support the crowding herds or sustain the long drives. Overstocking tumbled prices downward, and then nature intervened with a destructive finishing blow. Two severe winters, in 1885–1886 and 1886–1887, with a searing summer between them, stung and scorched the plains. Hundreds of thousands of cattle died, streams and grass dried up, princely ranches and costly investments disappeared in a season.

The open-range industry never recovered; the long drive disappeared for good. But the cattle ranches—with fenced-in grazing land and stocks of hay for winter feed—survived and grew and prospered, eventually producing more beef than ever.

## THE TAMING OF THE TRIBES

When the miners and cowmen sifted into the last frontier, they came face to face with its Indian inhabitants, and they had to advance against more determined and sustained resistance than whites had met anywhere else in the sweep across the continent. In the end the in-

vaders triumphed. The Indian tribes were broken and their members were forced to adapt themselves to an approximation of the white man's culture.

### The Plains Indians

On the rolling, semiarid, treeless plains, the Indians followed a nomadic life. Riding their small but powerful horses, which were descendants of Spanish stock, the tribes roamed the spacious expanses of the grasslands. Permanent abodes were rare; when a band halted, tepees carried on the journey were quickly pitched as temporary dwellings. The magnet that drew the wanderers and guided their routes was the buffalo, or bison. This huge grazing animal provided the economic basis for the plains Indians' way of life. Its flesh was their principal source of food, and the skin supplied materials for clothing, shoes, tepees, blankets, robes, and utensils. To the Indians, the buffalo was, as someone had said, "a galloping department store." They trailed the herds, estimated to number at least 15 million head in 1865, all over the plains. The plains Indians were almost uniformly martial, proud, and aggressive. Mounted on their horses, they were a formidable foe, whether armed with bow, spear, or rifle. They possessed a mobility enjoyed by no previous Indians, and students of war have ranked them among the best light cavalry in military history.

It was the traditional policy of the federal government to regard the tribes as independent nations (but also as wards of the Great White Father in Washington) and to negotiate agreements with them in the shape of treaties that were solemnly ratified by the Senate. This concept of Indian sovereignty was responsible for the attempt of the government before 1860 to erect a permanent frontier between whites and red men, to reserve the region west of the bend of the Missouri as permanent Indian country. But by the sixties the related principles of tribal independence and a perpetual line of division were breaking down before harsh realities. Administration of Indian matters was divided between the Bureau of Indian Affairs, located in the Department of the Interior, and the army. The bureau was vested with general powers to supervise the disposition of Indian lands, dis-

### The Slaughter of the Buffalo

This sketch, sardonically entitled "Sport on the Plains," shows the way in which the buffalo was often hunted. A wealthy hunter has employed a guide and a driver and carriage to take him out to get a trophy. (Culver)

burse annuities, and, through its agents in Western posts, distribute needed supplies. From top to bottom, the personnel was shot through with the spoils system. Although some agents were conscientious and able men, more were dishonest and incompetent.

The army came into the picture only when trouble developed—when bands of Indians attacked homes or stagecoach lines or when a tribe went on the warpath. In short, its principal function was to punish, not to police. The army of the frontier was an effective fighting body, and it was led by some able officers. Still, in its "wars" with the Indians the army frequently experienced rugged going. The mobile plains tribesmen were fully a match for cavalrymen armed with carbines. But soon the superior technology of the whites shifted the balance. The Colt repeating revolver gave the army increased firepower, the railroads facilitated quick troop concentrations, and the telegraph reported immediately the movements of hostile bands. Even so, the business of suppressing Indians was

frightfully expensive. Three wars in the sixties cost the government $100 million, and one official estimated that the cost per Indian killed was $1,000.

The subjection of the fierce plains Indians was accomplished by economic as well as orthodox warfare—by the slaughter of the buffalo herds that supported their way of life. After the Civil War the demand for buffalo hides became a national phenomenon. It was partly based on economics—a commercial demand for the hides developing in the East; and it was partly a fad—suddenly every one east of the Missouri seemed to require a buffalo robe from the romantic West. Gangs of professional hunters swarmed over the plains to shoot the huge animals, divided by the Union Pacific Railroad into southern and northern herds. Some hunters killed merely for the sport of the chase, though the lumbering victims did not present much of a challenge. The southern herd was virtually exterminated by 1875, and within a few years the smaller northern herd met the same fate. Fewer than a thousand of the magnificent beasts survived. The army and the Indian agents condoned and even encouraged the killing. With the buffalo went the Indians' source of food and supplies and their will and ability to resist the white advance.

## The Warriors' Last Stand

There was almost incessant Indian fighting on the frontier from the sixties to the eighties. During the Civil War the eastern Sioux in Minnesota, cramped on an inadequate reserve and exploited by agents, suddenly took to the warpath. Led by Little Crow, they killed over 700 whites before being subdued by a force of regulars and militia. Thirty-eight of the Indians were hanged, and the tribe was exiled to the Dakotas.

At the same time trouble flared in Colorado, where the Arapaho and Cheyenne had been re-stricted to the Sand Creek reserve. Bands of braves attacked stagecoach lines and settlements, provoking a concentration of territorial militia and threats from the army. The governor urged all friendly Indians to congregate at army posts before retribution fell on the hostiles. One Arapaho and Cheyenne band under Black Kettle came into Fort Lyon on Sand Creek and encamped nearby. Although some braves just off the warpath were undoubtedly members of the party, Black Kettle understood he was under official protection. Nevertheless, Colonel J. M. Chivington, apparently encouraged by the army commander of the district, led a militia force to the unsuspecting camp and massacred a disputed (but large) number of men, women, and children. The government then forced the Arapaho and Cheyenne to accept an even less desirable reservation, but the Senate neglected to ratify the treaty.

**Apache Warrior**

Geronimo (left, mounted) was not a chief, but he assumed the leadership of one of the Apache tribes and fought the whites fiercely until captured in Mexico in 1886. General N. A. Miles, who fought him, said that he was one of the cruelest Indians he had met in his frontier experience. (Culver)

At the end of the war against the southern rebels, wars against the western Indians flared up on several fronts. The most serious and sustained conflict was in Montana, where the army attempted to build a road, the Bozeman Trail, from Fort Laramie, Wyoming, to the mining centers. The western Sioux resented this intrusion into the heart of their buffalo range, and led by one of their great chiefs, Red Cloud, they so harried the soldiers and the construction party that the road could not be completed.

Meanwhile, Congress, shocked by the Chivington massacre and the continued hostilities, appointed a committee to investigate the situation on the scene, and after studying its report created an Indian Peace Commission, composed of soldiers and civilians, to recommend a permanent Indian policy. The commission called the southern tribes to council at Medicine Lodge Creek in 1867, and the following year it met with the northern tribes at Fort Laramie. At Medicine Lodge the Arapaho and Cheyenne and other tribes agreed to accept reserves in the Indian Territory. At Laramie the Sioux accepted a reserve in southwestern Dakota, with rights to hunt as far as the Big Horn Mountains in Wyoming; they insisted, however, that the government abandon the Bozeman road, marking probably the only instance in which whites formally yielded to Indians. The minor plains tribes and the mountain tribes consented to smaller reserves. For its part, the government pledged annuity payments and regular supplies. Some of the Arapaho and Cheyenne had another bad experience before being finally settled on their reserve. Black Kettle, who had escaped the Chivington massacre, and his Cheyennes, some of whom had taken the warpath, were caught on the Washita River, near the Texas border, by Colonel George A. Custer, and the chief was killed and his people slaughtered.

After 1870 the broad outlines of a new Indian policy began to take shape. The tribes were now concentrated in two large reserves, one in Dakota and the other in the Indian Territory. Thus restricted, they found their powers to wage war severely limited. An advisory civilian Board of Indian Commissioners counseled the government to continue the reservation program and to break down the tribal structure with a view to assimilating the Indians to white culture. Congress responded in 1871 by abolishing the practice of treating the tribes as sovereignties, a step calculated to undermine the collective nature of Indian life.

But Indian resistance was far from ended. A source of potential conflict smouldered on the northern plains, where the Sioux roamed from Dakota to Wyoming. It burst into flame in 1875 when many of the tribesmen, angered by the dealings of crooked agents and alarmed by the entrance of miners into the Black Hills, suddenly left the reserve. Commanded to return, they gathered in Montana under Crazy Horse, probably the greatest leader of the plains Indians, and Sitting Bull. Three army columns were sent to round them up. With the expedition as colonel of the famous Seventh Cavalry was the colorful and controversial George A. Custer, golden-haired romantic and alleged gloryseeker. At the Battle of the Little Bighorn (1876) the Indians surprised Custer with part of his regiment and killed every man. Custer has been accused of rashness, but he seems to have ridden into something that no white man would have believed possible. On this occasion the chiefs had concentrated at least 2,500 warriors, perhaps 4,000, the largest Indian army ever assembled at one time in the United States.

But the Indians did not have the political organization or the commissary to keep their troops united. Soon they drifted off in bands to elude pursuit or search for food, and the army ran them down singly and returned them to Dakota. The power of the Sioux was now broken. The proud leaders, Crazy Horse and Sitting Bull, accepted defeat and the monotony of agency existence, and both were later killed by reservation police after being tricked or taunted into a last pathetic show of resistance.

In 1877 one of the most dramatic episodes in Indian history occurred in Idaho. Here the Nez Percé, a small and relatively pacific and civilized tribe, refused to accept a smaller reservation and were, in effect, forced into resistance. When troops converged on them, their able leader, Chief Joseph, attempted to conduct the band to Canada. A remarkable chase ensued. Joseph moved with 200 warriors and 350 women, children, and old people. Pursued by four columns, he covered 1,321 miles in seventy-five days, but was caught just short of the Canadian border. Like so many other crushed tribes, the Nez Percé were shipped to the Indian Territory.

The last Indians to maintain organized resistance against the whites were the Apaches, who fought intermittently from the sixties to the late eighties. The two ablest chiefs of this fierce tribe were Mangas Colorados and Cochise. Mangas was murdered during the Civil War, and in 1872 Cochise agreed to peace and a reservation for his followers. But one leader, Geronimo, continued to lead a war faction. When he was finally captured in 1886, formal warfare between Indians and whites may be said to have ended.

A final, tragic encounter in 1890 was hardly a battle. As the Indians saw their culture and their glories fading, they turned to an emotional religion which emphasized the coming of a Messiah and featured "ghost dances," trances, and visions. Agents on the Sioux reservation, fearing the frenzy might turn into an outbreak, called for troops, and some of the Indians fled to the Badlands. They were pursued and slaughtered at a creek called, with an unpremeditated but curiously fitting symbolism, Wounded Knee.

In 1887 Congress finally moved to destroy the tribal structure that was the cornerstone of Indian culture. Although the motivation was partially a humanitarian impulse to help the Indian, the action was frankly designed to force him to become a landowner and farmer, to abandon his collective society and culture, to become, in short, a white man. The Dawes Severalty Act provided for the gradual abrogation of tribal ownership of land and the allotment of tracts to individual owners: 160 acres to the head of a family, 80 acres to a single adult or orphan, 40 acres to each dependent child.

## A White Defender of the Indians

Among the few voices raised to defend the Indians and criticize the government's policy toward them was that of Helen Hunt Jackson, a writer who lived in Colorado Springs, Colorado. She presented her views in *A Century of Dishonor* (1881):

*There is not among these three hundred bands of Indians [in the United States] one which has not suffered cruelly at the hands either of the Government or of white settlers. The poorer, the more insignificant, the more helpless the band, the more certain the cruelty and outrage to which they have been subjected. This is especially true of the bands on the Pacific slope. These Indians found themselves of a sudden surrounded by and caught up in the great influx of gold-seeking settlers, as helpless creatures on a shore are caught up in a tidal wave. There was not time for the Government to make treaties; not even time for communities to make laws. The tale of the wrongs, the oppressions, the murders of the Pacific-slope Indians in the last thirty years would be a volume by itself, and is too monstrous to be believed.*

*It makes little difference, however, where one opens the record of the history of the Indians; every page and every year has its dark stain. The story of one tribe is the story of all, varied only by differences of time and place; but neither time nor place makes any difference in the main facts. Colorado is as greedy and unjust in 1880 as was Georgia in 1830, and Ohio in 1795; and the United States Government breaks promises now as deftly as then, and with added ingenuity from long practice.*

*One of its strongest supports in so doing is the wide-spread sentiment among the people of dislike to the Indian, of impatience with his presence as a "barrier to civilization," and distrust of it as a possible danger. The old tales of the frontier life, with its horrors of Indian warfare, have gradually, by two or three generations' telling, produced in the average mind something like an hereditary instinct of unquestioning and unreasoning aversion which it is almost impossible to dislodge or soften.*

Adult owners were accorded the status of citizenship but, unlike other citizens, they could not alienate their property for twenty-five years. The act was hardly a success. The Indians were not ready for a wrenching change from a collective society to individualism. Congress attempted to facilitate the transition with the Burke Act of 1906. Citizenship was deferred until after the completion of the twenty-five-year period contemplated in the Dawes Act, but Indians who proved their adaptability could secure both citizenship and land ownership in a shorter period. Full rights of citizenship were conferred on all Indians in 1924. Even then many resisted white ways, and in the 1930s the government would make a notable attempt to restore some of the institutions of tribal culture.

## DECLINE OF THE FARMER

The development of an industrial and urban civilization would have been impossible without a great increase in the productivity of agriculture. Yet on the whole the nation's farmers, while producing more than ever, were getting less and less in both pecuniary and psychological reward for their effort. Those who tried farming on the last frontier soon discovered that the West no longer provided much of a way out for them.

### Farming on the Plains

Some farmers had drifted into the Great Plains during its first stages of development, following the miners and cattlemen, but the great rush of settlement came in the late seventies. In the next decade the relentless advance of the farming frontier would gradually convert the plains country to an agricultural economy. The surge of migration came at a time when for years in succession the rainfall was well above the average. People scoffed at the idea that the plains were the Great American Desert, and they looked forward to an indefinite era of prosperity. They scoffed too at the old cowmen who warned that the light soil of the plains should not be deprived of its protecting turf by cultivation.

But even under the most favorable conditions, farming on the plains presented problems not encountered in any previous region. First and most critical was the problem of fencing. The farmer had to enclose his land, if for no other reason than to protect it from the herds of the cattlemen. But the traditional wood or stone fences were impossible on the plains. The cost of importing the material was prohibitive, and besides, such barriers were ineffective against range cattle. In the mid-seventies two Illinois farmers, Joseph H. Glidden and I. L. Ellwood, solved this problem by developing and putting on the market barbed wire. Produced in mass quantities—40,000 tons a year—it sold cheaply, became standard equipment on the plains, and revolutionized fencing practices all over the country.

The second problem, present even when the rainfall was above average, was water. It became particularly acute after 1887, when a series of dry seasons began. One expedient resorted to was the use of deep wells and steel windmills, which assured a steady water supply for stock. Another was dry farming—a system of tillage designed to conserve moisture in the soil by covering it with a dust blanket—and the utilization of drought-enduring crops. In many areas of the plains, agriculture could not exist without irrigation. Large-scale irrigation, the only practicable kind, would have to be planned and supported by the government. The national government tried to hand the issue to the states, turning over to them in the Carey Act (1894) several million acres of public land to be reclaimed. The states made little progress, largely because the problems of reclamation cut across state boundaries.

Farming on the plains was always expensive and often risky. The uncertainty of rainfall and the danger of grasshopper plagues and tornadoes made every farm year a speculative experiment. Costs of operation ran high, partly because many supplies had to be imported into the region from distant points, but mainly because of the nature of plains farming. In all the farm areas of the country, machines were playing a larger part in the agricultural process, and they were especially vital on the plains, where grain farming was conducted on large land units.

The last West was not, as has so often been claimed, a refuge for the urban poor or a safety valve for proletarian unrest. The men who set-

**Threshing Wheat on the Great Plains**

This print of a Dakota field shows the magnitude of operations on a large landed unit and gives an idea of the high cost of farming on the plains. Here several steam-driven machines are in use. The average farmer could not afford even one thresher. In some areas owners of the machines went from farm to farm with hired crews during the harvest season. According to Raymond M. Wik in *Steam Power on the American Farm*, the total horsepower of these engines increased from 1,200,000 in 1880 to 3,600,000 by 1910. (The Bettmann Archive)

tled this area were mostly farmers, and they came from farms in the Middle West, the East, or Europe. In the booming eighties, with land values rising, credit was easy, and the farmers confidently expected to retire their obligations. With the advent of the arid years of the late eighties, the prospect changed with grim suddenness. There followed a reversal of the frontier movement, as many settlers retreated from the Great Plains. Those who remained gave an unintentional boost to the overproduction that caused farm prices to fall (wheat, which had sold for $1.60 a bushel at the end of the Civil War, dropped to 49 cents in the 1890s) and added to the distress of farmers elsewhere in the country.

## Changes in Agriculture

Americans had always liked to talk about the wonderful life of the farmer. According to the popular myth, he was a sturdy yeoman, a simple, honest, happy man who dwelt close to nature and embodied all the virtues. Producing most of the things he and his family required, he was independent, subsisting on his own labor, depending not on the market place, and owing no man. The myth may have had some basis in Jefferson's time, but its reality was being destroyed by one of the great agricultural changes of the nineteenth century, the shift from subsistence, or self-sufficient, farming to commercial farming.

In commercial husbandry, the farmer specialized in a cash crop, sold it in a national or world market, ceased making his household supplies and bought them at the town or village store. This kind of farming, when it was successful, raised the farmer's living standards. But now he was dependent on other people and on impersonal factors he could not control: bankers and interest rates, railroads and freight rates, national and European depressions, world supply and demand. In short, he had become a businessman—but with a difference. Unlike the capitalists of the industrial order, he could not regulate his production or influence the prices of what he sold.

Machines came to the aid of the farmer as to the manufacturer. The mechanization of agriculture had accelerated during the Civil War, when the government called thousands of laborers into military service and forced farmers to employ labor-saving devices. For example, approximately 100,000 reapers were in use at the beginning of the war but 250,000 at its close.

In the years after 1860 a host of new machines —and improved models of old ones—were unveiled. Among these were the chilled steel plow, perfected by James Oliver; the sulky, or riding, plow; the disc and gang plows; various improvements of the reaper, notably the twine binder, introduced by John F. Appleby, which cut and bound grain; the grain drill, the seed planter, the corn binder, the corn lister, the potato planter, the cream separator, and the poultry incubator. The effect of the machines on production and labor was revolutionary.

Before 1900 farmers were generally hostile to the theories and teachings of scientific agriculture, to what they scornfully termed "book learning." In 1887 Congress passed the Hatch Act, providing for a system of agricultural experiment stations; this was the only major agricultural legislation passed by Congress between 1865 and 1900. But farmers generally spurned the new information because they felt no need for its aid and could see no benefits for themselves in its lessons. American agriculture before 1900 was, as it always had been, extensive and wasteful.

The period between 1865 and 1900 witnessed a tremendous expansion of agricultural facilities, not only in the United States but all over the world: in Brazil and the Argentine in South America, in Canada, in Australia and New Zealand, and in Russia. World production increased at the same time that modern means of communication and transportation—the telephone, telegraph, cable, steam navigation, railroads— were welding the producing nations into one international market. The American commercial farmer, always augmenting his production, pro-

duced more than the domestic market could absorb and disposed of his surplus in the world market. Cotton farmers depended on export sales for 70 per cent of their annual income, and wheat farmers for 30 to 40 per cent; other producers relied on a smaller percentage—it might be 10 to 25—but it was large enough to make the difference between a year of profit and one of loss.

In the forty years after 1860 huge new areas of land were put under cultivation in America, machines became standard equipment on most farms, land values boomed, and production soared to ever higher levels. But while costs of operation increased, prices dropped after 1870. Meanwhile, though the proportion of people living on farms declined in relation to the total population, farm population increased by absolute standards. From 1860 to 1910 the number of farm families rose from 1.5 million to over 6 million. In 1860 agriculture represented 50 per cent of the total wealth of the country, in the early 1900s only 20 per cent. The farmer received 30 per cent of the national income in 1860 and 18 per cent in 1910. By the decade of the nineties, 27 per cent of the owned farms in the country were under mortgages, and by 1910, 33 per cent. In 1880, 25 per cent of all farms were operated by tenants; in 1910, 37 per cent. The agrarian scene as it presented itself in the 1890s hardly realized Jefferson's dream of sturdy and independent yeomen owning the land they tilled.

## The Farmers' Grievances

The farmers were painfully aware that something was wrong. They did not recognize—and it would have been strange if they had recognized—the intricate implications of national and world overproduction. Instead, they concentrated their attention and anger on more immediate and easily understood problems, problems that were in truth real and important to them, such as freight rates, interest charges, and an adequate currency.

The farmers' first and most burning grievance was that against the railroads. In all sections, and especially in the states west of the Mississippi, farmers depended on the railroads to carry crops to the markets. In many cases the roads charged higher rates for farm than for other shipments and higher rates in the South and West than in the Northeast. Freight rates sometimes consumed so much of the current price that farmers refused to ship their crops and either let them rot or used them as fuel. Railroads controlled elevator and warehouse facilities in buying centers and charged arbitrary storage rates.

In the farmers' list of villains the sources that controlled credit—banks, loan companies, insurance corporations—ranked second to the railroads. Commercial farming was by its nature expensive, and ambitious producers needed credit to purchase machines or enlarge holdings. Though eager to advance loans during the boom period of rising land values, the lenders insisted on high interest rates. The farmers were in no position to resist, and in the West and the South they had to submit to charges running from 10 to 25 per cent. Usually they borrowed money when it was cheap, or abundant, and then had to retire their debts when money had become dear, or scarce. According to one estimate, 1,200 bushels of grain would buy a $1,000 mortgage in the 1860s; twenty years later it took 2,300 bushels to repay the mortgage. With good reason, the farmers fought for an increase in the volume of currency.

A third grievance of the farmer concerned prices, both the prices he received for his products and the prices he paid for goods he bought. He disposed of his products as an individual in competition with countless other individuals in this and other countries. He possessed little or no advance information on the state of the market and probable price changes; he did not have storage facilities to hold his crop for a favorable price; and he was powerless to regulate his production. Instead of changing his marketing procedures, the farmer blamed his woes on personal villains—grain speculators in distant cities, international bankers, or regional and local middlemen. These operators, he became convinced (sometimes with justice), were combining to fix prices so as to benefit themselves while hurting him.

The farmer was also convinced that there was something of a conspiracy against him in the prices of the goods he purchased. He sold his crops in a competitive market but bought in a domestic market protected by tariffs and dominated by trusts and corporations. According to government reports, over one hundred articles purchased by farmers—farm machinery, tools, sewing machines, blankets, staple foods, clothing, plowshares, and others—were protected. On these necessary items the tariff added from 33 to 60 per cent to the purchase price.

Last on the agrarian catalog of grievances was a vague yet tremendous resentment. In part, this was an outgrowth of the isolation of farm life before the days of paved roads, automobiles, telephones, and radios. Farm families in some parts of the country, particularly in the prairie and plains region where large farms were scattered over vast areas, were virtually cut off from the outside world and from other human companionship during the winter months or protracted spells of bad weather. This enforced seclusion was only partially alleviated when the national government established rural free delivery of mail in 1896. The drabness and the dullness of farm existence, the lack of adequate educational, recreational, and medical facilities, and the absence of community culture and action—these things helped to account for the tremendous migration of young people from the farms to the cities. The farmer, once eulogized as the surest support of American democracy, was now ridiculed as a "hayseed." He was losing status, and he knew it.

## KNOWLEDGE FOR A NEW SOCIETY

While the farmer's ways declined in prestige, the urban environment increasingly made its influence felt upon the mind of the entire nation, despite the persistence of stereotypes from the rural past. The city's influence was spread through the educational system, which was being broadened and extended, and through the publishing industry, which centered in New York and reached out for a wider and wider readership.

### The Pragmatic Approach

Along with the economic and social changes of the time, there was a change in the philosophical assumptions of thinking Americans. This came

## Christian Science

One of the new religions that came into being in the 1870s was Christian Science, founded by a woman, Mary Baker G. Eddy. She explained the essence of her belief as follows:

*The Scriptures name God as good, and the Saxon term for God is also good. From this premise comes the logical conclusion that God is naturally and divinely infinite good. How, then, can this conclusion change, or be changed, to mean that good is evil, or the creator of evil? What can there be besides infinity? Nothing! Therefore the Science of good calls evil nothing. In divine Science the terms God and good, as Spirit, are synonymous. That God, good, creates evil, or aught that can result in evil,—or that Spirit creates its opposite, named matter,—are conclusions that destroy their premise and prove themselves invalid. Here is where Christian Science sticks to its text, and other systems of religion abandon their own logic. Here also is found the pith of the basal statement, the cardinal point in Christian Science, that matter and evil (including all inharmony, sin, disease, death) are unreal.*

about largely in response to the doctrine of evolution—the thesis that all living things had evolved from earlier forms and that the various species had resulted from a process of natural selection.

Here was a doctrine that challenged almost every tenet of the American faith. If Darwin and the scientists were right, man was not endowed with a higher nature, but was only a biological organism, another form of animal life —the highest form, it was true, but still like the other animals that had had their day in past ages. Instead of history's being the working out of a divine plan, it was a random process dominated by the fiercest or luckiest competitors.

All over the United States Darwinism became a subject of popular interest and an issue of debate. By 1900 the evolutionists had carried the day, except in the South and parts of the rural Midwest. Many Protestant ministers, especially those in urban centers, had managed a reconciliation between religion and science. Particularly in the cities and larger towns, more and more people accepted the basic principles of evolution. Science was enshrined in the university and college curriculums.

Out of the controversy over Darwinism there arose finally a new philosophy which was peculiarly American and peculiarly suited to America's changing material civilization. The name of the philosophy was pragmatism, and its principal formulators were Charles Peirce and William James in the period before 1900, and John Dewey later.

Pragmatism is difficult to define, partly because its advocates differed as to its meaning, but mainly because it avoided absolutes and dealt with relative standards. According to the pragmatists, who accepted the idea of organic evolution, the validity of human institutions and actions should be determined by their consequences. If the ends of an institution or the techniques of a group did not satisfy social needs, then a change was in order. In blunt terms, the pragmatists applied their one standard: Does it work? They employed the same test to truth. There were no final truths or answers, they contended, but a series of truths for each generation and each society. Truth, like institutions, had to be validated by consequences. Said James: "The ultimate test for us of what a truth means is the conduct it dictates or inspires."

## Toward Universal Schooling

Mary Antin, a Russian girl who came as an immigrant to the United States, had heard that in America everything was free. Best of all: "Education was free. That subject my father had written about repeatedly, as comprising his chief hope for us children, the essence of American opportunity, the treasure that no thief could touch, not even misfortune or poverty." Education in America after the Civil War was indeed free or in the process of becoming so— free, public, and almost universal.

In 1860 there were only 100 public high schools in the country, but by 1900 the number had reached 6,000; their total enrollment, however, was not more than 200,000. The most spectacular expansion occurred at the elementary or grade school level. Below the elementary level appeared the kindergartens, the first of which was established in St. Louis in 1873. By 1900 compulsory school attendance laws were in effect, although not always enforced, in thirty-one states and territories. In the expansion of school facilities, the Northeast led, the Middle West followed, and the South trailed behind.

Most of the elementary schools and many of the high schools in all sections were, by modern standards, small, inadequate, and unattractive. Dominating the curriculum were the traditional three R's—reading, writing, and arithmetic—with history and a few other subjects holding a secondary place. Also traditional were the textbooks used, among them the Webster Spellers and the McGuffey Readers.

Teaching was not yet regarded as a profession. In 1900 the average annual salary was a mere $325, less than the average wage of unskilled workers. Thousands of teachers, with only a high school or elementary education, knew little more than their pupils. Nevertheless, real progress was achieved in establishing the idea that teaching was a profession and education a science. In 1865 there were only twelve teacher-training institutions, or normal schools, as they were called, in the country. By 1900 every state supported at least one such school, and in some of the leading universities, Chicago, Harvard, Columbia, Stanford, and others, schools of education had been set up. The states created boards or commissions of education to raise standards, and in 1867 the national government manifested its interest by establishing the office of Commissioner of Education to collect and disseminate educational information. By the turn of the century one in every five of the elementary teachers was a graduate of a professional school.

In the 1880s a number of innovations in educational methods began to make their influence felt. New, more up-to-date textbooks were introduced, and the curriculum was expanded to include more science and practical or vocational courses. At the same time German educational doctrines, stressing the necessity of arousing the student's desire to learn, stirred the attention of American educators. Among those impressed by the German theories was John Dewey, one of the pragmatic philosophers and a member of the faculty of the school of education of the University of Chicago. In lectures and essays in the 1890s, Dewey proposed that education should be considered as a part of the social process, that its purpose should be to prepare students to live in modern society, and that pupils should learn by doing instead of by the traditional rote or drill method. His program of progressive education had its greatest impact after 1900.

## Expanding Higher Education

Powerfully stimulating the expansion of higher learning were huge new financial resources made available by the national government and private benefactors. The national government, by the Morrill Land Grant Act of the Civil War period, donated land to states for the establishment of colleges to teach, among other subjects, agriculture and mechanical arts. After 1865, particularly in the West and the South, states began to exploit the possibilities of the act to strengthen existing institutions or to found new ones. In some cases the proceeds went to a single state university with an agricultural and mechanical division, and in other cases to a separate college for the practical arts. In all, sixty-nine "land grant" institutions came into existence, among them the universities of Wisconsin, California, Minnesota, and Illinois.

Supplementing the resources of the government were the millions of dollars contributed by business and financial tycoons, who endowed private institutions. The motives of the magnates were various: they were influenced by the gospel of wealth; they thought that education would blunt class differences; they realized that the demands of an industrial society called for specialized knowledge—or they were simply vain. Men like Rockefeller and Carnegie gave generously to such schools as Harvard, Chicago, Northwestern, Syracuse, Yale, and Columbia. Other philanthropists founded new universities and thereby perpetuated their family names—Vanderbilt, Johns Hopkins, Cornell, Tulane, and Stanford.

Taking over as president of Harvard in 1869 at the age of thirty-five, Charles W. Eliot pioneered a break with the traditional curriculum. The usual course of studies at American universities emphasized classical and humanistic courses: ancient languages, mathematics, ethics, and rhetoric; and each institution prescribed a rigid program of required courses. Under Eliot's leadership, Harvard dropped most of its required courses in favor of an elective system and increased its course offerings to stress the physical and social sciences, the fine arts, and modern languages. Soon other institutions in all sections of the country were following Harvard's lead.

Eliot also renovated the Harvard medical and law schools, raising the requirements and lengthening the residence period, and again the Harvard model affected other schools. Improved technical training in other professions accompanied the advances in medicine and law. Both state and private universities hastened to establish schools of architecture, engineering, education, journalism, and business. The leading center for graduate study, based on the German system with the Ph.D. degree as its highest award, was the Johns Hopkins University (founded in 1876). In 1875 there were only 399 graduate students in the United States, but by 1900 the number had risen to more than 5,000.

Two groups in American society—women and Negroes—did not receive the full benefits of higher education. Before the Civil War, girls had been generally admitted on an equal basis to elementary and secondary schools, but the doors of most colleges were closed to them. A few private colleges for women had been founded, and a very few schools (three, to be exact) admitted girls to study with boys. After the war a number of additional women's colleges came into existence, generally as the result of donations from philanthropists: Vassar, Wellesley, Smith, Bryn Mawr, and Goucher. In addition, some of the largest private universities established on their campuses separate colleges for women. But the greatest educational opportunities for women opened in the Middle West, where the state universities began to admit women along with men.

Negroes reaped the fewest advantages from the educational renaissance. In the South, and

### Booker T. Washington on Negro Education [1895]

Washington rose from slavery to the leadership of his people. Founding Tuskegee Institute in Alabama, he advocated that the Negro improve his economic status before reaching for political rights. To that end Washington, in a speech in 1895, advocated a vocational type of education, which prompted some Negroes to accuse him of subordinating the race's struggle for equal rights:

*Our greatest danger is that in the great leap from slavery to freedom we may overlook the fact that the masses of us are to live by the productions of our hands, and fail to keep in mind that we shall prosper in proportion as we learn to dignify and glorify common labour and put brains and skill into the common occupations of life; shall prosper in proportion as we learn to draw the line between the superficial and the substantial, the ornamental gewgaws of life and the useful. No race can prosper till it learns that there is as much dignity in tilling a field as in writing a poem. It is at the bottom of life we must begin, and not at the top. Nor should we permit our grievances to overshadow our opportunities.*

also in most parts of the North, they attended segregated elementary and secondary schools that were nearly always poorer than the white schools. Negroes desiring a higher education were almost universally barred from white institutions and had to attend one of the colleges established for their race by Northern philanthropy: Howard University, in Washington; Fisk University, in Nashville; Straight University, in New Orleans; or Shaw University, in Raleigh. Some Negro leaders were disturbed by the tendency of their people to seek a "classical" education that did not fit them for the economic position they occupied in the South. For the transitional period after emancipation, these leaders believed, an industrial education, stressing vocational training and the dignity of labor, was preferable. The result of their thinking was the establishment, with aid from private sources, of the Hampton Normal and Industrial Institute in Virginia and the Tuskegee Institute in Alabama, the latter presided over by Booker T. Washington, the most influential Negro leader of his times.

Many adults sought learning through agencies other than colleges. Summer after summer, thousands flocked to the Chautauqua Institution in western New York to hear lectures on a variety of subjects. Chautauqua offered a concentrated short course for teachers and others in residence; it also provided extension courses and a four-year home reading program for nonresident clients. In addition Chautauqua companies toured rural America bringing music and lectures to people who received no other exposure to such culture.

Public libraries appeared in increasing numbers, especially in the cities and larger towns. Andrew Carnegie gave $45 million of his steel fortune for the construction of public libraries, wisely stipulating that communities taking his money had to maintain the institutions. Through the benefactions of men like Carnegie and through public support, over 9,000 free libraries had come into being by 1900.

## The Publishing Business

Newspapers and magazines provided the reading matter for most Americans. During the period 1870–1910 the circulation of daily newspapers had a nearly ninefold increase (from less than 3 million to more than 24 million), which was over three times as great as the increase in population.

Meanwhile, journalism changed in various ways: (1) Newspapers became predominantly news organs, while editorial opinion and the editorial page declined in importance. (2) The nature of news changed. Politics received less attention, and there was an increasing emphasis on what was called the "human-interest" story. (3) Journalism became a recognized and respected profession. Salaries of reporters doubled.

Able and educated men were attracted to the profession, and schools of journalism were begun on university campuses. (4) With the passing of personal journalism, newspapers became corporations, impersonal business organizations similar to those emerging in industry, their worth often reckoned in millions of dollars. At the same time, they tended to become standardized. The press services furnished the same news to all their subscribing papers, and syndicates came into existence to provide their customers with identical features, columns, editorials, and pictures. By the turn of the century there were several newspaper chains, harbingers of a development that would become stronger in the future. Thus the newspapers conformed to and reinforced the trend toward uniformity that characterized American society as a whole. (5) There was a distinct improvement in the physical appearance of newspapers. The traditional pages of poorly and closely printed columns, each with its own headlines, disappeared; in their place came something resembling the modern paper, complete with varied make-up, pictures, cartoons, and imaginative advertising.

For almost twenty years after the Civil War, the principal magazines in the country were monthlies and weeklies that reached only a limited number of readers. Essentially, they were literary journals run by literary men. They were always genteel and in good (but often dull) taste; they sold for 35 cents a copy (a high price for those times); and the circulation of the largest did not exceed 130,000. The leading monthlies were *Harper's Magazine* and the *Atlantic Monthly*, both of which antedated the war, *Scribner's Monthly*, which was founded in 1870 and became the *Century* in 1881, and *Scribner's Magazine*, established in 1887. Somewhat similar were the weeklies: the *Nation*, the *Independent*, and *Harper's Weekly*, all published in New York.

During the decade of the eighties, a new type of magazine appeared—the popular magazine, designed to appeal to the masses and to achieve a mass circulation. One of the important pioneers of the popular journal was Edward W. Bok, who took over the *Ladies' Home Journal* in 1889 and, by employing writers who produced material to appeal to female readers, built the circulation of the magazine to over 700,000. Following Bok was Frank A. Munsey, the greatest of the popular publishers, who utilized the techniques of mass production and technology—cheap but attractive printing, low prices, and lavish advertising—to make *Munsey's Magazine* one of the most widely read organs in the country. The older *Saturday Evening Post* adopted many of the new methods and, by catering to the standards of the middle class, it led all other journals in circulation. The popular magazines were priced at 5 to 15 cents and had circulations of a half million to a million.

Book publishing became a business, and, in line with the trend in industry, a big business. The corporation replaced the individual publisher, and publishing became more impersonal and increasingly commercial. For approximately twenty years after the war most publishing houses, of whom the American Publishing Company of Hartford, Connecticut, was a leading example, sold books only by subscription. But gradually this type of organization was supplanted by the large firm that sold its products to book stores and reached the public through advertising techniques. By 1900 most of the big publishing houses were centered in New York City, the recognized publishing capital of the country and also the largest literary market. The passage by Congress in 1891 of an International Copyright Law prevented American publishers from pirating foreign books without payment (and also prevented foreign pirating of American books). The result was that publishers had to rely more on American authors and pay them better.

## CULTURE IN THE GILDED AGE

In a novel, *The Gilded Age* (1873), Mark Twain and Charles Dudley Warner satirized the men and manners of industrial society and thus provided a name that is sometimes applied to the last decades of the nineteenth century. The novel deals with greedy men and their get-rich-quick schemes. It suggests that American life, though showy on the surface, was essentially acquisitive and corrupt. Its authors thus reflected the economic and social changes of the time. Different writers responded to these

changes in a variety of ways. Some faced up to the realities of the industrializing and urbanizing trend; others sought a vicarious escape for themselves and for their readers.

## Reflections in Literature

Though New York City was the publishing center, the production of literature—the actual writing—was done all over the country. A literary renaissance began in the West and the South as well as the East. Writers in each section, describing their home scenes in local-color stories, found a national market for their wares.

Writers of the local-color school thought of themselves as realists. Rebelling against the sentimentality of the tear-jerking popular novelists like Mary Jane Holmes (whose thirty-nine novels sold more than 2 million copies), they insisted on careful reporting, real people and real plots, and an honest rendition of such things as dialect, dress, food, and manners. Usually, however, they were content with an accurate surface description that did not come to grips with fundamental problems, and on occasion some of them wrote sentimental nonsense.

In New England, Sarah Orne Jewett and Mary E. Wilkins Freeman portrayed the disappearing social order of their section: its rural scenes and ways, its isolated farms, and its decaying seaport towns. Of the two, Miss Jewett was the finer artist; her *The Country of the Pointed Firs* (1896) was far above the reportorial level of the average local-color author. In the South, George Washington Cable affectionately described the antebellum Creole life of Louisiana but was so outspoken on the race question that he had to take refuge in the North. Most famous of the Southern writers was Joel Chandler Harris, who recorded Georgia folk tales and Negro life in *Uncle Remus* (1880). Thomas Nelson Page extolled in fiction the old Virginia aristocracy. In the Middle West, Edward Eggleston presented an honest account of early Indiana life in *The Hoosier Schoolmaster* (1871), and James Whitcomb Riley gave a folksy view of contemporary Indiana life in his popular verse. In the Far West, Bret Harte wrote sentimental stories of the mining frontier. Mark Twain, while living in California, burst into

**Mark Twain With His Friends**

The author sat regally at the head of the table at a dinner given him on his seventieth birthday in the famous and garish Delmonico's restaurant in New York City. (Library of Congress)

national prominence with a humorous sketch, "The Celebrated Frog of Calaveras County," and he portrayed aspects of the last frontier in *Roughing It* (1872).

Mark Twain (born Samuel Clemens) began his career on a newspaper, and he long considered himself to be a journalist. The public long insisted on regarding him as merely a humorist, but he was probably the greatest American novelist in the era between 1865 and 1900. His first important success, *The Innocents Abroad* (1869), a tale of American tourists in Europe, was a loud and scornful laugh at Old World decay and hypocrisy—and also at American worship of European institutions. His literary fame, however, rests primarily on *The Adventures of Tom Sawyer* (1876) and *The Adventures of Huckleberry Finn* (1885), sensitive and sympathetic accounts of life in rural mid-America.

Not all the writers were concerned with depicting departing cultures. Some viewed with misgiving the culture of their own times, and deplored its materialism and economic inequalities. Gradually there developed a literature of protest, expressed chiefly in the medium of the problem novel. The dissenters attacked their targets from many and varied angles. A few, like Henry Adams in *Democracy* (1880) and John Hay in *The Breadwinners* (1884), spoke for the old aristocracy, the former ruling class; in criticizing the crassness of the new rich, they merely expressed the resentment of their group at being dethroned. No novelist of stature voiced the aspirations of labor, although Stephen Crane in *Maggie: A Girl of the Streets* (1893) described slum conditions and urban poverty with somber realism. For rural America and its small towns, Hamlin Garland and Edgar W. Howe grimly performed a similar descriptive job. Garland, smashing the traditional idyllic picture of pastoral culture, exposed in *Main-Travelled Roads* (1891) the ugliness, isolation, and drudgery of farm life, and Howe in *The Story of a Country Town* (1883) starkly painted the narrow, provincial nature of the American village.

A few literary critics of the American scene retreated from its vigor and materialism and found refuge in Europe. Preeminent among them was Henry James, who studied and described his country from England. In such novels as *The American* (1876), *An International Episode* (1878), and *Daisy Miller* (1879), he detailed the impact of Europe's ancient culture upon visiting Americans. In his coldly realistic volumes, the Americans are usually frustrated or defeated by Europe, but nearly always they appear more virile than the civilization they cannot understand. During his later years, James confessed he wished he had remained in America.

The greatest realistic novelist of the period, ranking second only to Twain in the hierarchy of letters, was William Dean Howells. His realism was confined to the common and the average; shunning the abnormal, he was the most painstaking literary historian of what was normal in the America of his age. In *The Rise of Silas Lapham* (1884), he portrayed shrewdly and in not completely flattering terms the psychology of the self-made businessman. His later novels, written during the social upheaval and labor strife of the nineties, dealt with social problems and social injustices.

## Art and Architecture

American attitudes toward the arts in the Gilded Age paralleled those manifested toward literature. Popular tastes, largely determined by the middle class, admired paintings that told a conventional story, pointed a moral, or photographically reproduced familiar people and scenes. The artists whose works were most widely viewed were the illustrators for the popular magazines and the weeklies.

But Americans also had opportunities to see the best painting and sculpture of Europe's past. The newly rich business magnates set out with vigorous determination to patronize art and artists and to acquire, as part of their process of acquiring culture, the finest collections their money would buy. They purchased, regardless of cost, many of the art treasures of Europe, which possessed, their agents taught them, the only art worthy of the name, and installed them in their palace homes. Sometimes they did more —they established public art galleries or muse-

ums of fine arts, and eventually nearly all of the private collections found their way into public depositories. At the close of the Civil War not a single American city could boast of a good art gallery, but by 1900 there was a gallery or museum of at least adequate status in every metropolitan center. Thousands of Americans could and did see the best paintings and sculpture of Europe's past.

In the years after the Civil War most American painters received their training in Europe. Some remained there as expatriates (like the writer Henry James), among them James McNeill Whistler and John Singer Sargent. Whistler, who is often ranked as the greatest genius in the history of American art, was equally proficient in several media—oil, watercolor, etching—and with several themes—portraits and his so-called "nocturnes," impressionistic sketches of moonlight on water and other scenes. He was one of the first to appreciate the beauty of Japanese color prints and to introduce Oriental concepts into Western art. Equally versatile but not as talented was Sargent, who built his international reputation on his portraits.

Breaking away from European influences was a small group of artists, of whom the ablest were John La Farge, Winslow Homer, and Thomas Eakins. La Farge's experiments with light and color anticipated the Impressionists. He worked with both landscapes and portraits, was our first important muralist, and probably is still America's most distinguished stained-glass artist. Homer, who began as a magazine illustrator, was vigorously and almost blatantly American. All of his powerful and rugged paintings dealt with native scenes and people; his best pictures were of the sea and maritime life on the New England coast.

American sculpture in the years immediately following the Civil War was dominated by Italian influences and the neoclassical tradition. When American sculptors made statues of American leaders, they produced figures that resembled Roman senators and indeed were often clothed in flowing robes or togas. But gradually France supplanted Italy as an influence, and American sculptors, many of whom were trained in Paris, began to work out an art form distinctively American. One of the first to break from the Italian tradition was John Quincy Adams

Ward with his statues of Indians and Negroes. Another was Daniel Chester French, who produced a number of realistic statues of great Americans, the most famous being the imposing Lincoln in the Lincoln Memorial at Washington. Incomparably the greatest American sculptor of the period was Augustus Saint-Gaudens, an Irish shoemaker's son who did more than any native artist to free American sculpture from its European bonds. His statues of General Grant and Sherman and of Admiral Farragut and, above all, his Lincoln in Lincoln Park, Chicago, were authentically American and impressively beautiful.

Before the Civil War the dominant influence in American architecture had been the classic Greek. Public buildings and dwellings throughout the country copied the lines of ancient Greek edifices. By 1860, however, the so-called Greek revival had spent its force, and another style, also a revival, had appeared. It became the rage of the Gilded Age. This was Gothic or, more accurately, an American version of the Gothic, with generous borrowings from other styles and some original native techniques added.

One of the first Americans to break with the Gothic tradition was Richard Morris Hunt, who designed dozens of homes for the business tycoons and became known as the architect of fashionable society. Although his houses were as large and elaborate as the Gothic edifices, they sprang from a different influence and reproduced a different mood—the light and lavish spirit of the French Renaissance. French chateaux and townhouses by Hunt dotted the rural resort areas of the East and its cities. Another rebel against the Gothic was Henry Hobson Richardson, the best-known architect of the period, who attempted to adapt the Romanesque form of France and Spain to the American scene. His public buildings, of which his churches are the most famous, and his houses were marked by solid but often graceful arches, heavy, short pillars, and simple carving; in their low-lying strength they resembled nothing so much as forts. Still another dissenting note was sounded by C. F. McKim, of the New York firm of McKim, Mead, and White, who endeavored to revive the Renaissance style by fitting it to American needs.

These men, however large their talents, were essentially imitative and derivative. They copied and adapted European forms, and their designs had little relevance to the facts of American life and little utility for the needs of the American scene, especially for the growing urban centers. Both the virtues and the faults of American architecture were demonstrated at the Chicago World's Fair of 1893. Most of the buildings shown were in the classical style; although they possessed a certain stately beauty, they revealed fully the unimaginative character of American architecture and the strength of the European bonds holding it. But there also emerged from the Fair an authentic genius, the first great original American architect—Louis Sullivan. Sullivan, who designed the Transportation Building for the Fair, denounced the work done there by most of his colleagues as mere copies rather than creations, "a naked exhibition of charlatanry . . . conjoined with expert salesmanship of the materials of decay."

## New Uses of Leisure

Many Americans, especially those of the urban middle and professional classes, found that they had more leisure at their command, and they had incomes sufficient to gratify their demands for pleasure. Even the workers had more free time, and they too sought satisfactory forms of recreation. The late nineteenth century witnessed the rise of organized spectator sports, the presentation of athletic events as entertainment for large audiences, and the organization of sports as a business.

Most popular of all the organized sports and well on its way to becoming the national game was baseball. Its origins probably stretched back to 1839, when Abner Doubleday, a civil engineering student, laid out a diamond-shaped field at Cooperstown, New York, and attempted to standardize the rules governing the playing of such games as town ball and four old cat, the ancestors of baseball. By the end of the Civil War, interest in the game had grown rapidly. Over 200 teams or clubs existed, some of which toured the country playing rivals; they belonged to a national association of "Baseball Players" that had proclaimed a set of standard rules.

These teams were amateurs or semi-professionals, but as the game waxed in popularity, it offered opportunities for profit, and the first professional team, the Cincinnati Red Stockings, appeared in 1869. Other cities soon fielded professional teams, and in 1876 the present National League was organized, chiefly by Albert Spalding. Soon a rival league appeared, the American Association. Competition between the two was intense, and in 1883 they played a postseason contest, the first "world's series." The American Association eventually collapsed, but in 1900 the American League was organized.

The second most popular game, football, arose in the colleges and universities. At first football had been played by rival student groups at the same school. Then in 1869 occurred the first intercollegiate game in this county, between Princeton and Rutgers, with twenty-five men on each side. Soon other Eastern schools fielded teams, organized a conference, the American Intercollegiate Football Association, and attempted to standardize the rules.

As football grew in popularity, it spread to other sections, notably to the Middle Western state universities, soon destined to overthrow the Eastern schools as the powers of the game. It also began to exhibit those taints of profes-

### An Early Football Game

Here, in an 1889 contest between Cornell and Rochester, the ball is being put into play by a "scrum," similar to that of rugby. The ball was placed on the ground, and a circle of players tried to kick it out to their respective teammates. The "father of American football," one-time Yale star Walter Camp, led in modernizing the game. He persuaded the rulemakers to reduce the number of players to eleven on each side, to permit the offensive team to put the ball into play from a line of scrimmage, with a quarterback, and to require the team to advance the ball five yards in three plays (and then, later, ten yards in four plays) or give it up to the opposing team. Camp also helped to eliminate excessive roughness from what had been a remarkably brutal sport. He selected the first "All-American" eleven. (Library of Congress) sionalism that have marked it ever since. Some schools employed as players "ringers," tramp athletes who were not even registered as students. In an effort to eliminate such abuses, Amos A. Stagg, athletic director and coach at the University of Chicago, led in forming the Western Conference, or Big Ten, in 1896.

A game that would eventually become one of the great spectator sports, basketball, was invented in 1891 at Springfield, Massachusetts, by Dr. James A. Naismith. It is the only major sport that is completely American in origin.

Boxing did not become a respectable sport until the 1880s. Before that time prize fights were illegal in practically every state, and bouts had to be conducted in isolated places beyond the reach of law officials. The existing rules were few and encouraged brutality. Contestants fought without gloves, a round ended when one man was knocked down, and a fight continued until one of the participants was unwilling or unable to go on. In the 1870s the Marquis-of-Queensberry rules were introduced in England and later in the United States. By these regulations, fighters were required to wear padded gloves, a round was limited to three minutes, and certain rough practices and types of blows were ruled out. The first American boxer to adopt the new rules was John L. Sullivan, who had become heavyweight champion of the world in 1882. Although Sullivan occasionally returned to bare-knuckle fighting, he invested the sport with a respectability it had never known. It was raised to a higher plane by James J. Corbett, "Gentleman Jim," who dethroned Sullivan in 1892. Five years later Corbett dropped the title to Bob Fitzsimmons, who in turn was knocked out by James J. Jeffries in 1899.

Before 1900 golf and tennis were almost completely participant rather than spectator sports. The first modern golf course in the United States was laid out at Yonkers, New York, in 1888, and the first golf tournament in the country was played at Newport, Rhode Island, six years later. The only courses were at exclusive private clubs, and until after 1900 the game was restricted to the rich. Much the same was true of tennis, first played at Eastern resorts frequented by the wealthy. The United States Lawn Tennis Association was organized in 1881 to standardize the rules and encourage the game, and in 1897 American tennis players engaged an English team in the first international match.

In the small towns and villages of rural America, recreation continued to follow more traditional patterns. People came together for entertainment at county fairs, political rallies, and court sessions. Always a big event in a rural community was the arrival of a Chautauqua company with its tent and array of lecturers, musicians, and other luminaries. Even more colorful was the circus with its display of exotic wonders, amazing to rural people who had never traveled far from their birthplace. To send a circus across the country was expensive, and many smaller companies could not stand the cost. By 1900 the circus industry was dominated by two large firms, Barnum and Bailey, and Ringling Brothers.

The nineties saw the birth of the bicycle craze. Bicycling was both a recreation and, for many people in urban areas, a convenient method of transportation. The bicycle in the 1880s, with a high wheel in front, often pitched the rider over the handlebars for a "header" in the dirt. It was too dangerous for practically everyone except the most daring young men. The "safety" bicycle of the 1890s, with two wheels of equal size and with pneumatic tires, invited riders of both sexes and all ages. By 1900 an estimated 10 million Americans, mostly adults, were riding bicycles. While it lasted, the mania had some influence on American life. It brought into being a new industry for the manufacture of the vehicles. The cyclists, organized in the League of American Wheelmen, spurred local governments to improve highways. And cycling changed clothing styles as many young women put on blouses and moderate-length skirts in place of the former dragging street dresses, which got in the rider's way.

The bicycle prepared the way for the coming of the automobile. The two-wheeler not only brought some good roads for the first cars to run on; it also provided essential components of the early models, such as tubular steel, wire wheels, pneumatic tires, and the chain-and-sprocket drive. Many of the pioneers among American automobile builders, such as Henry Ford, once had been bicycle mechanics.

# Selected Readings

**Frontier Interpretations and Miscellany** F. J. Turner, *The Frontier in American History* ° (1920); H. N. Smith, *Virgin Land: The American West as Symbol and Myth* ° (1950); W. P. Webb, *The Great Plains* ° (1931); J. C. Malin, *The Grassland of North America* (1947); H. R. Lamar, *The Far Southwest, 1846–1912* (1966); R. M. Robbins, *Our Landed Heritage: The Public Domain, 1776–1936* ° (1942); E. S. Pomeroy, *The Territories and the United States, 1864–1890* (1947); Wayne Gard, *The Great Buffalo Hunt* (1959).

**Mining** W. S. Greever, *The Bonanza West: The Story of the Western Mining Rushes, 1848–1900* (1963); R. W. Paul, *Mining Frontiers of the Far West, 1848–1880* (1963); C. H. Shinn, *Mining Camps: A Study in American Frontier Government* ° (1885); Wayne Gard, *Frontier Justice* (1949).

**Cattle and Sheep Raising** E. S. Osgood, *The Day of the Cattleman* ° (1929); E. E. Dale, *The Range Cattle Industry* (1930); Lewis Atherton, *The Cattle Kings* (1961); J. B. Frantz and J. E. Choate, Jr., *The American Cowboy: The Myth and the Reality* (1955); Philip Durham and E. L. Jones, *The Negro Cowboy* (1965); E. N. Wentworth, *Shepherd's Empire* (1945).

**Farming** F. A. Shannon *The Farmer's Last Frontier, 1860–1897* (1945); G. C. Fite, *The Farmer's Frontier, 1865–1900* (1966); Everett Dick, *The Sod-House Frontier, 1854–1890* (1937).

**The Indians** F. G. Roe, *The Indian and the Horse* (1955); H. H. Jackson, *A Century of Dishonor* ° (1881); L. G. Priest, *Uncle Sam's Stepchildren: The Reformation of the United States Indian Policy, 1865–1887* (1942); H. E. Fritz, *The Movement for Indian Assimilation, 1860–1890* (1963); Robert Utley, *Last Days of the Sioux Nation* ° (1963); J. C. Olson, *Red Cloud and the Sioux Problem* (1965); Stanley Vestal, *Warpath and Council Fire* (1948) and *Sitting Bull* (1957); F. F. Van de Water, *Glory Hunter* (1934), on Custer; Jay Monaghan, *Custer* (1959);

M. D. Beal, *"I Will Fight No More"* (1963), on Chief Joseph.

**Education** Frederick Rudolph, *The American College and University: A History* ° (1962); L. R. Veysey, *The Emergence of the American University* (1965); Richard Hofstadter and Walter Metzger, *The Development of Academic Freedom in the United States* (1955); L. A. Cremin, *The Transformation of the School: Progressivism in American Education, 1876–1957* ° (1961).

**Religion** C. H. Hopkins, *The Rise of the Social Gospel in American Protestantism, 1865–1915* (1940); A. I. Abell, *The Urban Impact on American Protestantism, 1865–1900* (1943); H. F. May, *Protestant Churches and Industrial America* (1949).

**Literature** Van Wyck Brooks, *New England: Indian Summer, 1865–1915* ° (1940); Larzer Ziff, *The American 1890's: Life and Times of a Lost Generation* (1966); Everett Carter, *Howells and the Age of Realism* (1954); Bernard De Voto, *Mark Twain's America* ° (1932); Justin Kaplan, *Mr. Clemens and Mark Twain* (1966); Elizabeth Stevenson, *Henry Adams* ° (1955); R. B. Perry, *The Thought and Character of William James* (2 vols., 1935); F. O. Matthiessen, *The James Family* (1947).

**Architecture** W. A. Starrett, *Skyscrapers and the Men Who Built Them* (1928); John Szarkowski, *The Idea of Louis Sullivan* (1957).

**Popular Culture** Ray Ginger, *The Age of Excess: The United States from 1877 to 1914* (1965); R. O. and Victoria Case, *We Called It Culture: The Story of Chautauqua* (1958); J. D. Hart, *The Popular Book* ° (1950); F. L. Mott, *A History of American Magazines*, vol. 3, *1865–1885* (1938), and vol. 4, *1885–1905* (1957); D. C. Seitz, *Joseph Pulitzer* (1924); J. K. Winkler, *W. R. Hearst* (1928); F. R. Dulles, *America Learns to Play* (1940); J. A. Krout, *Annals of American Sport* (1924).

---

° Titles available in paperback.

JUNE 6 1891     PRICE 10 CENTS

# Judge

ENTERED AT THE POST OFFICE AT NEW YORK AS SECOND-CLASS MATTER.     COPYRIGHT 1891 BY THE JUDGE PUBLISHING CO.

# Chapter 19
# The Swell of Agrarian Protest

In the 1880s the major parties in the United States were like two bottles that had different labels but otherwise were identical—and both were empty. So it seemed to the Englishman James Bryce, the most perspicacious of all foreign commentators on American institutions next to the Frenchman Alexis de Tocqueville. "Tenets and policies, points of political doctrine and points of political practice, have all but vanished," Bryce wrote in *The American Commonwealth* (1888). "All has been lost, except office or the hope of it."

In American society there were serious problems arising out of the development of big business and monopoly, the organization of labor and the resulting industrial conflict, the decline of agricultural prices and the worsening position of the farmer, and the defects in the economic system that caused it to collapse every twenty years or so (in 1873 and again in 1893). But the leaders of the major parties evaded these problems as best they could.

Politics was more highly professionalized than ever, and the politicians played it like a game that had little to do with economic and social realities. With the politicians the object was to win power and jobs. In many cities or entire states a political boss headed a machine (organization) that operated as an "invisible government" controlling the official government of the city or state. The machine bought votes and sold governmental favors. The national parties looked to the boss and the machine to provide the votes with which to win elections.

The parties depended for support not only on the patronage of government but also on contributions from business. It took the assassination of a President to shock the politicians into accepting a partial reform of the spoils system. After that, the parties had to depend more and more on corporation gifts. The president of the sugar trust testified before a congressional investigating committee that during the 1892 campaign his company had contributed money to both the Republicans and the Democrats. "The American Sugar Refining Company has no politics of any kind," he concluded. "Only the politics of business?" he was asked. "Only the politics of business," he replied.

Already, in the early 1890s, a tide of protest was swelling and dashing against the politics of business. It was headed by discontented farmers, but it included other dissatisfied groups whose numbers were increased by the onset of the depression. It encountered the forces of conservatism and partially recoiled before them but recovered to reach a roaring climax in the election of 1896. Thereafter the protest movement re-

---

**A Party of Patches**

This satirical and anti-Populist cartoon depicts the People's party as a balloon made up of patches from previous radical parties. Operating it are Terence Powderly of the Knights of Labor, "Sockless" Jerry Simpson of Kansas, Senator William A. Peffer of Kansas, and Ben Butler, the old radical Republican who had turned Greenbacker. (Brown Brothers) ceded, as the economic system demonstrated its capacity to enlarge the general well-being, and the political system showed its ability to absorb dissenters into the traditional two parties. Meanwhile, the protesters had displayed a moral fervor and a class bitterness that frightened and appalled the more secure and sober elements of society. "It was a fanaticism like the crusades," wrote a Kansas editor (William Allen White).

## THE POLITICS OF COMPLACENCY

It has sometimes been thought that political parties ought to define and discuss issues as sharply as do debating clubs. But the major parties in the United States have seldom divided on fundamental principles except in times of crisis (as during the 1850s and the 1890s). More commonly the parties have been concerned with confusing issues rather than clarifying them, with harmonizing interests rather than antagonizing them. The politics of the years from 1877 to 1888 illustrate in extreme form this function of the parties.

### Republicans and Democrats

Republicanism was almost a religion in the North. The Republican party, the Grand Old Party of Abraham Lincoln and the boys in blue, had saved the Union and freed the slaves. In election after election, long after Appomattox, Republican campaigners continued to recall the war record of their own party and attack the opposition as the party of treason and slavery. Related to this, as another reminder of the war, was the practice, every four years (except in 1884), of nominating as the Republican presidential candidate a veteran officer of the Union army.

Flights of campaign oratory thinly masked the economic composition and goals of the dominant party. Even more powerful in the party's councils than in the prewar era was the business element, composed of manufacturers, bankers, investors, and government bondholders—more powerful because business was forging ahead of agriculture in the indices of national wealth and because industry was reaching out into every area and raising up champions in the West and South, which had been solidly agricultural. But still influential in the party was the farming wing, particularly because the farmers

had more votes than businessmen. Other important elements of the party were the veterans of the Union armies, numbering perhaps a million and organized in potent pressure groups such as the Grand Army of the Republic, which found the Republicans cordial to the idea of soldier pensions, and which served as an auxiliary of the party.

In its economic composition the Democratic organization was, much as it had been in Jackson's time, largely a party of farmers and laborers—of small property holders. But it was a party without clear direction or goals, and here probably is the principal reason for its minority condition. The important Eastern wing, representing importing interests, was willing to accept the traditional Democratic low-tariff policy, but on other issues, and particularly on the question of a "sound" currency, it was as conservative as the Republicans. Any Democratic move to challenge the Republicans on economic issues was certain to scare off the Easterners. Even on the tariff, the Democrats failed to demonstrate unity or take a firm position. As industry moved into the West and South, islands of protection appeared in these once free-trade regions to divide a once cohesive public opinion. In many elections the Democrats adopted an ambiguous tariff plank that hardly differed from that of their opponents, causing wags to quip that the party of Jefferson and Jackson stood for "a protective tariff for revenue only." In short, the party failed to devise a program that distinguished it from the Republicans, failed to offer a set of issues to those groups who were alarmed by the rise of big business, failed, above all, to be a party of opposition. It was a "me too" party asking for votes on the grounds that it could do what the Republicans were doing—only better and with less corruption.

Although the Republicans in a general sense represented the upper and middle income groups and the Democrats the average and lower groups, neither spoke for a precise economic interest. Both included people from all economic levels, and both embraced business and agricultural elements. When economic legislation was considered in Congress, the votes usually followed sectional rather than party lines; Western Republicans and Southern Democrats, for example, were likely to unite behind a measure of benefit to the agricultural interests.

Although the Republicans usually dominated the Presidency, they did not always control Congress. The Democrats, with the solid South behind them and with the support of highly organized machines in Northern cities and states, sometimes managed to secure a majority in one or both houses of the legislative branch and thereby block Republican programs. When a Democrat sat in the White House, the converse was often true: the Republicans ruled at least one house and voted down Democratic measures. The failure of either party to control consistently all branches of the government is, of course, another reason for the absence of firm issues and the relative paucity of positive legislation.

Of the three branches of government, Congress was predominant. Retaining most of the powers and prerogatives it had seized in the struggle with Andrew Johnson, it easily overshadowed the Presidency and the judiciary. Nor did it encounter any serious challenge from its traditional rival, the executive arm. None of the Presidents elected between 1868 and 1888, with the possible exception of Grover Cleveland, was a strong political leader.

The Republicans Matt Quay in Pennsylvania and Roscoe Conkling in New York were outstanding examples of the boss type. Tall, handsome, and flamboyant, Conkling ruled the Republican party in New York and swayed its councils in the United States Senate. To him politics was a game for professionals, not for amateur "carpet knights," and it was a rough game: "Parties are not built by deportment, or by ladies' magazines, or gush."

When Benjamin Harrison won the Presidency in 1888, he ascribed his victory to Providence. Matt Quay knew better. "Providence hadn't a damn thing to do with it," he announced. He wondered if the candidate knew how many men

**The Stalwart Boss of the Republicans**

Handsome Roscoe Conkling, senator from New York, led the Stalwart faction of the Republicans. Blaine, who despised him, described Conkling as a "majestic, supereminent, overpowering, turkey-gobbler strut." In this cartoon Conkling is casting covetous eyes at the Republican presidential nomination for 1880, represented by the eagle. The smaller bird looking doubtfully at the boss is the independent vote. From *Harper's Weekly* (1879).

had approached the gates of the penitentiary to make him President. Harrison soon learned the facts of political life. "When I came into power," he said later, "I found that the party managers had taken it all to themselves. I could not name my own Cabinet. They had sold out every place to pay the election expenses." The machines sustained their position by various techniques: making alliances with business interests and securing campaign contributions and other subsidies, assessing officeholders a share of their salaries, and employing gangs of vote "repeaters" or "floaters" or using other fraudulent methods to carry elections.

## Hayes and the Patronage

Before the end of Rutherford B. Hayes' administration two groups—the Stalwarts, led by Conkling of New York, and the Half-Breeds, captained by James G. Blaine of Maine—were competing for control of the Republican party, and threatening to split it. Only a subtle difference separated the factions. The Stalwarts, consisting of state bosses like Conkling and Oliver P. Morton of Indiana and Zachariah Chandler of Michigan, stood for machine politics and the allocation of political and material spoils to the victor. They were professional operators who believed in politics for its own sake. The Half-Breeds had practically the same concept of the functions of parties, but circumstances—specifically, the fact that the Stalwarts at first were stronger—forced them to adopt a more circumspect and sanctimonious role. They rendered lip service to such issues as civil service and governmental efficiency, although most of them were no more interested in reform than the Stalwarts.

Although Hayes awarded some offices to the machine elements of his party, he consistently held up merit as the primary standard of appointment. His cabinet, headed by William M. Evarts as secretary of state, John Sherman as secretary of the treasury, and Carl Schurz as secretary of the interior, was an exceptionally able one; but four of the members had bolted the party in the Liberal defection of 1872 and one was a Southern Democrat. Hayes' patronage policy horrified the Stalwarts and hardly pleased the Half-Breeds; at the same time, it was sufficiently political to raise doubts among the civil-service reformers. The President yielded up much of his power to influence any faction of his party when he announced early in his administration that he would not be a candidate for reelection. To complete Hayes' handicaps, the Democrats controlled the House when he entered office, and two years later they captured the Senate too.

After settling the Reconstruction issue to his satisfaction, Hayes turned to the problem of governmental reform. Long an advocate of civil service, he instructed his executive deputies that he wished appointments awarded on the basis of merit, that assessments of salaries of employees for political purposes must stop, and that the party activities of officials should be limited. Schurz placed the Interior Department on a merit basis, and Treasury Secretary Sherman and a few other department heads also made some effort to comply with their chief's wishes. Others ignored or evaded them. The strength of the spoils system was so great that

**President and Mrs. Hayes**

This photograph catches the dignity and sincerity that were the hallmark of Hayes' character. His wife was strongly opposed to the drinking of intoxicating liquors and did not permit any to be served at White House functions. Critics dubbed her "Lemonade Lucy." (Library of Congress)

Hayes could not force the executive branch to accept his policy. He had even less luck with Congress. Despite repeated appeals by the President, the legislators refused to appropriate money to renew the civil service commission created under Grant.

Hayes' persistent advocacy of civil service precipitated his biggest fight with Congress. As part of his campaign to reform the spoils-ridden Treasury bureaucracy, he removed from office two prominent officials in the New York custom house, Chester A. Arthur and Alonzo B. Cornell. Both men were leaders in Roscoe Conkling's organization, and the senator interpreted their removal as an attempt to undermine his machine. Striking back with the arrogance of a great state boss, he persuaded the Senate to deny confirmation of the men Hayes had named to replace Arthur and Cornell. Stubbornly the President refused to retreat, and kept on transmitting new appointments until finally the Senate ratified his choices. Hayes was the first President since 1865 to resist successfully the constant attempts of Congress to encroach on executive prerogatives.

## The Martyrdom of Garfield

Fortunately for the faction-rent Republicans, prosperity had returned by the time of the election of 1880. An increased export trade and an upward spurt in industrial and agricultural production signaled the end of the depression and the beginning of another boom period. But the Republican leaders knew that not even prosperity could guarantee victory: they had to patch up their dissensions and settle on a nominee who could unite the party for another contest. Grant, backed by Conkling and the Stalwarts, was again a candidate, while the Half-Breeds were divided between Blaine and Sherman. At the Republican convention Grant led for thirty-five ballots but could not reach a majority. Then the anti-Grant forces united to nominate a "dark horse," James A. Garfield, a veteran member of the House of Representatives from Ohio. As Garfield was known as a Half-Breed, the convention, to conciliate the Stalwarts, gave the second place on the ticket to Chester A. Arthur, the Conkling henchman just dismissed from office by Hayes.

With the ancient and ill Tilden unavailable, the Democrats were without a leader. They acted as though they were also without hope of victory. As their candidate, they selected General Winfield Scott Hancock, who had won some fame as a corps commander in the Union army but was hardly a commanding national figure. Their apparent purpose was to refute the usual Republican charges of Democratic disloyalty in the Civil War. Also, having witnessed the success of the Republicans in running generals, they wanted to try their luck with a Democratic officer against Garfield, who had been a volunteer general. Although the platform called for a revenue tariff, it emphasized the "great fraud" of the election of 1876 as the paramount issue. As usual, the Democrats were harking back to the past instead of looking to the future.

During the bitter campaign, which revolved around such questions as Garfield's complicity in the Crédit Mobilier scandal and alleged errors committed by Hancock in the war, the Democratic candidate was pressed for a statement on the tariff. He replied that it was entirely a "local issue." As a description of how tariff schedules were arrived at in Congress, his phrase was reasonably accurate, but it constituted a virtual repudiation of the platform and removed the tariff as a campaign issue. In November Garfield piled up a decisive electoral majority of 214 to 155. But his popular vote was only about ten thousand more than his rival's: 4,454,000 to 4,444,000. The Republicans also captured both houses of Congress.

Up to the time of his accession to the Presidency, the career of James A. Garfield had been a perfect example of the American success legend. Born in humble Ohio surroundings, in fact, in a log cabin, he worked from boyhood up, once laboring as a mule-driver on the Ohio Canal—"from the tow-path to the White House" was a theme the Republicans emphasized in the 1880 election. He worked his way through college, became a teacher, studied law and was admitted to the bar. In 1863 he was elected to the House of Representatives, where he served with increasing distinction until he became the Republican standard-bearer.

During his brief tenure of office, Garfield gave evidence that he intended to conduct a moderate Half-Breed administration. He appointed Blaine as secretary of state, and as postmaster-general (the cabinet official having the most to do with patronage) Thomas L. James, a civil-service champion. Almost immediately James exposed a scandal in his department—the so-called "star-route" frauds. In many areas of the West mail was carried by stages or riders and assigned to contractors; on the postal list these routes were designated by stars. If a contractor could demonstrate that his costs had increased, his compensation could be raised without re-opening the agreement. Investigation disclosed that collusive contracts had been awarded to certain Republican politicians, who then had secured increased payments for their services. Despite protests from some leading Republicans, Garfield backed up James in his inquiry. In dispensing patronage, Garfield gave the important jobs to Half-Breeds. He provoked a fight with Conkling by naming his own followers to federal positions in New York. When the President appointed a bitter Conkling foe as collector of the port of New York, the senator tried to prevent Senate confirmation. Failing this, he and his colleague, Platt, resigned and asked the New York legislature to reelect them. Their purpose was to awe Garfield into submission, but the legislators, in a fine display of perversity, selected two other men.

While the unseemly quarrel was dragging on, the evils of the spoils system were dramatically brought home to the American people. On July 2, 1881, after only four months in office, President Garfield was in the Washington railroad station, about to leave for a holiday trip, when a man in the crowd fired two pistol shots at him. As Garfield fell, the man with the gun shouted: "I am a Stalwart and Arthur is President now!" The assassin, Charles J. Guiteau, held a grudge because Garfield had refused to give him a government job (though evidently insane, Guiteau was hanged). Actually, Arthur was not yet President; Garfield lingered for nearly three months before dying. At his death, people concerned about the menace of machine politics were doubly grieved. Even some Republicans echoed the sentiment of the man who groaned: "Chet Arthur President of the United States! Good God!"

## Arthur and Reform

For all of his political lifetime Chester A. Arthur had been a devoted, skilled, and open spoilsman. Before the assassination of Garfield, he had gone to Albany to lobby for the reelection of his benefactor and mentor, Conkling. But on becoming President, he pursued an independent course between the Republican factions, affiliating with neither and being dominated by neither, and he worked zealously and with partial success for the cause of reform. Undoubtedly he had been deeply affected by the grisly circumstances that brought him to the Presidency. It may be that realizing he now stood in the spotlight of history, he guided his actions accordingly.

The revelation of the "new" Arthur dismayed most of the party bosses. Although the President reorganized the cabinet, he left the majority of Garfield's appointees in office. He vigorously pushed the prosecution of the star-route Republicans, who managed, however, to escape punishment. He vetoed a huge river and harbors bill on the grounds it was "pork-barrel" legislation, but Congress overrode him. In his first message to Congress he recommended a civil-service law, and he kept prodding the legislators to act. Although the spectacle of the great spoilsman championing reform seemed incongruous, Arthur was undoubtedly sincere, and his course was smart politics. With the public shocked by Garfield's assassination and disgusted by the postal frauds, sentiment for civil service was running high, and some kind of legislation would have been enacted whether Arthur had intervened or not.

Responding to popular as well as presidential pressure, Congress passed in 1883 the first national civil-service measure, the Pendleton Act. By its terms a limited number of federal jobs were to be "classified": applicants for them were to be chosen on the basis of competitive written examinations. The law also forbade assessment of office-holders for political purposes. To administer the act, a bipartisan Civil Service Commission, headed by reformer Dorman B. Eaton, was established. At first only about 14,000 of some 100,000 offices were placed on the classified list. But the act provided that future Presidents might by executive order enlarge the number of positions subject to civil service. Every chief executive thereafter extended the list, primarily to "blanket" his appointees into office and prevent their removal by his successor. By this piecemeal and partisan process, the government finally achieved by the 1940s a system in which the majority of the people working for it were under the merit system.

## Return of the Democrats

The election of 1884, with its absence of issues and its emphasis on the personal qualities of the candidates, epitomized the politics of the era of complacency. Arthur would have accepted the Republican nomination, but his independent course had pleased neither Half-Breeds nor Stalwarts. Ignoring him and other aspirants, the

**Blaine and Gould**

In this bitter Nast cartoon of the campaign of 1884, Jay Gould offers Blaine, with plumes in his hat, a partnership, saying that he thinks Blaine will be more useful than his late colleagues, Jim Fisk and "Boss" Tweed. Blaine is willing, if "let in on the ground floor." From *Harper's Weekly* (1884).

Republican convention nominated its most popular man and most vulnerable candidate, James G. Blaine, known to his adoring admirers as "the plumed knight" but to thousands of other Americans as "Old Mulligan Letters." His selection split the party badly. To the Stalwarts he was anathema; Conkling, asked if he intended to campaign for Blaine, snapped that he did not engage in criminal practice. The independent reform faction, now called the Mugwumps, announced they were prepared to bolt the party and support an honest Democrat. Rising to the bait, the Democrats nominated Grover Cleveland, the reform governor of New York. The platforms of the two parties were almost identical. Both endorsed revision of the tariff without endangering domestic industries, both approved and claimed credit for civil service, and both, taking account of popular rumblings against big business, spoke vaguely about subjecting corporations to some kind of national regulation.

With no real issues between the parties, the election was essentially a struggle for office, and

the campaign developed into a mud-slinging contest involving the personal fitness, or more accurately, unfitness of the candidates. Eagerly the Democrats went to work on the plumed knight's unsavory record, reprinting the Mulligan correspondence and uncovering new damning letters. At torchlit rallies the Democrats chanted:

> Blaine! Blaine! James G. Blaine!
> Continental liar from the state of Maine!

Frantically the Republicans researched Cleveland's brief political career as mayor of Buffalo and governor of New York for evidence of corruption—a politician had to be corrupt, they seemed to assume—but found nothing. They did discover a juicy personal item. As a young man Cleveland had been accused of fathering an illegitimate child, and whether guilty or not, he had agreed to support the infant. He did not specifically deny the imputation when the Republicans brought it into the campaign. Thereafter at their rallies the Republicans roared out:

> Ma! Ma! where's my Pa?
> Going to the White House. Ha! Ha! Ha!

In addition to sex, the canvass featured the bloody shirt, waved vigorously by Blaine; freedom for Ireland from the British rule, held out to the Irish voters by Republican orators; and religion, a last-minute issue that may have decided the election. In the closing days of the campaign a delegation of Protestant ministers called on Blaine in New York City; their spokesman, Dr. Samuel Burchard, in the course of his remarks referred to the Democrats as the party of "Rum, Romanism, and Rebellion." Apparently Blaine, whose mother was a Catholic, did not catch the statement or notice its linking of elements. Soon the Democrats were spreading the news through New York and other Eastern cities that Blaine had countenanced a slander on the Catholic Church, and his denial came too late to counteract the charge. The so-called Burchard incident may have swung New York State to the Democrats, and New York was the pivotal state in what turned out to be an extremely close election. Cleveland had 219 electoral votes to Blaine's 182; the popular vote showed 4,875,000 for Cleveland and 4,852,000 for Blaine, a Democratic plurality of only 23,-000.

Grover Cleveland was the ablest President between Lincoln and Theodore Roosevelt. Short and corpulent, brusque in manner, boldly beardless in a hirsute age, he was far from being an appealing figure. He did possess character, courage, and integrity. In his brief career in prominent offices—he had been elected mayor of Buffalo in 1881 and governor of New York in 1882—he had fought politicians, grafters, pressure groups, and Tammany Hall. He had become famous as the "veto mayor" and the "veto governor," as an official who was not afraid to say "No." This ability to be honestly negative was the most positive feature of his political personality; it was at once his greatest strength and his most distressing weakness as a political

**Grover Cleveland**

Cleveland was the first Democrat to be elected President since the Civil War. Honest, courageous, and stubborn, he was extremely conservative and unable to understand some of the new economic problems emerging in his administration. A bachelor when elected, he married while in the White House. (Library of Congress)

leader. It enabled him to withstand pressure from any quarter, to oppose the spoilsmen, and to uphold high standards of official probity. It also rendered him tragically incapable of understanding the problems of an industrial society or the role of government in a changing economic order.

## Cleveland Finds an Issue

When Cleveland became President, he was absorbed with plans to improve the administrative machinery of the government, to install business standards in its operations, and to purify its processes. Issues such as the currency and the tariff did not greatly interest him, nor was he concerned with the problems of the farmer and the laborer. His knowledge of economics was slender and his economic philosophy almost primitively simple. He was sincerely opposed to a paternalistic and positive government that extended special favors to any group. Let all stand equal, the giant corporation and the worker, he proclaimed, never comprehending that there were vital power-differences between contesting economic interests. He summed up his faith in a veto of an appropriation of $10,000 for drought-stricken farmers. The lesson must never be forgotten, he moralized, that "though the people support the Government, the Government should not support the people."

Although Cleveland was known as a civil-service reformer, in dealing with patronage he had to proceed with due partisan caution. After years of wandering in the political wilderness, the Democrats were hungry for offices, and they expected the President to throw the Republican "rascals" out—immediately and in wholesale lots. Instead, the President compromised in a manner that did not completely satisfy either his own party or his Mugwump followers. He added approximately 12,000 offices to the classified list, but of the jobs not under civil service he removed two-thirds of the incumbents and replaced them with deserving Democrats. Determined to check extravagance and congressional raids on the surplus, Cleveland vetoed a river and harbors bill, and attempted to introduce principles of economy and honesty into the awarding of soldier pensions.

On the pension issue, he stirred up a hornet's

nest. For years real or alleged veterans of the Union army—who could not qualify under the existing general pension laws—had had no difficulty in getting Congress to enact private pension bills for their benefit. Many of the claims were fraudulent but nobody ever examined them. Cleveland actually took the trouble to read them, and, outraged by what he found, vetoed over 200 such measures. When Congress, responding to pressure from the powerful Grand Army of the Republic (GAR), passed a Dependent Pension Bill to grant pensions to all veterans suffering from disabilities, no matter when or how contracted, he killed it with a veto. In reality, Cleveland was sympathetic to the claims of genuine veterans, and the total appropriation for pensions increased during his administration. But his vetoes enabled Republican and GAR orators to remind the voters of the peril of placing a Southern-dominated Democrat in the White House.

On another front of battle against corruption, Cleveland instructed his secretary of the interior to inspect past grants of public lands in the West to railroad, lumber, and cattle interests, and where the lands had been obtained on fraudulent or false ground to institute suits to recover them. Eventually some 81 million acres were restored to the government. Although businessmen bellowed that the President was acting like a radical, he was only being consistently conservative: no special favors to any group.

Cleveland himself precipitated one economic issue into the political arena. Always mildly dubious of the high tariff, he concluded after thorough study that the existing rates were responsible for the annual surplus that tempted Congress to reckless legislation. Once convinced, he acted with sudden and startling vigor. In December 1887 he devoted almost all of his annual message to the lawmakers to discussing the tariff and demanding its downward revision. Although he spoke bitingly of the great fortunes that had been built on protective duties and of the inflated living costs of the poor, he rested his case on immediate and practical considerations: the tariff was bringing in an unneeded surplus and the piling up of this surplus would eventually depress the economy. In a phrase that intrigued the public, he said: "It is a *condition* that confronts us, not a theory." Characteristically, he assured Congress that reductions could be made without endangering the interests of American manufacturers.

Immediately, the Southern and Western Democrats, who had been moving rapidly to a low-tariff position, responded to the President's leadership. They pushed the Mills Bill through the House, incorporating Cleveland's recommendations and providing for moderate reductions. Only four Democrats voted against it, and doubtless some of the Easterners went along in the knowledge that the Republican Senate would kill the measure. In the Senate the Republican leaders, believing that they could sell the tariff to the voters, met the issue head-on. As an alternative to the Mills Bill they enacted a protective measure. Action was deadlocked for the moment, and the tariff was squarely before the people as an issue in the election of 1888.

As the tariff fight swirled to a climax, the Democrats again named Cleveland as their standard-bearer, although some machine bosses and some Easterners, disgusted by his stand on civil service and lower duties, would have preferred another candidate. The platform emphasized the tariff question and pledged support to the President's policy of moderate revision. The Republicans had in protection what they were certain was a winning issue, but they were hard put to find an acceptable and available nominee. They finally decided on Benjamin Harrison of Indiana, who was relatively obscure and formidably respectable, and in their platform endorsed protection for American producers and generous pensions for Union veterans.

The campaign of 1888 was the first since the Civil War that was fought out on a definite issue, the first that involved a question of economic difference between the parties. It was also one of the most corrupt campaigns in American political history. Both parties employed the usual fraudulent methods of the day, but the Republicans, with a campaign fund contributed by apprehensive business interests and amounting to several million dollars, were the worse offenders.

When the votes were counted, it was obvious that the people had not registered a clear decision or authorized a definite mandate. Harrison had an electoral majority of 233 to 168, but Cleveland's popular vote exceeded Harrison's, 5,540,000 to 5,440,000.

## THE FARMERS ORGANIZE

Most farmers had always been strong individualists. But many of them eventually concluded that they could solve their problems—high costs, increasing debts, falling prices, declining status—only by overcoming their traditional individualism. They would have to organize and act in politics as a group.

### The Grangers and the Railroads

The first farm organization to appear after the Civil War was established in boom times as a social association and was turned into an agency of agrarian protest at the onset of the 1873 depression.

On a tour through the South, Oliver H. Kelley, a clerk in the Department of Agriculture at Washington, became impressed with the isolation and drabness of rural life. In 1867 he and other department employees founded the National Grange of the Patrons of Husbandry, to which Kelley devoted years of labor as secretary. Local lodges of the order were called granges, and the organization is commonly known as the Grange. Its announced purposes were social, cultural, and educational. By bringing farm men and women together in groups, it aimed to diffuse knowledge of scientific agriculture, machines, and markets, to furnish a community feeling hitherto absent in rural society, and to keep agriculture in "step with the music of the age." Recognizing that human nature is intrigued by secrecy and ceremony, the founders provided for an elaborate system of initiation and ritual.

At first the Grange grew slowly. It filled an obvious rural need, but farmers were not attracted to it in large numbers while times were good. Then the depression of 1873 struck, and suddenly the farmers saw benefits to be achieved through organization. By 1875 the Grange claimed over 800,000 members and 20,000 local lodges. These appeared in almost every state but were most numerous in the staple-producing sections of the Middle West and the South.

As membership increased, the lodges in the Middle West turned to economic issues. They stressed the necessity of collective action by farmers to eliminate the middleman—through the organization of cooperatives—and the urgency of political action to curb the monopolistic practices of the railroads and warehouses. All over the midlands on Independence Day 1873, the "Farmers' Fourth of July," embittered yeomen assembled to hear Granger orators read "The Farmers' Declaration of Independence." The resolutions proclaimed that the time had come for farmers, "suffering from long continued systems of oppression and abuse, to rouse themselves from an apathetic indifference to their own interests." The declaration also vowed that the farmers would use "all lawful and peaceful means to free [themselves] from the tyranny of monopoly."

The Grangers launched the first major cooperative movement in the United States, though successful collective societies had existed earlier in England and other countries. The Grangers set up cooperative stores, creameries, elevators, warehouses, insurance companies, and factories that turned out machines, stoves, and other items. Some 400 enterprises were in operation at the height of the movement, but eventually most of them failed because of the inexperience of the operators and the opposition of middleman interests. Not all business groups fought the cooperatives; some sought their trade, and one corporation was formed specifically in 1872 to meet the wants of the Grangers, Montgomery Ward and Company, which brought the mail-order business into existence.

In political action the Grangers labored to elect to state legislatures candidates pledged to their program. Usually they operated through the existing Republican and Democratic parties, only occasionally putting up nominees under such party labels as "Antimonopoly" or "Reform." Marshaling their votes in the local lodges, they were able to gain control of the legislatures in most of the Middle Western states. Their purpose, openly and angrily announced, was to subject the railroads to social controls.

Between 1870 and 1874 the legislatures of Illinois, Iowa, Minnesota, and Wisconsin enacted laws to regulate railroads and warehouse and elevator facilities. These "Granger laws" authorized maximum rates for passenger and freight traffic, provided rules and rates for the storing of grain, and prohibited a number of alleged discriminatory practices. They were to be administered and enforced by special state commissions.

The railroads contested the legality of the laws, and eventually fought them from the state courts up to the United States Supreme Court. In 1877 the highest tribunal handed down a decision in the first of the "Granger cases," the case of *Munn* v. *Illinois*, involving the right of a state to fix storage rates for warehouses. Other cases concerned state laws establishing maximum rates for railroads.

Chief Justice Morrison R. Waite spoke for the Court in the Munn case, and his opinion formed the basis for the decisions on the railroad laws. The complainants, the warehouses and railroads, had rested their cause on two points: (1) the laws infringed the power of Congress to regulate interstate commerce; and (2) they violated the due-process clause of the Fourteenth Amendment, namely, that a state could not deprive a "person" of property without due process of law. The plaintiffs were contending not only that a corporation was a person within the meaning of the Fourteenth Amendment, but also that expected income was property and that any regulation reducing income was deprivation of property within the meaning of the amendment. The Court rejected their arguments and validated the Granger laws. It held that a state in the exercise of its police power could regulate private property devoted to public use and affecting the general community; it conceded the right of a state to regulate interstate commerce in the absence of national regulation; and it dismissed "due process" with the observation that it was not intended to restrict the police power.

The Grange soon lost its position as a major force in the agricultural scene. By 1880 its membership had shrunk to 100,000. The collapse of its cooperative experiments and the ineffectiveness of its railroad laws drove some members away. Above all, it was weakened by a return of prosperity in the late seventies. The embattled farmers, who once had shouted for collective action, soon left the fold and resumed their old and familiar individualistic ways.

## The Farmers' Alliances

In the 1880s the prices of the great staples again declined, hard times returned to the South and the West, and the farmers of those regions, more embittered and frustrated than the Grangers, turned to more militant forms of organization. From the Carolinas to the Dakotas a multitude of farm societies bearing a variety of names mushroomed into existence, but by the end of the decade they had been combined into two major organizations: the National Farmers' Alliance, centering in the prairie states west of the Mississippi, and the Farmers' Alliance and Industrial Union, largely restricted to the South and known as the Southern Alliance. Loosely affiliated with the Southern order was a Negro branch, the Colored Farmers' Alliance. Of the two main alliances, the Southern was the more tightly knit and the larger, numbering over a million members.

At their beginning both alliances toyed with the same kind of objectives that had intrigued the Grange: social and educational activities and cooperative enterprises. But almost immediately they shifted their emphasis to politics —and to a program designed to save the farmer by state and national legislation rather than improved business techniques. The Northern leaders decided that farmers could expect nothing from the Democrats or Republicans and would have to create their own political organization. In the elections of 1890 they ran candidates for national and state office under diverse party labels in all the prairie states. The Southern Alliance turned to politics more reluctantly, but by 1890 it too was ready for action, though not in the form of a third party. Fearful that a new party would split the solidity of the one-party South and endanger white supremacy, the Southerners, heeding the counsel of such farm leaders as Benjamin F. Tillman of South Carolina, set their sights on capturing control of the Democratic party from its conservative Bourbon rulers. In 1890 Alliance-backed candidates competed with Bourbon aristocrats in every corner of the former Confederacy.

The farmers startled conservatives and surprised themselves with their success in 1890. The farm forces won partial or complete control of the legislatures in twelve states, eight in the South and four in the West, and elected six governors, three senators, and approximately fifty congressmen. The magnitude of the agrarian sweep was not, however, as great as it seemed. In the South, where the triumph was most complete, the farmers had stuck fast to the Democratic party. Over forty of the farm congressmen were Southern Alliance-endorsed Democrats; the one Southern representative to admit a third-party affiliation was Georgia's Thomas E. Watson.

## The People's Party

After the elections of 1890, the leaders of the Northern Alliance were certain that the time was ripe for the formation of a national farmer-labor party. Some of the Southern leaders—the fiery Watson, consumed with an emotional hatred for monopoly, and Leonidas L. Polk of North Carolina, perhaps the ablest mind in the agrarian movement—were coming to the same conclusion. Reluctantly the Southerners recognized that their local successes would have no weight whatsoever in determining the course of the national Democratic party.

Plans for a third party were laid at meetings in Cincinnati (May 1891) and in St. Louis (February 1892), attended by many representatives of the Northern Alliance, some Southerners, and spokesmen of the fading Knights of Labor. Then in July 1892, 1,300 excited and exultant delegates poured into Omaha, Nebraska, in the heart of the plains country, to proclaim the new party, approve an official set of principles, and nominate candidates for the Presidency and Vice Presidency. By common consent the party already had a name, one first used by the Kansas agrarians—the People's party—from which, by way of Latin, were derived the terms Populist and Populism.

In a spirit of dedicated idealism reminiscent of the antislavery crusade, the delegates at Omaha adopted a platform. To achieve their ends, they were willing to invest government with powers that would horrify business conservatives: "We believe that the power of government—in other words, of the people—should be expanded . . . as rapidly and as far as the good sense of an intelligent people and the teachings of experience shall justify, to the end that oppression, injustice, and poverty shall eventually cease in the land."

The Populist platform demanded national government ownership and operation of the railroad, telephone, and telegraph systems (a significant advance on the state regulation urged by the Grangers); a flexible national currency issued by the government and not by the banks; the free and unlimited coinage of silver; government-operated postal savings banks; a graduated income tax; the subtreasury plan, an arrangement whereby farmers could deposit nonperishable produce in government warehouses and borrow in United States treasury notes up to 80 per cent of the current value of their commodities (thus enabling farmers to withhold crops from sale until the price was right); prohibition of alien land ownership; and reclamation of lands held by railroads and other corporations "in excess of their actual needs." Bidding for the support of labor, the platform also demanded shorter hours for workers and restrictions on immigration, and denounced the employment of private detective agencies as strikebreakers in labor disputes. Other planks called for new political techniques to place government more directly under democratic control: the Australian, or secret, ballot; the popular election of United States senators; the initiative, a device whereby state legislation could be introduced or enacted by the voters; and the referendum, a method whereby the voters could veto actions of state legislatures.

"It is a struggle," cried one Populist orator, "between the robbers and the robbed."

Populism was strong in only three geographic centers: the South, the plains and prairie region (but chiefly Kansas, Nebraska, and North and South Dakota), and the Rocky Mountain states. The Populists evoked little response in the old Granger states of the Middle West. In this previous center of protest, diversified techniques, emphasizing dairying and a corn-hog complex,

# Where Historians Disagree

## The Meaning of Populism

The historical literature on Populism is of comparatively recent origin. The first scholarly study of the movement appeared in 1931, when J. D. Hicks published *The Populist Revolt*. It is still the only general treatment of Populism, and as a full and factual account it remains the standard work. Its viewpoint has, however, in recent years been subjected to question and possible modification.

That viewpoint is summarized in Hicks' statement that Populism represented "the last phase of a long and perhaps a losing struggle—the struggle to save agricultural America from the devouring jaws of industrial America." Hicks wrote at a time when scholars tended to see certain evils in American industrial society and definite virtues in the older agrarian America of the previous century; inherent in his pages was an assumption that the reforms proposed by the Populists were good. He seemed to lament the failure of the Populist dream, and yet he conceded that parts of the dream eventually became reality when, in later years, many Populist proposals were enacted into law.

This favorable view of the Populists prevailed for over twenty years. Then, in 1955, Richard Hofstadter put forth a different thesis and unleashed an attack on the Populists in *The Age of Reform*. Hofstadter represented a new school of history, one having its roots in an urban society and having certain doubts about the older rural order. He argued that important aspects of Populism had been overlooked by Hicks and previous writers. Thus Populism had a soft side. It was essentially romantic and did not face up to the hard problems of a modern society. It proposed simple solutions and favored returning to an older and simpler America. Moreover, it had a dark side. Many Populists denounced international bankers, some of whom were Jewish, and therefore the movement displayed anti-Semitic tendencies. Other writers expanded this charge to say that Populism possibly reflected a fascist psychology.

The Hofstadter view caught on with many historians. But almost immediately it was challenged vigorously. In *The Populist Response to Industrialism* (1962), Norman Pollack argued that the Populists had a sophisticated and mature view of society, that they accepted the modern world and proposed sensible ways of dealing with its problems. And W. T. K. Nugent, in *The Tolerant Populists* (1963), refuted the charge of religious or ethnic bias.

At present there is no one or accepted view of the meaning of Populism. It is still a subject to excite research and thought, for both historians and students.

**"Sockless" Jerry Simpson**

The Kansas Populist, the "Socrates of the prairies," is here shown riding a bicycle. Note that the rear tire seems to be flat and that Simpson seems to be wearing socks. (Brown Brothers)

had brought a new prosperity and induced a new conservatism. Even in the South the hold of Populism was tenuous and temporary. Populist leaders, seeking to unite poor white and black people in politics, encountered the unyielding barriers of race. They could not, except for short periods and in a few states, persuade the white masses that class was paramount to color, and they could not overcome the traditional white loyalty to the Democratic party.

The Populists also failed to unite under their standard the forces of urban protest. Despite the brave platform talk about the common interests of rural and city workers, the Populists had no real interest in effecting such a combination. In any event, no realistic basis for an alliance between Populist farmers and urban dissenters existed. The Knights of Labor endorsed the new party, but the Knights were a dying organization.

Hardly any of the party leaders were dirt farmers. The great majority were of the rural middle class; they were professional men, editors and lawyers, or professional politicians and agitators. Only a handful had held office or exercised the responsibility of power. James B. Weaver, the party's presidential nominee in

1892, had run the political gamut. He had begun as a Democrat and deserted that party because it was controlled by the slavocracy, had joined the Republicans and left them because they were dominated by the business plutocracy, and had then become successively a Greenbacker and a Populist. Despite his seemingly erratic course, Weaver was a man of balance and ability and a fine sense of justice.

Many Populist leaders gave an impression of personal failure, of brilliant instability, of brooding communion with mystic forces. The matchless orator, Ignatius Donnelly of Minnesota, wrote one book locating the lost isle of Atlantis, another proving that Bacon wrote Shakespeare's plays, and a novel purporting to describe a Populist utopia. Georgia's Tom Watson, author of biographies of Jefferson and Napoleon (he referred curiously to the latter as a "great Democratic despot"), once championed political union across racial lines but ended his career baiting Negroes and Jews. Jerry Simpson of Kansas ridiculed a rival candidate for wearing silk socks and won the undying title of "Sockless Jerry, the Socrates of the prairies."

Despite the weaknesses of the People's party, its leaders and adherents looked forward enthusiastically to the election of 1892.

## A NEGATIVE RESPONSE

At first the regular politicians gave a rather negative response to the demands of the organizing farmers. Although, yielding to pressure, Congress provided for the federal regulation of railroads, for the time being the government was given little real power to control rates. Then Congress passed an act to prohibit monopolies, but the government made no more than a halfhearted effort to enforce this law. And when Congress got around to acting on the tariff—that "mother of trusts"—it finally revised the rates, but it revised them in more an upward than a downward direction.

### Regulating the Railroads

After the Supreme Court had upheld the Granger laws—by which some of the states were attempting to regulate railroad rates—the railroad companies continued to test the validity of these laws in the courts. Eventually the railroads won out. The undoing of the statutes came after new justices friendly to an expanded notion of property rights and willing to strike down state powers ascended to the Supreme Court.

The first step came in 1886 in the so-called Wabash case (*Wabash, St. Louis, and Pacific Railway Co.* v. *Illinois*). Involved was a statute prohibiting higher rates for a "short haul" than a "long haul" between points in Illinois and New York City. The Court held that the statute attempted to regulate interstate commerce and infringed on the exclusive power of Congress. Interstate rates were thus removed from state control, but within its own limits a state could still regulate railroads if the regulations did not directly affect interstate commerce. Later the roads eliminated even this regulatory power of the states by persuading the Court to accept the due-process clause as a "substantive" restriction on state authority. That is, due process, previously conceived of as guaranteeing the accused certain procedural rights, came to be defined as a limitation on the power of states to regulate private property or vested rights—with the judiciary acting as the guardian of property and reviewing the acts of legislatures. The Court arrived at this position gradually and with some indirection. It affirmed it in essence, although not explicitly, in *Chicago, Milwaukee and St. Paul Railroad* v. *Minnesota* (1890) and thereafter in starkly specific terms. Constant judicial review of state decrees meant, of course, that state regulation had become a mockery.

The only solution to the problem was national regulation. Since the 1870s demands had been voiced in and out of Congress for some kind of supervisory legislation, and revelations of such railroad practices as pooling, rebates, and other discriminatory devices stirred public support for action. Even some railway operators, alarmed by the fierce competition in their industry, were willing to accept regulation. Sentiment became so strong that Congress was finally forced to act. In 1887 it passed the Interstate Commerce Act, a measure described by its sponsor, Senator Shelby M. Cullom, as "conservative legislation."

The Interstate Commerce Act prohibited rebates, pools, long-short haul discriminations, and drawbacks. It required railroads to publish their rate schedules and file them with the government. It provided that all charges in interstate rail transportation should be "reasonable and just," but failed to furnish a standard or method to determine the justness of a rate. To administer the act, a five-man agency, the Interstate Commerce Commission was created, with powers to hear complaints from shippers, examine witnesses, and inquire into the books and accounts of railroads. The law did not clearly authorize the commission to fix rates. After investigating a complaint, the commission could issue a cease-and-desist order to a carrier to lower its charges. If the road refused, the commission had to take its case to the courts and justify its decree, a cumbersome procedure that militated against effective regulation.

For almost twenty years after its passage, the Interstate Commerce Act was without practical effect; it did not accomplish widespread rate reduction or eliminate discrimination. No wonder an attorney general of the United States advised a railroad president not to ask for repeal of the act: "It satisfies the popular clamor for government supervision of the railroads at the same time that that supervision is almost entirely nominal."

## Disposing of the Trusts

Benjamin Harrison, the victor in the close and corrupt election of 1888, assumed the Presidency the following year in the nation's centennial inauguration. Just forty-eight years before, his grandfather, William Henry Harrison, had entered the same office and died almost immediately, leaving no trace of his influence on the Presidency. Benjamin Harrison served out his term, but he left behind a record of negative accomplishment. Intelligent and honest, he was colorless in personality, cold in manner, and singularly aloof—from people, from the new currents of social change, and from the more sordid realities of politics. In White House annals his administration is notable for the wiring of the executive mansion for electricity.

Harrison's cabinet was, like himself, competent but drab. Secretary of State Blaine was the only member who rose above the level of average ability. Though known as a moderate civil-service supporter, Harrison extended the classified list but slightly. He permitted his Postmaster General, John Wanamaker, a hefty contributor to his campaign fund, to sweep 30,000 postmasters out of office in a year. One of his worst appointments was that of "Corporal" James Tanner as commissioner of pensions. While his actions wrung from some people the prayer, "God help the surplus," Tanner replaced Cleveland's policy of careful examination of pension claims with a reckless generosity that delighted politicians and veterans alike.

Harrison exerted little effort to influence legislation. With slender majorities in both houses, the Republicans could carry through a program only by submitting to rigid leadership and acting as a disciplined unit. The leadership came from Maine's Thomas B. Reed, Speaker of the House and a master of parliamentary law and savage wit. Some fruits of his control were a Dependent Pensions Act that almost doubled the number of pensioners and even stunned the GAR, and a flood of appropriations bills for internal improvements, subsidies to steamship lines, and naval expansion.

Public opinion forced the Reed Congress to consider legislation affecting broad areas of the economy, and in 1890 important measures dealing with big business and the tariff were enacted. Some fifteen Western and Southern states had adopted laws prohibiting combinations that restrained competition. But corporations found it easy to escape limitations by incorporating in states that offered special privileges (New Jersey and Delaware were notorious examples). Acceptance by the Supreme Court of the argument that a corporation was a "person" before the law and entitled to the protection of the due-process clause of the Fourteenth Amendment in *Santa Clara County v. Southern Pacific Railroad* (1886) meant that any form of state control was subject to judicial negation. If antitrust legislation was to be effective, it would obviously have to come from the national government. In 1888 both parties promised to curb monopolies.

With little debate and by almost unanimous votes in both houses of Congress, the Sherman Antitrust Act became law in July 1890. Its pro-visions and phraseology were determined by the fact that the only basis for national action against trust derived from the power of Congress to regulate interstate commerce. The heart of the measure was in the first two sections: (1) "Every contract, combination in the form of trust or otherwise, or conspiracy, in restraint of trade or commerce among the several States, or with foreign nations, is hereby declared to be illegal"; (2) "Every person who shall monopolize, or attempt to monopolize . . . any part of the trade or commerce among the several States, or with foreign nations, shall be deemed guilty of a misdemeanor. . . ."

Even though the law on paper prohibited all combinations "in restraint of trade," Congress in passing it was making no very serious effort to break up monopolies. As one senator explained, his colleagues merely wanted to get up "some bill headed 'A bill to Punish Trusts' with which to go to the country" and get themselves reelected. Congress was making a gesture to appease popular discontent without changing the realities of contemporary economic life. The antitrust people now had their law, and business continued to have its trusts.

For over a decade after its passage there was little attempt to enforce the Sherman Act. Before 1901 the Justice Department instituted only fourteen suits under the law against business combinations, and failed to obtain convictions in almost every one. The courts, uniformly hostile to the law, proceeded to emasculate it. The crowning decision came in *United States* v. *E. C. Knight Co.* (1895), a case in which the government charged that the defendants controlled 98 per cent of the manufacture of refined sugar in the country. Chief Justice Melville W. Fuller, speaking for the Supreme Court, threw out the government's case with a curious distinction between manufacturing and commerce. He admitted that the present combination was a trust to monopolize the refining of sugar but denied that it was therefore illegal: the trust was not in interstate commerce but in manufacturing. The Knight decision created a "twilight zone" between state and national powers, an area of economic life outside the authority of any agency of government.

## Revising the Tariff

Having made an effort to dispose of the trust question, the Republicans turned with anticipation to the subject that most interested them and their business backers and that had been the paramount issue in the campaign of 1888, the tariff. William McKinley of Ohio, a rising party luminary and chairman of the House Ways and Means Committee, and Senator Nelson W. Aldrich of Rhode Island framed, with the assistance of the tariff lobbies, the highest protective measure yet offered to a Congress. It became law in October 1890 as the McKinley Tariff Act.

Seldom in American political history has a party in power suffered such a stunning reverse as befell the Republicans in the mid-term elections of 1890. Their majority in the Senate was slashed to 8, and in the House they could count only 88 seats to 235 for the Democrats and 9 for the Alliance-Populists. Popular revulsion against the McKinley duties, pictured by the Democrats as raising the living costs of the masses, was an undoubted factor in causing the Republican debacle; McKinley himself was among those going down to defeat. But the elections registered more than condemnation of a tariff. They reflected the deep anxieties of millions of Americans who were beginning to question the fundamental justice of the economic order.

In the presidential election of 1892 Benjamin Harrison was again the Republican nominee and Grover Cleveland the Democratic. Once more the platforms of the two parties were almost identical except for the tariff, with the Republicans upholding protection and the Democrats pledging reduction. Both parties in their official pronouncements ignored the pulsing currents of unrest in the country. Only the Populists, with James B. Weaver as their candidate, advocated economic reform. Cleveland amassed 277 electoral and 5,557,000 popular votes as compared to Harrison's 145 and 5,176,000 votes. For the first time since the Civil War the Democrats won a majority of both houses of Congress. Weaver polled 22 electoral votes from six mountain and plains states and over a million popular votes and the Populists elected at least a dozen senators and congressmen.

Despite Cleveland's negative record, a large proportion of the people who had voted for him expected him to devise some original approach to the new problems troubling America. His inaugural address rudely disillusioned them, as he reaffirmed his devotion to laissez faire: "The lessons of paternalism ought to be unlearned and the better lesson taught that while the people should . . . support their Government its functions do not include the support of the people."

Cleveland called on his party to redeem its pledge to lower the existing tariff rates. In the House William L. Wilson of West Virginia introduced a bill in 1894 designed to accomplish moderate downward revision and yet provide adequate protection for domestic producers. To get Populist support and to compensate for an anticipated loss in revenues, the bill provided for an income tax with a 2-per-cent levy on incomes over $4,000. When the Wilson bill reached the Senate, the customary lobbying and log-rolling began. Eastern Democrats, directed by Maryland's Arthur P. Gorman and abetted by Republicans, added 634 amendments, most of them altering Wilson's duties upward. Strong pressure from the Democratic leadership induced the House to accept the Senate version. Cleveland denounced it as a violation of the party's platform but allowed it to become law without his signature.

The Wilson-Gorman Tariff reduced the general scale of duties only 10 per cent, and its duties on raw and refined sugar and other items afforded ample protection to the sugar trust and every other trust. Far from the kind of tariff the Democrats had promised the country, the act seemed to confirm the Populist contention that tariff-making was a sham battle between the major parties.

Even the one crust thrown to the Populists, the income tax, was shortly snatched away by the courts. In a case testing the right of the government to levy an income tax (*Pollock* v. *The Farmer's Loan and Trust Co.*, 1895), the Supreme Court declared in a 5-to-4 decision that a tax on incomes was a "direct" tax and hence had to be apportioned among the states according to population. Since an income tax, by its

## The Supreme Court Denounces Protest

When the Pollock case was argued before the Court, the lawyers appearing against the income tax passionately appealed to the Court to preserve the sanctity of property and halt the onward march of radicalism. Some of the justices responded with opinions more sociological than legal. One wrote:

*The present assault upon capital is but the beginning. It will be but the stepping stone to others, larger and more sweeping, till our political contests will become a war of the poor against the rich; a war constantly growing in intensity and bitterness.*

very nature, would be effective only if applied on a basis of individual wealth and would have no reality if reckoned on the distribution of population, the Court had made it impossible to levy such a tax.

## "BATTLE OF THE STANDARDS"

The Populists had done fairly well in 1892, and they were encouraged by the events that soon followed—the depression, the Pullman strike, and the growing bitterness of workers as well as farmers. In the state and local elections of 1894 the Populists added to their earlier victories. Then they looked hopefully toward the election of 1896.

But that year one of the major parties, the Democratic, adopted the most appealing of the Populist programs, free silver. Even so, the Democrats went down in defeat, and the People's party soon disappeared.

This short-lived party nevertheless left its mark on American history. One or both of the major parties sooner or later adopted other things, besides free silver, that the Populists had stood for. Some of these, in one form or another,

became accepted features of American government—notably the income tax, a flexible (managed) currency, crop loans to farmers, the secret ballot, and the direct election of United States senators.

## The Panic of 1893

The Cleveland administration was hardly settled in office when the Panic of 1893 struck the country. There followed one of the most severe depressions up to that time. Its causes were various and complicated. The eighties had been a typical boom period, featuring overexpansion and overinvestment in railroads and industrial combinations. Depressed prices in agriculture since 1887 had weakened the purchasing power of a substantial section of the population. Depression conditions that had begun earlier in Europe were resulting in a loss of American markets abroad, a decline in the export trade, and a withdrawal by foreign investors of gold invested in this country. Whatever the causes of the depression, over 8,000 business concerns failed in a period of six months, 156 railroads went into receivership, and 400 banks suspended operations. Agricultural prices tumbled to new lows, and perhaps as many as a million workers, 20 per cent of the laboring force, were thrown out of jobs.

Jacob S. Coxey, a Massillon, Ohio, businessman and Populist, proposed two lines of action: (1) Congress should issue $500 million in legal-tender notes to be used in the construction of roads throughout the country; and (2) local governments wishing to undertake public improvements should be authorized to issue noninterest-bearing bonds which could be exchanged at the federal Treasury for legal-tender notes. Coxey's ideas were hooted at in conservative circles. (But the notion of creating jobs by a building program would appeal to a later generation afflicted by depression. At the onset of the next great depression in the 1930s the government would inaugurate a public works program. Coxey, who lived until 1951, thus saw his scheme finally put into effect.)

Seeking to dramatize his program, Coxey organized a march of the unemployed on Washington to present a petition for work relief to Congress. Only 500 of "Coxey's army" were able to make their way to Washington, and they were barred from the Capitol by armed police. Coxey was arrested on a trumped-up charge of walking on the grass, and the marchers were herded into camps because their presence supposedly endangered public health.

## The Silver Question

The financial panic deranged the government's monetary system, and in the minds of people like Cleveland the silver policy became the primary cause of the depression. This money question had a long history.

Since the beginning of the republic the country had been on a bimetallic standard: the government purchased and coined all the gold and silver offered to it for sale. At first the relative value of the two metals had been set by commercial demand for them, but eventually the government fixed a legal ratio. Back in Andrew Jackson's period the ratio had been placed at sixteen to one, meaning that the silver dollar had sixteen times as much silver as the gold dollar did gold. For sound economic reasons, hardly any silver dollars were coined. Because of the relative scarcity of silver bullion, the price of gold in the open market was almost never sixteen times the price of silver, so that what silver was mined was sold for commercial purposes. Nobody objected when in 1873 Congress enacted a measure that, while keeping existing silver money in circulation, removed the silver dollar from the coinage list. Soon the inflationists, charging a banker conspiracy, would be calling this act the "Crime of '73."

Almost immediately there occurred a drastic change in the supply of silver. The discovery of huge new deposits of the metal in the Far West, notably in Nevada, increased the amount in the domestic market; at the same time, several European countries went on the gold standard, melting their silver coins and swelling the world supply. The inevitable result was that the price of silver plunged downward and fell far below the legal ratio. Silver-mine owners, pinched by the dropping price, joined the discontented farmers in demanding that the government return to the bimetallic system, that it purchase all the silver brought to the mint—"the free and unlimited coinage of silver."

In 1878 the inflationists, a coalition of Democrats and Republicans from the Middle West, South, and Far West, attempted to pass a free-silver measure through Congress. They were forced, however, to accept a compromise, the Bland-Allison Act, which provided that each month the government must purchase not less than $2 million and not more than $4 million worth of silver and convert it into dollars at the ratio of 16 to 1. The inflation forces had won only a partial victory.

Later, in 1890, the Sherman Silver Purchase Act directed the Treasury to buy 4.5 million ounces of silver each month, an amount esti-

### The Currency Issue

**The Republican Platform:**
The Republican party is unreservedly for sound money. It caused the enactment of a law providing for the redemption [resumption] of specie payments in 1879. Since then every dollar has been as good as gold. We are unalterably opposed to every measure calculated to debase our currency or impair the credit of our country. We are therefore opposed to the free coinage of silver, except by international agreement with the leading commercial nations of the earth, which agreement we pledge ourselves to promote, and until such agreement can be obtained the existing gold standard must be maintained.

**The Democratic Platform:**
We demand the free and unlimited coinage of both silver and gold at the present legal ratio of 16 to 1 without waiting for the aid or consent of any other nation. We demand that the standard silver dollar shall be a full legal tender, equally with gold, for all debts, public and private, and we favor such legislation as will prevent for the future the demonetization of any kind of legal-tender money by private contract.

mated to be the maximum domestic production, and to pay for the purchased bullion in treasury notes. The purchased silver was not to be coined. The amount of money in circulation did not increase materially, and the price of silver continued to drop. Creditors and conservatives still argued for the adoption of a single metallic standard; debtors and inflationists still agitated for the unlimited coinage of silver at the rate of 16 to 1.

The Populists at first did not emphasize silver. But as the party developed strength, the money question came to overshadow all other issues. Currency reform was already a popular issue with debtor farmers, who with some reason believed that inflation would ameliorate their ills. Besides, the Populists desperately needed money to finance their campaigns, and the only source of help was the silver-mine owners who insisted on an elevation of the money plank and the subordination of other proposals.

The influence of silver on the thinking of Populists, agrarian Democrats, and farmers was graphically illustrated by the enormous popularity of a small and not particularly profound book, *Coin's Financial School*, written by William H. Harvey and published in 1894. "Professor Coin" ran a school, an imaginary institution specializing in finance, and the book reproduced his lectures and his dialogues with his students. The professor clearly indicated the marvelous restorative qualities of free silver: "It means the reopening of closed factories, the relighting of fires in darkened furnaces; it means hope instead of despair; comfort in place of suffering; life instead of death."

Ever since the Resumption Act of 1875 the Treasury had aimed to maintain a minimum gold reserve of $100 million to redeem its paper and silver dollars. During the prosperous eighties the reserve increased, and it reached the figure of $190 million by 1890. But in the last two years of the Harrison administration it fell off sharply. The prohibitive duties of the McKinley Tariff reduced imports and hence revenue; the pension and internal improvements appropriations ate up the surplus; and the Sherman Silver Purchase Act forced the government to buy increased amounts of silver and issue new treasury notes that the Treasury insisted on redeeming in gold. Holders of greenbacks and silver certificates, jittery at rumors the government might be swept off the gold standard, demanded gold, and when Cleveland assumed office in 1893, the reserve had shrunk to a little over $100 million.

The panic intensified the rush for gold, and soon the reserve sank below the minimum deemed necessary to sustain the gold standard. Cleveland had always disliked the Sherman Silver Purchase Act, and now he was convinced that it was the chief factor draining gold from the Treasury and that, if allowed to stand, it would force the country off the gold standard and impair the government's financial honor. In one of his rare moods of leadership, the President summoned Congress into special session and demanded the repeal of the Sherman Act. He worked his will, but only by swinging the patronage lash hard on recalcitrant Democrats and enlisting the support of Eastern Republicans. Western and Southern Democrats fought repeal to the last, and in defeat were incredibly bitter. A historic party split was in the making.

The President had his victory, but the financial crisis deepened. In 1895, Cleveland approached the big New York bankers for help. A banking syndicate headed by J. P. Morgan agreed to take up a $65 million bond issue and to use the influence of the financial community to check the flow of gold to Europe. As a result, public faith that the government would maintain the gold standard was strengthened. The stampede to redeem notes eased. To agrarian Democrats and Populists, however, it seemed that Cleveland had sold out to Wall Street and concluded a crooked deal with the money lenders. Actually, there had been no deal and no corruption, though the bankers undoubtedly turned an excessive profit.

The Cleveland administration ended amidst flaming portents of social unrest. The Democratic party was bitterly divided. The President's gold policy had aligned the Southern and Western Democrats in a solid phalanx against him and his Eastern followers.

## "A Cross of Gold"

As the election of 1896 approached, Republicans were confident of victory.

Marcus A. Hanna, boss of the Ohio machine

**The Cross of Gold**

This Republican cartoon illustrates the deep bitterness that Bryan aroused in conservative people. It depicts him as an enemy of religion, because he had used the figure of the cross in his speech at the Democratic convention. (Culver)

and soon to be national boss of the party, was a wealthy industrialist who aspired to be a President-maker. He represented a new type in politics, the businessman who held office and actively manipulated parties instead of remaining in the background and paying out money for services rendered. He had picked out his man and had been grooming him carefully since 1890. The man was William McKinley, governor of Ohio, who as a congressman had been the author of the tariff act of 1890. Hanna's support of McKinley included providing him with generous campaign contributions, bailing him out of a threatened bankruptcy, and advertising his availability to Republican bosses in other states.

By the time the convention met, Hanna had lined up enough Middle Western and Southern delegations to nominate McKinley. Everywhere and on every occasion he presented his candidate as "Bill McKinley, the advance agent of prosperity" and the champion of protection for American producers.

The platform as finally framed endorsed the protective tariff, ignored completely such ques-

tions as the income tax, railroad and trust abuses, and labor injunctions, and opposed the free coinage of silver except by international agreement with the leading commercial nations. As other countries, and particularly Great Britain, were unlikely to abandon the gold standard, the Republicans were supporting gold. Thirty-four delegates from the mountain and plains states walked out when the currency plank was adopted. Their obvious destination was the Democratic party.

The Democrats met amid scenes of drama seldom equaled in American politics. The Southern and Western delegates came to the convention determined to seize control of the party from the Easterners. Alarmed by the rise of Populist strength in their sections, they intended to write free silver and other planks of the third party into the platform and to nominate a silver candidate.

The resolutions committee presented to the convention two reports. The majority platform demanded tariff reduction, endorsed the principle of the income tax, denounced the issue of currency notes by the national banks, condemned the use of injunctions in industrial disputes, pledged a "stricter control" of trusts and railroads, and—this was the issue that headlined the platform—called for free silver: "We demand the free and unlimited coinage of both silver and gold at the present legal ratio of 16 to 1, without waiting for the aid or consent of any other nation." The minority resolution opposed the free coinage of silver except by international agreement, a stand identical to that of the Republicans.

Six speakers debated the resolution, three for gold and three for silver. The defenders of gold had the better of the oratorical tournament—up to the final address. Then from the Nebraska delegation a strikingly handsome young man walked to the platform to close the debate. He was William Jennings Bryan, thirty-six years of age. His political experience was limited to two terms in the House of Representatives, but he was widely known in the plains country as a magnetic orator, and he eagerly hoped for the presidential nomination. Through the farthest reaches of the vast hall now rang his magnificent organ-like voice.

### The Orator of the Silver Crusade

America has produced many orators who could sway crowds with the magic of their voices, but it is generally agreed that in power and persuasiveness William Jennings Bryan was without an equal. This picture shows him at a later date than 1896. Although no longer the Boy Orator of the silver campaign, he was still a young man, in the political sense, and at the height of his career. (Brown Brothers)

He ended with a peroration that brought the delegates and the spectators to their feet in a frenzied tumult of passion and that was declaimed by later generations of schoolboys all over rural America: "If they dare to come out in the open and defend the gold standard as a good thing, we will fight them to the uttermost. Having behind us the producing masses of this nation and the world, supported by the commercial interests, the laboring interests and the toilers everywhere, we will answer their demand for a gold standard by saying to them: 'You shall not press down upon the brow of labor this crown of thorns; you shall not crucify mankind upon a cross of gold.' "

The majority platform was adopted. The agrarians had found their leader, and the following day Bryan was nominated on the fifth ballot. It is doubtful if he understood the technical implications of the money problem that he discussed so eloquently before the convention. It is even more dubious if he realized the full import of the protest movement or the Populist program. He seized on one Populist plank, free silver, the most superficial of the various protest proposals, and erected it into a personal and political obsession.

One Republican (Joseph Foraker), when asked if he thought Bryan's title, the Boy Orator of the Platte, was an accurate phrase, replied that it was, because the Platte River was six inches deep and six miles wide at the mouth. More descriptive was another designation applied to Bryan: the Great Commoner. Born in Illinois of typical middle-class stock, he had attended a small sectarian college, had practiced law with only average success, and then, repeating a normal American pattern, had moved to Nebraska, a frontier area, to try his fortunes. Almost completely he represented the feelings and emotions of rural, middle-class America.

The choice of Bryan and the nature of the Democratic platform placed the Populists in a cruel quandary. They had expected both of the major parties to adopt conservative programs and nominate conservative candidates, leaving the Populists to represent the growing forces of protest. But now the Democrats had stolen much of the Populists' thunder. The Populists faced the choice of naming their own candidate and splitting the protest vote, or endorsing Bryan and losing their identity as a party. When the party assembled, the convention voted to approve Bryan but nominated its own vice-presidential candidate, Tom Watson, whom the Democrats were expected to adopt but whom they ignored.

## Bryan Is Beaten

There has never been another campaign quite like the one of 1896. It had unequaled drama, intense excitement, a clean-cut issue, and a David and Goliath theme: the boy orator Bryan contending against the powerful boss Hanna. The boss had the great advantage of ample funds to spend on organization. The business and financial community, frightened beyond reason at the prospect of Bryan's sitting in the White House and taking advice from John P. Altgeld and Ignatius Donnelly, pressed contributions upon Hanna. Just how much money

Hanna had to dispense has been disputed, but the lowest estimate is $3.5 million and the highest is $7 million. The Democrats, by contrast, reported expenditures of only $300,000, a sum only slightly larger than the contribution of one firm, Standard Oil, to the Republican war chest. With his almost inexhaustible resources, Hanna organized the most lavish propaganda machine yet to operate in American politics.

Shrewdly, Hanna kept McKinley off the hustings, knowing better than to pit his solemn candidate against the matchless Bryan. From his home at Canton, Ohio, McKinley conducted a dignified "front-porch" campaign. To Canton came pilgrimages of the Republican faithful, organized and paid for by Hanna, to offer tribute to the standard-bearer. They came every day but McKinley always had a speech ready for them, and always he stressed one theme: the Republican party was the only agency that could bring prosperity to the country.

No such decorous restraint marked the campaigning of the young and vital Bryan. Joyously bearing the brunt of the battle for his party, he inaugurated techniques never before witnessed in American political contests. Previous candidates had addressed audiences in campaigns

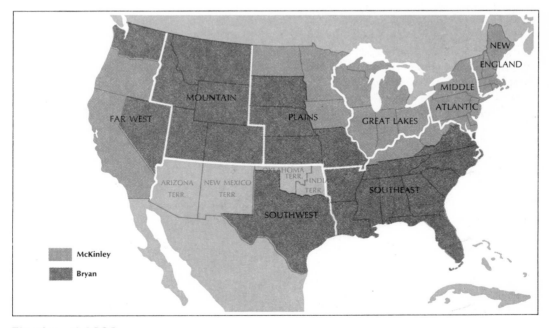

Election of 1896

and had even toured the country to speak at a few selected points. But Bryan was the first to stump systematically every section, to appear in villages and hamlets, the first, really, to say frankly to the voters that he wanted to be President. He traveled 18,000 miles, speaking several times a day, and addressed an estimated 5 million people.

As Bryan's campaign mounted in intensity, cold fear gripped the East. Employers told their workers not to report for work in case of a Democratic victory: industry would have to close down in anticipation of being taken over by the government. Some employers threatened to dismiss workers who voted for Bryan. The banks let it be known that farmers supporting the Democratic candidate probably would have their mortgages foreclosed or at least not renewed.

Everything broke right for the Republicans in the closing weeks of the election. Crop failures abroad brought an increased demand for American products, and on the eve of the election the price of wheat almost doubled.

On election day, McKinley polled 271 electoral votes to Bryan's 176. The popular vote was 7,105,000 to 6,503,000. Bryan won the Confederate South plus Missouri, swept the plains and mountain states with the exception of North Dakota, but lost California and Oregon on the Pacific coast. In short, he carried only the mining regions and the areas where staple farming was predominant and agricultural prices were lowest. He went down to defeat in all the Granger states in the Middle West. The Democratic program, like that of the Populists, had been designed to serve the needs of one segment of one class, the most depressed fraction of agriculture, and this was too narrow an appeal to win a national election.

## McKinley and Prosperity

William McKinley, a shrewd political operator, was the last of a long list of officer veterans of the Union army (beginning with Grant) to sit in the White House. Friendly, kindly, and lovable, he was inclined to defer to stronger characters like Hanna and to act in harmony with his party's leaders. He and they realized the dangers inherent in the currency issue. Silver had

many adherents, as evidenced by Bryan's huge popular vote, and the Republican party numbered many silverites in its Western wing. Impulsive action might divide the party in its hour of victory.

Postponing action on the money problem until a more propitious time, the administration turned to an issue on which Republicans were agreed, the necessity for higher tariff rates. Immediately after assuming office, McKinley summoned Congress into special session to consider tariff revision. With record brevity the Republican majority whipped into shape and passed the Dingley Tariff, raising the duties to an average of 57 per cent, the highest in history.

On the currency question the administration proceeded in accordance with the party's platform pronouncement that bimetallism could not be established except by international action. McKinley sent a commission to Europe to explore the possibility of a silver agreement with Great Britain and France. As he and everyone else anticipated, Britain refused to abandon her gold standard, thus effectively ending any hopes for international bimetallism. The administration could now argue that if the United States embarked on a silver program alone it would be economically isolated from the rest of the world, and the argument was hard to refute. Believing that their position was unassailable, the Republicans finally moved to enact currency legislation. The Currency, or Gold Standard, Act of 1900 legalized the gold standard and enlarged the redemption fund, which was to be maintained as a separate and special charge to protect the supply of gold from depletion.

And so the "battle of the standards" ended in victory for the forces of conservatism. Economic developments seemed to prove that the conservatives had been right in the struggle. In 1898 prosperity returned to America. Foreign crop failures enlarged the farmer's market and sent farm prices surging upwards. At the same time business entered another cycle of booming expansion. Prosperity and gold had come hand in hand—the lesson seemed obvious.

But it was not quite that simple. Bryan and the silverites were essentially right in demanding currency inflation. In the quarter century before 1900 the countries of Western civilization had experienced a spectacular augmentation of productive facilities and population. Yet the supply of money had not kept pace with economic progress, because the supply was tied to gold and the amount of gold remained practically constant. A committee of the British House of Lords, hardly a radical agency, reported after a careful investigation that the world's economy required a larger money supply.

It so happened that the supply was vastly increased soon after the Republicans took over the government in 1897. A new technique for extracting gold from low-content ores, the cyanide process, made it possible to work mines previ-

ously considered marginal or unprofitable. At the same time huge new gold deposits were discovered in Alaska, South Africa, and Australia. In 1898 two and a half times as much gold was produced as in 1890, and the currency supply soon was inflated far beyond anything proposed by Bryan. The price level, which had been declining since 1865, started on an upward swing.

With McKinley, then, there came a tariff increase, the gold standard, and prosperity. There also came a new departure in foreign policy, as the nation entered upon the path of overseas imperialism and took its place among the "great powers" of the world.

# Selected Readings

**Overviews** W. A. White, *Masks in a Pageant* (1928); Matthew Josephson, *The Politicos, 1865–1896*° (1938); D. J. Rothman, *Politics and Power: The United States Senate, 1869–1901*° (1966).

**Republican Politics** Harry Barnard, *Rutherford B. Hayes and His America* (1954); R. G. Caldwell, *James A. Garfield, Party Chieftain* (1931); D. S. Muzzey, *James G. Blaine, a Political Idol of Other Days* (1934); D. B. Chidsey, *The Gentleman from New York: A Life of Roscoe Conkling* (1935); G. F. Howe, *Chester A. Arthur* (1934); A. B. Sageser, *The First Two Decades of the Pendleton Act* (1935); H. J. Sievers, *Benjamin Harrison, Hoosier Statesman* (1959).

**Cleveland and the Democrats** Allan Nevins, *Grover Cleveland: A Study in Courage* (1932); H. S. Merrill, *Bourbon Leader: Grover Cleveland and the Democratic Party* (1957) and *Bourbon Democracy of the Middle West, 1865–1896* (1953); J. R. Hollingsworth, *The Whirligig of Politics: The Democracy of Cleveland and Bryan* (1963); G. H. Knowles, *The Presidential Campaign and Election of 1892* (1942); J. A. Barnes, *John G. Carlisle* (1931), Cleveland's Secretary of the Treasury.

**Agrarian Protest** S. J. Buck, *The Granger Movement*° (1913); J. D. Hicks, *The Populist Revolt*° (1931); Norman Pollack, *The Populist Response to Industrial America*° (1962); W. T. K. Nugent,

*The Tolerant Populists* (1963); R. F. Durden, *The Climax of Populism*° (1965); Theodore Saloutos, *Farmer Movements in the South, 1865–1933*° (1960); R. B. Nye, *Midwestern Progressive Politics: A Historical Study of Its Origins and Development, 1870–1958*° (1958); C. V. Woodward, *Tom Watson, Agrarian Radical*° (1938); F. B. Simkins, *Pitchfork Ben Tillman* (1944); Stuart Noblin, *Leonidas Lafayette Polk* (1949); Martin Ridge, *Ignatius Donnelly* (1962).

**Economic Policies** F. W. Taussig, *The Tariff History of the United States* (1931); Milton Friedman and A. J. Schwartz, *Monetary History of the United States, 1867–1900* (1963); D. R. Dewey, *Financial History of the United States* (1934); F. B. Webeg, *The Background of the Panic of 1893* (1929); D. L. McMurry, *Coxey's Army* (1929).

**Bryan and McKinley** S. L. Jones, *The Presidential Election of 1896* (1964); P. W. Glad, *The Trumpet Soundeth* (1960) and *McKinley, Bryan, and the People*° (1964); P. E. Coletta, *William Jennings Bryan, Political Evangelist, 1860–1908* (1964); H. W. Morgan, *William McKinley and His America* (1963); Margaret Leech, *In the Days of McKinley* (1959); Herbert Croly, *Marcus Alonzo Hanna* (1912).

---

°Titles available in paperback.

# Chapter 20
# Emergence of
# a World Power

In the 1890s the United States took what seemed like a startling new departure in foreign affairs when it began to acquire possessions overseas. From the very beginning, however, the republic had been expansionist. As the American people moved relentlessly westward across the continent, their government from time to time acquired new lands for them to occupy: the trans-Appalachian region (in the treaty ending the Revolutionary War), the Louisiana Territory, Florida, Texas, a part of the Oregon country, California and New Mexico, Alaska.

Almost all these acquisitions—the fruits of what might be called the old Manifest Destiny—were contiguous with existing territories of the United States. Desired mainly as places for settlement by Americans seeking farms, these acquisitions represented a kind of agricultural imperialism. And they were expected to be organized as territories and ultimately as states, the equals of all the rest.

The expansionism of the 1890s, the new Manifest Destiny, was in some respects different. It meant acquiring island possessions, some of which were already thickly populated, were not suitable for settlement by migrants from the United States, and were expected to be held indefinitely as colonies, not as states or even territories. The new expansion was motivated largely (though not entirely) by considerations of trade. Thus it represented a kind of commercial imperialism.

Some Americans had begun to interest themselves in overseas acquisitions—Cuba, the Hawaiian Islands—as early as the 1850s, but the sectional controversy had intervened to frustrate that expansionist movement. In 1867 the United States annexed tiny Midway Island in the Pacific, and a few years later President Grant tried in vain to annex Santo Domingo in the Caribbean. The nation was not yet ready for the new imperialism.

By 1900 the United States had finally become an empire. It was now recognized as a "world power," though in fact it had been one of the great nations of the world for some time. As such, it pursued three basic and long-standing foreign policies—one for each of three broad areas of the globe. With respect to Europe, the aim (often inaccurately called "isolation") was to promote commerce while avoiding diplomatic involvements. With respect to the Americas, the purpose was expressed in the Monroe Doctrine, as supplemented by the idea of Pan-Americanism. With respect to Asia, the slogan came to be the Open Door, signifying opportunity for American commercial interests in China. The Monroe Doctrine and the Open Door were reaffirmed and strengthened by events of the

---

**The Victors of San Juan Hill**

Colonel Roosevelt (center with glasses) and the Rough Riders stand on San Juan Hill. Roosevelt and his men received more newspaper publicity than any unit in the army, and to some readers it must have seemed that T.R. was winning the war single-handed. When Roosevelt announced that he was going to write a book about his war experiences, Mr. Dooley suggested as a title *Alone in Cuba*. (Library of Congress) late nineteenth century. The policy of "isolation" began to be questioned, however, on the grounds that it was inconsistent with imperial obligations, with the responsibilities of "world leadership," and with the spirit of Anglo-American friendship which, by the end of the century, was about to prevail.

## IMPERIALIST STIRRINGS

In the two decades after 1870 the American people seemed to have forgotten the expansionist impulse of the prewar years. They were occupied with things closer to home—reconstructing the South, settling the last frontier, building a network of railroads, and expanding their great industrial system. By the 1890s they were ready —indeed, eager—to try imperialism, to resume the course of Manifest Destiny that had impelled their forebears to wrest an empire from Mexico in the expansionist forties.

### The New Manifest Destiny

Various developments subtly played a part in shifting the attention of Americans from their own country to lands across the seas. The passing of the frontier gave rise to a feeling that resources would soon become scarce and that they must be sought abroad. The depression beginning in 1893 seemed to confirm the fear of certain businessmen that industry had been overbuilt and was producing more goods than customers at home could buy. The bitter class protests of the time—the Populist movement, the free-silver crusade, the bloody labor disputes— led many people to believe that the nation was threatened with internal collapse. Some politicians advocated a more aggressive foreign policy to divert the popular mind from dissensions at home.

The swelling volume of American exports to other countries altered the nature of our trade relations and directed the attention of political leaders to the importance of foreign markets— and to the possible necessity of securing foreign colonies. The value of American exports in 1870 was approximately $392 million; in 1890 the figure was $857 million, and by 1900 it had leaped to $1,394,000,000. "But today," Senator Albert J. Beveridge of Indiana cried in 1899, "we are raising more than we can consume. Today, we are making more than we can use. Therefore, we must find new markets for our produce, new occupation for our capital, new work for our labor."

In the century's closing years the powers of Europe partitioned most of Africa among themselves and then turned eager eyes on the Far East and the feeble Chinese empire. Imperialism was in the air, and a leading American expansionist, Senator Henry Cabot Lodge of Massachusetts, warned that the United States "must not fall out of the line of march."

A philosophic justification for expansionism was provided by historians, professors, clergymen, and other intellectuals, who found a basis for imperialism in Charles Darwin's theories. These thinkers contended that, among nations, or "races," as well as biological species, there was a struggle for existence and only the fittest could survive. If the strong dominated the weak, that was in accordance with the law of nature.

One of the first to argue this proposition was the popular writer John Fiske, who predicted in an article in *Harper's Magazine* (1885) that the English-speaking peoples would eventually control every land that was not already the seat of an established civilization. Support for Fiske's position came from Josiah Strong, a Congregational clergyman and champion of overseas missionary work. In a book entitled *Our Country: Its Possible Future and Its Present Crisis* (1885), Strong declared that the Anglo-Saxon "race," and especially its American branch, represented the great ideas of civil liberty and pure Christianity and was "divinely commissioned" to spread its institutions over the earth. John W. Burgess, founder of Columbia University's School of Political Science, gave the stamp of scholarly approval to imperialism. In his *Political Science and Comparative Law* (1890), he flatly stated that the Anglo-Saxon and Teutonic nations possessed the highest political talents. It was the duty of these nations, he said, to uplift less fortunate peoples, even to force superior institutions upon them if necessary: "There is no human right to the status of barbarism."

The ablest and probably the most effective apostle of imperialism was Alfred Thayer Mahan, an officer in the navy. Mahan presented his philosophy in three major works: *The Influence of Sea Power upon History, 1660–1783* (1890); *The Influence of Sea Power upon the French Revolution and Empire, 1793–1812* (1892); and *The Interest of America in Sea Power* (1897). His thesis may be briefly stated. The sea-power nations were the great nations of history, and the United States, a huge island, had to build its greatness on sea power. The essential links in sea power were a productive domestic economy, foreign commerce, a merchant marine to monopolize national trade, a navy to defend the trade routes and national interests, and colonies to provide raw materials and markets and to serve as bases for the navy. Specifically, Mahan advocated that the United States construct a canal across the isthmus of Central America to join the oceans, acquire defensive bases on both sides of the canal in the Caribbean and the Pacific, and take possession of Hawaii and other Pacific islands. "Whether they will or no," he proclaimed, "Americans must now begin to look outward."

Mahan doubted that the United States would achieve its destiny, because its navy was not large enough to play the role he envisioned for it. But he did not accurately gauge the progress of the naval construction program launched in the Garfield-Arthur administration and continued by every succeeding administration. By 1898 the United States had advanced to fifth among the world's naval powers, and by 1900 to third.

## Hemispheric Hegemony

The most ardent practitioner of the new, assertive diplomacy was Harrison's Secretary of State, James G. Blaine, who in 1889 was beginning his second tour of duty in the foreign office. He believed that his country was destined to dominate the Caribbean and the Pacific. His expansionist policy was based largely on his conviction that the United States had to find enlarged foreign markets for its surplus goods. The most likely foreign outlet, he believed, was Latin America, with whose countries he wanted friendly commercial relations.

During his first term of office (1881), Blaine had invited the Latin nations to a Pan-American conference at Washington to discuss trade matters and arbitration of disputes. But after Garfield's death Blaine left office, and his cautious successor withdrew the invitations. Shortly before the Harrison administration took office, however, Congress authorized the convoking of a conference, and the State Department issued the invitations. With delegates from nineteen American nations in attendance, the first Pan-American Congress assembled in 1889. Blaine tried to persuade the conference to endorse his two principal objectives: (1) to draw the United States and Latin America into a customs union and (2) to create machinery to arbitrate controversies between the hemispheric nations. The Latin delegates rejected both proposals. They preferred to buy in the cheaper European market, and they feared the dominance of the United States in arbitration. Still, the meeting was not entirely a failure. Out of it arose the Pan-American Union, an agency in Washington that became a clearing house for distributing information to the member nations, and other congresses would meet in the future to discuss common hemispheric matters.

When, after the election of 1892, the Democrats took over, the change in personnel meant no break in the new self-assertive diplomacy. Indeed, in 1895 President Cleveland and his Secretary of State, Richard Olney, in a dispute with Great Britain over the boundary of Venezuela, carried the country close to the brink of war.

For years Britain and Venezuela had argued about the boundary between Venezuela and British Guiana, the dispute assuming new importance when gold was discovered in the disputed area. Both Cleveland and Olney, as well as the American public, were disposed to sympathize with Venezuela as the little, underdog country confronting the great power. The President and Congress publicly expressed hopes that Britain would see fit to arbitrate the matter. When the English government took no action, Olney drafted a note to Lord Salisbury of the foreign office protesting that Britain was violating the Monroe Doctrine. Any European interference with hemispheric affairs—and a bound-

## Olney's Statement on the Venezuela Crisis [1895]

Acting on Cleveland's instructions, Secretary Olney sent the British government a note deliberately framed in belligerent language:

*Today the United States is practically sovereign on this continent, and its fiat is law upon the subjects to which it confines its interposition. Why? It is not because of the pure friendship or good will felt for it. It is not simply by reason of its high character as a civilized state, nor because wisdom and justice and equity are the invariable characteristics of the dealings of the United States. It is because, in addition to all other grounds, its infinite resources combined with its isolated position render it master of the situation and practically invulnerable as against any or all other powers.*

ary dispute constituted interference—came within the scope of the famous doctrine, said the secretary. In bellicose language designed to make England sit up and listen, he declared: "Today the United States is practically sovereign on this continent, and its fiat is law upon the subjects to which it confines its interposition."

After months of delay Salisbury replied to Olney. With firm finality and a touch of condescension, he informed the secretary that the Monroe Doctrine did not apply to boundary disputes or the present situation and was not recognized as international law anyway. Britain was not going to arbitrate. Cleveland was enraged. In December 1895 he sent a special message to Congress reviewing the controversy. He asked for authority to create a special commission to determine the boundary line, and declared that if Britain resisted the commission's decision the United States should fight.

Enthusiastically Congress voted support for Cleveland's plan, and war talk flamed all over the country. Belatedly the British government realized that it had stumbled into a genuine diplomatic crisis. The last thing in the world that England wanted or could afford was a war with the United States. Suddenly the British backed down and agreed to arbitration.

However clumsy the Cleveland-Olney techniques had been, they had produced the desired results. The prestige of the United States was enhanced, the Monroe Doctrine was vitalized, and the bonds of friendship between the two great English-speaking nations were actually strengthened by strain.

## Hawaii and Samoa

The first area into which the United States directed its expansionist impulse after the Civil War was the vast Pacific Ocean region.

The islands of Hawaii in the mid-Pacific had been an important stopover station for American ships in the China trade since the early 1800s. The first American settlers to reach Hawaii were New England missionaries, who, like their fellows in Oregon at approximately the same time, advertised the economic possibilities of the islands in the religious press. Soon other Americans arrived to become sugar planters and to found a profitable new industry. Eventually, officers of the growing navy looked longingly on the magnificent natural base of Pearl Harbor on the island of Oahu.

The American residents of Hawaii came to dominate the economic life of the islands and also the political policies of the native ruler. Commercial relations were inexorably pushing Hawaii into the American orbit and making it, as Blaine accurately contended, a part of the American system. A treaty signed in 1875 permitted Hawaiian sugar to enter the United States duty-free and bound the Hawaiian kingdom to make no territorial or economic concessions to other powers. The trade arrangement tied the islands to the American economy, and the political clauses meant that, in effect, the United States was guaranteeing Hawaii's independence, and hence was making the islands a protectorate. In 1887 a new treaty renewed the existing arrangements and granted the United States exclusive use of Pearl Harbor as a naval station. The course of events was rendering outright political union almost inevitable.

Sugar production in Hawaii boomed, and

prosperity burgeoned for the American planters. Then the McKinley Tariff of 1890 dealt the planters a bad blow; by removing the duty on foreign raw sugar and giving domestic producers a bounty, it deprived Hawaii of its privileged position in the American sugar market. Annexation seemed the only alternative to economic strangulation. At the same time there ascended to the throne a new ruler, Queen Liliuokalani, who was determined to eliminate American influence in the government.

The American residents decided to act at once. They started a revolution (1893) and called on the United States for protection. At a critical moment the American minister, John L. Stevens, an ardent annexationist and friend of Blaine, ordered 160 marines from a warship in Honolulu harbor to go ashore to aid the rebels. The Queen yielded her authority, and a delegation representing the triumphant provisional government set out for Washington to negotiate a treaty of annexation. They found President Harrison highly receptive, but before the resulting treaty could be acted on by the Senate he was succeeded by Cleveland.

However disposed Cleveland was to upholding American rights under the Monroe Doctrine, he had old-fashioned ideas about taking other people's property. Suspicious of what had happened in Hawaii, he withdrew the treaty and sent a special representative to the islands to investigate. When this agent reported that Americans had engineered the revolution, Cleveland endeavored to restore the Queen to her throne. But the Americans were in control of the kingdom and refused to budge. Reluctantly the President had to accord recognition to their government as representing the "republic" of Hawaii. Cleveland, actuated by honorable motives but opposing the course of history, had only delayed the inevitable. In 1898, with the Republicans again in power and with the United States, as we shall see, constructing a colonial empire in both oceans, Hawaii was annexed by joint resolution of both houses of Congress.

Three thousand miles to the south of Hawaii, the Samoan Islands dominated the sea lanes of the south Pacific and had long served as a way station for American ships in the Pacific trade.

As American commerce with Asia increased after the completion of the first transcontinental railroad in 1869 and the extension of a steamship line from San Francisco to New Zealand, certain business groups regarded Samoa with new interest, and the navy eyed the harbor of Pago Pago on the island of Tutuila. In 1872 a naval officer visited the islands and negotiated a treaty granting the United States the use of Pago Pago, but the Senate rejected it. President Grant nevertheless dispatched a special representative to Samoa to encourage American trading and business interests. The familiar chain of events leading to involvement was being set in motion. In 1878 a native prince was brought to Washington, where he signed a treaty, which was approved by the Senate, providing for an American naval station at Pago Pago and binding the United States to employ its "good offices" to adjust any differences between a foreign power and Samoa. This indicated that the American government meant to have a voice in Samoan affairs.

The opportunity for expressing that voice soon came. Great Britain and Germany were also interested in the islands, and they hastened to secure treaty rights from the native princes. For the next ten years the three powers scrambled and intrigued for dominance in Samoa, playing off one ruler against another and coming dangerously close to war. In 1889 warships of the contending nations appeared in one Samoan harbor, and a clash seemed imminent. But a tropical hurricane dispersed the vessels, and the German government, not wishing to antagonize the United States, suggested a conference of the interested powers in Berlin to settle the dispute. Germany and Britain would have preferred a division of the islands, but Secretary Blaine insisted on preserving native Samoan rule. The result was that the conferees agreed on a tripartite protectorate over Samoa, with the native chiefs exercising only nominal authority.

The three-way arrangement proved unsatisfactory, failing altogether to halt the intrigues and rivalries of the signatory members. It was abrogated in 1899 when the United States and Germany divided the islands between them, with Britain being compensated elsewhere in the

Pacific. Germany obtained the two largest islands, but the United States retained Tutuila with its incomparable harbor of Pago Pago. Everyone was satisfied—with the possible exception of the Samoans.

## WAR WITH SPAIN

Though imperialist ambitions had begun to stir the United States, American imperialism did not flower until the coming of the war with Spain in 1898.

### Controversy Over Cuba

The immediate background of the Spanish-American War lay in the Caribbean island of Cuba, which with nearby Puerto Rico comprised nearly all that was left of Spain's once extensive Latin American empire. The Cubans had long resented Spanish rule, and they had engaged in a notable attempt to overthrow it between 1868 and 1878 (the Ten Years' War). During that revolt the American people were strongly sympathetic to the Cuban cause, but their feelings did not go beyond expressions of support. The government maintained a position of strict neutrality, despite the provocation offered by Spain. In 1873 the Spanish authorities captured a Cuban-owned, arms-running ship, the *Virginius,* and executed fifty-three of her crew. Because the vessel had flown an American flag and some of her seamen were Americans, popular indignation was intense. But Secretary of State Hamilton Fish avoided a crisis by inducing the Spanish government to return the *Virginius* and pay an indemnity to the families of the executed men.

In 1895 the Cubans rose up again. Not only the continuing Spanish misrule but also the American tariff policy created conditions of misery that prepared the way for revolt. Cuba's principal export was sugar, and the bulk of the crop went to the United States. The Wilson-Gorman Tariff in 1894, with its high duties on raw sugar, shut off the island's chief source of wealth and prostrated its economy.

From the beginning the struggle took on aspects of ferocity that horrified Americans. The Cubans deliberately devastated the island to force the Spaniards to leave. To put down the insurrection, the Spanish resorted to methods equally extreme. General Valeriano Weyler—or "Butcher" Weyler, as he soon came to be known in the American press—confined the entire civilian population of certain areas to hastily prepared concentration camps, where they died by the thousands, victims of disease and malnutrition.

Many of the same savage techniques had been employed earlier in the Ten Years' War without shocking American sensibilities. But in the nineties a wave of anger ran through the American public. The revolt of 1895 was reported more fully and floridly by the American press than the former outbreak—and so reported as to give the impression that all the cruelties were being perpetrated by the Spaniards.

At this time Joseph Pulitzer with his New York *World* and William Randolph Hearst with his New York *Journal* were revolutionizing American journalism. The new "yellow press" specialized in lurid and sensational news; when such news did not exist, editors were not above creating it. To Hearst and Pulitzer, engaged in a ruthless circulation war, the struggle in Cuba was a journalist's dream. Both sent batteries of reporters and illustrators to Cuba with orders to provide accounts of Spanish atrocities. "You furnish the pictures," Hearst supposedly told a too scrupulous artist, "and I'll furnish the war."

The mounting storm of indignation against Spain left President Cleveland unmoved. Convinced that both sides in Cuba were guilty of atrocities and that the United States had no interests justifying involvement in the struggle, he issued a proclamation of neutrality and attempted to arrest the numerous filibustering expeditions being organized by a "junta" of Cuban refugees in New York City. When Congress, in a state of excitement, passed a resolution favoring recognition of Cuban belligerency, he ignored the action. His only concession to the demands for intervention was to offer America's good offices to mediate the conflict, a proposal which Spain declined.

When McKinley took over the Presidency in 1897, he renewed the American mediation offer, which was again refused. Taking a stronger line than his predecessor, he protested to Spain

# Part Three
# The Course of
# American Art

Continuing a pattern that began during the colonial period, American artists after the Civil War looked to European models for inspiration. By imitating what was fashionable and accepted abroad, these artists hoped to give their work an aesthetic value they felt lacking in provincial America. As the nineteenth century progressed, this interest focused increasingly on Paris where the influential École des Beaux Arts epitomized the accepted, academic tradition in painting, sculpture, and architecture. Many American artists studied at the Paris school and several returned to this country to produce elegant and fashion-

*Plate 1*
**The Breakers.**
Richard Morris Hunt. (Sandak)

Plate 2

**"Anahita."**

William Morris Hunt. (Courtesy of the Pennsylvania Academy of the Fine Arts)

able works fully in keeping with the Beaux Arts tradition. Others, with more imagination, rejected French precedents and sought to develop a style more expressive of the realities of an increasingly industrial and urban America. The conflict between these two groups of European trained artists provided the main focus of American art during the second half of the nineteenth century.

Although nearly all American artists came into contact with the Beaux Arts tradition—either at home or abroad—some evolved a completely personal style, unrelated to and unaffected by European influence. Others went to France and discovered revolutionary movements (such as Impressionism) more meaningful and exciting. But the American public was unwilling to accept the unorthodox, and these artists were forced to live as expatriates. As a result, their influence was very limited.

The Beaux Arts style, with its elaborate decorative forms and monumental scale, derived from a variety of historical styles.

It appealed particularly to the growing American upper class. Influential in establishing this style among the very wealthy was the architect, Richard Morris Hunt (1827–1895), who introduced into his designs a variety of eclectic motifs, in particular the French Renaissance Chateau style. The central hall of the Breakers, a "cottage" built at Newport, Rhode Island, for the Vanderbilts in 1892 (*Plate 1*), shows this eclecticism at its most opulent. The hall incorporates the lavish use of marble, colonnades, and ornamental detail common to that mode of architecture. Hunt's eclecticism reflected the academic concern for accuracy in borrowing fostered by the French school.

Richard's brother, William Morris Hunt (1824–1879), was likewise trained in the French academic tradition, but preferred painting to architecture. Anxious to raise the level of American art, he produced large murals representing lofty themes and depicting symbolic forms. "Anahita" (*Plate 2*), one of his last works

(1878), derived from a Persian allegory about the forces of darkness being dispelled by knowledge. The forms are large, stylized, and elegant—characteristics of the Beaux Arts style. Hunt's paintings were very popular and established this style in American painting.

In sculpture, the Beaux Arts tradition was exemplified by the work of Daniel Chester French (1850–1931). One of the most popular of late nineteenth century sculptors, he is best known for his statue of Lincoln at the Lincoln Memorial. French commonly produced massive, dignified monuments. His "Alma Mater," built at Columbia University in 1903 (*Plate 3*), shows the use of large and symbolic forms to express an allegorical theme—an approach taught him at Paris.

Not all American artists embraced the

*Plate 3*
**"Alma Mater."**
Daniel Chester French.
(M. Warman)

Beaux Arts concepts with equal fervor. Henry Hobson Richardson (1838–1886), for example, though trained in Paris, sought to develop a more versatile eclecticism. His design for Sever Hall, built at Harvard University between 1878 and 1880 (*Plate 4*), though utilizing some Romanesque elements, is not an exact copy of any historical style. Richardson adapted Sever Hall to the surrounding buildings of Harvard Yard, substituting red brick for the stone with which he often worked, and adding long bands of windows that suggested the classroom function of the hall. Although more personal and free in his use of borrowed motifs, Richardson remained an eclectic architect, using traditional materials and conventional structural methods.

Then, during the 1890's, there developed a new attitude towards architecture involving experimentation with both materials and structural techniques. Louis Sullivan (1856–1924) was born in Boston and later traveled to France. He rejected the academic precepts to which he was exposed, and desired instead to produce a simple architecture in which a building would express both its function and the urban environment in which it was placed. In Chicago he developed an "aesthetic of the skyscraper," utilizing such materials as structural steel to pro-

*Plate 4*

**Sever Hall.**

Henry Hobson Richardson. (Sandak)

*Plate 5*

**Carson-Pirie-Scott Department Store.**

Louis Sullivan. (Hedrich Blessing)

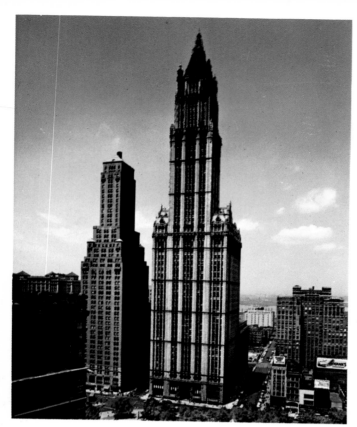

*Plate 6*

**The Woolworth Building.**

Cass Gilbert. (Sandak)

*Plate 7*

**"Country School."**

Winslow Homer. (City Art Museum of St. Louis)

duce a "proud and soaring thing." In his early work, such as the Wainwright Building in St. Louis, Missouri (1890–1891), Sullivan manipulated his forms to place great stress on the vertical. The column-like exterior gave a great feeling of height but reflected Sullivan's concept of the skyscraper rather than the functional structure of the building. The Carson-Pirie-Scott Department Store in Chicago, designed in 1899 (*Plate 5*), shows the ways in which Sullivan developed his earlier ideas. Instead of emphasizing the vertical, the building equally stresses vertical and horizontal lines, and clearly reflects the steel grid on which it is structured. A major innovation

were the "Chicago windows" whose fixed center panels and movable sides allowed a large amount of light to enter the upper stories. As in the Wainwright Building, decorative elements were treated as a necessary but separate aspect of the design. Instead of borrowing specific historical motifs, Sullivan fused a variety of forms into an intensely personal decorative vocabulary.

The concept of the skyscraper was received with admiration by the American public, but Sullivan's sparse and functional approach was rejected by most architects of his day. The abundance of large, lavishly decorated classical buildings at the Chicago World's Fair of 1893 established a new eclectic style that superseded both the Romanesque revival and Sullivan's attitude toward design. Urban architects, unwilling to abandon traditional Beaux Arts attitudes, produced skyscrapers such as the Woolworth Building, erected in New York City in 1913 (*Plate 6*). Here, classical forms were supplanted by a Gothic exterior that included unrestrained use of gargoyles and other medieval decorative forms. The architects seized on these linear forms to heighten the size of the building. The

desired effect was to create a "Cathedral of Commerce."

The majority of late nineteenth-century architects were forced to respond to the public taste or lose their commissions. This was not true of painting, where the smaller scale and limited amount of patronage allowed for more individual variations. While some artists, like William Morris Hunt, preferred the Beaux Arts style, many others rejected this tradition as restricting and unsatisfying. Among these was Winslow Homer (1836–

*Plate 8*
**"Moonlight Cove."**
Albert Pinkham Ryder. (Smithsonian Institution)

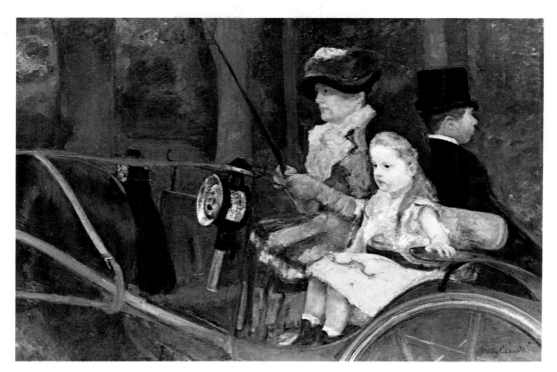

Plate 9
**"Woman and Child Driving."**
Mary Cassatt. (Philadelphia Museum of Art: W. P. Wilstach Collection)

1910), who traveled in Europe but never studied in Paris. His first job as an illustrator for *Harper's Weekly* trained him to observe details accurately and to reproduce a great variety of subjects in a simple, linear style. In his early painting he remained closely linked to the genre tradition, preferring narrative scenes of rural and frontier life. But, as can be seen in "Country School," painted in 1871 (*Plate 7*), he did not idealize his subjects. Through the clarity of his visual approach, he was able to communicate with honesty of detail the affection he felt for what was familiar in American life.

The works of Albert Pinkham Ryder (1847–1917) provide a sharp contrast. Ryder rejected all traditions, both European and American, and evolved instead an intensely personal style of painting. A self-taught artist, he concentrated on developing a technique of applying paint that would express his unique vision. The sea was his constant subject, and in

paintings such as "Moonlight Cove" (late 1880's) (*Plate 8*), he uses a heavy impasto technique to impart a brooding, mystic quality.

Although very few artists imitated Ryder's introspective approach, many were motivated by a search for a meaningful, personal style outside the Beaux Arts tradition. In Paris, Mary Cassatt (1845–1926) discovered the Impressionists. She studied with Degas, whose influence is most apparent in her experiments with perspective—approaching the subject from above or below. Her work was further characterized by its genre subject matter, and by the relative sharpness of her colors as is typified in "Woman and Child Driving" (1881) (*Plate 9*). The first American to work in the Impressionist style, Cassatt was not immediately recognized in this country, where the public was slow to accept innovations in the arts. However, she was able to awaken a few individuals to the new French art and to inspire them to start collections that are now in many American museums.

By the end of the century, American painters, as well as the general public, had discovered Impressionism, many years after it had been developed and at a time when the Post-Impressionists, Fauves, and Cubists were already at work in Europe. Increasingly, it was felt that the Beaux Arts tradition was trite, and new artistic precedents were sought. Childe Hassam (1859–1935) was one of several artists who found in Impressionism the right combination of freshness of approach and already-accepted aesthetic value. Scenes of rural and urban life, such as "Rainy Day in Boston" (1885) (*Plate 10*), were treated with the lightness and fragility typical of early Impressionist painting.

As has been shown, throughout the last decades of the nineteenth century the majority of American artists were reacting—either positively or negatively—to styles and aesthetic values imported from

*Plate 10*

**"Rainy Day in Boston."**

Childe Hassam. (The Toledo Museum of Art,
Toledo, Ohio; Gift of Florence Scott Libbey, 1956)

Europe. But the work of Frank Lloyd
Wright, at the turn of the century, reveals that there was a uniquely American
tradition available to those with insight
enough to perceive it. Wright's early
work, exemplified by the Robie House
built in Chicago in 1909 (*Plate 11*), is
related more to the "Salt Box" houses of
the colonial period than to any of the
eclectic buildings of his day. Wright
sought to design a house that would simultaneously reflect its location, communicate such symbolic and typically

American themes as openness and freedom, and utilize modern materials and forms appropriate to twentieth century American design. Thus, the horizontal lines suggest the flatness of the prairie, while the interior plan gives a feeling of openness and allows for a mingling of interior and exterior spaces. The materials are varied and many are native to the area in which the building is placed; the construction techniques are highly inventive. Wright, through the development of the "Prairie Style," paved the way for a reevaluation and reacceptance of American themes and values in the art of this country.

*Plate 11*
**The Robie House.**
Frank Lloyd Wright. (Sandak)

against her "uncivilized and inhuman" conduct. The Spanish government, alarmed that McKinley's course might forebode American intervention in Cuba, recalled Weyler, modified the concentration policy, and took steps to grant the island a qualified autonomy. At the end of 1897, with the insurrection losing ground, it seemed that war might be averted.

If there was any chance of a peaceful settlement, it was extinguished by two dramatic incidents in February 1898.

A Cuban agent in Havana stole a private letter written by Dupuy de Lôme, the Spanish minister in Washington, and thoughtfully turned it over to the American press. First published in Hearst's New York *Journal*, the minister's letter described McKinley as a weak man and "a bidder for the admiration of the crowd." This was no more than many Americans, including some Republicans, were saying about their

President—Theodore Roosevelt described McKinley as having "no more backbone than a chocolate éclair"—but when a foreigner made such a remark it was a national insult. Popular anger was intense, and Dupuy de Lôme resigned before the outraged McKinley could demand his recall.

While the excitement was still at fever pitch, even more sensational news hit the front pages: the battleship *Maine* had been blown up in Havana harbor with a loss of over 260 lives. This vessel had been ordered to Cuban waters in January on a "friendly" visit, but the real reason for its presence was to protect American lives and property against possible attacks by Spanish loyalists. Many Americans jumped to the conclusion that the Spanish had sunk the ship—"an act of dirty treachery," Theodore Roosevelt announced—and the imperialists and the jingoists screamed for war. This opinion seemed con-

**Wreck of the *Maine***

During the night after the explosion, the *Maine* settled down into the mud on the harbor bottom, so that only the wrecked superstructure remained visible, as shown here. Soon afterward, divers examined the hull; from their findings and from other evidence a naval court of inquiry concluded that an underwater mine had exploded, setting off explosions in the ship's powder magazines. Years later, in 1911, the wreck was raised so that

it could be examined for a second court of inquiry. This court agreed with the first one on the essential point— that there had been both external and internal explosions—but disagreed on certain significant details. Finally, the hulk was towed out to sea and sunk in water too deep to permit another examination. (National Archives) firmed when a naval court of inquiry reported that an external explosion by a submarine mine had caused the disaster. As war hysteria swept the country, Congress unanimously appropriated $50 million for military preparations. "Remember the *Maine*" became a national chant for revenge.

After the *Maine* episode there was little chance that the government could keep the people from war, although McKinley did not wish to resort to force. In March 1898, he asked Spain to agree to an armistice, with negotiations for a permanent peace to follow, and an immediate ending of the concentration system. After a slight delay, Spain essentially accepted the American demands on April 9. Two days later McKinley asked Congress for authority to use military force to end the hostilities in Cuba—in short, for a declaration of war. After reviewing the reasons that impelled him to recommend war ("in the name of humanity, in the name of civilization, in behalf of endangered American interests") he mentioned only casually, at the end of the message, that Spain already was capitulating to his requests.

It is doubtful whether any emphasis he might have given Spain's submission would have influenced Congress. That body, reflecting the people's will, was not going to be cheated out of a war by anything Spain might yield at the last minute. By huge majorities Congress passed a joint resolution declaring Cuba free and authorizing the President to employ force to expel the Spanish from the island. Added to the resolution, which was really a declaration of war, was the Teller Amendment, disclaiming any intention on the part of the United States to annex Cuba.

## "A Splendid Little War"

The Spanish-American War was, in the words of Roosevelt's friend John Hay, "a splendid little war." Indeed, to all Americans, with the possible exception of the enlisted men who fought it, it was almost an ideal conflict. It was the last small, short, individualistic war before the huge, protracted, impersonal struggles of the twentieth century. Declared in April, it was over in August. Newspaper readers easily and eagerly followed the campaigns and the heroic exploits of American soldiers and sailors. Only 460 Americans were killed in battle or died of wounds, but some 5,200 perished of disease: malaria, dysentery, typhoid, and other ills.

Blithely and confidently the United States embarked on a war it was not prepared to fight. The regular army, numbering only 28,000 troops and officers scattered around the country at various posts, was a tough little force, skilled at quelling Indian outbreaks, but with no experience in large-scale warfare. Hastily Congress directed the President to increase the army to 62,000 and to call for 125,000 volunteers. It was expected that the National Guard, the state militia, would furnish the bulk of the volunteers, and in addition the President was authorized to accept directly into the national service three volunteer cavalry regiments. By far the most colorful of the cavalrymen were the Rough Riders, nominally commanded by Leonard Wood but actually by Theodore Roosevelt, who was about to burst onto the front pages as a war hero. The services of supply, manned by elderly bureaucratic officers, proved incapable of meeting the modest wants of the forces raised during the war. On hand were enough Krag-Jorgensen repeating rifles, using smokeless powder, for the regulars, but the volunteers had to make do with the old black-powder, single-shot Springfields. American soldiers campaigning in tropical regions were clothed in the traditional heavy blue uniforms and fed canned rations that they called "embalmed beef."

The Spanish army numbered almost 130,000 troops, of whom 80,000 were already in Cuba at the beginning of the war. Despite its imposing size, it was not an efficient force; its commanders seemed to be paralyzed by a conviction of certain defeat. The American navy, fifth largest in the world, was far superior to the Spanish in ships, gunnery, and personnel.

The greatest weakness in the American military system was that no agency in it, either in the army or the navy, was charged with strategic planning. Only the navy had worked out an objective, and its objective had little to do with freeing Cuba.

The Assistant Secretary of the Navy in the McKinley administration was Theodore Roosevelt, ardent imperialist and proponent of war.

**The Spanish-American War: Pacific Front**

In consultations with naval officers, Roosevelt prepared to seize Spain's Philippine Islands in the far Pacific. He strengthened the Asiatic squadron and instructed its commander, Commodore George Dewey, in event of war to attack the Philippines. Immediately after war was declared, Dewey left the China coast and headed for Manila, where a venerable Spanish fleet was stationed. On May 1 he steamed into Manila Bay, and as his ships prepared to pass down the line of anchored enemy vessels he uttered the first slogan of the war: "You may fire when ready, Gridley." When the firing was finished, the Spanish fleet was completely destroyed, one American sailor lay dead—of a heat stroke—and George Dewey, immediately promoted to admiral, had become the first hero of the war.

The Spaniards still held Manila city, and Dewey had no troops with which to attack them.

While he waited nervously, the government assembled an expeditionary force to relieve him and take the city. Not until August 13 did the Americans receive the surrender of Manila.

In the rejoicing over Dewey's victory, few Americans paused to note that the character of the war was being subtly altered. What had begun as a war to free Cuba was becoming a war to acquire colonies.

But Cuba was not to be left out of the war picture. Late in April it was known in the United States that a Spanish fleet under Admiral Pascual Cervera had sailed for the west, presumably for a Cuban harbor. Cervera's antique armada was no match for the powerful American Atlantic squadron, as the Spanish government well knew. The Atlantic squadron, commanded by Admiral William T. Sampson, with Commodore W. S. Schley second in command, was expected to intercept and destroy Cervera before he reached his destination. (The squadron was " as strong as Sampson and as Schley as a fox," newspapers happily assured their readers.) But the Spaniard turned out to be the fox. Easily eluding his pursuers, he slipped into Santiago harbor on the southern coast of Cuba, where he was not discovered by the Americans until ten days after his arrival. Immediately the Atlantic fleet moved to bottle him up.

While the navy was monopolizing the first phases of the war, the War Department was trying to mobilize and train an army. The volunteer and National Guard units were collected near Chattanooga, Tennessee, while the regulars, plus the Rough Riders, were assembled at Tampa, Florida, under the command of General William R. Shafter. The entire mobilization process was conducted with remarkable inefficiency. There were appalling shortages of arms, ammunition, food, clothing, and medical supplies.

The army's commanding general, Nelson A. Miles, veteran of the Civil War, had planned to train the troops until autumn, then to occupy Puerto Rico and in conjunction with the Cuban rebels attack Havana. But with a Spanish naval force at Santiago, plans were hastily changed. It was decided to send Shafter with his force of 17,000 to take Santiago. So in June the expedition left Tampa, the Rough Riders, for want of

**The Spanish-American War: Caribbean Front**

transport space, having to leave their horses behind. The embarkation was accomplished amidst scenes of fantastic incompetence, but it was efficiency itself compared to the landing. Five days were required to put the army ashore, and this with the enemy offering no opposition.

Once landed, Shafter moved his army toward Santiago, planning to surround and capture it. On the way he fought and defeated the Spaniards at two battles, El Caney and San Juan Hill. In both engagements the Rough Riders were in the middle of the fighting and on the front pages of the newspapers. Colonel Roosevelt rapidly emerged as a hero of the war. Shafter was now before Santiago, but his army was so weakened by sickness that he feared he might have to abandon his position. When he besought Sampson to unite with him in a joint attack on the city, the admiral answered that mines in the harbor made it too dangerous to take his big ships in.

At this point disaster seemingly confronted the Americans, but unknown to them the Spanish government had decided that Santiago was lost. On July 3 Cervera, acting under orders from home, broke from the harbor to attempt an es-

cape that he knew was hopeless. The waiting American squadron destroyed his entire fleet. Shafter then pressed the Spanish army commander to surrender, and that official, after bargaining for generous terms, including free transportation back to Spain for his troops, turned over Santiago on July 16. While the Santiago campaign was in its last stages, an American army landed in Puerto Rico and occupied it against virtually no opposition.

Spain was whipped and knew it. Through the medium of the French ambassador in Washington she asked for peace, and on August 12 an armistice ended the war.

## Decision for Imperialism

In agreeing to a preliminary peace, the United States had laid down terms on which a permanent settlement must be based: Spain was to relinquish Cuba, cede Puerto Rico to the United States, cede also to the victor an island in the Ladrones, midway between Hawaii and the Philippines (this turned out to be Guam), and permit the Americans to hold Manila pending the final disposition of the Philippines. The last clause reflected the confusion in the McKinley administration as to what to do about the islands where its forces had won a foothold. The demands for Puerto Rico and Guam showed how quickly the war to free Cuba had assumed an imperialist character. Aroused by the excitement of military victory and a heady sense of mastery, the American government and people were disposed to keep what American arms had won.

In October 1898, commissioners from the United States and Spain met in Paris, to determine a permanent peace. With little protest Spain agreed to recognize Cuba's independence, to assume the Cuban debt, and to cede Puerto Rico and Guam to the victor. Then the American commissioners acting under instruction from McKinley, startled the conference by demanding the cession of all the Philippines. The President later said that he had arrived at his decision as a result of divine guidance. Probably such mundane factors as the swelling sentiment for annexation in the country and the pressure of the imperialist leaders of his party influenced his thinking more. Stubbornly the Spanish resisted the American demand, although they realized they could retain the islands only by resuming the war. They yielded to the inevitable when the United States offered a money payment of $20 million. The Treaty of Paris was signed on December 10, 1898, and sent to the United States for ratification by the Senate.

When the treaty was submitted to the Senate, it encountered immediate and fierce criticism and occasioned in that body and throughout the country one of those "great debates" that frequently precede a departure in American foreign policy. The chief point at issue was the acquisition of the Philippines, denounced by many, including prominent Republicans, as a repudiation of America's high moral position in the war and a shameful occupation of a land that wanted to be free. Favoring ratification were the imperialists, the big navy lobby, the Protestant clergy, who saw in a colonial empire enlarged fields for missionary enterprise, and most Republicans. Business, which had opposed the war, swung over to support the treaty, converted by the notion that possession of the Philippines would enable American interests to dominate the Oriental trade. In the forces opposing the treaty were old-fashioned Americans who objected to their country's annexing other people against their will, traditionalists who feared that a colonial empire would necessitate large armaments and foreign alliances, a majority of the intellectuals, economic interests like the sugar growers who foresaw colonial competition, and most Democrats.

After weeks of bitter wrangling, the treaty was ratified, February 6, 1899, but only because it received an unexpected assist from William Jennings Bryan, who expected to be his party's candidate again in the election of 1900. Bryan persuaded a number of Democratic senators to vote for ratification. It has been charged that he was looking for a campaign issue, and in his defense it has been said that he thought the question of the Philippines should be decided by a national referendum: if the Democrats won in 1900 they would free the islands.

In 1900 Bryan ran against McKinley again, and this time Bryan went down to a crushing defeat. Although the Republicans claimed a popular mandate for imperialism, other factors had helped to determine the outcome. The victors had again exploited the money and tariff issues; they had harped on the continuing prosperity in the country under a Republican administration; and they had displayed to the voters the colorful personality of their vice-presidential candidate, the hero of San Juan Hill, Colonel Theodore Roosevelt.

## THE REPUBLIC AS AN EMPIRE

The new colonial empire was extensive enough to warm the heart of the most ardent imperialist. Stretching from the Caribbean to the far reaches of the Pacific, it embraced Puerto Rico, Alaska, Hawaii, a part of Samoa, Guam, the Philippines, and a chain of minor Pacific islands.

With the empire came new problems. Many of the predictions of the anti-imperialists proved accurate. Ultimately, as a colonial power, the United States had to maintain large armaments, concern itself with the complexities of Far Eastern international politics, and modify its traditional policy of holding aloof from alliances.

## Governing the Colonies

Immediately, the nation faced the problem of how it was to govern its dependencies, and here a host of perplexing questions arose. Did Congress have to administer the colonies in accordance with the Constitution? Did the inhabitants of the new possessions have the rights of American citizens? Could Congress levy tariff duties on colonial imports? Or, in a phrase that pleased the public fancy, did the Constitution follow the flag? The Supreme Court pointed to a solution in the Insular Cases (*De Lima* v. *Bidwell*, *Downes* v. *Bidwell*, and others, 1900–1904), involving duties on colonial trade. In a series of decisions the Court distinguished, in extremely technical language, between "incorporated" and "unincorporated" territories. In legislating for the latter—the insular possessions—Congress was not bound by all the limitations in the Constitution applicable to incorporated territories, although some restrictions did apply. What the Court was saying was that the Con-

stitution followed the flag only if Congress so decided and that the government could administer its colonies in almost any way it saw fit.

Three of the dependencies—Hawaii, Alaska, and Puerto Rico—were given territorial status as quickly as Congress considered them ready for it. For Hawaii, with its large American population and close economic ties with the United States, a basis for government was provided by an act of 1900. This measure granted American citizenship to all persons who were citizens of the Hawaiian republic, authorized an elective two-house legislature, and vested executive authority in a governor appointed from Washington.

Alaska was being governed by appointed civil officials. The discovery of gold there in 1896 caused the first substantial influx of Americans, and in 1912 Alaska received territorial status and a legislature, and its inhabitants were given the rights of citizenship. In Puerto Rico the people readily accepted American rule. Military occupation of the island was ended and civil gov-

### McKinley Measures Uncle Sam for a New Suit

Tailor McKinley is fitting Uncle Sam with a new suit— one to go with his new imperialist proportions. Anti- expansionist Carl Schurz offers some reducing

medicine, but Sam scornfully says that he has never taken any of the stuff and does not intend to begin. From *Puck* (1900). (Culver) ernment was established by the Foraker Act in 1900. The governor and upper house of the legislature were to be appointed from Washington, while only the lower house was to be elected. The act did not declare the Puerto Ricans to be American citizens, this privilege being deferred until 1917.

Smaller possessions in the empire were dealt with more arbitrarily. Such places as Guam and Tutuila were placed under control of naval officials, and many of the small islands, containing only a handful of inhabitants, experienced no form of American government at all.

American military forces, commanded by General Leonard Wood, remained in Cuba until 1902, the occupation being protracted to enable American administrators to prepare the island for the independence promised in the peace treaty of 1898. The vigorous occupiers built roads, schools, and hospitals, reorganized the legal, financial, and administrative systems, and introduced far-reaching sanitary reforms.

At Wood's urging a convention assembled to draft a constitution for independent Cuba. This document contained no provisions concerning relations with the nation responsible for Cuba's freedom. The United States, with its expanding interests in the Caribbean, expected to exercise some kind of control over the island republic. Therefore, in 1901, Congress passed the Platt Amendment, as a rider to an army appropriation bill, and pressured Cuba into incorporating the terms of the amendment into her constitution. The Platt Amendment stated that Cuba should never impair her independence by treaty with a foreign power (this was equivalent to giving the United States a veto over Cuba's diplomatic policy); that the United States had the right to intervene in Cuba to preserve its independence, life, and property; and that Cuba must sell or lease to the United States lands for naval stations. The amendment left Cuba only nominally independent. With American capital taking over the island's economy—investments jumped from $50 million in 1898 to $220 million by 1914—Cuba was in fact, if not in name, an American appendage.

Among the possessions in the imperial system, only the Philippines offered resistance to American rule. The Filipinos, rebellious against

Spain before 1898, had hailed Dewey and the expeditionary force sent to Manila as their deliverers from tyranny. When the hard fact sank in that the Americans had come to stay, the Filipinos resolved to expel the new invaders. In 1899 they resorted to war (rebellion, by the American definition) and, ably led by Emilio Aguinaldo, they fought the army of occupation from island to island until 1901. In the end the Americans repressed the uprising, but only after employing methods unpleasantly reminiscent of Weyler's tenure in Cuba, including the use of concentration camps, and at a cost of $170 million and 4,300 American lives. Civil government began taking over from the military in 1901, and the Filipinos, with great adaptability, began the process of adjusting to American culture. Thus they started on the long road that would lead, in 1946, to the independence they so ardently desired.

## The Open Door

The acquisition of the Philippines made the United States an Asian power. American interest in the Far East, already aroused by our growing trade with China, reached a new intensity immediately after 1898. Other nations more experienced in the ways of empire were casting covetous eyes on China, ancient, enfeebled, and seemingly open to exploitation by stronger countries. By the turn of the century the great European imperialistic powers—England, France, Germany, and Russia—and one Asian power, Japan, were beginning to partition China into "spheres of influence." One nation would force the Chinese government to grant it "concessions" to develop a particular area; another would use pressure to secure a long-term lease to a region. In some cases the outside powers even asserted ownership of territory. The process, if continued, threatened to destroy American hopes for a vast trade with China.

The situation posed a delicate problem for the men directing American foreign policy. Knowing that public opinion would not support any use of force, they had to find a way to protect American interests in China without risking war. McKinley's Secretary of State, John Hay, attempted an audacious solution. In September 1899 he addressed identical notes to England,

Germany and Russia, and later to France, Japan, and Italy, asking them to approve a formula that became known as the "Open Door." It embodied three principles: (1) each nation with a sphere of influence was to respect the rights and privileges of other nations in its sphere; (2) Chinese officials were to continue to collect tariff duties in all spheres (the existing tariff favored the United States); and (3) each nation with a sphere was not to discriminate against other nations in levying port dues and railroad rates.

Hay could hardly have expected an enthusiastic response to his notes, and he got none. Russia declined to approve the Open Door, and the remaining powers gave evasive replies. Each one stated in effect that it approved Hay's ideas in principle but could make no commitment until the others had acted. Apparently the United States had met a humiliating rebuff, but Hay boldly announced that since all the powers had accepted the principle of the Open Door, his government considered their assent to be "final and definitive." Although the American public applauded his diplomacy, Hay had won little more than a theoretical victory. The United States could not prevent any nation that wanted to violate the Open Door from doing so—unless it was willing to resort to war.

Almost immediately after the diplomatic maneuvering over the Open Door ended, a secret Chinese society known as the Boxers instigated an uprising against foreigners in China. The movement came to a blazing climax when the Boxers and their supporters besieged the entire foreign diplomatic corps in the British embassy in Peking. At this point the powers with interests in China decided to send an international expeditionary force to rescue the diplomats. The situation seemed to offer a perfect excuse to those nations with ambitions to dismember China.

The United States contributed 2,500 troops to the rescue force, which in August 1900 fought its way into Peking and broke the siege. McKinley and Hay had decided on American participation in order to secure a voice in the settlement of the uprising and to prevent the partition of China. Again Hay sent a note to the world powers. This time he called for the Open Door not only in the spheres of influence but in "all parts of the Chinese Empire." He also called for the maintenance of China's "territorial and administrative integrity." This—the integrity, or independence, of China—thus became a corollary of the Open Door policy. He persuaded England and Germany to approve his views, and then with their support he induced the participating powers to accept a money indemnity as satisfaction. The sum allotted to the United States amounted to almost $25 million, which greatly exceeded damages, but later the American government reduced the obligation and even remitted the unpaid balance. China gratefully used part of this money to educate Chinese students in the United States.

## A Modern Military System

The war with Spain had revealed glaring deficiencies in the military system. The greatest weakness had appeared in the army, but there had been an absence of coordination in the entire military organization that might have resulted in disaster had the United States been fighting a first-rate power. The army, now being called upon to police the new colonial possessions, obviously needed a thorough overhauling. To do the job McKinley appointed Elihu Root, an extremely able administrator, as secretary of war in 1899. Between 1900 and 1903 Root put into effect, by congressional authorization or by executive order, a series of reforms that gave the United States what amounted to a new military system.

The Root reforms may be conveniently listed in summary form:

1. An enlarged regular army, with a maximum size of 100,000.

2. Federal supervision of the National Guard, provided by the Dick Act of 1903.

3. The creation of a system of officer-training schools, crowned by the Army Staff College (later the Command and General Staff School) at Fort Leavenworth, Kansas, and the Army War College at Washington.

4. The establishment in 1903 of a General Staff headed by a Chief of Staff, who would replace the former commanding general of the army and act as military adviser to the Secretary of War.

While Root was intent on improving the professional quality and the efficiency of all segments of the army, his primary concern was to provide it with a central planning agency modeled on the example of European staffs. The General Staff was charged with many functions (it was to "supervise" and "coordinate" the entire army establishment) but one of its most important branches was to devote its whole work to planning for possible wars. To ensure interservive strategic cooperation, an Army and Navy Board, representing both services, was created.

Whatever the shortcomings of the Root reforms, they invested the army with a new and needed competence. The United States entered the twentieth century with something resembling a modern military system.

## LIFE IN THE IMPERIAL REPUBLIC

The acquisition of a far-flung empire did not noticeably affect the daily lives of the American people, who numbered nearly 76 million according to the census of 1900. But the lives of the people were being profoundly affected by other developments that went on contemporaneously with overseas expansion.

### Automobiles and Airplanes

As the twentieth century opened, great changes were under way in communication and transportation, changes that were to make the new century very different from the preceding one. The telephone was becoming a familiar feature of the home as well as the office. In 1900 the Bell system operated 677,000 telephones; by 1915 the number was nearly 6 million, and coast-to-coast lines were in operation. Radio was in its infancy. In 1901 the Italian inventor, Guglielmo Marconi, flying a kite aerial in Newfoundland, caught signals from Cornwall, England. The next year the Marconi Wireless Telegraph Company of America was established, and by 1910 all large ships were equipped with radios.

At the beginning of the new century, the day of the radio as a familiar part of American life still lay a few decades in the future, and so did the day of the airplane. But the day of the automobile was already arriving. Since the introduction of railroads, men had been intrigued with the idea of installing some kind of engine in carriages or cars that would run on roads. Throughout the nineteenth century, inventors had experimented with engines driven by steam or electric power, but the vehicles thus propelled all demonstrated impossible mechanical drawbacks. In the 1870s designers in France, Germany, and Austria began to develop the internal-combustion engine using the expanding power of burning gas to drive pistons, and the gasoline engine soon prevailed over all other types. France seized the lead in the early automotive industry, introducing such terms as "garage," "chassis," and the word "automobile" itself.

Meanwhile, in the United States, inventors— the Duryea brothers (Charles E. and J. Frank), Elwood Haynes, Ransom Olds, and Henry Ford —were busily designing their own models. In 1893 the Duryeas built and operated the first gasoline-driven motor vehicle in the United States. Three years later Ford produced the first of the famous cars that would bear his name, a two-cylinder, four-horsepower affair. Other "firsts" followed in rapid succession. In 1898 the first automobile ad in the country appeared in the *Scientific American;* its headline read: "Dispense with a horse." The first automobile salesroom was opened in New York in 1899, and the next year the first automobile show was held at Madison Square Garden. In 1901 Ransom Olds built 1,500 curved-dash Oldsmobiles, thus becoming the first mass-producer of automobiles.

The first automobiles were built in various Eastern cities, but gradually production came to center at Detroit, Michigan. Detroit offered several attractions: it had an established carriage industry that could construct automobile bodies, and it was close to supplies of iron ore and lumber. In 1900 the automobile companies turned out over 4,000 cars, but the big development of the industry had to wait until the first decade of the new century.

A number of factors held back production. For one thing, the country's roads were not adequate for automobile transportation. Only 150,-000 miles, 7 per cent of the total mileage, were

**Herald Square    1910**

By the first decade of the century, both electric trolley cars and automobiles were beginning to take over from the horse-drawn vehicles. New York City had entered the electric age with arc lights and illuminated signs. (Museum of the City of New York)

### The Wright Brothers Making Their First Flight

On December 17, 1903, on the side of Kill Devil Hill at Kitty Hawk, North Carolina, Orville and Wilbur Wright became the first men to fly in a motor-driven machine heavier than air. Their airplane had a wing span of 40 feet; its two propellers were driven by an engine producing about 12 horsepower. "After running the motor for a few minutes to heat it up," Orville Wright later wrote, "I released the wire that held the machine to the track, and the machine started forward into the wind. Wilbur ran at the side of the machine, holding the wing to balance it on the track. . . . Wilbur was able to stay with it till it lifted from the track after a forty-foot run. One of the Life Saving men snapped the camera for us, taking a picture just as the machine had reached the end of the track and had risen to a height of about two feet." It traveled a little over 120 feet. Later Wilbur Wright stayed aloft 59 seconds and flew 852 feet. Only three papers bothered to print the news the next morning. (Official U.S. Air Force photo)

improved with gravel, oil, shell, or other forms of surfacing; by contrast, there were over 2 million miles of dirt roads. The greatest deterring force was the expense involved in the manufacturing process, which resulted in a car priced too high for the mass market. The first builders had to order their parts from many sources, including sewing-machine and bicycle companies, and then begin the job of assembling; but soon they turned to assembly-line techniques and mass-production methods.

There had been only four automobiles on the American highways in 1895; by 1917 there were nearly 5 million, and the automobile was beginning to remake American life. Automobiles then had become commonplace among upper-middle-class families, just as telephones were almost essential in middle-class homes.

In 1903 the Wright Brothers made their first flight at Kitty Hawk, North Carolina. It lasted only twelve seconds and covered a distance less than the wing span of the largest airplanes of fifty years later. Soon the Wrights and other inventors and pilots, in the United States and Europe, were busy improving the airplane, making longer flights with it, and even putting it to a few practical uses. In 1909 the Wrights delivered the first military plane to the United States Army. World War I stimulated rapid developments in aircraft design, especially in Germany and France. As early as 1914 a plane had begun to carry passengers on daily flights in Florida, and in 1918 regular air-mail service was started between New York City and Washington, D. C. For the time being, however, flying remained in an essentially experimental stage.

## Mass Production

Middle-class Americans, as they self-consciously greeted the twentieth century, congratulated themselves upon the enormous technical achievements that had advanced the United States to a position of preeminence in the world. The steel furnaces of Pittsburgh outproduced those of England and Germany and functioned with such efficiency and low cost that Carnegie could have sold steel rails at a profit in Birmingham, England. New manufacturing marvels of every sort were giving Americans the highest average level of living in the world's history.

In the factories, the new era meant acceleration of the introduction of labor-saving machin-

ery. There was, for example, a bottle-making machine patented in 1903 that virtually eliminated the hand blowing of glass bottles, and another that ended manual production of window glass. The invention of a rotating kiln in 1899 made possible the cheap, standardized production of Portland cement at about the time a demand for paved highways was gaining momentum. A shift toward electric power was already well advanced. The first 5,000-horsepower alternating-current generator had been installed at Niagara Falls in 1895; within a few years steam generators of 100,000 horsepower were commonplace. Electricity was entering the home, but even more important, it was becoming a great new source of efficient industrial motive

### The Ford Assembly Line

In August 1913, at the main Ford plant in the Detroit suburb of Highland Park, it took twelve and one-half man-hours of labor to assemble every Model T chassis. Then the world's first moving assembly line for automobiles was installed; instead of the workers moving to the stationary work, the moving work came to the workers. Within six months, each chassis was being assembled in only one hour and thirty-three minutes.

This picture, taken in 1914, shows a portion of the final assembly line where the radiator and the wheels were placed on the Model T chassis. At this time the company employed about 12,000 men in making cars, and another 1,000 men in making better tools to use in making cars—a fact that shows how the technical revolution in modern industry had been institutionalized and made continuous. (Ford Motor Company) power. In 1899 it ran only 5 per cent of the machinery; by 1919, 55 per cent; by 1925, 73 per cent. Large-scale electric power also made possible electrolytic processes in the rapidly developing heavy chemical industry.

In the automobile and other industries, new principles of scientific management found spectacular application. Scientific management began with the work of an engineer, Frederick Winslow Taylor, who helped revolutionize the machine-tool industry with carbon steel high-speed cutting edges. As soon as Taylor learned how to manufacture tools that could cut efficiently while running white hot, he began to insist that machinists operate their lathes at correspondingly fast speeds. Taylor was beginning to apply the same sort of scientific techniques to management as to machinery. At first he looked upon workmen much as he did at machines. Fewer and fewer men could perform simpler tasks at infinitely greater speed; if not, Taylor would discard them as unhesitatingly as he had discarded the poorer cutting steel.

The new system, "Taylorism," meant less need for skills among workmen and more monotonous tasks for them. At first organized labor rebelled, and won at least a minor victory when it persuaded Congress in 1915 to forbid the introduction of efficiency systems into government arsenals or navy yards. But Taylor and his followers regarded themselves as scientific seekers after higher production and thus a higher living standard. He talked of the greatest good for the greatest number, including the workers. Indeed, if Taylorism were used to eliminate the intolerable inefficiencies in many industries, it could mean not only lower prices for consumers but also higher wages for employees. By the 1920s some unions recognized this and were cooperative.

American industrialists, usually ready to try new techniques, increasingly undertook Taylor "scientific management" studies of workers' motions. They also brought scientists and engineers into their plants to engage in research for new tools and products. A few years earlier any industrialist who established a laboratory would have been looked upon as a crackpot. Now laboratories became accepted, partly because of the phenomenal success of some of the pioneer-

ing ones. There was, as every schoolboy could proudly cite, the industrial laboratory of Thomas A. Edison at Menlo Park, New Jersey, out of which had come the incandescent lamp, the phonograph, the motion picture, and scores of other devices. By 1913 Bell Telephone, Du Pont, General Electric, Eastman Kodak, and about fifty other companies had established laboratories with budgets totaling hundreds of thousands of dollars per year.

Out of these new methods and machines came mass production. It required the technology, raw materials, transportation, and markets that the United States could supply in the twentieth century. Precision manufacturing made possible interchangeability of parts even in assembling a machine as complicated as the automobile. Ford began with stationary assembly, earlier used in manufacturing guns, clocks and the like, then gradually changed by 1914 to the moving assembly line. This revolutionary technique cut the time for assembling a chassis from twelve and a half hours to an hour and a half. While Ford raised the wages and lowered the hours of his workers, he cut the base price of his Model T car from $950 to $290. Other industrialists, following his example, soon took over the assembly line and mass production for their plants also.

By 1914 American manufacturers were producing 76 per cent more goods than in 1899. They were doing so with only 36 per cent more workers and 13 per cent more establishments. The greater output of goods reflected the rising living standards and the growth of population at home as well as the growth of the foreign market.

## Social and Cultural Advances

In other ways, too, the United States took giant strides into the twentieth century. Medical advances helped bring about marked improvement in public health. The Caribbean adventures of the United States led to great discoveries in tropical medicine. In 1900 Dr. Walter Reed and his associates proved conclusively the hypothesis of a Cuban doctor that a striped variety of mosquito transmitted yellow fever. During the digging of the Panama Canal (1904–1914), Major William C. Gorgas applied the new knowledge so thoroughly that not one case of

**The Duryea Car**

J. Frank Duryea sits at the tiller of his automobile
after winning the first motor vehicle race in America
in 1895. With him is one of his umpires.
(Automobile Manufacturers Association)

yellow fever originated there, and malaria was virtually eradicated. In Puerto Rico, Major Bailey K. Ashford discovered that the cause of the widespread anemia was hookworm, and developed an inexpensive cure.

All this knowledge was valuable in the southern United States. In 1909 Rockefeller gave $1 million for the eradication of hookworm in the South, where almost 60 per cent of the school children had some infestation. With chemicals and vaccines, some of which were important European developments, the nation made encouraging progress in combating venereal diseases, typhus, typhoid, and diphtheria. Sanitariums and a national association successfully combated tuberculosis. Campaigns against mosquitoes and flies, improvements in sanitation, the inspection of milk, and, beginning in 1908, the chlorination of water supplies reflected the new vigor of the state and municipal boards of health. To cap the entire program, the old marine hospital service was expanded in 1902, and in 1912 became the United States Public Health Service. The death rate dropped from 17 per thousand in 1900 to 13.2 in 1920; life expectancy increased from 49 years in 1901 to 56 in 1920.

The number of public high schools nearly doubled between 1900 and 1914; the number of students increased two and a half times. In higher education, enrollment more than doubled (to 216,493), while professional and graduate schools were greatly strengthened. In many fields, American universities at last rivaled those of Europe. Nevertheless, much remained to be accomplished in education. In 1900 the average child in elementary school attended a one-room school about half the time during a 143-day school year, to be taught by rote by an untrained young woman who received $38 per month. By 1914, he might attend 86 days out of 158, and be taught rather better by a woman receiving $66. American children went to school an average of only 6.16 years.

In increasing numbers people purchased the new popular newspapers, sending their circulation soaring, making them also big business. Several newspaper chains developed; the most powerful, that of William Randolph Hearst, by 1914 already numbered nine newspapers and two magazines. Most of the papers used their new wealth for greatly improved reporting, sprightly features and cartoons, and increased pictures. As papers drew more of their news from the Associated Press and the new United Press, founded in 1907, they became more standardized.

Before 1898 few American novels had sold 100,000 copies; by 1901 a number were doing so. Edwin Westcott's homespun *David Harum* (1898) eventually sold more than a million copies, and two historical novels by the American Winston Churchill, *Richard Carvel* and *The Crisis,* 420,000 and 320,000 respectively. By 1904 the craze for historical fiction gave way to a vogue for the adventure stories of Jack London and Rex Beach, the sentimentalism of Kate Douglas Wiggin and Alice Hegan Rice, and the shrewd portrayal of American life, whether middle-class or genteel, of Booth Tarkington and Edith Wharton. Popular fiction was for the most part American in theme, and some of it became progressive in overtone. London lost much of his audience when he turned from adventure to socialism, but Churchill kept his when he attacked the railroads in *Mr. Crewe's Career* (1908). Tarkington's first best seller, *The Gentleman from Indiana* (1899) portrayed an idealistic small-town editor, almost the progressive prototype.

The literary pioneers of the period, the so-called naturalists, drew for inspiration upon the French writer Emile Zola and European literary movements, but presented American realities harshly, in the spirit of rural and urban revolt. Theodore Dreiser's blunt, powerful *Sister Carrie* (1900) dealt so frankly with sex that it was suppressed by its publisher; it was not until 1911 when the public attitude had changed that his

next novel appeared. Then in *The Financier* (1912) and *The Titan* (1914) he portrayed a ruthless Chicagoan who destroyed his business competitors. Frank Norris also wrote of unscrupulous businessmen, California railroad barons in *The Octopus* (1901) and Chicago grain speculators in *The Pit* (1903).

The new poets either extolled the common man or wrote about him with realism. Carl Sandburg, in free verse, applied the themes of Whitman to Chicago; Vachel Lindsay wrote chants like *The Congo,* full of mysticism and rhythm. In Chicago, Harriet Monroe founded *Poetry* magazine in 1912. In New England, Edward Arlington Robinson seemed to represent a fading afterglow of Puritanism and transcendentalism; his verses in the *Outlook* received the praises of President Roosevelt. Robert Frost, writing in a quiet, almost vernacular way about the rural folk and nature of New England, failed at first to find an audience. In 1915 he returned from England, where he had published two books, to take his place as an accepted poet. Closer to European movements than American, Ezra Pound, an expatriate from Idaho, proclaimed the techniques of the Imagists. Among them were Amy Lowell of Boston and later T. S. Eliot of St. Louis, who in 1914 moved permanently to London. The Imagists discarded rhyme from their work as an obstacle in the way of creating a pure image of everyday life.

A similar ferment stirred other branches of the arts. In 1908 a group of eight young American painters—including John Sloan, George Luks, and George W. Bellows—rebelled against conventional academicians and painted urban life as Dreiser wrote about it. Conservatives dismissed these realists as the "Ash Can School," but were even more shocked by the Armory Show of 1913 which exhibited the American moderns and brought French Post-Impressionism to America. Modernistic architecture began with the low-lying "prairie houses" of Frank Lloyd Wright, whose designs influenced Europe more than the United States until the late 1920s. Well-to-do Americans did not accept Wright but reverted to graceful colonial styles for their homes.

The expanding theatrical business was dominated by a syndicate which nationally booked romantic plays and popular vaudeville. It was the heyday of the matinee idol. Experimental realism began, but only in the realm of little-theater groups like the Provincetown Players and in the "47 Workshop" of Professor George P. Baker of Harvard. These could hardly appeal to wide audiences. The real threat to the great theatrical producers like David Belasco and the mediocre playwrights who served them came from the motion picture. At first the idea of movies competing with the stage was ludicrous. The first film telling a continuous story was a melodrama, *The Great Train Robbery*, produced in 1903. By 1905 stores were being converted into "nickelodeons," which still seemed no threat to the stage, but by 1915 the lengthy, impressive feature film had arrived with *The Birth of a Nation*. This motion picture was as significant in marking the coming of age of a new art form as it was deplorable in its glorification of the Ku Klux Klan. A motion-picture monopoly movement began in 1909 and was smashed by the government in 1914, but the cinema was becoming a multimillion-dollar industry, and movies were being shown in large and impressive theaters.

## High Noon of Monopoly

Twentieth-century industrialism brought evil as well as good. Populists, socialists, and the relative few who had followed reform theoreticians like the single-taxer Henry George and the utopian Bellamy no longer were alone in proclaiming that the American economic system was in need of reform. Even the thoroughly conservative Judge Peter S. Grosscup, who had issued the injunction to help break the Pullman strike, proclaimed in 1905 that the modern corporation was destroying the opportunity for the individual to participate in the proprietorship of the country. This was the recurring complaint of the middle class.

Monopolies could lead to higher prices and higher profits, which were often the basic reasons for the creation of combinations. (Their promoters argued the reverse, that they led to greater efficiency, lower prices, and a higher living standard.) Furthermore, the monopolists could use their great economic strength to wield proportionately great political power.

Despite all the agitation against "trusts," American industry moved toward greater consolidation and monopoly. From 1887 to 1897 there had been only 86 industrial combinations, and the capitalization of all of these combined had been less than $1.5 billion. By 1904 there were 318 so-called trusts with a capitalization of over $7 billion. These combinations included basic industries like copper, oil, and steel, and industries directly affecting the consumer like sugar and tobacco. Six financial groups controlled 95 per cent of the nation's railway mileage. In the highly competitive steel industry, twenty-one significant mergers between 1898 and 1901 prepared the way for a large-scale struggle between Carnegie and Morgan. When Carnegie announced plans for plants that might be ruinous to Morgan and his associates, they chose to buy him out at his own inflated figure of $447 million and they then established the nation's first billion dollar corporation, United States Steel. It was able to set standard prices for steel everywhere in the United States—prices from which none of the smaller steel companies dared to deviate.

Whatever pride Americans might have felt over the emergence of these industrial giants was mingled with serious misgivings. The United States Industrial Commission reported in 1902: "In most cases the combination has exerted an appreciable power over prices, and in practically all cases it has increased the margin between raw materials and finished products. Since there is reason to believe that the cost of production over a period of years has lessened, the conclusion is inevitable that the combinations have been able to increase their profits." Whether or not monopolies were to blame, prices were rising so rapidly between 1897 and 1913 that the cost of living went up about 35 per cent.

## The Rich and the Poor

For millions of Americans the economic system meant personal poverty and misery. There was a vast disparity between the incomes of the wealthy few and those of the poor multitudes. One per cent of the families owned nearly seven-eighths of the wealth; seven-eighths of the families owned only one-eighth of the wealth. While a fifth of the families were comfortable or even rich, four-fifths lived precariously. A careful estimate in 1904 indicated that about one-eighth of the people, or a total of 10 million, lived in poverty.

At the top, Carnegie had earned an estimated $23 million from his steel company alone in the one year 1900. It had paid him an average of $10 million a year during the previous five years. On none of this did he have to pay a cent of income tax. Carnegie lived comparatively modestly and devoted his millions to worthy causes, but many of the very rich created sensational headlines through their ostentatious living. The Vanderbilts, like a clan of feudal barons, maintained, in addition to their many country estates, seven mansions in seven blocks on Fifth Avenue in New York City.

These wealthy few often spent incredible sums on parties, accounts of which fascinated but also angered readers of yellow journals. The most notorious was the ball upon which Mrs. Martin Bradley spent $250,000; it created such a furor that she and her husband fled to exile in England. A less exceptional dinner, served on gold plates at the old Waldorf-Astoria in 1899, cost $10,000 for forty people, or $250 apiece. At this time, $250 was six months' wages for the average workingman. In part the millionaires were able to get their huge incomes because of the low cost of labor in their factories, and to afford their huge estates and townhouses because of the low cost of servants. Middle-class families also benefited from cheap labor. While they did not enjoy the great variety of household appliances of later generations, they were able with the aid of servants to maintain large homes.

Servants at least were entitled to meals and garret rooms. Working girls could not count upon even these. One woman in five worked, and often for wages as low as $6 or $8 per week. Unless a girl lived at home, it was almost impossible for her to exist upon these wages. The popular magazine writer O. Henry (William Sidney Porter) was reflecting the widespread indignation of contemporary Americans when he described in his short stories how strong the temptation was for these nearly starving girls to succumb to predatory men. Advocates of a minimum wage law to protect women created a

sensation in Chicago by bringing several women to a hearing to testify that low pay and poverty had driven them to prostitution. Nevertheless, the Illinois legislature failed to enact the desired law.

Child labor, which had always existed in the United States, was becoming an increasingly serious problem by the early 1900s. At least 1.7 million children under sixteen were employed in

**Child at Spindles in a Carolina Textile Mill   1909**

According to the 1900 census, one out of three of the employees in Southern cotton mills was a child under sixteen. Under strong pressure from within, Southern states gradually passed laws prohibiting the worst of the abuses. In North Carolina, manufacturers drafted a law, passed in 1907, prohibiting children under sixteen from working more than sixty-six hours per week, banning children under fourteen from night work, and allowing children of twelve to work only as apprentices. As a means of obtaining graphic evidence of violations of even this lenient law, the secretary of the National Child Labor Committee brought Lewis Hine, a documentary photographer of city slums, into some of the worst of the mills. Hine's pictures, of which this one is representative, were instrumental in arousing public indignation against child labor abuses.
(Photograph by Lewis Hine, George Eastman House Memorial Collection)

factories and fields. Ten per cent of the girls between ten and fifteen, and 20 per cent of the boys, were gainfully employed. At least thirty-eight states had laws to protect children, but these typically applied only to children employed in factories, and set a minimum age of twelve years and a maximum workday of ten hours. Sixty per cent of the child workers were employed in agriculture, which could mean a twelve-hour day picking or hoeing in the fields. In the cotton mills of the South, children working at the looms all night were kept awake by having cold water thrown in their faces. In canneries, little girls cut fruits and vegetables sixteen hours a day. Some children worked at dangerous machines without safety devices. As these young workers became exhausted at the end of a long day, or night, they might become careless as they leaned over a loom to retie broken threads, have their hair caught in machinery, and be scalped as it suddenly started up again.

Industrial accidents were commonplace. For most laborers, whether children, women, or men, working conditions were far from ideal. Many women labored in dark, cold, dirty factories or sweatshops without restrooms or fire escapes. For men, working conditions were even worse. As early as 1877 Massachusetts had required safety devices on elevators and machinery; some states also required mine inspection. But there was little effective enforcement of the laws, if indeed personnel for enforcement existed. In American factories and mines, and on the railroads, the accident rate was higher than in any other industrial nation in the world. As late as 1907 an average of twelve railroad men a week were killed. In factories, not much had been done to prevent occupational diseases such as phosphorus and lead poisoning.

Nor was there economic incentive for employers to improve working conditions. Under the common law, if an accident was due, even in part, to the negligence of an employee himself or a fellow employee, the employer bore no responsibility. Even if the employer was liable under the common law, the courts were slow, and often too expensive for the maimed worker or his widow. Until 1911 there were almost no state workmen's compensation laws.

Cheap labor was one of the reasons for high profits; unrestricted immigration was one of the reasons for cheap labor. At the same time that the big industrialists fought against a lowering of the tariff bars, they welcomed and even recruited the low-paid workers of Europe. While the flow of the "old immigrants" from northern and western Europe continued, a new flood, comprising about 72 per cent of the total immigration between 1900 and 1910, poured in from southern and eastern Europe. For the most part they were Italians, Slavs, and Jews. In the single year 1905, over 1.2 million arrived. In most big cities of the North, immigrants and their children outnumbered the native-born. Bewildered at being thrust into an alien culture, living under conditions far below the level of native Americans (except Negroes), they filled most of the backbreaking unskilled jobs in the new heavy industries, on the railroads, and around the cities. The Jews, many of whom brought their skill with the needle, went into the garment trade, but under just as wretched circumstances.

The American Federation of Labor (whose

## "The Steerage" by Alfred Stieglitz

When Stieglitz (1864–1946), crossing the Atlantic in 1907, took this photograph of immigrants crowded in the cheapest quarters, his intent was not documentary, nor was his object to publicize the misery of these passengers. Rather, he was trying to utilize photography as a form of creative expression —an art in itself rather than an imitation of other arts. Picasso remarked of "The Steerage," "This is exactly what I have been trying to say in paint."

Stieglitz demonstrated the way in which an art form could take advantage of technical advances (in this instance, photographic emulsions) by taking unparalleled night photographs and capturing the feeling of rainstorms and snow. He also helped change American taste in painting. Between 1905 and 1917 at his New York gallery he displayed, in addition to photographic art, the paintings of French impressionists and their successors at that time unknown in the United States, from Cézanne through Picasso. He became associated with an equally advanced group of American artists, including John Marin, Max Weber—and Georgia O'Keeffe, whom he married. (Collection Museum of Modern Art)

president, Samuel Gompers, was himself an immigrant) fought to cut off this flood of cheap, unskilled foreign labor, which was said to keep wages down and hamper unionization. Many Americans, both conservative and progressive, were susceptible to the popular dogma of Anglo-Saxon superiority and joined in the anti-immigration movement. They feared the high birth rate among immigrants as compared with the low birth-rate among natives in the higher-income groups; Theodore Roosevelt warned darkly against "race suicide." They blamed the squalor of the slums and the power of the political bosses largely upon the immigrants, and felt that through restriction could come improvement. In 1907 they succeeded in stopping the immigration of Japanese to the agricultural lands of the Pacific Coast through the "gentleman's agreement" that Roosevelt negotiated with the Japanese government. A series of restrictive laws prohibited various undesirables, ranging from ex-convicts to alcoholics, from entering the United States. In 1917, over the veto of President Wilson, Congress passed a law setting up a literacy test as a means of reducing the number of immigrants.

For all those, immigrant or native, who were crowded into city tenements, life was far from enviable. Jacob Riis, the crusading journalist, thought that by 1900 the worst of the New York slums were gone. In their place were a scattering of parks and playgrounds; in some of the worst remaining areas there were privately financed settlement houses to aid the poor. Nevertheless, for millions of city dwellers, housing was barely tolerable. In New York City, two-thirds of the 3.5 million people lived in tenement houses. Most of these had direct light and air in only four rooms of the fourteen on each floor.

# Selected Readings

**The New Great Power** E. R. May, *Imperial Democracy: The Emergence of America as a Great Power* (1961); Walter LaFeber, *The New Empire: An Interpretation of American Expansion, 1860–1898°* (1963); J. A. S. Grenville and G. B. Young, *Politics, Strategy, and American Diplomacy: Studies in Foreign Policy, 1873–1917* (1966); Dexter Perkins, *The Monroe Doctrine, 1867–1907* (1937).

**Imperialist Stirrings** A. F. Tyler, *The Foreign Policy of James G. Blaine* (1927); D. M. Pletcher, *The Awkward Years: American Foreign Relations under Garfield and Arthur* (1962); G. R. Dulebohn, *Principles of Foreign Policy under the Cleveland Administration* (1941); S. K. Stevens, *American Expansion in Hawaii, 1842–1898* (1945); W. E. Russ, Jr., *The Hawaiian Revolution* (1959) and *The Hawaiian Republic* (1961); G. H. Ryden, *Foreign Policy of the United States in Relation to Samoa* (1933).

**War With Spain** J. W. Pratt, *Expansionists of 1898°* (1936); Walter Millis, *The Martial Spirit°* (1931); Frank Freidel, *The Splendid Little War* (1958), a pictorial history; F. E. Chadwick, *The Relations of the United States and Spain: The Spanish-American War* (2 vols., 1911); Orestes Ferrara, *The Last Spanish War* (1937), a Spanish view; Theodore Roosevelt, *The Rough Riders* (1899).

**The Colonies** J. W. Pratt, *America's Colonial Experiment* (1950); G. A. Grunder and W. E. Livezey, *The Philippines and the United States* (1951); J. F. Guggenheim, *The United States and Cuba* (1934).

**The Open Door** Tyler Dennett, *John Hay, from Poetry to Politics* (1933); C. S. Campbell, Jr., *Special Business Interests and the Open Door Policy* (1951) and *Anglo-American Understanding, 1898–1903* (1957); L. M. Gelber, *The Rise of Anglo-American Friendship* (1938).

**The Army and the Navy** P. C. Jessup, *Elihu Root* (2 vols., 1938); J. D. Hittle, *The Military Staff* (1949); Harold and Margaret Sprout, *The Rise of American Naval Power, 1776–1918°* (1939); R. S. West, Jr., *Admirals of the American Empire* (1948); W. R. Herrick, *The American Naval Revolution* (1966).

**Automobiles and Airplanes** J. B. Rae, *The American Automobile* (1965); D. L. Cohn, *Combustion on Wheels* (1944); Allan Nevins and F.

E. Hill, *Ford: The Times, the Man, the Company* (1954); Douglas Rolfe, *Airplanes of the World From Pusher to Jet, 1490–1954* (1955); C. H. Gibbs-Smith, *The Aeroplane: An Historical Survey* (1960) and *The Invention of the Aeroplane* (1965).

**Technology** Siegfried Giedion, *Mechanization Takes Command* (1948); Samuel Haber, *Efficiency and Uplift: Scientific Management in the Progressive Era, 1890–1920* (1964); M. J. Nadworny, *Scientific Management and the Unions, 1900–1932* (1955); H. G. J. Aitken, *Taylorism at Watertown Arsenal* (1960); Kendall Birr, *Pioneering in Industrial Research: The Story of the General Electric Research Laboratory* (1957).

**Society and Culture** Mark Sullivan, *Our Times* (6 vols., 1926–1935); F. L. Allen, *The Big Change°* (1952); H. F. May, *The End of American Innocence* (1959); Van Wyck Brooks, *The Confident Years: 1885–1915* (1952); W. L. O'Neill, *Divorce in the Progressive Era* (1968); Albert Rees, *Real Wages in Manufacturing, 1890–1914* (1961).

———

°Titles available in paperback.

# Chapter 21
# The Progressive Movement

In the opening years of the twentieth century a new political impulse—which came to be known as "progressivism"—aroused a large number of Americans. Those who thought of themselves as "progressives" saw with great concern the nation's rapid technological development and growing involvement in international affairs. They wanted to make sure that the United States, as an industrial giant and a world power, held on to the democratic ideals that it had inherited from the past.

There were many wrongs to be righted, and the progressives differed among themselves in both their aims and their methods. To some, the main evil was monopoly; to others, corruption in city government; to still others, the unequal status of women. And so it went. Various groups combined and cooperated, or they divided and worked against one another, on certain issues. For example, some favored and others opposed imperialism. Thus progressivism may be considered as an aggregate of causes rather than a single movement. Still, most progressives had in common the following convictions: (1) "the people" ought to have much more influence in government, and the "special interests" much less, and (2) government ought to be stronger, more active, and more efficient in serving the public welfare.

In certain respects, progressivism was a continuation of Populism. Progressives advocated some (though not all) of the reforms that the Populists had proposed, and some of the former Populists joined the progressive movement. But progressivism and Populism differed in important respects. The People's party members had been mostly distressed farmers of the Southern and the Great Plains and Rocky Mountain states. The progressive ranks included men and women from all parts of the country, but especially from the Northeast and the Midwest, and prominent among the progressives were persons of the urban middle class. The progressives had a broader concept of both "the people" and the public welfare than the Populists had had.

A third party took the name "Progressive," but the movement was too broad to be confined by party lines. Active in it were both Republicans and Democrats, though the Republicans were the more numerous. For most of them, regardless of party, the path of reform led from the city hall to the state capitol to the chambers of Congress and the White House. Many conspicuous evils of the time, incapable of cure by local or state authorities, required action by the federal government. Prominent figures of both major parties brought progressivism into national politics. Among the leading Republicans were Robert M. La Follette, Theodore Roosevelt, and William Howard Taft; among the Democrats, William Jennings Bryan and Woodrow Wilson. From 1901 to 1916, politics and government largely reflected the opinions and ambitions of these men—especially Roosevelt and Wilson—and their respective followings.

---

**Suffragettes in Action**

In the early 1900s, many young women became political activists seeking the right to vote, but their efforts were not realized until 1920 when the Nineteenth Amendment was passed. (Culver)

## LOCAL AND STATE BEGINNINGS

Progressivism in some of its phases got its start in the cities. Here it took two main forms: a movement for "social justice" and another for governmental reform. The proponents of governmental reform soon directed their attention also to the evils of statewide politics.

### The Urban Progressives

Progressive leaders were largely members of the urban middle class and were to a remarkable extent college-educated and self-employed professional men or small businessmen, of native-born Protestant background. For the most part they were about forty years old, financially secure civic leaders who had earlier been McKinley Republicans.

Following these leaders was a middle class, like them still clinging to the traditional agrarian values, but caught up in the social whirlpool of the new industrial age. The older segment of the middle class—the independent professional and business men from which such a high proportion of progressive leaders came—somewhat more than doubled between 1870 and 1910. This meant it grew as rapidly as the population as a whole, which increased about two and a third times. The working class (including farm laborers) trebled; farmers and farm tenants doubled. But there was another group, a new middle class of white-collar workers—the clerks, sales people, and technicians who worked for corporations or service enterprises. This group increased almost eight times, from 756,000 to 5,609,000 people, thus reaching a number almost double the size of the older middle class.

While members of this new white-collar class did not provide leadership for the progressive movement, they did help to provide it with voting strength. Political action was their only outlet for economic protest, since they did not belong to unions or trade associations. Often it was they, on their fixed salaries, who were worst caught by rising prices. And basically, like the older middle class, they were urbanites who still expressed the emotions of their rural backgrounds. These two groups, the white-collar class and the older middle class, combined to form the respectable element of the towns and cities who, along with many of the more successful farmers and some of the laborers, were ready to accept the new progressive creed.

Middle-class people were frightened by urban political bosses, not only because of their corrupt ties with the industrial moguls but also because of their hold over the ignorant laboring masses (often largely immigrants) of the cities. Moreover, these middle-class people had some fear of the new rising labor unions. Populist farmers had shared these suspicions of the moguls and the masses. One of the Populist papers had said the purpose of the party was to serve as a "bulwark against the anarchy of the upper and lower scums of society." Progressives continued the same prejudices.

Theodore Roosevelt in his *Autobiography* has stated clearly the reasoning that led him, a conservative young plutocrat of the upper middle-class gentry, to enter politics. The men Roosevelt knew best, cultivated clubmen, warned him that politics was a cheap affair of saloon keepers and horsecar conductors, which gentlemen should shun. "I answered," Roosevelt wrote, "that if this were so it merely meant that the people I knew did not belong to the governing class, and that the other people did—and that I intended to be one of the governing class."

Many progressives were converted to the cause by the writings of the so-called "muckrakers." The muckrakers were the many journalists who dramatized the need for reform by writing exposés of the unsavory in business and government. They began to attract attention toward the end of 1902 and were at their peak of popularity in 1906. There long had been a literature of exposure, from the *Harper's Weekly* crusade against the Tweed Ring through Henry Demarest Lloyd's denunciation of Standard Oil in *Wealth against Commonwealth* (1894). What was new was the scale of the revelations and the rapid attraction of a wide audience. Muckraking began almost by accident in about ten of the new popular magazines, selling for 10 or 15 cents, which were then building mass circulation. *McClure's*, already a magazine of broad appeal, began publishing Ida Tarbell's series on Standard Oil. The publisher, S. S. McClure, sent a new editor, Lincoln Steffens, out to see the

# Where Historians Disagree

## The Nature of Progressivism

The first historians of the progressive movement were men who had lived through it and enthusiastically hailed its achievements. Sometimes in their writings they fell little short of some progressive memoirists who remembered the movement as the coming of the millennium.

One of the first and best interpretations, sympathetic but balanced, was that of Charles and Mary Beard, who in a notable chapter of *The Rise of American Civilization* (1927) linked Populism and progressivism as a single heroic surge toward social democracy. In the *Quest for Social Justice* (1931), Harold U. Faulkner embellished this theme. "To many thoughtful men in the opening years of the twentieth century it seemed that America in making her fortune was in peril of losing her soul," wrote Faulkner. "Crude and chaotic as was this civilization in many respects, its essential soundness became manifest in the next decade and a half as the rising social consciousness of the people directed the national energy into fresh and nobler channels."

This optimistic, and rather agrarian-based view of progressivism as a triumph of the Jeffersonian tradition dominated academic thinking into the 1940s. It persisted even as, in the depression years of the thirties, several disillusioned popular writers, especially John Chamberlain, whose *Farewell to Reform* appeared in 1932, began to attack progressivism as a basically conservative exercise in futility. Chamberlain went so far as to assert that progressivism had been "preparing the ground for an American Fascism."

The economic determinist views of Chamberlain and others preceded skeptical scholarly appraisals of progressivism, which began to appear after World War II. George Mowry and Richard Hofstadter emphasized the middle-class urban background of the progressive leaders. In *The Age of Reform* (1955), Hofstadter suggested that these leaders were drawn to progressivism as a means of regaining the political status and power which had been draining away from their class, and that rising prices created a consumer consciousness that "gave mass appeal and political force to many Progressive issues and provided the Progressive leaders with a broad avenue of access to the public."

A succeeding group of historians, members of the New Left, believed, on the contrary, that progressivism meant no more than a successful maneuver on the part of businessmen to obtain government regulation that would further their own economic interests. The most vigorous of these historians, Gabriel Kolko, in *The Triumph of Conservatism* (1963), wrote: "Progressivism was initially a movement for the political rationalization of business and industrial conditions, a movement that operated on the assumption that the general welfare of the community could be best served by satisfying the concrete needs of business. But the regulation itself was invariably controlled by leaders of the regulated industry, and directed toward ends they deemed acceptable or desirable."

The debate continues as to whether progressivism was liberal or conservative, idealistic or self-seeking.

country first-hand; this experience led Steffens to begin a series on municipal corruption. At the same time, Ray Stannard Baker contributed an article denouncing a union for wrongdoing during a coal strike.

At the height of the muckraking movement, ten journals with a combined circulation of about 3 million were devoting considerable space to the literature of exposure. In addition some books like Upton Sinclair's *Jungle* (1906), an exposure of the meat-packing industry, sold over 100,000 copies. Many newspapers, most notably the New York *World* and the Kansas City *Star*, printed articles by muckrakers. It was exciting for a while, but by 1912 it was over. This was due partly to the hostility of business, which at times withheld credit and advertising from the muckraking magazines.

## Social Justice

The social-justice movement was already well advanced by the turn of the century. It had its roots in European, especially English, reform movements. Almost every prominent English reformer visited the United States, and conversely almost every American progressive leader fell under the influence of the British. Young Jane Addams had worked at the newly established Toynbee Hall in the Limehouse section of London; in 1889 she returned to the United States to establish Hull House, a slum relief center, in Chicago. Settlement houses, slum clearance agitation, and a great variety of other English reforms quickly had their counterpart in the United States.

The Salvation Army, which had recently come to the United States from England, by 1900 boasted a corps of 3,000 officers and 20,000 privates. It offered aid as well as religion to the dregs of the cities. So did ministers, priests, and rabbis who by the nineties were working in the slums. These men were united in their determination to improve the existence of the miserable people around them in addition to saving their souls. "One could hear human virtue cracking and crushing all around," Walter Rauschenbusch wrote of Hell's Kitchen (a slum section) in New York City. To him the way of salvation for these human souls seemed to be a Christian reform of the social and economic system. Thus many an American Protestant minister arrived at the "social gospel." Catholics like Father John Augustine Ryan joined in the fight for social justice under the authority they found in Pope Leo XIII's encyclical *Rerum Novarum*. This declared that "a small number of very rich men have been able to lay upon the masses of the poor a yoke little better than slavery itself. . . . No practical solution of this question will ever be found without the assistance of religion and the church."

Close behind the ministry were middle-class and upper-class women. In the 1890s many of them had seemed restless and discontented, reading more widely than their husbands or brothers, joining literary circles and women's clubs. By the early 1900s these clubs were beginning to display a remarkable growth. The General Federation of Women's Clubs, from a membership of 50,000 in 1898, grew to over 1 million by 1914. In the new era, the members of the clubs were quick to take up the fight for

---

### Chicago's "Ghetto": Jefferson and 12th Streets    1906

Typical of the residents in this area were a Russian man and his wife who earned $2 a day finishing coats. Their household was thus described: "Three small children and the grandmother constitute the family, the latter dying of a cancer without medical attendance of nursing. Man has been 18 years in this country and owns a populous frame tenement house. He also owns the wretched rear cottage, on the second floor of which his family lives. His work room contains a bed, an upright piano, dining table, sewing machine and the couch on which his mother lies dying. The filth and smell are intolerable. He does only the finest custom work and was

making a valuable coat. Most of the year he has been making police uniforms." (Top right, Courtesy Chicago Historical Society)

### Slum Dwellers in a Tenement Room, About 1910

For years Riis, originally an immigrant from Denmark, struggled to try to eradicate living conditions such as these. By the turn of the century, the worst of the tenements were gone; but as pictures like this testify, Riis and the progressives had ample reason to continue their battle against the slums. (Bottom right, The Jacob A. Riis Collection, Museum of the City of New York)

the ballot and legal equality for themselves, and for a wide array of reforms on behalf of children and working women.

Another small but mighty social-justice group consisted of those who gathered careful data and statistics on the need for reform. They were often social-welfare workers who prepared articles for *Survey* magazine, or they were frustrated crusaders working for federal or state agencies. In many states before 1900 there were bureaus of labor which compiled great quantities of data on deplorable working and living conditions.

## Municipal Reform

*The Shame of the Cities* was the title Lincoln Steffens gave to his notable series of exposés which first appeared in *McClure's*, and shame was what civic-minded progressives felt. They tried to wrest control of their city governments away from the machines, reorganize the governments scientifically, and use them as instruments of economic and social reform.

Arrayed in opposition were the bosses, and behind them those interests so abhorrent to the progressives, the saloons, brothels and various businesses that could gain more from the bosses than from clean government. Allied with the bosses were some newspapers, which ridiculed the progressives as either killjoys or scoundrels. Finally, there was the great constituency of city working people, mostly of immigrant origins. To them the bosses were friends who could be counted upon to help them when they violated the law in some minor way, or were in need of jobs or food. Progressives, on the other hand, seemed to be do-gooders who were trying to take away the saloon—the poor man's club— and to deprive him of his amusements from prize-fighting to Sunday baseball.

Many progressives, finding it difficult to grasp the relationship between the bosses and their constituents, saw the problem in simple moral and legal terms. Bad government, they thought, came from bad charters. Reformers should seize the municipal governments and, by remaking the charters, usher in the urban millennium.

Municipal reform began in response to a tragedy in Galveston, Texas, where the old, ineffective government broke down in the wake of a tidal wave. The citizens replaced it with a commission of five, whose members were jointly enacting ordinances and singly running the main city departments by 1908. In 1907 Des Moines adopted the commission plan with modifications to make it more democratic, and other cities followed. Another variation was the city-manager plan which placed a trained expert, similar to the manager of a business, in charge of the city, and made him responsible to the commission or the mayor and council. Staunton, Virginia, hired a city manager in 1908, and the new device attracted national attention when Dayton, Ohio, adopted it in 1913 to speed rehabilitation from a serious flood. By the end of the progressive era approximately 400 cities were operating under commissions, and another 45 under city managers.

Whether through old or new city machinery, progressives fought to destroy economic privilege on the municipal level. This meant primarily trying to prevent the sale of streetcar franchises, or to force exorbitantly high fares downward. The most notable of the reform mayors was Tom Johnson of Cleveland, who had invented the streetcar fare box. He was a traction magnate converted to the ideas of Henry George. As mayor, Johnson fought to raise the ridiculously low assessments upon railroad and utility property, introduce city planning, and above all, lower streetcar fares to 3 cents. After his defeat and death, his brilliant aide, Newton D. Baker, was elected mayor and helped maintain Cleveland's position as the best governed American city.

Many of the urban gains of progressivism were permanent, but in some cities, as soon as progressives relaxed, the old forces recaptured the city hall. In other municipalities, state control over city government made reform almost impossible. Cities derived all of their powers from the state, and many state legislatures granted new charters only reluctantly or controlled a large city within the state through special legislation. In the state of New York, which functioned this way, the reform mayor of Schenectady complained: "Whenever we try to do anything, we run up against the charter. It is an oak charter, fixed and immovable." Consequently, a municipal home-rule movement spread, to try to obtain state laws allowing cities to write their own charters. Much of the difficulty with state legislatures was even more serious. Many a reformer, like Johnson in Cleveland, or Joseph W. Folk in St. Louis, found himself helpless in the cities because the trail of corruption led back to the legislature.

## In the Statehouse

Hiram Johnson in California, Folk in Missouri, and other progressives moved on from cities, where they had been crusading district attorneys, to become progressive governors. Only by taking this step could Folk, for example, break the bosses. Johnson's avowed purpose as governor of California was to end the political hold of the Southern Pacific Railroad upon the state.

At the state level, progressives enacted a wide array of legislation to increase the power of crusading governors, give the people more direct control over the government, and decrease the functions of legislators. These ill-paid, relatively inconspicuous men were being exposed by muckrakers as the villains in many states. William Allen White in *McClure's*, December 1905, wrote of Missouri: "The legislature met biennially, and enacted such laws as the corporations paid for, and such others as were necessary to fool the people, and only such laws were enforced as party expediency demanded." This view of the legislatures led progressives to circumscribe and circumvent them in almost every conceivable way. The most important of the devices, the initiative and the referendum, were first enacted in Oregon in 1902 as a result of the quiet but persistent advocacy of the secretary of several voters' organizations, William S. U'Ren. The initiative enabled voters to short-circuit the legislature and vote upon measures at general elections; the referendum forced the return of laws from the legislature to the electorate. By 1918 twenty states had adopted these schemes.

Progressives also tried to obtain better officials. They tried to eliminate machine choice of candidates through the direct primary, first instituted in Mississippi in 1902 and adopted in some form by every state by 1915. Unfortunately, machines often dominated the primaries.

Another way many progressives hoped to thwart the machines was through giving the vote to women, who presumably would bring purity to politics. For decades the suffrage had been the main objective of the women's rights movement, since women felt that once they obtained this they could vote in their other rights. As early as 1897 Colorado women obtained the right to vote, at a time when those of Kentucky still could not legally even make wills. By 1914 women could vote in twelve states, all west of the Mississippi; in 1916 Montana elected the first woman to the House of Representatives. During World War I, Congress finally gave in to the suffragists, and in 1919 the Nineteenth Amendment was added to the Constitution. It seemed to make no spectacular change in voting patterns.

A more controversial and less used device for improving officials was the recall, which made possible their removal at a special election to be called after sufficient numbers of the electorate had signed petitions. This became a national issue when President Taft vetoed a bill admitting Arizona as a state because its constitution authorized recall of judges. Horrified conservatives approved of the veto, but soon after Arizona entered the Union without the offensive provision, the state's voters restored it.

Undoubtedly all these devices did bring about a greater degree of democratization. Progressives used them to obtain control of states, and then eradicated corruption and passed reform legislation. Robert M. La Follette in Wisconsin obtained firm regulation of railroads, compensation for workmen injured in industrial accidents, and graduated taxation of inheritances. Charles Evans Hughes in New York obtained a commission to regulate public utilities. In New Jersey, when Woodrow Wilson, fresh from the presidency of Princeton University, became governor in 1911, he obtained from the legislature a substantial array of measures to transform the state from the backward "mother of trusts" into a model of progressivism.

Much of the sorely needed legislation came only late and after a hard struggle. New York, for example, adopted factory-safety laws only when shocked into action by the Triangle Shirtwaist Factory fire (1911), which trapped and killed 148 persons, most of them young women, in New York City.

Progressive legislators in the states ran the risk that the Supreme Court would invalidate their handiwork. The Court made one great, although temporary, shift toward progressivism. This came in 1908 when Louis D. Brandeis argued in support of an Oregon law to limit women workers to a ten-hour day. He presented a brief in which he devoted only 2 of 104 pages to the legal precedents and the remainder to proofs that Oregon's police power was necessary to protect the health and general welfare of the mothers, and thus of all mankind. The Supreme Court accepted this argument and thus moved toward the "sociological jurisprudence" which Dean Roscoe Pound of the Harvard Law School had been developing. This, Pound explained, was intended to adjust "principles and doctrines to human conditions they are to govern rather than to assumed first principles."

Progressives seeking state reforms looked not only to the Supreme Court but also to Congress and the White House. Here obviously rested the ultimate power for the control of the many problems that crossed state lines. Reformers obtained from Congress in 1910 several laws to reinforce state legislation. The Webb-Kenyon Act, passed over Taft's veto, prohibited the interstate shipment of liquor into dry areas. The Mann Act outlawed the interstate transportation of "white slaves" and thus helped in the fight to break up prostitution syndicates, one of the main sources of underworld income.

At the state level, progressives fought to liberalize the United States Senate through the direct election of senators. State legislatures were occasionally open to bribery, and much too often they elected conservatives who did not represent the public choice. David Graham Phillips in his senatorial articles, "The Treason of the Senate," scourged the body as a rich men's club; a California senator replied that there were only ten millionaires in the Senate.

By 1902 the House of Representatives had already passed resolutions five times for a constitutional amendment for direct election of senators; each time the Senate blocked the amendment. Impatient progressives in various states provided in effect for direct election by means of preferential votes for senators; the legislatures were obligated to choose the candidate whom the voters preferred. By 1912 twenty-nine states had adopted these devices. In 1911 Governor Wilson of New Jersey gained renown by blocking the legislative election of a party boss. At the same time, in New York, Franklin D. Roosevelt, just twenty-nine, won his political spurs by leading legislative insurgents against Tammany's hand-picked candidate, a Buffalo traction magnate. That same year, the Senate ousted one of its members, Boss William E. Lorimer of Chicago, for vote-buying. In the wake of the public indignation that followed, the Senate in 1912 passed the Seventeenth Amendment, for the direct election of senators, and by 1913 the requisite number of states had ratified it. The new amendment did not startlingly modify the nature of the Senate, since most progressive states had already elected senators of a new mettle.

Neither did another progressive reform measure, the preferential presidential primary, have much consequence. This was begun in Oregon in 1910 and spread to twenty states by 1920, but it by no means eliminated the maneuvering in conventions. Its main effect was to provide a series of state-wide popularity contests among leading candidates in the months before the convention.

## The Neglected Negro

The Negro was the forgotten man of the progressive era. He made few gains except in literacy—between 1900 and 1910 the percentage of Negroes who could read and write increased from about 65 to 70. In the South, despite the "separate but equal" theory, Negro schools were far inferior to those of the whites. In the nation as a whole there were, as late as 1910, only 8,251 Negroes attending high school.

In some respects the plight of black Americans worsened, and progressives themselves were largely to blame for this in the Southern states. Progressive leaders there concluded that political reform was hopeless so long as the Negro remained a potential voter, for their opponents could argue that the progressive movement, by dividing the whites and disrupting the solid South, would lead to "Negro domination." Hence progressives joined in the popular de-

## W. E. B. Du Bois and the New Negro

In the early 1900's many Negroes, and some whites as well, began to criticize Booker T. Washington's gradual approach to the racial problem. These people contended that Washington's emphasis on education and economic progress was inadequate, and they advocated more militant methods. At first they expressed themselves through a somewhat loose organization known as the Niagara Movement. But in 1909, after a race riot in Springfield, Illinois, they came together to establish the National Association for the Advancement of Colored People. Although most of the officers of the new society were whites, the guiding spirit was a Negro, W. E. B. Du Bois. Fiery and articulate, Du Bois demanded nothing less than an equal place for the Negro in American life. He directly challenged Washington's position as leader of the race. Washington's leadership, Du Bois claimed, "has tended to make the whites, North and South, shift the burden of the Negro problem to the Negro's shoulders and stand aside as critical and rather pessimistic spectators; when in fact the burden belongs to the nation, and the hands of none of us are clean if we bend not our energies to righting these great wrongs." In the years after 1909 the NAACP was to spearhead the drive for equal rights, using as its principal weapon lawsuits in the federal courts.

event led directly to the rise of the first effective nationwide oganization for Negro rights.

The emerging leader in the cause was William E. Burghardt Du Bois, a Negro historian and sociologist with a Harvard Ph.D. Du Bois openly challenged Booker T. Washington as the spokesman for their race. Washington taught Negroes that they must be patient and submissive until they had proved their worth, and thus he "tended to make the whites, North and South, shift the burden of the Negro problem to the Negro's shoulders and stand aside as critical and rather pessimistic spectators," Du Bois charged; "when in fact the burden belongs to the nation, and the hands of none of us are clean if we bend not our energies to righting these great wrongs."

At first Du Bois and a group of like-minded reformers, black and white, met from time to time in a fellowship known as the Niagara Movement. Then, on Lincoln's Birthday in 1909, they organized the National Association for the Advancement of Colored People. White men were named to most of the offices of the NAACP, but Du Bois as its director of publicity and research remained the guiding spirit. From 1909 on, the NAACP worked slowly but steadily for equal rights, mainly through legal strategy, through filing and winning one lawsuit after another in the federal courts.

## THE SQUARE DEAL

After intervening on behalf of striking coal miners (in 1902), President Roosevelt said he had tried to give them a "square deal." He also used this expression in reference to other reforms he sponsored, and it came to be a catch phrase for the domestic policies of his administration.

### The First Roosevelt

Theodore Roosevelt gave the muckraking movement its name. At a banquet shortly after the appearance of David Graham Phillip's shocking articles on "The Treason of the Senate," Roosevelt arose to liken the writer to the man in *Pilgrim's Progress* who was so busy raking the muck at his feet that he could not see the heavenly crown that was offered him from above. The

mand to remove the Negro, finally and completely, from politics.

Meanwhile Negroes suffered more and more at the hands of lynching mobs in the South and rioters in both the South and the North. In 1908, while the city's leaders were planning a 1909 celebration of the centennial of Abraham Lincoln's birth, a bloody race riot broke out in Springfield, Illinois, Lincoln's home town. This

**President Theodore Roosevelt in Yosemite Valley**

Seen here with John Muir, the naturalist, Roosevelt dramatized his interest in conservation when he visited Yosemite and later succeeded in bringing it under federal administration. It became a national park in 1906. (The Bettmann Archive)

cynical, conservative Speaker of the House, "Uncle Joe" Cannon, is supposed to have replied to Roosevelt: "Yes, you're the chief muckraker." This was true. The great role of the muckraker was to publicize the need for reform. No one succeeded better than Roosevelt in dramatically arousing the indignation of the progressives and leading them toward political action on a national scale.

Roosevelt was an "accidental" occupant of the White House. As Vice President, he had taken over the Presidency after McKinley's assassination in September 1901. The assassin, who shot McKinley at an exposition in Buffalo, New York, was a young drifter named Leon F. Czolgosz, who proclaimed himself an anarchist and said he had had an urge to kill a "great leader." He was electrocuted.

At the news of McKinley's death, his friend and mentor Mark Hanna exclaimed: "Now look, that damned cowboy is President of the United States!" Actually, as a rather uncertain fledgling President, only forty-two years old when he took office, Roosevelt had little inclination to put a vigorous progressive program into operation. He later admitted: "I cannot say that I entered the presidency with any deliberately planned and far reaching scheme of social betterment." His greatest ambition obviously was to be elected President in his own right.

Even had Roosevelt possessed a detailed plan of legislation, he could have done little to forward it in the fall of 1901. Congress, like most of the governmental machinery in the United States from the municipalities up, was under the control of old-style politicians. "Uncle Joe" Cannon, as speaker of the House, operated under the autocratic powers "Czar" Reed had seized in 1890. Though genial, Cannon so firmly controlled appointments to committees and debates on legislation that the few progressives beginning to appear in the House were obliged either to cooperate or to sit as impotent witnesses to Cannon's dictatorship. The Senate was under the domination of an intelligent and competent oligarchy of conservatives. The most commanding of them was tall, austere Nelson Wilmarth Aldrich, a wealthy banker of Rhode Island.

Roosevelt realized how futile it would be to thrust his spear single-handedly against the conservatives in Congress. For the time being, therefore, he was cautious and conciliatory toward their leaders. As he planned his first annual message to Congress, his strategy obviously was to try to attract a wide following without alienating these powerful men. "Before I write my message," he wrote Aldrich in 1901, "I should like to have a chance to go over certain subjects with you." Roosevelt wrote to Senator Chauncey Depew of the New York Central Railroad: "How I wish I wasn't a reformer, oh, Senator! But I suppose I must live up to my part, like the Negro minstrel who blacked himself all over!"

Roosevelt dispensed patronage throughout the Middle West in a manner calculated to break Hanna's control over the party, although the policies of the two men were in reality basically similar. It made little difference whether these appointments took Roosevelt to the left or right. In Kansas he backed a former Populist against Hanna's GAR supporter. From Wisconsin, to the chagrin of La Follette, he chose Henry Clay

Payne of the Old Guard to be postmaster general. Payne, through his wide distribution of spoils, helped rally right-wing Republicans and Democrats behind Roosevelt. Finally, Roosevelt cemented alliances with businessmen in the North and reshuffled the unstable Republican organizations in the South. In the South, he reversed Hanna's "lily-white" policy, to appoint some qualified Negroes to office. Indeed, it was to discuss appointments that Roosevelt took the sensational step of inviting Booker T. Washington to the White House in the fall of 1901.

While playing the game of political patronage, Roosevelt markedly improved the quality of officeholders. Gradually he was able to pull into public service a group of distinguished men, both old and young, of a sort that previously had shunned government work. Henry L. Stimson, who had been earning enormous fees as a corporation lawyer, became United States attorney for the New York City area and brought into his office a group of brilliant and idealistic young lawyers, including Felix Frankfurter.

Partly because Roosevelt had attracted into the government progressives of stature, bound to him by strong ties of personal loyalty, and even more because he had won over or neutralized the Republican machines, he was in firm control of the party by 1904. He had not made it progressive, but he had made it answerable to him. Hanna died early in the year; had he lived and felt the inclination, he could have mustered little strength against Roosevelt at the convention.

In 1904 the Democrats abandoned Bryan to nominate Cleveland's former law partner, Alton B. Parker. When Roosevelt, fearing that Wall Street was putting $5 million behind Parker, allowed his campaign manager to tap the trusts, the money came pouring in. Businessmen might call Roosevelt the "mad messiah," but they were not really afraid of him. E. H. Harriman personally contributed $50,000 and J. P. Morgan, $150,000; far more came from their associates. The steel, beef, oil, and insurance trusts, and the railroads all aided. Roosevelt was not aware of the source of all the donations, nor did he feel he was putting himself under obligation.

After a dull campaign, he won by a popular majority of 2.5 million votes. While businessmen

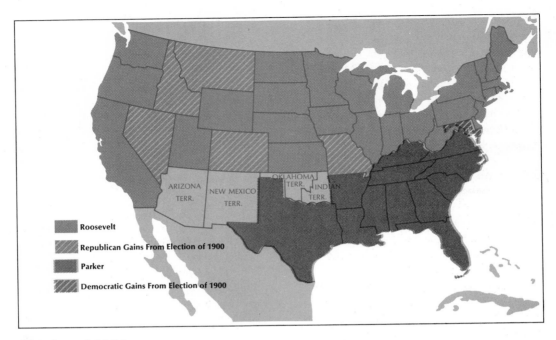

Roosevelt
Republican Gains From Election of 1900
Parker
Democratic Gains From Election of 1900

**Election of 1904**

were convinced he was safe, progressives were confident he would lead in reform. In state elections throughout the nation, progressives were generally victorious. As a sidelight, the Socialists under Eugene V. Debs (often regarded as a left-wing offshoot of the progressives), received 400,-000 votes, four times as many as in 1900. The growth of Socialist feeling gave Roosevelt a convincing argument that sane and slow reform was essential to forestall a violent upheaval.

## Trust Busting

While Roosevelt was quietly taking over the Republican machinery, he was spectacularly building an excited national following. He launched a series of attacks upon the corporate plutocracy—attacks that were vigorous but at the same time moderate.

In his first annual message to Congress, December 3, 1901, he set forth his basic policy toward trusts: "There is a widespread conviction in the minds of the American people that . . . trusts are in certain of their features and tendencies hurtful to the general welfare. This . . . is based upon sincere conviction that combination and concentration should be, not prohibited, but

supervised and within reasonable limits controlled; and in my judgment this conviction is right." Roosevelt's position on trusts was ready-made for burlesque by Finley Peter Dunne's character, Mr. Dooley: "Th' trusts, says he, are heejoous monsthers built up be th' enlightened intherprise iv th' men that have done so much to advance progress in our beloved country, he says. On wan hand I wud stamp thim undher fut; on th' other hand not so fast."

Specifically, Roosevelt asked for legislation to give the government the right to inspect and examine the workings of great corporations, and subsequently to supervise them in a mild fashion. What he desired first was the power to investigate them and publicize their activities; on the basis of these data, Congress could later frame legislation to regulate or tax the trusts. Consequently he requested the establishment of a Department of Commerce and Labor, containing a Bureau of Corporations to carry on investigations. Congress set up such a department in 1903.

The establishment of a great railroad monopoly in the Northwest, after a bitter and spectacular stock-market battle in 1901, gave Roosevelt an opportunity to begin prosecution under the Sherman Antitrust Act. And so he did, even though his avowed purpose had been to regulate, not destroy, and to stamp underfoot only "malefactors of great wealth," while sparing large corporations that were benign. The new Northern Securities Company had emerged out of the struggle for control of the Northern Pacific between E. H. Harriman of the Union Pacific on the one side and James J. Hill of the Great Northern and J. P. Morgan on the other. In the eyes of progressives, these men were malefactors.

Morgan, feeling his position challenged, hastened to the White House, accompanied by Senators Hanna and Depew. According to Roosevelt, Morgan declared: "If we have done anything wrong, send your man to my man and they can fix it up." Morgan, Roosevelt later remarked, "could not help regarding me as a big rival operator, who either intended to ruin all his interests or else could be induced to come to an agreement to ruin none." Roosevelt was not set upon ruining Morgan, but to the joy of progressives, he was using his power as President to discipline industry.

When, in 1904, Roosevelt won the case and the Supreme Court dissolved the Northern Securities combine, it in no material way injured Harriman, Hill, or Morgan. But it convinced progressives that Roosevelt, however cautious his avowed policies might be, was a heroic "trust buster."

Trust busting was popular and proceeded rapidly. Roosevelt's attorneys obtained twenty-five indictments altogether and instituted suits against the beef, oil, and tobacco combinations. In these, the government was ultimately successful, but the Supreme Court instituted a "rule of reason," declaring in effect that the Sherman Act prohibited only unreasonable restraints upon trade. Even though President Taft initiated ninety more suits and obtained forty-three additional indictments, the results of trust busting were disappointing.

Although Roosevelt's followers believed he was leading them into the millennium, the panic of 1907 illustrated the serious flaws still present in the American economic structure—and the President's unwillingness to go very far in trying

## The Supreme Court and the Sherman Act

**U.S. v. E. C. Knight Co. (1895):**
In this case involving a monopoly in the manufacture of sugar, Chief Justice Melville W. Fuller declared: "Commerce succeeds to manufacture, and is not a part of it." Since the Sherman Act was based on the constitutional power of Congress to regulate commerce, this narrow interpretation left the sugar trust untouched.

**U.S. v. Trans-Missouri Freight Association (1897):**
The Court 5 to 4 applied the Sherman Act to dissolve a railroad combination. Justice Edward D. White, dissenting, protested that the combination was valid because its "contract does not unreasonably restrain trade." The principle on which he based his dissent was known as the "rule of reason."

**Addyston Pipe and Steel Co. v. U.S. (1899):**
The Court unanimously decided against a combination of manufacturers of cast-iron pipe because it was setting prices in interstate commerce.

**Northern Securities Co. v. U.S. (1904):**
By a 5 to 4 vote, the Court ordered a railroad holding company dissolved. The dissenters, including Justice Oliver Wendell Holmes, again stated the "rule of reason."

**Standard Oil Co. v. U.S. (1911):**
The Court broke the Standard Oil combination, but the majority accepted Chief Justice White's "rule of reason": trusts were not to be dissolved unless they unreasonably restrained trade.

**U.S. v. United States Steel (1920):**
The Court refused to dissolve the corporation although it was the largest in its field, holding that it had not engaged in unlawful conduct.

to remedy them. Speculation and mismanagement during the boom years since the Spanish-American War led to a sharp break in prosperity in 1907. Roosevelt was quick to conciliate Wall Street. Judge Elbert H. Gary and Henry C. Frick called upon him one morning to tell him that unless United States Steel took over shares of the Tennessee Coal and Iron Company, this company would fail and its failure would threaten a widespread industrial smash-up. Gary and Frick desired assurance that the government would not consider the purchase a violation of the Sherman Act. Roosevelt tacitly agreed. United States Steel was thus able to buy out a vigorous competitor at a bargain price, thus reducing competition and holding back the development of the iron and steel industry in the South.

## Government and Labor

Presidential intervention in labor disputes was nothing new—there had been, for example, the Pullman strike—but the government had usually acted as a strikebreaker for the employers. Now Roosevelt was ready to make the government an impartial arbiter instead. Here again, as in dealing with capitalists, he wished the government to be paramount over the conflicting economic forces and neutral in dealing with them. Organized labor, as long as it was well-behaved, did not frighten the progressives nearly as much as did organized capital. The unions were comparatively weak; despite the great upsurge of the American Federation of Labor in the 1890s, by 1900 only about 4 per cent of the working force, even excluding agricultural laborers, was organized.

Injustice toward workers was most extreme in anthracite coal mining. Eight coal railroads under Morgan's domination held a virtual monopoly over the industry. Wages were substandard, hours long, and the accident rate shockingly high. The workers, under John Mitchell, struck in May 1902, for an eight-hour day, a 20-per-cent wage increase, and recognition of the union. Mitchell so effectively presented the miners' claims, and George F. Baer, spokesman for the operators, was so truculent, that public sympathy was aligned with the strikers. Baer foolishly asserted the divine right of the operators

to deal with miners as they saw best. He remained adamant when Roosevelt called operators and miners to the White House early in October to ask them to accept arbitration. In contrast, Mitchell was quite willing to accept. Roosevelt eventually persuaded Morgan to force arbitration upon the operators. Even so, the miners after their long strike failed to gain union recognition and obtained only a 10-per-cent wage increase.

The coal strike and its settlement were evidence of "a honeymoon period of capital and labor," stretching from McKinley's inauguration through Roosevelt's first term. Union membership jumped from less than a half million to over 2 million. Monopolistic companies could well afford to deal liberally with unions, since the companies could thus avoid work stoppages in prosperous periods and pass on increased labor costs to the consumers. It was altogether fitting that Hanna, the high priest of modern big business, should assume the presidency of the National Civic Federation, which was founded in 1901 to bring about friendly relations between capital and labor, and that Samuel Gompers should become vice president.

Not all laborers were ready to accept the assumption of leaders like Gompers and Mitchell that differences with capitalists could easily be adjusted around a conference table. The Socialist minority within the American Federation of Labor succeeded in capturing unions of machinists and miners. Socialists won municipal elections in Milwaukee, Schenectady, and Berkeley. Militant western miners in 1905 founded the Industrial Workers of the World, which tried to organize the great masses of unskilled workers, mostly immigrants, whom the AFL ignored. The IWW, a syndicalist organization, aimed ultimately to form "one big union" including all workers, hold one big strike, and thus paralyze and then take over the government. Its members, popularly known as "Wobblies," were accused of responsibility for acts of violence. Employers and state and local authorities certainly did not hesitate to use violence against the Wobblies. Two episodes, neither the work of the IWW, especially outraged orderly progressives. These were the murder of a former governor of Idaho and the dynamiting of the plant of

**Poor People Waiting for Coal   1902**

In the crisp October days of 1902, poor people began to suffer from the effects of the coal shortage. The price of coal was soaring, and it was becoming so scarce that people had to stand in queues to obtain a few pounds. Schools in the Northeast were running out of coal and would soon have to close. (Culver)

the Los Angeles *Times,* which was militantly antiunion.

Such episodes prompted many progressives to listen to the antiunion slogans of the National Association of Manufacturers and kindred organizations. The NAM, which proclaimed itself against union recognition in 1903, was predominantly made up of men who ran small plants and were dependent upon low labor costs to survive in highly competitive markets. It called the open shop the "American Plan," and the independent workman (strikebreaker) the "American hero." President Charles W. Eliot of Harvard gave formidable support by asserting that nothing was "more essential to the preservation of individual liberty" than protection of the independent workman.

The manufacturers had the backing of federal judges. The most spectacular court blow against collective bargaining grew out of the Danbury Hatters' strike of 1902. The courts held that the union's efforts to obtain a nationwide boycott of Loewe hats was a violation of the Sherman Act and assessed triple damages of $240,000 against the union. In another boycott case, involving the Buck's Stove and Range Company of St. Louis, a federal court issued a sweeping injunction that forbade the AFL to carry on the boycott, to include the company in a "We Don't Patronize" list in its newspaper, or even to mention the dispute orally or in writing. When Gompers and other AFL officials defied the injunction by mentioning the dispute, they were sentenced to prison for contempt of court. The sentences were never served, but the principle of the injunction stood. Union officials began a concerted and vigorous campaign to exempt labor organizations from the Antitrust Act and to outlaw antilabor injunctions.

Gompers and his followers demanded an end

to governmental discrimination against them; they were not asking for welfare laws. To some extent Roosevelt sympathized with them. He denounced the Buck's Stove decision and inveighed against court abuse of injunctions. But he was more interested in paternalistic legislation for labor, similar to that being proposed in many state legislatures. He asked Congress for laws to regulate the hours and working conditions of women and children, establish employers' liability for accident compensation, and improve railroad safety measures. For the moment he made no headway.

## Regulation and Conservation

Roosevelt accepted his 1904 victory as a mandate for progressive reform. He was now free from his earlier preoccupation with winning reelection, having announced that he would not seek another term. He continued to operate from the political center, offending big businessmen who had contributed to his campaign, and at the same time offending Midwestern progressives who took up what he called "the La Follette type of fool radicalism."

While leaving the tariff alone, Roosevelt now exercised his presidential leadership to obtain more effective railroad-rate regulation. The courts had practically nullified the Interstate Commerce Act of 1887. By a series of intricate maneuvers, Roosevelt managed to force a new regulatory law through Congress. At one point he seemed to join Senator Robert M. La Follette, the recent reform governor of Wisconsin, in demands for really drastic regulation of railroads. La Follette wished to give the ICC power to evaluate railroad property as a base for determining rates. He felt betrayed when Roosevelt abandoned him. Although the Hepburn Act of June 1906 was in La Follette's eyes only half a loaf, it was at least the beginning of effective railroad regulation. It empowered the ICC to put into effect reasonable rates, subject to later court review; extended its jurisdiction to cover express, sleeping car, and pipeline companies; separated railroad management from other enterprises such as mining; prescribed uniform bookkeeping; and forbade passes and rebates.

It was a large half-loaf, and La Follette and

his supporters in Congress soon were able to obtain the remaining part. In 1910 insurgent Republicans and Democrats passed the Mann-Elkins Act, abolishing the "long-and-short-haul" evil, further extending the jurisdiction of the ICC, and strengthening other features of the Hepburn Act. The ICC could now suspend proposed new rates up to ten months, and could demand proof from the railroads that they would be reasonable. Finally, in 1913, La Follette's long agitation resulted in passage of a law authorizing the ICC to evaluate railroads and to set rates that would give a fair return of profit.

One of the many reasons for the clamor for lower freight rates had been to lower the rising cost of lumber. The forests of the Great Lakes area were depleted, and the increasing amounts of lumber coming from the Pacific Northwest had to bear the heavy cost of transportation eastward. Furthermore, trees were being felled faster than they were being grown. At this point, conflict developed between progressives in the West and those in the East. Westerners wanted the government to aid in the rapid development of their resources. Easterners were more interested in preserving the remaining wilderness; their concern was esthetic and recreational.

Roosevelt, ardent sportsman and naturalist that he was, along with his Chief Forester, Gifford Pinchot, and most Eastern progressives, felt that the United States must develop great national forests like those of the European countries. For years Major John Wesley Powell, explorer of the Grand Canyon, and other experts had been advocating new policies for husbanding the public domain.

A beginning had come with the passage of the Forest Reserve Act of 1891; under its provisions 47 million acres had been set aside as national forests. Roosevelt, clothing his actions with the terminology of the progressive struggle against the vested interests, rapidly extended the government reserves. In 1907 Western congressmen succeeded in attaching a rider (unrelated amendment) to an appropriation bill, prohibiting him from withdrawing further lands. Roosevelt could not veto the appropriations bill without calamitous effects. So he quickly withdrew practically all remaining forests in the

### Robert M. La Follette Campaigning in Wisconsin

"Battling Bob" La Follette (1855–1925) in the 1880's was a Republican congressman sufficiently regular to help prepare the McKinley tariff. Although he remained in the party during the 1890's, he began to champion reforms of a Populist nature. In 1901, pledged to fight for a direct primary, tax reform, and railroad control, he was elected governor of Wisconsin. His advice came from experts at the University of Wisconsin, his votes largely from a rural constituency. In 1905, he finally obtained a legislature that would enact his program. Although he had already been elected United States Senator, he remained governor until the end of the year when his proposals had become law. In Washington he advocated a similar national program, especially rigorous regulation of railroads. It brought him into conflict with both the Old Guard and President Roosevelt; he entitled a chapter of his autobiography "Alone in the Senate." Roosevelt, La Follette wrote, "acted upon the maxim that half a loaf is better than no bread. I believe that half a loaf is fatal whenever it is accepted at the sacrifice of the basic principle sought to be attained." Although nationally La Follette was at times isolated in his advanced agrarian progressive position, in Wisconsin he and his sons commanded so loyal a following that they dominated the state politically for nearly forty years. (State Historical Society of Wisconsin)

public domain and then signed the bill. Altogether he added about 125 million acres to the national forests, and reserved 4.7 million acres of phosphate beds and 68 million acres of coal lands—all the known coal deposits in the public domain.

At the same time, Roosevelt prepared the way for a new government policy on electric power by reserving 2,565 water-power sites, which expanding private utility companies were interested in obtaining. Further, he vetoed a bill to permit private exploitation of the power at Muscle Shoals on the Tennessee River, which a generation later became the heart of the Tennessee Valley Authority (TVA). The way was open for government development of huge power projects, a program as popular in the West as the withdrawal of other land was unpopular.

It was not the President but a Democratic senator from Nevada, Francis G. Newlands, who proposed an extensive federal reclamation program for the West. Roosevelt endorsed it and was able to win much of the credit for the Newlands Reclamation Act of 1902. This provided that money from the sale of Western lands should go into a revolving fund to undertake irrigation projects too large for private capital or state resources. Eventually, the government built huge dams for the development of power and storage of water, and extensive systems of canals to carry the water to arid lands. By 1915 the government had invested $80 million in twenty-five projects, of which the largest was the Roosevelt Dam on the Salt River of Arizona. The principle of government aid in irrigation and power development in the West had become firmly established.

Progressives undertook to legislate the nation into better health after muckrakers had made the public aware of the disgusting and dangerous substances that were being sold and eaten as food. None created a more shocked reaction than Upton Sinclair, who wrote a powerful novel of protest against exploitation of immigrant labor in the stockyards, and incidentally included nauseating descriptions of the preparation of meats. When *The Jungle* appeared in 1906, it hit Americans' stomachs as much as their consciences.

Roosevelt himself was horrified, and when a commission verified the descriptions in *The Jungle*, he sought reform. Two pieces of legislation were passed in June 1906. One was the Meat Inspection Act, which eventually did much to bring about the eradication of some animal diseases, especially tuberculosis. The other was the Pure Food and Drug Act, which bore the impressive descriptive title: "An Act for preventing the manufacture, sale, or transportation of adulterated or misbranded or poisonous or deleterious foods, drugs, medicines, and liquors, and for regulating traffic therein, and for other purposes."

## The Sausages [1906]

*There was never the least attention paid to what was cut up for sausage; there would come all the way back from Europe old sausage that had been rejected, and that was mouldy and white—it would be dosed with borax and glycerine, and dumped into the hoppers, and made over again for home consumption. There would be meat that had tumbled out on the floor, in the dirt and sawdust, where the workers had tramped and spit uncounted billions of [tuberculosis] germs. There would be meat stored in great piles in rooms; and the water from leaky roofs would drip over it, and thousands of rats would race about on it. It was too dark in these storage places to see well, but a man could run his hand over these piles of meat and sweep off handfuls of the dried dung of rats. These rats were nuisances, and the packers would put poisoned bread out for them; they would die, and then rats, bread, and meat would go into the hoppers together.—Upton Sinclair,* The Jungle *(Garden City, N.Y.: Doubleday, 1906).*

## A RIFT IN REPUBLICAN RANKS

As early as 1904 Roosevelt had tentatively decided that his good friend William Howard Taft, then secretary of war, would make an excellent successor as President. But after Taft's election the two were to fall out and, in doing so, were to split the Republican party.

### Taft and the Tariff

Taft was known for his achievements as one of the first viceroys of the new American empire. Between 1900 and 1908, he traveled over 100,000 miles on assignment to Manila, Rome, Panama, Cuba, and within the United States. His achievements were almost all in the realm of colonial or foreign policy; he had little to do with Roosevelt's domestic policies, although privately he subscribed to almost every one of them. If he was to the right of Roosevelt, it was only by a hairline. The great distinction was that while he regarded Roosevelt's objectives as justifiable, he felt, as he commented in 1910, that Roosevelt "ought more often to have admitted the legal way of reaching the same ends." This colorless way of saying things marked another contrast between Taft and Roosevelt.

In 1908 Roosevelt had no difficulty in securing the nomination of Taft. The smooth-running Republican machinery followed Roosevelt's bidding and gathered the votes of the delegates: organization men, officeholders, and Southern Republicans.

Business moguls preferred the gingerly progressive Republican candidate to the more forthright William Jennings Bryan, running forlornly for a third time. Rockefeller wired Taft congratulations on the nomination; Morgan remarked, "Good! good!" Carnegie sent a campaign contribution of $20,000. This did not mean that Taft had capitulated to Wall Street; indeed he was more careful about accepting corporate campaign contributions than Roosevelt had been in 1904.

Taft campaigned as the champion of smaller business interests. In his acceptance address he promised that he would perfect the machinery for restraining law-breakers and at the same time interfere with legitimate business as little as possible. Most important, he appealed to small-business and middle-class concern over the rising cost of living by firmly promising a reduction in the tariff.

The election result was a foregone conclusion, a sweep for Taft. The electoral vote was 321 to 162, but there were portents of national unrest in the victory. Taft's lead over Bryan was only half the size of Roosevelt's plurality in 1904; several Western states shifted to Bryan, and several others in the Middle West elected Democratic governors even though they gave their electoral votes to Taft. Republican progressives, pleased at the outcome, proclaimed: "Roosevelt has cut enough hay; Taft is the man to put it into the barn." Republican conservatives rejoiced that they were rid of the "mad messiah."

Certainly Taft's intention was to load Roosevelt's hay into the barn, but the hay soon was drenched by violent political storms. Taft seemed incapable of negotiating with the Old

**Election of 1908**

**"New Wine in Old Bottles"**

(J. N. "Ding" Darling in the Des Moines *Register*)

Guard, as Roosevelt had done, without giving the impression that he had joined them. To the progressives Taft seemed guilty of betrayal.

The first of his betrayals in the eyes of progressives was the fiasco that occurred when Taft called Congress into special session to enact a lower tariff. "I believe the people are with me," he had written, "and before I get through I think I will have downed Cannon and Aldrich too." But having proclaimed a tariff crusade, he remained behind while Middle Westerners carried their lances into battle. They were not "free traders" like some Southern Democrats, but they did want to weaken trusts by exposing them to foreign competition. The way to do this, they thought, was to lower tariff rates substantially. They thought the President was behind them, but he failed to send Congress a fighting message or to intervene with his patronage powers when congressmen began to succumb to the blandishments of lobbyists and logrollers.

The Payne-Aldrich tariff passed Congress over the votes of Midwest Republicans and was signed by Taft on August 5, 1909. He said it was not a perfect bill but represented "a sincere effort on the part of the Republican party to make a downward revision." Also it provided for a Tariff Commission which was to make scientific studies of rates—an appealing idea to some progressives, who felt that the tariff, like most problems, should be determined scientifically and taken out of politics.

Nevertheless, the Payne-Aldrich tariff seemed to favor Senator Aldrich's New England at the expense of the rest of the country. On a tour around the country in the fall of 1909, Taft tried to defend the new tariff in a hastily prepared speech delivered in the heart of the area of resentment, Winona, Minnesota. One line from that speech made damaging headlines against the President. He said: "On the whole . . . the Payne bill is the best bill that the Republican party ever passed." The remainder of the trip through the Midwest, wrote a reporter, was "a polar dash through a world of ice."

In 1911 Taft further alienated Middle Westerners when he submitted to the Senate a reciprocal trade agreement with Canada, an agreement that would have lowered tariffs on both sides and in effect would have brought the two countries into an economic union. Many Eastern manufacturers, seeing larger Canadian markets for their goods, were enthusiastic, but the Middle Westerners, fearing a flood of competing Canadian farm products and raw materials, were bitterly hostile. La Follette complained: "It singles out the farmer and forces free trade upon him, but it confers even greater benefits upon a few of the great combinations sheltered behind the high rates found in the Payne-Aldrich tariff." He and his cohorts formed a strange alliance with die-hard members of the Old Guard but were defeated by Eastern Republicans and Southern free-trade Democrats. The Senate approved the reciprocity arrangement, 55 to 27. But the Canadian parliament refused to act, for many Canadians feared that tariff reductions might somehow lead to Canada's being annexed by the United States.

## T. R. Against Taft

The progressive Republicans of the Midwest had cut loose from Taft. They blamed him, unjustly, for their failure to oust Speaker Cannon in 1909. By 1910, without the presidential blessing, they were strong enough to resume the effort. Under the leadership of George W. Norris they breached Cannon's formidable parliamentary defenses and opened a fierce debate that raged for nearly thirty hours. It ended with Cannon's removal from the Rules Committee, which henceforth was to be elected by the House. He remained as House speaker, but he was no longer the obstacle he had been to progressive legislation.

Meanwhile, through the sensational Ballinger-Pinchot controversy, Taft lost the sympathy of most of Theodore Roosevelt's following in the urban East and the Far West. Taft had replaced Roosevelt's secretary of the interior with a man who wished to distribute to private interests the natural resources in the public domain. The viewpoint of the new secretary, Richard Ballinger, was dominant among businessmen of the West, who wished themselves to prosper and to see their region grow. But Taft had left in charge of the Forestry Service in the Department of Agriculture Roosevelt's ardent admirer, Gifford Pinchot of Pennsylvania, who, like most Eastern nature lovers and sportsmen, was zealous to preserve the public domain unspoiled, as a part of the nation's heritage. A violent clash between these two men was almost inevitable.

The occasion was the spectacular charge that Ballinger was conniving to turn over valuable coal lands in Alaska to a Morgan-Guggenheim syndicate. Taft, accepting Ballinger's rebuttal, publicly exonerated him. Immediately Roosevelt progressives throughout the country championed Pinchot as the defender of the national domain against the corrupt onslaught of big business. Pinchot, by going over the President's head directly to Congress, provoked Taft to discharge him for insubordination. A congressional committee investigated and, since the Old Guard dominated it, reported in favor of Ballinger. To the end, Taft stood by his Secretary of the Interior, whom he correctly considered to be an honorable man. But in refusing to dismiss Ballinger as an anticonservationist, Taft opened a rift between himself and the Roosevelt following that was as wide and deep as the one separating him from the La Follette supporters.

As early as the tariff fiasco in 1909, progressives had begun to look to the African jungle for their next presidential candidate. In the middle of June 1910, loaded with trophies from Africa and fresh impressions of reform from Europe,

**"Revising the Tariff Downward (?)"**
(J. N. "Ding" Darling in the Des Moines *Register*)

Roosevelt returned. Observers noted that his first hello was to Pinchot and that he turned down Taft's invitation to the White House. Indeed, he had already met Pinchot in Europe, bearing messages from progressives, and had come to the conclusion that Taft had "completely twisted around the policies I advocated and acted upon."

Furious with Taft for helping bring about the split in the party, Roosevelt determined to do all he could to reunify it. He told reporters he was seeing all Republicans—"regulars and insurgents, party men and independents." But at Osawatomie, Kansas, on September 1, he delivered a speech that returned him to command of the progressives. At Osawatomie, he proclaimed the doctrines of the New Nationalism, emphasizing that social justice could be attained in the nation only through strengthening the power of the federal government so that the executive could be the "steward of public welfare." Men thinking primarily of property rights and personal profits "must now give way to the advocate of human welfare, who rightly maintains that every man holds his property subject to the general right of the community to regulate its use to whatever degree the public welfare may require it." Going beyond these generalizations, frightening enough to the Old Guard, Roosevelt listed some specific proposals: graduated income and inheritance taxes, workmen's accident compensation, regulation of the labor of women and children, tariff revision, and firm regulation of corporations through a more powerful Bureau of Corporations and Interstate Commerce Commission. From the Mississippi westward, progressives were ready to acclaim him as the next presidential candidate, but among his right-wing enemies, Lodge warned him, he was regarded as "little short of a revolutionist."

Progressive Republicans of the Middle West hoped they could wrest the presidential nomination from Taft in 1912. In January 1911, a group of them formed the National Progressive Republican League to work for the nomination of La Follette. But a great majority of the progressive Republicans continued to hope that Roosevelt could be persuaded to run.

With Roosevelt receptive, many of La Fol-

lette's supporters switched to him with indecent haste after La Follette on February 2, 1912, exhausted and worried, delivered a rambling, repetitious talk. Roosevelt thus acquired new recruits, but he also won the undying hatred of La Follette and his loyal Middle Western progressive following. Nevertheless, in the primaries Roosevelt demonstrated that he was overwhelmingly the presidential choice of Republican voters.

The nomination at the Republican convention would depend upon the seating of the delegates; more than a third of the seats were contested. The Republican National Committee, made up almost entirely of loyal Taft supporters, allowed Roosevelt only 19 out of 254 contested seats, and thus in advance counted him out of the nomination.

Roosevelt had come in person to the convention to direct his forces, and the night before it opened, he told a hysterically cheering throng of 5,000 that he would not be bound by the convention if it failed to seat his contested delegates. He concluded thunderously: "We stand at Armageddon, and we battle for the Lord." As good as his word, he bolted, leaving the conservatives in complete command at the Republican convention. With Roosevelt's one-time friend Elihu Root presiding, Warren G. Harding, one of the most regular of the regulars, mellifluously nominated Taft, who was chosen on the first ballot.

During the Republican convention, Roosevelt had agreed to the formation of a new, Progressive party when Frank Munsey, the newspaper magnate, and George W. Perkins, of United States Steel and International Harvester, promised him financing. Announcing his willingness to run, Roosevelt said he was as fit as a bull moose, giving the party a symbol as well as a name. When the Progressives met at Chicago in August to nominate Roosevelt formally, the conclave was far more symbolic of progressivism than of ordinary American politics. Missing were La Follette and his following, five of seven governors who had signed a call for Roosevelt in January, and such notable Republican insurgents as Norris of Nebraska and William E. Borah of Idaho.

The convention was more like a camp meet-

**Woodrow Wilson and Champ Clark**

Speaker Clark seemed an almost certain nominee at the 1912 Democratic convention, at one point receiving well over a majority of the delegates' votes, 556 to 350½, but it took two-thirds to nominate. When finally he lost to Wilson he went to Sea Girt, New Jersey, where Wilson was spending the summer, to demonstrate his party support. (Culver)

ing than the gatherings to which Roosevelt was accustomed. The delegates sang "Onward Christian Soldiers" and closed the convention with the "Doxology." Roosevelt seemed bewildered as he acknowledged their almost fanatical, hymn-singing welcome, for "they were crusaders; he was not."

Roosevelt's program would accept big business but would regulate it through a national industrial commission. And a Federal Securities Commission would police stocks and bonds. In the program there was much to appeal to the progressives of the cities, whether reformers or businessmen, but little of interest to farmers, and much paternalism but no guarantee of collective bargaining for organized labor. In an effort to win disgruntled Southern businessmen away from the Democratic party, Roosevelt endorsed a lily-white (excluding Negroes) Progressive party for the South.

## THE NEW FREEDOM

Between the time Roosevelt bolted the Republican convention and the time he received the Progressive nomination, the Democrats met in Baltimore and exulted in the knowledge that, though theirs was a minority party, they were almost certainly choosing the next President.

## Woodrow Wilson Wins

In Baltimore, Bryan, who long had dominated the party, stood aside while four contenders battled for the nomination. These were Governor Woodrow Wilson of New Jersey, Speaker Champ Clark of Missouri, the right-wing Governor Judson Harmon of Ohio, and Representative Oscar W. Underwood, of Alabama, the champion of Southern conservatives and a low tariff. Wilson's spectacular reform achievements in New Jersey had made him the favorite of Democratic progressives in Eastern cities, and he took a quick lead for the nomination as he crisscrossed the nation to make hundreds of inspiring speeches denouncing special privilege and heralding the new progressive order. Yet, in 1912, he emerged from the primaries and state conventions with only 248 delegates to Clark's 436. Underwood swept most of the South.

It was little short of a miracle that Clark, who had the rural Democrats and most of the bosses behind him, and who obtained more than a majority of the votes on ballot after ballot, nevertheless failed to win the nomination. The main reason for the miracle was that the Wilson and Underwood forces stood firm, blocking Clark's nomination, while Wilson's managers negotiated deals with the machines and with Underwood's following. To some extent Clark's defeat may

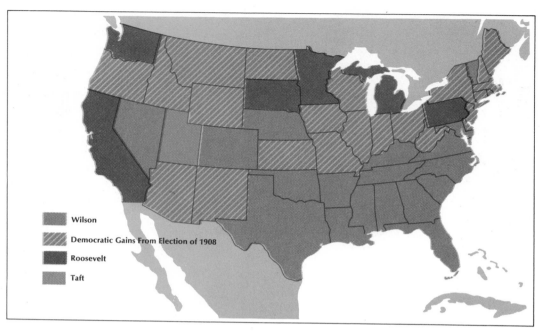

**Wilson**

**Democratic Gains From Election of 1908**

**Roosevelt**

**Taft**

**Election of 1912**

have been due to Bryan, who threw his support to Wilson at a critical moment in the convention struggle.

A crusade requires a crusader, and the Democrats obtained one at last on the forty-sixth ballot when they nominated Wilson. This lean, lantern-jawed son of a Southern Presbyterian preacher looked as well as acted the part. His aspiration had always been to become a political leader, but when he found the road rough as a beginning lawyer in Atlanta, he took a Ph.D. degree at Johns Hopkins, became a professor of political economy, and then served as president of Princeton University.

Both as president of Princeton and as governor of New Jersey, Wilson demonstrated the courageous strength and alarming weaknesses that would characterize his Presidency. He had the vision to inspire multitudes but was dogmatic and distant with individuals. He could lecture an opponent in high moral terms, but his sense that he and he alone was absolutely right prevented him from stooping to necessary political negotiations.

Wilson had won the nomination without

badly splitting the party. Backed by a progressive platform, he appeared before the electorate in armor at least as brightly shining as Roosevelt's. The distance between the positions of the Democratic party and the new Progressive party was not as great as campaign oratory made it out to be, just as personality more than principles separated Wilson from Roosevelt. Nevertheless, the differences in platform were significant in the campaign and in Wilson's future program as President.

Wilson's program, called the New Freedom, emerged as the campaign unfolded. His conversion to progressivism had come only two or three years before, and he had continued to cling to the state-rights position that the task of the federal government was the purely negative one of destroying privilege. Thus Wilson hoped to restore the good old days, which in reality had never existed, by recreating full opportunity for the small enterprise. Roosevelt's New Nationalism, Wilson charged, would mean the federal licensing of the juggernauts of big business to crush the American people. In contrast, Wilson proclaimed his New Freedom as the fight for emancipation of the small businessman, the "man on the make." He proclaimed: "If America is not to have free enterprise, then she can have freedom of no sort whatever."

Wilson was able to win over Bryan's rural and small-town following with the same religious appeal, the same denunciation of the Wall Street money trust, that the "Great Commoner" had always used. Some well-educated people who had always scorned Bryan as a fool came to worship Wilson as a saint.

Thus Wilson was able to hold Democratic progressives, while Roosevelt was able only to pull progressives out of the Republican party. As for Taft, after several sad speeches, so conservative that they might have been written by Aldrich, he lapsed into silence. The Socialists, at the peak of their strength under Eugene V. Debs, criticized all three major candidates as defenders of capitalism. The main effect of the Socialists was to serve as a bugaboo for progressive leaders, who could warn that the only alternative to their own safe, moderate programs would be the drastic remedies of Socialism. Even in 1912, their heyday, the Socialists attracted only 901,000 votes, 6 per cent of the total votes cast.

Because of the three-cornered contest, Wilson carried the electoral college overwhelmingly, with 435 votes to 88 for Roosevelt and only 8 for Taft. Wilson had received less than 42 per cent of the popular vote, fewer votes than Bryan in any of his three campaigns. Yet, considering the combined Democratic and Bull Moose totals, the newly elected President had an overwhelming progressive mandate.

## Presidential Leadership

Few Presidents have taken more seriously their electoral mandate or worked more effectively to transform it into law than did Wilson. He brought back into the White House a strong belief in firm, positive presidential leadership.

The closest of Wilson's advisers was the shrewd and ubiquitous Colonel Edward M. House, who virtually shared presidential powers as Wilson's alter ego until 1919. House served as an agent for Wilson in negotiations first with the men of economic power in America, and later with those of political power in Europe. His dis-

cretion and anonymity were so consummate that one contemporary remarked: "He can walk on dead leaves and make no more noise than a tiger."

Wilson's official advisers, the members of his cabinet, were less influential. Bryan had to be offered the post of Secretary of State in recognition of his long leadership of the party. Representative William B. Wilson, former secretary-treasurer of the United Mine Workers, became the first Secretary of Labor, establishing a twenty-year precedent that the office should be filled by a labor leader. It was the most Southern cabinet since the Civil War; half of its members were Southerners, at least by birth.

Wilson promptly undertook what Roosevelt had avoided and Taft had failed to achieve—a substantial lowering of the tariff. On the day he took office he called a special session of Congress. When it met, he did what no other President since Jefferson had done: he appeared before Congress in person. His short graphic message was aimed less at congressmen than at their constituents. It brought to a blaze the sentiment for real tariff reform. With the President's active support, Underwood introduced a bill in the House providing for tariff cuts substantial enough to bring European manufacturers into competition with Americans.

To make up for the loss of revenue under the new tariff, Representative Cordell Hull drafted a section for the bill, providing for a graduated income tax under the Sixteenth Amendment. Hull cautiously set the rates exceedingly low. Then, to his delight, progressive Republican and Democratic senators forced substantially higher rates upon the conservatives and the administration. This first modern income tax imposed a 1-per-cent tax upon individuals and corporations earning over $4,000, and an additional 1-per-cent tax on income over $20,000, ranging up to a maximum of 6 per cent on income over $500,000. This income tax was the beginning of a great change in the American tax structure. Although more slowly than England and some other nations, the United States was beginning to place a proportionately greater share of the cost of government upon the rich. In so doing, it was beginning to chip away at the enormous disparity in incomes in the United States.

## The Trusts Again

Rather than lose momentum, President Wilson held Congress in session through the sweltering summer to begin work on banking reform. In 1911 he had declared: "The great monopoly in this country is the money monopoly. So long as that exists, our old variety and freedom and individual energy of development are out of the question." Early in 1913, a House investigating committee headed by a Democrat, Arsene Pujo, published frightening statistics to back Wilson's accusation. These figures, to which Louis D. Brandeis gave wide circulation in a series of articles entitled "Other People's Money," indicated that small banks were depositing their surpluses with larger ones, which in turn deposited with a few great investment bankers concentrated on Wall Street. These bankers with their enormous capital, representing the aggregate savings of millions of people, were able to demand control over corporations in

### The Credit Monopoly [1913]

*Far more dangerous than all that has happened to us in the past in the way of elimination of competition in industry is the control of credit through the domination of these groups over our banks and industries. . . .*

*Whether under a different currency system the resources in our banks would be greater or less is comparatively immaterial if they continued to be controlled by a small group. . . .*

*If the arteries of credit now clogged well-nigh to choking by the obstructions created through the control of these groups are opened so that they may be permitted freely to play their important part in the financial system, competition in large enterprises will become possible and business can be conducted on its merits instead of being subject to the tribute and the good will of this handful of self-constituted trustees of the national prosperity.* —Report of the Pujo Committee, February 28, 1913.

return for granting them financing, "the life blood of business." The Morgan-Rockefeller empire held "in all, 341 directorships in 112 corporations having aggregate resources or capitalization of $22,245,000,000." This was in 1913, when the entire national wealth was estimated at less than ten times this figure.

To Wilson, there was clearly a need to break the money trust. At the same time, paradoxically, one of the serious ills of the American banking system was its decentralization and independence, except for the loose tie of urban clearing houses. This, and the defective functioning of the national banking system, meant that in time of financial crisis and deflation it was hard for banks to draw upon their reserves or to expand their currency. With Wilson's encouragement, Congress responded to the need for banking reform.

The Federal Reserve Act (1913) created twelve regional banks. Each was to serve and be owned by the banks of its district. The Federal Reserve Bank would rediscount their notes, issue a new type of paper currency—Federal Reserve notes—and fulfill other banking functions for member banks and for the government. The act required national banks to become members and encouraged other banks to do so. Nearly half the nation's banking resources were represented in the system within its first year of operation, and four-fifths by the late 1920s. Bankers had no cause to fear the Federal Reserve Board, which governed the system, and to which Wilson appointed conservative, sympathetic men. The system was a notable advance in banking regulation, providing as it did for a more elastic currency, though it did not destroy the "money trust."

There remained the problem of the great business combinations. As several antitrust bills began to move through Congress in 1914, Wilson gave his support to one bill prohibiting unfair trade practices and establishing a Federal Trade Commission to watch out for them. He accepted the Clayton Antitrust Act, though it was not quite as strong a measure as he had desired. Conservatives in Congress put qualifying clauses around the sections outlawing interlocking directorates or stockholdings and exclusive selling contracts, so that the clauses, as progressive Republican senator complained, did not have enough teeth to masticate milk toast. Labor gained nothing of practical importance from the bill, which did, however, contain a platitude that labor was not a commodity and declared that unions were not conspiracies in restraint of trade. President Gompers of the AFL chose to hail the Clayton Act as "Labor's Magna Carta" and to insist that organized labor was now exempted from antitrust prosecution. This assumption served merely to make bitterness and resentment greater when courts continued in the twenties to follow their earlier inclinations. The Sherman and Clayton acts, though ineffective for breaking up business monopolies, were stout clubs for disciplining boycotters and strikers.

The debate over antitrust legislation during the first half of 1914 coincided with a decline in prosperity. This came because the United States, still a debtor nation easily affected by European money markets, suffered from credit restrictions growing out of European pessimism over the Balkan wars and the likelihood of a bigger war. Within this country, businessmen blamed the recession upon the Underwood tariff, and the other legislation of the New Freedom. Wilson tried to placate business titans through friendly conferences and mild administration of his new reform legislation. He assured the leaders that he only opposed businesses that expanded "by methods which unrighteously crushed those who were smaller."

## Retreat and Advance

Through 1914 and 1915, to the disappointment of many advanced progressives, Wilson again and again applied the brakes to reforms. With a state-rights answer he turned aside the plea for female suffrage. He condoned the actions of his Southern cabinet members when they introduced Jim Crow practices (discriminating against Negroes) into the administration to an unprecedented degree. Only the angry protests of Northern liberals brought some reversal. He opposed a bill to establish federally-backed land banks to ease credit to farmers, declaring it went beyond the proper scope of the government. He gave no aid to a child-labor bill because he thought it unconstitutional. Only with reluc-

tance did he sign the La Follette Seamen's bill of 1915, the work of the eloquent president of the Seamen's Union, Andrew Furuseth, which improved safety regulations and working conditions for men in the merchant marine.

For Wilson, the New Freedom might be complete, but not for the progressive Democrats in Congress. At times they expressed their sharp dismay, though they did not have to engage in warfare with him as the Republican insurgents had done with Taft. When the election year 1916 opened, two things were apparent. The Progressive party, which had never been much more than a Roosevelt vehicle, was disintegrating. Unless the Democrats, who were normally a minority, presented a new, strong progressive program, they would be swamped at the polls by the reunited Republicans. Wilson saw this danger and again became an enthusiastic reformer, going beyond the New Freedom and allying himself with the progressives, farmers, and laborers to accept a series of laws that in many respects enacted the Progressive party program of 1912. From a negative policy of restriction he moved to a positive one of vigorous federal economic and social intervention. Curiously, this came at a time when Roosevelt had moved to the far right and no longer supported his 1912 proposals.

In January 1916, Wilson named Louis D. Brandeis to the Supreme Court and weathered the conservative storm in order to obtain Senate confirmation. Brandeis was both liberal and Jewish, the first man of his faith to serve on the highest bench.

In May the President accepted a farm-loan bank system in the Federal Farm Loan Act. At the urging of progressives, he applied pressure upon the Democratic leaders in the Senate to obtain a workmen's compensation system for federal employees and the first federal child-labor law. The child-labor law, the Keating-Owen Act of 1916, prohibited the shipment in interstate commerce of products manufactured by children. It marked not only a significant reversal on the part of Wilson but also a new assumption of federal control over manufacturing through the commerce clause. When the Supreme Court invalidated the law by a 5-to-4 decision in 1918, Congress passed an act levying a heavy tax on the products of child labor. This too President Wilson signed, and the Supreme Court ultimately invalidated, with Chief Justice Taft writing the decision.

Despite the setback in regard to child labor, this second wave of legislation of the Wilson administration significantly restored and enlarged the regulatory function of the federal government. After Wilson had failed to mediate a dispute between the railroad brotherhoods and the railroads, he signed an emergency measure, the Adamson Act, to prevent a nationwide railroad strike that would have paralyzed commerce. The measure provided for an eight-hour day at the previous ten-hours' pay for all railroad workers.

Other lesser known pieces of legislation brought about even greater changes. Without attracting much attention, they undermined state rights by granting subsidies on a dollar-matching basis for states to undertake various types of programs. These laws, in combination with the new income tax, took money out of the wealthier Northeastern areas and redistributed it in the South and West. The first such law was the Smith-Lever Act of 1914, which provided money for states to establish extension work in agricultural education. This formalized and nationalized the new system of county agents to advise farmers, and facilitated the rise of the powerful American Farm Bureau Federation. It was followed by the Smith-Hughes Act of 1917 which subsidized vocational courses in secondary schools. Most important of all, the Federal Highway Act of 1916 appropriated $75 million to be spent for road-building over a period of five years.

Wilson was justified in his boast that the Democrats had come close to carrying out the Progressive party's platform as well as their own.

# Selected Readings

**Synthesis and Interpretations** Richard Hofstadter, *The Age of Reform*° (1955); Eric Goldman, *Rendezvous with Destiny: A History of Modern American Reform*° (1952); R. H. Wiebe, *Businessmen and Reform* (1962) and *The Search for Order, 1877–1920*° (1967); Christopher Lasch, *The New Radicalism in America, 1889–1963* (1965); Gabriel Kolko, *The Triumph of Conservatism* (1963); J. R. Chamberlain, *Farewell to Reform*° (1932).

**Progressive Journalism** C. C. Regier, *The Era of the Muckrakers* (1932); Walter Johnson, *William Allen White's America* (1947); Charles Forcey, *The Crossroads of Liberalism: Croly, Weyl, Lippmann, and the Progressive Era, 1900–1925*° (1961); Herbert Croly, *The Promise of American Life*° (1909); Lincoln Steffens, *Autobiography* (2 vols., 1931).

**States and Cities** G. E. Mowry, *California Progressives*° (1951); R. S. Maxwell, *La Follette the Rise of Progressivism in Wisconsin* (1944); H. L. Warner, *Progressivism in Ohio, 1897–1917* (1964); R. M. Abrams, *Conservatism in a Progressive Era: Massachusetts Politics, 1900–*

*1912* (1946); Jane Addams, *Forty Years at Hull House*° (1935); A. F. Davis, *Spearheads of Reform: The Social Settlements and the Progressive Movement, 1890–1914* (1968); Ray Lubove, *The Progressives and the Slums: Tenement House Reform in New York City, 1890–1917* (1962).

**Roosevelt** G. E. Mowry, *The Era of Theodore Roosevelt*° (1958) and *Theodore Roosevelt and the Progressive Movement*° (1946); H. F. Pringle, *Theodore Roosevelt* (1931); W. H. Harbaugh, *Power and Responsibility*° (1961); J. M. Blum, *The Republican Roosevelt*° (1954); J. A. Garraty, *Right Hand Man: The Life of George W. Perkins* (1960), a leading Bull Mooser.

**Taft and the Insurgents** H. F. Pringle, *The Life and Times of William Howard Taft* (2 vols., 1939); Kenneth Hechler, *Insurgency: Personalities and Policies of the Taft Era* (1940); James Holt, *Congressional Insurgents and the Party System, 1909–1916* (1967).

**Wilson** A. S. Link, *Wilson: The Road to the White House* (1947), *Wilson: The New Freedom* (1956), and *Woodrow Wilson and the Progressive Era, 1910–1917*° (1954); A. C. Walworth,

*Woodrow Wilson* (2 vols., 1958); J. M. Blum, *Woodrow Wilson and the Politics of Morality*° (1956) and *Joe Tumulty and the Wilson Era* (1951); W. E. Leuchtenberg, ed., *Wilson: The New Freedom*° (1961), containing selections from Wilson's writings.

**Progressives and Conservatives** Belle and Fola La Follette, *Robert M. La Follette* (2 vols., 1953); R. M. La Follette, *Autobiography*° (1913); Richard Lowitt, *George W. Norris: The Making of a Progressive, 1861–1912* (1963); C. G. Bowers, *Beveridge and the Progressive Era* (1932); A. T. Mason, *Brandeis: A Free Man's Life* (1946); F. L. Allen, *The Great Pierpont Morgan* (1949); N. W. Stephenson, *Nelson W. Aldrich* (1920); Richard Leopold, *Elihu Root and the Conservative Tradition*° (1954).

**Conservation and Health** S. P. Hays, *The Gospel of Efficiency: The Progressive Conservation Movement, 1890–1920*° (1959); E. R. Richardson, *The Politics of Conservation: Crusade and Controversies, 1897–1913*° (1962); O. E. Anderson, *The Health of a Nation: Harvey W. Wiley and the Fight for Pure Food* (1958).

**Socialists and Unions** Ray Ginger, *The Bending Cross: A Biography of Eugene Victor Debs* (1949); Ira Kipnis, *The American Socialist Movement, 1897–1912* (1952); D. A. Shannon, *The Socialist Party of America* (1955); Marc Karson, *American Labor Unions and Politics, 1900–1918* (1958); R. J. Cornell, *The Anthracite Coal Strike of 1902* (1957).

**The Negro** I. A. Newby, *Jim Crow's Defense: Anti-Negro Thought in America, 1900–1930* (1965); E. M. Rudwick, *W. E. B. DuBois: A Study of Minority Group Leadership*° (1960); R. S. Baker, *Following the Color Line*° (1908); E. S. Redkey, *Black Exodus: Black Nationalism and Back-to-Africa Movements, 1890–1910*° (1969).

---

°Titles available in paperback.

# Chapter 22
# The War
# to End War

While Americans clung to the old idea of keeping out of Europe's quarrels, the nation drifted toward the twentieth-century maelstrom of world conflict. The industrial developments in Europe had brought, along with increased material abundance, a heightened competition for markets, sources of raw materials, places for investment, and sheer national prestige. To the great powers came not only social gains but also military ambitions, with an arms race that grew more and more frightening as Europe divided into two hostile alliances.

As the foremost of all industrial nations, the United States could scarcely remain unaffected by world events for long. Its emergence from the Spanish-American War with Pacific and Caribbean colonies intensified the risks of involvement. So did certain phases of the progressive spirit itself, which stimulated increased activity in foreign affairs. Some progressives aspired not only to revitalize democracy at home but also to extend it abroad. Finally, World War I brought the greastest challenge in a hundred years to the time-honored policy of neutrality and diplomatic independence.

For three years, from 1914 to 1917, the United States remained at peace, and then it joined in the hostilities. Its entrance hardly meant that the traditional policy had failed, for strict neutrality had not been tried. The American people had closer ties of kinship and commerce with one set of European belligerents than with the other. The prosperity of this country had come to depend on swollen wartime trade with the one side, which needed supplies in order to continue the war. Both groups of warring countries attempted to cut off the other's imports, and both used methods that were contrary to international law as the United States had long interpreted it. But now the American government drew a sharp distinction between the violations of neutral rights on the one side and on the other. In the one case this government protested long-windedly and perfunctorily; in the other, it took a stern and threatening stand, demanding a "strict accountability."

According to this country's constitutional system, one man has the ultimate responsibility for war or peace—the President. In 1917 President Wilson made the decision for war. He saw it as a war to end war, to bring about an international organization for keeping the future peace, and thus to "make the world safe for democracy." After the military victory had been won, however, the Senate refused to accept his plan for a League of Nations, despite his pleas that the United States must join the League if a second world war were to be prevented. At the height of his struggle for the League, he suffered a stroke that left him a partially paralyzed as well as a deeply embittered man.

---

**World War I Recruiting Poster**

James Montgomery Flagg's portrayal of Uncle Sam was one of the most popular posters of the era. (The Bettmann Archive)

# PROGRESSIVISM BY THE SWORD

Progressive foreign policy, as practiced by Roosevelt, Taft, and Wilson, from 1901 to 1917, was rather aggressive, particularly in dealings with Latin America and the Far East.

## T. R. and World Politics

As much as any other progressive, Theodore Roosevelt liked to engage in moralizing about the position of the United States in the world. His most often repeated theme was, as he once put it: "The just war is a war for the integrity of high ideals. The only safe motto for the individual citizen of a democracy fit to play a great part in the world is service—service by work and help in peace, service through the high gallantry of entire indifference to life, if war comes on land." This kind of talk rallied the support of many progressives, even those who were revolted by Roosevelt's blatant militarism—his equally incessant extolling of the soldierly virtues as "the most valuable of all qualities." Despite his bombast, he conducted foreign affairs with a sure hand.

Roosevelt's concept of the role of the United States in world politics emphasized sea power. Now that the United States had colonies, it needed to build a navy powerful enough to keep the sea lanes open to them. It also needed to build an Isthmian canal so that naval units could sail quickly from one ocean to another, and not have to make a long and difficult voyage around Cape Horn, as the *Oregon* had done during the Spanish-American War. In addition it needed to protect the Caribbean approaches to the canal from encroachment. All this predicated a strong naval policy at a time when the key to strength in the world was a powerful fleet. This meant a navy second only to that of Great Britain.

Such were the views of President Roosevelt at the time when Kaiser Wilhelm II was launching Germany upon a gigantic naval race with Great Britain. As Britain began construction of the first dreadnought (large modern battleship) in 1905, both Germany and the United States were building more and larger warships, amid growing alarums of war. Urged on by Roosevelt, the most effective of naval lobbyists, Congress voted appropriations for ten battleships and four armored cruisers between 1902 and 1904. These were more powerful and more widely ranging than the relatively light vessels of the nineties, which had been designed primarily to defend the American coast. By 1906 the American navy was second only to the British, but in the next few years was surpassed by the German navy.

Roosevelt liked to quote an African proverb: "Speak softly and carry a big stick." This certainly characterized his action in the Far East, as well as in the Caribbean. He hoped to make the Open Door policy effective against Russian expansion in Manchuria. For a moment in 1903 he expressed such indignation over the "treachery" and "mendacity" of Russia that he toyed with the idea of going to "extremes" with her. His practical policy, however, was to encourage Japanese efforts to check the Russian drive. When the Japanese made a surprise attack upon the Russian fleet at Port Arthur, Manchuria, in 1904, he was inclined to cheer, as were most Americans. He warned the French and Germans against aiding Russia, but he did not wish to see the Japanese totally victorious, since this might "possibly mean a struggle between them and us in the future."

Roosevelt pursued this same policy in the peace negotiations. Though the Japanese won a series of spectacular victories, they faced such serious financial difficulties that they asked Roosevelt to mediate. He agreed and called a peace conference at Portsmouth, New Hampshire, in the summer of 1905. But he soon offended the Japanese by opposing their demands for an enormous indemnity. He lost their good will even though he approved their territorial gains at the conference—control over Korea and South Manchuria and annexation of the southern half of Sakhalin Island, which had belonged to Russia.

Japanese-American relations, thus suddenly made worse, were not much improved by a secret Japanese-American agreement which was effected at the time of the Portsmouth conference. President Roosevelt had dispatched Secretary of War Taft from Manila to Tokyo to reach a Far Eastern understanding with the Japanese. In the resulting Taft-Katsura memorandum of July 1905, the Japanese prime minister acknowledged American sovereignty in the Philippines, and the American President recognized the suzerainty of Japan over Korea.

Roosevelt's role in helping to negotiate the 1905 Treaty of Portsmouth won for him the Nobel Peace Prize. His actions did indeed contribute to preservation of the peace by maintaining a power balance between Russia and Japan on the Asian mainland. But in Asian waters, Japan had risen to a new ascendancy through its destruction of the Russian fleets. Japan repaired and refloated many of the vessels and rapidly built new ships in the following years. Japan undoubtedly had become powerful enough to seize the Philippines (which Roosevelt came to regard as an Achilles heel) because the American fleet would have had trouble fighting effectively so far from home. Unfortunately, at this same time, the people of Japan and the United States became angry with each other.

In October 1906, within a year after Japan's victory over a great European power, the San Francisco school board ordered the segregation of Oriental schoolchildren. This step was taken in response to the feelings of Californians against the 500 to 1,000 Japanese immigrants coming in each year, feelings which were intensified by lurid "Yellow Peril" articles in the Hearst and other newspapers. Resentment in Japan flared high, and jingoes in each country fanned the flames still higher.

Roosevelt worked skillfully to douse the flames. He persuaded San Francisco to desegregate its schools, and in return in 1907 he negotiated a "Gentlemen's Agreement" with Japan to keep out agricultural laborers. Then, lest the Japanese government think he had acted through fear, he launched a spectacular naval demonstration. He sent sixteen battleships of the new navy, "the Great White Fleet," on an unprecedented 45,000-mile voyage around the world. It gave the navy invaluable experience in sailing in formation while demonstrating the danger of dependence on foreign-owned coaling stations. The Japanese invited this formidable

armada to visit Yokohama and gave it a clamorous welcome. Thus Roosevelt came to feel that through brandishing the big stick he had helped the cause of peace.

For the moment, the United States had demonstrated sufficient naval strength to restore an unsteady balance in Asian waters. In 1908, before the fleet had returned home, Japan and the United States negotiated the comprehensive Root-Takahira Agreement. Both countries agreed to support the Open Door in China. The United States tacitly seemed to give Japan a free hand in Manchuria (where rivalry with Russia continued) in return for an explicit guarantee of the status quo in the Pacific. This precarious equilibrium might be destroyed by any future upset in the naval ratios.

At the same time that he was directly engaged in balancing the powers in the Pacific, Roosevelt was participating somewhat less directly in trying to maintain a balance in Europe. American relations with Great Britain were increasingly cordial. In 1903, the British agreed to refer a troublesome dispute over the boundary between Alaska and Canada to a tribunal of three Americans, two Canadians, and one Englishman. To cultivate the friendship of the United States, the English member of the tribunal voted against the Canadians and in favor of the American claim. Then the British government made another concession by pulling its naval units out of the Caribbean and leaving it as virtually an American lake.

When Germany and France quarreled over Morocco, Roosevelt was reluctant to involve the United States. "We have other fish to fry," he told Taft in 1905. Nevertheless, he resolved to try "to keep matters on an even keel in Europe." Consequently he intervened on behalf of the German Kaiser to persuade France and England to attend an international conference for establishing the status of Morocco. Germany was protesting because the French had set up a protectorate there. At the conference, which met in Algeciras, Spain, in 1906, the American delegates sided with the British and the French to keep France dominant in Morocco while making some concessions to appease Germany. For the moment the United States had helped avert, or at least postpone, a war into which it might ultimately be dragged.

## The Iron-Fisted Neighbor

Roosevelt's preoccupation with the American strategy of defense in the Caribbean—especially his almost obsessive fear of German penetration—betrayed him into acting like an iron-fisted neighbor toward small countries to the south. He first used his might impetuously to start work on a canal in Panama.

Before Roosevelt became President, the McKinley administration was negotiating with England to remove an old obstacle, the 1850 treaty agreeing that the two countries would jointly construct, operate, and defend any canal to be built in Central America. In 1901 the British, eager to court American friendship, consented in the Hay-Pauncefote treaty to exclusive American construction, operation, and fortification of a canal.

The next question was where to locate the canal. There were two possible routes. The shortest one would be across the Isthmus of Panama, but the rights there were owned by a French company, the successor of an earlier company which had tried and failed to dig a canal. For its franchise, the French company wanted $109 million, which would make a Panama canal more expensive than a Nicaraguan one. Consequently, both Congress and President Roosevelt favored the Nicaraguan route. But the French company had expert agents— Philippe Bunau-Varilla, its chief engineer, and William Nelson Cromwell, an attorney who had contributed heavily to the Republican campaign fund in 1900—who hastily cut the price of their rights to $40 million. Unless sold to the United States and sold quickly, the rights would be worthless, for they would expire in 1904. This price cut and able lobbying caused Congress and the President to change their minds.

Impatient to begin construction, Roosevelt put pressure upon Colombia, which owned Panama, to conclude a treaty authorizing the United States to dig a canal there. In January 1903, Secretary of State Hay and the Colombian chargé d'affaires Tomas Herrán signed a treaty that was most unfavorable to Colombia. It authorized the United States to construct a canal in

**"Here No One Dares Lay a Hand but Myself"**

This is an Argentinian cartoonist's conception of T.R.'s interpretation of the Monroe Doctrine. (Mayol in Buenos Aires *Caras y Caretas*)

return for a payment of only $10 million and an annual rental of $250,000, as compared with the $40 million the French company was to receive. The Colombian Senate, as it had every right to do, rejected the treaty.

Roosevelt was too furious to give thought to niceties or to the value of a friendly policy toward Latin America. Fuming that the Colombians were "inefficient bandits," he considered seizing Panama through twisting a technicality in an 1846 treaty with Colombia (then New Granada) guaranteeing the neutrality and free transit of the Isthmus. Roosevelt's intended seizure became unnecessary, because Bunau-Varilla helped organize a Panamanian revolution. There had been many previous revolts, all failures. But at the outset of this one, the United States landed troops from the U.S.S. *Nashville*, and, invoking the 1846 treaty obligation to maintain order, prevented Colombian forces from putting down the rebellion. Three days later the United States recognized the new republic of Panama and, soon after that, negotiated a treaty paying

Panama the sum Colombia had rejected, in return for the grant of a zone ten miles wide. The minister from Panama who arranged the treaty was Bunau-Varilla.

Work on the canal proceeded smoothly and efficiently. The elimination of tropical diseases in the area, the digging of the tremendous cuts, and the installation of huge locks at a total cost of $375 million filled Americans with patriotic enthusiasm, though some were ashamed of Roosevelt's ruthlessness. In 1911 he boasted: "I took the Canal Zone and let Congress debate; and while the debate goes on, the Canal does also." It opened in 1914.

Meanwhile Roosevelt was enlarging the Monroe Doctrine. In 1902 he had written to a German friend: "If any South American country misbehaves toward any European country, let the European country spank it." Germany, along with Italy and Great Britain, proceeded to spank Venezuela by blockading her coast. The object was to force the Venezuelan dictator to pay his country's debts to European bankers.

By 1903 Roosevelt had changed his mind. Americans were angered at the news of the German bombardment of a Venezuelan port, and he himself was beginning to fear that the Germans planned to establish a permanent base in Venezuela. He warned the Germans (according to his own later account) that Admiral Dewey had his fleet in the Caribbean and was ready to act in case they tried to acquire any territory. The Germans finally withdrew—as the British and Italians already had done—and agreed to submit the debt question to arbitration.

The Venezuela incident led to a new Caribbean policy usually called the "Roosevelt Corollary" of the Monroe Doctrine. The Hague Court declared that the powers that had threatened Venezuela had prior claim on payment of their debts; this increased the likelihood of future European intervention in the Western Hemisphere. For Roosevelt, who still believed that small nations must pay their just debts, the only way out seemed a drastic new device. If these little countries could not behave themselves, the United States reluctantly would police them and collect debt payments from them in order to forestall European intervention.

### Theodore Roosevelt's Latin American Policy [1905]

*It cannot be too often and too emphatically asserted that the United States has not the slightest desire for territorial aggrandizement at the expense of any of its southern neighbors, and will not treat the Monroe Doctrine as an excuse for such aggrandizement on its part. . . . Moreover . . . we do not intend to permit the Monroe Doctrine to be used by any nation on this Continent as a shield to protect it from the consequences of its own misdeeds against foreign nations. . . . On the one hand, this country would certainly decline to go to war to prevent a foreign government from collecting a just debt; on the other hand, it is very inadvisable to permit any foreign power to take possession, even temporarily, of the custom houses of an American Republic in order to enforce the payment of its obligations; for such temporary occupation might turn into a permanent occupation. The only escape from these alternatives may at any time be that we must ourselves undertake to bring about some arrangement by which so much as possible of a just obligation shall be paid. . . . The justification for the United States taking this burden and incurring this responsibility is to be found in the fact that it is incompatible with international equity for the United States to refuse to allow other powers to take the only means at their disposal of satisfying the claims of their creditors and yet to refuse, itself, to take any such steps.—Annual Message to Congress, December 5, 1905.*

Uncle Sam would act as a bill collector for European bankers. Roosevelt declared to Congress in 1904 that the United States might be forced, "however reluctantly, in flagrant cases of . . . wrongdoing or impotence, to the exercise of an international police power."

The occasion for putting the Roosevelt Corollary into operation was the defaulting of Santo Domingo on about $22 million of its debt to European nations. France and Italy threatened to intervene. In effect, the United States established a receivership, taking over Dominican customs, paying 45 per cent of the receipts to the Dominican government, and paying the rest to foreign creditors.

As a part of an American strategy of Canal defense, Roosevelt's Caribbean policy was doubtless successful. As a means of securing the support and cooperation of nations to the south, it left much to be desired. Roosevelt's tactics inspired fear rather than friendship.

## Taft and Dollar Diplomacy

President Taft was no readier in foreign affairs than at home to exert strong personal leadership as Roosevelt had done. For the most part he left the State Department to his Secretary of State, a former corporation lawyer, Philander C. Knox. Taft and Knox made no real effort to maintain a balance of power in either Europe or Asia. Instead, they concentrated upon promoting American banking and business interests overseas.

In Far Eastern relations, this policy brought to the forefront young Willard Straight, an agent of American bankers, formerly consul general at Mukden, Manchuria. He argued that dollar diplomacy was the financial expression of the Open Door policy, that it would make "a guaranty for the preservation, rather than the destruction of China's integrity." Taft, therefore, was ready to ignore Roosevelt's tacit arrangement with Japan that the United States would stay out of Manchuria, and to support the right of Americans to invest both there and in China. When British, French, and German bankers formed a consortium to finance railroads in China, Secretary Knox insisted that Americans should also participate. In 1911 they were admitted. Then Knox proposed that an international syndicate purchase the South Manchurian Railroad in order to neutralize it. This led the rivals Russia and Japan to sign a treaty

of amity in 1910, thus closing the Manchurian door in Taft's face.

In the Caribbean there were no other great powers to block the amateurish American operations. As a result, a new pattern emerged there of interventions going far beyond Roosevelt's limited ones, to establish firm military, political, and, above all, economic control over several unstable republics to the south. Advocates of this program argued that American investors must be invited in to replace European investors, who otherwise might eventually bring about European intervention. This was a logical step beyond the Roosevelt Corollary.

The new policy began in 1909 when Knox tried to arrange for American bankers to establish a financial receivership in Honduras. He persuaded New York bankers to invest in the National Bank of Haiti. Then he sent marines to Nicaragua to protect revolutionaries, sponsored by an American mining company, who were fighting to overthrow a hostile dictator. Knox negotiated a treaty with the new friendly government giving the United States financial control, but the United States Senate failed to approve it. American bankers, less reluctant, accepted Knox's invitation to move in. By 1912 the new pro-American government was so unpopular that a revolt broke out. Taft sent marines to crush the uprising, and some of them remained as late as 1925.

Even more than Roosevelt's policies, those of Taft alienated the neighboring countries to the south.

## Wilsonian Intervention

President Wilson brought to the determination of foreign policy a flair for idealistic pronouncements. He was never unsure of his moral position but was often uncertain how to reach it. He and his Secretaries of State and the Navy, William Jennings Bryan and Josephus Daniels, were all devoutly religious, war-hating men of good will, who disapproved of the exorbitant money-making sometimes connected with dollar diplomacy. But the temptation to make use of the force at their disposal to uplift their brothers to the south was too great to resist. The need to do so seemed compelling to them, because like their predecessors they felt that they must maintain an American-sponsored stability in the Caribbean as a vital part of national defense.

Wilson expounded his new policies in a speech at Mobile, Alabama, in the fall of 1913. He disavowed imperialist intent. "The United States will never again seek one additional foot of territory by conquest," he declared. Rather, he sought "the development of constitutional liberty in the world."

The Wilson administration not only regularized through treaty the continuing occupation of Nicaragua, but also initiated new interventions in Santo Domingo and Haiti—to head off a supposed threat of German intervention. In spite of American customs control, revolution after revolution had swept through and impoverished Santo Domingo. The United States took over all Dominican finances and the police force, but the Dominicans would not agree to a treaty establishing a virtual protectorate. In 1916 Wilson established a military government. During the eight years that this government continued, the United States forcibly maintained order, trained a native constabulary, and promoted education, sanitation, and public works.

On the other end of the island of Hispaniola, the Negro republic of Haiti was even more revolution-wracked, the violence culminating in 1915 when a mob tore an unpopular president limb from limb. Wilson again sent in the marines, established another military government, and began the task of improving living conditions in Haiti. The marines demonstrated their efficiency in 1918 when they supervised an election to ratify a new American-sponsored constitution. The vote for it was 69,377 to 355. Nevertheless, that year they had to put down a serious revolt, killing some hundreds of Haitians in the process.

There was a persistent fear that the Germans might try to acquire the Danish West Indies. In 1902 the Senate ratified a treaty for their purchase, but the Danish parliament rejected it. Finally in 1917 the United States acquired the poverty-stricken islets, which were then renamed the Virgin Islands, for an exorbitant $25 million. Their value was negative: the

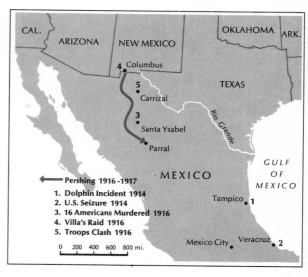

**The U.S. in Mexico   1914–1917**

United States wanted to make sure they were not in the possession of any potentially hostile power.

## Making Mexico Behave

American business interests had invested about $1 billion in Mexico during the regime of a friendly dictator, Porfirio Díaz. They owned over half the oil, two-thirds of the railroads, and three-fourths of the mines and smelters. Popular though Diaz was in the United States, he came to be hated in Mexico because, while he encouraged foreigners to amass huge profits, he suppressed civil liberties and kept the masses in peonage. For the average Mexican, there was little of the progress toward democracy or economic security that President Wilson desired. In 1910 the aged Díaz was overthrown by a democratic reform leader, who in turn was murdered and succeeded by the reactionary Victoriano Huerta just before Wilson took office. Wilson turned a deaf ear to American investors who saw in Huerta's presidency an opportunity to return to the "good old days." Rather, he refused to recognize "the government of butchers."

Years of tedious complications followed. Wilson hoped that, by refusing recognition to Huerta's government, he could bring about its collapse and the development of constitutionalism in Mexico. He offered in June 1913 to mediate between Huerta and the opposing Constitutionalists of Venustiano Carranza. Both sides refused.

For several months Wilson pursued a policy of "watchful waiting," but when Huerta established a full military dictatorship in October 1913, Wilson began to bring increasing pressure against him. First he persuaded the British (who were obtaining most of their naval oil from Mexico) to stop supporting Huerta. Next he offered to send American troops to the aid of Carranza, but again he was rebuffed, since all Carranza wanted was the right to buy arms in the United States. Wilson granted this in February 1914 by lifting President Taft's arms embargo, but still the Carranzists did not win.

Wilson was in a dilemma: he might have to choose between recognizing Huerta, stronger than ever, or intervening with armed force, which could mean war against all the Mexican factions. Off the coast of Mexico, the commanders of American fleet units, engaged in watchful waiting, became increasingly restless. The precipitate action of one of them gave Wilson a way out. In April 1914 one of Huerta's officers arrested several sailors of the U.S.S. *Dolphin* who had gone ashore at Tampico; a superior officer quickly released them and apologized. But the American admiral demanded a twenty-one gun salute to the United States flag in addition. At this Huerta balked. Wilson, deciding to back the admiral, sent all available warships to Mexican waters and asked Congress for authority to take drastic action. Then, anxious to prevent a German ship loaded with munitions from reaching Huerta's forces, Wilson, without waiting for Congress to act, ordered the navy to seize Vera Cruz. It did so, on April 21 and 22, 1914, but not in the bloodless way that Wilson had anticipated. The Mexicans suffered 126 killed and 195 wounded; the Americans, 19 killed and 71 wounded.

At this difficult point, Argentina, Brazil, and Chile offered to mediate. With relief, Wilson accepted, and sent his delegates to confer with Huerta's at Niagara Falls, Canada, from May to July, 1914. As the negotiations went on and on, the Carranzists advanced on Mexico City, finally bringing the result Wilson wished, the abdication of Huerta.

Under Carranza's presidency, the Mexican muddle did not clear up but got worse. By September 1914 civil war was again devastating Mexico, as a former general of Carranza's, Francisco ("Pancho") Villa, tried to overthrow him. In October 1915 the United States gave de facto recognition to Carranza's government.

This antagonized Villa, who was still roaming northern Mexico. He tried to bring about a war between the United States and Mexico by shooting sixteen Americans he seized from a train in January 1916. When that failed, in March he raided Columbus, New Mexico, just across the border, killing nineteen more Americans. Wilson retaliated by ordering a punitive expedition under Brigadier General John J. Pershing to hunt down Villa. For this, Wilson had the permission of Carranza, but as Villa drew the American forces 300 miles into Mexico, two skirmishes with Carranza's army almost led to war. Again the peace forces outweighed the jingoes in the United States, and again Wilson accepted compromise. On July 4, 1916, Carranza suggested the appointment of a Joint High Commission to consider the problem. The commission debated into January 1917, when it broke up without establishing a basis for the withdrawal of American troops. By then the United States was so close to war with Germany that Wilson nevertheless withdrew the troops and in March 1917 gave recognition to Carranza's government.

Nothing but trouble had come out of Wilson's long and muddled intervention in Mexico. His bad tactics had aroused a hostility among the Mexican people which did not dissipate for years.

In other respects Wilson and his Secretary of State were slightly more successful in improving relations between the United States and Latin America. During 1913 and 1914 they negotiated a treaty with Colombia expressing "sincere regrets" for the Panama incident and paying an indemnity of $25 million. Roosevelt thundered that it was a "blackmail treaty," and his Republican friends in the Senate blocked it until after his death. In 1921 Congress voted to pay the indemnity but omit the apology.

## UNNEUTRAL NEUTRALITY

Wilson had been elected President on a program of domestic reform, the New Freedom. Shortly before his inauguration he remarked: "It would be the irony of fate if my administration had to deal chiefly with foreign affairs." But so it was to be.

### War in Europe

Bryan, before he took office as secretary of state, suggested to Wilson a scheme for "cooling off" treaties with all the nations of the world. These would provide that disputes should go to permanent commissions for a one-year investigation before either party could strengthen its armaments or go to war. This proposal was in keeping with the progressive theory that war was unthinkable and that all disputes could be settled through reasonable discussion. Bryan negotiated thirty such treaties with large and small nations —but none with Germany.

The problem of the European balance gave Wilson at least slight concern in May 1914 when he authorized Colonel House to sail abroad to try to bring an end to the arms race. Within a few months, Europe became Wilson's greatest cause for anxiety, as fate directed his administration toward an overwhelming concern with foreign affairs.

Americans paid little attention to the minor alarms that followed the assassination of the Austrian Archduke in Sarajevo, Bosnia, at the end of June. Balkan crises were familiar and boring news; events in Mexico where Carranza was driving out Huerta seemed more sensational. Even when Austria-Hungary declared war on Serbia on July 28, Americans were not shocked, but the week that followed left them stunned. The declaration of war against Serbia triggered a chain reaction of threats and counterthreats, commitments and countercommitments among the alliances. It detonated an explosion no one seemed really to want, but no one seemed able to avoid. By August 5, England, France, and Russia were at war with Germany and Austria-Hungary. The explosion had blown to bits the comfortable, optimistic Europe that had seemed so safe and stable.

Bewildered Americans congratulated themselves that at least the explosion could not extend to their shores; the New World was still secure. A sizable number, who were of German ancestry or had been educated in German universities, automatically saw the war as a valiant German struggle against the cruel despotism of Czarist Russia. And most Irish-Americans sympathized with Germany as the foe of their ancient oppressor, England. But the vast majority of the people, with greater educational, economic, or sentimental ties to England and France, were shocked by the German invasion of Belgium in defiance of a treaty. They were pro-Allied without being at all sure what the war was about. None of them in August 1914 envisaged American entrance into the war. There was no clear call for an American democratic crusade.

With the outbreak of war in Europe, Wilson feared that Japan would take advantage of the preoccupation of the Western powers to expand in the Orient. He reverted to a balance-of-power policy to try to stem the Japanese tide as much as possible. Japan declared war upon Germany and seized the German holdings on the Shantung peninsula of China; this the United States could not criticize. Next Japan tried to impose upon the Chinese a treaty embodying twenty-one demands that would have made China virtually a protectorate. At this point (in 1915), the American government with the aid of the British, exerted such strong pressure that Japan abandoned the treaty.

But the United States appeased Japan in the Lansing-Ishii Agreement of November 2, 1917. This recognized that Japan had "special interests in China, particularly in the part to which her possessions are contiguous." The Japanese were pleased, because in translating the ambiguous document into Chinese they could give the impression that the United States approved their policy. Secretary of State Lansing was satisfied because he felt he had protected China for at least the duration of the European war. For both nations, if they held to their policies, there was trouble ahead.

### Blockade and Submarine Warfare

In 1914 President Wilson had proclaimed neutrality and, going beyond that, had called upon the American people to remain impartial in thought as well as in action. Yet from the beginning he himself took one attitude toward the Allies and quite a different attitude toward Germany.

The immediate problem for Wilson was domestic: to bolster the economy, which was staggering under the impact of war. As European nations sought to liquidate their investments in the United States, Wilson closed the stock exchange to prevent panic and discouraged loans to belligerents in order to preserve the gold reserve. (Secretary Bryan asserted that such loans by banks would be unneutral.) Then war orders began to turn the panic into a boom.

Americans soon learned that the nation in control of the seas would countenance no neutral trade with the enemy. President Wilson acquiesced, though not without protests, as the British developed and tightened their system of control. The United States could have retaliated with an embargo, but this would have created serious economic distress among American farmers and it would have hurt industry. Besides, the basically pro-Allied sympathies of the administration and a great majority of the people made so drastic a step unthinkable. Hence, the United States accepted the British blockade of the Central Powers but was not so ready to accept a German counter-blockade.

Blockade warfare became essential to the strategy of both the British and the Germans. The development of rapid-firing cannons and of machine guns made frontal assault prohibitively expensive, so the war in Europe settled down into an exhausting trench warfare between the combatants. The counterpart on the high seas was the blockade. From the outset, Great Britain made use of her superior navy to wage economic warfare against Germany. Gradually she extended the "contraband" list. She even seized American vessels carrying foodstuffs to neutral countries, on the grounds that such shipments might release supplies that could go to Germany. Americans complained that the British were using the controls to benefit British firms at the expense of American business.

On the whole, the British blockade proved to be no economic handicap for the United States, since by early 1915 heavy war orders were arriving which more than filled the trade gap it

had created. While trade with the Central Powers almost came to an end, that with the Allies between 1914 and 1916 jumped from $824 million to $3,214 million—a staggering figure for that time. In March 1915 the government relaxed its regulations to allow the Allies to float huge loans in the United States for financing their purchases. In effect the United States, embarking upon the greatest boom in its history, was becoming the great arsenal for the Allies.

This the Germans could not permit. During the first weeks of the war they imposed no blockades but concentrated upon trying to win a decision in France. The German armies drove deep but were halted short of Paris in the Battle of the Marne in September 1914. While on the Russian front great armies continued to move back and forth for several years, in the west the war turned into the grinding attrition of trench combat along lines extending from the North Sea to Switzerland. As a stalemate developed along the Western Front, Germany turned toward the submarine as a possible means of breaking the British blockade. Submarines had the advantage of surprise but were so vulnerable to attack by an armed ship that they could scarcely follow the accepted rules of international law. These rules called for visit and search of enemy merchantmen and allowed sinking only if provision were made for the safety of passengers and crew. The sinking of merchant vessels without warning seemed to Americans to add a new and frightful dimension to warfare.

Beginning on February 4, 1915, Germany announced that she would sink enemy vessels in a broad zone around the British Isles. This policy, the Germans explained, was in retaliation for the British food blockade, which they claimed would starve women and children in Germany. President Wilson declared on February 10 that he would hold Germany to "strict accountability" for unlawful acts.

A serious crisis came when, on May 7, 1915, a submarine fired a torpedo without warning into the Cunard liner *Lusitania*. The ship went down in eighteen minutes, drowning 1,198 people, among them 128 Americans. "An act of piracy," Theodore Roosevelt called it.

A few days earlier, April 22, the Germans had

# Where Historians Disagree

# The Causes of American Entrance Into World War I

In the 1920s, as soon as historians began to write about American entrance into World War I, they divided into two schools of interpretation. One stressed (as this chapter does) the complex problems that the policy decisions of the belligerents created for the Wilson administration, which was trying to defend the neutral rights of the United States. This group of historians also considered the larger elements of world politics.

Paying scarcely any attention to the actions of other nations, the other school focused upon economic factors within the United States. These factors, they asserted, were critical in bringing about an unnecessary and unwise American involvement in the struggle. This economic determinist view was widely popularized in the 1930s and became an important historical factor in molding the neutrality legislation intended to keep the nation out of World War II, which was clearly imminent. Walter Millis, a journalist, expressed this view in a best seller, *Road to War, 1914–1917* (1935). Millis emphasized the effectiveness of British propaganda and the emotional ties of Wilson and much of the public with Britain and France as well as the machinations of bankers and munitions makers as factors leading to the misguided decision to intervene. The most vehement scholarly argument along these lines was that of Charles C. Tansill in *America Goes to War* (1938). In more recent years, sophisticated historians critical of Wilson have put less emphasis on economic factors: instead they stress the President's misplaced concern for moral and legal questions rather than for the basic national interest. This was the view of George F. Kennan, a diplomat-turned-historian, and of the political scientist Hans J. Morgenthau, author of *In Defense of the National Interest* (1951).

Historians of the opposing school based their early defense of the Wilson administration on the widely read extracts of diaries and letters in the volumes on Ambassador Walter Hines Page and Colonel House, published in the 1920s. Charles Seymour, editor of *The Intimate Papers of Colonel House* (4 vols., 1926–1928), in subsequent writings in the 1930s emphasized that submarine warfare alone had brought American intervention. Wilson's biographer, Arthur Link, in numerous writings since World War II has stressed that Wilson was realistic as well as idealistic. Ernest May, in *The World War and American Isolation* (1959), analyzing internal factors in the warring powers as well as the United States, points out how limited the options were that Wilson faced as he met one incident after another, until by 1917 there seemed to him and to his cabinet no alternative to war.

launched against the Allied lines at Ypres a new weapon of frightfulness, poison gas. On May 13 American newspapers carried lengthy excerpts from an official British report on almost unprintable alleged German atrocities in Belgium. Although it bore the respected name of the former ambassador to the United States, Lord Bryce, this report contained fabrications. Yet few Americans questioned its authenticity, for by this time most people were ready to believe almost anything against Germany. Even in their revulsion, however, they were not ready to fight.

Wilson came close to the point of coercion over the *Lusitania* incident, in the ensuing exchange of notes with Germany. In his first note he virtually demanded that Germany end its submarine blockade. When the Germans sent an argumentative reply, he drafted a still-stronger second note—so strong that the peace-minded Secretary Bryan resigned rather than

sign it. Wilson appointed the Counselor of the State Department, Robert Lansing, an expert in international law, to be the new secretary. Lansing was ready to take an adamant position. Wilson had said: "There is such a thing as a man being too proud to fight." Yet he was ready to risk war rather than surrender to Germany what he considered to be American maritime rights.

New trouble developed in the early months of 1916 when the Allies began arming merchantmen and ordering them to attack submarines. On February 10, 1916, Germany gave notice that she would sink them without warning. Wilson reiterated his doctrine of "strict accountability," and on March 24, when the channel steamer *Sussex* was torpedoed, he threatened to break off diplomatic relations if Germany did not abandon her unrestricted submarine campaign. He made the threat at a time when Germany still lacked sufficient submarines to maintain a tight blockade and did not wish to bring

**The *Lusitania* Sailing From New York City**

On May 1, 1915, newspapers carried both the Cunard advertisement that the *Lusitania* was sailing that day and an unusual German warning: "Vessels flying the flag of Great Britain, or any of her allies, are liable to destruction . . . and . . . travelers sailing in the war zone on ships of Great Britain or her allies do so at their own risk." Passengers and crew discussed the announcement, but the *Lusitania* sailed on time, and by May 6

was proceeding along the coast of Ireland much as in peacetime, at a slow pace and not zigzagging. The commander of the German submarine U-20, seeing a large ship, fired a torpedo. Almost immediately the ship listed so sharply that few lifeboats could be launched; then it sank. As its bow went high in the air, the U-boat commander for the first time read on the ship the name *Lusitania*. (Brown Brothers) the United States into the war. Consequently, on May 4, the German foreign office pledged that submarine commanders would observe rules of visit and search. The President had won a diplomatic victory, and relations with Germany became less tense during the eight months that followed.

## Preparedness—or Pacifism?

With the outbreak of war, generals and admirals, who in peacetime attracted little attention, began to gather followings as they raised a hue and cry for increased defenses. President Wilson through his pacifist Secretary of the Navy, Josephus Daniels, was able to muzzle the navy rather effectively. Its demands for a huge fleet-building program and its warnings of the catastrophe that faced America if the British Grand Fleet collapsed appeared for the most part indirectly through friendly politicians and publicists. Roosevelt's close friend, Major General Leonard Wood, who had just finished a term as Chief of Staff, was not so easy to silence. The Secretary of War, Lindley M. Garrison, was a zealous advocate of preparedness, and several influential civilians like Roosevelt constantly made the headlines with their warnings.

The army was much less ready than the navy to fight a major war. The establishment of the General Staff and other administrative reforms had come into effect in the Roosevelt administration, but the older officers were still antagonistic toward such changes. The Quartermaster Corps in 1913 was thinking about using trucks, but as yet not seriously testing them. The air force, consisting of seventeen planes, was part of the Signal Corps; its 1913 appropriation was $125,000. The army numbered less than 80,000 men, a large part of whom were required to maintain the posts within the United States. The National Guard was somewhat larger, but was scarcely professional.

Wilson opposed new armaments, and so did public opinion, until the crisis over submarine sinkings frightened the nation into preparedness. In November 1915 the President proposed a long-range program which by 1925 would give the United States a navy second to none and would reorganize the army and provide a reserve force of 400,000 men. This proposal touched off a hot debate in Congress and throughout the country. Large numbers of those who had been agrarian progressives of the West and South rallied behind the House majority leader, Claude Kitchin of North Carolina, to block the army program. Throughout the country, the pleas of Bryan and peace organizations strongly appealed to farmers and workingmen. Wilson took the issue to the country in a series of speeches in January and early February 1916, but the House would not budge.

Wilson had to compromise. He accepted the resignation of Secretary of War Garrison, and appointed in his place Newton D. Baker, an able Ohio progressive who had opposed preparedness only a few weeks earlier. Ultimately Congress passed legislation providing for substantial increases in the army, the navy, and merchant shipping. The Merchant Marine Act of 1916 established the United States Shipping Board, which was empowered to own and operate vessels and regulate shipping.

Conservatives wished to finance the defense expenditures through bonds, but the administration proposed new, heavier taxes. Progressives denounced the tax proposals as falling too heavily upon the masses. In Congress the progressives fought through a tax measure frankly aimed at making the wealthy, whom they blamed for preparedness demands, pay the bill. The Revenue Act of 1916 levied income and inheritance taxes heavily upon the rich for the first time in American history.

In 1916 Democrats and Republicans fought the presidential campaign over the issue of foreign policy before a seriously divided people. At the Democratic convention, the keynoter began citing Wilson's interchanges with Germany, and the crowd whooped with enthusiasm. "What did we do? What did we do?" the delegates chanted, and the keynoter responded: "We didn't go to war, we didn't go to war." Out of the convention came the slogan (which Wilson himself never used): "He kept us out of war." The Democrats went into the campaign far stronger than had been expected of a minority party battling against the reunited Republicans. Many of the former Bull Moosers, Republican farmers in the Midwest, and workers who had once voted for a full dinner pail now

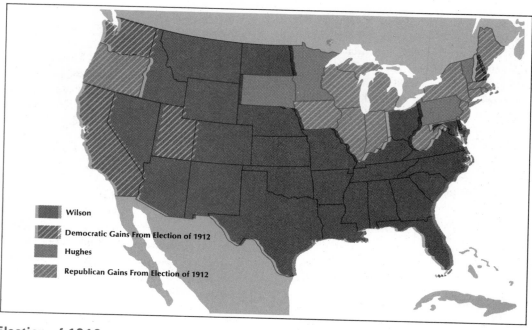

**Election of 1916**

favored the Democrats. In part they did so because of Wilson's progressive domestic policy
but still more because of their hope that the
President could continue to keep the country
out of the war.

As for the Republicans, they persuaded
Charles Evans Hughes, who had an impeccable
progressive record, to resign from the Supreme
Court and accept the nomination. Primarily because of the whooping of Roosevelt and others
on the sidelines, the Republicans gradually began to look like the war party. Hughes, under
pressure from militant Republicans, wired
Roosevelt congratulations on warlike speeches.
This and Hughes' own remarks led voters to believe that he was more likely than Wilson to
adopt a militant policy.

Wilson warned that a Republican victory
would mean intervention in Mexico and war in
Europe. The lure of progressivism and peace
were still so irresistible in 1916 that the Democratic party, though normally a minority,
squeezed through to victory. On election night
returns from the East were almost solidly for
Hughes; he appeared elected. Then, as returns
from the West came in, the picture began to
change, though it was not until Friday that Wil-

son's election was certain. The Democrats also
retained a precarious control over both houses
of Congress.

## "A Fearful Thing"

So far as elections can be regarded as national
plebiscites, Wilson had received a narrow mandate to continue along the path of progressivism
and peace. Undoubtedly he intended to follow
such a course. Since the outbreak of the war he
had repeatedly sought means to bring the warring nations into a peace conference. But both
sides had invested too heavily in the conflict,
and were still too hopeful of gaining from their
investment, to talk of a negotiated peace.

Immediately after the election, in November
1916, Wilson renewed negotiations looking toward a settlement. The Germans, successful on
the Russian front, for a while appeared to be
willing. But the top German generals did not
want any conference at all. Nevertheless, on
January 22, 1917, Wilson spread his plan before
the Senate, calling for a lasting peace that the
American people would help maintain through
a league of nations. It would be a peace with
freedom of the seas, disarmament, national self-
determination for subject peoples, and equality

among nations. "Peace among equals"—a lasting peace—could come only through "peace without victory."

On January 9 the military leaders of Germany had decided upon one final cast of the iron dice. They had resolved to return to unrestricted submarine warfare even though it would bring the United States into the war. They hoped that they could crush France on land and starve Britain from the sea before America could make her weight felt. On January 31 the German ambassador announced that, beginning the following day, submarines would sink all ships, enemy or neutral, in a broad zone around the British Isles.

President Wilson now faced a dilemma of his own making. He had in effect during the previous eighteen months drawn a narrow line—the right of American citizens and vessels to travel on the high seas in time of war—and threatened Germany with war if she transgressed it. How could Wilson take the United States into a war against Germany for such a limited end, and still bring about the sort of peace he wanted, a just peace among equals, a peace without the victor dictating to the vanquished?

Gradually events carried Wilson toward war. On February 25 the British turned over to him an intercepted note from the German foreign secretary, Arthur Zimmerman, proposing that in the event of war, Mexico should attack the United States and receive in return her lost provinces north of the border. Americans were infuriated. At about the same time, the Russian revolution eliminated one of the moral problems in Wilson's mind by replacing a despotism among the Allies with a constitutional monarchy. (This government lasted only until November 1917, when Lenin and the Communists came into power.)

On March 18, 1917, news came that submarines had torpedoed three American ships. On March 20 the cabinet unanimously advised the President to ask Congress for a declaration of war. On the evening of April 2, 1917, President Wilson delivered his war message to Congress. After enumerating the German transgressions of American neutral rights, he declared: "It is a fearful thing to lead this great peaceful people into war, into the most terrible . . . of all

wars. . . . But the right is more precious than peace, and we shall fight for the things which we have always carried nearest our hearts—for democracy, . . . for the rights and liberties of small nations, for a universal dominion of right by such a concert of free peoples as shall bring peace and safety to all nations and make the world itself at last free." Four days later, Congress passed the war declaration and the President signed it.

## WAR WITHOUT STINT

President Wilson had called for war "without stint or limit." In this spirit the American government proceeded to mobilize economic resources on a grand scale, to launch massive campaigns against German submarines in the Atlantic and against German armies in France, and to indoctrinate the American people for enduring the burdens and the sacrifices of the total war.

### Controlling the Economy

Clumsily at first, but steadily and impressively, the unprepared nation built a gigantic war machine. Nearly 5,000 government agencies were set up to see that men, money, and materials were directed toward the war effort. These agencies brought an unprecedented degree of regulation and control to American economic life.

Troops had to be raised, the army enormously enlarged. Theodore Roosevelt, elderly and ill, still seemed to think in terms of the Spanish-American War; backed by a clique of Republican senators, he fought for permission to take a volunteer division to the Western Front. Speaker Champ Clark was so incensed at the prospect of a draft that he asserted from the floor of the House during debate: "In the estimation of Missourians there is precious little difference between a conscript and a convict." For weeks the debate went on, but in the end Roosevelt was turned down, and the Selective Service Act was passed.

During the debate it had become clear what a large figure in both money and men the President must write into the blank check which

Congress (and the American people) had signed. In April British and French missions arrived and made clear for the first time their desperate need for money, men, and ships if they were to stave off imminent defeat. Congress soon authorized the Treasury Department to borrow $7 billion, of which $3 billion were to go as loans to the Allies.

In financing the war, Secretary of the Treasury William G. McAdoo raised about one-third of a $32 billion total through taxation. He felt that additional taxes would put too heavy a burden on low-income groups. The War Revenue Act of 1917 imposed a great variety of excise taxes and income taxes steeper than any before —so steep as to take two-thirds of a $2 million income. Altogether, the taxes on individual and corporate incomes, excess profits, and inheritances provided 74 per cent of the war tax revenues. There was one conspicuous loophole:

many corporations distributed to their stockholders stock exempt from taxes, rather than giving them dividends.

In his borrowing policy, McAdoo tried, again, to keep the burden of the war from falling too heavily upon the poorer people. He sought to sell as many Liberty Bonds as possible to them so that they, not richer people, would reap the ultimate profit. Despite McAdoo's efforts, those with moderate incomes (under $2,000 a year) probably purchased no more than 30 per cent of the $23 billion worth of bonds sold.

During the preparedness period, in August 1916, Congress had approved the establishment of a Council of National Defense, consisting of six cabinet members, and an Advisory Commission made up of representatives of industry, transportation, business, and labor. In July 1917 the council set up a centralized War Industries Board to coordinate government purchases.

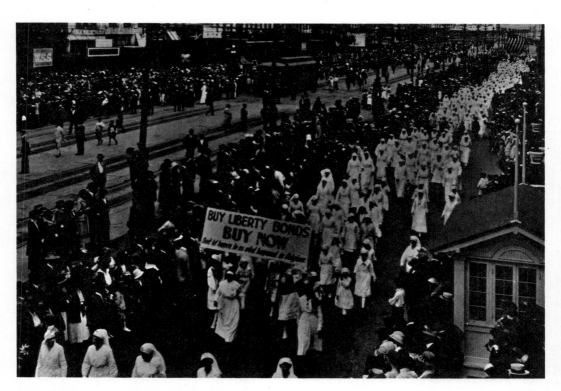

**Fourth Liberty Loan Parade, New Orleans**

Coming shortly before the armistice, in October 1918, the Fourth Liberty Loan drive set out to raise $6 billion. American heroes, celebrities, and volunteer workers all did their bit; the news from the Western Front was exciting. Again the loan was oversubscribed. (National Archives)

Wilson reorganized this board, conferred upon it sweeping powers over industry, and appointed as chairman a Wall Street broker, Bernard Baruch.

Food was almost as vital as munitions for the Allies. At the suggestion of the Council for National Defense, a Food Administration was set up by the President. After vigorous debate, it was later authorized by Congress, in the Lever Act of August 10, 1917. Its administrator was one of the most spectacular civilian heroes of the war, an American mining engineer, Herbert Hoover, who had supervised the relief feeding of Belgium. His task was to increase food production, cut waste, substitute plentiful for scarce foods, and protect consumers from speculators. Hoover, in keeping with his experience in Belgium, wished to be an administrator, not a dictator, and to run his program on a voluntary basis as far as possible. To a remarkable degree he was able to enlist the patriotic support of the public in conserving food and observing meatless and wheatless days. His slogan, seen on widely distributed posters, was "Food will win the war."

The shortage of wheat was especially critical because 1916 had been a bad crop year. Hoover encouraged wheat production by guaranteeing the purchase of the entire 1917 crop at $2.20 per bushel, a figure high enough to assure farmers a substantial profit. Wheat acreage jumped from 45 million in 1917 to 75 million in 1919, and the land produced bumper crops.

Hoover opposed retail price-fixing, which he thought would lead to black markets, but he did protect consumers from speculation. Food prices went up gradually.

The Lever Act which established the Food Administration also authorized a Fuel Administration, which fixed the price of coal high enough to bring submarginal coal mines into operation and increase bituminous coal production by about 50 per cent. In spite of this increase, the fuel shortage became so acute that the Fuel Administration had to order a series of coal holidays for Eastern industries in the early months of 1918.

In order to guarantee war production in German-owned factories in this country, especially those producing chemicals, these and all other German assets came under the custody of an Alien Property Custodian, A. Mitchell Palmer. The Trading-With-the-Enemy Act of October 1917, provided for their seizure and administration. Palmer obtained additional authority to sell German property, which he utilized especially to license dye and chemical patents to American industry. This was punitive toward the Germans, immensely profitable for some American businessmen, and helpful for the development of a strong chemical industry in the United States.

The Aircraft Production Board failed to produce a promised 22,000 airplanes by July 1918 —a ridiculous figure, since neither side on the Western Front ever had as many as 2,500 planes at one time. The failure to fulfill this over-optimistic promise led to harsh criticism. By the time the armistice was signed, the United States had delivered to France 1,185 De Haviland bombers and 5,460 Liberty motors.

In April 1918 President Wilson established the National War Labor Board, to serve as a sort of supreme court for labor disputes. Labor and industry each provided five representatives for the board; the two chairmen represented the public. The War Labor Board would not countenance strikes or lockouts, but recognized the right of unions to organize and bargain collectively. It favored the eight-hour day, the establishment in any given area of the wages prevailing in it, the maintenance of a basic living standard for workers, and equal pay for women who did equal work. Like some other war agencies, it had to function through persuasion or use of the President's war powers.

President Gompers of the AFL did much during the war to enhance the prestige of organized labor. He sat with industrialists on the Council of National Defense and pledged to see that there would be no strikes, in return for recognition of unionism and wage increases. He also cooperated in the government onslaught against labor radicals, which meant the Industrial Workers of the World, who were engaging in sabotage in the West. The IWW almost disappeared, while membership in other unions jumped from 2,716,900 in 1914 to 3,104,600 in 1917 and 4,169,100 in 1919. Still, this was no more than one-eighth of all wage earners.

## Delivering the Goods

Increased production and stringent economy within the United States would be of no avail unless supplies could be delivered to Europe. Into the winter of 1917–1918, transportation difficulties plagued the nation. Railroads could not get raw materials to Eastern factories or munitions to ports, even through cooperation with a voluntary Railroad War Board. On December 28, 1917, Wilson put the railroads under a Railroad Administration headed by Secretary of the Treasury McAdoo. He utilized expert railroad men to run the lines as one unified system. Railroads could draw upon a half-billion-dollar revolving fund for improvements, and received rent equivalent to their average earnings in 1914–1917. The transportation snarl was so effectively untangled that a freight-car shortage of 150,000 in 1917 was transformed into a surplus of 300,000 by the end of 1918.

Shipping was a still greater and more persistent problem. By the summer of 1917, submarines had sunk nearly a quarter of the British merchant fleet; that of the United States was relatively small, and mainly committed to coastal trade. The Emergency Fleet Corporation under the Shipping Board eventually began to make remarkable progress in building new shipyards to turn out 1,700 ships of steel and 1,000 of wood.

War vessels escorted fleets of transports and supply ships across the Atlantic to protect them from submarine attacks. At first, the British admiralty had opposed the use of such convoys and kept most of its destroyers as a curtain to protect the Grand Fleet and the channel ferries. Eventually, however, United States Admiral William S. Sims broke down the resistance of the admiralty, so that a convoying system was well established by August 1917.

Sinkings, which had totaled nearly 900,000 tons in April 1917, dropped to 350,000 tons by December 1917, and to only 112,000 tons by October 1918. This was primarily a British achievement, but the United States contributed to it substantially. The British provided 70 per cent of the escorting ships, the French 3 per cent, and the Americans 27 per cent.

The American navy grew enormously in size and efficiency. By the time the armistice was signed it had 200,000 men and 834 vessels convoying across the Atlantic or serving in European waters. It had grown in overall size to 533,000 men and 2,000 ships. It performed great feats in moving men and supplies across the Atlantic.

## Peace Ideals and War Hatreds

Ever since the hesitant entrance of the United States into the war, official agencies and private groups, from President Wilson and the Committee on Public Information to the yellow press, had sought to mold the minds of Americans. In conflicting ways they tried to explain the significance of the war, encourage Americans in its vigorous pursuit, and prepare them for the peace to follow. As is all too easy in such circumstances, Americans learned readily to hate the Germans and German sympathizers but prepared themselves less well to assume a commanding role in maintaining a just peace in the postwar world. This in the end was to be the tragedy of President Wilson, of the American people, and consequently of all mankind.

Even before America entered the war, President Wilson had begun a series of idealistic addresses outlining the nature of the postwar world he wished to see emerge. He talked then of "peace without victory" and the right of the several submerged nationalities in Europe to organize governments of their own choosing. He asserted too that the American people would be willing to join a postwar association of nations. Many Americans of good will, like the members of the League to Enforce Peace, thrilled to Wilson's words. But his speeches remained merely words, since Wilson had not bound the Allies to his conditions as a basis for American intervention. And he seemed to reinforce the distinction between the United States and the Allies through the fiction that we were fighting Germany separately as an "associated power."

After American entrance Wilson had discovered that the Allies had made secret treaties among themselves. These treaties divided among the Allies the enemy's colonies as spoils of the war. The new Bolshevik government of Russia publicized some of the treaties; their terms seemed to run counter to the idealism for which Wilson was exhorting Americans to fight.

Wilson was sure that in time he could counteract the treaties and force the British and French to accept a just peace. On January 8, 1918, he expounded his own war aims, under fourteen headings, in a speech before a joint session of Congress.

His Fourteen Points, coming at a time when all the belligerent peoples were overwhelmingly weary of the war, met with an enthusiastic response among liberals and working people in the United States, in the Allied nations, and throughout the world. Even many Germans welcomed them and a later clarification of them, "the five particulars," as the promise of a democratic Germany that could assume a position of equality in the community of nations. They were the most stirring and effective piece of propaganda the war produced.

It was not clear that Wilson had the American people behind him, even though his Committee on Public Information had been engaged in a large-scale effort to sell the war. George Creel, a progressive newspaperman who had worked in the 1916 presidential campaign, headed the committee. He persuaded newspapers to engage in voluntary self-censorship, an idea not entirely palatable to them. The committee disseminated countless tons of propaganda, and enlisted the services of 150,000 writers, lecturers, actors, and artists. Throughout the country, 75,000 such volunteers arose to speak on almost every conceivable occasion. Throughout the United States and the world, 75 million pieces of printed matter carried the American view of the war. Much of what the Creel Committee disseminated was idealistic, in keeping with Wilson's speeches and the Fourteen Points, depicting the war as a great crusade for humanity. Much also, unfortunately, appealed more to fear and hate than to a spirit of altruistic sacrifice.

Throughout the country spread a hysterical hatred of all that seemed unpatriotic. Congress reflected and encouraged the hysteria by passing stern laws for the suppression of dissent. The Espionage Act of June 15, 1917, provided penalties running up to a $10,000 fine and twenty years' imprisonment, not only for those engaged in espionage, sabotage, and obstruction of the war effort, but even for those who should

"willfully cause or attempt to cause insubordination, mutiny, or refusal of duty" or "willfully obstruct the recruiting or enlistment service." The law also empowered the postmaster general to ban from the mails any matter which in his opinion was seditious. The Trading-With-the-Enemy Act of October 1917, established censorship over international communications and the foreign-language press (in addition to authorizing various types of economic warfare against the Germans).

These measures were vigorously, and at times capriciously, enforced, but the administration sought still greater punitive powers to discipline the disloyal. Congress responded with the Sabo-

### The Sedition Act [1918]

Be it enacted. . . . *Whoever, when the United States is at war, shall wilfully make or convey false reports or false statements with intent to interfere with the operation or success of the military or naval forces of the United States . . . or . . . obstruct the sale by the United States of bonds . . . or incite . . . insubordination, disloyalty, mutiny, or refusal of duty in the military or naval forces of the United States, or shall wilfully obstruct . . . the recruiting or enlistment service . . . [or] wilfully utter, print, write, or publish any disloyal, profane, scurrilous, or abusive language about the form of government of the United States, or the Constitution of the United States, or the military or naval forces of the United States, or the flag . . . or the uniform of the Army or Navy of the United States . . . or shall wilfully . . . urge, incite, or advocate any curtailment of production in this country of any thing or things . . . necessary or essential to the prosecution of the war . . . and whoever shall wilfully advocate, teach, defend, or suggest the doing of any of the acts or things . . . enumerated . . . shall be punished by a fine of not more than $10,000 or imprisonment for not more than twenty years, or both. . . .*

tage Act of April 20, 1918, aimed primarily at the IWW, and the Sedition Act of May 16, 1918. The Sedition Act, modeled after a Montana statute for suppressing the IWW, was harsh beyond any previous legislation in American history. The enforcement of these laws was almost as stern as any lynch mob could desire. Over 1,500 were arrested for seditious utterances, though only 10 were taken into custody for sabotage. The force of the laws continued unabated after the armistice. In the fall of 1918, after a four-day trial, the Socialist leader, Eugene V. Debs, who had been pacifist, not pro-German, was sentenced to ten years in a federal penitentiary under the Espionage Act; in March 1919 the Supreme Court upheld his conviction.

Whatever pacifist or pro-German offenders escaped the federal net were likely to be caught in the meshes of state sedition laws, or to suffer the wrath of vigilantes. The furor was rather ludicrous in some ways, as sauerkraut became "liberty cabbage," and hamburger, "liberty sausage." It was a bit less funny to ban all German music, the teaching of the German language, or the keeping of German books in public libraries, as was done in many places. And it was frightening when a vigilance committee in Minnesota, having forbidden a pastor to speak German, caught him praying at the bedside of a dying woman who spoke only German, tarred and feathered him and rode him out of town on a rail.

## The AEF in France

American strategic plans were drawn up after the country entered the war, and essentially these plans were developed in France at the headquarters of the commanding general of the American Expeditionary Force (AEF), John J. Pershing, a highly intelligent officer and a driving personality.

Pershing's goal was to build an American force in France numbering 1 million men by June 1, 1918. Many obstacles stood between him and his objective, as he came to realize after he arrived in Paris on June 14, 1917. The dispirited Allies stood on the defensive against the desperately aggressive enemy; they needed fresh American troops but wished to use them piecemeal as reinforcements along their own weary lines. They did not like Pershing's insistence that the Americans should operate as a separate army; they had no reason to trust the untried American soldiers or officers. In truth, there had been nothing in American military activities during the Spanish-American War and the Mexican intervention to warrant confidence. But General Pershing stood firm, with President Wilson behind him.

In the winter of 1917–1918 the Germans knocked the Russians out of the war. Lenin and his followers in Russia overthrew the constitutional government of Kerensky and opened peace negotiations. Meanwhile, the Germans along with the Austrians delivered a near-fatal blow to the Italians at Caporetto. The stunned Allies organized a Supreme War Council and looked desperately to the United States for manpower. Pershing gradually had been building port facilities, running railroads across France, and constructing training camps and supply dumps. As a trickle of troops began to arrive, he tried to give them three months' training before putting them into combat. While the number was small, he was willing to brigade his units temporarily among the Allies to give them experience and to meet emergencies. Thus the First Division went into action with the French in Lorraine in October 1917 and took over a quiet sector of its own near Toul in January 1918.

In the early months of 1918 Germany moved troops from the east and slammed them against the Allies in a series of great offensives designed to end the war before a significant number of Americans could arrive. The Germans had not succeeded by July 1, when Pershing had his million soldiers in France.

On May 30 the Germans had crossed the Marne River at Château-Thierry and threatened Paris fifty miles away. American and French troops, under the French command, fought to blunt the German drive. After a week of bitter counterattacking, the Americans recaptured Belleau Wood and thus helped stabilize the line. A little further south at Reims, in the great bulge toward Paris, the Germans tried on July 15, the morning after Bastille Day, to crash through the French lines. Some 85,000 American troops helped repel the German thrust. By July 18 the

## Captain Edward V. Rickenbacker and Other Pilots of the 94th Pursuit Squadron

The "hat-in-the-ring" squadron, as it was popularly known, was the first American-trained squadron to engage in combat. It began operations on April 3, 1918. The overall record of the Americans, who engaged for the most part in individual combat against German aviators flying the superior Fokker planes, was not impressive. At the armistice they constituted only 10 per cent of the Allied air power. Individually they were brave to the point of foolhardiness—they refused to wear parachutes. The exploits of the seventy-one American aces (those who shot down five or more enemy airplanes) were followed eagerly at home by newspaper readers hungry for heroes. Captain Rickenbacker (center), who shot down at least twenty-six German planes, became more famous than most generals. (National Archives)

German offensive was over; and the Allies began a counteroffensive, with American divisions participating, to liquidate the Marne salient (outward projection in the battle line). By August 6 it was gone.

In the months that followed, as American troops disembarked at a rate averaging 263,000 per month, the reinvigorated Allies pressed the exhausted Germans from Lorraine to the North Sea. On August 12 Pershing for the first time launched an offensive under his own command. He directed the First Army, consisting of 550,-000 American troops, against the St. Mihiel salient protruding south of Verdun. Within thirty-six hours the drive had succeeded.

On September 26, 1918, the Americans began to advance along a 24-mile front in the Argonne Forest, as part of a grand, 200-mile-wide offen-

NORTH SEA

ENGLAND

London

Dover   Dunkirk

Calais   Ypres

ENGLISH CHANNEL

Dieppe   Amiens

Le Havre

Rouen

Seine R.

Paris

NETHERLANDS

Antwerp

Bruges   Ghent

Scheldt R.

Brussels

BELGIUM   Liége

Lys R.   Lille

Arras

Namur

Meuse R.

Somme R.

St. Quentin

Cantigny
Montdidier
Noyon

BELLEAU
WOOD

Chateau Thierry

Oise R.

Aisne R.

Reims

ARGONNE FOREST

Marne R.

Cologne

Rhine R.

Liége

Sedan

LUX.

Moselle R.

GERMANY

Verdun   Metz

Saar R.

St. Mihiel

Strasbourg

FRANCE

- - - Farthest German Advance 1914
——— Battle Line March 21, 1918
▰ German Gains
1. Somme    March 21–April 6
2. Lys    April 9–27
3. Aisne    May 27–June 6
4. Noyon-Montdidier   June 9–15
5. Champagne-Marne   July 15–18

0    25    50    75 mi.

**Major German Offensives   1918**

sive, which was to continue for a total of forty-seven days. The American troops fought through what Pershing described as a "vast network of uncut barbwire, the deep ravines, dense woods, myriads of shell craters, and a heavy fog." The Allied high command had not imagined the Americans could make much progress against these obstacles, but after October 4 the regrouped army advanced. By the end of the month it had overrun almost all of the enemy's fixed positions, was beyond the Argonne Forest, and was driving toward vital German communications. On November 7 the Americans established bridgeheads across the Meuse River, planted their guns looking down on the famous fortress of Sedan, and cut the railroad that carried German supplies to the front. It had been the greatest battle in which American troops had ever fought. The 1.2 million soldiers had used a greater weight of ammunition than had all of the Union forces through the four years of the Civil War.

During the Argonne fighting, other American divisions were deployed elsewhere along the front. All together, Americans participated in

thirteen major operations, of which only two were under Pershing's command. By early November the weight of American troops was becoming irresistible; 2 million of them were serving in France.

All along the line, millions of Allied troops had pushed back the Germans, whose reserves were gone, regiments weakened, and communications threatened. They faced an invasion of their own country. They began to seek an armistice, a temporary cease-fire. Pershing, convinced that the Allies should demand a surrender instead, would have liked to push on to Berlin, to make the Germans really feel the war. The day after the Americans reached Sedan, German envoys crossed the lines to meet the Allied Commander in Chief, the French General Ferdinand Foch, and receive armistice terms from him— terms so stiff that a resumption of hostilities would be impossible. The Germans accepted, and on November 11, 1918, the armistice went into effect.

Rejoicing Americans credited their armies with winning the decisive battles—"We won the war." Beyond question they had supplied the

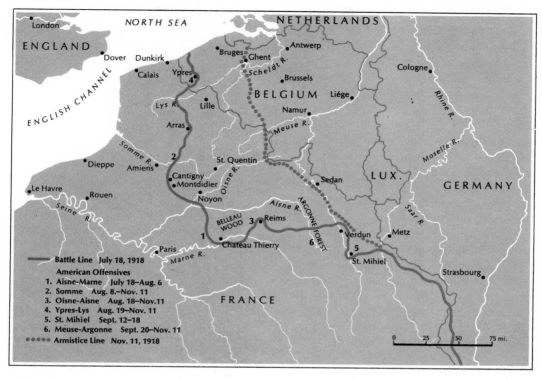

**U.S. Participation in Allied Offensives    1918**

margin of victory. Still, the really crushing burden of the war had not fallen upon the American troops or the American people. The United States lost 112,000 men from enemy action or disease; 237,000 more were wounded. By comparison 1,385,000 French and 900,000 British died. Only 7 per cent of the soldiers from the United States were casualties, compared with 73 per cent of those from France and 36 per cent of those from the British Empire.

## A FRUSTRATED PEACE

Wilson planned to attend the peace conference in person, and there he hoped to represent the masses of the world. Before the conference began, however, he had cause to wonder whether he would have even the people of the United States behind him.

### Repudiation at the Polls

Though the war had raised the income of millions of previously low-paid Americans, the Wilson administration failed to get the approval of a majority of the voters in the congressional elections of 1918. Throughout the war, Wilson had faced dissension within his own party as some of his congressional leaders of agrarian progressive background fought drastic war measures, helped impose heavy taxation on the more well-to-do, and hurried through wartime prohibition and a prohibition amendment to the Constitution. City Democrats were particularly unhappy over losing their beer. Southern Democrats prevented the limiting of the price of cotton while the price of wheat was controlled. The Midwestern grain belt, as a result, reacted angrily against all Democrats.

Even before the 1918 elections, it seemed likely that conditions at home would influence voters more than policies abroad. Nevertheless, with the war obviously almost over, the President put the election on the basis of high international policy. On October 24 he declared: "The return of a Republican majority to either house of the Congress would . . . be interpreted on the other side of the water as a repudiation of my leadership." This outraged those Republicans who had supported him in his foreign policy, since he had earlier declared "politics is adjourned" for the duration of the war. The fact that the Republicans captured both houses of Congress in 1918 would itself have a serious effect on foreign policy; the effect was exaggerated by Wilson's ill-considered appeal.

## The Armistice

Repudiation at the polls created a sad atmosphere for Wilson's assumption of peace negotiations. The President, like the nation, was tense and tired, but he was ready to drive ahead. He strove to pull his own country and the reluctant Allies with him in his determination to make the Fourteen Points and especially the fourteenth—the League of Nations—a reality.

The pulling and hauling with the Allies went on through most of October 1918, during the negotiations which led to the armistice. The Germans sought through Wilson an armistice based on the Fourteen Points. The Allies denied even knowing what these points were, for the Allies were by no means ready to give up their claims for reparations and annexations. Only after Wilson had twice threatened to negotiate a separate peace were they willing to present a united facade. The Allies seemed to agree to the Fourteen Points in entirety, except for explicit reservations on reparations and freedom of the seas, and this apparent agreement led the Germans to expect generous treatment. Further misunderstanding developed because, while the Allies laid down military and naval terms that would make it impossible for the Germans to resume warfare, they used the term "armistice," which meant a negotiated pause in hostilities, rather than the word "surrender." What followed at Versailles was a conclave of victors dictating to a vanquished country, not a negotiated peace or the peace without victory that Wilson had once recommended.

The armistice that went into effect on November 11, 1918, provided that the Allies would negotiate peace on the basis of the Fourteen Points. The Germans agreed to withdraw their forces from France and Belgium and to surrender huge quantities of matériel. They accepted what was virtually the unconditional surrender of their fleet. While the peace was being drafted, the Allied blockade continued.

### Summary of the Fourteen Points [1918]

*I. Open covenants of peace, openly arrived at. . . .*

*II. Absolute freedom of navigation upon the seas. . . .*

*III. The removal, so far as possible, of all economic barriers, and the establishment of an equality of trade conditions among all the nations consenting to the peace and associating themselves for its maintenance.*

*IV. Adequate guarantees given and taken that national armaments will be reduced to the lowest point consistent with domestic safety.*

*V. A free, open-minded, and absolutely impartial adjustment of all colonial claims. . . .*

*VI. The evacuation of all Russian territory. . . .*

*VII. Belgium, the whole world will agree, must be evacuated and restored. . . .*

*VIII. All French territory should be freed and the invaded portions . . . and . . . Alsace-Lorraine . . . [restored].*

*IX. A readjustment of the frontiers of Italy should be effected along clearly recognizable lines of nationality.*

*X. The peoples of Austria-Hungary . . . should be accorded the freest opportunity of autonomous development.*

*XI. Rumania, Serbia, and Montenegro should be evacuated . . . Serbia accorded free and secure access to the sea. . . .*

*XII. The Turkish portions of the present Ottoman Empire should be assured a secure sovereignty, but the other nationalities . . . should be assured . . . autonomous development, and the Dardanelles should be permanently opened. . . .*

*XIII. An independent Polish state should be erected . . . which should be assured free and secure access to the sea. . . .*

*XIV. A general association of nations must be formed. . . .*

To the Allies as they assembled in Paris, there seemed no need to consult Germany on the nature of the peace. Indeed, the only obstacle to the kind of postwar world they had planned in their secret treaties was President Wilson. He made the unprecedented decision to leave the United States and attend the peace conference in person. Colonel House and other advisers urged him not to go.

Wilson seriously miscalculated in refusing to take with him as one of the peace commissioners a leading Republican like Elihu Root or William Howard Taft. He would have done well, too, to include one of the powerful Republican senators, since it would take many Republican votes to muster the requisite two-thirds majority for the treaty in the Senate. Nevertheless, Wilson took only a nonpolitical Republican diplomat, Henry White, and relied neither upon him nor upon the other commissioners.

Arriving in Europe in December 1918, before the other European leaders were ready to confer, Wilson toured France, Italy, and England. Wherever he went hysterically cheering crowds greeted him; everywhere boulevards and plazas were renamed for him. The cheering millions reinforced his feeling that he was the spokesman for humanity. He was not aware that in each nation these masses looked to him to obtain for them much that ran contrary to the Fourteen Points. A little later, when he fought against some of their national claims, their adulation evaporated into disillusion.

## Wilson at Versailles

The sessions at Paris began January 12, 1919, in an atmosphere of idealism tinctured with national aggrandizement, amidst glittering scenes reminiscent of the Congress of Vienna. To the east, however, there was an urgency born of imminent starvation and the threatening spread of Communism. Hoover, trying to get food into central Europe to fend off both threats, declared: "The wolf is at the door of the world." One of the greatest difficulties was that Russia, where Red Bolsheviks were still fighting White counterrevolutionaries, was entirely unrepresented.

At the outset Wilson had to struggle to pre-vent a division of spoils under the secret treaties. He tried to block the Japanese from obtaining permanently the German treaty rights in the Shantung peninsula of China and the former German islands north of the Equator in the Pacific, which could be Japanese strongholds. He had to give way, however, to the insistence of the British that they honor the treaty promises with which they had lured the Japanese into the war. Wilson with more success persuaded the Allies to hold former German colonies and Turkish territories on a basis of trusteeship responsible to the League of Nations. This was the new and unprecedented "mandate" system.

Simultaneously, Wilson worked on the drafting of the League Covenant. He insisted that it form the first part of the treaty and be inseparable from it, and he labored long and hard to draft it in meticulous detail. In the League Covenant he saw the one possible way of overriding the vengeful selfishness that seemed dominant among the victorious nations. Whatever imperfections and inequities there were in the treaty he thought could be rectified through the League: through it and it alone, the world could avoid future wars. In the League he envisaged a potentially powerful (but not armed) international organization through which the nations of the world could share responsibility in maintaining the security of all against any aggressor.

At the end of February 1919, as Congress prepared to adjourn, Wilson came home to sign bills. He brought with him the League Covenant, determined that he would force the Senate to accept it without compromise. The acclaim with which Bostonians greeted him; the friendliness of editorials in most newspapers, and the energy with which large and influential organizations advocated the League, all encouraged him to think public sentiment was overwhelmingly behind him. When Colonel House warned him he must be prepared to compromise with the Senate, he retorted: "I have found that you get nothing in this world that is worth-while without fighting for it."

A stiff fight was taking form. In the Senate, on March 4, 1919, Henry Cabot Lodge produced a round robin signed by thirty-nine senators, a number sufficient to block the treaty, announcing that they would not accept the

Covenant in its existing form. Wilson, about to reembark for Paris, retorted angrily. But back at the conference he did obtain some of the amendments upon which the Senate would obviously insist. These provided that a nation need not accept a mandate against its will, that a member could withdraw with two years' notice, that the League would not regulate immi-

gration and other internal matters, and that it would not infringe upon the Monroe Doctrine. The Republican senators, however, were not appeased. Many of them saw in the struggle over the Covenant a means of embarrassing Wilson, stripping him of some of his glory, and developing a winning issue for the campaign of 1920.

## The Big Four in Paris

The council of four of the peace conference participants photographed at the Paris home of President Wilson, 11 Place des Etats-Unis, May 27, 1919. Left to right: David Lloyd George, Prime Minister of Great Britain; Vittorio E. Orlando, Premier of Italy; Georges Clemenceau, Premier of France; and President Wilson. A thirty-five-year-old British economist at the conference, John Maynard Keynes, described Wilson with a caustic pen: "He had no plan, no scheme, no constructive idea whatever for clothing with the flesh of life the commandments which he had thundered from the White House. . . . He not only had no proposals in detail, but he was in many respects, perhaps inevitably, ill-informed as to European conditions. And not only was

he ill-informed—that was true of Mr. Lloyd George also —but his mind was slow and unadaptable." Keynes concluded: "It was harder to de-bamboozle this old Presbyterian than to bamboozle him." These stereotypes clung to Wilson for decades, although the British foreign secretary, Arthur Balfour, who sat at the meetings of the Big Four, declared that Wilson was "firm, modest, restrained, eloquent, well-informed, and convincing." To Balfour's surprise, Wilson was "as good round a table as he was on paper." General Jan Smuts of South Africa declared that Wilson was "the noblest figure, perhaps the only noble figure in the history of the war." (National Archives)

While Wilson was obtaining revisions to the Covenant, the conference was also grappling with the critical problem of Germany and the remaking of the European map. Together with the British prime minister, Lloyd George, Wilson resisted the French proposal to break up western Germany into buffer states. He did sanction the return of Alsace-Lorraine to France, and the establishment of a strong Poland and Czechoslovakia on Germany's borders, all in keeping with the national self-determination clauses of the Fourteen Points. He also supported German demilitarization, long-term Allied occupation of the west bank of the Rhine, and an Anglo-French-American mutual defense pact (which was never ratified). If maintained, these security provisions should have prevented the resurgence of Germany as a military menace to the West.

Elsewhere the remapping of Europe proceeded rather fitfully. Italy obtained the Brenner Pass area, in which 200,000 Austrians lived, then was outraged at not also receiving Fiume, which Wilson felt must be a port for the new nation of Yugoslavia. In this region and others, the economic needs of nations conflicted with the principle of national self-determination of peoples. Back in the United States, ethnic groups were ready to clamor for more for their native countries. The Irish in the United States insisted that Wilson should fight for national self-determination for Ireland, wracked by civil war. Wilson took up the matter privately with Lloyd George but did not make a public stand.

Wilson's most important departure from the Fourteen Points was his acceptance of British and French demands for heavy reparations from the Germans. Even before the armistice, he had partly accepted the demands that Germany pay for civilian damages. At the conference, he permitted these demands to cover even pensions for veterans; the astronomical sum was to be set later by a reparations commission. Meanwhile, though Wilson himself for years had taken an economic-determinism view of the origins of the war, the other powers insisted that Germany must accept sole responsibility for starting it. The "war-guilt" clause and the reparations bill embittered the German people. Even in the United States, the harsh peace meted out against Germany disillusioned many

liberals and alienated them from Wilson. They regarded the treaty as a "hell's brew" which would ultimately lead to another war.

## The League Rejected

Wilson returned to the United States confident that the Senate, despite the difficulties Lodge was stirring up, would ratify the treaty. On July 10, 1919, when he presented it to the Senate, he asked rhetorically: "Dare we reject it and break the heart of the world?"

Through a combination of coercion and compromise he might have brought about ratification. But he was suffering from hardening of the arteries and, while in Paris, had been so ill that he may have been close to a stroke. His physical condition robbed him of political suppleness; instead of using patience and tact, he was more likely to shower his opponents with self-righteous anger.

Wilson's opponents in the Senate were moved by both principle and partisanship. The fourteen "irreconcilables" were men of conscience, of Middle Western or Far Western progressive tradition, like Republicans William E. Borah of Idaho, Hiram Johnson of California, and Robert M. LaFollette of Wisconsin, and Democrat James Reed of Missouri. They acted from a deep conviction that their nation could best be served by staying out of the League. Other opponents with less conviction were more concerned with constructing a winning issue for the Republicans in the 1920 election than they were with assuring the future of the world. Senator Lodge, applying all his brilliant intellect to his loathing for Wilson, was ready, as chairman of the Senate Foreign Relations Committee, to use every possible tactic to obstruct, delay, and defeat the treaty. Public sentiment seemed to favor ratification, and Lodge needed time to marshal forces against it. Consequently, he spent the first two weeks after it reached the committee reading aloud every word on its nearly three hundred pages. Next, he held six weeks of public hearings, listening to the complaints of every disgruntled minority.

From the White House, Wilson did some conferring with Republican senators. He explained to them that he considered the collective-security provision of Article X (according to which League members guaranteed one another's territorial integrity) to be more of a moral obligation upon the United States than a legal one—but to Wilson moral obligations were the more important. The senators were not impressed; it began to appear that Wilson would have to accept some of Lodge's reservations if he wished to obtain ratification. When one senator told him this, he retorted: "Never! Never! . . . I'll appeal to the country!"

So Wilson, at the end of his physical resources, against the stern warnings of his physician, undertook a cross-country speaking tour, writing his speeches as he went along, delivering them night after night. In twenty-two days he traveled over 8,000 miles, giving thirty-six addresses averaging an hour in length. At first the halls were not entirely filled nor were his speeches always well polished. As the tour proceeded, he gained larger and more enthusiastic audiences and grew more eloquent in his moral fervor. Had it been possible to sway the United States Senate through public opinion, the tour might have been a success. But Wilson became more and more frail. Finally after speaking at Pueblo, Colorado, September 25, he suffered such acute headaches that he had to cancel the tour and return to Washington.

Then he suffered an acute stroke which partially paralyzed his left side. For two weeks he was close to death, and for six more weeks so seriously ill that he could attend only to what little business his devoted wife and doctor thought would not unduly upset or fatigue him. When some officials tried to see the President on vital matters, Mrs. Wilson turned them away, saying: "I am not interested in the President of the United States. I am interested in my husband and his health."

At this critical juncture the Senate Foreign Relations Committee finally reported the treaty, recommending forty-five amendments and three reservations. Lodge managed to marshal the Republican senators so well that in November he obtained adoption of fourteen reservations. By this time Wilson had recovered sufficiently to give stern directions to the Democratic minority: they must vote only for the treaty without any reservations whatsoever. Although none of the Lodge reservations would have devitalized the League, Wilson preferred no ratification of the treaty to ratification with reservations. While he was by no means his old self, he was able to exert power enough to maintain discipline over the loyal Democrats. When the vote came on November 19, 1919, forty-two Democrats joined with the thirteen Republican irreconcilables to vote down the treaty with reservations. Next, the Senate voted on ratification of the treaty without reservations. There were thirty-eight senators, all but one of them a Democrat, who voted for it; fifty-five voted against it.

On the day of the final vote, March 19, 1920, when the Senate considered the treaty with fifteen reservations, it came within 7 votes of receiving the requisite two-thirds majority. By this time, President Wilson was looking to the election of 1920 as a "solemn referendum" on the League issue.

# Selected Readings

**T. R. and the Far East** H. K. Beale, *Theodore Roosevelt and the Rise of America to World Power*° (1956); C. E. Neu, *An Uncertain Friendship: Theodore Roosevelt and Japan, 1906–1909* (1967); R. A. Esthus, *Theodore Roosevelt and Japan* (1966); T. A. Bailey, *Theodore Roosevelt and the Japanese-American Crisis* (1934); Tyler Dennett, *Roosevelt and the Russo-Japanese War* (1924); P. J. Treat, *Diplomatic Relations Between the United States and Japan, 1895–1905* (1938); E. H. Zabriskie, *American-Russian Rivalry in the Far East, 1895–1914* (1946); W. R. Braisted, *The United States Navy in the Pacific, 1897–1909* (1958).

**Caribbean Policy** Dexter Perkins, *The United States and the Caribbean* (1947); D. G. Munro,

*Intervention and Dollar Diplomacy in the Carib-bean, 1900–1921* (1964); W. H. Callcott, *The Caribbean Policy of the United States, 1890–1920* (1942); Gerstle Mack, *The Land Divided: A History of the Panama Canal and Other Canal Projects* (1944); D. C. Miner, *The Fight for the Panama Route* (1940); D. F. Healy, *The United States in Cuba, 1898–1902* (1963); G. K. Lewis, *Puerto Rico: Freedom and Power in the Caribbean°* (1967).

**Mexican Relations** D. M. Pletcher, *Rails, Mines, and Progress: Seven American Promoters in Mexico, 1867–1911* (1959); C. C. Clendenen, *The United States and Pancho Villa: A Study in Unconventional Diplomacy* (1961); R. E. Quirk, *An Affair of Honor: Woodrow Wilson and the Occupation of Vera Cruz* (1962).

**Wilsonian Diplomacy** Harley Notter, *The Origins of the Foreign Policy of Woodrow Wilson* (1937); A. S. Link, *Wilson the Diplomatist°* (1957); N. G. Levin, Jr., *Woodrow Wilson and World Politics: America's Response to War and Revolution* (1968); R. E. Osgood, *Ideals and Self-Interest in America's Foreign Relations* (1953).

**Going to War** E. R. May, *The World War and American Isolation, 1914–1917°* (1959); E. H. Buehrig, *Woodrow Wilson and the Balance of Power* (1955); Charles Seymour, *American Diplomacy During the World War* (1934) and *American Neutrality, 1914–1917* (1935); Walter Millis, *Road to War: America, 1914–1917* (1935); E. M. Borchard and W. P. Lage, *Neutrality for the United States* (1937); C. C. Tansill, *America Goes to War* (1938); Armin Rappaport, *The Navy League of the United States* (1962); R. H. Heindel, *The American Impact on Great Britain, 1898–1914* (1940); Bradford Perkins, *The Great Rapprochement: England and the United States, 1895–1914* (1968).

**Combat** E. M. Coffman, *The War to End All Wars: The American Military Experience in World War I* (1969); H. A. De Weerd, *President Wilson Fights His War: World War I and the American Intervention* (1968); D. F. Trask, *The United States in the Supreme War Council: American War Aims and Inter-Allied Strategy, 1917–1918* (1961); J. G. Harbord, *The American Army in France, 1917–1919* (1936); Frank Freidel, *Over There: The Story of America's First Great Overseas Crusade* (1964), a pictorial history; E. E. Morison, *Admiral Sims and the Modern American Navy* (1942); J. J. Hudson, *Hostile Skies: A Combat History of the American Air Service in World War I* (1968).

**The Home Front** F. L. Paxson, *American Democracy and the World War* (3 vols., 1936–1948); S. W. Livermore, *Politics Is Adjourned: Woodrow Wilson and the War Congress, 1916–1918* (1966); D. R. Beaver, *Newton D. Baker and the American War Effort, 1917–1919* (1966); Margaret Coit, *Mr. Baruch* (1957); B. M. Baruch, *American Industry in the War* (1941); H. N. Scheiber, *The Wilson Administration and Civil Liberties, 1917–1921* (1960); H. C. Peterson and G. C. Fite, *Opponents of War, 1917–1918* (1957); J. R. Mock and Cedric Larson, *Words That Won the War* (1939); H. C. Peterson, *Propaganda for War* (1939).

**Peacemaking** R. J. Bartlett, *The League to Enforce Peace* (1944); H. R. Rudin, *Armistice, 1918* (1944); L. E. Gelfand, *The Inquiry: American Preparations for Peace, 1917–1919* (1963); T. A. Bailey, *Woodrow Wilson and the Lost Peace°* (1944) and *Woodrow Wilson and the Great Betrayal°* (1945); L. W. Martin, *Peace Without Victory: Woodrow Wilson and the British Liberals* (1958); D. F. Fleming, *The United States and the League of Nations, 1918–1920* (1932); J. M. Keynes, *Economic Consequences of the Peace* (1919); Herbert Hoover, *The Ordeal of Woodrow Wilson* (1958); J. A. Garraty, *Henry Cabot Lodge* (1953).

---

° Titles available in paperback.

VOL. LXXVI....No. 25,319.　　•　•　•　　　　　　　　　　NEW YORK, SATURDAY, MAY 21, 1927.　　　　　　　　TWO CENTS In Greater | THREE CENTS | FOUR

# LINDBERGH SPEEDS ACROSS NORTH ATLANTIC, KEEPING TO SCHEDULE OF 100 MILES AN HOUR; SIGHTED PASSING ST. JOHN'S, N. F., AT 7:15 P. M

## LOWMAN GETS POST AS ANDREWS QUITS IN BIG DRY SHIFT

### Mellon, in Same Stroke, Names Chief Chemist Doran Commissioner in Place of Haynes.

### STEP TO CHECK FRICTION

### Andrews Will Retire Aug. 1 With Work Completed—Haynes Is Forced Out in Shake-Up.

### MOVE SATISFIES ALL SIDES

Both Nominees Are on Record as Prohibition Advocates and Are Acceptable to Dry League.

*Special to The New York Times.*
WASHINGTON, May 20.—In the most dramatic overturn in the history of dry enforcement, which is expected to lead to further changes in the Washington headquarters as well as in the field, Secretary Mellon at one stroke today accepted the resignation of General Lincoln C. Andrews of New York, as Assistant Secretary of the Treasury in charge of prohibition enforcement, and appointed a successor in Major Roy A. Haynes of Ohio, the Acting Commissioner of Prohibition.

Mr. Mellon designated Seymour W. Lowman, former Lieutenant Governor of New York, for Presidential appointment to the post of General Andrews and named Dr. James M. Doran of North Dakota, now Chief Chemist of the Prohibition Unit, to be Prohibition Commissioner in place of Major Haynes.

Mr. Lowman is expected to enter upon his duties as Assistant Secretary on Aug. 1, assuming jurisdiction over the Customs and Prohibition Bureaus and the Coast Guard. Dr. Doran will take charge of the Prohibition Unit at once.

**End of Factionalism Expected.**

Hope was expressed today by Administration officials that the retirement of General Andrews and Major Haynes would end the factionalism in the Prohibition Bureau, which, in their opinion, has tended to lessen the efficiency of enforcement. Major Haynes, a former officer of the Anti-Saloon League, has frequently been at odds with Treasury superiors for years and the law enforcement work of General Andrews has been frequently criticized by Wayne B. Wheeler and others associated with the Anti-Saloon League.

Major Haynes's failure to lead the Prohibition Commissionership is regarded here as a defeat for the Anti-Saloon League and a victory for dry leaders who do not train with the Wheeler organization. At the same time league officials take comfort from the prospective retirement of General Andrews, whom they have long regarded as "unfriendly" to their purposes.

**Party Chiefs Sponsored Lowman.**

Mr. Lowman was endorsed for the appointment today by National Commissioner Hilles and Ogden L. Mills, Under Secretary of the Treasury. He was the running mate of Mr. Mills on the Republican gubernatorial ticket in New York last year, and has a record as a dry that makes him acceptable to most of the dry leaders. He was originally considered for Commissioner of Prohibition, but a switch was made when General Andrews gave notice of his resignation.

It is assumed here that Secretary Mellon consulted with the President before he announced his designation of Mr. Lowman. Mr. Lowman will come into authority on June 1 to familiarize himself with the duties of his new office, but he does not expect to be sworn in until General Andrews quits on Aug 1.

No provision has been made for Major Haynes to remain in the dry service and he is expected to resign forthwith. He is now functioning as "Acting Commissioner" under a temporary arrangement that became effective under the reorganization law on April 1.

Major Herbert D. White, special investigator, probably will be named Assistant Commissioner. James R. Jones and L. G. Nutt, who were appointed Deputy Commissioners last April, will remain in those positions at least for the present.

**Mellon Stresses Promotion System.**

In announcing the appointment of Dr. Doran, Secretary Mellon stated that because of his long service and intimate knowledge of the work, Dr. Doran was well qualified for the post of Commissioner.

He declared it to be a sound principle of administration to promote men

*Continued on Page Twelve.*

---

## 'Too Old,' Says Hughes at 65, To Run for the Presidency

Declaring that he was "too old to run for President," Charles Evans Hughes, after heading in the morning papers yesterday of a movement to start a Hughes boom in the event that President Coolidge should decide not to become a candidate for re-election, issued a statement declaring he would not accept a nomination. He was 65 years old April 11.

"I know nothing of the movement to which reference is made," Mr. Hughes said. "There should be no doubt as to my own attitude. I am for President Coolidge, first, last and all the time, and I believe that he will be renominated and re-elected. I do not wish my name to be used in any contingency. I am too old to run for President and I would neither seek nor accept the nomination."

---

## SINCLAIR SENTENCED TO 3 MONTHS IN JAIL

### Oil Man Is Also Ordered to Pay $500 Fine for Refusing to Reply to Senators.

### APPEALS AND GIVES BOND

### Littleton Argues in Vain That His Client Exercised His Constitutional Rights.

*Special to The New York Times.*
WASHINGTON, May 20.—Harry F. Sinclair, oil operator, under indictment with former Secretary Fall for conspiracy to defraud the Government, was sentenced today to serve three months in jail and to pay a fine of $500 on a charge of contempt of the Senate committee which investigates the naval reserve oil leases. Immediately after sentence was pronounced the sentence in the District of Columbia Supreme Court, Sinclair gave bond in the sum of $5,000 pending appeal to the Appellate Court.

The penalty was imposed notwithstanding the plea by Martin W. Littleton, Sinclair's counsel, that the Court nothing which would humiliate, shame, disgrace, mortify or worry his client, and despite Mr. Littleton's argument that the entire proceedings, beginning with Mr. Sinclair's appearance before the Senate committee March 22, 1924, and ending with the sentence, were "irregular."

Mr. Sinclair was originally charged with refusing to answer nine questions of the Senate committee regarding the lease of the Teapot Dome reserve in Wyoming by the Mammoth Oil Company. Sinclair's counsel filed a demurrer, and the number of questions was reduced to ten.

A special appeal was then allowed, but the progress of this was blocked by the Walsh bill, initiated by Senator Walsh of Montana, "prosecutor" for the Senate committee, and designed to prevent appeals from interlocutory orders of the criminal courts. Following the passage by Congress of the Walsh bill, Sinclair was tried in April and was convicted. The number of questions involved was reduced at the trial to four.

**No Crime, Says Littleton.**

When Sinclair stood up for sentence, he declared that he had nothing to say. Mr. Littleton, however, raised the history of similar cases, and stated that when he advised Mr. Sinclair to refuse to answer the Senate committee's questions he was not giving his client a "horseback opinion," but an opinion which was founded on substantial law.

"My client has done nothing to warrant this procedure," Mr. Littleton declared. "The question of the right of either house of Congress, acting separately or together, to compel a citizen to testify here must definitely by decided and, in fact, the United States Supreme Court in the case of Kilbourne versus Thompson deliberately refused to decide that question.

"The committee which summoned my client has denied nothing, nor did he impose a single obstruction in the path of the committee. There is no crime committed here, no offense committed, moral turpitude—merely a citizen of the United States who had and exercised a right which belongs to every American gentleman."

**The Four Questions Asked.**

The four questions which Mr. Sinclair declined to answer, on advice from Mr. Littleton, and which were included in the indictment, follow:

By Senator Walsh—Mr. Sinclair, I want to interrogate you about a matter concerning which the committee has no knowledge of or reliable infor-

*Continued on Page Twelve.*

---

## LINDBERGH LEAVES NEW YORK AT 7:52 A. M.

### With Cool Determination He Braves Death to Get Off in the Misty Dawn, Winning Out by Luck and Skill.

### PLANE FALTERS AND THEN RISES AND IS OFF

### Hundreds Gasp as Unconquerable Youth by Sheer Wizardry Lifts Machine Carrying 5,200-Pound Load, With Failure a Few Yards Off.

**By RUSSELL OWEN.**
Staff Correspondent of The Times, Who Reported the Polar Flights of Byrd and Amundsen.

*Copyright, 1927, by The New York Times Company.*

A sluggish gray monoplane lurched its way down Roosevelt Field yesterday morning, slowly gathering momentum. Inside sat a tall youngster, eyes glued to an instrument board or darting ahead for swift glances at the runway, his face drawn with the intensity of his purpose.

Death lay but a few seconds ahead of him if his skill failed or his courage faltered. For moments, as the heavy plane rose from the ground, dropped down, staggered again into the air and fell, he gambled for his life against a hazard which had already killed four men.

And then slowly, so slowly that those watching it stood fascinated, as if by his indomitable will alone, the young pilot lifted his plane. It dipped and then rose with renewed speed, climbing heavily but steadily toward the distant trees.

The spirit of unconquerable youth had won, and "Slim" Lindbergh was on his way to Paris.

All the romance which had surrounded this boy since his meteoric flight from the Pacific Coast a week ago reached its climax in that take-off. The uncertainty of it, the frightful disaster which threatened him, the quick recoveries which showed a cool, keen mind fighting for mastery, made veteran pilots gaze in fascination.

"God be with him!" exclaimed Commander Byrd fervently, when at last it seemed that Lindbergh was safely on his way.

The boyish, smiling lad, with the quiet confidence of bravery and belief in his own ability, has won the hearts of every one who came near him. Until two weeks ago he was hardly considered a factor in the race to be first through the air to Paris, that long, treacherous flight of 3,600 miles. And then he came on with speed of the wind, making only one stop between the Pacific Coast and New York, and while rival camps squabbled over money or worked through long, tedious tasks, Lindbergh rolled his plane out in the gray dawn and got away, all alone.

**Youth Breaks All Barriers.**

It may not have been the safest kind of flying; perhaps it was only a daring gesture, but it was magnificent. It was youth refusing to admit obstacles, breaking down barriers, and it brought him luck. For even as Lindbergh prepared his plane the fog that had choked his path to Newfoundland rolled back, and all the way from New York to Europe stretched a clear path of fair weather, with gentle favoring winds. Even the sun came out as he started, and it seemed that the fates which deal with brave men's lives were smiling at the youth who had defied them.

When Lindbergh made his decision to start just before midnight on Thursday, it seemed the height of folly. Heavy fog settled over Roosevelt Field under inky black skies which dripped slow drops of rain. It was dismal and threatening. But the young pilot, who has guided his temerity with a keen and thoughtful mind, saw in the late weather reports the possibility that the skies might clear to the north. All he needed was one look at Newfoundland before he left the land for his long, weary flight across the sea which had already claimed Nungesser and Coli.

The huge hangar in which his plane was housed was closed to every one except the mechanics, who went over the plane with zealous care and partly filled the gasoline tank. Lindbergh, after a parting word with them, went to the Garden City Hotel at midnight for a brief sleep. He lay down with orders that he be called at 2:15 o'clock in the morning, but before 2 o'clock he was downstairs.

While he had been resting weather reports indicated that the fog was lifting all along the coast, although it was depressingly wet at the field. The clouds had opened and poured down a short deluge, which left puddles in which shone the glare of many lights. Through a small opening in the hangar door the silver nose of Lindbergh's plane gleamed through the glancing rain drops.

Hundreds of people had gathered at midnight, but the rain drove many of them away. There were still about 500 standing patiently, disdaining soaked feet and drenched clothing, in the hope that they might see one of the great dramas of the air

*Continued on Page Two.*

---

### CAPTAIN CHARLES A. LINDBERGH.

The First American Flyer to Start on the Flight Between New York and Paris.

---

### LINDBERGH'S STORY FOR THE TIMES

When next heard from, Lindbergh will write the story of his great exploit especially for readers of The Times and certain associated world newspapers. It will appear in New York exclusively in The Times.

---

## BELLANCA FLIGHT HELD BACK BY WIND

### Hop, Set for Dawn, Is Called Off After All Preparations— Bertaud Writ Thown Out.

*Copyright, 1927, by The New York Times Company.*
*Special Cable to The New York Times.*

With Captain Lindbergh well on his way to Paris last night, those connected with the Columbia Aircraft Company's Bellanca monoplane Columbia made arrangements for a hop-off from Roosevelt Field at a o'clock this morning. Before midnight Charles A. Levine, backer of the company, made a definite statement that the Bellanca plane would start at daylight.

At 1:30 A. M., however, Clarence Chamberlin, senior pilot of the monoplane, announced that there would be no start today.

The weather report shown northwest winds, which would give us a head wind all the way to Newfoundland," he said. "We will not make the attempt today."

Levine's statement earlier in the evening was supplemented by additional information from a spokesman for him.

"After a conference at the Hotel Biltmore tonight between Charles A. Levine, Chairman of the Board of Directors of the Columbia Aircraft Corporation, and ex-Senator Charles Lockwood, representing Clarence D. Chamberlin, Mr. Levine decided that as a purely sporting proposition the flight should be made at once," the spokesman said.

He refused to reveal the name of the navigator who had been selected to replace Lloyd Bertaud and accompany Chamberlin on the flight.

"The navigator," he said, "will not be announced until just before the flight."

Lloyd Bertaud was definitely grounded and eliminated from the flight by the decision of Supreme Court Justice Mitchell May in the Brooklyn Supreme Court yesterday

*Continued on Page Four.*

---

## LONE FLIGHT GRIPS FRENCH IMAGINATION

### Lindbergh's Ocean Hop Appeals to Paris as Nothing Else Could Have Done.

*Copyright, 1927, by The New York Times Company.*
*Special Cable to The New York Times.*

PARIS, May 20.—Captain Charles Lindbergh's lone attempt to cross the Atlantic in a single jump from New York to Paris has appealed to the French as none other would have done. Of this entire people he has tonight the best wishes and prayers for his success and safety.

His calm courage and his quiet and efficient preparation, unaccompanied by fiery publicity, recalls to French minds that picture of "a real American" they found among the doughboys of the Marne, St. Mihiel and the Argonne and had, for sundry causes, almost forgotten since.

To welcome him there may not be so huge a crowd as would have greeted Captains Nungesser and Coli in New York. (Le Bourget is too far out of town for that.) But in the fortunes of this "Flying Fool" all France is tonight sharing America's anxiety and waiting eagerly tomorrow for that success which was denied their own two fliers but to which Captain Lindbergh's courage makes so great a claim.

As fully as possible all preparations have been made for Captain Lindbergh's reception. Unfortunately, the weather forecast in France is not so entirely favorable as it has been for some days past, though it is not unfavorable. For tomorrow the prediction is sunshine, with clouds followed by showers and a rising temperature. The wind will stay in the southwest, which will help to the full the airman on the last stage of his long struggle. Visibility will be the only essential varying along the coast and inland.

American Ambassador Herrick is

*Continued on Page Three.*

---

## GETS HIS BEARINGS IN NEWFOUNDL

### With the First Leg of His Flight Paris Over, He Puts to Sea and Heads for Ireland

### ALL OF THE "BREAKS" ARE IN HIS

### Fog Disperses, Weather Clears and Go Following Winds Help to Speed Him Along on His Hazardous Venture.

*Copyright, 1927, by The New York Times Company.*

ST. JOHN'S, N. F., May 20.—Captain Lindbergh's ai passed over St. John's at 8:15 o'clock tonight [7:15 New Daylight Saving Time]. It was seen by hundreds an appeared seaward, heading for Ireland. It is assumed passed over Cape Race and places south of this in the fog which prevailed there all day.

It was flying quite low between the hills near St. J and went east over the Signal Hill Station, following the of Hawker and Greeve and also of Alcock and Brown e first transatlantic flights eight years ago.

There was intense excitement during the passage of bergh's plane, and citizens motoring in the suburbs or str on the country roads are coming back with tales of its tr Many noted the fact that the flier seemed to be gettin bearing before setting out on the second leg of his flight.

Michael Sullivan, member of the Newfoundland Cu saw the plane while motoring and followed its progress car on the road that leads to the signal station, keeping sight for several minutes, but when he reached the sum had passed from sight, so great was its speed.

Robert Job, principal of the firm of Job Brothers, shi merchants, also saw it and watched its course over the He could see it so distinctly as to notice that it had some le on its side, though he could not make out words.

**Strong Wind Is in His Favor.**

By The Associated Press.
ST. JOHN'S, N. F., Saturday, May 21.—Strong we breezes, approaching gale force, were blowing here earl night and marine authorities declared that they should grant assistance to Captain Lindbergh in his transat crossing.

It was estimated here that he might reach the Irish by daylight.

**Leaves American Continent.**

*Copyright, 1927, by The New York Times Company.*
*Special to The New York Times.*

SYDNEY, N. S., May 20.—Captain Lindbergh got hi sight of the American continent at 5 o'clock [4 o'clock Ea Daylight Saving Time] this afternoon when he passed ou the Atlantic over Main-a-dieu, Cape Breton. The plane we ing low and at great speed, and her number, 211, was p visible to watchers with powerful glasses.

Should Lindbergh succeed in navigating through a s dense curtain over the Newfoundland banks he will have weather across the North Atlantic, ships at sea reporting visibility with no indications of a storm within the next tw four hours.

By The Associated Press.
HALIFAX, N. S., May 20.—Captain Lindbergh passed Mulgrave on the Strait of Canso, which separates the main of Nova Scotia from Cape Breton Island, at 4:05 P. M. Atl Day Time [3:05 o'clock Eastern Daylight Saving Time]. was flying high and the markings on his gray monoplane c not be seen.

**Reaches Nova Scotia Coast.**

*Copyright, 1927, by The New York Times Company.*
*Special to The New York Times.*

YARMOUTH, N. S., May 20.—Captain Lindbergh pa over New Tusket, about forty miles from here, at 12:45 o this afternoon [11:45 Eastern Daylight Time]. He was fl low, but traveling very fast.

By The Associated Press.
MIDDLEBORO, Mass., May 20.—A monoplane, believe be that of Captain Lindbergh, was seen over West Middle about 9:15 this morning flying northeasterly.

Chester Rice, clerk at the Middleboro police station, c not make out the letters on the wings, but is sure the num were 211.

**Lindbergh Keeps to Schedule.**

*Copyright, 1927, by The New York Times Company.*

On the basis of the above dispatches, "Slim" Lindberg keeping as closely to his schedule as an express train at a s

# Chapter 23
# The Illusion
# of Normalcy

"America's present need is not heroics, but healing; not nostrums, but normalcy." The year was 1920, and the speaker, with a fine sense of alliteration as well as a feeling for the spirit of the time, was Warren G. Harding, soon to be President of the United States. "The world needs to be reminded that all human ills are not curable by legislation."

Harding's remarks provided a catch phrase for the period following World War I. The American people, or at least the majority of them, were tired of legislation, tire of wartime restrictions, tired of progressive reforms. They wanted a return to "normalcy," to the good old days, to the days that never had existed except in nostalgic reverie.

The days that were to come in the 1920s were old in some respects but new in others. They were old—like those of the late nineteenth century—in respect to the position of big business, which again dominated both government and society. Indeed, business was more sanctified than ever. "The business of America is business," said Calvin Coolidge, who succeeded Harding in the Presidency. In *The Man Nobody Knows* (1925), a best seller of the period, Bruce Barton described Jesus Christ as "a startling example of business success," the author of "the most powerful advertisements of all time," and "the founder of modern business."

But much was new in the decade of the twenties. This was the time when the automobile came into its own, with production increasing from 1.5 million cars in 1921 to 4.75 million in 1929, by which year the automotive industry was responsible, directly or indirectly, for the employment of more than 3 million persons. It was the time of the coming of numerous household gadgets: the radio, the refrigerator, the vacuum cleaner, and many others. It was an age when the federal government sought to impose a species of morality by prohibiting the manufacture, sale, or transportation of intoxicating beverages—and an age of what seemed to many like unprecedented license in speech and behavior, the age of "flaming youth" and of unrestrained dances like the "bunny hug" and the "Charleston."

From 1923 to 1929 it was also a time of remarkable prosperity (for most but by no means all Americans). The people generally assumed—and experts in business, economics, and government told them—that this was veritably a new era in human history. The country had reached a "permanent plateau" of prosperity and need never worry again about the possibility of a serious slump. But prosperity, like "normalcy," proved to be an illusion. Eventually the country fell into much the worst economic depression it had ever known.

---

**"Lindbergh Speeds Across North Atlantic"**

On May 20, 1927, Charles Lindbergh began the first solo nonstop flight from New York to Paris. The trip, which took almost thirty-three and a half hours, made Lindbergh a national hero. (© 1927 by The New York Times Company. Reprinted by permission.)

## THE POSTWAR REACTION

In the immediate postwar years, prices rose and people complained of the "h. c. l.," the high cost of living. Suddenly, in 1921, prices dropped and a brief recession followed, giving way to full recovery by 1923. Meanwhile, fears of radicalism, heightened by the spread of Communism in Russia and elsewhere in Europe, provoked a hysterical spirit of reaction in America.

### The Red Scare

Union workers tried to preserve their wartime economic gains by striking for higher wages as living costs went upward. In 1919 a great wave of strikes spread across the country, involving about 4 million workers. In many of these strikes —such as those conducted by longshoremen, printers, and laborers in the clothing, textile, telephone, and other industries—the strikers succeeded in raising their living standards. In the process they alienated much of the public, which was quick to accept the industrialists' explanations that higher wages were responsible for higher prices, and that the strike leaders were radicals.

The outbreak of a steel strike in September 1919 brought antilabor feelings to a boil. The grievances of the workers were serious. They were working an average of nearly sixty-nine hours per week for bare subsistence wages and were becoming so discontented that the AFL's organizing committee made rapid headway among them. United States Steel discharged all union men and refused to negotiate with Gompers or any other union official. Some 343,-000 men struck in the Chicago area, and additional workers left their jobs in other areas. Despite the workers' valid claims, United States Steel was able to swing public sentiment away from the strikers by claiming that the leaders were Communists. The chief organizer, William Z. Foster, once a follower of Bryan, was to emerge in 1924 as the presidential candidate of the Communist party. The company brought in Negro strikebreakers, and state and federal troops prevented picketing. In rioting at Gary, Indiana, eighteen strikers were killed. Within a few weeks tens of thousands of strikebreakers under armed protection were operating the plants at three-quarters capacity, and by January the workers were starved out.

Public opinion turned even more firmly against organized labor when a police strike broke out in Boston. The policemen were working long hours on prewar salaries under unpleasant conditions. After their organization, the Boston Social Club, obtained an AFL charter and threatened to strike, a Mayor's Citizens Committee prepared to meet their demands except for recognition of their union. The police commissioner, responsible only to the governor, refused and dismissed nineteen leaders. In response, the police struck. As mischief-makers and rowdies took over, horrified citizens put on their military uniforms and, armed with rifles and shotguns, began patrolling the streets. The mayor mobilized state troops and restored order. The following day Governor Calvin Coolidge, who had done nothing to prevent the strike or preserve the peace, suddenly acted. He ordered in troops and backed the decision of the police commissioner never to reemploy any of the strikers. When President Gompers of the AFL appealed to Coolidge, the governor wired back: "There is no right to strike against the public safety, anywhere, anytime." This one telegram made Coolidge a formidable contender for the Republican presidential nomination in 1920.

In Washington Attorney General A. Mitchell Palmer was becoming prominent through his war on both labor and radicals. When the new president of the United Mine Workers, John L. Lewis, took the bituminous coal workers out on strike in November 1919, Palmer smashed the strike with federal court injunctions.

Palmer attracted even more attention with his crusade against Reds. Throughout the country the violent suppression of alleged pro-German activities during the war had been continued in the persecution of the Industrial Workers of the World (IWW), the Socialists, and all other left-wingers. Both Congress and the New York state legislature denied seats to Socialists. By 1920 one-third of the states had enacted criminal syndicalist laws to punish radicals. The New York law prohibited "advocating, teaching, or aiding and abetting the commission of crime and sabotage, or unlawful acts of force and violence or unlawful methods of terrorism as a means of accomplishing a change in industrial ownership or control, or affecting any political change."

Bombings and attempted bombings captured the headlines. A bomb damaged the front of Palmer's home in June 1919; bombs addressed to a number of government leaders were discovered in the mails; a year later an explosion on Wall Street killed thirty-eight people. Four members of the newly founded American Legion were killed in an attack on IWW head-

quarters in Centralia, Washington, on Armistice Day 1919. These incidents furnished the material out of which the newspapers, with some aid from Palmer, built a great national panic. Within the country there were very few radicals to undertake a revolution: IWW membership was down to 35,000 and continued to decline; the Socialist party numbered 39,000 and was not revolutionary anyway; the Communist-Labor party (left wing Socialists) had 10,000 to 30,000 members; and the Communist party, or-

### Sacco and Vanzetti Being Taken Into Court    1927

When Sacco and Vanzetti were brought before Judge Webster Thayer on April 9, 1927, they were allowed to speak. Sacco said: "I never knew, never heard, even read in history anything so cruel as this Court. . . . I know the sentence will be between two classes, the oppressed class and the rich class, and there will always be collision between one and the other." Vanzetti said: "I am suffering because I am a radical and indeed I am a radical; I have suffered because I was an Italian, and indeed I am an Italian . . . but I am so convinced to be right that you can only kill me once but if you could execute me two times, and if I could be reborn two other times, I would live again to do what I have done already." Judge Thayer then sentenced them to death.

One of the counsel for the two men who did not "belong even remotely to [their] school of thoughts," warned after the execution of "minds that are closed by deep prejudice or transient passion." "If," he declared, "the local hostility was inflamed by foolish words of their sympathizers or wicked deeds of their exploiters, this also is a fact to be recollected." The publisher of the conservative Boston *Herald*, which had called for an impartial commission to review the case, asserted: "The momentum of the established order required the execution of Sacco and Vanzetti, and never in your life or mine, has that momentum acquired such tremendous force." (Brown Brothers) ganized September 1, 1919, had 30,000 to 60,000.

Palmer's goal was to ferret out and eliminate the Communists. He proposed a sedition bill so drastic that Congress would not enact it, then he proceeded anyway without it. The Labor Department had already arrested and deported to Finland 249 Russian Communists. Nevertheless, Palmer, without advance notice to the Labor Department, conducted a great Red roundup on January 1, 1920, jailing some 6,000 suspects. Communists who were United States citizens he turned over to states for prosecution. The aliens came under the jurisdiction of the Labor Department, which gave them fair treatment. Only 556 proven Communists were deported.

In Massachusetts, a payroll robbery and murder in April 1920 led to the trial and conviction of two anarchists, Nicola Sacco and Bartolomeo Vanzetti. Many believers in civil liberties felt that the two men were being prosecuted more on the basis of their radicalism than on the criminal evidence. Ultimately throughout the country and even in western Europe, outraged liberals and radicals demanded the release of the two men, but in August 1927 they were executed. The Sacco and Vanzetti case was a *cause célèbre* of the 1920s.

## The KKK and the Negro

If there had been a blaze of revolution, which was improbable, it was indeed under control, but the backfire of intolerance swept out of control and began to sear the country. Not only radicals, but labor organizers, aliens, Catholics, Jews, and Negroes became its victims.

Intolerance was organized in the Ku Klux Klan, which in 1915 had been revived in Atlanta, Georgia, and soon spread throughout the country, claiming 5 million members at its height in the 1920s. White-robed and hooded Klansmen used fiery crosses, threats, torture, and murder to intimidate minority groups and other people they considered un-American or immoral. The Klan became a political power in many states, most notably in Indiana, where a Klansman made himself governor and virtually dictator for a time.

**The Ku Klux Klan Parading in Washington, D.C.**

In 1926 the Ku Klux Klan was still so powerful that it could march down Pennsylvania Avenue with the Capitol in the background. It professed to be a patriotic organization, but was openly anti-Negro, anti-Catholic, anti-Semitic, anti-foreigner, and anti-Union. (Culver)

No group suffered more severely than the Negroes. For hundreds of thousands of them, the war had offered an opportunity to break out of the narrow caste structure of the South. Some 400,000 served in the army, half of them in Europe, where the local people usually drew no color line. Several hundred thousand more moved into the industrial North, where there was less discrimination against them than in the South. Even in the North, however, they suffered from wretched housing, low pay, and the animosity of unskilled white workers who feared their competition.

In both North and South, Negroes faced explosive resentment against them. In order to intimidate them back into their former subservience, Southerners resorted to the terrorism of the Klan and to lynchings, which increased from thirty-four in 1917 to more than seventy in 1919. Terrible race riots broke out, beginning in July 1919, in twenty-six towns and cities, mostly in the North. Hundreds of persons were killed or wounded, and millions of dollars' worth of property was destroyed. The worst of the outbursts began on a Chicago bathing beach and continued through thirteen days of pillaging ·and burning in the Negro district; 23 blacks and 15 whites were killed, 500 were injured, and 1,000 families, mostly Negro, were left homeless.

These terrors led millions of Negroes to follow a persuasive charlatan, Marcus Garvey, founder of the Universal Negro Improvement Association. In return for their contributions, he promised to take them home to an African empire. In 1923 Garvey was convicted of swindling and sentenced to federal prison, but Negro nationalism nevertheless persisted.

## Persisting Progressivism

Some Americans—not radicals but old progressives—would have liked to see the continuation of wartime government regulation or even ownership. At the close of the war the government owned most of the nation's commercial radio facilities (used as yet only for sending messages), commanded a vast merchant fleet, and controlled the railroads.

The call for nationalization, which frightened many Americans, went beyond the old progressive bounds. Congress was not willing to go so

far but did pass the Esch-Cummins Transportation Act of 1920, establishing as tight federal control over railroad rates and securities as any progressive had ever visualized. Railroads suffered from the new rigorous competition of motor vehicles and other carriers and were seldom able to earn the 6-per-cent return the Interstate Commerce Commission allowed.

Shipping remained partly under direct government ownership, because private operation had to be heavily subsidized one way or another in order for American companies to compete successfully with those of other countries. These companies were subsidized by low prices and easy terms in buying government-owned ships and by generous mail contracts under the Merchant Marine Act of 1920. Congress refused to allow the navy to continue operating commercial radio communications, and so the navy reluctantly sold its stations to the newly established Radio Corporation of America.

Western progressives obtained two measures to stave off corporate onslaughts. One, the General Leasing Act, was intended to protect the naval oil reserves from oil companies that for some years had been trying to obtain them. It also authorized the leasing of other mineral and oil lands on terms favorable to the government. The other measure, the Water Power Act of 1920, was a first tentative step toward federal regulation of power. It established a Federal Power Commission (consisting of the secretaries of war, the interior, and agriculture) to license the construction and operation of hydroelectric plants on public lands and to regulate rates on power from these plants when it passed across state boundaries.

Soon after the war Congress helped bring to fruition two other progressive dreams. In June 1919 it approved the women's suffrage (Nineteenth) amendment, which was ratified in August 1920. In October 1919, over the veto of President Wilson, Congress passed the drastic Volstead Act implementing the prohibition (Eighteenth) amendment, submitted by Congress in December 1917 and ratified by January 1919. Several states had passed laws outlawing hard liquor but permitting the sale of weak beer, which might have been an adequate sop to the millions of urban opponents of prohibition. The

Volstead Act prohibited all liquors containing more than .5 per cent of alcohol. To jubilant members of the Anti-Saloon League and the Women's Christian Temperance Union—the two groups most responsible for bringing about prohibition—this meant the enforcement of morality. To opponents it meant an unjustifiable infringement on personal liberty.

## REPUBLICAN PROSPERITY

Though progressivism persisted, it had to yield to conservatism during the boom years of the 1920s. The wartime production miracles and the postwar writings of public relations experts and advertising men gave most Americans a renewed faith in business. The heroes of the time were the leaders of the great industries, and their interests were reflected by the dominant Republicans in politics.

### The Harding Tragedy

In 1920 domestic politics made impossible a solemn referendum on a League of Nations; only an ill man sequestered from the flow of events, as President Wilson was, could have expected such a thing. A Democratic victory was so improbable that Republican leaders felt no compulsion to put forth any of their strong candidates.

The two leading contenders were Leonard Wood and Frank O. Lowden. General Wood, an ardent conservative nationalist, commanded most of Roosevelt's former following and collected a campaign chest of startling proportions ($1,773,000), with which he battled Lowden for delegates. Lowden, favorably known as an efficient governor of Illinois, also commanded large campaign funds, totaling $414,000. Progressive Republican charges that both contenders were deeply indebted to big business helped induce party managers to ignore them when the two deadlocked at the convention. Late one night in a smoke-filled hotel room a cabal of senators led by Henry Cabot Lodge turned to one of the most regular and pliable of their colleagues, Warren G. Harding of Ohio. The convention nominated Harding on the tenth ballot and chose as his running mate the Massachusetts governor, Calvin Coolidge. These two were thoroughly conservative candidates running on a thoroughly conservative platform.

The Democrats, assembling at San Francisco, were rather confused because President Wilson, who could have easily designated a candidate, seemed to be waiting with pathetic coyness to be renominated for a third term. This was out of the question. For thirty-eight ballots, two of Wilson's cabinet members, his efficient son-in-law William G. McAdoo and his superpatriotic Attorney General, A. Mitchell Palmer, battled for the nomination. In the end the urban bosses stepped in and secured the nomination of an antiprohibition candidate who might salvage their city tickets for them. This was the former progressive governor of Ohio, James M. Cox. As a gesture toward the Wilsonians, Assistant Secretary of the Navy Franklin D. Roosevelt was nominated for Vice President.

Cox and Roosevelt campaigned arduously to make the election the League referendum that Wilson wished it to be. Harding, following the advice of his managers, made few speeches and took few positions on the issues of the day except to promise a return to what he earlier had called "normalcy." He displayed an ambivalence that was politically most successful. On the League he at first gave the impression that he favored adherence, then as city resentment against it flared, gave the impression he was against it. Lest Cox's crusade win away Republican votes, thirty-one distinguished Republicans signed a statement declaring that a vote for Harding was a vote for American entrance into the League with reservations.

The landslide exceeded even the expectations of the Republicans. Harding received 16,152,000 popular votes, 61 per cent of the total, and carried every state outside of the solid South. He even won Tennessee. Cox received only 9,147,000 popular votes. Eugene V. Debs, running on the Socialist ticket while in the Atlanta penitentiary, received 920,000 votes. The sweep brought a Republican majority of 22 in the Senate and 167 in the House.

In voting against Wilsonianism, the electorate brought into power a weak, amiable conservative. Alice Roosevelt Longworth, daughter of a President and wife of the speaker of the House,

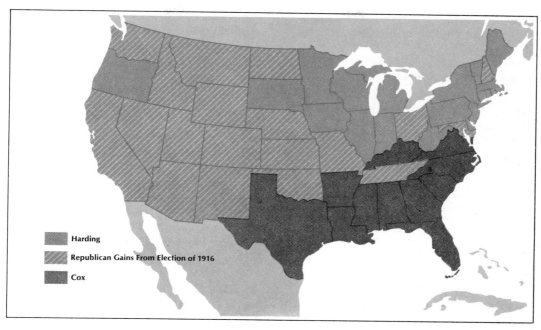

Harding

Republican Gains From Election of 1916

Cox

## Election of 1920

reared in the genteel tradition of Republican politics, could not forget the sight of a poker session in the President's study. "Harding was not a bad man," she reminisced. "He was just a slob."

President Harding wished to surround himself with the best-qualified men, and in part he succeeded. When he was persuaded that his friend Albert B. Fall was not of a caliber to be secretary of state, he placed Fall, a notorious anticonservationist, in charge of the Interior Department. He then appointed the brilliant and distinguished Charles Evans Hughes to be secretary of state. He placed Herbert Hoover, the friend of small enterprise and expert on efficiency, in charge of the Commerce Department, and made Henry C. Wallace, spokesman for the Midwest farmers, secretary of agriculture. Andrew W. Mellon represented big business as secretary of the treasury. These able men, pulling in several directions, together with the congressional leaders, developed government policies.

The President seemed to be carrying out his campaign slogan: "Less government in business and more business in government." The Democrats made strong gains in the 1922 elections, reflecting the hard times that followed the war,

but the return of prosperity soon afterwards heightened Harding's popularity. He occasionally was even vigorous in his humanity. He took a step Wilson had curtly declined; on Christmas Day, 1921, he pardoned the Socialist Debs. At the urging of Hoover, he pressured the steel companies into granting an eight-hour day to their workers. The press of the country, overwhelmingly Republican, created the illusion that Harding was an exceptionally fine President.

Behind the façade, rot had set in. With singularly bad judgment, Harding had placed a number of his poker-playing and drinking companions into positions of trust, where they betrayed him and the American people. Probably Harding never knew in detail how shockingly they were looting the government, but he knew enough to be heartsick. One of the "Ohio Gang," Attorney General Harry Daugherty's friend Jesse Smith, had been engaging in large-scale "fixing" in the Department of Justice. After Harding ordered him out of Washington, Smith committed suicide. The director of the Veterans' Bureau, Charles R. Forbes, engaged in such colossal thievery that the total loss ran to nearly $250 million. When Harding received intimations of the corruption, he allowed Forbes to flee the country and resign. Ultimately Forbes served a two-year penitentiary sentence for defrauding the government.

The most spectacular fraud involved the rich naval oil reserves at Teapot Dome, Wyoming, and Elk Hills, California. Secretary of the Interior Fall persuaded Harding to transfer the oil reserves to his department, then secretly leased them to Harry F. Sinclair and Edward L. Doheny. Fall, who had been in financial straits, suddenly became affluent. An investigation headed by Senator Thomas J. Walsh of Montana during the fall and winter of 1923 and 1924 uncovered the reason. Sinclair had loaned Fall $308,000 in cash and government bonds and a herd of cattle for his ranch; Doheny had loaned him $100,000 more. In 1929 Fall was convicted of bribery, fined $100,000, and sentenced to a year in a federal penitentiary.

In the summer of 1923 Harding journeyed to Alaska. Tired and depressed, he responded wanly to the cheering throngs, who had no inkling of the mess in Washington. He never had to face the exposure of the mess because upon his return to Seattle he became ill. It was reported that he had been poisoned by seafood, but actually he had suffered a serious heart attack. He seemed to improve, so he continued to San Francisco. There he had a second attack and suddenly died. In the months that followed, as exposure after exposure crowded the headlines, his reputation collapsed.

## Keeping Cool With Coolidge

It was the singular good fortune of Calvin Coolidge to become President of the United States at a time when his largely negative custodial approach to the Presidency could bring him popularity rather than disaster. He had reached the office through a curious mixture of luck, political regularity, and Yankee shrewdness. Unlike Harding, he had a clear-cut conservative philosophy. He always cooperated wholeheartedly with the big interests because he believed in them.

To the older circle in Washington, Coolidge's personality was not especially appealing. To the American public, however, there was an infinite appeal and security in his folksy virtues, so lavishly detailed and praised in the nation's press. Coolidge reinforced this appeal with little homilies drawn from his Vermont boyhood—exhortations (in which he fervently believed) to thrift, hard work, and respect for business.

Under this comforting moral leadership, the men of power in the United States could take a calm and even incredulous view of the Harding scandals as they came to light one by one in the winter of 1923–1924. Indeed, the respectable press showered indignation less upon the corrupt officials than upon those pressing the investigations. The two progressive Democratic senators, Thomas J. Walsh and Burton K. Wheeler, appeared to *The New York Times* to be "assassins of character."

Under Coolidge the Republicans seemed so patently incorruptible that the exposures appeared if anything to backfire against the exposing Democrats. Ultimately Coolidge forced Attorney General Daugherty to resign and helped clean up the scandals. As the election of 1924 approached, the revelations seemed to be doing no appreciable harm to the Republican party. The nation appeared ready to heed the party's campaign slogan: "Keep cool with Coolidge."

In 1924 the Democratic party was badly split between its rural and urban wings. Rural Democrats were backing as their candidate William Gibbs McAdoo, the competent heir to Wilsonianism. Strangely, the Teapot Dome scandal, which did no harm to the Republicans, tarnished McAdoo's reputation because he had served as a lawyer for Doheny, the California oil magnate. As for the urban wing of the party, it was advancing the candidacy of the equally competent liberal governor of New York, Alfred E. Smith, who was the son of Irish immigrants and had made his way upward from the Lower East Side of New York. Because of his background, and because he was a Catholic and a "wet" (an opponent of prohibition) he was the idol of many new Americans but an anathema to rural Democrats.

Finally both contenders withdrew, and on the 103rd ballot at the convention in Madison Square Garden the exhausted delegates nominated a compromise candidate, John W. Davis. Originally a West Virginian, Davis as solicitor general under Wilson had ably defended the legislation of the New Freedom before the Supreme Court. In the years since, he had become a lawyer for J. P. Morgan and some of the great corporations and had amassed a fortune.

While the Democratic convention dragged on, insurgent Republicans and allied representatives of labor held a third convention to organize a Progressive party and nominate Robert M. La Follette and Burton K. Wheeler. Their platform took an advanced progressive position, attacking monopoly and promising reforms for the farmers and workingmen. The party's support came from farmers, chiefly on the Great Plains, who had earlier formed the Nonpartisan League and the Farmer-Labor party, and from the Railroad Brotherhoods and the AFL.

This third party apparently was a real contrast to the Republican and Democratic tickets, and it served as a made-to-order target for the Republicans. They campaigned to frighten the electorate into choosing Coolidge as the only alternative to the "red radicalism" of La Follette. Before election day, labor became lukewarm toward La Follette; Republican farmers, as crop prices rose, decided to stay within the party. In its last thrust, the old Midwestern insurgency carried only Wisconsin and secured

but 16.5 per cent of the popular vote throughout the country. Coolidge polled 54 per cent, and Davis only 28.8 per cent.

In his inaugural, March 4, 1925, President Coolidge, declaring that the nation had achieved "a state of contentment seldom before seen," pledged himself to the maintenance of things as they were. During the prosperous years of the Coolidge era, as revenues came pouring in, the federal government did not greatly enlarge its services. It spent nothing in such areas as public housing, and little for farm relief or public works. Arms expenditures were a relative pittance. Consequently, the budget varied little between 1923 and 1929. Meanwhile, the national debt dropped by nearly a quarter.

## Favored Business

Big business had a special friend in the government during the 1920s. Andrew Mellon, the Pittsburgh aluminum baron who served as secretary of the treasury from Harding's inauguration into the Hoover administration, was widely hailed as the greatest secretary of the treasury since Alexander Hamilton. His main function seemed to be to preside over tax cuts; cartoonists routinely pictured Mellon slicing a tax

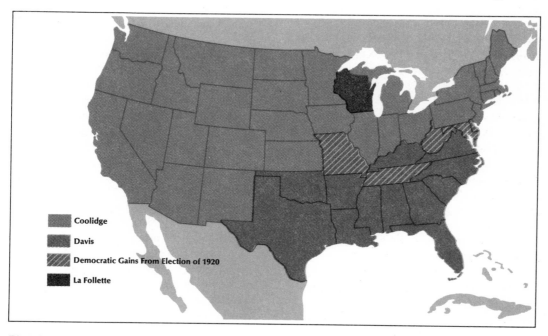

Coolidge

Davis

Democratic Gains From Election of 1920

La Follette

**Election of 1924**

melon. So far as he could do so, as a matter of principle, he divided these cuts among the wealthy to give them the incentive to earn more money.

Smaller businessmen also had a strong champion in the government, Secretary of Commerce Hoover. In his own spectacular rise as an international mining engineer, Hoover epitomized the self-made businessman. Denouncing both the radicalism and reaction he had seen in Europe, Hoover set forth his own credo in 1922 in a small book entitled *American Individualism*. It extolled the equality of opportunity that enabled Americans to succeed on their own merits, and the "rising vision of service" that led them to develop community responsibility rather than merely to seek "the acquisition and preservation of private property." This had been Hoover's own way of life.

Hoover made Commerce the most active of the departments, as he sought to help small business become as efficient and profitable as big business. Through commercial attachés whom he sent to American embassies, he solicited foreign orders for American industry at the same time that he favored the tariff to protect it from overseas competition. Through the National Bureau of Standards, he performed innumerable other services for industry, such as standardizing products and eliminating waste.

The most significant of the ways to help small business was the sponsorship of voluntary trade associations similar to the committees of the War Industries Board. By 1921 some 2,000 were in operation. These associations, free from government regulation, could establish codes of ethics, standardize production, establish efficiency, and make substantial savings. They could serve even better than government prohibition of evil practices, Hoover had pointed out, to secure "cooperation in the business community to cure its own abuses." They could also arrive indirectly at higher standard prices which would bring them good profits. Their real value to highly competitive smaller businesses was to eliminate competition through setting up standardized schedules of quality and prices.

Voluntarism was at the heart of all of Hoover's projects. As the new field of commercial radio broadcasting began to develop, Hoover fostered voluntary self-regulation for it. When the efforts to keep stations off each other's wave lengths completely broke down, he moved toward compulsory government regulation through the Federal Radio Commission, established in 1927. In the same way, the Department of Commerce finally took over regulation of commercial aeronautics through the Air Commerce Act in 1926.

On the whole, business thrived from 1923 to 1929. In part this was due to benign governmental policies. Hoover's laudable efforts to bring about increased standardization and efficiency took the economy further away from free competition and contributed to the increased profits of business and consequently to the concentration of wealth. Secretary Mellon's tax policies helped the rich to become richer, while incomes of poorer people advanced little if at all. The tendency of the courts to frown upon trade-association price schedules helped stimulate mergers. And mergers helped to sustain the trend toward concentration of business which had begun after the Civil War. During the twenties, 8,000 mining and manufacturing companies disappeared into combinations, and 5,000 public utilities were swallowed, mostly by holding companies. By 1929 chain stores were selling more than a quarter of the nation's food, apparel, and general merchandise. The 200 largest nonfinancial corporations owned nearly half of all corporate wealth, and 22 per cent of all national wealth. The 503 persons with the highest incomes received as much money as the total wages of 615,000 automobile workers.

## The Decline of Unions

The onslaught against all Americans who did not conform, against any who might disturb the status quo, reacted strongly to the advantage of business leaders, who already basked in the public favor. These leaders were able to reestablish in the minds of many people the feeling that unionism was somehow un-American. In 1920 they began a great open-shop movement to break unions and reduce wages, under the alluring title, "The American Plan."

The paternalistic policies of welfare capitalism, together with the antiunion campaign, led to a decline in union membership during the

1920s. Many companies greatly improved working conditions by installing safety devices and improving sanitation. They raised their workers' morale by building attractive cafeterias and promoting athletic teams. Company welfare workers looked into the workers' family problems. By 1926 nearly 3 million workers could look forward to pensions upon retirement. In some companies they could buy stock below market value. Altogether they owned less than 1 per cent, but even this did much to change some workers' attitudes. Further, they could voice their grievances through company unions or workers' councils, which were often effective safety valves for the employer. Through devices like these, companies helped fend off unionism from the new mass-production industries like automobile manufacturing.

Within the skilled crafts, the AFL continued quietly and conservatively under the presidency of William Green. Its leaders seemed more interested in maintaining labor monopolies, especially in the building trades, than in organizing industrial workers. Membership in the United Mine Workers dwindled after unsuccessful strikes in 1922. Union membership declined from over 5 million in 1920 to around 4.3 million in 1929.

In some industries, like coal mining and textiles in the South, hours were long and wages were pitiful. At Elizabethton, Tennessee, in 1929, mill girls were working fifty-six hours a week for 16 to 18 cents an hour. Behind the harried workers was always the threat of legal action if they sought to help themselves through unions. Federal courts were granting injunctions to break boycotts, or to enforce antiunion ("yellow dog") contracts. For most workingmen, however, conditions of labor had improved and living standards were up. Real wages increased about 26 per cent between 1919 and 1929. They still were far from adequate. The average was less than $1,500 a year at a time when it was estimated that $1,800 was required to maintain a minimum decent living standard.

## No Parity for Farmers

While the income of most Americans advanced during the 1920s, that of the farmers drastically declined. In 1920 they lost their price supports

at the same time that the bloated wartime European market contracted. At home, as machines released men from heavy manual labor, consumption of starches sharply dropped.

Within agriculture there were great variations. Truck gardening more than doubled, and dairying and citrus growing increased a third, reflecting the shifts in eating habits. Many such farmers enjoyed satisfactory incomes. At the same time, those on marginal or submarginal lands suffered so acutely that in the five years after 1919 13 million acres were abandoned. Poor farmers were unable to compete with large landowners using new, expensive machinery, which especially helped contribute to the glut of wheat. The number of tractors in use increased from 230,000 in 1920 to 920,000 in 1930, displacing 7,450,000 horses and releasing an additional 35 million acres of land for crops. On the Great Plains, speculators bought the lands of bankrupt farmers, and grew wheat on it with improved tractors and combines. In the Texas Panhandle alone, nearly 3 million new acres were ploughed.

The success of the big operators made the desperation of small farmers even more acute. In the year ending June 30, 1927, the average income of all the 6.3 million farmers was only $548, and out of this farmers had to meet a variety of pressing obligations. Farm income in 1920 was 15 per cent of the national total; by 1929 it was only 9 per cent. The agricultural population dropped 3 million between 1921 and 1928. Many of those who remained on the farms ceased to own them and became tenants. Distressed farmers, both owners and renters, began to agitate militantly for relief.

Even during the bonanza years of the war, agrarian agitation had stirred the Great Plains. In 1915 wheat growers of North Dakota had organized the Nonpartisan League, pledged to strict regulation of railroads and banks, and state ownership of grain elevators and farm credit agencies. The league won control of the North Dakota government in 1916, then began to organize in adjacent states, and in 1920 joined with other radical groups to form the Farmer-Labor party. The new party had some success in the congressional election of 1922, but by 1924 even La Follette would not accept its support. It

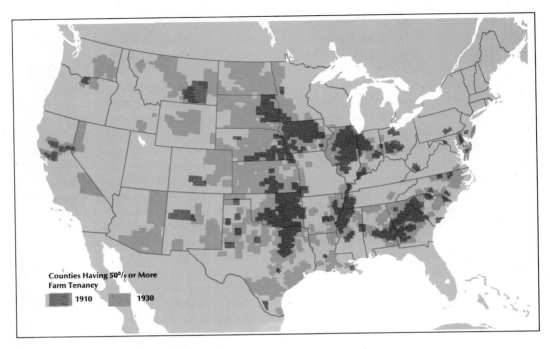

Counties Having 50% or More
Farm Tenancy
■ 1910        ▨ 1930

**Farm Tenancy:    1910 and 1930**

was too radical for farmers who were earning $1,000 to $4,000 a year.

These men, the middle 40 per cent of the farmers in terms of income, produced 46 per cent of the farm products, and were solid citizens in their communities. Often acting through the Farm Bureau Federation or the Grange, they sought government price supports. From the outset they had powerful strength in the Congress. During the special session of Congress in the spring of 1921, Midwestern congressional leaders from both parties, meeting in the offices of the Farm Bureau Federation, organized a farm bloc.

One price-raising scheme came to dominate the farmers' thinking. Behind the tariff barrier, the American protected price for crops should be raised to a "fair exchange value" based on the price of the crop during ten prewar years as compared with the general average of all prices during the same period. This was the "parity" price. The means of obtaining parity for farmers would be for the government to buy up the surplus at the high American price and sell it abroad at whatever it would bring on the world market. To make up for the loss, an equalization fee or tax would be charged the farmers on their entire crop.

Between 1924 and 1928 Senator Charles L. McNary of Oregon and Representative Gilbert Haugen of Iowa promoted this scheme in Congress. In 1924 the McNary-Haugen bill covered only grain, and was defeated in the House, but in 1926 the addition of cotton, tobacco, and rice brought Southern support. In 1927 Congress passed it, but President Coolidge coldly vetoed it as being preferential legislation contrary to the principles of laissez faire. (On the the same day he signed an order raising the tariff on pig iron 50 per cent.) A year later Congress again passed the McNary-Haugen bill, and Coolidge again vetoed it.

## THE RESURGENCE OF ISOLATIONISM

The task of developing Republican alternatives to Wilsonian foreign policy fell largely on the shoulders of Secretaries of State Charles Evans Hughes (1921–1925) and Frank B. Kellogg (1925–1929).

## Steps Toward Peace

Hughes' policy involved first of all ending the war with Germany by an act of Congress, which was signed July 2, 1921. Hughes then negotiated separate peace treaties with the former Central Powers, to secure for the United States the benefits without the responsibilities of the Paris treaties. In time, Hughes permitted American delegations to participate in League conferences on minor matters as long as they did not make commitments. Throughout his years as secretary of state he was chilly toward every European proposal for collective security. He did, in February 1923, persuade President Harding to recommend that the United States join with reservations the World Court, an almost completely powerless body. But the World Court was an instrument of the League, and while internationally minded Americans ardently favored joining, the irreconcilables in the Senate violently fought it. Each succeeding President through Franklin D. Roosevelt advocated American adherence to the League; each time, through 1935, the Senate blocked it.

Through the Washington Arms Conference, Republicans made it appear that they were taking positive steps to preserve the peace. This was in effect a Republican substitute for entrance into the League. In May 1921 Senator Borah had introduced a resolution calling for a conference to reduce armaments, but the basic impetus for the meeting came from the British, who feared a three-way naval race with the Americans and the Japanese. Japan had emerged from the war stronger than before in China and with troops still stationed in Siberia. It threatened to expand still further, to shut the "Open Door" in China, and to arm its new island possessions in the Pacific. American public opinion saw an even more serious threat in the Anglo-Japanese alliance. Hence the British, wishing to strengthen their amicable relations with the United States, proposed the conference. Hughes seized the initiative and President Harding issued invitations.

The arms conference opened on November 12, 1921, the day after burial rites for the Unknown Soldier at the Arlington Cemetery. Hughes in his opening speech startled the delegates and won enormous acclaim by dramatically presenting a concrete plan for the reduction in size of the fleets of the United States, Great Britain, and Japan. He proposed a ten-year moratorium on capital-ship construction (battleships, cruisers, and carriers) and the scrapping by the three powers of nearly 1.9 million tons of ships already built or under construction. A British observer declared: "Secretary Hughes sank in thirty-five minutes more ships than all the admirals of the world have sunk in a cycle of centuries."

In the negotiations that followed, Japan agreed to limit her capital ships to a total of approximately 300,000 tons compared with 500,000 tons each for the United States and Great Britain. In addition the United States pledged itself not to increase its fortifications in Guam and the Philippines. Japan and Great Britain made similar pledges. Thus the Five Power Pact of 1922 provided a ratio of 5:5:3 for the United States, Great Britain, and Japan, and 1.75:1.75 for France and Italy, stopping what otherwise could have become a disastrous armaments race. Two other treaties aimed at guaranteeing the status quo in the Far East. The Nine Power Pact pledged a continuation of the Open Door policy in China. Afterwards Japan restored full sovereign rights to China in the Shantung peninsula and promised to withdraw the Japanese troops from Siberia. The Four Power Pact —among the United States, Great Britain, France, and Japan—represented a mutual recognition of insular rights in the Pacific. Upon its ratification, Japan relinquished her alliance with Great Britain.

These Washington treaties lowered the tension between the United States and Japan for nearly a decade. Their one unfortunate result was that the United States relinquished the physical force with which to impose its will in the Far East but retained its moral, economic, and political objectives in that area. The Senate came close to rejecting the Four Power Pact for fear it would commit the United States to some collective security arrangement in the Orient. On the other hand, the popularity of the Naval Limitation Treaty (Five Power Pact) is shown by the fact that only one senator voted against its ratification.

During the Coolidge administration millions

of Americans signed petitions urging the United States to promote a multilateral treaty outlawing war. The French foreign minister, Aristide Briand, proposed a treaty of this sort between France and the United States. Secretary Kellogg responded by suggesting that other countries be invited to join. So, at Paris in 1928, most of the great nations including the United States signed a treaty solemnly renouncing war as an instrument of national policy, but providing no machinery whatever for enforcement. The treaty evoked much enthusiasm in the United States, for it seemed to offer collective security without any risks.

Hughes tried to extend the good will of the United States toward Latin America. During his first months in office, he was decidedly influenced by Sumner Welles, later one of the chief molders of the Good Neighbor policy. By 1924 Hughes had ended the marine occupation of Santo Domingo and prepared for its end in Nicaragua. He felt that the occupation was still necessary in Haiti.

Hughes moved away from the progressive policy of intervention and tried wherever possible to substitute the nonrecognition of undesirable governments for the landing of the marines. Neither he nor his successor in the Coolidge administration was ready to give up intervention entirely. For a time during the Coolidge administration, trouble with Mexico over the rights of American oil companies and renewed marine intervention in Nicaragua seemed to indicate a retreat to the old policies.

## Economic Nationalism

In European affairs a persisting and troublesome issue was that of reparations and war debts. The failure of the United States to join the League of Nations had most serious repercussions on this problem, since the League's Reparations Commission, which was not under the chairmanship of an American as had been expected, set astronomically high sums for Germany to pay. Reparations payments depended to a considerable degree upon American private loans to Germany; war-debt payments from the Allies to the United States depended, in turn, almost entirely upon reparations. The American public insisted that the Allies should repay the $10 bil-

lion the United States had loaned during the war. Coolidge later epitomized the popular view when he remarked simply: "They hired the money, didn't they?"

The United States pressured the former Allies, through a World War Foreign Debt Commission, to negotiate long-term schedules of debt payments. Between 1923 and 1926 the commission reached agreements with the Allies in regard to their debts (which the United States government insisted bore no relationship to German reparations payments). The administration did not worry as to how Germany, France, Italy, and the other debtors could make payments over the high tariff wall that the United States was raising against their exports.

What kept the payments going during the twenties was the huge total of private American loans pouring into German governmental units or corporations—about $2.5 billion between 1923 and 1930. Germany paid about $2 billion in reparations, and the former Allies about $2.6 billion in war-debt payments. Thus the Germans were paying the Allies, and the Allies were paying the United States, with dollars which Americans were lending to the Germans.

As soon as the Republicans had come into power in 1921, they enacted an emergency tariff measure to raise the low Underwood rates. In 1922 they passed the Fordney-McCumber Act providing protection especially for agriculture, the chemical industry, and manufacturers threatened by Japanese and German competition. The tariff gave agriculture little real protection, but it provided industrialists with several benefits. It accepted the principle that, when foreign firms had costs of production lower than their American competitors, the tariff should be high enough to offset the differential. It prohibited most competing imports and led to higher prices at home. Other nations followed the American lead in economic nationalism; by 1928 some sixty countries had raised their tariffs.

## Immigration Restriction

Along with high walls against competing goods, Congress finally succeeded in erecting barriers against incoming foreigners. The movement to curtail immigration came to a spectacularly successful climax with the beginning of the Harding

# Part Four
# The Course of American Art

At the beginning of the twentieth century, the turbulent growth of the nation was expressed by a new school of painters, called "The Eight," who challenged the academic idealism of the European establishment. Like Homer and Eakins, these men chose to depict the spontaneity and action of contemporary life but took their subjects from the crowded urban world. Their leader, Robert Henri, rejected the sentimental narrative and polished surfaces of academic painting in an attempt to depict the vigor of the city and its people. In his portrait of "Eva Green," painted in 1907 (*Plate 1*), Henri's bold brush tech-

*Plate 1*
**"Eva Green."**
Robert Henri. (Roland P. Murdock Collection, Wichita Art Museum)

Plate 2
**"The Nighthawks."**
Edward Hopper. (The Art Institute of Chicago)

nique is reminiscent of the seventeenth century Dutch master, Frans Hals. The girl's bright, alive face—enframed by a dark hat—shines out from an equally dark background. The explosive highlights on her face and her red ribbon intensify the frankness of her gaze as she looks directly at the viewer. Henri, through his painting, writing, and teaching, influenced not only The Eight but other American artists as well. Although the public was disturbed by the roughness of the group's work—derisively calling them "The Ash Can School"—the drama with which they depicted the life around them aptly expressed a period in American life when the melting pot was at a constant boil.

One of the "other" artists, who in his youth had studied with Henri, was Edward Hopper. Although his early works echo The Eight in their subject matter, in 1906 he was drawn to Paris by the experimental paintings of the Fauves and Cubists. These avant-garde movements, which were first introduced to the American public seven years later at the Armory Show, were to have a profound influence on many young American artists. Hopper, however, rejected the abstract subjectivity of contemporary European painting and replaced it with an objectivity rooted in reality. Like The Eight, Hopper concentrated on the American city. But, where for Henri the city was a background for a human drama, for Hopper the subject was the city itself. He shows its complexity of shapes and forms, illuminated either by intense sunlight or by the eerie glow of electric lights, often conveying a feeling of loneliness. In "The Nighthawks," painted in 1942 (*Plate 2*), he sets four figures in an all-night coffee shop. The painting is composed of strongly accented horizontal lines, and Hopper enhances the sensation that his figures are caged by encasing them within the brilliant glare of a plate glass window. The darkness that otherwise surrounds them intensifies the quality of isolation.

World War I was a devastating blow to many of the avant-garde European movements. The isolationism that developed in American politics was seen in painting as well. A strong sense of introspection led many American artists to reject European modernism, especially abstraction, in favor of a realistic narrative style. Some artists concentrated on the dislocation effected by the Depression, while others focused on the areas of American abundance. These latter artists, know as "The Regionalists," took their subject matter from the folk legends and topography of the Midwest. One of their leaders was Thomas Hart Benton, who, like many American artists of his generation, had dabbled in Cubism but rejected it in favor of his sinuous, linear, and highly individual style. "The Ballad of the Jealous Lover," painted in 1934 (*Plate 3*), is an illustrative narrative of a famous American folksong. Three musicians sing of the tragic events that appear as though at the end of a curved road of music behind them. Although strongly realistic in subject, the painting

*Plate 3*

**"The Ballad of the Jealous Lover."**

Thomas Hart Benton. (Courtesy of the University of Kansas Museum of Art)

is filled with an intense emotionalism that is characteristic of the artist's expressionist desire.

Although some artists, like Benton, continued to paint in this Regionalist style, the events of World War II and the unsettled nuclear peace that followed demanded a new approach. This period saw the development of a uniquely American invention, based on abstraction and reflecting the emotional intensity of the times. One of the innovators of this style (a former student of Benton who actually posed for the harmonica player in "The Ballad of a Jealous Lover") was Jackson Pollock. Pollock had moved to New York from the Midwest in the early 1940's and there came

in contact with a number of painters who had fled from Nazi Germany. These artists belonged to the school of Surrealism, which advocated the virtues of "automatic painting"—a technique in which the artist allows his subconscious mind to dictate the spontaneous execution of his painting. Pollock utilized this concept in his development of "action painting." For such works as "Number 27," (*Plate 4*) he placed the canvas directly on the floor and walked around it, applying paint from all sides. The paint was applied by dipping a small household brush into a can and then, with rapid wrist and body movements, allowing the paint to fall in weaving rhythms over the surface. To Pollock,

*Plate 4*
**"Number 27."**
Jackson Pollock. (Collection Whitney Museum of American Art, New York)

*Plate 5*
**"Odalisk."**
Robert Rauschenberg.
(Collection Mr. & Mrs. Victor Ganz)

Plate 6

**"200 Campbell Soup Cans."**

Andy Warhol. (Collection Mr. & Mrs. John Powers)

the "act of painting," with its acceptance of the accidental and its fundamental expression of freedom, became the artist's primary goal.

Other artists rebelled against the painterly technique and emotional impact inherent in an Abstract Expressionist canvas. Robert Rauschenberg is a transitional figure between action painting and the almost impersonal style of Pop Art. In Rauschenberg's search for new subject matter, he focused on his immediate environment and incorporated such objects as photographs and newspaper clippings into his paintings. In this regard his works are similar to the collage experiments tried by European artists earlier in the century. Rauschenberg, however, continues to use the ex-

pressive brushwork of the Abstract Expressionists, along with the everyday images, in elaborate constructions he calls "combines." In his combine entitled "Odalisk, painted from 1955 to 1958 (*Plate* 5), a stuffed rooster is perched atop a box balanced on a pedestal which, in turn, rests on a pillow. The disparate elements, including photographs and comic strips, are all part of the contemporary environment and provide a kaleidoscope of images from which the artist creates a harmonious whole.

Andy Warhol, another pioneer of the Pop movement, has moved further away from the personal gesture of the action painter and concentrates on the specific products of our culture. Warhol drew heavily on his experience in commercial art technique. Using the silkscreen process and the mechanical repetition of images, he strives to eliminate the hand of the artist from the work. In his 1962 painting of the "200 Campbell Soup Cans" (*Plate 6*), Warhol transforms a familiar object into a symbol of American popular culture by using huge scale and clarity of line and color. Although Warhol's painting has been described as satirical, it is rather a depiction of the life and images of our time without comment.

In contrast to Warhol, a number of contemporary artists have used the vocabulary of our environment to express a humorous or satirical intent. Marisol, a young Venezuelan living in New York, works in a variety of materials, combin-ing wood, plaster, photos, and paint in a single piece. In her 1964 Pop assemblage entitled "The Visit" (*Plate 7*), three carved and painted figures sit on an upholstered sofa next to which stands the figure of a child. Their stiff and separate presences suggest that they are making their annual visit to the dentist. What seems to be a conventional genre subject is transformed into a satirical experience by the ambiguity of the various parts of the composition. From the barrel that serves as the first lady's chest to the real coat and handbag of the third figure, Marisol has communicated a feeling of isolation while poking fun at contemporary American conventions.

While painting moved swiftly away from European influence, American

*Plate 7*
**"The Visit."**

Marisol. (Courtesy, Sidney Janis Gallery)

architecture continued to be dominated by eclecticism. At the Columbian Exposition of 1893, a number of eastern architectural firms popularized the classical idiom for public buildings. The "Imperial facade," was an attempt to satisfy the *nouveaux-riches* with an architectural coating resplendent with historical tradition. The medieval mode also had its adherents among eclectic architects. Because of its emphasis on the vertical, Gothic design was seen as appropriate for skyscrapers with the result that a number of New York towers are capped by replicas of cathedrals or chateaux. One of the leading firms designing in the Gothic mode was Cram, Goodhue, and Ferguson. In 1914, Bertram Goodhue left the firm to develop a more individual style based on contemporary French design with its smooth polished surfaces and combinations of curved and cubic forms. He utilized this style, called "the Moderne," for the Nebraska State Capitol in Lincoln, completed in 1924 (*Plate 8*). Although the tall central tower seems out of place in the Great Plains, Goodhue's design was a

*Plate 8*
**Nebraska State Capitol.**
Bertram Goodhue. (Sandak)

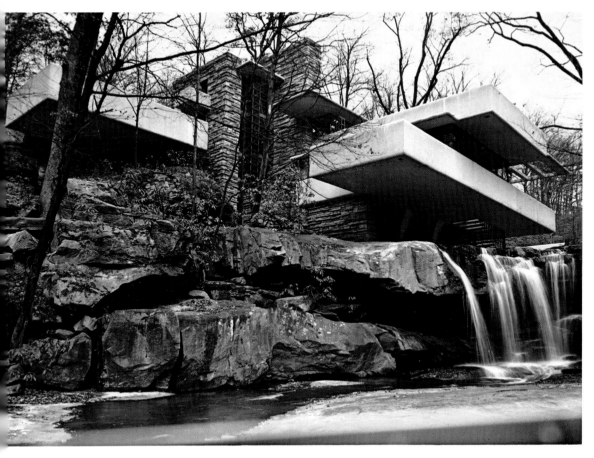

*Plate 9*
**Fallingwater.**

Frank Lloyd Wright. (Sandak)

daring break from the classical style that had dominated state capitol buildings since the erection of the federal capitol in the early nineteenth century.

While Goodhue sought to popularize a streamlined aesthetic, Frank Lloyd Wright continued to evolve his own architecture. Wright's early work had little influence in America, but had a profound impact on European architects including Gropius, Mies van der Rohe, and Le Corbusier. By 1930, Wright had become aware of the innovations of the men he had influenced and attempted to

integrate their contributions into his own work. In Fallingwater—built in 1936 in Bear Run, Pennsylvania (*Plate 9*)—Wright remained committed to an organic architectural solution, relating the building to its rocky hillside site and using the native stone as building material. However, the smooth, clean lines of the reinforced concrete cantilevers, as well as the thin skin of iron and glass, derive their inspiration from the International style.

The principles of the International style, particularly with regard to the use

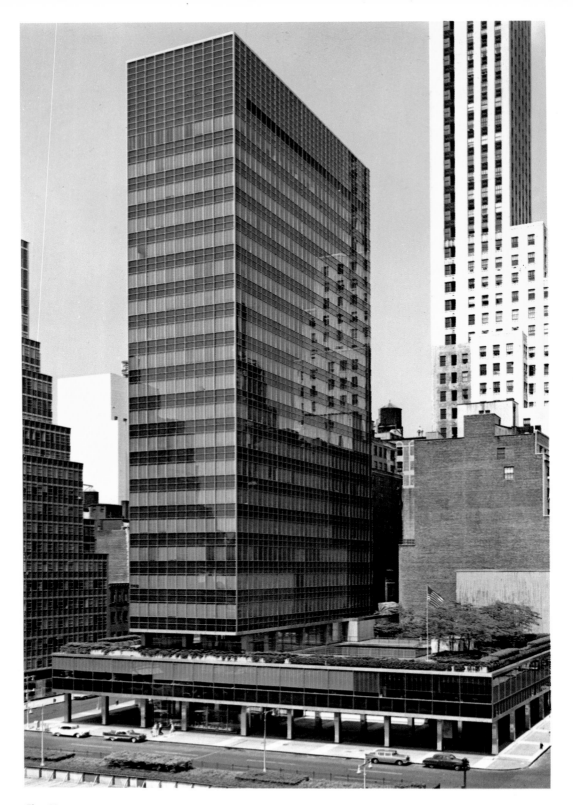

*Plate 10*

**The Lever House.**

Skidmore, Owings and Merrill.

of the steel frame, were most successfully interpreted in skyscraper design. The Lever House, designed by the firm of Skidmore, Owings and Merrill in 1952 (*Plate 10*), rises as a steel grid sheathed in a "curtain wall" of glass. Its primary aesthetic impact derives from the absolute clarity of the building's functionalism.

As a reaction to the severe linearity of the International style, in the 1950's a number of architects attempted to develop a more sculpturesque aesthetic. Eero Saarinen, in his T.W.A. Terminal at Kennedy International Airport (*Plate 11*), rejected his earlier, functional style in favor of a design utilizing reinforced concrete forms built on four intersecting shells. The interior shell rises to a height of 50 feet and spans over 300 feet of floor space. The bands of skylights that articulate the form of the vault increase the sense of lightness in the building. The sweeping curves of the terminal suggest a bird and the dynamism of flight.

As Saarinen's wing-like structure is symbolic of the qualities of flight, some contemporary sculptors have also searched for meaningful symbols in biomorphic forms. Seymour Lipton's large metal sculpture, "Earth Forge II" (*Plate 12*), derives its shape from the

*Plate 11*

**T.W.A. Terminal.**

Eero Saarinen. (Ezra Stoller)

unfolding, convoluted petals of a plant. Juxtaposed with this botanical imagery, Lipton has included the machine-like energy characterized by the aggressive thrust of the internal screw.

The last few years have been filled with a succession of movements and counter-movements in the arts. The United States is at the center of a world-wide cultural explosion that has fostered a phenomenal increase in museum building and attendance as well as the publication and purchase of art books. The growing public awareness of art and its relationship to society has stimulated artists to search for symbols of our age.

*Plate 12*
**"Earth Forge II."**
Seymour Lipton. (Brooklyn Museum, Dick S. Ramsay Fund)

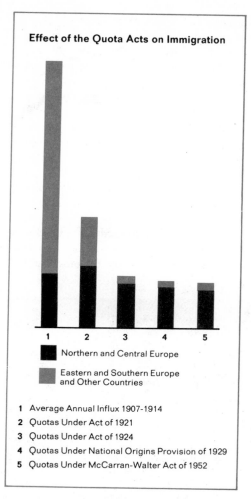

**Effect of the Quota Acts on Immigration**

|   |   |   |   |   |
|---|---|---|---|---|
| 1 | 2 | 3 | 4 | 5 |

◼ Northern and Central Europe

▬ Eastern and Southern Europe and Other Countries

1  Average Annual Influx 1907-1914
2  Quotas Under Act of 1921
3  Quotas Under Act of 1924
4  Quotas Under National Origins Provision of 1929
5  Quotas Under McCarran-Walter Act of 1952

The bars above illustrate how drastically the legislation of the 1920s and after cut off immigration from all Old World areas except Northern and Central Europe. The chart does not include immigration from other American nations, which continued unrestricted.

administration. Racist objections to the "new immigrants," and the unionists' fear that the newcomers were perpetuating a pool of cheap labor in the United States, were reinforced by the new allegation that some of them were radicals. This led employers who had previously favored immigration to switch to the restrictive side.

In 1921 Congress passed an emergency immigration act, setting up a quota system: immigrants from any country could not exceed 3 per cent of the number of persons of their nationality who had been in the United States in 1910. This cut the number of immigrants from 800,000 in the year ending June 30, 1921, to about 300,000 in the following twelve months. Racists still were not satisfied, so Congress in 1924 enacted the National Origins Act. This measure not only banned the people of East Asia entirely, but set a quota of 2 per cent for Europeans, and this on the basis of the 1890 census. It cut the yearly total to 164,000, heavily weighted in favor of those from northwestern Europe. On July 1, 1929, an overall limit of about 150,000 immigrants a year went into effect, but during the entire depression decade of the thirties the total net immigration was less than 70,000. The great flood of so many decades had been cut to a few drops.

Excluding all aliens ineligible to become citizens meant excluding the Japanese in particular. It was an unnecessary insult to the Japanese, since the Gentlemen's Agreement had worked well, and the application of a quota system to Japan would have allowed only a tiny trickle of immigrants. Indignation in Japan against the act of 1924 was so extreme that Hughes lamented privately: "It has undone the work of the Washington Conference and implanted the seeds of an antagonism which are sure to bear fruit in the future."

## LIFE IN THE TWENTIES

For those who shared in the prosperity, the decade of the twenties was a wonderful era. The wealth of the United States, as newspapers never tired of reminding their readers, was almost as great as that of all Europe. "My God, how the money rolls in!" went the words of a popular song. And some of the money was spent in remarkable ways.

### The Jazz Age

It was the era when Florida real-estate salesmen hired the famous orator William Jennings Bryan to lecture on the climate. Even though only an infinitesimal portion of Americans bought real estate in Florida during the land boom of 1924–1925, the impression was that most people were dabbling in the speculation. So too with the stock market later in the decade. Millions shared in the national frenzies, but most of them did so only vicariously while living sober, quiet lives.

The average middle-class American family owned an automobile. There were 23 million cars in use by 1929, and on Sundays it seemed as though they were all out on the new concrete highways. At home, people listened to the radio. The first commercial station, KDKA, broadcast the news of Harding's election in November 1920. By 1924 the National Broadcasting Company had organized a nationwide network of stations, and by 1930 over 12 million American families had radios. Millions also had electric vacuum cleaners and washing machines; many were beginning to buy electric refrigerators. Household appliances were supplanting the

housemaid and the hired girl. Food and clothing accounted for only 44 per cent of the family expenditures, compared with 58 per cent in 1899 —a clear indication of the rising living standards.

The prosperity of the twenties spilled over into the educational system. The per-pupil expenditure jumped from $24 in 1910 to $90 in 1930. Free elementary education had become established throughout the nation; illiteracy dropped from 7.7 per cent to 4.3 per cent. Enrollment in high schools increased 400 per cent, and enrollment in colleges and universities grew almost as fast.

Much money went to bootleggers, the dealers in illicit liquor, a new multi-million-dollar business. The first prohibition commissioner had

**Prohibition Officers at Detroit on the Seized Tug *Geronimo*    June 1928**

"Although it is impossible to calculate how much liquor was actually smuggled into America, the liquor revenues of the Canadian government increased four times during prohibition, while the consumption of spirits by the Canadian population almost halved. . . . [General Lincoln C. Andrews, head of the Prohibition Bureau] calculated that the law enforcement agencies caught only one-twentieth of the liquor smuggled into America. If his estimate was accurate, the flow of liquor into America can be calculated at between five and ten million gallons a year."—Andrew Sinclair, *Prohibition, The Era of Excess* (Boston: Atlantic-Little, Brown, 1962). (National Archives) optimistically announced his determination to see that alcoholic beverages were "not manufactured, nor sold, nor given away, nor hauled in anything on the surface of the earth or under the earth or in the air." But with an insufficient budget and only a few thousand poorly paid agents—and with little or no cooperation from state and local authorities—the commissioner had an almost impossible task in patrolling 18,000 miles of coastline, guarding against the diversion of any of the 57 million gallons of industrial alcohol, overseeing hundreds of millions of medical prescriptions, and checking on 20 million homes to prevent the concoction of home brew, wine, or "bathtub gin."

Gangsters turned to the large-scale smuggling or manufacture and distribution of liquor. In Chicago, "Scarface" Al Capone built an underworld empire that was based on beer and extended out into slot machines, laundries, and labor unions; it grossed about $60 million per year. He guarded it against interlopers with an army of 700 to 1,000 gunmen. Between 1920 and 1927 over 250 men were killed in Chicago gang warfare. Capone miraculously survived both his rivals and the forces of the law, until finally in 1931 he was convicted of federal income tax evasion.

New ways of life, alarming to the older generation, swept America. Men wore wrist watches and smoked cigarettes, both of which had seemed rather effeminate before the war. Women seemed to have lost their modesty as they bobbed their hair, applied lipstick, donned short skirts and silk stockings, and unblushingly began using words previously reserved for males. Younger people talked frankly and openly about sex. It was talk that frightened their elders, and was made doubly frightening by the disappearance of chaperons and the availability of automobiles. Compounding the evil in the eyes of elders were the many new road houses and speakeasies, where young people flouted prohibition by drinking beer or cocktails. There too they listened to jazz and danced the new steps like the Charleston, which some preachers denounced to their flocks as lascivious. It seemed to many critics that Gertrude Stein had correctly labeled this the "lost generation"; these people could not believe that in time the "flam-

ing youth" would mature into censorious middle age.

Motion pictures flamboyantly heralded the new moral code and together with tabloid papers helped fabricate false stereotypes of the period. An estimated 50 million people a week went to theaters to see the "it" girl, Clara Bow, the glamorous Rudolph Valentino, the comedian Charlie Chaplin, gangster pictures, Westerns, and great spectacles like the first film version of *The Ten Commandments.* These helped standardize American habits, and not always in the most edifying way. Further, since nine-tenths of the world's motion pictures were made in the United States, they brought curiously distorted notions of American culture to other countries. In 1927 a revolution struck the motion picture industry when the first important all-talking picture, *The Jazz Singer,* starring Al Jolson, was a phenomenal success. Motion pictures also began to carry American speech around the world.

In journalism, the twenties brought an even greater sensationalism than the nineties in some mass-circulation city papers. From England came the idea of the half-sized tabloid, which led to the founding of the *News, Mirror,* and *Graphic* in New York City, and similar papers throughout the country. Tabloid journalism came to mean what "yellow journalism" had meant earlier, with the addition of a strong emphasis upon serial comic strips and sensational photographs. Millions of readers followed the gang wars in Chicago and murder trials in New York and elsewhere. Even *The New York Times* had to capitulate its dignity to reader demands and lavish front-page space upon one spectacular murder trial, the Hall-Mills case, concerning the murder of a minister and a choir singer.

Among magazines, the *Saturday Evening Post,* with its conservative editorials and well-written stories, mirrored the era as faithfully as did President Coolidge. Close behind it in capturing the popular spirit was a reprint magazine founded in 1921, *Reader's Digest,* which filled its readers with inspiration and optimism, and guided them effortlessly through what they might consider difficult, serious subjects. It was the beginning of predigested reading. Much the same formula went into *Time,* the first of the news magazines, founded in 1925. In its cleverness, *Time* was one of the magazines tailored for the college graduates of the twenties. Another was the gay, sophisticated *New Yorker*, founded in 1925, which, with its clever cartoons and polished articles and stories, soon eclipsed the older *Life* and *Judge*. But the magazines that best typified the iconoclastic spirit of the intelligentsia and its rejection of middle-class values were *Smart Set* and the *American Mercury*. Their editors, Henry L. Mencken and George Jean Nathan, ridiculed the shibboleths of the decade, but more than that introduced to their readers many of the most vigorous writers of the era.

## Writers, Artists, Musicians

Seldom before in American history has such a remarkable galaxy of new writers appeared at one time. There was as much negativism from the expatriates in Paris as there had been before the war from Greenwich Village; many took perverse delight in damning the United States as a dollar-grubbing philistine civilization. De-

spite this spirit, it was not a generation lost to letters, nor were the voices of protest ignored.

Sherwood Anderson, giving up his paint factory, wrote tart Freudian sketches of small-town America in *Winesburg, Ohio* (1919). Sinclair Lewis more spectacularly exploited the same vein in his satiric *Main Street* (1920) and *Babbitt* (1922). His onslaught against business philistinism, in a long series of novels, at times verged close to caricature, but in time brought Lewis a Nobel Prize. With far more pessimism, utilizing experimental episodic techniques, John Dos Passos dissected the life of the metropolis in *Manhattan Transfer* (1925). Theodore Dreiser came into his own in 1925 with *An American Tragedy*, which analyzed with compassion both the psychological and environmental factors that led a young man to consider drowning his mistress.

The novelist who best embodied the jazz age in both his personal life and his writing was F. Scott Fitzgerald, catapulted to success with *This Side of Paradise* (1920). Young novelists who helped set patterns for later decades were

**The Sinclair Lewises Go Camping**

In 1916 Lewis bought a Model T Ford, and with his wife, Grace Hegger Lewis, embarked on a four-month trip from Sauk Center, Minnesota, to San Francisco.

Lewis wanted to see firsthand more of the small-town life about which he wished to write a novel. This photograph was taken in Duluth. (Brown Brothers)

Ernest Hemingway and William Faulkner. Hemingway stated the reaction against war most vigorously in his novel of disillusion, *A Farewell to Arms* (1929), which also helped set a new literary style. Faulkner, analyzing the South with morbid intensity in novels like *The Sound and the Fury* (1929) and *Sanctuary* (1931), developed an abstruse stream-of-consciousness technique which profoundly influenced other writers.

In drama these were the golden years of Eugene O'Neill, who drew from Ibsen, Strindberg, and Freud to develop American plays that were both critical and popular successes. *The Emperor Jones* (1920), *Anna Christie* (1922), *Strange Interlude* (1928), and other plays won O'Neill three Pulitzer Prizes in the decade, and helped maintain him in the forefront of American dramatists a decade later. A number of other young playwrights wrote for the experimental stage, which flourished at scores of colleges and cities, even while motion pictures were superseding the old legitimate theater circuits.

In poetry, two of the most significant writers were expatriates from the United States. These were T. S. Eliot in London, whose *The Waste Land* appeared in 1922, and Ezra Pound, who settled in Italy where he wrote *Cantos* and embraced Fascism. At home, Edna St. Vincent Millay typified the twenties with her hedonistic love poetry, while Robinson Jeffers turned to dark naturalistic themes. Older poets like Edwin Arlington Robinson and Robert Frost continued to write in established veins, and numerous young poets experimented with innovations in techniques and topics.

American artists continued to produce along lines that in many cases had been pioneered before the war. Architects filled the great cities with skyscrapers and were active in city planning. Some of the surplus wealth of the twenties poured into European painting; Mellon matched his ingenuity in keeping taxes down with his lavish purchases of old masters, some of them from the dollar-hungry Soviet Union. By 1930 American art galleries owned $2 billion worth of paintings. Along with this went a rapidly widening popular appreciation of fine art.

In music the twenties were notable for the rise of jazz, "the most important musical ex-

## T. S. Eliot on Expatriates of the Twenties

*The situation is different for the young men of today compared with the earlier part of this century. I don't know what Prohibition had to do with it. Certainly it was easier then for youngsters to earn a living overseas. And the American literary scene didn't offer them much encouragement. That was a very dull period.*

*In Europe there was a desire to aid younger people. Pound introduced me to Yeats. I got to know Virginia Woolf. People were interested in my poetry. I had never experienced such interest at home. But now the trend seems to be in the other direction. Young Americans go back and find they can make a living teaching in colleges, that there is genuine interest in them. A young writer needs the society of other writers, both his contemporaries and benevolent older writers whom he can respect. There are more of these now in the United States.—* The New York Times, *March 30, 1959.*

pression that America has achieved." It had originated among Negro musicians in the South, particularly in New Orleans, who drew upon their African heritage in composing and playing tunes with improvised harmonies and a syncopated beat. Among the outstanding black creators of jazz were the guitar-playing singer Huddie Ledbetter ("Leadbelly") and the bandconductor William C. Handy, the "father of the blues," whose compositions include *St. Louis Blues* (1914). The new music first became widely known when jazzmen moved with the general black migration northward during and after World War I. The great trumpet-player Louis ("Satchmo") Armstrong, for example, went from New Orleans to Chicago in 1922 to join a band that helped spread jazz through phonograph recordings. Meanwhile, white musicians had begun to take up the new form, modify it, and make it increasingly popular and even respectable by treating it as serious music. Prominent among them were the composer George

Gershwin, who incorporated jazz elements in his *Rhapsody in Blue*, and the conductor Paul Whiteman, whose band presented a pioneering jazz concert in New York City in 1922.

## A Search for Values

In letters, the arts, and learning, there was a seeking for values that would be something more than the advertising man's paeans to mass-production cultures, as expressed in Bruce Barton's *The Man Nobody Knows*. This seeking is the reason so many of the younger writers were rejecting the popular values of the United States for those of Europe, which did not seem to them as yet caught in the new commercial maelstrom. Others were trying to interpret the new society with the psychoanalytical approach suggested by Sigmund Freud, or the economic determinism stemming from Karl Marx.

Among ministers, publicists, philosophers, and economists seeking to interpret the new order, there was some confusion. The fundamentalist ministers went on much as before, although in some quarters they were subjected to ridicule in 1925 when their champion, William Jennings Bryan, matched wits with the agnostic Clarence Darrow in the famous Scopes trial involving a Tennessee law forbidding the teaching of evolution. Ministers to the middle class who earlier had so exuberantly preached the social gospel or the great crusade in Europe had been beaten down in 1919 when they took up the cause of the striking steel workers. Many businessmen were ready to adopt paternalistic policies and label them "Christian industrialism," but they denounced the militant social gospel as Bolshevism. Ministers further lost their hold on their following as middle-class reaction spread against two of the causes in which they had been so deeply involved—the war in Europe and prohibition. Many ministers tended, consequently, to concentrate upon the building of fine churches and the development of a sophisticated theology embracing the new psychological concepts.

Many of the most popular publicists were negative in their view of government. Mencken and Irving Babbitt launched some of their most scathing attacks against the American democratic system. Walter Lippmann, who had been

**H. L. Mencken [1933]**

As columnist for the Baltimore *Sun*, and especially as editor of the *Smart Set* and the *American Mercury*, Mencken exercised great influence for the fifteen years following World War I. Often regarded as an iconoclast whose value was purely negative, Mencken actually used the grace and taste of the eighteenth-century aristocracy as a standard to condemn the "booboisie" he saw around him. Outstanding for his pioneering studies of the American language, for his opposition to censorship and prohibition, and for his championing of such writers as Joseph Conrad, Theodore Dreiser, and Ring Lardner, he wrote a virile and sinewy prose. His wit (and his scorn for American politicians) shows in his obituary for Calvin Coolidge, published in April 1933:

*In what manner he would have performed himself if the holy angels had shoved the Depression forward a couple of years—this we can only guess, and one man's hazard is as good as another's. My own is that he would have responded to bad times precisely as he responded to good ones—that is, by pulling down the blinds, stretching his legs upon his desk, and snoozing away the lazy afternoons. . . . He slept more than any other President, whether by day or by night. Nero fiddled, but Coolidge only snored. . . . Counting out Harding as a cipher only, Dr. Coolidge was preceded by one World Saver and followed by two more. What enlightened American, having to choose between any of them and another Coolidge, would hesitate for an instant? There were no thrills while he reigned, but neither were there any headaches. He had no ideas, and he was not a nuisance.*

deeply involved in the New Nationalism and the New Freedom, became aloof and brilliantly analytical in his observation of American society. The Socialist candidate for President in 1928, Norman Thomas, remarked: "The old reformer has become the Tired Radical and his sons and daughters drink at the fountain of the *American Mercury.*"

Nevertheless, some of the most influential philosophers and social scientists continued to write in modified progressive terms. John Dewey, at the peak of his influence, was expounding a socialized pragmatism: man through science and technology could develop an organized social intelligence which could plan a rational and fruitful future society. The aged Thorstein Veblen was placing a similar faith in science: the engineers in contrast to the businessmen could bring forth an economic utopia. This doctrine, carried to its ultimate conclusion, engendered the technocracy movement of the early thirties. Other economists would not go this far, but some of them accepted Veblen's emphasis upon craftsmen and technicians, who, unlike businessmen, would not raise prices and restrict markets. Around them could develop an economy of still greater abundance. Agricultural economists, who were thinking in opposite terms of restriction, also looked forward to an age of social and economic planning.

Charles A. Beard was disseminating some of these ideas among a wider group of readers. In his and Mary Beard's *Rise of American Civilization* (1927), expressing mild economic determinism and emphasizing social and cultural factors, he did much to perpetuate progressive thinking among the new generation of intellectuals. Vernon L. Parrington's *Main Currents of American Thought* (1927), tracing the same themes in literature, helped create a Jeffersonian cult. Writing on a popular level, Claude Bowers developed similar ideas. Franklin D. Roosevelt, reviewing Bowers' *Jefferson and Hamilton* in 1925, commented: "Hamiltons we have today. Is a Jefferson on the horizon?"

## THE GREAT DEPRESSION

"I do not choose to run in 1928," President Coolidge had announced. The way to perpetuate Coolidge prosperity, it seemed to Republicans, was to elect Herbert Hoover, the "Great Engineer," whose policies as secretary of commerce promised a continuation of businessmen's government. The Republicans nominated him on the first ballot. In accepting the nomination, he proclaimed: "Given a chance to go forward with the policies of the last eight years, we shall soon with the help of God be in sight of the day when poverty will be banished from the nation."

## Election of 1928

Among Democrats, the experienced politicians were still almost as badly divided as in 1924, but they saw no reason to turn their convention into another brawl when their candidate had no chance of winning against Republican prosperity. Even those who were ardently dry and Protestant raised no barrier against the wet, Roman Catholic governor of New York, Alfred E. Smith. He was nominated to run on a platform not much more positive than that of the Republicans. It did, however, include a plank offering farmers the McNary-Haugen plan. More important, Smith promised to relax the Volstead Act for enforcing the Eighteenth Amendment. This brought prohibition to the forefront of the campaign. There was little except that and religion to campaign about.

Both Hoover and Smith were self-made men and proud of it. Hoover's path, from an Iowa farm through Stanford University, had been marked by a phenomenally successful rise as a business and government executive. Smith's path led from the East Side of New York through the Fulton Fish Market and the Tammany hierarchy to the governorship of New York. There he had demonstrated a consummate political and administrative skill. He had reorganized the state government, fought to build schools, parks, and parkways, and struggled for public development of the great power sites.

In the campaign, Hoover stressed prosperity, which was popularly translated into the notion of a chicken in every pot and two cars in every garage. Smith evoked more enthusiastic loyalty and venomous hatred than any candidate since Bryan. Millions of the urban masses, mostly of immigrant and Catholic background themselves, saw in Smith their spokesman, their great hero. Millions of Protestants in the rural South, where belief in prohibition was strong and the Ku Klux Klan boisterous in its anti-Catholicism, looked

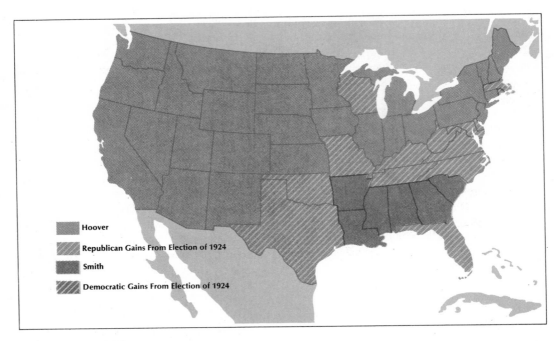

**Election of 1928**

upon him as a threat to their way of life. Fiery crosses greeted him near Oklahoma City, where he courageously denounced the Klan. But his cause was hopeless. The Republican landslide exceeded expectations, as Hoover received a popular vote of 21 million to 15 million for Smith.

## The Wall Street Crash

President Hoover, the prophet of permanent prosperity, had been in office scarcely six months when the Great Depression began. It was touched off by a collapse of the stock market. For several years stock prices had been rising so rapidly that they ceased to have much relation to the actual earning power of corporations. The New York Stock Exchange had become for many speculators a great national gambling casino, where everyone won almost all the time. By the summer of 1929, however, there were many disquieting signs that the prosperity, so long gone for the farmers, was coming to an end for businessmen also. Construction had passed its peak and was declining rapidly; automobiles were filling dealers' garages; business inventories of all sorts were three times larger than a year before; freight carloadings, industrial produc-

tion, and wholesale prices were all slipping downward.

On October 21, 1929, the stock market dropped sharply, and two days later the big crash began. Temporarily, J. P. Morgan and Company and other big bankers managed to stave off disaster, but on October 29 their efforts failed. That day 16 million shares were sold. Total losses for the month reached $16 billion. For two weeks more the market continued to drop, until stocks had lost over 40 per cent in value.

The stock market collapse, though not the cause of the depression, precipitated it by replacing the inflationary spiral with a deflationary one even harder to stop. It brought to an end a decade of business optimism and opened one of almost unquenchable pessimism. Bewildered businessmen saw their only hope in retrenchment, and the more they retrenched, the worse conditions became.

For years afterward, economists, businessmen, and political leaders debated the causes of the depression. Certainly there had been serious defects in the economy of the 1920s. As production rose, too little of the profits went to farmers, others producers of raw materials, or workers.

Too much went into the building of new industrial plants. So long as the expansion of capital facilities continued, new investments stimulated the economy, but the investments created more plant space than could be profitably used. By 1929, factories were pouring out more goods than consumers could purchase. This did not mean that Americans would not have consumed more had they had more income, for even in 1929 only one family in six had an automobile, only one in five a fixed bathtub or electricity, and only one in ten a telephone.

Government had played the wrong role in the economic system during the twenties. Taxes, by sparing the rich, had added to the inequality of incomes. High tariffs had discouraged foreign trade; large exports could have continued only so long as Americans kept on lending abroad. Failure to break up or regulate big business had encouraged concentration and resulted in rigidly high prices. Nothing had been done to check speculation or supervise the securities market, and nothing effective had been done to restore the buying power of farmers.

## The Hoover Program

In the view of critics a generation later, the government continued to do the wrong things in facing the depression. It concentrated upon balancing the budget and maintaining the gold standard, both of which were deflationary, at a

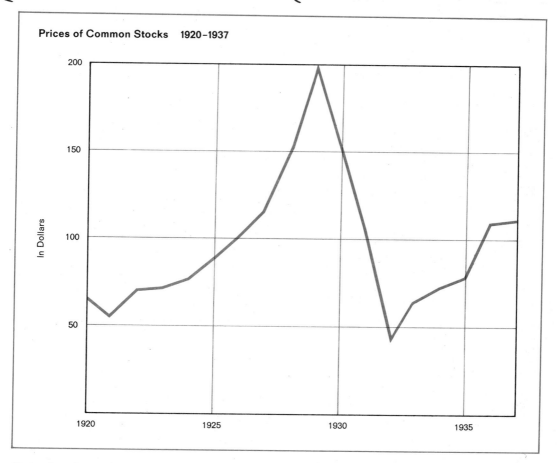

**Prices of Common Stocks 1920–1937**

In Dollars

The stock market crash marked only the beginning of the price decline. Stocks stayed low in the 1930s and even relatively low in the 1940s. By the Korean War the great bull market was underway and continued with only brief interruption until the 1960s. The stock prices shown above are based on the Dow-Jones stock averages.

time when the country was already suffering from too much deflation. Blame for these policies should not fall solely upon President Hoover. They were the ancient formulas for the conduct of government during a depression; they were urged upon the President by leaders of both parties and of business and by experts in economics.

Actually, President Hoover was far more energetic and imaginative than any previous American President in trying to combat the depression. His Secretary of the Treasury, Mellon, was a "leave-it-alone liquidationist" who thought a thoroughgoing cycle of bankruptcy and deflation would be healthful. Hoover did not agree. He determined that the government should intervene positively but in a very limited way, seeking the voluntary cooperation of business and labor.

First, to restore confidence, Hoover declared: "The fundamental business of this country, that is, production and distribution of commodities, is on a sound and prosperous basis." Most of the business leaders echoed him. Next, he held a number of highly publicized meetings of business, farm, and labor leaders in an effort to rally the country to adopt a voluntary program. Businessmen pledged themselves not to cut payrolls or production; labor leaders, not to ask for better wages or hours. Hoover also announced a significant tax cut and arranged for the Federal Reserve to provide increased bank credit. He asked Congress for an increase of $423 million in public works—a huge sum for the period—and called upon mayors and governors to engage in the "energetic yet prudent pursuit" of public construction.

Already, in April 1929, Hoover had called Congress into special session to provide farm relief and raise the tariff. His farm program, embodied in the Agricultural Marketing Act of 1929, set up large-scale government machinery to aid the farmer. The program, as Hoover insisted, was voluntary and did not include any of the price-fixing schemes for which farm organizations were lobbying. It encouraged the voluntary combination of farmers to help themselves under government auspices. A Farm Board of eight members administered a revolving fund of $500 million, from which the board could make loans to national marketing cooperatives or establish corporations to buy surpluses and thus raise prices.

Within six months the depression precipitated farm prices toward new lows. Until the summer of 1931, the Wheat Stabilization Corporation and the Cotton Stabilization Corporation were able to keep prices a bit above world levels. By 1932 their funds were spent, their warehouses full, and grain prices at the lowest point since the founding of the American colonies. The Farm Board had operated on too small a scale, and it had lacked power to limit production. When President Hoover later called for voluntary reduction of the wheat crop, acreage dropped only 1 per cent in Kansas. The Farm Board experiment thus underscored the futility of a voluntary crop-control program and prepared the way for a more drastic measure.

Congress, taking President Hoover's advice to raise agricultural tariffs, prepared an overall measure, the Hawley-Smoot bill, which contained 75 increases on farm products, and 925 on manufactured goods. It raised the average duty from the 26 per cent of the Fordney-McCumber Act to a new high of 50 per cent. By the time it was ready for the President's signature in the spring of 1930, a thousand members of the American Economic Association had signed a petition urging him to veto it as an unwise piece of economic nationalism. He ignored such warnings and signed the measure. Other nations in reprisal placed new restrictions on American goods. In a time of world depression, rampant economic nationalism was perhaps inevitable, but it was unfortunate that the United States led the way.

The worsening depression gave Democrats a political issue. In the fall of 1930 they won a bare majority in the House of Representatives and, with the aid of Republican progressives, took effective control of the Senate. From this point on, Congress began seriously to harass Hoover, demanding that he move from voluntary measures to large-scale federal relief and spending. He refused to budge. By the spring of 1931 conditions seemed to be improving, and Hoover and others thought the worst was over. But the American economy took another downturn in consequence of a European financial

## Hoover Dam

Conservationists for years urged the construction of a huge dam on the Colorado River to utilize its large flow for irrigation and power production and to prevent disastrous flooding of the Imperial Valley in California. Only the federal government was large enough to provide sufficient funds for the project. Through the 1920s, Hoover worked as chairman of the Colorado River Commission to reconcile conflicting claims of the seven states in the Colorado basin and to obtain President Coolidge's reluctant approval of preliminary surveys. Hoover himself insisted that the power be sold as falling water to keep the government even out of the business of generating electricity. Work on the dam began in the Hoover administration.

It was the first of the great self-liquidating public works to be constructed during the depression, directly employing 4,000 workers, and indirectly aiding thousands more. The dam and power houses cost $108 million; in addition, the cities of southern California constructed a $220 million aqueduct to carry part of the water 259 miles to the Pacific coast. The dam, 726 feet high, created an artificial lake stretching 115 miles up the river, holding enough water to cover the state of Connecticut to a depth of 10 feet. When the dam was finished in 1935, two years ahead of the contract date, it was dedicated by President Franklin D. Roosevelt. (National Archives)

panic. By May 1931 the largest bank in Austria had collapsed, and the disaster threatened to wreck the banking and monetary systems of Germany and other nations of Europe.

To avert this, President Hoover proposed a one-year moratorium on reparations and war-debt payments, but France destroyed much of the good effect through her delay in accepting the plan. By September, England and most other nations of the world had gone off the gold standard. The crisis in western Europe caused European gold to be withdrawn from American banks, and European holdings of American securities to be dumped on the market. As other nations devalued their currency in going off the gold standard, American trade with them declined disastrously.

By December 1931, when Congress met, conditions were so frightening that President Hoover abandoned his reliance upon voluntary measures and proposed direct governmental action of an unprecedented sort to combat the depression. In January 1932 Congress created a giant loan agency, the Reconstruction Finance Corporation, which during 1932 loaned $1.5 billion, mostly to banks, railroads, and other businesses. Hoover, trying to parry criticism that he had set up a bread line for big business, asserted that his purpose was to stop deflation and thus increase employment, mainly by helping relatively small companies. Congress also provided for banks, together with further capital for existing loan banks, to help prevent mortgage foreclosures.

On the issues of very large-scale public works and direct relief for the unemployed, the President clashed bitterly with Republican progressives and Democrats in Congress. In July 1932 he vetoed their bill as being impractical and dangerous; he felt that direct relief was a state and local responsibility. Subsequently, he signed a bill he himself had recommended, authorizing the RFC to lend $300 million for relief, and another $1.5 billion for self-liquidating public works.

Hoover believed that, while people must not go cold and hungry, feeding them was a voluntary and local responsibility. "If we start appropriations of this character," he had declared, "we have not only impaired something infinitely valuable in the life of the American people but have struck at the roots of self-government." It was hard for desperate people to appreciate such niceties of thought. Hoover, who had been one of the most popular of American heroes, became the scapegoat for the depression.

To some observers the 1928 election had seemed to be a great national referendum in favor of prohibition, yet prohibition was not to last much longer than prosperity. Though Hoover had referred to it as a "noble experiment," enforcement was breaking down so badly that Congress stiffened the penalties for violating the Volstead Act and authorized the new President to appoint a National Law Enforcement Commission. This commission, headed by a former Attorney General, George Wickersham, ultimately reported in 1931 that prohibition was not only unenforced but virtually unenforceable.

Rampant gangsterism and the open flouting of the law by millions of otherwise respectable citizens convinced many thoughtful Americans that prohibition was not worth its price in lawlessness. With the coming of the depression, some well-to-do people, already banded into antiprohibition organizations, redoubled their efforts in the hope that repeal would bring lower income taxes and greater prosperity. In February 1933 Congress submitted to the states the Twenty-first Amendment, repealing prohibition; by December it had been ratified, and the experiment was at an end.

## Deepening Despair

As the depression deepened, there were surprisingly few signs of social disorder or outbursts of violence within the United States. Communists agitated, won a few converts

---

**Shacks of the Unemployed,
New York City    1932**

Robert Bendiner has written: "To a New Yorker . . . the signs of collapse were aggressive. Along the Hudson, below Riverside Drive, I daily passed the tarpaper huts of a Hooverville, where scores of families lived the lives of reluctant gypsies, cooking whatever they had to cook over open fires within sight of passengers on the double-decker Fifth Avenue buses. Dozens of such colonies had sprung up in the city . . . but not nearly enough to accommodate the swelling army of the jobless and dispossessed." (Top right, Culver)

**An Apple Seller in New York City**

In the fall of 1931 and 1932, a number of unemployed tried to gain a pittance for themselves by selling apples. President Hoover later wrote: "One incident of these times has persisted as the eternal damnation of Hoover. Some Oregon or Washington apple growers' association shrewdly appraised the sympathy of the public for the unemployed. They set up a system of selling apples on the street corners in many cities, thus selling their crop and raising their prices. Many persons left their jobs for the more profitable one of selling apples. When any left-winger wishes to indulge in scathing oratory, he demands, 'Do you want to return to selling apples?' " (Bottom right, Culver)

among intellectual leaders, but made almost no impact upon the masses.

The chain reaction of unemployment slowly spread from 1930 into 1933. At first those in marginal or poorer jobs were hit hardest, as those who had been in better jobs moved downward. In time millions who had never been unemployed for any length of time were jobless and unable to find work of any sort. They were bewildered, for they had been brought up in the sturdy tradition of self-reliance and had accepted the doctrine of rugged individualism—that opportunities were limitless if only one had the ambition and energy to take advantage of them. Now these people were humiliated and baffled at not being able to provide for themselves and their families. As they remained idle for months and then years, they were in danger of losing their skills as well as their morale. Physical and moral erosion threatened.

Care of the unemployed had always been a responsibility primarily of private charity, and for several years the President and governors exhorted citizens to contribute to the Red Cross or to emergency funds. But the task soon became far too great for private charity to handle. By 1931, the Red Cross could provide only 75 cents a week to feed each hungry family in southern Illinois.

Although several European nations had maintained unemployment insurance programs for decades, not a single state in the United States enacted such a law until January 1932, when Wisconsin passed one. Even as the distress grew, many magazines and newspapers proclaimed that any permanent system of direct unemployment relief like the British dole would bankrupt the government and undermine the moral fiber of the recipients. Not until September 1931 did the New York legislature at the insistence of Governor Franklin D. Roosevelt establish the first relief organization of any state, the Tem-

porary Emergency Relief Administration, which became the model for other states and the prototype of the later federal relief agency.

To some of the unemployed who had recently moved to cities, the solution seemed to be to return to the farm; the migration away from farms was now reversed. But farm prices fell so low that once again, on parts of the plains, farmers burned corn to keep warm. A rancher sold seven lambs in the Denver livestock market and, after paying commissions and fees, received a check for 75 cents. In a railroad diner, two lamb chops cost the same amount. Prices of manufactured goods were relatively so high that it took ten bushels of wheat to buy a cheap pair of shoes. In drought areas farmers lacked even sufficient food.

Some bewildered farmers around Sioux City, Iowa, in 1932 embargoed milk bound for the city because they were receiving 2 cents a quart and it retailed for 8 cents. Many more Iowa farmers participated in Milo Reno's militant Farmers' Holiday Association to block all farm products from the market until prices rose.

Through the summer of 1932, some 12,000 to 14,000 unemployed veterans congregated in Washington to demonstrate for the immediate payments of their bonus for wartime service, not due until 1945. For weeks they lived in squalor in abandoned tenements and in shanties on the mud flats of the Anacostia River. After Congress failed to pass a bonus bill, about half of them, discouraged, went home. The continued presence of the rest alarmed Hoover and many Washingtonians. After a riot, the President called upon the army to oust the veterans. Under the personal command of General Douglas MacArthur, with tanks, gas masks, and fixed bayonets, the army did so. "That was a bad looking mob," MacArthur declared, expressing the alarm of conservatives. "It was animated by the essence of revolution."

# Selected Readings

**Surveys and Interpretations** J. D. Hicks, *Republican Ascendancy, 1921–1933*° (1960); W. E. Leuchtenberg, *The Perils of Prosperity, 1914–32*° (1958); George Soule, *Prosperity Decade: From War to Depression, 1917–1929* (1947); A. M. Schlesinger, Jr., *The Crisis of the Old Order*° (1957).

**Aspects of Life** G. H. Knoles, *The Jazz Age Revisited* (1955); F. L. Allen, *Only Yesterday*° (1931); R. S. and H. M. Lind, *Middletown*° (1929); N. F. Furniss, *The Fundamentalist Controversy, 1918–1931* (1954); Ray Ginger, *Six Days or Forever?*° (1958), about the Scopes trial; Erik Barnouw, *A Tower in Babel: A History of Broadcasting in the United States*, vol. 1: to 1933 (1966); W. R. Ross, *The Last Hero: Charles A. Lindbergh* (1967).

**Radicalism and Reaction** W. Preston, Jr., *Aliens and Dissenters: Federal Suppression of Radicals, 1903–1933* (1963); R. K. Murray, *The Red Scare*° (1955); Zechariah Chafee, Jr., *Free Speech in the United States* (1941); S. Coben, *A. Mitchell Palmer, Politician* (1963); G. L. Joughin and E. M. Morgan, *The Legacy of Sacco and Vanzetti*° (1948); David Brody, *Labor in Crisis: The Steel Strike of 1919*° (1965); Irving Bernstein, *The Lean Years: A History of the American Worker, 1920–1933*° (1960); David Chalmers, *Hooded Americanism*° (1965), on the Klan; E. D. Cronon, *Black Moses: The Story of Marcus Garvey*° (1955).

**The Eighteenth and Nineteenth Amendments** J. H. Timberlake, *Prohibition and the Progressive Movement, 1900–1920* (1963); Andrew Sinclair, *Prohibition: The Era of Excess*° (1962); Charles Merz, *Dry Decade* (1931); Virginius Dabney, *Dry Messiah: The Life of Bishop Cannon* (1949); A. S. Kraditor, *The Ideas of the Woman Suffrage Movement, 1890–1920* (1965).

**Literature** Alfred Kazin, *On Native Grounds: An Interpretation of Modern American Prose Literature*° (1942); Edmund Wilson, *The Shores of Light*° (1952) and *The American Earthquake*° (1958); Frederick Hoffman, *Freudianism and the Literary Mind*° (1947); Mark Schorer, *Sinclair Lewis*° (1961); M. K. Singleton, *H. L. Mencken and the American Mercury Adventure* (1962).

**Harding and Coolidge** S. H. Adams, *Incredible Era: The Life and Times of Warren G. Harding*° (1939); Andrew Sinclair, *The Available Man* (1965), on Harding; Burl Noggle, *Teapot Dome: Oil and Politics in the 1920's* (1962); J. L. Bates, *The Origins of Teapot Dome: Progressives, Parties, and Petroleum, 1909–1921* (1963); W. A. White, *A Puritan in Babylon*° (1938), on Coolidge; D. R. McCoy, *Calvin Coolidge, the Quiet President* (1967); H. H. Quint and R. H. Ferrell, eds., *The Talkative President: The Off-the-Record Press Conferences of Calvin Coolidge* (1964).

**Foreign Affairs** J. C. Vinson, *The Parchment Peace* (1955); M. J. Pusey, *Charles Evans Hughes* (2 vols., 1951); Dexter Perkins, *Charles Evans Hughes and American Democratic Statesmanship* (1953); R. H. Ferrell, *Peace in Their Time* (1952); R. J. Maddox, *William E. Borah and American Foreign Policy* (1969).

**Political Opposition** K. C. Mackay, *The Progressive Movement of 1924* (1947); J. J. Huthmacher, *Massachusetts People and Politics, 1919–1933*° (1959); Frank Freidel, *Franklin D. Roosevelt: The Ordeal* (1954); Oscar Handlin, *Al Smith and His America*° (1958); E. A. Moore, *A Catholic Runs for President* (1956); R. C. Silva, *Rum, Religion, and Votes: 1928 Re-examined* (1962).

**Hoover and the Depression** A. U. Romasco, *The Poverty of Abundance: Hoover, the Nation, the Depression*° (1965); H. G. Warren, *Herbert Hoover and the Great Depression* (1959); Herbert Hoover, *Memoirs: The Great Depression, 1929–1941* (1952); J. H. Shideler, *Farm Crisis, 1919–1923* (1957); Theodore Saloutos and J. D. Hicks, *Twentieth Century Populism: Agricultural Discontent in the Middle West, 1900–1939*° (1951); J. K. Galbraith, *The Great Crash*° (1955); Milton Friedman and A. J. Schwartz, *The Great Contraction, 1929–1933*° (1965).

---

°Titles available in paperback.

# Chapter 24
# Experimenting
# With a
# New Deal

During 1917 and 1918 the government of the United States, in order to win a war, had undertaken to control nearly all aspects of the economy. But never before the 1930s had the government intervened in so many ways in order to overcome a depression. Between 1933 and 1938, under the leadership of President Franklin D. Roosevelt, the government launched a bewildering variety of programs and set up a jumble of "alphabetical agencies"—AAA, NRA, TVA, and so on—to administer them. Some of these were intended to provide immediate relief for people facing a loss of income or property. Others were expected to stimulate economic activity and bring about recovery from the depression. Still others were designed to reform the economic system in order to reduce poverty and insecurity and avoid future depressions. Some of the programs served two or all three of these aims. All together, the series of measures constituted the New Deal.

The "three R's" of the New Deal, then, were Relief, Recovery, and Reform. Its conservative critics, among them former President Hoover, contended that it involved also a "fourth R," namely, Revolution. Certainly the New Deal, which at first was rather cautious, emphasizing short-term measures of relief and recovery, gradually became somewhat more daring and placed greater emphasis on lasting reforms. All along, however, the programs were directed toward patching up and preserving, not destroying, the political and economic institutions that President Roosevelt and the American people had inherited. The programs were mostly improvisations that were drawn up to meet the needs of the moment. They were based on previous American experience. A precedent for practically every one of them can be found in something that had been proposed or tried out earlier. The New Deal was revolutionary only in the sense that it embodied a larger number of undertakings at one time and carried them to greater lengths than other comparable movements, such as the New Freedom, had done.

The New Deal failed to bring about full recovery; not until after 1941 did war, the greatest of public works, take up the slack in the employment of human and other resources. But the relief measures enabled both the people and the economic system to survive the depression, and the reform measures made significant and enduring changes in the system itself. The role of government in economic life was vastly increased (and was to be increased still further by the ensuing war). The nation had become a welfare state. Henceforth the principle was to be generally accepted—though not always completely realized—that it was the government's duty to "provide for the general welfare" by controlling business and agriculture, maintaining full employment, and assuring at least a basic economic security to all members of society.

---

**The NRA Eagle**

General Johnson chose a blue eagle as the NRA emblem. "He is the Thunder Bird," Johnson explained, "—an Amerindian ideograph of unmeasured antiquity." (National Archives)

## A CHANGE OF LEADERSHIP

In 1932 Republicans meeting in Chicago renominated Hoover in a spirit far from jubilant; they had little illusion about the outcome of the election. The Democrats, assembling later in an excited, expectant mood, saw almost certain victory after twelve years out of power. Almost anyone they nominated was sure to be elected.

### The Interregnum of 1932–1933

Well over a majority of the delegates came pledged to vote for Governor Franklin D. Roosevelt of New York. Roosevelt had been working astutely for the nomination for years. To a considerable degree he bridged the gulf between the urban and rural Democrats. He was ready to emphasize economic issues and ignore the earlier divisions over prohibition and religion.

Breaking precedent, Roosevelt flew immediately to Chicago to deliver his acceptance address before the convention. He endorsed the Democratic platform, which except for a promise of prohibition repeal was not much bolder than that of the Republicans. He declared: "I pledge you, I pledge myself, to a new deal for

the American people." Thus the Roosevelt program acquired a name before the electorate had more than the haziest notion what it might embody.

Nor did the voters learn much during the campaign, for Roosevelt shrewdly confined himself to warm generalities which would offend few and yet would bring him the enormous vote of protest against Hoover. Through Roosevelt's speeches ran many of the old progressive themes, together with new suggestions of economic planning. An able team, largely of university professors under the leadership of Raymond Moley, helped devise policies and draft speeches for him. Newspapermen dubbed his group of advisers the "brain trust." At the Commonwealth Club in San Francisco, Roosevelt broke furthest from the past by insisting that the government must assist business in developing a well-regulated economic system. Everyone, he said, had a right to a comfortable living; the nation's industrial and agricultural mechanism could produce more than enough. If need be, to achieve this end, government must police irresponsible economic power. Roosevelt felt he was doing no more than restating the objectives of

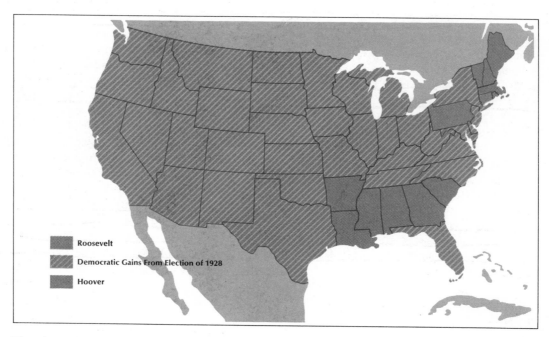

Roosevelt

Democratic Gains From Election of 1928

Hoover

**Election of 1932**

Jefferson and Wilson in terms of the complexities of the thirties when he proposed that the government should act as a regulator for the common good within the existing economic system. So far as Roosevelt explained the New Deal during the campaign, this was its essence.

President Hoover, tired and grim, took to the road in October to warn the populace that without his program things might be infinitely worse. His speeches, though earnest, were dull and dreary in both style and delivery compared with Roosevelt's breezy, optimistic performances. Hoover was the last of the Presidents to scorn the aid of speech writers.

Some voters, disappointed because they could detect little difference between Roosevelt's program and Hoover's, turned to Norman Thomas and the Socialists or to William Z. Foster and the Communists. Yet, even in this year of despair, the Socialists polled only 882,000 votes, and the Communists only 103,000. Roosevelt received 22,822,000 popular votes (57.4 per cent), Hoover 15,762,000 (39.7 per cent). The Democrats carried both houses of Congress by top-heavy majorities. Roosevelt had won an overwhelming mandate—but for what?

Actually, there had been discernible differences between the two candidates and their programs—besides the obvious difference that Hoover was a worn, discredited President, and Roosevelt a buoyant candidate. Hoover had seen the depression as world-wide in origin and development; rather inconsistently he was ready to combat it internationally through currency stabilization, and nationally, through raising the tariff still higher if need be. Roosevelt chose to regard the depression as domestic, specifically Republican, in origin. During the campaign Hoover had forced him to equivocate on the old Democratic low-tariff position. Roosevelt was ready (as both his record as governor and his speeches indicated) to move toward economic nationalism. But he agreed with Hoover on the need for government thrift and a balanced budget.

President Hoover faced an agonizing four months before Roosevelt would take office on March 4: the Twentieth ("lame duck") Amendment to end this long carry-over of a defeated President and Congress was not ratified until February 1933. There had been a brief economic upswing in the spring months of 1932, reaching a peak in July. (Economists later ascribed this to Hoover's own brief plunge into deficit financing through public works spending and Reconstruction Finance Corporation loans.) Hoover felt he was bringing an end to the depression and that only the threat of unsettling measures from Roosevelt was preventing continued recovery. Hence, in a series of interchanges with Roosevelt during the winter of 1932–1933, he tried to bind the President-elect to economic orthodoxy.

Hoover favored the reestablishment of an international gold standard. He hoped that the United States and other nations would agree to this at an economic and monetary conference that was scheduled to meet in London after Roosevelt's inauguration. But Roosevelt would make no commitment.

By February 1933 an acute banking crisis had developed. Bank resources and deposits had been declining at an alarming rate. In the previous three years, 5,000 banks had failed, and now one after another was collapsing as depositors lined up to withdraw their deposits. To stop the run on the banks, governors began proclaiming banking holidays in their states. By March 4 banking was at a halt or drastically restricted in all states but one.

President Hoover wrote a letter to Roosevelt, charging that the crisis was caused by "steadily degenerating confidence" in the President-elect, and calling upon him to give prompt public assurance that there would be no tinkering with the currency, no heavy borrowing, no unbalancing of the budget. Roosevelt had not the slightest intention of adopting Hoover's views.

## F. D. R. Takes Command

When Roosevelt was inaugurated, on March 4, 1933, most of the nation's banks were closed. At least 13 million people were unemployed, some of them so close to starvation that they were scrabbling for food scraps in garbage dumps. Millions of farmers were on the brink of foreclosure; many others had fallen over the brink.

In his inaugural address, President Roosevelt spoke with vigor and confidence. "This great

**Roosevelt and Hoover En Route to Roosevelt's Inauguration    March 4, 1933**

Roosevelt never forgot the awkwardness of his ride to the Capitol with the grim, unresponsive Hoover, exhausted from grappling with the banking crisis. No one would have guessed in the black days before March 4, 1933, that the incoming President would set his mark on the age as have few Chief Executives. He alarmed even those closest to him with his amiability, his ready acceptance of suggestions, his quick "Fine, fine, fine." New Yorkers, fearful that his jaunty buoyancy, his facility at compromise, and his skill at political maneuver were a façade for weakness, had sometimes referred to him as "the Grin" or the "Boy Scout Governor." They did not as yet see the energy and persistence with which he applied himself, or the

cold iron sometimes not far beneath the charm. His physical courage they realized, for after his polio attack in 1921 he had indomitably stayed in politics, refusing to surrender to his infirmity. He had subordinated it so thoroughly that most people regarded him only as somewhat lame and never thought of him as using a wheelchair. Again he demonstrated his self-possession at Miami in February 1933, by remaining astoundingly calm when an insane assassin missed him but mortally wounded the mayor of Chicago sitting beside him. Somehow Roosevelt was able to transmit some of his courage to the nation in March 1933. (United Press International)

Nation will endure as it has endured, will revive and will prosper," he declared. "So, first of all, let me assert my firm belief that the only thing we have to fear is fear itself." Somehow these words, although they said nothing new, helped inspire the American people. From their depths of helplessness they were ready for the moment

to be commanded, and in Roosevelt they saw someone ready to take strong leadership. Such leadership he promised. If Congress did not act, he announced, he would ask for "broad executive power to wage a war against the emergency, as great as the power that would be given to me if we were in fact invaded by a foreign foe."

Few Presidents have been better trained for the White House. Roosevelt had served in the New York state senate, been wartime assistant secretary of the navy, and had been twice elected governor of New York. He was skilled in both legislative and administrative techniques as well as in practical politics. As a youth he had spent much time in Europe, and maintained a continuing interest in foreign affairs. Roosevelt's ideology was progressive, influenced by his wife's uncle, Theodore Roosevelt, whom he admired, and his former chief, Woodrow Wilson, whom he revered.

Neither the new President nor his advisers were clearcut in their thinking. What was important was that Roosevelt, while basically rooted in the older economics and the social-justice tradition of the progressives, was ready to experiment. His program would be flexible, not doctrinaire; the new economic theories would grow from it, not it from the theories. When one of the brain-trusters warned of perils ahead, Roosevelt declared: "There is nothing to do but meet every day's troubles as they come." This was his political pragmatism, and out of it grew the New Deal economic policies.

With the banking crisis at its height, he might well have taken drastic steps such as nationalization of the banks. But he seemed bent above all upon restoring the confidence of businessmen. His initial program differed little from what they had been advocating. He met the banking crisis in a manner pleasing to the banking community. He issued a proclamation on March 6, 1933, closing all banks and stopping transactions or exports in gold for four days until Congress could meet in special session. On March 9 he sent in a conservative bill which would bolster the stronger banks. It authorized the Federal Reserve System to issue notes against their assets, and the Reconstruction Finance Corporation to make them loans. The bill dealt a death blow to weaker banks; inspectors would deny them licenses to reopen. It stopped the ebb of gold from the Treasury and the country through prohibiting hoarding and exportation. In effect, the country went off the gold standard (officially it did so April 19, 1933). Congress passed the bill within four hours of its introduction. In the House, a rolled-up newspaper substituted for it, since there had not been time to print copies.

On March 12, in the first of his "fireside chats" over the radio, the President, speaking in a warm, intimate manner, told the American people that the crisis was over. "I can assure you," he declared, "that it is safer to keep your money in a reopened bank than under the mattress." And so indeed it was; by his legislation and his confident leadership, Roosevelt had averted the threat to banks and the capitalist system. Three-fourths of the banks in the Federal Reserve System reopened within the next three days, and a billion dollars in hoarded currency and gold flowed back into them within a month. Practically all unsafe banks were now out of business; there were very few new failures in the years that followed.

On the morning after the passage of the Emergency Banking Act, Roosevelt further reassured business by sending Congress an economy bill, to balance the budget by cutting salaries of government employees and pensions of veterans as much as 15 per cent. This, Roosevelt declared, was the only way to avoid a billion-dollar deficit. This bill too passed almost instantly, although with such fierce opposition from veterans' organizations that it carried the House only with Republican votes. Pressure from veterans soon led Congress to rescind the pension cuts over Roosevelt's veto, but the President drastically slashed the regular expenditures of the government.

On March 13, 1933, Roosevelt proposed legalizing beer that had a 3.2 per cent alcoholic content, pending repeal of the prohibition amendment. This, he felt, would stimulate recovery and bring in needed taxes. (It also rescued millions of law violators from the rigors of home brew and gangster-made beer.)

Thus far, except for the gold clause in the Emergency Banking Act, the program of the new administration might have been that of a Hoover with a smile. It restored the confidence of bankers and businessmen, the stock market going up 15 per cent. But this was anticipatory of the real recovery to follow; for the moment nothing had been improved but the confidence of the American nation.

## TENTATIVE BEGINNINGS

During his first hundred days in office, keeping Congress in special session, Roosevelt put through a series of laws and began to take steps that led him away from the "sound" position—so reassuring to bankers and other businessmen—that he originally had assumed.

### Emergency Relief

The first step was to feed the millions of hungry unemployed. While Roosevelt subscribed to his predecessor's maxim that relief was primarily the task of states and communities, he proposed that the federal government provide grants rather than loans to states. Congress established

the Federal Emergency Relief Administration, and appropriated an initial half-billion dollars for it. Roosevelt appointed the director of the New York state relief agency, Harry Hopkins, whom he hardly knew as yet, to run the federal program. Hopkins was a dedicated social worker with a lively tongue and a keen sense of professional ethics. He ardently believed in work relief rather than direct relief, but in the spring of 1933 everyone hoped recovery was at hand so that relief would be needed only for a few months.

But recovery lagged, and some new way had to be found to care for the unemployed through the winter of 1933-1934. Relief administrator Hopkins persuaded the President to establish a

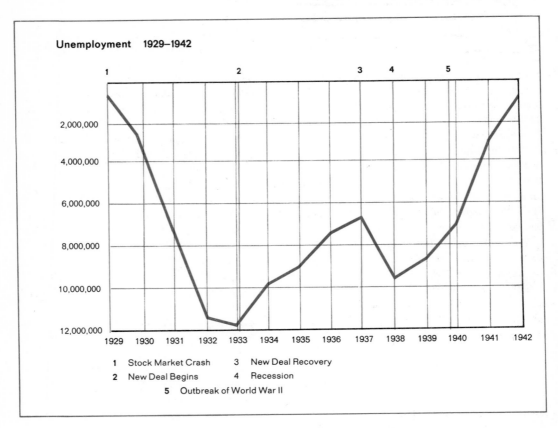

Unemployment 1929–1942

1 Stock Market Crash 3 New Deal Recovery
2 New Deal Begins 4 Recession
5 Outbreak of World War II

Unemployment was especially high among young people, those who lived in areas where the textile mills and coal mines had been closed, and among the minority groups. The rate of unemployment changed drastically with the acute shortage of labor during the war years.

Although the 1942 employment figures were up to the 1929 high, this chart does not reflect the proportionate population growth.

temporary work relief program, the Civil Works Administration. Between November and April it put 4 million people to work at emergency projects. Sometimes it was made-work like leaf raking, to which critics applied an old Texas term, "boondoggling." Some of the projects, despite lack of funds for materials and tools, made substantial improvements. The output was of secondary importance; the work raised the morale of the unemployed and increased their buying power by $950 million. The purchasing power thus injected into the economy was probably responsible for the wavering recovery, as the index of production rose from 71 in November 1933 to 86 in May 1934. But soon Roosevelt capitulated to fierce conservative criticism and liquidated the program.

Congress also created an organization that reflected Roosevelt's keen interest in preserving natural as well as human resources, the Civilian Conservation Corps. It received a grant of $300 million to enroll 250,000 young men from relief families and 50,000 veterans and woodsmen, to work at reforestation and flood control. Ultimately the CCC enrolled 500,000 young men, but this was only a fraction of the unemployed youths in the nation.

Mortgage relief was a pressing need of millions of farm owners and home owners. Roosevelt quickly consolidated all farm credit organizations into a new Farm Credit Administration, Congress voted such large additional funds for it that within two years it had refinanced a fifth of all farm mortgages in the United States. The Frazier-Limke Farm-Bankruptcy Act of 1933 enabled some farmers to regain their farms even after the foreclosure of mortgages. Unfortunately, these measures came too late to save all farmers; by 1934 a quarter of them for one reason or another had lost their property. A comparable Home Owners' Loan Corporation, established in June 1933, in a three-year period loaned $3 billion to refinance the mortgages of over a million distressed householders. Altogether it carried about a sixth of the nation's urban mortgage burden. A year later Congress established a Federal Housing Administration to insure mortgages ·for new construction and home repairs—more properly a recovery than a relief agency. All these mortgage agencies not only rescued mortgage holders, but also eased the burden on banks and insurance companies, thus filling a recovery function.

Under the New Deal, the Reconstruction Finance Corporation continued to function as the key loan agency for relief to business. The Democratic Congress inveighed against the RFC policy of making large loans only to big businesses and not to individuals. Congress therefore broadened the RFC's lending power so that it could, and indeed did, also lend to small businessmen. Under the conservative management of a shrewd Texan, Jesse Jones, it continued to make most of its loans to large enterprises, including banks, and to governmental units, on sound security and with a high percentage of ultimate repayment.

## The First AAA

The Agricultural Adjustment Administration, created in May 1933, marked the triumphant conclusion of the farmers' long struggle to get government aid for raising farm prices. Henceforth the farmers, who continued to be a declining fraction of the whole population, received preferential treatment from the government.

Roosevelt was mainly interested in the relatively substantial farmers, such as the 300,000 who even in 1933 were paying dues of $10 a year or more to the Farm Bureau Federation. These and the Grange members desired a program to limit crops. Poorer members of other farm organizations like the Farmers' Union and the National Farmers' Holiday Association opposed production cuts, seeking instead direct relief and, above all, inflation. Roosevelt hoped to develop a program that would fit the Farm Bureau formula and yet would not drive poorer farmers into new revolt. He let the various farm organization leaders devise their own plan. Fifty of them met in Washington early in March 1933 and drafted an omnibus bill that contained scraps and reworkings of most of the old schemes. It provided for a "domestic-allotment" system. Producers of seven basic commodities (wheat, cotton, corn, hogs, rice, tobacco, and milk and dairy products) were to receive benefit payments if they cut acreage or production. Funds for these payments would come from a

### A Sharecropper's Family   1936

"Total family incomes in a good year . . . averaged on the efficient plantations $312 for croppers and $417 for other share tenants. . . . The 18,000,000 bale crop of 1937 so reduced the price that it is probable that the average cropper did not have more than $75 in net cash at the end of the year and the lowest fourth either came out in debt or did not have enough to replace the overalls and brogan shoes worn out in working the crop. Living standards as expressed in the miserable shacks that croppers and other share tenants occupy, the shoddy clothing they wear, and the inadequate diet they consume are indefensible. Here are over a million families who cannot in any real sense be considered a part of the American market. They live in a climate which will produce an amazing variety of sustenance. Yet they can barely exist in good years and know hunger in poor years."—T. J. Woofter, Jr., and Ellen Winston, *Seven Lean Years* (Chapel Hill: University of North Carolina Press, 1939). (Library of Congress)

tax upon the processing of commodities—for example, a tax on the milling of wheat. The tax would be added to the price of the flour or other product, and so it would be passed on to the consumer, who would thus indirectly pay the farmer for growing less. Farm prices were to be brought up to "parity," that is, a level that would provide the same price relationship of farm products to manufactured goods as during the period 1909–1914.

Because the 1933 farm season was well under way when the AAA began operations, large-scale destruction was necessary to cut surpluses. Six million pigs and 220,000 sows about to farrow were slaughtered. Nine-tenths of their weight was inedible and processed into fertilizer, but they nevertheless provided 100 million pounds of pork for needy families. Bad weather so drastically cut the wheat crop that the AAA did not have to intervene to reduce it. Cotton farmers ploughed under a quarter of their crop —but it was the poorest quarter and they so intensively cultivated the rest that 30 million acres produced more than 36 million had done the previous year.

Despite continued high cotton production, a short textile boom sent the price up from 5.5 cents per pound to 10.6 cents in the summer. Then the price began to sag again and was held to 9.6 cents only through another device. A subsidiary of the AAA, the Commodity Credit Corporation, loaned 10 cents per pound to cotton farmers who would agree to take additional land out of production the next year. Since the loan was in excess of the market value of cotton, the government in effect was buying the crop at a premium price in return for the promise of drastic cuts in production. In this way cotton farmers received double the cash in 1933 that they had in 1931.

Farmers in other crop-reduction programs did not fare as well, although corn producers too could obtain commodity loans in the fall of 1933. Drought more than crop limitations reduced the output of wheat, corn, and hogs. Rising prices of manufactured goods canceled out most of the farmer's gain in real income. Yet on the whole his relative position improved somewhat.

The AAA actually hurt many of the farmers on the least productive farms, especially in the cotton belt. At times the AAA indirectly dispossessed them because planters, in reducing their acreage, sometimes evicted tenants and fired field hands. Unintentionally the AAA stimulated the great migration away from sharecropper cabins, at a time when city jobs no longer awaited the migrants. Rapid mechanization of farms and destructive wind storms on the Great Plains gave the great migration its impetus.

## The NRA

Hard-pressed businessmen sought measures providing for government stabilization of business. Since 1931 leaders of the United States Chamber of Commerce and others had been urging an antideflation scheme that involved price fixing through trade associations. This plan would have necessitated suspension of the antitrust laws. President Hoover, who earlier had

given strong support to the trade association movement, indignantly opposed price-fixing schemes. His attorney general forced five leading trade associations to dissolve, and the Federal Trade Commission compelled revision of the trade association codes for sixty-two industries.

In the spring of 1933, businessmen sought from Roosevelt what Hoover had refused them. Many of them also demanded government enforcement of their agreements in order to raise prices and stabilize production. The New Deal was ready to give them what they wanted if they would accept wages-and-hours regulation and other concessions for labor. As a consequence of such an arrangement, prices and wages would go up. Consumers' buying power might lag and thus defeat the scheme. Therefore the New Dealers drafting the great recovery bill added another ingredient for which there was much pressure: a large-scale public works spending program to prime the economic pump. This was the genesis of the National Industrial Recovery Act, which passed Congress in June 1933.

A new era of government alliance with business for the common good seemed to be opening. Roosevelt as he signed the act called it "the most important and far-reaching legislation ever enacted by the American Congress." On the same day, the President appointed as administrator the volatile, colorful General Hugh S. Johnson, who pictured himself as a sort of benign dictator presiding over the economy.

The President turned over the $3.3 billion for public works to Secretary of the Interior Harold L. Ickes, who slowly and methodically began to gather plans for projects, checking each carefully to make sure it would be really worthwhile. The need was for heavy spending in the next few months, but it was four years before Ickes' Public Works Administration pumped appreciable amounts of money into the economy.

President Roosevelt and NRA administrator Johnson called upon an excited nation to accept an interim blanket code, providing minimum wages of 30 cents or 40 cents an hour, maximum working hours of thirty-five or forty per week, and the abolition of child labor. Employers who agreed with the code were to display the NRA blue-eagle symbol; consumers who cooperated were to sign pledges that they would buy only from blue-eagle establishments. In much the spirit of 1917, the nation participated in NRA parades and rallies. As Johnson began negotiating codes with big industries, recovery seemed really imminent.

By the beginning of September 1933, specific codes for most of the big industries were in operation. In the drafting of the codes, Johnson had tried to serve as arbiter to balance the conflicting interests of business, labor, and the consumer. All three were represented at the bargaining table and received some degree of protection. Nevertheless, the real power in drawing up the regulations went to the businessmen themselves, to the leaders within each industry. They flocked to Washington and in the urgency of the moment rewrote their old trade association agreements into new NRA codes. These codes often contained provisions that were difficult for small units in the industry to maintain. Most of them provided for limiting production and, though often in disguised form, for price fixing.

Production, after a sharp rise, skidded downward during the fall of 1933, from an index figure of 101 in July to 71 in November, even as prices began to creep upward. The brave words and great NRA demonstrations of the spring and summer had not brought recovery. The New Deal honeymoon was over, and as General Johnson had predicted, the dead cats began to fly.

In the spring of 1934 a National Recovery Review Board under the famous iconoclastic lawyer, Clarence Darrow, reported that the NRA was dominated by big business; he hinted that what was needed was socialism. In the ensuing storm of vituperation between Johnson and Darrow, the NRA lost still more prestige.

A case involving the National Recovery Administration finally reached the Supreme Court. The constitutional basis for the NRA was the power of Congress to regulate commerce among the states, but the test case involved alleged code violations by the Schechter brothers, who were operating a wholesale poultry business confined to one locality, Brooklyn. Among the charges against them were the selling of poultry

in poor condition and the unfair treatment of employees. The Court (1935) unanimously held that the Schechters were not engaged in interstate commerce, and that Congress had unconstitutionally delegated legislative power to the President to draft the codes.

The "sick chicken" decision outraged Roosevelt. Seeing in it a threat to the whole New Deal, he lashed out at the judges for thinking in terms of the horse-and-buggy era. Actually, the decision proved to be more a blessing than a catastrophe for the New Deal, since it ended the decrepit NRA code system with its tacit suspension of the antitrust laws. "It has been an awful headache," Roosevelt confessed privately.

## TVA and Conservation

Increasingly New Dealers turned their attention to measures that would remedy conditions they felt had helped bring on the depression. Their indignation burned especially hot against the private power interests, which they felt had gulled investors and overcharged consumers. The spectacular collapse of the great Insull utility empire in the Middle West lent credence to their charges. Hence the first and most far-reaching of the New Deal reform measures was the creation of the Tennessee Valley Authority.

Through the twenties, millions of progressive Americans of both parties had shared the dream of Senator George Norris of Nebraska that the government might develop the nation's great water resources to provide cheap electric power. Millions of others accepted the educational program of the utilities companies, which spent $28 million to $35 million per year combating the idea of a national power program. The battle centered on the great dam that had been started at Muscle Shoals on the Tennessee River but had not been finished in time to provide nitrates during the war. Coolidge and the conservatives wished to sell it to Henry Ford for private development. Norris and his cohorts in Congress blocked them. Norris wished to make Muscle Shoals the center for developing the resources of the area and bringing abundance to millions of people living in poverty. His bill was vetoed by Coolidge and again by Hoover but was approved by Roosevelt in May 1933.

Basically, the TVA aimed to prevent the dev-

**The Tennessee Valley Authority**

astating floods that all too frequently had rolled down the rivers of the area, and to provide cheap, plentiful electricity as a yardstick for the measurement of private rates. More than this, the project became a great experiment in regional planning and rehabilitation.

Under a three-man board of directors with wide powers, the TVA in the next twenty years improved five existing dams and constructed twenty new ones. It stopped floods in the largest heavy-rainfall region in the nation and, by holding back the water, provided an inland waterway system with a nine-foot channel 652 miles long, soon heavy with traffic. From water power, and increasingly from steam plants, the TVA became the greatest producer of electricity in the United States. It also manufactured low-cost phosphate fertilizers. It taught farmers how to use them, how to restore the fertility of their soil, and how to end erosion by means of contour plowing and reforestation. TVA worked no miracles, but it did bring a higher living standard to the farmers of the area. It brought new light industry and increased business. When World War II came, the new power plants provided indispensable electricity for the production of munitions, aluminum, and plutonium.

In its "yardstick" function, TVA drove down the price of power in the area from 10 cents a kilowatt hour to 3 cents. Throughout the country, because of TVA and other pressures, the average residential rate dropped from 5.52 cents in 1933 to 3.67 cents in 1942. To private power companies the "yardstick" seemed grossly unfair, and they claimed that the TVA did not set its rates on the basis of true costs, including taxes. Its officials replied that its payments to local and state governments were comparable to the taxes assessed against private power companies.

Other great public power and irrigation developments were under way in the West during the same years. On the Colorado River, the Hoover Dam (begun during the Hoover administration) was finished in 1936, and on the Columbia River the Bonneville Dam was constructed in 1937 and the Grand Coulee Dam in 1942. In 1937 Norris proposed the creation of six additional regional authorities like the TVA; Congress failed to act, and the debate over public versus private development of power continued.

To combat drought conditions in the West, Roosevelt in 1934 by executive order set aside $15 million to build a "shelter belt" of trees on the Great Plains, to break the wind, collect moisture, and harbor wildlife. Critics scoffed, but somehow the trees grew where no one had believed they would. A Soil Erosion Service (later Soil Conservation Service), using much Civilian Conservation Corps manpower, was active, especially in the West. Homesteading on the range, which meant dry-farming under almost insuperable difficulties, came to an end with the passage of the Taylor Grazing Act of 1934, which withdrew overgrazed land and set regulations for the use of public rangeland. Spoliation of Indian lands came to at least a temporary halt with the passage of the Indian Reorganization Act of 1934, intended to preserve the tribal domain, customs, and civil liberties of the Indians.

## Money and Banking

Much of the New Deal was aimed at raising prices as a means of stimulating recovery. One way was to cut down production, as the AAA tried to do for agriculture and the NRA for industry. Another way was to put money into circulation through government spending, as was done in the relief programs (though recovery was not the primary aim of these). Still another way—at least in theory—was to manipulate the currency so as to increase the money supply.

By the summer of 1933, Roosevelt was ready to follow the reasoning of two Cornell University agricultural economists, who contended that if the price of gold were raised, the prices of other commodities would rise in rough proportion. The government needed only to purchase quantities of gold and cut the gold content of the dollar (as authorized by Congress). When financially orthodox Treasury officials refused to make the purchases, Roosevelt turned to the head of the Farm Credit Administration, Henry Morgenthau, Jr., who began buying gold every day along with wheat, corn, and oats. Soon Morgenthau was made secretary of the treasury.

The silver-purchase program had much the same object as the gold-purchase program. From the seven silver-producing states with their four-

teen senators came strong pressure, reminiscent of that of the Populist era, culminating in the Silver Purchase Act of 1934. This measure nearly tripled the price of silver at home. It also sent up the world silver price and wrought havoc in nations whose currency was on a silver standard. It did little or nothing to raise prices in the United States.

Roosevelt explained to a critical congressman: "I have always favored sound money, and do now, but it is 'too darned sound' when it takes so much of farm products to buy a dollar." In January 1934 he fixed the gold content of the dollar at 59.06 per cent of the former amount. The resort to managed currency created new precedents for government action and thus, like the income tax a generation earlier, helped bring about an important change in the relationship of government and the economy. But it had little immediate effect upon recovery.

Through other legislation the government acquired new powers over the banks, including the power to manage the supply of bank credit through increased control over the Federal Reserve System. In June 1933 Roosevelt signed the Glass-Steagall Act aimed at curbing speculation by banks. This also established the Federal Deposit Insurance Corporation, which he had not favored. The FDIC guaranteed small deposits up to $2,500 and functioned so successfully that the guarantee was raised by successive stages, eventually reaching $15,000. It was a longer task to work out a comprehensive overhauling and strengthening of the Federal Reserve System to remedy the defects that had appeared during the depression. This was accomplished through the Banking Act of 1935, which established a seven-man board of governors with direct power over interest rates. By lowering the rates, the board could encourage borrowing from banks, and this would ordinarily have an inflationary (price-raising) effect.

To protect investors further, Congress passed the so-called "Truth in Securities" Act of 1933, requiring corporations floating new securities to register them with the Federal Trade Commission, and provide full and accurate information on them. In June 1934 Congress went further and established the Securities and Exchange Commission to police the stock markets. Wall

Streeters protested, but their complaints lost some of their effect when a former head of the New York Stock Exchange was sentenced to Sing Sing for larceny.

# A SHIFT TO THE LEFT

Though President Roosevelt originally wished to provide for the welfare of each of the main economic and political groups in the nation, realities forced him to become the champion of the new political coalition of farmers, laborers, and the underprivileged in general. Roosevelt shifted partly because he felt that large business had defected, that it had betrayed his recovery program and was fighting politically to destroy the New Deal. Aligned against him were about 70 per cent of the newspaper publishers and most of the large contributors of campaign funds.

Far more important was the threat from the left; this was mainly responsible for the gradual change in emphasis of the New Deal. In undermining this threat, Roosevelt's political pragmatism combined with his humanitarian inclinations to carry him even farther than the progressives had dared venture toward positive government action for the general welfare.

## The Pressure of Politics

Through 1934 the President was still trying to hold the support of businessmen and bankers. As late as October he told the American Bankers' Association: "The time is ripe for an alliance of all forces intent upon the business of recovery. In such an alliance will be found business and banking, agriculture and industry, and labor and capital. What an all-American team that would be!" There was little chance of it. In August 1934 conservative businessmen and self-styled Jeffersonian Democrats founded the American Liberty League to fight for free enterprise, state rights, the open shop, and an end to New Deal bureaucracy.

As the congressional elections of 1934 approached, conservatives within the Liberty League and without campaigned against the New Deal on the grounds that it was destroying the Constitution and driving the country toward

bankruptcy. All they succeeded in doing was to drive the dispossessed millions closer to the New Deal. Instead of losing ground to the Republican party—which would have been normal in a midterm election—the Democrats gained an additional ten seats in the Senate and also in the House.

Throughout the nation leaders arose who promised much to those despairing people whom the New Deal had not yet rescued. An elderly physician in California, Dr. Francis E. Townsend, attracted a following of 5 million destitute old people with his plan to obtain a federal pension of $200 per month for everyone over sixty. This would have cost nearly half the national income. The Townsendites claimed, however, that since the pensions would have had to be spent within the month, "the velocity of money" would have ended the depression. The immediate realities of the movement were that its promoters raised nearly a million dollars in two years and commanded a formidable bloc of votes.

Among restless people in Northern cities, Father Charles Coughlin's politico-religious broadcasts attracted a wide following. Starting with a mixture of Papal encyclicals and Populism, he at first supported, then went far beyond, Roosevelt. Coughlin advocated silver inflation and nationalization of banks, utilities, and natural resources. Ultimately in 1938 he founded the antidemocratic, anti-Semitic Christian Front. In January 1935 he was able to demonstrate his power by inspiring an avalanche of letters and telegrams to senators protesting against the World Court. His program was vague, but the discontent he was able to tap was concrete.

From the South, Senator Huey P. Long of Louisiana succeeded in launching a far more telling assault upon the New Deal. A skillful politician, he built a powerful organization in Louisiana and a rapidly growing following that spilled out first into neighboring states, then by 1935 into the Middle West, the Pacific Coast, and indeed every part of the country. Within Louisiana, he had delighted his poverty-stricken supporters by immobilizing their traditional enemies through his strong-armed techniques. Within the state, he had built bridges, roads, hospitals, and a modern educational system. It was an era of dictators in Europe, and it was easy to assail the self-styled Louisiana Kingfish with ambitions to be a Fuehrer, although his techniques were the time-honored ones of the American political boss. Ambitious to become President, he lured the masses by offering them more than Roosevelt. His "Share Our Wealth" program promised through confiscatory taxes on great fortunes to provide every family with what in those depression years seemed in itself a fortune: an income of $2,500 per year and a homestead worth $5,000. Even in Iowa, farmers guffawed when he called the Secretary of Agriculture "Lord Corn Wallace." The New Dealers' political tactician, Postmaster General James A. Farley, estimated in the spring of 1935 that Long could poll 3 or 4 million votes on a third-party ticket and possibly could throw the 1936 election to the Republicans.

The "thunder from the left" was so ominous early in 1935 that many despairing New Dealers, chafing at Roosevelt's apparent inertia, predicted defeat in 1936. Roosevelt, who never liked to explain his tactics, remarked confidentially that he had no intention of engaging in public debate with the leaders of the "lunatic fringe." Rather, he quietly went about stealing their thunder with the reform programs the New Dealers had long been planning.

## The Workers' Welfare

Frances Perkins, the first woman cabinet member, had accepted the office of labor secretary only with Roosevelt's pledge that he would support a social-security program. For several years, she and a group of New Dealers sought to win converts in the cabinet, in Congress, and throughout the country to their view that social insurance would not only aid the unemployed but also help prevent future depressions.

The Social Security Act of 1935 provided two types of assistance for the aged. Those who were destitute could receive federal aid up to $15 per month, depending upon the matching sums which the states provided. Those who were working could receive upon retirement annuities provided from taxes upon their earnings and their employer's payroll. The 1935 law specified

payments, to begin in 1942, ranging from $10 to $85 per month, and excluded wide categories of workers from the program—but it was a beginning. The act also provided for unemployment insurance, aid for the blind and crippled, and assistance for dependent mothers and children, all such funds to be administered by the states in keeping with minimum federal standards. A Social Security Board supervised the entire system.

Social security could not immediately help those already unemployed in 1935; to aid them, Congress in April voted $5 billion to supplant direct relief with the Works Progress Administration. Work relief was more expensive but was essential to prevent the moral erosion, and if possible to save the skills, of the unemployed. The WPA under Harry Hopkins did much to "help men keep their chins up and their hands in." It enrolled an average of 2.1 million workers between 1935 and 1941 on a wide variety of projects. Since the WPA workers were, theoretically at least, the least employable segment of the working force, and since almost all WPA money went for wages rather than tools and materials, its undertakings could not compare in efficiency with private construction projects. Many people tended to forget this and regard WPA as a politically inspired paradise for loafers. Nevertheless, WPA built nearly 600 airports and built or rebuilt 110,000 public buildings, more than a half-million miles of roads and streets, over 100,000 bridges, a half-million sewers, and over a million privies. In the realm of art, music, and the theater it gave opportunities to a remarkable proportion of the nation's talented people; its writers, for example, produced a useful set of state guidebooks.

The National Youth Administration, established in June 1935, as a sort of "junior WPA," aided young people between sixteen and twenty-five, seven-eighths of whom received student aid in schools and colleges.

Meanwhile, improved living quarters were being provided for working-class families. From the outset in June 1933, the Public Works Administration (PWA—not the same as WPA), through an Emergency Housing Division, began federal sponsorship of public housing. It cleared

**Workers Balloting at a National Labor Relations Board Election, Ford Plant   1941**

Congress authorized the National Labor Relations Board to hold elections in plants to determine the employees' choice of collective-bargaining representatives. By secret ballot they could designate the union of their choice or vote "No union." The lists of eligible voters were compiled from the payrolls of a few weeks preceding. The elections, however, were decided by a majority of those voting rather than by a majority of those eligible because employers sometimes frightened away from the polls half or more of the eligible employees. (Library of Congress)

some of the nation's most notorious slum blocks, replacing them with about fifty developments containing almost 22,000 family units. The rent was an average of $26 per month, too high during these years for many previous slum dwellers to meet. Congress in 1937 finally passed Senator Wagner's bill creating the United States Housing Authority, which with $500 million (later in 1941 increased to $1.6 billion) took over and expanded the housing program to 511 projects with 161,000 units intended for the truly poor. Almost one-third of the units went to Negroes— one of the largest pieces of federal aid they had ever received.

## Encouraging Unions

For those fortunate enough to be employed, Roosevelt preferred a paternalistic program of wages-and-hours guarantees and social security benefits. Union leaders wanted to use collective bargaining to gain these advantages for their workers, so they would look to the unions, not to the government.

Labor leaders had gained much of what they wanted just before the advent of the New Deal, with the passage in 1932 of the Norris-LaGuardia Act. This prohibited the courts from issuing injunctions against most ordinary collective-bar-

gaining practices, and it made unenforceable
any "yellow-dog contracts"—pledges from employees that they would not join unions. The
Norris-LaGuardia Act stopped federal courts
from interfering on behalf of employers in
struggles with employees. It left management
and the unions free to bring economic pressure
upon each other as best they could in collective-
bargaining procedures.

In the depression years, however, employers
were usually stronger than unions. Besides,
strikes could interfere with economic recovery.
Hence in 1933 Section 7a of the National Industrial Recovery Act affirmed the right of labor to
bargain collectively, and led to the establishment
of a government agency—the National Labor
Board—to settle disputes arising under Section
7a. The relatively weak board was at first favorable to employers.

While Roosevelt had always maintained cordial relations with labor leaders, he was little
inclined to give them firm collective-bargaining
guarantees in place of the weak Section 7a in the
Nation Industrial Recovery Act. Congress, under
the leadership of Senator Robert F. Wagner, felt
differently. In May 1935 the Senate passed
Wagner's bill providing strong government protection for the unions. Roosevelt, bowing to the
inevitable, signed the measure. What he had reluctantly accepted became one of the mainstays
of the New Deal. The Wagner Act, passed at a
time when unions were relatively weak, outlawed a number of the "unfair practices" by
which management had been bludgeoning them,
and created a powerful National Labor Relations
Board to police the employers. Militant labor
thus obtained the governmental backing essential to a drive to unionize the great mass-production industries.

Even before the adoption of the Wagner Act,
union membership had risen from a depression
low of less than 3 million to 4.2 million. A group
of leaders of industrial unions (which offered
membership to everyone within an industry) had
chafed over the conservatism of the craft unions
(which took in only those working at a given
trade). In 1934 men like the head of the United
Mine Workers, John L. Lewis, and the leaders
of the two great garment unions, Sidney Hillman
of the Amalgamated Clothing Workers and

### The Wagner Act [1935]

The National Labor Relations Act
made it unlawful for employers to
engage in the following unfair labor
practices:

1. To interfere with employees in
their right to self-organization, to
form, join, or assist labor organizations, to bargain collectively through
representatives of their own choosing,
and to engage in concerted activities,
for the purpose of collective bargaining or other mutual aid or protection.

2. To dominate or interfere with
the formation or administration of any
labor organization or contribute financial or other support to it.

3. By discrimination in regard to
hire or tenure of employment or any
term or condition of employment to
encourage or discourage membership
in any labor organization.

4. To discharge or otherwise discriminate against any employee because he has filed charges or given
testimony under this Act.

5. To refuse to bargain collectively
with the representatives of his employees duly chosen pursuant to other
provisions in the Act.

David Dubinsky of the International Ladies'
Garment Workers, had forced President William
Green of the AFL and the craft unionists to
agree to charter new industrial unions in the big
unorganized industries.

In 1935 organization of these industries began. It led to violent opposition not only from
the corporations but also from the AFL craft
unions, which feared they would be submerged
by the new giant unions. Jurisdictional fights led
to a schism between the AFL leadership and the
industrial unionists, who formed a Committee
for Industrial Organization (within the AFL) in
November 1935. Industrial warfare followed, as
both the AFL and the CIO mounted great rival
organizational drives.

President Roosevelt and a few industrial leaders favored industrial unionism. Gerald Swope of General Electric told Roosevelt that his company could not conceivably negotiate with a large number of craft unions but might find advantages in contracting with a single industrial union. Generally, however, in the spring of 1936 the point was still far off when big business could see advantages in big labor. Vigorous young organizers had to battle it out, often by physical force, with "loyal" strong-arm squads, occasionally with the police, and sometimes with rival organizers. The great difference between this and earlier periods of labor warfare was the aid the federal government provided unions through the National Labor Relations Board.

Through 1936 the United Automobile Workers gained recruits despite vigorous company opposition. There was good reason, for in 1934, at about the time the organizing drive began, nearly half of the auto workers were receiving less than $1,000 per year. General Motors alone, in an effort to keep down union organization, spent almost $1 million on private detectives between 1934 and 1936. In the first two months of 1937, workers closed seventeen General Motors plants through the new device of the sitdown strike, the workers staying by their machinery inside the plants. General Motors soon recognized the UAW, and other automobile companies gradually did the same. Rubber and other industries were similarly organized. Newspapers saw in the sit-down strikes a menace to private property, and much of the public became thoroughly alarmed.

Bloody warfare in the steel industry heightened the alarm. In 1936 the CIO voted a $500,-000 fund to organize the industry and began its great onslaught, winning tens of thousands of workers from company unions. United States Steel chose to capitulate rather than face a long strike just as prosperity seemed to be returning. In March 1937, to the amazement of the nation, one of the company's subsidiaries signed a contract with the Steel Workers' Organizing Committee. For the first time, "Big Steel" was unionized. But three of the "Little Steel" companies, under the leadership of Tom Girdler of Republic Steel, resisted furiously. At the Republic plant in South Chicago on Memorial Day 1937, the police killed ten strikers. Republic

Steel, according to the prolabor La Follette committee, was the largest purchaser of tear gas and sickening gas in the United States; Youngstown Sheet and Tube Company owned an arsenal of over a thousand weapons. The Republic strikers lost completely, to the relief of middle-class Americans who, like the newspapers they read, blamed the strife upon the unions and the New Deal.

Yet organized labor continued to grow. By 1941 union membership totaled about 9.5 million.

## More for Farmers

In January 1936 the Supreme Court held that it was unconstitutional for the AAA to regulate farm production or to impose a tax for such a purpose. Congress hastily passed a law (the Soil Conservation and Domestic Allotment Act) to meet the Court's objections and yet continue the crop-reduction effort. Under the new law, Congress appropriated money to pay farmers for conserving the soil by leaving part of their land uncultivated. The law provided that landlords must share with their tenants and sharecroppers the payments for withdrawing land from production. Nevertheless, in 1937, while the average plantation operator was grossing $8,328, of which $833 came from the soil conservation program, the average tenant family received only $385, of which $27 came from the government.

Agricultural interests pressed for a new AAA to cope with an enormous threatened surplus. The end of the drought, increased mechanization, and other improvements like the rapid spread of hybrid corn in the Middle West outmoded the crop controls of the 1936 legislation. The Agricultural Adjustment Act of 1938—the "second AAA"—provided a number of devices to cut back production: soil conservation payments, marketing quotas, export subsidies, and crop loans. Surpluses of five nonperishable commodities upon which farmers received federal loans would be stored under government seal until needed in lean years, thus creating what Secretary Wallace termed an "ever normal granary." The surpluses so stored were to be of vital aid in feeding allies during the war years. The 1938 act also established a Surplus Market-

**Father and Sons Walking in the Face of a Dust Storm, Cimarron County, Oklahoma**

Beginning late in 1933, years of extreme drought and high winds further afflicted the depression-plagued farmers of the Great Plains. The worst-hit area, centering around the panhandles of Texas and Oklahoma, eastern Colorado and New Mexico, and western Kansas, came to be known as the "Dust Bowl." "Only those who have been caught out in a 'black blizzard' can have more than a faint conception of its terrors," Lawrence Svobida, a Kansas wheat farmer, has written. "The dust begins to blow with only a slight breeze. . . . The wind increases its velocity until it is blowing at forty to fifty miles an hour. Soon everything is moving—the land is blowing, both farm land and pasture alike. The fine dirt is sweeping along at express-train speed, and when the very sun is blotted out, visibility is reduced to some fifty feet; or perhaps you cannot see at all, because the dust has blinded you and even goggles are useless to prevent the fine particles from sifting into your eyes."—Lawrence Svobida, *An Empire of Dust* (Caldwell, Idaho: The Caxton Printers, 1940). (Library of Congress)

ing Administration to channel surpluses to needy persons and provide food for school lunches.

To improve the condition of the poorer farmers, those on submarginal soil, the government undertook to resettle them on better land. The Resettlement Administration (1935) and its successor, the Farm Security Administration (1937), made short-term loans for rehabilitation and long-term loans for purchasing farms but succeeded in moving only a few thousand farm families.

The more fortunate farmers were benefited by the Rural Electrification Administration, which was established in 1935 to extend power lines to farms through cooperatives. Since its activities also stimulated private power companies to extend into the country, it was effective both directly and indirectly. Power lines had reached only 4 per cent of the farms in 1925; they reached 25 per cent by 1940.

## Less for Big Business

After the NRA had been declared unconstitutional, parts of the law were reenacted piecemeal and with alterations to form a "little NRA." As early as February 1935, in response to the Supreme Court invalidation of legislation to prevent the overproduction of oil, Congress passed the Connally Act prohibiting the shipment of "hot oil" (oil produced in excess of state limitations) in interstate commerce. The Guffey Act of August 1935 virtually reenacted the NRA bituminous-coal code, fixing prices, limiting production, and protecting labor. When the Supreme Court threw out the new coal-control law in 1936, Congress passed the second Guffey Act of 1937. Roosevelt feared a wages-and-hours law would be unconstitutional, but he signed the Walsh-Healey Act of August 1936, setting minimum wages and maximum hours for work done on federal contracts. In order to protect small retailers, the Robinson-Patman Act of 1936 prohibited wholesalers or manufacturers from giving preferential discounts or rebates to chain stores or other large buyers; the Miller-Tydings Act of 1937 fortified state "fair trade" price-fixing laws.

As yet, Roosevelt did not resort to vigorous use of the antitrust laws, but he advocated tightening the regulation of big business. In March 1935 he recommended passage of an act to prohibit after five years the pyramiding of utility holding companies, which had led to flagrant abuses in the 1920s. In the 1930s thirteen companies still controlled three-fourths of the nation's electric power. They fought desperately through the summer of 1935 against what they viewed as a threatened "death sentence." One company alone spent $700,000 lobbying against the measure. In the Holding Company Act of 1935, the companies gained a partial victory; it permitted two strata of holding companies above the operating companies.

Between 1935 and 1940 Congress passed a series of other laws stiffening federal regulation. These strengthened the Federal Power Commission, brought trucks and carriers on inland waterways under the supervision of the Interstate Commerce Commission, created a new Maritime Commission to subsidize and regulate a merchant fleet, and set up a Civil Aeronautics Authority (later Board) to regulate airlines.

One of the most effective ways to regulate was to tax, and in 1935 Roosevelt proposed democratizing the federal tax structure by placing far higher levies upon big corporations and wealthy people. He pointed out that a person receiving $6,000 per year paid twice as high a tax as one receiving $4,000, yet the tax upon a $5 million income was only about five times as high as on $1 million. Conservative newspapers immediately attacked this proposal as a "soak the rich" tax scheme, but it passed Congress. It wiped away the last vestiges of Secretary Mellon's influence on tax policy, as it established the highest peacetime rates in history at the top: a maximum 75 per cent income tax, 70 per cent estate tax, and 15 per cent corporate income tax. It was an important step toward the redistribution of American income.

Big business seemed to have grown bigger through New Deal inadvertence. The NRA relaxation of the antitrust laws had given it an opportunity to thrive at the expense of smaller business. In the two years after the end of the codes, the Attorney General initiated even fewer antitrust suits than during the NRA period.

Then, in April 1938, the President sent Congress a message vehemently denouncing the unjustifiable concentration of economic power. Less than 5 per cent of all corporations in 1935 owned 87 per cent of all the assets, he declared. This was leading to such a serious maldistribution of income, he pointed out, that in 1935–1936 the upper 1.5 per cent of the population had a share of the national income as great as the 47 per cent at the bottom—and these had less than $1,000 per year per family. The remedy, Roosevelt proposed, was to study economic concentration and enact more modern antitrust laws to cope with the newer techniques of monopoly. In response, Congress established the Temporary National Economic Committee under the chairmanship of Senator O'Mahoney. It conducted lengthy public hearings and published thirty-nine volumes of reports and forty-three scientific monographs by the end of 1941. By that time the national attention was entirely engrossed elsewhere; legislation never followed.

Meanwhile, Roosevelt launched an immediate trust-busting program through Thurman Arnold, whom he appointed head of the Antitrust Division of the Department of Justice. Arnold, who felt there was nothing wrong with existing legislation, made new and sophisticated use of the Sherman and Clayton acts as he undertook 215 major investigations and 92 test cases.

## THE LIMITS OF REFORM

In 1936 Roosevelt was at the zenith of his popularity and power. But soon he was to run into stronger political opposition than ever, and by 1938 he was to turn his attention from domestic reform to foreign policy and military defense.

### Mandate From the People

Roosevelt's vigorous reform program, enacted in its main outlines by 1936, made him a sure winner in the election of that year. Many millions felt that their personal lot had been improved by the New Deal. The violent attacks upon it from the right, and the cries of anguish over such measures as the "soak the rich" taxes, convinced them even more that Roosevelt was their friend. Despite the misgivings of many conservatives within the party, the Democratic convention in 1936 renominated him by acclamation. His control was so complete that he even obtained abrogation of the two-thirds rule

through which minorities had often hamstrung conventions.

As for the Republicans, they nominated their strongest candidate. Ignoring former President Hoover and the right wing, which was crying calamity, they chose a one-time Bull Mooser who had never strayed far from the 1912 Progressive position. This was the competent governor of Kansas, Alf M. Landon. His running mate was another Bull Mooser who had moved well to the right, the Chicago publisher Frank Knox. The Republican platform promised to do most of what the New Deal was undertaking— but more competently, constitutionally, and without running a deficit. Landon's dry voice could not match Roosevelt's radio eloquence, and Landon was further handicapped because, though he was a moderate, he had to try to hold the militant Republican right.

The election demonstrated the extent to which the New Deal depended upon a coalition of farmers, union men, and the poor. The unions were the heaviest Democratic campaign contributors, providing $1 million. Negroes switched en masse from the party of Lincoln to that of Roosevelt. The "lunatic fringe" coalition against

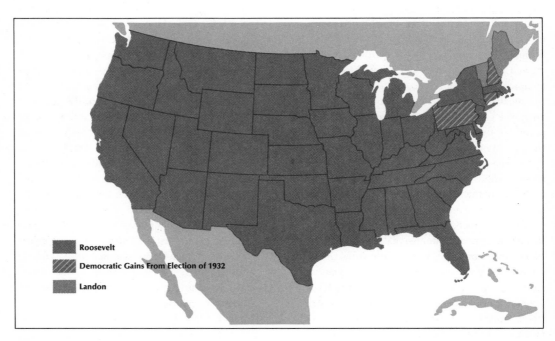

Election of 1936

**President Roosevelt's Second Inaugural Address [January 20, 1937]**

*I see a great nation, upon a great continent, blessed with a great wealth of natural resources. . . . I see a United States which can demonstrate that, under democratic methods of government, national wealth can be translated into a spreading volume of human comforts hitherto unknown, and the lowest standard of living can be raised far above the level of mere subsistence.*

*But here is the challenge to our democracy: In this nation I see tens of millions of its citizens—a substantial part of its whole population—who at this very moment are denied the greater part of what the lowest standards of today call the necessities of life.*

*I see millions of families trying to live on incomes so meager that the pall of family disaster hangs over them day by day.*

*I see millions whose daily lives in city and on farm continue under conditions labeled indecent by a so-called polite society half a century ago.*

*I see millions denied education, recreation, and the opportunity to better their lot and the lot of their children.*

*I see millions lacking the means to buy the products of farm and factory and by their poverty denying work and productiveness to many other millions.*

*I see one-third of a nation ill-housed, ill-clad, ill-nourished.*

Roosevelt stirred hardly a ripple. Huey Long had been assassinated the year before; the Union party candidate was "Liberty Bell" William Lemke—who was "cracked," said wiseacres. His ticket polled only 890,000 votes; the Socialists, 190,000; the Communists, under 80,000.

A preelection postal card poll by the *Literary Digest* had indicated that Landon would win by a big margin. How could it be so wrong? The names and addresses of those polled were taken from old telephone directories. A majority of people who could afford telephones and had not been forced to move favored Landon. In the election he received 16,680,000 popular votes, compared with 27,477,000 for Roosevelt, and got the electoral votes of only Maine and Vermont.

In the campaign Roosevelt had challenged his right-wing opponents—"economic royalists," he called them—and now he had not only received an overwhelming endorsement for himself but he had carried with him many congressmen pledged to his support. Nevertheless, those economic royalists would still have the upper hand so long as the Supreme Court continued to check New Deal laws. He felt he had a mandate from the people to do something about the obstructionist Court.

## Storm Over the Court

Foes of the Coal Act, the Holding Company Act, the National Labor Relations Act, and the Social Security Act were openly flouting these laws, confident that the Supreme Court would disallow them as it had already done the NRA and the first AAA. The Court, through its narrow interpretation of the federal power over commerce and taxation, and its broad interpretation of freedom of contract in the Fourteenth Amendment, seemed to have created an economic no man's land within which neither the federal nor the state governments could act.

Critics of the Court had been urging passage of some sort of constitutional amendment to provide the federal government with more extensive economic powers. Roosevelt's opinion (which subsequent Supreme Court decisions were to sustain) was that the Constitution granted adequate powers. All that was wrong was the Court's antiquated interpretation, he felt, but the four or five justices firmly opposed to the New Deal enjoyed excellent health and showed no signs of resigning. Consequently Roosevelt decided to propose adding to the Supreme Court—and to lower federal courts— new justices (presumably sharing his viewpoint) to match superannuated ones.

At this point Roosevelt's political sixth sense

deserted him and, instead of presenting his proposal frankly and firmly in terms of its economic implications, he enclosed it in a larger scheme. Without informing congressional leaders in advance, in February 1937 he sent a surprise message proposing a needed general overhauling of the federal court system and the appointment of as many as six new Supreme Court justices. His nearest approach to frankness was a statement that the addition of younger blood would revitalize the courts and help them meet the needs and facts of an ever-changing world.

There was no real question about the constitutionality of Roosevelt's proposal, since Congress had from time to time changed the number of justices on the Supreme Court. Nevertheless, the plan aroused a great furor throughout the country. Many thoughtful people who had supported Roosevelt in 1936 heeded the warning of conservatives that, through such constitutional shortcuts, dictators came into power. Within Congress, the controversy cut across party lines. Some Democrats fought against the "packing" of the Court, while the Republican progressive Senator Robert M. La Follette, Jr., supported the President. La Follette declared that the Court had already been "packed" for years "in the cause of Reaction and Laissez-Faire."

Some of the old-line Democratic leaders, especially from the South, had gone along with the New Deal mainly because of party loyalty and pressure from their constituents. Now that much of the electorate was turning against the administration, these conservatives broke loose. They joined with the bulk of the Republicans to form a new conservative coalition in Congress. Roosevelt fought back by using every device of party discipline to round up votes in Congress. He might have succeeded in obtaining at least a compromise measure, had not the Supreme Court itself eliminated the necessity for one.

The justices—including Louis D. Brandeis, the oldest and most liberal—had been indignant over charges that they were too old to handle the business of the Court. Chief Justice Charles Evans Hughes even wrote a letter insisting that they were not falling behind in their work. Four of them, far to the right, were of no disposition to take a broader view of the Constitution.

Three of them took a more progressive if not a New Deal view. Chief Justice Hughes on occasion voted with them, while Justice Owen J. Roberts more often voted with the conservative four.

Just before the President sent his court plan to Congress, Roberts joined with Hughes and the three more liberal justices in the case of *West Coast Hotel* v. *Parrish* to validate, by a 5-to-4 decision, a state minimum-wage law. This reversed a 5-to-4 decision of the previous year invalidating a similar law. "You may have saved the country," Hughes jubilantly told Roberts. The decision was announced on March 29, 1937. Two weeks later, the Court, again 5-to-4, upheld the Wagner Act, and in May, the Social Security Act. Since there no longer seemed to be any pressing need for judicial reform, the new conservative alliance in Congress easily dealt Roosevelt a personal defeat by voting down his court plan. At the same time, the shift of the Supreme Court's interpretation of the Constitution was a significant victory for Roosevelt and the New Deal.

Almost at once the older justices began retiring, and Roosevelt replaced them one by one with his appointees. In the next decade the Roosevelt Court rewrote large sections of constitutional law. The new justices sharply divided among themselves, but usually upon technical matters. In the main they interpreted the commerce and tax clauses so broadly and the Fourteenth Amendment so narrowly that there remained few restrictions upon economic regulation by either the federal or the state governments. For several years the judges tended to restrict governments in their interference with organized labor, but by the end of a decade, labor too was subject to firm restraints. Thus almost all constitutional impediments to government regulation of the economic system were removed.

### Recovery and Recession

A sharp recession developed in the fall of 1937. It came just as many economists were fearing than an inflationary boom might get out of hand. There had been a remarkable recovery. The national income, which had dropped from $82 billion in 1929 to $40 billion in 1932, was back

# Where Historians Disagree

## The Nature of the New Deal

Unlike some of the debates among historians over foreign policy in the twentieth century, there have been no clear-cut arguments over two contrasting points of view toward the New Deal. Historians were writing tentatively about the New Deal before the end of 1933 and have been writing about it at great length ever since. There was little real discussion over whether the New Deal represented an evolutionary or revolutionary development, since the consensus was that it had evolved out of the progressive movement. Arthur Link, the biographer of Wilson, agrees with the leading brain truster, Raymond Moley, that the New Deal was no more than the enactment of an enlarged progressive program. Richard Kirkendall has marshaled much of the vast literature on the New Deal in support of a similar contention, that the New Deal was no watershed in American history.

There was an outpouring of contemporary popular attacks upon the New Deal, but no other scholar went so far as Edgar Eugene Robinson in *The Roosevelt Leadership, 1933–1945* (1955). He saw in the program a sharp, disastrous break with the past: "Within the nation in these twelve years was developed a distrust of the basic democracy of the republic, as well as a social philosophy that included within its practices, if not in its pronouncements, many of the primary leveling objectives of communism. A whole generation of youth was cut off from the past by an eloquent proponent of revolutionary change." Other scholars, including Richard Hofstadter and Arthur Schlesinger, Jr., saw in the New Deal a break with the past, a movement beyond progressivism, but hailed the changes as salutary. Schlesinger's monumental study, *The Age of Roosevelt* (1957–     ), takes almost the reverse view of Robinson's, holding the Republican "old order" of the 1920s to have been bankrupt in its economic leadership. Schlesinger, while critical in detail, is in general highly favorable to the New Deal as offering a liberal, humane governmental solution to the problem of maintaining balance in an intricate industrial civilization. In *Roosevelt: The Lion and the Fox* (1956), James Mac-Gregor Burns, though generally favorable toward Roosevelt, takes him to task for not having been more Keynesian. Through heavy spending, Burns contends, Roosevelt could have ended the depression without raising the troublesome constitutional questions that caused him to run afoul of the Supreme Court.

Recent writings on Roosevelt and the New Deal tend to be more critical of the achievements of the man and the program; at the end of the sixties, few younger historians are ready to view the New Deal as being nearly as daring, innovative, or decisive as it had seemed to contemporaries.

up to nearly $72 billion. Yet there were still 7.5 million unemployed and nearly 4.5 million families on relief. And there had been no upsurge of capital investment and business expansion as in the 1920s.

Recovery had come because of the enormous sums spent on work relief, the gradual momentum of the public works program, the loans to farmers, and the payment in 1936 (over Roosevelt's veto) of the veterans' bonus. All this government spending had powerfully stimulated the economy. Out of this experience emerged new economic theories, centering upon the concept that the government could help pull the nation out of a depression by liberal expenditures. As a corollary, the government could help curb inflationary booms by means of restrictive policies. These new economic theories came to be known as Keynesianism, after the famed British economist John Maynard Keynes.

In 1937 Roosevelt as much as his Republican opponents abhorred a deficit and worried about the mounting national debt, which had risen to $30 billion. He actually feared another disastrous crash like that of 1929. Acting in terms of the older economics, he had the Federal Reserve tighten credit even though the upswing had been sound rather than speculative. More important, he tried to balance the budget by drastically reducing government spending. Between January and August, 1937, he cut the WPA in half, sending 1.5 million workers on unpaid "vacation."

And since, with the ending of the drought, a huge farm surplus was again imminent, produce prices fell sharply. The fragile new boom collapsed and sent the economy plummeting. The index of production dropped from 117 in August 1937 to 76 in May 1938; 4 million additional workers were thrown out of employment. It seemed like 1932 all over again.

In October 1937 the President called Congress into special session to renew heavy public spending and to reform the "selfish interests" he blamed for the recession. Congress passed an emergency appropriation of $5 billion; the public works and work relief programs once again poured these large sums into the economy, and by June 1938 recovery was under way. The "spending school" had scored a point, and the

## The New Deal: Relief, Recovery, and Reform [1933–1938]

In their New Deal program, President Roosevelt and his advisers sought to achieve three objectives at once: to provide relief for those suffering from the depression, to bring about the recovery of business and agriculture, and to make reforms in the economic system. Not all the measures can be separated and put in neat categories according to the immediate objectives of relief and recovery and the long-range objective of reform; some measures were intended to accomplish more than one of these aims. Nevertheless, the following lists may facilitate an understanding of the complex and multifarious legislation of the period:

### Relief and Recovery

Emergency Banking Act, 1933
Economy Act, 1933
Civilian Conservation Corps, 1933
Federal Emergency Relief Administration, 1933
Civil Works Administration, 1933
Public Works Administration, 1933
National Recovery Administration, 1933
Agricultural Adjustment Administration, 1933
Farm Credit Administration, 1933
Federal Housing Administration, 1934
Works Progress Administration, 1935

### Reform

Tennessee Valley Authority, 1933
Federal Securities Act, 1933
Glass-Steagall Act, 1933
Gold Reserve Act, 1934
Reciprocal Trade Agreements Act, 1934
Public Utilities Holding Company Act, 1935
Social Security Act, 1935
National Labor Relations Act, 1935
Soil Conservation and Domestic Allotment Act, 1936
National Housing Act, 1937
Farm Security Administration, 1937
Fair Labor Standards Act, 1938

government seemed to have assumed a new role in warding off threatened economic disaster.

Thus the New Deal entered into its final stage of reform, combining what was as new as Keynesianism with what was as old as progressivism. The trend had been toward big business, and now big government had come with the active intervention of the New Deal in so many aspects of the economy. The number of civilian government employees swelled from 588,000 in 1931 to 1,370,000 in 1941.

Since questions of constitutionality no longer seriously interfered after the changes in the Supreme Court, New Dealers fought the Fair Labor Standards Act through Congress in 1938. This established a minimum wage of 25 cents an hour (to be raised gradually to 40 cents by 1945) and a maximum work week of forty-four hours (to be lowered to forty) for most laborers, excepting agricultural, domestic, and maritime workers. It also forbade employment of children under sixteen in most areas except agriculture. Low though these standards were, they raised the pay of 300,000 workers and shortened the work week for 1.3 million. In subsequent years the standards were raised repeatedly, and the scope of the law was broadened to include additional categories of workers.

Roosevelt worried about the strong negative power the conservative coalition was developing in Congress. In many states, the Democratic party was under the leadership of conservatives. Postmaster-General Farley, in charge of patronage, had done little to aid New Dealers who tried to challenge this leadership. In 1938 Roosevelt intervened in several primaries, mostly in the South, to try to defeat powerful conservative Democrats who headed congressional committees. Since these men had strong organizations behind them, and the New Deal candidates were relatively unknown, the conservatives won in almost every contest. The 1938 elections reflected the degree to which the prestige of Roosevelt and the New Deal were waning. The Republicans gained eighty seats in the House and seven in the Senate. Together with the conservative Democrats, the Republicans could dominate Congress.

By the end of 1938 the New Deal was close to its limits. The threat of a second world war was beginning to overshadow even the most critical domestic problems. The President could drive Congress with its Southern committee chairmen in the direction of strong defense legislation and a vigorous foreign policy only if he conciliated them by abandoning reform.

## CULTURE IN THE DEPRESSION

Both the depression and the government's efforts to combat it left a mark on the cultural life of the time. Unemployment left many people with unaccustomed leisure, which they used either to protest against or to escape from unpleasant realities. The federal government became a patron and promoter of culture on a scale it had never attempted before.

### Expression and Escape

Even before the establishment of the Federal Art Project, which eventually enrolled 5,000 persons, the government had aided artists through an earlier relief project and the commissioning of extensive murals for new public buildings. Some of these artists expressed leftist themes comparable to those of the highly popular Mexican muralists. Many turned their attention, sometimes satirically, to the American scene. This was the heyday of Grant Wood, with his patterned Iowa landscapes and austere rural portraits, and of Thomas Hart Benton, who with dramatic sympathy portrayed sharecroppers and Negroes. In sculpture, responding to the new government aid and the resurgent nationalism, Gutzon Borglum finished the enormous heads of Washington, Jefferson, Lincoln, and Theodore Roosevelt which were carved on a rocky mountainside in the Black Hills. Altogether, thousands of artists and sculptors worked during the depression years; never before had America possessed so many who were competent and promising.

Appreciation of the arts took a strong upturn, partly through art classes sponsored by the Federal Art Project, partly through the opening of new art museums. In 1941, the National Art Gallery in Washington opened, displaying collections of European art valued at $35 million, the gift of Andrew W. Mellon. Samuel H. Kress

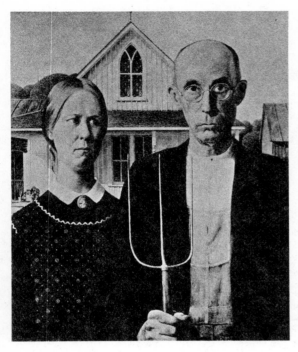

**"American Gothic" by Grant Wood**

Wood brought back to Cedar Rapids, Iowa, the bright colors and stylized forms with which he had experimented during his art studies in Paris. His careful, sympathetic interpretation of the Iowa countryside and people was easy for his generation to understand and won him wide acclaim during the 1930s. His "American Gothic" was the most popular painting at the Chicago Century of Progress Exposition of 1933. The art historian Oliver W. Larkin has written: "If his faces looked rather stony and his rounded hills monotonous and hard, Iowans explained that these qualities were indigenous ones in a country where a hen's shadow at noon fell sharp as a cut silhouette on the barnyard." (The Art Institute of Chicago)

added 400 Italian paintings. More people than ever before visited galleries and bought reproductions of the old masters and of the French impressionists, especially Vincent Van Gogh.

Although jazz more than held its own, interest in classical music increased. The Federal Music Project employed 15,000 persons. They brought concerts to 100 million people and gave free music lessons to over a half-million pupils, most of whom could have afforded neither concerts nor lessons. Much of the music they played was that of American composers, such as Roy Harris'

Third Symphony, and Aaron Copland's *Music for the Theatre*. Through new high-quality radio receivers and recordings, many additional millions listened to fine music, especially the symphony broadcasts conducted by Arturo Toscanini and the Metropolitan Opera performances. In 1940 listeners contributed over $300,000 to help "save the Met." Many millions more mourned the death in 1937 of young George Gershwin, composer of *Porgy and Bess* and *Rhapsody in Blue*. To the great mass of Americans, music still meant either sweet popular songs played by bands like Guy Lombardo's, or jazz like Benny Goodman's which came surging back into favor in 1934.

After depression and competition from motion pictures had thrown most actors and old vaudeville performers out of employment, the Federal Theater Project found employment for 12,500 of them. It brought performances to millions who had never previously seen a stage production. Some of these were highly successful as entertainment, some were of an advanced experimental nature, and some were so far to the left that they kindled the wrath of Congress, which killed the project in 1939. Many of the Broadway playwrights, impervious to congressional hostility, also took a critical look at social problems, as did Lillian Hellman in *The Little Foxes*. Robert E. Sherwood, who illustrated another trend, stopped writing light comedies and dramatized the impotence of the intellectual (*The Petrified Forest*, 1936) and the menace of war (*Idiot's Delight*, 1936). Later, in the pressure of world events, he reversed themes, and glorified the intellectual fighting totalitarian aggression (*There Shall Be No Night*, 1940). Meanwhile, Thornton Wilder wrote *Our Town* (1938) and Eugene O'Neill, who in 1936 won a Nobel Prize, labored quietly on a long-continuing cycle of plays.

Novelists likewise divided into those who, like William Faulkner, seemed to be largely unaffected by the era, and others like Ernest Hemingway, who paralleled Sherwood's cycle from 1929 (*A Farewell to Arms*) to 1940 (*For Whom the Bell Tolls*). Thomas Wolfe richly and poetically portrayed the world swirling around him, in his *Of Time and the River* (1935) and his posthumous *You Can't Go Home Again* (1940).

Many other novelists turned out proletarian themes from Marxist molds. John Steinbeck sentimentalized his suffering protagonists in his best-selling novel about the Oklahoman trek to California, *The Grapes of Wrath* (1939). The lure of romantic escape and the bargain of the sheer bulk helped make best-sellers of Hervey Allen's *Anthony Adverse* (1933) and Margaret Mitchell's *Gone With the Wind* (1936).

Reading was one of the most inexpensive pursuits of the depression years, and although libraries suffered from slashed funds, book circulation increased considerably. Depression likewise cut the cost of radios and enlarged the size of audiences. In 1929 12 million families owned radios; by 1940 28 million families, comprising 86 per cent of the population, owned them. This in part explains why Roosevelt, the master of the radio "fireside chat," campaigned so successfully with at least 70 per cent of the metropolitan newspaper circulation opposing him. A radio serial, *Amos and Andy*, was so popular that Huey Long took the name of one of its characters, the Kingfish, as his sobriquet. Motion picture audiences dropped one-third early in the depression, then by 1939 boomed to a yearly box-office average of $25 per family. Like radio serials, motion pictures dispensed mostly escapist themes—because of the vigor of the Catholic-led Legion of Decency, founded in 1934, it was a less sexy escape than in the twenties. Theaters also dispensed two movies rather than one and offered give-aways of a wide variety in order to bolster the box office. As yet, the coming threat to the movies, television, was still in the engineering laboratory—a curiosity exhibited at the New York World's Fair of 1939. It was too expensive for commercial development during the depression.

## Education and the Professions

The two depression factors of lack of funds and excess of leisure also operated in education. It was estimated in 1935 that one-third of the unemployed were young people. Many went to school for lack of an alternative, and high school enrollment increased by one-third between 1929 and 1935. In spite of this, economy-minded chambers of commerce and citizens' commit-

tees led a drive for cuts so deep that they carved out educational sinew along with the fat. Colleges and universities dropped in enrollment until 1935, then more than recuperated but continued to suffer budgetary crises. Vocational education was strongly emphasized on both the high school and the college level. Serious students explored social and economic questions so energetically that frightened civic and patriotic organizations warned that "pinks" were taking over the educational systems.

Alarmists feared pinks were taking over the churches also, for ministers responded as enthusiastically to the new demands for human welfare as they once had responded to the "social gospel." Of 20,000 ministers polled in 1934, nearly one-third favored socialism, and three-fifths, a "drastically reformed capitalism." The main intellectual current among ministers was toward neoorthodoxy. Reinhold Niebuhr, without disavowing political and social liberalism, found powerful psychological pressures driving man toward sin, from which man could be rescued only by faith, that is, submission to God.

Though the depression seriously cut funds for medical research, the thirties were another decade of advance in medical knowledge. Ironically, by 1935, when the American Medical Association was warning that 20 million people were suffering malnutrition or were close to it, highly publicized discoveries in vitamin research were leading the well-fed to consume a variety of vitamin-fortified foods and to swallow vitamin pills in quantities second only to laxatives. Sulfa drugs, typhus vaccine, blood plasma, and the "artificial lung" all came into use. Life expectancy increased from fifty-six years in 1920 to sixty-four in 1940, but malnutrition, illness, and sometimes lack of good medical care wrought a heavy toll during the depression. Army medical examiners rejected almost half of the first 2 million young men Selective Service called up in 1940–1941.

Yet doctors were ill-paid (even in 1929 half of them netted less than $3,000) and were idle much of the time. When some relief units and the Farm Security Administration offered medical aid to the destitute, the demand was overwhelming. Senator Wagner in 1938 introduced a national health bill, but it met stern opposition from the American Medical Association. Voluntary group health and hospitalization plans spread rapidly in some sixty cities and gained 3 million or more subscribers.

While scientists suffered temporary cuts in research funds, university budgets and industrial resources for research were back at a peak level by 1936; federal expenditures, by 1940. Thus the decade was one of increasing scientific investigation. The need for reorganization and reinvigoration of some of the government's scientific agencies led to the creation in 1933 of a Science Advisory Board, which futilely tried to obtain a New Deal for science. In 1935 the National Resources Committee (succeeding several similar planning agencies) took over the problem and prepared a study, *Research—A National Resource* (1940). The way was being prepared for centralized scientific planning in the future.

The thirties were years of marked scientific achievement in both basic and applied research in many fields. A series of discoveries by men of many nationalities opened the way to the possibility of nuclear fission. In 1931 Harold C. Urey of Columbia discovered a heavy isotope of hydrogen—deuterium—which, combined with oxygen atoms, formed heavy water. Bombardment of deuterium atoms by various types of atom smashers brought new knowledge about the nature of the atom, knowledge that could lead to revolutionary applications. Science, a neglected stepchild of the New Deal, was to become the nation's savior in time of war.

# Selected Readings

**Roosevelt and the New Deal** Basil Rauch, *History of the New Deal*° (1944); A. M. Schlesinger, Jr., *The Age of Roosevelt: The Coming of the New Deal*° (1959) and *The Politics of Upheaval*° (1960); W. E. Leuchtenberg, *Franklin D. Roosevelt and the New Deal, 1932–1940*° (1963); Frank Freidel, *Franklin D. Roosevelt: The Triumph* (1956); J. M. Burns, *Roosevelt: The Lion and the Fox*° (1956); R. G. Tugwell, *The Democratic Roosevelt* (1957); Frances Perkins, *The Roosevelt I Knew*° (1946).

**Some New Dealers** J. R. Kearney, *Anna Eleanor Roosevelt: The Evolution of a Reformer* (1968); H. L. Ickes, *The New Democracy* (1934); Thurman Arnold, *The Folklore of Capitalism*° (1937); Raymond Moley, *After Seven Years* (1939); J. M. Blum, *From the Morgenthau Diaries: Years of Crisis, 1928–1938* (1959); J. J. Huthmacher, *Senator Robert F. Wagner and the Rise of Urban Liberalism* (1968); O. L. Graham, *An Encore for Reform*° (1967).

**Relief, Recovery, Reform** S. F. Charles, *Minister of Relief: Harry Hopkins and the Depression* (1963); J. A. Salmond, *The Civilian Conservation Corps, 1933–1942* (1967); Roy Lubove, *The Struggle for Social Security, 1900–1935* (1968); Jesse Jones, *Fifty Billion Dollars* (1951), on the RFC; M. L. Eccles, *Economic Balance and a Balanced Budget* (1940), on spending for recovery; H. S. Johnson, *The Blue Eagle from Egg to Earth* (1935); E. W. Hawley, *The New Deal and the Problem of Monopoly* (1966); D. E. Lilienthal, *TVA: Democracy on the March*° (1953); R. F. de Bedts, *The New Deal's SEC: The Formative Years* (1964); P. K. Conkin, *Tomorrow a New World: The New Deal Community Program* (1959); Richard Polenberg, *Reorganizing Roosevelt's Government* (1966).

**The Farmers** H. A. Wallace, *New Frontiers* (1934); J. L. Shover, *Cornbelt Rebellion: The Farmers' Holiday Association* (1965); C. M. Campbell, *The Farm Bureau and the New Deal* (1962); R. S. Kirkendall, *Social Scientists and Farm Politics in the Age of Roosevelt* (1966); D. E. Conrad, *The Forgotten Farmers: The Story of Sharecroppers in the New Deal* (1965); Sidney Baldwin, *Poverty and Politics: The Rise and Decline of the Farm Security Administration* (1968).

**The Unions** Irving Bernstein, *New Deal Collective Bargaining Policy* (1950); H. A. Millis and E. C. Brown, *From the Wagner Act to Taft-Hartley* (1950); Herbert Harris, *Labor's Civil War* (1940); Walter Galenson, *The CIO Chal-*

lenge to the AFL (1960); J. S. Auerbach, *Labor and Liberty: The La Follette Committee and the New Deal* (1966).

**Opposition From Left and Right** D. R. McCoy, *Angry Voices: Left-of-Center Politics in the New Deal Era* (1958) and *Landon of Kansas* (1966); T. H. Williams, *Huey Long* (1969); C. J. Tull, *Father Coughlin and the New Deal* (1965); Abraham Holtzman, *The Townsend Movement* (1963); F. A. Warren, *Liberals and Communism: The "Red Decade" Revisited* (1966); George Wolfskill, *Revolt of the Conservatives* (1962), on the Liberty League; J. T. Patterson, *Congressional Conservatism and the New Deal: The Growth of the Conservative Coalition in Congress, 1933–1939* (1967).

**The Supreme Court** E. S. Corwin, *Court over Constitution* (1938); R. H. Jackson, *The Struggle for Judicial Supremacy* (1941); C. H. Pritchett, *The Roosevelt Court* (1948).

**Aspects of Life** F. L. Allen, *Since Yesterday* (1940); R. S. and H. M. Lind, *Middletown in Transition* (1935); Leo Gurko, *Angry Decade* (1947); Dorothea Lange and P. S. Taylor, *An American Exodus: A Record of Human Erosion in the Thirties* (1969); G. B. Tindall, *The Emergence of the New South, 1913–1945* (1967); D. T. Carter, *Scottsboro: A Tragedy of the American South* (1969).

**Literary Expression** Harvey Swados, ed., *The American Writer and the Great Depression*° (1966); Daniel Aaron, *Writers on the Left*° (1961); J. D. Mathew, *The Federal Theatre, 1935–1939* (1967).

---

° Titles available in paperback.

# Chapter 25
# The
# Abandonment
# of Isolation

Having fought a war to end war and make the world safe for democracy, Americans of the 1920s were generally optimistic about the prospects whenever they gave thought to international affairs. True, the United States had failed to join the League of Nations, the organization that was intended to keep the peace. But this country took the lead in bringing the nations of the world to renounce war in the Kellogg Pact (1928), which many people hailed as the sign of a warless future. Henceforth, said admirers of the pact, aggressive war was illegal.

Optimism faded after the great depression struck. During the 1930s, Japan under fanatical militarists, Germany under Hitler and the Nazis, and Italy under Mussolini and the Fascists each launched programs of domestic tyranny and foreign conquest. Opposed to these aggressive nations were the contented powers of Europe—Great Britain, France, and the Soviet Union—which disagreed on many things but had a common interest in maintaining the status quo.

The American government faced a choice between two broad lines of policy. On the one hand, the United States might back Great Britain, France, and the Soviet Union (if they could manage to get together themselves) in the hope that all somehow could and would provide for their "collective security," enforce the Kellogg Pact, prevent aggression, and maintain peace—though in this there was the real risk of hastening a general war. On the other hand, the United States might follow a policy of so-called "isolation." That is, this country might strengthen its position in the Western Hemisphere and concentrate on keeping out of war instead of preventing it.

Most of the American people favored the second of these alternatives. They were preoccupied with the depression and were determined to set their own country to rights, regardless of what might go on in the rest of the world. They were disillusioned about their earlier effort to bring peace through war—more than 70 per cent of them, according to an opinion poll in 1937, thought it had been a mistake to go to war in 1917—and they were in no mood to go on a second crusade.

Ever regardful of public opinion, President Roosevelt hesitated to come out openly and clearly in favor of collective security even after the long-expected war had broken out in Europe in 1939. He continued to talk the language of isolationism, representing his policy as one of keeping out of war, while he committed the country to greater and greater support of Great Britain and her allies. The issues became more and more confused as the debate between "interventionists" and "isolationists" grew hotter. Suddenly, on December 7, 1941, the debate was stilled.

---

**"A Good Time to Look at Them"**

In this cartoon of the 1930s, J. N. "Ding" Darling, appalled as he was by the threats of the dictators, expressed the widespread American view that the United States must not become involved in another war. (Des Moines *Register*)

## DEPRESSION DIPLOMACY

Herbert Hoover—a Quaker, an engineer, and a man of wide experience in international affairs—was impressed by the wastefulness of war as a human enterprise. As President, he held the United States to a rather modest and cautious role in world politics. Franklin D. Roosevelt, an admirer of his cousin Theodore Roosevelt's bold and vigorous approach, favored an active role for the United States, but during his first term he was restrained by his preoccupation with the New Deal as well as by his concern for public opinion.

### Hoover-Stimson Policies

With regard to Latin America, Hoover continued the movement that under his successor became the Good Neighbor policy. Before his inauguration he toured much of the hemisphere, promoting good will; during his administration he prepared for the removal of marines from Haiti and finally withdrew them from Nicaragua. He refused to intervene in Cuba, which was restless under a dictatorship. Throughout Latin America, as depression toppled about half the regimes, he recognized de facto rulers without questioning the means by which they had come into power. Even when several countries defaulted on their obligations in October 1931, he did not press them to pay or threaten to seize their customs houses.

With reference to Europe, policy became increasingly concerned with economic conditions as the depression deepened. The moratorium on war-debt and reparations payments, begun in June 1931, aided Europe temporarily. Secretary of State Henry L. Stimson wished it to lead to a general cancellation of these obligations but could not convince the President, who considered them sacred. Soon Germany ceased reparations payments, and nations owing money to the United States, except for Finland, began to default or make mere token payments.

With regard to the Far East, policies were aimed at safeguarding American rights while preserving peace. As unstable conditions in China continued throughout the 1920s, the United States could do little to protect China from the encroachments of strong nations. As

Russia became stronger, she built up her forces in eastern Siberia, and in 1929, when China tried to oust her from northern Manchuria, Russia fought an undeclared war to retain her foothold. Stimson tried to invoke the Kellogg-Briand Pact, which outlawed war, and to bring about mediation; he failed, demonstrating the weakness of the pact.

Japanese military leaders, feeling that their treaty rights in southern Manchuria were being threatened both by the Russians and by the Chinese Nationalists under Chiang Kai-shek, wrested the initiative from the Japanese foreign office in a manner little short of mutiny. In September 1931 they launched a large-scale military campaign in Manchuria at a time when the United States and Great Britain were preoccupied with the monetary crisis. For several weeks Stimson was moderate, in the hope that the civilians in the Japanese cabinet could regain control; the British were even less disposed to pursue a strong policy. The Japanese foreign office engaged in conciliatory talk but was unable to alter events as the army plunged deeper into Manchuria. By January 2, 1932, the conquest was complete.

As early as October 1931, Stimson had felt the United States might have to cooperate with the League of Nations in imposing economic sanctions against Japan even though these might lead to war. Hoover strongly opposed such action and, in cabinet meetings, discouraged Stimson by referring to the Washington treaties and the Kellogg-Briand Pact as scraps of paper. He learned from the British that they too opposed sanctions. Hoover was willing to allow Stimson to exert moral suasion against the Japanese, and suggested that he apply the doctrine of nonrecognition against territorial changes brought by force of arms. Stimson did so on January 7, 1932.

The American people were eager to see the United States assume moral leadership—and nothing more—against aggression. Their ideal was international disarmament, not policing. Hoover himself took the same view.

After the Geneva Conference of 1927 had failed to extend quotas to detroyers, cruisers, and submarines, the United States had threatened to begin a substantial building program. Hoover, fearing a naval race, called a

## The Stimson Doctrine [1932]

*The American Government . . . can not admit the legality of any situation de facto nor does it intend to recognize any treaty or agreement entered into between those governments, or agents thereof, which may impair the treaty rights of the United States or its citizens in China, including those which relate to the sovereignty, the independence, or the territorial and administrative integrity of the Republic of China, or to the international policy relative to China, commonly known as the open-door policy; and . . . it does not intend to recognize any situation, treaty, or agreement which may be brought about by means contrary to the covenants and obligations of the pact of Paris of August 27, 1928, to which treaty both China and Japan as well as the United States, are parties.*

Identical notes were sent to Japan and China, January 7, 1932.

## Seeking Friends and Customers

President Roosevelt inherited from the Hoover administration the questions of war-debt settlements, disarmament, and currency stabilization. He did not share Hoover's view that the proper settlement of these was a key to recovery. In April 1934 he signed an act sponsored by Senator Hiram Johnson, forbidding private loans to any defaulting nations; from then on all war-debt payments, except those from Finland, stopped altogether. Meanwhile, the United States continued to assert a strong moral position to try to bring about substantial disarmament. But Hitler was bent upon rearming, not disarming, and in October he withdrew from both the Geneva Conference and the League of Nations. A new arms race was under way.

In the same months that hopes for an arms settlement collapsed, so did those for international economic stabilization, and the blame this time was assessed against Roosevelt. He had agreed to cooperate in the World Economic Conference which President Hoover had called to meet in London in June 1933. He gave vague assurances to the representatives of eleven countries who visited him in advance that he favored currency stabilization, which he announced on May 16 was essential to "establish order in place of the present chaos." This was the policy under which Secretary of State Cordell Hull, a firm believer in international economic cooperation, and the American delegation went to London. After their arrival, President Roosevelt changed his mind, deciding that currency stabilization would be disadvantageous until the dollar had fallen to a competitive position on the world market. Whatever chance of agreement there had been disappeared when Roosevelt on July 3, 1933, cabled Hull a "bombshell message" disavowing currency stabilization.

The hope of stimulating foreign trade led Roosevelt to recognize Soviet Russia in November 1933. Since the revolution of November 1917, the Russian government had gone unrecognized while a number of irritating questions between the two nations continued to fester. Americans, hungry for what they unrealistically dreamed would be a substantial Russian

conference which opened in London in January 1930. There the United States, Great Britain, and Japan agreed not to build the capital ships authorized under the Washington treaty, and even to scrap some existing ships. They also agreed to ratios on smaller ships, to continue until 1936.

The United States participated vigorously in the World Disarmament Conference that opened under League sponsorship at Geneva in February 1932. With the Japanese attacking Shanghai, and Hitler daily winning new converts to his militaristic Nazi movement in Germany, the French firmly demanded an international army and compulsory arbitration rather than disarmament. In June 1932 Hoover tried to break the deadlock with a proposal to abolish immediately all offensive weapons, such as bombing planes and tanks, and to cut all land and naval forces approximately 30 per cent. Despite much enthusiasm for the proposal, nothing came of it.

### Secretary of State Cordell Hull

Secretary Hull (1871–1955), born in a log cabin in
backwoods Tennessee, was first elected to Congress
in 1907. Except for two years as chairman of the
Democratic National Committee, he served in one
or the other house of Congress until 1933, strongly
advocating lower tariffs. William L. Langer and
S. Everett Gleason in *The Challenge to Isolation*
have analyzed his policies this way: "Even earlier
than Mr. Roosevelt, he had sensed the dangers in
the world situation and had warned the country of
them. As a man of great integrity and high principle
he was especially disturbed by the rapidly progressing breakdown of international law and morality.
His prescription against this menace was reaffirma-
tion of traditional standards of justice and fair dealing, insistence on the value of peaceful methods to
settle international differences, and return to more
liberal trade relations as the only way to alleviate the
existing world tension. His was a somewhat rigid,
doctrinaire approach, criticized by those who felt
that his constant harping on general principles revealed a disinclination to come to grips with concrete, practical problems. Mr. Hull was a man of the
people and as such easily moved to that moral indignation characteristic of the American people when
confronted by the iniquities of foreigners."
(New York: Harper & Row, 1952.) (Karsh, Ottawa)

trade, were eager for recognition. The Russians
had even stronger motives for obtaining recognition, for they were afraid of being attacked by
Japan. Maxim Litvinov, the Russian foreign
minister, after discussions with Roosevelt at the
White House, agreed that Russia would end its
propaganda activities in the United States,
guarantee religious freedom and protection in
the courts to Americans resident in Russia, and
negotiate a settlement of debts and claims.

By January 1934 Roosevelt was ready to listen
seriously to Hull's homilies on the necessity of
lowering tariff barriers in order to improve
foreign trade. With Roosevelt's support, Congress (in June 1934) passed Hull's cherished
program, the Reciprocal Trade Agreements Act.
It authorized the administration to negotiate
agreements, lowering tariffs by as much as 50
per cent on specified goods coming in from individual nations in return for their reducing
tariffs on American goods.

The immediate effect of the reciprocal trade
agreements is difficult to estimate. During the
depression years they were drafted carefully to
admit only products not competitive with American industry and agriculture. By 1939 Hull had
negotiated agreements with twenty-one countries, ranging from Cuba to the United Kingdom. These lowered the tariff an estimated 29
per cent, at the same time that they gained concessions for American exporters, especially
growers of cotton and tobacco. By the end of
1938 American exports to the sixteen nations
with which it then had trade agreements had
increased nearly 40 per cent.

At the Inter-American Conference at Monte-
video in December 1933, Hull won such acclaim with his proposals for reciprocity that
President Roosevelt gave him full support upon
his return home. To small nations like Cuba, dependent upon exports to the United States, reciprocity seemed a way out of the depression.
While Hull offered economic succor, he reiterated to the people of Latin America at Monte-
video (and Roosevelt said the same thing in
Washington), that the United States was opposed to armed intervention in Latin America.
Hull even signed a convention declaring: "No
state has the right to intervene in the internal
or external affairs of another."

Thus Hull took the United States a step further than the Hoover administration, which had unofficially disavowed the Theodore Roosevelt Corollary to the Monroe Doctrine but had reserved the right to intervene in self-defense. This seemed to be the American policy, as late as the summer of 1933, when revolution exploded in Cuba. Sumner Welles, one of the chief draftsmen of the new Latin American policy, was sent into Cuba to offer the "good offices" of the United States. Welles helped bring pacification without calling in the marines. In 1934, when a more conservative government came into power in Cuba, the United States gave up its right of intervention under the Platt Amendment. It also withdrew the last marines from Haiti and negotiated a treaty (not ratified until 1939) relaxing the restrictions upon Panama.

The new Good Neighbor policy of nonintervention received a severe testing in 1938 when Mexico expropriated all foreign oil holdings, including property valued by its American owners at $200 million. The United States conceded the right of expropriation but at first contended that the price the Mexicans wished to pay was so trivial as to be confiscation. In 1942, after years of involved controversy, a commission evaluated the property at $24 million, and the State Department then told the protesting oil companies that they must accept the settlement or receive nothing. This renunciation of the right to intervene for the purpose of protecting American property in Latin America was a reversal of dollar diplomacy. In encouraging trade, the new policy was of immediate benefit. It came to be even more valuable in promoting mutual defense, as the threat of war in Europe increased.

As for the Philippines, primarily the depression and secondarily isolationism brought them the long-sought but economically dubious blessing of independence. American producers of sugar, fats, and oils were determined to push their Filipino competitors outside the tariff wall. Isolationists were also eager to drop this dangerous Far Eastern military commitment. The Tydings-McDuffie Act of 1934 thrust upon the Philippines complete independence rather than the dominion status they sought. In 1935 the Philippines entered upon a transitional commonwealth period; on July 4, 1946, they became a fully independent republic. The United States was demonstrating that it was trying to rid itself of possessions rather than seize new ones.

At the London Naval Conference of 1935, the Japanese withdrew after they failed to obtain equality with the Americans and British in place of the 5:5:3 ratio, and thus the way was opened for competitive naval building. The United States soon turned to building the fleet with which it was later to fight the opening battles of a Pacific war.

## Legislating Neutrality

With the breakdown of the naval status quo and the threatened aggressions in both Asia and Europe, most Americans felt that at all costs they must stay out of impending wars. Many leaders of the peace movement—dedicated Wilsonians and advocates of the League—had become disgusted with the League's inability to stop Japanese aggression. They reasoned that internationalism had failed to maintain the peace. Others, taking an economic-determinist view of wars, concluded that Wall Streeters and munitions makers, along with Wilson's legalistic insistence upon outmoded neutral rights on the high seas, had trapped the nation into World War I. Senate investigators, under the progressive Republican Gerald P. Nye of North Dakota, revealed exorbitant wartime profits and tax evasion and claimed that bankers had sought war to rescue their loans to the Allies. President Roosevelt, himself impressed by the Nye investigation, privately wrote his regret that Bryan had left the State Department in 1915.

The Nye Committee findings and similar sensational popular writings convinced a large part of the public that entrance into World War I had been a frightful mistake. The way to avoid its repetition seemed to be to legislate against the supposed causes. As Mussolini openly prepared to conquer Ethiopia in 1935, Americans feared that a general European war might develop. They felt that the way to avoid involvement was not to participate in strong deterring pressure against Italy, since Mussolini might strike back. Rather it was to isolate the nation by means of neutrality laws.

President Roosevelt also favored legislation, but he desired, as Hull had proposed in 1933, a law that would enable the President to embargo war supplies to the aggressor and allow their sale to the victim. But Congress passed a neutrality act providing a mandatory embargo against both aggressor and victim and empowering the President to warn American citizens that they might travel on vessels of belligerents only at their own risk. This first Neutrality Act of 1935, a temporary measure, was renewed in 1936 and again, with even stronger provisions, in 1937.

When the attack upon Ethiopia came, in October 1935, the League branded Italy an aggressor and voted sanctions against her. England and France made gestures against Italy but showed no inclination toward determined action. Hull imposed a "moral embargo" upon oil. Mussolini easily conquered his African empire, and then withdrew from the League. In October 1936 he joined with Hitler to form a new Rome-Berlin axis.

All this seemed to strengthen the determination of the American people to stay out of war. The new public opinion polls (based on samplings of only 1,500 to 3,500 people, with a probable error of 4 to 6 per cent) indicated top-heavy opinion against involvement. A typical poll in November 1935, after the attack on Ethiopia, queried: "If one foreign nation insists upon attacking another, should the United States join with other nations to compel it to stop?" The answer: yes, 28 per cent; no, 67 per cent; no opinion, 5 per cent.

This anti-involvement sentiment continued to be the mood of the nation when a new danger arose in July 1936, as General Francisco Franco and the Falangists (modeled after the Fascists) revolted against the republican government in Spain. Hitler and Mussolini sided with Franco; Russia, France, and, to a lesser extent, Great Britain favored the Loyalists. To prevent the Spanish Civil War from spreading into a general European conflict, England and France agreed to send no aid to either side. Roosevelt, trying to cooperate with France and England, persuaded Congress to apply the existing Neutrality Act to civil as well as international wars. The result was that the United States and other Western nations denied assistance to republican Spain. The republican government came to depend increasingly upon Russia for what little help it received.

As for Franco, he received massive aid from Mussolini and Hitler, and ultimately crushed the Loyalists.

American feelings became inflamed over the invasion of Ethiopia and the Spanish Civil War, but President Roosevelt voiced the majority attitude in August 1936, a month after the outbreak of the war in Spain, when he asserted: "We shun political commitments which might entangle us in foreign wars; we avoid connection with the political activities of the League of Nations. . . . We are not isolationists except in so far as we seek to isolate ourselves completely from war."

## WORLD WAR AGAIN

A great Japanese drive into the five northern provinces of China began in the summer of 1937. At first the State Department pursued a middle-of-the-road policy, favoring neither country. Japan avoided declaring war, and President Roosevelt did not invoke the Neutrality Act. Private American ships at their own risk could carry arms and munitions to both belligerents. The administration's purpose was to help the Chinese, who needed American supplies more than the Japanese did.

### Facing Japan and Germany

By October 1937 the administration was ready to take a firm position against Japan. The British proposed a joint arms embargo, which seemed to involve no great risk. At this time and during the next four years, the consensus of the experts was that Japan was a mediocre military power. Hull persuaded Roosevelt to make a statement to counteract isolationism. The President, speaking in Chicago, declared: "The peace-loving nations must make a concerted effort in opposition to those violations of treaties and those ignorings of humane instincts which today are creating a state of international anarchy, international instability from which there is no escape through mere isolation or neutrality." War, he asserted, was a contagion which must be quarantined by the international community.

There is evidence that Roosevelt had in mind nothing more drastic than a collective breaking off of diplomatic relations, that he did not favor economic or military sanctions. Immediate press reaction and White House mail was favorable, but within a few days, as the Chicago *Tribune* and Hearst press continued to draw sinister implications from the "quarantine" speech, it plunged the nation, as the *Tribune* reported, into a "hurricane of war fright." This set back Roosevelt in his thinking. In November 1937 he sent a delegate to an international conference in Brussels to consider the Japanese aggression—but instructed him neither to take the lead nor to be a tail to the British kite.

Japan had no need to fear economic or military reprisals from the United States. On December 12, 1937, young Japanese aviators bombed and sank the United States gunboat *Panay* on the Yangtze River. The aviators claimed they bombed it in error, but visibility was excellent and an American flag was painted on the deck. As at the sinking of the *Maine* in 1898, a wave of excitement swept the country, but this time it was fear that the nation might become involved in war. The United States quickly accepted the profuse Japanese apologies and offers of indemnity.

At the end of 1938, as the Japanese supplanted the Open Door with their so-called New Order in East Asia, they were making conditions almost untenable for Americans in China. But the threat of war in Europe overshadowed the Asian impasse.

The traditional American isolationism, as exemplified by Hearst editorials and the speeches of several senators, implied strict nonintervention in Europe but a considerably more active role in Asia—no sanctions, but an insistence upon the Open Door in China. Within the Western Hemisphere, these isolationists were ready to give the President almost a free hand toward both Canada and Latin America. Indeed there were no more devout exponents of the Monroe Doctrine than they.

Roosevelt took full advantage of these feelings to inaugurate, within the hemisphere, policies that he could later apply across the Atlantic and the Pacific. In December 1936 he traveled all the way to Buenos Aires to put his personal prestige behind a pact to enlarge the Monroe Doctrine into a mutual security agreement. Henceforth, if any outside power threatened the

American republics, instead of the United States acting unilaterally they would all consult together for their own protection. The understanding covered disputes among the republics themselves but was specifically aimed at meeting the threat of the Axis. It provided that the members would consult "in the event of an international war outside America which might menace the peace of the American Republics." In December 1938, with war in Europe imminent, the republics, at a meeting in Lima, Peru, established a means of consultation. Roosevelt also extended hemispheric security to the north when he issued a declaration of solidarity with Canada in August 1938.

By 1938 Hitler had rebuilt such a strong German army and air force that he was ready to embark upon a course of intimidation and conquest. In March he proclaimed union with Austria and paraded triumphantly through Vienna. This union put western Czechoslovakia into the jaws of a German vise. Hitler began tightening it with demands on behalf of the minority of 3.5 million Germans in Czechoslovakia. In September 1938 he brought Europe to the brink of war with his demands for the cession of the Sudeten area in which the minority lived. The Czechs, who had a strong army, were ready to fight rather than submit, but the people of other Western nations, appalled at the threat of another world conflict, were eager for a settlement on almost any terms. Roosevelt joined in the pleas to Hitler for a peaceful solution. At Munich on September 29 the French and the British signed a pact with Hitler granting his demands in Czechoslovakia. "This is the last territorial claim I have to make in Europe," he declared.

Within a few weeks, the once strong Czechoslovakia was whittled down to impotence. In March 1939 Hitler took over the remaining areas as German protectorates, thus demonstrating the worthlessness of his Munich pledge. In April, he began harassing Poland. The British and French, seeing clearly that appeasement had failed, gave firm pledges to Poland and to other threatened nations. They made half-hearted gestures toward Russia, which had been left out of the Munich settlement, but Stalin signed a nonaggression pact with Hitler in August. This freed Hitler to attack Poland if he could not frighten that country into submission. Poland stood firm, and Germany invaded her territory on September 1, 1939. Great Britain and France, true to their pledges, declared war on Germany on September 3. World War II had begun.

## Aiding the Allies

With the outbreak of war, Roosevelt issued a neutrality proclamation pointedly different from Wilson's 1914 plea for Americans to be impartial in thought as well as action. "This nation will remain a neutral nation," Roosevelt stated, "but I cannot ask that every American remain neutral in thought as well."

Promptly, Roosevelt called Congress into special session and, despite a heated debate, was able to muster the votes for a revision of the Neutrality Act. The 1939 measure still prohibited American ships from entering the war zones, but it allowed belligerents to purchase arms on a "cash-and-carry" basis. Had England and France been able to defeat Hitler with this limited assistance, Roosevelt probably would have been satisfied with it. Indeed, after the quick Nazi overrunning of Poland, overoptimistic American publicists during the quiet winter of 1939–1940 asserted that the Allies were calling Hitler's bluff and, after a long and boring blockade on sea and land, would triumph. During these months of the "phony war," American indignation flared hottest over the Russian invasion of Finland. The administration applied a tight "moral embargo" on shipments of munitions to Russia but went no further.

Optimistic illusions about Hitler's weakness turned into panic in the spring of 1940 when the Nazis invaded Denmark and Norway, then swept across Holland and Belgium deep into France. On May 16 Roosevelt asked Congress for an additional billion for defense expenditures and obtained it quickly. On the premise that the United States must build great air armadas to hold off the Nazis, he set a goal of at least 50,000 airplanes a year.

On June 10, 1940, Mussolini joined the Germans by attacking France. Roosevelt that evening asserted: "The hand that held the dagger has struck it into the back of its neighbor." And, with France tottering from the German on-

slaught, he proclaimed that the United States would "extend to the opponents of force the material resources of this nation." He was taking the United States from a status of neutrality to one of nonbelligerency on the side of the democracies.

Twelve days later France fell, and in all western Europe only the shattered remnants of the British army that had been retrieved from Dunkirk opposed the Nazis. Already the new prime minister, Winston Churchill, was showering Roosevelt with requests for destroyers and arms of all kinds to help the British man their bastion. The odds against the British were heavy, but Roosevelt made the bold and dangerous decision to "scrape the bottom of the barrel" and make it possible for the British to buy all available war materials. As the Germans, preparing for an invasion, began to bomb Britain from the air, Roosevelt gave Britain fifty overage destroyers in return for ninety-nine-year leases on eight bases to be located on British possessions ranging from Newfoundland to British Guiana in the Western Hemisphere. The "destroyer deal" was, as Churchill later wrote, "a decidedly unneutral act." Roosevelt also turned back to the factories government-purchased war planes to be resold to Britain. In September 1940 he gave an indication that aid would not be confined indefinitely to materials alone when he pushed through Congress the Burke-Wadsworth bill, which inaugurated the first peacetime conscription of men in American history.

Roosevelt threw the resources of the United States behind the British as completely as Congress would let him. He did so with the feeling that an Axis victory would mean disaster to the nation. A large part of the public suddenly seemed to agree. In March 1940 only 43 per cent of those polled thought a German victory would be a threat to the United States; by July, 69 per cent did. In May 1940 only 35 per cent favored aid to Britain at the risk of American involvement; four months later, 60 per cent did. Yet as late as November 1941 only 20 per cent of those polled favored a declaration of war against Germany. Roosevelt and the American public seemed to share incompatible aims. They wished to bring about the defeat of the Axis without involving the United States in a shooting

## Lindbergh's Isolationist Argument [1941]

*I know I will be severely criticized by the interventionists in America when I say we should not enter a war unless we have a reasonable chance of winning. . . . But I do not believe that our American ideals, and our way of life, will gain through an unsuccessful war. And I know that the United States is not prepared to wage war in Europe successfully at this time. . . .*

*There is a policy open to this nation that will lead to success—a policy that leaves us free to follow our own way of life, and to develop our own civilization. It is not a new and untried idea. . . .*

*It is based upon the belief that the security of a nation lies in the strength and character of its own people. It recommends the maintenance of armed forces sufficient to defend this hemisphere from attack by any combination of foreign powers. It demands faith in an independent American destiny. This is the policy of the America First Committee today. It is a policy not of isolation, but of independence; not of defeat, but of courage.—The New York* Times, *April 24, 1941.*

## "Stop Hitler Now!" [1940]

*We Americans have naturally wished to keep out of this war—to take no steps which might lead us in. But—*

*We now know that every step the French and British fall back brings war and world revolution closer to US— our country, our institutions, our homes, our hopes for peace.*

*Hitler is striking with all the terrible force at his command. His is a desperate gamble, and the stakes are nothing less than domination of the whole human race. . . .*

*WE CAN HELP—IF WE ACT NOW— before it is forever too late.*

*We can help by sending planes, guns, munitions, food. We can help to end the fear that American boys will fight and die in another Flanders, closer to home. . . .*

*The United States of America is still the most powerful nation on earth— and the United States of America is YOU!"—Advertisement written by Robert Sherwood for the Committee to Defend America by Aiding the Allies and widely published in June 1940.*

war. Sometime in the next eighteen months, Roosevelt probably came to feel that complete entrance into the war was desirable; the public never did.

## "Intervention" or "Isolation"?

The whole country was drawn into a great debate on the issue of neutrality as against all-out aid to the Allies. With a rather careless use of words on both sides, the advocates of neutrality called their opponents "interventionists," and the advocates of all-out aid responded with the term "isolationists."

William Allen White, the Kansas editor, headed the Committee to Defend America by Aiding the Allies, often called the White Committee. White himself (like a large percentage of Americans) favored merely aid, but a minority

wanted to go further and declare war. In April 1941 this group founded the Fight for Freedom Committee. On the anti-involvement side, a Yale student, R. Douglas Stuart, Jr., organized an America First Committee under the chairmanship of a leading Chicago businessman, General Robert E. Wood. It drew upon the oratorical talent of the aviation hero Charles Lindbergh, General Hugh Johnson, and Senators Nye and Wheeler. It won the editorial support of the Hearst and other large newspapers. It appealed to a considerable segment of patriotic Americans, and inevitably it also attracted a small fringe of pro-Nazi, anti-Semitic, and American Fascist fanatics. The debate was bitter, and through the summer and fall of 1940 it was complicated by a presidential election.

The Republicans met at Philadelphia in June,

at the time of the collapse of France. National defense suddenly became the most important issue. Roosevelt underscored this and stole headlines from the Republican convention by appointing to his cabinet two of the most distinguished Republicans. He made the elder statesman Henry L. Stimson, secretary of war, and the 1936 vice-presidential candidate and sharp critic of the New Deal, Frank Knox, secretary of the navy.

The chagrined Republicans at Philadelphia promptly read Stimson and Knox out of the party but could not ignore the defense issue. They succumbed to the grassroots pressure, which had been built up through a careful advertising campaign, and nominated a young internationalist, Wendell Willkie. This was a startling blow to the isolationist majority among the Republican politicians, but it provided them with a tousle-haired, personable candidate who could win hysterical devotion from the amateur party workers. Both the platform and the candidate pledged that the nation would be kept out of war but would aid peoples fighting for liberty.

By the time the Democrats met in mid-July, it was a foregone conclusion that they would

renominate Roosevelt. He was even able to force the Democratic politicians to swallow his choice for Vice President, Secretary of Agriculture Henry A. Wallace, who was considered an advanced New Dealer.

Willkie embarked upon an appealing but slightly amateurish campaign, whistle-stopping so vigorously that he nearly lost his voice, denouncing the bad management of the New Deal rather than its basic program, and always referring to his opponent as "the third-term candidate" (no President had ever run for a third term before). Numerous right-wing Democrats and even some early New Dealers like Moley and General Johnson supported him. John L. Lewis threatened to resign as president of the CIO if Willkie were not elected—a possibility that did not seem to frighten organized labor.

Roosevelt, a wily old campaigner, tried to give the appearance of not campaigning at all. Defense problems were so acute, he insisted, that he had to spend his time touring army bases, munitions plants, and shipyards. He followed routes that somehow took him through innumerable cities, where he cheerily greeted quantities of voters.

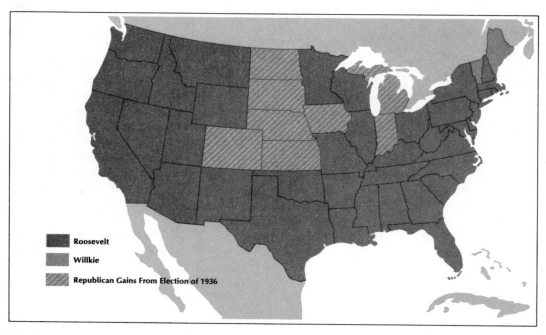

■ Roosevelt
▨ Willkie
▨ Republican Gains From Election of 1936

**Election of 1940**

Foreign policy was paramount. On this, both Willkie and Roosevelt had much the same views. Willkie approved of the destroyers-bases agreement. Both made fervent antiwar statements to placate the isolationists. Willkie declared that if Roosevelt's promise to stay out of a foreign war was no better than his pledge to balance the budget, the boys were "already almost on the transports." This was an effective campaign issue which cut into Roosevelt's support. In Boston, Roosevelt (making the mental reservation that any attack upon the United States would not be a foreign war) picked up the challenge in words the isolationists were to mock incessantly: "I have said this before, but I shall say it again and again and again: Your boys are not going to be sent into any foreign wars."

A large part of the vote of those opposing aid to the Allies went to Willkie. Those favoring vigorous aid or even intervention (including many who fervently opposed New Deal domestic policies) voted for Roosevelt. They preferred Roosevelt's sure leadership to Willkie's inexperience. It was a relatively close vote: 27,244,000 for Roosevelt, and 22,305,000 for Willkie; 449 electoral votes to 82. The combined third-party vote was less than 200,000. Within a few weeks Willkie was on his way to England with a letter from Roosevelt to Churchill in his pocket.

## Arsenal of Democracy

By mid-December, the British had so nearly exhausted their financial resources that they had practically stopped making new contracts, yet Churchill warned Roosevelt that their needs would increase tenfold in the future. The Neutrality Act of 1939 and the Johnson Act of 1934 forbade American loans; a request for repeal would have reawakened the old ill feelings about unpaid war debts. Roosevelt, cruising in the Caribbean after the election, thought of a formula. The United States, "to eliminate the dollar sign," should lend goods rather than money, while serving as an "arsenal of democracy."

A "Lend-Lease" bill went into the congressional hopper at the right moment to bear a significant number: it became House Resolution No. 1776. After fierce debate, the bill went through Congress by a wide margin and was signed by the President in March 1941. It empowered him to spend an initial $7 billion—a sum as large as all the controversial loans of World War I.

Lend-Lease formally committed the United States to the policy the President had been following since the fall of France, the policy of pouring aid into Great Britain to help her withstand the German onslaught. Since Lend-Lease shipments had to cross the Atlantic to be of aid, the United States acquired a vital interest in keeping the Atlantic sea lanes open against the formidable wolf packs of German submarines, which in the spring of 1941 were destroying a half-million tons of shipping a month, twice as much as could be replaced. The President did not dare to convoy vessels openly to England as Secretary Stimson urged; isolationists in Congress were too powerful. Instead he fell back upon the device of "hemispheric defense." The American republics had proclaimed an Atlantic neutrality zone in 1939; in 1941 Roosevelt extended it far to the east, almost to Iceland, and ordered the navy to patrol the area and give warning of aggressors. This meant radioing to the British naval and air forces the location of Nazi submarines. The United States occupied Greenland in April 1941 and began escorting convoys as far as Iceland in July.

In secret, the United States had gone even further, for in the spring of 1941 American and British officers in Washington reached agreement on the strategy to be followed if the United States should enter the war. President Roosevelt demonstrated publicly in August 1941 how close he had come to carrying the United States from nonbelligerency to cobelligerency with England when he met with Prime Minister Churchill off the coast of Newfoundland. Roosevelt refused to make military commitments but did join Churchill in signing a press release on mutual war aims—the Atlantic Charter. As Churchill later pointed out, Roosevelt, representing a nation not at war, subscribed to a document that referred to "the final destruction of the Nazi tyranny" as a war aim.

In June 1941 Hitler unleashed against Russia a surprise attack so powerful that American military leaders predicted that Russia would collapse in a few weeks or months. The Russians fell back before the deep Nazi invasion but continued to fight, and in September Roosevelt, again gambling, extended Lend-Lease to them. This made it even more imperative to patrol the seas effectively.

The German answer was to strike back with submarines. In May 1941 they sank the American ship *Robin Moor* off the coast of Brazil. The Nazis replied to protests by saying: "Germany will continue to sink every ship with contraband for Britain whatever its name." In September a submarine attacked but failed to hit the destroyer *Greer*, which was radioing the submarine's position to the British. President Roosevelt, who did not know or at least did not reveal what the *Greer* was doing, issued orders to the navy to "shoot on sight." In October another destroyer was hit, and the *Reuben James* was sunk. Congress voted legislation to arm merchantmen and allow them to sail to belligerent ports. Naval war with the Nazis was under way.

The Chief of Naval Operations, Admiral Harold R. Stark, wrote in his diary that Hitler "has every excuse in the world to declare war on us now, if he were of a mind to." But Hitler was not, and war came from the Pacific, not the Atlantic.

## Pearl Harbor

The Japanese saw in the European crisis an unparalleled opportunity to extend their empire. In the summer of 1939 they forced from Great Britain concessions that demonstrated their intentions. The United States promptly took a most serious step and gave the requisite six months' notice to terminate its 1911 commercial treaty with Japan. Beginning in January 1940, the United States was free to cut off its shipments of oil, scrap iron, and other raw materials.

The United States was determined to restrain Japan, even at the risk of a war. More was at stake than tin, rubber, and other vital raw materials. In September 1940 Japan signed a defensive alliance with Germany and Italy (the Tripartite Pact); any further Japanese thrusts would damage the world status quo to which the State Department was committed. The administration policy toward Japan was insep-

arably interrelated with and subordinate to that policy toward Germany.

Under the Export Control Act, by the fall of 1940 the United States had placed an embargo upon aviation gasoline and almost all raw materials with military potential, including scrap iron and steel. Already war was close. The Japanese government of Prince Konoye wished to conciliate the United States if it could do so without serious concessions. Negotiations began in the spring of 1941 and dragged on into December. At first the Japanese informally suggested rather generous proposals, but by May they were making formal ones that were unacceptable: the United States should ask Chiang Kai-shek to make peace on Japan's terms, should restore normal trade with Japan, and should help Japan procure natural resources in Southeast Asia.

The German attack upon Russia relieved the Japanese of one of their greatest worries, since they thought they no longer needed to fear interference from Siberia. They decided to move into southern Indochina and Thailand. The United States had broken the Japanese code and, through intercepted messages, knew this was probably a prelude to attacks upon Singapore and the Dutch East Indies. At the end of July 1941, when the Japanese occupied southern Indochina, the United States, acting firmly with the British and the Dutch, froze Japanese assets in their respective countries, so that the Japanese could not convert these assets into cash. This put the Japanese into such a desperate plight that they would either have to abandon their aggressions or attack British or Dutch East Indian possessions to get needed supplies.

Since the Japanese naval leaders wished to avoid a war they feared they might lose, the Japanese cabinet sought a compromise. Prince Konoye requested a personal meeting with Roosevelt at which Konoye was ready to make some concessions. (Simultaneously Japan prepared for war in case agreement could not be reached.) Roosevelt was enthusiastic, since Konoye was ready to promise that Japan would not expand further southward and would not attack the United States in the event of war with Germany. Hull was becoming discouraged because he feared Konoye could not bind the

# Where Historians Disagree

## The Background of Pearl Harbor

After the end of World War II a number of critics charged that the Roosevelt administration had deliberately brought the United States into the war by provoking the Japanese to attack Pearl Harbor. Charles A. Beard, for one, presented the case against the administration in his *President Roosevelt and the Coming of the War, 1941* (1948). According to Beard, the American government refused to compromise with Japan and allow her to buy the raw materials she needed for her military adventure in China. Hence Japan had little choice but to strike out in the southwest Pacific and take the necessary supplies by force, even at the risk of war with the United States. From decoded Japanese radio messages, Roosevelt and his advisers must have known, by late November, that Japan was about to begin hostilities. Indeed, as War Secretary Henry L. Stimson recorded in his diary, Roosevelt at a cabinet meeting "brought up the event that we were likely to be attacked" in the near future, for the Japanese were "notorious for making an attack without warning." Stimson added, significantly: "The question was how we should maneuver them into the position of firing the first shot."

In *Roosevelt from Munich to Pearl Harbor* (1950) Basil Rauch undertook to refute Beard's argument, yet Rauch conceded that the administration had had in mind a "maneuver" of sorts. "The question," he explained, "was whether the President should ask Congress for a declaration of war *prior* to a Japanese attack on the Philippines or Guam, in order to avoid giving Japan the advantage of a surprise attack, or wait until Japan attacked American territory, that is, 'maneuver' Japan into firing the first shot."

Disagreeing with both Beard and Rauch, R. N. Current contended in *Secretary Stimson: A Study in Statecraft* (1954) that Roosevelt and his advisers intended neither to provoke an attack on Pearl Harbor nor to await one on Guam or the Philippines. Stimson and the others were expecting the Japanese to move against Dutch or British but *not* American possessions. When Stimson said "we were likely to be attacked," he meant "we" in the sense of "our side," including the British and the Dutch. If he and his colleagues had really been anticipating a blow at Pearl Harbor, they obviously would not have had to worry about how to provoke the Japanese to attack there. The real question, as Stimson saw it, was how to make the Japanese *appear* to be firing on the United States—in the sense of threatening vital American interests—if and when they aggressed upon Dutch or British territory in the southwest Pacific. He assumed that such a "maneuver" as this would be necessary in order to persuade Congress to pass a war declaration, which he believed to be in the best interests of the United States.

The most thorough and scholarly study of the subject is *Pearl Harbor: Warning and Decision* (1962), by Roberta Wohlsetter, who on the whole is favorable to the Roosevelt policy. Today few if any historical experts hold to the Beard provocation thesis, but they continue to disagree among themselves in regard to the appropriateness of various American diplomatic and military measures preceding the attack.

Supreme Command. On Hull's advice, Roosevelt refused to meet Konoye without specific advance commitments about China, and these Konoye would not give.

Roosevelt and Hull seemed to make the foolish error of thinking Japan was bluffing when she was not. Instead of granting limited concessions that would have strengthened the Japanese moderates and postponed or avoided a war which the United States was in no position to fight in 1941, the American policy makers took an adamant moralistic position which played into the hands of the Japanese extremists. The Japanese made an even more grievous miscalculation by provoking a war that few of their leaders were sure they could win.

Each nation refused to budge on the question of China. On November 20, 1941, Japan offered a modus vivendi (temporary settlement) highly favorable to herself. Hull rejected it and replied in the basic American terms, insisting that Japan get out of China. He not only knew Japan would not accept these terms but knew also, through

intercepted Japanese messages, that she had made her last offer and that after November 29 things would happen automatically. "I have washed my hands of the Japanese situation," Hull told Stimson on November 27, "and it is now in the hands of you and Knox, the Army and Navy."

The United States knew that Japan was on the move and that war was imminent. A large Japanese convoy was moving southward through the China Sea. The administration thought an attack upon American territory unlikely. The commanders in Hawaii were routinely warned. Negligence there and in Washington, not diabolical plotting as was later charged, led to the disaster ahead. Meanwhile, on November 25, a Japanese naval task force had sailed eastward from the Kuriles.

At 7:55 on Sunday morning, December 7, 1941, the first wave of Japanese airplanes hit the United States naval base at Pearl Harbor, Hawaii; a second wave came an hour later. The attacks were successful beyond Japan's greatest

**The Magazine of the U.S.S. Shaw Exploding During the Japanese Raid on Pearl Harbor**

The destroyer *Shaw,* in a new floating drydock, went through the first attack unscathed. One of the second wave of bombers at 9:12 A.M. hit her badly, and fire spread to her forward magazine, which about 9:30 went up spectacularly, blowing off her bow and sinking the

dock. From the bridge aft the damage was so slight that the *Shaw* was refloated and a month later put in the same repaired dock to be fitted with a temporary bow. She steamed to the mainland to be rebuilt and later rejoined the fleet. (Official U.S. Navy photo) expectations. Within two hours the planes destroyed or severely damaged 8 battleships, 3 light cruisers, 4 miscellaneous vessels, 188 airplanes, and important shore installations. There were 3,435 casualties. The Japanese task force withdrew without being detected, having lost 29 airplanes, 5 midget submarines, and fewer than 100 men. In the first strike, the United States was rendered almost impotent in the Pacific, but the bitterly wrangling nation was suddenly unified for the global war into which it had been precipitated.

## THE BATTLE FOR PRODUCTION

"Yesterday, December 7, 1941—a date which will live in infamy—the United States of America was suddenly and deliberately attacked by the naval and air forces of the Empire of Japan." Thus President Roosevelt addressed Congress on the Monday after the debacle at Pearl Harbor. Within four hours, the Senate unanimously, and the House 388 to 1, voted for a war resolution against Japan. Three days later Germany and Italy declared war against the United States, and on the same day, December 11, Congress reciprocated without a dissenting vote.

Total war made the planning of industrial production as vital as military strategy. "War is no longer simply a battle between armed forces in the field," the Industrial Mobilization Plan of 1939 had stated, "—it is a struggle in which each side strives to bring to bear against the enemy the coordinated power of every individual and of every material resource at its command. The conflict extends from the soldier in the front line to the citizen in the remotest hamlet in the rear."

### Mobilizing for Defense

At the time of the Munich crisis in 1938, Roosevelt had ordered the armed forces to modernize their production plan. Just before the outbreak of war in Europe, he authorized the War and Navy departments to appoint a civilian advisory committee to survey the 1939 plan. This was the War Resources Board, made up of five leaders of big business together with the presidents of the Massachusetts Institute of Technology and the Brookings Institution, and an army colonel.

At this point politics began. The unfortunate use of the word "war" rather than "defense" in the title frightened the public, especially after the invasion of Poland when even the existence of such a body seemed a move toward involvement. The firmly anti-New Deal attitude of the board pained Roosevelt. He speedily disbanded the War Resources Board and submitted to the pressures against substituting any new defense agencies.

With the collapse of France in the late spring of 1940, Roosevelt could delay no longer, even though he was embarking upon a new presidential campaign and wished to temper isolationist hostility. Rather than ask Congress to create defense agencies, he drew upon a 1916 statute for authority and reestablished the Advisory Commission of the Council of National Defense. This time he used the word "defense" rather than "war," and carefully balanced all of the major national interests. He headed it with William Knudsen, of General Motors.

Out of this prototype grew the many defense agencies with their shifting or nebulous lines of authority and often ill-defined powers. Out of it came many of the heads of subsequent war agencies. Out of it too came one clear fact amid the many uncertainties: whatever war agencies developed, Roosevelt was of no disposition to abdicate or share his presidential powers. At its first meeting, Chairman Knudsen asked Roosevelt: "Who's boss?" The President replied: "I am."

In January 1941, after the Advisory Commission had almost broken down and had lost its control over priorities to the military, Roosevelt set up a new Office of Production Management. After American entrance into the war, he replaced this with a War Production Board under Donald Nelson, of Sears, Roebuck and Company. Though personable and a good organizer, Nelson was not strong enough to force civilian control over priorities, or a more equitable distribution of contracts among smaller manufacturers, or a well-balanced production plan. He lost much of his power when President Roosevelt persuaded Justice James F. Byrnes to resign from the Supreme Court and act as a sort of assistant president in charge of war production. Byrnes was at first head of the Office of

Economic Stabilization, then (after May 1943) of the Office of War Mobilization, which developed into an effective agency.

## Materials for Victory

Meanwhile, with the awarding of the first large government contracts in the summer of 1940, industry began to boom.

Some manufacturers, still thinking in depression terms of an economy of scarcity, were at first reluctant to build new plants, which they feared would lead to overproduction after the war. Still others would not accept contracts until they were sure of an adequate profit. It was the initial task of Knudsen, the production genius of General Motors, to persuade manufacturers that it was their patriotic duty to take contracts. As for the new war plants, even if later they should prove to be excess capacity, manufacturers need not worry about paying for them; the Reconstruction Finance Corporation received authorization from Congress (June 1940) to finance the construction, expansion, and equipment of plants and to lease them to contractors. Or, if manufacturers put their own capital into defense construction, they would receive a fast five-year tax write-off. This meant that instead of deducting a normal 5 per cent a year for depreciation from their taxes on wartime profits, they could deduct 20 per cent of the cost of the plant. Manufacturers who turned to war production were not to suffer financially.

Neither were the war workers. The manufacturers, backed by the War and Navy departments, wished to abrogate New Deal restrictions on government contracts in order to lengthen the hours of workers without paying overtime. Labor leaders, wishing to increase employment, fought bitterly for double shifts. Ultimately the government decreed a forty-hour week with time-and-a-half for overtime. Contractors had to comply with New Deal labor legislation—the Walsh-Healey, Fair Labor Standards, and Wagner acts.

At the time of Pearl Harbor, the United States still had little armament because so much had been shipped to Great Britain and because so many of the plants had only recently begun production. The new productive capacity was remarkably large. Despite errors and chaotic conditions, the United States was producing more combat munitions than any of the belligerents—indeed almost as much as Germany and Japan combined. Airplane production was up to a rate of almost 25,000 per year. The armed forces already had inducted and were training 2 million men. This mobilization was only a fraction of what was soon to come, for large scale construction of factories and training camps was under way. While the nation during the debate over neutrality had not built its defenses with the smoothness and speed that critics demanded, it had achieved a substantial degree of preparedness.

The Japanese attack on Pearl Harbor created almost as much chaos indirectly in American war production as it did directly in the fleet in the Pacific. The war agencies in Washington began ordering tremendous quantities—indeed far too much—of everything.

The problem of restoring some order to war production, then raising it to astronomical totals, was a joint one. The armed forces, the Maritime Commission, and other procurement agencies did the ordering. The War Production Board tried to control the size of the procurement program and to allocate materials between the armed forces and the civilians. The WPB was thus trying to control the entire economy and inevitably was coming into collision with the armed forces over the size and nature of war orders as opposed to what was to be reserved for

---

**The Mushrooming of War Plants**

These two pictures of a West Virginia valley taken from the same spot, the first in 1941 and the second in 1942, indicate the remarkable speed with which the Morgantown Ordnance Plant was built and went into production. This was typical of the mushrooming construction all over the nation. The plant was one of fifty-four built by Du Pont in thirty-two locations for the government at a total cost of $1,034,000,000. Du Pont received a total fee, after taxes and all applicable charges, of one-fifteenth of 1 per cent of the construction cost. (Du Pont)

civilians. Internecine conflict among the agencies and personality clashes among the administrators were unavoidable.

Out of the confusion a pattern gradually emerged. The first step, oddly enough, was to cut back the building of plants, although at times this created a furor throughout a region, as when the Higgins Shipyards in New Orleans were abandoned. After the middle of 1942, the amount of new construction being started declined sharply; in another six months, the larger part of the war plants and military facilities had been built.

The second step was to coordinate the various phases of the war-production program. As late as the summer of 1942, bottlenecks were halting some assembly lines. The vital shipbuilding program had to be cut back because of scarcities of raw materials like steel plate and glass, and of components like valves, turbines, and engines. The WPB eventually broke most of the bottlenecks through the Controlled Materials Plan, which established a balanced production of finished products and allocated precise quantities of raw materials to each manufacturer.

The shortage of rubber became so critical in 1942 that it required special attention. After the WPB failed to solve the problem, Roosevelt appointed a committee under Baruch to make a special report. This recommended sharp restrictions upon the use of motor vehicles, including a national speed limit of thirty-five miles per hour, and immediate construction of enormous synthetic rubber plants. Roosevelt ordered the restrictions, and appointed a Rubber Director in the WPB, William M. Jeffers, president of the Union Pacific Railroad, to construct the plants. By the end of 1943 the synthetic rubber industry was producing a third again as much rubber as the country had normally used before the war.

An indispensable adjunct of the war agencies was the Senate War Investigating Committee, headed by Harry S Truman, previously little known. The senators consciously patterned it after the Committee on the Conduct of the War of the Civil War period, but avoided the pitfalls of their predecessors by ruling out questions of military policy. Instead, they ferreted out incompetence and corruption in the war-production and military-construction programs: outrageous expense in building army camps, im-

proper inspection of airplane engines, a quixotic scheme to build an Arctic pipeline, and the like. The Truman Committee uncovered and stopped hundreds of millions of dollars of waste. In the wartime expenditure of $400 billion there was amazingly little corruption.

By the beginning of 1944 factories had turned out what seemed to be needed to win the war. The output was double that of all Axis countries combined. Cutbacks began but were haphazard and ill-planned, and when the armed forces met reverses, some turned out to have been premature. With the cutbacks came pressure for a resumption of the manufacture of civilian durable goods. The military leaders staunchly opposed this.

War needs even at their peak took only about one-third of American production. While manufacture of such goods as automobiles, most electrical appliances, and nondefense housing had come to a halt in 1942, production of food, clothing, and repair and maintenance goods was continued or even slightly increased.

## Transporting the Supplies

As war production grew, the problem of transporting the supplies within the country and overseas became acute. Inside the United States, the Office of Defense Transportation, established in December 1941, coordinated all forms of transport—railroads, trucking, airlines, inland waterways, and pipelines. In contrast to the system in World War I, railroads remained under private control, but functioned effectively, carrying double the traffic of 1939 with only 10 per cent more locomotives and 20 per cent more freight cars. Since they could not, however, transport sufficient oil to the East when German submarines began attacking coastal tankers in 1942, the government authorized construction of the Big Inch pipeline from Texas to eastern Pennsylvania.

Transporting troops and supplies overseas required one of the most spectacular construction programs of all. The Germans had sunk more than 12 million tons of shipping by 1942. To replace it, the United States Maritime Commission had to abandon its program of building fast, efficient ships requiring scarce turbines, valves, and electrical equipment. As early as July 1940,

Admiral Emory S. Land, head of the commission, and Knudsen recommended to the President mass production of a freighter that, while slow (sailing only eleven knots), would be simple to construct and would not require scarce components. By using the existing designs for an old-fashioned British tramp steamer with a reciprocating engine and steam winches, they saved six months in starting production. This "ugly duckling" was the Liberty ship. After a slow beginning, builders substituted welding for riveting and applied prefabrication and subassembly techniques in constructing it. In 1941 construction of a Liberty ship required an average of 355 days; by the end of 1942 the time had been cut to 56 days, and one of Henry J. Kaiser's companies completed one in 14 days. During 1942 alone 8 million tons of shipping were built; by 1945 the United States had over 36 million tons of ships afloat.

## Scientists Against the Axis

The most revolutionary changes for the future came out of laboratories, as scientists pooled their skill in a race against those of the Axis—above all the Germans—to turn the basic knowledge that was available to all into decisive weapons of war. Between the two wars, while the United States had neglected military research and development, Germany had sprinted far ahead, except in the field of radar. In the 1920s the Naval Research Laboratory in Washington had discovered the principle of radar by bouncing back a radio beam directed at a ship on the Potomac. The British had developed radar most highly, and it was their salvation during the air blitz of 1940–1941.

Other potential weapons were in the offing which, if the Germans developed them first, could mean Nazi victory in the war. (This was one of the reasons why the armed forces had decided to concentrate upon defeating Germany first.) The only way in which American scientists could catch up seemed to be through teamwork. The German threat brought the creation of a government scientific agency such as the New Deal had failed to produce. A leading scientist, Vannevar Bush, persuaded President Roosevelt to create a committee for scientific research in June 1940. A year later, under the direction of Bush, it became the Office of Scientific Research and Development, which mobilized scientists with such effectiveness that in some areas they outstripped their German opponents.

The Americans and the British developed superior radar, which not only detected enemy airplanes and ships but helped direct shells against them. In these shells, by 1943, were radio-directed proximity fuses that detonated the shells as they neared their targets. American rocket research produced weapons that enormously increased the fire power of airplanes, ships, and tanks. But the Americans still lagged behind the Germans, who before the end of the war were blasting London with enormous V-1 and V-2 rockets. The Germans also built the first jet airplanes and snorkel submarines, which would have been an even more serious menace if they had come into full production.

There was a danger, little publicized, that Germany might develop an atomic weapon. In the summer of 1939, a physicist, Enrico Fermi, and a mathematician, Albert Einstein, got word to President Roosevelt that German physicists had achieved atomic fission in uranium; what had long been theoretically possible had been accomplished. Next might come a bomb. The President authorized a small research project, and a race in the dark against the Nazis began.

In December 1942 physicists produced a controlled chain reaction in an atomic pile at the University of Chicago. The problem then became the enormous technical one of achieving this release of power in a bomb. Through the Manhattan District of the Army Engineer Corps, the government secretly poured nearly $2 billion into one project for producing fissionable plutonium and into another, under the supervision of J. Robert Oppenheimer, for building a bomb. This was an enormous and frightening gamble, against the hazards that the thing might not work and that the enemy might succeed first. Only after the war did the United States discover that the Germans were far from developing a usable atomic device. On July 16, 1945, after the end of the war in Europe, the first A-bomb was exploded, on a tower in New Mexico, producing the most blinding flash of light ever seen on earth, and then a huge billowing mushroom cloud.

## THE IMPACT ON CIVILIANS

No American could escape the impact of the war effort. Everybody was affected—and most people very deeply—by war jobs, wages, prices, rationing and other controls, taxes, and propaganda.

### Manpower and Womanpower

The nation, after grappling for years with the problem of millions of unemployed, found itself hard pressed for sufficient people to swell the fighting forces, man the war plants, till the fields, and keep the domestic economy functioning. There were periodic demands for national service legislation or a labor draft, but unions were so vehemently opposed that no such measure ever passed the Senate. The relatively weak War Manpower Commission tried to coerce workers into remaining at defense jobs at the risk of being drafted, but the war came to an end without any tight allocation of manpower comparable to that of materials. The armed forces had first call upon men through Selective Service, which had been in operation since the fall of 1940. Altogether draft boards registered 31 million men. Including volunteers, over 15 million men and women served in the armed forces during the war. Nevertheless the working force jumped from 46.5 million to over 53 million as the 7 million unemployed and many previously considered unemployable, the very young and the elderly, and several million women found jobs. The number of civilian employees of the federal government trebled.

This mobilization of manpower entailed the greatest reshuffling of population within such a short time in the entire history of the nation; altogether 27.3 million people moved during the war. It also meant a heavy weight of wartime tension on American families. With the return of prosperity and the impending departure of soldiers, both marriage and birth rates rose. In 1942 and 1943 about 3 million children were born each year, compared with 2 million a year before the war. But young wives and mothers fared badly in crowded housing near defense plants or army bases, or, after husbands had been shipped overseas, back home with parents. Draft boards deferred fathers as long as possible,

> **The Home Front [1942]**
>
> *That was the spring when women took to wearing slacks in the streets (a great blow to the human race), old toothpaste tubes had to be turned in for new ones, men's trousers were commanded to be cuffless, and a radio comedian named Bob Hope began to play soldiers' camps around the country. . . . That was the spring we first heard about sugar rationing, with gasoline rationing to come. Ice cream was reduced to ten flavors, and civilian suffering really hit its stride when the War Production Board banned the use of metals for asparagus tongs, beer mugs, spittoons, bird cages, cocktail shakers, hair curlers, corn poppers, and lobster forks. New York blacked out, and for days we talked about how beautiful the great city looked stark and naked, silhouetted against the moon and the stars. . . . Sex reared its pretty head in factories as an occupational hazard. Girls were requested to quit wearing sweaters, peekaboo waists, halters, and other revealing garments. The boys were rubbernecking themselves into too many accidents.—Paul Gallico in Jack Goodman, ed., While You Were Gone (New York: Simon and Schuster, 1946).*

but more than 1 million were ultimately inducted. More than 2.5 million wives were separated from their husbands because of the war. The divorce rate increased slowly. Because men in the armed forces could not be divorced without their consent, and many estranged wives stayed married in order to continue receiving allotment checks, a heavy backlog was built for postwar divorce courts.

When mothers were forced to work, children often suffered neglect, or were upset over the change. Court cases involving juvenile delinquency, especially among children from eight to fourteen, and among girls, the "bobby-soxers," increased 56 per cent. Even among the non-delinquents, a serious price had to be paid at the time and later for the disruption of more American families for a longer period of time than ever before.

As adolescents found jobs, the percentage of those between fourteen and nineteen who attended school dropped from 62 in 1940 to 56 in 1944. Teachers also left for the armed forces or better-paying war jobs. Universities kept functioning through military research projects and training programs.

The great migration to war plants was stripping the agricultural South of underprivileged whites and blacks alike, as 5 million people moved within the South, and another 1.6 million left the area completely. In the South this exodus led to the false rumor among outraged white housewives that the departing Negro domestics had formed "Eleanor Clubs," named after Mrs. Roosevelt, to "get a white woman in every kitchen by 1943." In the North, it led to explosive tension when Negroes, enjoying their new freedom, were jostled in crowded streetcars against indignant whites newly migrated from the South. A serious riot, in which twenty-five blacks and nine whites were killed, shook Detroit in June 1943. New York narrowly averted a similar disaster. At the very time when the United States was fighting a war against the racist doctrines of Hitler, many whites became resentful over the rapid gains Negroes were making.

In June 1941, after the head of the Pullman porters' union, A. Philip Randolph, had threatened a march on Washington, President Roosevelt established the Fair Employment Practices Committee. It worked diligently throughout the war against discrimination in employment. By 1944 2 million Negroes were at work in war industry, and many previous barriers to economic opportunities for Negroes were permanently cracked.

Not everyone shared in the new prosperity. Government economists reported in 1943 that 10 million families still received less than the $1,675 per year requisite for a minimum standard of living. Most Americans, however, were relatively more affluent than they had been. The living standard of working people ad-vanced rapidly. This was due less to wage increases than to payment of time-and-a-half for overtime beyond 40 hours. The average work week lengthened from 40.6 hours in 1941 to 45.2 in 1944. As living costs rose (on a 1935–1939 base of 100) from 100.4 in 1940 to 128.4 in 1945, gross weekly wages went up from $25.20 to $43.39. Working women and children created social problems, but they also brought additional prosperity to millions of families.

## Restraining Labor Unions

Labor unions rapidly grew in strength during the war, and their unpopularity among Americans of the middle and upper classes increased. Union membership rose with the rise in the working force, from about 10.5 million workers in 1941 to over 13 million in 1945. Keeping these workers satisfied was no easy matter. The administration was determined to prevent strikes and to restrain the formidable pressure of the labor unions from forcing wages, and thus all prices, upward. President Roosevelt followed the procedure of World War I by establishing a National Defense Mediation Board (March 1941) made up of representatives of management, labor, and the public. In November 1941 it broke down when the CIO members resigned over the refusal of the board to recommend a union shop (i.e., one in which all new workers hired must join the union) in coal mines. In January 1942 Roosevelt replaced it with the National War Labor Board, similarly constituted but much stronger. This board could set wages, hours, and working conditions, and through the war powers of the President it could enforce these in a final extremity by government seizure and operation of plants.

On the union-shop question, which was creating much hostility between management and labor, the board arrived at a compromise, the "maintenance of membership" clause. Non-members hired into a war plant did not have to join a union, but members had to remain in it, and the union remained the bargaining agent for the duration of the contract. Pressure for wage increases, which might contribute to inflation, was more serious. The board hit upon a solution in ruling upon the Little Steel cases in July 1942. Taking January 1, 1941, as the base date when workers had received a standard wage, it recognized a 15-per-cent rise in the cost-of-living index since then. Consequently, it felt that a proportionate increase for steel workers would be equitable. The Little Steel formula, except for those receiving substandard wages (like some textile workers), served thereafter as a wage ceiling.

Despite the no-strike pledges of the major unions, there were nearly 15,000 work stoppages during the war, involving the loss of more than 36 million man-days. These stoppages involved only one-ninth of 1 per cent of the working time (though they indirectly caused more damage than this). When John L. Lewis' United Mine Workers defied the government in their strike against the Little Steel formula in May 1943, Congress reacted by passing over Roosevelt's veto the Smith-Connally or War Labor Disputes Act (June 1943). This act required unions to wait thirty days before striking and empowered the President to seize a struck war plant.

## Price Controls, War Finance

At the beginning of the war, with a two-year supply of wheat, cotton, and corn stored in Secretary Wallace's ever-normal granary, there seemed no danger of food shortages in the United States. But within six months after Pearl Harbor, scarcities of many sorts began to develop. The United States felt the increased demand of the armed forces and its allies and the reduction of supplies due to the loss of fibers and oils from Southeast Asia. By 1942 meat production was half again that of depression years, but American consumers with their increased buying power were eager to buy even more. Consumer income in 1943 was 65 per cent above depression levels, and much of it was in the pockets of people who had not eaten adequately for years.

A food administrator did exist, Chester Davis, but he resigned in protest when his views (and those of the American Farm Bureau Federation) did not prevail; his successor was Marvin Jones. Neither man had the dictatorial powers to provide the scarce supplies and manpower that the dominant farm bloc in Congress would have liked to bestow upon agricultural producers.

Rather, farmers had to depend upon whatever the War Production Board would allocate to them, and upon a generous draft-exemption program they obtained from Congress. They also received legislation raising the ceiling on commodity prices to 110 per cent of parity. Since this came into conflict with the anti-inflation efforts of the administration, a dogged struggle developed between the President and the congressional farm bloc over farm prices. Neither side won entirely.

Pressures from business, farmers, and labor, combined with the scarcity of consumer goods and the burgeoning of buying power, created an almost irresistible trend toward inflation. During the defense period, the Office of Price Administration, under a vigorous New Dealer, Leon Henderson, lacked real coercive power and failed to halt inflation. Between the invasion of Poland and the attack on Pearl Harbor, prices of twenty-eight basic commodities rose by nearly one-fourth. Immediately thereafter, pressures became so acute that prices went up 2 per cent per month. Soon Congress hastily passed a bill authorizing only selective price fixing and setting ceilings with a preferential trap door for agriculture.

In April 1942 the OPA issued a General Maximum Price Regulation that froze prices of consumer goods, and of rents in defense areas only, at their March 1942 level. But the rise of uncontrolled farm prices toward 110 per cent of parity forced an upward revision of food prices. This gave ammunition to the labor unions' barrage against fixed wages. In October 1942 Congress, grudgingly responding to the President's demand, passed the Anti-inflation Act. Under its authority, Roosevelt immediately froze agricultural prices, wages, salaries, and rents throughout the country.

In July 1943 Roosevelt appointed a former advertising executive with remarkable administrative talents, Chester Bowles, to head the OPA. With a small enforcement staff, Bowles braved general unpopularity to hold the increase in living costs during the next two years to 1.4 per cent. Altogether, the price level went up less than 29 per cent from 1939 to the end of the war, compared with 63 per cent between 1914 and the armistice.

**Consumers Waiting to Purchase Meat**
After the Office of Price Administration issued
rationing books, the long lines in front of markets
when meats came in soon disappeared. (Wide World)

Consumers nonetheless suffered numerous
irritations and discomforts. The OPA, through
unpaid local volunteers manning 5,600 price and
rationing boards, administered the rationing of
canned goods, coffee, sugar, meat, butter and
other fats, shoes, tires, gasoline, and fuel oil.
The OPA could not, however, control deterioration of quality. Black-marketing and overcharg-
ing grew in proportions far beyond OPA policing
capacity; in 1943 Congress slashed the funds of
the enforcement division.

One of the most important inflationary controls was the sale of war bonds and stamps to
channel off some of the excess purchasing
power, which for the single year 1945 mounted
to nearly $60 billion. Throughout most of the
war, personal incomes were at least one-third
greater than the available civilian goods and services. The Treasury Department, through eight
war bond drives and its payroll deduction plans,
but with few of the lurid or coercive touches of
World War I, sold $40 billion worth of series
"E" bonds to small investors, and $60 billion
more to individuals and corporate entities other
than banks.

Had this been the total of government loans,
the effect would have been to quell inflation, but
the Treasury had to borrow $87.5 billion more
from Federal Reserve and commercial banks.
Since in effect the banks created new credits
which the government then spent, the result
was to inflate bank credits and money in circulation by over $100 billion.

Taxes did much more to drain off surplus purchasing power. The government raised 41 per
cent of its war costs through taxation, compared
with 33 per cent during World War I. The
Revenue Act of 1942, which Roosevelt hailed

as "the greatest tax bill in American history," levied a 94-per-cent tax on the highest incomes; the President had suggested that no one should net more than $25,000 per year during the war. Also, for the first time, the income tax fell upon those in lower income brackets. To simplify payment for these new millions, Congress enacted a withholding system of payroll deductions in 1943. Corporation taxes reached a maximum of 40 per cent on the largest incomes. In addition, excess profits were subject to a 90-per-cent tax, reclaiming for the government a large part of the return from war contracts. However, these taxes could be rebated to companies to aid them in reconversion (changing back to peacetime production), a provision of future significance. In effect, the government taxed away a large part of the profits of corporations, then returned it later when it was needed. Heavy excise taxes on transportation, communication, luxuries, and amusements completed the levies.

Between 1941 and 1945 the government raised $138 billion through taxation—nearly a $100 billion of it from income and excess profits taxes. Those in the top 5 per cent of the income scale suffered a serious relative economic loss, as their share of disposable income dropped from 26 per cent in 1940 to 16 per cent in 1944. Few persons or corporations were able to make fortunes out of the war, and a considerable amount of economic leveling—upward more than downward—had taken place. Despite the heavy taxation, by the end of the war consumers possessed an estimated $129 billion in liquid savings.

From 1941 to 1945 the federal government spent twice as much as the total appropriations from the creation of the government to 1941, and ten times as much as the cost of World War I—a total of $321 billion. The national debt rose from $49 billion in 1941 to $259 billion in 1945, yet the black warnings of national bankruptcy that had punctuated the New Deal years all but disappeared.

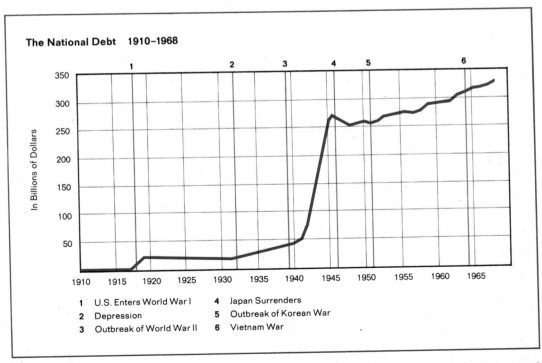

**The National Debt    1910–1968**

In Billions of Dollars

1  U.S. Enters World War I    4  Japan Surrenders
2  Depression                5  Outbreak of Korean War
3  Outbreak of World War II  6  Vietnam War

Taken by itself, the growth of the national debt could be interpreted as appalling. Compared with the even more rapid growth of the economy—as reflected in the Gross National Product, for example—the size of the national debt did not seem a cause for undue concern.

## Information and Misinformation

As an incentive for winning the war, advertisers presented a vision of a postwar America in which every husband would have a chrome-trimmed car and every wife a gleaming kitchen filled with wonder-working gadgets. President Roosevelt promised even more. "In the future days, which we seek to make secure," he told the people (January 1941), "we look forward to a world founded upon four essential freedoms." These were freedom of speech and worship, and freedom from want and fear. They were for the postwar future, not necessarily for the wartime present.

From Pearl Harbor on, there was the suspicion that through the Office of Censorship, almost immediately established under a competent Associated Press executive, Byron Price, the government was withholding information not because it was vital to the enemy but because it would be damaging to public opinion of the armed forces. Diligent newspapermen, aided by Price, exerted pressure on the armed forces to make censorship an instrument for security, rather than for the concealing of incompetence. Newspapers following Office of Censorship rules censored themselves to withhold local news that might be of value to the enemy.

The overlapping and conflict among government information agencies led to the establishment in June 1942 of the Office of War Information under a shrewd news commentator, Elmer Davis. Although the OWI consolidated four previous organizations, it coordinated rather than assumed the information function of domestic war agencies.

The OWI aroused the misgivings of Congress, partly because of internal feuding and the mass resignation of the pamphlet writers, but mainly because conservatives objected to several of the OWI pamphlets: one on the dangers of inflation, another on Negroes in the war, and another on the need for high taxes. A fourth pamphlet, intended only for overseas distribution, a cartoon biography of Roosevelt, especially worried antiadministration congressmen. They feared that the OWI might promote New Dealish policies and the 1944 candidacy of Roosevelt. In 1943 Congress cut funds for the domestic branch of the OWI so drastically that it had to stop producing propaganda.

Overseas, the OWI carried on a program employing 8,400 persons by V-E Day. Through Voice of America broadcasts begun in 1941 and propaganda of many sorts, it presented an idealistic view of American war aims and aspirations for a peaceful postwar world. As the symbol of this idealism it dramatized President Roosevelt. By the end of the war, Roosevelt was more of a hero overseas than at home, and American aims appeared more idealistic abroad than in the United States.

The war produced less hatred and vindictiveness at home than had World War I. The energy that had gone into crude vigilantism in the earlier war now went into serving as air-raid wardens and doing similar duties for the Office of Civilian Defense. People continued to eat hamburgers and sauerkraut and listen to Wagner. They demonstrated little animosity toward Americans of German background and practically none toward Italians. A few Nazi agents and American Fascists were jailed, but the most ambitious effort to punish them, a sedition trial of twenty-eight, ended in a mistrial after the defendants' lawyers had engaged in long weeks of delaying tactics. A few papers like Father Coughlin's *Social Justice* were barred from the mails. But Socialists went unpunished, and religious conscientious objectors who were willing to register went to Civilian Public Service camps rather than to prison.

In sad contrast to this moderation, the frenzy of public fury turned toward the Japanese. The fighting in the Pacific developed a fierce savagery, reflected in the public anger within the United States. On the Pacific Coast, hatred of Americans of Japanese background became extreme. Wild stories circulated about sabotage at Pearl Harbor and plots to aid a Japanese landing on the California coast—later proven completely untrue. Under public pressure, Roosevelt, in February 1942, authorized the army to remove all people of Japanese ancestry from the West Coast. Some 117,000 people, two-thirds of them United States citizens, were abruptly herded behind barbed wire, and later shipped into ten relocation centers in wild and disagreeable areas. They suffered the financial loss of at least 40 per cent of their possessions and for several years were barred from lucrative employment. Yet Japanese-Americans in Hawaii

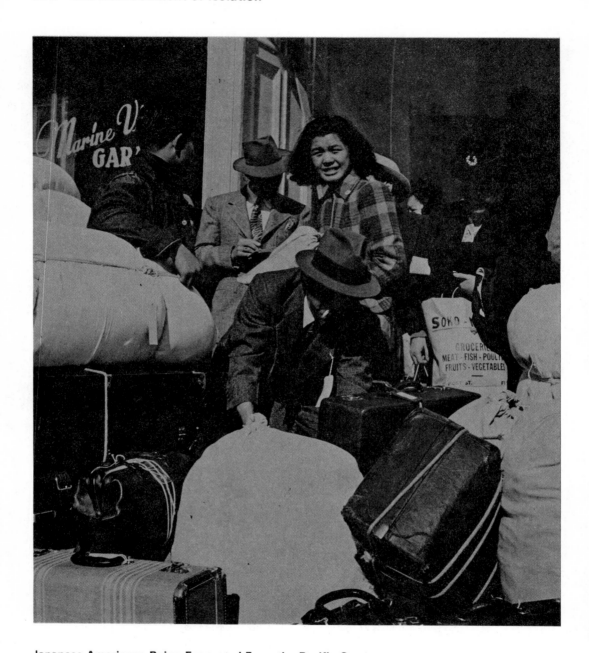

### Japanese-Americans Being Evacuated From the Pacific Coast

"Americans . . . have held up to scorn the crudities of the Fascist regimes. Yet the history of the evacuation policy could be an episode from the totalitarian handbook. The resident Japanese minority became the scapegoat of military defeat at Hawaii. Racial prejudices, economic cupidity, and political fortune-hunting became intertwined with patriotic endeavor. In the face of exact knowledge to the contrary, military officials propounded the theory that race determined allegiance. Civil administrators and the national legislature were content to rubber-stamp the military fiat. . . .

"The American Civil Liberties Union has called the Japanese evacuation 'the worst single wholesale violation of civil liberties of American citizens in our history.' Later judgment will probably not lower that estimate, though it has already been tempered in historical perspective as abrogated rights have been restored and most Japanese in America have returned with full status to normal life."—Morton Grodzins, *Americans Betrayed* (Chicago: University of Chicago Press, 1949). (National Archives) were left unmolested without incident throughout the war. There were 17,600 Japanese-Americans in the armed forces. Their units, especially in Italy, established outstanding records for bravery under fire.

The Supreme Court in 1944 validated the evacuation and, in other decisions as well, upheld military control over civilians. In time of war or national emergency, United States citizens apparently could expect no court protection of their civil rights from military or executive authority.

# Selected Readings

**Biographical Studies** E. E. Morison, *Turmoil and Tradition: A Study of the Life and Times of Henry L. Stimson* (1960); R. N. Current, *Secretary Stimson: A Study in Statecraft* (1954); R. E. Sherwood, *Roosevelt and Hopkins*° (1948); J. W. Pratt, *Cordell Hull, 1933–44* (1964); W. S. Cole, *Senator Gerald P. Nye and American Foreign Relations* (1962); E. D. Cronon, *Josephus Daniels in Mexico*° (1960).

**Depression Diplomacy** R. H. Ferrell, *American Diplomacy in the Great Depression* (1957); S. F. Bemis, *The Latin American Policy of the United States* (1943); Alexander De Conde, *Herbert Hoover's Latin American Policy* (1951); E. O. Guerrant, *Roosevelt's Good Neighbor Policy* (1950); Bryce Wood, *The Making of the Good Neighbor Policy*° (1961); A. W. Griswold, *The Far Eastern Policy of the United States* (1938); Dorothy Borg, *The United States and the Far Eastern Crisis of 1933–1938* (1964); R. P. Browder, *The Origins of Soviet-American Diplomacy* (1953); W. A. Williams, *American-Russian Relations, 1781–1947* (1952); R. P. Traina, *American Diplomacy and the Spanish Civil War* (1968); A. Guttmann, *The Wound in the Heart: America and the Spanish Civil War* (1962).

**Interventionists Versus Isolationists** Alexander De Conde, ed., *Isolation and Security: Ideas and Interests in Twentieth-Century American Foreign Policy* (1957); R. A. Devine, *The Illusion of Neutrality* (1962); M. L. Chadwin, *The Hawks of World War II* (1968); J. K. Nelson, *The Peace Prophets: American Pacifist Thought, 1919–1941* (1967); Manfred Jonas, *Isolationism in America, 1935–1941*° (1966); W. S. Cole, *America First* (1953); Walter Johnson, *Battle Against Isolation* (1944); Warren Moscow, *Roosevelt and Willkie* (1968).

**Steps Toward War** W. L. Langer and S. E. Gleason, *The Challenge to Isolation, 1937–1940* (1952) and *The Undeclared War, 1940–1941* (1953), comprehensive accounts; C. A. Beard, *American Foreign Policy in the Making, 1932–1940* (1946) and *President Roosevelt and the Coming of the War, 1941* (1948), highly critical of F. D. R.; Basil Rauch, *Roosevelt from Munich to Pearl Harbor*° (1950), an attempt to refute Beard; Herbert Feis, *The Road to Pearl Harbor*° (1950); Roberta Wohlsetter, *Pearl Harbor: Warning and Decision* (1962); R. J. C. Butow, *Tojo and the Coming of the War* (1961); P. W. Schroeder, *The Axis Alliance and Japanese-American Relations, 1941* (1958); W. F. Kimball, *The Most Unsordid Act: Lend-Lease, 1939–1941* (1969).

**War Production** Bureau of the Budget. *The United States at War* (1946); D. M. Nelson, *Arsenal of Democracy* (1946); Bruce Catton, *War Lords of Washington* (1946); Eliot Janeway, *The Struggle for Survival* (1951); H. M. Somers, *Presidential Agency: OWMR* (1950); L. R. Groves, *Now It Can Be Told* (1962), on development of the A-bomb; J. P. Baxter III, *Scientists Against Time* (1946); W. W. Willcox, *The Farmer in the Second World War* (1947); W. A. Nielander, *Wartime Food Rationing in the United States* (1947).

**Wartime Life** Jack Goodman, ed., *While You Were Gone: A Report on Wartime Life in the United States* (1946); W. F. Ogburn, ed., *American Society in Wartime* (1943); Reuben Hill, *Families Under Stress* (1949); E. S. Corwin, *Total War and the Constitution* (1947); Morton Grodzins, *Americans Betrayed: Politics and the Japanese Evacuation* (1949); M. Q. Sibley and P. E. Jacob, *Conscription of Conscience: The Conscientious Objector, 1940–1947* (1952).

---

° Titles available in paperback.

# Chapter 26
# Victory Without Peace

President Woodrow Wilson had turned from progressive reform to a foreign crusade, with disillusioning results. Similarly, President Franklin D. Roosevelt turned from the New Deal to national defense and then war abroad, but he hoped to escape the frustrations that had befallen his predecessor. In trying to avoid the "mistakes" that Wilson had made, Roosevelt pursued essentially the same objectives by almost exactly the opposite means, so that at times his policies appeared to be the very reverse of Wilson's.

Thus, during World War II, Roosevelt did not hold the United States somewhat aloof from its allies and call it merely an "associated" power, as Wilson had done during World War I. To the contrary, under Roosevelt this country took the initiative in drafting and signing a Declaration of the United Nations (January 1, 1942). The document set forth the war aims of the Atlantic Charter, committing the country's entire military and economic resources to the prosecution of the war, and pledging unlimited cooperation with the other signatories to fight on and make no separate peace. In effect, the United States was taking the lead in forming a grand alliance between the twenty-six original partners and the twenty more that signed before the war was over.

In peacemaking as in warmaking, Roosevelt followed a course quite different from Wilson's. True, the war aims he presented in the Atlantic Charter, which he cosigned with Prime Minister Winston Churchill, were vaguely reminiscent of those that Wilson had announced, unilaterally, in his Fourteen Points. But Roosevelt, with his slogan of "unconditional surrender," was determined to allow no armistice short of the enemy's utter defeat. And he was careful to keep from repeating the steps that had led the United States to a fiasco in relation to the Versailles Treaty and the League of Nations. This time there was to be no general peace conference comparable to the one at Versailles, and the new peacekeeping arrangement was to be kept quite separate from the political settlements to be made. The wartime alliance itself was to be converted into a peacekeeping body—the United Nations organization.

When, at the war's conclusion, the Senate approved American membership in the U. N. organization, many liberal Americans rejoiced that their country now was righting the wrong it presumably had done in rejecting the League. They assumed that, with the

---

**The Mushroom Cloud Over Nagasaki, Japan   August 9, 1945**

"When the atomic bomb exploded, an intense flash was observed first, as though a large amount of magnesium had been ignited, and the scene grew hazy with white smoke. At the same time at the center of the explosion, and a short while later in other areas, a tremendous roaring sound was heard and a crushing blast wave and intense heat were felt. The peo-ple of Nagasaki, even those who lived on the outer edge of the blast, all felt as though they had sustained a direct hit, and the whole city suffered damage such as would have resulted from direct hits everywhere by ordinary bombs."—Nagasaki prefectural report on the bombing. (Official U.S. Air Force photo)

United States as a member, the League would have prevented a second world war; surely the U. N. would prevent a third. This optimism soon passed. For Americans the consequences of the Second World War were to prove even more disillusioning than those of the First, as the people came to realize that the victory of the grand alliance had brought no real peace to the world.

## FIGHTING A GLOBAL WAR

In December 1941 neither the army nor the navy seemed very well prepared for the enormous tasks ahead, and the disaster at Pearl Harbor did not improve confidence in their commands. Enormous industrial production alone could not win the war. The military leaders must know what to order, and where and how to use it, on a scale they had not envisaged in their prewar establishments.

### The American War Machine

At the outset the navy possessed only 300 combat ships, but at the close of the war it had 1,167 and was employing only one of the prewar vessels in the final attacks on Japan.

The army in 1939 had in theory nine infantry divisions but actually only the equivalent of about three and a half at half strength. Nor could it organize tactical units larger than a division. By mid-1941 it had twenty-nine infantry and cavalry divisions at nearly full strength, organized into four field armies—still less than half a million men. The army air force, nominally under the army but in practice almost independent, had only 22,000 officers and men and 2,400 aircraft in 1939.

There was little hint of what was to come. The most important of the war plans, "Orange," devised to go into effect in case of conflict with Japan, had presumed primarily a naval war, with the army mobilizing over a million men. By 1940 the more comprehensive "Rainbow" plans superseded these; by December 1941 a substantial mobilization was under way, though it was still far short of wartime totals.

Vast increases in personnel and equipment forced rapid changes in planning and organization. General George C. Marshall, Chief of Staff of the Army, reorganized the army high command in March 1942. That same month, Admiral Ernest J. King, a clear-headed hard driver,

became Chief of Naval Operations. Together with General H. H. Arnold of the army air force, these men met with a personal representative of the President, Admiral William D. Leahy, to constitute the Joint Chiefs of Staff. They functioned as the overall command and represented the United States in combined planning with the British or occasional negotiations with the Russians.

Over the Joint Chiefs of Staff was the Commander in Chief, President Roosevelt, who bore

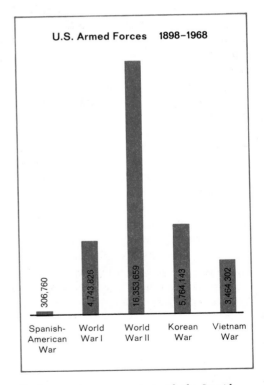

In the seventy years opening with the Spanish-American War, the United States was engaged in five major confrontations, yet the total deaths during this period were less than those in the Civil War. Much of the difference was due to improvements in military medicine and handling of casualties.

responsibility for the conduct of the war. Personally, and through assistants like Harry Hopkins and cabinet members, he coordinated the war planning of the Joint Chiefs with war production and manpower and with foreign policy. The War Plans Division of the Army General Staff had pointed out that civilians should decide the "what" of national policies, and the professional soldiers the "how." Roosevelt, who had always zealously guarded civilian control even in the Navy Department and the War Department, followed this course throughout the war. He depended heavily upon the advice of the Joint Chiefs of Staff and, once major policy had been decided, seldom interfered with their strategy.

The first of the great policy decisions had come in 1940 when the Americans decided that, even if Japan entered the war, their primary goal would be to defeat Germany with its superior military force, war production, and weapons development. The United States confirmed this priority in the initial wartime conference with the British at the end of December 1941. This decision did not mean neglecting the war against Japan. By August 1941, when the build-up, especially of airplanes, was under way in the Philippines, and later when General Douglas MacArthur received orders to fight, the strategy was shifting to a two-front war. The war against Germany was to be offensive, while that against Japan was to be defensive. It was difficult to hold to this policy as the Japanese tide in the Pacific swelled far beyond the bounds that the most pessimistic planners had anticipated. For the President, furious over Japanese treachery, and the navy, primarily responsible in the Pacific, it was not an easy decision to maintain. General MacArthur, the panic-stricken public on the Pacific Coast, and most Americans elsewhere clamored for prompt and stern action against the Japanese.

During the first chaotic months of shocking reverses, the armed forces allotted their men and supplies piecemeal to try to meet each new Axis threat. Top strategists emphatically warned that such dissipation of effort might lead to defeat. No one was more insistent than Dwight D. Eisenhower, who had been brought to Washington after Pearl Harbor as a Far Eastern ex-

pert, and who by the spring of 1942 was head of the Operations Planning Division under General Marshall. In emphatic memoranda, Eisenhower hammered away at the need to build up men and supplies in Europe for the invasion of North Africa that Roosevelt and Churchill had decided upon in their December 1941 meeting. Because of his vigor and his important role in developing an invasion plan, Eisenhower became the logical man to send to England (in June 1942) as commanding general in the European theater.

## On the Defensive    1941–1942

While the United States was building and equipping its fighting forces, it had to depend upon the Russians and the British to hold back the Germans as best they could. During the discouraging first six months of American participation, the American forces had to stand perilously on the defensive in both the Atlantic and the Pacific. There even seemed danger of a breakthrough in Egypt and the Caucasus which might enable the Germans and Japanese to join forces in the Middle East or India.

Ten hours after the strike at Pearl Harbor, Japanese airplanes hit the airfields at Manila, destroying half the American bombers and two-thirds of the fighter planes. That same day the Japanese sank two British warships off Malaya, the only Allied warships in the Far East. Three days later Guam fell; then, in the weeks that followed, Wake Island and Hong Kong. The great British fortress of Singapore in Malaya surrendered in February 1942, the Dutch East Indies in March, and Burma in April. In the Philippines on May 6 the exhausted Philippine and American troops, having made brave withdrawals to the Bataan peninsula and the Island of Corregidor in Manila Bay, ran down the last American flag in the Far East.

Only one weak outpost, Port Moresby in southern New Guinea, stood as a bulwark against the invasion of Australia. It seemed likely to fall, but there containment began through the efforts on land of Australian and American troops, and on the sea, of American aircraft carriers. In the Battle of Coral Sea on May 6–7, 1942, the Americans turned back Japanese invasion forces threatening Port Moresby. Under

General MacArthur, who had escaped from the Philippines, American and Australian troops began clearing the Japanese from New Guinea.

After the Battle of Coral Sea, the navy, having intercepted Japanese messages, knew the next move and rushed every available plane and vessel into the central Pacific. Near Midway Island, June 3–6, 1942, these forces inflicted heavy damage on a Japanese invasion fleet and headed off a drive to capture the island and neutralize Hawaii. The United States had achieved its goal of containment in the Pacific, and as men and supplies could be spared from the operations against the Nazis, it could assume the offensive against Japan.

In the Atlantic during the early months of 1942, the Nazis tried by means of submarines to confine the Americans to the Western Hemisphere. By mid-January the Germans had moved so many submarines to the Atlantic coast, where at night they torpedoed tankers silhouetted against the lights of cities, that they created a critical oil shortage. Against convoys bound for Europe they made attacks with devastating success. In the first eleven months they sank over 8 million tons of shipping—1.2 million more than the Allies meanwhile built—and threatened to delay indefinitely the large-scale shipment of supplies and men to Europe. Gradually the United States countered by developing effective antisubmarine vessels, air patrols, detecting devices, and weapons.

The submarines made it difficult to send assistance to the British and Russians in the summer of 1942 when they needed it most. The German *Afrika Corps* raced to El Alamein, only seventy-five miles from Alexandria, Egypt, threatening the Suez Canal and the Middle East. At the same time, German armies in Russia were plunging toward the Caucasus. In May the Russian foreign minister, Vyacheslav Molotov, visited Washington to demand an immediate second front that would divert at least forty German divisions from Russia; the alternative might be Russian collapse. Roosevelt promised to do everything possible to divert the Germans by invading France. But Churchill arrived the next month, when the Germans were threatening Egypt, and he strongly urged an invasion of North Africa instead.

## The Mediterranean Offensive

The overwhelming losses in the August 1942 raid on Dieppe, France, undertaken by experienced Canadian troops, indicated the wisdom of making the first American landing on a relatively unprotected flank. Through advance negotiations with officials of the Vichy government of defeated France, the Americans hoped to make a bloodless landing in French North Africa. At the end of October 1942 the British opened a counteroffensive at El Alamein which sent the *Afrika Corps* reeling back. On November 8, Anglo-American forces landed at Oran, Algiers, and Casablanca, Morocco, with some bungling and gratifyingly few losses. They met determined Vichy French resistance only at Casablanca.

Admiral Jean Darlan, earlier one of the most notorious collaborators with the Nazis, signed an armistice with the Allies on November 12. He ordered a cease-fire and promised the aid of 50,000 French colonial troops. Outraged American liberals protested against the deal with the Vichyites as opposed to the French resistance forces under General Charles de Gaulle. The critics quieted somewhat a few weeks later when Darlan was assassinated. Unsavory though it was to idealists, the Vichy gamble probably saved lives and speeded the liberation of North Africa.

The Germans tried to counter the invasion by ferrying troops from Sicily into Tunisia at the rate of a thousand a day. Early in 1943 the *Afrika Corps*, which had retreated westward across Tripoli, joined them and threw the full weight of its armor against the green American troops. The Americans lost heavily but with the aid of the British held onto their bases and gained in experience. Allied air power and the British navy so seriously harassed the Axis supply line from Sicily that Germany decided not to make a major stand in Tunisia. From March into May, the British army in the east and the armies in the west under Eisenhower gradually closed a vise on the German and Italian troops. On May 12, 1943, the last Axis troops in North Africa surrendered. The Mediterranean had been reopened, and the Americans had learned lessons that would be useful in the successful invasion of France.

That invasion, despite the continued clamor-

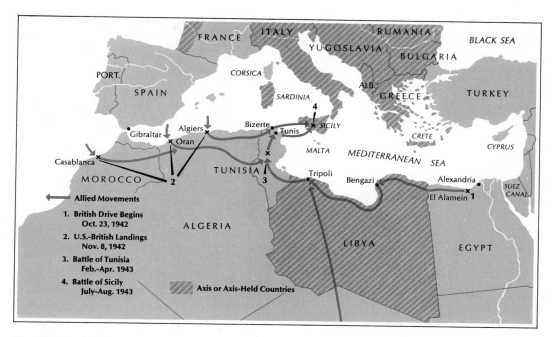

**The North African and Sicilian Campaigns**

Map legend:

**Allied Movements**

1. British Drive Begins Oct. 23, 1942
2. U.S.-British Landings Nov. 8, 1942
3. Battle of Tunisia Feb.-Apr. 1943
4. Battle of Sicily July-Aug. 1943

Axis or Axis-Held Countries

ing of the Russians, was not to take place immediately. The fighting in Tunisia had tied up too large a part of the Allied combat resources for too long. Nazi submarines were still taking too heavy a toll of the Allies' inadequate shipping. Some of the ships and production had to be diverted to the antisubmarine war, and others to the prosecution of the Pacific campaigns. Also, the planners in London had come to recognize that an enormous build-up was necessary for a successful cross-channel invasion. Fortunately for the Allies, the tide turned for the Russians also during the winter of 1942–1943, when they successfully held the Germans at Stalingrad in the Ukraine, eliminating an army of 250,000 men.

As early as mid-January 1943, Roosevelt and Churchill and their staffs, while conferring at Casablanca, looked ahead to the next move. This was to be an invasion of Sicily, even though General Marshall feared it might delay the invasion of France. Churchill argued persuasively that the operation in Sicily might knock Italy out of the war and lead the Germans to tie up many divisions in defense of Italy and the Balkans.

On the night of July 9, 1943, American and British armies landed in the extreme southeast of Sicily, where defenses were comparatively light. The Americans made grievous errors, the worst being to shoot down twenty-three planeloads of their own paratroops, but learned from their mistakes. In thirty-eight days the Allies conquered the island and looked toward the Italian mainland. Mussolini now fell from power, to be replaced by the pro-Allied Marshall Pietro Badoglio. At once Badoglio opened complicated negotiations to switch Italy to the side of the United Nations. As the negotiations went on, the Nazis moved eight strong divisions into northern Italy, concentrated other troops near Rome, and turned the country into an occupied defense bastion.

A limited but long and punishing campaign opened on the Italian peninsula on September 3, 1943. It started with the greatest optimism, for that same day the Italian government signed an armistice agreement, and the Allies quickly seized bases and airfields in southern Italy. But the Nazi defenders fought so fiercely from hillside fortifications that by early 1944 they had stopped the slow and deliberately moving Al-

### The Invasion of Normandy

A coast guard combat photographer, climbing beyond the Nazi trench in the foreground to the top of the cliff, looked out at this panorama of channel waters crowded with ships while landing craft were putting ashore men and supplies. The barrage balloons floated overhead to protect the ships from low-flying enemy strafers. One of them is resting on the deck of a LST (landing barge). Long lines of trucks were heading inland, carrying reinforcements for the battle for the Cotentin peninsula. (Official U.S. Coast Guard photo)

lies at Monte Cassino. When the Allies tried to break behind the line by landing at Anzio, south of Rome, they were almost thrown back into the sea. With relatively few divisions, the Nazis were tying down the Allies while concentrating their main effort upon Russia. Finally, in May 1944, the Allies captured Cassino, pressed on from the Anzio beachhead, and on June 4 captured Rome, just before the cross-channel invasion of France began.

### The Liberation of Europe

In the fall of 1943 Germany was already reeling under the incessant blows from the growing Allied air power. Great Britain had begun its mass bombing of German industrial centers in the late spring of 1942 with a thousand-plane night raid on Cologne. In August the Americans made their first experimental daytime raids on the Continent. Bombing almost around-the-clock began on a gigantic scale in February 1944. One of the objects of these bombing raids was to draw German fighter planes into battle. By the end of the war the Americans were flying over 7,000 bombers and 6,000 fighters in Europe, had dropped nearly a million and a half tons of bombs, and had lost nearly 10,000 bombers. British figures were similar. Especially in the last year of the war, the bombing drastically cut production and impeded transportation. As early as the winter of 1944 it had so seriously demoralized the German people that 77 per cent of them already regarded the war as lost.

The bombing attacks, first upon the aviation industry, then upon transportation, did much to

**The Normandy Landings**

clear the way for the invasion in the late spring. By May 1944 the *Luftwaffe* was incapable of beating off the Allied air cover for an invasion. As D-Day (invasion day) approached, the invasion was postponed from the beginning of May until early June despite the likelihood of worsening weather, in order to obtain an additional month's production of special landing craft. A sudden storm delayed the operation for a day, but on the morning of June 6, 1944, the invasion came, not at the narrowest part of the English Channel, where the Nazis expected it, but along sixty miles of the Cotentin peninsula on the Normandy coast. While airplanes and battleships offshore incessantly bombarded the Nazi defenses, 4,000 vessels, stretching as far as the eye could see, brought in troops and supplies.

Within two weeks after the initial landings, the Allies had put ashore a million men and the equipment for them. They also had captured Cherbourg, only to find that the Germans had blocked its harbor so skillfully that it could not be used until August.

Well into July, the Allies fought mile by mile through the Normandy hedgerows. The breakthrough came on July 25, 1944, when General Omar Bradley's First Army, using its armor as cavalry had been used in earlier wars, smashed the German lines in an enormous sweep southward, then eastward. The invasion on the Mediterranean coast, beginning on August 15, quickly seized new ports (also seriously blocked) and opened new supply lines for the Allies. On August 25 French forces rode into Paris, jammed with cheering throngs. By mid-September the Allied armies had driven the Germans from almost all of France and Belgium, including the port of Antwerp, and had come to a halt against a firm line of German defenses.

Cold weather, rain, and floods aided the Germans. In December they struck with desperate fury along fifty miles of front in the Ardennes Forest, driving fifty-five miles toward Antwerp before they were stopped (in the "Battle of the Bulge") at Bastogne.

While the Allies were fighting their way through France to the Westwall (German defense line) and up the Italian peninsula, the Russian armies had been sweeping westward into central Europe and the Balkans. The Russian armies advanced more rapidly than had been expected and, in late January 1945, launched an offensive of over 150 divisions toward the Oder River, far inside Germany.

After liquidating the German thrust into the Ardennes, which had almost exhausted the Nazi fighting capacity, the Allied armies pushed on to the Rhine. The Americans captured Cologne on the west bank March 6, 1945, and on the next day, through remarkable luck, captured a bridge across the Rhine at Remagen. Troops poured across it. By the end of March the last great drives were under way as the British commander Montgomery with a million troops pushed across the north while Bradley's army, sweeping through central Germany, completed the encirclement and trapping of 300,000 German soldiers in the Ruhr. Russian troops were about to mount a spring offensive only thirty-five miles from Berlin.

There were fears that the Nazis were preparing for a last stand in an Alpine redoubt centering on Berchtesgaden on the Austrian border. In fact, however, the German western front had been demolished. The only real questions were where the Americans would drive next and where they would join the Russians. The Americans, capable of moving much farther eastward than had been anticipated, could have beaten the Russians to Berlin and Prague. This would have cost American lives but would have reaped political gain in Europe. General Eisenhower decided, instead, to send American troops to capture the Alpine redoubt and then halt along the Elbe River in central Germany to meet the Russians.

On May 8, 1945, the remaining German forces surrendered unconditionally. V-E (Victory in Europe) Day arrived amidst monster celebrations in western Europe and in the United States. The rejoicing was tempered only by the knowledge of the continuing war against Japan.

## The Pacific Offensive

The offensive strategy against the Japanese involved amphibious warfare of a type that the marine corps had been developing since the early 1920s. In the Pacific these new tactics came to be so perfected that troops were able to cross and seize vigorously defended beaches when the United States could not by-pass them and immobilize advanced Japanese strong points. The American strategy was, whenever feasible, "Hit 'em where they ain't."

The southern Solomon Islands to the east of New Guinea were being developed as a Japanese base for air raids against American communications with Australia. In August 1942 the navy and marines opened an offensive against three of these islands, Gavutu, Tulagi, and

Guadalcanal. Around and on Guadalcanal a struggle of unprecedented ferocity developed as the United States and Japanese navies battled for control in a series of large-scale engagements. By the time the struggle was over, the United States and its allies had lost heavily in cruisers, carriers, and destroyers, but had sunk forty-seven Japanese vessels. The Japanese navy had lost its offensive strength and thereafter concentrated upon defensive operations.

During the months when the great naval battles had been going against the United States, the Americans had gained control of the air and thus were able to sustain the marines, and subsequently the army, in their precarious jungle onslaught. By February 1943 Guadalcanal had been won. Through the year the island-hopping continued all around the enormous Japanese-held perimeter: in the South Pacific through the northern Solomons to New Georgia, and in No-

vember to Bougainville; in the central Pacific, also in November, the marine landing on Makin and the bloody assault on Tarawa in the Gilberts; in the northern Pacific, the inexpert reconquest of Kiska and Attu in the Aleutians.

Victories in the Marshall Islands in February 1944 cracked the Japanese outer perimeter, and before the month was out the navy had plunged far within it to wreck the bastion at Truk and raid Saipan in the Marianas. American submarines were increasingly harassing Japanese shipping, and thus hampering the economy. In 1943 the Americans sank 284 ships; in 1944 they sank 492—necessitating by summer a cut of nearly a quarter in skimpy Japanese food rations and creating a crucial gasoline shortage. The inner empire of Japan was coming under relentless siege.

Meanwhile, in 1942, the Japanese forced General Joseph H. Stilwell out of Burma and

**The War in the Pacific**

brought their troops as far west as the mountains bordering on India. China was so isolated that the United States could send in meager supplies only through an aerial ferry over the "hump" of the Himalayas. On the return trip, the planes brought Chinese troops for Stilwell to train and arm. Through 1943, Stilwell with Chinese, Indian, and a few American troops fought back through northern Burma, constructing a road and parallel pipeline across the rugged mountains into Yunnan province, China. The Ledo or Stilwell road was not open until the fall of 1944, but meanwhile the Air Transport Command managed to fly in sufficient supplies to enable the Fourteenth Air Force (before Pearl Harbor, the "Flying Tigers") to harass the Japanese. The Command undertook a still larger task when B-29 bombers struck the Yawata steel mills in Japan from Chinese bases (June 1944). The Japanese retaliated in the next few months by overrunning the bases from which the bombers operated, and clearing the coastal area so they could bring supplies northward from Southeast Asia by rail or road. They drove so far into the interior that they threatened the Chinese terminus of the Ledo Road, and perhaps even the center of government at Chungking.

The great Japanese offensive precipitated a long-simmering crisis in Chinese-American affairs, centering upon the relations between General Stilwell and Chiang Kai-shek. Stilwell was indignant because Chiang was using many of his troops to maintain an armed frontier against the Chinese Communists and would not deploy them against the Japanese. In order to have bolstered Chiang adequately, the United States would have had to send such substantial immediate support that the campaigns against Germany and directly against Japan might have had to be slowed down or postponed.

During 1944 Japan came under heavy blockade from the sea and bombardment from the air. American submarines firing torpedoes and laying mines continued to make heavy inroads in the dwindling Japanese merchant marine.

In mid-June an enormous American armada struck the heavily fortified Mariana Islands, quickly but expensively capturing Tinian, Guam, and Saipan, 1,350 miles from Tokyo.

These were among the bloodiest operations of the war. In September the Americans landed on the western Carolines. The way was being prepared for the return to the Philippines. For weeks in advance navy craft swept the central Pacific, and airplanes ranged over the Philippines and Formosa. Finally, on October 20 General MacArthur's troops landed on Leyte Island in the Philippines. The Japanese, threatened with being fatally cut off from their new empire in Southeast Asia, threw their remaining fleets against the invaders in three major encounters—together comprising the decisive Battle of Leyte Gulf, the largest naval engagement in history—and lost almost all their remaining sea power.

## Atomic Triumph Over Japan

With remarkable speed but grievous losses the American forces cut still deeper into the Japanese empire during the early months of 1945. While fighting continued in the Philippines, the marines landed in February on the tiny volcanic island of Iwo Jima, only 750 miles from Tokyo. The Americans needed Iwo Jima to provide fighter cover for Japan-bound bombers and a landing place for crippled ones. The Japanese defended the island so grimly that the marines suffered over 20,000 casualties. It was the bloodiest battle in the history of the marine corps.

The battle for Okinawa, an island sixty-five miles long, beginning on April 1, 1945, was even bloodier. This island lies 370 miles south of Japan, and its conquest clearly would be a prelude to an invasion of the main islands. On land and from the air, the Japanese fought with literally a suicidal fury. Week after week they sent *kamikaze* suicide planes against the American and British ships, losing 3,500 of them but inflicting great damage. Ashore at night, Japanese troops launched equally desperate attacks on the American lines. The United States and its allies suffered nearly 50,000 casualties on land and afloat before the battle came to an end in late June 1945. The Japanese lost 110,000 killed and 7,800 prisoners.

This same sort of bitter fighting seemed to await the Americans when they invaded Japan —if indeed they should ever have to invade. There were signs that the Japanese might surrender, for they had almost no ships and few airplanes with which to fight. In July 1945 American warships stood offshore with impunity and shelled industrial targets, most of which were already in ruins from the heavy bombing attacks. Long since, moderate Japanese leaders had regarded the war as lost. Upon the invasion of Okinawa, the Emperor appointed a new premier and instructed him to sue for peace. The premier could not persuade the army leaders to lay down their arms, but nevertheless he, and in early summer the Emperor himself, tried to obtain mediation through Russia.

Apparently the Russians were determined, at their own time, to enter the war. But the atomic bomb rather than Russian intervention was to be decisive in bringing the war to an end. At a meeting of Allied leaders in Potsdam, Germany, in mid-July 1945, President Truman received word that the first atomic test was successful. He and Prime Minister Clement Attlee (who had succeeded Churchill) issued the Potsdam Declaration urging the Japanese to surrender or face utter devastation. The Japanese premier wished to accept the ultimatum, but the army leaders would not surrender. President Truman had set August 3 as the deadline; when it passed and the Japanese fought on, he ordered an atomic bomb to be dropped on one of four previously selected Japanese cities.

**Hiroshima, Japan, Looking Northeast    October 1945**

"A single atomic bomb, the first weapon of its type ever used against a target, exploded over the city of Hiroshima at 0815 on the morning of 6 August 1945. Most of the industrial workers had already reported to work, but many workers were enroute and nearly all of the school children and some industrial employees were at work in the open on the program of building removal. . . . The explosion came as an almost complete surprise, and the people had not taken shelter. Many were caught in the open, and most of the rest in flimsily constructed homes or commercial establishments. The bomb exploded slightly northwest of the center of the city. Because of this accuracy and the flat terrain and circular shape of the city, Hiroshima was uniformly and extensively devastated. Practically the entire densely or moderately built-up portion of the city was leveled by blast and swept by fire. . . . The surprise, the collapse of many buildings, and the conflagration contributed to an unprecedented casualty rate. Seventy to eighty thousand people were killed, or missing and presumed dead, and an equal number were injured."—Report, United States Strategic Bombing Survey. (National Archives)

On August 6, 1945, a B-29 dropped an atomic bomb on Hiroshima, destroying most of the hitherto undamaged city, and killing 80,000 people (according to American estimates) or 200,000 (according to the Japanese). Even after the horror of Hiroshima, the Japanese army remained adamant. Russia declared war on Japan as of August 9. That same day, the air force dropped a second atomic bomb, on Nagasaki. This was the final blow. After frantic negotiations, on August 14 the Japanese government agreed to give up. On September 2, 1945, aboard the battleship *Missouri* in Tokyo Bay, the articles of surrender were signed.

World War II was at an end. All together, some 14 million men under arms had been killed, and countless millions of civilians had died. In comparison, about 322,000 Americans had been killed or were missing; total United States casualties were about 1,120,000. Despite this frightful expenditure in lives and an astronomical cost in material resources, the American people faced a future made uncertain and perilous by the tensions with the Russians and the threat of future atomic wars.

## FRUSTRATIONS OF PEACEMAKING

Only the imminent threat of Axis victory had forced an uneasy and unsatisfactory form of cooperation between Russia and its Western allies, Great Britain and the United States. As the threat began to lift in 1943, it became increasingly difficult to keep the alliance cemented and to plan for a postwar world in which a decent peace could be maintained.

### The Dangerous Alliance

The difference between British and American strategy—the British opposing a cross-channel invasion and preferring campaigns in southern and eastern Europe—affected the two nations' dealings with the Russians. To a certain extent the United States seemed nearer to the Russians in insisting with them upon an early invasion of France. Roosevelt seemed at times to take a middle position between Stalin and Churchill.

As the Nazi tide receded, the postwar patterns began to emerge throughout eastern Europe, as they were already doing in Italy. Firm political agreements were necessary if these areas were not to fall entirely under Russian hegemony, just as firm military plans were essential to the achievement of final victory.

At Casablanca, Morocco, in January 1943, after previous consultation with Churchill, Roosevelt announced the doctrine of unconditional surrender by the Axis. What Roosevelt seemed to desire was to avoid the sort of negotiations that had marred the 1918 armistice, causing bickerings among the Allies at the time and German misunderstandings afterwards. As the war progressed, it became clear that "unconditional surrender" left the United Nations free to state to the Axis powers the peace terms the latter might expect. Roosevelt and Churchill both emphasized that the phrase did not mean, as the Nazi propagandists charged, that extremely severe terms would be imposed. Yet, after the war, some historians charged that the "unconditional surrender" doctrine seriously discouraged the anti-Nazi German underground movement, stiffened the Nazi will to fight, and thus lengthened the war.

In October 1943 Secretary Hull, although he was seventy-two and in precarious health, flew to Moscow to confer with the British and Russian foreign ministers. His faith in Wilsonian idealism almost limitless, Hull returned from Moscow elated because the Russians had agreed to a Declaration of Four Nations on General Security. (China was the fourth nation.) This was a pledge to continue the united action of war "for the organization and maintenance of peace and security" and to create, as soon as practicable, a general international organization.

With an air of optimism Roosevelt and Churchill traveled eastward in November 1943 for a long-awaited meeting with Stalin at Teheran, Iran. On the way they stopped at Cairo to confer with Chiang Kai-shek and to prepare a statement (released after the Teheran conference) drawing a map for the postwar Far East. They proposed stripping Japan of her empire in order to restore Manchuria, the Pescadores, and Formosa to China, and to create in due course a free and independent Korea. Japan was to lose,

### Stalin, Roosevelt, and Churchill at Teheran

"We—The President of the United States, the Prime Minister of Great Britain, and the Premier of the Soviet Union, have met these four days past, in this, the Capital of our Ally, Iran, and have shaped and confirmed our common policy.

"We express our determination that our nations shall work together in war and in the peace that will follow. . . .

"Emerging from these cordial conferences we look with confidence to the day when all peoples of the world may live free lives, untouched by tyranny, and according to their varying desires and their own consciences.

"We came here with hope and determination. We leave here, friends in fact, in spirit and in purpose."—From a joint statement issued December 1, 1943. (National Archives)

in addition, all other territory she had acquired since 1914.

At Teheran, Roosevelt undertook to establish a friendly, intimate relationship with Stalin of the sort he enjoyed with Churchill. Stalin reaffirmed his intention to bring Russia into the Pacific war soon after hostilities had ended in Europe, and expressed his satisfaction with the Cairo communiqué on Japan. In a cordial way the three leaders discussed the means, through an international organization, of keeping Germany from ever again becoming a menace. Stalin wished Russia to retain the areas she had seized in her period of collaboration with Germany, including eastern Poland as far as the so-called Curzon line proposed in 1919. Roose-

velt and Churchill agreed to the Polish boundary.

Roosevelt and Churchill seem not to have recognized realistically the nature of the peace that was being foreshadowed at Teheran. In the general rejoicing over the apparent accord among the Big Three, and in their assumption that Russia would be content within its new boundaries, they overlooked the appraisal that one of the American participants at Teheran wrote a few days later: "The result would be that the Soviet Union would be the only important military and political force on the continent of Europe. The rest of Europe would be reduced to military and political impotence."

It was unrealistic to expect, as Roosevelt apparently did, that the Russians would forbear from exploiting the great European and Asian power vacuums that the defeat of Germany and Japan would create. This miscalculation led the United States into a tragic triumph—a victory without peace.

## The Yalta Conference

Churchill's mood fluctuated with the ebb and flow of Russian good will. Upon leaving Moscow, after a visit in the fall of 1944, he wrote Stalin: "This memorable meeting . . . has shown that there are no matters that cannot be adjusted between us when we meet together in frank and intimate discussion." By January 1945 he was so badly disillusioned that he wrote Roosevelt concerning the forthcoming Yalta meeting: "This may well be a fateful Conference, coming at a moment when the Great Allies are so divided and the shadow of the war lengthens out before us. At the present time I think the end of this war may well prove to be more disappointing than was the last." Such was the bleak and unpromising setting for the great conference at Yalta in the Crimea (February 1945).

At that time American forces were having to reduce Germany mile by mile; there seemed no reason to think Japan would be different. General MacArthur insisted on the necessity for Russian aid, taking the position that otherwise the United States would have to fight a series of difficult and expensive campaigns to overcome the Japanese in Manchuria. Consequently the Joint Chiefs did not revise their timetable calling for the defeat of Japan eighteen months after German surrender, and they continued to regard Russian aid as indispensable. Roosevelt expressed to Stalin his hope that Japan could be bombed into submission without invasion— but the Americans could not count upon it.

These were the limitations upon the Americans in their bargaining at Yalta. In return for Stalin's reiterated promise to enter the Far Eastern war two or three months after German surrender, Roosevelt and Churchill promised him the Kurile Islands north of Japan and the restoration of "the former rights of Russia" lost in the Russo-Japanese War. This meant the return of southern Sakhalin Island, the return of

> ## Enlisting Russian Aid Against Japan at Yalta [1945]
>
> *I think there was the belief that Russia's entry into the war [against Japan] before we hit the islands would save hundreds of thousands of American casualties. . . . The disposition of Chinese territories, as you know, was subsequently embodied in the Soviet-Chinese Treaty of August 1945, which was almost universally hailed in this country, as well as, I believe, in China, as a great event, because this treaty involved the recognition by the Soviet Union of the sovereignty of the Chinese Nationalist Government over Manchuria. . . .*
>
> *The first reaction from the Chinese was not one that they had been sold, as it were, down the river. Mr. T. V. Soong in his negotiations in Moscow found the Yalta agreement of considerable use to him as a backstop.*
>
> *There are now, in retrospect, two valid criticisms of the agreement: First it was unnecessary, the war did not take the course predicted; and, secondly, it was done without the participation of the Chinese Government.—Testimony of Charles E. Bohlen (who had been an assistant to the Secretary of State and interpreter at Yalta), on his nomination as ambassador to Russia, before the Senate Committee on Foreign Relations, 1953.*

a lease on Port Arthur as a naval base and internationalizing of the port of Dairen, Manchuria (in both instances with recognition of Russia's preeminent interests), and joint operation with China of the Chinese Eastern and South Manchurian railroads feeding into the ports. China was to retain sovereignty over Manchuria, but Roosevelt did not clarify what "preeminent interests" meant. (For many months these clauses remained secret because Russia was still at peace with Japan.)

In its disposition of central European questions, the Yalta conference for the most part ratified previous decisions. Germany was to be divided into zones of occupation previously agreed upon. Since Berlin was to be deep in the Russian zone, the Americans and British proposed an accord providing freedom of transit into Berlin. The Russians held back, and in the general spirit of amity at Yalta, the matter was postponed. At the time, the Russian demands for heavy reparations in the form of German factories, goods, and labor seemed far more important. The British tried to scale down the Russian demand for $20 billion in such reparations, of which Russia was to obtain half. This would so strip and starve the Germans, Churchill pointed out, that the United States and Great Britain would have to feed them. Consequently he and Roosevelt agreed to the Russian figure only as a basis for discussion by a reparations commission. Already, in the light of reality, the West had left far behind the Morgenthau plan (initialed by Roosevelt and Churchill at Quebec in October 1944) for the pastoralization of Germany.

One of the touchiest questions was what would constitute a democratic government for Poland, a matter over which Russia and the West had negotiated for months. The Russians did not wish to allow the Polish government in exile in London or the Polish underground to assume any substantial share of power with a government the Russians had established at Lublin. At the beginning of August 1944, as the Red army drove within ten miles of Warsaw, the underground in the city arose against the Germans. The Russians halted, ignored the revolt, and despite the strong pleas of the United States and Great Britain, stood by while the Polish patriots were annihilated in sixty-three days of fighting. The Russian explanation was military exigency, but the situation seemed to show the sort of government Stalin was determined to establish in Poland.

At Yalta the West managed to obtain Stalin's agreement that the Lublin (Communist) government should be broadened to include democratic leaders from Poland and abroad. What the percentage should be was not specified. Subsequently the new government should hold "free and unfettered elections as soon as possible on the basis of universal suffrage and secret ballot."

It would have been a satisfactory arrangement for the West if the terms had been interpreted in their Western meaning. As for the Polish boundary, it was to follow the Curzon line in the east, and the Poles were to receive territorial compensation in the north and west.

For the rest of liberated or defeated Europe, the Big Three agreed to establish interim governments "broadly representative of all democratic elements" and to provide for free elections that would create "governments responsible to the will of the people."

In years after the war, disappointed Americans harshly criticized the Yalta agreements, especially for their violations of the Atlantic Charter. The morality of the Far Eastern arrangements is open to challenge. Their purpose was to obtain Russian aid, which top military leaders thought would shorten the war against Japan and perhaps prevent a million American casualties. The terms promised nothing to Stalin that he could not have taken anyway. The morality of the European arrangements (except perhaps for the ethnic dislocations wrought by the new Polish boundaries) would have been defensible if the terms had received their customary Western interpretation. Roosevelt may be most severely criticized for not insisting at every point upon absolutely clear, sharply defined agreements that could receive only one interpretation in Russia—the interpretation as understood by the West. This was especially true of the question of entry into Berlin. Experience with the Russians long before Yalta had pointed to the need for precise understandings.

Roosevelt was careless in this respect because he pinned his hopes upon the good faith of the Russians and their willingness to enter into and actively participate in an international organization for the preservation of the peace.

## The U. N. Organization

A few months before war broke out in Europe— and long before the attack at Pearl Harbor— Secretary Hull had taken the first step toward proposing a new international organization in which the United States would participate. In January 1940 he appointed an Advisory Committee on Problems of Foreign Relations. Its membership was composed of congressmen from both parties and distinguished experts from within and without the State Department. Several private organizations like the Council on Foreign Relations also prepared numerous studies for the State Department.

President Roosevelt, firmly determined to avoid Wilson's failure, encouraged Hull to include Republicans in the planning for the peace. However, Roosevelt did not consult Congress before making his most famous statements of war aims; Senator Robert A. Taft asserted in 1943 that he did not believe "we went to war to establish the 'four freedoms' or any other freedom throughout the world," nor "for the purposes set forth in the Atlantic Charter." The administration, to counter this sort of resentment, included prominent Republicans in at least sketchy briefings on wartime diplomacy and let them participate more fully in postwar planning of many kinds. In this way it won their support. In 1943 four senators, two Republican and two Democratic, none of whom were serving on the Foreign Relations Committee, introduced a resolution calling for American leadership in establishing a United Nations organization. Public opinion polls indicated a general enthusiasm for the resolution; the Senate passed a similar declaration 85 to 5. Senator Arthur H. Vandenberg of Michigan, previously one of the most forthright isolationists, assumed Republican leadership in helping mold a "bipartisan" foreign policy. He thus gained for himself and the Republican party new power and stature.

The Big Four powers, conferring in the summer and fall of 1944 at Dumbarton Oaks, a Harvard-owned estate in Washington, drafted tentative outlines for a new international organization. These were the starting points for the drafting of a United Nations charter at a conference of fifty nations in San Francisco, opening April 25, 1945. President Roosevelt had appointed a bipartisan delegation headed by his new Secretary of State, Edward R. Stettinius, Jr. One of its most effective members was Senator Vandenberg, who helped to wrest concessions from the Russians at San Francisco and to win the votes of reluctant Republicans for ratification in the Senate.

Basically the charter of the United Nations was a refurbishing of the old Wilsonian League covenant with the former American objections removed through giving a veto to each of the five main powers. The Americans and British, as well as the Russians, had insisted upon the veto as a seemingly necessary protection of their sovereignty. The American delegates, led by Vandenberg, succeeded in obtaining for the small nations in the General Assembly freedom to discuss and make recommendations—in effect creating "a town meeting of the world."

The Senate quickly ratified the charter (July 1945) by a vote of 80 to 2, in remarkable contrast to the slow and painful defeat it had administered to American membership in the League of Nations. But the great and growing gulf between Russia and the West destined the United Nations to be, like its predecessor, the League, a town meeting for international discussion or a sounding board for national views, rather than the forerunner of a world government.

## A Fourth Term for F. D. R.

With "bipartisanship" prevailing, there had been no serious disagreement between Democrats and Republicans on the issues of peace planning. But in regard to domestic questions there had been politics as usual. Indeed, despite all the platitudinous pleas to put aside politics in the interest of national unity, the struggles became even more virulent during the war.

Conservatives saw in the war an opportunity to eradicate hated remnants of the New Deal; some liberals regarded it as an opportunity to bring Wilson's ideas to fruition, and even go beyond them to establish a global New Deal. Every one of the great pressure groups in the country fought to maintain or improve its relative position; spokesmen for large business and small, farmers and labor, jockeyed for position in Washington. The tenor of Congress continued to be conservative, and it was sensitive as always to the demands of organized constituents. Throughout the war, key committee chairmen who were leaders of the conservative coalition dominated Congress and forced their will upon President Roosevelt. Through the election of 1942, as the United States and its allies suffered unparalleled military disasters and the war administration in Washington seemed to compound confusion, the criticism rose to a crescendo. In the election, the Republicans gained forty-seven seats in the House and ten in the Senate. Within both parties the trend was to the right.

President Roosevelt, in order to get crucial congressional support in prosecuting the war and planning the peace, continued to accept the sacrifice of New Deal measures. At a press conference in 1943 he announced that "Dr. Win-the-War" had replaced "Dr. New Deal."

Dissatisfaction with wartime regimentation and smoldering resentments still glowing from the prewar debate over intervention seemed to give the Republicans an opportunity in 1944. They had seen auguries of a national shift toward the right in the congressional election of 1942. In their vigorous young candidate, Governor Thomas E. Dewey of New York, who ran with Governor John W. Bricker of Ohio, they seemed to have an answer to Roosevelt and the aging New Dealers.

As for President Roosevelt, it was a foregone conclusion that he would be nominated for a fourth term if he so desired. There was none of the suspense that had preceded the third-term

nomination. Rather, since he was visibly aging, unwell, and thinning so that his clothes ill fit him, there was much speculation over his choice for the vice-presidential nominee. During the war, Vice President Wallace was the hero of most advanced New Dealers and much of the CIO membership. But he was sneered at by party bosses and some Southern Democrats as a visionary who wished to extend the New Deal to the entire globe, to bring "a quart of milk for every Hottentot." They rallied behind James M. Byrnes of South Carolina, who had been functioning ably as the unofficial assistant president—but Byrnes was unacceptable to organized labor. Out of the skirmishing among the rival factions within the Democratic party came Roosevelt's proposal of a compromise candidate acceptable to most of them, Senator Harry S Truman of Missouri. Truman had won newspaper approval as chairman of the Senate War Investigating Committee, was a consistent New Dealer in his voting record, and was from a border state. He was popular in the Senate.

In keeping with the bipartisan spirit, Republican and Democratic leaders had arranged for practically identical planks on foreign policy,

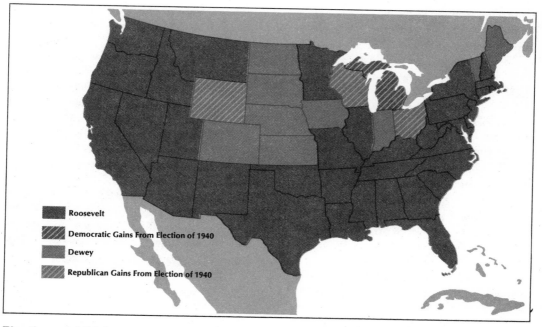

Roosevelt

Democratic Gains From Election of 1940

Dewey

Republican Gains From Election of 1940

**Election of 1944**

thus eliminating it as an issue in the campaign. Dewey had a good chance to make it an issue when he got word that American intelligence had broken the Japanese code before Pearl Harbor. With this information, he could have charged that the Roosevelt administration knew —or should have known—of the coming Japanese attack. But an envoy from General Marshall dissuaded Dewey from using the information, which if made public would have caused the Japanese to change their code (American intelligence was still exploiting it) and thus would have disadvantaged United States forces fighting in the Pacific. Even without this issue, the election promised to be close—partly because the vote was likely to be small, and presumably a light vote would aid the Republicans.

The possibility was like an injection of adrenalin into Roosevelt. At the end of September 1944, addressing a raucously appreciative audience of Teamsters Union members, he was at his sardonic best. He followed this triumph with a strenuous campaign in Chicago and throughout the East. This he climaxed with a day-long drive in an open car through New York City in a soaking rain.

Roosevelt's seeming capacity to serve four more years, his international leadership, and his promise to return to the New Deal after the war were a winning combination. Organized labor, working through the CIO Political Action Committee, brought out the workers' votes. The President defeated Dewey by a margin of 432 electoral votes to 99, and a popular vote of 25,602,000 to 22,006,000. The Democrats lost one seat in the Senate, but gained twenty in the House. The Democratic victory seemed to mean a revival of the New Deal at home, and the campaign promises of both parties indicated that the United States would continue to take a lead in international affairs.

But President Roosevelt lived to see neither the triumph in war nor the tragedy of peace. Already his vigor was draining away, and he could ill afford the exertions of the campaign or those of the grueling trip to Yalta. Addressing Congress on his return, he was very tired and for the first time he made public reference to his paralyzed legs and his heavy steel braces as he remained seated and spoke optimistically of the Yalta agreement—which he said contained no secret provisions. Suddenly, on the afternoon of April 12, 1945, he died of a cerebral hemorrhage at his private retreat in Warm Springs, Georgia.

## Truman Takes Over

Through no fault of his own, President Harry S Truman was unbriefed and poorly prepared for the task of concluding the war and making the peace. No one doubted his sincerity when he remarked to reporters the day after he had suddenly taken his oath of office: "I felt like the moon, the stars, and all the planets had fallen on me. I've got the most terribly responsible job a man ever had."

During the first phase of his relations with the Russians, Truman was moderately firm but tried to give the Soviet government no cause for protest. He was chagrined when in May 1945 the Foreign Economic Administration enforced his order ending Lend-Lease so precipitately as to call back some ships at sea. The British were the most hard-hit, but Stalin complained most bitterly.

At the Potsdam conference (July 1945) Truman could secure few satisfactory agreements on questions involving occupied and liberated countries. Despite the failure at Potsdam, Truman's Secretary of State, James F. Byrnes, continued in a conciliatory fashion to seek accommodation with the Russians.

The Potsdam conferees provided for a Council of Foreign Ministers to draft treaties with Italy and the former Axis satellites. During a tedious and depressing round of meetings of the council in London, Moscow, Paris, and New York (between September 1945 and December 1946), relations between the West and Russia steadily deteriorated, though five treaties were concluded. The one with Italy reflected Western demands; those with Finland, Hungary, Rumania, and Bulgaria in effect incorporated Soviet armistice terms. By ratifying the three latter treaties, the United States acquiesced in the Russian domination of these nations.

In Berlin a four-power Allied Control Council began sessions marked by the same blocking and delaying tactics that made other joint conferences with the Russians so dismal. The Western nations had visualized unified controls for Ger-

**Stalin and Truman at Potsdam**

Despite the smiles on their faces, there was little meeting of minds between Stalin and President Truman at the conference in July 1945. Much of the controversy centered around the Eastern European nations.

When Churchill accused Stalin of building an "iron fence" around them, Stalin responded, "All fairy tales." (Culver)

many to prevent its resurgence. But the Russians had no interest in a Germany reunified in a manner acceptable to the West. Germany was to remain split indefinitely.

Meanwhile in occupied Germany and Japan, the United States pursued firm but conflicting policies compounded of harshness and idealism. During the war the American people had come to hate the enemy leaders and were insistent that they be punished for their war crimes, especially those Nazis who were responsible for the maintenance of frightful concentration camps like Buchenwald and for the gas-chamber murder of millions of Jews. This led to the trials of thousands of Nazis and war criminals, capped by that of twenty-two key Nazi leaders before an International Military Tribunal at Nuremberg in 1945–1946. Eleven were sentenced to death.

There was also a sweeping purge of Japan, and a trial was held for twenty-five former top Japanese military and civil officials. Seven of them, including two premiers, were executed. The dangerous precedent seemed to be established,

as Churchill pointed out, that "the leaders of a nation defeated in war shall be put to death by the victors."

At first the Americans seemed bent on the pastoralization as well as reform of conquered Germany. They banned all industry directly or indirectly contributing to German war potential, including even the construction of seagoing ships, drastically cut steel and chemical production, destroyed munition plants, and allowed the dismantling of some factories for shipment to the Russians. They disbanded cartels and encouraged only agriculture and peaceful domestic industries. Along with this, they wished to foster American-style democracy in place of the repudiated Nazism. These economic policies, coming at a time when so much of German housing and industry was rubble, and when several million exiles were making their way from eastern Germany and from Czechoslovakia, reduced western Germany to a living standard not much better than that of a giant relief camp. The army undertook to feed the German people between 1945 and 1948 at a subsistence level of 950–1550 calories per day.

Even this near-starvation diet cost the British and Americans nearly half a billion dollars per year. The Russians were adding further to the economic burden by taking out of their zone (and from the western zones to the extent agreed at Potsdam) reparations totaling $1.5 to $3 billion dollars per year. They were siphoning out of Germany more than the Americans and British could pump in.

In Japan American occupation policy suffered fewer obstacles and profited from the initial errors in Germany. During the first critical weeks General MacArthur, the Supreme Commander for the Allied Powers (SCAP), set up an overwhelmingly American occupation, based on a directive radioed him from Washington on August 29, 1945. Truman refused Stalin's demand that Russians occupy part of the northern Japanese island, Hokkaido. The irritated Russians had a voice, but no real power, on an eleven-country Far Eastern Commission in Washington and on a four-power Allied Council to advise MacArthur in Tokyo.

The American occupation authorities in Japan acted rapidly to demilitarize and democratize the country. From the outset they recognized that Japan must be left with a healthy economy, but in practice—by limiting the nation's war potential—they reduced Japan like Germany to a relief state.

## POSTWAR READJUSTMENTS

The glad new day that wartime propaganda had foretold was not to dawn when the fighting stopped. Somehow, Americans had to readjust to the troublesome realities of postwar life. The most serious political problems had to do with the adaptation of the military establishment and the economic system to the new conditions —which were themselves uncertain.

### Military Reorganization

In the face of growing menaces in Europe and Asia, the United States speedily dismantled its army, air force, and navy. At the end of the war, there was a popular demand to "bring the boys back." In April 1945 President Truman announced that nearly 7 million men had been released from the army—"the most remarkable demobilization in the history of the world, or 'disintegration,' if you want to call it that." He proposed a system of universal military training, but Congress did no more between 1946 and 1948 than to pass limited Selective Service measures. The gradual whittling of the armed forces continued, until by the spring of 1950 the army was down to 600,000 men, and the ceiling on defense expenditures, to $13 billion. Lacking land armies, the United States sought to balance the Soviet power with atomic bombs and an air force that could deliver them.

Since September 1945 the administration had been ready to negotiate an agreement with Russia which would "control and limit the use of the atomic bomb as an instrument of war" and "direct and encourage the development of atomic power for peaceful and humanitarian purposes." Great Britain and Canada joined with the United States in proposing international control of atomic energy. The United Nations Assembly responded by creating the United Nations Atomic Energy Commission (January 1946), to which the American member, Bernard Baruch, submitted a plan. This proposed a thoroughgoing system of control and inspection of atomic energy development through a United Nations agency. When the system became effective, the United States would liquidate its stockpile and join in an international ban on atomic bombs.

The Russians refused to accept the Baruch plan for international inspection and control of atomic development; instead they constantly and vociferously demanded that the United States unilaterally destroy its atom bombs. Through their widespread propaganda the Russians tried to marshal world indignation against the United States while they rushed ahead with their own research on atomic weapons. American scientists and military leaders, not aware as yet of the successful Russian espionage, and underrating Russian scientific and technical proficiency, predicted that it would be many years before the Soviet Union could produce a successful bomb.

Meanwhile, Congress lengthily debated the

domestic control of American atomic energy. Democrats wished to vest control in civilians; Senator Vandenberg and the Republicans urged giving it to the heads of the armed forces. A compromise was reached in the Atomic Energy Act of 1946. This created a five-man civilian Atomic Energy Commission with complete control over research and development of fissionable materials; linked to it was a Military Liaison Committee.

Under the protection of an atomic umbrella, military leaders indulged in the luxury of a vigorous and prolonged controversy over unification of the various armed forces. This measure, proposed to bring greater efficiency and effectiveness, led instead to heightened rivalry, as the generals pushed for it, and the admirals feared for the loss of the marine corps and the relative weakening of the navy. Both sides brought the utmost pressure upon Congress. Finally, the National Security Act (July 1947) provided for a secretary of defense to preside over separate Departments of the Army, Navy, and Air Force, with the Joint Chiefs of Staff serving as advisers to him and to the President. To coordinate diplomacy and military planning, the 1947 act also provided for a National Security Council to consist of the President, certain cabinet members, and other advisers on foreign and military policy. This control was to be served by two other new agencies, a National Security Resources Board and a Central Intelligence Agency.

Within the reorganized Pentagon Building the old rivalries continued. Indeed, through the creation of a separate air force there now appeared to be three separate services where there had been only two before. The first Secretary of Defense, James V. Forrestal, exhausted by the struggle to make unification effective, resigned in 1949 and committed suicide. His successor, Louis A. Johnson, became embroiled in a violent quarrel over cancellation of construction of a huge new aircraft carrier, a quarrel culminating in the resignation of the Secretary of the Navy and the replacement of the Chief of Naval Operations. This crisis led to amendments to the National Security Act, forcing greater unification, and formally establishing a Department of Defense.

## Reconversion and Inflation

On September 6, 1945, only four days after the Japanese surrender ceremonies, the President sent to Congress a twenty-one-point domestic program outlining what he later termed the "Fair Deal." He called for the expansion of social security, the raising of the legal minimum wage from 40 to 65 cents an hour, a full employment bill, a permanent Fair Employment Practices Act, public housing and slum clearance, long-range planning for the protection of natural resources and building of public works (like TVA), and government promotion of scientific research. Within ten weeks he sent additional recommendations to Congress for federal aid to education, for health insurance and prepaid medical care, and for the St. Lawrence seaway project.

Congress acted upon several of the President's recommendations. The Maximum Employment Act became law in 1946. It established a three-man Council of Economic Advisers to aid the President and issue an annual economic report. Although the experts frequently disagreed, they became an integral part of the governmental machinery. They did much to accustom the public to the new economics that had been emerging during the New Deal and the war.

Congressional conservatives tried to steer Congress and the public away from the Fair Deal program by concentrating upon the reconversion of industry to peacetime production. Truman himself recommended, first, speedily removing all possible controls that would hamper reconversion and, second, preventing increases in prices, rents, and wages. The two aims could easily conflict.

After Germany surrendered, cutbacks in war orders began, and after Japan capitulated, $35 billion in contracts was suddenly cancelled. The War Production Board soon dropped controls, except on commodities that were still very scarce. Congress passed a new revenue bill cutting taxes nearly $6 billion. The War Assets Administration, established in January 1946, sold several hundred war plants, mostly to the corporations that had been operating them, and disposed of mountains of surplus, some of which enabled veterans with priorities to start small businesses. Members of the armed forces, who were being demobilized at an unparalleled pace, found their problems of readjustment to civilian life eased by the Servicemen's Readjustment Act of 1944 (the "G.I. Bill of Rights") which provided them with further education and training, or aid while unemployed or starting in business or farming.

Industry changed back to civilian production with more speed and less economic dislocation than had been expected. The gloomy forecasts of 8 million unemployed did not materialize. By the end of November 1945, peacetime employment was up to the end-of-the-war total, and 93 per cent of the war plants had been reconverted.

The expected glut of surplus goods did not materialize either. Instead, acute problems of scarcity arose. Shortages ranged from automobiles and appliances to men's suits, nylon stockings, and beef. Consumers commanded some $129 billion or more in savings and billions more in credit with which to back their demands. Added to these were the needs of the rest of the world. Against such pressures, it was impossible for the Office of Price Administration to hold prices down to the 1941–1942 level.

If prices were to be checked, wages must be also, and if wages were to be held down, so must prices be. It was a vicious circle. By January 1946 workers had gone on strike in a number of the nation's critical industries—steel, automobiles, electrical manufacturing, and others. When Philip Murray demanded a 25-cents-an-hour increase for the United Steelworkers to bring them up to their wartime take-home pay, President Benjamin F. Fairless of United States Steel, acting as spokesman for the industry, refused unless the government would allow a $7-per-ton increase in the price of steel. President Truman announced that labor was entitled to the 33 per cent that living costs had gone up since January 1941. The Wage Stabilization Board must approve the increase; but if it cut profits below the prewar level, the companies might obtain corresponding price increases. Ultimately there was a steel settlement allowing raises of 18½ cents an hour and $5 per ton. Throughout industry, the "bulge" led to a round of similar raises in wages and prices.

In April 1946 John L. Lewis precipitated a

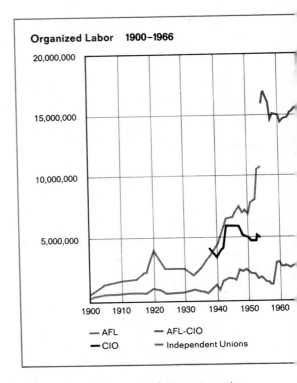

**Organized Labor   1900–1966**

Under the friendly Roosevelt administration, union membership soared during the New Deal and World War II. Note that CIO figures are not available for 1948–1950; from 1951 on, the chart indicates the combined AFL and CIO membership.

fresh crisis. He demanded that the bituminous coal workers receive, even before wage increases, drastic improvement in safety rules and substantial contributions to a health and welfare fund. Refusing White House suggestions of compromise, he led out 400,000 miners. Within six weeks, as coal supplies dwindled, much of the nation's industrial production had to be cut back. In mid-May Lewis allowed his workers back for twelve days' mining; in the interim a railroad strike threatened. The President, by broadcasting a warning that the army would run the railroads, managed to avert a new walk-out. The government took over the coal mines and provided the workers with most of what Lewis had demanded.

While unions were going on strike for higher wages, businessmen and farmers were exerting almost equal pressure upon Congress to obtain higher prices. Controls, they argued, were preventing full production, encouraging a black market, and robbing producers of a fair profit. After long debate, Congress passed a circumscribed price-control bill on June 27, 1946, just three days before the existing act was to expire. President Truman unexpectedly vetoed the bill as "a sure formula for inflation," and most price controls expired.

During the first sixteen days of July 1946, the index of prices of twenty-eight basic commodities jumped 25 per cent, compared with 13 per cent during the previous three years. On the first day of free trade at the Chicago stockyards, prime beef jumped from $18 to $22 per hundred weight. As prices soared, stock raisers, who had been holding back their cattle, rushed them to market. Congress quickly passed a new price-control bill only slightly stronger than the vetoed one, and on July 25 President Truman signed it. The decontrol board it created studied meat prices, decided they were unreasonable, and ordered prices rolled back to the old levels. Stockmen once again held back cattle until they could force abandonment of controls; angry consumers chafed in near-empty butcher shops.

For several weeks President Truman stood firm, but as public discontent focused on the Democratic party, politicians already fearful of the worst in the congressional elections of 1946 persuaded him to relent. On October 14 he announced the immediate ending of meat controls. Meat came back, but like many other commodities, with new price tags so high that the old black-market price seemed to have become the new legal standard. Millions of consumers on small, inflexible salaries or pensions were hurt. Real earnings dropped 12 per cent below those of July 1945.

## "Had Enough?"

All that the Republicans needed in the fall of 1946 was the slogan, "Had Enough? Vote Republican." They captured both houses of Congress, controlling the House 246 to 188, and the Senate, 51 to 45.

President Truman, accepting the returns as a mandate to liquidate regulations, dropped almost all remaining controls on wages and prices and on the channeling of construction into low-cost homes. Congress continued rent control to March 1, 1948, but allowed rents to go up 15

per cent. Retail prices moved upward 3 per cent per month, canceling the gains organized labor had won in the spring of 1946. Unions fought for and obtained a second round of increases in 1947, and in 1948 as prices still went upward, a third round. The spiral of inflation was creeping upward relentlessly. Workers and others in modest circumstances began to notice that it was taking place under a Republican Congress whose spokesmen had asserted that laissez faire would cure the nation's ills.

The Chairman of the House Appropriations Committee, John Taber, proclaimed that he would apply a "meat-axe to government frills." He did so. Congress refused to appropriate funds for public housing, even of the moderate sort championed by Taft. It would not aid education, or extend social security; it slashed budget allowances for reclamation and power projects in the West. It passed a tax bill that, as President Truman pointed out in vetoing it, reduced the taxes of families receiving $2,400 or less by only 3 per cent, but those of families receiving $100,000 or more, from 48 to 65 per cent.

One of the few noncontroversial domestic achievements of this Congress was authorization of a commission on reorganization of the executive departments. President Truman appointed former President Hoover chairman of the commission. Congress already had voted to improve its own procedures and to reorganize its committees, cutting those in the House from forty-eight to nineteen, and in the Senate from thirty-three to fifteen.

The principal positive handiwork of the Eightieth Congress was a new basic labor law to supplant the pro-labor Wagner Act of 1935. The Taft-Hartley Labor-Management Relations Act loosened some of the previous restrictions upon employers and added several prohibitions against the unions. It also provided for "cooling-off" periods before unions could strike. President Truman stingingly vetoed it on June 20, 1947. That same day Republicans and Southern Democrats in the House overrode his veto; the Senate followed three days later. In practice, the Taft-Hartley Act did not cripple organized labor, partly because of the skill of labor leaders and because of President Truman's appoint-

## Restrictions on Unions in the Taft-Hartley Act [1947]

Outlawed "closed shop" (which required that one must be a union member to be hired), but permitted "union shop" (which meant that if the contract so provided, one had to join the union after being hired).

Provided "cooling off" periods and empowered the President to issue injunctions to prevent strikes imperiling national safety or health.

Prohibited as "unfair" union practices: jurisdictional strikes, refusal to bargain in good faith, secondary boycotts, exaction of pay for work not performed, and union contributions to political campaign funds.

Prohibited certification of unions as bargaining agents with employers until officers had filed affidavits that they were not Communists.

Required unions to register with the Secretary of Labor and submit annual financial reports to him.

Allowed employers to present their side during organizational campaigns, petition the National Labor Relations Board for elections to determine bargaining agents, and sue unions for breach of contract.

ment to the National Labor Relations Board of members sympathetic toward labor. But the law did emphatically turn most of organized labor against the Republicans and back to the support of President Truman.

## Truman Beats Dewey

When the Republicans met in Philadelphia (June 1948) to nominate a presidential candidate, they rejected Senator Robert A. Taft, the vigorous leader of the Eightieth Congress. Though the idol of many businessmen, Taft was hampered by his prewar isolationism and his lack of glamor as a campaigner. The Republicans again nominated Governor Thomas E. Dewey, who favored the new role of the United States in world affairs, and whose stand on do-

mestic issues came closer to the Fair Deal than to the Republican record in Congress. His running mate was Governor Earl Warren of California, who was even more liberal. Their platform was a promise to continue all the things the Democrats had established, but to do them more efficiently and cheaply.

It seemed a winning ticket and program, especially since the Democratic party suffered from two schisms. A faction to the left followed Henry A. Wallace out of the party. Wallace ran on a "Progressive" ticket to fight for thoroughgoing reform at home and more friendly relations with Communists overseas. Around him rallied a sprinkling of Americans who felt that the Truman domestic policies were too slow and ineffective and who feared that the foreign policies would lead to a third world war. Around him also rallied the American Communists and fellow-travelers.

Despairing Democratic liberals organized as Americans for Democratic Action, sought some more glamorous candidate than President Truman. The one candidate they could be sure would win votes by the million, General Eisenhower, rejected their overtures. At their convention (July 1948) the Democrats gloomily accepted the inevitable, the nomination of President Truman. Certain of defeat, the liberals salvaged what they could by fighting through a platform containing a strong civil-rights plank that proposed federal legislation to prevent discrimination in employment, penalize lynching, and outlaw poll taxes. This platform was expected to help Northern and city Democrats in their local and state elections.

But it drove Southern Democrats, already angered by President Truman's espousal of a strong civil-rights program, into open revolt. Waving Confederate flags, a number of them met at Birmingham, Alabama (July 1948) to form the States Rights' Democratic Party and nominate Governor J. Strom Thurmond of South Carolina. They captured the party organization in Alabama, Louisiana, Mississippi, and South Carolina.

The defections on both the left and the right seemed to leave President Truman in a pathetically hopeless position; all the public opinion polls showed him trailing far behind. Governor

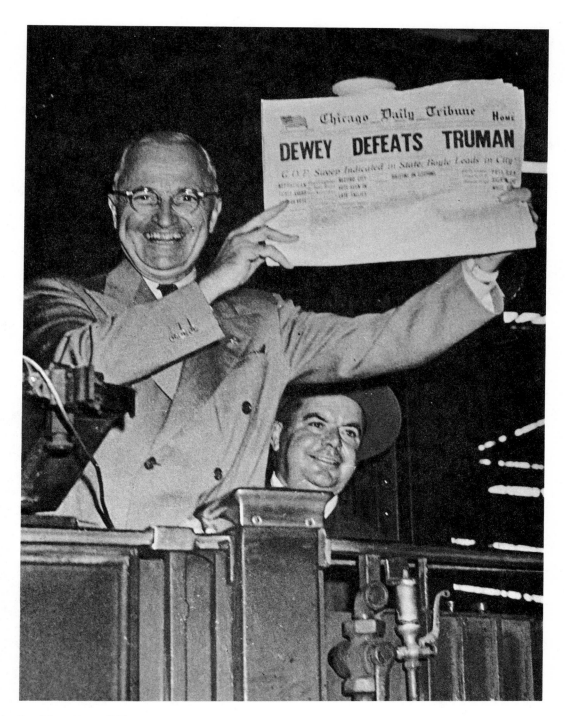

### President Harry S Truman

As a campaigner, President Truman apparently had no chance in 1948, but he was remarkably successful in his extemporaneous speaking at whistle-stops, which together with his policies had rallied behind him much of the farm and labor vote. On the morning after the election, he gleefully displayed a newspaper that had underestimated him—as indeed had much of the American public. (United Press International)

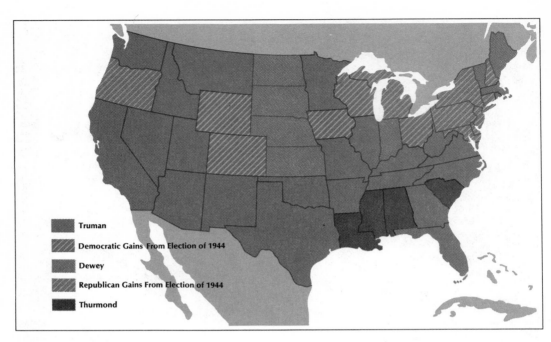

**Election of 1948**

Dewey, campaigning in a cold and formal way, aroused as little animosity as possible, and seemed to be delivering previews of his inaugural. Instead of campaigning against the impeccable Dewey, who stood for much the same in domestic and foreign policy, Truman launched his attack at the Republican Congress. Because he felt the press was giving a hostile impression of his administration, Truman embarked upon a strenuous personal tour of the United States, traveling 31,700 miles to speak 356 times directly to the American people. In this "whistle stop" tour, he spoke only a few times from manuscripts, preferring his far more effective, rather blunt extemporaneous style.

To all those groups who could be convinced they had a grievance against the Republican Congress, he appealed effectively, winning the strong support of organized labor, disgruntled farmers, and Northern Negroes.

On election day, to the amazement of everyone but himself, President Truman defeated Dewey, 24,106,000 to 21,969,000 in the popular vote, and 304 to 189 in the electoral vote. Thurmond's Dixiecrat ticket received 1,169,000 popular and 38 electoral votes. Wallace polled only 1,156,000. The Democrats also regained both houses of Congress by a margin of ninety-three seats in the House and twelve in the Senate.

# Selected Readings

**Military Operations** A. R. Buchanan, *The United States and World War II*° (2 vols., 1962); Winston S. Churchill, *Second World War* (6 vols., 1948–1953); Fletcher Pratt, *War for the World* (1950), a brief account; K. R. Greenfield, *American Strategy in World War II* (1963); S. E. Morison, *Strategy and Compromise*° (1958); M. S. Watson, *Chief of Staff: Prewar Plans and*

*Preparations* (1950); R. S. Cline, *Washington Command Post* (1951); H. L. Stimson and McGeorge Bundy, *On Active Service in Peace and War* (1948); Forrest Pogue, *George C. Marshall* (2 vols., 1963–1966); D. D. Eisenhower, *Crusade in Europe°* (1948); Chester Wilmot, *The Struggle for Europe°* (1952), critical of Eisenhower; H. H. Arnold, *Global Mission* (1949); O. N. Bradley, *A Soldier's Story°* (1951); S. E. Morison, *The Two Ocean War: A Short History of the United States Navy in the Second World War* (1963); E. J. King and W. M. Whitehill, *Fleet Admiral King* (1952).

**Wartime Diplomacy** J. L. Snell, *Illusion and Necessity: The Diplomacy of Global War, 1939–1945* (1967); Gaddis Smith, *American Diplomacy During the Second World War, 1941–1945* (1965); W. L. Langer, *Our Vichy Gamble°* (1947); W. R. Deane, *The Strange Alliance* (1947); H. W. Baldwin, *Great Mistakes of the War* (1950), critical of "unconditional surrender"; Anne Armstrong, *Unconditional Surrender* (1961); W. L. Neumann, *After Victory: Churchill, Roosevelt, Stalin, and the Making of the Peace* (1967); E. R. Stettinius, *Roosevelt and the Russians: The Yalta Conference* (1949); J. F. Byrnes, *Speaking Frankly* (1947); R. L. Walker and George Curry, *American Secretaries of State: E. R. Stettinius, Jr., James F. Byrnes* (1965); Herbert Feis, *Churchill, Roosevelt, Stalin°* (1957), *Between War and Peace: The Potsdam Conference°* (1960), *Japan Subdued* (1961), and *Contest over Japan* (1967); R. J. C. Butow, *Japan's Decision to Surrender°* (1954); John Hersey, *Hiroshima°* (1946); Gar Alperowitz, *Atomic Diplomacy: Hiroshima and Potsdam* (1965); R. A. Devine, *Second Chance: The Triumph of Internationalism in America During World War II* (1967), on the U. N.; R. B. Russell, *A History of the United Nations Charter: The Role of the United States, 1940–1945* (1958).

**Domestic Politics** A. H. Vandenberg, Jr., *The Private Papers of Senator Vandenberg* (1952); H. S Truman, *Memoirs°* (2 vols., 1955–1956); Roland Young, *Congressional Politics in the Second World War* (1955); Jonathan Daniels, *Frontier on the Potomac* (1946); Joseph Gaer, *The First Round: The CIO Political Action Committee* (1944); R. A. Lee, *Truman and Taft-Hartley* (1967); E. C. Brown, *From the Wagner Act to Taft-Hartley* (1950); L. V. Chandler, *Inflation in the United States, 1940–1948* (1951); Jules Abels, *Out of the Jaws of Victory* (1959), on the 1948 election; Irwin Ross, *The Loneliest Campaign: The Truman Victory of 1948* (1968); K. M. Schmidt, *Wallace: Quixotic Crusade* (1960); C. W. Mills, *The New Men of Power* (1948); Samuel Lubell, *The Future of American Politics°* (1952); E. F. Goldman, *The Crucial Decade: America, 1945–1955°* (1956); John Gunther, *Inside U. S. A.* (1951).

---

° Titles available in paperback.

# Chapter 27
# A Balance
# of Terror

In 1942 the American geopolitical expert Nicholas J. Spykman wrote that the United States had found itself in World War II because the balance of power on the opposite shores of both the Atlantic and the Pacific had been upset. So the American war aim should be to restore the balance, Spykman said. It should not be to annihilate either Germany or Japan, lest this leave Europe and the Far East exposed to Soviet domination. As for Europe: "A Russian state from the Urals to the North Sea can be no great improvement over a German state from the North Sea to the Urals." As for the Far East: "The danger of another Japanese conquest of Asia must be removed, but this does not inevitably mean the elimination of the military strength of Japan and the surrender of the Western Pacific to China or Russia."

In fact, however, the war was fought for "unconditional surrender," for total victory over the Axis, not for a restoration of the balance. The upshot was that Germany and Japan were eliminated as military powers for the time being. A "power vacuum" was left in Europe, and another in Asia. Only two really great powers remained in the world— the Soviet Union and the United States. Into the voids left by the war, the influence of the Russian Communists and later that of the Chinese Communists began to flow. The United States undertook to resist the spread of Communist power and thus came into collision with its recent allies, the Russians and the Chinese. It now sought new alliances not only with old associates like Great Britain and France but also with former foes, Germany (or a part of that country) and Japan, which it began to help revive and rebuild as strong nations. Such, in essence, was the "cold war" that commenced within two years after the end of World War II.

At first the United States appeared to hold the upper hand, for it had a monopoly of atomic weapons. But within a short time, in 1949, the Russians exploded an A-bomb of their own. The Americans got ahead again, in 1952, with the vastly more destructive hydrogen bomb, but the Russians produced an H-bomb, too, the following year. By 1957, when the Russians put into orbit the first artificial satellite, they seemed to have taken the lead in the capacity to deliver missiles with nuclear warheads. In any event, each of the great contestants now had the capability, quite literally, of destroying the other. A wholly new era had arrived, in which another world war could wipe out mankind itself. Nobody really knew whether the old rules of power politics had relevance any longer. If humanity was spared an all-out war, the reason was perhaps that the world had reached what *The New York Times* (in 1958) called a new "balance of terror."

---

**Eighth Army Fighting Chinese Communists**
On February 1, 1951, members of Company A and K, 35th Infantry Regiment, 25th Division, were keeping a lookout for movement in the Communist-held area where United Nations troops were dropping white phosphorus.
(Top left, Official U.S. Army photo)

**U.S.S. *New Jersey* Bombarding North Korean Installations**
Battleships, which had seemed outmoded at the end of World War II, became useful again during the Korean War when they fired salvos from their 16-inch guns against shore targets.
(Bottom left, Official U.S. Navy photo)

## START OF THE COLD WAR

As early as January 1946 President Truman, concerned over Russian delay in withdrawing troops from Iran and Russian threats against Turkey, had written his secretary of state: "Unless Russia is faced with an iron fist and strong language another war is in the making."

### Containment of Communism

Truman faced a peculiarly difficult task in trying to convince the American public that a truly deep and serious rift was developing between Russia and the West. For too many war years they had listened to publicists ranging from that advanced New Dealer Henry Wallace to the Republican president of the United States Chamber of Commerce, Eric Johnston, praising the Russians and picturing Stalin as a sympathetic figure. Many had come to imagine him as a benign, pipe-smoking sage, "good old Uncle Joe." In addition, idealists had too long placed all their hopes upon the "one world" of which Wendell Willkie had preached so eloquently.

Not even the revered Winston Churchill could shift American opinion. In March 1946, through Truman's arrangement, Churchill, speaking at Westminster College in Fulton, Missouri, proclaimed a grim warning: "From Stettin in the Baltic to Trieste in the Adriatic an iron curtain has descended across the Continent. . . . I do not believe that Soviet Russia desires war. What they desire is the fruits of war and the indefinite expansion of their power and doctrines. . . . From what I have seen of our Russian friends and allies during the war, I am convinced that there is nothing they admire so much as strength, and there is nothing for which they have less respect than for weakness, especially military weakness."

A new Truman policy for countering Communist aggression began to unfold in the spring of 1947. Already George F. Kennan, counselor of the American embassy in Moscow, was warning the administration that it faced "a political force committed fanatically to the belief that with the U.S. there can be no permanent *modus vivendi.*" The only answer, Kennan wrote anonymously in the July 1947 issue of *Foreign Affairs,* must be "a long-term, patient but firm

> ### Kennan on Containment [1947]
>
> *The Soviet pressure against the free institutions of the Western world is something that can be contained by the adroit and vigilant application of counterforce at a series of constantly shifting geographical and political points, corresponding to the shifts and maneuvers of Soviet policy, but which cannot be charmed or talked out of existence. The Russians look forward to a duel of infinite duration, and they see that already they have scored great successes. . . .*
>
> *But in actuality the possibilities for American policy are by no means limited to holding the line and hoping for the best. It is entirely possible for the United States to influence by its actions the internal developments, both within Russia and throughout the international Communist movement, by which Russian policy is largely determined. . . . It is . . . a question of the degree to which the United States can create among the peoples of the world generally the impression of a country which knows what it wants, which is coping successfully with the problems of its internal life and with the responsibilities of a World Power, and which has a spiritual vitality capable of holding its own among the major ideological currents of the time.—* ''X'' *[George F. Kennan],* Foreign Affairs, *July 1947.*

and vigilant containment of Russian expansive tendencies."

Russian pressure on Turkey and support of Communist guerrilla forces in Greece emphasized the immediacy of the Soviet threat. The British had been aiding the Greek government, but could no longer carry the burden. Unless Stalin were contained quickly, he might achieve the centuries-old Russian prize of the straits leading from the Black Sea into the Mediterranean. Russia already controlled Albania on the Adriatic.

On March 12, 1947, President Truman appeared before Congress to request $400 million to bolster the armed forces of Greece and Turkey, and to enunciate the doctrine that came to bear his name: "I believe that it must be the policy of the United States to support free peoples who are resisting attempted subjugation by armed minorities or by outside pressures." Senator Vandenberg again supported him, and the Republican Congress voted the Greek-Turkish Aid Act. The initial military aid and subsequent appropriations eased Russian pressure upon Turkey, and by the fall of 1949 brought to an end the long civil war against Communists in Greece.

Military aid was not enough. The Truman Doctrine logically led to a program of economic reconstruction to bolster the stability of Europe and help eradicate the misery out of which the Communist parties in western European countries were gaining recruits. In April 1947 Secretary of State George C. Marshall returned from the Conference of Foreign Ministers in Moscow convinced that the Russians were interested only in profiting from the economic plight of Europe, not in ameliorating it. The solution, he and President Truman agreed, lay in State Department plans to aid European nations that were willing to cooperate with each other in rebuilding their economies. Speaking at the Harvard University commencement in June 1947, Secretary Marshall offered aid to all those European nations (including Russia) who would join in drafting a program for recovery.

Russia denounced the Marshall Plan as American imperialism and intimidated the satellites and Finland and Czechoslovakia into staying away from the planning conference. Germany had no government, and Spain was not invited. Sixteen other nations of Europe joined a Committee of European Economic Cooperation, which in September 1947 presented specifications for reconstruction to create a self-sufficient Europe by 1951. Opposition formed in Congress, but it was embarrassed from the start by possessing as unwelcome allies the American Communists, and in February 1948 it was overwhelmed by a shocked and aroused public opinion when Czech Communists seized power in Prague. Congress in April established the Economic Cooperation Administration. It cut the

administration's request, but did vote an initial $4 billion.

Altogether over a three-year period the United States spent $12 billion through the ECA. This helped to stimulate a remarkable recovery in Europe. By the end of 1950 industrial production was up 64 per cent, economic activity was well above prewar levels, and Communist strength among voters in most areas was dwindling.

## The North Atlantic Alliance

In his inaugural address, January 20, 1949, President Truman challenged the nation to come to the aid of the "more than half the people of the world" who were "living in conditions approaching misery." Point Four of his foreign policy proposals was a plan for aiding them through technical assistance and the fostering of capital investment. The Point Four or Technical Cooperation program began in 1950 with an appropriation of only $35 million, but spent $400 million in the next three years.

Soviet leaders reacted vigorously against the American efforts for world economic recovery. They had organized their own Warsaw Alliance of nine satellite nations (September 1947) to combat "American imperialism." Through a new Cominform (Communist Information Bureau) they sought to eradicate traces of nonconformity throughout eastern Europe. Their greatest triumph was the successful coup in democratic Czechoslovakia in February 1948. Because it was as horrifying to western Europeans as it was to Americans, it helped unify the Western world against the Communist countries. Later in the year, the pressure of Stalin and the Cominform on Marshal Tito provoked him to pull Communist Yugoslavia out of their orbit, and with American aid to embark upon an independent course between Russia and the West. In western Europe, Communist parties tried to thwart the Marshall Plan, especially by calling out on strike the unions they controlled in Italy and France. Despite the strikes, progress continued.

Meanwhile, the United States moved with the British and the rather reluctant French toward the creation of a self-governing, economically strong West Germany. The culmination came on

June 7, 1948, when they announced plans for a new federal West German government with sovereignty over domestic matters and full membership in the European Recovery Program. They also reformed the currency to stop the inflationary flood of marks from the Soviet zone, which was hampering recovery.

The Russians retaliated. Taking advantage of a lack of a written guarantee of land transit across the Soviet zone, they clamped a tight blockade around the western sectors of Berlin. The object was to force the Western powers to abandon either Berlin or the proposed West German republic. President Truman, unwilling to risk war by ordering in armed convoys by land, ordered the supplying of Berlin by increasing on a massive scale the airlift begun in April. By the time bad weather hampered flights in the late fall, adequate stockpiles had been established in Berlin. Through the winter and into the spring of 1949, the airlift continued. It was a remarkable demonstration to Europeans—

especially to the Germans—of what the Americans and British could achieve. Altogether they flew over 277,000 flights to bring in nearly 2.5 million tons of food, fuel, and other supplies to maintain 2 million people. They carried in more than had previously been brought by train.

In the spring of 1949 the Russians backed down and ended the blockade. In October 1949 the German Federal Republic came into existence at Bonn in West Germany, and the Soviets established a German Democratic Republic for East Germany.

Russian intransigence led to the consolidation of the Western countries into a new grand alliance. The North Atlantic Treaty was signed April 4, 1949, by twelve nations, and subsequently also by Greece and Turkey. It declared that an armed attack against one would be considered an attack upon all, and provided for the creation of joint military forces. Under it, the signatory powers established the North Atlantic Treaty Organization to construct a defense force

**Divided Germany and Austria**

### The Berlin Airlift

"It was inspiring and somewhat heart-rending to witness the spontaneous visits of the women and children of Berlin to Tempelhof airport to show their appreciation of the airlift, bringing with them some precious last possession as a token of gratitude to the members of the air crews," wrote General Lucius D. Clay, military governor of the American zone. The pilots called the airlift "Operation Vittles," and some of them informally instituted "Operation Little Vittles," dropping candy tied to hankerchief parachutes to the children. "Berlin had kept its courage," Clay declared. Despite unemployment and an acute shortage of heat and electricity through the winter, "the determination of the people did not falter. They were proud to carry their burden as the price of their freedom."
(United Press International)

that, while not equal to that of the Russians, would be large enough to make an attack highly costly.

The United States began to shift from economic to military aid as the Mutual Defense Act of 1949 appropriated an initial billion dollars for armaments for the signatories. The governing body of NATO, the North Atlantic Council, established military headquarters near Paris early in 1951 under the supreme command of General Dwight Eisenhower. This was SHAPE (Supreme Headquarters, Allied Powers in Europe). The number of divisions and airplanes under NATO command began gradually to grow, but while its power was still relatively feeble, its chief significance was the commitment that the United States had made with the nations of western Europe to stand firm against Russian threats.

That these threats were not to be taken lightly became even clearer on September 23, 1949, when President Truman issued a press statement: "We have evidence that within recent weeks an atomic explosion occurred in the U.S.S.R." The years of relative safety for the American people were already at an end.

## China Turns Red

While the United States was struggling to contain Russia in Europe between 1947 and 1949, the Chinese Communists were destroying the armies of Chiang Kai-shek. To prevent civil war and to effect a coalition government, the Truman administration in December 1945 had sent General George C. Marshall to China. At first he obtained a cease-fire and encouraging signs of accommodation, but irreconcilable differences kept apart the two Chinese governments—the *Kuomintang* (Nationalists) and the Communists. Finally, in January 1947, Marshall returned to Washington disgusted with both governments and all factions except a handful of powerless *Kuomintang* liberals.

Full-scale war broke out. Although the Nationalist armies were larger and better equipped, they soon began to fall back before the better trained, more vigorous Communist forces. As the inept Chiang Kai-shek government failed both on the fighting front and at home, where inflation and inefficiency were rampant, it was plunging toward defeat.

President Truman now sent General Wedemeyer, who had been Chiang's chief of staff, to investigate. Wedemeyer warned that Communist control of China would imperil American interests, since the Communists were in fact closely tied to the Soviet Union. He believed that the United States could rescue Chiang only by sending 10,000 army officers and other advisors to introduce reforms, together with massive material support.

President Truman did not request large-scale aid for Chiang, and for this omission critics subsequently castigated him. But to do so might have interfered with the program of containment in Europe; it would have been unpopular and, in any event, would probably have been too late. Truman did ask Congress to provide $570 million; in April 1948 it voted $400 million, of which China could spend only $125 million for military supplies. Basically the administration decided, as Secretary Marshall made clear, that the United States could not salvage the Nationalist government so that it would be "capable of reestablishing and then maintaining its control throughout all of China." The collapse was rapid, and it came through lack of morale rather than shortages of arms and supplies. In October 1948 the Communists seized Mukden, Manchuria, and as Nationalist troops surrendered or defected, the Reds swept on with captured American arms into central and southern China. At the end of 1949, Chiang and the Nationalists fled to Formosa. All of China was under the new People's Republic, which ruthlessly consolidated its strength by liquidating several million dissidents, harrying out American businessmen, teachers, and missionaries, and proclaiming its propaganda to all of East Asia.

Though Great Britain and some of the western European nations recognized the new government of Red China, the United States refused to do so and blocked its entry into the United Nations. Also, beginning in 1947, the American government introduced new policies in Japan to strengthen that nation in a manner similar to the rebuilding of Germany.

The American occupation in Japan brought a democratization of the government, extension of rights to women and underprivileged groups, expansion of the educational system (from a starting point as high as the goal of educational reform in China), land reform that was as drastic as that in China, a curbing of the power of the monopolistic *zaibatsu* industrial system, and an improvement in the status of labor. In Japan, more than anywhere else in Asia, the United States helped develop a dynamic alternative to Communism. In 1949, to stimulate Japanese recovery, the United States ended its reparations and stopped the dismantling of industrial combinations.

Negotiation of a Japanese peace treaty began in 1950 through the skilled offices of a Republican, John Foster Dulles, whom President Truman appointed to undertake the task. Aside from the fact that it stripped Japan of all her recent conquests, it was a generous treaty, a "peace of reconciliation," as Dulles called it. By recognizing the right of the sovereign Japanese nation to self-defense, it opened the way to rearmament. Thanks partly to its negotiation by a Republican, the treaty easily received Senate ratification and went into effect in 1952. A security treaty, signed at the same time, permitted the United States to maintain armed forces in Japan. Two years later, a mutual-defense-assistance pact provided for Japanese rearmament with American aid, but the building of armed forces proceeded slowly. Disarmament had been one of MacArthur's most cherished reforms, and the American-imposed Japanese constitution had banned war forever. This encouraged such a strong pacifist sentiment that as late as 1957 only 100,000 Japanese had joined the armed forces. The task of defending Japan continued to rest largely with the United States.

Several nations to the south that had suffered either invasion or the threat of invasion during the war viewed with some concern the rebuilding of Japan as a military power. To reassure them, the United States in 1951 signed a security treaty with the Philippines, and the ANZUS pact with Australia and New Zealand.

While rebuilding Japan, the Truman administration refused to capitulate to the demands of the so-called China Lobby for military and naval aid to Chiang on Formosa which might lead the nation into a war against Red China. On the contrary, the State Department issued a white paper (1949) charging the Nationalists with responsibility for their debacle. In January 1950 Secretary of State Dean Acheson publicly outlined a Pacific defense perimeter which did not include Formosa or Korea. If these areas were attacked, he declared, the people invaded must rely upon themselves to resist, "and then upon the commitments of the entire civilized world under the charter of the United Nations."

Within a few months, East Asia became the focal point of American foreign policy as the cold war turned hot in Korea.

## Defending South Korea

During the hectic days at the end of the war in the Pacific, the United States had hastily proposed that Americans accept the surrender of the Japanese in the lower half of Korea, up to the 38th parallel, and that the Russians do the same in the northern half. At the moment the arrangement was useful to the United States. Afterwards, however, the Russians were willing to accept a reunited Korea only if it were Communist-dominated.

The 38th parallel became more and more an impenetrable barrier. To the north of it, the Communists developed a "peoples' government" with a strong aggressive army. To the south, the United Nations held elections that led to a government under the ardently nationalistic

Dr. Syngman Rhee, long an exile in the United States. Rhee would have liked to extend his government to the north, but the United States provided the South Korean army only with relatively light defensive weapons. Consequently when the United States withdrew its forces from below the 38th parallel in June 1949, South Korea was left militarily weaker than its even more aggressive northern twin.

On June 24, 1950, the North Koreans acted swiftly, launching a full-scale invasion that caught the South Koreans and Americans completely by surprise. Almost immediately President Truman and Congress reversed the policy of withdrawal from the Asiatic mainland. The President brought the question of the invasion before the United Nations Security Council. It could act more quickly than the Assembly, and at the moment the Russians were boycotting it, and hence had no representative present to vote a paralyzing veto. The Council on June 25 passed an American resolution demanding that the North Koreans withdraw behind the 38th parallel, and two days later called upon members of the United Nations to "furnish such assistance to the Republic of Korea as may be necessary to repel the armed attack." President Truman on June 27 sent United States air and sea forces to the aid of the South Koreans; on June 30 he ordered ground forces into Korea, and sent the Seventh Fleet to act as a barrier between the Chinese mainland and Formosa.

The Council of the United Nations on July 7, 1950, requested those nations providing troops to place them under a unified command headed by the United States. President Truman appointed General MacArthur commander in chief. Some fifteen nations besides the United States and the Republic of Korea provided troops, but these never comprised more than 9 per cent of the total fighting force. The United States sent about 48 per cent; South Korea mustered 43 per cent. What was officially a United Nations "police action" came to most Americans to seem a war on the part of the United States.

General MacArthur, who at first could draw upon only four understrength divisions in Japan, rushed in troop units piecemeal to slow the rapidly advancing North Koreans as they rushed southward past Seoul, threatening to envelop the entire tip of the peninsula. By thus sacrificing themselves, these forces gave MacArthur an opportunity to build stable defenses around the port of Pusan in the extreme southeast. When the North Koreans struck there in force early in August, strong army and marine reinforcements fresh from the United States hurled them back at each point of assault. As men and supplies poured into Pusan, marine officers devised a bold plan of attack which General MacArthur reluctantly accepted. Rather than try to push the North Koreans back mile by mile, on September 15, 1950, while the United Nations troops around Pusan opened a sharp counteroffensive, he launched an amphibious assault far behind the North Korean lines at Inchon, near Seoul. It caught the Communists almost completely unprepared. The United Nations troops quickly recaptured Seoul; within two weeks the North Korean armies, disrupted and demoralized, were fleeing as best they could to north of the 38th parallel.

## Retreat From North Korea

Amid jubilation, the United States and the United Nations had to make new decisions. Should they capitalize upon their spectacular victory and move into North Korea? The premier of Red China on October 1 warned that the Chinese would "not allow seeing their neighbors being invaded by imperialists." A few days later, he announced the Chinese would send troops, and dispatched a warning to the United Nations through India. These threats worried American strategists, but there was a possibility that China was bluffing, and there was the probability that the North Koreans, unless pursued, would recoup their strength and strike new blows.

The Joint Chiefs of Staff on September 27, 1950, ordered MacArthur to destroy the North Korean armed forces, but under no circumstances to cross the borders of China or Russia. The United Nations Assembly gave its sanction to the project on October 7, reiterating its aim to create "a unified, independent and democratic

Communist Forces
1. North Korean Attack June 25, 1950
2. U.N. Line of Defense Sept. 10, 1950

U.N. Forces
3. U.N. Landing at Inchon Sept. 15, 1950
4. Communist Line of Defense Nov. 24, 1950

**The Korean War    1950–1953**

Korea." Two days later, the United Nations forces poured across the 38th parallel toward the Yalu River, which marked the boundary with Manchuria.

For several weeks the advance into northern Korea went well. On October 19, the capital, Pyongyang, fell, and parachutists landed thirty miles beyond to trap much of the remaining North Korean army. Then, on October 26, a Chinese Communist soldier was captured; four days later, fourteen more were taken. By November 4, eight Chinese divisions had been identified, and Russian-made MIG fighter planes had briefly engaged the United Nations air force.

General MacArthur issued a special communiqué warning that "a new and fresh army now faces us," and he excoriated the Chinese for their international lawlessness in intervening without notice and "massing a great concentration of possible reinforcing divisions with adequate supply behind the privileged sanctuary of the adjacent Manchurian border." Both in

his private communications to the Joint Chiefs of Staff and in the encouragement he gave to pressure groups in the United States, MacArthur engaged in a vigorous campaign for permission to bomb this "privileged sanctuary." President Truman refused to allow all-out military action against China, because, he later explained, "if for no other reason . . . it was a gigantic booby trap."

In the two weeks after they first sighted Chinese troops, the United Nations forces marched into a serious trap. The Chinese suddenly appeared in overwhelming numbers, stalled MacArthur's offensive, and hurled back advance units. Through December 1950, in bitter weather, the outnumbered Eighth Army and X Corps fought a heroic withdrawal from North Korea. The United Nations tried to negotiate peace with the Chinese, but the Communists, as they swept below the 38th parallel and recaptured Seoul, set impossibly stiff terms. In March 1951 the Eighth Army counterattacked, for a second and final time capturing Seoul and

**Communist Forces**
5. Chinese-North Korean Attack Nov. 26, 1950
6. U.N. Line of Defense Jan. 12, 1951

**U.N. Forces**
7. U.N. Counterattack Jan. 25–Nov. 27, 1951
8. Armistice Line Nov. 1951–July 1953

recrossing the 38th parallel. President Truman was ready again to seek a negotiated peace.

General MacArthur, far from ready to accept the position of his commander in chief, repeatedly made public his eagerness to win total victory in Korea at the risk of full involvement in war with China. On March 20, 1951, he communicated his views to the Republican minority leader in the House of Representatives, Joseph W. Martin, concluding: "There is no substitute for victory."

President Truman clung to his thesis that, in the great struggle against Communism, western Europe with its concentration of heavy industry, not industrially weak Asia, was the main potential battlefield. He could not have won the support of western European partners in the United Nations for a more militant policy in Asia. He would not accept the arguments of the Asia-firsters that the United States should undertake unilateral action—"go it alone."

General MacArthur thus emerged as a major figure in American politics, trying to reverse the administration policies. Five days after Representative Martin released MacArthur's letter to the press. President Truman, on April 11, 1951, relieved General MacArthur of his commands. A groundswell of outrage swept the United States; a Gallup poll reported that 69 per cent of those interviewed favored the General, only 29 per cent the President. MacArthur upon his return was greeted hysterically wherever he appeared; millions watched their television sets as he addressed Congress.

Truman's policy of fighting a limited war of containment continued to baffle and exasperate a considerable part of the American people. It went against the American tradition of total victory. It was hard to explain to the public or to the soldiers fighting endlessly through the rice paddies and over the hilltops of Korea.

In June 1951 the Russian delegate to the United Nations hinted that settlement was possible. Armistice negotiations began on July 10, 1951, near the 38th parallel, and continued for many weary months at Panmunjom. They came to revolve around the difficult questions of locating the cease-fire line, enforcing the armistice, and repatriating prisoners of war. By the spring of 1952, agreements had been reached upon all but the last question. Finally, in October 1952, the negotiations were recessed. By then the nation was in the midst of a presidential campaign, and though there was no large-scale fighting in Korea, the interminable negotiations, endless skirmishing, and ever-growing casualties had worn out the patience of the American people.

## THE POLITICS OF FRIGHT

In the disappointing months and years that followed World War II, as warm friendship toward Russia turned into apprehension and alarm, the American public became increasingly afraid that traitors within the government were betraying it to the Communists.

### Hysterical Loyalty

During the period of the New Deal and the war there had been some Communists and Communist sympathizers in the government. At a time when the Russians and the United States were allies this seemed of little consequence, but in 1942 and 1943 President Roosevelt established loyalty checks. By 1946 Russia seemed more a potential enemy than an ally. The Canadian government discovered that at least twenty-three of its employees in positions of trust had turned over secrets, some of them concerning nuclear fission, to Russian spies. Several of the spy rings had operated across the boundary in the United States.

The federal government began extensive efforts to ferret out Communists. President Truman established a Temporary Commission on Employee Loyalty (November 1946) to recommend loyalty investigation systems and safeguards of fair hearings. This led to the establishment of loyalty boards (March 1947) to undertake a sweeping investigation of all federal employees. In August 1950 the President authorized the dismissal in sensitive departments of even those deemed no more than "bad security risks." By 1951 more than 3 million government employees had been cleared, over 2,000 had resigned, and 212 had been dismissed.

Against the recommendations of the Departments of Defense and Justice and of the

Central Intelligence Agency, Congress overrode the President's veto and passed the McCarran Internal Security Act (September 1950). This did not outlaw Communist organizations but required them to publish their records. It barred Communists from employment in defense plants and denied them passports.

Already, in 1948, the Attorney General had obtained indictments against eleven key Communist leaders for violation of the Smith Act of 1940, which prohibited conspiring to teach the violent overthrow of the government. During their nine-month trial in 1949, the Communists engaged in elaborate harassing tactics, which further aroused the public against them. They were convicted. In the 1951 case of *Dennis* v. *United States*, the Supreme Court in a 6-to-2 decision rejected their appeal. Chief Justice Fred Vinson held that advocating or teaching revolution in the existing state of the world, or even conspiring to do so, fell within Justice Holmes' earlier definition of what was punishable—that it constituted a "clear and present danger." In dissenting, Justice Hugo Black remarked: "There is hope that in calmer times, when the present pressures, passions, and fears subside, this or some later court will restore the First Amendment liberties to the high preferred place where they belong in a free society."

While the Supreme Court was solemnly deciding that civil liberties must be circumscribed to protect the modern state, some less careful politicians were capitalizing upon the growing public hysteria over several spectacular cases. Above all there was the case of Alger Hiss, in which these politicians seemed to put on trial and condemn a whole generation of liberal intellectuals. Hiss, a handsome and ambitious young man, had risen rapidly in the government during the 1930s to become a high-ranking official of the State Department. He was present as a clerk at the Yalta conference, but in no way influenced policy there. In 1947 he resigned to head the Carnegie Endowment for International Peace. Whittaker Chambers, a self-avowed former Communist agent, had denounced Hiss as early as 1939, but because he provided no details and no supporting evidence, Chambers was ignored. In 1948 he repeated his accusations be-

fore the House Un-American Activities Committee. When Hiss sued him for slander, Chambers produced microfilms of classified State Department documents that Hiss allegedly had given him in 1937 and 1938.

Hiss was brought to trial for perjury (the statute of limitations prevented indictment for espionage). He called upon a number of the nation's most distinguished liberals to bear witness to his character. The first trial ended with a hung jury (July 1949); the second ended with conviction (January 1950).

More important in convincing Americans that a real Communist menace existed was the revelation, in February 1950, that a young British scientist, Dr. Klaus Fuchs, had turned over to Russian agents full details on the manufacture of atomic bombs. His confession led to the trial and ultimate execution of Julius and Ethel Rosenberg, Americans who were alleged to have been his accomplices—and who were hailed as martyrs by Communists throughout the world.

### Senator McCarthy Attacks the State Department [1950]

*In my opinion the State Department, which is one of the most important government departments, is thoroughly infested with Communists.*

*I have in my hand 57 [some of his listeners swore McCarthy said "205"] cases of individuals who would appear to be either card carrying members or certainly loyal to the Communist Party, but who nevertheless are still helping to shape our foreign policy.*

*One thing to remember in discussing the Communists in our Government is that we are not dealing with spies who get 30 pieces of silver to steal the blueprints of a new weapon. We are dealing with a far more sinister type of activity because it permits the enemy to guide and shape our policy.—Senator Joseph R. McCarthy, at Wheeling, W. Va., February 12, 1950.*

Among the politicians who capitalized upon the public's fears, none was more sensational in his rise than Senator Joseph McCarthy of Wisconsin. Already some other politicians were winning fame through crusading against Communism. Representative Richard Nixon, who had helped keep the Hiss affair alive until Chambers produced the incriminating microfilms, was on his way to the Senate and a national reputation. McCarthy decided to exploit the same issue. In February 1950 he charged that a large number of Communists and men loyal to the Communist party were still shaping foreign policy in the State Department. When a subcommittee of the Senate Foreign Relations Committee took up his charges, they found not a single Communist or "fellow-traveler" (sympathizer).

An excited public numbering many millions eagerly swallowed McCarthy's new claims as he went on from sensation to sensation more rapidly than his detractors could refute his unsubstantiated charges. Millions wanted to believe McCarthy when he attacked as Communists the "whole group of twisted-thinking New Dealers" who had "led America near to ruin at home and abroad." McCarthy was providing a troubled nation with a scapegoat, and the Republican party with a winning issue.

## A Troubled Electorate

In 1950 the voters were disturbed by the charges of subversion, by the Communist victory in China, and by the Korean War. Many were led to believe that the events in China and Korea had resulted from a conspiracy in the State Department. When Hiss was convicted in January, his former acquaintance Secretary of State Dean Acheson declared that he would not turn his back on him; meaning, Acheson later explained, that he was following "Christ's words setting forth compassion as the highest of Christian duties." But Acheson's remark, together with President Truman's early reference to the Hiss case as a red herring, served as Republican campaign texts. Representative Nixon declared: "Traitors in the high councils of our own government have made sure that the deck is stacked on the Soviet side of the diplomatic tables."

Bipartisanship in foreign policy disappeared

as the Republicans pressed their issue. They did not capture Congress in November 1950, but they gained twenty-eight seats in the House and five in the Senate. Neoisolationists, heartened by the election results and no longer restrained by Senator Vandenberg, who was fatally ill, opened a "great debate" in the Senate over foreign policy. They succeeded in passing a resolution (April 1951) restraining the President from sending troops to western Europe without congressional authorization.

Meanwhile, President Truman made but little headway with his Fair Deal. Congress passed the Displaced Persons Act of 1950, liberalizing the 1948 legislation that the President had denounced as discriminatory against Catholics and Jews because its quotas were unfavorable to people from southern and eastern Europe. The new law increased the number of persons to be admitted from 205,000 to 415,000—but even this latter figure was a total for a three-year period, not a yearly number. Congress also implemented some of Truman's proposed reforms. The National Housing Act of 1949 provided for the construction over the succeeding six years of 810,000 housing units for lower-income families, together with a subsidy for forty years to bridge the gap between costs and the rents the tenants could afford to pay. It also provided grants for slum clearance and rural housing. Congress voted increased appropriations for power development and reclamation in the West, for TVA and for the Farmers' Home Administration (which carried on the rehabilitation work of the earlier Resettlement Administration and Farm Security Administration). In contrast, the Fair Deal health-insurance program went down to crashing defeat under the vigorous opposition of the American Medical Association, which raised a $3 million fund to combat it. Federal aid for education failed because of dissension over whether aid should go to parochial schools.

Republicans undermined the Truman administration with charges of favor-peddling and corruption, which implicated men in the White House though not the President himself. The President's military aide had received as a gift a $520 deep-freeze unit; the wife of an examiner of loans for the Reconstruction Finance Corporation had acquired a $9,540 mink coat. These became the symbols of a moral malaise in Washington. Apparently go-betweens, in return for a 5-per-cent fee, could obtain contracts, arrange RFC loans, and take care of tax difficulties in the Bureau of Internal Revenue. President Truman reorganized the RFC and reformed the Bureau of Internal Revenue and the Department of Justice, but much too slowly to satisfy his Republican critics.

As the election of 1952 approached, there was no indication that the majority of voters wished to reverse either Truman's foreign policy or his domestic program. They did want to "clean up the mess in Washington," and above all they wanted to see an end to the drawn-out, wearying Korean War.

## Eisenhower Elected

It was not surprising that in times so troubled the voters overwhelmingly turned to a successful and popular general who they felt could lead them to security in a frightening world. They turned not to MacArthur but to Dwight D. Eisenhower, who was closely linked to the military and foreign policies of the Roosevelt and Truman administrations.

Partly this was the logic of politics. The wing of the Republican party holding to the views of MacArthur was committed to Senator Robert A. Taft—but it was a minority with the party, even though it controlled the Republican National Committee. The majority (knowing they could count upon the votes of most of the minor-

### Eisenhower Versus Taft

Two factions in the Republican party, the more internationalist and the more isolationist, polarized around General Dwight D. Eisenhower and Senator Robert A. Taft in the early months of 1952.

General Eisenhower, born in 1890 in Texas and raised in Kansas, had graduated from West Point and risen steadily in the army, mainly through staff positions. After serving as Supreme Commander in World War II, he was briefly president of Columbia University, then returned to uniform as head of the new NATO command. He was the symbol both of victory during the war and collective security through the United Nations afterward. The only inkling of his political views lay in his speeches while a civilian, which were little

homilies reminiscent of his roots in the rural life of a simpler era. They appealed to the yearnings of his listeners without giving them much idea how he could cope with the complexities of the 1950s. Politically this was all to the good.

Eisenhower said privately that he was willing to run only in order to prevent the nomination of Taft and a resurgence of isolationism. Yet in September 1952, he had to invite Taft to confer with him at the president's house on the Columbia University campus. Taft promised to do everything possible, short of sacrificing friends and principles, to help Eisenhower win. (United Press International)

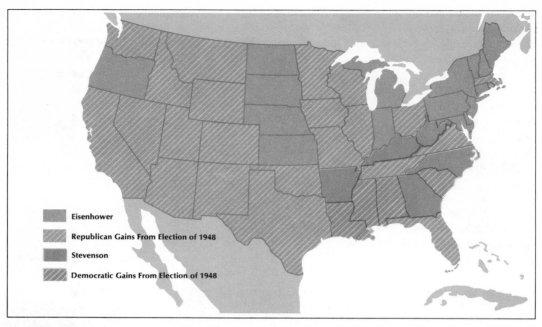

Eisenhower

Republican Gains From Election of 1948

Stevenson

Democratic Gains From Election of 1948

**Election of 1952**

ity) sought a candidate who could pull strong support from many who had favored the Democratic foreign and domestic policy. Consequently, they looked to General Eisenhower —whom some liberal Democrats had sought to draft in 1948.

In the struggle for delegates, Eisenhower easily carried the East, and Taft the Middle West. Later, in a violent struggle on the floor of the convention, the Eisenhower forces won contested delegations and, with them, the nomination on the first ballot. Senator Richard M. Nixon of California, who was acceptable to conservative Republicans, was nominated for the Vice Presidency. The platform was ambiguous enough to cover disagreements between the two wings of the party. Early in September Eisenhower went still further to mollify the Midwestern Republicans by conferring with Taft. He promised patronage to the Taft followers and avowed that the main issue of the campaign was "liberty against creeping socialization"—but he did not compromise on foreign policy. Later in Wisconsin he was conciliatory toward Senator McCarthy. Thus he was able to campaign with

the diverse factions of the party unified behind him.

As for the Democrats, the Northern wing of the party was in control at the convention. President Truman had announced that he would not run again. The most vigorous campaigner in the primaries, Senator Estes Kefauver of Tennessee, won little support among party leaders; Vice President Alben Barkley was deserted by labor spokesmen, who declared that he was too old. So the Northern leaders drafted Governor Adlai E. Stevenson of Illinois, who had earlier declared he would not run. His running mate was the liberal Senator John J. Sparkman of Alabama. The platform stated the positions of the Northern Democrats: endorsement of the Truman foreign policies, civil rights, repeal of the Taft-Hartley Act, and high price supports for farmers.

Governor Stevenson began delivering speeches brilliant in their eloquence, clever in their wit, and startling in their candor. As he promised to "talk sense to the American people," he drew the hearty support of most intellectuals, whose critics derisively called them "eggheads." But General Eisenhower appealed much more effectively to businessmen and the masses by promising to end their various frustrations.

Republican campaigners played upon the triple theme of "Communism, corruption, and Korea." Speaking in Detroit on October 24, 1952, Eisenhower promised to bring the war to "an early and honorable end." To help do so, he promised he would make a personal trip to Korea. The response at the polls was overwhelming: Eisenhower getting 33,936,000 votes to 27,315,000 for Stevenson. Despite Eisenhower's victory, the Republicans failed to gain complete control of Congress. They won a majority of eight seats in the House and only an even split in the Senate. The Republican candidate was far more popular than his party.

## NEW HANDS AT THE HELM

John Foster Dulles, the Republican expert in foreign policy, had criticized the Democratic program of "containment" as a passive one that left the initiative to the Communist side. Dulles proposed, instead, a program of "liberation" that would lead to a "roll-back" of Communist expansion. As secretary of state in the Eisenhower administration, he continued to talk of new approaches. Yet the Eisenhower-Dulles policy was to be essentially a continuation of the Truman-Acheson policy.

### A Korean Armistice

Before his inauguration President-elect Eisenhower flew to Korea to talk to commanders

**Secretary of State John Foster Dulles Reporting to President Eisenhower    May 17, 1955**

The Eisenhower administration made extensive use of television to dramatize its actions among the American people. For the first time the President's press conferences were televised, and on several occasions like this, Secretary Dulles reported to the President in front of the television cameras. He had just returned from Europe, where he had signed the treaty restoring sovereignty to Austria. (U.S. Department of State) about means of obtaining an honorable truce. There he issued a press statement asserting: "We have no panaceas, no trick ways of settling any problems." In his inaugural he committed himself to a firm policy in Korea and elsewhere in the struggle against Communists. "In the final choice," he declared, "a soldier's pack is not so heavy a burden as a prisoner's chains." He informed Congress that the United States would encourage the strengthening of the South Korean armed forces, and would no longer use the Seventh Fleet to shield Red China from Chiang Kai-shek.

Less than two months after President Eisenhower took office, Stalin died. This opened the possibility of an end to the Korean War and perhaps some moderation of the cold war. When the new Soviet Premier, Georgi Malenkov, seemed conciliatory, the President called upon the Russians to show their good faith by signing an Austrian peace treaty and supporting an armistice in Korea. Through the spring of 1953 negotiations for an armistice proceeded rather smoothly. By June, when they were almost completed, President Rhee disrupted them by freeing 27,000 North Korean troops who did not wish to be repatriated. Nevertheless, on July 27, 1953, a final armistice agreement was signed at Panmunjom. It provided for a cease-fire and withdrawal of both armies about a mile and a half back of the existing battle line, which ran from coast to coast, from just below the 38th parallel in the west to thirty miles north of it in the east.

A conference was to be held to seek peaceful reunification of Korea, but at the Geneva meeting (1954) no agreement was reached. The armistice turned into an uneasy and indefinite armed truce. In 1957, after the Communists had long been violating armistice prohibitions against introducing new armaments, the United States announced it was also sending more modern weapons into South Korea. The United States not only continued to face a threat from North Korea, but had to restrain President Rhee, who bitterly threatened to unify Korea by force. The Senate ratified a mutual defense treaty in 1954, but warned that the United States would not support South Korean military aggression.

The Korean War (officially only a "police action") had lasted more than three years and cost the United States alone 25,000 dead, 115,000 other casualties, and $22 billion. For Americans who liked to think in terms of total victory, it all seemed painfully inconclusive. The fighting had settled no problems in the Far East except to prevent the Communist conquest of South Korea.

## "Massive Retaliation"

As secretary of state from 1953 to 1959, Dulles gave the impression of formulating policy decisions on his own. A sturdy moralist, a skilled and stubborn advocate, and a tireless worker, he seemed to feel that he must participate personally in innumerable top-level negotiations all over the globe. Since as secretary he flew 479,286 miles outside of the United States, his detractors liked to wisecrack that he was demonstrating an infinite capacity for taking planes. Assuming many of the normal functions of State Department officials, diplomats, and even the President, he dominated the making of foreign policy.

The Eisenhower administration had come into office firmly committed to existing collective-security arrangements and a Europe-first priority. Nevertheless, it maintained a tenuous compromise with the ardently nationalistic Asia-first wing of the party. This group was exploiting at home the thesis that setbacks in Asia were due to internal subversion in the Truman administration, that Communist aggression in Asia must be met with military force, and that economic aid to remove the grievances the Communists were exploiting was a waste of money. The hero of the Asia-firsters was Chiang Kai-shek, and their special villain, Red China, which they insisted must be curbed or destroyed at all costs. Concurring with this group at some points were the business leaders dominant in the Eisenhower administration, who were determined that defense expenditures must fit within a balanced budget.

The pressures of these groups helped lead to crucial decisions in 1953. Again, as before the Korean War, a movement began to reduce the military establishment. At the same time, the Eisenhower administration wished to meet the Communist challenge in Indochina and elsewhere. The solution seemed to lie in a "new look" in defense policy, equally pleasing to the secretaries of defense, the treasury, and state. This meant cutting the expensive army ground forces and basic scientific research. Secretary of Defense Charles E. Wilson, an expert on practical matters of automobile production, said basic research was what you do "when you don't know what you are doing." The United States would depend especially upon its thermonuclear weapons and their delivery by the air force. Popularized, this was the policy of "more bang for a buck."

A new diplomatic and strategic approach was necessary to make the "new look" in defense operate adequately. Secretary of the Treasury George M. Humphrey, looking at it from a standpoint of cost, asserted that the United States had "no business getting into little wars." If the nation had to intervene, he declared, "let's intervene decisively with all we have got or stay out." This was the economic basis for Secretary of State Dulles' proposal of "massive retaliation." The United States would depend less on local defense, he declared in an address on January 12, 1954, and depend more on "the deterrent of massive retaliatory power . . . a great capacity to retaliate instantly, by means and at times of our own choosing."

Occasionally, Dulles declared two years later, this policy brought the United States close to war, but he said it produced the desired results. In January 1956, *Life* magazine quoted him: "The ability to get to the verge without getting into the war is the necessary art. If you cannot master it, you inevitably get into war. If you try to run away from it, if you are scared to go to the brink, you are lost." Critics of Dulles, within the United States and abroad, suggested that "brinkmanship" had not worked in this salutary fashion. Rather, they suggested, war-weariness on both sides and mutual fear of atomic retaliation led to compromise solutions averting all-out war. Despite Dulles' words, the Eisenhower administration did not rely on "massive retaliation" or even the threat of it.

## China and Indochina

The Indochina crisis of 1954 offered the first test of the new approach. Under the leadership of Ho Chi Minh the people of Indochina, a French colony that had fallen to Japan in World War II, had been fighting for their independence—against the Japanese and then against the French. The end of the Korean War enabled the Chinese Reds to give indirect aid to the Indochinese nationalists, who were largely Communists, at a time when the French were tottering on the edge of military disaster. In 1954 the rebels besieged an army of 12,000 Frenchmen and friendly Indochinese in the frontier fortress of Dienbienphu. Already the United States was paying 70 per cent of the French war costs, thus supporting colonialism as an alternative to Communism. Now, it appeared, the United States would also have to send direct military aid if Dienbienphu and all of Indochina were not to fall under Communist control.

At a press conference, President Eisenhower likened the nations in Southeast Asia to a row of dominoes. The moral was implicit; the first domino must not be allowed to fall. Many of the President's advisers favored at least bombing the beseiging army with carrier-based planes, but Dulles failed to gain support among allied nations. Congressional leaders had no stomach for an intervention that might soon involve more ground troops than the Korean War, and in which the United States might have to fight alone. The United States did not intervene; there was no "massive retaliation." Dienbienphu fell on May 7, 1954. At a conference in Geneva, the United States, stripped of bargaining power (except for the threat of unilateral intervention), had to stand by, neither associating itself with negotiations with Red China, nor approving the agreements of July 1954, which provided for a cease-fire and the partitioning of Indochina into three independent nations.

After the Geneva conference, Secretary Dulles succeeded in building a Southeast Asia Treaty Organization (SEATO) to serve as a counterpart of NATO and help contain Communism. SEATO (established September 1954) was far less impressive, since the terms of the Geneva conference kept Nationalist China and nations of Indochina (Vietnam, Laos, and Cambodia) from participating. Several of the most important Asian states (India, Ceylon, Burma, and Indonesia) refused to join because they were committed to neutralism. This left only three nations of Southeast Asia—Pakistan, Thailand, and the Philippines—to join with the United States, Great Britain, France, Australia, and New Zealand. They drew up a pact, weaker than the North Atlantic Treaty, providing only that an attack upon one would be regarded as a threat to the others. SEATO opened the way for economic and military aid, but without the key nations of Southeast Asia participating, it remained a relatively ineffective organization.

The United States continued to function in Asia as best it could on a virtually unilateral basis. Trouble with Communist China developed over some offshore islands that Chiang continued to garrison—Quemoy and Matsu and Tachen Islands. Occasionally Chiang's air force attacked the Communists from them. Since the Mutual Defense Treaty with Chiang, signed at the end of 1954, did not include these islands, Red China in January 1955 began air attacks upon the Tachens and bombardment of Quemoy. Before invasion could follow, Congress granted President Eisenhower rather indefinite emergency powers to aid Chiang. These sufficed to maintain a precarious status quo.

Intermittently, the Chinese Communists renewed their pressure upon Quemoy and Matsu. In August 1958 they began another serious bombardment. Secretary Dulles, although not always clear in what he said, implied repeatedly that the United States would help Chiang defend the islands. But the United States could not count upon the support of other Western nations if a large-scale struggle with Red China developed. The militant Chinese Communists in 1959 pressed on other borders. After crushing a revolt in Tibet, they pushed troops across several ill-defined frontiers into areas claimed by India. Of much more serious concern to the United States, they backed a Communist penetration deep into Laos, one of the nations of Indochina.

In the involved and unending struggle with Communist China, the American arsenal of atomic weapons was of relatively little effect even against a nation that as yet did not possess any. Against Russia, with its rapidly expanding nuclear strength, the threat of massive thermonuclear retaliation was still less effective.

## Our German Ally

Fortunately, the United States and its allies did not depend upon nuclear power alone. The concept of the North Atlantic Treaty Organization was embodied in its emblem of a sword and a shield. The sword stood for atomic weapons, the striking force, and the shield for conventional ground forces, to deter or withstand attack. During the Korean War the United States began to rebuild its military establishment at home and gradually to pour funds into NATO, to strengthen its defenses in terms of ground forces as well as atomic weapons.

Europeans worried over the slowness of the United States to provide arms and men, its failure (partly because of constitutional limitations) to commit itself clearly in advance to resist any armed attack on western European nations, and its desire to rearm Germany.

While the French were still afraid of the Germans, the Germans themselves were so war-weary that it was difficult to persuade them to arm again. Between 1950 and 1954 they were able to win back step by step almost all their sovereignty in return for rearming. During these years the vexing problem was how the new western European defense force would be constituted. The French proposed a European Defense Community consisting of France, Italy, the Benelux countries (Belgium, The Netherlands, and Luxemburg), and West Germany. This community would build a supranational army in which no division would have more than 12,000 men from the same country. The army would be under the NATO supreme command. This fragmentation of national forces would circumvent the building of a large German army. But the United States and Germany favored larger national army units, and succeeded in obtaining a provision that integration would be at the level of army corps made up of several divisions. The specter of a resurgent German army led the French Communist deputies and the right wing nationalists in the French Assembly to unite and subsequently defeat ratification of the European Defense Community treaty (August 1954).

Some new way had to be found to make the rearming of Germany acceptable to France. In October 1954 Great Britain placated the French by promising to keep four divisions and a tactical air force on the Continent as long as its allies wanted them. With this reassurance, France agreed to a treaty that same month restoring full sovereignty to Germany (except for the stationing of allied troops in West Berlin until Germany was reunified). To take the place of the European Defense Community, a weak and limited treaty organization, which had been created earlier, was expanded and strengthened into the Western European Union, including all the European Defense Community nations plus Great Britain. National armies were not to be scrambled as had been earlier planned, but the West German army was to be limited to twelve divisions, which would be supplied to NATO. Germany promised not to seek reunification or extension of her boundaries through force, and was prohibited from manufacturing nuclear, biological, or chemical weapons. Germany joined NATO and thus directly became a military ally of the United States. In 1957 she contributed her first forces—five divisions totaling 120,000 men.

## The Geneva Spirit

After the death of Stalin in 1953, there were increasing signs that new Russian policies might lead to some enlargement of freedom behind the Iron Curtain and some relaxation of tensions with the Western powers. Russia extended a peace overture to Tito of Yugoslavia, returned a key base to Finland, recognized the Federal Republic of West Germany, and signed a peace treaty with Japan. Above all, the Soviet Union joined with the Western powers in signing a peace treaty with Austria, making it a neutral state, and terminating the long military occupation.

The softening of Soviet policy and the increase in international exchanges led to demands from Europeans, Asians, and even Americans for a conference among the heads of state—a "summit conference"—to consider means of easing international tensions. But the greatest single motive for such a meeting was the knowledge that both the United States and Russia were manufacturing hydrogen bombs of staggering destructive power.

In August 1953 the Russians had set off a hydrogen explosive. President Eisenhower warned a few weeks later that the physical security of the United States had "almost totally disappeared before the long-range bomber and the destructive power of a single bomb." The meaning of this became dramatically clear in the spring of 1954 when the United States announced that it had exploded in the Pacific a bomb powerful enough to destroy or put out of commission all of New York City.

Against this background, the American people, after an initial wariness, became enthusiastic about the meeting of the heads of the United States, Great Britain, France, and Russia in Geneva (July 1955). President Eisenhower, hopeful that he could wage "a war for peace," proposed at the meetings that the Russians and the United States exchange blueprints of their armed forces and permit inspection of their military installations from the air. He declared to Premier Nicolai A. Bulganin: "The United States will never take part in an aggressive war." Bulganin replied: "Mr. President, we believe that statement."

The affability of the Russians at Geneva immensely relieved the American people, who were hopeful for the moment that a real change of policy had come about. This "Geneva spirit," as newspapermen called it, led to a general feeling on the part of most Western nations that a nuclear war between Russia and the United States would not develop. Secretary Dulles declared, however, that the conference had avoided "creating an illusion that all was now so well that we could safely relax our efforts to build individual and collective self-defense." All proposals from both sides had been referred to a future foreign ministers' conference. Even before it met, several nations began to scale down their NATO contributions.

President Eisenhower upon his return from Geneva warned: "We must never be deluded into believing that one week of friendly, even fruitful negotiations can wholly eliminate a problem arising out of the wide gulf that separates East and West." The American public, less inclined to caution, greeted the President with unrestrained acclaim.

The subsequent foreign ministers' conference failed dismally to agree upon German unification, disarmament, or lowering of trade barriers. Even before it adjourned, the "Geneva spirit" rapidly evaporated throughout the West.

## Menace in the Middle East

Soon a new Russian drive was launched toward the Middle East, where the United States had long been deeply involved because of its conflicting interests in the people of the new state of Israel and in the oil of the Arab states.

During World War II, the British, in order not to offend the Arabs, had continued restrictions upon immigration to Palestine; both political parties in the United States favored lifting these restrictions and creating a Jewish state. After the war, the British brought the problem to the United Nations, which recommended partitioning Palestine between Jews and Arabs. The Jews successfully fought off military attacks by the Arabs and, on the day the British mandate ended, May 14, 1948, proclaimed a new government. President Truman recognized it within a few minutes, thus ending United Nations proposals to put Palestine under a temporary trusteeship. The new nation, Israel, fought off armies from surrounding Arab countries until the United Nations established an unstable truce in 1949. Although the United States tried to promote amity, relations between Israel and its neighbors continued close to the point of explosion, and other quarrels in the Middle East persisted.

Gradually the United States won over some of the Arab nations to the Western defense system. This country leased air bases from Saudi Arabia; and through the Baghdad Pact of 1955 Secretary Dulles managed to bring the northern bloc of Arab states—Iraq, Iran, and Pakistan—into the defense arrangement.

Dulles' diplomacy was less successful with Egypt, which for years had quarreled with the British over the Sudan and British bases along the Suez Canal. The United States tried to mediate; in 1954 the British agreed to remove their troops from the Suez area. After Gamal Abdel Nasser came to power, the State Department tried to woo him, although he proclaimed emphatic neutralist and Arab nationalist policies, and strove for leadership of the entire Arab world. Secretary Dulles tried to win him with offers of economic aid—even the sum needed to construct an enormous dam on the Nile. Meanwhile, the Russians concluded a deal, made public in September 1955, by which they gave Nasser large quantities of armaments in exchange for cotton.

With sufficient Communist arms Nasser might destroy Israel. He could also threaten the security system the United States was trying to build in the Middle East. With the arms that went to Nasser and his close ally, Syria, would also go Russian experts to show Egyptians how to use them. Secretary Dulles met the challenge. Instead of continuing to be conciliatory toward Egypt, in July 1956 he suddenly withdrew his promise to provide funds for a dam. A week later Nasser retaliated by seizing the Suez Canal, purportedly to obtain money for the Nile project. This action gave him a stranglehold on the main oil line to Europe, since two-thirds of the proven oil reserves of the world were in the Middle East, and four-fifths of the oil for western Europe flowed from there.

During the tedious months of negotiations with Nasser that followed, Great Britain, France, and Israel all came to feel that they were not obtaining as much support as they should from the United States. Meanwhile, the armed strength of Egypt was growing rapidly. On October 29, 1956, Israeli forces struck a preventive blow at Egypt; the next day the British and French intervened to drive the Egyptian forces from the Suez Canal zone. They were militarily successful, but not before the Egyptians had thoroughly blocked the canal. The United States led the United Nations in denouncing the military intervention; the Western alliances seemed in danger of dissolving; Russia threatened to send "volunteers" to the aid of Egypt. Under these pressures, the British and French issued a cease-fire order on November 6. Another prolonged truce between Egypt and Israel began under the supervision of the United Nations.

The power vacuum in the Middle East in the weeks after the Suez cease-fire created new opportunities for the spread of Communism. Once again the American public was alarmed and incensed, since coincident with the Suez crisis came brutal Soviet suppression of an uprising in Hungary. Because of the nuclear stalemate, the United States could not intervene in Hungary. It limited itself to fostering United Nations resolutions of censure and to admitting tens of thousands of refugees.

In the Middle East more positive action afterward seemed possible. The public was receptive when the President appeared before Congress on January 5, 1957, to enunciate what came to be called the "Eisenhower Doctrine." He asked Congress to authorize military and economic aid "to secure and protect the territorial independence" of Middle Eastern nations "against overt armed aggression from any nation controlled by international communism." Congress authorized the President to use armed force as he deemed necessary, and to spend $200 million on economic aid in the area.

As an instrument of pressure upon Egypt, the Eisenhower Doctrine was of little effect. Nasser reopened the Suez Canal on his own terms, and with Soviet aid continued penetration of his neighbors. In April 1957 American policy seemed more successful when the United States rushed its Sixth Fleet to the eastern Mediterranean to bolster the government of Jordan. Three other states, Saudi Arabia, Iraq, and Lebanon, seemed to give at least tacit support to the Eisenhower Doctrine.

Soviet penetration in the next few months, both through feeding Arab nationalism and through providing arms to Egypt, Syria, and Yemen, effectively countered the American policy. In August 1957 the Russians negotiated a $500 million arms-and-aid pact with Syria. In its aftermath, a pro-Soviet army clique seized power. Since the clique of course did not ask for American aid, the Eisenhower Doctrine was inoperative in Syria, but the State Department, declaring that Syria's neighbors were alarmed, sent them weapons. The strong tone of the United States led to an unfavorable reaction among the Arab nations, and they reaffirmed their solidarity.

Egypt and Syria, combining to form the United Arab Republic, continued to exert pressure on their neighbors. When a pro-Nasser clique took over Iraq (July 1958), it appeared that Lebanon and Jordan might also come under Nasser's domination. The pro-Western government of Lebanon requested aid against rebels, and the United States rushed in troops. At the same time Great Britain sent forces into Jordan. In the fall of 1958, when conditions became stabilized in Lebanon, the United States withdrew its troops. Iraq, however, continued to be a serious problem. Secretary Dulles, in order to balance its loss from the Baghdad Pact mutual defense organization, announced that the United States would assume full partnership in the alliance. But the withdrawal of Iraq from the alliance did not lead the country into Nasser's United Arab Republic as expected. The elements favoring this course soon fell from power in Iraq, and the danger in 1959 and after seemed to be that the country would swing into the Communist bloc. Reacting against the Communist trend in Iraq, Nasser veered back toward the West, and the United States again began plying him with favors. Conditions were thus unstable and uncertain in much of the Middle East.

## THE COMMUNISTS GAIN

The Eisenhower administration was hard pressed to contain the expansion of Communist power in the world, even without attempting the "roll-back" of which Dulles once had spoken. Indeed, before the end of the administration, the Communists appeared to be making further gains.

### The Rocket Race

The onslaught of Communist ideology and power was especially frightening because of the apparent failure of the United States to keep pace with the Soviet Union in the development of intercontinental ballistic missiles, a failure that the Russians tried to exploit throughout the world. In early 1957 the United States had appeared to be abreast or ahead of Russia in the development of guided missiles with nuclear warheads. Because of the potential horror of these weapons, both nations seemed ready to reach disarmament agreements during seven months of discussions in 1957 at a meeting of the United Nations subcommittee in London. The United States insisted upon schemes of strict inspection, including proposals for aerial photography over strips of each other's territory. To this the Soviet Union would not agree.

Then, in August, Russia announced that she had successfully tested an intercontinental ballistic missile. In contrast, the United States had successfully tested only intermediate-range missiles that had traveled from 1,500 to 3,000 miles. The Russian claims received sobering confirmation in October when Soviet scientists, using a rocket booster engine more powerful than any yet developed in the United States, launched the first successful satellite, the "sputnik."

Khrushchev, who in a series of bold moves had just consolidated his power in the Kremlin, now issued a series of strong statements. The intent of his "sputnik diplomacy" was clearly to shake the Western alliance and impress neutral nations. The reaction within the United States, especially when the first American attempt to launch a much smaller satellite failed, was more one of angry fear than of congratulations to the Russian scientists. Three months later the United States began launching its own, smaller satellites.

As an indication of his concern, President Eisenhower, although recuperating from a mild stroke, flew to Paris (December 1957) to lend strong moral support at a NATO conference. In January 1958 he devoted almost his entire annual message to Congress to the armaments crisis and to the need to surpass Russia in providing aid for underdeveloped countries. He called upon an acquiescent Congress for heavy additional expenditures to rush development and construction of long-range missiles and of submarines and cruisers that could launch missiles. The first task confronting the nation was "to ensure our safety through strength," he pointed out. "But we could make no more tragic mistake than merely to concentrate on military strength. For if we did only this, the future would hold nothing for the world but an age of terror."

Meanwhile, extensive nuclear testing after 1954 by both the United States and Russia, climaxed by the Russian explosion of several "dirty" bombs, greatly increased the fallout of radioactive isotopes. Throughout the world there was a fear of possible harmful effects. "Any dose, however small, produces some biological effect and . . . this effect is harmful," the Joint Congressional Committee on Atomic Energy granted in a 1959 report. If testing were to continue at the same rate as that of the previous five years over the next two generations, the report warned, the predicted average concentration of radioactive strontium in the bones would be close to what scientists had estimated would be the maximum permissible body burden. This threat, well before 1959, was bringing popular pressure for the curtailing of nuclear tests.

In the spring of 1958 Khrushchev announced a unilateral abstention from nuclear tests by Russia. This left Eisenhower faced with the choice of two courses. He could follow the reasoning of most officials in the Defense Department, who held that nuclear weapons were the only way in which the United States could counter the enormous land armies of Russia and China—and continue tests. Or he could promise to stop tests on the condition that Russia would agree to adequate inspection.

He decided upon the latter course and announced that the United States and its allies would suspend tests for one year beginning October 31, 1958. The suspension would continue on a year-to-year basis, provided a proper system of control could be developed and substantial progress could be made on disarmament negotiations. Russia, proclaiming that this was a Western trick, announced that it would resume testing. Nevertheless, President Eisenhower declared that for the time being the United States would continue its suspension of tests as it sought some workable agreement with the Soviet Union. Representatives of the United States, Great Britain, and Russia met in Geneva and slowly, laboriously, tried to construct a regulatory treaty.

In 1959 Khrushchev made much propaganda use of the failure of the United States to catch up with Russia in astronautical feats. These feats

# Where Historians Disagree

## Origins of the Cold War

In the years immediately following World War II, while Stalin was still in power in the Soviet Union, the generally accepted view of the cold war in the United States was that altruistic American policy, bent on establishing democratic governments and healthy economies throughout the world, had been blocked by sinister Russian expansionism. The onus for starting the cold war was placed squarely upon the Russians. Containment of the Communists and maintenance of collective security were hailed as American achievements. By the beginning of the sixties, some years after the death of Stalin, revisionist historians began to appear; by the end of the sixties, in the wake of disillusion over the Vietnam War, the earlier, simple view of the cold war origins was undergoing serious reappraisal.

The cold war was a continuation of the policy of suspicion and hostility toward Russia going back as far as the Bolshevik seizure of power in 1917, Denna Frank Fleming charges in *The Cold War and Its Origins, 1917–1960* (2 vols., 1961). In *The Tragedy of American Diplomacy* (1962), William Appleman Williams, in terms reminiscent of Charles Beard, blames the cold war largely upon American shortcomings. Gar Alperovitz, in *Atomic Diplomacy: Hiroshima and Potsdam* (1965), suggests that the United States dropped atomic bombs on a Japan already seeking a way to surrender, partly because no alternative was seriously considered and partly to make the Soviet Union more manageable. Herbert Feis expresses quite different views—more favorable to American policy makers—in a revision of his *Japan Subdued, The Atomic Bomb and the End of World War II* (1967). In a detailed essay exploring both sides of the debate, "Origins of the Cold War," *Foreign Affairs* (October 1967), Arthur Schlesinger, Jr., takes to task those who blame the impasse solely upon the United States. "The Cold War could have been avoided only if the Soviet Union had not been possessed by convictions both of the infallibility of the communist world and of the inevitability of a communist world," writes Schlesinger. "One might wish that America had preserved the poise and proportion of the first years of the Cold War and had not in time succumbed to its own forms of self-righteousness. But the most rational of American policies could hardly have averted the Cold War."

More recent writings are taking into account the complexities Schlesinger suggests. For example, Walter LaFeber in *America, Russia, and the Cold War, 1945–1966* (1968) examines internal policies of nations on both sides of the iron curtain and suggests the motives for their moves and countermoves. This is a balanced work, but in the revisionist tradition. Historians are now at least agreed that both sides in the cold war share part of the blame.

### Launching the First American Satellite

On January 31, 1958, four months after the Russians launched the first satellite—three months after they sent up one so big that it contained a dog—the United States, using a Jupiter-C launching vehicle, put into orbit the first American satellite, called Explorer I. It was 80 inches long, 6 inches in diameter, and weighed 30.8 pounds. In it were devices for measuring temperature, cosmic rays, and the frequency of meteorite particles, and radios for transmitting the measurements.
(Official U.S. Army photo)

obscured the fact that the "missile gap" between the two nations was not as great as had been feared two years earlier. The United States was successfully producing and testing its own missiles and developing plans for hiding and spreading the launching sites so that it would require ten times as many Russian missiles to destroy them. The success of the navy in constructing atomic-powered submarines that could launch missiles, and in bringing the submarines up through the ice at the North Pole, was a dramatic example of American achievement. The naval development of "Project Tepee," a radio-monitoring system that could detect any missile launchings anywhere in the world, was an indication of the technical advance of American defense.

If the Russians were to attack the United States, they could not expect their own cities to remain unscathed. The reverse held equally true—that American nuclear power would be incapable of destroying all the sites from which the Russians could launch missiles. The Congressional Joint Committee on Atomic Energy reported in August 1959 that an attack upon the United States, if it came, might kill 50 million people, seriously injure 20 million more, and destroy or render unusable for months half of the dwellings in the country. Crops would be contaminated and swept by fire. The only hopeful note was the assurance that bomb shelters for the entire population could reduce casualties by 25 or 30 per cent.

## Friendly Overtures Fail

Suddenly, in November 1958, Khrushchev precipitated a new crisis over Berlin, where the West's position was, as always, vulnerable. He asserted that conditions had changed so markedly in Berlin since the end of the war that the occupation agreements no longer applied. In six months he proposed to sign a separate peace treaty with the government of East Germany, turning over to it all the Russian occupation functions in Berlin including control over the access routes that stretched 110 miles to West Germany.

The United States insisted that its treaty rights still held and undertook the twofold task of trying to maintain unity among its Western

### President Eisenhower on Berlin [1961]

*Berlin is not so much a beleaguered city or threatened city as it is a symbol—for the West, of principle, of good faith, of determination; for the Soviets, a thorn in their flesh, a wound to their pride, an impediment to their designs.*

*The Soviets want to banish the Allies from West Berlin because, first, it is to them an unwelcome show place of Western freedom and prosperity in a region otherwise completely regimented and impoverished; and, second, because the opportunity it creates for the unhappy East Germans to escape to freedom emphasizes to the outside world the emptiness of the phrase 'people's democracies.'' In the meantime, they use it as a pretext to create and intensify tensions and to try to divide the West.—Saturday Evening Post, December 9, 1961.*

allies and of getting from the Soviet government concessions that would correspond to any that the United States might make. Neither task was easy. Russia made alternate proposals that were as unacceptable as the first demand had been, and Khrushchev manipulated the issue to try to force a summit meeting. The United States was not willing to go further than a foreign ministers' conference unless the Russians became more conciliatory. The Geneva sessions beginning in May 1959 were discouragingly unfruitful.

Meanwhile, the burden of conducting American foreign policy had shifted to a new Secretary of State, Christian Herter, when Dulles, dying of cancer, resigned in April 1959. Herter was a strong successor. He had capped his foreign service record as a young man with a successful career in politics. But he did not continue the one-man determination of foreign policy that had distinguished Dulles. President Eisenhower now assumed a larger measure of responsibility, and this pointed toward new interchanges at the top with the Russians.

Exchanges at lower levels had been going on at an increasing rate since the Geneva thaw of 1955. One of its few positive effects had been personal and cultural interchanges of musicians, dancers, students, and delegations of all kinds, climaxed in the summer of 1959 by a visit to the United States of Anastas Mikoyan, a Soviet deputy premier, and to Russia of Vice President Nixon. The Russians demonstrated their wares at a fair in New York City, and the Americans at a corresponding fair in Moscow showed crowds of Russians the components of the high standard of living in the United States. While Nixon was at the fair, he engaged in informal debate with Khrushchev. The Russian press was for the most part hostile, but the crowds were friendly, and Khrushchev himself, while holding dogmatically to Soviet positions, seemed to demonstrate a keen interest in things American.

In August 1959 President Eisenhower announced that he would exchange visits with the Russian leader. The purpose in inviting Khrushchev, Eisenhower explained, was "to give him the opportunity to see what Americans are like" and "to give him, face to face, the basic convictions of our people on the major issues of the day." Khrushchev, during his travels in the United States, received on the whole a hearty welcome, despite the coldness of most American officials and the hostile demonstrations of certain groups, especially those sympathizing with the Hungarian rebels of 1956. He impressed Americans with his energy, toughness, and—except for a few petulant outbursts—good humor. Eisenhower, postponing his return visit, made tours of western Europe, southern Asia, and Latin America, to the cheers of enthusiastic crowds at almost every stop.

A second "summit" conference, to meet in Paris, was scheduled for May 1960. On May 1 an unarmed American U-2 plane was downed inside the Soviet Union. The American government at first denied, then acknowledged and attempted to justify the fact that the plane had

**Broadcasting a Voice of America Program**

These visitors are listening to a broadcast for Burmese audiences. In addition to broadcasting in thirty-six languages through short-wave transmitters in the United States and at strategic points throughout the world VOA "packaged" taped programs in sixty-two languages were being broadcast by more than 3,000 local stations throughout the non-Communist world.

been engaged in aerial reconnaissance of a kind the United States had been carrying on, systematically but secretly, for some time. At the Paris meeting, unsatisfied by Eisenhower's belated promise to discontinue flights over Russian territory, Khrushchev made the U-2 incident an occasion for denouncing Eisenhower and breaking up the conference.

Khrushchev also took back his invitation for Eisenhower to go to the Soviet Union. Eisenhower, having planned to stop in Japan on the way home from Russia, went ahead with arrangements for a Far Eastern trip in June. A new security pact, authorizing continued American bases in Japan, awaited ratification. Communist agitators now played upon the pacifism of the Japanese people, a pacifism that American occupation policies earlier had stimulated. In Tokyo mobs began wild demonstrations against the pact, against Premier Nobusuke Kishi, who sponsored it, and against the Eisenhower visit. At the last minute, after the President had reached as far as Manila, his Japan appearance was called off. The Kishi government managed to put the unpopular treaty into effect; but throughout the world the Eisenhower administration could scarcely avoid a serious loss to American prestige, which already had been weakened by the administration's handling of the spy-plane affair.

## Disgruntled Neighbors

The incessant threats against areas close to the Communist perimeter so occupied the American government and people that they paid scant attention to an area of vital worth to the United States and of growing vulnerability to Communist influence—the area to the south. One of the minor ironies of this hectic age was the erosion of the Good Neighbor feeling between Latin American nations and the United States during the very years when this country was extending much of the Good Neighbor policy to Europe and Asia.

On paper there was no deterioration. Quite the contrary; the Latin American nations signed new pacts and received additional forms of aid. They all became members of the United Nations. In 1947, at a conference at Rio de Janeiro,

they drafted an Inter-American Treaty of Reciprocal Assistance, and the following year established an Organization of American States. The United States had abandoned the old unilateral Monroe Doctrine by entering into pacts and organizations providing for mutual action whether in defense, settlement of disputes, or economic cooperation.

Yet the overwhelming military and economic power of the "colossus of the North" remained. Latin Americans were not pleased when the United States brought its prestige to bear against the totalitarian dictator of Argentina, Juan D. Perón, in 1946–1947, even though the pressure failed. They were not much more pleased when the United States successfully brought pressure against a pro-Communist regime in Guatemala in 1954. But in the late fifties, when many of the nations overthrew dictators, the more common complaint was that the United States had been too friendly toward despots, as in Venezuela, and not enthusiastic enough about rebels like Fidel Castro, who came into power in Cuba in 1959, and who thereafter devoted himself to denunciations of "Yankee imperialism."

Above all, the problems from which Latin American peoples were suffering were economic. After the close of World War II, they could no longer sell raw materials from their farms and mines to the United States in such large quantities or at such favorable prices as before. The soaring costs of the American manufactured goods they imported further hurt them. At home they were undergoing a rapid industrial revolution, an accompanying social evolution, and an explosive population increase at the highest rate in the world, as much as 2.5 per cent per year. Already their combined population had passed that of the United States. All these factors helped create acute internal problems.

Inevitably the United States would have to be involved in the solution of economic questions because the hostility of neighbors to the south would be potentially ruinous, and because the two areas had become increasingly interdependent economically. Trade with Latin America exceeded $8 billion a year by the end of the fifties, and accounted for a third of the imports and a quarter of the exports of the United

States. In Latin America 80 per cent of the foreign capital was American; it had a book value of about $9.5 billion. (This figure was second only to the $13 billion invested in Canada, which was also unhappy about its economic relations with the United States.)

It seemed to Latin Americans that, despite these close economic ties, the United States was doing little specifically to help them solve their problems—to provide adequate capital for large-scale development, to stabilize raw materials at a profitable level, and to conquer inflation. They felt neglected as the American government poured billions into Europe and Asia while giving Latin America only a comparative pittance. Secretary Dulles was occupied elsewhere, and the Eisenhower administration, under the influence of two successive conservative secretaries of the Treasury, was cold to requests for government loans for development. The festering economic ills and other grievances that could easily be focused against the United States were ready-made for the Communists. Exercising an influence out of proportion to their small numbers, they were active from Cuba to Guatemala and Argentina.

Despite riots and disorders, the Latin American discontent received little notice in the United States until May 1958, when Vice President Nixon was mobbed in Lima and Caracas. In the aftermath of the national shock, the State Department speeded changes in policy which were already slowly under way. This country helped Latin American nations negotiate export quota pacts among themselves to raise the price of coffee and some metals, and it expedited negotiations toward the establishment of a regional common market among the republics. When, in June 1958, the President of Brazil called for an Operation Pan-America to speed economic development, the American government agreed to furnish nearly half the capital for a new billion-dollar Inter-American Bank to make development loans. It also tried to improve public relations in a way Nixon had suggested by giving no more than a correct handshake to dictators but offering a warm embrace to democratic leaders.

The administration was increasing its attention to Latin America none too soon, since it was obvious that the well-disciplined, widely pervasive Communist activities throughout the area were receiving direction from Russia. Early in 1959 Latin American Communist leaders returned from attending the twenty-first party congress in Moscow and began the systematic denunciation of every point of the new United States program.

The full import of the Communist challenge to the south became clear in 1960. Fidel Castro, whose revolutionary accession to power had been cheered by Americans at the beginning of 1959, turned his administration increasingly to the left and indulged in shrill tirades against the United States. The Eisenhower administration, acting with restraint, was slow to retaliate economically until, in the summer of 1960, Castro systematically confiscated a billion dollars' worth of American property. At this point the United States stopped importing Cuban sugar at a subsidized price. Castro complained to the United Nations Security Council that the United States was engaging in economic aggression.

The Soviet leader Nikita S. Khrushchev proclaimed that the Monroe Doctrine was dead and that, if the United States were to intervene militarily, Soviet artillerymen could "support Cuba with rocket fire." In the fall of 1960 tension heightened as Castro tried to spread his revolution to neighboring republics. President Eisenhower established a naval patrol to prevent an invasion of Guatemala or Nicaragua. At the same time, secretly, Americans were training an anti-Castro Cuban force at a camp in Guatemala. In January 1961 Castro ordered the staff of the United States embassy in Havana cut from eighty-seven to eleven. The United States then severed diplomatic relations with Cuba. Soviet influence clearly extended to within ninety miles of the United States.

# Selected Readings

**The Eisenhower Administration** D. D. Eisenhower, *The White House Years°* (2 vols., 1963–1965); E. J. Hughes, *The Ordeal of Power* (1963); Richard Nixon, *Six Crises°* (1962); J. R. Beals, *John Foster Dulles* (1959); Richard Goold-Adams, *J. F. Dulles: A Reappraisal* (1962); Louis Gerson, *American Secretaries of State: John Foster Dulles* (1967).

**The Cold War** G. F. Kennan, *American Diplomacy, 1900–1950°* (1951); J. W. Spanier, *American Foreign Policy Since World War II°* (1962); W. G. Carleton, *The Revolution in American Foreign Policy: Its Global Range°* (1963); Norman Graebner, *Cold War Diplomacy: American Foreign Policy, 1945–1960°* (1962); M. F. Herz, *Beginnings of the Cold War* (1960); D. F. Fleming, *The Cold War and Its Origins, 1917–1960* (2 vols., 1961), critical of the U.S.; L. S. Wittner, *Rebels Against War: The American Peace Movement, 1941–1960* (1969); David Wise and Thomas Ross, *The U-2 Affair* (1962).

**Nuclear Power and Military Policy** H. A. Kissinger, *Nuclear Weapons and Foreign Policy* (1957); L. L. Strauss, *Men and Decisions* (1962); R. G. Hewlett and O. E. Anderson, Jr., *The New World* (1962); Herman Kahn, *On Thermonuclear War* (1960); M. D. Taylor, *The Uncertain Trumpet* (1960); H. L. Nieburg, *Nuclear Secrecy and Foreign Policy* (1964).

**Communism and Anti-Communism** E. L. Shils, *The Torment of Secrecy* (1956); J. A. Wechsler, *The Age of Suspicion* (1953); Whittaker Chambers, *Witness* (1952); Alger Hiss, *In the Court of Public Opinion* (1957); R. H. Rovere, *Senator Joe McCarthy°* (1959); C. P. Curtis, *The Oppenheimer Case* (1955).

**Germany** L. D. Clay, *Decision in Germany* (1950); Drew Middleton, *The Struggle for Germany* (1949); R. H. Jackson, *The Nürnberg Case* (1947); Eugene Davidson, *The Death and Life of Germany: An Account of the American Occupation* (1959); J. E. Smith, *The Defense of Berlin* (1963).

**The Far East** E. O. Reischauer, *The United States and Japan°* (1957); R. A. Fearey, *Occupation of Japan* (1950); F. S. Dunn, *Peace-Making and the Settlement with Japan* (1963); Herbert Feis, *The China Tangle°* (1953); Tang Tsou, *America's Failure in China, 1941–1950* (1963); David Rees, *Korea: The Limited War* (1964); Carl Berger, *The Korea Knot: A Military-Political History* (1957); G. D. Paige, *The Korea Decision, June 24–30, 1950°* (1968); J. W. Spanier, *The Truman-MacArthur Controversy and the Korean War°* (1959); A. D. Biderman, *March to Calumny* (1962), on "brain-washed" American prisoners; Melvin Gurtov, *The First Vietnam Crisis: Chinese Communist Strategy and United States Involvement, 1953–1954* (1967).

**The Near East** Nadav Safran, *The United States and Israel* (1963); Hugh Thomas, *The Suez Affair* (1967); Herman Finer, *Dulles over Suez* (1964).

**Latin America** M. S. Eisenhower, *The Wine is Bitter: The United States and Latin America* (1963); B. F. Smith, *The United States and Cuba: Business and Diplomacy, 1917–1960* (1960).

---

°Titles available in paperback.

# Chapter 28
# The Politics
# of Plenty

Though the peril of nuclear annihilation hung over them, the majority of the American people, in the phrase of the time, "never had it so good." They were riding a wave of prosperity much higher and longer-lasting than any previous one in the history of the country. The boom, beginning in the 1940s, continued through the 1950s and the 1960s, with an occasional recession or minor slump but with no real depression. A generation grew up that had never experienced such a calamity and could not believe it possible.

Yet there was much to be apprehensive about, at home as well as abroad. The prosperity was largely due to the foreign dangers, for it was stimulated by government spending for defense, and there was reason to wonder how long the good times would last if by some chance there should be a sudden "outbreak of peace." And even while the prosperity lasted, a large minority of the people, perhaps as many as 30 million of them, had little or no share in it.

A Swedish sociologist, Gunnar Myrdal, well acquainted with life in the United States, was moved to write: "I draw the conclusion that the common idea that America is an immensely rich and affluent country is very much an exaggeration. American affluence is heavily mortgaged. America carries a tremendous burden of debt to its poor people. That this debt must be paid is not only a wish of the do-gooders. Not paying it implies a risk for the social order and for democracy as we have known it."

Especially disadvantaged were the Americans of African descent. They suffered from limitations on equality and liberty in a country that professed devotion to the creed of liberty and equality. This contradiction between profession and practice was the theme of an elaborate study, *An American Dilemma* (2 vols., 1944), which Myrdal and a team of American scholars had made of the Negro's place in the United States. Myrdal had warned that, after the war, Negro Americans could be expected to demand the rights that so long had been systematically denied them.

In the war black troops fought along with white for the declared object of creating an international order in which the "four freedoms" would be secure. Then, in the cold war, the United States sought the support of dark-skinned peoples throughout the world. These peoples, emerging from colonialism in their own lands of Asia and Africa, provided inspiration for blacks in America who began to insist upon the freedom they had not yet fully won a century after their emancipation had been officially proclaimed.

With his "Fair Deal," President Truman had made an abortive effort to solve some of the most pressing of the domestic problems. President Eisenhower announced no comparable program, but his successors John F. Kennedy and Lyndon B. Johnson proposed reforms going beyond Truman's.

---

**President John F. Kennedy**

President Kennedy would jab at the air in staccato fashion as he earnestly expounded the New Frontier program. (Albert Crenshaw)

## THE "MIDDLE OF THE ROAD"

In the 1950s the majority of the voters seemed more interested in preserving their own economic gains than in remaking society. Viewing themselves as moderates, they gave wholehearted support to the moderate President, Dwight D. Eisenhower. As early as 1949 Eisenhower had indicated his own approach when, as president of Columbia University, he addressed the American Bar Association. "The path to America's future," he then said, "lies down the middle of the road between the unfettered power of concentrated wealth . . . and the unbridled power of statism or partisan interests."

### Businessmen in Government

Once in office, President Eisenhower set up a businessmen's administration. To his cabinet he appointed one of the highest paid corporation lawyers in the country (Secretary of State John Foster Dulles), the president of General Motors (Secretary of Defense Charles E. Wilson), the president of Mark Hanna's former firm M. A. Hanna and Company (Secretary of the Treasury George Humphrey), a New England manufacturer, two automobile distributors, a conservative specialist in farm marketing, and the wife of a wealthy Texas publisher (Mrs. Oveta Culp Hobby, who had been wartime commander of the WAC's and who was named to head the Department of Health, Education, and Welfare when it came into existence in 1953). Something of an exception was the Secretary of Labor, Martin P. Durkin, the president of the plumbers' union, who had backed Adlai Stevenson in the 1952 campaign. "Eight millionaires and a plumber," the *New Republic* disrespectfully remarked. At the hearing on his appointment, Wilson played into the hands of Democratic critics by testifying that he had long assumed that "what was good for our country was good for General Motors, and vice versa." A few days later, Stevenson declared: "While the New Dealers have all left Washington to make way for the car dealers, I hasten to say that I, for one, do not believe the story that the general welfare has become a subsidiary of General Motors."

President Eisenhower's system of administering the government gave special importance to this cabinet made up preponderantly of businessmen. Borrowing from earlier army experience, he established his assistant, Sherman Adams, former governor of New Hampshire, as a sort of chief of staff, and from Adams down through the cabinet he extended a chain of command. Through the cabinet, and through numerous new committees, administrators arrived at important policy decisions that they referred to the President, who relied heavily upon these recommendations.

### "Eisenhower Prosperity"

At the beginning of the new administration, Secretary of the Treasury George Humphrey undertook to restrict bank credit and thus prevent inflation. By the fall of 1953 the threat was one of deflation instead. When the economy slackened, Secretary Humphrey and the Federal Reserve Board reversed the scarce-money policies and eased credit. The Republican administration's first venture with the expedients of Keynesian economics (manipulating money and credit to control the business cycle) was a success. By the summer of 1955 the American economy was again booming.

In order to avoid strikes that might unsettle economic conditions, several large industries, led by the automobile manufacturers, made new concessions to organized labor. As early as 1948 Walter Reuther, the president of the United Automobile Workers, had obtained from General Motors, and later from other manufacturers, an "escalator clause" in contracts, providing for automatic increases or decreases in wages every three months as the consumers' price index rose or fell. In 1955 he demanded from the Ford Motor Company a guaranteed annual wage. Ford compromised by agreeing that workers should receive 65 per cent of their net weekly wages for the first four weeks they were unemployed, and 60 per cent for the next twenty-two weeks. General Motors followed. A few months later, steel workers received from the American Can Company and the Continental Can Company the first guarantee of an annual wage.

The round of wage raises continued through 1956. After a five-week strike, steel workers won a substantial gain, and the United Mine Workers without a strike obtained a 30 cents-an-hour increase. Factory workers' wages went up to approximately $80 per week. These wage increases, together with other factors, led to widespread wholesale price rises and a renewed threat of inflation.

In December 1955 the American Federation of Labor and the Congress of Industrial Organizations merged at the top into a new giant federation, the AFL-CIO. The powerful Teamsters' Brotherhood in 1957 became the focal point of a congressional investigation into labor racketeering. A Senate committee charged the president of the Teamsters, David Beck, with the misappropriation of over $320,000 in union funds. When Beck appeared before the committee, he refused to answer questions, invoking the constitutional protection of the Fifth Amendment against self-incrimination. Ultimately the committee brought forth so much evidence against Beck that he declined to run for reelection as president of the Teamsters. But at their convention the Teamsters defiantly elected, as their new president, James Hoffa, also under attack by the committee. His election resulted in the eviction of the Teamsters, the largest union in the United States, from the AFL-CIO. The congressional investigation led to the Labor Reform Act of 1959, which was intended to promote honest elections of union officials, safeguard union funds, ban Communist leaders, and restrict boycotting and picketing.

The great staples piled up in surplus, and from 1948 to 1956, farm prices dropped a third while the national income went up by half. In 1948 farmers received 8.9 per cent of the national income; in 1956, only 4.1 per cent. Farm population declined steadily, to 22,300,000 in 1956—only a ninth of the nation. In that single year, one out of every eleven of the farm population either moved to a city or was absorbed in an expanding city. While farm produce prices fell, consumer food prices continued to rise. Mainly this was because distribution costs were steadily going up. The farmer was caught in a squeeze, as prices for his produce slipped while prices of what he bought gradually increased.

As surpluses of such agricultural staples as wheat and cotton piled up, the government sought to bolster the prices through $8 billion worth of purchases. In 1954 President Eisenhower and Secretary of Agriculture Benson proposed a shift away from rigid price supports to a flexible sliding-scale program. The purpose was to cut government losses and end artificiality in production and distribution. The 1955 harvest was the first to be grown under the new flexible system, but already Democratic politicians were denouncing flexible supports as ones that could only "flex" downward. Seeking to win the farm vote, in 1956 they wrote a bill providing for high price supports and a subsidy for farmers who let land lie fallow. They thought they had put President Eisenhower in an impossible position, and as they expected, he vetoed the bill. But in May 1956 he pulled out of the vetoed bill the provision for a "soil bank" of fallow land and threw it back at the congressional Democrats. In this form, Congress passed the bill and it became law. Under the 1956 program, farmers took 12.3 million acres out of production in return for payments of over $250 million.

In the realm of public power development, the administration demonstrated its friendliness toward private enterprise. The President in 1953 referred to expansion of the Tennessee Valley Authority as "creeping socialism." The administration sought to circumvent the TVA by contracting with the Dixon-Yates syndicate in 1954 to build a huge steam power plant on the banks of the Mississippi. The administration declared that the contract would save taxpayers an immediate $100 million in construction costs, but opponents pointed to the large profits that the syndicate would collect over many years. The power would cost the government $3.5 million per year more than TVA power. Ultimately in 1955, when the city of Memphis, Tennessee, offered to build the plant, the President retreated to the principle of decentralization and canceled the Dixon-Yates contract.

The Eisenhower administration proposed federal "partnership" with local public or private enterprise in power construction. Secretary of the Interior McKay thus permitted a private power company to plan three small power dams in Hell's Canyon on the Snake River, rather than obtain appropriations for one large federal multipurpose dam. In keeping with his feeling that development of resources should be decentralized, President Eisenhower signed a bill turning over to states offshore oil lands along the Gulf of Mexico and the Pacific coast.

While the Eisenhower administration moved toward the right, conciliating the Taft wing of the Republican party in Congress, the President retained the basic general welfare programs that had been enacted during the previous twenty years. He took a firm stand against so-called "socialized medicine" but proposed a public health insurance program that would involve little more than limited underwriting of private insurance companies issuing health policies. Congress passed no health-insurance legislation, but in 1954 extended social security to 10 million more people, and unemployment compensation to an additional 4 million. In 1956 Congress authorized a ten-year highway building program for which it would allocate $24,825,000,000.

This concept of the limited role of the federal government in providing for the general welfare was what Eisenhower referred to as "dynamic conservatism." It appealed to many members of Congress. During his first two years in office, when Congress was narrowly Republican, the President was supported more often than not by a coalition of liberal Republicans and Democrats. Of eighty-three key issues brought to a vote in the 1953 session of Congress, the administration won seventy-four, but succeeded in fifty-eight of these only through Democratic support. After the elections of 1954 the Democrats controlled both the House and the Senate.

## An End to McCarthyism

Only slowly after the Korean armistice was the nation relieved from the excesses of McCarthyism. The hunt for subversives in the government, begun during the Truman years, was intensified early in the Eisenhower administration. Large numbers of employees resigned or were dismissed—a total of 2,200 according to an official report. But most of the serious security risks had already been removed in the Truman purge. A study of some 400 of the Eisenhower administration cases by the Fund for the Republic of the Ford Foundation indicated that in a majority of them the charges had been insup-

portable, and often reinstatement ultimately followed. In July 1955 the Congress established a bipartisan Commission on Government Security to reevaluate the security program.

Senator Joseph McCarthy himself plummeted from the national limelight to relative obscurity. His downfall followed his serious blunder in obliquely attacking President Eisenhower and directly assailing Secretary of the Army Robert Stevens, in January 1954. The attacks led to congressional hearings, which turned into a great national spectacle viewed by millions over television. Many people for the first time saw McCarthy in action, as for thirteen days he bullied and harried Secretary Stevens, evading issues through irrelevant countercharges and insinuations, and interrupting to object at every point. As the public watched, McCarthy seemed to change from a national hero into something of a villain, then into a low buffoon. In December 1954 the Senate voted 67 to 22 to condemn him for conduct unbecoming a senator. He no longer had much of a following when he died in May 1957.

Remnants of the attitudes that had made possible the rise of McCarthy remained. There was, for example, the case of a consultant to the Atomic Energy Commission, J. Robert Oppenheimer, who had directed the wartime laboratory at Los Alamos that made the first atomic bomb. In 1950 he had opposed the development of a hydrogen bomb. The FBI in 1953 distributed to the White House and several government departments a report on Oppenheimer detailing his prewar associations with Communists. On order from President Eisenhower, a "blank wall" was placed between Oppenheimer and government secrets, pending hearings. A three-man board voted 2 to 1 against granting him security clearance; the AEC ratified the decision 4 to 1. Scientists were bitterly split over the wisdom of the decision.

The Supreme Court, as a result of the appointments of the Republican President, seemed to be moving toward a more liberal rather than conservative policy. In one case in 1957 it ruled that the government could not use secret FBI evidence against a defendant unless it was made available to his lawyers. Congress quickly passed legislation safeguarding FBI files. In four other cases the Court protected individuals who were suspected of being subversive against undue encroachment by federal or state power. In 1958 the Court ruled 5 to 4 that the State Department, in the absence of an act of Congress, was exceeding its authority in refusing passports to persons who failed to file affidavits "with respect to present or past membership in the Communist party." These decisions attracted relatively little attention compared with the Supreme Court rulings on desegregation.

## Desegregation Begins

A series of cases before the Supreme Court breaking down bit by bit racial segregation in public schools had been pressed by the National Association for the Advancement of Colored People since the late 1930s. Their target was a Supreme Court decision of 1896, *Plessy* v. *Ferguson*, which had interpreted the Fourteenth Amendment clause requiring that states give "equal protection of the laws" to mean that separate but equal facilities could be furnished to Negroes. Finally, the Supreme Court reversed this doctrine in the case of *Brown* v. *Board of Education of Topeka* in May 1954. Chief Justice Earl Warren (who had been appointed by President Eisenhower in 1953, after the death of Chief Justice Vinson) delivered the unanimous opinion of the Court: "We conclude that in the field of public education the doctrine of 'separate but equal' has no place. Separate educational facilities are inherently unequal." The Court called for the desegregation of schools "with all deliberate speed."

Some Southern and border states resorted to every possible legal device to avoid mixed schools. Each September mob action against integration in a few communities within the South attracted widespread attention throughout the world. By the fall of 1957, of some 3,000 biracial school districts in the South, a total of 684 had begun desegregation. Schools within these districts in large cities in the upper

**Desegregation in Washington, D.C.**

In the fall of 1954, following the Supreme Court decision against school segregation, McKinley Technical High School quietly opened on a basis of equality for all students regardless of color. Before this date, public schools in the nation's capital were segregated. (Wide World)

*Brown* et al. v. *Board of Education of Topeka* et al. [1954]

*In approaching this problem, we cannot turn the clock back to 1868 when the [Fourteenth] Amendment was adopted, or even to 1896 when* Plessy v. Ferguson *was written. We must consider public education in the light of its full development and its present place in American life throughout the Nation. Only in this way can it be determined if segregation in public schools deprives these plaintiffs of the equal protection of the laws.*

*Today, education is perhaps the most important function of state and local governments. Compulsory school attendance laws and the great expenditures for education both demonstrate our recognition of the importance of education to our democratic society. It is required in the performance of our most basic public responsibilities, even service in the armed forces. It is the very foundation of good citizenship. Today it is a principal instrument in awakening the child to cultural values, in preparing him for later professional training, and in helping him to adjust normally to his environment. In these days it is doubtful that any child may reasonably be expected to succeed in life if he is denied the opportunity of an education. Such an opportunity where the state has undertaken to provide it, is a right which must be made available to all on equal terms.*

*We come then to the question presented: Does segregation of children in public schools solely on the basis of race, even though the physical facilities and other 'tangible' factors may be equal, deprive the children of the minority group of equal educational opportunities? We believe that it does.*
—*Excerpt of opinion of the Supreme Court delivered by Chief Justice Earl Warren.*

South or the border area, like Washington, Baltimore, Louisville, and St. Louis, opened quietly on an integrated basis. But 2,300 districts, including all those in the deep South and in Virginia, remained racially separate. Some districts attempted desegregation on a very slow, "token" basis. One of these was Little Rock, Arkansas, where intervention by the governor and threats by a mob led President Eisenhower to send federal troops to maintain order.

Pressure from growing blocs of Negro voters in the North, and from Negroes rising in economic status in the South, helped bring other changes. President Eisenhower completed the desegregation of the armed forces and tried to bring about greater integration in the government and the District of Columbia. "There must be no second-class citizens in this country," he wrote the Negro Representative Adam Clayton Powell. Representative Powell, ironically, was instrumental in killing President Eisenhower's school-aid program of 1956, which provided for grants of $250 million a year for five years to match state funds. Powell succeeded in amending the bill to ban racial segregation; Southern segregationists aligned themselves with Northern conservatives to defeat the bill.

Congress in August 1957, after debating sixty-three days, passed a new civil rights law—the first since Reconstruction—to give federal protection to Negroes wanting to vote. In eight Southern states with an adult Negro population of over 3,750,000, only 850,000 or 25 per cent were registered and still fewer went to the polls. In a 1955 election in Mississippi, only about 1 per cent of the adult Negroes had voted. The Civil Rights Act empowered the federal government to remove some of the obstacles that state and local officials were placing in the way of Negro registration and voting. Federal judges were authorized to enjoin state officials from refusing to register qualified persons. The judges could fine recalcitrant officials up to $300 and could sentence them to forty-five days in jail, without a jury trial.

With the Supreme Court ruling out school segregation and the Congress legislating for civil rights, it seemed that a "second Reconstruction" was beginning, one that would complete the task of emancipation left unfinished in 1877.

### State of South Carolina, Resolution on Desegregation [1956]

*For almost sixty years, beginning in 1896, an unbroken line of decisions of the [Supreme] Court interpreted the Fourteenth Amendment as recognizing the right of the States to maintain racially separate public facilities for their people. If the Court in the interpretation of the Constitution is to depart from the sanctity of past decisions and to rely on the current political and social philosophy of its members to unsettle the great constitutional principles so clearly established, the rights of individuals are not secure and government under a written Constitution has no stability. . . .*

*The educational opportunities of white and colored children in the public schools of South Carolina have been substantially improved during recent years and highly satisfactory results are being obtained in our segregated schools. If enforced, the decision of the Court will seriously impair and retard the education of the children of both races, will nullify these recent advances and will cause untold friction between the races.—Excerpt from Joint Resolution, February 14, 1956.*

## A Second Term for Ike

In 1955 President Eisenhower was at the height of his popularity. Only the anti-third-term Twenty-second Amendment, ratified in 1951 as a belated slap at Roosevelt, seemed to bar him from staying in the White House as long as he chose. Apparently his health was excellent, but while vacationing in Colorado, on the morning of September 24, he suffered a heart attack.

The President began to make a promising recovery, but no one expected him to run for another term. During his long hospitalization in Denver and his convalescence in Gettysburg, he began to "ease" rather than "bulldoze" his way back into his presidential duties.

A panel of doctors met with the press in February 1956 to state that the scar on the President's heart muscle had healed. It was almost an anticlimax when Eisenhower announced that he would run again. In June, stricken a second time, he was operated upon for ileitis. Although the operation was serious, Eisenhower's advisers never let the question arise whether or not he would continue as a candidate—and except among some Democrats it seemed a matter above debate. At the Republican convention in San Francisco at the end of August, he and Vice President Nixon were renominated by acclamation. The proceedings seemed to some observers to reflect more the atmosphere of a coronation than a party convention. Even while the President was recuperating from his heart attack, public-opinion polls attested to his overwhelming popularity. Regardless of this, Adlai Stevenson and Estes Kefauver fought vigorously for the Democratic nomination in state primary after primary. In the end, Stevenson triumphed at the Democratic convention and Kefauver became the vice-presidential nominee.

It was a rather dull campaign. Stevenson sought an issue by proposing that the United States agree to end hydrogen bomb tests. The average voter, relieved because the stalemate in nuclear weapons seemed to rule out a third world war, refused to worry about international affairs until actual shooting in the Suez area just before election day sent him to seek refuge with Eisenhower as commander in chief. Altogether, about 58 per cent of the voters marked their ballots for Eisenhower, although he was sixty-six, the oldest man ever to be reelected to the Presidency, and had suffered two serious illnesses in little more than a year past. He received more than 35 million votes to only 26 million for Stevenson and carried forty-one states. It was not much of a triumph for the Republican party. The prestige of the President pulled some Republican congressmen to narrow victories, but the Democrats continued to control both houses of Congress.

During President Eisenhower's second administration, domestic policies were little changed. In 1957 Congress occupied itself largely with trying to slash the President's $71.8 billion budget, the largest in peacetime history.

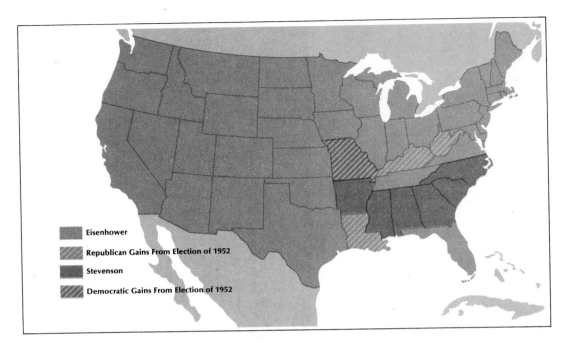

Eisenhower

Republican Gains From Election of 1952

Stevenson

Democratic Gains From Election of 1952

### Election of 1956

Even Secretary of the Treasury Humphrey (who resigned a few months later) joined in the onslaught against the "terrific" expenditures.

At the close of 1957 the nation skidded into the most serious recession since the war. By late spring of 1958 industrial production had dropped 14 per cent below the level of a year earlier, and approximately 5 million workers were unemployed. Again the so-called "built-in stabilizers" of the economy, such as unemployment insurance payments to those out of work, somewhat softened the blow of the recession.

As Republicans prepared for the congressional campaign of 1958, they were handicapped by the persistence of economic trouble. Some of the more conservative Republican candidates, most notably Senate Minority Leader William Knowland, running for governor of California, centered their campaigns around attacks on organized labor. In some states they sought "right-to-work" laws to outlaw union shops (plants in which every employee hired must join the union). This onslaught, in most states, succeeded only in insuring a large labor vote for Democratic candidates. The Republican party was also weakened by the revelation in the

spring of 1958 that Sherman Adams, in effect the President's chief of staff, had received gifts from a New England textile manufacturer. Adams resigned in September, too late to benefit the party.

The result on November 4, 1958, was a Democratic landslide of impressive proportions. The Democrats won 13 additional seats in the Senate, giving them a 62 to 34 majority. They gained an added 47 seats in the House of Representatives, providing a majority of 282 to 153—the largest margin since Roosevelt's 1936 victory.

The voter reaction in 1958 had slight effect upon the national administration in the two years that followed. President Eisenhower presented Congress in January 1959 with a $77 billion budget, which he promised would be in balance—a budget that northern Democrats decried as not sufficiently large in an expanding economy and not providing the services the nation needed. At first the Democrats in Congress gave promise of pushing far beyond the President's limited requests. As prosperity returned in the spring of 1959, however, public opinion began to react to the incessant warnings of the President and of conservative publicists that budget balancing was the only way to avoid another ruinous round of inflation. Eisenhower, acting more vigorously than in previous years, was able to marshal much public support and congressional voting strength for his conservative course, and Speaker Sam Rayburn and Senate Majority Leader Lyndon B. Johnson were more disposed to compromise than to throw their large Democratic majorities against him. As a result, Eisenhower succeeded in keeping down expenditures for inexpensive public housing for families displaced from slums and for other social services. He also succeeded in ending the 1960 fiscal year with a billion-dollar surplus. In the following year, he repeated the battle over the 1961 budget, which proposed expenditures of $70.8 billion and a surplus of $4.2 billion. But by the fall of 1960 the economy had again stalled into a recession; tax revenue declined, and the fiscal year ended with a serious deficit.

In his final State of the Union message, in January 1961, President Eisenhower granted that problems of recession and unemployment left little room for complacency. But he pointed out that during his eight years in office the inflationary spiral had all but ceased and that the nation's output of goods and services had increased 25 per cent; the income of the average American family, 15 per cent; and the real wages of workers, 20 per cent. "In a united determination to keep this nation strong and free and to utilize our vast resources for the advancement of all mankind," he asserted, "we have carried America to unprecedented heights."

## THE "NEW FRONTIER"

"The world is very different now," said President John F. Kennedy in his inaugural address, January 20, 1961, "for man holds in his mortal hands the power to abolish all forms of human poverty and all forms of human life." To achieve the promise and avoid the peril was the twofold challenge of the time. This was what Kennedy called the "New Frontier"—a new challenge to the old pioneering instincts of Americans.

## Kennedy Over Nixon

The presidential election of 1960 was notable both for its remarkable closeness and for the relative sobriety with which the two major candidates addressed themselves to the issues.

Kennedy won the Democratic nomination only after a vigorous struggle in the primaries. A forty-three-year-old senator from Massachusetts and a Roman Catholic, he was thought to be handicapped by his youth and his religion. In the primaries he had to dispose of a fellow senator, Hubert Humphrey of Minnesota, who was considered more liberal than he. Then, at the convention in Los Angeles, he had to overcome the powerful opposition of Lyndon B. Johnson of Texas, the Senate majority leader. In the 1930s, Johnson had been one of the coterie of ardent New Dealers. By 1960, without entirely abandoning his earlier allegiances, he had become the most respected spokesman of the industrialized and conservative South. When Kennedy won the presidential nomination, he offered the vice-presidential nomination to Johnson, who accepted and campaigned energetically.

The Republican nomination went almost by default to Vice President Richard M. Nixon, whom President Eisenhower favored. Nixon's only rival, Governor Nelson Rockefeller of New York, dropped out of the contest months before the primaries. Henry Cabot Lodge, ambassador to the United Nations, was nominated for Vice President.

Kennedy and Nixon represented the broad moderate position within their respective parties, though Kennedy was slightly to the left of center and Nixon slightly to the right. As Vice President, Nixon had enjoyed eight years on the front pages and had even argued with Khrushchev in Moscow. Thus he was able to offer a continuation of President Eisenhower's "peace and prosperity," and—though he was only four years older than Kennedy—mature leadership.

When Kennedy challenged Nixon to a series of television debates, Nixon's advisers thought Kennedy would be no match for their man, and they agreed to four joint appearances. In the first debate, however, everything went wrong for Nixon. Not yet recovered from an illness, he appeared tired, haggard, and heavy-jowled, in contrast to Kennedy, who seemed relaxed, self-confident, and well-informed—before an estimated 70 million television viewers. From then on, Kennedy seemed to take the lead from Nixon.

The business recession also hurt the Republicans. Nevertheless, in the closing days of the campaign, a vigorous Republican campaign drive, with the aid of President Eisenhower, brought a hairline decision at the polls. Out of 68,836,000 votes cast, Kennedy received 34,-227,000 or 49.7 per cent, and Nixon, 34,109,000 or 49.5 per cent. (The remaining 502,000 votes were divided among thirteen minor candidates.)

Before the election, Kennedy had hoped that on taking office he could push through Congress a legislative program as sweeping as that of Franklin D. Roosevelt during the first hundred days of the New Deal. Kennedy did not abandon his reform plans, but the closeness of the decision led him to move with caution. Unlike the Eisenhower cabinet, which had predominantly represented business, the Kennedy cabinet balanced the economic and political as well as the regional interests in the nation. The most controversial of the appointments was that of Kennedy's thirty-five-year-old brother and campaign manager, Robert F. Kennedy, as attorney general.

### Two Presidential Candidates Debate on Television

Before an estimated audience of 70 million viewers, the 1960 Republican nominee, Vice President Richard M. Nixon, and the Democratic nominee, Senator John F. Kennedy, participated in an unprecedented series of televised debates. Until then, the lesser-known Kennedy had seemed the underdog. "It was the sight of the two men side by side that carried the punch," Theodore H. White has written. "There was, first and above all, the crude, overwhelming impression that side by side the two seemed evenly matched—and this even matching in the popular imagination was for Kennedy a major victory. Until the cameras opened on the Senator and the Vice President, Kennedy had been the boy under assault and attack by the Vice President as immature, young, inexperienced. Now, obviously, in flesh and behavior he was the Vice President's equal."—*The Making of the President 1960* (New York: Atheneum, 1961), p. 288. (NBC)

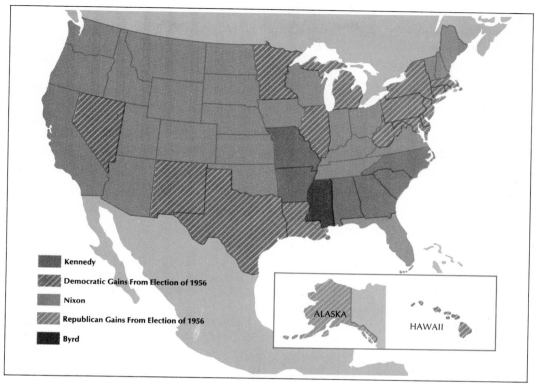

**Election of 1960**

## The Kennedy Program

President Kennedy—the youngest man, except for Theodore Roosevelt, ever to occupy the White House—sent a record number of messages, twenty-five, to the first session of the Eighty-seventh Congress. Some called for long-range national undertakings: economic recovery and growth, health care for the aged, federal aid for schools, conservation and use of natural resources, highway construction, housing and community development.

The existence of a Democratic majority in each house did not mean that Kennedy could count upon an easy enactment of his program, since many Democrats were conservative and frequently voted with the Republicans.

By dint of persuasion and compromise he managed to obtain considerable legislation. An improvement in the minimum-wage law failed in its first version. The final bill provided considerably less coverage than the President had wished, but it did bring an additional 3,624,000

workers under the law. It raised the minimum hourly pay rate, effective in several steps over two to four years, from $1.00 to $1.25. Another measure increased social security benefits substantially along the lines of the President's recommendations. The Housing Act of 1961 fully embodied his proposals, authorizing $4.9 billion in federal grants or loans over a four-year period for the preservation of open spaces in cities, the development of local mass transit systems, and the construction of middle-income housing. Congressional conservatives dealt the President two sharp setbacks when they defeated his bills to provide medical care for the aged and federal aid for school construction and teachers' salaries.

Kennedy obtained from Congress additional expenditures for unemployment compensation and aid to depressed areas—appropriations totaling $900 million. The only other large additions to the federal budget were $4 billion in defense spending to meet new challenges from Russia and large amounts of farm crop subsidies that had to be paid by virtue of earlier legislation. These expenditures were sufficient to bring about, well before the end of 1961, a substantial economic recovery.

But employment improved only slightly; in a time of record prosperity over 5 per cent of the working force had no job. Out of a total of approximately 4.4 million unemployed (as of March 1962) between 1 and 2 million were formerly connected with eight industries in which the total number of jobs had declined from 7.5 million to 5 million in the years since World War II. Among these industries were textiles, coal, automobiles, and aircraft. The Kennedy administration tried to eliminate such unemployment through the retraining of dismissed workmen under the Manpower Training Bill and through the establishment of new industries in chronically depressed areas under the Area Redevelopment Act.

During his first two years in office, Kennedy emphasized that, because of the inflationary danger, the budget must be kept balanced. He also used his presidential power vigorously to try to prevent inflationary moves on the part of labor and industry. In the spring of 1962 he persuaded the United Steel Workers to accept a contract granting only small wage increases. When, almost immediately, United States Steel and most other companies unexpectedly announced 3.5-per-cent price increases, the President exploded with anger. During the three days that followed, he brought every variety of pressure he could muster, until the steel companies returned to their old prices. The cost to Kennedy was the hostility of the business community, which vented its anger upon him and blamed him for a stock-market drop a few weeks later. A year afterward, in the spring of 1963, when steel companies announced limited increases in prices, the President commented only that the companies had shown some restraint; he hoped the steel union and steel users would do likewise.

By January 1963 Kennedy had become convinced that the only way to stimulate economic growth and to reduce unemployment was a bold tax cut. He proposed to Congress a reduction of $13.5 billion in income taxes over a period of three years.

Kennedy was also becoming convinced that the government must do more than it had done for the Negroes—to whose votes he owed his narrow victory in the 1960 election. Nearly a decade after the Supreme Court's historic decision against segregation, the equal-rights movement was making little or no progress.

The National Association for the Advancement of Colored People (NAACP), which had led the cause, was still pressing lawsuits and seeking court orders, but more and more Negroes were growing impatient with its methods and were embittered by white obstruction of the cause. Blacks began to form more militant organizations. A desperate minority of perhaps 200,000 joined the Black Muslims and, in a spirit reminiscent of the Garvey black nationalism of the 1920s, proclaimed black supremacy and demanded a complete separation of the races. Others continued to struggle for integration but turned to direct action through new organizations such as the Congress of Racial Equality (CORE) and the Southern Christian Leadership Conference. The SCLC was led by an eloquent young Baptist minister, Dr. Martin Luther King, who had gained national and international fame as an advocate of passive resistance and, for his work, was to win the Nobel Peace Prize in 1964.

In the South, beginning in 1960, youthful blacks with some white sympathizers engaged in "sit-ins" to demand the right to eat in restaurants or at lunch counters or the right to use books in the main public libraries rather than in segregated branches. Negroes and whites went on "freedom rides" to desegregate interstate buses and terminals. Thousands engaging in mass demonstrations accepted arrest; on several occasions the jails of Southern cities were filled to overflowing. Demonstrations spread to the North in mass attacks against de facto segregation in schools and housing and against the exclusion of all but a handful of Negroes from various kinds of employment. By the summer of 1963 the movement had reached such a peak that it was being proclaimed by news magazines as the "Negro revolution." More than 200,000 demonstrators (10 to 15 per cent of them white) participated in a "March on Washington," converging on the Lincoln Memorial.

In areas where federal power could be invoked, those protesting against segregation

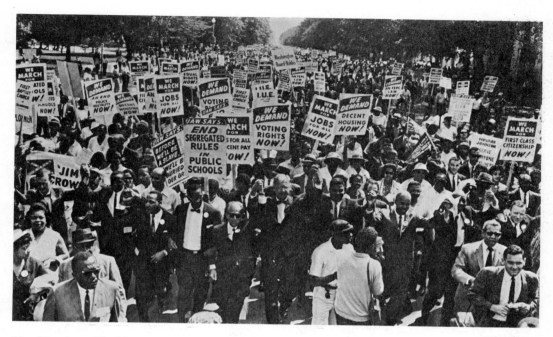

## The March on Washington

At the end of the summer of 1963, which had been marked by demonstrations and some violence in both South and North, advocates of civil rights participated in a spectacular one-day "March on Washington." In the first line of demonstrators are Walter Reuther, president of the UAW; Roy Wilkins of the NAACP; and the Reverend Martin Luther King, Jr., who declared: "We subpoenaed the conscience of the nation." (Wide World)

received the support of the Kennedy administration. Attorney General Robert F. Kennedy mustered federal force behind the integration of interstate transportation, and the President sent troops to the University of Mississippi to protect a Negro, James Meredith, who had been enrolled by order of a federal court. Throughout the South campaigns were under way to enroll Negro voters under the protection of the civil rights legislation of 1957. As pressure intensified in 1963, President Kennedy threw the prestige of his administration behind the most comprehensive civil rights bill ever presented to Congress.

## "Let Us Continue"

In the fall of 1963, though congressional conservatives were blocking enactment of the two major bills in the New Frontier program, the civil rights and tax-cut measures, President Kennedy felt optimistic. He was looking ahead to the election of 1964, which most observers thought would result in his own reelection by a comfortable margin. He hoped that the election would bring to Washington a more liberal Congress.

To court Southern support, Kennedy visited Florida and then Texas in November 1963. The Texas trip began well. On Friday, November 22, as he drove through the streets of Dallas, to the cheers of an enthusiastic crowd, the wife of Governor John Connally of Texas remarked to him: "You can't say that Dallas isn't friendly to you today." As Kennedy started to reply, he was hit in the neck by a bullet; another bullet struck the back of his head. His bleeding head cradled in the lap of his wife Jacqueline, he was rushed to a hospital.

An assassin, shooting three times in quick succession from a sixth-floor window, had killed President Kennedy and seriously wounded Governor Connally. Police arrested Lee Harvey Oswald, a self-styled Marxist who had once tried to expatriate himself in Russia, and charged him with the murder both of the President and a po-

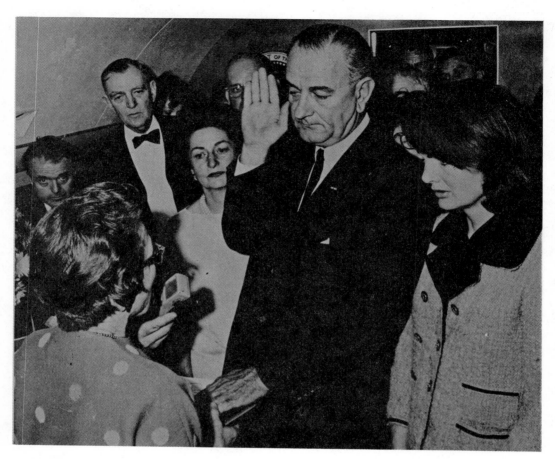

### President Johnson Takes the Oath of Office

With Mrs. Johnson (left) and Mrs. Kennedy at his side,
Lyndon Baines Johnson took his oath of office as
President on the afternoon of November 22, 1963,
before Judge Sarah T. Hughes aboard the presidential
airplane at Dallas, Texas. Johnson, born on a cattle
ranch near Stonewall, Texas, on August 27, 1908, was
of Confederate forebears, but considered himself
more a Westerner than a Southerner. He had to bear
the handicap of being regarded as a Southerner in
national politics, even though he pointed with pride to
his grandfather, who had been a Populist member of
the Texas legislature, and his father, who had also
served in the legislature and had been a firm opponent
of the Ku Klux Klan. Johnson taught elementary school
for a year after graduating from Southwest Texas State
Teachers College, then became secretary to a Texas
congressman. An ardent New Dealer, he was Texas
director of the National Youth Administration and,
after his election to the House of Representatives in
1937, a protégé of President Roosevelt. When
Roosevelt died, Johnson said: "He was just like a daddy
to me always." After an initial defeat, Johnson won
election to the United States Senate in 1948 by a
primary margin of eighty-seven votes. As senator from
a state in which new business and industrial interests
were increasingly powerful, Johnson came to be known
less for his liberalism (which he continued to avow)
than for his moderation. He liked to quote, as had his
father, the words of the prophet Isaiah: "Come, let us
reason together." An unparalleled master of the arts of
political persuasion, Johnson rose to the position of
Senate majority leader. Again and again he managed
to bring together and to compromise the differences
among Democratic senators from South and North.
As Vice President, Johnson lacked the opportunity to
practice these arts; he spent much of his time on
missions outside the United States. When he was
suddenly elevated to the Presidency, he pointed out to
the Congress that he had taken the leadership in
obtaining the civil rights acts of 1957 and 1960. Once
again he undertook to bridge divisions of opinion in
order to obtain constructive legislation. (Wide World)

liceman. Piece after piece of circumstantial evidence seemed to tie Oswald to the murders, but through hours of questioning he continued to protest his innocence. Two days after the shooting, while he was in the Dallas city jail, on his way to be transferred to the county jail, he was himself murdered by a Dallas night-club operator, before an incredulous national television audience. Inevitably rumors spread concerning the possibility that a ramifying plot lay behind President Kennedy's assassination. In an effort to eliminate uncertainties, a presidential commission headed by Chief Justice Warren sifted through the evidence and several months later reported to the American people that Oswald had been a lone assassin.

About two hours after the assassination, Vice President Lyndon B. Johnson was sworn in as the thirty-sixth President of the United States. When he addressed a joint session of Congress on November 27, President Johnson expressed his main theme in the words "let us continue." The most fitting memorial to Kennedy, he reminded Congress, would be the enactment of the civil rights and tax bills and, indeed, the whole agenda of the New Frontier.

The Eighty-eighth Congress responded and, in its 1964 session, enacted not only several vital measures of the New Frontier program but also one of President Johnson's own recommendations, an antipoverty bill. In getting the program adopted, the new President utilized to the utmost the formidable political skills he had perfected earlier as Senate majority leader. Not only did he conciliate and persuade congressional majorities; he also built a great national following. Like other vigorous Presidents in the twentieth century, he emphasized that he was President of all the American people and sought the support of all of them.

From the outset, Johnson assiduously courted businessmen. Most of them were Republicans, and the proposal of a tax cut deliberately creating a deficit in the budget at a time of prosperity went diametrically against their economic thinking. Nevertheless, after Congress passed the legislation early in 1964, the reduction of taxes seemed to stimulate an unprecedented continuation of prosperity and economic growth. By the beginning of 1965, the United States had experienced four years of boom without recession, a peacetime record since 1945. The rate of unemployment had dropped to about 5 per cent for the first time in years.

To the delight of many businessmen, Johnson accompanied the lowering of taxes with the presentation of a federal budget smaller than they had anticipated for the 1965 fiscal year. Roger Blough of United States Steel, who had been a firm antagonist of President Kennedy, declared it was "a step in the right direction." Johnson dramatized to the public his economy-mindedness by turning off excess electric lights in the White House, but the sums involved in the budget amounted to billions of dollars. Despite the overall cutback, he was able to increase expenditures on health, education, and welfare, through sharp limitation of the defense budget. The expensive modifications of the armed forces that the Kennedy administration had ordered in 1961–1963 had largely been achieved, and new efficiencies were saving further sums.

While courting business, the administration remained on cordial terms with labor leaders. Workingmen shared in the boom as take-home pay rose 4 per cent in 1964, and automation did not seem to be reducing jobs as rapidly as had been feared. In one major sector of the economy where unions had most vigorously fought automation, the railroads, the President met his greatest success. For five years the unions had disputed the railroad effort to eliminate almost a third of the 200,000 union workers. Arbiters had finally ruled that railroads would be allowed gradually to drop some 40,000 firemen working on diesel engines, which had no fires to stoke. A nationwide railroad strike threatened, and it could have punctured the national prosperity. In April 1964 the President's mediators succeeded in reaching a settlement that would provide benefits for workers and yet enable railroads to save an estimated $300 million a year.

To aid those who were not sharing in the national prosperity, the President in January 1964 called upon Congress to enact a thirteen-point program that would declare "unconditional war on poverty." In August 1964 the antipoverty bill was passed. It called for the establishment of VISTA, a volunteer corps of social workers, and for remedial education, vocational training, part-time employment for teenagers and students, and federal grants to states or communities for local attacks on poverty. The initial budget was almost a billion dollars.

## Commitment to Equal Rights

Throughout the nation the problem of civil rights was closely related to that of poverty. A large proportion of the very poor were Negroes, unable either South or North to obtain adequately paid, secure employment. In cities like New York, Negroes (together with Puerto Ricans) filled a large number of badly paid service positions and jobs not requiring skill. The average Harlem family received $2,000 a year less in income than its white neighbors. Of the Negroes (largely youths) 13 per cent were unemployed, since the poorer jobs were the sort being most rapidly eliminated by automation. Either through discrimination or through lack of

training, young people were barred from more highly skilled work. Many Northern Negroes were crowded into substandard housing, and their children were enrolled in poor schools integrated only in name.

A number of young Northerners went to Mississippi in the summer of 1964 to enroll several thousand young Negroes in "Freedom Schools" and to conduct drives registering Negroes to vote. Three of the first civil rights workers to arrive disappeared; after some weeks the FBI found their bodies buried deep beneath an earthen dam.

As the struggle intensified, President Johnson threw his weight behind the comprehensive civil rights bill that Kennedy had presented to Congress. Bipartisan leadership in the Senate finally overcame Southern opposition. In June 1964, for the first time in history, the Senate voted to end a filibuster, so that the bill could be passed. The Civil Rights Act of 1964 strengthened

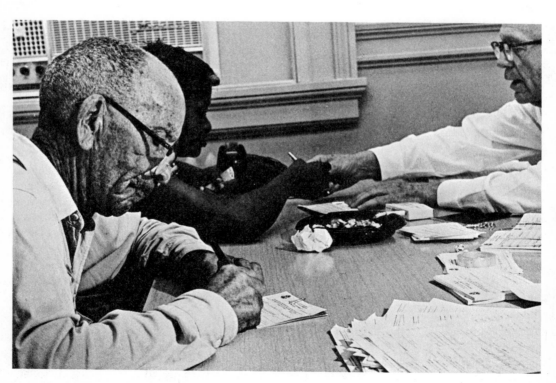

**Voter Registration, Selma, Alabama**

In the aftermath of the passage of the Civil Rights Act of 1964, large numbers of black voters began to enroll.

They made a significant change in Southern politics. (Dominic Capezza)

earlier legislation to protect the voting rights of Negroes and to expedite the desegregation of schools. It also prohibited discrimination in public accommodations and facilities and in private employment.

After the act went into effect, Negroes ate with whites for the first time in some restaurants in the deep South, stayed in some hotels and motels, sat in "white only" sections of motion picture theaters, and swam in previously segregated swimming pools. Compliance was not universal, and several test cases challenging the constitutionality of the law were brought before federal courts. Senator Allen J. Ellender of Louisiana, who had opposed passage of the bill, nevertheless called upon Southern whites to accept the measure with "calm and reason." Illegal defiance, he warned, would be "foolhardy and indefensible—much more indefensible and dangerous than it might have been at some other time in our nation's past."

The act did little to alleviate the plight of Negroes in the North. A few days after its passage, the shooting of a fifteen-year-old boy by a police lieutenant set off angry protests in Harlem against police brutality. The protests quickly became riots as teenagers and young men jeered police, smashed store windows, and engaged in widespread looting. For more than a week the rioters defied the efforts of local and national Negro civil rights leaders to restore order. Riots also occurred in Brooklyn and other Northern cities.

Early in 1965 violence again erupted in the South, especially in Selma, Alabama, where masses of Negroes and a few white sympathizers demonstrated in protest against registration procedures which kept Negroes off the voting rolls. The state police brutally broke up a parade, and assassins (said to be Klansmen) murdered two white civil rights workers from the North. To protect the demonstrators, President Johnson called up the Alabama National Guard. He also urged upon Congress a bill to guarantee the right to vote in presidential, senatorial, and congressional elections. This bill provided for federal registration of voters in those states where there were literacy or other special tests for registering and where fewer than half of the people of voting age actually went to the polls.

## One Man, One Vote

Meanwhile, constitutional amendments and court decisions were affecting, actually or potentially, the political rights of many Americans, both Negro and white.

The Twenty-third Amendment (1961) gave the franchise in presidential elections to residents of the District of Columbia. Home rule for Washington, which had the highest percentage of Negroes of any city in the country, continued to be withheld by Congress.

The Twenty-fourth Amendment (1964) gave symbolic, if not much practical, aid to Negro voters by providing that the right to vote in any primary or other federal election should not be abridged for failing to pay a poll tax. Most states in the deep South were using other methods to try to disfranchise Negroes.

An issue involving the rights of representation of a large part of the American electorate came before the Supreme Court in 1962, in a case involving the apportionment of legislative districts in Tennessee. Although the state constitution called for reapportionment every ten years, none had taken place since 1901, with the result that rural dominance in the legislature was out of all proportion to population. Moore County, with a population of 3,454, sent one legislator; Shelby County (Memphis), with 627,019 residents, sent only three. A vote in Moore County was worth more than sixty times as much as one in Shelby County. By a 6-to-2 decision, the Supreme Court gave the federal district court a mandate to order reapportionment if it found a violation of the Constitution. Similar inequities existed in a surprising number of other states; in all but six states, fewer than 40 per cent of the population could elect a majority of the legislature. As a result of the Tennessee decision, many states quickly made some reapportionment of their legislative districts, either as a result of court action or as a means of forestalling it.

An even more important Supreme Court decision (in *Reynold* v. *Sims,* 1964) held that congressional districts within a state also must be substantially equal in population. The case before the court involved the congressional district containing the city of Atlanta, Georgia, a district that had a population of 820,000 as compared with the population of 270,000 in another Georgia district. Several state legislatures quietly initiated a counteraction by endorsing a constitutional amendment (proposed by the National Legislative Conference) which would negate federally enforced reapportionment. Within a few years, thirty-three legislatures had approved it. If one more should act, Congress would be required, according to the Constitution, to call a national convention to consider submitting the proposal to the states for their ratification. The movement lost its chief congressional sponsor, however, when Senator Everett Dirksen of Illinois died in 1969.

## THE "GREAT SOCIETY"

As he took up and expanded the Kennedy program, President Johnson restated the objective as the creation of the "Great Society." "For half a century we called upon unbounded invention and untiring industry to create an order of plenty for all our people," he declared in May 1964. "The challenge of the next half century is whether we have the wisdom to use that wealth to enrich and elevate our national life—and to advance the quality of American civilization."

But President Johnson himself was to jeopardize the "Great Society" program when, in 1965, he committed the country to large-scale war in far-away Vietnam.

### Johnson Thrashes Goldwater

In the presidential campaign of 1964 the moderate liberalism for which Johnson had spoken confronted extreme conservatism.

In the years following the collapse of McCarthyism, militant conservatives in the United States had organized a number of action groups. The best known was the John Birch Society, whose founder, Robert Welch, called for the impeachment of Chief Justice Earl Warren and seemed to suspect the loyalty of even President Eisenhower. Senator Barry Goldwater of Arizona, though not himself a member of the so-called "radical right" organizations, became the hero of most of these groups.

By 1964, Goldwater was on record as having said that the graduated income tax was "a con-

fiscatory tax." He added: "Artificial devices for enforcing equality among unequal men must be rejected." As for welfare programs: "Let welfare be a private concern." In the Senate he voted against tax reduction and against both the antipoverty and civil rights bills. As for the United Nations: "Frankly, I think the fact that it is proven to be unworkable is ground enough for us to quit wasting our money on it." He opposed efforts to negotiate disarmament with Russia as "a dangerous exercise in complete and total futility," and he voted against ratifying the test-ban treaty. He consistently criticized the Kennedy and Johnson administrations for what he considered to be insufficient militancy, and he favored giving to an army commander discretion to use tactical nuclear weapons.

At the Republican convention in San Francisco, the Goldwater forces were in complete command from the outset. They produced a platform conforming to their conservative philosophy and making no concessions to the moderate and liberal wings of the party. When Governor Nelson A. Rockefeller of New York tried to obtain a stronger civil rights plank they hooted him down. Nor did Goldwater try to "balance the ticket" in his vice-presidential choice—Representative William E. Miller of New York stood staunchly to the right. Goldwater received tumultuous applause when, in his acceptance address, he declared: "I would remind you that extremism in the defense of liberty is no vice! And let me remind you also that moderation in the pursuit of justice is no virtue!"

As Senator Goldwater carried the Republican party far to the right, President Johnson tried to preempt not only the center of the road but also a wide strip to both the right and the left of it. Although he had been President for only nine months when the Democratic convention met at Atlantic City late in August 1964, he was firmly in control of his party. His main concern seemed to be to achieve as broad a consensus as possible in the platform. His supporters worked to minimize differences between the North and the South, especially over the seating of delegates. Delegates from Mississippi and Alabama were denied votes unless they pledged themselves to support the party's candidates in the November election, and most of them departed. Two votes were given to a Negro delegation representing the new Freedom Democratic party of Mississippi. In addition, the convention voted that in 1968 it would seat only those delegations that were chosen in a nondiscriminatory way.

The only drama in the convention concerned the question of whom President Johnson would ask the delegates to nominate for Vice President. Earlier he had eliminated one of the party's favorites, Attorney General Robert Kennedy, brother of the assassinated President. When Johnson, in person, revealed his choice to the convention, it was Senator Hubert Humphrey of Minnesota, identified with the liberal wing of the Democratic party.

Paradoxically, the campaign was one of the most hectic and yet one of the dullest ever to weary the electorate. In contrast to the comparatively precise debates of four years earlier, neither candidate ever went much beyond his acceptance speech. Yet each campaigned in-

cessantly, often spanning the continent by jet in a day's appearances. Much of the Goldwater campaign centered upon charges of corruption and moral malaise in Washington. In mid-October, Johnson's chief White House aide was forced to resign because of personal scandal, but that same week the American people were even more startled by news of the precipitate removal of Nikita Khrushchev from the leadership of the USSR. New uncertainties abroad seemed to help drive the voters toward the President. Throughout the campaign President Johnson was as wary of making specific, detailed promises as Eisenhower had been in 1956 and Roosevelt in 1936; his best strategy seemed to be merely to gather the votes against Goldwater.

And gather them he did. He received more votes, over 42 million, and a larger plurality than any other candidate in history. On election night he told the American people that he regarded the overwhelming victory as a "mandate for unity." It gave him and the Democratic majority in Congress an opportunity to move on

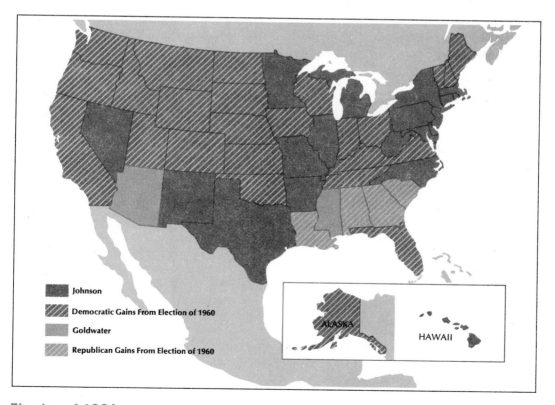

Election of 1964

toward what he had been describing as the "Great Society," a society as free as it could be from poverty, prejudice, ignorance, and ugliness.

## The Johnson Program

When the Eighty-ninth Congress convened, President Johnson presented to it comprehensive proposals to make a beginning toward his long-range goals. Acting with caution in order to preserve the vast national consensus he had obtained in his election, he gave the impression in advance that what he would propose would be moderate indeed. He appeared before Congress at the evening hour when most television sets would be turned on and in his State of the Union message outlined his goals in broad, appealing terms:

"I propose we begin a program in education to ensure every American child the fullest development of his mind and skills.

"I propose we begin a massive attack on crippling and killing diseases.

"I propose we launch a national effort to make the American city a better and more stimulating place to live.

"I propose we increase the beauty of America and end the poisoning of our rivers and the air we breathe.

"I propose we carry out a new program to develop regions of our country now suffering from distress and depression.

"I propose we make new efforts to control and prevent crime and delinquency.

"I propose we eliminate every remaining obstacle to the right and opportunity to vote.

"I propose we honor and support the achievements of thought and the creation of art.

"I propose we make an all-out campaign against waste and inefficiency."

With unprecedented speed, almost all of this far-ranging program became law. In the six weeks that followed the message, the President sent a series of messages to Congress spelling out the specifics of each of these recommendations. Although some of these included notable innovations, Congress acted rapidly. The overwhelmingly Democratic majorities in Congress, which had accompanied the landslide victory over Goldwater, were Johnson's to command. In commenting on the President's annual message,

a Republican congressional leader realistically declared: "He's got the votes. There's not much we could do to stop his program if we tried." Nor could conservative Democratic committee chairmen stop the trend. When the Congress was organized, liberal Democrats in the House (aided by some Republicans) succeeded in transferring to the speaker of the House, who was receptive to White House suggestions, some of the power that the Rules Committee had used to obstruct legislation. The committee could no longer indefinitely block a vote on administration legislation; after twenty-one days, the speaker, if he had a majority approval, could call up to the floor of the House a bill that had been awaiting clearance in the committee. Thus Johnson's message on immigration, almost identical to Kennedy's, received speedy action.

The new immigration legislation, in response to the demands of urban and minority groups in America, abolished the inequities of the quota system established in the 1920s. The quota for England and Ireland of 83,000 persons per year had been seldom filled; that for Greece was only 308 persons. Gradually the government eliminated these quotas and began to allot visas not on a basis of national origins but giving preference on a basis of education and skills. Soon there were complaints that only an elite of professionals could enter the United States and that other nations, especially underdeveloped ones, were suffering a "brain drain" of their doctors, engineers, and highly educated specialists. In 1966 relatives of United States citizens began to receive preference, and a quota of 17,000 was set for professionals. Immigration from northwestern Europe declined and that from southern Europe and Asia increased.

Massive sustained federal aid to education at last began. President Johnson succeeded in circumventing the impasse in Congress over the question of whether parochial schools should receive a share of federal funds. He called for grants for text and library books for students in both public and parochial schools—and significantly the grants were to be made on the basis of the needs of individual students, not schools, a formula which the Supreme Court had approved when it applied to federal funds that were to provide milk or transportation to students. The Elementary and Secondary Education Act of 1965 and subsequent legislation gave aid to schools in both urban and rural areas in proportion to the number of poverty-stricken students in them. Federal funds purchased textbooks and library materials, financed special programs for adults and for the handicapped, and strengthened state educational agencies. Total federal expenditures in education and technical training rose from less than $5 billion in 1964 to more than $12 billion in 1967.

The establishment of Medicare for the 19 million Americans over sixty-five through the Medicare-Social Security Act of 1965 altered the lives of old people and had great impact upon American medicine. The debate over Medicare, which had been so bitter for twenty years, ended as the program went into effect. Expected resistance did not materialize. In the South, where hospitals had to accept desegregation in order to obtain funds, nearly nine-tenths of the hospitals complied. But numerous practical problems arose that made future adjustments likely. It was particularly difficult to institute the program in an era of rapidly rising costs. Objections to complicated paper work led more than half the nation's doctors to force patients to pay directly; patients were required to submit receipted bills for government reimbursement. The irritations were serious, but less important than the fact that large numbers of older people were receiving care that they could not previously have obtained or that would have exhausted their savings.

Rising costs also created problems for the Medicaid program, which was launched in 1968 to provide financial assistance to persons who were not old enough to qualify for Medicare but were too poor to pay their own medical bills. Under the Medicaid law each state was to set up its own plan, determining payments and standards of eligibility for them, and the federal government was to contribute from 50 to 80 per cent of the expense. During the first year, however, the program cost the federal government more than ten times as much as had been expected. Congress and the state legislatures therefore changed their definition of the needy so as to make the benefits available to fewer people than had originally been covered.

## War on Poverty

Both Medicare and Medicaid were parts of the effort to eradicate the explosive pockets of poverty within the prosperous nation. President Johnson continued to press for new programs, often harking back to the depression years. Speaking in San Antonio, Texas, in 1966, he remembered "seeing little Mexican children (1935) go up to the garbage can outside that cafeteria and take the grapefruit hulls . . . and try to get enough food in their body to sustain them by hulling the hulls. I saw that with my own eyes and I have not forgotten it."

In May 1967 a team of doctors found hundreds of similar Negro children in the South. One doctor testified before a Senate committee: "We do not want to quibble over words, but 'malnutrition' is not quite what we found; the boys and girls we saw were hungry—weak, in pain, sick . . . They are suffering from hunger and disease and directly or indirectly are dying from them—which is exactly what 'starvation' means."

More than 9 million people classified as poor were receiving no aid from federal food programs, a Senate subcommittee learned. Figures were incomplete. There was hunger in great cities, in Appalachia, the deep South, the Southwest, and on Indian reservations. Yet over 5 million people were receiving aid through federal food programs; either they were given food or could purchase it with reduced-cost stamps. Many millions were receiving other types of relief. While a considerable proportion of Negroes were desperately poor, they numbered only a quarter to a third of the poverty-stricken people. In addition to the acutely poor, there were the many families living on substandard incomes. By the end of 1967, the Bureau of Labor Statistics estimated that a family of four living in a city required $9,000 a year in order to maintain a moderate living standard—a rise of 50 per cent in the previous eight years.

The poverty program of President Johnson, continuing and expanding that of Kennedy, approached the problem in numerous ways. By 1966 the Office of Economic Opportunity, established in 1964, had put about two-fifths of its budget into a variety of Community Action Programs. Another two-fifths went into youth pro-

grams—the Job Corps, Neighborhood Youth
Corps, and College Work Study. Most of the re-
maining funds went into the Work Experience
Program. VISTA (Volunteers in Service to
America) accounted for only 1.5 per cent of the
budget, although it attracted much attention.

While social security aided the considerable
proportion of the poor who were aged, the
Office of Economic Opportunity placed its emphasis upon helping the great numbers of poor
among the young. The 1,000 core Community
Action Programs were locally proposed and
operated, in part by poor people themselves.
Some of these programs came under blistering
attack, but many of them not only gave poor
people an opportunity to help themselves but
gave them some feeling of political power.
Southern congressmen were concerned because
of Negro participation in the programs; many
Northern congressmen favored such programs
because they seemed to ease tensions that might
lead to riots. Congressional critics asserted that
Community Action projects should give more attention to job training and less to social action.
Yet the job-training programs proved more expensive and less effective than had been predicted.

Especially among the urban Negro unemployed, the job-training programs were a disappointment. Although Negroes began to penetrate the ranks of the white-collar workers, the
total numbers were small. Nominally, union
restrictions against them no longer existed, yet
few could gain employment as skilled, highly
paid construction workers. Industries that might
have hired Negroes were moving out of the
cities, away from where they lived. The training
programs could not easily provide the overall
education and motivation that most of these
unemployed Negroes lacked. A New York Negro
woman declared in despair, "We are being
trained for the unemployed." By the beginning
of 1968 the unemployment rate for Negroes,
which since the Korean War had been double
that of whites, was climbing even higher. President Johnson asked Congress to provide funds
to subsidize industry to train and employ 250,-
000 of the 500,000 hard-core unemployed in the
cities. Another possible solution was that which
the Commission on Technology, Automation

and Economic Progress in 1965 recommended
—a "program of public service employment,
providing that the Government be an employer
of last resort." Large-scale remedial measures
did not come in 1965 or the years immediately
thereafter. Impatient urban Negroes, disappointed at the meager return that cooperation
seemed to have brought them, began increasingly to turn toward other possible solutions:
black power, separatism, or even violence.

With increasing rapidity after 1964, the
United States moved into a double crisis, compounded of rioting in the poverty-stricken Negro areas in Northern cities and escalation of
the intervention in Vietnam into a major—but
stalemated—military confrontation. Each crisis
interacted with the other. White college and
university students and Northern liberals shifted

**Black Power: SNCC Paper**

*If we are to proceed toward true liber-
ation, we must cut ourselves off from
white people. We must form our own
institutions, credit unions, co-ops,
political parties, write our own histories, . . .*

*. . . on whatever level of contact . . .
blacks and whites come together, that
meeting or confrontation is not on the
level of the blacks but always on the
level of the whites. This only means
that our everyday contact with whites
is a reinforcement of the myth of white
supremacy. Whites are the ones who
must try to raise themselves to our
humanistic level. We are not, after all,
the ones who are responsible for a
genocidal war in Vietnam; we are not
the ones who are responsible for neo-
colonialism in Africa and Latin America; we are not the ones who held a
people in animalistic bondage over 400
years. We reject the American dream
as defined by white people and must
work to construct an American reality
defined by Afro-Americans.—Position
paper by members of SNCC, 1966.*

their efforts from the civil rights drive in the South to concentrate on protest against the Vietnam War. Negroes in the rural South, and even more in the urban North, increasingly sought to take their destiny into their own hands through their own organizations, independent of aid or funds from whites. Simultaneously, the enormous cost of the Vietnam War eliminated whatever possibility there might have been of mounting a massive war against poverty within the United States.

## Black Power

The threatened catastrophe implicit in the riots of the mid-sixties forced the American nation to appraise the black revolution that had taken place since World War II. The monumental *Report of the National Advisory Commission on Civil Disorders,* published in 1968, focused on the rapid changes. The Negro population had been increasing more rapidly than the white population and had been shifting from the rural South to the cities throughout the nation, especially in the North. In 1910 only about a quarter of the Negroes lived in cities, and only a tenth outside the South; by 1966 15 million Negroes, 69 per cent of the Negro population, were living in metropolitan areas; 45 per cent of all Negroes were living outside the South. In several of the largest cities, the proportion of Negroes at least doubled between 1950 and 1968. Negroes constituted at least 30 per cent of the population of seven of these cities and 66.6 per cent of the population of Washington, D.C. A corresponding exodus of whites from the cities to the suburbs dramatically increased the areas of residential and school segregation in the "black ghettos."

While urban Negroes were sharing in the national prosperity, their proportional gains were decidedly less than those of the whites. Indeed, the gap between their incomes and those of whites was growing wider. The number of Negroes enjoying well-paid, highly skilled employment giving them exceptional status doubled in the sixties, while the lowest-income group grew smaller. Yet 20 per cent of all Negroes, the 2 million "hard-core disadvantaged" living in cities, were making no significant economic gains. They seemed trapped, and were ready to blame their entrapment upon the whites. The Commission on Civil Disorders reported: "What white Americans have never fully understood—but what the Negro can never forget—is that white society is deeply implicated

### Black Power: Commission's Report

*What is new about "Black Power" is phraseology rather than substance. . . . The decade after World War I—which saw the militant, race-proud "new negro," the relatively widespread theory of retaliatory violence, and the high tide of the Negro-support-of-Negro-business ideology—exhibits striking parallels with the 1960's. . . .*

*Black Power rhetoric and ideology actually express a lack of power. The slogan emerged when the Negro protest movement was slowing down, when it was finding increasing resistance to its changing goals, when it discovered that nonviolent direct action was no more a panacea than legal action. . . . This combination of circumstances provoked anger deepened by impotence. Powerless to make any fundamental changes in the life of the masses—powerless, that is, to compel white America to make those changes —many advocates of Black Power have retreated into an unreal world, where they see an outnumbered and poverty-stricken minority organizing itself independently of whites and creating sufficient power to force white America to grant its demands. . . .*

*The Black Power advocates of today consciously feel that they are the most militant group in the Negro protest movement. Yet they have retreated from a direct confrontation with American society on the issue of integration and, by preaching separatism, unconsciously function as an accommodation to white racism.—* Report of the National Advisory Commission on Civil Disorders, *1968.*

in the ghetto. White institutions created it, white institutions maintain it, and white society condones it."

An explosive mixture, the commission declared, had been accumulating in the cities since the end of World War II. The prime ingredients were the chronic discrimination and segregation in employment, education and housing; the growing concentration of Negroes in the cities; and the oppressive effects upon the young of the black ghettos "where segregation and poverty converge . . . to destroy opportunity and enforce failure." The result was "crime, drug addiction, dependency on welfare, and bitterness and resentment against society in general and white society in particular." These young people, failing to share in the unprecedented prosperity spread before their eyes, through television especially, became increasingly resentful.

The gradual shift from white participation and leadership to Negro domination of civil rights organizations was one indication of the new mood. The Congress of Racial Equality (CORE), founded in 1941–1942, had long been the most interracial of the organizations, but by 1962 was predominantly Negro; after 1965 CORE allowed only Negro leadership in its chapters. At their height these organizations through direct action did succeed in obtaining some votes for Negroes and political participation, even in Alabama and Mississippi. In the North they helped force open new, desirable employment opportunities for adequately educated Negroes. But they could not change the inferior conditions under which most Negroes suffered. Their failure helped stimulate feelings of separateness and militancy among Negro youth in the large cities.

Out of James Meredith's march southward from Memphis, Tennessee, to Jackson, Mississippi, in June 1966 there grew the concept of black power. Politically it meant separate action through which blocs of Negro voters would win control in Northern ghettos or the Southern black belt. Economically it meant creating Negro business to serve Negroes. CORE and SNCC (the Student Nonviolent Coordinating Committee) became associated with the concept of black power—of Negro separateness. In some respects black power seemed to critics to be retrogressive, a harking back to the proposals of Booker T. Washington; it seemed to propose a withdrawal comparable to that which white racists had been demanding. Black militants replied that Negroes by themselves must attain economic and political parity with the white population before effective integration could take place.

## Resort to Riot

On August 11, 1965, a Negro crowd gathered in Watts, a Los Angeles suburb, to protest a traffic arrest; a policeman hit a bystander with his club, and several days of violence were touched off. Before the rioting was over, thirty-four people had been killed, hundreds wounded, and some $35 million in property destroyed. White Americans, hopeful that the civil rights movement was solving Negro problems, were shocked out of their optimism. There was cause for their shock.

Events of the summer of 1966 demonstrated that a new pattern of rioting and violence was taking over. There were forty-three outbreaks, with especially serious trouble in Chicago and Cleveland. In the summer of 1967 there were eight major riots. In the worst of these, at Detroit, forty-three persons (thirty-three Negroes, and ten whites) were killed. On their television screens, the people of the nation saw alarming scenes of arson, plunder, and military action. President Johnson, calling for law and order, warned also that the only genuine long-range solution must be an attack upon the conditions that were causing despair and violence. He appointed a group of distinguished citizens to a commission to investigate the disorders and recommend preventive measures for the future.

The report of the Commission on Civil Disorders, which appeared in the spring of 1968, went much further than had been expected. It deflated numerous wild stories circulating during the riots: there had been few black snipers, and no organized conspiracy instigating and directing the riots. It pointed to the complexities of the problems facing the occupants of the Negro ghettos, and it recommended massive spending to erase these ghettos and the inequities their occupants suffered. "Only a commitment to national action on an unprece-

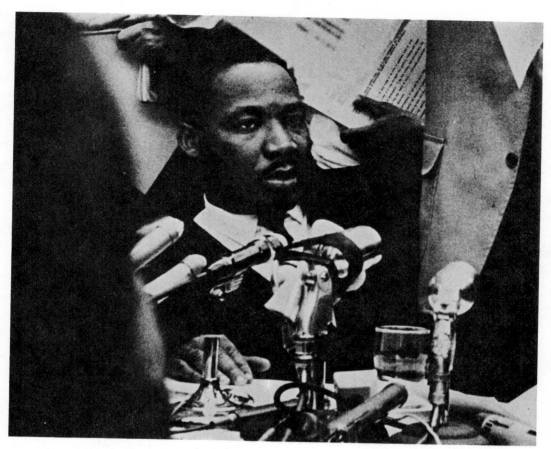

**Martin Luther King Holding a Press Conference
at Birmingham, Alabama   1963**

Throughout his years as head of the Southern Christian Leadership Conference, King insisted that the civil rights movement must be nonviolent. He stated his vision most vividly for America in August 1963 when during the "March on Washington" he asserted from the steps of the Lincoln Memorial: "I have a dream that one day this nation will rise up and live out the true meaning of its creed: 'We hold these truths to be self-evident, that all men are created equal.' . . . I have a dream that my four little children will one day live in a nation where they will not be judged by the color of their skin, but by the content of their character. This is our hope. This is the faith that I go back to the South with—with this faith we will be able to hew out of the mountain of despair a stone of hope." (Magnum)

dented scale can shape a future compatible with the historic ideals of American society," the commission concluded. "The major need is to generate new will—the will to tax ourselves to the extent necessary to meet the vital needs of the nation."

Congressional leaders and their constituents throughout the nation were not in a mood to fight for these enormous expenditures. Frightened by overseas crisis in Vietnam in the spring of 1968 and by a serious depletion of the na-

tion's gold supply, they were more disposed to cut drastically the existing poverty programs than to augment them. Community action programs in Northeastern cities were cut 7 per cent, and Head Start aid for preschool children, 14 per cent.

In April 1968 the assassination of Dr. Martin Luther King shocked the nation but scarcely altered the mood of Congress. King, whose insistence upon Gandhi-like nonviolent techniques seemed old-fashioned to black militants, was to lead a protest march on behalf of striking garbage workers in Memphis, Tennessee. While standing on a motel balcony, he was struck by a sniper's bullet and died within a few minutes. King's death touched off the most widespread rioting the nation had yet undergone in the Negro areas of cities from coast to coast. Looting and arson were endemic; forty persons were killed. Washington was the worst hit, as fires gutted buildings within sight of the Capitol and the White House. Yet within the Negro districts, innumerable residents worked doggedly to end the disorders.

Simultaneously, the nation was preoccupied with mourning the assassinated leader, as King was given a funeral bringing together an assemblage of notables and receiving television coverage exceeded only by that of President Kennedy.

Within a week Congress responded by enacting the Civil Rights Act of 1968, which had been pending for two years. It outlawed racial discrimination in the sale and rental of four-fifths of all homes and apartments. But as poor people assembled in Washington a few weeks later in the campaign that King had been planning at the time of his death, Congress was preoccupied with economy and little disposed to provide economic aid for them.

# Selected Readings

**Eisenhower** F. M. Shattuck, *The 1956 Presidential Campaign* (1960); Samuel Lubell, *The Revolt of the Moderates* (1956); R. H. Rovere, *Affairs of State: The Eisenhower Years* (1956); M. J. Pusey, *Eisenhower the President* (1956), very favorable; M. W. Childs, *Eisenhower, Captive Hero* (1956), rather critical; E. T. Benson, *Crossfire: The Eight Years with Eisenhower* (1962).

**J. F. K. and L. B. J.** J. M. Burns, *John Kennedy: A Political Profile°* (1959); T. H. White, *The Making of the President, 1960°* (1961); A. M. Schlesinger, *A Thousand Days: John F. Kennedy in the White House°* (1965); T. C. Sorensen, *Kennedy°* (1965); William Manchester, *Death of a President°* (1967); Tom Wicker, *JFK and LBJ: The Influence of Personality upon Politics* (1968); T. H. White, *The Making of the President, 1964°* (1965); Rowland Evans and Robert Novak, *Lyndon B. Johnson: The Exercise of Power°* (1966), critical; Robert Sherrill, *The Accidental President* (1967), critical.

**Prosperity and Poverty** H. G. Vatter, *The U. S. Economy in the 1950's°* (1963); Walter Heller, *New Dimensions of Political Economy* (1966); Gabriel Kolko, *Wealth and Power in America* (1962); Michael Harrington, *The Other America: Poverty in the United States* (1962); H. P. Miller, *Rich Man, Poor Man°* (1964); Oscar Lewis, *La Vida: A Puerto Rican Family in the Culture of Poverty—San Juan and New York°* (1966); H. M. Caudill, *Night Comes to the Cumberlands* (1963), on poverty in the Appalachians; J. D. Donovan, *The Politics of Poverty* (1967); Sar Levitan, *The Great Society's Poor Law: A New Approach to Poverty* (1969).

**The Supreme Court** A. T. Mason, *The Supreme Court from Taft to Warren* (1958); J. D. Weaver, *Warren: The Man, the Court, the Era* (1967); W. F. Murphy, *Congress and the Court°* (1962); R. G. Dixon, Jr., *Democratic Representation: Reapportionment in Law and Politics* (1968); R. B. McKay, *Reapportionment: The Law and Politics of Equal Representation* (1965); Loren Miller, *The Petitioners: The Story of the Supreme Court of the United States and the Negro* (1964); I. A. Newby, *Challenge to the Court: Social Scientists and the Defense of Segregation, 1954–1966* (1968).

**Black Voices** M. L. King, Jr., *Stride Toward Freedom°* (1958) and *Why We Can't Wait°* (1964); James Baldwin, *The Fire Next Time* (1963); L. E. Lomax, *The Negro Revolt°* (1963) and *When the Word Is Given: A Report on Elijah Muhammad, Malcolm X, and the Black Muslim World* (1963); *The Autobiography of Malcolm X°* (1966); James Farmer, *Freedom— When?* (1966); Stokely Carmichael and C. V. Hamilton, *Black Power: The Politics of Liberation in America°* (1967).

**Civil Rights and Civil Disorders** Anthony Lewis, *Portrait of a Decade: The Second American Revolution* (1964); Louis Harlan, *Separate and Unequal°* (1961), on segregated schools; A. P. Blaustein and C. C. Ferguson, *Desegregation and the Law°* (1962); J. W. Silver, *Mississippi: The Closed Society°* (1964); J. W. Anderson, *Eisenhower, Brownell, and the Congress: The Tangled Origins of the Civil Rights Bill of 1956–1957* (1964); D. M. Berman, *A Bill Becomes Law: The Civil Rights Act of 1960* (1962); A. I. Waskow, *From Race Riot to Sit-In: 1919 and the 1960's* (1966); James Peck, *Freedom Ride* (1962); D. R. Matthews and J. W. Prothro, *Negroes and the New Southern Politics°* (1966); N. V. Bartley, *The Rise of Massive Resistance: Race and Politics in the South During the 1950's* (1969); M. A. Schwartz, *Trends in White Attitudes Toward Negroes* (1967); Lee Rainwater and W. L. Yancey, *The Moynihan Report and the Politics of Controversy°* (1967); *Report of the National Advisory Committee on Civil Disorders°* (1968).

° Titles available in paperback.

# Chapter 29
# National
# Security
# in the 1960s

"We face a hostile ideology—global in scope, atheistic in character, ruthless in purpose, and insidious in method. Unhappily the danger it poses promises to be of indefinite duration." So said President Eisenhower in the farewell address he directed to the American people shortly before leaving office in 1961. "A vital element in keeping the peace is our military establishment. Our arms must be mighty, ready for instant action, so that no potential aggressor may be temped to risk his own destruction."

While warning of dangers from outside, President Eisenhower also drew attention to a possible threat arising within the nation. This was the threat of undue power accruing to the "military-industrial complex" that had developed to provide for the national defense. For the first time in their history, the American people had in their midst, on a permanent basis, the "conjunction of an immense military establishment and a large arms industry." Eisenhower did not fully describe the complex, but the military establishment consisted of the Armed Services, the Central Intelligence Agency, and other bodies provided for in the National Security Act of 1947. The arms industry included not only manufacturers of traditional armaments but also producers of a bewildering variety of new aviational, aerospace, electronic, chemical, and biological supplies. Supporting the industry and supported by it were certain labor unions and numerous scientific groups, many of these in universities that had government research contracts.

Under President Eisenhower's successors—Kennedy, Johnson, and Nixon—the United States continued to face a "hostile ideology" abroad. And the military-industrial complex continued to grow. It seemed to gain a greater and greater role in the determination of policy. Certainly it took a larger and larger share of the federal budget, leaving less and less for domestic needs, though these became increasingly serious. "The control of military arms is undoubtedly the most important political question in the world today," James Reston wrote in The New York Times, March 16, 1969, "for the arms race devours the money and influences all other questions of poverty, race, jobs, and housing, both here and abroad."

How to provide for the national security while preserving and promoting individual freedom and opportunity—how to defend democracy without destroying it in the process—this was the basic dilemma that the American people had to grapple with as they made their way through the decade of the 1960s and into the decade of the 1970s.

---

**Peace March   1968**

This peace march held in San Francisco in October 1968 was typical of the nationwide demonstrations against the Vietnam War. Students conducted frequent all-night teach-ins at their universities protesting the war; others went so far as to burn their draft cards. The varied backgrounds of the demonstrators was illustrated by the trial of several representative marchers ranging from a graduate student to one of the most prestigious physicians in the country, Dr. Benjamin Spock. (Photoreporters)

## THE KENNEDY APPROACH

President Kennedy's domestic program, the New Frontier with its proposed reforms, soon yielded priority to what seemed to be the requirements of foreign policy. Even his efforts to stimulate economic growth were subordinated to these needs. He repeatedly emphasized that a strong economy was a prerequisite for maintaining national defense and providing adequate aid to underdeveloped countries.

## Continuing Foreign Aid

Since the inception of the Truman Doctrine (1947) and the Marshall Plan (1948), the United States had depended on economic aid as well as military power to defend many areas of the world against Communism. For both strategic and humanitarian reasons, President Eisenhower year after year requested and received huge appropriations for the mutual security program.

Most of the new, emergent nations in Asia and Africa were suffering from poverty and

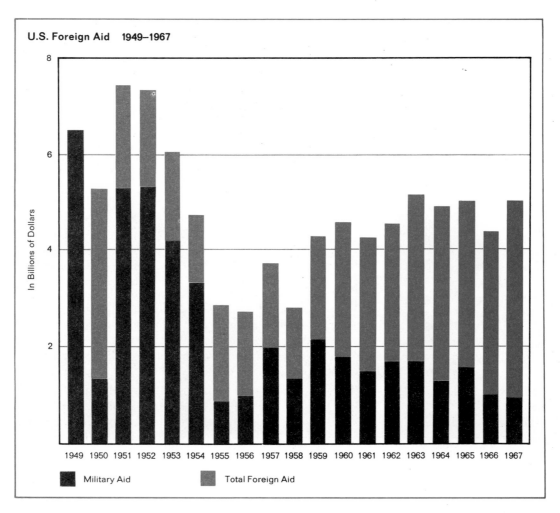

U.S. Foreign Aid 1949–1967

In Billions of Dollars

Military Aid    Total Foreign Aid

About three-quarters of all foreign aid is expended for military purposes; the remaining one-quarter provides technical assistance, machinery, food, and capital loans. The tendency of the aid program is toward providing capital with which nations can develop their own enterprises.

While foreign aid totals remained high, the percentage of the country's Gross National Product being spent on aid steadily declined.

ignorance and from a growth in population so explosive that it canceled out gains in living standards. Even the mere provision of rudimentary medical aid in many of these areas had cut the death rate more drastically than other aid could increase agricultural and industrial productivity. As of 1950 the per capita income was $50 per year in Asia compared with $1,100 in North America. Yet the population of underdeveloped areas, where two-thirds of the people were living in misery, was growing faster than their gross national product. The world population was increasing at the rate of 2 per cent per year, the National Academy of Sciences reported in 1963, "faster than any other period in man's history." By the year 2000, the world's population would double to a total of 6 billion. Had this rate been operating since the time of Christ, there would already be one hundred persons for every square foot of earth. "Either the birth rate of the world must come down," the academy warned, "or the death rate must go back up."

To suggestions that the United States help underdeveloped areas control population growth, President Eisenhower in 1959 asserted that he could not imagine anything more emphatically not the business of the government; if other countries wished aid, they should seek it from private professional groups. This remained government policy under President Kennedy until 1962 when an American spokesman informed a United Nations committee: "While we will not advocate any specific policy regarding population growth to any other country, we can help other countries, upon request, to find potential sources of information and assistance on ways and means of dealing with population problems."

Most of the underdeveloped nations, preoccupied with their own problems and neutralist in theory, were ready to accept aid from the United States at the same time that they were also receptive both to aid and to propaganda from Communist Russia and Communist China. Even before the end of the Eisenhower administration, the United States was no longer insisting that these countries firmly align themselves on the Western side. Their right to be neutral in the cold war was conceded.

President Kennedy continued and in some ways elaborated upon the policy of financial assistance abroad. He established the Agency for International Development (AID) to coordinate various projects and to explore means of making them more effective. He sponsored the so-called Alliance for Progress, which was not really an alliance but a set of agreements between the United States and Latin American governments for cooperative undertakings in Latin America. He also brought about the establishment of the Peace Corps, which trained and sent abroad thousands of specialists, mostly young people, to work for two years in underdeveloped areas.

The returns from foreign aid were debatable. The most successful of the programs—and the least expensive—was probably the Peace Corps. With few exceptions, the youthful volunteers seemed to make friends everywhere, whether teaching school in Nigeria or raising poultry in India. "If there is a problem here," Kennedy said in 1962, after the first year of the program, "it is that we cannot supply the spontaneous and mounting demand."

The Alliance for Progress was criticized by businessmen in the United States on the grounds that the administration's demands for tax and land reforms, as prerequisites to aid, were frightening investors away from Latin America. The Alliance was opposed by businessmen and landowners in Latin America on the grounds that, by demanding reforms, the United States was encouraging Communism. A friendly critic, Senator Hubert Humphrey, reported to Congress in 1963: "In terms of where it was a year ago, the Alianza para el Progreso has taken a great leap forward. In terms of where it has yet to go, it has taken only a short faltering step."

Foreign aid appeared to help in counteracting Russian influence in the emerging nations of Africa. Despite innumerable Russian missions, these countries by the mid-sixties had been oriented more toward the United States and its European allies than toward the Soviet Union. In the Congo, when civil war broke out resulting in independence in 1960, United Nations forces intervened to prevent the secession of Katanga, the richest of the provinces. By 1963 the Congo was both quiet and non-Communist, though bloody fighting was later to break out anew.

In 1963 a presidential study commission

headed by General Lucius D. Clay recommended stricter management of the foreign-aid programs. The United States, Clay reported, was trying to do "too much for too many too soon." Nevertheless, Clay later testified before a congressional committee that, of forty-one countries which had been receiving substantial assistance since 1945, thirty-three were achieving marked economic progress.

## Reshaping Defense Policies

At the time Kennedy took office, the military establishment of the United States was spending half of the federal budget and nearly a tenth of

### The Military Establishment and Arms Industry [ 1961]

*[The] conjunction of an immense military establishment and a large arms industry is new in American experience. The total influence—economic, political, even spiritual—is felt in every city, every state house, every office of the federal government. We recognize the imperative need for this development. Yet we must not fail to comprehend its grave implications. Our toil, resources and livelihood are all involved; so is the very structure of our society.*

*In the councils of government, we must guard against the acquisition of unwarranted influence, whether sought or unsought, by the military-industrial complex. The potential for the disastrous rise of misplaced power exists and will persist.*

*We must never let the weight of this combination endanger our liberties or democratic processes. We should take nothing for granted. Only an alert and knowledgeable citizenry can compel the proper meshing of the huge industrial and military machinery of defense with our peaceful methods and goals, so that security and liberty may prosper together.—Dwight D. Eisenhower, Farewell Address, January 18, 1961.*

the gross national product; it was directly employing 3.5 million people. The incoming President and his new Secretary of Defense, Robert McNamara, were as determined as President Eisenhower had been in his farewell address that this vast establishment should protect but not dominate the American nation. From the outset, McNamara established firm control over the enormous and complex Department of Defense. Despite the distress of some high-ranking officers and many congressmen, he brought in brilliant young civilians who, employing computers and cost-analysis techniques, plotted policy changes. He was accused of relying more upon civilian skills and problem-solving machines than upon military experience.

Since World War II, policy planning and weapons research and development had become major responsibilities, and astronomically expensive ones, of the Department of Defense. Upon the correctness of this planning rested the security of the nation both in the present and in years to come. The 1950s had brought two revolutionary changes in weapons systems, each change enhancing the potency of the other— the introduction of the hydrogen bomb and the development of the long-range missile. Upon the basis of these innovations, defense planning took new directions in the sixties.

President Kennedy and Secretary McNamara built their plans upon the theory that the strength of thermonuclear weapons on the part of both the United States and Russia was sufficiently great to constitute a "mutual deterrent" against war. During the campaign of 1960 Kennedy had warned that the United States lagged behind Russia; soon after he took office his secretary of defense reported that the missile gap, if there was one, favored the United States. This nation, possessing sufficient striking power to destroy the Soviet Union several times over, was committed to staying ahead of Russia in missile and nuclear development. The new administration speeded the placing of nuclear-armed missiles in underground sites and the building of nuclear-armed Polaris submarines to rove the seas. These retaliatory weapons would guarantee that, if the United States suffered destruction, so would the attacking nation.

Unlike the Eisenhower administration, which

had thought only in terms of an all-out nuclear attack in the event of war, the Kennedy administration envisaged a broad range of options. Secretary McNamara even suggested that a Russian nuclear attack might spare cities. "It would certainly be in their interest as well as ours to try to limit the terrible consequences of a nuclear exchange," he asserted. "Considering what is at stake, we believe it is worth the additional effort on our part to have this option." Many defense experts thought no such option could exist.

There was the assumption, however, that under the umbrella of the mutual deterrence of countering nuclear forces, the Communists would seek to gain new territories by subversion or by conventional warfare. Experts pointed to areas like South Vietnam to illustrate what

## Two Views of the "Nuclear Stalemate"

### Secretary of Defense Robert McNamara:

*[The Russians] as well as we recognize that with the kind of weapons now becoming increasingly available, a global nuclear war would be disastrous to both sides. Indeed, there is ample evidence that the Soviet leadership believes that local wars are also becoming too dangerous because, in Mr. Khrushchev's words, such a local war "might develop into a world thermonuclear rocket war."*

### General Maxwell D. Taylor, Chairman, Joint Chiefs of Staff:

*The clearly evident major Soviet efforts in space, missiles, nuclear submarines, nuclear weapons development and air defense systems will require unremitting effort on the part of the United States. We must not think in terms of static nuclear stalemate, but in terms of dynamic progress and flexible adaptation in meeting the changing requirements for superiority in the strategic nuclear field. — Testimony before the Senate Defense Appropriations Subcommittee, April 1963.*

they meant; nuclear deterrents were of no value there. So the President wished to develop forces expert in guerrilla and jungle warfare and equipped with special arms. A million American men were thus trained in "counterinsurgency." In addition, United States military missions aided other countries in establishing their own programs. During its first two years the administration also committed more of its defense expenditures to increasing its conventional forces. It raised the number of army combat divisions from eleven to sixteen and air force tactical wings from sixteen to twenty-one.

President Kennedy appointed as chairman of the Joint Chiefs of Staff General Maxwell D. Taylor, who, as Chief of Staff of the Army in the Eisenhower administration, had unavailingly recommended strengthening conventional forces to meet the threat of Communist tactical power. General Taylor now warned that the United States must engage in a constant race to maintain its balance with Russia in both conventional and nuclear forces. These policies, intensified by a series of frightening crises, increased the military budget to approximately $50 billion a year.

## PERILOUS ENCOUNTERS

In his inaugural address, President Kennedy had advised: "Let us never negotiate out of fear. But let us never fear to negotiate." In the ensuing months and years, as Russia pressed the United States over the issues of Berlin, Cuba, and nuclear testing, the spirit of negotiation was put to severe trials.

### Heightening Tension

The Cuban dictator Fidel Castro was drawing closer to Russia, heaping invective upon the United States, and exporting "Fidelismo" throughout Latin America. President Kennedy had declared: "Communist domination in this hemisphere can never be negotiated."

Once in office, Kennedy and his advisers faced the question of whether to go ahead with a project that the Eisenhower administration had begun. Under the direction of the Central Intelligence Agency, anti-Castro Cubans were secretly being trained and equipped in Central America for a landing in Cuba. They were intended to overthrow the Castro regime with the aid of discontented groups still on the island. Kennedy decided to authorize the invasion but refused to provide United States air support. On the morning of April 17, 1961, a force of about 2,000 rebels landed at the Bay of Pigs. No accompanying revolt, such as had been expected, took place in Cuba, and the invading rebels were left to the mercy of the Cuban army and air force. Within two days the beachhead was wiped out.

Throughout Latin America, and in many allied and neutral nations as well as Communist countries, the United States was the object of condemnation. This country reaped all the disadvantages and none of the potential advantages of the invasion attempt. President Kennedy retorted on April 20: "We do not intend to abandon [Cuba] to the Communists." But Castro moved rapidly toward aligning Cuba fully with the Soviet Union, proclaiming that it was a "socialist" state.

In the somber aftermath of the Bay of Pigs fiasco, President Kennedy in June 1961 met Premier Khrushchev in Vienna for a frank interchange of views. It was not encouraging. According to reports, Kennedy told Khrushchev that Russia wanted to trade an apple for an orchard, but the United States did not do business that way.

An ominous sequel to the conference was renewed Russian pressure upon Berlin, bringing with it the serious threat of nuclear war. On June 15, 1961, Khrushchev, who was then back in Russia, set a deadline for the settlement of the Berlin issue. "The conclusion of a peace treaty with Germany cannot be postponed any longer," he declared. "A peaceful settlement in Europe must be attained this year." With or without the Western powers, he proposed to conclude a peace treaty with the East German government (the "German Democratic Republic"), which would then control access routes to West Berlin. As he well knew, the NATO powers did not possess conventional forces of sufficient strength to defend West Berlin and its access routes with any certainty of success. The defense of Berlin must rest upon the use of nu-

clear power, and Khrushchev acted as if he thought the United States would not risk the danger of world holocaust to defend Berlin.

What was pushing the Soviet Union toward this dangerous confrontation was the spectacular success of West Berlin as a "showcase of democracy" behind the Iron Curtain. East Germans could easily slip into West Berlin, though barbed wire and minefields prevented fugitives from crossing the rest of the border between Communist countries and western Europe. West Germany with its higher living standards and its demands for skilled workers and professional men was an irresistible lure to the poor, regimented East Germans.

Suddenly, before dawn on August 13, 1961, the East German government closed the border between East and West Berlin and in the next few days began erecting elaborate concrete block and barbed wire barriers. East Germany was transformed into a vast concentration camp and West Berlin into a beleaguered island. Khrushchev had thus gained by a single act of force much that he had been seeking unsuccessfully at the conference table. The United States protested but was not ready to use armed force to destroy the new wall. Fears of thermonuclear war ran so high throughout the United States that the nation faced seriously for the first time the problem of trying to construct fallout shelters sufficient to protect the entire population. There was much controversy about shelters in ensuing months and little actual construction, despite the encouragement of the federal and state governments.

Russia kept up the pressure on the West by announcing an extensive series of nuclear tests. During the autumn Russia exploded approximately fifty nuclear devices, one with an estimated force of sixty-five megatons—3,000 times more powerful than the Hiroshima bomb. The series as a whole produced double the amount of fallout of all previous atomic tests.

The United States, fearing it would fall behind in the nuclear race, announced it would resume tests underground and in outer space. These tests would not add to fallout, but unaligned nations took as censorious a view toward the United States as toward Russia, ignoring the fact that Khrushchev had broken the test truce.

Most American experts concluded that Russia had made important weapons advances through testing, perhaps had even developed an anti-missile missile, and that the United States in consequence must conduct atmospheric tests.

## Confrontation Over Cuba

The Berlin crisis slowly subsided during the autumn of 1961, to be succeeded a year later by a new, more frightening encounter, this time in regard to Cuba. In mid-July 1962, shiploads of Russian technicians and equipment began arriving on the island, and in August more than thirty Soviet ships unloaded two thousand technicians and instructors, together with fighter planes, surface-to-air missiles, and patrol boats with missiles. Photographic reconnaissance, which the United States was carrying out secretly around the periphery of Cuba, indicated, as Kennedy announced on September 4, that the armaments were solely defensive. "Were it otherwise," he declared, "the gravest issues would arise."

Refugees from Cuba brought reports, however, that Russia was also introducing offensive missiles into the island. Kennedy authorized

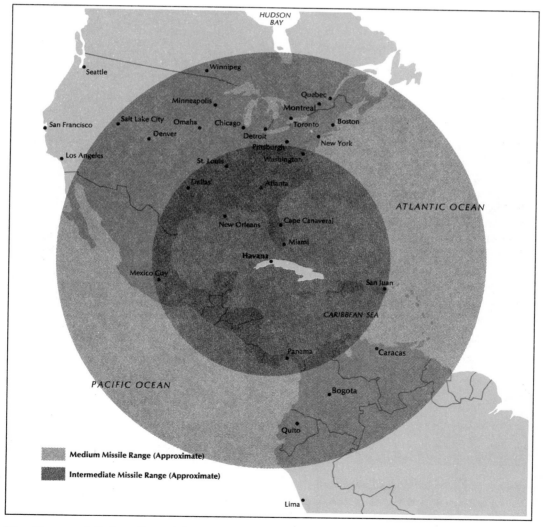

The Range of Cuban-Based Soviet Missiles

photographic reconnaissance of all Cuba to ascertain if this was true. On October 14, a U-2 plane brought back incontrovertible evidence—photographs of new missile sites being rushed to completion. Why were the Russians engaged in this dangerous and expensive gamble? This was the first question that President Kennedy's advisers pondered as they began deliberations on October 16. The Russian move would more than redress the missile balance that had favored the United States. According to the London *Observer* (October 28, 1962): "Seen from the Pentagon, the two most alarming features of the missile build-up [in Cuba] were proximity and speed. Radar would give 15 minutes' warning of a missile attack from Russia, but only two–three minutes from Cuba. Medium-range missile bases can be constructed in hours or days. Within a month, if the U. S. sat tight, Russia could get 200–300 missiles in position—enough, at least in theory, to knock out a large part of the U. S. retaliatory forces in a surprise 'pre-emptive' attack."

How could the United States counter the Russian move? One of the two main alternatives was to strike the bases from the air; the other was to blockade Cuba. The President and his advisers decided upon a "quarantine"—a blockade. Meanwhile, on October 18, Soviet Foreign Minister Gromyko called upon the President to assure him that Soviet assistance to Cuba was solely defensive.

On October 22, President Kennedy was ready to act. Appearing on television, he presented the photographic evidence of the missile sites and announced that the United States would establish a quarantine on all offensive weapons bound for Cuba. "This secret, swift and extraordinary build-up of Communist missiles—in an area well known to have a special and historical relationship to the United States and the nations of the Western hemisphere—is

**A Cuban Medium-Range Ballistic Missile Launch Site**

This photograph shows the site at San Cristobal, Cuba, on October 25, 1962, at the height of the crisis. Allen Dulles, former head of the Central Intelligence Agency has hinted that the requisite skill in identifying Soviet missile sites from photographs had been acquired through data gathered by U-2 flights over Russia. (U.S. Department of Defense) a deliberately provocative and unjustified change in the status quo which cannot be accepted by this country, if our courage and our commitments are ever again to be trusted by either friend or foe."

Several days of acute tension followed as the United States instituted its naval and air blockade, uncertain what would happen if a Soviet vessel among the twenty-five bound for Cuba should refuse to stop and should be sunk. Some of the Soviet ships changed course or stopped. But low-flying Navy P-8U planes brought back evidence that work on the Soviet bases continued at top speed.

This evidence made especially unacceptable to the United States a proposal issued by U Thant, acting secretary general of the United Nations, after strong urging by unaligned nations. U Thant requested Russia to suspend arms shipments, and he requested that the United States suspend the blockade for two or three weeks while negotiations took place. Khrushchev accepted U Thant's suggestion, but Kennedy declined.

All week long the United States negotiated with Russia, and behind the stand of each side was the threat of nuclear force. The United States left no doubt that it was in earnest. The navy established a 2,100-mile ring about Cuba, employing 180 ships, including 8 aircraft carriers. The Strategic Air Command began "massive airborne" alerts on October 22, keeping quantities of its heavy nuclear-armed B-52 bombers in the air at all times. Behind these were 156 intercontinental ballistic missiles in combat readiness and a fleet of Polaris submarines. Soviet miscalculation could bring a holocaust.

Late on the evening of October 26, President Kennedy received a long, rambling letter from Khrushchev in which he compared the United States and the Soviet Union to two men tugging on a rope, pulling a knot tighter and tighter until it could be cut only by a sword. In effect, the letter said that if Kennedy would cease tugging on his end, Khrushchev would do likewise. The letter seemed to imply that Russia would remove the missile bases provided the United States would promise not to invade Cuba. The next morning Moscow radio broadcast quite a different proposal from Khrushchev—that Russia would dismantle the bases in Cuba if the United States would withdraw its missile bases from Turkey.

Time was running out for the United States, and meanwhile in Cuba antiaircraft fire had downed one American plane and menaced others. Under these tense conditions, the President decided to accept Khrushchev's first offer and to ignore the second: if Khrushchev would remove the missiles, Kennedy proposed, the United States would end the blockade and not invade Cuba. The next day, October 27, Khrushchev accepted.

Though an armed clash had been avoided, trouble over Cuba by no means had been brought to an end. The Soviet Union did indeed remove the missiles and dismantle its bases, but Castro refused to allow on-the-spot inspection. Thousands of Soviet technicians remained, and although President Kennedy pressured Khrushchev to remove them, their return to Russia was slow. Cuban refugee groups, bewildered and angered by the no-invasion pledge, engaged in plots of their own against Castro and were resentful when the United States restrained them. In the immediate aftermath of the crisis, the national sentiment was one of profound relief, and President Kennedy's popularity rose to unprecedented heights.

## Loosening of Alliances

With the onset of the cold war in 1947, world politics had become largely polarized between two power blocs: the United States and its allies, and the Soviet Union and its satellites. Though some countries, such as India, attempted to remain neutral, most of the nations of the world aligned themselves on one or the other of the two sides. By the early 1960s, however, both of the great alliances had begun to loosen somewhat. Strains were developing in the relations between the Soviet Union and Red China and in those between the United States and some of its former friends. These developments presented both new opportunities and new problems for American diplomacy.

In the fall of 1962, at the time of the Cuban crisis, Red China launched surprise offensives along the Indian frontier. The light and poorly armed Indian troops were pushed back until, at one point, the Chinese were only 300 miles from Calcutta. Though the Himalayan border was in dispute, China in 1954 had pledged respect for the territorial integrity of India. China's motives in attacking may have been to lower Indian prestige in Southeast Asia and also to embarrass the Soviet Union, which had been providing economic aid to India.

The United States did not stand passively by while the Chinese forces advanced. Despite American preoccupation with Cuba, John Kenneth Galbraith, the ambassador to India, succeeded in obtaining commitments of military aid, and within a few days air force "flying boxcars" were ferrying weapons and supplies to the Himalayan front. Indian-Chinese negotiations toward a border settlement got under way, but the government of India looked upon the difficulties with China as likely to last a long time. Meanwhile, as Prime Minister Jawaharlal Nehru pointed out, Indo-American relations had seldom been as close and cordial. "The deep sympathy and practical support received from the United States in meeting the Chinese aggression has created a wealth of good feeling," he declared, "and, apart from that, there is much in common between us on essentials."

Meanwhile, the most notable of the American aid programs, the Marshall Plan, had helped stimulate a recovery in western Europe so remarkable that these nations in the 1960s were not only more prosperous than ever before in their history but in percentage of annual growth were in several instances outstripping the United States. Their new economic power meant that, if they chose, they could either insist upon a more equal partnership or break loose to form a "third force" between the United States and Russia, such as some French leaders had long envisaged.

President Kennedy emphasized the need for a transatlantic community. In 1962 he obtained from Congress the Trade Expansion Act, enabling him better to negotiate with the European Common Market. This act authorized him to reduce duties as much as 50 per cent in the following five years, and to eliminate tariffs entirely on many types of goods exported by both the United States and Common Market nations.

Then, at the beginning of 1963, in the aftermath of the Cuba crisis, the hopes for closer cooperation between the United States and western Europe were jolted by President Charles de Gaulle of France. Unexpectedly, De Gaulle vetoed the British application to join the Common Market and did so because of the close British ties with the United States. At almost the same time, he proclaimed his opposition to American plans for creating a multination nuclear force within the North Atlantic Treaty Organization. De Gaulle insisted upon creating a separate small nuclear force for France, in order to gain an independent voice in European policy. Later he recognized Red China, thus asserting an independent position in Asian affairs as well.

In the summer of 1963, perhaps in part because of growing trouble with China, the Soviet Union, after years of negotiation, agreed to a treaty banning atmospheric (but not underground) tests of nuclear weapons. The treaty, the first definite step in the direction of international arms reduction since the onset of the cold war, was ratified by almost every important country except Red China (which was preparing to test its own nuclear bomb), France, and Cuba. A notable thaw in the cold war followed. President Kennedy announced that the United States would be willing to sell large quantities of surplus wheat to the Russians who were suffering from a shortage.

By 1964 many Americans were thinking hopefully of the prospect at last for a "detente," a relaxation of tensions, in relations with the Soviet Union. But these prospects soon declined as the United States became more and more deeply involved in an anti-Communist crusade far from home in Southeast Asia.

## JOHNSON'S DILEMMAS

During the presidential campaign of 1964 the Republican candidate, Senator Goldwater, urged that the United States take a much more active part in the war then going on between Communist North Vietnam and non-Communist South Vietnam. But President Johnson specifically repudiated the Goldwater policy. "There are those that say you ought to go north and drop bombs, and try to wipe out the supply lines, and they think that would escalate the war," Johnson declaimed in a campaign speech. "We don't want our American boys to do the fighting for Asian boys. We don't want to get involved in a nation [China] with 700 million people and get tied down in a land war in Asia."

In fact, Johnson himself was already preparing to enlarge the American role in Vietnam, and soon he was ordering bombs dropped on the north and was sending American boys by the hundreds of thousands to fight in that faraway land. As a consequence he lost all possibility of maintaining the "consensus" he had desired and of achieving the "Great Society" he had proclaimed. Never before had a President been elected by such a large popular majority, and never before had a President seen his popularity dwindle away so fast and so completely.

## Dominican Intervention

While undertaking to prevent the spread of Communism in distant Asia, President Johnson faced what seemed like a new Communist threat much closer to home, in the Caribbean. There appeared to be a danger that a Castro-type government might be imposed upon the Dominican Republic, thus making that country a second Cuba. Johnson acted quickly to forestall the supposed Communist coup. In doing so, he laid himself open to charges of fostering imperialism and right-wing dictatorship.

After the assassination of the dictator General Rafael Trujillo in 1961, the Dominican Republic was slowly and painfully emerging from three decades of economic exploitation and political repression. The government of the democratically elected President, Juan Bosch, who was leftist though not Communist, floundered. In 1963 a conservative military junta overthrew Bosch and, faring little better, became itself the target of unrest. There were rumors of Communist infiltration into the island. In the spring of 1965 when young military men sympathetic to Bosch rebelled against the junta, there was rioting, shooting, and looting in the streets of the capital, Santo Domingo. Conservative groups in the armed forces counterattacked. Officials in Washington sympathized with the

### A Critique of the Dominican Intervention

The Center for Strategic Studies of Georgetown University assembled a distinguished committee of experts with differing views on Latin American affairs to evaluate the intervention. It concluded:

1. There was a serious threat to foreign nationals that justified the first landings on April 28, 1965.

2. Growing chaos and the number of persons seeking evacuation required landing reinforced troops on April 29, 1965.

3. "A coup had been planned for a later date, but was precipitated by a series of unforeseen events. Communists were linked with the earlier planning. Although surprised by the timing of the rebellion they quickly assumed a leading role in the disorders that broke out. Progress in the Communist effort to dominate the revolt became increasingly evident." The third stage of American action was based upon this threat and a resolution of the Council of the Organization of American States, calling for a cease-fire and the establishment of a neutral zone between the fighting forces.

4. "The United States should have attempted to make earlier use of the machinery available to the OAS for collective action. Such efforts would have reduced the possibility of suspicion and misunderstanding of U.S. action."

5. "The reasons for U.S. landings were ineptly explained to the public. The failure to communicate effectively the rationale for its actions had damaging effects in the United States and throughout Latin America."—Center for Strategic Studies, Georgetown University, *Dominican Action—1965; Intervention or Cooperation?* July 1966.

conservatives. When the conservatives seemed about to be defeated, President Johnson, acting on the basis of lurid reports of widespread slaughter, ordered United States troops ashore, ostensibly to protect American citizens. Later, President Johnson declared: "Of course, we knew of the forces at work in the Dominican Republic. We were not unaware that there were Communists that were active in this effort. But 99 per cent of our reason for going in there was to try to provide protection for these American lives and the lives of other nationals."

Within the next few days, United States forces numbering 30,000 ashore and afloat helped restore order. In reply to criticisms that the United States had acted unilaterally, the President and Secretary of State Dean Rusk insisted that they had held preliminary consultations with other American states and that the need for sudden intervention to prevent loss of life arose too quickly for further reliance upon the Organization of American States. It was at this point that President Johnson warned of a Communist threat. He put this most pungently while speaking informally to White House visitors: "We don't expect to sit here on our rocking chairs with our hands folded and let the Communists set up any government in the Western Hemisphere. We are not the interveners in the Dominican Republic. The people who intervened in the Dominican Republic were people trained outside the Dominican Republic in guerrilla warfare to overthrow the government and have a Communist seizure of that country."

The OAS did authorize the establishment of an Inter-American Peace Force. American troops, together with token forces from several other republics, donned blue and yellow OAS armbands, and served under the command of a Brazilian general. Bloody fighting continued for some days before order could be restored. More than a year later, on June 1, 1966, in a new presidential election, Bosch was defeated by a moderate candidate. The Peace Force was withdrawn in September 1966.

The United States achieved stabilization of the Dominican Republic only at the cost of much Latin American good will. In June 1965 a professor at the National University of Mexico wrote: "The way Juan Bosch has been treated

and the clumsy invasion of the Dominican Republic have created more hatred toward the United States in Latin America than the combined anti-colonial propaganda of China and Russia."

## Involvement in Vietnam

The involvement of the United States in Vietnam had developed so slowly that when it began spectacularly to grow, in 1964 and 1965, few Americans could remember how it had originated.

After the close of World War II, Vietnamese nationalists, seeking independence from France, rallied around Ho Chi Minh, a Communist who during the war had led the anti-Japanese resistance and had cooperated with the Americans. Ho issued a declaration of independence echoing the American Declaration of 1776 and began negotiations with France. When negotiations broke down, Ho and his followers resorted to arms. The American government was little concerned until the fall of Nationalist China and the outbreak of the Korean War. Then the Truman administration looked upon the French as manning a bastion to check the spread of Communism in Southeast Asia and began to send substantial aid. The Eisenhower administration increased the economic assistance and, when the French forces faced disaster in 1954, considered sending large-scale military aid as well. Eisenhower held back, however, because of the opposition of Congress and because of the refusal of Great Britain to cooperate.

There followed the 1954 settlements at Geneva, establishing Laos and Cambodia, and temporarily splitting Vietnam into a Communist north and non-Communist south until free elections could be held to unify the new nation. The United States did not participate in the negotiations or sign the agreements. It promised not to use force to upset them, but warned that "it would view any renewal of the aggression in violation of the . . . agreements with grave concern and as seriously threatening international peace and security." Subsequently, the State Department threw its influence against free elections: they were never held.

The Eisenhower administration sought new arrangements to contain the Communists in

Southeast Asia. Within two months of the Geneva agreements, Secretary Dulles succeeded in establishing the Southeast Asia Treaty Organization (SEATO), whose members agreed to consult one another regarding not only their own security but also the security of Laos, Cambodia, and South Vietnam. On October 23, 1954, President Eisenhower wrote the premier of South Vietnam, not only promising aid in return for certain reforms, but offering "to assist the Government of Viet-Nam in developing and maintaining a strong, viable state, capable of resisting attempted subversion or aggression through military means." The SEATO treaty and President Eisenhower's letter were subsequently cited as the American commitments to assist South Vietnam—even though Dulles himself had told the Senate Foreign Relations Committee, when seeking its approval of SEATO, that if there should be a "revolutionary movement" in Vietnam, the SEATO members "would

consult together as to what to do about it . . . but we have no undertaking to put it down; all we have is an undertaking to consult."

While the United States sought stabilization, it claimed that North Vietnam continued to seek through guerrilla activity the conquest of Laos and South Vietnam. Political turbulence and the economic dissatisfaction of many South Vietnamese made possible the successful growth of bands of Vietcong (short for Viet Communists), which by 1959 at least, were receiving training and supplies from North Vietnam. At the end of 1960, the Vietcong established the "National Front for the Liberation of South Vietnam." Making its forays at night, murdering headmen and terrorizing villages, the Vietcong succeeded in controlling large parts of the countryside. The government of South Vietnam was confined to the cities and main lines of communication.

Gradually the United States sent increasing aid to Vietnam. Between 1954 and 1959, of $2.3

**Training Vietnamese Troops to Combat Communist Guerrillas**

One of the most vital of the programs to counter Communist nibbling tactics was established in South Vietnam where a joint military assistance advisory group of the United States armed forces intensively trained Vietnamese armed forces in the use of American

weapons and of limited warfare tactics against the Vietcong troops. Army Chief Warrant Officer Richard Parsons (standing right) instructs Vietnamese infantrymen on how to board an H-21C helicopter.
(Official U.S. Army photo)

billion in aid, only two-fifths was military. American military advisers helped train the South Vietnam army. President Kennedy, inheriting the problem, tried to build more effective resistance in Vietnam, not only through military counterinsurgency, but also through gaining the support of the peasants. Vice President Johnson, visiting Saigon in May 1961, recommended aid but warned against direct military involvement: "American combat troop involvement is not only not required, it is not desirable. . . . Possibly Americans fail to appreciate fully the subtlety that recently colonial peoples would not look with favor upon governments which invited or accept the return this soon of Western troops."

As political and military conditions in Vietnam continued to deteriorate, President Kennedy, despite his misgivings, added to the number of military advisers; by the time of his assassination in November 1963, the American personnel in that country had reached a total of 15,500. Reports from American officials in Vietnam were optimistic, though internal troubles there caused newspapermen to cable home dark predictions. A new era of even greater instability began in the fall of 1963 when the South Vietnamese army seized control of the government from the aristocratic nationalist Ngo Dinh Diem.

## Escalating the War

Despite growing difficulties in Vietnam, in the summer of 1964 they were overshadowed by the political campaign in the United States. The number of military advisers was up to 20,000, and on its way to 25,000. Then, in August, there occurred an episode that was to give legal grounds for the reshaping of the war: American destroyers on patrol in international waters in the Gulf of Tonkin reported that they had been attacked by North Vietnamese torpedo boats. (In 1968 Senator Fulbright, chairman of the Foreign Relations Committee, held hearings and sharply inquired about what had happened in the Tonkin Gulf. He raised the question of whether there actually had been an attack.) In 1964 President Johnson and Congress were in a mood to take stern measures. Congress at the request of the President passed by a vote of 88 to 2 in the Senate and 416 to 0 in the House, a joint resolution "To promote the maintenance

> ### The Tonkin Gulf Resolution [August 1964]
>
> *. . . The Congress approves and supports the determination of the President, as Commander in Chief, to take all necessary measures to repel any armed attack against the forces of the United States and to prevent further aggression.*
>
> *The United States regards as vital to its national interest and to world peace the maintenance of international peace and security in Southeast Asia. Consonant with the Constitution and the Charter of the United Nations and in accordance with its obligations under the Southeast Asia Collective Defense Treaty, the United States is, therefore, prepared, as the President determines, to take all necessary steps, including the use of armed force, to assist any member or protocol state of the Southeast Asia Collective Defense Treaty requesting assistance in defense of its freedom. . . .*

of international peace and security in Southeast Asia." The resolution authorized the President to "take all necessary measures" to protect American forces and "prevent further aggression" in Southeast Asia. Senators Wayne Morse and Ernest Gruening, the only two men in Congress to vote against the resolution, opposed it as being a "predated declaration of war power." Subsequently it did serve as legal authorization for the escalation of the conflict.

By the beginning of 1965 the Vietcong, aided not only by supplies but also by military units coming from North Vietnam along the jungle "Ho Chi Minh trail" through Laos, were in ascendancy. The American "advisers" had gradually become combatants and were already suffering serious casualties. At this point the United States began a rapid build-up of troops in Vietnam and the launching of regular bombing attacks upon supply depots, army camps, and transportation lines in North Vietnam. In 1965 United States armed forces in Vietnam grew

**Vietnam**

from 23,000 to over 180,000; in 1966, the number was doubled; by the end of 1967, it was approaching an authorized half-million. Air sorties were intensified until the tonnage of bombs being dropped exceeded that in Europe during World War II. Casualties mounted. By every statistic, the Vietnam War was becoming one of the most serious in United States history.

The purpose of this enormous effort was to try to bring an end to the Communist threat. In the spring of 1965, speaking at Johns Hopkins University, President Johnson, in answer to sharp criticism from unaligned nations (and from within the United States) outlined four main points:

1. "Our objective is the independence of

South Vietnam, and its freedom from attack. . . . We will not withdraw, either openly or under the cloak of a meaningless agreement."

2. A peaceful settlement must provide for "an independent South Vietnam—securely guaranteed and able to shape its own relationships to all others—free from outside interference—tied to no alliance—a military base for no other country."

3. "We will never be second in the search for . . . a peaceful settlement in Vietnam . . . and we remain ready, with this purpose for unconditional discussions."

4. The United States invited the countries of Southeast Asia, together with the United Nations and the Soviet Union to join in "a greatly expanded cooperative effort for development."

North Vietnam and Communist China through their spokesmen retorted that Johnson's offer was "overflowing with lies and deception . . . a big swindle . . . a mystification and a huge hoax." North Vietnam stepped up its direct action and its aid to the Vietcong; in turn it received arms from Red China and the Soviet Union. Behind Ho Chi Minh was the threat that Red China might at some point, if the war escalated too far, enter as it had into the Korean conflict. In 1964 China exploded its first nuclear device and by 1967 had successfully tested a hydrogen bomb. The rift between China and Russia had widened. The Soviet Union made no serious threats against the United States, but apparently refrained from trying to bring North Vietnam to the negotiating table. Indeed, by late 1969 the Soviet Union was supplying North Vietnam with more sophisticated weapons.

On occasions, the United States limited or halted its bombings and other offensive actions in efforts to persuade the North Vietnamese to begin negotiations. Each time North Vietnam refused, for the most part adhering to the position that the United States must unconditionally and permanently end all bombing. At times a further stipulation was attached to this condition: all American forces were to leave Vietnam.

President Johnson and his advisers refused to end the bombing unconditionally and permanently. They pointed out that during each bombing halt at the time of a holiday truce the North Vietnamese rushed men and supplies southward

or prepared for new attacks. Military leaders, following a policy of seeking out and destroying enemy forces, were confident at the beginning of 1968 that given sufficient men and matériel they could eventually triumph.

## Deescalation Begins

In the United States, where television brought pictures of the cruelty and destruction of the war into every living room, the war became more and more unpopular. Liberals and university students participated vigorously in demonstrations, "teach-ins," and "sit-ins." Some young men burned their draft cards. Senator Fulbright and a group of his colleagues became bitter critics of President Johnson and Secretary of State Rusk. Public opinion polls indicated that a majority of Americans still supported the Vietnam War, but it had become the transcendent issue in the nation.

Heavy war costs brought inflationary pressures in 1965. Two years later, President Johnson sought to obtain from Congress a 10-percent increase in income taxes; leaders in the House of Representatives refused to vote it unless he cut drastically his requests for domestic expenditures. Johnson refused to make cuts as deep as they wished, and the tax increase was not voted. The outpouring of funds intensified the balance-of-payments gap that long had been plaguing the United States. As the war escalated, speculators and several European nations exchanged dollars for American gold, trying to force it from the fixed price of $35 per ounce. President de Gaulle of France was eager to see the world domination of the dollar come to an end, a return to an international gold standard with Paris once again a dominant money center. In the spring of 1968 the United States and six European nations (not including France) stemmed the gold outflow temporarily by establishing a two-price system. They retained the $35-per-ounce price for transactions among themselves and stopped the sale of gold to private buyers. Outside of their own gold holdings, they agreed to allow a free market to operate, on which the price of gold could rise and fall like that of any other commodity.

The drain of enthusiasm for the Vietnam War accelerated rapidly in the early months of 1968. During a truce in the fighting to observe Tet—

the Chinese New Year—the Vietcong suddenly struck in almost every city of South Vietnam. They were dislodged only after days of bitter fighting, great devastation, and heavy casualties. The single blow destroyed the homes of a half-million South Vietnamese. The Tet offensive intensified pressure against the war among a growing segment of the American voters.

In the fall of 1967 Senator Eugene McCarthy of Minnesota began what seemed to be a futile protest campaign for the Presidency. He had behind him only a handful of liberals and a growing group of enthusiastic students. In the first of the primary campaigns in New Hampshire, some of the young men cut their long hair and shaved their beards before ringing doorbells for McCarthy. In the voting, McCarthy was startlingly strong against Johnson, winning almost all of the delegates to the convention. The next day, Senator Robert Kennedy of New York, also a critic of the Vietnam War, announced his candidacy. There were indications that the challenge to President Johnson would be so strong that he might not be able to win renomination.

For months President Johnson had been considering a change in his course of action. On the evening of March 31, 1968, in a telecast to the nation, he suddenly announced that he was ordering a halt in the attacks upon the populous areas of North Vietnam and was inviting the North Vietnamese to join him in a "series of mutual moves toward peace": "Tonight in the hope that this action will lead to early talks, I am taking the first step to de-escalate the conflict. We are reducing—substantially reducing—the present level of hostilities. And we are doing so unilaterally, and at once." At the close of his talk he made an announcement that removed any possibility that the deescalation could be looked upon as a political gesture: "I shall not seek and I will not accept the nomination of my party for another term."

The North Vietnamese government accepted President Johnson's invitation, and in May 1968 lengthy, difficult negotiations began in Paris.

## NIXON'S INHERITANCE

By the time Johnson left office, the national consensus that he had sought, and that his tremendous majority of 1964 had promised, was completely shattered. His successor inherited his problems but received no such endorsement at the polls.

## Election of 1968

During 1967 and 1968, the issues of the Vietnam War and urban violence became the focus of the preconvention presidential campaigns.

Significantly, the successful Republican contender, Richard Nixon, took no clearcut stand on Vietnam. According to public opinion polls, Nixon was running so far ahead in the first of the primary campaigns in New Hampshire that his principal opponent, Governor George Romney of Michigan, withdrew before the balloting. Nixon easily fended off last-minute threats from Governor Ronald Reagan of California on the right, and Governor Nelson Rockefeller of New York to the left, to win nomination on the first ballot. He chose Spiro Agnew, governor of Maryland, as his running mate.

The Vietnam debate, by contrast, wracked the Democratic party. After Johnson made his announcement not to run for another term, only Eugene McCarthy and Robert Kennedy (holding much the same views on Vietnam and domestic problems) were left to battle each other in the Democratic primaries. In late April, too late to become embroiled in the primaries, Vice President Humphrey entered the campaign. So many Democratic leaders in states without primaries backed Humphrey that he became an immediate favorite to win the nomination. Public attention focused on the primary contests. Kennedy won Indiana, lost Oregon to McCarthy, and then in the last primary in California, won again. At a Los Angeles hotel, on June 5, just after he had exhorted his cheering followers to seek victory with him at the Democratic convention, he was shot and killed by an assassin. National mourning for Kennedy brought a temporary cessation in the campaigning.

At the Democratic convention in Chicago, McCarthy (and some Kennedy followers backing Senator George McGovern of South Dakota) were unable to prevent the nomination of Humphrey on the first ballot. The critics of Humphrey, heir to administration policies, were bitter. Adding to their bitterness were the rough tactics of the Chicago police who shoved and harassed delegates and spectators to the conven-

### The 1968 Democratic Candidates

After President Johnson announced that he would
not be a candidate for reelection, three candidates
battled through the spring of 1968 for the nomination. Senator Eugene McCarthy, whose eloquent
opposition to the Vietnam War brought him the
support of large numbers of young people, contended with Senator Robert Kennedy, whose views
were almost identical. After the assassination of
Kennedy, it was McCarthy alone who opposed Vice
President Hubert Humphrey, who had not entered
the primaries, and who (despite privately expressed
misgivings about the war) defended the administration record. (Photoreporters)

tion, and before television cameras, clubbed and manhandled demonstrators in the streets of Chicago. An investigating committee subsequently referred to the violent police reactions to the taunts and attacks by the demonstrators as a "police riot." Through the campaign, Humphrey (although he had been distinguished for his liberalism throughout his political career) received little support from those who had followed McCarthy and Kennedy.

The candidate who evoked the most enthusiastic responses and violent heckling wherever he spoke throughout the country was former Governor George Wallace of Alabama, running with General Curtis LeMay on the American Independent party ticket. "We are not talking about race," Wallace declared again and again, as he whipped up enthusiasm among audiences largely made up of white workers. General LeMay, who had been Chief of Staff of the Air Force, favored a hard line toward Vietnam. Public opinion polls showed Wallace at one

point to be the favorite of a fifth of the voters; he hoped to throw the election into the House of Representatives. By election day his support had dropped substantially.

Neither of the major candidates evoked much enthusiasm. Nixon, campaigning methodically in almost computerized fashion, seemed far ahead from the outset. On the two main issues —law and order at home, and the Vietnam War —Nixon favored conciliation from a position of strength. He declared in his acceptance address that he would heed "the voice of the great majority of Americans, the forgotten Americans, the non-shouters, the non-demonstrators, that are not racists or sick, that are not guilty of the crime that plagues the land." Regarding the Vietnam War, he pointed out that at every point he had been a critic of the administration, and Humphrey its defender; beyond that comment he made little commitment.

In contrast to Nixon's campaign, Humphrey's seemed lacking in both planning and finance. On

Election of 1968

### President Nixon

After phenomenal early success, Richard M. Nixon underwent serious adversity, yet he succeeded in coming back spectacularly to win election as President in 1968. Born in California, educated at Whittier College and Duke Law School, he served as a lieutenant-commander in the navy during World War II. He entered politics as an energetic conservative Republican in 1946, winning election over a New Dealer incumbent, whom he criticized for his endorsement by the CIO. In Congress he helped draft the Taft-Hartley Act and the Mundt-Nixon bill, much of which was later incorporated in the McCarran Internal Security Act. As a member of the House Un-American Activities Committee, he became famous through his persistence in keeping the Alger Hiss affair alive. In 1950 he ran for the Senate from California against a woman supporter of the Fair Deal and won by a huge plurality. In 1952 at the age of thirty-nine, he was elected Vice President, and in 1960 received the Republican nomination for President by acclamation. Adversity followed. He lost to John F. Kennedy by less than 119,000 votes, and two years later when he ran for governor of California was again defeated. He moved to New York where he devoted himself to his law practice, but was still the most vigorous of Republican campaigners. As late as 1966 he remarked that "as a practical political realist," he was sure he would not again be a candidate for President. Nevertheless, in 1968 he carried both Republican primaries and the convention to win nomination, and in November he was elected President. (NBC)

Vietnam, he and his opponent differed little, but on the problem of poverty he pledged federal aid for a massive "Marshall Plan for the cities" in contrast to Nixon's insistence that private capital must help the poor to help themselves. During the last weeks of the campaign, Humphrey's standing in the public opinion polls increased markedly, and the statements of both candidates became sharper. Yet, as the front runner, Nixon refused to debate on television, and many of the positions of the two men did not seem sharply different. Both were occupying middle positions with Nixon to the right and Humphrey to the left of center.

By a fairly narrow margin of some 500,000 votes, out of more than 73 million cast, Nixon defeated Humphrey. The electoral vote was far more decisive, 302 for Nixon to 191 for Humphrey and 45 for Wallace.

## Appeal for Consensus

In his victory statement, Nixon returned to a theme he had frequently touched upon during the campaign and asserted that "the great objective of this Administration at the outset" would be "to bring the American people together." In the weeks that followed, as he began to develop policies and announce appointments, he emphasized moderation and open-mindedness. Indeed this seemed to be the extra dimension to which he frequently referred as he introduced the twelve appointees to his cabinet in a television broadcast. All were Republicans, none a Negro or a woman, and none was very far to the left or the right, or notable for doctrinaire views. They seemed ready to take a pragmatic approach to the problems of the cities and foreign affairs.

Nixon had kept his options open. He had asserted in one of his campaign speeches on the nature of the Presidency some suggestion of what his course might be:

"We stand at a great turning point—when the nation is groping for a new direction, unsure of its role and its purposes, caught in a tumult of change. And for the first time, we face serious, simultaneous threats to the peace both at home and abroad. . . . The next President must unite America. He must calm its angers, ease its terrible frictions, and bring its people together

once again in peace and mutual respect. He has to take *hold* of America before he can move it forward."

In his inaugural address Nixon appealed once again for a national consensus. With respect to foreign affairs he promised: "I shall consecrate my office, my energies, and all the wisdom I can summon to the cause of peace among nations." And with regard to domestic policies he declared: "No man can be fully free while his neighbor is not. To go forward at all is to go forward together. This means black and white together, as one nation, not two. The laws have caught up with our conscience. What remains is to give life to what is in the law."

The new President also urged the people to be reasonable, to lower their voices. And the people were inclined to respond. During the first few months of his administration, Nixon was fairly free from criticism. He seemed to be making no serious mistakes, and the country seemed to be suffering no new disasters—nothing like the Bay of Pigs fiasco of 1961 or the Tet offensive of 1968. Opinion polls indicated that, for the time being, Nixon had the support of a large majority of the people, a much larger number than had voted for him. He was, after all, a minority President, one who had received less than a majority of the votes cast in the 1968 election. But he now appeared to have a good chance of gaining a fair approximation of the consensus that he sought.

As more months went by, however, a larger and larger number of Americans grew impatient. Though Nixon had apparently managed to "take *hold* of America," he had not yet clearly shown that he could "move it forward." The Vietnam War dragged on, and no solutions were in sight for the domestic problems that the war either caused or aggravated.

## Revising the Constitution

One of the new President's first significant proposals was a plan for reorganizing the electoral college. The need for reform had been underscored by the recent election, when the Wallace vote, if it had been a little larger in one or two states, would have deprived Nixon of his electoral majority and left the final decision to the House of Representatives. A further reminder of defects in the existing system came when a North Carolina elector, who had run on the Republican ticket, cast his vote for Wallace instead of Nixon—there was nothing in the Constitution to prevent any elector from disregarding the will of the voters who had elected him. An opinion poll indicated that 81 per cent of the people favored a direct popular choice of Presidents in the future. Going beyond Nixon's recommendation, the House approved a constitutional amendment that would do away with the electoral college. The amendment would give the Presidency to the candidate with the largest number of popular votes if these were at least 40 per cent of the total, and it would require a run-off between the two leading candidates if no one received the minimum percentage. Nixon endorsed this measure.

While seeking to amend the Constitution, Nixon also hoped to change the interpretation of it. He wanted to alter the direction of the Supreme Court, which under Chief Justice Earl Warren had been actively enlarging the sphere of both personal liberty and civil rights. The Warren Court's decisions on civil rights had antagonized conservatives, especially in the South, and the decisions on personal liberty had aroused advocates of "law and order" (one of Nixon's themes in the 1968 campaign) all over the country. Especially resented were the *Miranda* and *Escobeda* cases, in which the judges had limited the power of the police to extract confessions from persons accused of crimes. As Chief Justice Warren approached retirement, President Johnson had tried to replace him with Abe Fortas, whom Johnson earlier had appointed as an associate justice. Fortas, a liberal, could have been expected to keep the Court on essentially the same track it had been following under Warren. The Republicans in the Senate blocked the Fortas appointment and thus gave Nixon an opportunity to choose his own chief justice.

Nixon—who insisted that it was "the job of the courts to interpret the law, not make the law"—chose a conservative strict-constructionist who agreed with him. This was Warren Burger, who had served for thirteen years on the United States Court of Appeals for the District of Columbia, and who had spoken out against what he considered the Supreme Court's protection of the rights of criminals. Burger's appointment received the prompt approval of the Senate.

Nixon soon had a chance to put another man of his choice on the Supreme Court, but this time he ran into difficulty and embarrassment. The opening occurred when Justice Fortas resigned after the revelation that he had received a salary payment from a foundation whose donor was under indictment for fraud. To take Fortas' place, Nixon named a federal circuit court judge from South Carolina, C. F. Haynsworth, who had the endorsement of the American Bar Association, but whose past decisions showed that he lagged considerably behind the Warren Court in devotion to civil rights. Spokesmen for Negro organizations and for labor unions vociferously opposed the nomination of Haynsworth. Eventually they were joined by others, including prominent members of Nixon's own party, when it was revealed that Haynsworth had sat on cases involving corporations in which he himself had a financial interest. His critics now said he was even more insensitive to possible conflicts of interest than Fortas had been. The Senate finally rejected the Haynsworth appointment, and Nixon then named G. Harrold Carswell, a judge of the Florida federal appeals court, whom the Senate also rejected. The Senate finally accepted the appointment of Harry A. Blackmun of Minnesota, who also had a reputation as a conservative jurist.

## The General Welfare

In dealing with poverty and with segregation, Nixon appeared to pursue a zigzag course down the middle. To head the Department of Health, Education, and Welfare, he appointed Robert H. Finch, who was known as a liberal and a zealous advocate of civil rights. But when Finch selected for a top department post a physician whom the conservative American Medical Association opposed, Nixon failed to support Finch's choice. In an economy drive, Nixon cut back the Johnson poverty program by closing more than half of the Job Corps training centers. He then asked Congress to enact a law that would give state and local governments the prime responsibility in job training for the poor.

Later (August 1969) Nixon proposed drastic alterations in the national welfare system, which had remained essentially unchanged since the time of the New Deal. Among the most serious faults of the existing program was the following: it provided no benefits for the poor who were employed, and thus it discouraged welfare recipients from accepting jobs. Under Nixon's plan, every unemployed family of four would receive at least $1,600 a year. The working poor would get this minimum and would be allowed to keep part of their pay until their earned income reached $4,000, when the benefits would be discontinued. To be eligible for relief, the able-bodied (women as well as men) would be required to work. The plan would add about 6 million people to the welfare rolls, and it would increase federal spending by about $4 billion annually. Increased responsibility for the administration of the program would be turned over to the states, under a principle that Nixon labeled the "new federalism." He later proposed that 400,000 poverty-stricken marginal farmers be made eligible for welfare payments, so that crop controls could be lifted and farmers allowed to compete for a larger share of the world market.

The Nixon welfare recommendations provoked immediate controversy. Some experts hailed them as promising a great improvement in the condition of the poor; others denounced them as inadequate and even retrogressive. The program, in fact, would increase welfare payments in much of the rural South but would add little or nothing to those, already supplemented by state funds, in most of the large cities of the North. There was little prospect that Congress would approve the plan without making drastic changes in it.

To lessen poverty among Negroes, Nixon advocated the encouragement of "black capitalism" through both public and private assistance to Negro-owned business enterprises. No conspicuous progress was made along this line. Yet, while poverty persisted among the Negro masses, the summer of 1969 was spared the worst of the racial violence that had been erupting annually in the cities. The urban black communities had apparently come to the conclusion that rioting did them more harm than good.

In school integration, 1969 promised to be a crucial year. During 1968–1969—a decade and a half after the Supreme Court's historic decision outlawing segregation—only 20 per cent of the black children in the South were attending mixed schools. The percentage was expected to double, however, with the beginning of the next school year. Secretary Finch talked as if he were determined to make the most of the government's power to withhold federal aid from schools whose authorities permitted no more than token integration. He indicated that he would not be satisfied with "freedom of choice" plans, which required the Negro child or his parents to take the initiative in seeking entrance to a school attended by whites. Then, in September 1969, the Nixon administration suddenly pulled back, ceased to insist on immediate steps toward integration, and granted Mississippi an additional delay in eliminating its dual school system. But several weeks later the Supreme Court overruled the administration and called for an immediate end to all racially identifiable public schools. It remained to be seen how effective the Court's edict would be.

Not only black Americans but also the nearly 5 million people of Mexican ancestry, mostly living in the Southwest, suffered from discrimination, though they were not consigned to separate schools. The Mexican-Americans acquired a hero in Cesar Chavez, leader of a four-year-old strike of California farm workers. As a means of bringing pressure upon employers, Chavez and his followers appealed for a nationwide boycott of California table grapes. The boycott had the support of millions of sympathizers throughout the country, but got no assistance from the federal government, which increased its purchases of grapes to be sent to American troops in Vietnam.

Aside from "law and order" (to put down "crime in the streets") the main concern of the average, white, middle-class American during 1969 was, with regard to domestic affairs, the condition of the nation's economy. Consumer prices kept on rising and the purchasing power of the dollar falling faster than at any other time since the Korean War. Interest rates soared to unprecedented levels, making it difficult for young couples to finance house purchases and for cities to borrow the funds they desperately needed for the maintenance and improvement of transportation, sewerage, and other public services. While most prices rose, the value of corporation stocks declined.

To slow down the galloping inflation, the Nixon administration adopted a deliberate policy of tight money—raising interest rates through the operations of the Federal Reserve System. Nixon also urged Congress to keep taxes high and to extend the income surtax that Johnson had persuaded Congress to adopt. The House of Representatives was willing to maintain a high level of taxation but only on the condition that the tax structure be reformed to lessen the burden of the poor and to increase that of corporations and wealthy individuals, especially that of the oil interests who enjoyed a generous "depletion" allowance (an exemption of much of their oil income, justified on the ground that, without this exemption, insufficient capital would go into the highly uncertain business of petroleum exploration). Administration spokesmen begged the House to go easy on the rich, including the oil men.

In another anti-inflationary move, Nixon cut down on the spending of a number of federal agencies, including the National Institute of Health. He also called upon the states to postpone their construction plans. Yet he endorsed federal spending for subsidizing an airplane manufacturer in the development of a supersonic transport (SST), a large plane that would carry passengers faster than the speed of sound and would compete with aircraft under construction by the Soviet Union and, cooperatively, by Great Britain and France. President Kennedy had put the government into the SST project, and by 1969 some $300 million of federal funds had already been contributed to it. President Nixon asked Congress to appropriate another $96 million for 1969–1970.

Before the end of 1969 there were signs that the anti-inflationary measures were having some effect. Not only was the stock market wavering, but much business activity appeared to be slowing down. Large corporations were deferring plant improvements, the construction industry was in the doldrums, and more and more wage earners where being thrown out of work. Nixon's Secretary of the Treasury, the Chicago banker

D. M. Kennedy, told a congressional committee that an unemployment rate as high as 4 per cent of the working force would be quite tolerable. By the spring of 1970 it had reached 4.8 per cent, and among Negroes it was considerably higher than that.

The strains on the economy and the increase in joblessness made up a part of the price that the nation was paying for the Vietnam War. Many Americans had hoped that, once the war was finally ended, public funds would be available for reconstructing cities, wiping out poverty, and improving the conditions of life in general. But Nixon's special adviser on urban and poverty problems, Daniel P. Moynihan, dispelled those hopes when he announced that other expenditures for the defense program would take up the slack after the Vietnam spending had ceased.

## The Doomsday Game

Like his predecessors for a whole generation, President Nixon preoccupied himself mainly with foreign affairs. His cabinet advisers in this field were Secretary of State William P. Rogers, a successful lawyer, and Secretary of Defense Melvin R. Laird, a former congressman. Closer to the President was his personal adviser on matters of diplomacy, Henry Kissinger, a university scholar.

Early in his administration, Nixon took a fling at top-level diplomacy when he traveled to Southeast Asia and to Europe, stopping in Rumania as the first President to visit an "iron curtain" country. His European trip accomplished little except to show, through the popular reaction to it, that Americans for the moment were not greatly concerned about European questions. The people were more anxious about Vietnam policy, but the President's Asian travels produced only a series of ambiguous statements, except for promises of firm support to the generals' regime in South Vietnam. Meanwhile he sent Governor Nelson Rockefeller of New York as his personal representative on a fact-finding tour of Latin America. The main fact that Rockefeller found, as practically every visit touched off an anti-American riot, was the existence of strong popular hostility in that part of the world. Capitalizing upon this sentiment, new military governments in Peru and Bolivia seized the property of American corporations. Later in the year the President received as his official guest the head of the Israeli government, Prime Minister Golda Meir (who once had taught school in Milwaukee). Mrs. Meir requested additional warplanes for Israel to balance those that the Soviet Union was furnishing the Arab nations, as sporadic fighting continued between Israel and her neighbors.

World peace still depended, as it had done since the start of the cold war, mainly on the relations between the Soviet Union and the United States, the two superpowers that were backing opposite sides in Vietnam, the Middle East, and elsewhere. The growing conflict between the Russians and the Chinese, as seen in repeated border clashes, suggested that the Soviet Union might have an increasing interest in an accommodation with the United States. At the same time, the economic strains, social tensions, and war weariness in this country led many Americans to renew their demands for a detente with the Soviet Union.

A necessary first step toward such a detente would be an agreement on the limitation of nuclear arms. The two superpowers were engaged in a "doomsday game" of competition in the development of new weapons and new delivery systems. Both nations were testing the MIRV (multiple independently targeted reentry vehicle), a device that could be sent into orbit and then directed back into the earth's atmosphere above the enemy's territory, where it would drop separate nuclear warheads on widely scattered targets. In June 1969 the Republican Senator Edward Brooke of Massachusetts led thirty-nine colleagues of both parties in sponsoring a resolution that called upon the American government to halt its development of the MIRV on the condition that the Russian government would do the same.

The Nixon administration meanwhile carried ahead plans for the construction of an ABM (antiballistic missile) system, which was intended to protect the United States from attack by ICBMs (intercontinental ballistic missiles). In the ABM system, nuclear "antimissile missiles" would be launched to intercept and explode approaching enemy missiles before these could reach their targets. Originally the administration planned to locate the ABMs near popu-

lation centers to protect the large cities, but this aroused strong objections from people who feared the ABMs as a terrible potential hazard in themselves.

The administration then modified the plan so as to reduce the number of ABM installations and to locate them in thinly populated areas—beginning on the northern Great Plains—as a means of protecting the nation's own ICBM launching sites. Opposition again arose. Congressmen were already exposing flagrant cases of extravagance and waste in military procurement. Critics of the ABM proposal denounced this as another expensive and useless project of the military. They maintained that it would be ineffective even against enemy ICBMs to say nothing of MIRVs. They also argued that it would antagonize the Soviet Union (which already had installed a comparatively primitive ABM system around Moscow) and thus jeopardize the chances for a Russian-American agreement to limit nuclear arms. Defense Secretary Laird defended the plan against all criticisms while hinting darkly at the "first-strike" capabilities and intentions of the Soviet Union. President Nixon, making the issue a test of his leadership, used all his resources of patronage and persuasion to induce Congress to approve the plan. Apparently he eased the pressure for school desegregation in order to get Southern support. He finally obtained legislation for beginning ABM construction, though the Senate concurred by the majority of only a single vote.

The long awaited Russian-American arms discussions finally began on November 17, 1969, in Helsinki, Finland. Secretary of State Rogers said the United States was seriously interested in curbing the competition in nuclear armaments, and he thought the Russians also were. But he cautioned: "We should not confuse a beginning with success."

## A Way Out of Vietnam?

Regarding Vietnam, President Nixon said in May 1969 that he hoped to achieve "a peace we can live with and a peace to be proud of." He did not specify the kind of peace he had in mind, but presumably it would be one that kept in power the anti-Communist generals' regime of Saigon. Whatever the details, his kind of peace like Lyndon B. Johnson's remained unacceptable to the Ho Chi Minh government of Hanoi. In Paris the talks went on—among the representatives of the United States, South Vietnam, North Vietnam, and the National Liberation Front—but rumors of progress toward a settlement proved disappointing again and again. In South Vietnam the fighting continued, and by early 1970 American casualties totaled over 40,000 dead and 300,000 wounded—exceeding the number of American casualties in World War I. The demise of Ho Chi Minh, late in the summer, had no visible effect on either the Paris negotiations or the Vietnam bloodshed.

After Nixon had taken office the war's critics in the United States remained rather quiet for a time. They were willing to wait and see what would come of his plan for ending the war, the plan he had hinted at but had not revealed while campaigning for the Presidency. As the months passed and no end to the fighting appeared in sight, "Johnson's war" began to be looked upon as "Nixon's war," and its critics in Congress and throughout the country grew in number and in determination. By the summer's end an opinion poll showed a clear majority of the people judging the involvement in Vietnam a mistake. Youthful peace advocates, former campaigners for Eugene McCarthy, were planning a series of nationwide "Vietnam moratorium" demonstrations to occupy one day in October, two days in November, three in December, and so on until the war was over. Nixon turned opinion in favor of his Vietnam policy, however, by a televised speech on November 3, 1969. He said the "silent majority" agreed with him that a "precipitate withdrawal" would be disastrous for the "future of peace." Vice President Agnew afterwards gave a series of blunt speeches in which he denounced the peace demonstrators as an "effete corps of impudent snobs" and criticized newspaper and television commentators for questioning the Nixon policy. By the end of the year, opinion polls indicated that most Americans were willing to wait somewhat longer for the policy's results.

Meanwhile, Nixon was making concessions to the opponents of the war. In June 1969 he announced the beginning of partial troop withdrawals, which he said would reduce by 60,000, within a few months, the United States force of about 540,000 men in Vietnam. These withdrawals, he explained, were steps toward the "Vietnamization" of the war. That is, the South Vietnamese themselves would be trained and equipped to take over the defense of their country as the American fighting men were gradually pulled out.

Nixon also sought to lessen opposition by reforming the draft, which because of its uncertainties and inequities added to the difficulty of justifying the bloodshed in Vietnam. To its critics, the draft seemed all the worse because of the high-handed way in which it was administered by General Lewis Hershey, who had been director of the Selective Service System since its founding in 1941. Hershey persisted in advising local draft boards to punish antiwar demonstrators by conscripting them, even after a federal court had held this to be illegal. (Early in 1970 the Supreme Court declared it unconstitutional.) Nixon announced the removal of Hershey and recommended to Congress that the conscription law be changed to provide for a "draft lottery" that would take only nineteen-year-olds and would take them at random on a national basis. A draft lottery went into effect at the beginning of 1970.

The American people were further reassured when, in April 1970, the President informed them that his Vietnamization plan was going well and that, within a year or so, he would bring home 150,000 additional men. Suddenly, just ten days later, he broke the startling news that he had ordered American troops to cross into neutral Cambodia and, in cooperation with their South Vietnamese allies, to seize military bases that the enemy had been using for operations in South Vietnam. He explained that "increased military aggression" in Cambodia had begun to jeopardize the continuing success of the Vietnamization program.

All at once the languishing peace movement in the United States came to life with a more desperate and determined spirit than ever. On campuses all over the country, during May, youthful protesters demanded that the universities close down in a "strike" against the government's war policy. A radical minority resorted to violence, smashing windows and fire-bombing buildings. Policemen and national guardsmen arrived to face rock-throwing mobs, which they tried to disperse with tear gas and, in a few instances, with gunfire. Four students (all white) were shot and killed at Kent State University in Ohio, and two (both black) at Jackson State University in Mississippi. Opposition to the Cambodian venture spread far beyond the academic communities, though there were also demonstrations in support of the Nixon policy, especially on the part of New York City construction workers.

On the eve of a peace rally to be held in Washington, Nixon declared at a nationally televised news conference: "Those who protest want peace. I know that what I have done will accomplish the goals that they want." He promised to withdraw the American ground forces from Cambodia by the end of June. But his assurances failed to satisfy Senate leaders, including some members of his own party, who resented his failure to consult the Senate before sending troops beyond the South Vietnamese border. Congressional opponents of the war, headed by J. William Fulbright, chairman of the Senate foreign relations committee, renewed their efforts to limit the President's war-making power. They concentrated on proposals to repeal the 1964 Gulf on Tonkin resolution (which

had served as authorization for escalating the war) and to cut off funds for continuing Cambodian operations after the time limit that Nixon himself had set.

Even if these operations were to end on schedule, and even if troop withdrawals from Vietnam were to be speeded up, the prospects for real peace in Southeast Asia would remain rather dim. In neighboring Laos the United States was using its air force, though reportedly no ground troops as yet, in an anti-Communist campaign that paralleled the one in Vietnam. Next door to Laos, in Thailand, the United States maintained a strong military presence. In South Korea, sixteen years after the signing of the truce at Panmunjom, 55,000 American soldiers were still stationed. The North Koreans engaged them in continual border skirmishes and occasionally took more provocative action, such as the seizure of the American spy ship *Pueblo* (in 1968) and the shooting down of an American observation plane (in 1969). According to the United States Army Chief of Staff, General William Westmoreland, a renewal of the Korean War was "certainly a possibility."

# Selected Readings

**Diplomacy in General** Seyom Brown, *The Faces of Power: Constancy and Change in United States Foreign Policy from Truman to Johnson* (1968); Gabriel Kolko, *The Roots of American Foreign Policy: An Analysis of Power and Purpose* (1969), a radical view; Crane Brinton, *The Americans and the French* (1968).

**Foreign Aid** E. S. Mason, *Foreign Aid and Foreign Policy* (1964); D. A. Baldwin, *Economic Development and American Foreign Policy, 1943–1962* (1966); M. K. O'Leary, *The Politics of American Foreign Aid* (1967); W. D. Rogers, *The Twilight Struggle: The Alliance for Progress and the Politics of Development in Latin America* (1967).

**Cuba and Santo Domingo** H. B. Johnson, *The Bay of Pigs* (1964); Elie Abel, *The Missile Crisis* (1966); Henry Pachter, *Collision Course* (1963), on the missile crisis; J. B. Martin, *Overtaken by Events* (1966), on the Dominican intervention;

Dan Kurzman, *Santo Domingo: Revolt of the Damned* (1966).

**Vietnam** David Halberstam, *The Making of a Quagmire* (1956); M. G. Raskin and B. B. Fall, eds., *The Vietnam Reader* ° (1965); J. W. Fulbright, ed., *The Vietnam Hearings* ° (1966); R. N. Goodwin, *Triumph or Tragedy: Reflections on Vietnam* (1966); G. M. Kahin and J. W. Lewis, *The United States in Vietnam* (1967); A. M. Schlesinger, Jr., *The Bitter Heritage: Vietnam and American Democracy, 1941–1966* (1967); Robert Shaplen, *Time Out of Hand: Revolution and Reaction in Southeast Asia* (1969).

**Recent Politics** Stewart Alsop, *The Center: People and Power in Political Washington* (1968); T. H. White, *The Making of a President, 1968* (1969).

---

°Titles available in paperback.

# Chapter 30
# Entering the
# Space Age

On Sunday, July 20, 1969, slowly, cautiously, a white-clad figure climbed down from his spacecraft and extended a heavy, well-insulated boot toward the surface of the moon, while hundreds of millions of people throughout the world followed his movements on television or radio. As the astronaut, Neil Armstrong, placed both feet on the strange, finely powdered lunar soil, he said: "That's one small step for a man, one giant leap for mankind." A human being was standing where none had ever stood before—on land beyond the earth. A new age of interplanetary exploration had begun.

Most Americans rejoiced in the event as a triumph for humanity in general and for the United States in particular. "In a thousand years there will be few things remembered," a physicist predicted, "but this will be one of them." A political scientist disagreed. "It's a very proud and fine day for all Americans," he said, "but it's an event apart from the main flow of history." And there were other voices of dissent. Some Americans, especially among those of African ancestry, argued that the billions of dollars spent on traveling to the moon might better have been used for eliminating poverty from the earth. A Black Panther leader, Eldridge Cleaver, from his exile in Algeria, dismissed the lunar voyage as "a circus to distract people's minds from the real problems, which are here on the ground."

Certainly the moon landing, the result of cooperative effort by thousands of scientists and technicians, provided a spectacular illustration of what sociologists call "cultural lag," that is, the failure of social and political development to keep up with technological advances. Man was acquiring the ability to visit other worlds before he had the capacity to put his own in order, with peace and plenty for its inhabitants. Another example of cultural lag was the exploitation of nuclear energy with no adequate arrangement of human power to control it. Still other examples were to be found in new production techniques that brought the promise of greater abundance and leisure without assuring that these benefits would be well-distributed and without making sufficient provision for the protection of the natural environment. Improvements in communication—the spread of the "mass media," especially television—only made the masses of the people even more aware of the stark contrast between affluence and poverty. Humanity needed inventions and achievements in society and government that would match those in science and technology.

This had been the main challenge of the nineteenth and twentieth centuries, and all signs indicated that it would be still more urgent in the twenty-first century. Many of the country's leaders-to-be of the year 2000 were already in school or college. The future would be largely up to them.

---

### ". . . One Giant Leap for Mankind"

Astronaut Edwin "Buzz" Aldrin poses for a historic portrait photographed by the Apollo 11 Commander, Neil Armstrong. The surrealism of the fiction-like spacesuit and the starkness of the moon's landscape are brought to life by the astronauts' footprints and the reflection of the photographer and the lunar module as seen in Aldrin's visor. (NASA)

## THE CROWDING COUNTRY

In 1967 the demographic clock of the Census Bureau officially passed the 200 million mark, quite possibly the population had actually reached that figure several years earlier. Contrary to the predictions in the depression years of the thirties, the population in the decades since World War II had not moved toward a level of stabilization, but had increased rapidly. Affluent Americans married younger and had larger families. There was such a baby boom that pessimists predicted that within 800 years, at the rate of population growth in the 1950s, each American would have only one square foot of land upon which to stand. Then, in the 1960s, the birth rate dropped rapidly until it was somewhat below the depression percentage, at a level that would lead to moderate rather than spectacular growth in population. In contrast, the world population was growing at an explosive rate, which could be of serious consequence for the United States. In many of the developing nations population increases were offsetting whatever economic gains American aid might stimulate.

### Levels of Living

Within the United States people did not face famine or even a decline in living standards, but rather a lowering of the quality of life. As the sociologist Dennis H. Wrong pointed out, "the costs of American population growth are traffic jams, spreading urban and suburban blight, the overcrowding and destruction of beaches, parks and other outdoor recreational facilities, water shortages, air pollution, deterioration in professional and social services resulting from shortages of trained personnel."

For an increasing proportion of Americans, the city or suburbs rather than the country was home. The migration from farms, which had been so heavy for decades, intensified. While 7.5 million people moved to cities during the wartime decade of the forties, nearly 10 million more followed during the fifties. During the 1950s the number of farms decreased by one-third. A second shift in population was from the central sections of the big cities into the suburbs. In 1920, there were twice as many city

dwellers as suburbanites; by 1960 the numbers were almost equal. There was also a westward shift in people, dramatized by the emergence of California as the most populous state.

The occupations of Americans were likewise shifting from agricultural and unskilled labor toward skilled and professional work. Since 1900, the proportion of farmers had dwindled to a sixth, of manual laborers, to a half. The percentage of white-collar workers more than doubled, and of professional men, nearly tripled.

Most Americans were enjoying a living standard far beyond any they had previously known. The output of goods and services had more than doubled since the 1920s. Even allowing for inflation and heavy taxation, the average person was better off than ever before. Family income had more than tripled since the boom year 1918. Many statistics indicated the affluence of the American people, yet there was still substantial poverty. The Conference of Economic Progress, reporting in 1962 on a study by Leon H. Keyserling, an economist, asserted:

"An American family living on less than $4,000 per year is in a state of poverty and an American family living on less than $6,000 per year is in a state of deprivation. For unrelated individuals, under $2,000 constitutes poverty and under $3,000 is considered deprivation. When that definition is overlaid on an income distribution based on 1960 data, 77 million Americans—roughly 40% of the population—lived in either poverty or deprivation. Specifically, in 1960, 38 million lived in poverty, 39 million in deprivation."

Labor's share in the national income rose from 18 per cent in 1929 to 29 per cent by 1956, while the average workweek decreased from forty-four to forty hours. Counting such benefits as liberal vacations and paid holidays, the industrial worker enjoyed fifteen or twenty hours a week more free time than his father or grandfather had at the turn of the century. Unlike them, upon retirement he could look forward to a pension; welfare and pension plans had increased twentyfold since 1929. Because of their higher income, workers were spending a smaller percentage of their wages for food, clothing, and housing, and more for automobiles, medical care, recreation, and vacations. Although mil-

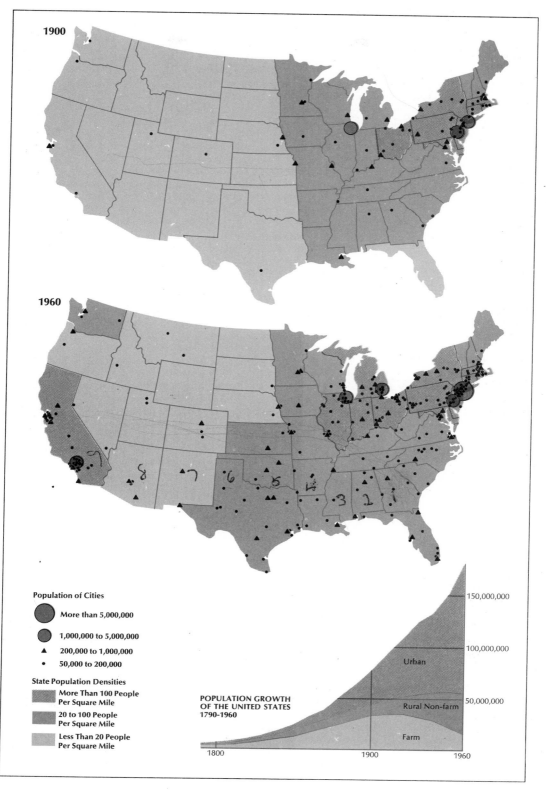

**1900**

**1960**

**Population of Cities**

- ⬤ More than 5,000,000
- ● 1,000,000 to 5,000,000
- ▲ 200,000 to 1,000,000
- • 50,000 to 200,000

**State Population Densities**

- More Than 100 People Per Square Mile
- 20 to 100 People Per Square Mile
- Less Than 20 People Per Square Mile

**POPULATION GROWTH OF THE UNITED STATES 1790-1960**

150,000,000

100,000,000

Urban

50,000,000

Rural Non-farm

Farm

1800     1900     1960

**Population Density of the United States 1900 and 1960**

lions of families lived in poverty and deprivation, 93 per cent of American homes (1964) contained television sets, and almost 60 per cent of families with incomes less than $4,000 (1960) owned automobiles.

The movement of women into employment continued. Since the turn of the century they had been entering the working force in increasing numbers. In 1900, half the women in the United States had never held jobs in their lives; by the 1950s, one-third of all females over fourteen were working and nine-tenths had worked at one time or another. Between 1950 and 1964, while the number of employed men increased only 8 per cent, the number of employed women jumped 39 per cent. In 1900, only one clerical worker in four was a woman; by the 1960s, two out of three were women. Although women were filling an increasing number of professional positions, they still were not being trained in keeping with their potentialities. Only a quarter of those capable of finishing college were doing so; only 1 in 300 of those qualified was earning a Ph.D. The old-fashioned career woman, refusing marriage, was nearly gone; only 7 per cent of women failed to marry. Increasing numbers of married women worked, especially after their children entered school or were grown. The modern counterpart of the girls who had worked before marriage in the Lowell textile mills of the 1830s were the airline hostesses of the 1960s; on one of the largest airlines they stayed an average of only 26 months, and 85 per cent of them left to be married.

## The Rise of the Megalopolis

The rapid growth of metropolitan areas intensified and developed new ramifications. In several parts of the United States these areas began to expand until they met one another. From north of Boston to south of Washington, a megalopolis was coming into being; the future outlines of several others were already discernible. The concentration of population in these areas would make the problems of housing, pollution, and transportation even more acute. Increasing size was intensifying these problems faster than answers could be devised.

The proper governing of these areas was a key problem since many solutions seemed likely to come only through state or federal intervention and aid. States had continued to legislate extensively for metropolitan areas, but increasingly as federal programs developed, more important relationships developed directly between cities and the federal government. Adding infinitely to the complications was the white escape beyond city jurisdictions and tax collectors to the suburbs. Even while the Negro ghettos were expanding rapidly in the major cities, necessitating drastic financial aid, the tax base of the cities was growing only slowly or even declining.

Because individual metropolitan problems transcended city and sometimes state lines, special governmental authorities to deal with matters like harbor development or transit had often come into existence. Together with traditional governments they led to a multiplicity of governmental agencies. Within the 212 standard metropolitan areas in the 1960s there were some 18,000 units of government, ranging from counties to school boards. There was little cooperation among them: most of these governments were ready to give little or no aid to the ailing cities. Many state, county, and suburban officials resisted the establishment of the federal Department of Housing and Urban Development, even though in 1961 President Kennedy had pointed out to Congress: "The city and its suburbs are interdependent parts of a single community, bound together by the web of transportation and other public facilities and by common economic interests. Bold programs in individual jurisdictions are no longer enough. Increasingly, community development must be a cooperative venture toward the common goals of the metropolitan region as a whole."

To some authorities the solutions to the metropolitan governmental problems seemed to lie in cooperation among the numerous local governmental units rather than in their centralization. There was a traditional abhorrence to running everything from Washington, yet local programs

**Two Kitchens**

Nothing illustrates more sharply the contrasting ways of life among the American people than these two kitchens of the late 1960s. (Top right, *House Beautiful;* bottom right, Department of Real Estate, The City of New York)

depended heavily upon federal aid. From Washington might come the funds; from local units or even committees, democratically run by the poor as well as the middle class, might come the administration. One of Nixon's advisers, Daniel P. Moynihan, suggested: "The diffusion of the middle-class ideal of participation in public decision-making will add a considerable and, in a sense, unanticipated utility to the complexity of the American government structure, which requires such great citizen participation in order to operate. . . . To the extent that the many small units of government in the present system represent genuine interests, the skill and energy with which those interests are sure to be defended by a middle-class electorate are such as to suggest further that there will be a minimum of consolidation."

The problems with which the citizens of the metropolis and the emerging megalopolis had to grapple were those long faced by city dwellers: improvement of housing, transportation, living conditions, educational and cultural opportunities, and above all the economic base for both the family and community; conversely, the elimination of pollution, blight, crime, and violence. The size of the new metropolitan areas made these problems far larger and sometimes more complex than in earlier generations. Simple solutions often did not exist; tentative beginnings were sometimes too small to be effective and often had to be modified as experience pointed in different directions.

Federally sponsored housing, which had originated three decades earlier in the New Deal era, together with the urban renewal programs developed after World War II, were good examples. Proponents of housing hoped through combining public and private funds to wipe out the blighted core of the metropolis; erect beautiful, modern structures; and in addition provide comfortable housing that families of varying incomes could afford. Much was achieved, but reality sometimes ran counter to the dream.

Federal aid in one form or another had helped make possible the vast growth of suburbia since 1945—and then the white exodus from cities into suburbs. By 1963, 5 million families owned houses built with FHA aid; millions more lived in houses financed through the GI Bill of Rights.

Federal guarantees had helped 27 million home owners to borrow money for repairs. The government encouraged the deposit of money in savings and loan associations which issued millions of mortgages, by insuring the deposits.

## Urban Renewal and Reform

Simultaneously with the growth of suburbs, attempts were made to rejuvenate decaying central cities through federal aid. Urban renewal projects were to transform slums into business and cultural areas and above all into attractive apartment complexes. The new buildings were expected to bring a fivefold increase in taxes, thus helping to solve urban financial problems.

A small beginning during the New Deal had involved federal clearing of slums and construction of public housing. From 1937 on, the federal government helped cities in the undertaking. The 1949 legislation provided for a bold departure. The federal government would help cities finance the purchase of slum land, which would then be sold to private entrepreneurs at reduced costs. Federal loans or mortgage insurance gave these builders a further profit incentive. Thus private enterprise would be persuaded to rebuild the cities.

For five years the program made little progress and thereafter seemed most effective in producing profits for the entrepreneurs. There were numerous complaints that it was the land where the poorest people (often Negroes) lived that was being taken over, and that these people seldom received adequate housing elsewhere at rents they could afford. Sometimes land was cleared and left idle for years while builders were sought. Sometimes the new construction was a complex of luxury apartments, as in the West End of Boston. In *The Federal Bulldozer* (1964), Martin Anderson, an urban expert who became a Nixon adviser in 1968, enumerated all of the defects of the urban renewal program and called for its repeal. On the contrary, Charles Abrams, another urban specialist, suggested, "What the program needs is amplification, not abolition, a complementary housing program to make it workable, and an enlargement of its basic concept to do what its name implies."

Beautification, cleanliness, and safety were

**Some Favorable Aspects
of Metropolitan Development**

*The American urban pattern, in which
cities merge in great metropolitan
belts, developed as a consequence of
the efforts of economically free agents
to maximize profits and amenities. In
North America, therefore, the city is
especially an economic entity. The
American city is free, in an economic
if not a political sense, to push its
boundaries outward. It can preserve a
kind of density balance in which individuals' preferences for space are
accommodated and technology is used
both to concentrate a high intensity
of activities and to disperse places of
residence. Given the extraordinary
heterogeneity of the American population, it is possible that the sprawling
development of American cities has
actually relieved tension and reduced
intergroup conflict by substituting a
stratified spatial order for a genuine
social accommodation.—John W.
Dyckman, ''Some Conditions of Civic
Order in an Urbanized World,'' Daedalus, Summer 1966, p. 800.*

also problems requiring community and even
national action. Cities in an affluent society produced ever-increasing quantities of waste. Keeping streets and vacant lots clean was relatively
simple compared with disposing of the innumerable tons of sewage, garbage, and trash. In 1920
the average person threw away less than 3
pounds of refuse per day; by the mid-sixties he
was discarding 4.5 pounds. Urban and industrial
waste had turned many of the nation's rivers into
huge sewers; Lake Erie, for example, was called
the most polluted body of water in the world.
Pollution of the air by industries, automobiles,
incinerators, and burning dumps created acute
smog hazards in widespread areas. An estimated
360,000 tons a day of gaseous waste were spew-
ing into the atmosphere.

Control of pollution was possible, but not
politically popular. Of 7,300 communities suffering from air pollution, in 1965 only 90 had what
the Public Health Service considered substantial
control programs. Only about 20 communities
were spending as much as the 35 cents a person
per year that seemed the minimum for an adequate program. Yet control depended primarily
upon community action, backed by limited federal aid. The Clean Air Acts of 1963 and 1965
asserted federal jurisdiction only over interstate
pollution and control of automobile exhaust
fumes. The price of clean air did not seem prohibitively high. Gladwin Hill, a newspaperman,
estimated that the entire program for the Los
Angeles area in controlling car fumes, trash
burning, and industrial pollutants averaged only
$3 a year per capita over a decade.

Water pollution posed similar problems. Allied to all pollution was the need for better
means of disposing of wastes. A few communities were experimenting with the transformation
of waste into salable products: fly ash from incinerators as an ingredient for concrete, the manufacture of fertilizer from garbage and sewage,
and the retrieval of metals from dumps. Future
solutions should be no more impossible than
those earlier urbanities had to devise. Richard
Neutra points out: "Plans for public garbage
collection, incineration, and elaborate sewage
disposal first appeared as doctrinary, idealistic
dreams conceived in a vacuum of any possible
'financial facts' and altogether devoid of practical sense. . . . The most ordinary sewer systems
of today would have seemed like black fantastic
nightmares to the taxpayers of only one hundred
years ago."

Maintenance of safety also was a continuation of an old problem that each generation
faced anew, as appalled as though crime, delinquency, and violence were recent innovations.
It became a national political issue in the presidential campaign of 1964, particularly among
conservatives who objected to the decisions of
the Supreme Court protecting the civil rights of
those accused of crimes. *Uniform Crime Reports*
published by the FBI showed the crime rates increasing year by year. In 1967 the President's
Commission on Crime declared that there was
far more crime than ever reported to the police
—three times as many burglaries, half again

**Air Pollution in New York**

In any major American city the camera could underscore what gauges recorded: the serious pollution of the air, especially troublesome on windless days when an atmospheric inversion (a blanket of warmer air several hundred feet up) kept the pollutants from being dispersed. (New York *Daily News*)

more robberies, double the number of assaults. In 1965 more than 2 million offenders entered prison or juvenile training schools. Since a disproportionately large number of crimes were committed by youth, and the number of young people in the population was rising rapidly, crime statistics were likely to rise also. Inflation was also a factor in the continued rise in the number of larcenies over the figure of $50, set by law long before when it was a far more serious amount of money.

The public was so crime-conscious, the commission reported, that, "The existence of crime, the talk about crime, the reports of crime, and the fear of crime have eroded the basic quality of life of many Americans." The Commission on Crime suggested numerous means of reducing crime, ranging from the prevention of social conditions that led to crime to the better administration of justice. Nevertheless, some specialists were not sure that per capita crime rates had really risen. They did not doubt that crime rates were high, but were also skeptical whether any substantial reduction in crime could be achieved. As the commission made clear, the causes of crime grew out of the flaws in America's free society. Consequently, crime was likely to continue to worry Americans, and it might become a substantial political issue.

## Transportation

Another urban headache was transportation. Increasingly older modes of conveyance deteriorated; streetcars, which had taken over America in the early years of the twentieth century, almost completely disappeared, to be supplanted by buses or additional subways. Transit lines, unable to meet rising costs with revenues that failed to keep pace, faced bankruptcy; government-owned systems ran heavier and heavier deficits. Between 1955 and 1965 the number of riders on public transit lines declined 25 per cent. Railroads, to cut losses, tried to drop commuter services. The number of passengers commuting by train declined 45 per cent between 1929 and 1963. City dwellers and suburbanites depended more and more upon automobiles, which were quicker and more convenient.

**Urban Transportation
[1907–1966]**

*In 1907 it was found that the average
speed of horse-drawn vehicles through
the city's streets was 11.5 miles per
hour. In 1966 the average speed of
motor vehicles through the central
business district was 8.5 miles per
hour—and during the mid-day crushes
slower still.—A. E. Palmer, Jr., New
York City Transportation Administrator, before a Senate subcommittee,
November 16, 1967.*

But automobiles required six to forty-five times
more space on highways per passenger than did
buses, and multiple-unit rail cars were even
more efficient.

While public transportation languished, the
federal government helped subsidize the building of 6,000 miles of expressways; this forced
the leveling of countless blocks of urban buildings (including a disproportionate amount of
poor peoples' housing), and other buildings were
leveled to provide parking lots. As a consequence, still more automobiles poured into the
cities, compounding traffic problems and, during
public transportation strikes, creating chaos. An
opposite approach at both the local and federal
level was to try to improve public transit or even
to develop new systems as, most spectacularly,
in the San Francisco Bay region. In 1966 Congress created a new Department of Transportation.

National transportation problems were interrelated, as railroad passenger service rapidly
declined, and trucks became an increasingly important factor in carrying freight. The large-
scale program of turnpike building that marked
the first decade after World War II came to an
end as thousands of miles of toll-free super-
highways were built, beginning with the Interstate Highway Act of 1956, which set standards
for the roads (no grade crossings, for example)

and provided federal funds for 90 per cent of
the cost. For public transportation, Americans
had to depend either upon buses or airlines.

By the mid-fifties, airlines, which had been
luxury transportation before World War II,
were carrying over 30 million passengers per
year; by the mid-sixties, the figure had nearly
quadrupled and was expected to double again
within a decade. Especially along the northeast
coast, the air lanes were so crowded that at
the height of the evening rush, about 100 planes
would be landing or about to land at the three
major New York area airports, while another 250
private planes were also taking off or landing at
these and smaller fields. Despite an occasional
collision, and numerous near-collisions, the airlines were able to boast a remarkable safety record. But the congestion of people at the major
airports worsened with the appearance, in 1970,
of the "jumbo jet" carrying more than twice as
many passengers as any previous airliner.

For the future, when airlines might not be
able to meet the passenger demands along the
northeast corridor between Washington and
Boston, the federal government was fostering
high-speed train service which it hoped ultimately would carry passengers at 160 miles an
hour. The Metroliner, with a speed of 120 miles
an hour, was operating between New York and
Washington by 1969. There might be a future
along a few congested routes for rail passenger
service of this sort.

## LEISURE AND LEARNING

Never had so many people participated so fully
and enthusiastically in the arts. Patronage of the
arts flourished—attendance at the theater, concerts, and exhibitions increased, and participation in theatrical and musical groups and "Sunday painting" also became more popular. Sales
in paperback of both good books and the most
popular, of original paintings and reproductions,
and of inexpensive phonograph records from
classics to rock-'n'-roll, all mounted astronomically.

Government offered its formal sponsorship
and some slight aid to the arts through the establishment in 1966 of the Federal Arts and
Humanities Endowments and a Federal Council

on the Arts. Each state established its own council or commission on the arts, and some of them, like the federal government, made substantial grants. Private foundations continued to be even more substantial benefactors.

## Television

Television changed the leisure habits of the American people, made them better informed on the news and issues of the day, and even modified the patterns of American politics. In 1947 fewer than 10,000 people owned television sets with which they could view programs a few hours a day from a handful of stations. A decade later over 40 million sets in homes, hotels, and bars were tuned in to 467 stations. Motion picture attendance dropped from a wartime high of 90 million a week to about 40 million. Not until the sixties did Hollywood begin to recuperate, by producing pictures that were better than before, or at least bolder.

Television even more than radio meant mass communication to a nationwide audience. One musical show, telecast on 245 stations one night in March 1957 reached an estimated audience of 100 million—enough people to fill a Broadway theater every night for 165 years. Beginning with the 1952 campaign, television remade presidential elections as candidates began to make extensive and expensive use of the new medium. Radio was far from superseded, especially in the transistorized portable form that took over not only the United States but the entire world during these years. Within the United States, CBS found, 98.1 per cent of those over eighteen listened to the radio.

Advertisers paid for the vast outpouring from commercial television and radio stations. They spent enormous sums to compete for the attention of the average television viewer who, surveys indicated, sat in front of his set as much as six hours a day. The manufacturers of one headache remedy, for example, spent nearly $750,000 in one month in 1958; their two nearest competitors spent a combined total of nearly $1 million that same month. In consequence, programs were patterned to draw the largest number of viewers, and when surveys indicated that the sets were tuned in elsewhere, the programs were ruthlessly pruned. One critic, Richard

Schickel, commented that to literate people, television was "an unparalleled purveyor of trash," nevertheless "we sit there, eyes glued to the set, watching this explication of the obvious in hateful fascination." A Canadian scholar, Marshall McLuhan, won a large following by extolling in confusing but thought-provoking prose the new era of mass media.

Foundations and the federal government tried to further the positive role of television. The Carnegie and Ford foundations suggested that educational stations be substantially expanded as a means of furthering the great educational and cultural potential of the medium. Congress in 1967 enacted the Public Broadcasting Act, which authorized but did not finance a noncommercial television network. President Johnson in signing the measure expressed his hope that out of it would come a marshaling of technology to establish by means of computers and satellites an electronic "network of knowledge" not only for the United States but for most of the world. Already, educational television stations from coast to coast were demonstrating through their production of good theater, distinguished musical performances, and high-level lecture courses what the potential of television might be.

Commercial television at times triumphed in special programs prepared with lavish budgets. Its comprehensive news coverage and analysis, often emphasizing violence, at its best was far-ranging and thorough in its presentation of background. Television for better or worse was the great outlet for the newly acquired leisure of many people; it was also the most important factor in keeping Americans better informed than ever before and in molding their attitudes.

## Music

Music flourished in variety and abundance. The composer Virgil Thomson once commented, "The United States is the one country in all the world that produces all the kinds of music that there are. Only here do composers write in every possible style and does the public have access to every style."

Just as jazz had developed out of humble origins, so after World War II, rock-'n'-roll grew out of a rediscovery of folk songs. American youth neglected the piano for the guitar and by the millions became devotees of the new music, modifying it from the folk songs made popular by Woody Guthrie, Pete Seeger, and others. As it was transformed into rock-'n'-roll, the intense beat almost drowned out the lyrics—words that often took the form of protest against war, poverty, and the older generation.

Much semiclassical and classical music continued, as in the thirties, to grow out of American themes. Many of the most prestigious composers had made their reputations then, producing works that remained in the repertoire of symphony orchestras and chamber music groups. Aaron Copland's music, combining European techniques and American themes, continued to be popular; little of Roy Harris' work was heard, except for his Third Symphony. Walter Piston, Samuel Barber, Virgil Thomson, and Roger Sessions, all differing in their styles, were laden with honors.

New energy and direction came into postwar music through the influence of European composers, who had fled to America during the years of Nazi ascendancy. Arnold Schönberg, who arrived in 1931, brought the twelve-tone system.

Paul Hindemith and Kurt Weill, whose music had been banned in Germany, Igor Stravinsky, Béla Bartók, and Darius Milhaud all came to America and made their contributions to the development of younger composers. None of these had emerged to unquestioned preeminence by the sixties, but many had achieved solid reputations and might ultimately, like Charles Ives, appear to have been giants in their time. Many were atonalists of the Schönberg school; some were traditionalists; and some were eclectic, seeking still newer directions. One of the most energetic of the experimenters was John Cage, born in 1912, who worked beyond the twelve-tone scale by modifying pianos and developing new instruments to produce percussive sounds. Others experimented with tape recorders and electronic devices.

Ambitious composers sought to write original American operas, but few of these survived beyond initial performances. A notable Negro composer, William Grant Still, working with the music of his race, together with the Negro poet Langston Hughes as librettist, wrote *Troubled Island* (1938), an opera set in Haiti. The New

**The Robert Joffrey Ballet**

By the end of the 1960s a number of brilliant young companies were bringing both technical perfection and innovation to American ballets. (Isadora Bennett)

York City Center produced it in 1949. The most successful composer of operas was Gian Carlo Menotti, who wrote *The Medium* in 1947 and *The Consul* in 1950. NBC commissioned him to write an opera for television, *Amahl and the Night Visitors:* it was so successful that it has been replayed every Christmas season since the initial 1951 appearance. Musical comedies seemed to be the most successful American medium, perhaps the answer to the quest for popular opera. Every few years a truly outstanding one made its appearance: *Oklahoma!* by Richard Rodgers and Oscar Hammerstein in 1943, *My Fair Lady* by Frederick Loewe and Alan Lerner in 1956, and *West Side Story* by Leonard Bernstein in 1957.

The major contribution of technical innovation to music was in the development of high-fidelity electronic recording at the opening of the forties and of stereophonic sound at the close of the decade. These opened the way to a mass distribution of inexpensive long-playing records. Together with television and both AM and FM radio, they provided good music to an audience vastly larger than that attending opera houses and concert halls.

American ballet broke away from classic traditions and developed beyond the spectacle into styles combining the most modern forms of music and the visual arts. Martha Graham, a vital figure in the 1930s, interweaving the old and the new, was still presenting new dances in the 1960s. Merce Cunningham, who left his company in 1944, worked with the composer John Cage to develop dances that broke as sharply with the past as did Cage's percussive music. Some young dancers carried their performances to the point at which they might best be labeled "happenings" or events. During the same years three distinguished ballet companies emerged: the New York City Ballet, which came to be established in new Lincoln Center; the American Ballet Theater, begun in 1939 and reorganized in 1959; and the Robert Joffrey group, which first went on tour in 1956.

## Art and Architecture

Art, especially painting, flourished, and to the pride of many critics, by 1955 seemed to be dominating the world as it drew from European sources and rushed into new directions. Abstract expressionism flourished, then gave way to the excitement over Pop and Op art. It was still a serious question whether these directions were leading to art of enduring greatness. Certainly they were in key with the times, reflecting the technical, mass production aspects of the age, and at times something of the detachment or alienation of postwar Americans. Pop art might be a satire on mass media, but perhaps it was only another manifestation of the media.

Modern architecture was finally ascendant in the postwar years. The indefatigable Frank Lloyd Wright, having survived decades of earlier vicissitudes, became a familiar public figure and even appeared on television. He designed many of his most important structures between the erection of the administration building for the Johnson Wax Company in 1939 and the completion of the Guggenheim Museum in the year of his death, 1959. Wright became increasingly sculptural and vigorous in his use of circles and whorls; the great spiral of the Guggenheim Museum seemed to some critics more a monument to the architect than a setting for art exhibits.

In the same years that the individualistic Wright came into his own, his great European contemporaries—Ludwig Mies van der Rohe, Walter Gropius, and Marcel Breuer—had moved to America, and soon they were making an even larger impact upon American architecture. Together with other Europeans they had evolved the so-called International style, which like Wright's was an acceptance of the machine, but differed in its emphasis upon geometric construction, the use of the clean line, and the refinement of parts. Buildings designed by Mies and those of his school came to dominate the skylines of many American cities and indeed of cities all over the world. Younger architects like Philip Johnson, Minoru Yamasaki, and Edward Stone moved toward Neoclassicism while others like Eero Saarinen strived to achieve elaborate free-flowing structures.

Office buildings, colleges, churches, homes, and even public buildings (except for those in federal Washington) began to appear in the new styles. They accounted for only a small part of what was being built, but by the sixties, as two historians of American architecture, John Bur-

## American Interest in the Arts

The interest of Americans in the arts became so widespread that it was a significant factor in the economy. Statistics give some indication of the dimensions of the interest. Between 1953 and 1960, expenditures on the arts rose by 130 per cent, totaling $3 billion. (By comparison, advertisers in 1964 spent $2.25 billion on television). Total expenditures on the arts were soaring toward $7 billion a year by the end of the sixties. Americans were spending twice as much on the arts as on recreation in general and six times as much as on sports. In 1964 they bought more than $1 billion in books; spent $600 million on musical instruments; $200 million on paintings, prints, color reproductions, and art supplies; nearly $400 million to attend plays, operas, and concerts; and $300 million to maintain art museums.

On the other hand, two Princeton economists, W. J. Baumol and W. G. Bowen, in *Performing Arts: The Economic Dilemma* (1966) presented detailed statistics to show that there was little boom in the performing arts, except for the rise in costs and deficits. The nation was supporting only five full-time symphony orchestras; increase in attendance was "slightly slower than the increase in population." Over half the receipts for theatrical performances and nearly 40 per cent of those for musical performances were paid in New York alone. Audiences were made up almost entirely of those in the upper educational and financial brackets, people of white-collar occupations.

chard and Albert Bush-Brown, pointed out, something useful had been achieved: "This was that Americans could now see superior examples of what good building could be in any part of the land. There was enough brilliant architecture

and it was widely enough distributed so that Americans could easily learn what they would be able to do if they ever got around to wanting to do it."

## Writing

The most prestigious figures in American writing were those who had made their reputations in earlier decades. Through the fifties, Ernest Hemingway and William Faulkner were two of the patriarchs of literature for the Western world as well as for the United States. Faulkner retained his master's touch in portraying the deep South he knew so well and through it viewing the world. Hemingway at times seemed to be parodying his earlier, virile, trenchant style, but produced one work in these years, *The Old Man and the Sea* (1952), that seemed destined to endure. It was the brief tale of an aged Cuban striving heroically, and unsuccessfully, to protect from the forays of the sharks a huge fish he had caught. The poet Robert Frost seemed already a legendary figure before his death in 1963. After Eugene O'Neill's death in 1953, several of his previously unproduced plays ran for months on Broadway and on national tours.

By the sixties all these men of great reputation were gone. A large new generation of vigorous writers was attracting attention, but it was too soon to be sure which if any of them would win enduring top reputations. Among the novelists, their work ranged from the realism of John O'Hara and James Gould Cozzens, portrayers of the upper middle class, whose work seemed old-fashioned to younger critics, through a variety of newer styles and themes. The work of Robert Penn Warren, who won the Pulitzer Prize both in poetry and fiction, transcended Southern regionalism, but his most widely read novel, *All the King's Men* (1946), was a study of a political leader resembling Huey Long of Louisiana. In 1948 Norman Mailer produced the most acclaimed of the novels that came out of World War II, *The Naked and the Dead*, but in his subsequent work was more successful as a writer of nonfiction. J. D. Salinger through his account of the inward torture of an adolescent boy, *Catcher in the Rye* (1951), and subsequent stories about the precocious members of the

Glass family (*Franny and Zooey*, 1962) became the spokesman for the generation of the 1950s. John Barth in *The Sot-Weed Factor* (1961) established himself as the master of the mock-picaresque novel.

Through the writings of several of the novelists ran a theme of alienation from, or at least serious questioning of, their culture. Saul Bellow began his work in this vein with *Dangling Man* (1944) and continued it in a number of successful novels, including *The Adventures of Augie March* (1953) and *Herzog* (1964). Nelson Algren, no admirer of middle-class values, wrote with blunt clarity about the flotsam of society, the men and women who had never had a chance, in his stories and novels, most notably, *The Man With the Golden Arm* (1949). Several Negro writers fell within this pattern. The most famous was James Baldwin, perhaps at his best in works of nonfiction like *The Fire Next Time* (1963); the most bitter, the poet and playwright, LeRoi Jones, especially effective in his one-act plays; and the most distinguished, Ralph Ellison, for a single novel, *Invisible Man* (1952). When the New York *Herald Tribune Book Week* in 1965 queried some 200 critics, authors, and editors, their consensus was that the work of fiction of the previous two decades most memorable and most likely to endure was *Invisible Man*. It is the sweeping, at times fantastic, drama of a young Negro's quest for identity. The novel that the critics listed second as most memorable was the polished social satire *Lolita* (1955) written by a Russian émigré, Vladimir Nabokov.

Poetry, like painting, broke sharply with traditions after 1945. While poets like Frost and Carl Sandburg enjoyed fame in their old age, the liberal activism that moved poets like Archibald MacLeish during the depression and war years subsided after 1945. The newer poets moved away from public causes, toward the psychological and mythological, as did Randall Jarrell, or toward the autobiographical or confessional, as did Robert Lowell. Through much of this poetry ran a distaste for the established order. One critic, M. L. Rosenthal, suggests: "Behind it is the feeling, perhaps, that the humanistic way, which traditionally educated and romantic modern men still propose to protect, and indeed to project into a Utopian future, has

already been defeated and is now no more than a ghost. It is that feeling which Robert Lowell in one of his poems calls, self-ironically, 'our universal *Angst*'—a heart-heavy realization that remorseless brutality is a condition not only of the physical universe but also of man himself."

## Youth and Education

The refusal to yield to a world they did not accept became the prevalent attitude of participants in youth movements not only in the United States but in other nations. Those young Americans growing up in poverty were alienated because they felt they could not share in the prosperity of the middle classes. Some of those from middle-class families, often given personal freedom and economic security by their parents, were uneasy because they could not or would not accept the standards of the adult world. A few of these even went so far as to reject most of the accepted values and to live in the fifties as "beatniks" or in the sixties as "hippies." In the sixties, student movements and revolts rocked universities throughout the world. Within the United States, attention focused on the uprising at the University of California at Berkeley and, several years later, at Columbia University. Students participating in these strikes sought to force the universities to modify their policies in various ways and at times demanded a continuing share in the determination of policies.

Intimately related to the unrest of youth, and transcending it, was the task of all responsible citizens to improve the schools of the nation and to provide for rapidly increasing enrollments. Federal aid to education, while significant, was making no more than a start in coping with the problem. Upgrading was under way from the elementary level through graduate school. More and more young people were going on to college, and college for considerable numbers seemed to function mainly as preparation for graduate training. A sociologist, David Riesman, surveying higher education, concluded in 1968 that it was coming to be dominated by the graduate schools. Only through providing better teaching could the faculty and administrators of colleges and universities meet the internal pressures leading to college uprisings.

## Memorandum on Youth

*I would assume that adolescents today and tomorrow are struggling to define new modes of conduct which are relevant to their lives. . . . Yet, this is within the context of two culture factors which seem to be extraordinary in the history of moral temper. One is the scepticism of all authority, the refusal to define natural authority (perhaps even that of paternal authority) and a cast of mind which is essentially anti-institutional and even antinomian. . . . The second factor is an extraordinary hedonism—using the word in the broadest sense—in that there is a desacralization of life and an attitude that all experience is permissible and even desirable. . . . At the same time society imposes new forms of specialization, of extending training, of new hierarchies and organizations. Thus, one finds an unprecedented divorce between culture and the society. And, from all indications, such a separation will increase. . . . In this respect, assuming this hypothesis is true, the greatest strains will be on the youth. This particular generation, like its predecessors, may come back to some form of accommodation with the society as it grows older and accepts positions within the society. But the experiences also leave a ''cultural deposit'' which is cumulative consciousness and—to this extent I am a Hegelian—is irreversible, and the next generation therefore starts from a more advanced position of alienation and detachment.—Erik H. Erikson, Daedalus, Summer 1967, pp. 860–863.*

In viewing the world, American youth, especially those in college, were less preoccupied with frivolities and more actively concerned with trying to bring constructive changes than preceding generations had been. They were more aware of the injustices and inadequacies within the United States and without and were seeking means of redress. More young people than ever before were becoming activists; more were devoting themselves to advanced training, since in the age of electronics and mass media, a time of continuing crises, the demands upon the new generation were likely to increase rather than diminish.

At the same time, a growing number of youth were retreating from a world they disliked, instead of trying to change it. They were "turning on" (or, more correctly, turning off) by smoking marijuana, taking "mind-expanding" chemicals such as LSD, or injecting themselves with narcotics such as heroin. Surveys in 1970 showed that drug use was spreading at an alarming rate not only among college students but also among high school boys and girls. The majority of high schools in affluent suburbs as well as poverty-stricken inner cities were said to have a "hard drug" (heroin) problem. Marijuana smoking was even more widespread. Youthful advocates of marijuana claimed that it was less harmful than the tobacco and alcohol their elders were addicted to. Many authorities—though by no means all of them—were inclined to agree. In early 1970 the Senate passed a bill to reduce the penalties for possession and use of marijuana, and some observers thought they saw a possibility that the federal government might eventually legalize and regulate its sale.

## THE PROMISE OF TECHNOLOGY

Generation after generation, Americans had been preoccupied with material progress. Those of the late twentieth century saw technological achievements even more startling than those of earlier times. But people found it harder and harder to maintain the faith of their forefathers who had assumed that new inventions would almost automatically lead to a better life for everyone.

### Innovations and Resources

A future of increasing abundance for the American people seemed to be promised by the continuing development of technical innovations summed up in the term "automation." Yet automation, like earlier phases of technical change dating back to the eighteenth century, threatened to create unemployment and social upheaval. Continuous automatic production was older than the term "automation," which a Ford Motor Company executive coined in 1946 to describe a system Ford was installing for the automatic handling of parts.

Essential to automation as it developed after World War II were electronic controls and the development of computer systems. The first electronic computer went into operation in 1946; its name was descriptive: ENIAC, which stood for Electronic Numercial Integrator and Calculator. At first computers were large, cumbersome, and expensive, but the discovery that complicated electronic circuits, which had been assembled by hand, could be printed on cardboard or plastic and that compact durable transistors (invented in 1948) could replace fragile vacuum tubes made possible the rapid and spectacular advance in computer technology. By the end of the sixties, computers were a hundred times faster, ten times smaller in their

electronic components, and provided information in a thousandth the time of earlier ones.

Computers, capable of answering in a few minutes problems that would require a thousand man-hours of calculation, were bringing a revolution in information processing. Jerome B. Wiesner, who had been President Kennedy's science adviser, described the change this way: "The computer, with its promise of a millionfold increase in man's capacity to handle information, will undoubtedly have the most farreaching consequences of any contemporary technical development. The potential for good in the computer, and the danger inherent in its misuse, exceed our ability to imagine."

Computers could give answers to innumerable informational problems previously so complex as to be unmanageable. They were helping industry control inventories to eliminate the periodic scarcity or glut that had contributed to irregularities in the business cycle. They could fly jet planes, guide rockets to the moon, or control almost any sort of machinery. They could, critics feared, through data storage on every individual, destroy privacy; through the tasks

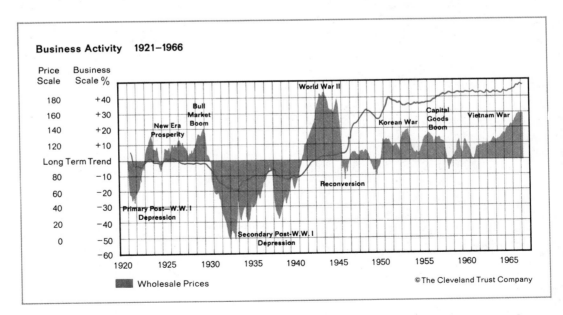

For the years 1921–1966, the index of business activity was computed on the basis of the following ten measures: commodity prices; imports; imports retained for consumption; government receipts; ship

construction; government expenditures; coal production; exports; iron exports; and tons of registered shipping in service.

they could guide, they might create serious unemployment.

In the age of automation, technicians and scientists could harness computers and other equipment to the mastering of almost any mechanical task. As early as 1955, Vannevar Bush explained to a House subcommittee that if a device were desired "to cause an automobile to follow a white line down the middle of a road automatically and even if the driver fell asleep . . . any number of concerns would stand ready to contract and build it. No real invention would be required. There are thousands of young men in the country to whom the design of such a device would be a pleasure. They would simply take off the shelf some photocells, . . . tubes, . . . , relays and, if urged, they would build what they would call a breadboard model, and it would work. The point is that the presence of a host of versatile, cheap, reliable gadgets and the presence of men who understand fully all their queer ways, has rendered the building of automatic devices almost straightforward and routine. It is no longer a question of whether they can be built, it is rather a question of whether they are worth building."

The bituminous coal industry was a spectacular example of what automation could mean. By the end of the 1940s, coal, being mined with some machinery, was being priced out of the market by cheaper petroleum and natural gas. In 1948 the United Mine Workers gave the operators freedom to automate in exchange for a royalty of 40 cents per ton to be paid into UMW welfare funds. The companies, investing $500 million in new machinery, automated the mines and laid off far more than half the workers. A quarter-million miners had lost their jobs; only 150,000 were kept at work. Yet the alternative, the president of the Princess Coal Company, pointed out, would have been bankruptcy for the bituminous coal industry. "We've lost major markets and must compete with other fuels that have tax advantages," he declared. "The fact that the price of coal at the mine has not gone up in the past ten years—during a period of inflation—is a major accomplishment."

Whether in the long run automation would mean chronic unemployment was not entirely clear. In agriculture and industry as well as mining, automatic machinery was displacing labor rather than creating jobs. Its effects upon other groups of workers—those employed as clerks, for example—remained to be seen. Yet overall, the first seven decades of the twentieth century had brought an enormous increase in output per man-hour without any corresponding rise in unemployment.

As production grew, the United States began to change from a "have" to a "have-not" nation in natural resources, but innovations eliminated the danger of many disastrous shortages. Between 1900 and 1950, the production of bituminous coal rose two and a half times, of copper three times, of iron ore three and a half times, and of crude oil thirty times. Although Gifford Pinchot, writing in the Progressive era, had feared that bituminous coal would soon be exhausted, exhaustion was still far off. In fact, the Department of the Interior was still researching new uses—such as liquefication and gasification—for bituminous coal. In 1877 Secretary of the Interior Carl Schurz warned of a "timber famine" only twenty years away, but according to a 1962 estimate forests at that time were growing at a rate that exceeded by 60 per cent the amount of timber cut. Synthetic substances, plastics, and metals had cut the demand for forest products. As the rich iron deposits began to dwindle, steel companies developed processes to make use of lower-grade ore. Once the huge investment had been made in plants that produced high-grade pellets from taconite ores, the steel companies reaped the advantage of higher productivity from furnaces into which they fed the pellets. New ore deposits were opened in Labrador. The United States became the largest importer of copper, lead, and zinc, leading to a flow of dollars overseas.

Already the United States was beginning to develop electric power from atomic energy. Two small power plants were completed in 1957. In the future nuclear reactors were likely to produce electric power at competitive rates. Already steam plants fueled by oil, gas, or coal could produce electric power more cheaply than could be expected at the few major hydroelectric sites remaining in the United States.

## Scientific Research

Applications of scientific knowledge, both civilian and military, were being developed at such a rapid pace that they created a sharp pressure for additional basic research. In 1957 a Department of Defense research officer declared: "We have been chewing up the findings of basic research since World War II at a speed faster than they are being produced in the laboratories and ivory towers."

The chief agency for promotion of basic scientific research was the National Science Foundation. In 1945 Dr. Vannevar Bush, who had been wartime director of the Office of Scientific Research and Development, proposed the establishment of a peacetime government agency to promote basic research. The United States could no longer depend upon Europe, Bush warned. In 1950 Congress established the National Science Foundation, but limited its annual appropriations to $15 million per year and appropriated less than that until the 1956 fiscal year. In the 1959 budget, after the sputnik crisis, President Eisenhower asked for $140 million for the National Science Foundation. Thereafter its budget, and its impact upon scientific research, increased significantly.

Overall federal expenditures on research and development—no more than a tenth of it for basic research—rose so spectacularly that by the end of the sixties they totaled more than the entire federal budget before Pearl Harbor:

| | | |
|---|---|---|
| 1940 | $ | 74,000,000 |
| 1950 | | 1,000,000,000 |
| 1955 | | 3,300,000,000 |
| 1965 | | 15,200,000,000 |

These sums were so large that many universities were dependent upon them for a considerable portion of their budgets. Concentration of expenditures in a few universities (68 per cent of federal research funds were going to twenty-five institutions) had important side effects.

Scientific and engineering work at Harvard and the Massachusetts Institute of Technology had helped attract science-based industry, especially in electronics, to Highway 128 ringing Boston; the University of California and Stanford had brought similar industry to the San Francisco Bay region. Understandably, there developed considerable pressure to allocate more scientific grants to the Middle West and other areas in the United States. The House Appropriations Committee forbade the granting of more than 10 per cent of the National Science Foundation fellowships to the residents of any one state.

The most comprehensive and spectacular of basic research enterprises, in which the United States cooperated with sixty-two other countries including Russia, was the International Geophysical Year, from July 1, 1957, to the end of 1958. It involved exploring the globe from pole to pole and from ionosphere to core, and included the launching of satellites and the establishment of an American base at the South Pole. The research in Antarctica developed into a long-range scientific program, centering in a permanent base at McMurdo Sound, which supplied a number of outlying stations. By international treaty, national territorial holdings and armaments were barred from the continent; the United States, the Soviet Union, and a number of other nations carried on scientific work and shared information without friction.

In medical research, the most important advance was the development of an effective polio vaccine by Dr. Jonas Salk of the University of Pittsburgh. The vaccine was first used on a large scale in 1955, and within two years the polio rate in the United States dropped 80 per cent. Many of the most spectacular innovations were made possible by electronic or atomic advances. The transplant of kidneys and even of a human heart were aided by chemical treatment and radiation to prevent rejection of the new organ. A number of mechanical and electronic inventions—among them artificial kidneys and miniature electronic generators to keep a heart beating at the right pace—helped to save lives. The laser beam, a ray of concentrated light, became a tool of eye surgery to repair damage to the retina.

Advances in medical research, extensive public health programs, private health insurance plans covering 73 per cent of the people, Medicare for those over sixty-five, and Medicaid for the poor—all contributed to a lengthening life span. In 1900 life expectancy at birth had been forty-nine years; by 1955 it was seventy years.

Most of the gain was in reducing the death rate among infants and children. Older people did not live much longer than before. In 1900 a sixty-four-year-old person had a remaining life span ahead of him that averaged about twelve years; in the 1960s it averaged fourteen years. Even if the two prime killers of the aged, heart disease and cancer, were to be eliminated, life expectancy would not be greatly increased. Since there was not likely to be much increase in the average life span, and since only a limited part of the population was middle-aged in the 1960s, there would not be any significant increase in the percentage of elderly people before the end of the twentieth century.

## The Space Race Begins

The American government had shown little interest in space exploration until October 1957, when the Soviet Union put its first satellite, Sputnik I, into orbit. Already the United States was carrying on a program of rocket research under the direction of Wernher von Braun, a German-born expert whose team had designed and built for the Hitler regime the V-2 rockets that devastated London during the final stages of World War II. As the Russians advanced into Germany in 1945, they captured a few of the top men and hundreds of the technicians engaged in the V-2 project. Von Braun and others turned themselves over to the United States Army. In the early postwar years, however, the Americans were slower than the Russians in using German expertise to produce ballistic missiles, and still slower in using it to develop space rockets.

"Our satellite program has never been conducted as a race with other nations," President Eisenhower declared as he congratulated the Soviet Union on the launching of Sputnik I. But most Americans, including prominent public figures, assumed that a race was indeed on, and the United States appeared to be lagging far behind. Sputnik II carried a dog into space in November 1957 while Von Braun and his co-workers were still trying to launch a tiny, three-pound sphere, which they did not succeed in orbiting until January 1958. In October of that year, twelve months after the appearance of Sputnik I, the American government set up the National Aeronautics and Space Agency

(NASA) to coordinate the nation's space efforts, but gave it only a small budget.

By 1961, when Kennedy took over the Presidency from Eisenhower, the United States appeared to be making some gains. This country was ahead of the Soviet Union in the number of satellites put into orbit—thirty-three to nine. The total weight of the nine Soviet satellites, however, was more than twice as great as that of all thirty-three American ones, and the Russians were rumored to be testing a five-ton spaceship that could take a man into orbit. To the Russians, Kennedy said in his inaugural: "Let us explore the stars together." But the Russians showed little interest in that. In April 1961 they sent the world's first cosmonaut, Yuri Gagarin, once around the earth. After reentering the atmosphere and parachuting to safety, Gagarin issued the boastful challenge: "Now let the other countries try to catch us."

Eight days after Gagarin's flight (and just one day after the Bay of Pigs fiasco in Cuba) President Kennedy directed a memorandum to Vice President Johnson, whom he had named as chairman of an advisory Space Council. "Do we have a chance of beating the Soviets," Kennedy asked, "by putting a laboratory in space, or by a trip around the moon, or by a rocket to land on the moon, or by a rocket to go to the moon and back with a man?" The best the United States could do for the time being was to propel Alan Shepard into a suborbital flight that went some 100 miles up to the edge of space and some 300 miles out into the Atlantic Ocean. Three weeks later, May 25, 1961, Kennedy appealed to Congress: "I believe this nation should commit itself to achieving the goal, before the decade is out, of landing a man on the moon and returning him safely to earth." Congress soon responded by making the first of the necessary appropriations.

The moon program, Project Apollo, was expected to cost $20 billion, ten times as much as the development of the atom bomb (but less than the Vietnam War was to cost for a single year). Advocates of the program maintained that it would be well worth the price on account of its scientific and economic benefits as well as its enhancement of national prestige. One space official declared: "Each improvement in our ability to fly unmanned and manned spacecraft results in a corresponding improvement in our ability to solve nature's mysteries." Vice President Johnson added: "Our space program is creating and helping create new basic industries for our economy." But there were doubters. *Science* (the journal of the American Association for the Advancement of Science) predicted: "Not more than a small fraction of the cost of the moon program will be recovered through technological fallout." Other critics objected to the diversion of funds from the improvement of society. "Some people say that we should take the money we're putting into space and put it into housing," President Kennedy expostulated (April 1963). "We have enough resources, in my opinion, to do what needs to be done in the field, for example, of education, and to do what needs to be done in space."

## To the Moon and Beyond

Until 1965 the United States continued to trail the Soviet Union in the launching of manned spacecraft, though not in the firing of unmanned satellites. A Russian cosmonaut circled the globe seventeen times (August 1961) before the first American, John Glenn, was put into space (February 1962), to return to earth after making only three orbits. Another and yet another American went around in one-man Mercury capsules similar to Glenn's, but the Russians kept the lead in flight endurance and took the lead in orbiting two vehicles close together, in launching two-man and then three-man craft, and in releasing a man from one of the ships to float in nothingness. But the United States was putting up, all together, more than twice as many satellites as was the Soviet Union. Some of these were intended for scientific purposes— to study solar radiation, the earth's magnetic field, and weather phenomena. Others, such as Telstar, facilitated around-the-world communication by telephone and television. Still others, such as the "eye in the sky" satellites Samos and Midas, gave the military new means of observation or espionage. Meanwhile, from 1963 to 1965, the Americans discontinued manned flights and concentrated on the design and construction of improved space vehicles.

By 1965 the Americans were ready to achieve some firsts of their own with men in space. The new two-man Gemini, unlike the latest Soviet spaceships, was maneuverable; it was equipped with small rockets that could change its course in mid-orbit, as its pilots demonstrated on their first flight. On a second flight an astronaut stepped into space and, with a small oxygen-spitting gun, pulled the vehicle about on a tether. The third of the Geminis, orbiting for nearly 191 hours, broke the endurance record that the Russians had set. On a later launching, in 1966, a Gemini succeeded in overtaking an orbiting craft and joining up or "docking" with it—a maneuver essential for a moon trip. The United States now appeared to hold the lead in manned as well as unmanned flights.

The next stage involved the Apollo, a three-man spacecraft which, with over 2 million parts, was far more complicated than the Gemini or the Mercury. The project was set back and the nation was stunned when, early in 1967, a fire killed the three astronauts while they were rehearsing for the first Apollo take-off. While the craft was being redesigned and retested, a succession of Surveyors, unmanned, were being rocketed to the moon and were sending back tens of thousands of pictures of the lunar surface. One of the Surveyors landed on the moon and then took off from it, as a manned vehicle was scheduled to do eventually. In late 1968, after Apollo 7 had carried three men around the earth, Apollo 8 carried three others around the moon, the first men to leave the earth's gravitational field. During the next few months, Apollo 9 tested a lunar module (the landing craft that was to leave and rejoin the mother ship) in an earth orbit, and Apollo 10 tested one in a moon orbit.

At last, in July 1969, Apollo 11 was blasted off on its epochal flight to land men on the moon. Ahead of them streaked a Russian spacecraft, Luna 15, heading for lunar orbit, but Luna carried no crew. Its launching seemed to show dramatically that, in space enterprises, the Soviet Union was still competing rather than cooperating—and now competing at a decided disadvantage. Not that sovereignty over the moon was at stake: by a treaty signed in 1966 the two superpowers had agreed that the moon should be a no man's land open to exploration and use by all nations. At issue were national prestige and (to the extent that the space programs yielded new techniques of warfare) military advantage.

The moon visit was a beginning, not an ending. The United States planned a series of lunar explorations, the second of which was launched in November 1969. Both the United States and the Soviet Union had been sending space probes far beyond the moon to Mars and Venus, and both could be expected sooner or later to start exploring the planets. The space race was not yet over. A joint Russian-American program seemed to be more and more needed, both for peace on this world and for progress toward other worlds. "The time will come, within ten years, when considerable amounts of equipment will be left on the moon and lunar bases established, and international cooperation will become essential," the famed British astronomer Sir Bernard Lovell predicted at the time of the Apollo 11 flight. "Otherwise, a very serious situation might arise, both scientifically and politically."

# Selected Readings

**Population** B. J. Wattenberg and R. M. Scammon, *The U.S.A. An Unexpected Family Portrait . . . Drawn from the Census* (1965); L. H. and A. T. Day, *Too Many Americans* (1965); Conrad and I. B. Taeuber, *The Changing Population of the United States* (1958).

**Interpretations of Society** David Riesman, *The Lonely Crowd*° (1950); D. M. Potter, *People of Plenty: Economic Abundance and the American Character*° (1954); J. K. Galbraith, *The Affluent Society*° (1958); C. W. Mills, *The Power Elite*° (1956); D. T. Bazelon, *Power in America* (1967); W. H. Whyte, *Organization Man*° (1956); Vance Packard, *The Hidden Persuaders*° (1957); Marshall McLuhan, *Understanding Media: The Extension of Man*° (1964) and *The Medium Is the Message* (1967).

**The City** Jean Gottman, *Megalopolis: The Urbanized Northeastern Seaboard of the United States* (1961); Martin Anderson, *The Federal Bulldozer: A Critical Analysis of Urban Renewal, 1949–1962*° (1965); Charles Abrams, *The City Is the Frontier*° (1965); R. C. Wood, *Suburbia: Its People and Their Politics* (1959); Wilfred Owen, *The Metropolitan Transportation Problem*° (1966); Claiborne Pell, *Megalopolis Unbound: The Supercity and the Transportation of Tomorrow* (1966); Frank Graham, *Disaster by Default: Politics and Water Pollution* (1966); J. R. Lowe, *Cities in a Race with Time: Progress and Poverty in America's Renewing Cities* (1967).

**Culture** Ronald Berman, *America in the Sixties; An Intellectual History* (1968); Bernard Rosenberg and D. M. White, eds., *Mass Culture* (1957); K. S. Lynn, ed., *The Professions in America*° (1965); John Burchard and Albert Bush-Brown, *The Architecture of America*° (1961); W. J. Baumol and W. G. Bowen, *Performing Arts: The Economic Dilemma* (1966); Richard Kostelanetz, ed., *The New American Arts*° (1965) and *On Contemporary American Literature*° (1964); Stephen Stepanchev, *American Poetry Since 1945*° (1965).

**Youth and Education** E. H. Erikson, *Identity: Youth and Crisis* (1968); Kenneth Keniston, *The Uncommitted: Alienated Youth in American Society* (1965); Christopher Jencks and David Riesman, *The Academic Revolution* (1968); S. M. Lipset and S. S. Wolin, eds., *The Berkeley Student Revolt: Facts and Interpretations*° (1965); J. B. Conant, *The American High School Today*° (1959) and *Slums and Suburbs* (1964).

**Science and Technology** D. K. Price, *The Scientific Estate* (1965); Gerald Holton, ed., *Science and Culture*° (1965); Herbert Simon, *The Shape of Automation* (1966); William Francois, *Automation: Industrialization Comes of Age*° (1964).

**To the Moon** Walter Sullivan, ed., *America's Race for the Moon*° (1962); Jay Holmes, *America on the Moon* (1962); Hugh Odishaw, ed., *The Challenges of Space* (1962); L. S. Swenson and others, *This New Ocean: A History of Project Mercury* (1966); R. L. Rosholt, *An Administrative History of NASA, 1958–1963* (1966).

---

°Titles available in paperback.

# Appendices

## The Declaration of Independence

*In Congress, July 4, 1776,*

The Unanimous Declaration of the Thirteen United States of America

When, in the course of human events, it becomes necessary for one people to dissolve the political bands which have connected them with another, and to assume, among the powers of the earth, the separate and equal station to which the laws of nature and of nature's God entitle them, a decent respect to the opinions of mankind requires that they should declare the causes which impel them to the separation.

We hold these truths to be self-evident, that all men are created equal; that they are endowed by their Creator with certain unalienable rights; that among these, are life, liberty, and the pursuit of happiness. That, to secure these rights, governments are instituted among men, deriving their just powers from the consent of the governed; that, whenever any form of government becomes destructive of these ends, it is the right of the people to alter or to abolish it, and to institute a new government, laying its foundation on such principles, and organizing its powers in such form, as to them shall seem most likely to effect their safety and happiness. Prudence, indeed, will dictate that governments long established, should not be changed for light and transient causes; and, accordingly, all experience hath shown, that mankind are more disposed to suffer, while evils are sufferable, than to right themselves by abolishing the forms to which they are accustomed. But, when a long train of abuses and usurpations, pursuing invariably the same object, evinces a design to reduce them under absolute despotism, it is their right, it is their duty, to throw off such government and to provide new guards for their future security. Such has been the patient sufferance of these colonies, and such is now the necessity which constrains them to alter their former systems of government. The history of the present King of Great Britain is a history of repeated injuries and usurpations, all having, in direct object, the establishment of an absolute tyranny over these States. To prove this, let facts be submitted to a candid world:—

He has refused his assent to laws the most wholesome and necessary for the public good.

He has forbidden his governors to pass laws of immediate and pressing importance, unless suspended in their operation till his assent should be obtained; and, when so suspended, he has utterly neglected to attend to them.

He has refused to pass other laws for the accommodation of large districts of people, unless those people would relinquish the right of representation in the legislature; a right inestimable to them, and formidable to tyrants only.

He has called together legislative bodies at places unusual, uncomfortable, and distant from the depository of their public records, for the sole purpose of fatiguing them into compliance with his measures.

He has dissolved representative houses repeatedly for opposing, with manly firmness, his invasions on the rights of the people.

He has refused, for a long time after such dissolutions, to cause others to be elected; whereby the legislative powers, incapable of annihilation, have returned to the people at large for their exercise; the state remaining, in the meantime, exposed to all the danger of invasion from without, and convulsions within.

He has endeavored to prevent the population of these States; for that purpose, obstructing the laws for naturalization of foreigners, refusing to pass others to encourage their migration hither, and raising the conditions of new appropriations of lands.

He has obstructed the administration of justice, by refusing his assent to laws for establishing judiciary powers.

He has made judges dependent on his will alone, for the tenure of their offices, and the amount and payment of their salaries.

He has erected a multitude of new offices, and sent hither swarms of officers to harass our people, and eat out their substance.

He has kept among us, in time of peace, standing armies, without the consent of our legislatures.

He has affected to render the military independent of, and superior to, the civil power.

He has combined, with others, to subject us to a jurisdiction foreign to our Constitution, and unacknowledged by our laws; giving his assent to their acts of pretended legislation:

For quartering large bodies of armed troops among us:

For protecting them by a mock trial, from punishment, for any murders which they should commit on the inhabitants of these States:

For cutting off our trade with all parts of the world:

For imposing taxes on us without our consent:

For depriving us, in many cases, of the benefit of trial by jury:

For transporting us beyond seas to be tried for pretended offences:

For abolishing the free system of English laws in a neighboring province, establishing therein an arbitrary government, and enlarging its boundaries, so as to render it at once an example and fit instrument for introducing the same absolute rule into these colonies:

For taking away our charters, abolishing our most valuable laws, and altering, fundamentally, the powers of our governments:

For suspending our own legislatures, and declaring themselves invested with power to legislate for us in all cases whatsoever.

He has abdicated government here, by declaring us out of his protection, and waging war against us.

He has plundered our seas, ravaged our coasts, burnt our towns, and destroyed the lives of our people.

He is, at this time, transporting large armies of foreign mercenaries to complete the works of death, desolation, and tyranny, already begun, with circumstances of cruelty and perfidy scarcely paralleled in the most barbarous ages, and totally unworthy the head of a civilized nation.

He has constrained our fellow citizens, taken captive on the high seas, to bear arms against their country, to become the executioners of their friends, and brethren, or to fall themselves by their hands.

He has excited domestic insurrections amongst us, and has endeavored to bring on the inhabitants of our frontiers, the merciless Indian savages, whose known rule of warfare is an undistinguished destruction of all ages, sexes, and conditions.

In every stage of these oppressions, we have petitioned for redress, in the most humble terms; our repeated petitions have been answered only by repeated injury. A prince, whose character is thus marked by every act which may define a tyrant, is unfit to be the ruler of a free people.

Nor have we been wanting in attention to our British brethren. We have warned them, from time to time, of attempts made by their legislature to extend an unwarrantable jurisdiction over us. We have reminded them of the circumstances of our emigration and settlement here. We have appealed to their native justice and magnanimity, and we have conjured them, by the ties of our common kindred, to disavow these usurpations, which would inevitably interrupt our connections and correspondence. They, too, have been deaf to the voice of justice and consanguinity. We must, therefore, acquiesce in the necessity which denounces our separation, and hold them as we hold the rest of mankind, enemies in war, in peace, friends.

We, therefore, the representatives of the United States of America, in general Congress assembled, appealing to the Supreme Judge of the world for the rectitude of our intentions, do, in the name, and by the authority of the good people of these colonies, solemnly publish and declare, that these united colonies are, and of right ought to be, free and independent states: that they are absolved from all allegiance to the British Crown, and that all political connection between them and the state of Great Britain is, and ought to be, totally dissolved; and that, as free and independent states, they have full power to levy war, conclude peace, contract alliances, establish commerce, and to do all other acts and things which independent states may of right do. And, for the support of this declaration, with a firm reliance on the protection of Divine Providence, we mutually pledge to each other our lives, our fortunes, and our sacred honor.

The foregoing Declaration was, by order of Congress, engrossed, and signed by the following members:

JOHN HANCOCK

**New Hampshire**
*Josiah Bartlett*
*William Whipple*
*Matthew Thornton*

**Massachusetts Bay**
*Samuel Adams*
*John Adams*
*Robert Treat Paine*
*Elbridge Gerry*

**Rhode Island**
*Stephen Hopkins*
*William Ellery*

**Connecticut**
*Roger Sherman*
*Samuel Huntington*
*William Williams*
*Oliver Wolcott*

**New York**
*William Floyd*
*Philip Livingston*
*Francis Lewis*
*Lewis Morris*

**New Jersey**
*Richard Stockton*
*John Witherspoon*
*Francis Hopkinson*
*John Hart*
*Abraham Clark*

**Pennsylvania**
*Robert Morris*
*Benjamin Rush*
*Benjamin Franklin*
*John Morton*
*George Clymer*
*James Smith*
*George Taylor*
*James Wilson*
*George Ross*

**Delaware**
*Caesar Rodney*
*George Read*
*Thomas M'Kean*

**Maryland**
*Samuel Chase*
*William Paca*
*Thomas Stone*
*Charles Carroll,*
   *of Carrollton*

**Virginia**
*George Wythe*
*Richard Henry Lee*
*Thomas Jefferson*
*Benjamin Harrison*
*Thomas Nelson, Jr.*
*Francis Lightfoot Lee*
*Carter Braxton*

**North Carolina**
*William Hooper*
*Joseph Hewes*
*John Penn*

**South Carolina**
*Edward Rutledge*
*Thomas Heyward, Jr.*
*Thomas Lynch, Jr.*
*Arthur Middleton*

**Georgia**
*Button Gwinnett*
*Lyman Hall*
*George Walton*

*Resolved,* That copies of the Declaration be sent to the several assemblies, conventions, and committees, or councils of safety, and to the several commanding officers of the continental troops; that it be proclaimed in each of the United States, at the head of the army.

# The Constitution of the United States of America[1]

WE the People of the United States, in Order to form a more perfect Union, establish Justice, insure domestic Tranquility, provide for the common defence, promote the general Welfare, and secure the Blessings of Liberty to ourselves and our Posterity, do ordain and establish this CONSTITUTION for the United States of America.

## Article I

Section 1. All legislative Powers herein granted shall be vested in a Congress of the United States, which shall consist of a Senate and House of Representatives.

Section 2. The House of Representatives shall be composed of Members chosen every second Year by the People of the several States, and the Electors in each State shall have the Qualifications requisite for Electors of the most numerous Branch of the State Legislature.

No Person shall be a Representative who shall not have attained to the Age of twenty-five Years, and been seven Years a Citizen of the United States, and who shall not, when elected, be an Inhabitant of that State in which he shall be chosen.

[Representatives and direct Taxes[2] shall be apportioned among the several States which may be included within this Union, according to their respective Numbers, which shall be determined by adding to the whole Number of free Persons, including those bound to Service for a Term of Years, and excluding Indians not taxed, three fifths of all other Persons.][3] The actual Enumeration shall be made within three Years after the first Meeting of the Congress of the United States, and within every subsequent Term of ten Years, in such Manner as they shall by Law direct. The Number of Representatives shall not exceed one for every thirty Thousand, but each State shall have at Least one Representative; and until such enumeration shall be made, the State of New Hampshire shall be entitled to chuse three, Massachusetts eight, Rhode-Island and Providence Plantations one, Connecticut five, New York six, New Jersey four, Pennsylvania eight, Delaware one, Maryland six, Virginia ten, North Carolina five, South Carolina five, and Georgia three.

When vacancies happen in the Representation from any State, the Executive Authority thereof shall issue Writs of Election to fill such Vacancies.

The House of Representatives shall chuse their Speaker and other Officers; and shall have the sole Power of Impeachment.

Section 3. The Senate of the United States shall be composed of two Senators

---

[1] This version, which follows the original Constitution in capitalization and spelling, was published by the United States Department of the Interior, Office of Education, in 1935.

[2] Altered by the Sixteenth Amendment.

[3] Negated by the Fourteenth Amendment.

from each State, chosen by the Legislature thereof, for six Years; and each Senator shall have one Vote.

Immediately after they shall be assembled in Consequence of the first Election, they shall be divided as equally as may be into three Classes. The Seats of the Senators of the first Class shall be vacated at the Expiration of the second Year, of the second Class at the Expiration of the fourth Year, and of the third Class at the Expiration of the sixth Year, so that one-third may be chosen every second Year; and if Vacancies happen by Resignation, or otherwise, during the Recess of the Legislature of any State, the Executive thereof may make temporary Appointments until the next Meeting of the Legislature, which shall then fill such Vacancies.

No Person shall be a Senator who shall not have attained to the Age of thirty Years, and been nine Years a Citizen of the United States, and who shall not, when elected, be an Inhabitant of that State for which he shall be chosen.

The Vice President of the United States shall be President of the Senate, but shall have no vote, unless they be equally divided.

The Senate shall chuse their other Officers, and also a President pro tempore, in the absence of the Vice President, or when he shall exercise the Office of President of the United States.

The Senate shall have the sole Power to try all Impeachments. When sitting for that purpose, they shall be on Oath or Affirmation. When the President of the United States is tried, the Chief Justice shall preside: And no person shall be convicted without the Concurrence of two thirds of the Members present.

Judgment in Cases of Impeachment shall not extend further than to removal from Office, and disqualification to hold and enjoy any Office of honor, Trust, or Profit under the United States: but the Party convicted shall nevertheless be liable and subject to Indictment, Trial, Judgment, and Punishment, according to Law.

Section 4. The Times, Places and Manner of holding Elections for Senators and Representatives, shall be prescribed in each State by the Legislature thereof; but the Congress may at any time by Law make or alter such Regulations, except as to the Places of Chusing Senators.

The Congress shall assemble at least once in every Year, and such Meeting shall be on the first Monday in December, unless they shall by Law appoint a different Day.

Section 5. Each House shall be the Judge of the Elections, Returns and Qualifications of its own Members, and a Majority of each shall constitute a Quorum to do Business; but a smaller number may adjourn from day to day, and may be authorized to compel the Attendance of absent Members, in such Manner, and under such Penalties, as each House may provide.

Each House may determine the Rules of its Proceedings, punish its Members for disorderly Behaviour, and, with the Concurrence of two thirds, expel a Member.

Each House shall keep a Journal of its Proceedings, and from time to time publish the same, excepting such Parts as may in their Judgment require Secrecy; and the Yeas and Nays of the Members of either House on any question shall, at the Desire of one fifth of those Present, be entered on the Journal.

Neither House, during the Session of Congress, shall, without the Consent of the other, adjourn for more than three days, nor to any other Place than that in which the two Houses shall be sitting.

Section 6. The Senators and Representatives shall receive a Compensation for their Services, to be ascertained by Law, and paid out of the Treasury of the United States. They shall in all Cases, except Treason, Felony, and Breach of the Peace, be privileged from Arrest during their Attendance at the Session of their respective Houses, and in going to and returning from the same; and for any Speech or Debate in either House, they shall not be questioned in any other Place.

No Senator or Representative shall, during the Time for which he was elected, be appointed to any civil Office under the Authority of the United States, which shall have been created, or the Emoluments whereof shall have been increased, during such time; and no Person holding any Office under the United States shall be a Member of either House during his continuance in Office.

Section 7. All Bills for raising Revenue shall originate in the House of Representatives; but the Senate may propose or concur with Amendments as on other bills.

Every Bill which shall have passed the House of Representatives and the Senate, shall, before it become a Law, be presented to the President of the United States; If he approve he shall sign it, but if not he shall return it, with his Objections, to that House in which it shall have originated, who shall enter the Objections at large on their Journal, and proceed to reconsider it. If after such Reconsideration two thirds of that House shall agree to pass the bill, it shall be sent, together with the objections, to the other House, by which it shall likewise

be reconsidered, and if approved by two thirds of that House, it shall become a Law. But in all such Cases the Votes of both Houses shall be determined by Yeas and Nays, and the Names of the Persons voting for and against the Bill shall be entered on the Journal of each House respectively. If any Bill shall not be returned by the President within ten Days (Sundays excepted) after it shall have been presented to him, the Same shall be a Law, in like Manner as if he had signed it, unless the Congress by their Adjournment prevent its Return, in which Case it shall not be a Law.

Every Order, Resolution, or Vote to which the Concurrence of the Senate and House of Representatives may be necessary (except on a question of Adjournment) shall be presented to the President of the United States; and before the Same shall take Effect, shall be approved by him, or being disapproved by him, shall be repassed by two thirds of the Senate and House of Representatives, according to the Rules and Limitations prescribed in the Case of a Bill.

Section 8. The Congress shall have Power To lay and collect Taxes, Duties, Imposts and Excises, to pay the Debts and provide for the common Defence and general Welfare of the United States; but all Duties, Imposts and Excises shall be uniform throughout the United States;

To borrow money on the credit of the United States;

To regulate Commerce with foreign Nations, and among the several States, and with the Indian Tribes;

To establish an uniform Rule of Naturalization, and uniform Laws on the subject of Bankruptcies throughout the United States;

To coin Money, regulate the Value

thereof, and of foreign Coin, and fix the Standard of Weights and Measures;

To provide for the Punishment of counterfeiting the Securities and current Coin of the United States;

To establish Post Offices and post Roads;

To promote the Progress of Science and useful Arts, by securing for limited Times to Authors and Inventors the exclusive Right to their respective Writings and Discoveries;

To constitute Tribunals inferior to the Supreme Court;

To define and punish Piracies and Felonies committed on the high Seas, and Offenses against the Law of Nations;

To declare War, grant Letters of Marque and Reprisal, and make Rules concerning Captures on Land and Water;

To raise and support Armies, but no Appropriation of Money to that Use shall be for a longer Term than two Years;

To provide and maintain a Navy;

To make Rules for the Government and Regulation of the land and naval forces;

To provide for calling forth the Militia to execute the Laws of the Union, suppress Insurrections and repel Invasions;

To provide for organizing, arming, and disciplining the Militia, and for governing such Part of them as may be employed in the Service of the United States, reserving to the States respectively, the Appointment of the Officers, and the Authority of training the Militia according to the discipline prescribed by Congress;

To exercise exclusive Legislation in all Cases whatsoever, over such District (not exceeding ten Miles square) as may, by Cession of particular States, and the acceptance of Congress, become the Seat of the Government of the United States, and to exercise like Authority over all Places purchased by the Consent of the Legislature of the State in which the Same shall be, for the Erection of Forts, Magazines, Arsenals, dock-Yards, and other needful Buildings;— And

To make all Laws which shall be necessary and proper for carrying into Execution the foregoing Powers, and all other Powers vested by this Constitution in the Government of the United States, or in any Department or Officer thereof.

Section 9. The Migration or Importation of such Persons as any of the States now existing shall think proper to admit, shall not be prohibited by the Congress prior to the Year one thousand eight hundred and eight, but a tax or duty may be imposed on such Importation, not exceeding ten dollars for each Person.

The privilege of the Writ of Habeas Corpus shall not be suspended, unless when in Cases of Rebellion or Invasion the public Safety may require it.

No bill of Attainder or ex post facto Law shall be passed.

No capitation, or other direct, Tax shall be laid unless in Proportion to the Census or Enumeration herein before directed to be taken.

No Tax or Duty shall be laid on Articles exported from any State.

No Preference shall be given by any Regulation of Commerce or Revenue to the Ports of one State over those of another: nor shall Vessels bound to, or from, one State, be obliged to enter, clear, or pay Duties in another.

No Money shall be drawn from the Treasury, but in Consequence of Appropriations made by Law; and a regular Statement and Account of the Receipts and Expenditures of all public

Money shall be published from time to time.

No Title of Nobility shall be granted by the United States: And no Person holding any Office of Profit or Trust under them, shall, without the Consent of the Congress, accept of any present, Emolument, Office, or Title, of any kind whatever, from any King, Prince, or foreign State.

Section 10.  No State shall enter into any Treaty, Alliance, or Confederation; grant Letters of Marque and Reprisal; coin Money; emit Bills of Credit; make any Thing but gold and silver Coin a Tender in Payment of Debts; pass any Bill of Attainder, ex post facto Law, or Law impairing the Obligation of Contracts, or grant any Title of Nobility.

No State shall, without the Consent of the Congress, lay any Imposts or Duties on Imports or Exports, except what may be absolutely necessary for executing its inspection Laws: and the net Produce of all Duties and Imposts, laid by any State on Imports or Exports, shall be for the Use of the Treasury of the United States; and all such Laws shall be subject to the Revision and Control of the Congress.

No state shall, without the Consent of Congress, lay any duty of Tonnage, keep Troops, or Ships of War in time of Peace, enter into any Agreement or Compact with another State, or with a foreign Power, or engage in War, unless actually invaded, or in such imminent Danger as will not admit of delay.

## Article II

Section 1.  The executive Power shall be vested in a President of the United States of America. He shall hold his Office during the Term of four years, and, together with the Vice-President,

chosen for the same Term, be elected, as follows:

Each State shall appoint, in such Manner as the Legislature thereof may direct, a Number of Electors, equal to the whole Number of Senators and Representatives to which the State may be entitled in the Congress: but no Senator or Representative, or Person holding an Office of Trust or Profit under the United States, shall be appointed an Elector.

[The Electors shall meet in their respective States, and vote by Ballot for two persons, of whom one at least shall not be an Inhabitant of the same State with themselves. And they shall make a List of all the Persons voted for, and of the Number of Votes for each; which List they shall sign and certify, and transmit sealed to the Seat of the Government of the United States, directed to the President of the Senate. The President of the Senate shall, in the Presence of the Senate and House of Representatives, open all the Certificates, and the Votes shall then be counted. The Person having the greatest Number of Votes shall be the President, if such Number be a Majority of the whole Number of Electors appointed; and if there be more than one who have such Majority, and have an equal Number of Votes, then the House of Representatives shall immediately chuse by Ballot one of them for President; and if no Person have a Majority, then from the five highest on the List the said House shall in the Manner chuse the President. But in chusing the President, the Votes shall be taken by States, the Representation from each State having one Vote; a quorum for this Purpose shall consist of a Member or Members from two-thirds of the States, and a Majority of all the States shall be necessary to a Choice. In every Case, after the Choice of the President, the

Person having the greatest Number of Votes of the Electors shall be the Vice President. But if there should remain two or more who have equal votes, the Senate shall chuse from them by Ballot the Vice-President.]4

The Congress may determine the Time of chusing the Electors, and the Day on which they shall give their Votes; which Day shall be the same throughout the United States.

No person except a natural-born Citizen, or a Citizen of the United States, at the time of the Adoption of this Constitution, shall be eligible to the Office of President; neither shall any Person be eligible to that Office who shall not have attained to the Age of thirty-five years, and been fourteen Years a Resident within the United States.

In Case of the Removal of the President from Office, or of his Death, Resignation, or Inability to discharge the Powers and Duties of the said Office, the same shall devolve on the Vice President, and the Congress may by Law provide for the Case of Removal, Death, Resignation, or Inability, both of the President and Vice President, declaring what Officer shall then act as President, and such Officer shall act accordingly, until the disability be removed, or a President shall be elected.

The President shall, at stated Times, receive for his Services a Compensation, which shall neither be increased nor diminished during the Period for which he shall have been elected, and he shall not receive within that Period any other Emolument from the United States, or any of them.

Before he enter on the execution of his Office, he shall take the following Oath or Affirmation:—"I do solemnly swear (or

4 Revised by the Twelfth Amendment.

affirm) that I will faithfully execute the Office of President of the United States, and will, to the best of my Ability, preserve, protect, and defend the Constitution of the United States."

Section 2. The President shall be Commander in Chief of the Army and Navy of the United States, and of the Militia of the several States, when called into the actual Service of the United States; he may require the Opinion, in writing, of the principal Officer in each of the executive Departments, upon any subject relating to the Duties of their respective Offices, and he shall have Power to Grant Reprieves and Pardons for Offenses against the United States, except in Cases of Impeachment.

He shall have Power, by and with the Advice and Consent of the Senate, to make Treaties, provided two thirds of the Senators present concur; and he shall nominate, and by and with the Advice and Consent of the Senate, shall appoint Ambassadors, other public Ministers and Consuls, Judges of the supreme Court, and all other Officers of the United States, whose Appointments are not herein otherwise provided for, and which shall be established by Law: but the Congress may by Law vest the Appointment of such inferior Officers, as they think proper, in the President alone, in the Courts of Law, or in the Heads of Departments.

The President shall have Power to fill up all Vacancies that may happen during the Recess of the Senate, by granting Commissions which shall expire at the End of their next Session.

Section 3. He shall from time to time give to the Congress Information of the State of the Union, and recommend to their Consideration such Measures as he shall judge necessary and expedient; he may, on extraordinary occasions, convene both Houses, or either of them, and in Case of Disagreement between them, with respect to the Time of Adjournment, he may adjourn them to such Time as he shall think proper; he shall receive Ambassadors and other public Ministers; he shall take care that the Laws be faithfully executed, and shall Commission all the Officers of the United States.

Section 4.   The President, Vice President and all civil Officers of the United States, shall be removed from Office on Impeachment for, and Conviction of, Treason, Bribery, or other high Crimes and Misdemeanors.

## Article III

Section 1.   The judicial Power of the United States, shall be vested in one supreme Court, and in such inferior Courts as the Congress may from time to time ordain and establish. The Judges, both of the supreme and inferior Courts, shall hold their Offices during good Behaviour, and shall, at stated Times, receive for their Services, a Compensation, which shall not be diminished during their Continuance in Office.

Section 2.   The judicial Power shall extend to all Cases, in Law and Equity, arising under this Constitution, the Laws of the United States, and Treaties made, or which shall be made, under their Authority;—to all Cases affecting ambassadors, other public ministers and consuls;—to all cases of admiralty and maritime Jurisdiction;—to Controversies to which the United States shall be a Party;—to Controversies between two or more States;—between a State and Citizens of another State;[5]—between Citizens of different States,—between

Citizens of the same State claiming Lands under Grants of different States, and between a State, or the Citizens thereof, and foreign States, Citizens or Subjects.

In all Cases affecting Ambassadors, other public Ministers and Consuls, and those in which a State shall be Party, the supreme Court shall have original Jurisdiction. In all the other Cases before mentioned, the supreme Court shall have appellate Jurisdiction, both as to Law and Fact, with such Exceptions, and under such Regulations as the Congress shall make.

The trial of all Crimes, except in Cases of Impeachment, shall be by Jury; and such Trial shall be held in the State where the said Crimes shall have been committed; but when not committed within any State, the Trial shall be at such Place or Places as the Congress may by Law have directed.

Section 3.   Treason   against   the United States, shall consist only in levying War against them, or in adhering to their Enemies, giving them Aid and Comfort. No Person shall be convicted of Treason unless on the Testimony of two Witnesses to the same overt Act, or on Confession in open Court.

The Congress shall have power to declare the Punishment of Treason, but no Attainder of Treason shall work Corruption of Blood, or Forfeiture except during the Life of the Person attainted.

## Article IV

Section 1.  Full   Faith   and   Credit shall be given in each State to the public Acts, Records, and judicial Proceedings of every other State. And the Congress may by general Laws prescribe the Man-

---

[5] Qualified by the Eleventh Amendment.

ner in which such Acts, Records and Proceedings shall be proved, and the Effect thereof.

Section 2.   The Citizens of each State shall be entitled to all Privileges and Immunities of Citizens in the several States.

A Person charged in any State with Treason, Felony, or other Crime, who shall flee from Justice, and be found in another State, shall on demand of the executive Authority of the State from which he fled, be delivered up, to be removed to the State having Jurisdiction of the crime.

No Person held to Service or Labour in one State, under the Laws thereof, escaping into another, shall, in Consequence of any Law or Regulation therein, be discharged from such Service or Labour, but shall be delivered up on Claim of the Party to whom such Service or Labour may be due.

Section 3.   New States may be admitted by the Congress into this Union; but no new State shall be formed or erected within the Jurisdiction of any other State; nor any State be formed by the Junction of two or more States, or parts of States, without the Consent of the Legislatures of the States concerned as well as of the Congress.

The Congress shall have Power to dispose of and make all needful Rules and Regulations respecting the Territory or other Property belonging to the United States; and nothing in this Constitution shall be so construed as to Prejudice any Claims of the United States, or of any particular State.

Section 4.   The United States shall guarantee to every State in this Union a Republican Form of Government, and shall protect each of them against Invasion; and on Application of the Legislature, or of the Executive (when the Legislature cannot be convened) against domestic Violence.

## Article V

The Congress, whenever two-thirds of both Houses shall deem it necessary, shall propose Amendments to this Constitution, or, on the Application of the Legislatures of two-thirds of the several States, shall call a Convention for proposing Amendments, which, in either Case, shall be valid to all Intents and Purposes, as part of this Constitution, when ratified by the Legislatures of three-fourths of the several States, or by Conventions in three-fourths thereof, as the one or the other Mode of Ratification may be proposed by the Congress; Provided that no Amendment which may be made prior to the Year One thousand eight hundred and eight shall in any Manner affect the first and fourth Clauses in the Ninth Section of the first Article; and that no State, without its Consent, shall be deprived of its equal Suffrage in the Senate.

## Article VI

All Debts contracted and Engagements entered into, before the Adoption of this Constitution, shall be as valid against the United States under this Constitution, as under the Confederation.

This Constitution, and the Laws of the United States which shall be made in Pursuance thereof; and all Treaties made, or which shall be made, under the Authority of the United States, shall be the supreme Law of the Land; and the Judges in every State shall be bound thereby, any Thing in the Constitution or Laws of any State to the Contrary notwithstanding.

The Senators and Representatives before mentioned, and the Members of the several State Legislatures, and all executive and judicial Officers, both of the United States and of the several States, shall be bound by Oath or Affirmation to support this Constitution; but no religious Test shall ever be required as a qualification to any Office or public Trust under the United States.

## Article VII

The Ratification of the Conventions of nine States shall be sufficient for the Establishment of this Constitution between the States so ratifying the same.

Done in Convention by the Unanimous Consent of the States present the Seventeenth Day of September in the Year of our Lord one thousand seven hundred and Eighty seven, and of the Independence of the United States of America the Twelfth. In Witness whereof We have hereunto subscribed our Names.[6]

George Washington
*President and deputy from Virginia*

**New Hampshire**
*John Langdon*
*Nicholas Gilman*

**Massachusetts**
*Nathaniel Gorham*
*Rufus King*

**Connecticut**
*William Samuel Johnson*
*Roger Sherman*

**New York**
*Alexander Hamilton*

**New Jersey**
*William Livingston*
*David Brearley*
*William Paterson*
*Jonathan Dayton*

**Pennsylvania**
*Benjamin Franklin*
*Thomas Mifflin*
*Robert Morris*
*George Clymer*
*Thomas FitzSimons*
*Jared Ingersoll*
*James Wilson*
*Gouverneur Morris*

**Delaware**
*George Read*
*Gunning Bedford, Jr.*
*John Dickinson*
*Richard Bassett*
*Jacob Broom*

**Maryland**
*James McHenry*
*Daniel of St. Thomas Jenifer*
*Daniel Carroll*

**Virginia**
*John Blair*
*James Madison, Jr.*

**North Carolina**
*William Blount*
*Richard Dobbs Spaight*
*Hugh Williamson*

**South Carolina**
*John Rutledge*
*Charles Cotesworth Pinckney*
*Charles Pinckney*
*Pierce Butler*

**Georgia**
*William Few*
*Abraham Baldwin*

---

[6] These are the full names of the signers, which in some cases are not the signatures on the document.

*Articles in Addition to, and Amendment of, the Constitution of the United States of America, Proposed by Congress, and Ratified by the Legislatures of the Several States, Pursuant to the Fifth Article of the Original Constitution[7]*

## [Article I]

Congress shall make no law respecting an establishment of religion, or prohibiting the free exercise thereof; or abridging the freedom of speech, or of the press; or the right of the people peaceably to assemble, and to petition the Government for a redress of grievances.

## [Article II]

A well regulated Militia, being necessary to the security of a free State, the right of the people to keep and bear Arms shall not be infringed.

## [Article III]

No Soldier shall, in time of peace, be quartered in any house, without the consent of the Owner, nor in time of war, but in a manner to be prescribed by law.

## [Article IV]

The right of the people to be secure in their persons, houses, papers, and effects, against unreasonable searches and seizures, shall not be violated, and no Warrants shall issue, but upon probable cause, supported by Oath or affirmation, and particularly describing the place to be searched, and the persons or things to be seized.

[7] This heading appears only in the joint resolution submitting the first ten amendments.

## [Article V]

No person shall be held to answer for a capital or otherwise infamous crime, unless on a presentment or indictment of a Grand Jury, except in cases arising in the land or naval forces, or in the Militia, when in actual service in time of War or public danger; nor shall any person be subject for the same offence to be twice put in jeopardy of life or limb; nor shall be compelled in any criminal case to be a witness against himself, nor be deprived of life, liberty, or property, without due process of law; nor shall private property be taken for public use, without just compensation.

## [Article VI]

In all criminal prosecutions, the accused shall enjoy the right to a speedy and public trial, by an impartial jury of the State and district wherein the crime shall have been committed, which district shall have been previously ascertained by law, and to be informed of the nature and cause of the accusation; to be confronted with the witnesses against him; to have compulsory process for obtaining witnesses in his favour, and to have the Assistance of Counsel for his defence.

## [Article VII]

In suits at common law, where the value in controversy shall exceed twenty dollars, the right of trial by jury shall be preserved, and no fact tried by a jury, shall be otherwise reexamined in any Court of the United States, than according to the rules of the common law.

## [Article VIII]

Excessive bail shall not be required, nor excessive fines imposed, nor cruel and unusual punishments inflicted.

## [Article IX]

The enumeration in the Constitution, of certain rights, shall not be construed to deny or disparage others retained by the people.

## [Article X]

The powers not delegated to the United States by the Constitution, nor prohibited by it to the States, are reserved to the States respectively, or to the people.

[Amendments I–X, in force 1791.]

## [Article XI][8]

The Judicial power of the United States shall not be construed to extend to any suit in law or equity, commenced or prosecuted against one of the United States by Citizens of another State, or by Citizens or Subjects of any Foreign State.

## [Article XII][9]

The Electors shall meet in their respective States and vote by ballot for President and Vice-President, one of whom, at least, shall not be an inhabitant of the same State with themselves; they shall name in their ballots the person voted for as President, and in distinct ballots the person voted for as Vice-President, and they shall make distinct lists of all persons voted for as President, and of all persons voted for as Vice-President, and of the number of votes for each, which lists they shall sign and certify, and transmit sealed to the seat

of the government of the United States, directed to the President of the Senate; —The President of the Senate shall, in the presence of the Senate and House of Representatives, open all the certificates and the votes shall then be counted;— The person having the greatest number of votes for President, shall be the President, if such number be a majority of the whole number of Electors appointed; and if no person have such majority, then from the persons having the highest numbers not exceeding three on the list of those voted for as President, the House of Representatives shall choose immediately, by ballot, the President. But in choosing the President, the votes shall be taken by states, the representation from each state having one vote; a quorum for this purpose shall consist of a member or members from two-thirds of the states, and a majority of all the states shall be necessary to a choice. And if the House of Representatives shall not choose a President whenever the right of choice shall devolve upon them, before the fourth day of March next following, then the Vice-President shall act as President, as in the case of the death or other constitutional disability of the President.—The person having the greatest number of votes as Vice-President, shall be the Vice-President, if such number be a majority of the whole number of Electors appointed, and if no person have a majority, then from the two highest numbers on the list, the Senate shall choose the Vice-President; a quorum for the purpose shall consist of two-thirds of the whole number of Senators, and a majority of the whole number shall be necessary to a choice. But no person constitutionally ineligible to the office of President shall be eligible to that of Vice-President of the United States.

---

[8] Adopted in 1798.
[9] Adopted in 1804.

## [Article XIII][10]

Section 1.   Neither slavery nor involuntary servitude, except as a punishment for crime whereof the party shall have been duly convicted, shall exist within the United States, or any place subject to their jurisdiction.

Section 2.   Congress shall have power to enforce this article by appropriate legislation.

## [Article XIV][11]

Section 1.   All persons born or naturalized in the United States, and subject to the jurisdiction thereof, are citizens of the United States and of the State wherein they reside. No State shall abridge the privileges or immunities of citizens of the United States; nor shall any State deprive any person of life, liberty, or property, without due process of law; nor deny to any person within its jurisdiction the equal protection of the laws.

Section 2.   Representatives shall be apportioned among the several States according to their respective numbers, counting the whole number of persons in each State, excluding Indians not taxed. But when the right to vote at any election for the choice of electors for President and Vice-President of the United States, Representatives in Congress, the Executive and Judicial officers of a State, or the members of the Legislature thereof, is denied to any of the male inhabitants of such State, being twenty-one years of age, and citizens of the United States, or in any way abridged, except for participation in rebellion, or other crime, the basis of representation therein shall be reduced in the proportion which the number of such male citizens shall bear to the whole number of male citizens twenty-one years of age in such State.

Section 3.   No person shall be a Senator or Representative in Congress, or elector of President and Vice-President, or hold any office, civil or military, under the United States, or under any State, who, having previously taken an oath, as a member of Congress, or as an officer of the United States, or as a member of any State legislature, or as an executive or judicial officer of any State, to support the Constitution of the United States, shall have engaged in insurrection or rebellion against the same, or given aid or comfort to the enemies thereof. But Congress may by a vote of two-thirds of each House, remove such disability.

Section 4.   The validity of the public debt of the United States, authorized by law, including debts incurred for payment of pensions and bounties for services in suppressing insurrection or rebellion, shall not be questioned. But neither the United States nor any State shall assume or pay any debts or obligation incurred in aid of insurrection or rebellion against the United States, or any claim for the loss or emancipation of any slave; but all such debts, obligations, and claims shall be held illegal and void.

Section 5.   The Congress shall have the power to enforce, by appropriate legislation, the provisions of this article.

## [Article XV][12]

Section 1.   The right of citizens of the United States to vote shall not be denied or abridged by the United States

---

[10] Adopted in 1865.
[11] Adopted in 1868.

[12] Adopted in 1870.

or by any State on account of race, color, or previous condition of servitude—

Section 2. The Congress shall have power to enforce this article by appropriate legislation.

## [Article XVI][13]

The Congress shall have power to lay and collect taxes on incomes, from whatever source derived, without apportionment among the several States, and without regard to any census or enumeration.

## [Article XVII][14]

The Senate of the United States shall be composed of two Senators from each State, elected by the people thereof, for six years; and each Senator shall have one vote. The electors in each State shall have the qualifications requisite for electors of the most numerous branch of the State legislatures.

When vacancies happen in the representation of any State in the Senate, the executive authority of such State shall issue writs of election to fill such vacancies: *Provided,* That the legislature of any State may empower the executive thereof to make temporary appointments until the people fill the vacancies by election as the legislature may direct.

This amendment shall not be so construed as to affect the election or term of any Senator chosen before it becomes valid as part of the Constitution.

## [Article XVIII][15]

Section 1. After one year from the ratification of this article the manufacture, sale, or transportation of intoxi-

cating liquors within, the importation thereof into, or the exportation thereof from the United States and all territory subject to the jurisdiction thereof for beverage purposes is hereby prohibited.

Section 2. The Congress and the several States shall have concurrent power to enforce this article by appropriate legislation.

Section 3. This article shall be inoperative unless it shall have been ratified as an amendment to the Constitution by the legislatures of the several States, as provided in the Constitution, within seven years from the date of the submission hereof to the States by the Congress.

## [Article XIX][16]

The right of citizens of the United States to vote shall not be denied or abridged by the United States or by any State on account of sex.

Congress shall have power to enforce this article by appropriate legislation.

## [Article XX][17]

Section 1. The terms of the President and Vice-President shall end at noon on the 20th day of January, and the terms of Senators and Representatives at noon on the 3d day of January, of the years in which such terms would have ended if this article had not been ratified; and the terms of their successors shall then begin.

Section 2. The Congress shall assemble at least once in every year, and such meeting shall begin at noon on the 3d day of January, unless they shall by law appoint a different day.

Section 3. If, at the time fixed for

[13] Adopted in 1913.

[14] Adopted in 1913.

[15] Adopted in 1918.

[16] Adopted in 1920.

[17] Adopted in 1933.

the beginning of the term of the President, the President elect shall have died, the Vice-President elect shall become President. If a President shall not have been chosen before the time fixed for the beginning of his term, or if the President elect shall have failed to qualify, then the Vice-President elect shall act as President until a President shall have qualified; and the Congress may by law provide for the case wherein neither a President elect nor a Vice-President elect shall have qualified, declaring who shall then act as President, or the manner in which one who is to act shall be selected, and such person shall act accordingly until a President or Vice-President shall have qualified.

Section 4.    The Congress may by law provide for the case of the death of any of the persons from whom the House of Representatives may choose a President whenever the right of choice shall have devolved upon them, and for the case of the death of any of the persons from whom the Senate may choose a Vice-President whenever the right of choice shall have devolved upon them.

Section 5.    Sections 1 and 2 shall take effect on the 15th day of October following the ratification of this article.

Section 6.    This article shall be inoperative unless it shall have been ratified as an amendment to the Constitution by the legislatures of three-fourths of the several States within seven years from the date of its submission.

## [Article XXI][18]

Section 1.    The eighteenth article of amendment to the Constitution of the United States is hereby repealed.

Section 2.    The transportation or importation into any State, Territory, or possession of the United States for delivery or use therein of intoxicating liquors, in violation of the laws thereof, is hereby prohibited.

Section 3.    This article shall be inoperative unless it shall have been ratified as an amendment to the Constitution by conventions in the several States, as provided in the Constitution, within seven years from the date of the submission hereof to the States by the Congress.

## [Article XXII][19]

No person shall be elected to the office of the President more than twice, and no person who has held the office of President, or acted as President, for more than two years of a term to which some other person was elected President shall be elected to the office of the President more than once.

But this Article shall not apply to any person holding the office of President when this Article was proposed by the Congress, and shall not prevent any person who may be holding the office of President, or acting as President, during the term within which this Article becomes operative from holding the office of President or acting as President during the remainder of such term.

This article shall be inoperative unless it shall have been ratified as an amendment to the Constitution by the legislatures of three-fourths of the several states within seven years from the date of its submission to the states by the Congress.

---

[18] Adopted in 1933.

[19] Adopted in 1951.

## [Article XXIII][20]

Section 1. The District constituting the seat of Government of the United States shall appoint in such manner as the Congress may direct:

A number of electors of President and Vice-President equal to the whole number of Senators and Representatives in Congress to which the District would be entitled if it were a State, but in no event more than the least populous State; they shall be in addition to those appointed by the States, but they shall be considered, for the purposes of the election of President and Vice-President, to be electors appointed by a State; and they shall meet in the District and perform such duties as provided by the twelfth article of amendment.

Section 2. The Congress shall have power to enforce this article by appropriate legislation.

## [Article XXIV][21]

Section 1. The right of citizens of the United States to vote in any primary or other election for President or Vice President, for electors for President or Vice President, or for Senator or Representative in Congress, shall not be denied or abridged by the United States or any state by reason of failure to pay any poll tax or other tax.

Section 2. The Congress shall have the power to enforce this article by appropriate legislation.

## [Article XXV][22]

Section 1. In case of the removal of the President from office or of his death or resignation, the Vice President shall become President.

Section 2. Whenever there is a vacancy in the office of the Vice President, the President shall nominate a Vice President who shall take office upon confirmation by a majority vote of both Houses of Congress.

Section 3. Whenever the President transmits to the President Pro Tempore of the Senate and the Speaker of the House of Representatives his written declaration that he is unable to discharge the powers and duties of his office, and until he transmits to them a written declaration to the contrary, such powers and duties shall be discharged by the Vice President as Acting President.

Section 4. Whenever the Vice President and a majority of either the principal officers of the executive departments or of such other body as Congress may by law provide, transmit to the President Pro Tempore of the Senate and the Speaker of the House of Representatives their written declaration that the President is unable to discharge the powers and duties of his office, the Vice President shall immediately assume the powers and duties of the office as Acting President.

Thereafter, when the President transmits to the President Pro Tempore of the Senate and the Speaker of the House of Representatives his written declaration that no inability exists, he shall resume the powers and duties of his office unless the Vice President and a majority of either the principal officers of the executive departments or of such other body as Congress may by law provide, transmit within four days to the President Pro Tempore of the Senate and the Speaker of the House of Representatives their written declaration that the Presi-

---

[20] Adopted in 1961.
[21] Adopted in 1964.
[22] Adopted in 1967.

dent is unable to discharge the powers and duties of his office. Thereupon Congress shall decide the issue, assembling within forty-eight hours for that purpose if not in session. If the Congress, within twenty-one days after receipt of the latter written declaration, or, if Congress is not in session, within twenty-one days after Congress is required to assemble, determines by two-thirds vote of both Houses that the President is unable to discharge the powers and duties of his office, the Vice President shall continue to discharge the same as Acting President; otherwise, the President shall resume the powers and duties of his office.

# Sovereigns of England and Great Britain, 1485–1820

The ruler was King (or Queen) of England until 1707, except for the interregnum of 1649–1660, during which Oliver Cromwell made himself Lord Protector. The ruler was King (or Queen) of Great Britain after the union of England and Scotland in 1707, and King (or Queen) of Great Britain and Ireland after 1800.

*Henry VII* 1485–1509
*Henry VIII* 1509–1547
*Edward VI* 1547–1553
*Mary I* 1553–1558
*Elizabeth I* 1558–1603
*James I* (VI of Scotland) 1603–1625
*Charles I* 1625–1649
   *Oliver Cromwell* 1650–1658
   *Richard Cromwell* 1658–1659

*Charles II* 1660–1685
*James II* 1685–1688
*William III and Mary II* 1689–1694
*William III* 1694–1702
*Anne* 1702–1714
*George I* 1714–1727
*George II* 1727–1760
*George III* 1760–1820

# Admission of States to the Union*

| | | | | |
|---|---|---|---|---|
| 1. | Delaware | Dec. 7, 1787 | 26. Michigan | Jan. 26, 1837 |
| 2. | Pennsylvania | Dec. 12, 1787 | 27. Florida | Mar. 3, 1845 |
| 3. | New Jersey | Dec. 18, 1787 | 28. Texas | Dec. 29, 1845 |
| 4. | Georgia | Jan. 2, 1788 | 29. Iowa | Dec. 28, 1846 |
| 5. | Connecticut | Jan. 9, 1788 | 30. Wisconsin | May 29, 1848 |
| 6. | Massachusetts | Feb. 6, 1788 | 31. California | Sept. 9, 1850 |
| 7. | Maryland | Apr. 28, 1788 | 32. Minnesota | May 11, 1858 |
| 8. | South Carolina | May 23, 1788 | 33. Oregon | Feb. 14, 1859 |
| 9. | New Hampshire | June 21, 1788 | 34. Kansas | Jan. 29, 1861 |
| 10. | Virginia | June 25, 1788 | 35. West Virginia | June 19, 1863 |
| 11. | New York | July 26, 1788 | 36. Nevada | Oct. 31, 1864 |
| 12. | North Carolina | Nov. 21, 1789 | 37. Nebraska | Mar. 1, 1867 |
| 13. | Rhode Island | May 29, 1790 | 38. Colorado | Aug. 1, 1876 |
| 14. | Vermont | Mar. 4, 1791 | 39. North Dakota | Nov. 2, 1889 |
| 15. | Kentucky | June 1, 1792 | 40. South Dakota | Nov. 2, 1889 |
| 16. | Tennessee | June 1, 1796 | 41. Montana | Nov. 8, 1889 |
| 17. | Ohio | Mar. 1, 1803 | 42. Washington | Nov. 11, 1889 |
| 18. | Louisiana | Apr. 30, 1812 | 43. Idaho | July 3, 1890 |
| 19. | Indiana | Dec. 11, 1816 | 44. Wyoming | July 10, 1890 |
| 20. | Mississippi | Dec. 10, 1817 | 45. Utah | Jan. 4, 1896 |
| 21. | Illinois | Dec. 3, 1818 | 46. Oklahoma | Nov. 16, 1907 |
| 22. | Alabama | Dec. 14, 1819 | 47. New Mexico | Jan. 6, 1912 |
| 23. | Maine | Mar. 15, 1820 | 48. Arizona | Feb. 14, 1912 |
| 24. | Missouri | Aug. 10, 1821 | 49. Alaska | Jan. 3, 1959 |
| 25. | Arkansas | June 15, 1836 | 50. Hawaii | Aug. 21, 1959 |

* In the case of the first thirteen states, the date given is that of ratification of the Constitution.

# Presidential Elections

| Year | Candidates | Parties | Popular Vote | Electoral Vote |
|------|-----------|---------|-------------|----------------|
| 1789 | **GEORGE WASHINGTON** *(Va.)*\* | | | 69 |
| | John Adams | | | 34 |
| | Others | | | 35 |
| 1792 | **GEORGE WASHINGTON** *(Va.)* | | | 132 |
| | John Adams | | | 77 |
| | George Clinton | | | 50 |
| | Others | | | 5 |
| 1796 | **JOHN ADAMS** *(Mass.)* | Federalist | | 71 |
| | Thomas Jefferson | Democratic-Republican | | 68 |
| | Thomas Pinckney | Federalist | | 59 |
| | Aaron Burr | Dem.-Rep. | | 30 |
| | Others | | | 48 |
| 1800 | **THOMAS JEFFERSON** *(Va.)* | Dem.-Rep. | | 73 |
| | Aaron Burr | Dem.-Rep. | | 73 |
| | John Adams | Federalist | | 65 |
| | C. C. Pinckney | Federalist | | 64 |
| | John Jay | Federalist | | 1 |
| 1804 | **THOMAS JEFFERSON** *(Va.)* | Dem.-Rep. | | 162 |
| | C. C. Pinckney | Federalist | | 14 |
| 1808 | **JAMES MADISON** *(Va.)* | Dem.-Rep. | | 122 |
| | C. C. Pinckney | Federalist | | 47 |
| | George Clinton | Dem.-Rep. | | 6 |
| 1812 | **JAMES MADISON** *(Va.)* | Dem.-Rep. | | 128 |
| | De Witt Clinton | Federalist | | 89 |
| 1816 | **JAMES MONROE** *(Va.)* | Dem.-Rep. | | 183 |
| | Rufus King | Federalist | | 34 |
| 1820 | **JAMES MONROE** *(Va.)* | Dem.-Rep. | | 231 |
| | John Quincy Adams | Dem.-Rep. | | 1 |

\* State of residence at time of election.

| Year | Candidates | Parties | Popular Vote | Electoral Vote |
|------|------------|---------|-------------|----------------|
| 1824 | **JOHN Q. ADAMS** *(Mass.)* | Dem.-Rep. | 108,740 | 84 |
|      | Andrew Jackson | Dem.-Rep. | 153,544 | 99 |
|      | William H. Crawford | Dem.-Rep. | 46,618 | 41 |
|      | Henry Clay | Dem.-Rep. | 47,136 | 37 |
| 1828 | **ANDREW JACKSON** *(Tenn.)* | Democrat | 647,286 | 178 |
|      | John Quincy Adams | National Republican | 508,064 | 83 |
| 1832 | **ANDREW JACKSON** *(Tenn.)* | Democrat | 687,502 | 219 |
|      | Henry Clay | National Republican | 530,189 | 49 |
|      | John Floyd | Independent | | 11 |
|      | William Wirt | AntiMason | 33,108 | 7 |
| 1836 | **MARTIN VAN BUREN** *(N.Y.)* | Democrat | 765,483 | 170 |
|      | W. H. Harrison | Whig | | 73 |
|      | Hugh L. White | Whig | 739,795 | 26 |
|      | Daniel Webster | Whig | | 14 |
|      | W. P. Mangum | Independent | | 11 |
| 1840 | **WILLIAM H. HARRISON** *(Ohio)* | Whig | 1,274,624 | 234 |
|      | Martin Van Buren | Democrat | 1,127,781 | 60 |
|      | J. G. Birney | Liberty | 7,069 | |
| 1844 | **JAMES K. POLK** *(Tenn.)* | Democrat | 1,338,464 | 170 |
|      | Henry Clay | Whig | 1,300,097 | 105 |
|      | J. G. Birney | Liberty | 62,300 | |
| 1848 | **ZACHARY TAYLOR** *(La.)* | Whig | 1,360,967 | 163 |
|      | Lewis Cass | Democrat | 1,222,342 | 127 |
|      | Martin Van Buren | Free-Soil | 291,263 | |
| 1852 | **FRANKLIN PIERCE** *(N.H.)* | Democrat | 1,601,117 | 254 |
|      | Winfield Scott | Whig | 1,385,453 | 42 |
|      | John P. Hale | Free-Soil | 155,825 | |
| 1856 | **JAMES BUCHANAN** *(Pa.)* | Democrat | 1,832,955 | 174 |
|      | John C. Frémont | Republican | 1,339,932 | 114 |
|      | Millard Fillmore | American | 871,731 | 8 |
| 1860 | **ABRAHAM LINCOLN** *(Ill.)* | Republican | 1,865,593 | 180 |
|      | Stephen A. Douglas | Democrat | 1,382,713 | 12 |
|      | John C. Breckinridge | Democrat | 848,356 | 72 |
|      | John Bell | Union | 592,906 | 39 |

| Year | Candidates | Parties | Popular Vote | Electoral Vote |
|------|-----------|---------|-------------|---------------|
| 1864 | **ABRAHAM LINCOLN** *(III.)** | Republican | 2,213,655 | 212 |
|  | George B. McClellan | Democrat | 1,805,237 | 21 |
| 1868 | **ULYSSES S. GRANT** *(III.)* | Republican | 3,012,833 | 214 |
|  | Horatio Seymour | Democrat | 2,703,249 | 80 |
| 1872 | **ULYSSES S. GRANT** *(III.)* | Republican | 3,597,132 | 286 |
|  | Horace Greeley | Democrat; Liberal Republican | 2,834,125 | 66 |
| 1876 | **RUTHERFORD B. HAYES** *(Ohio)* | Republican | 4,036,298 | 185 |
|  | Samuel J. Tilden | Democrat | 4,300,590 | 184 |
| 1880 | **JAMES A. GARFIELD** *(Ohio)* | Republican | 4,454,416 | 214 |
|  | Winfield S. Hancock | Democrat | 4,444,952 | 155 |
| 1884 | **GROVER CLEVELAND** *(N.Y.)* | Democrat | 4,874,986 | 219 |
|  | James G. Blaine | Republican | 4,851,981 | 182 |
| 1888 | **BENJAMIN HARRISON** *(Ind.)* | Republican | 5,439,853 | 233 |
|  | Grover Cleveland | Democrat | 5,540,309 | 168 |
| 1892 | **GROVER CLEVELAND** *(N.Y.)* | Democrat | 5,556,918 | 277 |
|  | Benjamin Harrison | Republican | 5,176,108 | 145 |
|  | James B. Weaver | People's | 1,041,028 | 22 |
| 1896 | **WILLIAM McKINLEY** *(Ohio)* | Republican | 7,104,779 | 271 |
|  | William J. Bryan | Democrat-People's | 6,502,925 | 176 |
| 1900 | **WILLIAM McKINLEY** *(Ohio)* | Republican | 7,207,923 | 292 |
|  | William J. Bryan | Dem.-Populist | 6,358,133 | 155 |
| 1904 | **THEODORE ROOSEVELT** *(N.Y.)* | Republican | 7,623,486 | 336 |
|  | Alton B. Parker | Democrat | 5,077,911 | 140 |
|  | Eugene V. Debs | Socialist | 402,283 | — |

* State of residence at time of election.

| Year | Candidates | Parties | Popular Vote | Electoral Vote |
|------|-----------|---------|-------------:|---------------:|
| 1908 | **WILLIAM H. TAFT** *(Ohio)* | Republican | 7,678,908 | 321 |
|      | William J. Bryan | Democrat | 6,409,104 | 162 |
|      | Eugene V. Debs | Socialist | 420,793 | — |
| 1912 | **WOODROW WILSON** *(N.J.)* | Democrat | 6,293,454 | 435 |
|      | Theodore Roosevelt | Progressive | 4,119,538 | 88 |
|      | William H. Taft | Republican | 3,484,980 | 8 |
|      | Eugene V. Debs | Socialist | 900,672 | — |
| 1916 | **WOODROW WILSON** *(N.J.)* | Democrat | 9,129,606 | 277 |
|      | Charles E. Hughes | Republican | 8,538,221 | 254 |
|      | A. L. Benson | Socialist | 585,113 | — |
| 1920 | **WARREN G. HARDING** *(Ohio)* | Republican | 16,152,200 | 404 |
|      | James M. Cox | Democrat | 9,147,353 | 127 |
|      | Eugene V. Debs | Socialist | 919,799 | — |
| 1924 | **CALVIN COOLIDGE** *(Mass.)* | Republican | 15,725,016 | 382 |
|      | John W. Davis | Democrat | 8,386,503 | 136 |
|      | Robert M. LaFollette | Progressive | 4,822,856 | 13 |
| 1928 | **HERBERT HOOVER** *(Calif.)* | Republican | 21,391,381 | 444 |
|      | Alfred E. Smith | Democrat | 15,016,443 | 87 |
|      | Norman Thomas | Socialist | 267,835 | — |
| 1932 | **FRANKLIN D. ROOSEVELT** *(N.Y.)* | Democrat | 22,821,857 | 472 |
|      | Herbert Hoover | Republican | 15,761,841 | 59 |
|      | Norman Thomas | Socialist | 881,951 | — |
| 1936 | **FRANKLIN D. ROOSEVELT** *(N.Y.)* | Democrat | 27,751,597 | 523 |
|      | Alfred M. Landon | Republican | 16,679,583 | 8 |
|      | William Lemke | Union and others | 882,479 | — |
| 1940 | **FRANKLIN D. ROOSEVELT** *(N.Y.)* | Democrat | 27,244,160 | 449 |
|      | Wendell L. Willkie | Republican | 22,305,198 | 82 |
| 1944 | **FRANKLIN D. ROOSEVELT** *(N.Y.)* | Democrat | 25,602,504 | 432 |
|      | Thomas E. Dewey | Republican | 22,006,285 | 99 |
| 1948 | **HARRY S TRUMAN** *(Mo.)* | Democrat | 24,105,695 | 304 |
|      | Thomas E. Dewey | Republican | 21,969,170 | 189 |
|      | J. Strom Thurmond | State-Rights Democrat | 1,169,021 | 38 |
|      | Henry A. Wallace | Progressive | 1,156,103 | — |

| Year | Candidates | Parties | Popular Vote | Electoral Vote |
|------|-----------|---------|--------------|----------------|
| 1952 | **DWIGHT D. EISENHOWER** *(N.Y.)* | Republican | 33,936,252 | 442 |
|      | Adlai E. Stevenson | Democrat | 27,314,992 | 89 |
| 1956 | **DWIGHT D. EISENHOWER** *(N.Y.)* | Republican | 35,575,420 | 457 |
|      | Adlai E. Stevenson | Democrat | 26,033,066 | 73 |
|      | Other |  |  | 1 |
| 1960 | **JOHN F. KENNEDY** *(Mass.)* | Democrat | 34,227,096 | 303 |
|      | Richard M. Nixon | Republican | 34,108,546 | 219 |
|      | Other |  |  | 15 |
| 1964 | **LYNDON B. JOHNSON** *(Tex.)* | Democrat | 43,126,506 | 486 |
|      | Barry M. Goldwater | Republican | 27,176,799 | 52 |
| 1968 | **RICHARD M. NIXON** *(N.Y.)* | Republican | 31,770,237 | 301 |
|      | Hubert H. Humphrey | Democrat | 31,270,533 | 191 |
|      | George Wallace | American Indep. | 9,906,141 | 46 |

# Presidents, Vice Presidents, and Cabinet Members,

| President | Vice President | Secretary of State | Secretary of Treasury | Secretary of War |
|---|---|---|---|---|
| 1. George Washington, Federalist 1789 | John Adams, Federalist 1789 | T. Jefferson 1789<br>E. Randolph 1794<br>T. Pickering 1795 | Alex. Hamilton 1789<br>Oliver Wolcott 1795 | Henry Knox 1789<br>T. Pickering 1795<br>Jas. McHenry 1796 |
| 2. John Adams, Federalist 1797 | Thomas Jefferson, Dem.-Rep. 1797 | T. Pickering 1797<br>John Marshall 1800 | Oliver Wolcott 1797<br>Samuel Dexter 1801 | Jas. McHenry 1797<br>John Marshall 1800<br>Samuel Dexter 1800<br>R. Griswold 1801 |
| 3. Thomas Jefferson, Dem.-Rep. 1801 | Aaron Burr, Dem.-Rep. 1801<br>George Clinton, Dem.-Rep. 1805 | James Madison 1801 | Samuel Dexter 1801<br>Albert Gallatin 1801 | H. Dearborn 1801 |
| 4. James Madison, Dem.-Rep. 1809 | George Clinton, Dem.-Rep. 1809<br>Elbridge Gerry, Dem.-Rep. 1813 | Robert Smith 1809<br>James Monroe 1811 | Albert Gallatin 1809<br>G. W. Campbell 1814<br>A. J. Dallas 1814<br>W. H. Crawford 1816 | Wm. Eustis 1809<br>J. Armstrong 1813<br>James Monroe 1814<br>W. H. Crawford 1815 |
| 5. James Monroe, Dem.-Rep. 1817 | D. D. Tompkins, Dem.-Rep. 1817 | J. Q. Adams 1817 | W. H. Crawford 1817 | Isaac Shelby 1817<br>George Graham 1817<br>J. C. Calhoun 1817 |
| 6. John Quincy Adams, Dem.-Rep. 1825 | John C. Calhoun, Dem.-Rep. 1825 | Henry Clay 1825 | Richard Rush 1825 | Jas. Barbour 1825<br>Peter B. Porter 1828 |
| 7. Andrew Jackson, Democratic 1829 | John C. Calhoun, Democratic 1829<br>Martin Van Buren, Democratic 1833 | M. Van Buren 1829<br>E. Livingston 1831<br>Louis McLane 1833<br>John Forsyth 1834 | Sam. D. Ingham 1829<br>Louis McLane 1831<br>W. J. Duane 1833<br>Roger B. Taney 1833<br>Levi Woodbury 1834 | John H. Eaton 1829<br>Lewis Cass 1831<br>B. F. Butler 1837 |
| 8. Martin Van Buren, Democratic 1837 | Richard M. Johnson, Democratic 1837 | John Forsyth 1837 | Levi Woodbury 1837 | Joel R. Poinsett 1837 |
| 9. William H. Harrison, Whig 1841 | John Tyler, Whig 1841 | Daniel Webster 1841 | Thomas Ewing 1841 | John Bell 1841 |
| 10. John Tyler, Whig and Democratic 1841 | | Daniel Webster 1841<br>Hugh S. Legare 1843<br>Abel P. Upshur 1843<br>John C. Calhoun 1844 | Thomas Ewing 1841<br>Walter Forward 1841<br>John C. Spencer 1843<br>Geo. M. Bibb 1844 | John Bell 1841<br>John McLean 1841<br>J. C. Spencer 1841<br>Jas. M. Porter 1843<br>Wm. Wilkins 1844 |

| President | Vice President | | | |
|---|---|---|---|---|
| 11. James K. Polk, Democratic<br>1845 | George M. Dallas, Democratic<br>1845 | James Buchanan  1845 | Robert J. Walker  1845 | William L. Marcy  1845 |
| 12. Zachary Taylor, Whig<br>1849 | Millard Fillmore, Whig<br>1849 | John M. Clayton  1849 | Wm. M. Meredith  1849 | G. W. Crawford  1849 |
| 13. Millard Fillmore, Whig<br>1850 | | Daniel Webster  1850<br>Edward Everett  1852 | Thomas Corwin  1850 | C. M. Conrad  1850 |
| 14. Franklin Pierce, Democratic<br>1853 | William R. D. King, Democratic<br>1853 | W. L. Marcy  1853 | James Guthrie  1853 | Jefferson Davis  1853 |
| 15. James Buchanan, Democratic<br>1857 | John C. Breckinridge, Democratic<br>1857 | Lewis Cass  1857<br>J. S. Black  1860 | Howell Cobb  1857<br>Philip F. Thomas  1860<br>John A. Dix  1861 | John B. Floyd  1857<br>Joseph Holt  1861 |
| 16. Abraham Lincoln, Republican<br>1861 | Hannibal Hamlin, Republican<br>1861<br>Andrew Johnson, Unionist<br>1865 | W. H. Seward  1861 | Salmon P. Chase  1861<br>W. P. Fessenden  1864<br>Hugh McCulloch  1865 | S. Cameron  1861<br>E. M. Stanton  1862 |
| 17. Andrew Johnson, Unionist<br>1865 | | W. H. Seward  1865 | H. McCulloch  1865 | E. M. Stanton  1865<br>U. S. Grant  1867<br>L. Thomas  1868<br>J. M. Schofield  1868 |
| 18. Ulysses S. Grant, Republican<br>1869 | Schuyler Colfax, Republican<br>1869<br>Henry Wilson, Republican<br>1873 | E. B. Washburne  1869<br>H. Fish  1869 | G. S. Boutwell  1869<br>W. A. Richardson  1873<br>B. H. Bristow  1874<br>L. M. Morrill  1876 | J. A. Rawlins  1869<br>W. T. Sherman  1869<br>W. W. Belknap  1869<br>A. Taft  1876<br>J. D. Cameron  1876 |
| 19. Rutherford B. Hayes, Republican<br>1877 | William A. Wheeler, Republican<br>1877 | W. M. Evarts  1877 | J. Sherman  1877 | G. W. McCrary  1877<br>A. Ramsey  1879 |
| 20. James A. Garfield, Republican<br>1881 | Chester A. Arthur, Republican<br>1881 | J. G. Blaine  1881 | W. Windom  1881 | R. T. Lincoln  1881 |
| 21. Chester A. Arthur, Republican<br>1881 | | F. T. Frelinghuysen  1881 | C. J. Folger  1881<br>W. Q. Gresham  1884<br>H. McCulloch  1884 | R. T. Lincoln  1881 |
| 22. Grover Cleveland, Democratic<br>1885 | T. A. Hendricks, Democratic<br>1885 | T. F. Bayard  1885 | D. Manning  1885<br>C. S. Fairchild  1887 | W. C. Endicott  1885 |
| 23. Benjamin Harrison, Republican<br>1889 | Levi P. Morton, Republican<br>1889 | J. G. Blaine  1889<br>J. W. Foster  1892 | W. Windom  1889<br>C. Foster  1891 | R. Proctor  1889<br>S. B. Elkins  1891 |
| 24. Grover Cleveland, Democratic<br>1893 | Adlai E. Stevenson, Democratic<br>1893 | W. Q. Gresham  1893<br>R. Olney  1895 | J. G. Carlisle  1893 | D. S. Lamont  1893 |
| 25. William McKinley, Republican<br>1897 | Garret A. Hobart, Republican<br>1897<br>Theodore Roosevelt, Republican<br>1901 | J. Sherman  1897<br>W. R. Day  1897<br>J. Hay  1898 | L. J. Gage  1897 | R. A. Alger  1897<br>E. Root  1899 |

| President | Vice President | Secretary of State | Secretary of Treasury | Secretary of War |
|---|---|---|---|---|
| 26. Theodore Roosevelt, Republican 1901 | Chas. W. Fairbanks, Republican 1905 | J. Hay 1901<br>E. Root 1905<br>R. Bacon 1909 | L. J. Gage 1901<br>L. M. Shaw 1902<br>G. B. Cortelyou 1907 | E. Root 1901<br>W. H. Taft 1904<br>L. E. Wright 1908 |
| 27. William H. Taft, Republican 1909 | James S. Sherman, Republican 1909 | P. C. Knox 1909 | F. MacVeagh 1909 | J. M. Dickinson 1909<br>H. L. Stimson 1911 |
| 28. Woodrow Wilson, Democratic 1913 | Thomas R. Marshall, Democratic 1913 | W. J. Bryan 1913<br>R. Lansing 1915<br>B. Colby 1920 | W. G. McAdoo 1913<br>C. Glass 1918<br>D. F. Houston 1920 | L. M. Garrison 1913<br>N. D. Baker 1916 |
| 29. Warren G. Harding, Republican 1921 | Calvin Coolidge, Republican 1921 | C. E. Hughes 1921 | A. W. Mellon 1921 | J. W. Weeks 1921 |
| 30. Calvin Coolidge, Republican 1923 | Charles G. Dawes, Republican 1925 | C. E. Hughes 1923<br>F. B. Kellogg 1925 | A. W. Mellon 1923 | J. W. Weeks 1923<br>D. F. Davis 1925 |
| 31. Herbert Hoover, Republican 1929 | Charles Curtis, Republican 1929 | H. L. Stimson 1929 | A. W. Mellon 1929<br>O. L. Mills 1932 | J. W. Good 1929<br>P. J. Hurley 1929 |
| 32. Franklin D. Roosevelt, Democratic 1933 | John Nance Garner, Democratic 1933<br>Henry A. Wallace, Democratic 1941<br>Harry S Truman, Democratic 1945 | C. Hull 1933<br>E. R. Stettinius, Jr. 1944 | W. H. Woodin 1933<br>H. Morgenthau, Jr. 1934 | G. H. Dern 1933<br>H. A. Woodring 1936<br>H. L. Stimson 1940 |
| 33. Harry S Truman, Democratic 1945 | Alben W. Barkley, Democratic 1949 | J. F. Byrnes 1945<br>G. C. Marshall 1947<br>D. G. Acheson 1949 | F. M. Vinson 1945<br>J. W. Snyder 1946 | R. H. Patterson 1945<br>K. C. Royall 1947<br>** |
| 34. Dwight D. Eisenhower, Republican 1953 | Richard M. Nixon, Republican 1953 | J. F. Dulles 1953<br>C. A. Herter 1959 | G. C. Humphrey 1953<br>R. B. Anderson 1957 | |
| 35. John F. Kennedy, Democratic 1961 | Lyndon B. Johnson, Democratic 1961 | D. Rusk 1961 | C. D. Dillon 1961 | |
| 36. Lyndon B. Johnson, Democratic 1963 | Hubert H. Humphrey, Democratic 1965 | D. Rusk 1961 | C. D. Dillon 1961<br>H. H. Fowler 1965 | |
| 37. Richard M. Nixon, Republican 1969 | Spiro T. Agnew, Republican 1969 | W. P. Rogers 1969 | D. M. Kennedy 1969 | |

** Lost cabinet status in 1947.

| | Attorney General | Postmaster General | Secretary of Navy | Secretary of Interior | Secretary of Agriculture | Other Members |
|---|---|---|---|---|---|---|
| *(1.) | E. Randolph 1789<br>Wm. Bradford 1794<br>Charles Lee 1795 | Samuel Osgood 1789<br>Tim. Pickering 1791<br>Jos. Habersham 1795 | Established<br>April 30, 1798 | Established<br>March 3, 1849 | | |
| (2.) | Charles Lee 1797<br>Theo. Parsons 1801 | Jos. Habersham 1797 | Benj. Stoddert 1798 | | | |
| (3.) | Levi Lincoln 1801<br>Robert Smith 1805<br>J. Breckenridge 1805<br>C. A. Rodney 1807 | Jos. Habersham 1801<br>Gideon Granger 1801 | Benj. Stoddert 1801<br>Robert Smith 1801<br>J. Crowninshield 1805 | | | |
| (4.) | C. A. Rodney 1809<br>Wm. Pinkney 1811<br>Richard Rush 1814 | Gideon Granger 1809<br>R. J. Meigs, Jr. 1814 | Paul Hamilton 1809<br>William Jones 1813<br>B. W. Crowninshield 1814 | | | |
| (5.) | Richard Rush 1817<br>William Wirt 1817 | R. J. Meigs, Jr. 1817<br>John McLean 1823 | B. W. Crowninshield 1817<br>Smith Thompson 1818<br>S. L. Southard 1823 | | | |
| (6.) | William Wirt 1825 | John McLean 1825 | S. L. Southard 1825 | | | |
| (7.) | John M. Berrien 1829<br>Roger B. Taney 1831<br>B. F. Butler 1833 | Wm. T. Barry 1829**<br>Amos Kendall 1835 | John Branch 1829<br>Levi Woodbury 1831<br>Mahlon Dickerson 1834 | | | |
| (8.) | B. F. Butler 1837<br>Felix Grundy 1838<br>H. D. Gilpin 1840 | Amos Kendall 1837<br>John M. Niles 1840 | Mahlon Dickerson 1837<br>Jas. K. Paulding 1838 | | | |
| (9.) | J. J. Crittenden 1841 | Francis Granger 1841 | George E. Badger 1841 | | | |
| (10.) | J. J. Crittenden 1841<br>Hugh S. Legare 1841<br>John Nelson 1843 | Francis Granger 1841<br>C. A. Wickliffe 1841 | George E. Badger 1841<br>Abel P. Upshur 1841<br>David Henshaw 1843<br>Thomas W. Gilmer 1844<br>John Y. Mason 1844 | | | |
| (11.) | John Y. Mason 1845<br>Nathan Clifford 1846<br>Isaac Toucey 1848 | Cave Johnson 1845 | George Bancroft 1845<br>John Y. Mason 1846 | | | |

* Numbers in parentheses indicate presidential administration.
** The postmaster general did not become a cabinet member until 1829.

| (No.) | Attorney General | Postmaster General | Secretary of Navy | Secretary of Interior | Secretary of Agriculture | Other Members |
|---|---|---|---|---|---|---|
| (12.) | Reverdy Johnson 1849 | Jacob Collamer 1849 | Wm. B. Preston 1849 | Thomas Ewing 1849 | | *Secretary of Commerce and Labor* Established Feb. 14, 1903. G. B. Cortelyou 1903 · V. H. Metcalf 1904 · O. S. Straus 1907 · C. Nagel 1909 · (Department divided, 1913) |
| (13.) | J. J. Crittenden 1850 | Nathan K. Hall 1850 / Sam D. Hubbard 1852 | Wm. A. Graham 1850 / John P. Kennedy 1852 | A. H. Stuart 1850 | | |
| (14.) | Caleb Cushing 1853 | James Campbell 1853 | James C. Dobbin 1853 | Robert McClelland 1853 | | |
| (15.) | J. S. Black 1857 / Edw. M. Stanton 1860 | Aaron V. Brown 1857 / Joseph Holt 1859 | Isaac Toucey 1857 | Jacob Thompson 1857 | | |
| (16.) | Edward Bates 1861 / Titian J. Coffey 1863 / James Speed 1864 | Horatio King 1861 / Montgomery Blair 1861 / William Dennison 1864 | Gideon Welles 1861 | Caleb B. Smith 1861 / John P. Usher 1863 | | *Secretary of Commerce* W. C. Redfield 1913 · J. W. Alexander 1919 · H. C. Hoover 1921 · H. C. Hoover 1925 · W. F. Whiting 1928 · R. P. Lamont 1929 · R. D. Chapin 1932 · D. C. Roper 1933 · H. L. Hopkins 1939 · J. Jones 1940 · H. A. Wallace 1945 · W. A. Harriman 1946 · C. W. Sawyer 1948 · S. Weeks 1953 · L. L. Strauss 1958 · F. H. Mueller 1959 · L. H. Hodges 1961 · J. T. Connor 1965 · A. B. Trowbridge 1967 · M. H. Stans 1969 |
| (17.)* | J. Speed 1865 / H. Stanbery 1866 / W. M. Evarts 1868 | W. Dennison 1865 / A. W. Randall 1866 | G. Welles 1865 | J. P. Usher 1865 / J. Harlan 1865 / O. H. Browning 1866 | Cabinet status since 1889. | |
| (18.) | E. R. Hoar 1869 / A. T. Ackerman 1870 / G. H. Williams 1871 / E. Pierrepont 1875 / A. Taft 1876 | J. A. J. Creswell 1869 / J. W. Marshall 1874 / M. Jewell 1874 / J. N. Tyner 1876 | A. E. Borie 1869 / G. M. Robeson 1869 | J. D. Cox 1869 / C. Delano 1870 / Z. Chandler 1875 | | |
| (19.) | C. Devens 1877 | D. M. Key 1877 / H. Maynard 1880 | R. W. Thompson 1877 / N. Goff, Jr. 1881 | C. Schurz 1877 | | |
| (20.) | W. MacVeagh 1881 | T. L. James 1881 | W. H. Hunt 1881 | S. J. Kirkwood 1881 | | |
| (21.) | B. H. Brewster 1881 | T. O. Howe 1881 / W. Q. Gresham 1883 / F. Hatton 1884 | W. E. Chandler 1881 | H. M. Teller 1881 | | |
| (22.) | A. H. Garland 1885 | W. F. Vilas 1885 / D. M. Dickinson 1888 | W. C. Whitney 1885 | L. Q. C. Lamar 1885 / W. F. Vilas 1888 | N. J. Colman 1889 | *Secretary of Labor* Established March 4, 1913. W. B. Wilson 1913 · J. J. Davis 1921 · W. N. Doak 1930 · F. Perkins 1933 · L. B. Schwellenbach 1945 · M. J. Tobin 1948 · M. P. Durkin 1953 · J. P. Mitchell 1953 · A. J. Goldberg 1961 · W. W. Wirtz 1962 · G. T. Shultz 1969 |
| (23.) | W. H. H. Miller 1889 | J. Wanamaker 1889 | B. F. Tracy 1889 | J. W. Noble 1889 | J. M. Rusk 1889 | |
| (24.) | R. Olney 1893 / J. Harmon 1895 | W. S. Bissell 1893 / W. L. Wilson 1895 | H. A. Herbert 1893 | H. Smith 1893 / D. R. Francis 1896 | J. S. Morton 1893 | |
| (25.) | J. McKenna 1897 / J. W. Griggs 1897 / P. C. Knox 1901 | J. A. Gary 1897 / C. E. Smith 1898 | J. D. Long 1897 | C. N. Bliss 1897 / E. A. Hitchcock 1899 | J. Wilson 1897 | |

**Secretary of Defense**
*Established July 26, 1947.*
J. V. Forrestal 1947
L. A. Johnson 1949
G. C. Marshall 1950
R. A. Lovett 1951
C. E. Wilson 1953
N. McElroy 1957
T. S. Gates, Jr. 1959
R. S. McNamara 1961
C. Clifford 1968
M. R. Laird 1969

**Secretary of Health, Education, and Welfare**
*Established April 1, 1953.*
O. C. Hobby 1953
M. B. Folsom 1955
A. S. Flemming 1958
A. A. Ribicoff 1961
A. J. Celebrezze 1962
J. W. Gardner 1965
W. J. Cohen 1968
R. H. Finch 1969

**Secretary of Housing and Urban Development**
*Established September 9, 1965*
R. C. Weaver 1966
G. Romney 1969

**Secretary of Transportation**
*Established October 15, 1966*
A. S. Boyd 1966
J. A. Volpe 1969

| | | | | | |
|---|---|---|---|---|---|
| (26.) | P. C. Knox 1901<br>W. H. Moody 1904<br>C. J. Bonaparte 1907 | C. E. Smith 1901<br>H. C. Payne 1902<br>R. J. Wynne 1904<br>G. B. Cortelyou 1905<br>G. von L. Meyer 1907 | J. D. Long 1901<br>W. H. Moody 1902<br>P. Morton 1904<br>C. J. Bonaparte 1905<br>V. H. Metcalf 1907<br>T. H. Newberry 1908 | E. A. Hitchcock 1901<br>J. R. Garfield 1907 | J. Wilson 1901 |
| (27.) | G. W. Wickersham 1909 | F. H. Hitchcock 1909 | G. von L. Meyer 1909 | R. A. Ballinger 1909<br>W. L. Fisher 1911 | J. Wilson 1909 |
| (28.) | J. C. McReynolds 1913<br>T. W. Gregory 1914<br>A. M. Palmer 1919 | A. S. Burleson 1913 | J. Daniels 1913 | F. K. Lane 1913<br>J. B. Payne 1920 | D. F. Houston 1913<br>E. T. Meredith 1920 |
| (29.) | H. M. Daugherty 1921 | W. H. Hays 1921<br>H. Work 1922<br>H. S. New 1923 | E. Denby 1921 | A. B. Fall 1921<br>H. Work 1923 | H. C. Wallace 1921 |
| (30.) | H. M. Daugherty 1923<br>H. F. Stone 1924<br>J. G. Sargent 1925 | H. S. New 1923 | E. Denby 1923<br>Curtis D. Wilbur 1924 | H. Work 1923<br>R. O. West 1928 | H. C. Wallace 1923<br>H. M. Gore 1924<br>W. M. Jardine 1925 |
| (31.) | W. D. Mitchell 1929 | W. F. Brown 1929 | C. F. Adams 1929 | R. L. Wilbur 1929 | A. M. Hyde 1929 |
| (32.) | H. S. Cummings 1933<br>F. Murphy 1939<br>R. H. Jackson 1940<br>F. Biddle 1941 | J. A. Farley 1933<br>F. C. Walker 1940 | C. A. Swanson 1933<br>C. Edison 1940<br>F. Knox 1940<br>J. V. Forrestal 1944 | H. L. Ickes 1933 | H. A. Wallace 1933<br>C. R. Wickard 1940 |
| (33.) | T. C. Clark 1945<br>J. H. McGrath 1949<br>J. P. McGranery 1952 | R. E. Hannegan 1945<br>J. L. Donaldson 1947 | J. V. Forrestal 1945<br>†† | H. L. Ickes 1945<br>J. A. Krug 1946<br>O. L. Chapman 1951 | C. P. Anderson 1945<br>C. F. Brannan 1948 |
| (34.) | H. Brownell, Jr. 1953<br>W. P. Rogers 1957 | A. E. Summerfield 1953 | | D. McKay 1953<br>F. Seaton 1956 | E. T. Benson 1953 |
| (35.) | R. F. Kennedy 1961 | J. E. Day 1961<br>J. Gronovski 1963 | | S. L. Udall 1961 | O. L. Freeman 1961 |
| (36.) | N. de Katzenbach 1965<br>W. R. Clark 1967 | L. F. O'Brien 1965<br>W. M. Watson 1968 | | | |
| (37.) | J. N. Mitchell 1969 | W. Blount 1969 | | W. J. Hickel 1969 | C. M. Hardin 1969 |

†† Lost cabinet status in 1947.

# Chief Justices
# of the United States

*John Jay*, N.Y. 1789–1795
*John Rutledge*, S.C. 1795
*Oliver Ellsworth*, Conn. 1795–1799
*John Marshall*, Va. 1801–1835
*Roger B. Taney*, Md. 1836–1864
*Salmon P. Chase*, Ohio 1864–1873
*Morrison R. Waite*, Ohio 1874–1888
*Melville W. Fuller*, Ill. 1888–1910

*Edward D. White*, La. 1910–1921
*William H. Taft*, Ohio 1921–1930
*Charles E. Hughes*, N.Y. 1930–1941
*Harlan F. Stone*, N.Y. 1941–1946
*Fred M. Vinson*, Ky. 1946–1953
*Earl Warren*, Calif. 1953–1969
*Warren E. Burger*, Minn. 1969–

# Speakers of the House
# of Representatives

*F. A. C. Muhlenberg*, Pennsylvania 1789–1791
*Jonathan Trumbull*, Connecticut 1791–1793
*F. A. C. Muhlenberg*, Pennsylvania 1793–1795
*Jonathan Dayton*, New Jersey 1795–1799
*Theodore Sedgwick*, Massachusetts 1799–1801
*Nathaniel Macon*, North Carolina 1801–1807
*Joseph B. Varnum*, Massachusetts 1807–1811
*Henry Clay*, Kentucky 1811–1814
*Langdon Cheves*, South Carolina 1814–1815
*Henry Clay*, Kentucky 1815–1820
*John W. Taylor*, New York 1820–1821
*Philip P. Barbour*, Virginia 1821–1823
*Henry Clay*, Kentucky 1823–1825
*John W. Taylor*, New York 1825–1827
*Andrew Stevenson*, Virginia 1827–1834
*John Bell*, Tennessee 1834–1835
*James K. Polk*, Tennessee 1835–1839
*R. M. T. Hunter*, Virginia 1839–1841

*John White*, Kentucky 1841–1843
*John W. Jones*, Virginia 1843–1845
*John W. Davis*, Indiana 1845–1847
*R. C. Winthrop*, Massachusetts 1847–1849
*Howell Cobb*, Georgia 1849–1851
*Linn Boyd*, Kentucky 1851–1855
*N. P. Banks*, Massachusetts 1856–1857
*James L. Orr*, South Carolina 1857–1859
*William Pennington*, New Jersey 1860–1861
*Galusha A. Grow*, Pennsylvania 1861–1863
*Schuyler Colfax*, Indiana 1863–1869
*James G. Blaine*, Maine 1869–1875
*Michael C. Kerr*, Indiana 1875–1876
*Samuel J. Randall*, Pennsylvania 1876–1881
*Joseph W. Keifer*, Ohio 1881–1883
*John G. Carlisle*, Kentucky 1883–1889
*Thomas B. Reed*, Maine 1889–1891
*Charles F. Crisp*, Georgia 1891–1895

*Thomas B. Reed,* Maine 1895–1899

*David B. Henderson,* Iowa 1899–1903

*Joseph G. Cannon,* Illinois 1903–1910

*Champ Clark,* Missouri 1911–1919

*Frederick H. Gillett,* Massachusetts 1919–1925

*Nicholas Longworth,* Ohio 1925–1931

*John Nance Garner,* Texas 1931–1933

*Henry T. Rainey,* Illinois 1933–1934

*Joseph W. Byrns,* Tennessee 1935–1936

*William B. Bankhead,* Alabama 1936–1940

*Sam Rayburn,* Texas 1940–1947

*Joseph W. Martin, Jr.,* Massachusetts 1947–1949

*Sam Rayburn,* Texas 1949–1953

*Joseph W. Martin, Jr.,* Massachusetts 1953–1955

*Sam Rayburn,* Texas 1955–1961

*John W. McCormack,* Massachusetts 1961–1970

# Population of the United States

| Division and State | 1790 | 1800 | 1810 | 1820 | 1830 | 1840 | 1850 | 1860 | 1870 |
|---|---|---|---|---|---|---|---|---|---|
| United States | 3,929,214 | 5,308,483 | 7,239,881 | 9,638,453 | 12,866,020 | 17,069,453 | 23,191,876 | 31,443,321 | 39,818,449 |
| **GEOGRAPHIC DIVISIONS** | | | | | | | | | |
| New England | 1,009,408 | 1,233,011 | 1,471,973 | 1,660,071 | 1,954,717 | 2,234,822 | 2,728,116 | 3,135,283 | 3,487,924 |
| Middle Atlantic | 952,632 | 1,402,565 | 2,014,702 | 2,699,845 | 3,587,664 | 4,526,260 | 5,898,735 | 7,458,985 | 8,810,806 |
| South Atlantic | 1,851,806 | 2,286,494 | 2,674,891 | 3,061,063 | 3,645,752 | 3,925,299 | 4,679,090 | 5,364,703 | 5,853,610 |
| East South Central | 109,368 | 335,407 | 708,590 | 1,190,489 | 1,815,969 | 2,575,445 | 3,363,271 | 4,020,991 | 4,404,445 |
| West South Central | | | 77,618 | 167,680 | 246,127 | 449,985 | 940,251 | 1,747,667 | 2,029,965 |
| East North Central | | 51,006 | 272,324 | 792,719 | 1,470,018 | 2,924,728 | 4,523,260 | 6,926,884 | 9,124,517 |
| West North Central | | | 19,783 | 66,586 | 140,455 | 426,814 | 880,335 | 2,169,832 | 3,856,594 |
| Mountain | | | | | | | 72,927 | 174,923 | 315,385 |
| Pacific | | | | | | | 105,871 | 444,053 | 675,125 |
| **NEW ENGLAND** | | | | | | | | | |
| Maine | 96,540 | 151,719 | 228,705 | 298,335 | 399,455 | 501,793 | 583,169 | 628,279 | 626,915 |
| New Hampshire | 141,885 | 183,858 | 214,460 | 244,161 | 269,328 | 284,574 | 317,976 | 326,073 | 318,300 |
| Vermont | 85,425 | 154,465 | 217,895 | 235,981 | 280,652 | 291,948 | 314,120 | 315,098 | 330,551 |
| Massachusetts | 378,787 | 422,845 | 472,040 | 523,287 | 610,408 | 737,699 | 994,514 | 1,231,066 | 1,457,351 |
| Rhode Island | 68,825 | 69,122 | 76,931 | 83,059 | 97,199 | 108,830 | 147,545 | 174,620 | 217,353 |
| Connecticut | 237,946 | 251,002 | 261,942 | 275,248 | 297,675 | 309,978 | 370,792 | 460,147 | 537,454 |
| **MIDDLE ATLANTIC** | | | | | | | | | |
| New York | 340,120 | 589,051 | 959,049 | 1,372,812 | 1,918,608 | 2,428,921 | 3,097,394 | 3,880,735 | 4,382,759 |
| New Jersey | 184,139 | 211,149 | 245,562 | 277,575 | 320,823 | 373,306 | 489,555 | 672,035 | 906,096 |
| Pennsylvania | 434,373 | 602,365 | 810,091 | 1,049,458 | 1,348,233 | 1,724,033 | 2,311,786 | 2,906,215 | 3,521,951 |
| **SOUTH ATLANTIC** | | | | | | | | | |
| Delaware | 59,096 | 64,273 | 72,674 | 72,749 | 76,748 | 78,085 | 91,532 | 112,216 | 125,015 |
| Maryland | 319,728 | 341,548 | 380,546 | 407,350 | 447,040 | 470,019 | 583,034 | 687,049 | 780,894 |
| Dist. of Columbia | | 14,093 | 24,023 | 33,039 | 39,834 | 43,712 | 51,687 | 75,080 | 131,700 |
| Virginia | 747,610 | 880,200 | 974,600 | 1,065,366 | 1,211,405 | 1,239,797 | 1,421,661 | 1,596,318 | 1,225,163 |
| West Virginia | | | | | | | | | 442,014 |
| North Carolina | 393,751 | 478,103 | 555,500 | 638,829 | 737,987 | 753,419 | 869,039 | 992,622 | 1,071,361 |
| South Carolina | 249,073 | 345,591 | 415,115 | 502,741 | 581,185 | 594,398 | 668,507 | 703,708 | 705,606 |
| Georgia | 82,548 | 162,686 | 252,433 | 340,989 | 516,823 | 691,392 | 906,185 | 1,057,286 | 1,184,109 |
| Florida | | | | | 34,730 | 54,477 | 87,445 | 140,424 | 187,748 |
| **EAST SOUTH CENTRAL** | | | | | | | | | |
| Kentucky | 73,677 | 220,955 | 406,511 | 564,317 | 687,917 | 779,828 | 982,405 | 1,155,684 | 1,321,011 |
| Tennessee | 35,691 | 105,602 | 261,727 | 422,823 | 681,904 | 829,210 | 1,002,717 | 1,109,801 | 1,258,520 |
| Alabama | | | | 127,901 | 309,527 | 590,756 | 771,623 | 964,201 | 996,992 |
| Mississippi | | 8,850 | 40,352 | 75,448 | 136,621 | 375,651 | 606,526 | 791,305 | 827,922 |

| | | | | | | | |
|---|---|---|---|---|---|---|---|
| **WEST SOUTH CENTRAL** | | | | | | | |
| Arkansas | | | | | | 209,897 | 435,450 | 484,471 |
| Louisiana | | 1,062 | 14,273 | 30,388 | 97,574 | 517,762 | 708,002 | 726,915 |
| Texas | | 76,556 | 153,407 | 215,739 | 352,411 | 212,592 | 604,215 | 818,579 |
| **EAST NORTH CENTRAL** | | | | | | | |
| Ohio | 45,365 | 230,760 | 581,434 | 937,903 | 1,519,467 | 1,980,329 | 2,339,511 | 2,665,260 |
| Indiana | 5,641 | 24,520 | 147,178 | 343,031 | 685,866 | 988,416 | 1,350,428 | 1,680,637 |
| Illinois | | 12,282 | 55,211 | 157,445 | 476,183 | 851,470 | 1,711,951 | 2,539,981 |
| Michigan | | 4,762 | 8,896 | 31,639 | 212,267 | 397,654 | 749,113 | 1,184,059 |
| Wisconsin | | | | | 30,945 | 305,391 | 775,881 | 1,054,670 |
| **WEST NORTH CENTRAL** | | | | | | | |
| Minnesota | | | | | | 6,077 | 172,023 | 439,706 |
| Iowa | | | | | 43,112 | 192,214 | 674,913 | 1,194,020 |
| Missouri | | 19,783 | 66,586 | 140,455 | 383,702 | 682,044 | 1,182,012 | 1,721,295 |
| North Dakota | | | | | | | | 2,405 |
| South Dakota | | | | | | | | 11,776 |
| Nebraska | | | | | | | 28,841 | 122,993 |
| Kansas | | | | | | | 107,206 | 364,399 |
| **MOUNTAIN** | | | | | | | |
| Montana | | | | | | | | 20,595 |
| Idaho | | | | | | | | 14,999 |
| Wyoming | | | | | | | | 9,118 |
| Colorado | | | | | | | 34,277 | 39,864 |
| New Mexico | | | | | | 61,547 | 93,516 | 91,874 |
| Arizona | | | | | | | | 9,658 |
| Utah | | | | | | 11,380 | 40,273 | 86,786 |
| Nevada | | | | | | | 6,857 | 42,491 |
| **PACIFIC** | | | | | | | |
| Washington | | | | | | 13,294 | 11,594 | 23,955 |
| Oregon | | | | | | 92,597 | 52,465 | 90,923 |
| California | | | | | | | 379,994 | 560,247 |

| Division and State | 1880 | 1890 | 1900 | 1910 | 1920 | 1930 | 1940 | 1950 | 1960 |
|---|---|---|---|---|---|---|---|---|---|
| UNITED STATES | 50,155,783 | 62,947,714 | 75,994,575 | 91,972,266 | 105,710,620 | 122,775,046 | 131,669,275 | 150,697,361 | 179,323,175 |
| GEOGRAPHIC DIVISIONS | | | | | | | | | |
| New England | 4,010,529 | 4,700,749 | 5,592,017 | 6,552,681 | 7,400,909 | 8,166,341 | 8,437,290 | 9,314,453 | 10,509,367 |
| Middle Atlantic | 10,496,878 | 12,706,220 | 15,454,678 | 19,315,892 | 22,261,144 | 26,260,750 | 27,539,487 | 30,163,533 | 34,168,452 |
| South Atlantic | 7,597,197 | 8,857,922 | 10,443,480 | 12,194,895 | 13,990,272 | 15,793,589 | 17,823,151 | 21,182,335 | 25,971,732 |
| East South Central | 5,585,151 | 6,429,154 | 7,547,757 | 8,409,901 | 8,893,307 | 9,887,214 | 10,778,225 | 11,477,181 | 12,050,126 |
| West South Central | 3,334,220 | 4,740,983 | 6,532,290 | 8,784,534 | 10,242,224 | 12,176,830 | 13,064,525 | 14,537,572 | 16,951,255 |
| East North Central | 11,206,668 | 13,478,305 | 15,985,581 | 18,250,621 | 21,475,543 | 25,297,185 | 26,626,342 | 30,399,368 | 36,225,024 |
| West North Central | 6,157,443 | 8,932,112 | 10,347,423 | 11,637,921 | 12,544,249 | 13,296,915 | 13,516,990 | 14,061,394 | 15,394,115 |
| Mountain | 653,119 | 1,213,935 | 1,674,657 | 2,633,517 | 3,336,101 | 3,701,789 | 4,150,003 | 5,074,998 | 6,855,060 |
| Pacific | 1,114,578 | 1,888,334 | 2,416,692 | 4,192,304 | 5,566,871 | 8,194,433 | 9,733,262 | 14,486,527 | 20,339,105 |
| Noncontiguous | | | | | | | | | 858,939 |
| NEW ENGLAND | | | | | | | | | |
| Maine | 648,936 | 661,086 | 694,466 | 742,371 | 768,014 | 797,423 | 847,226 | 913,774 | 969,265 |
| New Hampshire | 346,991 | 376,530 | 411,588 | 430,572 | 443,083 | 465,293 | 491,524 | 533,242 | 606,921 |
| Vermont | 332,286 | 332,422 | 343,641 | 355,956 | 352,428 | 359,611 | 359,231 | 377,747 | 389,881 |
| Massachusetts | 1,783,085 | 2,238,947 | 2,805,346 | 3,366,416 | 3,852,356 | 4,249,614 | 4,316,721 | 4,690,514 | 5,148,578 |
| Rhode Island | 276,531 | 345,506 | 428,556 | 542,610 | 604,397 | 687,497 | 713,346 | 791,896 | 859,488 |
| Connecticut | 622,700 | 746,258 | 908,420 | 1,114,756 | 1,380,631 | 1,606,903 | 1,709,242 | 2,007,280 | 2,535,234 |
| MIDDLE ATLANTIC | | | | | | | | | |
| New York | 5,082,871 | 6,003,174 | 7,268,894 | 9,113,614 | 10,385,227 | 12,588,066 | 13,479,142 | 14,830,192 | 16,782,304 |
| New Jersey | 1,131,116 | 1,444,933 | 1,883,669 | 2,537,167 | 3,155,900 | 4,041,334 | 4,160,165 | 4,835,329 | 6,066,782 |
| Pennsylvania | 4,282,891 | 5,258,113 | 6,302,115 | 7,665,111 | 8,720,017 | 9,631,350 | 9,900,180 | 10,498,012 | 11,319,366 |
| SOUTH ATLANTIC | | | | | | | | | |
| Delaware | 146,608 | 168,493 | 184,735 | 202,322 | 223,003 | 238,380 | 266,505 | 318,085 | 446,292 |
| Maryland | 934,943 | 1,042,390 | 1,188,044 | 1,295,346 | 1,449,661 | 1,631,526 | 1,821,244 | 2,343,001 | 3,100,689 |
| Dist. of Columbia | 177,624 | 230,392 | 278,718 | 331,069 | 437,571 | 486,869 | 663,091 | 802,178 | 763,956 |
| Virginia | 1,512,565 | 1,655,980 | 1,854,184 | 2,061,612 | 2,309,187 | 2,421,851 | 2,677,773 | 3,318,680 | 3,966,949 |
| West Virginia | 618,457 | 762,794 | 958,800 | 1,221,119 | 1,463,701 | 1,729,205 | 1,901,974 | 2,005,552 | 1,860,421 |
| North Carolina | 1,399,750 | 1,617,949 | 1,893,810 | 2,206,287 | 2,559,123 | 3,170,276 | 3,571,623 | 4,061,929 | 4,556,155 |
| South Carolina | 995,577 | 1,151,149 | 1,340,316 | 1,515,400 | 1,683,724 | 1,738,765 | 1,899,804 | 2,117,027 | 2,382,594 |
| Georgia | 1,542,180 | 1,837,353 | 2,216,331 | 2,609,121 | 2,895,832 | 2,908,506 | 3,123,723 | 3,444,578 | 3,943,116 |
| Florida | 269,493 | 391,422 | 528,542 | 752,619 | 968,470 | 1,468,211 | 1,897,414 | 2,771,305 | 4,951,560 |
| EAST SOUTH CENTRAL | | | | | | | | | |
| Kentucky | 1,648,690 | 1,858,635 | 2,147,174 | 2,289,905 | 2,416,630 | 2,614,589 | 2,845,627 | 2,944,806 | 3,038,156 |
| Tennessee | 1,542,359 | 1,767,518 | 2,020,616 | 2,184,789 | 2,337,885 | 2,616,556 | 2,915,841 | 3,291,718 | 3,567,089 |
| Alabama | 1,262,505 | 1,513,401 | 1,828,697 | 2,138,093 | 2,348,174 | 2,646,248 | 2,832,961 | 3,061,743 | 3,266,740 |
| Mississippi | 1,131,597 | 1,289,600 | 1,551,270 | 1,797,114 | 1,790,618 | 2,009,821 | 2,183,796 | 2,178,914 | 2,178,141 |

**WEST SOUTH CENTRAL**

| | | | | | | | | |
|---|---|---|---|---|---|---|---|---|
| Arkansas | 802,525 | 1,128,211 | 1,311,564 | 1,574,449 | 1,752,204 | 1,854,482 | 1,949,387 | 1,909,511 | 1,786,272 |
| Louisiana | 939,946 | 1,118,588 | 1,381,625 | 1,656,388 | 1,798,509 | 2,101,593 | 2,363,880 | 2,683,516 | 3,257,022 |
| Oklahoma | | 258,657 | 790,391 | 1,657,155 | 2,028,283 | 2,396,040 | 2,336,434 | 2,233,351 | 2,328,284 |
| Texas | 1,591,749 | 2,235,527 | 3,048,710 | 3,896,542 | 4,663,228 | 5,824,715 | 6,414,824 | 7,711,194 | 9,579,677 |

**EAST NORTH CENTRAL**

| | | | | | | | | |
|---|---|---|---|---|---|---|---|---|
| Ohio | 3,198,062 | 3,672,329 | 4,157,545 | 4,767,121 | 5,759,394 | 6,646,697 | 6,907,612 | 7,946,627 | 9,706,397 |
| Indiana | 1,978,301 | 2,192,404 | 2,516,462 | 2,700,876 | 2,930,390 | 3,238,503 | 3,427,796 | 3,934,224 | 4,662,498 |
| Illinois | 3,077,871 | 3,826,352 | 4,821,550 | 5,638,591 | 6,485,280 | 7,630,654 | 7,897,241 | 8,712,176 | 10,081,158 |
| Michigan | 1,636,937 | 2,093,890 | 2,420,982 | 2,810,173 | 3,668,412 | 4,842,325 | 5,256,106 | 6,371,766 | 7,823,194 |
| Wisconsin | 1,315,497 | 1,693,330 | 2,069,042 | 2,333,860 | 2,632,067 | 2,939,006 | 3,137,587 | 3,434,576 | 3,951,777 |

**WEST NORTH CENTRAL**

| | | | | | | | | |
|---|---|---|---|---|---|---|---|---|
| Minnesota | 780,773 | 1,310,283 | 1,751,394 | 2,075,708 | 2,387,125 | 2,563,953 | 2,792,300 | 2,982,483 | 3,413,864 |
| Iowa | 1,624,615 | 1,912,297 | 2,231,853 | 2,224,771 | 2,404,021 | 2,470,939 | 2,538,268 | 2,621,073 | 2,757,537 |
| Missouri | 2,168,380 | 2,679,185 | 3,106,665 | 3,293,335 | 3,404,055 | 3,629,367 | 3,784,664 | 3,954,653 | 4,319,813 |
| North Dakota | 36,909 | 190,983 | 319,146 | 577,056 | 646,872 | 680,845 | 641,935 | 619,636 | 632,446 |
| South Dakota | 98,268 | 348,600 | 401,570 | 583,888 | 636,547 | 692,849 | 642,961 | 652,740 | 680,514 |
| Nebraska | 452,402 | 1,062,656 | 1,066,300 | 1,192,214 | 1,296,372 | 1,377,963 | 1,315,834 | 1,325,510 | 1,411,330 |
| Kansas | 996,096 | 1,428,108 | 1,470,495 | 1,690,949 | 1,769,257 | 1,880,999 | 1,801,028 | 1,905,299 | 2,178,611 |

**MOUNTAIN**

| | | | | | | | | |
|---|---|---|---|---|---|---|---|---|
| Montana | 39,159 | 142,924 | 243,329 | 376,053 | 548,889 | 537,606 | 559,456 | 591,024 | 674,767 |
| Idaho | 32,610 | 88,548 | 161,772 | 325,594 | 431,866 | 445,032 | 524,873 | 588,637 | 667,191 |
| Wyoming | 20,789 | 62,555 | 92,531 | 145,965 | 194,402 | 225,565 | 250,742 | 290,529 | 330,066 |
| Colorado | 194,327 | 413,249 | 539,700 | 799,024 | 939,629 | 1,035,791 | 1,123,296 | 1,325,089 | 1,753,947 |
| New Mexico | 119,565 | 160,282 | 195,310 | 327,301 | 360,350 | 423,317 | 531,818 | 681,187 | 951,023 |
| Arizona | 40,440 | 88,243 | 122,931 | 204,354 | 334,162 | 435,573 | 499,261 | 749,587 | 1,302,161 |
| Utah | 143,963 | 210,779 | 276,749 | 373,351 | 449,396 | 507,847 | 550,310 | 688,862 | 890,627 |
| Nevada | 62,266 | 47,355 | 42,335 | 81,875 | 77,407 | 91,058 | 110,247 | 160,083 | 285,278 |

**PACIFIC**

| | | | | | | | | |
|---|---|---|---|---|---|---|---|---|
| Washington | 75,116 | 357,232 | 518,103 | 1,141,990 | 1,356,621 | 1,563,396 | 1,736,191 | 2,378,963 | 2,853,214 |
| Oregon | 174,768 | 317,704 | 413,536 | 672,765 | 783,389 | 953,786 | 1,089,684 | 1,521,341 | 1,768,687 |
| California | 864,694 | 1,213,398 | 1,485,053 | 2,377,549 | 3,426,861 | 5,677,251 | 6,907,387 | 10,586,223 | 15,717,204 |

**NONCONTIGUOUS**

| | | | | | | | | |
|---|---|---|---|---|---|---|---|---|
| Alaska | | | | | | | | | 226,167 |
| Hawaii | | | | | | | | | 632,772 |

# General Bibliography

**Guides to Further Reading**    The chapter bibliographies in this volume provide references to selected books bearing upon the subjects of the particular chapters. Most of the books listed here and on previous pages contain bibliographies of their own, useful for the further pursuit of any topic the student may be interested in. *The Harvard Guide to American History,*° edited by Oscar Handlin and others (1954), though seriously outdated, is still useful. The student should bear in mind, however, that any list of books becomes dated the moment it is published. John Higham, ed., *The Reconstruction of American History*° (1962), contains critical essays on the writings on key historical topics. A number of the pamphlets surveying interpretations and bibliography published by the Service Center for Teachers of History, 400 A Street, S.E., Washington, D.C. 20003, are in the field of American history. They are brought up to date from time to time. Also covering major themes, but at greater length, are the volumes in the *Crowell American History Series*, edited by Abraham Eisenstadt and J. H. Franklin. The *Journal of American History* (formerly the *Mississippi Valley Historical Review*) and the *American Historical Review* discuss recent books and publish lists of scholarly articles. *America: History and Life*, issued quarterly, contains abstracts of articles from a wide array of scholarly publications.

**Statistics**    The standard source for census and other data is *Historical Statistics of the United States, Colonial Times to 1957* (1960), which may be supplemented by *Continuation to 1962* (1965) and by the annual volumes of *Statistical Abstract of the United States*, both published by the Bureau of the Census.

**Maps**    The most comprehensive and attractive collection is *The American Heritage Pictorial Atlas of United States History* (1966); an older, standard work is C. O. Paullin, *Atlas of the Historical Geography of the United States* (1932). A briefer collection is C. L. and E. H. Lord, eds., *Historical Atlas of the United States* (rev. ed., 1953). An excellent, comprehensive collection of military maps is V. J. Esposito, ed., *The West Point Atlas of American Wars 1689–1953* (2 vols., 1959).

**Reference Dictionaries**    American history is told in brief lives of men who made it in the *Dictionary of American Biography*, edited by Allen Johnson and Dumas Malone (21 vols., 1928–1944), and in subsequent supplementary volumes, all abridged in the one-volume *Concise Dictionary of American Biography*, edited by J. G. E. Hopkins (1964). The *Dictionary of American History*,

° Titles available in paperback.

edited by J. T. Adams and R. V. Coleman (5 vols., 1940), is abridged in the *Concise Dictionary of American History,* edited by Wayne Andrews (1962). R. B. Morris, *Encyclopedia of American History* (rev. ed., 1961), is a useful outline, also containing data on 400 notable Americans.

**Source Collections**    A standard compilation, especially valuable for official records and court decisions is H. S. Commager, ed., *Documents of American History°* (8th ed., 2 vols., 1968). Major documents, beginning in 1765, are in Richard Hofstadter, ed., *Great Issues in American History°* (2 vols., 1958). D. J. Boorstin, ed., *An American Primer°* (2 vols., 1966), contains basic documents with commentary by eighty-three historians. Among the numerous collections of "readings" are: *Words That Made American History,* edited by R. N. Current and J. A. Garraty (rev. ed., 1965), and *Builders of American Institutions,* edited by Frank Freidel and Norman Pollack (1963).

**The Pictorial Record**    Pictures, which give a sense of reality to the past as nothing else can, are to be found abundantly in *The Pageant of America,* edited by R. H. Gabriel (15 vols., 1925–1929); the *Album of American History,* edited by J. T. Adams (4 vols., 1944–1948); and *Life in America,* edited by M. B. Davidson (2 vols., 1951).

**Geographical Influences**    E. C. Semple, *American History and Its Geographic Conditions* (rev. ed., 1933), though originally published more than half a century ago, is still useful as a general introduction. H. R. Brown, *Histor-ical Geography of the United States* (1949), traces in fascinating detail the interplay of environment and settlement, region by region. A special kind of geographical interpretation is that of Frederick Jackson Turner, who influenced the thinking of a whole generation of historians with his essays, gathered together in *The Frontier in American History°* (1920) and *The Significance of Sections in American History* (1932). What happened to the "free land," which Turner believed had determined the course of American history, is told by R. E. Robbins in *Our Landed Heritage* (1942). The most recent and thorough volume tracing the frontier movement is R. A. Billington, *Westward Expansion* (1967 ed.). See also T. D. Clark, *Frontier America* (1959).

**Histories: Comprehensive**    *The New American Nation Series,°* edited by H. S. Commager and R. B. Morris (1954–      ), approximately 40 volumes projected, undertakes to incorporate the latest scholarship and largely replaces *The American Nation: A History,* edited by A. B. Hart (28 vols., 1904–1916). The volumes in D. J. Boorstin, ed., *The Chicago History of American Civilization°* (1956–      ), are brief, up-to-date accounts of periods or topics. The *Chronicles of America* (50 vols., edited by Allen Johnson, 1918–1921; 6 additional vols., edited by Allan Nevins, 1950–1951) are written in a popular vein; some of the earlier volumes are now outdated. *A History of the South,°* edited (in part) by W. H. Stephenson and E. M. Coulter (12 vols., 1947–1967), is detailed and authoritative.

**Political and Constitutional**    R. H. Gabriel, *The Course of American Democratic Thought* (1956 ed.), and Louis

---

° Titles available in paperback.

Hartz, *The Liberal Tradition in America** (1955), interpret political philosophy. Two general accounts of constitutional history are A. H. Kelly and W. A. Harbinson, *The American Constitution* (1963 ed.), and C. B. Swisher, *American Constitutional Development* (1954 ed.). H. C. Hockett, *The Constitutional History of the United States, 1776–1826* (2 vols., 1939), is a detailed treatment of the first half-century. Charles Warren, *The Supreme Court in United States History* (2 vols., 1937 ed.), is comprehensive on the nineteenth century. R. G. McCloskey, *The American Supreme Court** (1960), is a brief interpretation. J. M. Smith and Paul L. Murphy, eds., *Liberty and Justice: A Historical Record of American Constitutional Development** (2 vols., 1958), is a collection of documents.

On the Presidency, see E. S. Corwin, *The President, Office and Powers** (1957), R. E. Neustadt, *Presidential Power** (1964), and L. W. Koenig, *The Chief Executive* (1966). A documentary collection is A. M. Schlesinger, Jr., and Fred Israel, eds., *The State of the Union Messages of the Presidents* (3 vols., 1966).

On parties, W. E. Binkley, *American Political Parties, Their Natural History* (1963 ed.); W. N. Chambers and W. D. Burnham, eds., *The American Party Systems; Stages of Development** (1967); Pendleton Herring, *The Politics of Democracy: American Parties in Action** (1965 ed.); R. F. Nicholas, *The Invention of the American Political Parties* (1967), which covers into the 1850's; and G. H. Mayer, *The Republican Party, 1854–1966** (1967 ed.).

**Diplomatic History**   Surveys include Alexander DeConde, *A History of Amer-*

ican Foreign Policy* (1963); R. W. Leopold, *The Growth of American Foreign Policy* (1962); J. W. Pratt, *A History of the United States Foreign Policy* (1965 ed.); S. F. Bemis, *A Diplomatic History of the United States* (1965 ed.); and T. A. Bailey, *A Diplomatic History of the American People* (1958) which pursues the thesis that public opinion determines foreign policy. Collections of documents are R. J. Bartlett, ed., *The Record of American Diplomacy* (1964 ed.), and W. A. Williams, *A Shaping of American Diplomacy** (2 vols., 1956). S. F. Bemis, ed., *American Secretaries of State and Their Diplomacy* (10 vols., 1927–1929), is being brought up to date in additional volumes edited by R. H. Ferrell. Area studies include Dexter Perkins, *A History of the Monroe Doctrine** (1955 ed.), S. F. Bemis, *The Latin American Policy of the United States** (1943), and A. W. Griswold, *The Far Eastern Policy of the United States* (1938).

**Military and Naval**   R. F. Weigley, *History of the United States Army* (1967), is outstanding; R. E. and T. N. Dupuy, *Military Heritage of Americans* (1956), is an able introduction; T. H. Williams, *Americans at War: The Development of the American Military System* (1960), is a brief interpretation. In *Arms and Men** (1956), Walter Millis puts the development of American strategy into the broad setting of technological and other changes. A. A. Ekirch, Jr., tells the story of the changing problems of civil and military relationships in *The Civilian and the Military* (1956); S. P. Huntington, *The Soldier and the State** (1957), is more analytical. G. T. Davis is somewhat critical in *A Navy Second to None* (1940); Harold and Margaret Sprout, more enthusiastic in *The Rise of American Naval Power* (1942) and *To-*

---

* Titles available in paperback.

*ward a New Order of Sea Power* (1943). C. C. Alden and Allan Westcott, *The United States Navy: A History* (1943), is a compact account.

**Economic**   *The Economic History of the United States* is told by experts in a series edited by Henry David and others (10 vols. projected, 1945–    ). Convenient summaries are H. U. Faulkner, *American Economic History* (rev. ed., 1954); E. C. Kirkland, *A History of American Economic Life* (rev. ed., 1951); and the analytic R. M. Robertson, *History of the American Economy* (1964). Aspects of the subject are treated with thoroughness by B. H. Meyer and others, *History of Transportation in the United States Before 1860* (1917); E. R. Johnson and others, *History of Domestic and Foreign Commerce of the United States* (2 vols., 1915); V. S. Clark, *History of Manufacturers in the United States* (3 vols., 1929); L. C. Gray, *History of Agriculture in the Southern United States to 1860* (2 vols., 1925); and P. W. Bidwell and J. I. Falconer, *History of Agriculture in the Northern United States, 1620–1860* (1925). The first three hundred years of American farming are well summarized by E. E. Edwards in the Department of Agriculture's *Yearbook of Agriculture* for 1940. Financial history is surveyed in W. J. Schultz and M. B. Caine, *Financial Development of the United States* (1937). Seymour Dunbar, *History of Travel in America* (4 vols., 1915) is both readable and authoritative. Sidney Ratner, *American Taxation: Its History* (1942) is comprehensive.

**Technological**   J. W. Oliver, *History of American Technology* (1956), is a fairly detailed and factual treatment, without illustrations. *A Popular History of American Invention*, edited by Waldemar Kaempffert (2 vols., 1924), is a useful introduction to the subject, though neither complete nor entirely accurate. Roger Burlingame relates technological invention to political and social history in *March of the Iron Men* (1938) and *Engines of Democracy* (1940). Siegfried Giedion, *Mechanization Takes Command* (1948), provocatively interprets the influence of technology upon the American home.

**Business and Labor**   The role of business in American history as a whole is emphasized by T. C. Cochran and William Miller in *The Age of Enterprise°* (1942). Business thinking, as well as general economic thought, is set forth in Joseph Dorfman, *The Economic Mind in American Civilization* (3 vols., 1946–1949). L. M. Hacker presents one interpretation of the stages of business development in *The Triumph of American Capitalism°* (1940), and N. S. B. Gras presents another interpretation in *Business and Capitalism* (1946). The worker's place in history is revealed through original records in the *Documentary History of American Industrial Society*, edited by J. R. Commons and others (10 vols., 1910–1911). Commons and his associates also are authors of the comprehensive *History of Labor in the United States* (4 vols., 1918–1935), which is based mainly on the documents cited above. An interpretive account of labor organization is Selig Perlman, *History of Trade Unionism in the United States* (1922). J. G. Rayback, *A History of American Labor°* (1959), is the standard one-volume account; Henry Pelling, *American Labor°* (1965), is a brief interpretation. A useful bibliography is Hen-

---

° Titles available in paperback.

rietta M. Larson, *Guide to Business History* (1948).

## Social

A pioneering cooperative work is *A History of American Life,* edited by A. M. Schlesinger and D. R. Fox (13 vols., 1927–1948). General accounts of church history are Winthrop Hudson, *Religion in America*° (1965); W. W. Sweet, *The Story of Religion in America* (rev. ed., 1939); W. L. Sperry, *Religion in America* (1946); and S. E. Mead, *The Lively Experiment; The Shaping of Christianity in America* (1963), an interpretation. A. W. Calhoun, *A Social History of the American Family* (3 vols., 1917–1919) is the only study of the subject; Andrew Sinclair, *Emancipation of the American Woman*° (1966), on women, is readable. Dixon Wecter, *The Saga of American Society* (1937), is on "high society." On leisure activities, see F. R. Dulles, *America Learns to Play*° (1965); and J. A. Krout, *Annals of American Sport* (1940). Other phases of social history are treated in F. R. Packard, *History of Medicine in the United States* (2 vols., 1931); J. H. Franklin, *From Slavery to Freedom: A History of American Negroes*° (rev. ed., 1967); and August Meier and E. M. Rudwick, *From Plantation to Ghetto* (1966). A good introduction to urban history is E. N. Glaab and A. T. Brown, *A History of Urban America* (1967).

## Immigration

This phase of social history receives a broad, general treatment in Carl Wittke, *We Who Built America*° (1940), which stresses the immigrant contribution. M. L. Hansen, *The Immigrant in American History*° (1940), is a collection of essays reinterpreting the

___
° Titles available in paperback.

subject. The same author's *The Atlantic Migration, 1670–1860*° (1940) was projected as the first volume of a comprehensive history, which Hansen's untimely death left uncompleted. Oscar Handlin, *The Uprooted*° (1951), reveals the heart and soul of the immigrants, especially those from Eastern Europe in the twentieth century. M. A. Jones, *American Immigration*° (1960) is a compact survey. The reaction of natives to immigrant arrivals is told by R. A. Billington, *The Protestant Crusade, 1800–1860* (1938); and John Higham, *Strangers in the Land* (1938), which takes up where Billington's book leaves off.

## Intellectual

Charles and Mary Beard, in *The Rise of American Civilization* (2 vols., rev. ed., 1933), make a brilliant effort to integrate the history of ideas with history in general. In *The American Spirit* (1942) the same authors elaborate upon their conception of what is distinctive in American ideas. Merle Curti, *The Growth of American Thought* (rev. ed., 1951), is a thorough, inclusive account. V. L. Parrington, *Main Currents in American Thought* (3 vols., 1927–1930), organizes the story biographically and presents it from the point of view of a Jeffersonian liberal. The history of schools is summarized by E. W. Knight, *Education in the United States* (rev. ed., 1951). See also A. E. Meyer, *An Educational History of the American People* (1957). Higher education is treated by Merle Curti, *Social Ideals of American Educators* (1935); and by Richard Hofstadter and W. P. Metzger, *The Development of Academic Freedom in the United States*° (1955). Both of these books are considerably broader than their titles indicate. Americans do not have the reputation of being a philosophical people, yet they have had their philosophers, as H. W.

Schneider shows in *A History of American Philosophy* (1946).

**Literary and Artistic**   H. L. Mencken, *The American Language* (3 vols., 1936–1948), deals lovingly and entertainingly with words and their history. Standard works on their respective subjects are F. L. Mott's *A History of American Magazines* (4 vols., 1930–1957) and his *American Journalism* (rev. ed., 1950). The history of literature and the fine arts may be traced in the following: R. E. Spiller and others, *Literary History of the United States* (3 vols., 1943); A. H. Quinn, *A History of the American Drama* (rev. ed., 1943); J. T. Howard, *Our American Music** (rev. ed., 1946); O. W. Larkin, *Art and Life in America* (1949); Alexander Eliot, *Three Hundred Years of American Painting* (1957); Edgar P. Richardson, *History of American Painting* (1956); S. M. Green, *American Art, An Historical Survey* (1966); E. P. Richardson, *Painting in America: The Story of 450 Years** (1956); John Burchard and Albert Bush-Brown, *The Architecture of America, A Social and Cultural History** (1966); and Wayne Andrews, *Architecture, Ambition, and Americans: A Social History of American Architecture** (1964).

---

* Titles available in paperback.

# Index

Abbey, Edwin A., 123
Abernethy, Thomas P., 255
*Ableman* v. *Booth,* 346
Abolitionists, 308–13, 323, 324
  historians' disagreements on,
    309
  sectionalism and, 345–46
  *see also* Antislavery
Abrams, Charles, 812
Adams, Charles F., 379, 383,
    384, 421
Adams, Henry, 484
Adams, John (1735–1826), 101
  Alien and Sedition Acts and,
    163
  "Boston Massacre" trial and,
    101
  death of, 223
  Declaration of Independence
    and, 113
  as diplomat, 122, 127–29,
    131
  election 1792 and, 148
  election 1800 and, 163–64
  and France, relations with,
    160–62
  on Great Britain, 106
  politics of, 114
  President, elected (1796),
    159–60
  revolt philosophy of, 101
  on Revolutionary War, 111
  war aims of, 112
  in Washington, D. C., 179–80
  X.Y.Z. affair and, 161
Adams, John Quincy (1767–
    1848), 244
  "corrupt bargain," 243–44
  as diplomat, 244
  election 1820 and, 214
  election 1824 and, 243–44

  election 1828 and, 246
  gag rule repeal, 324
  at Ghent, 208
  Indian trouble and, 245
  Latin America and, 238, 241,
    242, 245
  President, elected (1824),
    243–44
  as secretary of state, 213,
    214–15
  tariff of 1828 and, 245–46
Adams, Samuel (1722–1803)
  arrest orders for, 107
  "Boston Massacre" and,
    100–1
  committees of correspondence
    and, 106
  Shays' Rebellion and, 136
  "tea party" and, 105
  war aims of, 112
Adams, Sherman, 752, 758
Adamsites, *see* National Republi-
    cans
Adamson Act (1916), 572
Addams, Jane, 548
*Addyston Pipe and Steel Com-
    pany* v. *United States,* 557
Adult education, 482
Africa, aid to, 780–81
Agassiz, Louis, 296, 304
Agency for International Develop-
    ment (AID), 781
Agnew, Spiro, 804
Agricultural Adjustment Act
    (1938), 651–52
Agricultural Adjustment Adminis-
    tration (AAA), 641–43, 658
Agricultural Marketing Act
    (1929), 628
Agriculture
  Carey Act (1894), 475

  colonial, 38–39, 40, 62–63;
    *ill.* 41
  1860–1900, 477
  farm tenancy, *map* 616
  Federal Farm Loan Act (1916),
    571
  Great Depression and, 632,
    641–43
  Great Plains, 475–76
  Hatch Act (1887), 477
  Hoover and, 628
  McNary-Haugen bill, 616
  mechanization of, 477
  New Deal and, 641–43, 645–
    46, 651–52
  in 1920s, 615–16
  in Northeast, 280–81
  in Northwest, 281–83
  prices, 478, 616
    1948–1956, 753
    World War II, 686
  seed improvements, 282
  in South
    antebellum, 316–17
    New, 430–32
  technology and, 282–83
  in West, 281–83, 465
  World War I and, 591
  *see also* Farmers; Land
Aguinaldo, Emilio, 529
Air Commerce Act (1926), 614
Air pollution, 813; *ill.* 814
Airplanes, *see* Aviation
Alabama
  Reconstruction and, 410
  statehood (1819), 217, 234
Alamance, battle of, 95
Alamo, battle of the, 333
Alaska, 417–18, 528
Albany Plan, 85–86
Alcorn, James L., 413

Aldrich, Nelson W., 507, 555
Aldrin, Edwin, 807
Alexander I (Tsar of Russia, 1801–
   1825), 240, 421
Alger, Horatio, 452
Algiers, 185, 209–10
Algonquin Indians, 17–20
Algren, Nelson, 820
Alien and Sedition Acts (1798),
   163, 182
Allen, Frederick Lewis, 451
Allen, Hervey, 661
Allen, Ira, 131, 135
Allen, Levi, 131, 135
Alliance for Progress, 781
Allston, Washington, 160
Alperovitz, Gar, 743
Altgeld, John P., 459–60, 513
Amalgamated Association of Iron
   and Steel Workers, 457–58
America First Committee, 673
American Antislavery Society, 311
American Colonization Society,
   308–10, 311
American Dictionary of the English
   Language, An (Webster), 168
American Farm Bureau Federa-
   tion, 572
American Federation of Labor
   (AFL), 456, 540–42, 558,
   559, 615, 650
American Federation of Labor–
   Congress for Industrial Or-
   ganization (AFL-CIO), 753
American Fur Company, 215
American Independent Party, 797
American Journal of Science and
   Art, 296
American Liberty League, 647
American Magazine, 77
American Medical Association,
   662, 732
American Mercury, 622
American Peace Society, 307
American Philosophical Society,
   80
American Protective Association,
   447
American Publishing Company,
   483
American Railway Union, 458–59
American Revolution, see Revo-
   lutionary War

American Telephone and Tele-
   graph Company, 436
American Tobacco Company, 441
Americans for Democratic Action,
   716
Ames, Adelbert, 425
Ames, Oakes, 421
Amherst, Jeffrey, 92
Amnesty Act (1872), 423
Anarchism, 453
"Anarchist," 606–8
Ancient Order of Hibernians,
   455
Anderson, Martin, 812
Anderson, Robert, 363, 364–
   65
Anderson, Sherwood, 622
Andover Academy, 169
Andrews, Charles M., 83
Andrews, Lincoln C., 620
Andrews, Sidney, 438
Andros, Edmund, 50, 51–52
Anglican Church, see Church of
   England
Anglo-Dutch wars, 45
Anne (Queen of England, 1702–
   1714), 89
Antietam Creek, battle of, 390
Antifederalists, 146–48, 152
Antiinflation Act (1942), 686
Anti-Masonic party, 251, 265
Antin, Mary, 479
Anti-Saloon League, 610
Antislavery
   early crusades, 70–71
   Fugitive Slave Act, 345–46
   societies, 115, 311–12, 323
   Wilmot Proviso and, 340, 343
   see also Abolitionists
Antiwar movement, 307–8, 794,
   804; ill. 778
Apache Indians, 474
Appalachian Mountains, 16, 315
Appleby, John F., 477
Appomattox, 396
Arapaho Indians, 472, 473
Architecture
   colonial, 71; ills. 2, 54, 72,
   74
   Early Republican, ill. 155
   in Gilded Age, 486
   Greek Revival, ill. 263
   1900s, early, 537

post-World War II, 818–19
Revolutionary War, ill. 155
see also "The Course of American Art," Parts 1–4
Argentina, 240, 747
Argonne, battle of, 595–96
Arkansas
   Reconstruction in, 402, 403,
   410
   secession of, 365
Armed Forces
   1898–1968, chart 694
   v. Indians, 471, 472–74
   Jefferson and, 184–85
   modernization of, 530–31
   post-World War II demobilization of, 712–13
   unification of, 713
   see also specific wars
Armour, Philip D., 441
Arms race, see Cold War, arms
   race in
Armstrong, Louis, 623
Armstrong, Neil, 807
Army of the Potomac, 390, 394;
   ill. 350
Arnold, Benedict, 122, 126
   Canada invaded by, 120
   treason of, 125
Arnold, H. H., 694
Arnold, Thurman, 653–54
Aroostook War, 329
Art
   1820–1860, 295
   federal aid to, 815–16
   in Gilded Age, 485–86
   Great Depression and, 659–60
   in Jazz Age, 623
   post-World War II, 818, 819
   see also "The Course of Ameri-
   can Art," Parts 1–4
Arthur, Chester A., (1830–1896),
   494, 495, 496
Articles of Confederation, 115–17
Articles of Confederation, The
   (Jensen), 141
Artisans
   colonial, 63–64
   unions and, 234
Asbury, Bishop, 175
Asbury, Francis, 174
Ashburn, Lord, 329–30
Ashford, Bailey K., 536

Ashley, Andrew Henry, 215
Ashley, William Henry, 215
Asia, 4, 5, 6
    aid to, 780–81
Assemblies, colonial, see Legis-
    latures, colonial
Associated Press, 289, 537
Astor, John Jacob, 206, 215
Atlanta, Georgia, 395–96
Atlanta Compromise, 430
Atlantic Charter, 675, 693
Atlantic Monthly, 289, 482
Atomic bomb
    Cold War and, 712
    first, 683
    on Hiroshima, 703–4; ill. 703
    on Nagasaki, 704; ill. 692
    Soviet Union and, 725
    see also Cold War, arms race in
Atomic energy, for power, 823
Atomic Energy Act (1946),
    712–13
Atomic Energy Commission
    (AEC), 713
Attlee, Clement, 703
Attucks, Crispus, 103
Audubon, John J., 295
Austin, Stephen, 333
Automation, 177, 822–23
Automobile industry
    growth of, 531–33, 605, 620
    unionism in, 651
Aviation industry, 815
    Air Commerce Act (1926)
        and, 614
    first flight, 533
    in World War I, 587, 591,
        595
    in World War II, 698
Aztecs, 10–11

Babbitt, Irving, 624
Babcock, Orville E., 422
Bacon, Nathaniel, 41–42
Bacon's Laws, 42
Bacon's Rebellion, 42
Badoglio, Pietro, 697
Baer, George F., 558
Baffin's Land, 8
Bailyn, Bernard, 71
Baker, Mrs. Ebenezer, 51
Baker, George P., 538

Baker, Newton D., 550, 587
Baker, Ray Stannard, 548
Bakunin, Mikhail, 453
Balboa, Vasco de, 8; map 9
Baldwin, James, 820
Baldwin, Joseph G., 318
Balfour, Arthur, 600
Ballinger, Richard, 565
Baltimore, Lord, see Calvert,
    George
Baltimore and Ohio Railroad,
    230, 231, 286, 442, 443
Bancroft, George, 295
Bank of Augusta v. Earle, 274
Bank of the United States, 151,
    262; ills. 155, 263
    Biddle's presidency, 263–66
    constitutionality, 150, 151,
        152
    federal funds removed from,
        265
    land, sale of, 220
    McCulloch v. Maryland and,
        238
    second, 210
Banking
    crisis (1933), 637, 639
    farmers and, 478
    Federal Reserve Act (1913),
        570
    Glass-Steagall Act (1933), 646
    Great Depression, 628–29,
        637, 639
    national, see Bank of the United
        States
    National Bank Act (1863), 367
    New Deal and, 646, 647
    in South, New, 431
    W. Wilson and, 570
Banking Act (1935), 646
Baptists, 73, 174, 175, 351
Barbados, 93
Barbary Company, 15
Barbé-Marbois, 187
Barber, Samuel, 817
Barkley, Alben, 734
Barlow, Joel, 168, 172, 179
Barnes, Gilbert H., 309
Barnum, P. T., 295
Barnum and Bailey, 488
Barron, James, 198
Barron, Samuel, 185
Barth, John, 820

Bartok, Bela, 817
Barton, Bruce, 605, 624
Baruch, Bernard, 591, 682, 712
Baseball, 486–87
Baudelaire, Charles, 293
Baumol, W. J., 819
Bay of Pigs invasion (1961), 783–
    84
"Bay Psalm Book," 36
Beale, Howard K., 411
Bear Flag Revolution, 338
Beard, Charles A., 141, 178,
    361, 435, 547, 625, 677
Beard, Mary, 178, 361, 435,
    547, 625
Beaumarchais, Caron de, 123–
    24
Beauregard, P. G. T., 364–65,
    385, 387, 395
Beck, David, 753
Becker, Carl L., 119
Becknell, William, 335
Beecher, Catherine, 307
Belasco, David, 538
Belknap, William W., 422
Bell, Alexander Graham, 436
Bell, John, 362
Bellamy, Edward, 454
Bellow, Saul, 820
Bellows, George W., 537
Bendiner, Robert, 630
Benjamin, Judah P., 383
Bennett, James Gorden, 289
Bennington, Vermont, 122
Benson, Ezra T., 753
Benton, Thomas Hart, 257, 659
Bering, Vitus, 9
Berkeley, John, 46
Berkeley, William, 39–42, 43
Berlin airlift (1948), 724; ill.
    725
Berlin crisis (1961), 784
Berlin Decree (1806), 196, 199
Bernard, Henry, 302, 303
Bernstein, Leonard, 818
Bessemer, Henry, 437
Biddle, Nicholas, 263–66, 268
Bingham, George Caleb, 295
Birney, James G., 312, 331
Bishop of London, 73
Bissell, George H., 437
Black, Hugo, 731
Black Codes, 399, 408

Black Hawk War, 259
Black Hills, South Dakota,
     gold strike in, 467
     Indian rebellion in, 473
Black Kettle, 472, 473
Black Muslims, 762
Black power, 772, 773–76
Black Reconstruction (Du Bois),
     411
Blacks, see Negroes
Blackwell, Elizabeth, 307
Blaine, James G. (1830–1893),
     426, 493, 495
     election 1884 and, 497–98
     as secretary of state, 505, 519,
     521
Blair, Francis P., 256
Blair, James, 73
Bland-Allison Act (1878), 509
"Bloody Massacre," Boston,
     100–1; ills. 82, 103
Bloomer, Mrs. Amelia, 307
Blough, Roger, 765
Blount, William, 135
Board of Trade and Plantations
     (England), 84, 85
Bohlen, Charles E., 706
Bok, Edward W., 482–83
Boleyn, Anne, 13
Bolivar, Simon, 245
Bombings, 607
Bonds
     Confederate, 374–75
     United States, 368
Bonus Bill (1817), 213
Book publishing, 291
     colonial, 36, 77
     commercialization of, 483
     1800s, 171
     rise of, 291
     see also Literature
Boone, Daniel, 61, 131
Booth, John Wilkes, 359, 402–3
Bootlegging, 620–21
Boott Cotton Mills, 233
Borah, William E., 601, 617
Borden, Gail, 441
Borglum, Gutzon, 659
Bosch, Juan, 789, 790
Boston Manufacturing Company,
     211
Boston "Massacre," 100–1;
     ills. 82, 103
Boston News-Letter, 77

Bow, Clara, 621
Bowen, W. G., 819
Bowers, Claude, 625
Bowles, Chester, 686
Bowles, Samuel, 342
Boxer Rebellion, 530
Bozeman Trail, 473
Braddock, Edward, 90; map 87
Bradford, William, 26–27, 32
Bradley, Mrs. Martin, 539
Bradley, Omar, 700
Bragg, Braxton, 381, 392–93
Brandeis, Louis D., 552, 570,
     571, 656
Brandywine, battle of, 121
Braun, Wernher von, 825
Breckinridge, John C., 360
Breed's Hill, see Bunker Hill
Breuer, Marcel, 818
Briand, Aristide, 618
Bricker, John W., 709
Bridenbaugh, Carl, 74
Bright, John, 383
Brisbane, Albert, 305
Bristow, Benjamin H., 421–22
Brook Farm, 305
Brooke, Edward, 414, 803
Brooks, Preston, 354
Brougham, Lord, 211–12
Broughton, George Henry, 3
Brown, Charles Brockden, 171
Brown, John, 353, 359–60;
     ill. 359
Brown, Joseph, 376
Brown, Moses, 176
Brown, Robert E., 119, 141
Brown v. Board of Education of
     Topeka, 755, 756
Bruce, Blanche K., 414
Brush, Charles F., 436
Bryan, William Jennings (1860–
     1925), 619
     election 1896 and, 512–14
     election 1900 and, 527
     election 1908 and, 563
     election 1912 and, 567–69
     and Paris, treaty of, 527
     progressivism and, 545
     Scopes trial and, 624
     as secretary of state, 569, 580,
     583, 584–587
     and silver question, 511–12
Bryant, William Cullen, 294
Bryce, James, 491

Bryce, Lord, 586
Buchanan, James (1791–1868),
     345
     Kansas and, 356
     Ostend Manifesto and, 348
     President, elected (1856), 355
     Southern secession and, 363–
     64
Buell, Don Caralos, 386, 387,
     388
Buena Vista, battle of, 339
Buffalo
     extermination of, 471–72
     Indians and, 470, 471–72
Bulganin, Nicolai, 739
Bulge, battle of the, 700
Bull Run, battle of, 385
     second, 390
Bunau-Varilla, Phillippe, 578–79
Bunker Hill, battle of, 112, 120
Burchard, John, 818–19
Burcharel, Samuel, 497
Burger, Warren, 800
Burgess, John W., 518–19
Burgoyne, John, 121–22
Burke, Edmund, 101, 107
Burke-Wadsworth bill (1940),
     672
Burns, Anthony, 345
Burns, James MacGregor, 657
Burnside, Ambrose E., 390
Burr, Aaron (1756–1836), 184
     conspiracy and, 191–92
     election 1796 and, 159–60
     election 1800 and, 163–64
     election 1804 and, 182
     Hamilton, duel with, 191–92
     treason trial of, 192
Burritt, Elihu, 304
Burroughs, William S., 436
Bush, Vannevar, 683, 823,
     824
Bush-Brown, Albert, 819
Business
     activity
          1790–1839, chart 269
          1840–1879, chart 430
          1880–1920, chart 438
          1921–1966, chart 822
     Coolidge on, 605
     1820–1840, 231–32
     Eisenhower and, 752
     government favors to, 713–1
     Great Depression and, 643–4

L. B. Johnson and, 765
New Deal and
  aid to, 643–46
  opposition to, 647
  regulation of, 652–54
1923–1929, 613–14
in Northeast (1840–1860),
  278–80
politics and, 491–92
rise of, 436–44
  historians' disagreements on,
    439
and trade associations, voluntary, 614
see also Commerce; Industry;
  Manufacturing
Butler, Andrew P., 354
Butler, Ben, 490
Byrd, William, I, 69, 72
Byrd, William, II, 72, 77, 78
Byrd, William, III, 72
Byrnes, James F., 679–80
  election 1944 and, 709
  foreign policy of, 710

Cable, George Washington, 483
Cabot, John, 8
Cabral, Pedro, 6
Cadore letter, 200
Cage, John, 817, 818
Calhoun, John C. (1782–1850)
  banks and, 210, 264
  Bonus Bill and, 213
  on capitalism, 267
  on Compromise of 1850,
    343–44
  election 1824 and, 243
  Florida and, 214
  Jackson, break with, 256–59
  Missouri Compromise and, 236
  nullification and, 253–56,
    257–59, 260–62
  as secretary of state, 328–29
  as secretary of war, 213
  on slavery, 323, 324
  tariff of 1828 and, 245
  Texas annexation and, 333–34
  as Vice President, 243, 253–
    59
  War of 1812 and, 202, 206
  Whig party and, 266
California
  Bear Flag Revolution, 338

gold rush (1849), 340
Mexican War and, 337–39;
  map 337
slavery question, 340–41,
  341–44
statehood, 341–44 passim
United States expands into,
  335–36, 339; map 335
California Trail, map 334
Calvert, Cecilius, 37
Calvert, George (Lord Baltimore),
  37, 52
Calvert, Leonard, 37
Calvin, John, 12–13
Calvinists, 73
  see also Huguenots; Puritans
Camp, Walter, 487
Camp meeting, 175; ill. 173
Campbell, Alexander, 174
Campbell, Thomas, 174
Canada
  boundary disputes, 329, 330,
    418–19, 577
  Elgin treaty, 347
  French and Indian War and, 91,
    92
  Great Britain acquires, 93
  Great Lakes forts and, 129–30
  Indian support (1812), 201
  Quebec Act and, 105
  rebellion of 1837, 329
  Revolutionary War and, 120
  trade with, 564
  War of 1812 and, 201, 203–5;
    map 207
Canals
  Madison administration and,
    213
  New York system of, 226–29
  in Northeast, map 228
  in Ohio, 229
  Pennsylvania system of, 229
Canning, George, 241–42
Cannon, Joseph, 554, 555, 564–
  65
Cape Breton Island, 86–88
*Capital* (Marx), 453
Capital punishment, reform, 305
Capitalism
  corporate, 232
  critics of, 450–54
  industrial, 279–80
  Jackson and, 265–66
  laissez-faire economics and, 451

Lincoln on, 283
merchant, 232, 279–80
opposition to, 453–54, 607
and public welfare, 450–51
rationalizations for, 451–52
Social Darwinism and, 451–53
  see also Business; Imperialism;
    Industry; Monopoly
Capone, Al "Scarface," 621
Carey Act (1894), 475
Carlyle, Thomas, 294
Carnegie, Andrew (1835–1919),
  450, 451, 563
  finances, 539
  philanthropy and, 451–52, 480
  steel trusts and, 437, 538
  and unions, 457–58
Carnegie Steel Company, 457–58
Carolinas
  colonization of, 42–45; map 43
  in Revolutionary War, 125–26
  shipbuilding, 65
  slavery in, 63
  see also North Carolina; South
    Carolina
*Caroline* affair, 329, 330
Carpenter, Francis B., 293
Carpetbaggers, 413
Carranza, Venustrano, 482
Carribean
  Roosevelt Corollary and, 578–
    80
  Wilson and, 580–81
Carroll, Charles, 63, 174, 230
Carroll, John, 174
Carswell, G. Harrold, 800
Carteret, George, 46, 48
Cartier, Jacques, 8; maps 9, 87
Cartwright, Peter, 175
Caruthers, William Alexander, 317
Casas, Bartolomeo de las, 11
Cash register, 436
Cass, Lewis, 341, 345
Castro, Fidel, 747, 748, 783
Catholic Reformation, 13–14
Cattle industry
  colonial, 62
  in West, 467–70; map 469
Cavaliers, 29
Cavelier, Reni Robert, 86
Cayuga Indians, 18
Central Intelligence Agency (CIA),
  713, 783–84
Central Pacific Railroad, 367, 444

Cerro Gordo, battle of, 339
Cervera, Pascual, 525, 526
Chamberlain, John, 547
Chambers, Whitaker, 731, 732
Champlain, Samuel de, 20; *map* 87
Champlain Canal, 229; *map* 228
Chancellorsville, battle of, 390
Chandler, Zachariah, 494
Channing, William Ellery, 291–92
Charles I (King of England, 1625–
    1649), 29, 30, 31, 37
Charles II (King of England, 1660–
    1685), 29, 42, 45, 48, 49–
    50, 88–89
*Charles River Bridge* v. *Warren
    Bridge,* 274
Charleston, South Carolina, 44–
    45; *ill.* (1740) 67; *maps* 44,
    45
    population (1800), 179
    in Revolutionary War, 125
Chase, Salmon P., 367, 370
    as chief justice, 410–12, 422
Chase, Samuel, 184
Chastellux, Marquis de, 72
Chatham, Lord, *see* Pitt, William
Chattanooga, battle of, 392–93
Chattanooga, Tennessee, 387,
    392–93
Chautauqua Company, 488
Chautauqua Institution, 482
Chavez, Cesar, 801
Cherokee Indians, 18, 156, 245,
    260
Cherokee Nation, 260
*Cherokee Nation* v. *Georgia,* 260
Chesapeake Bay, 37–42
    War of 1812 and, *map* 207
*Chesapeake-Leopard* incident,
    196–98
Chesapeake and Ohio Canal, 229,
    231; *map* 228
Cheyenne Indians, 472, 473
Chiang Kai-shek (b. 1886), 70,
    704, 725–26, 736, 738
Chicago, 448; *ill.* 549
*Chicago, Milwaukee, and St. Paul
    Railroad* v. *Minnesota,* 505
Chickamauga, battle of, 392
Chickasaw Indians, 18, 156
Child labor, 232–33, 281, 539–
    40; *ill.* 539
    Keating-Owen Act and,
    571– 72

Chile, 239, 240
China
    civil war (1947), 725–26
    immigration regulation, 447
    Japan invades, 66–67, 671
    Lansing-Ishii Agreement, 583
    Nine Power Pact (1922), 617
    Open Door policy, 529–30
    Wanghia, Treaty of (1844),
    330
    in World War II, 702
    *see also* Communist China
Chisholm Trail, 468; *map* 469
Chivington, J. M., 472
Choctaw Indians, 18, 156
Christian, George M., 441
Christian Front, 647
Christian Science, 479
Church of England
    in colonies, 39, 73
    early 1800s, 174
    and Quebec Act (1774), 105
    and Scotch-Irish emmigration,
    60
    state constitutions and, 115
Churches (1800s), 172–75
Churchill, Winston (American),
    537
Churchill, Sir Winston (1874–
    1965)
    Allies, U. S. aid to, 672, 675
    on Cold War, 722
    on execution of officials, 711
    Roosevelt and, 675, 697
    second front and, 696, 697
    Teheran Conference, 704–6
    unconditional surrender doc-
    trine, 704
    Yalta Conference, 706–7
Cities
    conditions in, 447–50
    early, 179–80
    growth of, 225, 281–82, 445–
    50
    1840–1860, *chart* 284
    progressivism and, 550–55
    slavery in, 320
    transportation and, 448
    urban renewal and, 812–13
    *see also* Megalopolis
Citizenship
    Fourteenth Amendment and,
    408–9
    for Indians, 475

Civil liberties
    abolitionism and, 324
    Alien and Sedition Acts and,
    163
    in Civil War, 371, 374
    Japanese-American relocation,
    689–91
    under Nixon, 800, 801
Civil Rights Act (1957), 756
Civil Rights Act (1964), 766–67
Civil Rights Act (1968), 776
Civil Rights bill (1866), 408
Civil Rights cases (1883), 428–29
Civil rights movement, 762–63,
    766–67
    and black power, 773–76
Civil Service Commission, 419,
    496
Civil War
    armed forces recruitment
    in North, 369–70; *ill.* 350
    in South, 375
    blockade of South, 381–83
    campaigns, 384–96
    1861, 385
    1862
        Eastern theater, 388–90
        Western theater, 385–88
    1863
        East, 390–91
        West, 391–93
    casualties, 370; *chart* 369
    causes of, 364–65
        historians' disagreements on,
        361
    civil law in, 371, 374
    civilian role in, 381
    diplomacy in, 383–84
    economics of, 365–69, 374–
    75; *chart* 366
    financing
        in North, 368–69
        in South, 374–75
    historians' disagreements on,
    361
    maps
        Gettysburg campaign, 393
        Sherman's march, 395
        Vicksburg campaign, 391
        Virginia campaign, 394
        West, war in, 386
    as modern war, first, 379
    navies in, 381–83, 386, 387,
    391; *ill.* 382

Negroes in, 372; *ill.* 350
North in
    mobilization of, 367–73
    resources of, 365–67
opposition, in North, 370–73,
    381
peacemaking, 396–98; *see also*
    Reconstruction
resources compared, 365–67;
    *chart* 366
South in
    mobilization of, 373–76
    resources of, 365–67
strategy, 380–84
surrender, 396
transportation, 366
weapons, 382
Civil Works Administration, 640,
    658
Civilian Conservation Corps (CCC),
    641, 658
Clark, Champ, 567–68, 589
Clark, George Rogers, 125, 135,
    157
Clark, William, 190–91
Class, *see* Social class
Clay, Cassius M., 323
Clay, Henry (1777–1852)
    banking and, 210, 264–65
    Compromise of 1850 and, 343–
        44
    "Corrupt bargain," 243–44
    election 1824 and, 243–44
    election 1840 and, 273
    election 1844 and, 330–31
    at Ghent, 208
    Harrison administration and,
        328
    and Jackson, 266
    Missouri Compromise and, 236
    nullification and, 262
    as secretary of state, 244
    as war hawk, 202–3
Clay, Lucius D., 725, 782
Clayton, John, 40
Clayton Antitrust Act, 570–71
Clayton-Bulwer Treaty (1850), 347
Clean Air Acts (1963, 1965), 813
Cleaver, Eldridge, 807
Clemenceau, Georges, 600
Cleveland, Grover (1837–1908)
    Cuba and, 522
    domestic policies of, 498–99
    election 1888 and, 497–98

election 1892 and, 507
gold policy of, 510
Hawaii annexation and, 521
immigration and, 447
lands, public, 499
pension issue and, 498–99
Pullman strike and, 459–60
Sherman Silver Purchase Act,
    510
spoils system and, 498
tariffs and, 499, 507
Venezuela boundary dispute
    and, 519–20
Clinton, De Witt, 203, 227–28,
    235
Clinton, George, 182
Clinton, Henry, 124–26
Coal industry, 441
    automation and, 823
    1840–1860, 278
    1920s, 615
    strikes
        1902, 558
        post-World War II, 714
    World War I and, 591
Cobden, Richard, 383
Cochise, 474
Cochran, T. C., 439
Cockburn, George, 205
Coercive Acts (1774), 105
*Cohens* v. *Virginia*, 237–38
Colbert, Jean, 86
Cold War, 721
    arms race in, 739, 741–45,
        782–83, 803
    in Asia, 737–38
    atomic bombs and, 712
    Berlin airlift, 724; *ill.* 725
    Berlin crisis (1961), 745, 784
    Chinese Civil War and, 725–26
    containment policies, 722–23
    Cuba and, 747, 748
        invasion of (1961), 783–84
        missile crisis (1962), 785–
            87; *ill.* 786; *map* 785
    cultural interchanges, 746
    J. F. Dulles and, 736–37
    foreign aid and, 781
    Geneva Conference (1955),
        739–40
    Indochina crisis and, 737
    Japan as ally in, 726–27
    Korean War in, *see* Korean War
    in Latin America, 747–48

loyalty checks, 607–8, 730–
    32, 754–55
in Middle East, 740–41
North Atlantic Alliance, 723–25
nuclear testing and, 784–85
    treaty banning (1963), 788
origins, 705–7, 710–11
    historians' disagreements on,
        743
Vietnam War, 790–95, 803–4,
    *ill.* 790; *map* 793
World War II and, 705–7,
    710–11
Cole, A. C., 284
Coleridge, Samuel Taylor, 294
Colfax, Schuyler, 421
Colleges
    colonial, 78–80
    1880s, 168, 169–70
    first, 169–70
    social reform and, 303–4
Colombia, 240
    Panama Canal and, 578–79,
        582
Colonies
    agriculture, 38–39, 40, 62–63;
        *ill.* 41
    commerce, 35–36
    disunity among, 85–86
    Dutch, 45
    English, 14–27, 30–56 *passim;*
        *map* 96; *see also* Colonies,
        Great Britain and; Revolution-
        ary War
    exports and imports 1763–
        1776, *chart* 100
    French and Indian War, 89–91
    Great Britain, 82–85, 88–108,
        *see also* Revolutionary War
    immigrant groups, 58–60; *map*
        59
    King George's War and, 89
    King William's War and, 89
    legislatures of, 84–85
    population growth in, 58–60;
        *chart* 60
    Quaker, 46–49
    Queen Anne's War and, 89
    religion in, 73–76
    revolt of, *see* Revolutionary
        War
    self-government for, 83–85,
        92–93, 95–114, *passim*
    self-interest of, 95–96

Colonies (*Continued*)
  Spanish, 10–12
  Stamp Act and, 94, 97–98
  statehood for, 114–15
  taxation and, 92–93, 94, 97–107
  Tea Act and, 102–5
  Townshend Program in, 98–100
  unification, attempts at, 85–86
Colonies (United States), governing, 528–29
Colonization of Americas, 9–12, 14–27, 30–56
Colorado
  gold rush of 1859, 466
  Indian removal, 472
Colorados, Mangas, 474
Colored Farmers' Alliance, 501
Columbia and Philadelphia Railroad, 230
Columbia College, 78, 170
Columbus, Christopher (1451–1506), 4, 6–8; *map* 7
Comeriform, 723
Command of the Army Act, 410
Commerce
  colonial, 35–36, 65–69; *maps* 66, 68
  Constitution and, 145
  Constitutional Convention and, 144
  1800s, early, 178
  with Great Britain
    Treaty of 1815 and, 209
    War of 1812 affects, 210–12; *chart* 211
  interstate, regulation of, 238–39, 274, 505, 560
    Commerce Act, 505
    Supreme Court decisions on, 238–39, 644
  Jay's Treaty and, 158
  neutrality and, 195–96
  post-Revolutionary War, 131
Commerce and Labor Department, 556
Committee on the Conduct of the War, 381
Committee to Defend America by Aiding the Allies, 673
Committee of European Economic Cooperation, 723

Committee for Foreign Affairs (Revolutionary War), 122
Committee on Public Information, 593
Committees of correspondence, 106
Common law, 80
*Common Sense* (Paine), 112, 113
*Commonwealth* v. *Hunt,* 281
Communal societies, 304–5
Communism, loyalty checks for, 607–8, 730–32, 754–55
  *see also* Cold War
Communist China
  Cold War and, 737–38
  Indochina and, 737
  invades India (1962), 787–88
  Korean War and, 728–30
  origins of, 725–26
  Vietnam War and, 794
*Communist Manifesto,* 267
Communist party
  election 1932 and, 637
  election 1936 and, 655
  election 1948 and, 716
Community Action Programs, 771–72
Company of Merchant Adventurers, 14–15
Compromise of 1850, 343–45
Compromise of 1877, 407, 425–28
Computers, 822–23
Conciliatory Propositions, 107
Concord, battle of, 108
Confederate States of America
  constitution, 373
  diplomacy, 383–84
  economics, 374–75
  Europe and, 383–84
  formation of, 363
  government, 373–74
  navy, 382–83
  resources, 365–67, 374–75
  state rights and, 375–76
  *see also* Civil War
Confederation, under Articles, 129–36
  Constitutional Convention and, 143
  Constitution movement, 140–42
  debts and taxes, 135–36
  foreign affairs, 129–31

  Western plans, 133–35
Confederation of the United Colonies of New England, The, 34
Confiscation Act (1861), 372
Congregational Church, 31, 115, 173
  *see also* Puritans
Congress, Confederation, *see* Confederation, under Articles
Congress, Continental, *see* Continental Congress
Congress, United States
  Constitution and, 145
  Constitutional Convention and, 143–45
  first, 148–49
  Hayes' election and, 427
  Indian policy and, 473, 474–75
  judiciary acts (1789) of, 149
  Presidency and, 494–95
  progressivism and, 552
  Reconstruction and, 400, 402, 408–13
  reorganization of, 715
  Supreme Court and, 149
  *see also* specific Acts
Congress for Industrial Organization (CIO), 650–51
Congress of Racial Equality (CORE), 762, 774
Conkling, Roscoe, 420, 493, 494–96, 497
Connally Act (1935), 653
Connecticut
  colonization of, 31–32
  constitution of, 114
  Constitution ratified by, *chart* 146
  education in, 302
  population (1880s), 445
  religion in, 173
  in seventeenth century, *maps* 33, 45
Connecticut Yankee, 232
Conrad, Joseph, 624
Conscription, in Civil War, 369–70, 375
Conservation
  Ballinger-Pinchot controversy, 565
  Civilian Conservation Corps, 641
  Forest Reserve Act (1891), 560
  New Deal and, 651

Newlands Reclamation Act (1902), 562
  T. Roosevelt and, 554, 560–62
  Tennessee Valley Authority, 644–46
Conservation and Domestic Allotment Act (1936), 651
Conservatives
  reconstruction and, 400–1
  slavery and, 371
Constitution, English, 101
*Constitution* (vessel), 162, 203, 204
Constitution of the United States, 145–46
  amendments to, 149
  checks and balances in, 145
  Convention for, 139–45
  Eighteenth amendment, 609–10
  Electoral college amendment, 799–800
  Federalists *v.* Antifederalists, 146–48
  Fifteenth Amendment, 410, 425, 428
  Fourteenth Amendment, 408–9, 428
  historians' disagreements on, 141
  Kentucky and Virginia resolutions, 163
  as law, supreme, 145
  movement toward, 140–42
  Nineteenth Amendment, 609
  Presidency and, 144
  ratification, 146–48; *chart* 146
  Seventeenth Amendment, 552
  signing of, 145
  Supreme Court and, 145, 149, 183, 237–39
  Tenth Amendment, 149
  Thirteenth Amendment, 372, 398
  Twelfth Amendment, 182
  Twentieth Amendment, 637
  Twenty-first Amendment, 630
  Twenty-fourth Amendment, 767
  Twenty-third Amendment, 767
Constitutional Convention, 140–45; *ill.* 138
  delegates to, 142
  federalists *v.* nationalists, 143,

145
  Great Compromise, 144
  New Jersey Plan, 143
  slave *v.* free states, 144
  Virginia Plan, 142–44
Constitutional Union party, 360–62
Constitutions, state, 114–15
Continental Army, 118; *ills.* 110, 123
  *see also* Revolutionary War
"Continental Association," 106–7
Continental Congress
  First, 106–7
  Second
    Articles of Confederation, 115–17
    Declaration of Independence and, 113
    Revolutionary War and, 112–13, 117–18
Continental currency, 117, 135
Continental System, 196
Convention, first national nominating, 251
Conway Cabal, 118
Conwell, Russell H., 452
Coode, John, 52
Cooke, Jay, 368
Coolidge, Calvin (1872–1933)
  on business, 605
  election 1924 and, 612–13
  foreign policy, 617–19
  McNary-Haugen bill and, 616
  Mencken on, 624
  police strike and, 606
  Presidency, succeeds to, 612
  Tennessee Valley Authority and, 644
  on war debts, 618
Cooper, Anthony Ashley, 42–44
Cooper, James Fenimore, 292
Copland, Aaron, 660, 817
Copperheads, 370–71
Coral Sea, battle of the, 695–96
Corbett, James J., 488
Corinth, Mississippi, 387
Cornell, Alonzo B., 494
Cornwallis, Lord, 125–26
Coronado, 12; *map* 9
Corporations, rise of, 232
  1840–1860, 279–80
Cortes, Hernando, 10, 11; *map* 9
Cotton, John, 31

Cotton
  Civil War and, 383
  in Great Depression, 642–43
  Reconstruction and, 430–31
  Southern production, antebellum, 316–17; *map* 317
  Southwestern migration and, 217
Cotton gin, 177
Coughlin, Charles, 647, 689
Council of Economic Advisers, 713
Council of National Defense, 590–91
Council for New England, 26, 30, 33
Counter Reformation, 13–14
Courts
  J. Adams and, 164–65
  federal, structure of, 149
  T. Jefferson and, 182–84
Cowboys, 468
Cowpens, South Carolina, 62, 126
Cox, James M., 610
Cox, John, 411
Cox, La Wanda, 411
Coxey, Jacob S., 50–59
Cozzens, James Gould, 819
Craft societies, 234
Craftsmen, colonial, 63–64
Craig, James, 201
Crandall, Prudence, 312
Crane, Stephen, 484
Craven, Avery, 309, 361
Craven, Wesley Frank, 37, 52
Crawford, William H., 242–44
Crazy Horse, 473
Credit, 570
Credit Mobilier Company, 421
Creek Indians, 18, 135, 156, 205, 245
Creel, George, 593
*Creole*, 329, 330
Crime, 621, 813–814
Crittenden, John J., 363
Crittenden Compromise, 363–64
Cromwell, Oliver, 29, 49
Cromwell, William Nelson, 578
Crusades, 5
Cuba, 347, 348, 666, 669
  invasion of (1961), 783–84
  Lopez affair and, 347
  missile crisis (1962), 785–87; *ill.* 786; *map* 785
  Monroe Doctrine and, 241

Cuba (*Continued*)
  Platt Amendment and, 429
  property confiscated, U. S., 748
  Spanish-American War and,
    522–27
  trade with, 239
Cuffe, Paul, 308
Cullom, Shelby M., 505
Culpeper, John, 44
Culture, cities and, 449–50
Cumberland Road bill, 259
Cumberland Valley, 131
*Cumming* v. *County Board of Edu-
  cation,* 428
Cunningham, Merce, 818
Currency
  colonial, 67, 92–93, 94
  Confederate, 375
  Continental, 117
  greenback, 368, 416–17, 422–
    23
  National Bank Act and, 367–68
  Revolutionary War, 117
  F. D. Roosevelt and, 667
  silver question and, 509–12
  state issued, 136, 210
  *see also* Money
Currency Act (1764), 94
Currency Act (1900), 514
Curtis, George William, 419
Custer, George A., 473
Customs commissioners in Boston,
  100–1
  *see also* Tariff
Cutler, Manasseh, 134

Dale, Thomas, 24
Daniels, Josephus, 580, 587
Dare, Virginia, 21, 22
Darlan, Jean, 696
Darling, J. N., 564, 565, 665
Darrow, Clarence, 624, 644
*Dartmouth College* v. *Woodward,*
  237
Darwin, Charles, 296
Darwinism, *see* Social Darwinism
Daugherty, Harry, 611, 612
Davis, Chester, 686
Davis, David, 427
Davis, Elmer, 689
Davis, Henry Winter, 402
Davis, Jefferson (1808–1889)
  Black Hawk War and, 259

cabinet of, 374
civil rights and, 374
on Civil War, causes of, 365
as commander in chief, 380–
  381, 388
conscription and, 375
Gadsden Purchase and, 352
as President of Confederacy,
  373–74
Russell on, 373
as secretary of war, 345
surrender and, 396
Davis, John W., 612–13
Dawes, William, 108
Dawes Severalty Act (1887), 474–
  75
Deadwood City, South Dakota, 467
Deane, Silas, 124
Dearborn, Fort, 203
*De Bow's Review,* 314, 317
Debs, Eugene V., 594
  election 1904 and, 556
  election 1912 and, 569
  election 1920 and, 610
  pardoned, 611
  Pullman strike and, 458–60
Debt, public
  funding of, 150–51, 152
  under Jefferson, 184, 185
  1910–1968, *chart* 688
  post-Revolutionary War, 135–
    36
Debts, private
  Jay's Treaty and, 158
  post-Revolutionary War, 130,
    135–36
  reform and, 305
Decatur, Stephen, 204, 209–10
Declaration of the Causes and
  Necessity of Taking Up Arms,
  112
Declaration of Independence, 113–
  114
Declaratory Act (1766), 98, 99
Defense Department, 713, 782–
  83
De Gaulle, Charles, 696, 788, 794
Deism, 172
Delaware
  colonization of, 48
  Constitution ratified by, 148;
    *chart* 146
  in seventeenth century, *map* 45
De La Warr, Lord, 24

De Leon, Daniel, 453–54
Democracy, 250–53
  civilization and, 290–92
  Jackson and, 249, 250
  historians' disagreements on,
    255
  Jazz Age and, 624–25
  Tocqueville on, 249, 291
Democratic party, 265
  capitalism and, 266–67
  Civil War and, 372–73
  Compromise of 1850 and, 345
  economic composition of, 492–
    93
  1877–1888, 492–93, 497–98
  elections and, *see* Elections
  Great Depression and, 628
  Kansas-Nebraska Act and, 353
  progressivism and, 545
  Reconstruction and, 399–400,
    407
  silver question and, 509
  social reform and, 301, 571
  in South, 424–25
  split of, 351, 353, 360
  Supreme Court and, 656
  Wilson and, 571
  Young America Movement and,
    346
Democratic Republicans, 246
Dependent Pension bill, 499
Dependent Pensions Act, 506
Depew, Chauncey, 555
Depression
  Panic of 1819, 220–21
  Panic of 1837, 268–71; *ill.* 270
  Panic of 1857, 355
  Panic of 1873, 422–23, 500
  Panic of 1893, 508–9
  Panic of 1907, 557–58
  Great, 626–32, 637–63
    banking crises in, 628–29,
      637, 639
    causes of, 626–27
    culture in, 659–62
    foreign policy during, 666–
      71
    Hoover program, 627–30,
      637
    New Deal and, 635, 639–59
    public works during, 629, 630
    F. D. Roosevelt and, 635,
      639–59
    social order and, 630–31

unemployment and, 632
  Wall Street crash, 626–27;
    chart 627
Desegregation, 762–63
  Nixon and, 801
  in schools (1954), 755–56
Desert Land Act (1877), 465
Desert Trail, map 334
De Soto, Hernando, maps 9, 12
Dew, Thomas R., 323
Dewey, George, 525
Dewey, John, 479, 480, 625
Dewey, Thomas E.
  election 1944 and, 709–10
  election 1948 and, 716–18
Diaz, Bartholomeu, 6
Diaz, Porfirio, 581
Dick Act (1903), 530
Dickens, Charles, 291, 304
Dickinson, John, 101, 112
Dingley Tariff, 514
Disciples of Christ, 174
Discovery, voyages of, map 5
Discrimination, legalized, 428–30
  see also Civil rights; Segrega-
    tion
Disease, cities and, 448–49
Displaced Persons Act (1950), 732
District of Columbia, see Washing-
  ton, D.C.
Dix, Dorothea, 305
Dock St. Theater, 78
Dodd, C. T., 451
Doheny, Edward L., 612
Dolphin incident, 582
Dominican Republic, 789–90
Dominion of New England, 48–50
Donald, David, 309
Donelson, Fort, 387
Doniphan, A. W., 338
Donnelly, Ignatius, 504, 513
Doolittle, Amos, 107
Dorr Rebellion, 252
Dos Passos, John, 622
Doubleday, Abner, 486
Douglas, Stephen A., 288, 341,
  345
  Compromise of 1850 and, 344
  Kansas-Nebraska Act and, 352–
    53
  Lincoln debates with, 357–58
  popular sovereignty and, 356,
    358
  President, nominated for, 360

railroads and, 352
Douglass, Frederick, 310, 311,
  356
Downes v. Bidwell, 528
Drake, Edwin L., 437
Drake, Francis, 13; map 9
Drama, see Theater
Dred Scott v. Sanford, 355–56
Dreiser, Theodore, 537, 622, 624
Drew, Daniel, 443
Drugs, youth and, 821
Duberman, Martin, 309
Du Bois, W. E. B., 411, 553
Dubinsky, David, 650
Dudley, Charles, 483
Duke, James B., 441
Duke's Laws (New York), 46
Dulles, John Foster (1888–1959),
  726, 735, 736–41, 791
Dumond, Dwight L., 309
Dunne, Finley Peter, 556
Dunning, William A., 411
Duquesne, Fort, 89–90, 91
Durand, Asher B., 295
Durkin, Martin P., 752
Duryea, Charles E., 531
Duryea, J. Frank, 531; ill. 536
Dutch
  Anglo-Dutch wars and, 45
  colonization by, 20, 45
  explorations by, 8
  Spain, revolt against, 13–14
Dutch Reformed Church, 73
Dutch West India Company, 20,
  45
Dwight, Timothy, 172, 175
Dyckman, John W., 813

Eakins, Thomas, 485
Earl of Shaftesbury, see Cooper,
  Anthony Ashley
East Florida, 202
East India Company, 15, 103–5
Eastman Kodak, 535
Eaton, Dorman B., 496
Eaton, John H., 256
Eaton Affair, 256
Economic Cooperation Administra-
  tion (1948), 723
Economics
  Civil War, 365–67, 367–69,
    374–75; chart 366
  colonial, 61–69

sectionalism and, 278–83
  see also Business; Commerce;
    Depression; Foreign Trade
Economy Act (1933), 658
Eddy, Mary Baker G., 301, 479
Edict of Nantes (1598), 58
Edison, Thomas A., 436, 535
Education
  adult, 304, 482
  colonial, 35, 39, 77, 78–80
  1800s, 168–70; ill. 169
  federal aid to, 770–71
  graduate studies, 481
  in Great Depression, 661
  1900s, early, 536–37
  post-World War II, 820–21
  professional, 536
  progressive, 480
  public, see Public School Sys-
    tem
  social reform and, 302–4
  in South, antebellum, 318
  Virginia and, 39
  see also Colleges; Higher edu-
    cation
Edwards, Jonathan, 73, 75–78,
  294
Eggleston, Edward, 483
Egypt, 740–41
Einstein, Albert, 683
Eisenhower, Dwight D. (1890–
  1969), 824
  agriculture prices and, 753
  arms race and, 742–45
  Asia and, 737–38
  on Berlin crisis, 745
  business and, 752
  desegregation and, 756
  economic conditions under,
    752–53
  election 1948 and, 716
  election 1952 and, 733–35
  election 1956 and, 757
  foreign policy, 735–48, 790–
    92
  at Geneva, 739–40
  Japan and, 747
  Khrushchev and, 746–47
  Korean armistice and, 735–36
  Latin America and, 748
  J. McCarthy and, 754
  Middle East and, 741
  on military-industrial complex,
    779

Eisenhower, Dwight D. (*Continued*)
North Atlantic Treaty Organization (NATO) and, 725
population control and, 781
power development and, 753
President, elected
1952, 733–35
1956, 757
public welfare and, 754
second term of, 757–59
on space race, 825
Vietnam and, 790–92
in World War II, 695, 700
Eisenhower Doctrine (1957), 741
El Caney, battle of, 526
Elections
1789, 48
1792, 154
1796, 159–60
1800, 163–65; *map* 164
1804, 182, 199
1810, 202
1812, 203
1816, 213
1820, 214
1824, 242–44; *map* 243
1828, 246; *map* 246
1832, 265
1836, 267–68, *map* 268
1840, 272–73
1844, 330–31
1848, 340
1856, 355
1860, 360–62; *map* 362
1864, 372–73
1866, 409
1868, 415–17
1872, 421
1876, 425–28
1880, 495
1884, 496–98
1888, 493, 499–500
1892, 491, 507
1896, 491, 510–14; *map* 513
1900, 527
1904, 555–56; *map* 556
1908, 562–63; *map* 563
1912, 566–69; *map* 568
1916, 587–88; *map* 588
1920, 610; *map* 611
1922, 611
1924, 612–13; *map* 613
1928, 625–26; *map* 626
1932, 636–37; *map* 636

1936, 654–55; *map* 654
1940, 673–75; *map* 674
1942, 708–9
1944, 709–10; *map* 709
1946, 715
1948, 716–18; *map* 718
1950, 732
1952, 733–35; *map* 734
1956, 757; *map* 758
1958, 758
1960, 759–60; *map* 761
1964, 768–70; *map* 769
1968, 795–99; *map* 797
Electoral college, constitutional amendment, 799–800
Electoral Commission, 427
Electric power, 436
industry affected by, 534–35
nuclear, 823
Tennessee Valley Authority and, 644–45
Elementary and Secondary Education Act (1965), 771
Elgin treaty, 347
Eliot, Charles W., 481
Eliot, John, 34
Eliot, T. S., 537, 623
Elizabeth I (Queen of England, 1558–1603), 13–15, 21
Ellender, Allen J., 767
Ellison, Ralph, 820
Ellsworth, Oliver, 144
Ellwood, L. L., 475
Emancipation Proclamation, 372; *ill.* 371
Embargo of 1807, 198–99
Emergency Banking Act (1933), 639, 658
Emergency Fleet Corporation, 592
Emerson, Ralph Waldo, 292, 294, 300–1, 304, 360
Engels, Friedrich, 267
England
Anglo-Dutch wars and, 45
colonies and, 63–69 *passim*; *see also* Great Britain, colonies and
colonization by, 14–27, 30–56 *passim*
Constitution and, 101
Dutch and, 13–14, 45
explorations by, 8; *map* 9
exports and imports, 1763–1776, *chart* 100

*v.* France, 19–20
mercantile system and, 49
Protestantism *v.* Catholicism, 13
social class in, 69
*v.* Spain, 12–13, 19, 56, 89
war, 13–14
Tudor age in, 14
*see also* Great Britain
Enlightenment, Age of, 55
Entail and primogeniture, 115
Environmental pollution, 813
"Era of good feelings," 213–14
Ericson, Lief, 4
Ericson, John, 382
Erie Canal, 225, 227–29; *ill.* 227; *map* 228
Erie Railroad, 442, 443, 450
Erikson, Erik H., 821
Erlanger loan, 375
Esch-Cummins Transportation Act (1920), 609
*Escobeda* case, 800
Eskimos, 8
Espionage Act (1917), 593
Espy, James Pollard, 304
Essex Junto, 191
Ethiopia, 670
Europe
Civil War and, 383–84
in Middle Ages, 4–5
European Common Market, 788
Evans, Oliver, 177, 178
Evarts, William M., 494
Everett, Edward, 347, 362
Evolution, theory of, *see* Social Darwinism
Excise tax, 151, 152
Exeter Academy, 169
*Ex parte McCardle*, 412
*Ex parte Merryman*, 371
*Ex parte Milligan*, 371, 410
Exploration
age of, 6–9; *map* 9
early voyages of, *map* 5
lands seen by Columbus, *map* 7
sixteenth-century America, *map* 9
Export Control Act (1940), 616
Exports
imperialism and, 518
1763–1776, *chart* 100
1790–1820, *chart* 211
1840–60, 279
1870–1900, 518

Factory system, 175–77, 279
Fair Deal, 713, 732
Fair Employment Practices Committee, 685
Fair Labor Standards Act (1938), 658, 659
Fair Oaks, battle of, 388
Fairless, Benjamin, 714
Fall, Albert B., 611, 612
Fallen Timbers, battle of, 156
Family structure, colonial, 71
Far West, *see* West
Farley, James A., 648, 659
Farm Board, 628
Farm Bureau Federation, 616
Farm Credit Administration, 641, 658
Farm Security Administration, 652, 658
Farmer-Labor party, 615–16
Farmers
    credit and, 478
    decline of, 475–78
    Granger movement, 500–1
    Great Depression and, 641–43
    grievances of, 477–78
    income of (1920s), 615
    isolationism and, 478
    National Farmers' Alliance, 501–2
    New Deal and, 651–52
    organize, 500–4
    railroads and, 477–78
    Southern Alliance of, 501–2
Farmers' Alliance and Industrial Union, *see* Southern Alliance
Farming, *see* Agriculture
Farragut, David G., 386
Faulkner, Harold A., 547
Faulkner, William, 623, 660, 819
Federal Art Project, 659
Federal Deposit Insurance Corporation, 646
Federal Emergency Relief Administration, 640, 658
Federal Farm Loan Act (1916), 571
Federal Hall, New York, *ill.* 155
Federal Highway Act (1916), 572
Federal Housing Administration, 641, 658
Federal Music Project, 660
Federal Power Commission, 609
Federal Radio Commission, 614

Federal Reserve Act (1913), 570
Federal Securities Act (1933), 658
Federal Theater Project, 660
Federal Trade Commission, 570
*Federalist, The* (Hamilton, Madison, and Jay), 147
*Federalist Papers, The* (Hamilton), 183
Federalist party
    Constitution and, 146–48
    Constitutional Convention and, 143, 145
    downfall of, 159–65
    elections and, *see* Elections
    Embargo of 1807 and, 198–99
    French Revolution and, 152–53
    Jay's Treaty and, 158
    under Jefferson, 182–84, 186, 189
    Louisiana Purchase and, 186, 189, 191
    repression and, 162–63
    rise of, 152
    slavery and, 235–36
    War of 1812 and, 203, 206–8
Feis, Herbert, 743
Fenians, 418
Ferdinand II (King of Aragon, 1479–1516), 7
Fermi, Enrico, 683
Field, Cyrus W., 288–89, 436
Fifteenth Amendment, 410, 425, 428
Fight for Freedom Committee, 673
Fillmore, Millard (1800–1874), 
    election 1856 and, 355
    foreign affairs and, 347
    Presidency, succeeds to, 344
Finch, Robert H., 800
Finney, Charles G., 301, 311
First Conscription Act (CSA), 375
Fish, Hamilton, 417, 418–19, 522
Fisheries convention (1818), 209
Fishing industry, colonial, 64–65
Fiske, John, 141, 518
Fitch, John, 178
Fitzgerald, F. Scott, 622
Fitzhugh, George, 324
Fitzsimmons, Bob, 488
Five Power Pact (1922), 617
Flagg, James Montgomery, 575
Flagler, H. N., 438
Fleming, Denna Frank, 743

Florida
    Jackson invades, 214–15
    Louisiana Purchase and, 189
    real estate speculation in (1924–1925), 619
    Reconstruction and, 410
    Spanish control, 201–2, 214–15
    United States acquires, 215
    white supremacy, return of, 425
Florida Indians, *ill.* 20
Flour milling industry, 441
Floyd, John, 265
Foch, Ferdinand, 596
Folk, Joseph W., 551
Food Administration, 591
Football, 487–88; *ill.* 487
Foraker, Joseph, 512
Foraker Act (1900), 529
Forbes, John Murray, 280
Force Acts (1870–1871), 424
Ford, Henry A. (1863–1947), 488, 531, 535
Ford Motor Company, 752; *ill.* 534
Fordney-McCumber Act (1922), 618
Foreign Affairs, Department of, 122
Foreign aid
    J. F. Kennedy and, 781–82
    Marshall Plan for, 788
    1949–1967, *chart,* 780
Foreign policy
    Cleveland, 519–22
    Coolidge, 617–19
    Eisenhower, 735–48, 790–92
    election 1940 and, 675
    during Great Depression, 666–71
    Harding, 617
    Harrison, 519–21
    Hoover, 666–67
    L. B. Johnson, 788–90, 792–95
    Kennedy, 781–88, 792
    McKinley, 522–30
    1900s, early, 517–18
    Nixon, 802–4
    post-Revolutionary War failures, 129–31
    progressivism and, 576
    Revolutionary War and, 122–24

Foreign policy (*Continued*)
  F. D. Roosevelt, 667–79
  T. Roosevelt, 576–80
  Taft, 564, 580
  Truman, 710–11
  Wilson, 580–602 *passim*
  *see also* Cold War
Foreign trade
  China and, 330
  colonial, 65–69; *maps* 66, 68
  1800s, early, 178
  Embargo of 1807 and, 198–99
  imperialism and, 518
  Japan and, 347
  J. F. Kennedy and, 788
  post-Revolutionary War, 131
  F. D. Roosevelt and, 667–68
  1790–1820, *chart* 211
  War of 1812 and, 210–12
  *see also* Commerce; Tariff
Forest Reserve Act (1891), 560
Forrest, Edwin, 295
Forrest, Nathan Bedford, 320
Forrestal, James V., 713
Fortas, Abe, 800
Forterr, James, 308–10
Forts, *see* specific name
Foster, Stephen C., 295
Foster, William Z., 606, 637
Four Power Pact (1922), 617
Fourier, Charles, 305
Fourteen Points (1918), 593, 598
Fourteenth Amendment, 408–9, 428
Fowler, Orson, 306–7
Fox, George, 46–47
Fox Indians, 259
Frame of Government (Pennsylvania), 48
France
  Alliance Treaty (1778), 124
  Civil War and, 383–84
  colonies, American, and, 85–86
  colonization by, 19–20, 86–88; *map* 87
  Cuba and, 347
  Directory, 160
  election 1796 and, 159
  emigration from, 58
  exploration by, 8; *map* 9
  French and Indian War, 89–91

  *v.* Great Britain, 19–20, 85–86, 88–91, 124, 157, 196
  Holy Alliance and, 240–41
  Huguenots, 58
  A. Jackson and, 267
  Louisiana Purchase and, 185–89
  in Middle East, 740
  Monroe Doctrine and, 240–41
  in North America, *maps* 90–91
  quasi-war with, 160–62
  Revolution in, 153–54, 157
  Revolutionary War and, 113, 117, 123–29 *passim*
  San Ildefonso Treaty, 185
  and United States relations (1963), 788
  G. Washington and, 157
  World War I, *see* World War I
  World War II, *see* World War II
  X.Y.Z. affair, 161
Francis I (King of France, 1515–1547), 8
Franciscans, 12
Frankfurter, Felix, 555
Franklin, Benjamin (1706–1790), 60, 73; *ill.* 128
  Albany Plan of, 85–86
  Canada, negotiations with, 120
  as colonial agent, 84
  and Constitution, 147
  at Constitutional Convention, 142, 144, 145
  Declaration of Independence and, 113
  as deist, 172
  as envoy to France, 124
  as Federalist, 147
  T. Paine and, 113
  as peace delegate, 127–29
  as postmaster, 85
  as scientist, 79–80
  Stamp Act and, 99
  territorial imperialism and, 93
  writings of, 77, 85, 93
Franklin, John Hope, 411
Franco, Francisco, 670
Frazier-Lemke Farm Bankruptcy Act (1933), 641
Frederick the Great (King of Prussia. 1740–1786), 89–91
Fredericksburg, battle of, 390; *ill.* 397

Free Soil party, 341, 345
Freedmen's Aid Societies, 399
Freedmen's Bureau, 399, 408
Freedom Democratic party, 768
Freeman, Mary E. Wilkins, 483
Freeport Doctrine, 358
Frelinghuysen, Theodore J., 76
Frémont, John C., 336, 338, 355
French, Daniel Chester, 486
French and Indian War, 89–91
Freneau, Philip, 172
Freud, Sigmund, 624
Frick, Henry C., 437, 458, 558
Frobisher, Martin, 8; *map* 9
Frobisher's Bay, 8
Frontenac, Count, 86
Frontier
  last, 463–75; *map* 464
  securing, 154–56
  *see also* Northwest; West
Frost, Robert, 537, 819
Frye, Mrs., 51
Fuchs, Klaus, 731
Fuel Administration, 591
Fugitive Slave Act (1850), 344–46
Fulbright, W., on Vietnam War, 792, 794
Fuller, Melville W., 506
Fulton, Robert, 178, 179, 238
Fundamental Constitution for Carolina (1669), 43
Fundamental Orders of Connecticut, 32
Fundamental Orders of New Haven, 32
Fur Trade
  colonial, 64–65
  Far West, 215
Furuseth, Andrew, 571

Gadsden Purchase, 352
Gagarin, Yuri, 825
Gage, Thomas, 107, 120
Galbraith, John Kenneth, 788
Gallatin, Albert, 181, 184, 185, 206, 208, 212
Gallico, Paul, 684
Galloway, Joseph, 106
Gama Vasco da, 6
Gardoqui, Don Diego de, 131
Garfield, James A., (1831–1881), 495–96

Garland, Hamlin, 484
Garrett, John W., 443
Garrison, Lindley M., 587
Garrison, William Lloyd, 301, 304, 309, 310–11, 312
Garvey, Marcus, 609
Gary, Elbert H., 558
Gass, Patrick, 190
Gates, Horatio, 122, 125
Gates, Thomas, 24
General Electric, 436, 535
   unions and, 651
General Leasing Act (1920), 609
General Managers' Association, 459
General Motors, 752
   unions and, 651, 752
General Staff, United States Army, 530–31
Genet, Edmond, 157
Geneva Conference (1954), 739–40
Genovese, Eugene, 361
George, David Lloyd, 600, 601
George, Henry, 454
George I (King of England, 1714–1727), 84
George II (King of England, 1727–1760), 56, 84, 89, 102
George III (King of England, 1760–1820), 82, 91, 93–94, 98
   Coercive Acts of, 105
   and Continental Congress, 106
   peace treaty orders, 130
Georgia
   in Civil War, 394–95, 396
   colonization, 56; map 43
   constitution of, 114
   Constitution ratified, 148; chart 146
   Indians in, 245, 260
   land claims, 132–33
   Reconstruction and, 410
   in Revolutionary War, 125
   slavery in, 63
Georgia Platform, 345
Germantown, Pennsylvania, 64, 121
Germany
   immigration from, 58, 284
   post-World War II policies in, U.S., 711–12
   Samoan Islands and, 521–22
   Venezuela incident and, 579
   World War I, see World War I
   World War II, see World War II
   see also West Germany
Geronimo, 474; ill. 472
Gerry, Elbridge, 160–61
Gershwin, George, 624, 660
Gettysburg, battle of, 392; ill. 389; map 393
Ghent, Treaty of, 208–9
Gibbons v. Ogden, 238–39
"G.I. Bill of Rights," 714
Giddings, Joshua R., 345–46
Gilbert, Sir Humphrey, 21; map 9
Girdler, Tom, 651
Girondins, 157
Gladden, Washington, 453
Gladstone, William E., 139
Glass-Steagall Act (1933), 646, 658
Gleason, S. Everett, 668
Glenn, John, 826
Glidden, Joseph H., 475
Glorious Revolution (England), 29
   colonies affected by, 50–52
Gloucester, Massachusetts, 173
Godkin, E. L., 419
Gold mining, 515
   rush of 1849, 340; ill. 342
Gold Reserve Act (1934), 658
Gold standard
   Cleveland and, 510
   election 1896 and, 511
   in Great Depression, 639
   and Vietnam War, 794
   see also Money
Gold Standard Act (1900), 514
Goldwater, Barry G., 768–69, 788
Golf, 488
Goliad, battle of, 333
Gompers, Samuel (1850–1924), 456, 558, 559–60
   Clayton Antitrust Act and, 571
   immigration and, 542
   strikes and, 606
   World War I and, 591
Goodman, Benny, 660
Goodyear, Charles, 278
Gorgas, Josiah, 365
Gorgas, William C., 535–36
Gorges, Ferninando, 33–34
Gorman, Arthur P., 507
Gough, John B., 304
Gould, Jay, 443, 444, 450, 497
Government
   checks and balances, 145
   state, 114–15
Graham, Martha, 818
Graham, Sylvester, 306
Grand Army of the Republic, 499
Grandfather laws, 429–30
Granger movement, 500–1
Grant, Ulysses S. (1822–1885), 420
   cabinet of, 417
   in Civil War
      Chattanooga, battle of, 392–93
      as general in chief, 380–81; ill. 378
      in Kentucky, 387
      Lee, battles with, 394–95, 396
      at Shiloh, 387
      surrender to, 396
      Vicksburg campaign, 391
   corruption under, 421–22
   Democratic terrorists and, 425
   election 1868 and, 415–17
   election 1872 and, 421
   election 1876 and, 425
   election 1880 and, 495
   foreign affairs and, 417–19
   greenback question and, 422–23
   Liberal Republicans and, 421
   President, elected
      1868, 415–17
      1872, 421
   Reconstruction policies, 416, 419–20
   Tenure of Office Act, 413
   spoils system and, 417, 419
Grasse, Admiral de, 126
Gray, Asa, 296
Great American Desert, see Great Plains
Great Awakening, 75–76
Great Britain
   J. Adams, cooperation with, 161
   Aroostook War and, 329
   blockade of Europe, 196
   boundary dispute with, post-Revolutionary War, 130
   boycott against, 99–100
   California interests, 336

Great Britain (*Continued*)
Canada and
boundary dispute (1903), 577
Elgin treaty, 347
rebellion of 1837, 329
Central American interests, 347–48
Civil War and, 383–84, 418–19
Clayton-Bulwer Treaty, 347
colonies and, 82–85, 88–108; *maps* 87, 96; *see also* England, colonies and; Revolutionary War
Cuba and, 347
on democracy, 290–91
Embargo of
1774, 106–7
1807, 198–99
*v.* France, 85–86, 88–91, 124, 157, 196
French and Indian War and, 89–91
gold standard and, 514–15
Great Lakes forts and, 129–30
Hay-Pauncefote treaty, 578
impressment, 196–98
Indians, as allies of, 156, 201
Jay's Treaty, 158
Laird rams affair, 384
Latin American independence and, 239–40, 241
Maine boundary dispute, 329, 330
in Middle East, 740–41
ministry from, 156–57
Monroe doctrine and, 241–42
neutrality and, 157–58
in North America, eighteenth century, *maps* 90–91
Orders-in-Council, 196, 199
Oregon, partition of, 331–32
Paris Peace Treaty and, 129–31
post-Revolutionary War relations, 129–31
Samoan Islands and, 521–22
ship seizure by, 157, 158
slave trade, 313, 329, 330
*v.* Spain, 124
Texas interests, 333
textile industry, 175–76, 383
*Trent* affair, 384
United States relations with, 1837–1842, 329–30

Venezuela boundary dispute and, 519–20
War of 1812, 203–9
Washington, treaty of, 418
Webster-Ashburton Treaty, 329–30
World War I, *see* World War I
World War II, *see* World War II
*see also* England
Great Compromise (1787), 144
Great Depression, *see* Depression, Great
Great Lakes
British forts on, 129–30
War of 1812 and, 203–4; *map* 207
Great Plains, 215–16, 352
agriculture on, 475–76; *ill.* 476
settlement of, 464–65; *ill.* 467
Great Society, 768
Greek-Turkish Aid Act, 723–24
Greeley, Horace, 289, 421, 425, 445
Green, Wm., 615, 650
Greenbacks, 416–17, 422–23
Greene, Nathanael, 125–26
Greenville, Treaty of, 156
*Greer* incident, 676
Grenville, George, 94, 97
Grimké, Angelina, 311
Grodzins, Morton, 690
Gromyko, A., 786
Gropius, Walter, 818
Grosscup, Peter S., 538
Gruening, Ernest, 792
Guadalcanal, battle of, 701
Guadalupe Hidalgo, treaty of, 339
Guadeloupe, 86, 93, 186
Guam, 526–28
Guatemala, 747
Guffey Acts (1935), 653
Guilford Court House, battle at, 126
Guinea Company, 15
Guiteau, Charles J., 496
Guns, *see* Ordinance
Gunsmithing, colonial, 64
Guthrie, Woody, 817


Haiti, 580, 581, 618, 666, 669
Hakluyt, Richard, 15
Hale, John P., 345

Half-Breeds, 493–97
Half-Way Covenant, 36
Halleck, Henry W., 380–81, 387
Hamilton, Alexander (1815–1875)
beliefs of, 150–52
A. Burr, duel with, 191–92
Constitution and, 139, 140, 147
election 1796 and, 159
election 1800 and, 164
France and, 160
*v.* T. Jefferson, 150–54
neutrality and, 157
Paterson, New Jersey and, 176
secession and, 191
as secretary of treasury, 149–53, 157–58
Supreme Court and, 183
Whiskey Rebellion and, 154
Hamilton, Andrew, 80
Hamlin, Hannibal, 360
Hammerstein, Oscar, 818
Hampton Normal and Industrial Institute, 482
Hancock, John, 107
Hancock, Winfield Scott, 495
Handlin, Oscar, 449
Handy, William C., 623
Hanna, Marcus A., 510–11, 513, 514, 558, 752
T. Roosevelt and, 554, 555
Harding, Warren G. (1865–1923), 566, 605
cabinet of, 611
corruption under, 611–12
death of, 612
foreign policy of, 617
A. R. Longworth on, 610–11
President, elected (1920), 610
Harey, William H., 510
Hariot, Thomas, 22
Harkness, S. V., 438
Harmar, Josiah, 134
Harmon, Judson, 567
Harper, William, 313
Harpers Ferry, 390
raid on, 359
*Harper's Magazine*, 317, 2
*Harper's New Monthly Magazine*, 289
*Harper's Weekly*, 289, 371, 482, 546
Harriman, E. H., 450, 557
Harris, Joel C., 483

Harris, Roy, 660, 817

Harris, Townsend, 347

Harrison, Benjamin (1833–1901), 505–6
  election 1892 and, 507
  President, elected (1888), 499–500
  spoils system and, 493

Harrison, William H. (1773–1841)
  death of, 328
  election 1836 and, 268
  Indian fighting and, 200–1
  President, elected (1840), 272–73; *ill.* 272
  War of 1812 and, 204–5

Harrison Land Law, 200

Harrison's Landing, 389

Harte, Bret, 483

Hartford, Connecticut, 32

Hartford Convention, 206–8, 209

"Hartford Wits," 171–72

Harvard College, 78, 79, 303, 304; *ill.* 79
  elective system, introduces, 481
  in Revolutionary War, 168

Hasendever, Peter, 65

Hat Act (1732), 65

Hatch Act (1887), 477

Haugen, Gilbert, 616

Hawaii, 347
  annexed, 520–21
  as territory, 528

Hawke, David, 39

Hawley-Smoot bill (1930), 628

Hawthorne, Nathaniel, 292, 294, 305

Hay, John, 484, 529–30, 578

Hayes, Rutherford B. (1822–1893)
  patronage and, 493–95
  President, elected (1876), 426–28
  South and, 428

Haymarket affair, 456–57; *ill.* 457

Hayne, Paul Hamilton, 318

Hayne, Robert Y., 257–59

Haynes, Elwood, 531

Haynsworth, C. F., 800

Hay-Pauncefote Treaty (1901), 578

Health fads, 306–7

Hearst, William Randolph, 522, 537

Hellman, Lillian, 660

Helper, Hinton Rowan, 324

Hemingway, Ernest, 623, 660, 819

Henderson, Leon, 686

Henderson, Richard, 131

Henry, Fort, 387

Henry, Joseph, 295–96

Henry, O., 539

Henry, Patrick, 92–93
  Revolutionary War, need for, 106
  Stamp Act, speech of, 97

Henry VII (King of England, 1485–1509), 8

Henry VIII (King of England, 1509–1547), 13

Henry the Navigator, 6

Hepburn Act of 1906, 560

*Hepburn* v. *Griswold*, 422

Heriulfson, Biarni, 4

Herkimer, Nicholas, 122

Herrán, Tomás, 518

Hershey, Lewis, 804

Herter, Christian, 745

Hewitt, Abram S., 437

Hicks, J. D., 503

Higher education, 481–82, 536
  *see also* Colleges

Hill, Gladwin, 813

Hill, Isaac, 256

Hill, James J., 450, 557

Hillman, Sidney, 650

Hindemith, Paul, 817

Hine, Lewis, 539

Hiroshima, atomic bomb on, 703–4; *ill.* 703

Hispaniola, 8, 11

Hiss, Alger, 731, 732

Historians' disagreements on
  abolitionists, 309
  big business, rise of, 439
  Civil War, causes of, 361
  Cold War origins, 743
  Constitution, 141
  A. Jackson, 255
  New Deal, 657
  Pearl Harbor, 677
  Reconstruction, 411
  Revolutionary War, 119
  populism, 503
  progressivism, 547
  World War I, 585

Hitler, Adolf, 671, 672

Hobby, Mrs. Oveta Culp, 752

Ho Chi Minh, 737, 790, 794, 804

Hoe, Richard, 289

Hoffa, James, 753

Hofstadter, Richard, 255, 503, 547, 657

Holbrook, Josiah, 304

Holding Companies, 436

Holding Company Act (1935), 653

Holmes, Mary Jane, 483

Holmes, Oliver Wendell, 294

Holy Alliance, 240

Holy Roman Empire, 4

Home Owners' Loan Corporation, 641

Homer, Winslow, 485

Homestake Company, 467

Homestead Act (1862), 367, 465

Homestead strike, 457–58

Honduras, 580

Hood, John B., 396

Hooker, Joseph, 390, 392

Hooker, Thomas, 31–32

Hooper, Johnson J., 318

Hoover, Herbert (1874–1965)
  election 1932 and, 636–38
  Executive reorganization, 715
  farm program of, 628
  Food Administration and, 591
  foreign policy of, 666–67
  Great Depression and, 627–30, 637
  President, elected (1928), 625–26
  as secretary of commerce, 611, 614
  veterans and, 632

Hoover Dam, *ill.* 629

Hopkins, Harry, 640–41, 648

Hopkinson, Francis, 172

Hopkinson, Joseph, 172

Horseshoe Bend, battle of, 205

House, Edward M., 569, 583, 585, 599

House of Burgesses, 25, 39, 42

House of Delegates, 37–38

House of Representatives, Constitution and, 145
  *see also* Congress

Housing
  colonial, 71; *ills.* 2, 54, 72
  New Deal and, 648–49

Housing Act (1961), 761
Housing Authority, 649
Houston, Sam, 333
Howard, Oliver O., 399
Howe, Edgar W., 484
Howe, Elias, 278–79
Howe, William, 121, 124
Howells, William Dean, 485
Hudson, Henry, 8
"Hudson School," 295
Hudson's Bay Company, 331
Huerta, Victoriano, 581–82
Hughes, Charles Evans, 551, 656
    election 1916 and, 588
    as secretary of state, 611, 617–
        18
Hughes, Langston, 817–18
Hughes, Sarah T., 764
Huguenots, 58
Hull, Cordell
    income tax and, 569
    as secretary of state, 667, 668,
        670, 676–78, 704; ill. 668
    United Nations and, 707–8
Hull, William, 203
Humphrey, George M., 737, 752,
    758
Humphrey, Hubert, 781
    election 1960 and, 759
    election 1964 and, 769
    election 1968 and, 795–99
Hungarian revolution, 741
Hunt, Richard Morris, 486
Hutchinson, Anne, 32
Hutchinson, Thomas, 97
Hydrogen bomb, 739, 782
    see also Atomic bomb; Cold
        War, arms race in


Ice industry, 231
Ickes, Harold L., 643
Illinois, 445
    agriculture in, 280
    exploration of, 86
    Lincoln-Douglas debates, 357–
        58
    Quebec Act and, 105
    statehood (1818), 217
    as territory, 200
Immigration, ill. 276
    in Civil War, 367
    colonial, 58–60; map 59

Displaced Persons Act (1950)
    and, 732
1820–1840, 224–25
1830–1860, 284–85
1860–1900, 445–47
L. B. Johnson and, 770
labor force and, 281, 540–42
nativist movement and, 285
population and, 283, 445
prejudice against, 447
railroad construction and, 444
restricting, 447, 542, 618–19;
    chart 619
of Siberian tribes, 3–4
sources of, 445–47
voting and, 285
Immigration Act (1921), 619
Impeachment
    of A. Johnson, 412–13
    of judges, under Jefferson, 184
Imperialism, 517, 518–30
    rationalizations for, 518–19
    Spanish-American War and,
        522–27
    see also Business; Monopoly
Imports
    colonial, 99–100
    Hamilton and, 151–52
    1763–1776, chart 100
    1790–1820, chart 211
    see also Foreign trade
Impost amendment (1782), 140
Impressment, 196–98; ills. 194,
    197
Inca Indians, 10–11
Income tax
    Supreme Court and, 507–8
    W. Wilson and, 569
Indentured servants, 38, 56–57,
    72
Independent Treasury, 271–72,
    328, 340
India, 787–88
Indiana, 200, 217, 280
Indians, ills. 28, 47, 472
    Algonquin, 17–20
    Apache, 474
    Arapaho, 472, 473
    Army and, 471, 472–74
    Black Hawk War, 259
    buffalo and, 470, 471–72
    Burke Act (1906) and, 475
    Cayuga, 18
    Cherokee, 18, 156, 245, 260

Cheyenne, 472, 473
Chickasaw, 18, 156
Chirington massacre, 472
Choctaw, 18, 156
    citizenship for, 475
Creek, 18, 135, 156, 205, 245
Dawes Severalty Act, 474–75
    early, 3–4
English colonists and, 17–20,
    34
Fallen Timbers, battle of, 156
Florida, ill. 20
Fox, 259
in French and Indian War, 91
government policy, 470, 473–
    75
Horseshoe Bend, battle of, 205
Inca, 10–11
Iroquois, 18, 20, 91, 134–35
Jackson and, 259–60
Laramie council, Fort, 473
last stand, 472–75
Little Bighorn, battle of, 473
Massasoit, 26
Maya, 3–4
Medicine Lodge Creek council
    (1867), 473
Mohawk, 18
Muskogean, 18
New England colonies and, 34
Nez Percé, 473–74
North American, 17–20
Oneida, 18
Onondaga, 18
W. Penn and, 48; ill. 47
Pequot, 34
Plains, 470–75
Pontiac's Rebellion, 94
Sac, 259
Samoset, 26
Seminole, 18, 259–60
Seneca, 18
Shawnees, 201
Sioux, 472, 473, 474
Spanish colonization and, 10–
    11
Squanto, 26
"taming" of, 470–75
Thames, battle of, 204–5
Tippecanoe, battle of, 201
trade with, 216
treaties with, 47, 156, 200–1,
    245, 259
Tuscarora, 18

Indians (*Continued*)
Virginia and, 25, 40–42
Wampanoag, 34
War of 1812 and, 204–5
White man, greet, 18
Woods, 17–20
Wounded Knee, slaughter of, 474
Indian Affairs Bureau, 470–71
Indian Intercourse Act (1834), 259
Indian Peace Commission, 473
Indian Removal Act (1834), 259
Indian Reorganization Act (1934), 646
Indigo, 63
Indochina, 737
Industrial Mobilization Plan (1939), 679
Industrial Revolution, 175
Industry
accident rate in, 540
Civil War and, 365
colonial, 63–65
1800s, early, 175–77
1840–1860, 278–80
mass production and, 534–35
monopoly in, 538
in Northwest, 281
post-World War II, 713–14
rise of, 435–41
in South, 315
in South, New, 432
War of 1812, after, 211–12
working conditions in, 540
World War II and, 680–82
*see also* Business; Manufacturing
Inflation
Nixon and, 802
post-World War II, 715
Initiative, 551
Insular Cases, 528
Inter-American Conference (1933), 668
Inter-American Treaty of Reciprocal Assistance, 747
Internal Revenue Act, 368–69
International Copyright Law, 483
International Geophysical Year (1957–1958), 824
International Workers of the World (IWW), 558–59, 591, 594, 606–7

Interstate Commerce Act (1887), 505, 560
Interstate Commerce Commission, 505
Interstate Highway Act (1956), 815
Intolerable Acts (1774), 105
Inventions
1860–1890, 436
ca. 1900, 534–35
European, 6
industrial, 278–79
*see also* Technology
Iowa, 280
Ireland, immigration from, 58–60, 225, 284, 446–47
Iron Act (1750), 65
Iron industry, 231
colonial, 65
Iroquois Indians, 18, 134–35
Great Britain and, 20
French and Indian War and, 91
treaty with, 85
Iroquois League, 18
Irving, Washington, 292
Isabella I (Queen of Castile, 1474–1504), 7
Isolationism, 517–18
farmers and, 478
in 1920s, 616–19
World War II and, 669–70, 673–75
Israel, 740
Isthmus of Panama, explorations of, 8
Ives, Charles, 817
Iwo Jima, battle of, 702


Jackson, Andrew (1767–1845), 60, 248
banks and, 263–66
cabinet of, 256–57
Eaton affair and, 257
election 1824 and, 243–44
Florida invaded by, 214–15
France and, 267
historians' disagreements on, 255
inauguration of, 250
Indian policy of, 205, 259–60
laissez-faire and, 266–67
land sales and, 268–69

nullification and, 259, 260–62
President, elected (1828), 246
Proclamation of 1832, 262
South Carolina interposition and, 260–62
Specie Circular and, 269, 270, 271
spoils system and, 250–51
state rights and, 259, 260–62
Texas annexation and, 333
Union and, 259
vetoes, 259
in War of 1812, 205–6
Jackson, Claiborne, 385
Jackson, Frederick Turner, 463
Jackson, Helen Hunt, 474
Jackson, Rachel, 246
Jackson, Thomas J. ("Stonewall"), 388, 389, 390
Jacobins, *see* Federalist party
Jamaica, 93
James, Henry, 485
James, Thomas L., 495–96
James, William, 479
James I (King of England, 1603–1625), 15–16, 21–22, 24–26, 29, 37, 59
James II (King of England, 1685–1688), 29, 33, 45–46, 50–52, 88–89
Jameson, J. F., 119
Jamestown, 22–25
Japan
China invaded by (1937), 671
as Cold War ally, 726–27
Eisenhower and, 747
Lansing-Ishii Agreement, 583
Manchuria and, 666
Portsmouth, treaty of, 576–77
T. Roosevelt and, 576–77
Root-Thakahira Agreement, 577
trade with, 347
U. S. post-World War II policies, 711–12
in World War II, *see* World War II
Japanese-Americans
relocation of, 689–91; *ill.* 690
segregation of, 577
Jarrell, Randall, 820
Jay, John
Constitution and, 147
as envoy, 127–29, 158

Jay, John (*Continued*)
  as secretary for foreign affairs,
    131
Jay Cooke and Company, 422
Jay's Treaty, 158
Jazz, 623–24, 660
Jazz Age, 619–22
Jeffers, Robinson, 623
Jeffers, William M., 682
Jefferson, Joseph, 295
Jefferson, Thomas (1743–1826)
  Alien and Sedition Acts and,
    163
  armed forces reduction, 184–
    85
  on Bank of the U. S., 150
  Burr and, 192
  on constitutions, state, 114
  courts and, 182–84, 239
  death of, 223
  Declaration of Independence
    and, 113
  as deist, 172
  education and, 168–70
  election 1796 and, 159–60
  election 1800 and, 163–65
  Embargo of 1807 and, 198–99
  France and, 161, 185–89
  *v.* A. Hamilton, 150–54
  impressment and, 198
  inaugural address of, 180, 181
  Louisiana Purchase and, 185–
    89
  Missouri Compromise and,
    235–37
  on Monroe, 214
  Monroe Doctrine and, 242
  Napoleon and, 185–87
  neutrality and, 157
  Ordinance of 1784 and, 133–
    34
  Paris peace talks (1783) and,
    128
  political philosophy of, 114,
    153
  President, elected (1800), 180–
    82
  second term (1804), 182
  as secretary of state, 149
  sectionalism and, 234–36
  on Shays' Rebellion, 142
  slavery and, 115, 186
  state rights and, 139, 167,
    189
  Statute of Religious Liberty and,
    115
  Supreme Court and, 239
  and West, exploration of, 190–
    91
Jeffersonians, *see* Republican
    party
Jeffries, James J., 488
Jensen, Merrill, 141
Jerome I. Case factory, 283
Jesuits, 12, 86
Jewett, Sarah Orne, 483
Jews, 75
John Birch Society, 768
John Ward House; *ill.* 54
Johns Hopkins University, 481
Johnson, Albert Sidney, 387
Johnson, Andrew (1808–1875)
  election 1864 and, 372–73
  election 1866 and, 409
  impeachment of, 412–13; *ill.*
    412
  Reconstruction and, 403–4,
    408, 409, 412–13
Johnson, Hiram, 551, 601, 667
Johnson, Hugh, 635, 643–44,
    673, 674
Johnson, Louis A., 713
Johnson, Lyndon B. (b. 1908)
  biography of, 764
  black power and, 774
  budget and, 765
  business and, 765
  civil rights and, 766–67
  Dominican Republic interven-
    tion, 789–90
  election 1960 and, 759
  election 1964 and, 768–70
  election 1968 and, 795
  Eisenhower and, 759
  foreign policy of, 788–90,
    792–95
  Great Society and, 768
  New Frontier program and, 765
  Presidency, succeeds to, 764,
    765
  program enacted, 770–71
  on F. D. Roosevelt, 764
  space race and, 825, 826
  on television, 816
  unions and, 765
  Vietnam and, 788–89, 792–95
  War on Poverty, 765–66, 771–
    72
Johnson, Philip, 818
Johnson, Renerdy, 418
Johnson, Samuel, 77, 101
Johnson, Tom, 550, 551
Johnson Act (1934), 675
Johnson-Clarendon   Convention,
    418
Johnston, Eric, 722
Johnston, Joseph E., 385, 388,
    394, 395–396
Joliet, Louis, 86; *map,* 87
Jolson, Al, 621
Jones, Jesse, 641
Jones, John Paul, 126
Jones, LeRoi, 820
Jones, Marvin, 686
Joseph, Chief, 473–74
Josephson, Matthew, 439
Journalism, 289
  1870–1910, 482
  1920s, 621
  muckraking, 546–48
  yellow, 522
*Judge,* 622
Judiciary Act (1789), 149, 237–
    38
Judiciary Act (1801), 164, 182–
    83
Junto, 80

Kalm, Peter, 88
Kansas
  Lecompton constitution of,
    356–57
  legislature formation, 353
  migration to, 353
  slavery issue in, 353–54, 356–
    57
  statehood (1861), 465
  territorial organization, 352–53
Kansas City *Star,* 548
Kansas-Nebraska Act, 352–53
Kean, R. G. H., 374
Kearny, Stephen W., 338
Kefauver, Estes, 734, 757
Kelley, Oliver H., 500
Kellogg Pact (1928), 665
Kellogg, Frank B., 616, 618
Kelly, William, 437
Kemble, Fanny, 295
Kendall, Amos, 250, 256
Kennan, George F., 585, 722
Kennedy, D. M., 802

Kennedy, John F. (1917–1963)
  assassinated, 763
  Berlin crisis and, 784–85
  civil rights and, 762–63
  Cuba and, 783–87; *map* 785
  defense policies, 782–83
  foreign aid, 781–82
  foreign policy, 781–88, 792
  foreign trade and, 788
  inauguration, 759
  inflation, 762
  Khrushchev and, 784, 787
  on megalopolis, 810
  New Frontier, 759, 761–63
  population control and, 781
  President, elected (1960), 759–60
  and space race, 825–26
  Vietnam War and, 792
Kennedy, John Pendleton, 317
Kennedy, Robert F., 768, 795
  as attorney general, 760, 763
  election 1968 and, 795, 796
Kennesaw Mountain, battle of 395–96
Kent, James, 251–52
Kent Island, 37
Kentucky
  in Civil War, 387, 388
  land claims and, 133
  religion in, 175
  settlement of, 131
  statehood (1792), 156
  unconstitutionality resolution, 163
Kentucky rifle, 64
Key, Francis Scott, 205
Keynes, John Maynard, 600, 658
Keyserling, Leon H., 808
Khrushchev, Nikita S. (b. 1894), 769
  arms race and, 742–45
  Berlin crisis and, 745, 784
  Cuba and, 748, 784, 787
  Eisenhower and, 746–47
  J. F. Kennedy and, 784, 787
King, Ernest J., 694
King, Martin Luther, Jr., 762, 763 775–76
King, N., 180
King, Rufus, 213, 235
King George's War, 89
King Philip's War, 34
King William's War, 89

King's Mountain, battle of, 125–26
Kirkendall, Richard, 657
Kirkland, E. C., 439
Kishi, Nobusuke, 747
Kissinger, Henry, 802
"Kitchen Cabinet," 256–57
Kitchin, Claude, 587
Knights of the Golden Circle, 370
Knights of Labor, 504
Knights of the White Camelia, 424
Knowland, William, 758
Know-Nothing party, 285, 353, 355
Knox, Frank, 654–55, 674
Knox, Henry, 149
Knox, Philander C., 580
*Knox* v. *Lee*, 423
Knudsen, William, 679, 680, 682
Kolko, Gabriel, 547
Konoye, Fuminaro, 676–78
Korean War (1950–1952), 727–30, 735–36, 804; *chart* 369; *ill.* 720; *maps* 728, 729
Kress, Samuel H., 659
Ku Klux Klan, 407, 424, 608–9, 626; *ills.* 423, 424, 608
Ku Klux Klan Act (1871), 424

Labor
  child, 232–33, 281
    Keating-Owen Act, 571–72
    1900, 539–40; *ill.* 539
  immigration and, 540–42
  laws regulating, 281
  Lowell system and, 232
  New Deal and, 648–51
  Northeast (1840), 281
  social reform and, 301
  strikes, *see* Strikes
  supply, colonial, 56–58
  unions, *see* Unions
Labor Reform Act (1959), 753
Ladd, William, 307
*Ladies' Home Journal*, 482–83
La Farge, John, 485
Lafayette, Marquis de, 118, 123, 126, 223
LaFeber, Walter, 743
La Follette, Robert M., 551, 561, 656
  election 1912 and, 566
  election 1924 and, 613

progressivism and, 545
railroad regulation and, 560
Versailles Treaty and, 601
La Follette Seamen's bill, 571
Laird, Melvin R., 802, 803
Laird rams affair, 384
Lake Erie, 204
La Luzerne, 127
Lancaster, Pennsylvania, 64
Lancaster pike, 212
Land
  Act of 1796, 220
  Act of 1800, 220
  Act of 1804, 220
  Act of 1820, 220–21
  boundary settlements, 1818–1819; *map* 216
  Cleveland and, 499
  conservation of, *see* Conservation
  Desert Land Act (1877), 465
  Homestead Act (1862), 367, 465
  Harrison Land Law (1800), 200
  Morrill Act (1862), 367
  Northwest Ordinance (1787), 134
  Ordinance of 1734, 133, 134
  Ordinance of 1785, 133–34, 220; *map* 133
  in Revolutionary War, 118
  sale of, 220–21, 268–69
  Timber Culture Act (1873), 465
  Timber and Stone Act (1878), 465
  Western, state claims to, *map* 132
Land, Emory S., 683
Landon, Alf M., 654–55
Langer, William L., 668
Lansing, Robert, 583, 586
Lansing-Ishii Agreement, 583
Lardner, Ring, 624
Larkin, Oliver W., 660
Larkin, Thomas O., 335–36
La Salle, Sieur de, 86; *map* 87
Latin America
  Alliance for Progress and, 781
  Cold War in, 747–48
  Dominican Republic intervention, 790
  Good Neighbor policy, 668–69
  Hoover and, 666
  Hughes and, 618

Latin America (*Continued*)
  and U. S. imperialism, 519–20.
    522–27
  independence for, 239–42
  Rockefeller visit to, 802–3
  F. D. Roosevelt and, 668–69
  T. Roosevelt and, 578–80
  Taft and, 580
  Wilson and, 580–82
Latrobe, Benjamin H., 263
Laurens, Henry, 128
Law
  colonial, 80
  common, 80
  Constitution and, 145
  profession of, 170
Law, John, 88
League of American Wheelmen,
  488
League to Enforce Peace, 592
League of Nations, 575, 598,
  599–602, 610, 618
Leahy, William D., 694
Leclerc, Charles, 186, 187
Lecompton constitution, 356–57
Ledbetter, Huddie "Leadbelly,"
  623
Lee, Arthur, 123
Lee, Jason, 332
Lee, Robert E. (1807–1870); *ill.*
  378
  appointed to command, 381,
    388
  Chancellorsville, battle of, 390
  Eastern Theater (1862), 388–90
  at Gettysburg, 391–92
  Grant's battles with, 394–96
  surrender at Appomattox of, 396
Leeward Islands, 93
Legare, Hugh Sinton, 318
Legislatures
  colonial, 84–85, 102
  state, 114–15
Leisler, Jacob, 52
LeMay, Curtis, 797
Lemke, William, 655
Lend-Lease, 675–76
L'Enfant, P. C., 179
Leo XIII, Pope, 548
Levant Company, 15
Lever Act (1917), 591
Lewis, Grace Hegger, 622
Lewis, John L., 606, 650, 674,
  686, 714

Lewis, Meriwether, 190–91
Lewis, Sinclair, 622; *ill.* 662
Lewis, William B., 256
Lewis and Clark Expedition, 190–
  91; *ill.* 190; *map* 189
Leyte Gulf, battle of, 702
Lexington, battle of, 108; *ill.* 107
Liberal Republicans, 421
*Liberator, The,* 310–11
Liberia, 310
Liberty Bonds, 590
Liberty boys, *see* Sons of Liberty
Liberty party, 312, 331, 341
Libraries, 482
  colonial, 77
*Life,* 622
Life-span, 824–25
Liliuokalani, Queen, 521
Lincoln, Abraham (1809–1865),
  231
  assassinated, 402–3
  Black Hawk War and, 259
  cabinet, 370
  capitalism and, 283
  civil liberties and, 371, 374
  as commander in chief in Civil
    War, 380–81
    armed forces recruitment, 369
    Bull Run and, 385
    Eastern Theater (1862) and,
      388, 389, 390
    Fort Sumter and, 364
  Douglas debates with, 357–58
  Emancipation Proclamation of,
    372
  as free thinker, 175
  inauguration of, 364
  President, elected (1860), 360–
    62
  Reconstruction and, 401–3
  slavery and, 324, 358
Lind, Jenny, 295
Lindbergh, Charles A., 605, 672
Lindsay, Vachel, 537
Link, Arthur, 585, 657
Lippmann, Walter, 624–25
Lisa, Manuel, 215
Literacy
  colonial, 77
  test, 429–30
Literature
  1800s, early, 171–72
  1870–1900, 483–85
  ca. 1900, 537

Golden Age of, 292–93
  in Great Depression, 660–61
  in Jazz Age, 621–23
  in New England, 293–95
  post-World War II, 819–20
  South, in antebellum, 317–18
  *see also* Book publishing
Little Bighorn, battle of, 473
Little Crow, 472
Litvinov, Maxim, 668
Living standard, 1960s, 808–10
Livingston, Robert R., 178, 186–
  87, 238
Lloyd, Henry Demarest, 454, 546
Locke, John, 43, 102, 113
"Loco Focos," 267
Lodge, Henry Cabot, 599–600,
  601–2, 610, 759
Loewe, Frederick, 818
Log Cabin Campaign, 272–73
Logan Act, 161
Lombardo, Guy, 660
Lome, Dupuy de, 523
London, Jack, 537
London Company, 22–26, 37
Long, Crawford W., 296
Long, Huey P., 647–48, 655
Long, Stephen, 215–16
Long Parliament, 29
Longfellow, Henry Wadsworth,
  294
Longstreet, Augustus B., 318
Longworth, Alice Roosevelt, 610–
  11
Lopez, Narciso, 347
Lords of Trade, 50
Lorimer, William E., 552
Louis XIV (King of France, 1643–
  1715), 58, 86, 88–89
Louis XV (King of France, 1715–
  1774), 89
Louis XVI (King of France, 1774–
  1793), 123, 157
Louisbourg, Fort, 86–88
Louisiana (state)
  Black Code and, 399
  Reconstruction and, 402, 403,
    410
  statehood, 190
  white supremacy, return of, 425
Louisiana (territory)
  exploration of, 86; *map* 87
  French control of, 185–89
  settlement of, 88

in seventeenth century, *map* 87
Louisiana Purchase, 185–89; *map* 188–89
L'Ouverture, Toussaint, 186
Lovejoy, Elijah, 312
Lovell, Bernard, 827
Lowden, Frank O., 610
Lowell, Amy, 537
Lowell, Francis C., 211
Lowell, James Russell, 292, 294, 308
Lowell, Massachusetts, 233
Lowell, Robert, 820
Loyalists, 114, 118, 125, 130
Loyalty checks, *see* Communism
Lucas, Eliza, 63
Luks, George, 537
Lumber industry, 64
Lundy, Benjamin, 310
*Lusitania* incident, 584, 586
Luther, Martin, 12–13
Lyceum, 304
Lynn, Massachusetts, 64
Lyon, Mary, 303
Lyon, Nathaniel, 385

McAdoo, William G., 590, 592, 610, 612
MacArthur, Douglas, 632, 695, 696, 702, 706, 712, 727–30
McCarran Internal Security Act, 731
McCarthy, Eugene, 795–97
McCarthy, Joseph, 731, 732, 734, 754
McClellan, George B., 372–73, 380, 385, 388–89, 390
McClure, S. S., 546
*McClure's*, 546, 550, 551
McCormick, Cyrus H., 283
McCormick Harvester Company, 456
*McCulloch* v. *Maryland*, 238
McDonald, Forrest, 141
McDowell, Irvin, 385, 388
McGillivray, Alexander, 135, 156
McGovern, George, 795
McGuffey, William Holmes, 303
McHenry, Fort, 205
McHenry, Jerry, 345
McKay, Douglas, 753

McKim, C. F., 486
McKinley, William (1843–1901), 507
army reforms of, 530–31
assassinated, 554
election 1900 and, 527
gold standard and, 514–15
President, elected (1896), 511, 513–14
silver question and, 514
Spanish-American War and, 522–27
tariff and, 514
McKinley Tariff Act (1890), 507
McKitrick, Eric, 411
MacLeish, Archibald, 820
McLeod, Alexander, 329
McLoughlin, John, 331
McLuhan, Marshall, 816
McNamara, Robert, 782–83
McNary, Charles L., 616
McNary-Haugen bill, 616
Macon's Bill No. 2 (1810), 199–200
Macready, William Charles, 295
Madison, Dolley, 199
Madison, James (1751–1836), 142
bank constitutionality and, 152
Bonus Bill veto of, 213
Constitution and, 140, 143, 145, 147
election 1808 and, 182
Embargo of 1807 and, 198, 199
Florida annexation and, 202
Great Britain, relations with, 198–200
impressment and, 198
*Marbury* v. *Madison*, 183
Monroe Doctrine and, 242
nullification and, 254
political philosophy of, 153
President, elected (1808), 199
public debt and, 152
Republican party and, 152
as secretary of state, 181, 189
transportation and, 213
Virginia resolution of, 163
War of 1812 and, 203, 208
Magazines, 77, 171, 289, 291, 482–83, 621–22
Magellan, Ferdinand, 8, 11
Mahan, Alfred Thayer, 519

Mailer, Norman, 819
Maine
boundary disputes in, 329, 330
colonization of, 32–34
in seventeenth century, *map* 33
statehood for, 236
temperance movement and, 306
War of 1812 and, *map* 207
*Maine,* sinking of, 523–24
Makemie, Francis, 73
Malenkov, Georgi, 736
Malthus, Thomas, 60
Malvern Hill, battle of, 389
Manassas, battle of, 385
second, 390
Manchuria, 576, 580, 666
Manifest Destiny, 327, 331
new, 517, 518–19
Mann, Horace, 302, 303
Mann Act (1910), 552
Mann-Elkins Act (1910), 560
Manufacturing
colonial, 64–65
1840–1860, 278–80
War of 1812 and, 210–12
*see also* Business; Industry
Manumission Society, 235
Marbury, William, 183
*Marbury* v. *Madison*, 183–84
Marconi, Guglielmo, 531
Marcy, William L., 250, 345, 347, 348
Maria, Henrietta, 37
Marion, Francis, 125
Marquette, Father, 86; *map* 87
Marshall, George C., 694, 710, 723, 726
Marshall, John, 160–61, 260
Burr trial and, 192
v. Jefferson, 183, 184
nationalism and, 223
state rights and, 234, 237–39
Marshall Plan (1947), 723, 788
Martin, Joseph W., 730
Martineau, Harriet, 230, 290
Martinique, 186
Marx, Karl, 267, 453, 624
Mary II (Queen of England, 1689–1694), 29
Maryland
agriculture, 63
Constitution ratified by, *chart* 146
Glorious Revolution and, 52

Maryland (*Continued*)
  legislature of, 37–38
  political discontent in, 42
  religion in, 39, 75, 174
  settlement of, 37–38
  in seventeenth century, *map* 45
  slavery in, 57, 63
  tobacco and, 38–39
Maryland Toleration Act (1649),
  38
Mason, James M., 384
Mason, John, 33–34
Mason, John Y., 348
Mason, Lowell, 295
Mass production, 177, 534–35
Massachusetts, 30–36
  black militancy in, 310
  boycott of English goods, 99
  Coercive Acts (1774), 105
  committees of correspondence
    and, 106
  constitution of, 114
  Constitution ratified by, 148;
    *chart* 146
  debt, public, 152
  education in, 35, 39, 168–69,
    302, 303
  exodus from, 31–34
  fugitive slaves, 346
  General Court, 30, 32, 35, 50
  Glorious Revolution and, 50–51
  Great Britain, prerevolutionary
    resistance to, 93
  labor laws, 281
  Mutiny Act, and, 99
  Navigation Acts and, 50
  Negroes in, 312
  religion in, 173
  Revolutionary War, 125
  in seventeenth century, *maps*
    32, 45
  Shays' Rebellion, 136
  slavery in, 115
  social reform, 305
  temperance movement and, 306
  Townshend program and, 99
  voting reform in, 251
  witchcraft, 51
Massachusetts Bay Company, 30,
  45
Massasoit Indians, 26
Mather, Cotton, 51, 78, 305
Mather, Increase, 50, 51
Mathews, George, 202

Mathews, Shailer, 453
Maury, Matthew Fontaine, 296
Maximilian, Emperor, 417
May, Ernest, 585
Maya civilization, 3–4, 10–11
*Mayflower* (vessel), 26
Mayflower Compact, 26
Maysville Road bill (1830), 259
Meade, George G., 392, 394
Meat Inspection Act (1906), 562
Meat-packing industry, 441
Medicaid, 771
Medicare-Social Security Act
  (1965), 771
Medicine
  colonial, 78
  in Great Depression, 661–62
  ca. 1900, 535–36
  post-World War II, 824
  profession of, 170–71
Megalopolis, rise of, 810–12, 813
Meir, Golda, 803
Mellon, Albert, 628
Mellon, Andrew W., 611, 613–
  14, 623, 659
Melville, Herman, 292, 294
Memminger, Christopher G., 374
Mencken, Henry L., 622, 624
Menotti, Gian Carlo, 818
Mental institutions, reform of, 305
Mercantilism, 15, 49, 63, 83
Merchant marine, 178
  *see also* Shipping
Merchant Marine Act (1916), 587
Merchant Marine Act (1920), 609
Merchants, in South, 315
Meredith, James, 763, 774
*Merrimack* (vessel), 382
Methodist Church, 174–75, 351
Mexican War, 336–39; *map* 337
  casualties, *chart*, 369
  peace movement and, 308
Mexico
  California and, 335–36, 339
  France and, 384, 417
  Gadsden Purchase, 352
  independence recognized, 240
  oil expropriation, 669
  Spanish colonization of, 10–12
  Texas annexation and, 332–34
  U. S. in (1914–1917), 581–
    82; *map* 581
  war with U. S., *see* Mexican
    War

Mexico City, 339
Michigan, 200, 280
Michigan Central Railroad, 280
Middle colonies
  immigrant groups in, *map* 59
  in seventeenth century, *map* 45
Middle East (1948–1959), 740–
  41
Midway Island
  annexed, 418, 517
  battle of, 696
Migration, 332, 340; *ill.* 326;
  *map* 334
Mikoyan, Anastas, 746
Milan Decree (1807), 196, 199
Miles, Nelson A., 472, 525
Milhaud, Darius, 817
Military-industrial complex, 779,
  782
Millay, Edna St. Vincent, 623
Miller, William E., 301, 439, 768
Miller-Tydings Act (1937), 653
Millis, Walter, 585
Mills bill, 499
Mims, Fort, 205
Mining, 466–67; *ill.* 462
Minutemen, 107–8
*Miranda* case, 800
Missionaries, 332
Mississippi
  Reconstruction and, 410
  statehood (1817), 217
  white supremacy, return of, 425
  women's rights in, 307
*Mississippi* v. *Johnson*, 412
Mississippi Plan, 424–25
Mississippi River (Valley)
  in Civil War, 385–86
  exploration of, 86–88; *map* 87
  Indian fighting, 200–1
  navigation on, 226
  railroads in 1865–1873, 443
  settlement of, 217
  Spain and, 130, 156, 186
Missouri, 280, 385
Missouri Compromise, 234–37;
  *map* 235
Missouri Fur Company, 215
Mitchell, John, 558
Mitchell, Margaret, 661
Moderate Republicans, 401
Mohawk and Hudson Railroad,
  230
Mohawk Indians, 18

Molasses Act of 1733, 68, 94
Moley, Raymond, 657, 674
Molly Maguires, 455
Molotov, Vyacheslav, 696
Money
    colonial, 65–69, 92–93, 94
    Confederate, 375
    Continental, 117
    Constitution and, 145
    gold standard, 510, 514–15
    Gold Standard Act (1900) and,
        514
    New Deal and, 646–47
    silver question, 509–12, 514
    soft v. hard, 263–64
    see also Currency
Monitor (vessel), 382
Monopoly
    on credit, 570
    New Deal and, 653–54
    ca. 1900, 538
    rise of, 436–44
    T. Roosevelt and, 556–58
    Sherman Antitrust Act and, 506
    W. Wilson and, 570–71
Monroe, Fort, 388
Monroe, Harriet, 537
Monroe, James (1758–1831)
    Cumberland Road bill, 259
    election 1820 and, 214
    "era of good feelings," 213–14
    France, as envoy to, 158, 159
    impressment and, 198
    Jay's Treaty and, 158
    Jefferson on, 214
    Latin America and, 239, 242
    Louisiana Purchase, 187
    nationalism and, 223
    President, elected (1816), 213
Monroe Doctrine, 234, 240–42,
    517–18, 520
    Roosevelt Corollary and, 579–
        80
Montana, 465
Montcalm, Marquis de, 91, 92
Monterrey, 336–37
Montezuma II (Aztec emperor,
    c. 1502–1520), 10
Montgomery, Alabama, 373–74
Montgomery, B. L., 700
Montgomery, Richard, 120
Montgomery Ward and Company,
    500
Montreal, 88

Moon, men on, 807, 825–27;
    ill. 806
Moore, Thomas, 14, 299
Moore's Creek Bridge, 120
Morgan, E. S., 119
Morgan, J. P., 510, 563
    coal mine strike and, 558
    railroads and, 444, 557
    steel and, 538
    Wall Street crash (1929), 626
Morgan, Lewis H., 452–53
Morgan, William, 251
Morgantown Ordinance Plant, 681
Morgenthau, Hans J., 585
Morgenthau, Henry, Jr., 646
Morguer, Jacques Le Moyne de,
    20
Mormons, 339
Morocco, 185, 577–78
Morrell Land Grant Act (1862),
    367
Morrell Tariff Act, 367
Morris, Nelson, 441
Morris, Robert, 135
Morristown, N. J., 121
Morse, Jedidiah, 168
Morse, Samuel F. B., 160, 225,
    288
Morse, Wayne, 792
Morton, Oliver P., 420, 494
Motion pictures, 535, 538, 621,
    661
Motley, John Lothrop, 295
Mott, Lucretia, 307
Mount, William Sidney, 295
Mount Holyoke, 303
Mountain men, 215
Mowry, George, 547
Moynihan, Daniel P., 802, 812
Muckrakers, 546–48, 553–54
Mugwumps, 497
Muir, John, 554
Mulligan letters, 426, 497
Mun, Thomas, 15
Municipal reform, 550–51
Munsey, Frank, 483, 566
Munson, William Giles, 176
Murfreesboro, battle of, 388
Murray, Philip, 714
Muscovy Company, 15
Music, 295
    1800s, early, 172
    in Great Depression, 660
    jazz, 623–24

post-World War II, 816–18
Muskogean Indians, 18
Mussolini, Benito, 669, 670, 697
Mutiny Act (1765), 94, 98
Mutual Defense Act (1949), 725
Myers, Gustavus, 439
Myrdal, Gunnar, 751

Nagasaki, atomic bomb on, 704;
    ill. 692
Naismith, James A., 488
Napoleon I (Bonaparte, 1769–
    1821), 208
    Adams administration and, 161
    Berlin Decree (1806), 196, 199
    Cadore letter, 200
    Continental System and, 196
    Jefferson and, 185–87
    Louisiana Purchase and, 187,
        189
    Milan Decree (1807), 196, 199
Napoleon III (1852–1870), 383,
    384, 417
Nashville
    battle of, 396
    Southern rights convention,
        343, 345
Nasser, Gamal Abdel, 740, 741
Nast, Thomas, 407
Nathan, Jean, 622
National Aeronautics and Space
    Agency (NASA), 825
National Art Gallery, 659–60
National Association for the Ad-
    vancement of Colored People
    (NAACP), 553
National Bank Act (1863), 367–
    68
National Banking System, 367–68
National Broadcasting Company,
    620
National Civic Federation, 558
National debt, see Debt, public
National Farmers' Alliance, 501–2
National Grange of the Patrons of
    Husbandry, 500
National Greenback Party, 423
National Housing Act (1937), 658
National Housing Act (1949), 732
National Industrial Recovery Act
    (1933), 643–44, 650
National Labor Board, 650–51
National Labor Relations Act, 658

National Labor Union, 455
National Law Enforcement Commission, 630
National Origins Act (1924), 619
National Progressive Republican League, 566
National Republicans (Adamsites), 246, 265
National Recovery Administration, 643–44, 658
National Road, 212, 227, 245, 259
National Science Foundation, 824
National Security Act (1947), 713
National Security Council, 713
National Trades' Union, 234
National War Labor Board, 591, 685
National Youth Administration, 648
Nationalism, 223
  cultural, 290–96
  territorial expansion and, 327
Nationalist clubs, 454
Nationalists, 143, 145
Nationalization, 609
Native American party, see Know-Nothing party
Nativist movement, 285
Natural resources, depletion, 823
Naturalization Act repealed, 182
Naval Limitation Treaty, 617
Naval Observatory and Hydrographical Office, 296
Navigation Acts, 49–50, 84
  and foreign trade, colonial, 67–68
  supplements to, 83
Navy
  Algiers conflict, 209–10
  building, 162, 669
  Civil War, 381–83, 386, 387, 391; ill. 382
  Cold War and, 745
  Cuban missile crisis and, 787
  Department established, 161
  French conflict, 161
  Hoover and, 666–67
  Korean War, ill. 720
  1900, 519
  Revolutionary War, 126
  T. Roosevelt and, 576–77
  Spanish-American War, 524–25, 536
  Tripolian War, 185

War of 1812, 203–4; ill. 204
World War I, 587, 592
World War II, 675, 676, 695–96, 701–2
Nebraska
  statehood (1864), 465
  territorial organization, 352–53
Necessity, Fort, 90
Negroes
  Atlanta Compromise, 430
  black power, 772, 773–76
  civil disorder and, 774–76
  civil rights movement and (1960), 762–63, 766–67, 773–76
  in Civil War, 372, 398; ill. 350
  education for, 481
  discrimination against, legalized, 428–30; see also Segregation
  first arrivals, 25
  free, 322
  higher education for, 481–82
  Ku Klux Klan and, 608–9
  leadership, 413–14, 553
  Nixon and, 800, 801
  in North, 308–10, 312
  in post-Civil War South, 398
    see also Reconstruction
  post-World War I, 609
  progressivism and, 552–53
  Reconstruction and, 399, 400, 407, 413–15
  T. Roosevelt and, 555
  as slaves, 38–39 see also Slavery
  South, New, 413–32
  status, ca. 1960, 751
  Supreme Court and, 755
  voting rights, 253, 424–25, 429–30, 756, 766–67
  War on Poverty and, 772
  and white supremacy, 424–25
  World War II affects, 685
Nehru, Jawaharlal, 788
Nelson, Donald, 679
Netherlands, see Dutch
Neutra, Richard, 813
Neutrality
  Act of 1794, 157
  Act of 1935, 670
  Act of 1939, 672, 675
  Jay's Treaty and, 158
  Latin America and, 239

maintaining, 156–59
  ca. 1935, 669–70
  trade rights and, 195–96
  World War I and, 583–89
  World War II and, 669–70, 673–75
Nevada, 465–67
Nevins, Allan, 361, 439
New Amsterdam, 45
New Bern, 58
New Deal, 635, 639–59
  agriculture and, 641–43, 645–46, 651–52
  banking and, 646, 647
  business
    aid to, 643–44
    opposition from, 647
    regulation of, 652–54
  conservation, 644–46, 651
  Great Depression and, 635, 639–59
  historians' disagreements on, 657
  money, 646
  opposition to, 647–48
  recession of 1937 and, 656–59
  reform, 658
  relief measures, 641–46, 648, 658
  Supreme Court and, 644, 651, 653, 655–56
  Tennessee Valley Authority, 644–46
  workers' welfare and, 648
New England
  agriculture in, 62, 280–81
  Congregational Church, 115, 173
  colonization of, 25–27, 30–36
  commerce in, 35–36
  education in, 35, 168–69
  immigrant groups in, map 59
  King George's War and, 89
  King William's War and, 89
  literature in, 293–95, 483
  Louisiana Purchase and, 191
  manufacturing in (1840–1860), 278, 280
  Negro rights in (1850), 308
  population, 60
  secession threat, 191, 206–8
  in seventeenth century, maps 33, 45

shipping, 35–36, 65
slavery
  abolished, 277
  insurrections, 71
  trade in, 57–58
  social reform movement and,
    301
  Tariff of 1828 and, 245–46
  and taxation, post-war, 136
  textile industry, 211
  War of 1812 and, 195, 206–8
New England Antislavery Society,
  311
New England Confederation, 34
New England Emigrant Aid Company, 353
New France, 86–91
New Freedom, 568–69
New Frontier, 759, 761–63
  enacting, 765
  programs of, 759, 761–63
New Hampshire
  colonization of, 31–34
  Constitution ratified by, 148;
    chart, 146
  labor laws, 281
  migration from, 225
  religion in, 173
  in seventeenth century, map 33
New Jersey
  colonization of, 42, 47–48;
    map 43
  Constitution ratified by, 148;
    chart 146
  in seventeenth century, map 45
  women's rights in, 114
New Jersey Plan, 143
New Mexico
  American expansion into, 334–
    35, 336, 339
  boundary disputes, 342
  Mexican War and, 337–38;
    map 337
  slavery question, 340–41, 341–
    44
  statehood for, 341–44
  Texas claims, 342
New Netherland, 45; map 45
New Orleans
  acquisition of, 186–87
  battle of, 205–6
  in Civil War, 386
  founding, 88
  as port, 226

New York Central Railroad, 286,
  442
New York (city)
  draft riots, 370
  as national capital, 148
  Negroes in, 71, 308
  newspapers, 289
  1910, ill. 532
  population density (1894), 447
  rise of, 225
  transportation, 448; ill. 449
New York (colony)
  agriculture, 62, 63
  boycott English goods, 99
  as British colony, 51–52
  colonization of, 42, 45–46;
    maps 43, 45
  Glorious Revolution and, 51–52
  indentured servants in, 57
  Mutiny Act and, 98–99
  shipbuilding, 65
  Townshend program and, 98–
    99
New York (state)
  agriculture, 280–81
  canal system, 227–29
  Church of England and, 115
  citizenship in, 236
  Constitution ratified by, 148;
    chart 146
  Erie Canal, 227–29
  Negro rights in, 308
  population, 179, 445
  social reform movement and,
    301, 305
  Temporary Emergency Relief
    Administration, 632
  voting reform in, 251–52
  War of 1812 and, 205
New York and Erie Railroad, 286
New York Free School Society,
  169
New York World, 522
New Yorker, 622
Newcomen, Thomas, 175
Newlands Reclamation Act (1902),
  562
Newport, Christopher, 23
Newspapers, 77, 171, 289
  1870–1910, 482
  ca. 1900, 537
  tabloid, 621
  in World War I, 593
  in World War II, 689

Newton, Isaac, 55
Nez Percé, 473–74
Niagara Movement, 553
Niagara Suspension Bridge, ill.
  287
Nicaragua, 347–48, 580–81,
  618, 666
Nicholson, Francis, 51–52
Niebuhr, Reinhold, 661
Nina (vessel), 7
Nine Power Pact (1922), 617
Nineteenth Amendment, 609
Nixon, H. C., 318
Nixon, Richard M. (b. 1913)
  arms race and, 803
  biography, 798
  consensus, appeals for, 799
  economy and, 801–2
  election 1952 and, 734–35
  election 1960 and, 759–60
  electoral college and, 799–800
  foreign affairs, 802–4
  general welfare and, 800–2
  Hiss affair and, 732
  in Latin America, 748
  loyalty investigations and, 731,
    732
  President, elected (1968), 795–
    99
  Soviet Union, visits, 746
  Supreme Court and, 800
  Vietnam and, 803–4
Noble Order of the Knights of
  Labor, 455–56
Nonintercourse Law (1809), 199
Nonpartisan League, 615
Normandy invasion (1944), 698–
  70; ill. 698; map 699
Norris, Frank, 537
Norris, George W., 564, 644,
  645
Norris-La Guardia Act, 649–50
North
  abolitionists attacked in, 312–
    13
  antislavery, 345–46
  in Civil War, see Civil War
  Compromise of 1850 and, 340,
    342, 343–45
  Kansas-Nebraska Act, 352–53
  Negroes in, 308–10, 609
  and panic of 1857, 355
  Reconstruction and, 400–4,
    408–13

North (*Continued*)
Republican party in, 492
see also Northeast; Northwest
North, Lord, 100
Coercive Acts and, 105
Conciliatory Propositions, 107
peace offensive and, 124
resigns, 127–28
Tea Act and, 103–5
North, Simon, 278
North America, eighteenth century, *maps* 90–91
North Atlantic Alliance, 723–25
North Atlantic Treaty Organization (NATO), 724–25, 738–39
North Carolina
in Civil War, 396
Constitution ratified by, *chart* 146
immigrants to, 58
labor laws, 539
land claims, 132–33
migration from, 225
Reconstruction and, 410
Regulator movement, 95
secession of, 365
statehood (1789), 156
see also Carolinas
North Dakota, 465
*North Star,* 310
Northeast
agriculture, 280–81
business, 278–80
canals, *map* 227
railroads, 286
Northern Confederacy, 191
Northwest
agriculture, 281–83
Indians, 134–35, 156, 200–1
industry, 281
migration to, 216–17
see also Frontier
Northwest Ordinance (1787), 134
Northwest Territory, 134, 200
Northwestern Fur Company, 215
Noyes, John Humphrey, 305
Nuclear power plants, 823
Nuclear tests, 742, 784–85
treaty banning, 788
Nugent, W. T. K., 503
Nullification, 254–59, 260–62
Nullification Ordinance, 260–61
Nuremberg trials, 711

Nye, Gerald P., 669, 673

Oberlin College, 303
Office of Censorship, 689
Office of Defense Transportation, 682
Office of Economic Opportunity (OEO), 771–72
Office of Price Administration, 686–87
Office of Scientific Research and Development, 683
Office of War Information (OWI), 689
Office of War Mobilization, 680
Ogden, Aaron, 238
Oglethorpe, James, 56
O'Hara, John, 819
Ohio
agriculture, 280
Indian problems, 156
population, 445
statehood (1803), 200, 212
Ohio Company, 89, 134
Ohio River Valley
French claim to, 89–90
Great Britain and, 156
as migration route, 217
Oil, see Petroleum
Okinawa, battle of, 702
Olds, Ransom, 531
Olive Branch Petition, 112–13
Oliver, James, 477
Olney, Richard, 460, 519–20
O'Mahoney, Joseph C., 653
*On the Origin of Species* (Darwin), 296
Oneida Community, 305
Oneida Indians, 18
O'Neil, Peggy, 257
O'Neill, Eugene, 623, 660, 819
Onis, Don Luis de, 214–15
Onondaga Indians, 18
Opechancanough, Chief, 25, 40
Open Door Policy, 517–18, 529–30, 577, 617
Oppenheimer, J. Robert, 683, 754
Ordinance
Civil War, 365
1800, 177; *ill.* 176
manufacturing, 176
Revolutionary War, 111, 117

World War II, 680
Ordinance of 1784, 133, 134
Ordinance of 1785, 133–34, 220; *map* 133
Oregon
election 1844 and, 330
partition of, 331–32; *map* 332
slavery question, 341
Oregon Trail, 333; *map* 334
Organization of American States, 747, 790
Orinoco River, 8
Oriskany, New York, 122
Orlando, Vittorio E., 600
Osieola, Chief, 260
Osgood, Mary, 51
Ostend Manifesto, 348
O'Sullivan, John L., 331
Oswald, Lee Harvey, 763–64
Otis, James, 93, 102
Owen, Robert, 305
Oxford University, 79

Pacts, see Treaties
Page, Thomas Nelson, 483
Page, Walter Hines, 585
Pago Pago, 521
Paine, Thomas
religion and, 172
on Revolutionary War, 111
writings of, 112, 113
Painting, see Art; see also The Course of American Art, Parts 1–4
Pakenham, Edward, 205–6
Palatines, 58
Palmer, A. Mitchell, 591, 606–8, 610
Palmerston, Lord, 329
Panama Canal, 578–79
Pan-American Congress, 519
Pan-American Union, 519
*Panay* incident, 671
Panic of 1819, 220–21
Panic of 1837, 268–71; *ill.* 270
Panic of 1857, 355
Panic of 1873, 422–23
Panic of 1893, 508–9
Panic of 1907, 557–58
Paris, treaty of (1783), 127–30
Paris, treaty of (1898), 527
Parker, Alton B., 555–56
Parkman, Francis, 295

Parliament (England) *v.* King, 84
  *see also* England; Great Britain
Parrington, Vernon L., 625
Pastorius, Daniel, 48
Paterson, N. T., 176
Paterson, William, 143
Patriot party, 114, 118, 125
Patronage, *see* Spoils system
Patterson, Robert, 385
Paxton Boys, 95
Payne, Henry Clay, 555
Payne, John Howard, 295
Payne-Aldrich tariff (1909), 564
Peace Corps, 781
Peace Democrats, 370, 373
Peace movement, 307–8; *see*
  *also* Antiwar movement
Peace pacts, 617–18
Peale, Rembrandt, 166
Pearl Harbor, 520
  historians' disagreements on,
  677
  Japan attacks, 678–79; *ill.* 678
Peddlers, 231–32
Peffer, William A., 490
Peirce, Charles, 479
Pemberton, John C., 391
Pendleton, George, 416
Pendleton Act (1883), 496
Penn, William, 46–48; *ill.* 28, 47
Pennsylvania
  agriculture, 62–63, 280–81
  boycott of English goods, 99
  canal system, 229
  in Civil War, 392
  colonization of, 42, 48; *maps*
  43, 45
  constitution of, 114
  Constitution ratified by, 148;
  *chart* 146
  education in, 302
  immigration to, 58
  indentured servants in, 56–57
  labor laws, 281
  population, 60, 445
  religion, 74
  seventeenth century, *map* 45
  shipbuilding, 65
  slavery and, 115
  social reform, 305
  Whiskey Rebellion, 154–56
Pennsylvania Railroad, 286, 442–
  43, 450
Pennsylvania rifle, 64, 111

People's party, *see* Populist party
Pequot Indians and New England
  colonies (War), 34
Percy, George, 23
Perkins, Frances, 648
Perkins, George W., 566
Peron, Juan D., 747
Perry, Matthew C., 347
Perry, Oliver Hazard, 204
Perryville, battle of, 388
Pershing, John J., 582, 594–96
Peru, 240
Pestalozzi, Johann, 303
Petersburg, Virginia, 395, 396
Petroleum industry, 437–40
Philadelphia, 48
  Constitutional Convention at,
  140–45
  Continental Congress and, 106
  population, 179
  Revolutionary War, 121
Philadelphia-Pittsburgh Turnpike,
  227
Philanthropy, 451–52
Philip II (King of Spain, 1556–
  1598), 13–14
Philippines
  acquired, 527
  independence for, 669
  rebellion crushed, 529
  in Spanish-American War, 525
Phillips, David Graham, 552, 553
Phillips, Wendel, 360
Philosophy
  Darwinism, 479
  in Jazz Age, 624–25
  pragmatism, 479
Phonograph, 535
Phrenology, 307
Pickens, Andrew, 125
Pickens, Fort, 363
Pickering, John, 184
Pickering, Timothy, 160
Pickett's charge, 392
Piedmont plateau, 16
Pierce, Franklin (1804–1869)
  cabinet, 345
  foreign policy, 347–48
  Kansas-Nebraska Act and, 352
  and Kansas slavery issue, 353
  President, elected (1852), 345
Pike, Albert, 314
Pike, Zebulon Montgomery, 191,
  204; *map,* 189

Pike's Peak gold rush, 466
Pilgrims, 25–27, 30; *ill.* 2
Pillsbury, Charles A., 441
Pinchback, P. B. S., 414
Pinchot, Gifford, 560, 565–66,
  823
Pinckney, C. C., 160–61, 163–
  64, 182, 199
Pinckney, Thomas, 159–60
Pinckney's Treaty, 159, 186
Pinkerton Detective Agency, 458
*Pinta* (vessel), 7
Pioneer Village (Salem, Mass.),
  3; *ill.* 2
Piston, Walter, 817
Pitcairn, John, 107–8
Pitman, Isaac, 357
Pitt, William (Lord Chatham), 91,
  93, 94, 98, 101, 107
Pizarro, Francisco, 11; *map* 9
Plains of Abraham, 92
Plantation system, 431; *ill.* 298
Platt, Tom, 496
Platt Amendment, 529
Plattsburg, battle of, 205
*Plessy* v. *Ferguson,* 428, 429,
  755
Plymouth Company, 22, 25–27
Plymouth, Massachusetts, 25–27
Plymouth Plantation, 25–27
Pocahontas, 25
Poe, Edgar Allan, 292, 293
Poetry, 171–72
Point Iowa program (1950), 723
Poland, 672, 707
Political parties, 153–54, 253;
  *see also* specific parties
Polk, James K. (1795–1849)
  California and, 327, 336, 339
  Independent Treasury and, 340
  Mexican War, 336–39
  Oregon and, 327, 332
  post-war politics, 340–41
  President, elected (1844), 330–
  31
  slavery and, 340–41
  Tariff 1846 and, 340
  Texas boundary disputes and,
  334, 336, 339
Poll tax, 429
Pollack, Norman, 503
*Pollack* v. *The Farmers' Loan and
  Trust Company,* 507–8
Polo, Marco, 4, 7

Ponce De Leon, 6, 12; *map* 9
Pontiac's Rebellion, 94
Pools, business, 436
*Poor Richard's Almanac* (Franklin), 77
Pope, John, 389–90
Population
  centers, 1790–1860; *map* 279
  central, 781
  colonial, 58–60; *chart* 60
  density, 1900, 1960; *map* 809
  growth, *chart* 224
    colonial period, 58–60; *chart* 60
    1840–1900; *chart* 446
  immigration and, 283, 445
  rural *v.* urban, 1860–1910, 445
  1790–1800, 179
  1820–1840, 224–25
  1850–1860, 283
  1860–1900, 445
  1967, 808
Populist party
  election 1892 and, 502–4, 507
  election 1896 and, 512–513
  founding, 502
  historians' disagreements on, 503
  progressivism and, 545
*Populist Response to Industrialism, The* (Pollack), 503
  silver question and, 510, 512
Port Hudson, 391
Portsmouth, treaty of (1905), 576–77
Portugal, explorations by, 6–8; *map* 9
Post office, 85, 149
Potsdam Conference (1945), 710
Potsdam Declaration, 703
Pottawatomie Massacre, 353
Pound, Ezra, 537, 623
Pound, Roscoe, 552
Powderly, Terence, 490
Powell, Adam Clayton, 756
Powell, John Wesley, 560
Power development, 753
Powers, Hiram, 295
Powhatan, 23
Pragmatism, 479
Preble, Edward, 185
Prepared-foods industry, 441

Presbyterian Church, 73, 173–75
Prescott, William H., 295
Presidency
  Command of the Army Act and, 410
  Congress and, 494–95
  Constitution and, 145
  Reconstruction and, 400, 402, 410–13
  Tenure of Office Act and, 410
President's Commission on Crime, 813–14
Preston, Captain Thomas, 101; *ill.* 103
Price, Byron, 689
Price control, 686–87, 714–15
*Prigg* v. *Pennsylvania,* 312
Primaries, 551
Primogeniture and entail, abolition of, 115
Princeton, New Jersey, 121
Princeton College, 78, 168
Prison reform, 305
Privy Council, England, 84
Proclamation Line of 1763, 94; *map* 96
*Progress and Party* (George), 454
Progressivism, 545
  Congress and, 552
  election 1924 and, 613
  foreign policy and, 576
  and health, public, 562
  historians' disagreements on, 547
  middle class and, 546
  muckrakers and, 546–48
  municipal reform and, 550–51
  Populism and, 545
  post-World War I, 609–10
  T. Roosevelt and, 545, 546, 553–62, 566–67, 576–80
  state governments and, 551–52
  Supreme Court and, 552
  W. H. Taft and, 564–65
  W. Wilson and, 568–69, 571–72
Prohibition, 609–10, 620–21, 630
Prohibitory Act, 113
Propaganda, World War II, 689
Property
  confiscated in Revolutionary War, 118

state constitutions and, 115
  voting, 251–52
Prophet, The, 201
Prosser, Gabriel, 323
Protestant Episcopal Church, 174
Protestants
  Quebec Act and, 105
  Roman Catholicism and, 12–14
  social reform and, 300–1
Providence, R. I., 32
Provincial Company of Lexington, *see* Minutemen
Public Broadcasting Act, 816
Public school system, 168
  desegregation of, 755–56
  1860–1900, 479–80
  ca. 1900, 536–37
  1920s, 620
  social reform and, 302–3
Public Utilities Holding Company Act (1935), 658
Public Works Administration (PWA), 643, 648–49, 658
Publishing, *see* Book publishing
"Publius," 147
*Pueblo* incident, 804
Puerto Rico, 526–29
Pujo, Arsene, 570
Pulitzer, Joseph, 522
Pullman, George M., 442, 457, 458
Pullman strike, 457–60
Pure Food and Drug Act (1906), 562
Puritans, 73–75
  Anglican Church and, 15–16
  New England and, 25–27, 30–36
  Massachusetts Bay, 30–36
  Plymouth Plantation and, 25–27, 30

Quakers, 46–48, 73–74, 235
Quay, Matt, 493
Quebec, 88, 91, 120; *ill.* 92
Quebec Act (1774), 105
Queen Anne's War, 89
Quids, 182

Radar, 683
Radical Republicans
  Civil War and, 381

Grant and, 415, 419
Johnson's impeachment, 412–13
Reconstruction and, 401–4, 408–13
and slavery, abolition of, 371–73
Radio, 531, 620, 661
Radio Corporation of America, (RCA), 609
Railroad Administration, 592
Railroad War Board, 592
Railroads
  Adamson Act (1916), 572
  canals and, 231
  capitalizing, 288
  cattle industry and, 469; *map* 470
  in Civil War, 366, 367
  construction, 285–86; *map* 442–43
  costs and times, 287–88; *chart* 288
  development of, 285–88, 441–44; (1850) *map* 286
  elevated, 448; *ill.* 449
  farmers and, 477–78
  first, 229–30
  Granger Movement and, 500–1
  L. B. Johnson and, 765
  operative (1870), *map* 442–43
  Pullman strike, 458–60
  regulation of, 504–5
    Esch-Cummins Transportation Act (1920), 609
    Hepburn Act (1906), 560
    Mann-Elkins Act (1910), 560
    T. Roosevelt and, 560
    Sherman Antitrust Act, 556–57
  in South, 443
  technological improvements, 230–31
  transcontinental, 352, 443–44, 465
  union strikes (1877), 455
  *v.* water transportation, *chart* 288
  in World War I, 592
  in World War II, 682
Raleigh, Sir Walter, 21, 24
Randolph, A. Philip, 685
Randolph, Edmund
  as attorney general, 149

bank constitutionality and, 152
and Constitution, 145
at Constitutional Convention, 143
Jay's Treaty and, 158
as secretary of state, 158, 159
Randolph, John, 182, 184, 189, 245, 322
Rauschenbusch, Walter, 453, 548
Rayburn, Sam, 759
Raymond, Henry J., 289
Reagan, Ronald, 795
Reapportionment, 767–68
Recall, 551
Recession
  1937, 656–59
  1957–1958, 758
  1960, 759
  *see also* Depression
Reciprocal Trade Agreements Act (1934), 668
Reconstruction, 399–404, 407–15
  acts, 409–10
  Black Code, 399, 408
  carpetbaggers, 413
  Compromise of 1877, 407
  Congress and, 400, 402, 408–13
  corruption under, 415
  Fourteenth Amendment and, 408–9
  Grant's policies, 419–20
  historians' disagreements on, 411
  industry and, 432
  Johnson's policies, 403–4, 408, 409, 412–13
  Joint Committee on, 408
  Lincoln's policies, 401–3
  Radical Republicans and, 401–4, 408–13
  scalawags, 413
  Supreme Court and, 410–12
  Wade–Davis Bill and, 402
Reconstruction Finance Corporation, 630, 641, 680
Red China, *see* Communist China
Red Cloud, 473
Reed, James, 601
Reed, Thomas B., 506
Reed, Walter, 535
Reeve, Tapping, 170
Referendum, 551

Reform, *see* Social reform
Reformation, 12–14
Regulator movement, 95
Religion
  colonial, 73–76
  colonization and, 12–13, 15–16, 25–26, 30–34, 36, 39, 45–46, 50–51
  1800s, 172–75; *ill.* 173
  freedom of, 115
  Great Awakening, 75–76
  in Great Depression, 661
  Jazz Age, 624
  Second Awakening, 175
  social reform, 548
Remington Gun Company, 436
Renaissance, 5–6
Reno, Milo, 632
Rensselaer Polytechnic Institute, 304
*Report of the National Advisory Commission on Civil Disorders*, 773–75
Republican party (to 1828)
  *v.* Antifederalists, 153
  French Revolution and, 152–53
  Jay's Treaty and, 158
  rise of, 152
  slavery and, 235
  split of 1828, 246
  War of 1812 and, 202, 206
Republican party (after 1854)
  in Civil War, 367, 371–73
  Conservative, 371
  Coolidge and, 612
  courts and, 182–84
  economic composition (1877–1888), 492–93
  1877–1888, 492–97
  elections and, *see* Elections
  formation, 353
  Grant and, 419–21
  Half-Breeds, 493–97
  under Harrison, 506
  Liberal, 421
  neutrality and, 617
  progressivism and, 545
  Radical, *see* Radical Republicans
  Reconstruction and, 400–4, 407–15
  F. D. Roosevelt and, 708
  T. Roosevelt and, 555
  silver question and, 509

Republican party (after 1854)
(*Continued*)
  spoils system and, 493–96
  Stalwarts, 493–97
  state rights and, 167
  tariffs and, 507, 618
  Truman administration and,
    732–33
Republic Steel, 651
*Rerun Novarum* (Leo XIII), 548
Resettlement administration, 652
Reston, James, 779
Resumption Act (1875), 423
Retty, James, 436
Reuther, Walter, 752, 763
Revels, Hiram R., 414; *ill*. 414
Revenue Act (1916), 587
Revenue Act (1942), 687–88
Revere, Paul, 58, 64, 103, 108
Revivalism, *see* Great Awakening
RevolutionaryWar, 111–14, 117–
  29
  aims of, 112–13
  casualties, *chart* 369
  Concord, battle of, 108
  Continental Army Formation,
    118
  Continental Congress and,
    106–7
  cooperation for, 105–7
  education and, 168
  fighting to 1777, 120–22;
    *maps* 120, 121, 122
  financing, 117–18
  foreign aid and, 122–24
  historians' disagreements on,
    119
  Lexington, battle of, 108; *ill*.
    107
  maps
    British campaigns (1777),
      122
    in North, 120
    Washington's retreat, 121
    Yorktown Road, 125
  mobilization for, 117–18
  morale, 118
  motivation for, 119
  ordinance in, 111, 117
  peace negotiations, 127–29
  philosophy of, 101–2
  property seizure in, 118
*Reynold* v. *Sims*, 767
Rhee, Syngman, 727, 736

Rhode, James, 309, 361
Rhode Island
  colonization of, 31, 32
  constitution of, 114
  Constitution ratified by, 146–
    48; *chart* 146
  currency in, 136
  Dorr Rebellion, 252
  education in, 302
  impost amendment veto, 140
  religion, 74
  in seventeenth century, *maps*
    33, 45
  statehood for (1790), 156
  voting reform, 252
Rice, Alice Hegan, 537
Richardson, Henry Hobson, 486
Richmond, Virginia, 388, 389–
  90, 395, 396
Rickenbacker, Edward V., *ill*. 595
Riesman, David, 820
*Rights of Man, The* (Paine), 112
Riis, Jacob, 447–48, 542, 548
Riley, James Whitcomb, 483
Ringling Brothers, 488
Riots, 774–76
Rittenhouse, David, 168
River transportation, 178, 226
Roads, 212, 259, 815
  *see also* Turnpikes
Roane, Spencer, 239
Roanoke Island, 21, 22; *ill*. 13
Robert Joffrey Ballet, 818; *ill*.
  817
Roberts, Owen J.
Robertson, James, 131
Roberval, Jean Francois, 8
Robinson, Edgar Eugene, 657
Robinson, Edward Arlington, 537,
  623
Robinson-Patman Act (1936), 653
Rochambeau, Count de, 126
Rockefeller, John D., 450, 451
  petroleum industry and, 438–
    40
  as philanthropist, 480
Rockefeller, Nelson, 759, 768,
  795
  in Latin America, 802–3
Rockingham, Marquis of, 98
Rock'n'roll, 816–17
Rocky Mountain Fur Company,
  215
Roebling, John A., 287, 440

Rogers, Richard, 818
Rogers, William P., 802, 803
Rohe, Ludwig Mies vander, 818
Rolfe, John, 24, 25
Roman Catholic Church
  in colonial period, 74–75
  1800s, early, 174
  prejudice against, 225
  v. Protestantism, 12–14
  Quebec Act and, 105
Romney, George, 795
Roosevelt, Franklin D. (1892–
  1945), 552, 625
  banking and, 639, 646
  business
    aid to, 643–44
    regulation of, 653
  Churchill, meetings with, 675
  conservation and, 646
  currency stabilization and, 667
  death, 710
  election 1920 and, 610
  election 1932 and, 636–38
  election 1936 and, 654–55
  election 1940 and, 674–75
  farm relief and, 641–43
  foreign policy, 667–79
  Great Depression and, 635,
    639–59
  inauguration, 637–38
    second, 655
  loyalty investigations and, 730
  New Deal, 639–59; *see also*
    New Deal
  New York, as governor of, 632
  President, elected (1940), 674–
    75
  recession (1937) and, 658–59
  Soviet Union, recognizes, 667–
    68
  Supreme Court and, 655–56
  taxation and, 653
  trust busting, 653–54
  unions and, 649–51, 685–86
  United Nations and, 693, 708
  World War II and
    at Casablanca, 704
    as commander in chief, 694–
      95
    destroyer deal and, 672, 675
    industrial production and,
      682
    Japanese-American reloca-
      tion and, 689

Lend-Lease and, 675–76
mobilization and, 679–80
Negro discrimination and,
685
Pearl Harbor attack and, 676–
78
price controls and, 686
propaganda and, 689
Revenue Act (1942) and,
687–88
Teheran Conference, 704–6
unions and, 685–86
Yalta Conference, 706–7
Roosevelt, Theodore (1858–1919)
administration of, 555
coal mine strike and, 558
conservation and, 554, 560–
62
election 1912 and, 566–69
foreign policy, 576–80
v. M. Hanna, 555
and health, public, 562
Latin America and, 578–80
Moroccan question and, 577–
78
muckraking movement and,
553–54
Navy and, 576–77
Panama Canal and, 578–79
party machine, takes over,
555
Portsmouth, treaty of, 576–77
Presidency, succeeds to, 554–
55
President, elected (1904), 555–
56
as Progressive, 545, 546, 553–
62, 566, 576–80
as racist, 542
railroad regulation and, 556–
57, 560
San Juan Hill, 526; ill. 516
Spanish-American War, 523,
524, 526
Taft and, 563, 565, 566
trust busting, 556–58
unions and, 558, 560
World War I and, 589
Root, Elihu, 530–31, 566, 599
Root, R. M., 357
Root-Takahira Agreement, 577
Rosecrans, William S., 388, 392
Rosenberg, Julius and Ethel, 731
Rosenthal, M. L., 820

Rough Riders, 524, 525–26; ill.
516
Round Heads, 29
Royal African Company, 57
Royal Society of London, 40,
78–79
Ruffin, Edmund, 317
Rule of 1756, 157
Ruling class, capitalism and, 450
Rural Electrification Administra-
tion, 652
Rush, Benjamin, 170–71, 305
Rush, Richard, 241
Rush-Bagot agreement (1817),
209
Rusk, Dean, 790, 794
Russell, William Howard, 373
Russia
Alaska purchased from, 417–18
Civil War and, 383
Finland invaded by, 672
Holy Alliance and, 240–41
Monroe Doctrine and, 240–41
in North America, map 91
post-World War II settlements
and, 705–7, 710–12
recognition by U. S., 667–68
Vietnam War and, 794
War of 1812 and, 208
in World War I, see World
War I
in World War II, 706–7; see
also World War II
Ryan, John Augustine, 548

Saarinen, Eero, 818
Sabotage Act (1918), 593–94
Sac Indians, 259
Sacajawea, 190
Sacco, Nicola, 608
Saint-Gaudens, Augustus, 486
St. Leger, Barry, 121–22
Salem, Massachusetts, 3; ill. 54
witchcraft trials, 51
Salem Female Academy, 169
Salinger, J. D., 819–20
Salisbury, Lord, 520
Salk, Jonas, 824
Salt Lake City, 339–40
Salvation Army, ca. 1900, 548
Samoan Islands, 521–22
Samoset Indians, 26
Sampson, William T., 525

Sanborn, John D., 422
Sandburg, Carl, 537, 820
Sanford, J. F. A., 356
San Ildefonso, treaty of, 185
San Jacinto, battle of, 333
San Juan Hill, battle of, 526;
ill. 516
Santa Anna, Antonio Lopez de,
333, 339
Santa Fe, 335, 338
Santa Fe Trail, 335; map 334
Santa Maria (vessel), 7
Santo Domingo, 186, 187, 517,
580–81, 618
Saratoga, New York, 122
Sargent, John Singer, 485
Saturday Evening Post, 483, 621
Savannah, Georgia, 125, 396
Scalawags, 413
Schickel, Richard, 816
Schlesinger, Arthur M., Jr., 255,
361, 445, 657, 743
Schley, W. S., 525
Schonberg, Arnold, 817
Schurz, Carl, 494, 528, 823
Schuyler, Philip, 122
Science
applied, 295–96
in colonial times, 78–79
in Great Depression, 662
post-World War II, 824–25
World War II and, 683
Science Advisory Board (1933),
662
Scopes trial, 624
Scotland, 58–60
Scott, Dred, 356
Scott, Walter, 291
Scott, Winfield, 261, 329, 338–
39, 380
Scribner's Magazine, 482
Scribner's Monthly, 482
Sculpture, see Art; "The Course
of American Art," Parts 1–4
Seaman's Protection Paper. 196;
ill. 197
Secession
Confederate states, 362–65;
map 363
New England scheme, 191
South, 362–65; map 363
Southern movement (1850),
343
Second Awakening, 175

Sectionalism, 223
Compromise of 1850, 343–45
Democratic party division, 351, 353, 360
economics and, 278–83
Kansas and, 353–54
Kansas-Nebraska Act, 352–53
Missouri Compromise and, 234–37
origins, 277–90 *passim*
slavery and, 345–46, 347–48, 351, 353–54
Southernism and, 313–14
territorial expansion and, 339–41, 347–48, 351
Westward expansion and, 339–41, 347–48, 351
Securities and Exchange Commission, 646–47
Sedition Act (1798), 163, 182
Sedition Act (1918), 593, 594
Seeger, Pete, 817
Segregation, legalized, 428–30
see also Desegregation
Selective Service System, 804
Seminole Indians, 18
Seminole War, 259–60
Senate
Constitution and, 145
Constitutional Convention and, 144
reform of, 552
Senate War Investigating Committee. 682
Seneca Indians, 18
Separatists
Anglican Church and, 15
Plymouth Plantations and, 25–27
Sequoyah, 260
Servants, indentured, 38, 56–57; *ill.* 57
Servicemen's Readjustment Act (1944), 714
Sessions, Roger, 817
Settlers, frontier, 131–32
Seven Days, battle of, 389
Seven Pines, battle of, 388
Seven Years' War (1756–1763), 90–91
Seventeenth Amendment (1912), 552
Seventh-Day Adventists, 301

Sevier, John, 131, 135
Seward, William H., 268, 302, 344, 360, 370
as secretary of state, 383, 417–18
Seymour, Charles, 585
Seymour, Horatio, 370, 417
Shadrach, 345
Shafter, William R., 525–26
Shakers, 305
Sharecropper system, 431–32, 642
Shawnees, 201
Shays, Daniel, 136
Shays' Rebellion, 136, 142
Shelburne, Lord, 128
Shenandoah Valley, 388
Shepard, Alan, 825
Sherman, John, 494
Sherman, William T., 495
Georgia, march through, 394, 395–96; *map* 395
Sherman Antitrust Act (1890), 506, 557
Sherman Silver Purchase Act (1890), 509–10
Sherwood, Robert E., 660, 673
Shiloh, battle of, 387
Shipbuilding, 65
Shipping
colonial, 35–36
1800s, early, 178
post-World War I, 609
War of 1812 (affects), 210
World War I, 592
World War II, 682–83, 696
Shipping Board, 592
Shoe industry, 231
Sholes, Christopher, 436
Siberian tribes, immigration, 3–4
Silliman, Benjamin, 296, 437
Silver Purchase Act (1934), 646
Silver question, 509–12, 514
Simms, William Gilmore, 317–18
Simpson, Jerry, 490, 504
Sims, William S., 592
Sinclair, Andrew, 620
Sinclair, Harry F., 612
Sinclair, Upton, 548, 562
Singer, Isaac, 279
Single tax societies, 454
Sioux, 472, 473, 474

Sitting Bull, 473
Slater, Samuel, 176
Slavery
*Ableman* v. *Booth,* 346
abolitionism and, 308–13, 323, 324, 345–46
antislavery societies, 115
arguments for, 323–24
beginning, 25
California admission and, 340–41, 341–44
Civil War and, 371–72
colonial, 38–39, 43, 45, 57–58, 62, 63, 69–71, 72; *ill.* 70
Compromise of 1850, 343–45
Confiscation Act (1861), 372
Constitution and, 144
cotton gin affects, 177
*Creole* mutiny and, 329, 330
crusades against, 70–71
in District of Columbia, 342, 343–45
*Dred Scott* v. *Sanford,* 355–56
election 1860 and, 360
Emancipation Proclamation, 372
foreign, 320–22
Fugitive Slave Act, 344, 46
fugitives, 322–23, 342, 343, 344–45
Great Britain and, 329, 330
Great Compromise and, 144
importation prohibited, 115
indentured servants and, 38
Kansas and, 353–54
Kansas-Nebraska Act, 352–53
laws, 319
manumission and, 322
*map* (1850), 346
in Massachusetts, 115
New England abolishes, 277
New Mexico admission and, 340–41, 341–44
Northwest Ordinance and, 277
in Northwest Territory, 134
ownership of slaves, 314; *chart* 314
Paris Peace Treaty and, 130
post-Civil War, 399
Prices, 320
rebellions, 323
Reconstruction and, 399, 400

regiment of, 319–22; *ill.* 321
Santo Domingo revolt, 186
sectionalism and, 277, 345–
46, 347–48, 351, 353–54
slaves response to, 322–23
social reform and, 299
Southernism and, 313–14, 316
Spanish colonization and, 11
Supreme Court and, 346
Texas annexation and, 333–34
Thirteenth Amendment and,
372, 398
Wilmot Proviso, 340, 343
Slidell, John, 336, 384
Sloan, John, 537
Slums, *ill.* 549
Smet, Pierre Jean de, 332
Smith, Adam, 451
Smith, Alfred E., 612, 625–26
Smith, Henry Nash, 463
Smith, Jedediah S., 215
Smith, Jesse, 611
Smith, John, 23, 25, 38
Smith, Joseph, 301, 339
Smith, Mrs. Samuel H., 250
Smith, Sydney, 290
Smith-Connally Act (1943), 686
Smith-Hughes Act (1917), 572
Smith-Lever Act (1914), 572
Smithsonian Institution, 296
Smuts, Jan, 600
Social class
capitalism and, 538–39
colonial, 69–70
Jackson and, 249
Panic of 1837 and, 271
social reform and, 301
in South, 314–16
Social Darwinism
capitalism and, 451–53
imperialism and, 518–19
philosophy affected by, 479
*Social Destiny of Man* (Brisbane),
305
*Social Justice* (Coughlin), 689
Social protest
agrarian, 491–92
Coxey's army, 508–9
Granger movement, 500–1
Supreme Court denounces, 508
Social reform, 299–324
abolitionists, 308–13, 323, 324
antiwar movement, 307–8

communities, model, 304–5
education, 302–4
municipal, 550–51
ca. 1900, 548–50
origins, 300–1
Protestantism and, 300–1
at state level, 551–52
temperance movement, 305–6;
*ill.* 306
under W. Wilson, 571–72
women's rights, 307
Social Security Act (1935), 648,
658
Socialism, 453–54
Socialist Labor party, 453–54
Socialist party, 454, 606–7
election 1904 and, 556
election 1912 and, 569
election 1932 and, 637
election 1936 and, 655
labor and, 558
Societies, utopian, 304–5
Society of the Cinncinnati, 140,
163
Society of Freemasons, 251
Society of Friends, 46
*see also* Quakers
Society for the Promotion of Temperance, 306
Society for the Propagation of the
Gospel in Foreign Pacts, 73
Socioeconomic class, *see* Social
class
Soil Conservation and Domestic
Allotment Act (1936), 658
Sons of Liberty, 97, 98, 100–1,
106, 370
Soong, T. V., 706
Soulé, Pierre, 348
South
abolitionists and, 312, 323,
324, 345–46
banking in, 431
Black Codes and, 399, 408
child labor in, 539–40
colonization of, 21–25, 37–
38; *map* 59
Compromise of 1850 and,
342–45
cotton, *see* Cotton
economy of, 313–14
education in, 318
emigrants in, 285

Harpers Ferry raid and, 359–
60
industry in, 315, 432
Kansas-Nebraska Act, 352–53
literature of, 317–18, 483
merchants in, 315
Missouri Compromise, 234–37
Negroes in, 609
New, 430–32
nullification and, 254–56, 257–
59, 260–62
Panic of 1857 and, 355
population of (1850), 314
post-Civil War, 398–99; *see
also* Reconstruction
railroads, 286
Reconstruction, *see* Reconstruction
Republican control of, 423–25
secession, 343, 362–65; *map*
363
secret societies in, 423–25
sharecropping system in, 431–
32
slavery, *see* Slavery
social class in, 314–16
tariff of 1828 and, 245–46
voting reform, 252–53
white supremacy, return of,
423–32
World War II affects, 685
*see also* Civil War; Confederate
States of America
South Carolina, 410
in Civil War, 364, 396; *ill.* 397
at Constitutional Convention,
144
Constitution ratified by, *chart*
146
desegregation resolution, 757
migration from, 225
nullification and, 253–56, 260–
62
secession, 363
slavery in, 58, 71
white supremacy, return of, 425
*see also* Carolinas
South Dakota, 465
Southeast Asia Treaty Organization (SEATO), 737–38, 791
Southern Alliance, 501–2
Southern Christian Leadership Conference (SCLC), 762

Southern Railway, 443
Southernism, 313–14
Southwest
    Indian problems, 135, 156
    migration to, 217
    Spanish conspiracy in, 135
    territorial expansion into, *map* 335
    War of 1812 and, *map* 207
Soviet-Chinese Treaty of 1945, 706
Soviet Union, *see* Russia
Space
    moon, landing on, 807, 825–27
    race, 825–27
    satellites, first, 742, 825; *ill.* 744
Spain
    Armada of, 14
    Civil War (1936), 670
    colonization by, 10–12; *map* 87
    Columbus and, 7–8
    Cuba and, 347, 348
    explorations by, 7–8; *map* 9
    Florida and, 130, 202, 214–15
    Georgia and, 56
    *v.* Great Britain, 12–14, 19, 56, 89, 124
    Indians, as allies of, 156, 205
    Latin America and, 239
    Louisiana Purchase and, 185, 186, 189
    Mississippi River, closes, 130
    in North America, eighteenth century, *maps* 90–91
    Pinckney's Treaty and, 158–59
    Revolutionary War and, 124, 127–29
    Southwest and, 135
    treaty negotiations with, 131
    War with, *see* Spanish-American War
Spalding, Albert, 487
Spanish-American War, 522–27; *chart* 369; *maps* 525, 526
Spanish Civil War, 670
"Spanish Conspiracy," 135
Sparkman, John J., 734
Specie Circular, 269–71
Spencer, Herbert, 451

Spock, Benjamin, 779
Spoils system
    1800s, late, 491
    Garfield and, 495–96
    Harrison and, 493
    Hayes and, 494–95
    Jackson and, 250–51
    reform, 496
    in states, 253
Sports, 486–88
Springfield, Illinois, race riot, 553
Spykman, Nicholas, 721
Squanto Indians, 26
Stagg, Amos A., 488
Stalin, Joseph, 736
    Cold War and, 722
    at Potsdam, 711
    at Teheran Conference, 704–6
    at Yalta Conference, 706–7
Stalwarts, 493–97
Stamp Act (1765), 94, 97–98, 100
Stamp Act Congress, 97, 98
Stampp, Kenneth M., 411
Standard Oil, 450, 513, 546
    muckrakers and, 546
Standard Oil Company of Ohio, 438–40
*Standard Oil Company* v. *United States* (1911), 557
Stanton, Edwin M., 410
Stanton, Elizabeth Cady, 307
Stanton, William, 370, 412–13
Stark, Harold R., 676
Stark, John, 122
Starr, L. M., 289
State Department, 149
    Department of Foreign Affairs, precedes, 122
State rights, 139
    Calhoun and, 254–59, 260–62
    commerce regulation and, 505
    Confederacy and, 375–76
    Jackson and, 259, 260–62
    Jefferson and, 167, 189
    J. Marshall and, 234, 237–39
    Reconstruction and, 400
    Supreme Court and, 149, 274, 506
    W. Wilson and, 572
States
    banking in, 210
    constitutions of, 114–15

Constitution (U. S.) and, 142–45
    creation of, 133–34
    debts and, 135–36, 150–51, 152
    education in, 302
    free *v.* slave, 234
    funds to, federal surplus, 269
    governments of, 114–15
    land seizure by, 118
    legislatures of, 114–15
    progressivism and, 551–52
    voting requirement reform, 251–53
    Western land claims, *map* 132
States Rights' Democratic Party, 716
Steam engine, 178
Steamboat, 178, 179, 212, 226
Steel Industry
    growth of, 437
    Homestead strike, 457–58
    J. F. Kennedy and, 762
    labor, 685–86
    strike (1919), 606, 651, 714
Steel Workers' Organizing Committee, 651
Steffens, Lincoln, 546–58, 550
Stein, Gertrude, 621
Steinbeck, John, 661
Stephens, Alexander, 365, 373–74, 376, 400, 404
Stephens, Uriah S., 455
Stettinus, Edward R., 708
Steuben, Baron von, 118; *ill.* 123
Stevens, John, 230
Stevens, John L., 521
Stevens, Robert, 754
Stevens, Thaddeus, 169, 302, 371, 401, 410
Stevenson, Adlai
    election 1952 and, 734–35
    election 1956 and, 757
    on General Motors, 752
Stewart, A. T., 417
Stieglitz, Alfred, 540
Still, William Grant, 817–18
Stilwell, Joseph H., 701–2
Stimson, Henry L.
    as secretary of state, 666, 667
    as secretary of war, 674, 677
    as U. S. attorney, 555
Stimson Doctrine (1932), 667

Stock market crash 1929, 626–
27; *chart,* 627
Stockton, R. F., 338
Stockton and Darlington Railroad,
230
Stone, Edward, 818
Stone, Lucy, 307
Stone's River, battle of, 388
Story, Joseph, 250
Stowe, Harriet Beecher, 311
Straight, Willard, 580
Stravinsky, Igor, 817
Strickland, William, 263
Strikes
auto industry, 651
coal mine, 558
Danbury Hatters, 559
Homestead, 457–58
legalized, 281
police and, 606
post-World War II, 714
railroad, 455, 456
steel, 606, 651
World War II, 686
Strong, Josiah, 518
Stuart, Gilbert, 214
Stuart, J. E. B., 389
Stuart, Mary "Queen of Scots,"
13
Stuart, R. Douglas, Jr., 673
Student Nonviolent Coordinating
Committee (SNCC), 772, 774
Submarine warfare
Civil War, 382
World War I, 584–87, 589
World War II, 675, 676, 696,
697
Subversives, *see* Communism,
loyalty checks for
Suez Canal, Egypt seizes, 740–41
Suffrage, *see* Voting rights
Sugar Act (1764), 94, 98
Sullivan, John L., 488
Sullivan, Louis, 486
Sumner, Charles, 312, 371, 425
antislavery and, 345
Brooks' attack on, 354
Grant and, 419
Great Britain and, 418
Reconstruction and, 401
Sumner, William Graham, 453
Sumter, Fort, 363, 364–65
Sumter, Thomas, 125

Supreme Court
J. Adams and, 164–65
Agricultural Adjustment Administration and, 651
antitrust cases, 506, 557
appeals and, 237–38
communists, persecution of, 731
Constitution and, 145, 149
child labor and, 571–72
Civil Rights cases (1883), 428–
29
on currency, 422–23
defranchising laws and, 429–
30
desegregation, 755, 756
Granger cases, 501
income tax and, 507–8
Insular cases, 528
Japanese-American relocation,
691
Jefferson and, 182–84
Marshall as chief justice, 237–
39; *see also* Marshall, John
military trials and, 410–12
New Deal and, 644, 651, 653,
655–56
Nixon and, 800
progressivism and, 552
railroad regulation and, 501,
504–5
reapportionment and, 767–68
Reconstruction and, 410–12
F. D. Roosevelt and, 655–56
school desegregation and, 801
segregation validated by, 428–
30
Sherman Act and, 557
"sick chicken" decision, 644
slavery decisions, 312, 346
on social protest, 508
state rights and, 237–39, 274,
505, 506
subversives and, 754–55
Taney as chief justice, 273–74
Wabash case, 505
*see also* specific cases
Supreme Order of the Star
Spangled Banner, 285
Surplus Marketing Administration,
651–52
Sutter, John A., 336
Svobida, Lawrence, 652
Sweet, W. W., 174

Swift, Gustavus, 441
Swope, Gerald, 651
Sylvis, William H., 455
Symmes, John Cleves, 134


Taber, John, 715
Taft, Robert A., 708, 716, 733–
34
Taft, William Howard (1857–
1930), 599
Ballinger-Pinchot controversy
and, 565
Canada and, trade with, 564
election 1912 and, 655–59
foreign affairs and, 564, 580
President, elected (1908), 562–
63
progressivism and, 545, 564–
65
T. Roosevelt breaks with, 565,
566
trust busting and, 557
Taft-Hartley Labor-Management
Relations Act (1947), 715–
16
Talleyrand, Prince Charles, 160–
61, 187–88, 198
Tallmadge, James, Jr., 234
Talon, Jean, 86
Tammany Society, 163
Taney, Roger B., 265, 273–74,
356, 371
Tanner, James, 506
Tansill, Charles C., 585
Tappan, Arthur and Lewis, 301
Tarbell, Ida, 546
Tarkington, Booth, 537
Tariff
G. Cleveland and, 499, 507
Constitutional Convention and,
144
Dingley, 514
election 1880 and, 495
election 1888 and, 499
Fordney-McCumber Act (1922),
618
A. Hamilton and, 151–52
1789, 178
1792, 152
1816, 212
1828, 245–46, 254–56, 260–
62

Tariff (*Continued*)
  1842, 328
  1846, 340
  1860-1900, *chart* 368
  McKinley Tariff Act (1890), 507
  Mills bill, 499
  Morrill Act, 367
  Payne-Aldrich (1909), 564
  Reciprocal Trade Agreements
    Act (1934), 668
  W. Wilson and, 569
  Wilson-Gorman, 507
Taxation
  Articles of Confederation and,
    140
  Civil War and, 374
  colonial, 92–93, 94, 97–107
  Conciliatory Propositions, 107
  by consent, 101–2
  Constitution and, 145
  excise, 151, 152
  income
    first modern, 569
    Supreme Court and, 507–8
    W. Wilson and, 569
  Internal Revenue Act, 368–69
  internal taxes abolished 1802,
    184
  New Deal and, 653
  post-Revolutionary War, 135–
    36
  Revenue Act, 587
  Shays' Rebellion and, 136
  Stamp Act, 94, 97–98, 100
  Tea Act, 102–5
  Townshend program and, 98–
    100
  voting requirements and, 251–
    52
  War Revenue Act (1917), 590
  World War II and, 687–88
  see also Tariff
Taylor, Frederick Winslow, 535
Taylor, John, 239
Taylor, Maxwell D., 783
Taylor, Zachary (1784–1850),
    334, 336, 344
  California admission and, 341–
    44
  Mexican War and, 334, 336–
    39; *ill.* 338
  President, elected (1848), 341
Taylor Grazing Act (1934), 646
Tea Act (1773), 102–5

Teaching, as profession, 303,
    480
Teamsters' Brotherhood, 753
Teapot Dome Scandal, 612
Technical Cooperation program,
    723
Technology, 178
  business monopoly and, 436
  Civil War and, 379
  industry affected by, 175–77
  ca. 1900, 531–35
  post-World War II, 821–27
  railroads affected by, 441–42
  see also Science
Tecumseh, 200, 201, 204
Teheran Conference (1943),
    704–6
Telegraph, 288–89
Telephone, 436, 531
Television, 816
Temperance movement, 305–6;
    *ill.* 306
Temporary Emergency Relief Ad-
    ministration (N.Y.), 632
Temporary National Economic
    Committee, 653
Ten Years' War (Cuba), 522
Tenements, 447–48
Tennessee
  Civil War and, 387, 388, 392–
    93, 396
  Indian problems in, 156
  land claims and, 133
  Reconstruction and, 402, 403
  secession, 365
  settlement of, 131
  statehood for (1796), 156
  union, readmitted to, 409
Tennessee Valley Authority (TVA),
    644–46, 658; *map* 645
Tennis, 488
Tennyson, Alfred Lord, 293
Tenochtitlán, 10
Tenure of Office Act (1867), 410,
    412–13
Territorial expansion, 93, 517
  Alaska purchase, 417–18
  boundary settlements 1818–
    1819; *map* 217
  in California, 335–36, 339;
    *map* 335
  in Central America, 347–48
  Cuban consideration, 347, 348
  in Florida, 214–15

  Gadsden Purchase, 352
  Hawaii annexed, 520–21
  justifications, 518–19
  Louisiana Purchase, 185–89;
    *maps* 188–89
  Manifest Destiny and, 327, 331
  New, 518–19
  in Midway Islands, 418, 517
  in New Mexico, 334–35, 336,
    339
  Oregon boundary settlement,
    331–32; *map* 332
  in Philippines, 525, 526–27
  Pierce and, 347–48
  Polk and, 330, 334, 336, 339
  in Puerto Rico, 526–27
  in Samoan Islands, 521–22
  sectionalism and, 339–41,
    347–48, 351
  Spanish-American War, 522–
    27
  in Southwest, *map* 335
  Texas annexation, 332–34;
    *map* 335
  in Virgin Islands, 581
Territories
  planning for, 133–35
  slave v. free (1850); *map* 346
Tet offensive (1968), 794–95
Texas
  agriculture, 280
  annexation of, 332–34; *map*
    335
  boundary disputes, 342
  cattle industry in, 468
  election 1844 and, 330
  independence proclamation,
    333
  New Mexico claims, 342
  Reconstruction and, 410
  statehood (1845), 334
  *Texas* v. *White*, 412
Textile industry, 175–76; *ill.*
    233
  Civil War and, 383
  1800s early, 210–11
  1820–1840, 231
  1840–1860, 278
  1920s, 615
  England, Tudor Age, 14–15
  labor, 232–33
  in South, New, 432
  tariff of 1828 and, 245
Thames, battle of, 204–5

Thant, U, 787
Thayer, Webster, 607
Theater, 78
  1800s, 171
  1820–1860, 295
  ca. 1900, 537–38
  in Great Depression, 660
  Jazz Age, 623
Theresa, Maria (Austria), 89
Thomas, George H., 392
Thomas, Jesse B., 236
Thomas, John L., 309
Thomas, Norman, 624–25, 637
Thompson, Benjamin, 114
Thompson, J. Edgar, 443
Thomson, Virgil, 816, 817
Thoreau, Henry D., 292, 294, 308
Thumb, Tom, 295
Thurmond, J. Strom, 716–18
Tiebout, Cornelius, 204
Tilden, Samuel J., 426–27
Tillman, Benjamin, 501
Timber Culture Act (1873), 465
Timber and Stone Act (1878), 465
*Time*, 621–22
Timrod, Henry, 318
Tippecanoe, battle of, 201
Tobacco, 24, 38–39, 40, 67–68; *ill.* 41
Tocqueville, Alexis de, 249, 291, 299
Tonkin Gulf resolution (1964), 792
Tories, *see* Loyalists
Toscanelli, 7
Toscanini, Arturo, 660
Townsend, Francis E., 647
Townshend, Charles, 98–99
Townshend Program, 98–100; *chart* 100
Trade, *see* Commerce; Foreign trade
Trade Expansion Act (1962), 788
Trade unions, *see* Unions
Trading-With-the-Enemy Acts (1917), 591, 593
Trafalgar, battle of, 196
Transcendentalism, 300–1
Transportation
  canal, 227–29
  in cities, 448; *ill.* 449
  Civil War and, 366

1800s, early, 177–79
1955, 814–15
railroad, 229–31, 285–88, 352
river, 226
roads, 226–27
after War of 1812, 212–13
*see also* specific types
Trappers, 215
Treasury
  bond sales, 368
  creation of, 149
  greenback question and, 422–23
  independent, 271–72
    abolished, 328
    restored under Polk, 340
  National Bank Act and, 367–68
  World War II and, 687
Treaties
  Clayton-Bulwer, 347
  Elgin, 347
  Five Power Pact (1922), 617
  Four Power Pact (1922), 617
  French Alliance, 124
  Ghent, 208–9
  Guadalupe Hidalgo, 339
  Hay-Pauncefote (1901), 578
  Jay's, 158
  Louisiana Purchase, 185–89
  North Atlantic, 724–25
  Nine Power Pact, 617
  Nuclear test ban (1963), 788
  Paris (1783), 127–30
  Paris (1898), 527
  peace pacts, 617–18
  Pinckney's, 158–59, 186
  Portsmouth, 576–77
  San Ildefonso, 185
  trade, 347
  "Transcontinental," 215
  Versailles, 599–602
  Wanghia, 330
  Washington, 418
  Webster-Ashburton, 329–30
Tredegar Iron Works, 315
*Trent* affair, 384
Trenton, New Jersey, 121
*Trevett* v. *Weeden*, 136
Triangle Shirtwaist Factory fire, 551
*Tribune*, 289
Tripartite Pact, 676
Tripoli, 209

Tripolian War, 185
Trujillo, Rafael, 789
Truman, Harry S
  armed forces demobilization and, 712.
  atomic bomb and, 703–4
  Cold War and, 722–33
  election 1944 and, 709–10
  Fair Deal and, 713, 732
  foreign policy of, 710–11
  Korean War and, 727–30
  loyalty checks, 730–32
  at Potsdam, 710
  Presidency, succeeds to, 710
  price controls and, 715
  unions and, 714, 715–16
  War Investigating Committee and, 682
Truman Doctrine (1947), 723
Trumbull, John, 172
Trusts, 436–40, 538
  busting, 556–58
  *see also* Monopoly
"Truth in Securities" Act (1933), 646–47
Tucker, Nathaniel Beverly, 317
Tudor Age, 14
Tunis, 185, 209
Turner, Frederick Jackson, 255
Turner, Nat, 323
Turner, O., 218–19
Turnpikes, 178–79, 212
  *see also* Roads
Tuscarora Indians, 18
Tuskegee Institute, 481, 482
Twain, Mark, 483–84
Tweed Ring, 426
Twentieth Amendment, 637
Twenty-first Amendment, 630
Twenty-fourth Amendment, 767
Twenty-third Amendment, 767
Tydings-McDuffie Act (1934), 669
Tyler, Goody, 51
Tyler, John (1790–1862)
  banking and, 328
  election 1840 and, 273
  as President, 328–29, 330
  Texas annexation and, 333–34
Typewriter, 436
Tyron, William, 95

U-2 incident, 746–47
*Uncle Tom's Cabin* (Stowe), 311

Underground railroad, 323
Underwood, Oscar W., 567, 569
Unemployment, Great Depression,
    632; *chart* 640
Union League, 414
Union Pacific Railroad, 367, 421,
    444
Union party, 372–73, 655
Unions, 234
    boycotts and, 559
    collective bargaining, 559
    decline, 614–15
    formation of, 455–56
    growth of
        1900s, early, 558
        1900–1966, *chart* 714
        1950s, 752–53
    Haymarket affair, 456–57
    industrial, 650–51
    injunctions against, 559
    J. F. Kennedy and, 762
    Labor Reform Act (1959) and,
        753
    legalized, 281
    loyalty investigations and, 606
    New Deal and, 649–51
    in 1900, 460
    Norris-La Guardia Act (1932),
        649–50
    post-World War II, 714
    strikes, *see* Strikes
    Taft-Hartley Labor-Management
        Relations Act (1947), 715–
        16
    Taylorism and, 535
    Wagner Act (1935), 650
    World War I and, 591
    World War II and, 685–86
Unitarian Church, 173
United Automobile Workers, 651
United Mine Workers, 615, 686,
    753
United Nations, 693–94
    atomic energy and, 712
    chartered, 707–8
    declaration of, 693
    Korean War and, 727–30
United Press, 537
*United States* (vessel), 162, 204
United States Coast Survey, 296
*United States* v. *E. C. Knight Co.*,
    506, 557
United States Exploring Expedi-
    tion, 296

United States Industrial Commis-
    sion, 538
United States Military Academy,
    185, 304
United States Public Health Ser-
    vice, 536
United States Sanitary Commis-
    sion, 370
United States Shipping Board,
    587
United States Steel, 538, 557,
    558, 606, 762, 765
Universal Negro Improvement
    Association, 609
Universalist Church, 173
Universities, state, 303–4
University of Pennsylvania, 78,
    170
Urban renewal, 812–13
U'Ren, William S., 551
Urey, Harold, 662
Utah, 465
*Utopia* (Moore), 14, 299
Utopian communities, 304–5,
    454
Utrecht, treaty of (1713), 89


Valentino, Rudolph, 621
Vallandigham, Clement L., 371
Valley Forge, 117, 121; *ills.* 110,
    123
Van Buren, Martin (1782–1862)
    Canadian rebellion and, 329
    Eaton affair, 257
    election 1840 and, 273
    election 1844 and, 330
    election 1848 and, 340
    fiscal system, 271–72
    Panic of 1837 and, 271
    President, elected (1836), 267–
        68
    as secretary of state, 256–57
    Texas annexation application
        and, 333
Vance, Zebulon M., 376
Vandalia Company, 131
Vandenberg, Arthur H., 708,
    723, 732
Vanderbilt, Cornelius, 442, 539
Vanderbilt, William, 450
Vanzetti, Bartolomeo, 608
Veblen, Thorstein, 625
Venezuela, 519–20, 579

Vera Cruz, 339
Vergennes, Count de, 123–24,
    127–29
Vermont, 225
    seventeenth century, *map* 32
    statehood (1791), 156
Verrazano, Giovanni, 8, 18;
    *map* 9
Versailles, treaty of, 599–602
Vesey, Denmark, 323
Vespucius, Americus, 8
Veterans (1932), 632
Vicksburg, 391–92; *map* 391
Vietnam War, 790–95, 803–4;
    *ill.* 790; *map* 793
    deescalation, 794–95
    Eisenhower and, 790–92
    election 1968 and, 795–99
    escalated, 792–94
    L. B. Johnson and, 788–89,
        792–95
    J. F. Kennedy and, 792
    Nixon and, 803–4
    origins of, 790–92
    Tonkin Gulf Resolution (1964),
        792
    War on Poverty and, 772–73
Vikings, 4–5
Villa, Francisco "Pancho," 582
Vinson, Fred, 731
Virgin Islands, 581
Virginia
    agriculture, 280
    Civil War in, 385, 388–90,
        394–95; *ill.* 397; *map* 394
    colonization of, 21–25
    committees of correspondence
        and, 106
    Constitution ratified by, 148;
        *chart* 146
    Constitutional Convention and,
        142–43
    Continental Congress and, 106
    debt, public, 152
    Declaration of Rights, 115
    education in, 168–69
    Great Britain and, 92–93
    House of Burgesses, 25, 39,
        42, 97
    Indian Wars, 40–42
    land claims, western, 132–33
    peace conference (1861), 364
    political history, 39–42
    Reconstruction and, 403, 410

religion in, 39, 115, 174
Revolutionary War and, 125, 126
secession, 365
shipbuilding, 65
slavery in, 57, 58, 115
Statute of Religious Liberty, 115
tobacco, 38–39, 40
unconstitutionality resolution, 163
voting reform, 252
Virginia Company of London, see London Company
Virginia Dynasty, 213
Virginia Plan, 142–44
Virginia Resolves, 97
Voice of America, 746
Volstead Act (1919), 609–10
Voting
immigrants and, 285
initiative, 551
literacy test, 429–30
for Negroes, 424–25, 429–30, 756, 766–67
primaries, 551
property requirements, 114–15
referendum, 551
state constitutions and, 114
state reform, 251–53
universal suffrage, 114, 252
for women, 551, 609; ill. 544
Voyages of Discovery, map 5

Wade, Benjamin F., 371, 381, 402
Wade-Davis bill, 402
Wages, post-World War II, 714
Wagner Act (1935), 650
Waite, Morrison R., 501
Waldseemuller, Martin, 8
Walker, David, 310
Walker, Quork, 115
Walker, William, 347–48
Wallace, George, 797–99
Wallace, Henry A., 651, 674, 709, 716–18, 722
Wallace, Henry C., 611
Walpole, Robert, 84
Walsh, Thomas J., 612
Walsh-Healy Act (1936), 653
Wampanoag Indians, 34
Wanamaker, John, 506

Wanghia, treaty of (1844), 330
War Democrats, 370, 372
War Department, 149
War of 1812, 195, 203–9; map 207
casualties, chart 369
causes, 195–203
peace settlement, 208–9
War hawks, 202–3
War Industries Board, 590–91
War Labor Disputes Act (1943), 686
War Manpower Commission, 684
War on Poverty, 765–66, 771–73
Nixon and, 800
Vietnam War and, 772–73
War Production Board, 679, 680–82, 713
War of the Rebellion, see Civil War
War Resources Board, 679
War Revenue Act (1917), 590
Ward, John Quincy Adams, 485–486
Ward, Lester, 453
Warren, Earl, 716, 755, 756, 765, 800
Warren, Robert Penn, 819
Warsaw Alliance (1947), 723
Washburn, Cadwallader C., 441
Washburne, Elihu B., 417
Washington (statehood), 465
Washington (vessel), 212
Washington, Booker T., 430, 481, 482, 553
Washington, D. C., 179–80; ill. 180
as capital, 152
slavery in, 342, 343–45
War of 1812 and, 205
Washington, George
Bank of U. S. and, 152
cabinet appointments, 149
at Constitutional Convention, 142, 143; ill. 138
death, 171
"Farewell Address," 159
as Federalist, 147
foreign affairs, 156–59
in French and Indian War, 89–90
Indian trouble and, 156
neutrality proclamation, 157

political parties and, 153
policies of, 114
as President (1789), 148–50
Revolutionary War and,
appointed commander in chief, 118
retreat to Morristown, map 121
1778–1779, 125
at Trenton, 121
second term, 154
Senate and, 149
on Shays' Rebellion, 142
slavery and, 115
theater and, 171
on union, 351
Whiskey Rebellion and, 154–56
Washington, treaty of (1871), 418
Washington Arms Conference, 617
Washington Temperance Society, 306
Washoe gold strike, 465–66
Watauga settlements, 131
Water pollution, 813
Water power, 64
Water Power Act (1920), 609
Water transportation v. railroads, 287–88; chart 288; see also Canals; Rivers
Waterman, Thomas T., 72
Watson, Thomas E., 502, 504, 513
Watt, James, 175, 178
Watts riot (1965), 774
Wayne, Anthony, 156, 200
Weaver, James B., 504, 507
Webb-Kenyon Act (1910), 552
Webster, Daniel
banks and, 264
on capitalism, 267
Compromise of 1850, 344
Dartmouth College v. Woodward, 237
election 1836 and, 266–68
Gibbons v. Ogden, 239
Great Britain, treaty with, 329–30
Hayne debate with, 257–59; ill. 258
Hungarian revolt and, 346–47
industrial capitalists and, 280

Webster, Daniel (*Continued*)
  land speculation and, 269, 270
  *McCulloch* v. *Maryland,* 238
  McLeod case and, 329
  nullification and, 261, 262
  as schoolteacher, 169
  as secretary of state, 328–30,
    346–47
  on territorial expansion, 327
  voting requirements, 251
  War of 1812 and, 206
Webster, Noah, 168, 303
Webster-Ashburton Treaty (1842),
  329–30
Wedemeyer, Albert C., 726
Weill, Kurt, 817
Welch, Robert, 768
Weld, Theodore, 309, 311
Welfare, Nixon and, 801
Welles, Sumner, 669
Wellington, Duke of, 205
Wescott, Edwin, 537
Wesley, Charles, 75–76
Wesley, John, 75–76, 174
West
  agriculture, 281–83
  cattle industry in, 467–70
  Civil War in, 386–88; *map*
    386
  exploration, 190–91, 215–16;
    *map* 189
  fur trade, 215
  growth of, 225
  Indian removal in, 470–75
  land claims in, *map* 132
  last, 463–76, *map* 464
  literature, 483–84
  migration to, 131–32, 216–
    20, 332, 340; *ill.* 218–19,
    326; *map* 334
  mining, 466–67
  planning for, 133–35
  settlement, 131–33, 339–40,
    464–65; *ill.* 467
  trails to, *map* 334
West, Benjamin, 47, 160
*West Coast Hotel* v. *Parrish,* 656
West Florida, 189, 202
  *see also* Florida
West Germany, 723–24, 738–39
West Indies, 186, 187
West Point, 185
West Virginia, 131, 365, 385
Western Conference, 488

Western European Union, 739
Western Railroad, 230
Western Union Telegraph Com-
  pany, 288
Westinghouse, George, 442
Westinghouse Electric and Manu-
  facturing Company, 436
Westmoreland, William, 804
Westover; *ill.* 72
Wethersfield, Connecticut, 32
Weyler, Valeriano, 522, 523
Whaling industry, 231
Wharton, Edith, 537
Wheeler, Burton K., 612, 613,
  673
Wheelwright, John, 33
Whig party
  broadside of 1840, 272; *ill.*
    272
  capitalism and, 267
  composition of, 266
  disintegrates, 351, 353
  elections and, *see* Elections
  Kansas-Nebraska Act and, 353
  Log Cabin Campaign, 272–73
  Panic of 1837 and, 270
  slavery and, 345
  social reform and, 301
  under Tyler, 328
  *see also* Patriot party
Whiskey Rebellion, 154–56
Whistler, James McNeill, 485
White, Henry, 599
White, Hugh Lawson, 268
White, John, 22
White, Theodore H., 760
White, William Allen, 492, 551,
  673
White collar class, 546
White Committee, *see* Committee
  to Defend America by Aiding
  the Allies
Whitefield, George, 76
Whitehall, treaty of (1686), 89
Whiteman, Paul, 624
Whitman, Marcus, 332
Whitman, Walt, 292–93; *ill.* 293
Whitney, Eli, 177, 278
Whitney's Gun Factory, *ill.* 176
Whittier, John Greenleaf, 294–95
Wickersham, George, 630
Wiesner, Jerome B., 822
Wiggen, Kate Douglas, 537
Wik, Raymond M., 476

Wilder, Thornton, 660
Wilderness, battle of, 394–95
Wilderness Road, 131
Wilkes, Charles, 296, 384
Wilkes, George, 289
Wilkins, Roy, 763
Wilkinson, James, 135, 189,
  190, 192
Willard, Emma, 307
William of Orange (King of Eng-
  land, 1659–1702), 29, 50,
  52, 89
William & Mary College, 78, 79,
  168, 170, 303
Williams, Roger, 32, 34, 73
Williams, William Appleman, 743
*Williams* v. *Mississippi,* 430
Willkie, Wendell, 674–75, 722
Wilmot, David, 340
Wilmot Proviso, 340, 343
Wilson, Charles E., 737, 752
Wilson, William B., 569
Wilson, William L., 507
Wilson, Woodrow (1856–1924),
  693
  antitrust legislation and, 570–
    71
  election 1920 and, 610
  foreign policy, 580–602 *passim*
  Fourteen Points, 593, 598
  Latin America and, 580–82
  League of Nations, 575, 598,
    599–602
  Mexico and, 581–82
  New Freedom program, 568–
    69
  New Jersey, as governor, 551,
    552
  President, elected (1912), 567–
    69
  progressivism and, 545, 568–
    69, 571–72
  tariffs and, 569
  Versailles treaty and, 599–602
  World War I, *see* World War I
Wilson-Gorman Tariff Act (1894),
  507
Wilson's Creek, battle of, 385
Windsor, Connecticut, 32
Windward Islands, 93
Winston, Ellen, 642
Winthrop, John, 30–32, 36
Wirt, William, 265
Wisconsin, 280, 346

Wister, Owen, 468
Witchcraft, 51
Wobblies, see Industrial Workers of the World (IWW)
Wohlsetter, Roberta, 677
Wolfe, James, 91, 92
Wolfe, Thomas, 660
Wollen Act (1699), 65
Women
  education for, 303, 481
  employment for, 232, 233, 810
  reform for rights of, 114, 307
  social reform and, 548–50
  voting rights, 253, 551, 609; ill., 544
  working conditions (1900), 539
Women's Christian Temperance Union, 610
Wood, Grant, 659, 660
Wood, Leonard, 524, 529, 587, 610
Wood, Robert E., 673
Woodlands, North American Eastern, 16–17
Woodward, C. Vann, 411
Woofter, T. J., 642
Woolf, Virginia, 623
Woolman, John, 70–71, 78
Works Progress Administration (WPA), 648, 658
World Court, 617
World Disarmament Conference (1932), 667
World Economic Conference (1933), 667
World War Foreign Debt Commission, 618
World War I (1914–1918), 583–602
  aircraft in, 587, 591, 595
  armistice, 596, 598–99
  begins, 583
  blockades, 583–87
  casualties, 597; chart 369
  debts and reparations, 618
  land operations, 594–97; maps 596, 597

submarine warfare, 584–87, 589
United States
  armed forces strength, 587
  as arsenal, 584
  entry, 589
    historians' disagreements on, 585
  financing, 590
  peace ideals and war hatred, 592–94
  prepares for, 587, 589–90
Versailles, treaty of, 599–602
World War II
  allies, U. S. aid to, 672–73, 675–76
  bombings, 698–99
    atomic, 703–4; ill. 692, 703
  casualties, chart 369
  causes, 670–72
  civilians affected by, 684–85
  conferences
    Potsdam, 703, 710, 711
    Teheran, 704–6
    Yalta, 706–7
  European Theater, 698–700
  financing, 687–88
  France falls, 672
  Germany surrenders, 700
  industry, 680–82
  information, 689
  Japan surrenders, 704
  Japanese-Americans relocated in, 689–91; ill. 690
  Lend-Lease, 675–76
  maps
    Normandy invasion, 699
    North African and Sicilian campaigns, 697
    Pacific, War in, 701
  Mediterranean offensive, 696–98; map 697
  mobilization (allied), 679–80
  naval warfare, 695–96, 701–2
  ordinance production, 680–82
  Pacific front
    atomic bombings, 703–4

China and, 701–2
  1941–1942, 695–96
  1942–1945, 700–4; map 701
Pearl Harbor attacked, 678–79
price controls, 686–87
Russia in, 675–76
science in, 683
shipping in, 682–83
submarine warfare in, 675, 676, 696
unions and, 685–86
United States
  armed forces, 694–95; chart 694
  enters, 679
Wounded Knee, slaughter of, 474
Wright, Frank Lloyd, 537, 818
Wright, Orville and Wilbur, 533
Writs of Assistance, 93
Wrong, Dennis H., 808
Wyeth, N. C., 126
Wythe, George, 170

X. Y. Z. affair, 161

Yale College, 78, 79, 296, 303, 304
Yalta Conference, 706–7
Yamsaki, Minoru, 818
Yancey, William L., 322
"Yankee Doodle," 172
Yazoo land claims, 182, 237
Yellow fever, 171
York (Toronto), Canada, 204
York, Duke of, see James II
Yorktown, 124–26; map 125
Young, Brigham, 339, 340
Young America movement, 346
Youngstown Sheet and Tube Company, 651
Youth, 820–21
Yugoslavia, 723

Zenger, John Peter, 80
Zimmerman, Arthur, 589